YOUNG INDIA
(1919-1922)

YOUNG INDIA
(1919-1922)

MAHATMA GANDHI

GYAN

Published by

GYAN

Gyan Publishing House
5, Ansari Road
Daryaganj, New Delhi-110002
Phone: 011-47034999, 9811692060
E-mail: books@gyanbooks.com

Distribution Network
gyanbooks.com
India, USA, Canada, UK, Australia

ISBN: 978-93-7133-051-0 (PB)
First Published, 1924

2nd Impression 2025

Printed at: Gyan Press, Delhi.

YOUNG INDIA (1919-1922)
Author Mahatma Gandhi

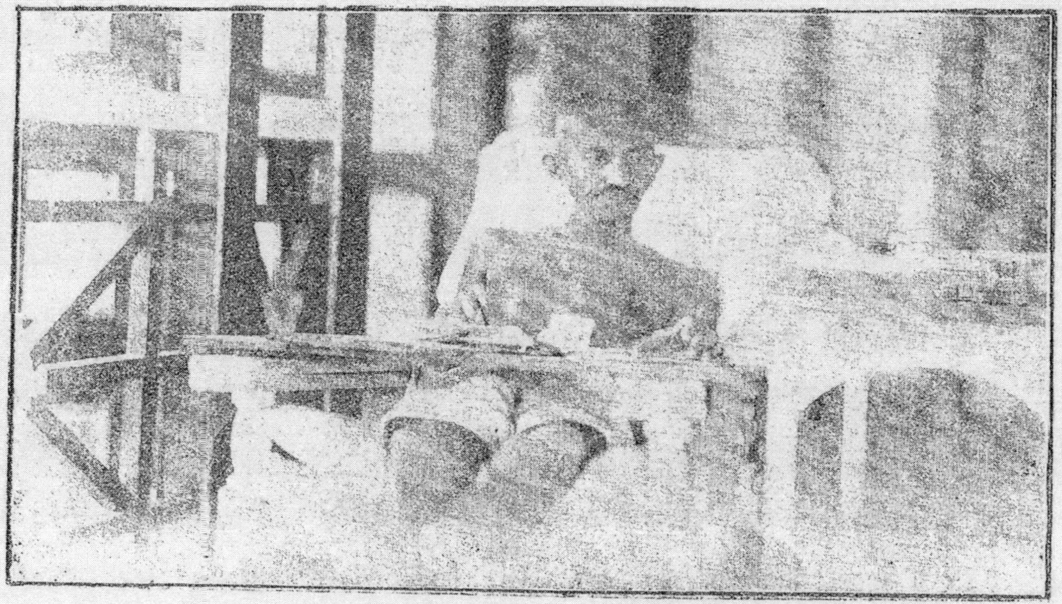

Mahatma Gandhi at Juhu

YOUNG INDIA

1919-1922

By MAHATMA GANDHI

WITH A BRIEF SKETCH OF
THE NON-CO-OPERATION MOVEMENT
BY
BABU RAJENDRA PRASAD

1924

CONTENTS

PART I

THE SATYAGRAHA MOVEMENT

PART II

TOWARDS NON-CO-OPERATION

TOWARDS NON-CO-OPERATION—(*Contd.*)

TOWARDS NON-CO-OPERATION—(*Contd.*)

PART III

THE PRINCIPLES OF NON-CO-OPERATION

CONTENTS

TOWARDS NON-CO-OPERATION (*Contd.*)

TOWARDS NON-CO-OPERATION—*(Contd.)*

PART III

THE PRINCIPLES OF NON-CO-OPERATION

THE PROGRAMME OF NON-CO-OPERATION—(Cnotd.)

PART V

THE NON-CO-OPERATION CAMPAIGN

THE PROGRAMME OF NON-CO-OPERATION—*(Contd.)*

PART VI

MISCELLANEOUS

MISCELLANEOUS—*(Contd.)*

MISCELLANEOUS—*(Contd.)*

PART VII

CONGRESS AND SWARAJ

CONGRESS AND SWARAJ—*(Contd.)*

PART VIII

TOWARDS CIVIL DISOBEDIENCE

TOWARDS CIVIL DISOBEDIENCE—*(Contd.)*

PART IX

ARREST AND TRIAL

PART X

APPENDICES

APPENDICES—*(Contd.)*

H.—SATYAGRAHA MANIFESTOES

SATYAGRAHA LEAFLETS

I.—MAHATMAJI'S EARLIER WRITINGS

PREFATORY NOTE

I

WITH the incarceration of Mahatma Gandhi, his writings in *Young India* have passed beyond the pale of polemical politics and entered the realm of the "classic" literature. Far more than their practical value to India, at present or hereafter, is their value to the world at large, embodying in them a philosophy of life and practical conduct elaborated by the experience of the lifetime of a soul which will undoubtedly rank in history as that of one of the world's greatest of men.

A few isolated articles are all that have so far been published in book form and the need for a systematic collection of *all* the articles, numbering hundreds, and their presentation in a carefully edited form, is the justification for this publication. The task of editing has not been easy. To have arranged the articles in a wholly chronological order would perhaps have been preferred by the few close followers of *Young India* who till recently have been comparatively few. On the other hand, the by far more numerous lay readers who pay serious and systematic attention to the writings for the first time—and their number is bound to grow—prefer, as experience proves, a logical arrangement. A wholly logical arrangement would, however, have required an amount of editing which would have been incompatible with the publisher's desire not to tamper with the original in any way. The result is a compromise whereby while the articles are sorted and grouped under ten sections, so as to facilitate the study of particular subjects, they are, within these sections, arranged exactly as they appeared in *Young India.** In all cases, where to have given the whole article would only have been unduly burdening the book, the articles have been carefully summarised and given as footnotes in appropriate places. As far as possible, even observations by the way, though on topics of but momentary interest, have, wherever they are in the nature of valuable *obiter dicta*, been also included. All endeavour has thus been made to give in this one volume the valuable writings of Mahatmaji and others in *Young India* from the date of its first publication in Ahmedabad, 1919 to the date of his imprisonment in 1922. Throughout, the writings have been approached as an earnest and reverent student in search solely of Truth would have done, so that the collection might be a reliable account of the Mahatmaji's views to all who desire seriously to study them.

The task has involved a considerable amount of labour and money and but for the fact that Mahatma Gandhi accepts no royalty or honorarium for his writings, it would have been altogether impossible to price the book so cheap.

II

A BIOGRAPHICAL NOTE

That Mahatma Gandhi's life was, as stated above, rich in experiences will be easily realised from the all too brief biographical note which is given below:

* The American *Federalist* which in importance and some other respects bears a close analogy to the *Young India* articles almost follows this arrangement.

Born at Porbandar on 2nd October, 1869; son of Karamchand Gandhi, Prime Minister first of Probandar and then of Rajkot; educated at Kathiawar High School, London University and the Inner Temple; married to Kasturibhai 1881, having been betrothed at the age of 8; Advocate, Bombay High Court, 1891; visits South Africa, 1893; enrolled as Advocate, Supreme Court in spite of White opposition; founded Natal Indian Congress, 1894; agitation in India on behalf of South African Indians, 1895; mobbed almost to death under the lead of Attorney-General Escombe on landing in S. Africa on return and saved by the heroism of the wife of the Police Superintendent; led the Indian Ambulance Corps in the Boer War, 1899, whose services were well appreciated in S. Africa as well as in England; returns to India to recoup health, 1901; attends the Calcutta Congress under the presidentship of Mr. Wacha; called to Natal to place the Indian case before Mr. Chamberlaim appointed to consider the question; helps Transvaal Indians in the same manner, though right of leading the deputation was refused by the White authorities; enrolled as Attorney of the Supreme Court of Transvaal; founds the Transvaal British Indian Association and becomes its Hony. Secretary and legal adviser; founds also the *Indian Opinion*; also the Phœnix settlement, 1904, under the influence of Ruskin and the experience of the conflict between Capital and Labour in S. Africa; anti-plague work in Johannesburg in 1904; led the Stretcher Bearer Corps in the Native Revolt in 1906; anti-Asiatic Law Agitation, 1906; Passive Resistance struggle; arrest and imprisonment; Gandhi-Smuts compromise; nearly killed by his own followers who thought the compromise was a betrayal of Indian interests; General Smuts's repudiation of the compromise;

the recommencement of the struggle; arrest and imprisonment; *Indian Home Rule* written, 1908; visit to England, 1909; 1911 settlement; Gokhale's visit to S. Africa; repudiation of promise to repeal the £ 3 poll tax, 1913; recommencement of the great Passive Resistance struggle; its success; visit to England, 1914; raises Ambulance Corps in London, 1914; return to India, 1915; other recent incidents referred to in the statement before the Court (See p. 1049); arrest and imprisonment.

III

A NOTE ON "YOUNG INDIA"

A few words about the journal *Young India* will, we think, be also of interest to the readers. The history of *Young India* has a piquant interest. It was started originally by Mr. Jamnadas Dwarkadas, a young Bombay politician, who, wavering between the lead of Mr. Gandhi and that of Mrs. Besant, ultimately accepted that of the latter and became one of the most uncompromising opponents of the Non-co-operation Movement. It then came into the hands of a syndicate of whom Mr. Shankerlal Banker was a member. When Mr. Horniman was deported and the *Bombay Chronicle* was put under censorship, public life in Bombay needed the services of Mahatmaji. *Young India* was, therefore, put under his charge. After the *Bombay Chronicle* got back its freedom, Mahatmaji found it necessary to shift it to Ahmedabad (see p. 1) for reason mentioned on p. 2 and take over complete charge of the paper. He stopped all advertisments through *Young India* and determined to carry it on only so long as it paid its way without them. The High Court of Bombay once tried to extort an apology from the Mahatmaji, which it was impossible for him to tender.* The High Court, therefore, prudently let him off with a reprimand 'behind his back' as the *Mahratta* put it.

Young India increased in its popularity as the Non-co-operation movement developed in its intensity. At first it failed to get even the minimum 2,500 which Mahatmaji wanted to keep it going, but subsequently its circulation rose till when Mahatmaji was arrested its weekly sale was about 40,000.

On the arrest and convicition of Mahatmaji and Mr. Banker, the paper was put in the hands of that young and faithful Mussalman Mr. Shuaib Qureshi. The Government soon prosecuted a second time all the workers connected with the paper and they were sent to jail for practically a year and a half. Professors Desai and Bhansali and the never tiring Swami Anandan of *Young India* and *Nava Jivan* were thus safely lodged in the Sabarmati jail along with Mr. Shuaib Qureshi.

The paper is now being conducted by Mr. C. Rajagopalachar of Salem, Madras, and Mahatmaji's son, Ramadas Gandhi, has taken upon himself the responsibility of publisher, printer and keeper of the press.

* *See* p. 55.

A BRIEF SKETCH OF THE NON-CO-OPERATION MOVEMENT

India and the War.—To understand the significance and causes of the Non-co-operation Movement one has to go back beyond the incidents which immediately led to its adoption by the Khilafat Conference and the Indian National Congress. When the Great European War broke out between England and Germany in August 1914, India rose as one man to help the British Government. Those very people, the educated classes, who had been regarded as opponents of the Government on account of their inauguration of and participation in all political movements of the country were the first to realise the significance of the German menace and to throw in the whole weight of their influence on the side of the Government. The country as a whole helped the Empire in its time of need by offering her sons to fight its battle and also by making monetary contributions. Her services were recognised and spoken of in most eulogistic terms not only by the Viceroy and other officials in this country but also by the Prime Ministers and other statesmen in England. The war aims which were declared to be nothing less than making the world safe for democracy, the protection of weak nationalities, and the conferment of the boon of self-determination on all peoples naturally roused great hopes in the minds of the people of India who began to see in the world-devastating war a chance of their deliverance from the humiliating position of a subject people and a hope of the elevation of their country to the status of an equal partner in the British Commonwealth.

The Montagu-Chelmsford Report.—In this hope they were encouraged by a declaration by the Secretary of State for India (Mr. E. S. Montagu) in August 1917 which, while promising full responsible government to India within the British Empire by a gradual transference of power to popular control and a larger association of Indians in the administration of the country, reserved to the British Parliament the right of determining the pace of progress towards full responsible government. It was followed in the cold weather of 1917-18 by a visit of Mr. Montagu to India for consulting Indian public opinion regarding the reforms proposed to be introduced as the first step in fulfilment of the promise made in the declaration of August 1917. After a tour through the country and after interviewing a large number of persons and receiving numerous deputations, Mr. Montagu and the Viceroy, Lord Chelmsford, issued their report on constitutional Reform on the 8th July 1918.

The Delhi War Conference.—Early in 1918 the war had been passing through a phase most threatening to the Allies and the big German offensive was in full progress. To secure greater support and a further concentration of effort, the Prime Minister (Mr. Lloyd George), on the 2nd of April, 1918, sent a message to India reminding her of "the intention of the rulers of Germany to establish a tyranny, not only over Europe, but over Asia as well" and asking "every lover of freedom and law" to play his part in preventing "the menace spreading to the East and gradually engulfing the world" and hoping that India "will add to the laurels it has already won" and "be the bulwark which will save Asia from the tide of oppression and disorder which it is the object of the enemy to achieve." The Viceroy in reply assured him on behalf of the people of India of the "fullest effort and the fullest sacrifice to safeguard the soil of the motherland against all attempts of a cruel and unscrupulous enemy and to secure the final triumph of those ideals of justice and honour for which the British Empire stands." This was followed by a War Conference at Delhi on April 27th, 1918, at which the King Emperor's message declared that "the need of the Empire is India's opportunity" and a series of similar Provincial Conferences.

Mahatma Gandhi joined the War Conference at Delhi and supported the resolution about loyalty. As a result, contributions in men and money increased on a large scale and recruitment went up. Some idea of the contribution of India to the success of the allies may be gathered from the following facts culled from official acknowledgments. India made a total combatant contribution of 9,85,000 men of whom 5,52,000 were sent overseas and of whom no less than 7,91,000 were enlisted during the War. Of non-combats India contributed 4,72,000 of whom 3,91,000 were sent overseas and no less than 4,27,000 were enrolled during the war. The total contribution of Indian personnel was thus 14,57,000 of whom 9,43,000 served overseas and no less than 1,06,594 suffered casualities. The number of animals sent was 1,75,000. During the war 1,855 miles of railway track, 229 locomotives, and 5,989 vehicles were sent out and 940 crafts of various descriptions for service on rivers and on seas were made available for war service. It is difficult to estimate accurately the contributions in money, but roughly they amounted in all to no less than 130 million pounds or nearly 200 crores.

The Rowlatt Acts Report and After.—While India was making such immense sacrifices for the sake of the Empire believing in the King Emperor's words that "the need of the Empire was India's opportunity," there were not signs wanting to the keen observer that the righteous war aims so pompously advertised were after all intended to secure the support of India in the war and would go the way of other similar declarations of British Policy in India in the past. The internment of Mrs. Besant gave a rude shock to the country at large and the internment and maltreatment of a large number of persons supposed to be dangerous under the Defence of India Act without any trial awakened the country to a sense of the mistake it had committed in giving its tacit consent to the passing of that Act and the prostitution of its provisions to secure political purposes as distinguished from protection of the country from the enemy's designs. On the top of it all came the Report of a Committee appointed under the Presidentship of Sir Sidney Rowlatt to report on the growth of revolutionary movement in the country and to suggest remedies.

The report was published on the 19th July, 1918 and recommended practically the perpetuation of the provisions of the Defence of India Act, taking away trials by juries and assessors in cases of seditious crimes, taking away the preliminary proceedings of commitment on the one hand and the right of appeal after conviction on the other, authorising trials *in camera* and admission of evidence not subjected to cross-examination and not recorded by the trial court under certain circumstances and, above all reserving to the Executive the right and power not only to restrict the liberty of the individual by demanding securities with or without sureties, by restricting his residence or requiring notification of change of residence and demanding abstention from certain acts, such as engaging in journalism, distributing leaflets, attending meetings, etc., but also to deprive him of it by arresting and confining him. The abuses to which similar provisions of the Defence of India Act and the rules promulgated under powers conferred by it had been put showed the country what these proposals meant and they naturally created consternation in the country and when armistice was declared in the autumn of 1918, India was seething with discontent at what she rightly considered to be a betrayal of her after the time of "the need of the Empire" had passed away. Suspicion was naturally roused that the promised Reforms would be postponed and the ordinary rights of the citizen to enjoy freedom of movement and sanctity of home and home life taken away on the pretext of the existence of a revolutionary conspiracy in the country. When at last on the 6th of February, 1919, the Rowlatt Bills, embodying the recommendations of the Rowlatt Committee, were introduced by Sir William Vincent into the Imperial Legislative Council at Delhi, the whole country rose like one man against this most unwarranted encroachment on the ordinary rights of free citizens. It was the beginning of an agitation throughout the country the like of which had never before been witnessed. Innumerable meetings were held in all parts of the vast peninsula, and in the Council itself not a single Indian was found to support its drastic provisions even with a silent vote. But all this was of no avail and the Government with the help of official votes passed one of the Bills into an Act in the third week of March, 1919.

The Hartal and the Disturbances.--The result of forcing the Act was some members of the Imperial Legislative Council resigned their seats in protest against this high-handed action of the Government, and when Mahatma Gandhi declared his intention of leading a Satyagraha campaign, he only voiced the feeling of India smarting under an insult and humiliation which was as undeserved of India as it was unbecoming and ungrateful of the British Government to offer. The Satyagraha pledge* which began to be signed in large numbers required the signatory to affirm that they would refuse civilly to obey those laws and such other laws as the Committee to be appointed later on might think fit and further that "in this struggle we will faithfully follow the truth and refrain from violence to life, person, or property." On the 23rd of March, Mahatma Gandhi issued his manifesto fixing the 6th of April for the observance of an All-India *Hartal* and as a day of fasting, prayer and penance. Under some mistake, the *Hartal* was observed at Delhi on the 30th March. And, as a result of a quarrel between some demonstrator on the one hand and the stall keeper at the Railway Station on the other, a riot ensued. Military police and a small military force were brought out and some people were shot. In other parts of the country, the *Hartal* on the 6th April passed off quietly without any untoward incident. It was a first demonstration in which all, rich and poor, high and low, educated or uneducated, village folks and town people took part. The people of India seemed to have broken their slumber of centuries and to have awakened to a sense of their hidden power. In one word, they re-discovered their soul.

* *See* Appendix.

Mahatma Gandhi was proceeding to Delhi on the 8th of April to relieve the sufferings of the people and to apply a healing balm to their lacerated hearts. He was however served with an order not to enter the Punjab or Delhi and on his refusal to obey the order he was arrested and turned back from a way side Railway Station by a special train to Bombay. The news created consternation throughout the length and breadth of the country and nowhere more than in the province of the Punjab where on account of the reactionary regime of Sir Michael O'Dwyer, people were already exasperated. To add fuel to the fire, under the order of Sir Michael O'Dwyer, on the 10th of April, two popular leaders of Amritsar, Drs. Kitchlew and Satyapal, were deported. Feeling was running very high when a large body of men proceeding towards the house of the Deputy Commissioner to make a representation for the release of the leaders was fired at and on its way back broke out in a serious riot burning and looting banks, the Post Office and some other Government offices, murdering some Europeans and assaulting two ladies. Quite was however soon restored but the atmosphere was surcharged with panic.

Jallianwalla Massacre.—General Dyer arrived at Amritsar on the night of the 11th and occupied the town. There was no incident either on the 11th or on the 12th. On the 13th a meeting was advertised to be held at a vacant space known as Jallianwalla Bagh. General Dyer prohibited any gathering of men on pain of death and hearing that a meeting was going to be held at Jallianwalla proceeded to the spot with his troops and machine guns. The place was full of men, women and children as it was an important Hindu festival day. Within 30 seconds of his arrival, he opened fire which continued for 10 minutes directing it where the crowd was thickest. The fire continued till ammunition was exhausted. Some 5 to 6 hundred people were killed outright and three times the number wounded. The place being surrounded on all sides by high walls no one could escape. There was no warning given before firing and no care taken of the dead and wounded after it. Subsequently, Martial Law was declared in Amritsar, Lahore, Gujrat, and Llyalpur districts and what may be fitly described as a reign of terror followed. Large numbers of people were arrested and tried under Martial Law. Even respectable people were arrested. Some were flogged, others made to crawl on their bellies and unutterable horror committed including bombing of unarmed crowds from aeroplanes.*

The news of Mahatma Gandhi's arrest led to riots at Ahmedabad and other places also. But Martial Law was not continued there for more than a few days.

The Indemnity Act and the Hunter Committee.—The news of these horrors in the Punjab did not go abroad as a strict censorship was maintained. In course of time, however, when some months later, Martial Law was withdrawn, the news began to leak-out and caused deep and widespread indignation throughout the country. A Committee of Enquiry was demanded and was ultimately appointed by the Government with Lord Hunter as its President. But before the Committee began its labours, the Government of India passed an Indemnity Act for the protection of its officers. There was a great deal of opposition to it in the Council, but Mahatma Gandhi, true to his principle of non-retaliation, supported the bill. When the Hunter Committee began to record evidence,

* For further details, *See* the Congress (the Punjab) Enquiry Report.

disclosures of facts and incidents of the most harrowing nature were made. The Congress Committee had appointed a sub-committee to lead evidence before the Hunter Committee. But on account of the refusal of the President to secure the temporary release of those Punjab leaders who were undergoing sentences, even for a short period, to enable them to collect the necessary evidence, the Congress Sub-Committee decided not to lead any evidence at all but to hold an independent enquiry and published its report on the 26th March, 1920, making recommendations which were regarded as much too lenient by the people. On the other hand, the report of the Hunter Committee was not unanimous, the Indian members appending a note of dissent differing from their European colleagues and holding that the promulgation of Martial law in the Punjab was not justified. The recommendations of the Committee as also the orders of the Goverement failed to satisfy Indian opinion and led immediately, along with another matter to be presently mentioned, to the inauguration of the Non-co-operation Movement.

The Khilafat Question.--The other question which had greatly exercised the mind of the Indian people was the question of the Khilafat. When war broke out between England and Turkey, Indian Mussalmans found themselves on the horns of a dilemma. Should they help the Turks and the Sultan who stood as the representative and Defender of their faith, or should they support the British power under which they had been living for more than a century? They decided to throw in their lot with the British in the hope and faith that their religious places would be kept under Muslim control and they would be able to secure for their Turkish co-religionists terms of peace which would be favourable to them. Their faith was based on declarations made by the Viceroy in India and the Prime Minister of England (Mr. Lloyd George) in which the former had pledged immunity of the holy places in Arabia, Mesopotamia and of Jeddah, and the latter had assured the Muslims— "Nor are we fighting to deprive Turkey of its capital or of the rich and renowned lands of Asia Minor and Thrace which are predominantly Turkish in race."

When the war came to an end and rumours about the severe nature of the terms proposed to Turkey got abroad, Mussalmans became naturally alarmed and representation began to be made to the authorities, insisting on the fulfilment of the pledge so unequivocally given by the Prime Minister. The First All-India Khilafat Conference met at Delhi on Nov. 23, 1919, which thanked Mahatma Gandhi and other Hindus for their deep interest in the Khilafat question, enjoined upon Indian Mussalmans to refrain from participating in Victory celebrations, and in the event of a satisfactory settlement of the Turkish question not taking place, to progressively withhold all co-operation from the British Government and to boycott British goods. And lastly, it decided to send a deputation to England with the object of acquainting the British ministers and others with the true sentiments of the Mussalmans regarding the Turkish settlement and the Khilafat question. The second Khilafat conference met at Amritsar in the Congress week. It affirmed the resolution regarding the deputation to England and America, resolved further to send a deputation to the Viceroy and another deputation to Turkey and reiterating the Moslem demands and directed the Central Khilafat Committee to collect funds. A representation signed by the Aga Khan, Syed Ameer Ali and a number of other gentlemen, Indian and European, was submitted to the Premier in December, 1919. The Khilafat question came further to the forefront in December, 1919, when Maulana Shaukat Ali and Mahammad Ali were released from their internment.

The Khilafat Deputations.—A deputation headed by Dr. Ansari accordingly waited on the Viceroy on January 19,1920. The reply which the Viceroy gave to the deputation was disappointing to a degree, and the Muslim leaders issued a statement recording their firm conviction that "should the peace terms result unfavourably to Muslim religion and sentiments, they would place an undue strain upon Muslim loyalty" and demanding that "Arabia as delimited by Muslim authority and the Holy places of Islam must remain under the control of the Khalif", and that the pledge given by Mr. Lloyd George should be fulfilled. The third Khilafat Conference met at Bombay in February, 1920, and expressed its confidence in the deputation going to England and issued a very important manifesto, laying down the Muslim demands and declaring that "any reduction of the claim would not only be a violation of the deepest religious feelings of the Muhammadans, but also a flagrant violation of the solemn declarations and pledges made or given by responsible statesmen, representing Allied and Associated Powers and given at a time when they were desirous of enlisting the support of Muslim people and soldiery, and warning them against the consequence of a wrong decision, particularly when not only the Mussalmans but also the entire Hindu population were joining them in their demand."

Their Failure.—The deputation which was headed by Maulana Muhammad Ali was received by Mr. Fisher on behalf of the Secretary of State for India, and it also waited upon the Prime Minister. It further requested permission to place its views before the Supreme Council of the Peace Conference but was refused. While the deputation was still in Europe, the proposed terms of peace with Turkey were made public on 14th May, 1920, and in India, they were accompanied with a message from the Viceroy to the Muslims of India, explaining those terms. The message recognised that the terms were such as must cause pain to the Muhamadans of India, but asked the Muslims of India to brace themselves to bear with patience and resignation the misfortunes of their Turkish co-religionists. The publication of the proposed peace terms caused the deepest indignation, and synchronising as it did with the publication of the Hunter Committee's report, the whole country was ablaze. The Khilafat Committee met at Bombay to deliberate upon Mahatma Gandhi's Non-co-operation project and adopted it on the 28th May, 1920, as the only means now left to the Muslims. On the 30th May, the All-India Congress Committee met at Benares to discuss the Hunter Report and the Turkish Peace terms. and after a long debate decided to hold a special session of the Congress to consider the question of Non-co-operation.

Non-co-operation Adopted.—On the 30th of June, there was a joint Hindu-Muslim Conference at Allahabad regarding the Khilafat question, and Non-co-operation was unanimously adopted to be resorted to after a month's notice to the Viceroy. Numerous meetings of all parties were held in the different parts of the country, strongly condemning the Hunter Report and demanding justice regarding the Punjab and the Khilafat. On the 22nd of June, a message signed by numerous Muhammadan leaders was submitted to the Viceroy, asking him to sceure revision of the Turkish Peace terms and, in the event of the British Cabinet failing to comply with the Muslim wishes, to make common cause with the Indian Mussalmans. It further warned him that, if he failed to adopt the suggestion, they would be obliged from the 1st August following to withdraw co-operation from the Government and to ask other Mussalmans and Hindus to do likewise. Mahatma Gandhi also addressed a letter to the Viceroy in which he explained his connection with the Khilafat question. He told him how he had noticed the growing anxiety of the Mussalmans and their distrust of British intention and how he had advised them not to give away to despair. He proceeded: "The terms violate ministerial pledges and utterly disregard Mussalman sentiment. I consider that as a staunch Hindu wishing to live on terms of the closest friendship with my Mussalman countrymen, I should be an unworthy son of India if I did not stand by them in their hour of trial. . . The report of the majority of the Hunter Committee and your Excellency's despatch thereon have aggravated the distrust. In these circumstances, the only course open to one like me is either in despair to sever all connection with British rule, or if I still retain the faith in the inherent superiority of British Constitution to all others at present in vogue, to adopt such means as will rectify the wrong done and thus restore confidence. I have not lost faith in such superiority and I am not without hope somehow or other, justice will yet be rendered if we show requisite capacity for suffering. It is then because I believe in British constitution that I have advised my Muslim friends to withdraw their support from your Excellency's Government, and the Hindus to join them."

The 31st of August was celebrated as a Khilafat day. A general hartal was declared and the Non-co-operation resolution began to be given effect to. Mahatma Gandhi, returning his medal in pursuance of the Non-co-operation resolution, wrote to the Viceroy: "Events have happened during the past month which have confirmed me in the opinion that the Imperial Government have acted in the Khilafat matter in an unscrupulous, immoral, and unjust manner and have been moving from wrong to wrong to defend their immorality. I can retain neither respect, nor affection for such Government. The attitude of the Imperial and your Excellency's Government on the Punjab question has given me additional cause for great dissatisfaction. Your Excellency's light-hearted treatment of official crime, your exoneration of Sir Michael ODwyer, Mr. Montagu's despatch and, above all, the shameful ignorance of the Punjab events and callous disregard of the feelings of Indians, betrayed by the House of Lords, have filled me with the gravest misgivings regarding the future of the Empire, have estranged me completely from the present Government and have disabled me from tendering, as I have hitherto wholeheartedly tendered, my loyal co-operation." The feeling in India became worse and worse, as the Government persisted more and more in its determination to disregard Muslim sentiments and as the House of Lords, in England, and the Anglo-Indians, residing in India, began more and more to support General Dyer who had perpetrated the Jallianwala Bagh massacre. The Europeans in India went so far as to open a Dyer appreciation fund and raised a large amount to be presented to him. Associations of Europeans and Ango-Indian papers vied with each other in extolling General Dyer's services.

The Calcutta Special Congress.—Mahatma Gandhi and Maulana Shaukat Ali toured through a great part of the country before the special session of the Congress which met at Calcutta, early in September, under the presidentship of Lala Lajpat Rai. After a long discussion, the Congress adopted the Non-co-operation resolution by a large majority. The resolution recited that, in view of the fact that in the matter of the Khilafat, Indian and Imperial Governments had signally failed in their duty towards the Mussalmans in India, that the Prime Minister had deliberately broken his pledged words and, further, in view of the fact that in the matter of the events of April, 1919, both the said Governments had grossly neglected or failed to protect the innocent people of the Punjab, punish officers guilty of unsoldierly and barbarous behaviour towords them, and had exonerated Sir Michael O'Dwyer and that the debate in the House of Lords betrayed a woeful lack of sympathy with the people of India and showed virtual support of the systematic terrorism and frightfulness adopted in the Punjab, the Congress was of opinion that there can be no contentment in India without redress of the two afore-mentioned wrongs, and the only effectual means to vindicate National honour and to prevent similar wrongs in future is the establishment of Swarajya.

The Congress was further of opinion that there was no course left open for the people of India, but to approve of and adopt the policy of progressive Non-violent Non-co-operation, until the said wrongs are righted and Swarajya is established. It accordingly advised: (*a*) surrender of titles and honorary offices and resignations from nominated seats in local bodies, (*b*) Refusal to attend Government levies, Darbars etc., (*c*)

Gradual withdrawal of children from schools and colleges owned, aided or controlled by Government, and the establishment of national schools and colleges in their place, (*d*) Gradual boycott of British Courts by lawyers and litigants, and establishment of private arbitration courts for the settlement of private disputes, (*e*) Refusal on the part of military, clerical and labouring classes to offer themselves as recruits for service in Mesopotamia, (*f*) Withdrawal by candidates of their candidature from the Reformed Councils and refusal on the part of the voters to vote for any candidate, and (*g*) Boycott of foreign goods. The Congress further advised adoption of Swadeshi in piece-goods on a vast scale and, to meet the requirements of the nation which could not be met by Indian Mills alone, it advised manufacture on a large scale by means of reviving hand spinning in every home and hand weaving on the part of millions of weavers who had abandoned their ancient and honorable calling for want of encouragement.

Mr. Bipin Chandra Pal's amendment which asked for a mission to be sent to the Prime Minister to lay before him a statement of Indian grievances, coupled with a demand for immediate autonomy, and in case of his refusal to receive this mission or to replace the Act of 1919 by a measure granting full autonomy to India, for the adoption of a policy of active Non-co-operation and, in the meantime, advising the consideration of Mahatma Gandhi's programme and the adoption of measures as preparatory to actual putting into practice of that programme, was, as stated above, thrown out in the Congress by a large majority.

The Non-co-operation Campaign.— The adoption of the Non-co-operation resolution by the Congress gave a great fillip to the Non-co-operation movement. To give effect to the Resolution of the Special Congress, a Sub-committee had been appointed in Calcutta to draft instructions. The report of the Sub-committee was considered by a meeting of the All-India Congress Committee on the 2nd October, and detailed instructions were issued. But some doubt was still entertained that at the annual sessions at Nagpur in December, the Congress would rescind the Non-co-operation resolution, passed at Calcutta. Mahatma Gandhi toured through the country amidst scenes of wild enthusiasm.

Mahatma Gandhi, accompanied by Maulana Mohammad Ali who returned from Europe in the first week of October, visited Aligarh on the 12th of October, and with this visit commenced that campaign againstGovernment-controlled educational institutions which became more and more intense for the following four or five months. An attempt was made to nationalise the M.A.O. College and a letter was addressed by some of the Non-co-operation leaders who were also trustees of the college to the other trustees, urging upon them the necessity of nationalising the institution. The trustees met on the 17th of October, 1920. Mahatma Gandhi also addressed a letter to them. They, however, decided to carry on the institution on the old lines, and a National Muslim University was inaugurated with Maulana Mohammad Ali as its Principal, under the presidentship of Sheik-ul-Hind Maulana Mohammad-ul-Hassan Sahib on the 29th of October. Mahatma Gandhi's visit to the Punjab created similar stir among students and there were whole-sale strikes and demand for nationalisation of the Lahore College, the Khalsa College and other educational institutions. On the 15th of November, the Gujrat National College was opened by Mahatma Gandhi and he was also appointed Chancellor of the Vidyapitha inaugurated there. Mr. Gidwani was appointed Principal of the College which started with 500 students. There was a strike at Benares among the students of the Hindu University. Early in December, Mahatma Gandhi visited Bihar and advised the opening of a National College which was done at Patna on the 5th of January, 1921. Tilak Mahavidyalaya was opened at Poona on the 11th of December.

The Nagpur Congress.—Things were going on in this way, when the Congress met again in its annual session at Nagpur under the presidentship of Mr. Vijiaraghava chariar. It changed its creed into the "attainment of Swarajya by the people of India by peaceful and legitimate means" and re-affirmed the resolution of Non-violent Non-co-operation, passed in Calcutta. It declared that the entire or any part of the scheme of Non-violent Non-co-operation with the renunciation of voluntary association with the present Government at one end and the refusal to pay taxes on the other should be put in force at a time to be determined by either the Indian National Congress or the All-India Congress Committee and that, in the meanwhile, to prepare the country for it effective steps should continue to be taken in that behalf by calling upon the guardians and parents of children under the age of 16 years and upon students of the age of 16 or over to withdraw them from Government-controlled educational institutions; by calling upon lawyers to make greater efforts to suspend their practice and to devote their attention to national service, including the boycott of law courts by fellow lawyers and litigants; by carrying out gradual boycott of foreign trade relations by encouraging hand spinning and hand weaving and generally calling upon every section and every man and woman in the country to make the utmost contribution of self-sacrifice; and, lastly, by organizing a committee in each village or group of villages with a Provincial Central Organization and a band of national workers to be called Indian National Service to be financed out of funds, called the All-India Tilak Memorial Swarajya Fund. The Congress further asked persons who had got themselves elected to the new Councils in spite of the deliberate abstention from the polls of an over-whelming majority of their constituents, to resign their seats and in the event of their failure to do so, it advised the people to studiously refrain from asking for any political service from such Councillors. The Congress recognized the growing friendliness between the police and soldiers and the people, and appealed to all people in Government employment, pending the call of the Nation for the resignation of their services, to help the national cause by importing greater kindliness and stricter honesty in their dealings with the people and fearlessly and openly to attend all popular gatherings, while refraining from taking any active part therein and more especially by openly rendering financial assistance to the National movement. The Congress laid special emphasis on Non-violence being an integral part of the Non-co-operation resolution and called upon public association to advance Hindu-Muslim unity and to settle all disputes between Brahmins and non-Brahmins, wherever they might be existing. It further called upon Hindus to rid Hinduism of the reproach of untouchability and respectfully urged the religious heads to help the growing desire to reform Hinduism in the matter of its treatment of the suppressed classes. The resolution was passed unanimously.

Thus closed the first phases of the Non-co-operation movement amidst scenes of great joy at the discovery of a means which the despairing people clasped with all their fervour as the only means of their delivery from the wrongs, oppression and humiliation to which they had been subjected for a series of years and which had culminated in the indescribable scene of the Punjab and the unspeakable betrayal of the Khilafat cause. The nation determined to win its way to Swarajya by suffering and, to-day, after twenty months have elapsed since that momentous decision was arrived at Nagpur, it may truly be said that the Nation has not flinched from any sacrifices which have been demanded of it by the course of events which will be presently described.

Progress of the Movement.—The months that followed were months of strenuous work. Never before in the history of India, since its connection with Britain, had popular indignation and popular enthusiasm been greater. Never before during this long period had the country secured the loving and unguiding services of so many of her sons. Never before had the faith of the people in themselves and in the country's ability to solve its own difficulties burned brighter.

As a result of the decision of the Congress, hundreds of lawyers throughout the country suspended practice in the law courts and began to devote themselves to the service of the country. Panchayats began to be organised and litigants began to avoid law courts. There was a great fall in the revenue from stamps throughout the country on account of the fall in the number of suits, instituted in the law courts. In regard to the educational programme, it may be safely asserted that thousands of college and school students withdrew themselves or were withdrawn from Government-controlled institutions by their guardians. Many a school became absolutely deserted. Mahatma Gandhi's appeal to the finer instincts of the youth of the country to devote themselves to its service and to shun the institutions which had been created and maintained to kill all manliness in them was responded to with enthusiasm. Nor was the work confined merely to boycott. National Universities, National Colleges, and National schools of all grades were started in different parts of the country. We have already referred to the student movement in the U.P., the Punjab, and the Bombay Presidency. Bengal was not behind hand and Calcutta witnessed one of those thrilling scenes which have not been few in the course of the last year and a half. About the middle of January, on an appeal by Desabandhu C. R. Das, thousands of students left their colleges and examinations. Mahatma Gandhi visited Calcutta and opened the National College on the 4th of February. He also visited Patna for a second time and formally opened the National College and inaugurated the Behar Vidyapith. Thus in the course of less than four months, the National Muslim University of Aligarh, the Gujrat Vidyapith, the Behar Vidyapith, the Benares Vidyapith, the Bengal National University, the Tilak Maharastra Vidyapith and a large number of national schools of all grades with thousands of students on the rolls were started in all parts of the country as a result of the great impetus given to National Education.

In the matter of the organisation of Swadeshi, the result achieved in popularising spinning wheels and the use of khaddar (hand spun and hand woven cloth) has been marvellous. In homes which had altogether forgotten even the name of charkha (spinning wheel) its musical hum can now be heard. It has invaded even the parlour of the rich, while it has given a source of livelihood to lakhs of poor women in the country.

Resignation of titles were few, but after all the title-holders form a class from whom from the nature of their position much was not to be expected. But there can be no doubt that nothing had lowered these titles in the estimation of the people so much as this movement. One thing which was not mentioned in the Congress resolution was spontaneously taken up by the people. People started a compaign against the evils of drink and a most marvellous progress was visible in all parts of the country, resulting in a great loss to the Government from Excise Revenue. Under the reformed constitution elections had, in the meantime, taken place, and His Royal Highness, the Duke of Cannaught, landed at Madras on 8th January and opened the Legislative Council there on the 12th. Under the Congress resolution, Mahatma Gandhi had advised a boycott of the Duke's visit, not by away of offering an insult to His Royal Highness, but as an expression of protest against the persistent refusal of the Government to listen to people's demands. Wherever the Duke went, the masses as a body and amongst the middle classes also most of those who were not directly concerned or connected with the Government observed hartals. His Royal Highness, after opening some of the Provincial Legislative Councils and the new Legislature at Delhi, left the country.

Non-violence.—Mahatma Gandhi had insisted on Non-violence as an essential feature of the movement and it was this insistence which had kept the people in spite of the great upheaval and the great indignation from committing acts of violence. Some incidents, however, occurred which, though not directly due to the N. C. O. movement, were, nevertheless, attributed to the stir and the awakening created by it. One of the earliest of these was the great agrarian movement in U. P. which had its origin in the agrarian trouble between landlords and tenants, on account of the latter's refusal to pay illegal and oppressive cesses. Large bodies of men collected at various place and several riots took place in several places. The police dispersed the mob by opening fire in some of these places, and it took more than a month to restore quiet. Another movement which having an independent origin was deeply affected by the N. C. O. movement has been the Akali movement of the Sikhs. Starting as a purely religious movement for the reform of the Sikh Gurdwaras,it has been more and more drawn into adopting the principles of the Non-co-operation movement by the conduct of the Government. In February occurred what is known as the Nankana tragedy in which nearly two hundred sikhs lost their lives amidst scenes of indescribable horror. The news created great indignation among Sikhs and others in all parts of the country and Mahatma Gandhi had to visit the Punjab early in March.

The Reaction of the Government to the Movement.—The Government had watched the growth of the movement. It first tried to pooh-pooh it. In August 1920, Lord Chelmsford had described it as "the most foolish of all foolish schemes". Subsequently the Government of India issued a communique on the 6th November 1920, stating that the Government had refrained from instituting criminal proceedings, because the promoters of the movement had advocated simultaneously with Non-co-operation, abstention from violence and that "they had instructed local Government to take action against those persons only who in furtherance of the movement had gone beyond the limits originally set by its organisers and had by speech or writing incited the public to violence or had attempted to tamper with the loyalty of the army or the police." This restriction was, however, not observed in practice and from the beginning of March onwards, the country passed through a tide of repression, culminating in the months of November and December in the suppression of volunteer organisations, the promulgation of the Seditious Meetings Act and the arrest and the incarceration of thousands of Indians. The first acts of repression were in connection with the anti-drink campaign. A large number of volunteers were sent to jail for alleged offences in connection with the picketing of liquor shops. Others were dealt with under secs. 107 and 108 of the Cr. P. C. and on their refusal to furnish security for good behaviour were sent to jail. Sec. 144 Cr. P. C. has been used with great effect, but with very doubtful legality in prohibiting public meetings and gagging individuals. The province of Behar was the first to witness repression on an extensive scale which was inaugurated with a circular, issued by the Government giving local officers a *carte blanche* in regard to any steps they might think necessary to counteract the movement which was described as revolutionary and anarchical. The Government of the Punjab and the U. P. were not slow to follow in their efforts to combat the movement and the Seditious Meetings Act and the provision of the ordinary law were freely resorted to, even where there was no justification for their use. One notable incident which deserves mention was the prohibition of N. C. O. meetings in the Malabar district and the subsequent arrest and imprisonment of Mr. Yakub Hassan and others, the former one of the most respected among the Mussalman leaders, for disobeying the prohibition order.

The Bezwada Programme.—It was at a time when the

Congress propaganda was making such rapid progress and the country passing through the first spell of repression that the All-India Congress Committee met at Bezwada in the last week of March 1921, and chalked out a programme of work for the following three months. It required that, before the 30th of June 1921, the Congress should raise one crore of rupees for the Tilak Swarajya Fund, enrol one crore of members for the Congress and see 20 lakhs of spinning wheels working in the country. On account of policy of repession started by the Government which was held by the Committee to be totally unwarranted by the situation in the country, there was a desire expressed by many of the members that Civil Disobedience should be resorted to. The Committee however held that the country was not yet sufficiently disciplined, organised or ripe for the immediate taking up of Civil Disobedience, and it advised all those upon whom orders might be served voluntarily to conform to them, trusting that new workers would take the place of those disabled by the Government and that the people at large, instead of becoming frightened or disheartened, would continue their work of quite organisation and construction. The following months witnessed tremendous efforts by the thousands of workers spread all over the country and engaged in organising it to fulfil the programme sketched out at Bezwada, and when the 30th of June was reached, Mahatma Gandhi could safely declare that the nation had collected the requisite sum, and although the number of members enrolled and charkhas was not accurately known, there was no doubt that the programme in this respect also had been nearly if not altogether fulfilled. Mahatma Gandhi himself had been as unremitting in his labours as ever, carrying the gospel of Non-co-operation and Non-violence from district to district wherever he went. Thousands of men and women assembled to have a glimpse of the great hero. Railway lines and stations were lined by thousands of spectators who showered their love in the shape of flowers and money wherever the train carrying the Mahatma happened to pass by them.

Malegaon and other Disturbances.—While the country was engaged in this constructive work, there occurred a riot at Malegaon in the Nasik district resulting in the death of several policemen and also some of the mob and acts of incendiarism. There was also a disturbance at Giridih in Behar in which, however, there was no loss of life. Early in May 1921, there was labour trouble in the tea province of Assam on account of low wages and a great exodus of about 12,000 coolies from tea gardens amidst scenes of great destitution and suffering. There was an attack on these coolies at Chandpur where they had congregated in large numbers by Gurkhas who had been drafted there by the Government. The news of this outrage caused great indignation in the country and led to a sympathetic strike among the Railway and steamer employees in Eastern Bengal which created a complete deadlock for nearly two months.

Gandhi-Reading Interview.—Another event which requires mention is the interview between Mahatma Gandhi and Lord Reading which extended over several hours and led to a great deal of speculation about its subject matter. Pandit Madan Mohan Malaviya and Lala Lajpat Rai also had similar interviews. The details of the interview have never been published, but one incident was the publication of an apology by the Ali Brothers for the "unnecessary heat" of some of the passages of their speeches which had been construed by some as having a tendency to incite to violence. They further gave an assurance that, so long as they were associated with the movement of Non-co-operation, they would not directly or indirectly advocate violence. The Government of India on the 30th May, issued a communique stating that they had suspended action against the Ali Brothers on account of their undertaking and apology. Lord Reading in a speech at the Chelmsford Club referred to this incident as a result of the interviews which he had with Mahatma Gandhi. The subject excited comment amongst friends and foes alike. The Non-co-operators saw in it a lapse from the high ideal of Non-co-operation, while opponents tried to discredit the brave brothers by reading in it an attempt to save their skins by offering an undertaking. It was not until Mahatma Gandhi had obtained the publication of an account of the interview * with the Viceroy's consent from which it was made clear that the Mahatma had agreed to secure an apology from the Ali Brothers for certain passages in their speeches calculated to incite to violence and that it was after the promise had been given that the proposal to institute criminal proceedings were mentioned by the Viceroy that the controversy came to a close.

The Karachi Khilafat Conference.—On the 8th of July, the All-India Khilafat Conference opened at Karachi with Maulana Mohamed Ali in the chair. The proceedings of the conference formed later on the subject matter of the prosecution of the Ali Brothers, Dr. Kitchlew, Jagat Guru Shankaracharya of Shardapeeth, Maulana Nisar Ahmed, Pir Gulam Mujadid and Maulvi Hussain Ahmed. While reiterating the Muslim demands, the Conference also passed a resolution declaring it "unlawful for any faithful Mussalman to serve from that day in the

* *See* p. 1107.

army or help or acquiesce in their recruitment." It also declared that, if the British Government fought the Angora Government, the Muslims of India would start Civil Disobedience and establish their complete independence and hoist the flag of the Indian Republic at the Ahmedabad session of the Indian National Congress.

The A. I. C. C. Meeting at Bombay.—On July 28 the All-India Congress Committee met again at Bombay. It was the first All-India Congress Committee elected under the new constitution adopted at the Nagpur Congress. The appearance of the members all clad in white *Khadi* was in keeping with the ideals of plain living held up before the country by the simple life of the Mahatma. The Committee passed a resolution declaring that it is the duty of every one, in terms and in virtue of the Non-co-operation Resolution passed by the Special Congress and reaffirmed at Nagpur, to refrain from participating in or assisting any welcome to H. R. H. The Prince of Wales. While tendering this advice, the Committee placed "on record its opinion that India bears no sort of ill-feeling against the person of H. R. H. and that the advice is tendered because the Committee regards the proposed visit as a political move calculated to give strength and support to a system of government that has resulted in breach of faith with the Mussalmans and atrocious injustice to the people of India, and the system that is designed to keep India as long as possible from her birthright of Swaraj." The 2nd resolution, after congratulating the nation on carrying out the Bezwada programme, asked it to concentrate its attention upon attaining complete boycott of foreign cloth by the 30th of September and manufacture of Khaddar by stimulating hand-spinning and hand-weaving and advised all persons belonging to the Congress to discard the use of foreign cloth from the first of August and all Congress organisations to collect foreign cloth from consumers for destruction or use outside India. It also invited Indian mill agents to support the national effort by regulating the price of their manufactures so as to bring them within the reach of the poorest and the importers of foreign cloth and yarn to co-operate with the nation by stopping foreign orders and by disposing of their stock as far as possible outside India. The 3rd resolution noted with satisfaction the growth of public opinion and the campaign against the use and sale of intoxicating liquors or drugs by peaceful picketing and warned the Government that in case of continued improper interference with peaceful picketing it would advise its continuance in disregard of such orders. It appealed to local Boards or Municipalities to follow the lead of the Thana District Board by passing resolutions on picketing and it invited keepers of liquor and drug shops to discontinue them. The 4th resolution deplored the excesses at Malegaon and in Aligarh even though under great provocation and advised Congress organisations to inculcate Non-violence as an essential part of Non-co-operation and congratulated the people upon their exercising complete self-restraint notwithstanding grave provocation by local authorities in Dharwar, Matiari, Guntur and other places. It congratulated the families of those who had lost their lives by the unprovoked fire of the authorities at several places and also those brave and innocent citizens who had been wounded or were suffering imprisonment. The resolution, while taking note of Government repression and of the reasonable desire of the workers to take up Civil Disobedience, held that Civil Disobedience should be postponed till after the completion of the Swadeshi programme which it regarded as a test of the measure of influence attained by the Congress and a guarantee of the stability of non-violent atmosphere. It, however, authorised the Working Committee to sanction Civil Disobedience in any place or province.

The Arrest of the Muslim Leaders.—The 31st July witnessed the burning of a huge pile of foreign-cloth at Bombay by Mahatma Gandhi. The following day was the death anniversary of the great Lokamanya Tilak and was celebrated all over the country. Mahatma Gandhi and Maulana Mahomed Ali started on a tour through Behar, Assam and Madras. It was in the month of August that the Moplah out-break which was not suppressed for several months broke out. The Mahatma and Maulana Mahomed Ali were going from Calcutta to Malabar to pacify the rioters, but they were not allowed and Maulana Mahomed Ali was arrested in the train at Waltair on the 14th September, 1921, under a warrant of the District Magistrate of Vizagapatam to show cause why he should not be bound over to keep the peace under sec. 107 or 108 Cr. P. C. On the 17th, he was however re-arrested under a warrant from Karachi and taken by special train. Maulana Shaukat Ali was arrested at Bombay, Dr. Kitchlew at Simla, and Pir Gulam Mujadid in Sindh, while Maulana Nisar Ahmed, Hassan Ahmed and Shree Shankaracharya were also brought under arrest. It became known that the arrests had been made on account of the resolution passed at the Karachi Khilafat Conference regarding the duties of Muslims not to serve the army which had been based on a *Fatwa* given by five hundred of the most respected Moslem Divines. On the 21st September, the Central Khilafat Committee and the Jamiat-ul-Ulema met at Delhi under the presidency of

Hakim Ajmal Khan and resolved to reprint the *Fatwa* for distribution and to repeat the Karachi resolution. Hundreds of meetings began to be held all over the country where the Karachi resolution was repeated, word by word, bv each member of the audience. On the 4th of October, Mahatma Gandhi and about 50 other prominent Congressmen issued a manifesto asserting the right of every citizen to express his opinion regarding the propriety or otherwise of individuals joining or remaining in the Civil or Military service of the Government. It further proceeded to state it as their opinion that it was contrary to national dignity for an Indian to serve as a civilian and more specially as a soldier under a system of government which had brought about India's economic, moral and political degradation and which had used the soldiery and the police for repressing national aspiration at home and for crushing the liberty of other nations, who had done no harm to India, abroad. It also expressed its opinion that it was the duty of every Indian soldier and civilian to sever his connection with the Government and find some other means of livelihood.

Their Trial and After.—The trial of the Ali brothers and others was held at Karachi and ended in the acquittal of Shree Shankaracharya on all the charges and the conviction and sentence of the other accused persons to two years rigorous imprisonment. The stand taken by the accused was that Muslims were forbidden by their religion from serving a State which had put itself in opposition to their religious injunction and it was the duty of every Mussalman to preach to his co-religionists to refrain from serving the Government. They were therefore bound by their religious creed to preach it, any secular or temporal laws to the contrary notwithstanding.

The Working Committee of the Congress met at

Bombay on the 5th October and practically affirmed the manifesto issued on the previous evening and advised a voluntary hartal on the day of landing of H. R. H. the Prince of Wales and a boycott of all public welcome during his visit to the different cities of India.

The A. I. C. C. Meeting at Delhi.—On the 4th of November, the All-India Congress Committee met at Delhi and endorsed the resolution of the Working Committee regarding the duty of Government servants whether civilians or soldiers. It passed another resolution authorising every province on its own responsibility to undertake Civil Disobedience including non-payment of taxes subject to the conditions that, in case of individual Civil Disobedience, the individual must know hand-spinning, must have fulfilled the part of the programme applicable to him, must be a believer in the unity of communities and in Non-violence as absolutely essential and if a Hindu must show by personal conduct that he regards untouchability as a blot upon nationalism. In the case of mass Civil Disobedience, it required the vast majority of the population of the area embarking upon Civil Disobedience to have adopted full Swadeshi and to believe in and practice all other items of Non-co-operation. It further laid down that civil resisters and their families should not expect to be supported out of public funds and it authorised the Working Committee to relax the condition in suitable cases.

The Prince's Visit and the Hartal.—On the 17th of November, 1921, H. R. H. the Prince of Wales landed in Bombay where he was received by Princes, officials, Europeans, Eurasians, Parsis and other rich persons. On the other hand, the middle and lower classes boycotted the welcome. Mobs got out of hand

and began to molest visitors to the reception. From small beginnings the riots assumed large proportions; mobs burnt tramcars, smashed liquor shops and even molested some Parsi ladies. Mahatma Gandhi who happened to be in Bombay holding a meeting in another part of the town rushed to the scene of occurrence to quieten the mob. He was deeply affected by the events and he determined to fast till the riots ceased. The riots lasted for several days and several persons were wounded and killed. The Mahatma declared that he had come deliberately to the conclusion that mass Civil Disobedience could not be started then as the atmosphere for it was absent and the cult of Non-violence had not been sufficiently imbibed by the masses. The hartal however in all the other cities and even in villages was not marred by any such incidents. No shops were opened, no vehicles for hire plied and even some public offices had to be closed on account of the inability of the officers to attend for want of conveyance.

Its Success and Results.—The success of the hartal produced great panic among all classes of Europeans and the Bengal Chamber of Commerce and the European Association of Calcutta pressed the Government to take immediate action. The Government of Lord Reading which had brought out the Prince in spite of the protests and warnings of the people felt sorely disappointed at the turn events had taken and decided to secure a welcome for the Prince at the point of the bayonet. On 19th November, the Government of Bengal declared the Khilafat and Congress Volunteer Corps and other similar bodies unlawful under sec. 16 of the Indian Criminal Law Amendment Act, 1908, which had been passed to suppress anarchical bodies and secret societies. The Non-co-operation leaders, on the other hand, issued a manifesto declaring that volunteer organisations had not interfered with the maintenance of law and order and as a challenge to the Government notification enrolled themselves as members of the volunteer corps. A long list of such civil resisters was published and an appeal was made to observe the 24th of December as a day of complete hartal on the occasion of the Prince's visit. Similar notifications declaring volunteer organisations unlawful were issued in the provinces of Delhi, the Punjab, the U. P., Assam and Bihar and Orissa and the challenge was similarly accepted by the people. In many places,the Seditious Meetings Act was also applied. The Working Committee of the Congress met at Bombay on the 22nd and 23rd and directed all Provincial Congress Committees to appoint Volunteer Boards in their respective Provinces for controlling and bringing under an uniform discipline all existing volunteer corps and gave them draft instructions for giving effect to it. It also suggested the form of a pledge to be signed by volunteers in which Non-violence was insisted upon and a promise made to observe instructions of superiors and to run all risks in the performance of their duties.

The Attack on Elementary Rights.—In the 1st week of December commenced what is known as the period of repression. Pandit Motilal Nehru, Mr. C. R. Das, Lala Lajpat Rai, Maulana Abul Kalam Azad, Mr. S. E. Stokes to mention some of the leaders only, and a large number of volunteers began to be arrested for violating the terms of the notification. Thousands of volunteers in different parts of the country offered themselves for arrest and were arrested and sentenced to various terms of imprisonment. There was a great flutter even in Moderate circles and their recognised leaders and association sent protests to the Government. Pandit

Madan Mohan Malaviya took a deputation to the Viceroy urging upon him the desirability of facing the situation and calling a Round Table Conference of the representatives of the people to make practical suggestions and recommendations to meet it. The deputation asked for a withdrawal of the notification under the Criminal Law Amendment Act and the Seditious Meetings Act and the release of the persons imprisoned under them. The Viceroy, however, was unable to accede to the request and repression went on. The Prince, in the midst of this after visiting various places where he had met with no popular welcome, arrived at Calcutta on the 24th December, which observed a complete hartal on the accasion. The Congress, the Khilafat, and the Muslim League also met at Ahmedabad in the same week.

The Ahamedabad Congress.—On account of the incarceration of Mr. C. R. Das who was the president-elect of the Congress, Hakim Ajmal Khan was elected to preside. The proceedings of the Congress did not last long and there was practically only one resolution passed by it. The Congress, after re-affirming the Non-co-operation resolution passed at its previous sessions, called upon all, in view of the repressive policy of the Government, to quietly and without any demonstration offer themselves for arrest by belonging to the Volunteer organisations and it further advised the holding of Committee meetings and even of public meetings under certain restrictions in spite of prohibitions. It declared that Civil Disobedience is the only civilised and effective substitute for armed rebellion* and

* Even political reactionaries should approve of this course if it becomes inevitable. "The Indian community . . . are struggling for the maintenance of a right and the removal of a degradation. Can we as Englishmen find fault with them for that? The only method of

advised Congress workers and others to organise individual and mass Civil Disobedience when the mass of the people have been sufficiently trained in the methods of non-violence. It called upon all students and the staff of national institutions to join the national volunteer corps. And, in view of the impending arrest of a large number of workers, the Congress, while requiring the ordinary machinery to remain in tact and to be utilised in the ordinary manner whenever feasible, appointed Mahatma Gandhi as the sole executive authority of the Congress and invested him with the full authority of the All-India Congress Committee and also with the power to appoint a successor in emergency, save that Mahatma Gandhi or any of his successors could not conclude any terms of peace with the Government without the previous sanction of the All-India Congress Committee to be finally satisfied by the Congress and that he could not change the creed. A resolution moved by Maulana Hasrat Mohani for a change in the creed of the Congress, so as to make complete independence the goal of the Congress, was thrown out by a large majority.

Intensive Repression.—In the following months, the repression policy of the Government was given full play and thousands of volunteers were sent to jail. Many of the leaders in several of the Provinces were also imprisoned and are still in jail. The history of these months is a history of unbridled arrests and incarcera-

---

protest, except that of violence and disorder, which is open to them, who have neither votes nor representation, is that of passive resistance. Can we find fault with them for that? Let him who blames them say what he would in similar circumstances. Is there one of us who, out of respect for the law, would submit meekly and without protest to deprivation of 'rights and social degradation?" *Lord Ampthill in his introduction to Doke's Life of Gandhi.*

ions on the one hand and a brave and undaunted acceptance of the challenge on the other. It can be truly asserted that the country had given an account of itself which is one to be proud of and even though the fruits of the sacrifice of 25,000 men and women are not yet visible, the sacrifice cannot have gone in vain.

Civil Disobedience and Chauri Chaura.—In the month of February, serious riots took place at a place called Chauri Chaura in the district of Gorakhpur and Mahatma Gandhi who had proceeded to Bardoli to lead a campaign of mass Civil Disobedience and had gone so far as to issue his message to the Viceroy* and Government intimating the initiation of mass Civil Disobedience had to suspend the campaign as consequence. On the 11th of February the Working Committee of the Congress met at Bardoli and suspended Civil Disobedience and called upon all Congress organisations to concentrate their efforts creating an atmosphere of non-violence and further strengthening the Congress organisations by improving the panchayats and national educational institutions established under it, by enrolling members for the Congress, by stimulating the use of spinning wheels and production of Khaddar, by the raising of suppressed classes by removing untouchability and by collecting money for the Tilak Swarajya Fund to carry on the Congress work. Mahatma Gandhi observed a five day's fast as a penance for the Chauri Chaura tragedy. The All-India Congress Committee met at Delhi on the 24th of February and practically affirmed the Bardoli resolutions of the Working Committee. With the Delhi session of the All-India Congress Committee, practically suspending Civil Disobedience, differences in the ranks of Non-co-operators

* *See* p. 966

began to manifest themselves. The Maharashtra Party moved what was a vote of censure on the Working Committee for the Bardoli resolutions and suggested a revision of the programme, but it was lost in the All-India Congress Committee. Many workers were dissatisfied with the suspension of Civil Disobedience and the constructive programme which chalked out a course of quiet and unostentatious work of organisation and consolidations of the national resources was regarded by many as throwing a wet blanket on the fire and fervour of the people.

The Mahatma's Arrest and After.—It was while things were moving on in this way that the Government had Mahatma Gandhi arrested on the 10th of March, tried for sedition and sentenced to six years' imprisonment. With the removal of Mahatma Gandhi from the scene of his labours where he had led the millions of India's masses, India has been deprived of the guidance of a world leader. The Congress Committees have been trying to carry on the constructive programme laid down at Bardoli. When the All-India Congress Committee met at Lucknow on the 7th of June, great dissatisfaction with the present programme and an earnest desire to resort to Civil Disobedience was expressed by many members. The Committee, however, ultimately appealed to the country to concentrate its efforts upon carrying out the constructive programme and asked the President to appoint a Committee to report on the situation in the country as regards its preparedness for Civil Disobedience at its next meeting. The Civil Disobedience Enquiry Committee appointed in terms of this resolution has been touring the country and is expected to issue its report in a few days to be considered by the All-India Congress Committee.

Here closes a narrative of events. The reader will find the principles, the faith and the inspiration of the N. C. O. movement and the Non-co-operators in the words of its originator in the pages of *Young India* reprinted hereinafter for the behoof of the growing number of persons desirous of imbibing the true spirit from its fountain source.

Conclusion.—Looking back at the history of the last 2 years one finds that the country as a whole has been roused more than ever before during the period of its occupation by Britain. Within a few months of the Nagpur Congress, there was hardly a village or hamlet to which the message of Swaraj had not been carried. The feeling of helplessness and despair gave place to one of buoyant hope and faith in the destiny of the country. People have for once realised their strength and feel that strong as the Government may appear with its armaments, it cannot but fall at the feet of a nation determined to be free and determined to suffer for attaining that freedom. They know that all their troubles and humiliations are of their own making, and the moment they are united and organised enough they can bring the Government to its knees. To this end, unity between Hindus, Mussalmans, Sikhs, Parsis, Christians, Jew and other races and communities of the country is regarded as the first and most important step. To this end a perfect organisation of Panchayats linking village to village, District to District, Province to Province and all these into one whole, is looked upon as a *sine qua non* of success in this momentous struggle. To this end also the production and propagation of Khaddar to free the nation from economical thraldom in respect of one of the necessaries of life is calculated to lead. And last, though not least, to this end, too, is directed the effort to purge society of social evils, such as drinking and litigiousness and of the sin of untouchability which condemns a vest proportion of the population to a position worse than that of lower animals. The movement is essentially a movement intended and expected to strengthen and purify the Indian people. It relies more and more upon the moral strength and superiority of the peoples of India —a strength and superiority born of the purity of their aims and purity of their methods—than upon naked brute force which is inherently weak. Therefore it is that it has made an irresistible appeal to India. May her efforts to relieve herself from the present position of bondage, humiliation and dishonour without recourse to arms be successful and thus pave the way for the freedom of a world sick with a state of things in which Justice, Truth, Honour and the divine virtue of Charity count for nothing before the imperious demands of Imperialism and Capitalism.

31st August, 1922. RAJENDRA PRASAD.

Supplementary Note to the Second edition.—The history of the Non-co-operation movement is so much the history of its inaugurator himself that no sooner was he sealed up within the prison walls of Yerowada than the movement showed signs of stagnation. The Government, after sounding the position carefully, appears to have concluded that with Gandhi's masterful personality once out of their way, they could go about with easy hearts dealing contemptuously with the minor fry in Indian politics by the well-known process of putting the steam-roller of repression into active and ruthless operation.

The Congress fully realised the significance of this and so callous and unjust had repression become that many advocated Civil Disobedience to be enforced forthwith. But Civil Disobedience, as Mahatma Gandhi was never tired of stating, required certain anterior conditions to be fulfilled and these conditions the Congress Civil Disobedience Committee found had not been fulfilled and would not, in the very near future, be fulfilled. That Committee found that while Mahatmaji's gospel had taken roots in exteriors, the people had lost sight of the essential spiritual foundations of the great movement. "The depression in the country" was acknowledged and so was the need for removing it. Only two courses, so it was held, could remove it. The immediate adoption of Civil Disobedience was the one; the modification of the rigid Programme, the other. The former was out of the question and the latter became, so to say, a virtual apple of discord among Indian politicians. The Civil Disobedience Committee itself could not come to any unanimous decision on the points referred to it, especially in regard to the vexed question of council entry. In regard to the others, it adopted the positive basis of the Gandhi programme, the constructive programme as it has come to be known, and the virtual suspension of its negative or the destructive portion.

The emergence of the Swarajya Party.—But the constructive programme lacked spice and eventually a party grew up, the Swarajya Party, within the Congress which sought to rouse up the drooping enthusiasm of the country by adopting the war cry of "entering the councils to destroy them" and of "bearding the bureaucracy in its own den." This Party's programme did not, of course, find favour with the strict followers of Mahatma Gandhi, for, it was so much opposed on principle to the Non-co-operation of which Mahatma Gandhi is the apostle. The wrangle between these two parties in the Congress, and the many makeshifts, compromises and understandings which were negotiated among these make up indeed the history of the Congress between the years 1922 and 1924. The Swarajists, led, as they were, by such self-sacrificing patriots as Pandit Motilal Nehru and Mr. C. R. Das, won their way to some kind of recognition of their position within the Congress and they managed to get a sort of benevolent neutrality for their programme from the Congress. This result was not easily brought about. The patch-up was the work of three notable consultations—the meeting of the All-India Congress Committee at Bombay, the Special Congress at Delhi and the session of the Congress held at Cocanada.

Mahatma's illness and release.—Now to revert to the story of Mahatma Gandhi, Mahatmaji had little knowledge of the trials the country was undergoing nor, the ideal prisoner that he was, did he seek to put himself in touch with these developments. Between 18th March

1922, when the prison walls closed on him and 5th February 1924, the date of his release, the politics of India were a sealed book for him. Nor did the outside world know much of his life within the jail. Occasional alarming rumours about his ill-health were quickly followed by official and non-official reassurances that he was all right. On the 13th of January, however, India was taken aback at the painful news that Mahatmaji had contracted appendicitis and that he had been operated upon successfully by Col. Maddock at the Sassoon Hospital, Poona, to whose courage, skill and defiance of red-tape, we in India owe a debt of gratitude which cannot be adequately repaid. In view of the illness, the Government released him from prison, of course unconditionally. He did not leave the hospital, however, till March 10th on the night of which date he was privately removed to Juhu, a seaside resort, a few miles from Bombay. He stayed at this station to recoup his health for nearly three months and, before he left for Ahmedabad Ashram, had resumed charge of his journals, *Young India* and *Navajivan*, and begun proclaiming his strict adherence to his original gospel.

Mahatma Gandhi on the situation in the country.—No sooner did Mahatma Gandhi complete his survey of the situation than he lost no time in proclaiming that he had no remedy for the ills of India other than his spiritual weapon of Non-co-operation. The tinkering of that weapon to suit the inclinations of the Swarajya Party found no favour with him. Not that he wished to impose his remedy on unwilling men. As ever, he laid emphasis on the quality of workers and deprecated evaluating work on the basis of numerical strength behind it. The Swarajists demurred to his view. He gave them full freedom of action on their own responsibility. The fact that the Congress and the country, the *intelligentsia* at any rate, had their faith in Non-co-operation in all its prestine purity on the wane pained him evidently, but it did not upset him. He gave them freedom of action to the full, but, like Galileo the Astronomer, repeated that he was right. He has again set himself to the task of re-educating the country; and India is pleased that from his journals have begun to pour forth week in and week out those virile thoughts of purity, strength, and consolation which they used to do before his incarceration.

Of the future fortunes of the movement, we cannot, of course, say, anything for certain, but it is significant, that Mahatma Gandhi is more confident than ever that in Non-violent Non-co-operation lies the ultimate salvation of India.

July 1924.

YOUNG INDIA

8th October, 1919

TO THE SUBSCRIBERS AND THE READERS

(By M. K. Gandhi)

"YOUNG INDIA" from this week* enters upon a new stage. It became a bi-weekly when Mr. Horniman was deported and the "Chronicle" was strangled. Ever since the "Chronicle's" re-birth, the syndicate and I have been considering the advisability of reverting to the weekly issue. The conversion of "Nava Jivan" into a weekly and its coming under my charge has hastened the decision. The burden of conducting a bi-weekly and a weekly is too great a strain on me and a weekly "Young India" will now serve almost as well as a bi-weekly. An endeavour will be made to give as much matter as was given in the bi-weekly. The annual subscription will now be Rs. 4 instead of Rs. 8 and the price of a single copy will be one anna instead of two without postage. Subscribers may either have the balance due to this change returned to them or the amount

* See Introduction for the past history of the paper.

may be credited to the next year's account. Those subscribers who may be dissatisfied with the change can have the proportionate payment refunded to them on application.

The headquarters of "Young India" have been transferred to Ahmedabad for better management, and in order to enable me to devote some time to the Satyagrah Ashram which, owing to my continued absence from it, was being somewhat neglected by me. Moreover, it was obviously uneconomical in every respect to edit two papers at two different places. This deprives me of the privilege of being with Bombay friends as much as I have lately been. But I hope they will forgive me, if the new arrangement results, as I hope it will, in greater service to the country.

"Young India" has hitherto been chiefly occupied in dealing with the Punjab affairs. But one may reasonably hope that the cloud will lift in the near future.

What will "Young India" then present to its readers? I frankly confess that to me, editing a newspaper in English, is no pleasure. I feel that, in occupying myself with that work, I am not making the best use of my time. And, but for the Madras Presidency, I should now leave the work of editing "Young India." It is true that I should at times like to make my views in matters of general interest known to the Government. But I do not need to control a newspaper merely for that purpose.

The editing of "Nava Jivan" has been a perfect revelation to me. Whilst "Young India" has a little more than 1,200 subscribers, "Nava Jivan" has 12,000. The number would leap to 20,000 if we would but get printers to print that number. It shows that a vernacular newspaper is a felt want. I am proud to think that I have numerous readers among farmers and workers. They make India. Their poverty is India's curse and crime. Their prosperity alone can make India a country fit to live in. They represent nearly 80 p.c. of India's population. The English journals touch but the fringe of the ocean of India's population.

Whilst therefore I hold it to be the duty of every English-knowing Indian to translate the best of the English thought in the vernaculars for the benefit of the masses, I recognise that for a few years to come, *i.e.*, until we have accepted Hindustani as the common medium among the cultured classes and until Hindustani becomes compulsory in our schools as a second language, educated India, especially in the Madras Presidency, must be addressed in English.

But I will not be party to editing a newspaper that does not pay its way. "Young India" cannot pay its way unless it has at least 2,500 paying subscribers. I must appeal to my Tamil friends to see to it that the requisite number of subscribers is found, if they wish to see "Young India" continued.

The more so now, because the proprietors of "Young India" have decided to give up all advertisements. I know that they have not been entirely, if at all, converted to my view that a newspaper ought to be conducted without advertisements. But they are willing to let me make the experiment. I invite those who wish to see "Young India" free from the curse of advertisements to help me to make the venture a success. The Gujarati "Nava Jivan" has already demonstrated the possibility of conducting a newspaper without advertisements soiling its pages. What a financial gain it would be to the country, if there was for each province only one advertising medium—not a newspaper—containing innocent, unvarnished notices of things useful for the public! But for our criminal indifference, we would decline to pay the huge indirect taxation by way of mischievous advertisements. Some readers who are interested in the purity of journalism recently sent me a most indecent advertisement extracted from a well-known newspaper. I have refused to soil the pages of "Nava Jivan" by reproducing it. But any one turning to the advertisement sheets of even leading journals can verify the aptness of my criticism.

A word as to the policy of "Young India." Apart from its duty of drawing attention to injustices to individuals, it will devote its attention to constructive Satyagraha as also sometimes cleansing Satyagraha. Cleansing Satyagraha is civil resistance where resistance becomes a duty to remove a persistent and degrading injustice such as the Rowlatt Act.

5th November, 1919

"RING OUT THE OLD, RING IN THE NEW"

We give below a translation of a leading article in the "Nava Jivan," dated 26th October, 1919, the Gujarati New Year Day:

It is difficult to strike the last year's balance. The War has ended but with little result. The hopes it nourished have remained unfulfilled. The Peace, which was expected to be a permanent one, has turned out to be one in name. The War which was greater than the *Mahabharat* War has been proved to be but a prelude to a still greater war. Wide-spread discontent hung all over France, America and England after the War—enough to bewilder one. All that has followed seems to be a huge enigma. Here, in India, we are faced with despair everywhere. It was confidently hoped that at the close of the

War, India would get something substantial, but the hope turned out to be false. For aught we know, the reforms * may not come. Even if they do, they will be worthless. The Congress-League Scheme, then the Delhi Congress Scheme and the subsequent schemes are now airy nothings. We have to wait and see. The Punjab has been a scene of most revolting episodes. Innocent lives have been lost. There reigned a reign of terror. The gulf between the rulers and ruled has been widened. In these matters it is impossible to strike a correct balance. What is the sum total on the credit side? Or is there something to be debited, and if so, what? Or is it that there is no credit side at all and we have simply to sum up the debit figures?

Was there any silver lining to such a thick, dark, cloud of despair? The sun of Satyagraha dawned all over India on the 6th of April. The clouds were scattered and the rays could be distinctly seen. But the sun underwent an eclipse in the Punjab and Ahmedabad and its shadows are still haunting us. And yet Satyagraha is again seen dawning on most minds, though slowly. There was *hartal* in many parts of India on the 17th of October, amid perfect peace and quiet. The Faithful passed that day in fasting and prayer. The Hindus participated in the Moslems' mourning, strengthened the latter's hopes and the bonds of union with them. It may now be very difficult to break the bonds.

If some one were to ask, "What was the greatest event of the last year?", we would unhesitatingly say, "It was the acceptance of Satyagraha,—however slightly, and consciously or unconsciously, both by the rulers

* The British Cabinet had announced that the grant of substantial constitutional reforms for India was under consideration.

and the ruled. And in proof of the statement we would cite *October the* 17*th*.

The hope of India lies in Satyagraha. And what is Satyagraha? It has often been described. But just as the sun cannot be *fully* described even by the myriad-tongued Sheshnaga,* so also the sun of Satyagraha cannot be adequately described. And though we always see the sun but know really very little of it, even so we do ever seem to see the sun of Satyagraha, but we know precious little about it.

The spheres of Satyagraha are Swadeshi, Social Reform and Political Reform. And in so far as these are based on Satyagraha, so far only, and no farther, is their permanence assured. The way of Satyagraha is distinct from the beaten track and it is not always easy to discover it. Few have ventured along that path and the footprints on it are few and far between and indistinct, and hence the people's dread of it. And still we clearly find people taking that course, be it ever so slowly.

He to whom Satyagraha means nothing more than Civil Disobedience has never understood Satyagraha. No doubt the rigid interpretation of Satyagraha does include within its meaning Civil Disobedience. But only he who has mastered the art of obedience to law knows the art of disobedience to law. Only he who thoroughly knows how to construct may destroy. The poet has sung:

"The path of Truth is the path of the brave,
It is beyond the power of the cowards."

Swadeshi is Satyagraha. It is beyond the power of

* The great snake in Hindu mythology on whom lies God Vishnu, the Protector in the Hindu Trinity. Shesha is reputed to possess a 1,000 tongues.

cowardly spirits to observe or to propagate Swadeshi. It is impossible for a coward to foster Hindu-Moslem Unity. It takes any one but a cowardly Musalman to receive a wound from a Hindu's dagger and *vice versa* and to preserve his mental balance. If both could master this much forbearance, Swarajya would be instantaneously obtained. There is none to forbid us the path of Satyagraha, and both Swadeshi and Hindu-Moslem Unity being in this essence religious, India would incidentally perform an act of religion. This then is our prayer for the New Year:

"Lord, lead India towards the path of Truth; this doing, teach her the religion of Swadeshi, and knit the Hindus, Musalmans, Parsis, Christians and Jews living in India closer together."

PART I

THE SATYAGRAHA MOVEMENT

PART I

THE SATYAGRAHA MOVEMENT

AN EXPOSITION AND GENERAL REVIEW.

THE following statement, submitted by Mr. Gandhi to the Hunter Committee, surveying the beginning of the Satyagraha Movement in India, was published in "Young India" of 5th November, 1919 and two or three consecutive issues:

General Principles.—For the past thirty years, I have been preaching and practising Satyagraha. The principles of Satyagraha, as I know it to-day, constitute a gradual evolution.

Satyagraha differs from Passive Resistance as the North Pole from the South. The latter has been conceived as a weapon of the weak and does not exclude the use of physical force or violence for the purpose of gaining one's end, whereas the former has been conceived as a weapon of the strongest and excludes the use of violence in any shape or form.

The term Satyagraha was coined by me in South Africa to express the force that the Indians there used for full eight years and it was coined in order to distinguish it from the movement then going on in the United Kingdom and South Africa under the name of Passive Resistance.

Its root meaning is holding on to Truth, hence Truth-force. I have also called it Love-force or Soul-force. In the application of Satyagraha, I discovered in the earliest stages that pursuit of Truth did not admit of violence being inflicted on one's opponent but that he must be weaned from error by patience and sympathy. For what appears to be Truth to the one may appear to be error to the other. And patience means self-suffering. So the doctrine came to mean vindication of Truth, not by infliction of suffering on the opponent, but on one's self.

But, on the political field, the struggle on behalf of the people mostly consists in opposing error in the shape of unjust laws. When you have failed to bring the error home to the law-giver by way of petitions and the like, the only remedy open to you, if you do not wish to submit to error, is to compel him by physical force to yield to you or by suffering in your own person by inviting the penalty for the breach of the law. Hence Satyagraha largely appears to the public as Civil Disobedience or Civil Resistance. It is civil in the sense that it is not criminal.

The law-breaker breaks the law surreptitiously and tries to avoid the penalty; not so the civil resister. He ever obeys the laws of the State to which he belongs, not out of fear of the sanctions, but because he considers them to be good for the welfare of society. But there come occasions, generally rare, when he considers certain laws to be so unjust as to render obedience to them a dishonour. He then openly and civilly breaks them and quietly suffers the penalty for their breach. And in order to register his protest against the action of the law givers, it is open to him to withdraw his co-operation from the State by disobeying such other laws whose breach does not involve moral turpitude.

In my opinion, the beauty and efficacy of Satyagraha are so great and the doctrine so simple that it can be preached even to children. It was preached by me to thousands of men, women and children commonly called indentured Indians with excellent results.

Rowlatt Bills.—When the Rowlatt Bills were published, I felt that they were so restrictive of human liberty that they must be resisted to the utmost. I observed too that the opposition to them was universal among Indians. I submit that no State, however despotic, has the right to enact laws which are repugnant to the whole body of the people, much less a government guided by constitutional usage and precedent such as the Indian Government. I felt too that the oncoming agitation needed a definite direction if it was neither to collapse nor to run into violent channels.

The 6th April.—I ventured therefore to present Satyagraha to the country, emphasising its Civil Resistance aspect. And, as it is purely an inward and purifying movement, I suggested the observance of fast, prayer and suspension of all work for one day—the 6th of April. There was a magnificent response throughout the length and breadth of India, even in little villages, although there was no organization and no great previous preparation. The idea was given to the public as soon as it was conceived. On the 6th April, there was no violence used by the people and no collision with the police worth naming. The *hartal* was purely voluntary and spontaneous. I attach hereto the letter* in which the idea was announced.

* The letter emphasised the purifying aspect of the movement and urged that absolutely no compulsion or pressure should be used.

My arrest.—The observance of the 6th April, was to be followed by Civil Disobedience. For that the Committee of the Satyagraha Sabha had selected certain political laws for disobedience. And we commenced the distribution of prohibited literature of a perfectly healthy type, *e.g.*, a pamphlet written by me on Home Rule, a translation of Ruskin's 'Unto this Last', 'The Defence and Death of Socrates', etc.

Disorder.—But there is no doubt that the 6th of April found India vitalised as never before. The people who were fear-stricken ceased to fear authority. Moreover, hitherto the masses had lain inert. The leaders had not really acted upon them. They were undisciplined. They had found a new force but they did not know what it was and how to use it.

At Delhi, the leaders found it difficult to restrain the very large number of people who had remained unmoved before. At Amritsar, Dr. Satyapal was anxious that I should go there and show to the people the peaceful nature of Satyagraha. Swami Shraddhanandji from Delhi and Dr. Satyapal from Amritsar wrote to me asking me to go to their respective places for pacifying the people and for explaining to them the nature of Satyagraha. I had never been to Amritsar and, for that matter, to the Punjab before. These two messages were seen by the authorities and they knew that I was invited to both the places for peaceful purposes.

I left Bombay for Delhi and the Punjab on the 8th April, and had telegraphed to Dr. Satyapal whom I had never met before to meet me at Delhi. But, after passing Muttra, I was served with an order prohibiting me from entering the province of Delhi. I felt that I was bound to disregard this order and I proceeded on my journey.

At Palwal, I was served with an order prohibiting me from entering the Punjab and confining me to the Bombay Presidency. And I was arrested by a party of Police and taken off the train at that station. The Superintendent of the Police who arrested me acted with every courtesy. I was taken to Muttra by the first available train and thence by goods train early in the morning to Siwai Madhupur, where I joined the Bombay Mail from Peshawar and was taken charge of by Superintendent Bowring. I was discharged at Bombay on the 10th April.

But the people of Ahmedabad and Viramgam and in Gujarat generally had heard of my arrest. They became furious, shops were closed, crowds gathered, and murder, arson, pillage, wire-cutting and attempt at derailment followed.

Causes—I had worked in the midst of Kaira raiyats just before and had mixed among thousands of men and women. I had worked at the instance of and with Miss Ansuya Sarabhai among the mill-hands of Ahmedabad. The mill-hands appreciated her philanthropic work and adored her. The fury of the labourers in Ahmedabad reached white heat when a false rumour was started that she too was arrested. Both of us had visited and interceded for the mill-hands of Viramgam when they were in trouble. And it is my firm belief that the excesses were due to the great resentment of the mobs over my arrest and the rumoured arrest of Miss Ansuya Sarabhai.

I have mixed with the masses in practically the whole of India and talked to them freely. I do not believe that there was any revolutionary movement behind the excesses. They could hardly be dignified by the term rebellion.

Measures.—And in my opinion the Government erred in prosecuting the offenders for waging war. This view has caused unmerited or disproportionate suffering. The fine imposed on poor Ahmedabad was heavy and the manner of collecting it from the labourers was unnecessarily harsh and irritating. I doubt the justice of inflicting on the labourers a fine so large as 1,76,000 (one hundred and seventy-six thousand) rupees. The imposition of the cost from the farmers of Barejdi and from the Banias and Patidars of Nadiad was totally unjustified and even vindictive. I think that the introduction of Martial Law in Ahmedabad was also unjustified and its thoughtless administration resulted in the loss of several innocent lives.

At the same time, and subject to the reservations mentioned by me, I have no doubt that in the Bombay Presidency the authorities acted with considerable restraint at a time when the atmosphere was surcharged with mutual suspicion and the attempt at wrecking the train which was bringing the troops to restore order had naturally angered the authorities.

MR. GANDHI'S ORAL EVIDENCE

Examination by Lord Hunter.

Q. I take it, Mr. Gandhi, that you are the author of the Satyagraha movement.

A. Yes, Sir.

Q. Will you explain it briefly?

A. It is a movement intended to replace methods of violence and a movement based entirely upon Truth. It is, as I have conceived it, an extension of the domestic law on the political field and my experience has led me to the conclusion that that movement and that alone can rid India of the possibility of violence spreading throughout the length and breadth of the land, for the redress of grievances.

Q. It was adopted by you in connection with the opposition to the Rowlatt Act. And in that connection you asked the people to sign the Satyagraha pledge.

A. Yes, Sir.

Q. Was it your intention to enlist as many men as possible in the movement ?

A. Yes, consistently with the principles of Truth and Non-violence. If I got a million men ready to act according to those principles, I would not mind enlisting them all.

Q. Is it not a movement essentially antagonistic to Government because you substitute the determination of the Satyagraha Committee for the will of the Government ?

A. That is not the spirit in which the movement has been understood by the people.

Q. I ask you to look at it from the point of view of the Government. If you were a Governor yourself, what would you say to a movement that was started with the object of breaking those laws which your Committee determined ?

A. That would not be stating the whole case of the Satyagraha doctrine. If I were in charge of the Government and brought face to face with a body who, entirely in search of Truth, were determined to seek redress from unjust laws without inflicting violence, I would welcome it and would consider that they were the best constitutionalists, and, as a Governor, I would take them by my side as advisers who would keep me on the right path.

Q. People differ as to the justice or injustice of particular laws ?

A. That is the main reason why violence is eliminated and a Satyagrahi gives his opponent the same right of independence and feelings of liberty that he reserves to himself and he will fight by inflicting injuries on his person.

Lord Hunter.—I was looking at it from the point of view of the continuance of Government. Would it be possible to continue the Government if you had set up against the Government a body of men who would not accept the Government view but the view of an independent Committee ?

A. I have found from my experience that it was possible to do so during eight years of continuous struggle in South Africa. I found General Smuts, who went through the whole of that campaign, at the end of it saying that if all conducted themselves as the Satyagrahis had done, they should have nothing to fear.

Q. But there was no such pledge in that campaign as is prescribed here ?

A. Certainly there was. Every Satyagrahi was bound to resist all those laws which he considered to be unjust and which were not of a criminal character, in order to bend the Government to the will of the people.

Q. I understand your vow contemplates breaking of laws which a Committee may decide.

A. Yes, my Lord. I want to make it clear to the Committee that that part of the vow was meant to be a restraint on individual liberty. As I intended to make it a mass movement, I thought the constitution of some such Committee as we had appointed was necessary, so that no man should become a law unto himself, and, therefore, we conceived the plan that the Committee would be able to show what laws might be broken.

Q. We hear that doctors differ, and even Satyagrahis might differ ?

A. Yes, I found it so to my cost.

Q. Supposing a Satyagrahi was satisfied that a particular law was a just law and that the committee did not obey this law, what is a Satyagrahi to do ?

A. He is not bound to disobey that law. We had such Satyagrahis in abundance.

Q. Is it not rather a dangerous campaign ?

A. If you will conceive the campaign as designed in order to rid the country of violence, then you will share with me the same concern for it. I think that at any cost a movement of this character should live in the country in a purified state.

Q. By your pledge are you not binding a man's conscience ?

A. Not according to my interpretation of it. If my interpretation of the pledge is found to be incorrect, I shall mend my error if I have to start the movement again. (Lord H.—No, No, Mr. Gandhi, I do not pretend to advise you.)

I wish I could disabuse the Committee of the idea that it is a dangerous doctrine. It is conceived entirely with the object of ridding the country of the idea of violence.

Lord Hunter here briefly detailed the circumstances preceding the passage of the Rowlatt Act, the widespread general Indian opposition to the Act, etc., and asked Mr. Gandhi to describe the essence of his objection to the legislation.

A. I have read the Rowlatt Committee's report to the end and the legislation foreshadowed in it, and I came to the conclusion that the legislation was not warranted by the facts produced by the Committee. I thought it was very restrictive of human liberty and that no self-respecting person or nation could allow such legislation. When I saw the debates in the Legislative Council, I felt that the opposition to it was universal. When I found the agitation against it, I felt that for me, as a self-respecting individual and a member of a vast Empire, there was no course left open but to resist that law to the utmost.

Q. So far as the objects of that legislation are concerned, have you any doubt that they are to put down revolutionary and anarchical crimes?

A. They are quite laudable objects.

Q. Your complaint, then, must be as regards the methods adopted?

A. Entirely.

Q. The method is, I understand, that greater power has been given to the executive than they enjoyed before.

A. That is so.

Q. But is it not the same power that the executive enjoyed under the Defence of India Act?

A. That is true, but that was essentially an emergency measure designed to secure the co-operation of everybody in order to put down any violence that may be offered by any section of the community in connection with the successful carrying on of the War. It was assented to with the greatest reluctance. The Rowlatt legislation is of a different character altogether, and now the experience of the working of the former Act has strengthened my objections to the Rowlatt Act.

Q. Mr. Gandhi, the Rowlatt legislation is only to operate if the local Government is satisfied that there is anarchy.

A. I would not, as a legislator, leave that power in the hands of an executive whom I have known to run mad in India at times.

Q. Then, really, your objection comes to this, that the Government of India, in the prosecution of a laudable object, adopted a wrong method. Therefore, is not the proper method of dealing with that, from a constitutional point of view, to endeavour to get the legislation remedied by satisfying Government of the inexpediency of it?

A. I approached on bended knees Lord Chelmsford, and pleaded with him and with every English officer I had the pleasure of meeting, and placed my views before them, but they said they were helpless, and that the Rowlatt Committee's recommendations had to be given effect to. We had exhausted all the methods open to us.

Q. If an opponent differs from you, you cannot satisfy him all of a sudden. You must do it by degrees. Is it not rather a drastic way of attempting it by refusing to obey the law?

A. I respectfully beg to differ from your Lordship. If I find that even my father has imposed upon me a law which is repugnant to my conscience, I think it is the least drastic course that I could adopt by respectfully telling him that I cannot obey it. By that course I do nothing but justice to my father, and, if I may say so without any disrespect to the Committee, I have myself followed that course with the greatest advantage and I have preached that ever since. If it is not disrespectful to say so to my father, it is not so to say so to a friend and, for that matter, to my Government.

Lord Hunter.—In the prosecution of your Satyagraha movement against the Rowlatt legislation you resolved upon a general *hartal* thoughout India. That *hartal* was to be a day when no business was to be done and people were generally to indicate by their attitude that they disapproved of the Government's action. A *hartal* means a general cessation of business througout the whole country. Would it not create a very difficult situation ?

A. Cessation for a great length of time would create a difficult situation.

Mr. Gandhi here explained how the observance of the *hartal* in some parts of the country on the 30th March, and all over the country on the 6th April, came about, not on account of any miscalculation, but on account of the people in one part coming to know of the Viceregal assent to the Act earlier than the people in other parts.

Q. You agree that the abstention from work should be entirely voluntary ?

A. Yes, entirely voluntary, in the sense that persuasion on the day of the *hartal* would not be allowed, whereas persuasion by means of leaflets and other propaganda work on other days would be perfectly legitimate, so long as no physical force was employed.

Q. You disapprove of people interfering with *tongas* on the day of the *hartal* ?

A. Certainly.

Q. You would not object to the police interfering in the cause of such a disapprovable interference on the people's part ?

A. I would not, if they acted with proper restraint and forbearance.

Q. But you agree that on the day of the *hartal* it was highly improper to jostle with other people and stop *tongas* ?

A. From a Satyagrahi's standpoint I would hold it to be criminal.

Lord Hunter.—Your leading lieutenant in Delhi, Swami Shraddhananda—(Mr. Gandhi interrupting :—I would not call him my lieutenant, but an esteemed co-worker). —Did he write you a letter on the subject, and indicate to you that after what had occurred in Delhi and the Punjab, it was manifest that you could not present a general *hartal* without violence inevitably ensuing?

A. I cannot recall the contents of that letter. I think he went much further and said that it was not possible that the law-breaking campaign could be carried on with impunity among the masses. He did not refer to *hartal* proceeding. There was a difference of opinion between me and Swami Shraddhananda when I suspended Civil Disobedience. I found it necessary to suspend it because I had not obtained sufficient control, to my satisfaction, over the people. What Swami Shraddhananda said was that Satyagraha could not be taken as a mass movement. But I did not agree with his view and I do not know that he is not converted to my view to-day. The suspension of Civil Disobedience was as much necessary as prosecution for offences against law I would like the committee to draw a sharp distinction between *hartal* and Civil Disobedience. *Hartal* was designed to strike the imagination of the people and the Government. It was a discipline for those who were to offer Civil Disobedience. I had no means of understanding the mind of India except by some such striking movement. *Hartal* was a proper indication to me how far I would be able to carry Civil Disobedience.

Q. If there is a *hartal* side by side with the preaching of Satyagraha, would it not be calculated to promote violence?

A. My experience is entirely to the contrary. It was an amazing scene for me to see people collected in their thousands—men, women and even little children and babies marching peacefully in procession. The peaceful *hartals* would not have been at all possible if Satyagraha was not preached in the right way.

But, as I have said, a *hartal* is a different thing from Civil Disobedience in practice.

In further reply to Lord Hunter, Mr. Gandhi recounted the incidents connected with his 'so-called arrest' at Palwal. He characterised the proceeding of his being detained at Palwal and turned back to Bombay under escort as, in form and in substance, an arrest and he was surprised to find his arrest described in some quarters as his "supposed arrest." At Palwal he was served with an order prohibiting him from entering the Punjab and confining him to the Bombay Presidency. The Police Officer who served him with the order was exceedingly courteous to him. When he resolved to disregard the order prohibiting him from entering the Delhi Province, the Police Officer reasoned with him pointing out how much inconvenience would result in his being arrested at a small wayside station. When he proceeded to Palwal, he saw the Superintendent of Police, Delhi, with his officers and men. The officer placing his hand on his shoulder said, "Mr. Gandhi, I arrest you." He was asked to remove quickly his luggage from the train and to point out the men of his party who wished to accompany him. This was done. He was placed under the watch of some police constables; and to show that it was nothing else but a proper arrest, Mr. Gandhi said, when he went to the side of the platform to clear his throat, an officer challenged him. He did not mean to imply that the officer did anything wrong. He was doing nothing more than his duty.

Mr. Gandhi then described how the officer arresting him had no knowledge as to how he was going to be proceeded with, how he was taken to Sawai Madhupur and there joined the Punjab Mail in which he was left in charge of Mr. Bowring, how at daybreak next day

Mr. Bowring, after consultation with an officer who had joined him, told him that he would be free in Bombay.

Lord Hunter.—All that was required of you was that you were not to proceed to Delhi or the Punjab ?

Mr. Gandhi.—No, by the time I was arrested, I had already committed an offence by proceeding to Palwal. Therefore, I was not asked to go back to Bombay, but I was escorted.

Lord Hunter.—Then it amounted to this, that in consequence of a Government order it was made clear to you that you would not be allowed to proceed to Delhi or the Punjab and that if you remained in the Bombay Presidency, you would be allowed perfect freedom ?

Mr. Gandhi.—Yes.

Lord Hunter.—That is a little different from arresting you and throwing you into the jail. Is it not so, Mr. Gandhi ?

Mr. Gandhi.—Nobody made that assertion. The only complaint against Government is that they had no business to turn me away from my mission of peace.

Lord Hunter.—If the Government honestly thought that it would be inexpedient to allow you to go to a place to propagate your doctrine which was already in an excited state on account of that doctrine; then would you object ?

Mr. Gandhi.—From that standpoint, I have absolutely nothing to say.

Lord Hunter.—Subsequent to your arrest, serious incidents occurred in Delhi and the Punjab and also in Ahmedabad ?

Mr. Gandhi—Yes.

Lord Hunter.—Now, the only matters that we have got to deal with here are as regards Ahmedabad itself.

In Ahmedabad, as we have been told, you enjoy great popularity among the mill workers ?

Mr. Gandhi.—Yes.

Lord Hunter.—And your arrest seems to have caused great resentment on their part and led to the very unfortunate actions of the mob on April 10, 11 and 12, in Ahmedabad and Viramgam ?

Mr. Gandhi.—Yes.

Lord Hunter.—So far as those incidents are concerned, you have no personal knowledge of them ?

Mr. Gandhi.—No.

Lord Hunter.—I don't know whether there is anything that you can communicate to us in connection with those events to help us to form an opinion.

Mr. Gandhi.—I venture to present the opinion that I considered that the action of the mob, whether at Ahmedabad or at Viramgam, was totally unjustified, and I think that it was a very sad thing that they lost self-control. But, at the same time, I would like to say that the people among whom, rightly or wrongly, I was popular, were put to a severe test by Government. They should have known better. I do not say that the Government committed an unpardonable error of judgment and the mob committed no error. On the contrary, I hold that it was more unpardonable on the part of the mob than on the part of Government.

Proceeding, Mr. Gandhi narrated how he endeavoured to do what he could to repair the error. He placed himself entirely at the disposal of the authorities. He had a long interview with Mr. Pratt and other officials. He was to have held a meeting of the people on the 13th, but he was told that it would not be possible to hold it that day, not on account of Colonel Fraser's order, because he was promised every assistance in connection with the meeting, but that the notice of the meeting would not reach all the people that day. The meeting took place on the 14th. There he adumbrated what had happened. There he had to use the terms "organised" and "educated", both of which terms had been so much quoted against him and against the people. The speech was in Gujarati. Mr. Gandhi explained, and hoped Sir Chimanlal Setalvad would bear him out on a reference to the Gujarati speech, that the word only means those who can read and write, and that he used the word and expressed the opinion as he sensed the thing at that time.

He emphasised it was not a previous organisation that he meant; he only meant to say, and there could be no mistaking the actual words in his speech, that the acts were done in an *organised manner*. He further emphasised that he was speaking of Ahmedabad only, that he had then no knowledge of what had happened even at Viramgam, and that he would not retract a single statement from that speech. In his opinion, said Mr. Gandhi, violence was done in an organised manner. It cannot be interpreted to mean a deep-laid conspiracy. He laid special emphasis on the fact that, while he used these expressions, he was addressing the people and not the police authorities.

If Mr. Guider stated that a single name of the offenders was not forthcoming from him, he was entirely mistaken about his mission and had put an improper valuation upon the term "organisation." The crimes committed by the mob were the result of their being deluded by the wicked rumour of the arrest of Miss Anasuya. There was a class of half-educated people who possessed themselves with false ideas from sources such as cinematographs and from silly novels and from political leaders. He knew that school. He had mixed with them and endeavoured to wean them. He had so far succeeded in his endeavours that there were to-day hundreds of people who had ceased to belong to the school of revolution.

Proceeding, Mr. Gandhi said he had now given the whole meaning of what he had said. He had never meant that there were University men behind the disturbances. He did not say they were incapable of those acts, but he was not aware of any highly educated man directing the mob.

Lord Hunter.—Do you imply that there was a common purpose on the part of the rioters.

Mr. Gandhi.—I don't say that. It would be exaggerating to say that, but I think the common purpose was restricted to two or three men or parties who instigated the crimes.

Q. Did the agitation take an anti-European character?

A. It was certainly an anti-Government movement. I would fain believe it was not anti-European, but I have not yet made up my mind as to that.

Lord Hunter.—I do not know whether you want to answer this or not. According to the Satyagraha doctrine, is it right that people who have committed crimes should be punished by the civil authorities?

Mr. Gandhi.—It is a difficult question to answer, because, through punishment, you anticipate pressure from outside. I am not prepared to say that it is wrong, but there is a better method. But I think, on the whole, it would be proper to say that a Satyagrahi cannot possibly quarrel with any punishment that might be meted out to an offender and therefore he cannot be anti-Government in that sense.

Lord Hunter.—But apparently it is against the doctrine

of Satayagraha to give assistance to Government by way of placing the information that a Satyagrahi has that would lead to the conviction of offenders?

Mr. Gandhi.—According to the principles of Satyagraha, it is inconsistent for the simple reason that a Satyagrahi's business is not to assist the police in the method which is open to the police, but he helps the authorities and the police to make the people more law-abiding and more respectable to authority.

Lord Hunter.—Supposing a Satyagrahi has seen one of the more serious crimes committed in these riots in his own presence. Would there be no obligation on him to inform the police?

Mr. Gandhi.—Of course I answered that question to Mr. Guider before and I think I must answer it to Your Lordship. I don't want to misguide the youth of the country, but even then he cannot go against his own brother. When I say brother, I do not, of course, make any distinction of country or nationality. A Satyagrahi is wholly independent of such a distinction. The Satyagrahi's position is somewhat similar to that of a counsel defending an accused. I have known criminals of the deadliest type and I may humbly claim to have been instrumental in weaning them from crimes. I should be forfeiting their confidence if I disclosed the name of a single man. But supposing I found myself wanting in weaning them, I would surely not take the next step to go and inform the police about them: I do not hesitate to say that for a Satyagrahi it is the straightest thing not to give evidence of a crime done even under his nose. But there can be only the rarest uses of this doctrine and even to-day I am not able to say whether I would not give evidence against a criminal whom I saw caught in the act.

Asked as regards his view of the general situation, Mr. Gandhi said the impression made on his mind was that there was martial-law and that he thought that the Government acted under the greatest restraint and forbearance. He said he could understand troops in a train, which was attempted to be derailed, being infuriated and he would find it in his heart to excuse those troops of mad acts of fury. He thought that the terms in which the military notice was couched was entirely capable of misrepresentation. He thought the people were fired on without notice. There were, say, nine men going along, and a tenth man met them not wanting to be the tenth man. It cannot be proper to fire on them and probably there was no use in giving notice to those who probably did not know of the military proclamation at all.

Asked as to his views on the work of the two tribunals, Mr. Gandhi said, in his opinion, the Government erred in prosecuting the offenders for waging war. He must admit that the work of the tribunals was consistent with the laws of civilised justice. The sections under which the prosecutions were undertaken ought not to have been brought into use. That hasty view had caused unmerited and disproportionate suffering. The fine imposed on poor Ahmedabad was heavy and the manner of collecting it from the labourers was unnecessarily harsh and irritating. And he ventured to differ there from Mr. Ambalal's opinion as expressed by Lord Hunter and he felt that Mr. Ambalal had erred grievously against his people. He thought the action of Government in imposing the additonal police on Nadiad and Barejadi was totally unjustified. The arguments urged by the Collector of Nadiad for inflicting that fine were totally irrelevant and vindictive. He was satisfied that the people of Nadiad were not in league with those who went to derail the train but gave every assistance to Government to trace the offenders and got a handsome acknowledgment and compliment from the Collector for their assistance.

Examination by Mr. Justice Rankin.

Mr. Justice Rankin said he wanted to get some dates from Mr. Gandhi. In reply to him, Mr. Gandhi said the Satyagraha vow was taken on the third week of February, and agreed that the Rowlatt Bill No. 2 had not yet been passed.

Mr. Justice Rankin.—But before it was passed, the country was ringing with suggestions as to methods of protest against it and one of the forms of protest suggested was refusal to pay the revenue?

A. Yes.

Q. The orders passed by Magistrates were also to be disobeyed?

A. I opposed the proposal. I had asked the people in observing the *hartal* or Civil Disobedience that all police orders should be scrupulously carried out.

Mr. Justice Rankin asked Mr. Gandhi if he could substantiate his statement by any of his public declarations and Mr. Gandhi agreed to furnish what documentary evidence there was in his possession.

Q. In going to Delhi, it was not your intention to come into collision with the authorities.

A. No. I had received a letter from Dr. Satyapal, and Swami Shraddhanandji had asked me to go to Delhi as the people there were getting unamenable.

Q. He was not inviting you to pacify the people who had got out of his hands, but to promote the Satyagraha movement?

A. No, not to promote the movement. He said, 'I have failed,' and that I should go to pacify people there.

I was not going there to disobey Government laws for the purpose of the Satyagraha vow. I was proceeding to help the authorities.

Here also Mr. Justice Rankin asked Mr. Gandhi to supply any documentary evidence in his possession, as to the pacific intention of his mission.

Mr. Justice Rankin.—Mr. Gandhi, you say in your speech of the 14th April, that the action of the mob prevented you from carrying out your idea of going again to Delhi for re-arrest. It was not a passing thought, I suppose?

A. It was not a passing thought. It was my intention.

Q. What was your object in seeking re-arrest?

A. My object was to seek imprisonment again and again until the objectionable Act was removed.

Q. That is not the object of a Satyagrahi as I understand it.

A. It is not always. I did it in order to invite self-suffering.

Mr. Justice Rankin.—Was it your idea that that would inflame the country and be effective in removing the legislation?

Mr. Gandhi.—Not at all. If it was, I would have proceeded to Delhi straight away. I had no idea of what had occurred at Amritsar and elsewhere and had urgent messages from Ahmedabad the day after my arrival in Bombay.

Mr. Gandhi then explained why Civil Disobedience was suspended, why he again thought of starting it, but, yielding to the desire of Lord Chelmsford conveyed through the Government of Bombay, he desisted from re-starting it. He emphasised that during the interval various attempts were made to educate the people and there was even devised another vow by which people were asked to pledge themselves to the Truth part and Non-violence part of the former vow.

Q. Do you think that for India as a whole, by a misinterpretation of your doctrine, there has been an undue tendency to sympathise with lawlessness?

A. I don't think that it is so.

Mr. Justice Rankin.—Pardon the question, Mr. Gandhi. Do you feel having done anything to damage the law-abiding instincts of the people in India?

Mr. Gandhi.—I feel guilty of having temporarily damaged that instinct in certain people.

Mr. Justice Rankin.—There are certain parts in India, *e.g.*, the Punjab, where people were more liable to misinterpret your doctrine?

Mr. Gandhi.—No. There were certain people so liable to misinterpret. As to the Punjab, I have found there people who can best understand Satyagraha, and wherever I have gone I have met people who sincerely regret the excesses.

Mr. Justice Rankin.—You said, Mr. Gandhi, finding the laws by a Committee was meant as a restraint. Did you intend that each Province would have a separate Committee?

A. Yes, each was to have a separate Committee. But I was made President everywhere, so that we should have the same policy everywhere. But, of course, I did contemplate the contingency of different laws being broken in different places.

Mr. Gandhi then explained the difference between passive Resistance and Civil Disobedience and said Passive Resistance did not exhaust the methods of protest.

Examination by Sir Chimanlal Setalvad.

Sir Chimanlal.—With regard to your Satyagraha

doctrine, so far as I understand it, it involves the pursuit of Truth and in that pursuit you invite suffering on yourself and do not cause violence to anybody else.

Mr. Gandhi.—Yes, Sir.

Q. However honestly a man may strive in his search for Truth his notions of Truth may be different from the notions of others. Who then is to determine the truth* ?

A. The individual himself would determine that.

* "*I should suffer too for conscience sake.*—Under the preceding heading, *Young India* of 21st January 1920, wrote; The discussion that took place the other day between Sir Chimanlal Setalvad and Mr. Gandhi as regards the determination of Truth and qualifications necessary for one to be able to determine Truth, was not mere casuistry. Sir Chimanlal's questions and the answers he expected, reveal a distinct attitude of mind. Sir Chimanlal would not only deny every human being's right to determine truth for himself but even his capacity to do so. And he found Rao Bahadur Ramanbhai to nod assent to his views. This invertebrate attitude of mind takes no count either of human nature or of history. In every age and clime there have not been found wanting men who suffered for their conscience. The thousands of Dukhobars who went through years of untold suffering did not need any great intellectual and moral equipment to determine that military service was a crime. And General Smuts also once frankly admitted that the passive resisters he had imprisoned were suffering for conscience' sake. If you do not posit the essential virtue in man to be able to determine Truth for himself which alone separates him from the brute, you deny all human progress, and our national leaders if they have any faith in national progress, can ill ignore this basic principle. We commend to them the words of Gen. Smuts from an interview with Mr. Gandhi that took place in 1911:

" Gen Smuts—What are you doing in Johannesburg ?

Mr. G.—Looking after the families of passive resisters.

Gen. S.—It has hurt me more than you to imprison these people. It has been the unpleasantest episode of my life to imprison men who suffer for their conscience. *I should do the same thing for conscience sake.*

Following at the controversy, *Young India* wrote on 14th February 1920: Sir Chimanlal Setalved in his examination of Mr. Gandhi, asked if it did not require high intellectual and moral equipment to

Q. Different individuals would have different views as to Truth. Would that not lead to confusion?

A. I do not think so.

---

apprehend truth Replying to this question directly, in its note on 'Satyagraha,' the *Indian Social Reformer* says: "The question in our opinion, betrays a strange ignorance of what Truth is. The test and credential of truth is that it can be apprehended by all." Another question of Sir Chimanlal was equally noteworthy. He asked: "Honestly striving after truth is different in every case. Would that not lead to confusion?" Mr. Gandhi replied: "That is why the non-violence part was a necessary corollary. Without that there would be a confusion and worse." These replies together make the basis of Satyagraha clear. In this connection the *Social Reformer* observes: "If the populace understood Satyagraha in the sense that Mr. Gandhi understands it, there will be no safer or more efficacious means of national salvation."

The tradition current in Northern India of the people having used Satyagraha against Aurangazeb in connection with a bathing ceremony at Mathura can be quoted as an example of the populace having understood Satyagraha 'in Mr. Gandhi's sense.' But such traditions which have not unfortunately found their place in the pages of history are classed with the Puranic stories. The story of Indian Satyagrahis in South Africa is explained away by some by attributing to special circumstances the understanding of Satyagraha by the masses. If we cite the recent peaceful Hartals, the credit is put to the account of the military force. English history has a precedent in the presecution of the Quakers and their success in getting their demands recognised by the Legislature The history of these brave sufferers also may not, we are afraid, be regarded as sufficient to warrant a generalisation for all nations, because, it may be argued, the English Dissenters were cultured enough to understand the non-violence part of their creed. Surely topping all these is, in point of conviction to those that demand a precedent in history, the touching history of the Doukhobors, a band of peasant Satyagrahis of Russia. Theirs, is an instance of a people, certainly not more cultured than our masses here. The descendants of the bravest of these Satyagrahis are at present in Canada our fellow citizens of the Empire. We admit that the capacity of the masses for suffering for Truth may be under certain circumstances limited. That, however, cannot detract from the fact of their possessing such a capacity.

Q. Honestly striving after Truth is different in every case.

A. That is why the non-violence part was a necessary corollary. Without that there would be confusion and worse.

Q. Must not the person wanting to pursue Truth be of high moral and intellectual equipment ?

A. No. It would be impossible to expect that from everyone. If A has evolved a truth by his own efforts which B, C, and other are to accept, I should not require them to have the equipment of A.

Q. Then it comes to this, that a man comes to a decision and others of lower intellectual and moral equipment would have to blindly follow him.

A. Not blindly. All I wish to urge is that each individual, unless he wants to carry on his pursuit of Truth independently, needs to follow some one who has determinded truth.

Q. Your scheme involves the determination of truth by people of high moral and intellectual equipment and a large number of people may follow them blindly, being themselves unable to arrive at similar conclusions by reason of their lower intellectual equipment.

A. I would exact from them nothing more that I would expect from an ordinary being.

Q. I take it that the strength of the propaganda must depend on the number of its followers.

A. No. In Satyagraha success is possible even if there is only one Satyagrahi of the proper stamp.

Q. Mr. Gandhi, you said you do not consider yourself a perfect Satyagrahi yet. The large mass of people are then even less so.

A. No. I do not consider myself as an extraodinary man. There may be people more capable of determining truth than myself. Forty thousand Indians in South Africa, totally uncultured, came to the conclusion that they could be Satyagrahis ; and if I could take you through those thrilling scenes in the Transvaal, you will be surprised to hear what restraint your countrymen in South Africa exhibited.

Q. But there you were all unanimous.

A. I have more solidity of opinion here than in South Africa.

Q. But there you had a clear-cut issue, not here.

A. Here too we have a clear-cut issue, *viz.*, the Rowlatt Act.

Mr. Gandhi then explained how he presented Satyagraha as an instrument of infinitely greater power than violence.

Q. Does not suffering and going on suffering require extraordinary self-control ?

A. No, no extraordinary self-control is required. Every mother suffers. Your countrymen, I submit, have got such a control and they have exhibited that in a very large measure.

Q. Take Ahmedabad. Did they exhibit control here ?

A. All I say is, throughout India where you find there isolated instances of violence, you will find a very large number of people who exercised self-restraint. Ahmedabad and other places show that we had not attained proper mastery over self. The Kaira people in the midst of grave provacation last year acted with the greatast self-restraint.

Q. Do you mean to say these acts of violence were mere accidents ?

A. Not accidents. But they were rare and would be rarer for a clear conception of Satyagraha. The country,

I think, has sufficiently well realised the doctrine to warrant a second trial. I do feel sure that the country is all the purer and better for having gone through the fire of Satyagraha.

Q. Ordinarily your doctrine contemplates co-operation with the Government and elimination of race-hatred and inviting self-suffering. Does not suffering create ill-will?

A. It is contrary to my thirty years' experience that people have by suffering been filled with any ill-will againt the Government. In South Africa, after a bitter struggle the Indians have lived on the best of terms with the Government, and Gen. Smuts was the recipient of an address which was voluntarily voted by the Indians.

Q. Is it possible to take part in the movement without taking the Satyagraha vow?

A. I would ask them to take part in the Non-Civil Resistance part of the movement. The masses unless they took the pledge were not to do the Civil Disobedience part of the pledge. For those who were not civil resisters, therefore, another vow was devised asking people to follow Truth at all costs and to refrain from violence. I had supsended Civil Resistance then; and as it is open to a leader to emphasise one part of the vow, I eliminated the Civil Resistance part which was not for that reason suited to the people and placed the Truth part before them.

Sir Chimanlal Setalvad then referred to the question whether disobedience of the Rowlatt Act also was contemplated in the vow and referred to Mrs. Besant's difference with Mr. Gandhi. Mr. Gandhi said that he had heard in Bombay that she had taken the vow less the Committee part of it. She said she had not done so.

Q. Did she not point out that to disobey the Rowlatt Act one would have to be an anarchist?

A. She has certainly advanced that ground.

Mr. Gandhi explained that the determining consideration was that the Rowlatt Act would not lend itself to active disobedience in a systematic manner.

Q. Is not the underlying idea embarrassment of Government?

A. Certainly not. A Satyagrahi relies not upon embarrassment but upon self-suffering for securing relief.

Q. Would not ordered government be impossible?

A. Ordered government cannot be impossible if totally inoffensive people break the laws. But I would certainly make government impossible, if I found it had taken leave of its senses.

Q. In your message you ask people to refrain from violence and still violence occurred. Does it not show that the ordinary mind finds it very difficult to practise the theory of non-violence?

A. After having used methods of violence for years it is difficult for them to practise abstention.

In reply to a question whether he had any evidence in support of the statement that the disturbances were organised, Mr. Gandhi replied in the affirmative and said he had no objection to place the materials he had before the Committee, although he would not disclose the names of the persons concerned.

Mr. Gandhi said they did not suggest any destruction of life but only of property. There was some organisation arranged on the 10th and on the 11th. He said he had the testimony of those who were told to do violence, and of those who did so, and of those who were witnesses of the scenes. He said he had direct evidence, he had people coming to him to surrender swords in their possession, but they had not the courage to do so. He said he could identify some of the informants, but it was impossible for him to identify all, as, for instance, there were people from neighbouring villages who came to him, and said they regretted what they had done and that what they had done was from pure love for me.

Asked as to how he could determine whether what they said was the truth, Mr. Gandhi said, he thought he was capable of discriminating an untruthful statement from a truthful one. They took advantage of the temper of the people and put those ideas into their heads. The Kaira derailment was committed by two or three individuals. They were drunkards, and he could not say that the act was a deliberately organised one. It was his conviction that the people in the town had no knowledge of the crime, and if they had, they would have prevented it. His view was based on the testimony of those for whom he had high regard. He could not tell whether the person covicted of the crime was the same who committed it, because he had not learnt his name.

Proceeding, Mr. Gandhi said he suspended the Civil Disobedience movement, because he realised that the movement as a mass movement under present circumstances was not advisable. He would not expect the people to realise the inwardness of the Satyagraha movement but he would expect them to realise that it was better for them, if they could not join the movement, at least to refrain from violence.

Here Sir Chimanlal asked Mr. Gandhi to read from a leaflet of his, entitled, 'When will Satyagraha be resumed?' and added if, when he was saying that they should be ready to resume Satyagraha because the military dispositions would then be complete, he was not desiring that military dispositions should be kept in all parts of the country in order that people may have the pleasure to indulge in breaking laws. Mr. Gandhi said that that was not the interpretation warranted by his words. He would not be guilty of saying such a thing. He did not re-start the campaign on the Ist of July as he had expected, much to the disappointment of his co-workers, only because the Viceroy and the Governor of Bombay asked him whether he wanted India to be an armed camp and to suspend the Satyagraha movement if he did not want her to be so, and he suspended it.

Asked as to the fine imposed on the Ahmedabad workmen, Mr. Gandhi said the manner of collection was wholly bad, the principle of taxation was bad and the time fixed for collection was inopportune for collection. The fine was imposed in certain cases upon those who had nothing to do with the disturbances. He added that he was not going to say anything regarding the exemptions, and that he was not prepared to dispute the discretion vested in the authorities. He said he would not be fair if he did not pay his testimony to the handsome manner in which the Collector of Ahmedabad had taken the measures he had thought necessary.

Examination by Pandit Jagat Narain.

Q. I presume, Mahatmaji, you are not against the Government's taking measures to put down anarchy?

A. Of course, not. But anarchical crimes can be punished under the ordinary law.

Q. How was it then that you objected to the Rowlatt Legislation?

A. My fundamental objection to the Rowlatt Act is that it constitutes a libel on the whole Indian nation.

Q. But you know there are safeguards?

A. As to the safeguards, I can say from experience they are not merely illusory but dangerous traps. The safeguards are but a delusion and make the executive still more irresponsible.

Q. It is alleged that the Satyagraha movement would embarrass the Government. Are you not afraid of any such result of your movement?

A. The Satyagraha movement is not started with the intention of embarrassing the Government, while ordinary political agitation is often started with that object. If a Satyagrahi finds his activities resulting in embarrassing the Government, he will not hesitate to face it.

Q. But you will agree with me that every political agitation depends for its success on the number of followers?

A. I do not regard the force of numbers as necessary in a just cause, and in such a cause every man, be he high or low, can have his remedy.

Q. But you would certainly try to have as many men in your movement as possible?

A. Not exactly so. A Satyagrahi depends only on truth and his capacity to suffer for truth.

Q. But in politics, Mahatmaji, how can a single man's voice be heard?

A. That is exactly what I have been attempting to disprove.

Q. Do you believe that an English officer will take any notice of isolated attempts?

A. Why, that is my experience. Lord Bentinck became an ordinary Mr. at the instance of Keshub Chandra Sen.

Q. Oh, you cite an example of an extraordinary man.

A. Men of ordinary abilities also can develop morality. No doubt I regard illiteracy among my people as deplorable and I consider it necessary to educate them, but it is not at all impossible to imbibe the Satyagraha principle in an absolutely illiterate man. This is my long-standing experience.

Here Mr. Gandhi briefly cleared the distinction between *hartal* and Satyagraha. *Hartal* was no integral part of Satyagraha. It should be resorted to only when necessary. He tried and tried it successfully in connection with the deportation of Mr. Horniman and the Khilafat movement.

Q. You can resort to no other remedy to oppose the irresponsible foreign officials, and that is why you have started this movement. Is it not?

A. I cannot say that with certainty. I can conceive the necessity of Satyagraha in opposition to the would-be full responsible self-government. Our ministers can never claim to defend themselves on the score of their ignorance, whereas such a defence is avilable to-day for the English officers.

Q. But with all the rights of self-government we shall be able to dismiss the ministers.

A. I cannot feel on that point so assured for ever. In England, it often happens that ministers can continue in the executive even though they lose all the confidence of the public. The same thing may happen here too, and therefore I can imgine a state of things in this country which would need Satyagraha even under Home Rule.

Q. Would you think that there should be no unrest coming after the Satyagraha movement?

A. Not only I do not think so, I would be disappointed if there were no unrest in case myself and Anasuyaben were arrested. But that unrest will not take the shape of violence. It pains a Satyagrahi to see others suffering and Satyagrahis will follow each other to jail. I do wish for such unrest.

Q. On your return to Bombay on the 11th April, why did you go to Pydhonie?

A: I went there as there was danger of violence breaking out.

Q. It is said that people there refused to listen to your advice.

A. It would not at all be correct to say that the crowd refused to listen to my advice. Those who heard me followed my advice implicitly.

Q. I have a report before me to the effect that you pretend to be ill although your steps are quick.

A. All that I can say is that it is all untrue.

Q. The report further says that you were so very terrified that you ran away and concealed yourself in a house.

A. That too is a lie. I was in the crowd to the last. I personally saw the charge of the mounted police on the crowd. I went to Mr. Griffiths to talk to him on this very thing.

Examination by Mr. Kemp.

Q. You say that martial law was not at all necessary in Ahmedabad?

A. Yes, that is my opinion.

Q. But, Mr. Gandhi, if the military officers said it was necessary, what will you say to that?

A. From the facts in my possession I concluded that they did not warrant such an order.

Q. You say some innocent men were killed.

A. That is my deliberate opinion.

Q. Can you say you have got any positive proof for that?

A. I have got proof enough to satisfy me.

Q. Did you write to Mr. Chatfield about this?

A. Yes, I did.

Q. Did he ask you to send the complainants to him?

A. Yes.

Q. Did you then take any steps?

A. I took no steps because martial law was withdrawn on the very day I wrote to Mr. Chatfield. I consider Mr. Chatfield, a noble officer. In very few officers have I seen his honesty and straightforwardness. I should be very sorry to say anything that would amount to a criticism of his conduct. I see his nobility even in his mistakes. But I should like you not to press this point further. I have granted that the sobriety with which the Bombay Government acted during the month of April, leaves nothing to complain of.

But when I have to analyse the whole situation, it is my duty to point the mistakes also with all the humility I can command. And I have done it. I do not want to make it a serious complaint by emphasising the fact that some innocent people were killed.

Mr. Kemp: I accept, Mr. Gandhi, that your evidence is fair and candid. I don't want to put you any more questions.

[Mr. Gandhi was also examined by Mr. Jivanlal Desai and Sahebzada Sultan Ahamed Khan, but, so far as Satyagraha is concerned, what has been given above seems sufficient.]

3rd December, 1919

DURGADAS ADWANI

(By M. K. Gandhi)

Durgadas Adwani is one of the best workers I have had the privilege of meeting. I came to know him through correspondence, immediately on my arrival in India in 1915. The occasion that gave rise to the correspondence showed the true man in Durgadas. He has been a consistent, conscientious and zealous worker in Sind for many years. He has now gone to gaol for one year with hard labour.* I have been asked to give my opinion on the judgment of the Appellate Court. In my humble opinion the judgment is unsound. The Court has erred in holding that "New Call" was a seditious leaflet and it has strained the analysis of evidence to record a finding against Durgadas. But in giving this opinion, I admit I may be biased in favour of Durgadas. I do not believe him to be capable of telling an untruth in order to avoid imprisonment. The evidence *may* bear the meaning placed upon it by the Appellate Court.

But as a friend and as a Satyagrahi, I must decline to condole with Durgadas or his family upon his incarceration. Durgadas has, after great deliberation, taken the Satyagraha pledge. And I seize the opportunity offered by this case of placing before the reader my views about such cases. We spend too much money in litigation and in appeals. We have an excessive dread of prisons. I have not a shadow of doubt that society will be much cleaner and healthier if there was less resort to law courts than there is. The rush after the best counsel is undignified. It is unpardonable when it is indulged in at public expense. But it is sinful when a Satyagrahi spends money after the best legal talent or after appeals. I was, therefore, pained when I heard of appeals in the "New Call" convictions. If one has committed an offence, he must plead guilty and suffer

* In connection with the printing of a pamphlet on passive Resistance in a Press of which he was the keeper.

the penalty. If he has not and is still found guilty, imprisonment for him is no disgrace. And if he is a Satyagrahi, he has no business to fear the hardships of gaol life.

We, in India, whilst we are living in an atmosphere surcharged with suspicion and distrust and in the midst of a secret police department unrivalled, perhaps, in the world for its duplicity and unscrupulousness, must use ourselves to the gaol life if we want to mend that department and remove distrust and suspicion.

The best and quickest way to deliverance from the distrust and secret police department is to rid the country of false fear and all violence. But till that far-off day arrives, the handful of Satyagrahis must be prepared to treat the prison as their second home.

I hope, therefore, that the friends of Durgadas will not advise him or his wife to petition for mercy nor add to the wife's unhappiness by commisserating with her. On the contrary, it is our duty to ask her to steel her heart and feel glad that her husband is in goal for no fault of his own. The truest service that we can render to Durgadas would be to offer Mrs. Durgadas such assistance, pecuniary or otherwise, as she may need. I understand that the "New Call" cases have cost nearly Rs. 15,000. The money could ocrtainly have been utilised to better purpose. It is not right to beggar ourselves by fighting against odds. It is hardly manful to be over-anxious about the result of political trials that involve no disgrace.

Here, in the Punjab,* I find mothers with stricken heart coming and shedding tears over the imprisonment of their sons whom they regard as innocent. I know I am

* Mahathma Gandhi incessantly wrote even while travelling. This article was written while n a visit to Punjab.

helpless. But it is so difficult to comfort them. To give them false hope would be a sin. To ask them patiently to endure what cannot be cured brings no comfort. I am, therefore, endeavouring to perform the uphill task of asking them to be Satyagyahis enough to realise that we shall only perpetuate political convictions so long as we fret and foam and worry over the imprisonment of our dear ones. Needless to say, I am not here thinking of imprisonments for acts of actual incendiarism or murder.

25th February, 1920

CLEAN UP!

The following interview, first published in the *Indian Witness* of Lucknow, was reproduced in "Young India" of February, 25:

As I talked with Mr. Ganbhi, I marvelled at the simplicity of his dress. He wore coarse white cloth, with a *kambal* thrown over his body to protect him from the cold. A little white cap was his only head covering. As he sat on the floor facing me, I asked myself, how can this little man, with his thin face and large protruding ears, and quiet brown eyes, be the great Gandhi about whom I have heard so much? All doubts were set aside, when we began to talk. I do not agree with all the methods that Mr. Gàndhi employs to bring about the desired end; but I do want to bear this personal testimony of the man himself. Mr. Gandhi is a spiritual man. He is a thinker. In my short interview, I had the same heart-to-heart fellowship with him as I have had scores of times with some of God's saints. I took knowledge that this man had been to the Source of Christian strength and had learned from the great Christ.

"Mr. Gandhi, what can nations of the West do in furthering the all-round development of the East, and particularly of India?" Mr. Gandhi answered the question indirectly: "India is just now in the state of unlearning. She has learned a lot that is useless and unprofitable. From my observation of the West, and particularly of your own country, I have learned two outstanding facts: First, cleanliness; second, energy. I am fully convinced that my people cannot advance spiritually, until they clean up. Your people are wonderfully energetic. To a large extent, it has been energy after things material. If Indian people could have that same amount of energy, rightly directed, they would receive a great blessing."

"Mr. Gandhi, will you kindly tell me how Christianity can best help India, in view of the spirit of nationalism that is abroad?" He replied, "What we need, most of all, is *sympathy*. When I was down in Africa, I found this illustration. I had to dig some artesian wells. In order to search the pure flowing streams, I had to dig deep. Many of the people who come out here to study my people only scratch the surface. If they would dig deep by means of sympathy, they would find a stream of life there pure and clear."

"And will you kindly tell me, Mr. Gandhi, what book or person has influenced you the most?" Of course, I was prepared to hear him say something about the Vedas and several other Indian books with which Christian people should be conversant; but I was not prepared to hear from the lips of this man the mention of three English books that had shaped his life and thought. He frankly confessed that he was not an omnivorous reader, but rather a careful selector of the very best. The order in which he spoke of the books was as follows: The Bible, Ruskin, Tolstoi. Speaking of the Bible, he said: "There have been many times when I did not know which way to turn. But I have gone to the Bible, and particularly the New Testament, and have drawn strength from its message."

I was anxious to know how our Meerut Graduates' Association, composed of the finest of the educated men in the city, could further the city's welfare. In reply to the question, he gave me this one word, "*Scavenger.*" He said, "I employ that word in all its meaning. If the members would get out and lend a helping hand to clean up the city, literally and morally, they would be doing a great work."

Meerut S. W. CLEMES.

23rd June, 1919

SOME PROOFS OF THE UNIVERSALITY OF SATYAGRAHA

It may be long before the law of love will be recognised in international affairs. The machineries of governments stand between and hide the hearts of one people from those of another. Yet if only we watched the latest international developments in Europe and Eastern Asia with an eye to essentials, we could see how the world is moving steadily to realise that between nation and nation, as between man and man force has failed to solve problems, but that the economic sanction of Non-co-operation is far more mighty and conclusive than armies and navies. The victories of war have only thrown fresh burdens on the nations that emerged out of the struggle as apparent victors. The food and the industries of the defeated nations are a source of anxiety as much to the victors as to themselves. All the ingenuity of the Governments of the Allied nations is directed to show, without detriment to the glory of the victors, they can make the vanquished people economically solvent, happy, and willing to work to keep the world going. Reading between the lines of the brief telegram*about the American Republican Party's international programme, one can see that the Far West is beginning to realise that the ultimate sanction of a league of nations should be, not the vicious chain of the might of arms again, but the might of international 'outlawry', *i.e.*, Non-co-operation of the nations. From this it would be an easy step to the complete recognition of the law of love. Till a new energy is harnessed and put on wheels, the captains of the older energies will treat the innovation as theoretical, impractical, idealistic, and so on. We may be certain that the steam engineer was laughed at by the horse-dealer, till he saw that even horses could be transported by the steam engine. The electrical engineer was, no doubt, called a faddist and a mad man in steam engine circles, till work was actually done over the wires. It may take long to lay the wires for international love, but the sanction of international Non-co-operation in preference to continued physical compulsion, as appears to have been conceived by the Republican Party of Amercia, is a distinct progress towards the ultimate and real solution.

The most striking news in this connection is a rumour of contemplated action in regard to the Irish situation. The "Observer" gives currency to the belief that the British Ministry is considering, as an alternative of martial law in Ireland, a policy of Non-co-operation.

* A General Election in America was proceeding at the time this article was written and the great Parties were engaged in the electioneering campaign, issuing manifestoes and programmes.

The disaffected interior of Ireland is to be entirely ignored until it comes to its senses. There would be no police, no troops, no trade, no education, no distribution of revenue, no railways. There would be complete administrative boycott. The beauty of Satyagraha, of which Non-co-operation is but a chapter, is that it is available to either side in a fight, that it has checks that automatically work for the vindication of truth and justice for that side, whichever it may be, that has Truth and justice in preponderating measure. It is as powerful and faithful a weapon in the hand of the capitalist as in that of the labourer. It is as powerful in the hands of the government, as in that of the people, and will bring victory to the government, if people are misguided or unjust, as it will win the battle for the people if the government be in the wrong. Quick disorganisation and defeat are bound to be the fate of bolstered up cases and artificial agitations if the battle is fought with Satyagraha weapons. Suppose the people are unfit to rule themselves, or are unwilling to sacrifice for a cause, then, no amount of noise will bring them victory in Non-co-operation. If the government be a good government, just, on the whole, and necessary for the people, and the grievance be false or unreal or is based on misconception or is not of such measure as to weigh against the virtues of the government in other vital respects then Non-co-operation has only to be adopted on either side, and, without rancour or bloodshed, the question will automatically be settled with unerring precision and justice. It may not be generally known, but it has long been maintained by Mr. Gandhi, that the Satyagrahic weapon of Non-co-operation is as available to government against the people as to the people against the government. The action said to be contemplated in regard to the Irish disorders would, if true, be a beautiful illustration of the universality of the principles of Satyagraha.

10th March, 1920

THE 6TH OF APRIL AND THE 13TH

(By M. K. Gandhi)

It is impossible for us to forget the 6th of April * which vitalized the whole of India and the 13th of April which, by the spilling of innocent blood, has made the Punjab a place of pilgrimage for the whole of India. The 6th of April saw the advent of Satyagraha. One may dissent from the Civil Disobedience·part of it, but no one can dissent from the essential doctrine of Truth and love or non-injury. With *Satya* combined with *Ahimsa* you can bring the world to your feet. Satyagraha in its essence is nothing but the introduction of truth and gentleness in the political, *i.e.*, the national life. And whether one takes the Satyagraha pledge or not, there can be no doubt that the spirit of Satyagraha has pervaded the masses. Any way, that is my experience of thousands of the Punjabis I met throughout my tour in the Punjab.

The 6th of April again saw the inauguration of a definite plan of Hindu-Moslem unity and Swadeshi.

It was the 6th of April which broke the spirit underlying the Rowlatt Act and made it a dead letter. The 13th of April saw not merely the terrific tragedy but in that tragedy Hindu-Moselm blood flowed freely in a mingled stream and sealed the compact.

How to commemorate or celebrate these two great

* The 6th April is being every year observed throughout India as Satyagraha Day, a day of prayer, one consecrated to self-purification.

national events? I venture to suggest that those who will, should devote the 6th April next to fast (twenty-four hours abstention from food) and prayer and that all over India at 7 p.m., public meetings should be held praying for the repeal of the Rowlatt Act and expressing the national belief that there will be no peace in the land till that Act is repealed. That the Act is a dead letter is not enough. Either it is a disgrace or it is not. If it is, the Act must be repealed. The repeal before the reforms will be a token of good-will on the part of the Government.

The whole of the week, beginning from the 6th, should be devoted to some work connected with the tragedy of the 13th. I therefore venture further to suggest that the week should be devoted to the collecting of funds for the Jallianwala Bagh memorial, it being remembered that the sum to be collected is ten lacs of rupees. Each village or town can devise its own plan of collection guarding against misappropriation and fraud. The collection should be finished by the evening of the 12th April.

Then the 13th. That day of days should be devoted to fasting and prayer. It should be free from ill-will or anger. We want to cherish the memory of the innocent dead. We do not want to remember the wickedness of the deed. The nation will rise by readiness to sacrifice, not by preparing to revenge. On that day I would also have the nation to remember the mass excesses and feel penitent for them. We close the week by meetings throughout India to pass resolutions urging the Government, both Imperial and Indian, to take effective steps to render a repetition of the tragedy impossible.

I would further urge that during the week each one does his or her best in his or her own person to realise more fully than ever the principles of Satyagraha, Hindu-Moslem unity and Swadeshi. In order to emphasise Hindu-Moslem unity I would advise joint meetings of Hindus and Mahomedans on Friday the 12th April at 7 p.m., urging that the Khilafat question be decided in accordance with the just Moslem sentiments.

Thus this national week should be a week of purification, self-examination, sacrifice, exact discipline and expression of cherished national sentiments. There should be no trace of bitterness, no violence of language, but absolute fearlessness and firmness.

Should there not also be a *hartal* on the 6th and the 13th? My answer is an emphatic no. This week is a Satyagraha week for those who believe in Truth and Non-violence. The *hartal* of the 6th was a Satyagraha *hartal* in the sense that it was a prelude to Satyagraha. The *hartal* of the 6th April last, though it was spontaneous, was not altogether free from undue pressure during the course of the day in the way of asking people not to use carriage, etc. I would therefore not advise *hartal* at all for this week of discipline and penance. Moreover, *hartal* must not be made cheap. It must be only for rare occasions.

I respectfully trust that all parties and all classes will see their way to take their full share in the observances of the national week and make it an event for the true and definite progress in national awakening.

24th March, 1920

CONTEMPT OF COURT

(By M. K. Gandhi)

The long expected hearing of the case against the editor and the publisher of "Young India" in connection with the publication of a letter* of the District Judge of Ahmedabad regarding Satyagrahi Lawyers and my comments thereon has been heard and judgment has been pronounced. Both the editor and the publisher have been serverely reprimanded. But the Court did not see its way to pass any sentence upon either of us. If I dwell upon the judgment it is only because I am anxious as a Satyagrahi to draw a moral from it. I wish to assure those friends who out of pure friendliness advised us to tender the required apology, that I refused to accept their advice, not out of obstinacy, but because there was a great principle at stake. I had to conserve a journalist's independence and yet respect the law. My own reading of the law was that there was no contempt committed by me. But my defence rested more upon the fact that I could not offer an apology if I was not prepared not to repeat the offence on a similar occasion. Because I hold that an apology tendered to a Court, to be true, has to be as sincere as a private apology. At the same time, I owed a duty to the Court. It was no light thing for me to refuse to accept the advice of the Chief Justice, especially when the Chief Justice was so very considerate in the correspondence with me. I was on the horns of a dilemma. I therefore decided not to offer any defence but simply to make a statement frankly and fully defining my position, leaving it to the Court to pass any sentence it thought fit in the event of an adverse decision. In order to show that I meant no disrespect of the Court and that I did not desire to advertise the case, I took extraordinary

* The letter called upon lawyers who took the Satyagraha pledge. See *supra*, Gandhi's evidence before the Hunter Committee, to explain why they should not be debarred from practice under the Legal Practitioner's Act for their act in taking the pledges defying Law.

precautions to prevent publicity and I venture to think that I succeeded eminently in convincing the Court that behind my disobedience, if it was disobedience, there was no defiance but perfect resignation, there was no anger or ill-will but perfect restraint and respect; that, if I did not apologise, I did not, because an insincere apology would have been contrary to my conscience. I hold that it was about as perfect an instance of Civil Disobedience as it ever has been my privilege to offer. And I feel that the Court reciprocated in a most handsome manner and recognised the spirit of civility that lay behind my so-called disobedience. The luminous judgment of Justice Marten lays down the law, and decides against me. But I feel thankful that it does not question the propriety of my action. Justice Hayward's judgment recognises it as an instance of Passive, *i.e.*, Civil Resistance and practically makes it the reason for not awarding any sentence. Here, then, we have an almost complete vindication of Civil Disobedience. Disobedience to be civil must be sincere, respectful, restrained, never defiant, must be based upon some well understood principle, must not be capricious and, above all, must have no ill-will or hatred behind it. I submit that the disobedience offered by Mr. Desai and myself contained all these ingredients.

31*st March*, 1920

THE SATYAGRAHA WEEK

(By M. K. Gandhi)

First and foremost in the programme for the holy National Week I put fasting and prayer. I have said enough to emphasise the necessity of both these for the unfoldment of our national life. I speak of these from personal experience. But writing to a friend on this very matter of prayer, I came across a beautiful thing from Tennyson which I present to the readers of "Young India" if perchance I might convert them to a definite belief in the efficacy of prayer. Here is the gem:

"More things are wrought by prayer
Than this world dreams of. Wherefore let thy voice
Rise like a fountain for me night and day.
For what are men better than sheep or goats
That nourish a blind life within the brain,
If, knowing God, they lift not hands of prayer
Both for themselves and those who call them friend?
For so the whole round earth is every way
Bound by golden chains about the feet of God."

Throughout my wanderings in India, I have had the privilege of mixing with men of all creeds, of mixing with thousands of women, hundreds upon hundreds of students. I have discussed with them national problems with a passion which I am unable to describe. I have found that we have not yet reached a conscious recognition of our national state. We have not had the discipline necessary for a realisation of that state and venture to say that there is nothing so powerful as fasting and prayer that would give us the requisite discipline, spirit of self-sacrifice, humility and resoluteness of will without which there can be no real progress. I hope therefore that millions throughout India will open the Satyagraha Week with sincere fasting and prayer.

I do not wish, during this week, to emphasise the Civil Resistance part of Satyagraha. I would like all to contemplate Truth and Non-violence, and to appreciate their invincibility. Indeed, if all of us regulated our lives by this eternal law of *Satya* and *Ahimsa*, there will be no occasion for civil or other resistance. Civil

Resistance comes into play when only a small body of men endeavour to follow Truth in the face of opposition. It is difficult to know what is truth, when to defend it to the point of Civil Resistance, and how to avoid error in the shape of violence in one's pursuit after Truth. There may well be differences of opinion as to the advisability of preaching Civil Resistance as a creed during a week devoted to national uplift, in which one seeks the co-operation of all without distinction of party, class or creed.

Beyond the prayer and fasting on the 6th and the 13th, we have the collection for the Jallianwala Bagh Memorial. I trust that complete organisation would be set up in every province, in every district, and every town or village.

The third part of the activity is represented by three meetings during the week all over India at the stated times, whereat I have suggested the passing of certain resolutions, *viz.*, on the Rowlatt Act which gave rise to the Satyagraha movement, the Khilafat question which by Hindu association cements Hindu-Moslem unity and what may be called the Jallianwalla Bagh resolution to be passed on the 13th April, calling upon the Government to take such measures as may be necessary to prevent a repetition of the tragedies that were witnessed during Martial Law regime and which were opened even before the inauguration of Martial Law by the unlawful massacre of the 13th. I suggest the following resolutions for acceptance:

For the 6th April.—This meeting of the citizens of . . . places on record its emphatic opinion that there will be no peace in the land until the Rowlatt Act is repealed and therefore appeals to the Government of India to introduce at the earliest opportunity a bill repealing that Act.

For the 9th April.—This meeting of Hindus, Mahomedans and others, the inhabitants of . . . trusts that the Khilafat question will be solved consistantly with the just demands of the Mussalmans of India and thus the solemn pledges of His Majesty's ministers and this meeting records its opinion that in the event of an adverse decision being arrived at, it will be the duty of every Indian to withdraw co-operation from the Government until the pledges are fulfilled and Mussalman sentiment conciliated.

For the 13th April.—This meeting of the inhabitants of . . . is of opinion that whilst mob excesses at Amritsar, although committed after grave provocation, were worthy of condemnation, the deliberate and calculated massacre, without warning, by General Dyer, of innocent, unarmed and otherwise defenceless men at Jallianwala Bagh was an unexampled act of barbarity and hopes that the Government of India and the Imperial Government will take such steps as will render impossible a repetition of such barbarity and other similar barbarities committed by responsible officers in the Punjab during the period of Martial Law administration and hopes that the recommendations made by the Punjab Sub-committee of the Indian National Congress will be carried out in their entirety.

28th April 1920

TO THE MEMBERS OF THE ALL-INDIA HOME RULE LEAGUE

(By M. K. Gandhi)

It is a distinct departure from the even tenor of my life for me to belong to an organisation that is purely and frankly political. But after careful deliberation and consultation with friends, I have joined the All-India Home Rule League and accepted the office of its President. Some friends whom I consulted told me that I should not join any political organisation and that if I did, I would lose the position of splendid isolation I enjoy at present. I confess that this caution had considerable weight with me. At the same time, I felt that if I was accepted by the League as I was, I should be wrong in not identifying myself with an organisation that I could utilise for the advancement of the causes in which I had specialised and of the methods which experience has shown me are attended with quicker and better results than those that are usually adopted. Before joining the League, I endeavoured to ascertain the opinion of those who were outside the Presidency and with whom I had not the privilege to come in such close contact as with co-workers in the Bombay Presidency.

The causes referred to by me are Swadeshi, Hindu-Moslem Unity with special reference to Khilafat, the acceptance of Hindustani as the *lingua franca* and a linguistic re-distribution of the Provinces. I would engage the League if I can carry the members with me in these actvities so that they occupy the largest part of the nation's time and attention.

I freely confess that Reforms take a secondary place in my scheme of national reorganisation. For I feel that the activities chosen by me, if they could but absorb national energy, would bring about all the Reforms that the most ardent extremists can ever desire, and so far as the desirability of full self-government at the earliest possible moment is concerned, I yield to none in my desire to hasten our progress. And it is because I feel that the progress towards self-government can be best accelerated by developing the activities I have mentioned that I keep them in the forefront of the national programme. I shall not treat the All-India Home Rule League as a party organisation in any sense of the term. I belong to no party and I wish to belong to none hereafter. I am aware that the constitution of the League requires it to help the Congress, but I do not consider the Congress as a party organisation, even as the British Parliament though it contains all parties and has one party or other dominating it, from time to time, is not a party organisation. I shall venture to hope that all parties will cherish the Congress as a national organisation providing a platform for all parties to appeal to the nation with a view to moulding its policy and I would endeavour to so mould the policy of the League as to make the Congress retain its non-party, national character.

This brings me to my methods. I believe that it is possible to introduce uncompromising truth and honesty in the political life of the country. Whilst I would not expect the League to follow me in my Civil Disobedience methods, I would strain every nerve to make Truth and non-violence accepted in all our national activities. Then we shall cease to fear or distrust governments and their measures. I do not wish however to develop the theme any further. I would rather let time solve the many questions that must arise from the bald statement I have made. My purpose just now is not to demonstrate the propriety of my action or the truth of the policy herein adumbrated but to take the members of the League into my confidence and to invite criticism of the programme herein set forth and any suggestions they may wish to make for the advancement of the welfare of the League.

23*rd March*, 1921

SATYAGRAHA WEEK

(BY M. K. GANDHI)

April 6th and 13th will be soon upon us. The 6th saw India one and awakened. The 13th was a black Sunday, when a diabolical attempt was made to crush the spirit of. a nation that had just become awakened. India observed the anniversary of the two days last year in a fitting manner, and the whole week commencing from the 6th was treated as a week of consecration. Would that the coming April will find us ready for greater consecration. We have every reason and every occasion for it. Last year we concentrated merely on securing subscriptions for paying the purchase price of the ground hallowed by innocent blood. It was a necessary and pious act. But greater things have happened since then. The nation has affirmed and re-affirmed its determination to redress the Khilafat and the Punjab wrongs and to establish Swaraj. The December Congress went further and declared its intention to acquire Swaraj within one year.*

We cannot, then, do better than consecrate ourselves for greater national effort in this direction. The school and the courts movements continue.† No special endeavour is now necessary on that score except on the part of those who have left educational institutions or law courts. They must search within and see how they are utilising their time. But there are six things in which we certainly need to make a very special effort.

Firstly, we must acquire greater mastery over ourselves and secure an atmosphere of perfect calm, peace, and

* For the Congress resolutions referred to above, *see* appendix.

† The national movement is explained and discussed at length *infra*.

goodwill. We must ask forgiveness for every unkind word thoughtlessly uttered or unkind deed done to any one.

Secondly, we must still further cleanse our hearts, and we, Hindus and Moslems, must cease to suspect one another's motives; and we should believe ourselves to be incapable of wronging one another.

Thirdly, we Hindus must call no one unclean or mean or inferior to ourselves, and must therefore cease to regard the 'Pariah' class to be untouchable. We must consider it sinful to regard a fellow-being as untouchable.

These three things are matters of inward transformation and the result will be seen in our daily dealings.

The fourth is the curse of drink. Happily, India seems to have voluntarily and spontaneously resolved to get rid of the curse. A supreme effort should be made during the week to induce, by respectful entreaty, the liquor-sellers to give up their licences and the habitual visitors to these shops to give up the habit. Every caste knows its own offenders and can handle them much more effectively than others. But I have suggested to the women of Ahmedabad that they should organise temperance bands and approach the liquor-sellers and the drinkers. In any case, no physical force should be used to attain the end. A determined peaceful campaign of persuasion must succeed.

The fifth thing is the introduction of the spinning wheel in every home, larger production and use of *khadi*, and complete giving up of foreign cloth.

The sixth thing is the systematic and ceaseless collection of subscriptions for the Tilak Swaraj Fund. If an organised endeavour is made in this direction, we should be able to finish the collection of even one crore rupees during the Satyagraha week. My incessant touring has convinced me that India is ready to pay much more than one crore. Only there are not enough honest collectors. Every district of India should be able to organise itself for this work to be done during the Satyagraha week.*

Hartals have become cheap, and are easily organised and, therefore, have lost much of their original value. But *hartals* for the two days have a significance all their own. And I would certainly advise *hartals* for both the sixth and the thirteenth April accompanied by fast. Needless to say that there should be no compulsion. The employees whether in mills, or elsewhere should not stop work if they cannot secure leave, and no undue pressure should be brought to bear on the tram management. We must rely upon the public not using public vehicles on the two days without just and urgent cause. The two days of fast should be utilised for special prayers and worship.

I would dissuade the public from passing any resolutions as to our demands. The week of consecration must be a week of self-examination and purification. We must rely upon our work to bring about the desired result. As soon as we have rendered ourselves fit no person on earth can prevent our establishing Swaraj and securing redress of the two great wrongs.

* These six points were accepted by the Congress. *See* Appendix.

PART II

TOWARDS NON-CO-OPERATION

PART II

TOWARDS NON-CO-OPERATION

24th March, 1920

THE MESSAGE OF THE PUNJAB

THE following free rendering of the address delivered in Hindi by Shrimati Sarala Devi Chaudhrani to the public of Ahmedabad on the 27th February was re-published in "Young India" for the benefit of its readers. The address was entitled "The Message of the Punjab."

The Message.—Bharat is a holy place; and in it, in many respects, Punjab, the land of the five rivers, may be considered the holiest. It has been called the ancient abode of the Rishis. When modern civilisation spreads its dazzling wares for our acceptances and tempts us by its speech and succeeds in making us entirely ashamed of our own, we seek shelter and comfort in exploring the treasured stores of those dwellers in the cottages on the banks of the Five Rivers and when we meet them face to face in their pastoral hymns, we are filled with pride about the glory of our own ancient civilisation that lies buried in the inexhaustible mines called the *Vedas*. The *Vedas* represent to us the word of God and the word was given, so the historians tell us, on the holy banks of the rivers of the Punjab. It is for that reason that the very name of the Punjab fills every Indian with a thrill of pride. It is that soil whose children found perfect joy and pleasure in learning from its wise men divine wisdom. It is that holy place where a Rishi's wife proudly said to her husband, "What have I to do with earthly riches that cannot rob death of its terror to me." She at last herself became a divine singer and to-day, throughout Hindu India, millions of Hindus sing those immortal verses which mean—"Lead me from Falsehood unto Truth, from Darkness unto Light, from Death unto Immortality. Reveal Thyself to me, O Lord. Protect me with Thy benign aspect." It is the same holy land where the youth Nachiketa, spurning long life and enjoyment of the world, immortalised himself by thus addressing the God of Death who had asked him to choose a boon, "Riches do not make a man great. I want no other boon. I want only knowledge of things eternal." It was in the ancient Punjab that the very gods, renouncing enjoyments lawful for them and elevated by the preaching of Divine Wisdom, sat at the feet of the sages and observed *Brahmacharya* for ages.

Thus we are beholden to this land of the Sacred rivers for all that is loftiest in Hinduism and it is on that account and that alone that we should think of the Punjab in our morning prayers. Not only did the Punjab lead the way in divine knowledge in the times of the Rishis but even during recent times it has been the birthplace of the Sikh Gurus. We bow our heads to the Punjab for the renunciation, the self-sacrifice and the spirituality that these Gurus expressed in their lives and held up before us as a pattern worthy of imitation by us. Alas! since then the Punjab seems to have remained in temporary oblivion of her ancient heritage. The present descendants of the Rishis of old, though they still prove their noble descent by their handsome Aryan features, seem to have misinterpreted the teaching of the ancients about Power. The Rishis have said—"Power is greater even than Science. Our man of power is more than a match for hundred scientists. Power sustains the earth, the ether, the sky, the mountains, the gods, mankind, beasts, birds, vegetation and insects—all these are also dependent upon this Power. Therefore worship It."

The Punjab of to-day has mistaken this great Power of the soul for physical power and put it on a pedestal. She seems to have forgotten that the sages sang not of the mere momentary body-force but that they sang of the invincible soul-force. It is said of this Power which sustains everything every where that eyes cannot see it, speech cannot describe it, mind cannot comprehend it. Of the same Power Herbert Spencer has said—"The Power which the Universe manifests to us is utterly inaccountable . . An Infinite and Eternal energy from which all things proceed." This Soul-Power is beneficent and in its beneficence has its distinctive character from the power of the brute or the body-force. It has the force with which Vasishta over-powered Vishwamitra. Could the Punjab have been ensnared by the dazzle of the Western worship of brute-force? There are two distinctive qualities which characterise brute-force—tyranny and cowardice—to terrorise the week and to fear the strong, whereas the characteristic of soul-force are protection of the weak and fearlessness before the tyrant. But the same immortal Rishis tell us that *the choice lies with us.* They alone achieve the better way whom the gods choose—and the gods forgot the

Punjab for a while. When however they remembered that holy land once more, there came a voice from above:

> Awake, arise, approach the great ones,
> And learn wisdom from them.

The one who was to awaken the Punjab was in Gujarat. He had never seen the Punjab but he had a message for her as for the rest of India. Many read it, some only understood it. The result was that there was a kind of stimulation. The people of the Punjab did not sign his pledge. They did not grasp the inwardness of Satyagraha, nevertheless its freedom-giving spirit permeated the Punjab and the Punjab was vitalised. A new power came into being—the power of suffering—and so the citzens of Lahore received bullets in their breasts without retaliating. Only to-day the news has been received that the 21 men, who were under heavy sentences including death penalty, had their appeals dismissed by the Privy Council. I have no doubt that the people of the Punjab with their eyes fixed on Truth will, even like Mirabai, acquire the power to drink this poison as if it was nectar. For many an innocent man, including the leaders, has suffered imprisonment, many have lost their all, many families have been deprived of their bread-winners, hundreds are dependent on public charity.* But save for a few, the sufferers have borne their suffering with a brave heart. The message of Satyagraha has taken effect. Happi-

*As a result of the so-called "rebellion" in the Punjab martial law was introduced in the administration of which hundreds of Indians were imprisoned, unjustly in most cases. Some of the following articles reveal the nature of the summary courts sentences. The origin of the rebellion itself is briefly summarised in Gandhi's evidence before the Hunter Committee and in the Introduction. *See supra.*

ness and misery, prison and palace, life and death are to-day different aspects of the same thing. If we are filled with Truth, why need we fear an O'Dwyer or a Dyer? The Truth in us shall make us free. The Punjab says to-day—"The weak shall not find the soul within." And if the Punjab forgives, it will be a forgiveness which adorns the strong—it will not be the deceitful refuge of the coward. I venture thus to sing for you the words of the "Message of the Punjab."

The Message in Verse.—And the speaker sang, on the beautiful bank of the Sabarmati just after sunset, to the vast audience of the citizens of Ahmedabad who listened in perfect respectful silence, the verses composed by Pandit Rambhuj Dutt Chowdhry,* that were sung by her to the Amritsar Congress. We give a free translation of these verses.

1

Never lose heart,
  What though the very life be in danger?
Let us not lose heart
  Though the body may perish.

2

Whether it be through lightning, fire
  water, flood, hurricane or earthquake,
    Never lose heart.

3

Let the shell from the gun riddle you,
Let the edge of the sword cut you in twain,
    Never lose heart.

* The speaker's husband, one of the leaders of the Punjab and victims of the "firm" policy.

4

Let confiscation, forced sale impoverish you,
Let hard words pierce you,
Let the gallows or transportation be your lot,
Never lose heart.

5

Let Islam, let Hinduism,
Let knowledge, let strength of the strong
sustain you,
Never lose heart.

6

By the valour of the Majhas,*
By the lustiness of the Malwas,*
By the voice of the friends,
Never lose heart.

7

By the people of Dhana,† Potdhar,*
Sandalbar,* and Jhangsy,*
Never lose heart.

8

O Ram, through love,
Through peace, through patience.
And by the grace of True God,
Never lose heart.

Mahatma Gandhi's Remarks.—Mr. Gandhi who was in charge of the usual vote of thanks to the speaker and the chair in a humourous little speech said that

* Majhas and Malwas are warrior tribes living in the Punjab.

† Names of places in the Punjab.

it was somewhat embarrassing for him to speak of one who was not only his valued guest, but had become as dear to him as his own sister. During his privileged residence under Sarla Devi's roof whilst she was separated from her husband, he had had many a rich experience of her devotion to her husband. He knew how like a lioness she had fought for securing justice for her husband but never till that evening had he so fully realised that she was husband-mad. The audience might think that she had delivered the message of the Punjab which was the message of Satyagraha in the words of some ancient Rishis, for they had heard so much that evening of the Rishis of old. If they were labouring under any such delusion it was his duty to undeceive them. He was certainly proud to think that the message of Satyagraha had been delivered in a beautiful sweet song. But his pride was mixed with grief because he noticed that under the cover of delivering the message of Satyagraha, Sarala Devi had done nothing else than glorifying her husband. For Ram, the author of the song, was no other than Pandit Rambhuj Dutt Chowdhry. He did not mind the glorification of a husband by a husband-mad wife. But he resented such glorification under false colours. The speaker hoped that the audience would join him in his resentment by enthusiastically carrying the vote he had the honour of moving and that the sisters of Ahmedabad whom he saw among the audience would show their appreciation of the gifts of the guest of the evening by copying her wonderful devotion to her husband.

15th October, 1921

A PUNJAB VICTIM

(BY M. K. GANDHI)

Behari Lal Sachdeva is a young man of twenty-four with a young wife and an aged father seventy-two years old. He belongs to the Gujranwala batch and was sentenced to transportation with forfeiture of property. He had "waged war against the king." So said the prosecution and so found the court. His Honour the Lieut.-Governor has commuted the sentence to that of four years' imprisonment. Poor comfort to a prisoner who is innocent or to his father who is on the verge of death.

And so poor Behari Lal Sachdeva has sent another petition* as "he believes that through some serious mistake his case has not been carefully gone into." The petition is convincing enough. It is so well drawn that it will repay perusal. It is almost free from rhetoric or superfluous adjectives and is brief enough even for a busy reader.

A friend told me the other day that after forty years of life devoted to the praising of British justice, the Punjab had undeceived him. He no longer believed in British justice. He added with distinct energy, 'I do not care a straw for your reforms; what can they do for us if our lives and our honour be not safe and we stand in peril of being wrongly imprisoned?"

Well, the case of Behari Lal Sachdeva seems to be one such. It is probably one of mistaken identity. The young man would appear to be perfectly innocent. The prisoner is not stated to have been connected with or present at the meeting on the 4th and the 5th April or

* Not included in this collection.

on the 12th or the 13th April. The principal witness's evidence is merely hearsay. The other evidence is stated to be tainted, and, even if true, the facts sworn to do not disclose any offence. The evidence given for the prisoner by respectable and impartial witnesses was discarded by the court. The reader has by this time known sufficient of the Punjab judgments* not to feel surprised at such attitude of the special courts. What is however surprising is the fact that even now when perfect quiet reigns in the Punjab these cases of injustice do not receive the attention they deserve at the hands of the Lieut.-Governor. No government deserves respect which holds cheap the liberty of the subject as the Punjab Government seems to do.

29th October, 1919

ANOTHER MARTIAL LAW CASE FROM THE PUNJAB

(BY M. K. GANDHI)

Mr. Purshotam Singh, son of Mr. Jamiat Singh Bagga of Wazirabad, has sent me a statement of his father's case, and what is miscalled a record of his case and judgment. Mr. Jamiat Singh Bagga is a merchant and banker of Wazirabad. He is 62 years old and suffering from a bad cataract in the eye. He was sentenced to 18 months' rigorous imprisonment and a fine of Rs. 1,000 or in default to undergo further rigorous imprisonment for 6 months. I have no hesitation in saying that the judgment is utterly unworthy of anybody calling himself a judge. It is devoid of reasoning and full of imputations and bad logic, and if the facts set forth in the

* The monstrous sentences awarded by the special courts had scandalised the Indian public at the time.

son's statement are true, the convicting Magistrate is utterly unfit to sit as a judge. Mr. Jamiat Singh's crime seems to have been that he was present at the mosque meeting and advocated *hartal*, and that he was a rich man, for, the Magistrate disbelieves the testimony of impartial witnesses, because "Jamiat Singh is a rich man." It is sufficient for the Magistrate that the accused was with the mob that stoned the troopers, that "if he prevented boys from breaking fencing, there may have been some other reason, but he certainly was in the mob." Thus everything in favour of the accused is deliberately disregarded by the Magistrate. The reader must go through the judgment to feel the force of my remarks regarding its incoherence. But the son's statement makes what seems apparently to be an injustice appear blacker still. Is it true that the Magistrate confiscated the accused's property without a moment's notice, that the inmates were subjected to the treatment described in the statement, and if it is true, was it not a lawless act? Is it true that the witnesses cited for the defence were not called, that the defence counsel was not allowed to appear, when the charge was framed against the accused? So much for the precious judgment.

The treatment received by the accused before and after judgment seems to have been in keeping with the proceedings of the court. It was an inhuman act to make him walk handcuffed with his bedding under his arm-pit. It reminds one of General Hudson's speech about the hand and knee order, which, by the way, should be, according to the correction made by Pandit Jawahirlal Nehru, described as the crawling order. It is evident that the proceedings taken by the authorities were intended, like the crawling order, to produce an impression on the people. It is difficult on any other ground to understand the insulting and cruel treatment to which the accused was subjected. Even the help he rendered the Government during the war period by subscribing the largest amount in Wazirabad to the war loan, and by recruiting, was of no avail. The *Sanad* granted to him for his loyal services was of no service to him when he was put in the dock, and treated as a common felon.

I cannot congratulate the Punjab Government on the reduction of the sentence to six months, when the accused seems clearly to be entitled to a full discharge. The case, as appears from the statement, is now to be investigated by the Revision Judges. I have already ventured to express my misgivings about this Revision Tribunal. Its composition cannot inspire any confidence or hope. If the Government fail to repair the irreparable mistakes, create tribunals merely in order to cover themselves, they will forfeit all title to respect and intelligent co-operation. The dead are buried and gone, but it is intolerable that the living, who are now suffering undeserved punishment, are not given an opportunity of showing their innocence before a tribunal in which they and the public can have full confidence.

19*th November*, 1919

BHAI PARAMANAND

(By. M. K. Gandhi)

Mr. Andrews has dealt with the case of Bhai Paramanand * in pathetic language in the columns of the

* In 1915 Bhai Paramanand was convicted under Sections 121, 121-A (abetment of waging war against the King), and 124-A., I.P.C.

Tribune. Bhai Paramanand belongs to the band of Indians daily growing in numbers who have set apart their lives for India's service and have accepted comparative poverty as their lot. It was in that spirit that under the influence of Lala Hansaraj that he joined the D. A. V. College at Lahore as a professor. By his unassuming manners, industry and sterling character he made himself popular with the students as also the staff. He then paid a visit to South Africa and preached on the necessity of religion as a factor in life-building. He left on my mind a deep impression as a man full of truth and nobility. He came in close touch with me during his visit to that sub-continent, and was nearly a month my honoured guest. I had many a chat with him on various matters, and I believe that his patriotism was of a lofty type, a patriotism that would disdain to use violence to serve national ends. He went to England from South Africa. There he came in touch with the school of violence headed by Pandit Shyamji Krishnavarma. But the truth in him burnt as brightly as ever even in the midst of temptation. His frank and fearless

(Sedition) and sentenced to the extreme penalty of law by a Special Tribunal consisting of three Commissioners in what is known as the Lahore Conspiracy Case. On the recommendation of one of the Commissioners, the sentences was commuted to one of transporation for life and forfeiture of property. The evidence on which he was convicted was based on the story of unreliable approvers and was so flimsy that, earlier in the proceedings, the Government Advocate recommended the withdrawal of proceedings against him. "If we could have manufactured any evidence," said Mr. Bevan Petman, the Government Advocate, who was subsequently raised to the High Court Bench, we could have done so against Bhai Paramanand, whom we all along suspected and were anxious to get in. But all that the principal approvers say against him amount to this—that he had no knowledge of the conspiracy." Sir M. O'Dwyer, however, persisted and got a conviction against Paramanand!

statement before the court shows that he has hidden nothing. He has made admissions which are damaging to him. He was not bound to make any statement, but he would not flinch. He felt that he would hide nothing even though his statement involved a conviction. His statement itself provides no material for a conviction. But the special court tacked to it other evidence and condemned him.

The able petition presented by his wife, and reproduced elsewhere,* contains a convincing analysis of the case. I do not propose to refer to it for the moment. My purpose is to show that the Government have grievously erred in treating an honourable man as a common felon. Assume his guilt. It was still wrong to send him to the Andamans. It was easy, if he was an enemy, to turn him into a friend by humane treatment. If he was really dangerous it was right to deprive him of his liberty. But it was cruel to herd him with ordinary prisoners or to send him to the Andamans. I have taken care to ask many men in Lahore and elsewhere about Bhai Paramanand. Not one man believed in his guilt. Every one of them considers him to be innocent of the crime imputed to him. A government that exists by terror does not deserve to exist at all. For such a government Bhai Paramanand has been long enough in jail. His wife and children were deprived (I think illegally) of their personal effects under the order of forfeiture. His letters show that Bhai Paramanand, instead of being embittered, has been leading in the Andamans a life of religious introspection. It is not right for the Government to keep such a man in prison. I trust that His Honour the Lieutenant-Governor of the Punjab will examine the case, and what

*Omitted in this collection.

is more, inquire about Bhai Paramanand's record in the Andamans and discharge him without delay. I trust, too, that the public and the press will study this case and urge the Government to release Bhai Paramanand.

26th May, 1920

A HARD CASE

(BY M. K. GANDHI)

I have received the following telegram from the families of Messrs. Bugga and Ratanchand:

"Bugga and Ratto under orders transfer Andamans. Bugga suffering hernia and piles since ten years. Was operated upon. Ratto aged over forty and therefore should not be sent Andamans under Jail Manual Rule 721."

The readers will remember that these were the accused on whose behalf appeals were made to the Privy Council in common with others and whose appeals were rejected on technical grounds. The Hon'ble Pandit Motilal Nehru has analysed the cases and shown that they are no more guilty than the others who have been discharged. But several who were originally sentenced to death had their sentences commuted to imprisonment and are now set free. What is it that distinguishes these two cases from the others? Is it the fact of the appeal itself? If they had not appealed or rather a philanthrophic lawyer out of pity had not taken up their case, fought for them against tremendous odds, they would not have escaped the hangman's horse. H. H. the Lieut.-Governor of the Punjab has been showing a generous discretion in releasing many who suffered between April and June last year. Although he had the opportunity, after the dismissal of the appeal, to hang Messrs. Bugga and Ratanchand, H. E. the Viceroy, it is equally true, has commuted the sentence of death to one of transportation. But I venture to submit that if the Royal Proclamation is to be given effect to in the fullest measure, Messrs. Bugga and Ratanchand are entitled to their liberty. They are no more a danger to the State than Lala Harkishenlal, Pundit Rambhuj Dutt Chaudhri and others of that distinguished company. But for the time being, strong as the case is for their discharge, I am pleading not for a complete release but for keeping them in the Punjab and, if they have been sent away already, for bringing them back, if for nothing else, out of consideration for the wives of these poor men. Let not the public think that the acts of the Government of the day are dictated only by fear and expediency, not by logic and high principles of justice.

31st December, 1919

THE ROYAL PROCLAMATION

(BY. M. K. GANDHI)

The Proclamation* issued by the Sovereign on the 24th instant is a document of which the British people have every reason to be proud, and with which every Indian ought to feel satisfied. Coming on the top of the dis-

* In giving assent to the Indian Reform Act of 1919, the King-Emperor issued a Proclamation, surveying the progress of the Reform movement, calling upon the people and the officials to co-operate with one another in an early advance towards free institutions, and directing the Viceroy to amnesty political prisoners as far as public safety permitted.

closures made before Lord Hunter's Committee, the Proclamation gives one an insight into the true British character. For as the Proclamation shows it at its best, General Dyer's inhumanity shows it at its worst. The Proclamation is the evidence of the intention to do justice, as General Dyer's deed is proof of man becoming devil under fear and excitement. I believe that the juxtaposition of the two events is a pure accident. The Proclamation was the inevitable consequence of the great measure which has received Royal assent. It was the finishing touch. The Reforms Act coupled with the Proclamation is an earnest of the intention of the British people to do justice to India. And it ought to remove suspicion on that score. But that does not mean that we may sit with folded hands and may still expect to get what we want. Under the British constitution no one gets anything without a hard fight for it. No one for a moment believes the statements made in the Parliament that the Reforms have not been granted because of the agitation. We must lay to heart the advice of the President of the Congress that we shall gain nothing without agitation. We would have been nowhere if there had been no Congress to agitate for the rights of the people. Agitation means no more than movement towards something. But just as all movement does not mean progress, so does all agitation not mean success. Undisciplined agitation which is a paraphrase of violence of speech or deed, can only retard national growth and bring about even unmerited retribution such as the Jallianwalla Bagh massacre. Disciplined agitation is the condition of national growth. The most correct agitation, therefore, consists in the most correct action and we have little doubt that the Royal Proclamation and the Reforms mean not less agitation and less work but more agitation and more work of the correct type.

The Reforms are undoubtedly incomplete, they do not give us enough; we were entitled to more, we could have managed more. But the Reforms are not such as we may reject.* On the contrary they are such as to enable us to expand. Our duty therefore is not to subject them to carping criticism but to settle down quietly to work, so as to make them a thorough success and thus anticipate the time for a full measure of responsibility. Our work, therefore, may now well consist in agitation turned inward. Let us concentrate on ridding ourselves of social abuses, on producing a strong electorate and on sending to the councils men who would seek election not for self-advertisement but for national service.

There has been much mutual distrust between us—the English and ourselves. General Dyer forgot the dignity of man and became unmanly because he was seized with distrust and consequent fear. He feared that he might be 'assaulted.' The Proclamation more than the Reforms replaces distrust by trust. It remains to be seen whether the trust will filter down the Civil Service. But let us assume that it will, and let us respond in the fullest measure. We cannot be wrong in so doing. To trust is a virtue. It is weakness that begets distrust. The best satisfaction we can show is undoubtedly to work gracefully and ungrudgingly. Our honest work will constitute the best guarantee for the quickening of progress towards the goal.

Throughout all these years, the one figure that has laboured for India without, for a single moment, turning

* Subsequently, Mr. Gandhi had to change his views on the subject. See *infra*.

back is Mr. Montagu. We have had many Secretaries of State who have adorned their office. But no Secretary has so well adorned it as Mr. Montagu. He has been a true friend of India. He has earned our gratitude. And for Lord Sinha? He has added lustre to his country. Indians have every reason to be proud of him.

10*th December*, 1919

THE KASUR INCIDENT

If we may generalise from a particular instance, the Kasur incident of which the description is given in a letter to the *Tribune*, reproduced elsewhere,* and

* A correspondent from Kasur wrote to the *Tribune* under date 27th November:—Accompanied by Dr. Parsram, Mr. Gandhi visited Kasur yesterday in order to see two Indians who were said to have been assaulted by Mr. Marsden, the S. D. O., on Friday last. They gave Mr. Gandhi written statements of what had actually taken place. One of them, Kader Bux, a vegetable dealer, was assaulted rather severely because he was suspected of having stuck up on his wall a Khilafat placard. Another, a storekeeper named Goolam Mahamad also made a statement, saying that he was struck for the same thing. The notices in question were removed. But Mr. Marsden quickly realised that he had made a mistake. He found out that the notices were quite inoffensive and that they were put at the instance of Mr. Goolam Mahay-ud-Din, the well-known pleader of Kasur. He at once apologised and paid Kader Bux ten rupees as compensation. During his stay at Kasur, Mr. Gandhi saw Mr. Marsden at his invitation and discussed the incident with him. Mr. Marsden authorised Mr. Gandhi, who was to address a public meeting of the people of Kasur the same afternoon, to express his regret for the hasty action he had taken under the belief that the placards in question were of an inflammatory character. Mr. Gandhi consequently announced to the meeting the handsome manner in which Mr. Marsden had apologised for the mistake made by him. The meeting was attended by over three thousand men, and two to three hundred ladies were also present. After referring to the unfortunate incident, Mr. Gandhi explained why

fully confirmed by Mr. Gandhi shows that officers in the Punjab are prone to use force on the merest shadow of provocation. But the significance of the incident, small

---

the Congress Sub-committee had decided to withdraw co-operation from Lord Hunter's Committee and invited those who had not already made their statements before the Sub-committee to do so now. The speaker also dwelt strongly on the excesses committed by the mob and said that India's deliverance lay through resistence of wrong by quiet, dignified, suffering. Truth and fearlessness were necessary for removal of all wrongs.

The following account given by Mr. Gandhi of the Kasur incident fully corroborates the account given by the correspondent to the "Tribune": "I had received a telegram from Kasur that a Musalman was severely beaten by the Sub-divisional officer there, for a Khilafat placard stuck on his wall. The man had not stuck the placard at all, and it was harmless. I thought this was a serious affair. That British officers should take the law in their own hands and commit a criminal offence should be intolerable. I therefore visited Kasur in company with Dr. Parasaram and took the statements of two Musalmans who were beaten by the Sub-divisional officer. In the meantime, I received a note from Mr. Marsden, the S. D. O., asking me to see him. He said in the course of his conversation that he had apologised to the Musalman and paid Rs. 10 to him as compensation. I told him that as he had publicly beaten the Musalman he should also publicly apologise. He agreed to my publicly expressing his regret. The notices were also restored on the wall. Just after this visit I had to address a big public meeting attended by about three thousand men and women. I expressed to them Mr. Marsden's unconditional regret and the people were greatly satisfied". Mr. Gandhi also refers to a visit to Wazirabad where the people were so very much fear stricken that they would not even accommodate him and his friends and they had at last to put up in a Sikh temple! There was a surprise in store for him, he says, at Nizamabad, a small village over fifty milles from Lahore where an industrious population of blacksmiths manufacture cutlery which is reputed to be the best in India, beautiful handles for sticks and fine rifles. He was very sorry that fine craftsmanship lay thus hidden and unknown in distant villages and that even he with his deep interest in Swadesh did not know of this village.

though it was, lies elsewhere. Mr. Marsden did no doubt take the law into his own hands, but hastened to make what reparation he could. He did not resent the presence of Mr. Gandhi as an unwarranted interference into local affairs, had not only the grace to invite Mr. Gandhi to explain the matter, but the further grace to accept Mr. Gandhi's suggestion that the reparation he had made was not adequate, unless there was a public expression of regret, for an offence committed in public and the still further grace to authorise Mr. Gandhi to publish his regret for what he had done. On the other hand, the public expression of regret was sufficient to satisfy the people, who welcomed it, and have not only forgiven the officer and forgotten the incident, but probably think more highly of him than before. The moral is obvious. Patient truth must tell. The public, instead of taking any precipitate action, calmly pointed out to the officer his mistake; he had to admit it and made sufficient amends for it. For the ruling class there could be no better instance of the triumph of regard for truth. Mr. Marsden had committed, no doubt, a grave mistake, but having admitted the mistake found a public ready to respect him all the more.

If instances as these were more common in India, good-will between the rulers and the ruled would be the rule, and ill-will and consequent disturbances a thing of the past.

11th February, 1920

TWO PICTURES

The following has been received by Shrimati Sarladevi Chaudhrani from the Government of India:

GOVERNMENT OF INDIA
ARMY DEPARTMENT, DELHI,
Dated 8th Dec., 1919.

Madam,

I am directed to refer to the list published with the *Gazette of India*, dated the 29th July, 1919, in which you were mentioned for valuable services rendered in India in connection with the War, 1914—1919 and to forward as a souvenir and a mark of appreciation of the Government of India the war badge enclosed.

I am,
Your obedient servant,
(Sd.) G. H. BINGLEY, *Major-General*,
Secretary to the Government of India.

TO MRS. DUTT CHAUDHARI.

She was instrumental in sending many a Bengali youth to the war. It is said that it was her poetry, her touching songs and addresses that appealed to the masses and inspired them to offer their services and co-operation. Hence the badge she has only just had the honour of receiving.

Now turn to the other picture.

To

THE COMMITTEE OF THE LAHORE PURDAH CLUB,
Government House, Lahore.
17-4-19

As President of the Lahore Purdah Club, I wish to let you know that the names of Chaudhari and Chaudhrani Rambhuj Dutt have been taken off the Government House list.

I should like the Committee of the Purdah Club here to consider at once the desirability of first giving the Chaudhrani the opportunity of resigning her membership of our Purdah Club before taking steps to remove her name from the list of our members.

It is obvious that the wife of the Lieutenant-Governor cannot belong to the same club as the wife of Chaudhari Rambhuj Dutt.

As Mrs. Richey is away and has appointed no one to take her place, I am taking upon myself to act as secretary and I am writing to Mrs. Richey to that effect so as not to waste time and if the members, English and Indian, agree and sign enclosed, the notice from our Lahore Purdah Club can be sent to the Chaudhrani in a day or two.

I am,
Yours sincerely
(Sd.) ANNA O'DWYER.

SIMLA,
April 22nd, 1919.

Dear Madam,

I am requested by the Committee, Lahore Purdah Club, to ask you to send in your resignation of membership of this Club and to forward to you the enclosed notice.

Yours faithfully,
(Sd.) M. RICHEY,
Hon. Secy., Purdah Club.

[The notice sent to Shrimati Sarladevi is the draft notice referred to in the following.—Ed. Y. I.]

Notice from the President of the Committee of the Lahore Purdah Club sent to Chaudhrani Rambhuj Dutt, dated 2nd April 1919.

We, the English and Indian members of the Committee of the Lahore Purdah Club, in consequence of what has happened, consider that your name should no longer appear among its members and understand from this that you will not in future be welcome to any of our meetings.

(Sd.) M. RICHEY,
Secy., Purdah Club.

Copies of member signatures—
Anna O'Dwyer (*President*)
Mildred Kitchin
Mrs. B. J. Rustomjee
Mrs. K. Rustomjee
Begum Zulfiquar Ali Khan
A. N. Mahomed Shafi
Marie Woolver
Mrs. K. Niamatullah
Mrs. Thapar
P. W. Thapar
F. R. Sirajuddin Mohini Mayadas
F. B. Ahmed Hussain
Nancy Ewing Lucas.

Let it be remembered that Pandit Rambhuj Dutt Chaudhari was simply deported along with other Lahore leaders on mere suspicion. There was nothing proved against him. The trial followed a considerable time later. But the day after his doportation, his and Mrs. Chaudhari's names were removed from the Government House list. The same day Lady O'Dwyer hastened to circulate the letter and procure the signatures of the members of the Purdah Ladies Club. It is painful to find cultured Indian ladies being so terror-struck as to easily expose themselves to ridicule and insult. For, in sending the notice they did to Sarladevi Chaudhrani, they insulted not Mrs. Chaudhari but themselves.

Shrimati Sarladevi is a member of the Bengal aristocracy, wife of a noted leader of the Punjab and, what is more, one of the few highly educated and gifted ladies India possesses. It was the Club that was honoured by her being its member. We have no desire to give undue prominence to this indiscretion of Lady O'Dwyer, 'blazing' though it was. We hope, now that everybody seems to be regaining sanity, either Lady Maclagan or the members themselves would right this wrong they have done to themselves and to society.

3rd March, 1920

THE AMRITSAR APPEALS

(By M. K. Gandhi)

So these appeals* have been dismissed in spite of the advocacy of the best counsel that were obtainable. The Privy Council has confirmed lawless procedure. I must confess that the judgment does not come upon me quite as a surprise, though the remarks of the judges as Sir John Simon was developing his argument on behalf of the appellants, led one to expect a favourable verdict. My opinion based upon a study of political cases is that the judgments, even of the highest Tribunals, are not unaffected by subtle political considerations. The most elaborate precautions taken to procure a purely judicial mind must break down at critical moments. The Privy Council cannot be free the limitations of all human institutions which are good enough only for normal

* Some 20 victims of martial law administration of the Punjab appealed to the Privy Council on the ground that the Viceroy had no power to issue the Martial Law ordinances and that the procedure followed by the summary courts was irregular.

conditions. The consequences of a decision favourable to the people would have exposed the Indian Government to indescribable discredit from which it would have been difficult to free itself for a generation.

Its political significance can be gauged from the fact that as soon as the news was received in Lahore all the preparations that were made to accord a fitting welcome to Lala Lajpatrai were immediately cancelled and the Capital of the Punjab was reported to be in deep mourning. Deeper discredit, therefore, now attaches to the Government by reason of the judgment, because rightly or wrongly the popular opinion will be that there is no justice under the British constitution when large political or racial considerations are involved.

There is only one way to avoid the catastrophe. The human and especially the Indian mind quickly responds to generosity. I hope that without the necessity of an agitation or petitions the Punjab Government or the Central Government will immediately cancel the death sentences and, if at all possible, simultaneously set the appellants free.

This is required by two considerations each equally important. The first is that of restoring public confidence which I have already mentioned. The second is fulfilment of the Royal Proclamation to the letter. That great political document orders the release of all the political offenders who may not by their release prove a danger to society. No one can possibly suggest that the twenty-one appellants will, if they are set free, in any shape or form constitute a danger to society. They never had committed any crimes before. Most of them were regarded as respectable and orderly citizens. They were not known to belong to any revolutionary society. If they committed any crimes at all, they were committed only under the impulse of the moment and under what to them was grave provocation. Moreover, the public believe that the majority of the convictions by the Martial Law Tribunals were unsupported by any good evidence. I, therefore, hope that the Government, which have so far been doing well in discharging political offenders even when they were caught in the act, will not hesitate to release these appellants and thus earn the good-will of the whole of India. It is an act of generosity done in the hour of triumph which is the most effective. And in the popular opinion this dismissal of the appeal has been regarded as a triumph for the Government.

I would respectfully plead with the Punjab friends not to lose heart. We must calmly prepare ourselves for the worst. If the convictions are good, if the men convicted have been guilty of murders or incitements to murder, why should they escape punishment? If they have not committed these crimes as we believe most at least have not, why should we escape the usual fate of all who are trying to rise a step higher? Why should we fear the sacrifice if we would rise? No nations have ever risen without sacrifice and sacrifice can only be spoken of in connection with innocence and not with crime.

26th May, 1920

SAVARKAR BROTHERS

(By M. K. Gandhi)

"It is My earnest desire at this time that so far as possible any trace of bitterness between My people and those who are responsible for my Government should be obliterated. Let those who in their eagerness for political progress had broken the law in the past, respect it in the future. Let it become possible for those who are charged with the maintenance of peaceful and orderly Government to forget the extravagances which they have had to curb. A new era is opening. Let it begin with a common determination among My people and officers to work together for a common purpose. I therefore direct My Viceroy to exercise in My name and on My behalf My Royal clemency to political offenders in the fullest measure which in his judgment is compatible with the public safety. I desire him to extend it on this condition to persons who, for offences against the State or under any special or emergency legislation, are suffering imprisonment or restrictions upon their liberty. I trust that this leniency will by justified by the future conduct of those whom it benefits and that all My subjects will so demean themselves as to render it unnecessary to force the laws for such offences hereafter".—*The Royal Proclamation of 24th December*. 1919.

The Proclamation from which the above extract has been copied was published in December last. Thanks to the action of the Government of India and the Provincial Governments, many of those who were undergoing imprisonment at the time have received the benefit of the Royal clemency. But there are some notable "political offenders" who have not yet been discharged. Among these I count Savarkar brothers. They are political offenders in the same sense as men, for instance, who have been discharged in the Punjab. And yet these two brothers have not received their liberty although five months have gone by after the publication of the Proclamation.

Mr. Ganesh Damodar Savarkar, the elder of the two, was born in 1879, and received an ordinary education. He took a prominent part in the Swadeshi movement at Nasik in 1908. He was sentenced to transportation for life with confiscation of property under sections 121, 121-A, 124-A and 153-A on the 9th day of June 1909, and is now serving his sentence in the Andamans. He has therefore had eleven years of imprisonment.

Section 121 is the famous section which was utilised during the Punjab trials and refers to "waging war against the King." The minimum penalty is transportation for life with forfeiture of property. 121-A is a similar section. 124-A relates to sedition. 153-A relates to promotion of enmity between classes 'by words either spoken or written' or 'otherwise.'" It is clear therefore that all the offences charged against Mr. Savarkar (senior) were of a public nature. He had done no violence. He was married, had two daughters who are dead, and his wife died about eighteen months ago.

The other brother was born in 1884, and is better known for his career in London. His sensational attempt to escape the custody of the police and his jumping through a port-hole in French waters, are still fresh in the public mind. He was educated at the Fergusson College, finished off in London and became a Barrister. He is the author of the proscribed history of the Sepoy Revolt of 1857. He was tried in 1910, and received the same sentence as his brother on 24th December, 1910. He was charged also in 1911 with abetment of murder. No act of violence was proved against him either. He too is married, had a son in 1909. His wife is still alive.

Both these brothers have declared their political opinions and both have stated that they do not entertain any revolutionary ideas and that if they were set free they would like to work under the Reforms Act, for they consider that the reforms enable one to work thereunder so as to achieve political responsibility for India. They both state unequivocally that they do not desire independence from the British connection. On the contrary, they feel that India's destiny can be best worked out in association with the British. Nobody has questioned their honour or their honesty, and in my opinion the published expression of their views ought to be taken at its face value. What is more, I think, it may be safely stated that the cult of violence has, at the present moment, no following in India. Now the only reason for still further restricting the liberty of the two brothers, can only be 'danger to public safety,' for, the Viceroy has been charged by His Majesty to exercise the Royal clemency to political offenders in the fullest manner which in his judgment is compatible with public safety. I hold therefore that unless there is absolute proof that the discharge of the two brothers who have already suffered long enough terms of imprisonment, who have lost considerably in body-weight and who have declared their political opinions, can be proved to be a danger to the State, the Viceroy is bound to give them their liberty. The obligation to discharge them, on the one condition of public safety being fulfilled, is in the Viceroy's political capacity just as imperative as it was for the Judges in their judical capacity to impose on the two brothers the minimum penalty allowed by law. If they are to be kept under detention any longer, a full statement justifying it is due to the public.

This case is no better and no wrose than that of Bhai Paramanand who, thanks to the Punjab Government, has after a long term of imprisonment received his discharge. Nor need his case be distinguished from that of Savarkar brothers in the sense that Bhai Paramanand pleaded absolute innocence. So far as the Government are concerned, all were alike guilty because all were convicted. And the Royal clemency is due not merely to doubtful cases but equally to all cases of offences proved up to the hilt. The conditions are that the offence must be political and the exercise of Royal clemency should not, in the opinion of the Viceroy, endanger public safety. There is no question about the brothers being political offenders. And so far the public are aware there is no danger to public safety. In answer to a question in the Viceregal Council in connection with such cases the reply given was that they were under consideration. But their brother has received from the Bombay Government a reply to the effect that no further memorials regarding them will be received and Mr. Montagu has stated in the House of Commons that in the opinion of the Government of India they cannot be released. The case however cannot be so easily shelved. The public are entitled to know the precise grounds upon which the liberty of the brothers is being restrained in spite of the Royal Proclamation which to them is as good as a royal charter having the force of law.

17*th December*, 1919

THE RAMNAGAR TRAGEDY

Mr. Purshotamdas Tandon's public letter flatly contradicting the allegation that any effigy of the King-Emperor was burnt at Ramnagar* still remains unchall-

* Under the direction of Pandits Malaviya and Nehru, Mr. Tandon, a vakil of the Allahabad High Court and leader, investigated the occurrences in the Punjab, about August 1919. He wrote to *Young India*, of 15th October that, as a result of his investigation, he found there was no truth at all in the story which was built up as an after-thought on the fact of a few boys holding a demonstration against the Rowlat Bill on the 15th April, and that the people knew obsolutely nothing about the alleged investigation into the affair by two special officers who are said to have confirmed the finding of the Magistrate O'Brien.

enged. Indeed, Pandit Jagat Narayan's and Sahebzada Sultan Ahmed's examination of Col. O'Brien entirely corroborates all the statements in that letter. Colonel O'Brien admitted that in the first report of the trouble at Ramnager he had received, there was no mention of the burning of the effigy of the King-Emperor there. He also admitted that he tried the case which involved the examination of about 130 witnesses and gave the accused the full sentence that he could give and maintained that the accused had a fair trial. What doubt can there be that the accused had a fair trial when they were convicted and sentenced on the sole evidence of "two Hindus and one Muhammadan"—out of the whole host of one hundred witnesses disposed of by him—"who gave evidence as to the burning of the effigy as also to the casting of ashes into the river?" The Commissioners, we hope, do know what value they should attach to the finding of a colonel who even before them is not ashamed to boast that 'he made the arrests whether he was powered or not.'

Mr. Gandhi has since visited Ramnagar and after his inquiries, he is convinced that the people there are absolutely innocent, that they have been unjustly imprisoned, abused and insulted. And yet no less than twenty-eight respectable citizens at Ramnagar are still rotting in jail for the alleged burning of an effigy of the King-Emperor.

14th July, 1920.

A SUPERINTENDENT'S ORDER

Mr. Gandhi writes to the Press:

The Hon'ble Pandit Madan Mohan Malaviya has handed to me an order signed by Mr. F. A. Heron, the

Superintendent of Police, Gujranwala (Punjab). The Panditji has given it to me for publication with such criticism as I could offer out of my experience of the Gujranwala district, the whole of which I visited during my stay in the Punjab. The order is dated the 5th June, 1919. It may be recalled that Superintendent Heron it was who directed the firing when one of the Railway bridges was set fire to by a Gujranwala crowd on the 14th April, 1919. Here is the order in question:

ORDER

Gujranwala, dated 5th of June, 1919.

TO THE SUB-INSPECTOR OF POLICE—

It is now practically certain that Martial Law will be taken off in this district, from those towns upon which it is still in force in a few days. The result of this will be that only those cases actually at the time of removal of Martial Law then under trial before the Martial Law Commissions will be allowed to continue to be tried under Martial Law.

All other cases whether under investigation or under trial before a Summary Court will have to be dropped and can then only be tried under the ordinary law. This will mean greatly prolonging these cases as under the ordinary law cases will proceed slowly in court and there will be appeals, etc. It is therefore imperative that all cases now ready for trial in the Summary Courts should be sent up for trial immediately and that all cases still under investigation which can be completed rapidly should be completed immediately and sent up for trial. In this district so far the police have sent up compartively few cases for trial and so there must be many persons who are guilty and against whom there is proof available who should be sent up for trial without delay.

Great efforts must now be made to complete all pending cases at once. Identification parades should be held immediately and every endeavour must be made to call up new witnesses, etc., who can help in proving the guilt of the accused.

Proper attention has not so far been paid to securing the arrests of absconders. This must now be done. Constables, Sufedposhes, etc., should now be sent out immediately after absconders and every effort made to capture them at once. It is not sufficient merely to send a Ruqua to some police stations for their arrests.

*I need not impress upon my officers the great necessity of completing their cases at once and of getting a sufficient number of accused dealt with before Martial Law is removed. This district in point of view of numbers sent up for trial is far behind other districts and this naturally arouses criticisms on the efficiency and energy shown by the police here. Something can still be done to improve matters and if all my officers put their hearts into the work there is no reason why the reputation of all the investigating staff here should suffer in comparison with those who have investigated in Lahore and Amritsar, but should the number sent up for trial continue so small all concerned will undoubtedly not receive the *Qader* and respect they are in some instances entitled to.

5-6-1919

(Sd.) F. A. HERON,
Superintendent of Police,
Gujranwala.

Scores of witnesses in the district gave evidence before the Congress Sub-committee that during the last days of Martial Law, batches after batches of prisoners were hurried to the Summary Courts so-called. The presiding officer sat late at night and without even examining defence witnesses condemned absolutely innocent men to varying terms of imprisonment. One of the officers who thus conducted trials was Col. O'Brien, and the other was Mr. Bosworth Smith. The order reproduced above adds emphasis to the evidence recorded by the Congress Committee and throws a lurid light on the way in which prosecutions took place. And it was in this summary and hasty manner that men who were absolutely innocent of any crime were harrassed and imprisoned at Akalgarh, Ramnagar and other places, and still these officials retain their offices and the power of doing evil.

18*th November*, 1920

JALLIANWALA BAGH

(BY M. K. GANDHI)

There was an unfortunate hitch about the purchase of this Bagh* for the nation. Thanks to the efforts of the

* Mr. Gandhi, in a letter to the *Navajivan*, thus speaks about the Jallianwalla Bagh: The name 'Jallianwalla Bagh' is a misnomer. 'Jallian' is a surname, and the original owner of the place was a 'Jallian.' The 'Bagh' is to-day the joint property of about 40 partners. It is not a 'Bagh' or garden, but a dunghill. It is hemmed in on all sides by the back walls of houses and people have made it a convenient place to throw house-refuse in from back windows. It is an open space with three trees and a tomb, and is accessible by a narrow lane. General Dyer used this land to approach the Bagh. The people who were attending the meeting in the Bagh on the 13th

Hon'ble Pundit Madan Mohan Malaviya, Sanyasi Swami Shri Shraddhananda and the local leaders, it has now become the property of the nation, subject to the full payment of the purchase price within three months from the 6th instant. The purchase price is Rs. 5,36,000. And the amount must be raised within the prescribed period.

It is, therefore, necessary to examine the propriety of making this purchase on behalf of the nation, especially as it has been questioned even in enlightened quarters. With the Cawnpore Memorial before us the attitude is not to be wondered at. But with all respect to objectors, I cannot help saying that if the Bagh had not been acquired, it would have been a national disgrace. Can we afford to forget those five hundred or more men who were killed although they had done nothing wrong either morally or legally? If they had died knowingly and willingly, if, realising their innocence, they had stood their ground and faced the shots from the fifty rifles, they would have gone down to history as saints, heroes and patriots. But even as it was, the tragedy became one of first class national importance. Nations are born out of travail and suffering. We

---

April were thus penned up, and had no way of escape except at three or four places by jumping walls. Thousands escaped with their lives by jumping the walls on that fateful day.

Torrents of innocent blood have hallowed this ground. Attempts are being made to purchase it for public purposes and if we do not succeed, it will be a shame to us.

We may add to this the *Times of India* correspondent's description: "Thousands are paying visits to Jallianwalla Bagh which is a large open space surrounded on all sides by dwelling houses with two or three bottle-necked entrances to it. Some of the walls of houses round about bear marks of the bullets fired from the machine guns and attract the attention of the sightseers visiting the scene."

should forfeit all title to be considered a nation, if we failed to treasure the memory of those, who in our battle for political freedom might, innocently or for the crimes of others, lose their lives or otherwise suffer. We were unable to protect our helpless countrymen when they were ruthlessly massacred. We may decline, if we will, to avenge the wrong. The nation will not lose if we did. But shall we—can we afford to—decline to perpetuate the memory and to show to the surviving members of the families of the dead that we are sharers in their sufferings, by erecting a national tombstone and by telling the world thereby that in the death of these men each one of us has lost dear relations? If national instinct does not mean at least this much kinship, it has no meaning for me. I hold it to be our duty to tell the present generation and generations yet unborn that in our march towards true freedom we must be prepared for repetitions of the wrongs such as the Jallianwala Bagh massacre. We must provide against them, we must not seek them, but we must be ready to face them if they came again. I would not have us flinch from the battle of national life. The supreme lesson of the Amritsar Congress* was that the sufferings of the Punjab did not dishearten the nation but that the nation treated them as a matter of course. Some of us made stupid mistakes and the innocent suffered for them. We must in future try to avoid the mistakes, but in spite of our best effort, we may fail to convert every one to sanity. We must, therefore, be ready for the repetition of the sufferings of the guiltless by telling the country now that they and theirs shall not be forgotten but that the memory of the innocent dead shall be regarded as a sacred trust and that the surviving relations shall have the right to look to the

*For the resolutions of this Congress, *see* Appendix.

nation for maintenance in case of need. This is the primary meaning of the memorial. And has not the blood of the Mahomedan mixed with that of the Hindu? Has not the blood of the Sikh mixed with that of the Sanatanist and the Samajist? The memorial should be a national emblem of an honest and sustained effort to achieve Hindu-Muslim unity.

But the objector's objection still remains unanswered. Will not the memorial also perpetuate bitterness and ill-will? It will depend upon the trustees. And if I know them, I know that that is not their intention at all. I know that such was not the intention of the vast assembly. I go not wish to convey that bitterness was not there. It was there not in any way suppressed. But the idea of the memorial had nothing of bitterness in it. The people want to, they must be encouraged to, forget the doer and his madness. What General Dyer did we may all do if we had his irresponsibility and opportunity. To err is human and it must be held to be equally human to forgive if we, though being fallible, would like rather to be forgiven than punished and reminded of our misdeeds. Nor does this mean that we may not ask for General Dyer's dismissal. A lunatic cannot be kept in a position from which he can do harm to his neighbours. But just as we do not bear ill-will towards a lunatic, so too may we not bear ill-will even towards General Dyer. I would therefore eschew from the memorial all idea of bitterness and ill-will, but treat it as a sacred memory and regard the Bagh as a place of pilgrimage to be visited by all, irrespective of class, creed or colour. I would invite Englishmen to appreciate our feeling in the matter, ask them by subscribing to the memorial in the spirit of the Royal Proclamation to make common cause with us in our endeavour to regain consciousness, to realise the same freedom that they enjoy under the same constitution and to realise Hindu-Muslim unity without which there can be no true progress for India.

31*st March*, 1920

THE PUNJAB NON-OFFICIAL REPORT

The much expected report is published. The Commissioners may congratulate themselves on the methodical manner in which they have approached their work and the moderation with which they have handled their difficult task. The status of the Commissioners must give added weight to a report which is otherwise capable of standing on its merits. The Commissioners have not travelled beyond the evidence they had in their possession. The reader is, therefore, if he is so minded, able to test the conclusions for himself. The recommendations are neither wild nor weak. The Commissioners boldly ask for the recall of the Viceroy, and the dismissal from service of Sir Michæl O'Dwyer, General Dyer and other officers. These are the two recommendations against which there may be some opposition. But the Commissioners have given clear and unimpeachable reasons for each recommendation. And if the veracity of the facts set forth by them is not challenged, their recommendations are unchallengable.

It is not without much pain that we find ourselves in agreement with the recommendation for the Viceroy's recall. We believe His Excellency to be a cultured English gentleman, meaning well by India and anxious to do the right thing. But these are not the sole qualifications for the high Viceregal office. Lord Chelmsford has undoubtedly shown a lack of imagination. He has applied to his Indian office the traditions of a colonial constitutional Governor who has invariably to be guided by the advice of his ministers, is politically precluded from taking the initiative and affects colonial policies, if he affects them at all, not in virtue of office but through subtle influence and social intercourse. A Governor in the self-governing colonies acts by making gentle suggestions, never pressing them on his ministers, and tries to move public opinion, not by exercise of authority but by making indirect friends at social and semi-political functions. The very qualities therefore that enable a Colonial Governor to makes a success of himself disqualify Lord Chelmsford for the Viceregal office. The Viceroy of India has immense powers, he is an autocrat, he dominates the Executive Council. A mere suggestion from him is like a legal sanction. He initiates and gives effect to policies. He supervises, with the very tangible right of intervention, the administration of the provinces. He has, therefore, to be a strong ruler, with great imagination, with popular sympathies which he is never afraid to show. With all the qualities of the heart Lord Chelmsford has shown himself to be weak at critical junctures. Instead of leading his colleagues he has allowed himself to be ruled by them. He has allowed his provincial administrators to do as they have liked. The result was a variety of policies—level-headedness, or conciliation in Bombay even under provocation; repression, persecution and intolerance without provocation in Punjab. Such a contrast should be impossible under a Central Government with a chief at the centre who knows his mind and who knows how to impose his will on his subordinates. Lord Chelmsford has signally failed and so we believe that the Commissioners would have failed in their duty if they had hesitated to advise, with the facts before them, the recall of His Excellency the Viceroy.

With reference to the findings too, the Commissioners have 'if anything' erred on the side of moderation. But perhaps it would be better for the public to discuss the findings after the publication of the report of the official Committee. So far as the evidence collected by the non-official Commissioners goes, we feel that no other findings were possible. Indeed going through the evidence we can see a studious attempt to refrain from stating conclusions which could not be absolutely supported by overwhelming array of facts.

7th April, 1920

THE PUNJAB SENTENCES

(BY M. K. GANDHI)

The Commissioners appointed by the Congress Punjab Sub-committee have in their report accused His Excellency the Viceroy of criminal want of imagination. His Excellency's refusal to commute two death sentences out of five is a fine illustration of the accusation. The rejection of the appeal by the Privy Council no more proves the guilt of the condemned than their innocence could have been proved by quashing the proceedings before the Martial Law Tribunal. Moreover, these cases clearly come under the Royal Proclamation in accordance with its interpretation by the Punjab Government. The murders in Amritsar were not due to any private quarrel between the murderers and their victims. The offence, grave though it was, was purely political and committed under excitement. More than full reparation has been taken for the murders and arson. In the circumstances, commonsense dictates reduction of the death sentences. The popular belief favours the view that the condemned men are innocent and have not had a fair trial. The execution has been so long delayed that hanging at this stage would give a rude shock to Indian society. Any Viceroy with imagination would have at once announced commutation of the death sentences—not so Lord Chelmsford. In his estimation, evidently, the demands of justice will not be satisfied, if at least some of the condemned men are not hanged. Public feeling with him counts for nothing. We shall still hope that either the Viceroy or Mr. Montagu will commute the death sentences.

But if the Government will greviously err, if they carry out the sentences, the people will equally err if they give way to anger or grief over the hanging if it has unfortunately to take place. Before we become a nation possessing an effective voice in the councils of nations, we must be prepared to contemplate with equanimity, not a thousand murders of innocent men and women but many thousands before we attain a status in the world that shall not be surpassed by any nation. We hope therefore that all concerned will take rather than lose heart and treat hanging as an ordinary affair of life.*

[Since the above was in type, we have received the cruel news. At last H. E. the Viceroy has mercilessly given the rude shock to Indian society. It is now for the latter to take heart in spite of the unkindest cut.—Ed. Y. I.]

* *Sir Rabindranath's Message.*—The third and last of the series of public meetings in celebration of the National week was held in the open space near the French Bridge, Bombay, on the 13th, Mr. M. A. Jinnah presiding. The meeting was convened under the joint auspices

9th June, 1920

POLITICAL FREEMASONRY

(By M. K. Gandhi)

Freemasonry is a secret brotherhood which has, more by its secret and iron rules than by its service to humanity, obtained a hold upon some of the best minds. Similarly there seems to be some secret code of conduct governing the official class in India before which the

---

of the Bombay branches of the Home Rule League and the National Union.

The President at the outset announced that Sir Rabindranath Tagore was unable to be present but had sent a message, which he called upon Mr. C. F. Andrews to read.

Mr. Andrews thereupon read the message which ran as follows:

"A great crime has been done in the name of law in the Punjab. Such terrible eruptions of evil leave their legacy of the wreckage of ideals behind them. What happened in Jallianwalla Bagh was itself a monstrous progeny of a monstrous war, which for four years had been defiling God's world with fire and poison, physical and moral. The immenseness of the sin through which humanity had waded across its blood-red length of agony has bred callousness in the minds of those who have power in their hands with no check of sympathy within, or fear of resistance without. The cowardliness of the powerful who owned no shame in using their machines of frightfulness upon the unarmed and unwarned villagers, and inflicting unspeakable humiliations upon their fellow-beings behind the screen of an indecent mockery of justice, and yet not feeling for a moment that it was the meanest form of insult to their own manhood, has become only possible through the opportunity which the late war had given to man for constantly outraging his own higher nature, trampling truth and honour under foot. This disruption of the basis of civilsation will continue to produce a series of moral earthquakes, and men will have to be ready for still further sufferings. That the balance will take a long time to be restored, is clearly seen by the suicidal ferocity of vengefulness ominously tinging red the atmosphere of the peace deliberations.

flower of the great British nation fall prostrate and unconsciously become instruments of injustice which as private individuals they would be ashamed of perpetrating. In no other way is it possible for one to understand the majority report of the Hunter Committee, the despatch of the Government of India and the reply thereto of the Secretary of State for India. In spite of the energetic protests of a section of the Press to the personnel of the Committee, it might be said that on the

---

" But we have no place in these orgies of triumphant powers rending the world into bits according to their own purposes. What most concerns us is to know that the moral degradation not only pursues the people, inflicting indignities upon the helpless, but also their victims. The dastardliness of cruel injustice confident of its impunity is ugly and mean, but the fear and impotent anger which they are apt to breed upon the minds of the weak are no less abject. Brothers, when physical force, in its arrogant faith in itself, tries to crush the spirit of man, then comes the time for him to assert that his soul is indomitable. We shall refuse to be afraid and to own moral defeat by cherishing in our hearts foul dreams of retaliation. The time has come for the victims to be the victors in the field of righteousness.

"When brother spills the blood of his brother and exults in his sin, giving it a high sounding name; when he tries to keep the blood stains fresh on the soil as a memorial of his anger, then God in shame conceals it under His green grass and the sweet purity of His flowers. We who have witnessed the wholesale slaughter of the innocent in our neighbourhood, let us accept God's own office and cover the blood stains of iniquity with our prayer:

'Rudra yat te dakshinam mukham tena mam pahinityam'

'With Thy graciousness, O, Terrible, for ever save us.'

For the true grace comes from the Terrible, who can save our souls from the fear of suffering and death in the midst of terror and from vindictiveness in definance of injury. Let us take our lesson from His hand, even when the smart of the pain and insult is still fresh—the lesson that all meanness, cruelty and untruth are for the obscurityof oblivion, and only the Noble and True are for eternity. Let those,

whole the public were prepared to trust it, especially as it contained three Indian members who could fairly be claimed to be independent. The first rude shock to this confidence was delivered by the refusal of Lord Hunter's Committee to accept the very moderate and reasonable demand of the Congress Committee, that the imprisoned Punjab leaders might be allowed to appear before it to instruct counsel. Any doubt that might have been left in the mind of any person has been dispelled by the report of the majority of that Committee. The result has justified the attitude of the Congress Committee. The evidence collected by it shows what Lord Hunter's Committee purposely denied itself.

The minority report stands our like an oasis in a desert. The Indian members deserve the congratulation of their countrymen for having dared to do their duty

---

who wish, try to burden the minds of the future with stones, carrying the black memory of wrongs and their anger, but let us bequeath to the generations to come memorials of that only which we can revere,—let us be grateful to our fore-fathers, who have left us the image of our Buddha, who conquered self, preached forgiveness, and spread his love far and wide in time and space."

The Resolution.—Mr. Gandhi then moved the following resolution: "This meeting of the citizens of Bombay, is of opinion, that whilst mob excessess at Amritsar although committed after grave provocation were worthy of condemnation, the deliberate and calculated massacre without warning by General Dyer of innocent, unarmed and otherwise defenceless men at Jallianwala Bagh was an unexampled act of barbarity, and hopes that the Government of India and the Imperial Government will take such steps as to render impossible a repetition of such barbarity and other similar barbarities committed by responsible officers in the Punjab during the period of the martial law administration and hopes that the recommendations made by the Punjab Sub-Committee of the Indian National Congress will be carried out in their entirety."

The resolution was passed and the meeing was dissolved.

in the face of heavy odds. I wish that they had refused to associate themselves even in a modified manner with the condemnation of the Civil Disobedience form of Satyagraha... The defiant spirit of the Delhi mob on the 30th March, can hardly be used for condemning a great spiritual movement which is admittedly and manifestly intended to restrain the violent tendencies of mobs and to replace criminal lawlessness by civil disobedience of authority, when it has forfeited all title to respect. On the 30th March, Civil Disobedience had not even been started. Almost every great popular demonstration has been hitherto attended, all the world over, by a certain amount of lawlessness. The demonstration of 30th March and 6th April, could have been held under any other aegis as under that of Satyagraha. I hold that without the advent of the spirit of civility and orderliness, the disobedience would have taken a much more violent form than it did even at Delhi. It was only the wonderfully quick acceptance by the people of the principle of Satyagraha that effectively checked the spread of violence throughout the length and breadth of India. And even to-day it is not the memory of the black barbarity of General Dyer that is keeping the undoubted restlessness among the people from breaking forth into violence. The hold that Satyagraha has gained on the people—it may be even against their will—is curbing the forces of disorder and violence. But I must not detain the reader on a defence of Satyagraha against unjust attacks. If it has gained a foothold in India, it will survive much fiercer attacks than the one made by the majority of the Hunter Committee, and somewhat supported by the minority. Had the majority report been defective only in this direction and correct in every other, there would have been nothing but praise for it. After all, Satyagraha is a new experiment in political field. And a hasty attributing to it of any popular disorder would have been pardonable.

The universally pronounced adverse judgment upon the report and the despatches rests upon far more painful revelations. Look at the manifestly laboured defence of every official act of inhumanity except where condemnation could not be avoided through the impudent admissions made by the actors themselves; look at the special pleading introduced to defend General Dyer even against himself; look at the vain glorification of Sir Michæl O'Dwyer, although it was his spirit that actuated every act of criminality on the part of the subordinates; look at the deliberate refusal to examine his wild career before the events of April. His acts were an open book of which the Committee ought to have taken judicial notice. Instead of accepting everything that the officials had to say the Committee's obvious duty was to tax itself to find out the real cause of the disorders. It ought to have gone out of its way to search out the inwardness of the events. Instead of patiently going behind the hard crust of official documents, the Committee allowed itself to be guided with criminal laziness by mere official evidence. The report and the despatches, in my humble opinion, constitute an attempt to condone official lawlessness. The cautious and half-hearted condemnation pronounced upon General Dyer's massacre and the notorious crawling order only deepens the disappointment of the reader as he goes through, page after page, of thinly disguised official whitewash. I need, however, scarcely attempt any elaborate examination of the report or the despatches which have been so justly censured by the whole national press whether of the moderate or the extremist hue. The point to consider is how to break down this secret—be the secrecy ever so unconscious—conspiracy to uphold official iniquity. A scandal of this magnitude cannot be tolerated by the nation, if it is to preserve its self-respect and become a free partner in the Empire. The All-India Congress Committee has resolved upon convening a special session of the Congress* for the purpose of considering, among other things, the situation arising from the report. In my opinion, the time has arrived when we must cease to rely upon mere petitions to Parliament for effective action. Petitions will have value, when the nation has behind it the power to enforce its will.† What power then have we? When we are firmly of opinion that grave wrong has been done us and when

* The Congress met at Calcutta in special session in September. For a summary of its work, *see* Appendix.

† Mr. Gandhi has no faith in a Declaration of Rights. *Young India* of June 30th, writes as under: *Our Political Security.*

It is not difficult to discover in the Secretary of State's despatch issued in connection with the Hunter Committee Report the various attempts made to pass over the offences on the part of the Government officials. One of these attempts is easily detected when the despatch passes in almost an apologetic tone a halting criticism on some of the mistakes during the Martial Law period and abruptly goes on to propose arrangements for the future to be incorporated in a Martial Law Manual which the Government of India have at present under consideration. This Martial Law Manual may be an attempt to respond to the general demand for the future security. But we cannot compromise ourselves with any manual that does not fall in with the demands stated in the Congress Sub-committee's report. To fatten the statute book with any such manual without removing the Rowlatt Act from it would mean to endeavour to nourish a man without removing the poison in his system. If the Rowlatt Act is not repealed, the Government of India's manual can least satisfy those who are urging the British Parliament to pass a statute to secure the civil rights of His Majesty's Indian subjects, because the civil rights and the Rowlatt Act cannot at

after an appeal to the highest authority we fail to secure redress, there must be some power available to us for undoing the wrong. It is true that in the vast majority of cases, it is the duty of a subject to submit to wrongs on failure of a usual procedure, so long as they do not affect his vital being. But every nation and every individual has the right, and it is their duty, to rise against an intolerable wrong. I do not believe in armed risings. They are a remedy worse than the disease sought to be cured. They are a token of the spirit of revenge and impatience and anger. The method of violence cannot do good in the long run. Witness the

---

the same time remain on our statute book. The Rowlatt Act detracts from our rights whereas the Declaration of Rights recognises them in law."

Will the Declaration suffice to secure our liberties? We do realise the importance of the Declaration of Rights, but we are not much enamoured of the Declaration of Rights business. The Declaration will be of little avail if we have not the strength to have it well administered. Unless we become manly and fearless, no number of rights showered upon us can secure us our liberties. It is not unlikely that progress in legislation may outrun the administrative order. It required generations for Englishmen to harmonize their legislation and administration in this respect. Their Magna Charta (1215), the Petition of Right (1628), the Grand Remonstrance (1641) and the Bill of Rights (1689) record the continued progress of Englishmen for not less than full five centuries. The significance of this series of legislation does not so much lie in what each of them adds to the preceding law, but in each confirming the foregoing law. King after king violated the liberties of his subjects. But with greater determination than the kings, came forward heroes from amidst the people who fought these violations and successfully secured the writ of Habeas Corpus. We need not require the same long period to achieve freedom of person. But we cannot escape similar fights and sacrifice if we would have the fundamental principles of freedom engraved on our hearts. We emphasise the necessity of such preparation as of greater moment than the Declaration itself.

effect of the armed rising of the allied powers against Germany. Have they not become even like the Germans, as the latter have been depicted to us by them?

We have a better method. Unlike that of violence it certainly involves the exercise of restraint and patience; but it requires also resoluteness of will. This method is to refuse to be party to the wrong. No tyrant has ever yet succeeded in his purpose without carrying the victim with him, it may be, as it often is, by force. Most people choose rather to yield to the will of the tyrant than to suffer for the consequence of resistance. Hence does terrorism form part of the stock-in-trade of the tyrant. But we have instances in history where terrorism has failed to impose the terrorist's will upon his victim. India has the choice before her now. If, then, the acts of the Punjab Government be an insufferable wrong, if the report of Lord Hunter's Committee and the two despatches be a greater wrong by reason of their grievous condonation of these acts, it is clear that we must refuse to submit to this official violence. Appeal to the Parliament by all means, if necessary, but if the Parliament fails us, and if we are worthy to call ourselves a nation, we must refuse to uphold the Government by withdrawing co-operation from it.

23rd June, 1920

THE DUTY OF THE PUNJABEE

(BY M. K. GANDHI)

The Allahabad *Leader* deserves to be congratulated for publishing the correspondence on Mr. Bosworth Smith who was one of the Martial Law officers against whom the complaints about persistent and continuous ill-treatment were among the bitterest. It appears from the correspondence that Mr. Bosworth Smith has received promotion instead of dismissal. Sometime before Martial Law Mr. Smith appears to have been degraded. "He has since been restored", says the *Leader* correspondent, "to his position of a Deputy Commissioner of the second grade from which he was degraded and also been invested with powers under Sec. 30 of the Criminal Procedure Code. Since his arrival, the poor Indian population of the town of Ambala Cantonment has been living under a regime of horror and tyranny." The correspondent adds: "I use both these words deliberately for conveying precisely what they mean." I cull a few passages from this illuminating letter to illustrate the meaning of horror and tyranny. "In private complaints he never takes the statement of the complainant. It is taken down by the reader when the court rises and got signed by the magistrate the following day. Whether the Report (received upon such complaints) is favourable to the complainant or unfavourable to him it is never read by the magistrate, and complaints are dismissed without proper trial. This is the fate of private complaints. Now as regards police challans. Pleaders for the accused are not allowed to interview under-trial prisoners in police custody. They are not allowed to cross-examine prosecution witness. . . . Prosecution witnesses are examined with leading questions. . . . Thus a whole prosecution story is put into the mouth of police witnesses. Witnesses for the defence though called in are not allowed to be examined by the defence counsel. . . . The accused is silenced if he picks up courage to say anything in defence. . . . Any Cantonment servant can write down the name of any citizen of the Cantonment on a chit of paper and ask him to appear the next day in court. This is a summons. . . . If any one does not appear in court who is thus ordered, criminal warrants of arrest are issued against him." There is much more of this style in the letter which is worth producing but I have given enough to illustrate the writer's meaning. Let me turn for a while to this official's record during Martial Law. He is the official who tried people in batches and convicted them after a farcical trial. Witnesses have deposed to his having assembled people, having asked them to give false evidence, having removed women's veils, called them 'flies, bitches, she-asses' and having spat upon them. He it was who subjected the innocent pleaders of Shekhupura to indescribable persecution. Mr. Andrews personally investigated complaints against this official and came to the conclusion that no official had behaved worse than Mr. Smith. He gathered the people of Shekhupura, humiliated them in a variety of ways, called them *anvarlog, Gandi makkhi.* His evidence before the Hunter Commission betrays his total disregard for truth and this is the officer who, if the correspondent in question has given correct facts, has been promoted. The question however is why he is at all in Government service and why he has not been tried for assaulting and abusing innocent men and women.

I notice a desire for the impeachment of General Dyer and Sir Michael O'Dwyer. I will not stop to examine whether the course is feasible. I was sorry to find Mr. Shastri joining this cry for the prosecution of General Dyer. If the English people will willingly do so, I would welcome such prosecutions as a sign of their strong disapproval of the Jallianwalla Bagh atrocity, but I would certainly not spend a single farthing in a vain pursuit after the conviction of these men. Surely the public has received sufficient experience of the English mind. Practically the whole English Press has joined the conspiracy to screen these offenders against humanity. I would not be party to make heroes of them by joining the cry for prosecution private or public. If I can only pursuade India to insist upon their complete dismissal, I should be satisfied. But more than the dismissal of Sir Michæl O'Dwyer and General Dyer is necessary the peremptory dismissal, if not a trial, of Colonel O'Brien, Mr. Bosworth Smith, Rai Shri Ram and others mentioned in the Congress Sub-committee's Report. Bad as General Dyer is, I consider Mr. Smith to be infinitely worse and his crimes to be far more serious than the massacre of Jallianwalla Bagh. General Dyer sincerely believed that it was a soldierly act to terrorise people by shooting them. But Mr. Smith was wantonly cruel, vulgar and debased. If all the facts that have been deposed to against him are true, there is not a spark of humanity about him. Unlike General Dyer he lacks the courage to confirm what he has done and he wriggles when challenged. This officer remains free to inflict himself upon people who have done no wrong to him, and who is permitted to disgrace the rule he represents for the time being.

What is the Punjab doing? Is it not the clear duty of the Panjabees not to rest until they have secured the dismissal of Mr. Smith and the like? The Punjab leaders have been discharged in vain if they will not utilise the liberty they have received, in order to purge the administration of Messrs. Bosworth Smith and Company. I am sure that if they will only begin a determined agitation they will have the whole India by their side. I venture to suggest to them that the best way to qualify for sending General Dyer to the gallows is to perform the easier and the more urgent duty of arresting the mischief still continued by the officials against whom they have assisted in collecting overwhelming evidence.

14*th July*, 1920

GENERAL DYER

(BY M. K. GANDHI)

The Army Council has found General Dyer guilty of error of judgment and advised that he should not receive any office under the Crown. Mr. Montagu has been unsparing in his criticism of General Dyer's conduct. And yet somehow or other I cannot help feeling that General Dyer is by no means the worst offender. His brutality is unmistakable. His abject and unsoldier-like cowardice is apparent in every line of his amazing defence before the Army Council. He has called an unarmed crowd of men and children—mostly holiday-makers—'a rebel army.' He believes himself to be the saviour of the Punjab in that he was able to shoot down like rabbits men who were penned in an enclosure. Such a man is unworthy of being considered a soldier. There was no bravery in his action. He ran no risk. He shot without the slightest opposition and without warning. This is not an 'error of judgment'. It is paralysis of it in the face of fancied danger. It is proof of criminal incapacity and heartlessness. But the fury that has been spent upon General Dyer * is, I am sure,

*In *Young India* of March 16, 1921, Gandhi further explains the attitude of India towards General Dyer. He writes, in reply to a friend who asked him why the Jallianwallah Bagh and the Crawling Lane incidents were frequently recalled :

The answer is simple. To forgive is not to forget. There is no merit in loving an enemy when you forget him for a friend. The

largely misdirected. No doubt the shooting was 'frightful', the loss of innocent life deplorable. But the slow torture, degradation and emasculation that followed

---

merit lies in loving in spite of the vivid knowledge that the one that must be loved is not a friend. Ali, that Bayard of Islam, would not retaliate whilst the memory of a vile affront was still fresh in his mind and although he was more than a match for his adversary. India seeks, not punishment of the criminals Sir Michael O'Dwyer and General Dyer, but dismissal of servants who have proved unworthy of the trust reposed in them. And they are not fully dismissed so long as they receive any pension from the Indian treasury. A father is not only not bound to feed an unrepentant son but participates in his crime if he continues to support him.

The Congress Commissioners had their choice either to advise impeachment and prosecution or mere dismissal. They chose the latter on the ground of humanity and not on that of expedience. The reader may be led into the secret that the Commissioners passed many an anxious hour over the matter. The report was finally shaped at Kashi within a stone's throw of the waters of the Ganges. The recommendation was hotly debated among them and they came to the unanimous conclusion that India could only gain by refraining from prosecution. Mr. Das in a notable speech at Patna recently referred to the compact then made between the Commissioners that, whilst and if they reduced their recommendation to a minimum, they must solemnly resolve to enforce them at the risk of their lives. The Commissioners are therefore Non-co-operators as a matter of simple duty. But they chose to waive the right of punishment. It is true that the whole of India has not yet deliberately accepted the doctrine of humanity, *i.e.*, forgiveness. One often hears the talk of hanging the murderers and so on. But India does not yet feel strong as against British Governers and Generals. She still fears them. Forgiveness of Sir Michael O'Dwyer and General Dyer is therefore a meaningless term. But India is daily gaining strength and qualifying for forgiveness. When an Indian talks of punishment of the Punjab criminals, he talks in impotent rage. But I am convinced that if India was to-day free, *i. e.*, strong enough to punish them, she would refrain. She only wants her deliverance from possibilities of Jallianwala. The whole campaign of Non-co-operation has been conceived in a spirit not of revenge but of justice.

was much worse, more calculated, malicious and soul-killing, and the actors who performed the deeds deserve greater condemnation than General Dyer for the Jallianwalla Bagh massacre. The latter merely destroyed a few bodies but the others tried to kill the soul of a nation. Who ever talks of Col. Frank Johnson who was by far the worst offender? He terrorised guiltless Lahore, and by his merciless orders set the tone to the whole of the Martial Law officers. But what I am concerned with is not even Col. Johnson. The first business of the people of the Punjab and of India is to rid the service of Col. O'Brien, Mr. Bosworth Smith, Rai Shri Ram and Mr. Malik Khan. They are still retained in the service. Their guilt is as much proved as that of General Dyer. We shall have failed in our duty if the condemnation pronounced upon Goneral Dyer produces a sense of satisfaction and the obvious duty of purging the administration in the Punjab is neglected. That task will not be performed by platform rhetoric or resolutions merely. Stern action is required on our part if we are to make any headway with ourselves and make any impression upon the officials that they are not to consider themselves as masters of the people but as their trustees and servants who cannot hold office if they misbehave themselves and prove unworthy of the trust reposed in them.

29th September, 1920

MR. PENNINGTON'S OBJECTIONS ANSWERED

(BY M. K. GANDHI)

I gladly publish Mr. Pennington's letter* with its

* Under date 25th August, Victoria Road, Worthing, Sussex, Mr. J. B. Pennington, I.C.S. (*Rtd.*), wrote to Mr. Gandhi questioning his

enclosure just as I have received them. Evidently Mr. Pennington is not a regular reader of "Young India," or he would have noticed that no one has condemned mob outrages more than I have. He seems to think that the article he has objected to was the only thing I have ever written on General Dyer. He does not seem to know that I have endeavoured with the utmost impartiality to examine the Jallianwala massacre. And he can see any day all the proof adduced by my fellow-commissioners and myself in support of our findings of the massacre. The ordinary readers of "Young India" knew all the facts and therefore it was unnecessary for me to support my assertions otherwise. But unfortunately Mr. Pennington represents the typical Englishman. He does not want to be unjust; nevertheless he is rarely just in his appreciation of world events because he has no time to study them except cursorily and that through a press whose business is to air only party views. The average Englishman therefore, except in parochial matters, is perhaps the least informed though he claims to be well-informed about every variety of interest. Mr. Pennington's ignorance is thus typical of the others and afford the best reason for securing control of our own affairs in our own hands. Ability will come with use and not by waiting to be trained by those whose

---

condemnation of General Dyer's conduct and suggesting that the General was acting *bona fide* as a good and only responsible servant of Government on the spot in shooting down some hundreds of people ("some of them *perhaps* innocently mixed up with an illegal assembly") and in thus saving "the city from falling in the hands of a dangerous mob." "As a mere seeker after truth," Mr. Pennington asked for an account of the happenings at Amritsar on 10th April and the following days, adding, "mere abuse is not convincing, as you so often observe in your generally reasonable paper." The text of the letter is omitted in this collection.

natural interest is to prolong the period of tutelege as much as possible.

But to return to Mr. Pennington's letter, He complains that there has been no proper trial of any one. The fault is not ours. India has consistently and insistently demanded a trial of all the officers concerned in the crimes against the Punjab.

He next objects to the 'violence' of my language. If truth is violent, I plead guilty to the charge of violence of language. But I could not, without doing violence to truth, refrain from using the language I have regarding General Dyer's action. It has been proved out of his own mouth or hostile witnesses:

(1) That the crowd was unarmed.

(2) That it contained children.

(3) That the 13th was the day of Vaisakhi fair.

(4) That thousands had come to the fair.

(5) That there was no rebellion.

(6) That during the intervening two days before the massacre' there was peace in Amritsar.

(7) That the proclamation of the meeting was made the same day as General Dyer's proclamation.

(8) That General Dyer's proclamation prohibited not meetings but processions or gatherings of 4 men on the streets and not in private or public places.

(9) That General Dyer ran no risk whether outside or inside the city.

(10) That he admitted himself that many in the crowd did not know anything of his proclamation.

(11) That he fired without warning the crowd and even after it had begun to diperse. He fired in the backs of the people who were in flight.

(12) That the men were practically penned in an enclosure.

In the face of these admitted facts I do call the deed a 'massacre.' The action amounted, not to 'an error of judgment,' but its 'paralysis in the face of fancied danger.'

I am sorry to have to say that Mr. Pennington's notes, which too the reader will find published elsewhere,* betray as much ignorance as his letter.

Whatever was adopted on paper in the days of Canning was certainly not translated into action in its full sense. 'Promises made to the ear were broken to the hope,' was said by a reactionary Viceroy. Military expenditure has grown enormously since the days of Canning.

The demonstration in favour of General Dyer is practically a myth.

No trace was found of the so-called Danda Fauj dignified by the name of bludgeon-army by Mr. Pennington. There was no rebel army in Amritsar. The crowd that committed the horrible murders and incendiarism contained no one community exclusively. The sheet was found posted only in Lahore and not in Amritsar. Mr. Pennington should moreover have known by this time that the meeting held on the 13th was held,

* Under the heading, "Is India worth keeping?" Mr. Pennington wrote to Mr. Gandhi that the answer to the question depended on how England governed India. Prussianism was impossible and had not been countenanced by Government since the days of Canning *when equal justice for all* was adopted. There must be justice for the European as well as the Indian, but General Dyer had not got justice. A rebel gang, it was proclaimed by the mob at Amritsar, was operating against the Europeans and Dyer by his action saved the situation as acknowledged by the loyal Sikhs at the time who demonstrated in General Dyer's favour. People, however, confusing necessary punitive measures with "Massacre", condemned Dyer unheard and on the strenth of some of his statements made in an unguarded moment. The text of the Notes is not included in this collection.

among other things, for the purpose of condemning mob excesses. This was brought out at the Amritsar trial. Those who surrounded him could not stop General Dyer. He says he made up his mind to shoot in a moment. He consulted nobody. When the correspondent says that the troops would have objected to being concerned in "what might in that case be not unfairly called a 'massacre'," he writes as if he had never lived in India. I wish the Indian troops had the moral courage to refuse to shoot innocent, unarmed men in full flight. But the Indian troops have been brought up in too slavish an atmosphere to dare do any such correct act.

I hope Mr. Pennington will not accuse me again of making unverified assertions because I have not quoted from the books. The evidence is there for him to use. I can only assure him that the assertions are based on positive proofs mostly obtained from official sources.

Mr. Pennington wants me to publish an exact account of what happened on the 10th April. He can find it in the reports, and if he will patiently go through them he will discover that Sir Michæl O'Dwyer and his officials goaded the people into frenzied fury—a fury which nobody, as I have already said, has condemned more than I have. The account of the following days is summed up in one word, *viz.*, 'Peace' on the part of the crowd disturbed by indiscriminate arrests, the massacre and the series of official crimes that followed.

I am prepared to give Mr. Pennington credit for seeking after the truth. But he has gone about it in the wrong manner. I suggest his reading the evidence before the Hunter Committee and the Congress Committee. He need not read the reports. But the evidence will convince him that I have under-stated the case against General Dyer.

When however I read his description of himself as "for 12 years Chief Magistrate of Districts in the South of India before reform by assassination and otherwise became so fashionable," I despair of his being able to find the truth. An angry or a biased man renders himself incapable of finding it. And Mr. Pennington is evidently both angry and biased. What does he mean by saying, "before reform by assassination and otherwise became so fashionable?" It ill becomes him to talk of assassination when the school of assassination seems happily to have become extinct. Englishmen will never see the truth so long as they permit their vision to be blinded by arrogant assumption of superiority or ignorant assumption of infallibility.

11*th August*, 1920

MR. MONTAGU *vs.* MRS. NAIDU

In the course of a letter to Mr. Gandhi, dated 15th July, 1920, London, Mrs. Sarojini Naidu wrote:

"I am in very bad health. But the twin questions of the Punjab and the Khilafat absorb all my energies and emotions. But it is vain to expect justice from a race so blind and drunk with the arrogance of power, the bitter prejudice of race and creed and colour, and betraying such an abysmal ignorance of Indian conditions, opinions, sentiments and aspirations. The debate on the Punjab in the House of Commons last week shattered the last remnants of my hope and faith in British justice and good-will towards the new vision of India. The discusssion in the House was lamentable and indeed tragic. Our friends revealed their ignorance, our enemies their insolence—and the combination is appalling and heart-breaking.

"Mr. Montagu has proved a broken reed. I enclose copy of my correspondence* with him on the subject of the outrages committed during the Martial Law regime upon women as embodied in the Congress Sub-committee's report and evidence. I naturally assume that no single statement contained in the evidence has been accepted without the most vigorous and persisting scrutiny. But the general attempt seems to be to discredit the Congress Sub-committee's findings and to shift the responsibility of such outrages which cannot be denied to Indian shoulders, such as Indian police officials—the skin-game with a vengeance. Speaking at a mass meeting the other day, I said that what we Indians demanded was reparation and not revenge, that we had the spiritual force and vision that ennobled us to transcend hate and transmute bitterness into some-

* At a public meeting held at Kingsway Hall, London, on 3rd June, 1919, Mrs. Naidu, lecturing on the Punjab and Khilafat wrongs, stated: " My sisters were stripped naked; they were flogged; they were outraged " On 9th July, the India Office called upon Mrs. Naidu to quote authority for her statements which it maintained " are of course absolutely untrue." On 10th July the India Office, realising that the Congress Committee report contained some evidence on the matter, again wrote to Mrs. Naidu stating that the allegation in the Congress report was against the Indian Police and not against " Martial Law Authorities" and calling upon her to state publicly that she was speaking, not about Martial Law authorities, but about the Indian Subordinate Police. Mr. Montagu concluded the second letter with the mollifying statement that he had directed the Government of India to enquire into the matter. Mrs. Naidu wrote to Mr. Montagu on the 12th July, expressing her surprise at his attempts to distinguish the Martial Law authorities from the Police. She stated that the Police were working under the Martial Law authorities and perpetrated the atrocities to secure evidence for the Martial Law tribunals. She also drew Mr. Montagu's attention to the several cases of ill-treatment of women complained of before the Congress Enquiry Committee. The text of the letters is omitted in this collection.

thing that might mean redemption both for ourselves and the British race, but that freedom was the only true reparation for the agony and shame of the Punjab . . . The specialists think that my heart-disease is in an advanced and dangerous state; but I cannot rest till I stir the heart of the world to repentance over the tragedy of martyred India."

Commenting on the above, "Young India" wrote under the heading, "Outrages on women": "The correspondence between Mr. Montagu and Mrs. Naidu, published elsewhere,* gives one a glimpse into Mr. Montagu's mentality. A member of the House of Commons spoke in insulting tones of Mrs. Naidu regarding her charges against Martial Law authorities about outrages on women. Mr. Montagu hastily wrote to Mrs. Naidu accusing her of making untrue statements and challenging her to quote her authority or publicly withdraw her statement. The very next day he had to qualify himself by admitting that some authority did exist in the Congress Committee's report, but that it had reference to police torture. Mrs. Naidu had an easy task before her. We must refer the reader to Mrs. Naidu's crushing reply. And now we hear that Mr. Montagu has caused inquiries to be made into the statements published in the Congress Committee's report. We may invite the reader's sttention to the fact that Mr. Montagu's attempt to confine ill-treatment of women to the Indian police also failed. The Manianwala cases quoted by Mrs. Naidu refer to Mr. Bosworth Smith. The charge was investigated by Mr. Anderws himself and then by Mr. Labhsingh, Barrister-at-Law. Mr. Montagu comes out thoroughly discredited. Mrs. Naidu is now naturally anxious about the statements made in the Congress Report. The com-

* *See* foot-note on the previous page.

missioners have themselves described the way in which they have recorded evidence. In any event, Mrs. Naidu stands entirely absolved. The Congress Report may be trusted to take care of itself."

6th October, 1920

HOW THE VICEROY DISCHARGES HIS TRUST

(BY M. K. GANDHI)

The reader will find reproduced elsewhere * the Viceroy's cablegram to Mr. Montagu in refutation of Shrimati Sarojini Naidu's allegations regarding the ill-treatment of women in the Punjab during the Martial Law period, as also Shrimati Sarojini's spirited reply. It seems that every responsible statement made by His Excellency only strengthen the opinion of the public that he is totally unfit for the great trust which has been reposed in him. I do not wish to add one word to what Shrimati Sarojini has said in condemnatien of the Viceroy's attitude; but I would draw the reader's attention to the ignoring of some very material allegations that were made by the Shrimati. Even assuming the propriety of rejecting the evidence of prostitutes because they are engaged in the unfortunate traffic, what has His Excellency to say regarding the evidence of the many women of Manianwalla against whom, in so far as I am aware, not a word of reproach has been whispered? I give below in full the statement of Guredevi, the widow of Mangal Jat. That statement was corroborated by several other women. This is the statement:

* On 12th August 1919, the Viceroy, replying to the Secretary of State *re*: Mrs. Naidu's allegations, stated that the allegations made were made by low-caste prostitutes, belonging to criminal tribes, who were notorious liars, and that their evidence was not worthy of notice.

"One day, during the Martial Law period, Mr. Bosworth Smith gathered together all the males of over 8 years at the Dacca Dalla Bungalow, which is some miles from our village, in connection with the investigations that were going on. Whilst the men were at the Bungalow, he rode to our village, taking back with him all the women who met him on the way carrying food for their men at the Bungalow. Reaching the village, he went around the lanes and ordered all women to come out of their houses, himself forcing them out with sticks. He made us all stand near the village Daira. The women folded their hands before him. He beat some with his stick and spat at them and used the foulest and most unmentionable language. He hit me twice and spat in my face. He forcibly uncovered the faces of all the women, brushing aside the veils with his own stick.

"He repeatedly called us she-asses, bitches, flies and swines and said: 'You were in the same beds with your husbands; why did you not prevent them from going out to do mischief? Now your skirts will be looked into by the Police Constables.' He gave me a kick also and ordered us to undergo the torture of holding our ears by passing our arms round the legs, whilst being bent double.

"This treatment was meted out to us in the absence of our men who were away at the Bungalow."

If the facts set forth are true, can anything be more brutal or more loathsome? And yet the perpetrator of the crime will probably receive a pension from the Government treasury. The curious reader will find in the evidence collected ample material in proof of the depravity of the officer concerned. The evidence was first collected by Mr. Andrews. Mr. Labhsingh, M.A., Bar-at-law, was specially deputed to go to Manianwalla to see the ladies concerned. He held a kind of public enquiry which any body was free to attend.

Mr. Montagu had his attention drawn to these statements when he hastily rebuked Shrimati Sarojini for her so-called recklessness of speech. And it was due to this that Mr. Montagu pompously ordered an inquiry. The Viceroy seems quietly to have ignored the instructions issued to him, and has held no inquiry. He has laid down a new canon of evidence, hitherto unknown, and the law upon it that the evidence of prostitutes is not to be trusted. In other words, the legitimate corollary to be drawn from the viceregal pronouncement is that prostitutes may not get justice done to them, unless their complaint is supported by other evidence. Anyway, Mr. Montagu has evidently accepted the Viceroy's explanation, and has thus strengthened the cause of Non-co-operation. * Can India for one moment associate herself with a Government that condones offences of a most barbarous nature committed against her own folk by its officers?

*In an earlier issue of *Young India*, dated September 1st, 1920, Gandhi wrote, criticising the Viceroy's speech, opening the Indian Legislative Council, under the heading, "The Viceregal Pronouncement":

It may be that having lost faith in His Excellency's probity and capacity to hold the high office of Viceroy of India, I now read his speeches with a biased mind, but the speech His Excellency delivered at the time of opening of the council shows to me a mental attitude which makes association with him or his Government impossible for self-respecting men.

The remarks on the Punjab mean a flat refusal to grant redress. He would have us to 'concentrate on the problems of the immediate future'! The immediate future is to compel repentance on the part of the Government on the Punjab matter. Of this there is no sign. On the contrary, His Excellency resists the temptation to reply to his critics, meaning thereby that he has not changed his opinion on the many vital matters affecting the honour of India. He is 'content to

22nd October, 1919

KHILAFAT DAY

The 17th October will long be remembered as a great day in Indian history. That a big demonstration like the one organised for the 17th instant, should have

---

leave the issues to the verdict of history'. Now this kind of language, in my opinion, is calculated further to inflame the Indian mind. Of what use can a favourable verdict of history be to men who have been wronged and who are still under the heels of officers who have shown themselves utterly unfit to hold offices of trust and responsibility? The plea for co-operation is, to say the least, hypocritical in the face of the determination to refuse justice to the Punjab. Can a patient who is suffering from an intolerable ache be soothed by the most tempting dishes placed before him? Will he not consider it mockery on the part of the physician who so tempted him without curing him of his pain?

His Excellency is, if possible, even less happy on the Khilafat. "So far as any Government could", says this trustee for the nation, "we pressed upon the Peace Conference the views of Indian Moslems. But notwithstanding our efforts on their behalf, we are threatened with a campaign of Non-co-operation because, forsooth, the allied Powers found themselves unable to accept the contentions advanced by Indian Moslems." This is most misleading if not untruthful. His Excellency knows that the peace terms are not the work of the allied Powers. He knows that Mr. Lloyd George is the prime author of the terms and that the latter has never repudiated his responsibility for them. He has with amazing audacity justified them in spite of his considered pledge to the Moslems of India regarding Constantinople, Thrace and the rich and renowned lands of Asia Minor. It is not truthful to saddle responsibility for the terms on the allied Powers when Great Britain alone has promoted them. The offence of the Viceroy becomes greater when we remember that he admits the justness of the Muslim claim. He could not have 'pressed' it if he did not admit its justice.

I venture to think that His Excellency by his pronouncement on the Punjab has strengthened the nation in its effort to seek a remedy to compel redress of the two wrongs before it can make anything of the so-called Reforms.

passed off without a hitch reflects the greatest credit on the organisers and is indeed a triumph of Satyagraha. People have come to realise that not by violence but by peaceful combination and sustained effort are great causes to be won. As soon as the people cease to fear force, so soon will Government find it to be useless, and only those free themselves from that fear who are positively unwilling to use it themselves. Those in authority as a rule like some exercise of violence from the people. The art of government generally consists in having at one's disposal sufficient force to overawe people into submission. And a government is an instrument of service only in so far as it is based upon the will and the consent of the people. It is an instrument of oppression when it enforces submission at the point of the bayonet. Oppression therefore ceases when people cease to fear the bayonet. And this is Satyagraha—to hold on to truth in the face of overwhelming odds, whether in the shape of the brute force of a government or the unreasoning prejudice or the petty tyranny of a caste.

The organisers of Khilafat Day seem to have recognised the cardinal principle. They would have played themselves into the hands of their opponents if they had directly or indirectly prompted violence or, as a matter of fact, violence had ensued from the demonstration. The cause of Islam has gained by the peaceful nature of the demonstration. And if Bombay be any index to the police arrangements in the other places, the police undoubtedly deserve the highest praise, for in Bombay, as in Ahmedabad, so far as the public were concerned, there appeared to be no special precautions taken. There was absence of all show of force. The presence of an extraordinary police force or the military always irritates a mob. The organisers deserve equal credit for avoiding mass meetings and everything tending to bring together large crowds of ignorant and irresponsible people. The Khilafat is a difficult question. It has been rendered more complex by secret treaties. But it is not yet beyond hope. Eight millions of human beings, when justice is on their side, can make themselves felt anywhere. Our Mahomedan friends have therefore to recognise their own strength. The Friday demonstration, great though it was, may easily be frittered away if it is not followed up by sustained and intelligent effort. The Government must realise what the Mahomedan feeling is. And they will only realise it, when they see earnest effort and a due measure of suffering on the part of those who claim to feel so intensely. Continued pressure of enlightened public opinion can but help His Majesty's ministers, if they wish to be helped, in securing an honourable settlement of this knotty question. There must be no bluster, no theatricals, no declamation, no self-advertisement. There must be quiet and honest work.

There were resolutions passed at some meetings to the effect that Mahomedans will be unable to participate in peace rejoicings if the Khilafat question is not settled on principles of justice, or rather in accordance with the Mahomedan sentiment. This is the right of the subject. But if it is the general wish, it must be clearly expressed, and not at unorganised meetings.

There was too the question of boycott brought up by some. We have expressed ourselves on this matter in no uncertain terms. We do not believe in boycott, because it breeds ill-will and it is mostly ineffective. Boycott of goods is a subterfuge for boycott of the Government. We hate all subterfuge. If a case is made out for boycotting the Government, we would not hesitate to support it. But boycott then spells disloyalty. Loyalty is not an immutable principle. It is mutual understanding. A government that is loyal to the governed commands their loyalty as a matter of course. When our Government ceases to be loyal, *i.e.*, it becomes systematically unjust or oppressive, we should unhesitatingly declare our disloyalty and withdraw and advise withdrawal of all forms of support of the Government. That is a form of boycott which we would deem it a duty to proclaim, should the occasion arise. But boycott of British goods, whilst we retain the British connection, is, in our opinion, a blunder of the first magnitude.

But our Mahomedan friends have far too sacred a cause to be trifled with the use of a questionable weapon like boycott. And they and the world now know that theirs is a cause not of the eight crore Mahomedans, but of the twenty-two crore Hindus also. For the Seventeenth October has shown that the Hindu-Mahomedan bond is a reality and that it is a bond that is ever growing tighter. And a strong and united India cannot fail to be listened to with respect and attention by the allies of Great Britain.

3rd December, 1919.

ALL-INDIA KHILAFAT CONFERENCE

Mr. Gandhi, presiding over the joint session of the All-India Khilafat Conference held at Delhi on 24th November, addressed the audience in Urdu of which the following is a translation:

"It ought not to appear strange for Hindus to be on the same platform as the Mahomedans in a matter that specially and solely affects the Mahomedans. After all, the test of friendship is true assistance in adversity, and whatever we are, Hindus, Parsis, Christians or Jews, if we wish to live as one nation, surely the interest of any of us must be the interest of all. The only deciding consideration can be the justice of a particular cause. The Prime Minister of England and a whole host of distinguished ex-officials are witnesses to the justice of the Moslem cause. We talk of the Hiudu-Mahomedan unity. It would be an empty phrase if the Hindus hold aloof from the Mahomedans when their vital interests were at stake. Some have suggested that we, Hindus, can assist our Mahomedan countrymen only on conditions. Conditional assistance is like adulterated cement which does not bind. The only question, therefore, is how to help. The Khilafat Conference has come to the decision not to participate in the forthcoming peace celebrations. I think that it is a proper decision. Peace celibrations can have no meaning for India whilst a vital part of the peace, affecting one-fourth of India's population, remains undeclared. Eight crores of Mahomedands are deeply interested in the peace terms affecting the Khilafat. It is improper to ask them to celebrate peace whilst the fate of the Khilafat hangs in the balance. To ask India to celebrate peace whilst the Khilafat question remains uusettled is like expecting France to celebrate peace, pending the settlement of Alsace-Lorraine. That Turkey is outside India does not affect the comparison. England is as much a Mahomedan and Hindu power, as it is a Christian power, bnd if India be a partner in the Empire, then Mahomedan sentiment deserves as much placating as any other. It would, therefore, be the most seeming thing for his Excellency, the Viceroy, to postpone the peace celebrations pending a satisfactory settlement of the Khilafat question.

England's honour at stake.—It is a question which indeed affects the honour of England—the pledged word of the Primer Minister. What are riches, power, and military renown worth, if that honour become sullied ? I was, therefore, deeply pained to see the telegraphic summary of the Prime Minister's speech which seemed unnecessarily to wound Muslim susceptibility and to forecast a settlement of the Khilafat question in contradiction of his own solemn word, given with due deliberation and at a time when that word steadied the Mahomedan loyalty and possibly stimulated recruiting among the war-like Mahomedans. I shall still hope that wiser counsels will prevail and justice done to the Mahomedan claim. Should, however, the worst happen, the Khilafat Committee last night * decided to advise Mahomedans to withdraw co-operation from the Government. I was privileged to be present at both the Subject Committee and the general meetings. I take the liberty of warning the Government of the solemnity of the occasion and the seriousness of the decision. I know that withdrawal of co-operation is a grave thing and a big thing. It requires ability to suffer. I know too that it is the right of a citizen to withdraw his co-operation from the state, when that co-operation means his degradation. It is a tangible form of showing one's displeasure at the acts of one's Government.

Question of Boycott.—One may, therefore, hope that the Imperial Government will recognise the gravity of the situation. But from Non-co-operation to Boycott is a descent from the sublime to the ridiculous.

The Committee took last night a decision by a majority

* 25th November, 1919.

of votes in favour of boycott of British goods, if the Khilafat question was not satisfactorily settled. Boycott is a form of revenge, and talking of its being able to help us to secure a just solution we have to create a world opinion. I venture to suggest to my Mahomedan friends that they will not create a world opinion in their favour by proclaiming boycott of British goods for other goods, and in practice it is bound to break down. Moreover, the suggested boycott is a confession of weakness. You want strength, not weakness, to be able successfully to deal with all the questions. I, therefore, hope that the Khilafat Committee will retrace its steps and after mature consideration cancel the boycott resolution. In tackling this big question, calmness, patience and the strictest adherence to facts are needed. It is not enough that there is no violence. Indeed, a violent speech is often as injurious as a violent deed. And I am sure that you will not spoil a cause that is just and sacred by any hasty word or action.

The Punjab Grievance.—It remains for me to examine a position suggested by some friends. It has been contended that the Punjab grievance too is a good reason for refraining from the peace celebrations. I venture to differ from that view. However grievous the wrong done in the Punjab, it is after all a domestic affair and it would show on our part a want of sense of proportion to bring in the Punjab grievances to justify our Non-co-operation in the Imperial celebration. The Punjab grievance does not arise out of the peace terms as does the Khilafat question. We must isolate the Khilafat question if we wish to give it its proper place and value. In my humble opinion, it is not open to us to refuse to share the peace celebrations on grounds other than those that arise directly out of the peace and that touch the vital parts of our national existence. The Khilafat question alone satisfies these two tests.

10*th December*, 1919

KHILAFAT AND THE COW QUESTION

Mr. Gandhi has sent a long letter this week to the *Navajivan*. It contains in full his lecture at the Khilafat Conference at Delhi on 23rd November, of which he had supplied only a summary to the Associated Press. Two points not dealt with in detail in the English summary may here be noted. He said:

"Mr. Asafali, the Secretary of the Conference, has intimated in the papers circulated by him that the *Goraksha* problem and the Punjab matter will also be considered. I submit that the Hindus may not open the *Goraksha* question here. The test of friendship is assistance in adversity, and that too, unconditional assistance. Co-operation that needs consideration is a commercial contract and not friendship. Conditional co-operation is like adulterated cement which does not bind. It is the duty of the Hindus, if they see the justice of the Mahomedan cause, to render co-operation. If the Mahomedans feel themselves bound in honour to spare the Hindus' feelings and to stop cow-killing, they may do so, no matter whether the Hindus co-operate with them or no. Though, therefore, I yield to no Hindu in my worship of the cow, I do not want to make the stopping of cow-killing a condition precedent to co-operation. Unconditional co-operation means the protection of the cow.

"As regards the Punjab matter too, I venture to differ from many of you. I have probed deeply into the Punjab wounds. They may have deeply distressed others. I will not however say that they can distress any one more deeply than they do me, and yet I think that we cannot bring in here the Punjab grievance. However grievous the wrong done in the Punjab, I think we cannot abstain from the Imperial Celebrations on that score. We cannot say that the Punjab wrong is unredressed to justfy our absention. For we still expect redress. The Hunter Committee is still at work. Our own committee is equally busy. Only if we are dissatisfied or suspicious about a matter directly arising out of the peace terms, can we decide upon abstention.

"Such a one is only the Khilafat question. It arises out of the Khilafat question and not only are we in the dark about it but we fully apprehend that it may not be settled to our satisfaction. We shall be accused of having been thoughtless and without sense of proportion if we bring in the Punjab to justify abstention, and it will damage both the Khilafat and the Punjab question. The Khilafat question is a very serious one, and needs immediate remedies. We must isolate it if we wish to give to it its proper place and value."

"Moulana Abdul Bari Sahab in proposing a vote of of thanks to the chair said: 'Mahatma Gandhi may say anything as regards the bringing in of the *Goraksha* question. That does credit to him and to our Hindu brethren. But the Musalman's *Khandani* would be at stake if they forgot the co-operation of Hindus. I, for my part, will say that we should stop cow-killing, irrespective of their co-operation, because we are children of the same soil. As a Moulvi I say that, in voluntarily stopping cow-killing, we shall not offend against the canons of our religion. Nothing has so helped the Hindu-Moslem unity as the Hindus' Co-operation with us in the question of Khilafat.' The whole meeting greeted the words with 'Amen'."

28th *January*, 1919

THE KHILAFAT

(By. M. K. Gandhi)

The question of questions to-day is the Khilafat question, otherwise known as that of the Turkish peace terms. His Excellency the Viceroy deserves our thanks for receiving the joint deputation* even at this late hour, especially when he was busy preparing to receive the heads of the different provinces. His Excellency must be thanked for the unfailing courtesy with which he received the deputation and the courteous language in which his reply was couched. But mere courtesy, valuable as it is at all times, never so valuable as at this, is not enough at this critical moment. 'Sweet words butter no parsnips' is a proverb more applicable to-day than ever before. Behind the courtesy there was the determination to punish Turkey. Punishment of Turkey is a thing which Muslim sentiment cannot tolerate for a moment. Muslim soldiers are as responsible for the result of the War as any others. It was to appease them that Mr. Asquith said when Turkey decided to join the Central Powers that the British Government had no designs on Turkey and that His Majesty's Government would never think of punishing the Sultan for the misdeeds of the Turkish Committee. Examined by that

* A deputation of the Khilafat Conference consisting of Hindus and Muslims waited on Lord Chelmsford in the last week of January, 1920, to request facilities for an Indian deputation to England and support for Muslim cause.

standard, the Viceregal reply is not only disappointing but it is a fall from truth and justice.

What is this British Empire? It is as much Mahomedan and Hindu as it is Christian. Its religious neutrality is not a virtue, or if it is, it is a virtue of necessity. Such a mighty Empire could not be held together on any other terms. British ministers are, therefore, bound to protect Mahomedan interests as any other. Indeed, as the Muslim rejoinder* says, they are bound to make the cause their own. What is the use of His Excellency having presented the Muslim claim before the Conference? If the cause is lost, the Mahomedans will be entitled to think that Britain did not do her duty by them. And the Viceregal reply confirms the view. When His Excellency says that Turkey must suffer for her having joined the Central Powers, he but expresses the opinion of the British ministers. We hope, therefore, with the framers of the Muslim rejoinder, that His Majesty's ministers will mend the mistakes if any have been committed and secure a settlement that would satisfy Mahomedan sentiment.

What does the sentiment demand? The preservation of the Khilafat with such guarantees as may be necessary for the protection of the interests of the non-Muslim races living under Turkish rule and the Khalif's control over Arabia and the Holy Places with such arrangement as may be required for guaranteeing Arab self-rule, should the Arabs desire it. It is hardly possible to state the claim more fairly than has been done. It is a claim backed by justice,† by the declarations of British

* Not included in this collection.

†Mr. Gandhi reiterated this view subsequently. In the meeting held in Bombay on Saturday, 31st January, Mr. Hayat, Secretary to the Khilafat Deputation, read a telegram from Mr. Gandhi addressed to

ministers and by the unanimous Hindu and Muslim opinion. It would be midsummer madness to reject or whittle down a claim so backed.

10*th March*, 1920

THE QUESTION OF QUESTIONS

Mr. Gandhi writes to the Press as follows:

The Khilafat question has now become a question of questions. It has become an imperial question of the first magnitude.

The great Prelates of England and the Mahomedan leaders combined have brought the question to the fore. The Prelates threw down the challenge. The Muslim leaders have taken it up.

I trust that the Hindus will realize that the Khilafat question overshadows the Reforms and everything else.

If the Muslim claim was unjust apart from the Muslim scriptures, one might hesitate to support it merely on scriptural authority. But when a just claim is supported by scriptures, it becomes irresistible.

Mr. Shaukat Ali from Lahore in which it was stated: "Deputation has sacred mission. It has to appeal not merely to Imperial Government and British opinion but has to win world opinion. Its strength lies in its ability to appeal to reason and justice. It must therefore be moderate in presentation and firm in demand. Odds from a worldly stand-point seem heavily against us, but in Prophet's words minority of two when it has God on its side can face overwhelming numbers with confidence and hope. In my opinion Hindu India is solidly on your side, for your cause is not merely scripturally true, but it is morally just, and presently England will be on our side when through Deputation Englishmen learn that *British honour is at stake* in this question; for we are asking nothing more than what British Ministers have pledged themselves to give. May God guide Deputation."

Briefly put, the claim is that the Turks should retain European Turkey subject to full guarantees for the protection of non-Muslim races under the Turkish Empire and that the Sultan should control the Holy places of Islam and should have suzerainty over Jazirat-ul-Arab, *i.e.*, Arabia as defined by the Muslim Savants, subject to self-governing rights being given to the Arabs if they so desire. This was what was promised by Mr. Lloyd George and this was what Lord Hardinge had contemplated. The Mahomedan soldiers would not have fought to deprive Turkey of her possessions. To deprive the Khalif of the suzerainty of Arabia is to reduce the Khilafat to a nullity.

To restore to Turkey subject to necessary guarantees what was hers before War is a Christian solution. To wrest any of her possesssions from her for the sake of punishing her is a gun-powder solution. The Allies or England in the hour of triumph must be scrupulously just. To reduce the Turks to impotence would be not only unjust. It would be a breach of solemn declarations and promises. It is to be wished that the Viceroy will take his courage in both his hands and place himself at the head of the Khilafat agitation as Lord Hardinge did at the time of the South African "passive-resistance" struggle and thus like his predecessor give a clear and emphatic direction to an agitation which, under impulsive or faulty leadership, may lead to disastrous consequences.

But the situation rests more with us Hindus and Mahomedans than with the Viceroy and still more with the Muslim leaders than with the Hindus or the Viceroy.

There are signs already of impatience on the part of Muslim friends, and impatience may any day be reduced to madness and the latter must inevitably lead to violence. And I wish I could persuade every one to see that violence is suicide.

Supposing the Muslim demands are not granted by the Allies or say England! I see nothing but hope in Mr. Montagu's brave defence of the Muslim position and Mr. Lloyd George's interpretation of his own declaration. True, the latter is halting but he can secure full justice under it. But we must suppose the worst and expect and strive for the best. How to strive is the question.

What we may not do is clear enough.

(1) There should be no violence in thought, speech or deed.

(2) Therefore there should be no boycott * of British goods, by way of revenge or punishment. Boycott, in my opinion, is a form of violence. Moreover, even if it were desirable, it is totally impracticable.

*In *Young India* of March 17, 1920, under the heading, "Khilafat," Mr. Gandhi explained why Boycott should not be resorted to. Pointing out the confusion into which the *Leader* of Allahabad had fallen over Boycott and Non-co-operation, Mr. Gandhi wrote: "I had thought that my meaning was clear and that there was no inconsistency. Boycott is a punishment and is conceived in a vindictive spirit. The idea of boycotting British goods is that, although British goods may be better than, say, Japanese, I should not buy the former because I want to revenge myself upon the British people for a wrong done to me by British ministers, or for utterly irresponsible and insolent language of some Englishmen regarding the Khilafat. I hold that Boycott under such circumstances is a form of violence. Non-co-operation stands on a different footing. If the Government do wrong, I become a participator in its wrong-doing by co-operating with it and thus making it possible for them to do the wrong. It is my duty, not by way of punishment or by way of revenge but to the end that I may not make myself responsible for the wrong-doing, to withdraw my support off that Government. Indeed I should be justified in bringing that Government to a standstill. It is clear to me therefore that Non-co-operation is as different from Boycott as an elephant from an ass."

(3) There should be no rest till the minimum is achieved.

(4) There should be no mixing up of other questions with the Khilafat, *e.g.*, the Egyptian question.

Let us see what must be done:

(1) The cessation of business on the 19th instant and expression of the minimum demands by means of one single resolution is a necessary first step provided that the *hartal* is absolutely voluntary and the employees are not asked to leave their work unless they receive permission from their employers. I would strongly urge that the mill-hands should be left untouched. The further provison is that there should be no violence accompanying the *hartal*. I have been often told that the C. I. D. sometimes promote violence. I do not believe in it as a general charge. But even if it be true, our

The only way to retain peace is, he added, for the Hindu to join hands with the Muslim, offer Satyagraha and prevent Muslims from becoming desperate. He wrote: "I still believe that for the moment I consider that I am alone capable of offering Satyagraha in its fine form. But if that belief were to deter me from making experiments, Satyagraha would never make headway. But here, there is the further fallacy of the ambiguous middle. Satyagraha in the form of Civil Resistance has possibilities of mischief. But *hartal* is no new weapon and *hartal* may or may not be Satyagraha. When the Hon'ble Pandit Madan Mohan Malaviya resigned his membership on the Imperial Council or when Sir Rabindranath Tagore asked to be relieved of his distinction, they did not do so as Satyagrahis. Of course there is danger in widespread Non-co-operation. But that is merely stating a truism. The one thing to be remembered is that for the Mahomedans the Khilafat is a question of life and death. It is essential for them to secure a proper solution. It is the sacred duty of the Hindus to give their all for the sake of their brothers so long as they work along the lines of non-violence. And I know no better way of keeping them on that path save by all Hindus, Christians, Parsees and Jews who have made India their own, whole-heartedly supporting them and suggesting to them forcible methods of attaining redress without resort to violence."

discipline should make it impossible. Our success depends solely on our ability to control, guide and discipline the masses.

Now a word as to what may be done if the demands are not granted. The barbarous method is warfare, open or secret. This must be ruled out if only because it is impracticable. If I could but persuade every one that it is always bad, we should gain all lawful ends much quicker. The power that an individual or a nation forswearing violence generates is a power that is irresistible. But my argument to-day against violence is based upon pure expedience, *i.e.*, its utter futility.

Non-co-operation is, therefore, the only remedy left open to us. It is the cleanest remedy as it is the most effective, when it is absolutely free from all violence. It becomes a duty when co-operation means degradation or humiliation or an injury to one's cherished religious sentiment. England cannot accept a meek submission by us to an unjust usurpation of rights which to Mussalmans mean a matter of life and death. We may therefore begin at the top as also the bottom. Those who are holding offices of honour or emolument ought to give them up. Those who belong to the menial services under Government should do likewise. Non-co-operation does not apply to services under private individuals. I cannot approve of the threat of ostracism against those who do not adopt the remedy of Non-co-operation. It is only a voluntary withdrawal which is effective. For voluntary withdrawal alone is a test of popular feeling and dissatisfaction. Advice to the soldiers to refuse to serve is premature. It is the last, not the first step. We should be entitled to take that step when the Viceroy, the Secretary of State and the Premier leave us. Moreover, every step in withdrawing co-operation has to be taken with the greatest deliberation. We must proceed slowly so as to ensure retention of self-control under the fiercest heat.

Many look upon the Calcutta resolutions * with the deepest alarm. They scent in it a preparation for violence. I do not look upon them in that light, though I do not approve of the tone of some of them. I have already mentioned those whose subject-matter I wholly dislike.

"Can Hindus accept all the resolutions?" is the question addressed by some. I can only speak for myself. I will co-operate whole-heartedly with the Muslim friends in the prosecution of their just demands so long as they act with sufficient restraint and so long as I feel sure that they do not wish to resort to or countenance violence. I should cease to co-operate and advise every Hindu and for that matter every one else to cease to co-operate, the moment there was violence actually done, advised or countenanced. I would therefore urge upon all speakers the exercise of the greatest restraint under the gravest provocation. There is certainty of victory if firmness is combined with gentleness. The cause is doomed if anger, hatred, ill-will, recklessness and finally violence are to reign supreme. I shall resist them with my life even if I should stand alone. My goal is friendship with the world and I can combine the greatest love with the great opposition to wrong.

28th April, 1920

WHY I HAVE JOINED THE KHILAFAT MOVEMENT

(BY M. M. GANDHI)

An esteemed South African friend who is at present

* A Khilafat Conference held at Calcutta passed resolutions accepting Non-co-operation. For the implications of the letter see *infra*.

living in England has written to me a letter from which I make the following excerpts :

"You will doubtless remember having met me in South Africa at the time when the Rev. J. J. Doke was assisting you in your compaign there and I subsequently returned to England deeply impressed with the rightness of your attitude in that country. During the months before War I wrote and lectured and spoke on your behalf in several places which I do not regret. Since returning from military service, however, I have noticed from the papers that you appear to be adopting a more militant attitude . . . I notice a report in "The Times" that you are assisting and countenancing a union between the Hindus and Moslems with a view of embarrassing England and the Allied Powers in the matter of the dismemberment of the Ottoman Empire or the ejection of the Turkish Government from Constantinople. Knowing as I do your sense of justice and your humane instincts I feel that I am entitled, in view of the humble part that I have taken to promote your interests on this side, to ask you whether this latter report is correct. I cannot believe that you have wrongly countenanced a movement to place the cruel and unjust despotism of the Stamboul Government above the interests of humanity, for if any country has crippled these interests in the East it has surely been Turkey. I am personally familiar with the conditions in Syria and Armenia and I can only suppose that if the report which "The Times" has published is correct, you have thrown to one side, your moral responsibilities and allied yourself with one of the prevailing anarchies. However, until I hear that this is not your attitude I cannot prejudice my mind. Perhaps you will do me the favour of sending me a reply."

I have sent a reply to the writer. But as the views expressed in the quotation are likely to be shared by many of my English friends and as I do not wish, if I can possibly help it, to forfeit their friendship or their esteem, I shall endeavour to state my position as clearly as I can on the Khilafat question.* The letter shows

* Asked by Mr. Andrews to define his position more fully and publicly, Mr. Gandhj wrote in *Young India* of July 21, 1920, under the heading, "Mr. Andrews' difficulty": "I should clear the ground by

what risk public men run through irresponsible journalism. I have not seen *The Times* report referred to by my friend. But it is evident that the report has made the writer to suspect my alliance with "the prevailing anarchies" and to think that I have "thrown to one side" my "moral responsibilities."

It is just my sense of moral responsibilities which has made me take up the Khilafat question and to identify myself entirely with the Mahomedans. It is perfectly true that I am assisting and countenancing the union between Hindus and Moslems, but certainly not with "a view of embarrassing England and the Allied Powers in the matter of the dismemberment of the Ottoman Empire." It is contrary to my creed to embarrass Governments or anybody else. This does not

---

stating that I reject any religious doctrine that does not appeal to reason and is in conflict with morality. I tolerate unreasonable religious sentiment when it is not immoral. I hold the Khilafat claim to be both just and reasonable and therefore it derives greater force because it has behind it the religious sentiment of the Musulman world." Dealing with Mr. Mahomed Ali's letter to the Sultan promising the support of the Indian Moslems in regard to Khilafat, Mr. Gandhi wrote: "Mr. Andrews considers that Mr. Mahomed Ali's language goes to show that he would resist Armenian independence against the Armenians and the Arabian against the Arabs. I attach no such meaning to it. What he, the whole Musulmans and therefore I think also the Hindus, resist is the shameless attempt of England and the other Powers under cover of self-determination to emasculate and dismember Turkey. If I understand the spirit of Islam properly, it is essentially republican in the truest sense of the term. Therefore if Armenia or Arabia desired independence of Turkey they should have it. In the case of Arabia, complete Arabian independence would mean transference of the Khilafat to an Arab chieftain. Arabia in that sense is a Musulman trust, not purely Arabian. And the Arabs, without ceasing to be Musulman, could not hold Arabia against Muslim opinion. The Khalifa must be the custodian of the Holy places and therefore also the routes to them. He must

however mean that certain acts of mine may not result in embarrassment. But I should not hold myself responsible for having caused embarrassment when I resist the wrong of a wrong-doer by refusing assistance in his wrong-doing. On the Khilafat question I refuse to be party to a broken pledge. Mr. Lloyd George's solemn declaration is practically the whole of the case for Indian Mahomedans and when that case is fortified by scriptural authority it becomes unanswerable. Moreover, it is incorrect to say that I have "allied myself to one of the prevailing anarchies" or that I have wrongly countenanced the movement "to place the cruel and unjust despotism of the Stamboul Government above the interests of humanity." In the whole of the Mahomedan demand there is no insistence on the retention of the so-called unjust despotism of the Stamboul Government;

---

be able to defend them against the whole world. And if an Arab chief arose who could better satisfy that test than the Sultan of Turkey, I have no doubt that he would be recognised as the Khalifa.'' "The solution of the question", he added, "lies not in our academic discussion of the ideal position. It lies in an honest appointment of a mixed commission of absolutely independent Indian Musulmans and Hindus and independent Europeans to investigate the real wish of the Armenians and the Arabs and then to come to a *modus vivendi* whereby the claims of the nationality and those of Islam may be adjusted and satisfied". "If is common knowledge," concluded Mr. Gandhi, "that Smyrna and Thrace including Adrianople have been dishonestly taken away from Turkey and that mandates have been unscruplously established in Syria and Mesopotamia and a British nominee has been set up in Hedjaj under the protection of British guns. This is a position that is intolerable and unjust. Apart therefore from the questions of Armenia and Arabia, the dishonesty and hypocrisy that pollute the peace terms require to be instantaneously removed. It paves the way to an equitable solution of the question of Armenian and Arabian independence which in theory no one denies and which in practice may be easily guaranteed if only the wishes of the people concerned could with any degree of certainty be ascertained."

on the contrary, the Mahomedans have accepted the principle of taking full guarantees from that Government for the protection of Non-Muslim minorities. I do not know how far the condition of Armenia and Syria may be considered an 'anarchy,' and how far the Turkish Government may be held responsible for it. I much suspect that the reports from these quarters are much exaggerated and that the European powers are themselves in a measure responsible for what misrule there may be in Armenia and Syria. But I am in no way interested in supporting Turkish or any other anarchy. The Allied Powers can easily prevent it by means other than that of ending Turkish rule or dismembering and weakening the Ottoman Empire. The Allied Powers are not dealing with a new situation. If Turkey was to be partitioned, the position should have been made clear at the commencement of the War. There would then have been no question of a broken pledge. As it is, no Indian Mahomedan has any regard for the promises of British Ministers. In his opinion, the cry against Turkey is that of Christianity *vs.* Islam with England as the leader in the cry. The latest cablegram from Mr. Mahomed Ali* strengthens the impression, for he says that unlike as in England his deputation is receiving much support from the French Government and the people.

Thus, if it is true, as I hold it is true, that the Indian Musalmans have a cause that is just and is supported by scriptural authority, then for the Hindus not to support them to the utmost would be a cowardly breach of brotherhood and they would forfeit all claim to consideration from their Mahomedan countrymen. As a

* Mahomed Ali was at the time in England as head of the Indian Khilafat Delegation.

public-server, therefore, I would be unworthy of the position I claim, if I did not support Indian Mussalmans in their struggle to maintain the Khilafat in accordance with their religious belief. I believe that in supporting them I am rendering a service to the Empire, because by assisting my Mahomedan countrymen to give a disciplined expression to their sentiment it becomes possible to make the agitation thoroughly orderly and even successful.

12*th May*, 1920

KHILAFAT

(BY M. K. GANDHI)

"As I told you in my last letter, I think Mr. Gandhi has made a serious mistake in the Khilafat business. The Indian Mahomedans base their demand on the assertion that their religion requires the Turkish rule over Arabia; but when they have against them in this matter, the Arabs themselves, it is impossible to regard the theory of the Indian Mahomedans as essential to Islam. After all if the Arabs do not represent Islam, who does? It is as if the German Roman Catholics made a demand in the name of Roman Catholics with Rome and the Italians making a contrary demand. But, even if the religion of the Indian Mahomedans did require that Turkish rule should be imposed upon the Arabs against their will, one could not, now-a-days, recognise as a really religious demand, one which required the continued oppression of one people by another. When an assurance was given at the beginning of the war to the Indian Mahomedans that the Mahomedan religion would be respected, that could never have meant that a temporal sovereignty which violated the principles of self-determination would be upheld. We could not now stand by and see the Turks reconquer the Arabs (for the Arabs would certainly fight against them) without grossly betraying the Arabs to whom we have given pledges. It is not true that the Arab hostility to the Turks was due simply to European suggestion. No doubt, during the War we availed ourselves of the Arab hostility to the Turks to get another ally, but the hostility had existed long before the War. The non-Turkish Mahomedan subjects of the Sultan in general wanted to get rid of his rule. It is the Indian Mahomedans who have no experience of that rule who want to impose it on others. As a matter of fact, the idea of any restoration of Turkish rule in Syria or Arabia seems so remote from all possibilities that to discuss it seems like discussing a restoration of the Holy Roman Empire. I cannot conceive what series of events could bring it about. The Indian Mahomedans certainly could not march into Arabia themselves and conquer the Arabs for the Sultan. And no amount of agitation and trouble in India would ever induce England to put back Turkish rule in Arabia. In this matter it is not English Imperialism which the Indian Mahomedans are up against, but the mass of English Liberal and humanitarian opinion, the mass of the better opinion of England, which wants self-determination to go forward in India. Supposing the Indian Mahomedans could stir up an agitation so violent in India as to sever the connection between India and the British Crown, still they would not be any nearer to their purpose. For to-day they do have considerable influence on British world-policy. Even if in this matter of the Turkish question their influence has not been sufficient to turn the scale against the very heavy weights on the other side, it has weighed in the scale. But apart from the British connection, the Indian Mahomedans would have no influence at all outside India. They would not count for more in world politics than the Mahomedans of China. I think it is likely (apart from the pressure of America on the other side, I should say certain) that the influence of the Indian Mahomedans may at any rate avail to keep the Sultan in Constantinople. But I doubt whether they will gain any advantage by doing so. For a Turkey cut down to the Turkish parts of Asia Minor, Constantinople would be a very inconvenient capital. I think its inconvenience would more than outweigh the sentimental gratification of keeping up a phantom of the old Ottoman Empire. But if the Indian Mahomedans want the Sultan to retain his place in Constantinople, I think the assurances given officially by the Viceroy in India now bind us to insist on his remaining there and I think he will be there in spite of America."

This is an extract from the letter of an Englishman,

enjoying a position in Great Britain, to a friend in India. It is a typical letter, sober, honest, to the point and put in such graceful language that whilst it challenges you, it commands your respect by its very gracefulness. But it is just this attitude based upon insufficient or false information which has ruined many a cause in the British Isles. The superficiality, the one-sidedness, the inaccuracy and often even dishonesty that have crept into modern journalism, continuously mislead honest men who want to see nothing but justice done. Then there are always interested groups whose business it is to serve their ends by means fair or foul. And the honest Englishman wishing to vote for justice but swayed by conflicting opinions and dominated by distorted versions, often ends by becoming an instrument of injustice.

The writer of the letter quoted above has built up convincing argument on imaginary data. He has successfully shown that the Mahomedan case, as it has been presented to him, is a rotten case. In India, where it is not quite easy to distort facts about the Khilafat, English friends admit the utter justice of the Indian Mahomedan claim. But they plead helplessness and tell us that the Government of India and Mr. Montagu have done all that was humanly possible for them to do. And if now the judgment goes against Islam, Indian Mahomedans should resign themselves to it. This extraordinary state of things would not be possible except under this modern rush and preoccupations of all responsible people.

Let us for a moment examine the case as it has been imagined by the writer. He suggests that Indian Mahomedans want Turkish rule in Arabia in spite of the opposition of the Arabs themselves and that if the Arabs do not want Turkish rule, the writer argues, no false religious sentiment can be permitted to interfere with self-determination of the Arabs when India herself has been pleading for that very status. Now the fact is that the Mahomedans, as is known to everybody who has at all studied the case, have never asked for Turkish rule in Arabia in opposition to the Arabs. On the contrary, they have said that they have no intention of resisting Arabian self-government. All they ask for is Turkish suzerainty over Arabia which would guarantee complete self-rule for the Arabs. They want Khalif's control of the Holy Places of Islam. In other words, they ask for nothing more than what was guaranteed by Mr. Lloyd George and on the strength of which guarantee Mahomedan soldiers spilt their blood on behalf of the Allied Powers. All the elaborate argument therefore and the cogent reasoning of the above extract fall to pieces based as they are upon a case that has never existed. I have thrown myself heart and soul into this question because British pledges, abstract justice, and religious sentiment coincide. I can conceive the possibility of a blind and fanatical religious sentiment existing in opposition to pure justice. I should then resist the former and fight for the latter. Nor would I insist upon pledges given dishonestly to support an unjust cause as has happened with England in the case of the secret treaties. Resistance there becomes not only lawful but obligatory on the part of a nation that prides itself on its righteousness.

It is unnecessary for me to examine the position imagined by the English friend, *viz.*, how India would have fared had she been an independent power. It is unnecessary because Indian Mahomedans, and for that matter, India, are fighting for a cause that is admittedly just; a cause in aid of which they are invoking the whole-hearted support of the British people. I would however venture to suggest that this is a cause in which mere sympathy will not suffice. It is a cause which demands support that is strong enough to bring about substantial justice.

19*th May*, 1920

PLEDGES BROKEN

(By M. K. Gandhi)

The long-expected peace terms* regarding Turkey have been received. In my humble opinion, they are humiliating to the Supreme Council, to the British ministers, and if as a Hindu with deep reverence for Christianity I may say so, a denial of Christ's teachings. Turkey broken down and torn with dissentions within may submit to the arrogant disposal of herself, and Indian Mahomedans may out of fear do likewise. Hindus out of fear, apathy or want of appreciation of the situation, may refuse to help their Mahomedan brethren in their hour of peril. The fact remains that a solemn promise of the Prime Minister of England has been wantonly broken. I will say nothing about President Wilson's fourteen points, for they seem now to be entirely forgotten as a day's wonder. It is a matter of deep sorrow that the Government of India *communique* † offers a defence of the terms, calls them a fulfilment of Mr. Lloyd George's pledge of 5th January, 1918, and yet apologises for their defective nature and appeals to the Mahomedans of India as if to mock them that they would accept the terms with quiet resignation. The

* The terms subsequently forced on Turkey at Sevres.

† Not included in this collection.

mask that veils the hypocrisy is too thin to deceive anybody. It would have been dignified if the *communique* had boldly admitted Mr. Lloyd George's mistake in having made the promise referred to. As it is, the claim of fulfilment of the promise only adds to the irritation caused by its glaring breach. What is the use of the Viceroy saying, "The question of the Khilafat is one for the Mahomedans and Mahomedans only and that with their free choice in the matter Government have no desire to interfere," while the Khalif's dominions are ruthlessly dismembered, his control of the Holy places of Islam shamelessly taken away from him and he himself reduced to utter impotence in his own palace which can no longer be called a palace but which can be more fitly described as a prison? No wonder His Excellency fears that the peace includes "terms which must be painful to all Moslems." Why should he insult Muslim intelligence by sending the Mussalmans of India a message of encouragement and sympathy? Are they expected to find encouragement in the cruel recital of the arrogant terms or in a remembrance of "the splendid response" made by them to the call of the King "in the day of the Empire's need?" It ill becomes His Excellency to talk of the triumph of those ideals of justice and humanity for which the Allies fought. Indeed, the terms of the so-called peace with Turkey, if they are to last, will be a monument of human arrogance and man-made injustice. To attempt to crush the spirit of a brave and gallant race, because it has lost in the fortunes of war, is a triumph not of humanity but a demonstration of inhumanity. And if Turkey enjoyed the closest ties of friendship with Great Britain before the war, Great Britain has certainly made ample reparation for her mistake by having made the largest contribution to the humiliation of Turkey. It is insufferable, therefore, when the Viceroy feels confident that with the conclusion of this new treaty that friendship will quickly take life again and a Turkey regenerate, full of hope and strength, will stand forth in the future as in the past a pillar of the Islamic faith. The Viceregal message audaciously concludes: "This thought will, I trust, strengthen you to accept the peace terms with resignation, courage and fortitude and to keep your loyalty towards the Crown bright and untarnished as it has been for so many generations." If Muslim loyalty remains untarnished, it will certainly not be for want of effort on the part of the Government of India to put the heaviest strain upon it, but it will remain so because the Mahomedans realise their own strength—the strength in the knowledge that their cause is just and that they have got the power to vindicate justice in spite of the aberration suffered by Great Britain under a Prime Minister whom continued power has made as reckless in making promises as in breaking them.

Whilst therefore I admit that there is nothing either in the peace terms or in the Viceregal message covering them to inspire Mahomedans and Indians in general with confidence or hope, I venture to suggest that there is no cause for despair or anger. Now is the time for Mahomedans to retain absolute self-control, to unite their forces and, weak though they are, with firm faith in God to carry on the struggle with redoubled vigour till justice is done. If India—both Hindu and Mahomedan—can act as one man and can withdraw her partnership in this crime against humanity which the peace terms represent, she will soon secure a revison of the treaty and give herself and the Empire at least, if not the world, a lasting peace. There is no doubt that the struggle would be bitter, sharp and possibly prolonged, but it is worth all the sacrifice that it is likely to call forth. Both the Mussalmans and the Hindus are on their trial. Is the humiliation of the Khilafat a matter of concern to the former? And if it is, are they prepared to exercise restraint, religiously refrain from violence and practise Non-co-operation without counting the material loss it may entail upon the community? Do the Hindus honestly feel for their Mahomedan brethren to the extent of sharing their sufferings to the fullest extent? The answers to these questions, and not the peace terms, will finally decide the fate of the Khilafat.

26th May, 1920

MR. CANDLER'S OPEN LETTER

(By M. K. Gandhi)

Mr. Candler* has favoured me with an open letter on this question of questions. The letter has already appeared in the press. I can appreciate Mr. Candler's position as I would like him and other Englishmen to appreciate mine and that of hundreds of Hindus who feel as I do. Mr. Candler's letter is an attempt to show that Mr, Lloyd George's pledge is not in any way broken by the peace terms. I quite agree with him that Mr. Lloyd George's words ought not to be torn from their context to support the Mahomedan claim. These are Mr. Lloyd George's words as quoted in the recent

* Mr. Edmund Candler, a well-known English journalist and war correspondent, was at the time Publicity Officer in the Punjab and wrote some open letters to Mr. Gandhi, questioning his attitude towards the Khilafat problem.

Viceregal message: "Nor are we fighting to destroy Austria-Hungary or to deprive Turkey of its capital, or of the rich and renowned lands of Asia Minor and Thrace which are predominantly Turkish in race." Mr. Candler seems to read 'which' as if it meant 'if they,' whereas I give the pronoun its natural meaning, namely, that the Prime Minister knew in 1918, that the lands referred to by him were 'predominantly Turkish in race.' And if this is the meaning, I venture to suggest that the pledge has been broken in a most bare-faced manner, for there is practically nothing left to the Turk of 'the rich and renowned lands of Asia Minor and Thrace.'

I have already given out my view of the retention of the Sultan in Constantinople. It is an insult to the intelligence of man to suggest that 'the maintenance of the Turkish Empire in the home-land of the Turkish race with its capital at Constantinople' has been left unimpaired by the terms of peace. This is the other passage from the speech which I presume Mr. Candler wants me to read together with the one already quoted:

"While we do not challenge the maintenance of the Turkish Empire in the home-land of the Turkish race with its capital at Constantinople, the passage between the Mediterranean and the Black Sea being inter-nationalised, Armenia, Mesopotamia, Syria and Palestine are in our judgment entitled to a recognition of their separate national condition."

Did that mean entire removal of Turkish influence, extinction of Turkish suzerainty and the introduction of European-Christian influence under the guise of Mandates? Have the Moslems of Arabia, Armenia, Mesopotamia, Syria and Palestine been committed, or is the new arrangement being super-imposed upon them by Powers conscious of their own own brute-strength rather than of justice of their action? I for one would nurse by every legitimate means the spirit of independence in the brave Arabs, but I shudder to think what will happen to them under the schemes of exploitation of their country by the greedy capitalists protected as they will be by the mandatory Powers. If the pledge is to be fulfilled, let these places have full self-government with suzerainty to be retained with Turkey as has been suggested by the *Times of India.* Let there be all the necessary guarantees taken from Turkey about the internal independence of the Arabs. But to remove that suzerainty, to deprive the Khalif of the wardenship of the Holy Places is to render Khilafat, a mockery which no Mahomedan can possibly look upon with equanimity. I am not alone in my interpretation of the pledge. The Right Hon'ble Ameer Ali calls the peace terms a breach of faith. Mr. Charles Roberts reminds the British public that the Indian Mussalman sentiment regarding the Turkish Treaty is based upon the Prime Minister's pledge regarding Thrace, Constantinople and Turkish lands in Asia Minor, repeated on 26th February last with deliberation by Mr. Lloyd George. Mr. Roberts holds that the pledge must be treated as a whole, not as binding only regarding Constantinople but also binding as regards Thrace and Asia Minor. He describes the pledge as binding upon the nation as a whole and its breach in any part as a gross breach of faith on the part of the British Empire. He demands that, if there is an unanswerable reply to the charge of breach of faith, it ought to be given and adds the Prime Minister may regard his own word lightly if he chooses, but he has no right to break a pledge given on behalf of the nation. He concludes that "it is incredible that such pledge should not have been kept in the letter and in the spirit." He adds: "I have reason to believe that these views are fully shared by prominent members of the Cabinet."

I wonder if Mr. Candler knows what is going on to-day in England. Mr. Pickthall,* writing in *New Age*, says: "No impartial international enquiry into the whole question of the Armenian massacres has been instituted in the ample time which has elapsed since the conclusion of armistice with Turkey. The Turkish Government has asked for such enquiry. But the Armenian organisations and the Armenian partisans refuse to hear of such a thing, declaring that the Bryce and Lepssens reports are quite sufficient to condemn the Turks. In other words, the judgment should be given on the case for prosecution alone. The inter-allied commision, which investigated the unfortunate events in Smyrna last year, made a report unfavourable to Greek claims. Therefore, that report has not been published here in England, though in other countries it has long been public property." He then goes on to show how money is being scattered by Armenian and Greek emissaries in order to popularise their cause and adds: "This conjunction of dense ignorance and cunning falsehood is fraught with instant danger to the British realm," and concludes: "A Government and people which prefer propaganda to fact as the ground of policy—and foreign policy at that—is self-condemned."

I have reproduced the above extract in order to show that the present British policy has been affected by propaganda of an unscrupulous nature. Turkey which

* Mr. Marmaduke Pickthall, an English Muslim, journalist and novelist, subsequently appointed editor of the *Bombay Chronicle*. His close and intimate knowledge of the Near East is unrivalled among Englishmen.

was dominant over two million square miles of Asia, Africa and Europe in the seventeenth century, under the terms of the treaty, says the *London Chronicle*, has dwindled down to little more than 1,000 square miles. It says: "All European Turkey could not be accommodated comfortably between the Landsend and the Tamar, Cornwal alone exceeding its total area, and but for its alliance with Germany, Turkey could have been assured of retaining at least sixty-thousand square miles of the Eastern Balkans." I do not know whether the *Chronicle* view is generally shared. Is it by way of punishment that Turkey is to undergo such shrinkage, or is it because justice demands it? If Turkey had not made the mistake of joining Germany, would the principle of nationality have been still applied to Armenia, Arabia, Mesopotamia and Palestine?

Let me now remind those who think with Mr. Candler that the promise was not made by Mr. Lloyd George to the people of India in anticipation of the supply of recruits continuing. In defending his own statement, Mr. Lloyd George is reported to have said:

"The effect of the statement in India was that recruiting went up appreciably from that very moment. They were not all Mahomedans but there were many Mahomedans amongst them. Now we are told that was an offer to Turkey. But they rejected it, and therefore we were absolutely free. It was not. It is too often forgotten that we are the greatest Mahomedan power in the world and that one-fourth of the population of the British Empire is Mahomedan. There have been no more loyal adherents to the throne and no more eflective and loyal supporters of the Empire in its hour of trial. *We gave a solemn pledge and they accepted it.* They are disturbed by the prospect of our not abiding by it."

Who shall interpret that pledge and how? How did the Government of India itself interpret it? Did it or did it not energetically support the claim for the control of the Holy Places of Islam vesting in the Khalif? Did the Government of India suggest that the whole of Jazirat-ul-Arab could be taken away consistently with that pledge from the sphere of influence of the Khalif, and given over to the Allies as mandatory Powers? Why does the Government of India sympathise with the Indian Mussalmans if the terms are all they should be? So much for the pledge. I would like to guard myself against being understood that I stand or fall absolutely by Mr. Lloyd George's declaration. I have advisedly used the adverb 'practically' in connection with it. It is an important qualification.

Mr. Candler seems to suggest that my goal is something more than merely attaining justice on the Khilafat. If so, he is right. Attaining of justice is undoubtedly the corner-stone, and if I found that I was wrong in my conception of justice on this question, I hope I shall have the courage immediately to retrace my steps. But by helping the Mahomedans of India at a critical moment in their history, I want to buy their friendship. Moreover, if I can carry the Mahomedans with me, I hope to wean Great Britain from the downward path along which the Prime Minister seems to me to be taking her. I hope also to show to India and the Empire at large that, given a certain amount of capacity for self-sacrifice, justice can be secured by peacefullest and cleanest means without sowing or increasing bitterness between English and Indians. For, whatever may be the temporary effect of my methods, I know enough of them to feel certain that they alone are immune from lasting bitterness. They are untainted with hatred, expedience or untruth.

2nd June, 1920

KHILAFAT: FURTHER QUESTIONS ANSWERED

(By M. K. Gandhi)

I have been overwhelmed with public criticism and private advice and even anonymous letters telling me exactly what I should do. Some are impatient that I do not advise immediate and extensive Non-co-operation; others tell me what harm I am doing the country by throwing it knowingly in a tempest of violence on either side. It is difficult for me to deal with the whole of the criticism, but I would summarise some of the objections and endeavour to answer them to the best of my ability. These are in addition to those I have already answered:

(1) Turkish claim is immoral or unjust and how can I, a lover of truth and justice, support it?

(2) Even if the claim be just in theory, the Turk is hopelessly incapable, weak and cruel. He does not deserve any assistance.

(3) Even if Turkey deserves all that is claimed for her, why should I land India in an international struggle?

(4) It is no part of the Indian Mahomedans' business to meddle in this affair. If they cherish any political ambition, they have tried, they have failed and they should now sit still. If it is a religious matter with them, it cannot appeal to the Hindu reason in the manner it is put, and in any case Hindus ought not to identify themselves with Mahomedans in their religious quarrel with Christendom.

(5) In no case should I advocate Non-co-operation which in its extreme sense is nothing but a rebellion, no matter how peaceful it may be.

(6) Moreover, my experience of last year must show

me that it is beyond the capacity of any single human being to control the forces of violence that are lying dormant in the land.

(7) Non-co-operation is futile because people will never respond in right earnest, and reaction that might afterwards set in will be worse than the state of hopefulness we are now in.

(8) Non-co-operation will bring about cessation of all other activities, even working of the Reforms, and thus set back the clock of progress.

(9) However pure my motives may be, those of the Mussalmans are obviously revengeful.

I shall now answer the objections in the order in which they are stated.

(1) In my opinion, the Turkish claim is not only not immoral and unjust, but it is highly equitable, if only because Turkey wants to retain what is her own. And the Mahomedan manifesto has definitely declared that whatever guarantees may be necessary to be taken for the protection of non-Muslim and non-Turkish races, should be taken so as to give the Christians theirs and the Arabs their self-government under the Turkish suzerainty.

(2) I do not believe the Turk to be weak, incapable or cruel. He is certainly disorganised and probably without good generalship. He has been obliged to fight against heavy odds. The argument of weakness, incapacity and cruelty one often hears quoted in connection with those from whom power is sought to be taken away. About the alleged massacres a proper commission has been asked for, but never granted. And in any case security can be taken against oppression.

(3) I have already stated that, if I were not interested in the Indian Mahomedans, I would not interest myself

in the welfare of the Turks any more than I am in that of the Austrians or the Poles. But I am bound as an Indian to share the sufferings and trials of fellow-Indians. If I deem the Mahomedan to be my brother, it is my duty to help him in his hour of peril to the best of my ability, if his cause commends itself to me as just.

(4) The fourth refers to the extent Hindus should join hands with the Mahomedans. It is therefore a matter of feeling and opinion. It is expedient to suffer for my Mahomedan brother to the utmost in a just cause and I should therefore travel with him along the whole road so long as the means employed by him are as honourable as his end. I cannot regulate the Mahomedan feeling. I must accept his statement that the Khilafat is with him a religious question in the sense that it binds him to reach the goal even at the cost of his own life.

(5) I do not consider Non-co-operation to be a rebellion, because it is free from violence. In a larger sense, all opposition to a Government measure is a rebellion. In that sense, rebellion in a just cause is a duty, the extent of opposition being determined by the measure of the injustice done and felt.

(6) My experience of last year shows me that, in spite of aberrations in some parts of India, the country was entirely under control, that the influence of Satyagraha was profoundly for its good and that where violence did break out there were local causes that directly contributed to it. At the same time I admit that even the violence that did take place on the part of the people and the spirit of lawlessness that was undoubtedly showing in some parts should have remained under check. I have made ample acknowledgment of the miscalculation I then made. But all the painful experience that I then gained

did not in any way shake my belief in Satyagraha or in the possibility of that matchless force being utilised in India. Ample provision is being made this time to avoid the mistakes of the past. But I must refuse to be deterred from a clear course, because it may be attended by violence totally unintended and in spite of extraordinary efforts that are being made to prevent it. At the same time I must make my position clear. Nothing can possibly prevent a Satyagrahi from doing his duty because of the frown of the authorities. I would risk, if necessary, a million lives so long as they are voluntary sufferers and are innocent, spotless victims. It is the mistakes of the people that matter in a Satyagraha campaign. Mistakes, even insanity, must be expected from the strong and the powerful, and the moment of victory has come when there is no retort to the mad fury of the powerful but a voluntary, dignified and quiet submission but not submission to the will of the authority that has put itself in the wrong. The secret of success lies therefore in holding every English life and the life of every officer serving the Government as sacred as those of our own dear ones. All the wonderful experience I have gained now during nearly 40 years of conscious existence, has convinced me that there is no gift so precious as that of life. I make bold to say that the moment the Englishmen feel that, although they are in India in a hopeless minority, their lives are protected against harm not because of the matchless weapons of destruction which are at their disposal, but because Indians refuse to take the lives even of those whom they may consider to be utterly in the wrong, that moment will see a transformation in the English nature in its relation to India, and that moment will also be the moment when all the destructive cutlery that is to be had in India will begin to rust. I know that this is a far-off vision. That cannot matter to me. It is enough for me to see the light and to act up to it, and it is more than enough when I gain companions in the onward march. I have claimed in private conversations with English friends that it is because of my incessant preaching of the gospel of non-violence and my having successfully demonstrated its practical utility, that so far the forces of violence, which are undoubtedly in existence in connection with the Khilafat movement, have remained under complete control.

(7) From a religious stand-point, the seventh objection is hardly worth considering. If people do not respond to the movement of Non-co-operation, it would be a pity, but that can be no reason for a reformer not to try. It would be to me a demonstration that the present position of hopefulness is not dependent on any inward strength or knowledge, but it is hope born of ignorance and superstition.

(8) If Non-co-operation is taken up in earnest, it must bring about a cessation of all other activities including the Reforms, but I decline to draw therefore the corollary that it will set back the clock of progress. On the contrary, I consider Non-co-operation to be such a powerful and pure instrument that, if it is enforced in an earnest spirit, it will be like seeking first the Kingdom of God and everything else following as a matter of course. People will have then realised their true power. They would have learnt the value of discipline, self-control, joint action, non-violence, organisation and everything else that goes to make a nation great and good, and not merely great.

(9) I do not know that I have a right to arrogate greater purity for myself than for our Mussalman

brethren. But I do admit that they do not believe in my doctrine of non-violence to the full extent. For them it is a weapon of the weak, an expedient. They consider Non-co-operation without violence to be the only thing open to them in the war of direct action. I know that, if some of them could offer successful violence, they would do so to-day. But they are convinced that, humanly speaking, it is an impossibility. For them, therefore, Non-co-operation is a matter not merely of duty but also of revenge. Whereas I take up Non-co-operation against the Government as I have actually taken it up in practice against members of my own family, I entertain very high regard for the British constitution. I have not only no enmity against Englishmen, but I regard much in English character as worthy of my emulation. I count many as my friends. It is against my religion to regard any one as an enemy. I entertain similar sentiments with respect to Mahomedans. I find their cause to be just and pure. Although therefore their view-point is different from mine, I do not hesitate to associate with them and invite them to give my method a trial, for, I believe that the use of a pure weapon even from a mistaken motive does not fail to produce some good, even as the telling of truth, if only because for the time being it is the best policy, is at least so much to the good.

28th July, 1920

MR. MONTAGU ON THE KHILAFAT AGITATION

(BY M. K. GANDHI)

Mr. Montagu does not like the Khilafat agitation that is daily gathering force. In answer to questions put in the House of Commons,* he is reported to have said that, whilst he acknowledged that I had rendered distinguished services to the country in the past, he could not look upon my present attitude with equanimity and that it was not to be expected that I could now be treated as leniently as I was during the Rowlatt Act agitation. He added that he had every confidence in the central and the local Governments, that they were carefully watching the movement and that they had full power to deal with the situation.

This statement of Mr. Montagu has been regarded in some quarters as a threat. It has even been considered to be a blank cheque for the Government of India to re-establish the reign of terror if they chose. It is certainly inconsistent with his desire to base the Government on the good-will of the people. At the same time, if the Hunter Committee's finding be true and if I was the cause of the disturbances last year, I was undoubtedly treated with exceptional leniency. I admit too that my activity this year is fraught with greater peril to the Empire as it is being conducted to-day than was last year's activity. Non-co-operation in itself is more harmless than Civil Disobedience, but in its effect it is far more dangerous for the Government than Civil Disobedience. Non-co-operation is intended so far to paralyse the Government, as to compel justice from it. If it is carried to the extreme point, it can bring the Government to a standstill.

A friend who has been listening to my speeches once asked me whether I did not come under the sedition

* Mr. Montagu, then Secretary of State for India, threatened the Khilafat agitation with suppression. His statement, to which the article is a reply, is omitted in this collection.

section of the Indian Penal Code. Though I had not fully considered it, I told him that very probably I did and that I could not plead 'not guilty' if I was charged under it. For I must admit that I can pretend to no 'affection' for the present Government. And my speeches are intended to create 'disaffection' such that the people might consider it a shame to assist or co-operate with a Government that had forfeited all title to confidence, respect or support.

I draw no distinction between the Imperial and the Indian Government. The latter has accepted, on the Khilafat, the policy imposed upon it by the former. And in the Punjab case, the former has endorsed the policy of terrorism and emasculatian of a brave people initiated by the latter. British ministers have broken their pledged word and wantonly wounded the feelings of the seventy million Mussalmans of India. Innocent men and women were insulted by the insolent officers of the Punjab Government. Their wrongs not only remain unrighted, but the very officers who so cruelly subjected them to barbarous humiliation retain office under the Government.

When at Amritsar last year I pleaded with all the earnestness I could command for co-operation with the Government and for response to the wishes expressed in the Royal Proclamation, I did so because I honestly believed that a new era was about to begin, and that the old spirit of fear, distrust and consequent terrorism was about to give place to the new spirit of respect, trust and good-will. I sincerely believed that the Mussalman sentiment would be placated and that the officers that had misbehaved during the Martial Law regime in the Punjab would be at least dismissed and the people would be otherwise made to feel that a

Government that had always been found quick (and rightly) to punish popular excesses would not fail to punish its agents' misdeeds. But to my amazement and dismay, I have discovered that the present representatives of the Empire have become dishonest and unscrupulous. They have no real regard for the wishes of the people of India and they count Indian honour as of little consequence.

I can no longer retain affection for a Government so evilly manned as it is now-a-days. And for me, it is humiliating to retain my freedom and be witness to the continuing wrong. Mr. Montagu however is certainly right in threatening me with deprivation of my liberty, if I persist in endangering the existence of the Government. For that must be the result if my activity bears fruit. My only regret is that inasmuch as Mr. Montagu admits my past services, he might have perceived that there must be something exceptionally bad in the Government if a well-wisher like me could no longer give his affection to it. It was simpler to insist on justice being done to the Mussalmans and to the Punjab than to threaten me with punishment so that the injustice might be perpetuated. Indeed I fully expect it will be found that, even in promoting disaffection towards an unjust Government, I had rendered greater services to the Empire than I am already credited with.

At the present moment, however, the duty of those who approve of my activity is clear. They ought on no account to resent the deprivation of my liberty, should the Government of India deem it to be their duty to take it away. A citizen has no right to resist such restriction imposed in accordance with the laws of the State to which he belongs. Much less have those who sympathise with him. In my case, there can be no question of sympathy. For I deliberately oppose the Government to the extent of trying to put its very existence in jeopardy. For my supporters, therefore, it, must be a moment of joy when I am imprisoned. It means the beginning of success if only the supporters continue the policy for which I stand. If the Government arrest me, they would do so in order to stop the progress of Non-co-operation which I preach. It follows that, if Non-co-operation continues with unabated vigour, even after my arrest, the Government must imprison others or grant the people's wish in order to gain their co-operation. Any eruption of violence on the part of the people even under provocation would end in disaster. Whether therefore it is I or any one else who is arrested during the campaign, the first condition of success is that there must be no resentment shown against it. We cannot imperil the very existence of a Government and quarrel with its attempt to save itself by punishing those who place it in danger.

23rd March, 1921

THE KHILAFAT

(BY M. K. GANDHI)

The proposed change* in the Treaty of Sevres cannot satisfy Indian Muslims. And that is saying a great deal. It is not Turkey merely that Great Britain has to placate. It is India that has to be pacified. In my opinion, if the demands of the Muslims of India are

* There was at the time a proposal to revise the Sevres Treaty whereby Turkey would retain Asia Minor, including Smyrna, with Constantinople. The effect of it would be to dismember the Ottoman Empire, but to retain with the Sultan Turkey proper alone of which the population consisted solely of Turks.

conceded, it will not much matter whether Turkey's are satisfied or not. And this for two reasons. The Khilafat is an ideal and when a man works for an ideal, he becomes irresistible. The Muslims, who represent the ideal, have behind them the opinion of the whole mass of the Indian people.

It is wrong to say that Muslims are fighting merely for Turkey. They will abandon her to-day, if she went wrong, if, to take a foolish illustration, she demands her restoration to the status that she occupied during the reign of Suleiman the Magnificent. Similarly, the Muslims cannot abandon a claim based on the Koranic injunctions, because a weak and helpless Turkey cannot sustain it.

Whilst every good Muslim must strive to retain the temporal power of Turkey, it is obligatory on him to see that unequivocal Muslim control is retained over the 'Island of Arabia' which includes Mesopotamia, Syria, and Palestine as well, and the spiritual sovereignty over them of the Caliph whoever he may be for the time being. No other terms, however good otherwise they may be, can possibly satisfy Muslim opinion. They will not tolerate any non-Muslim influence direct or indirect over the holy places of Islam.

The most thorny part of the question is, therefore, Palestine. Britain has made promises to the Zionists. The latter have, naturally, a sacred sentiment about the place. The Jews, it is contended, must remain a homeless wandering race unless they have obtained possession of Palestine. I do not propose to examine the soundness or otherwise of the doctrine underlying the proposition. All I contend is that they cannot possess Palestine through a trick or a moral breach. Palestine was not a stake in the war. The British Government could not dare have asked a single Muslim soldier to wrest control of Palestine from fellow-Muslims and give it to the Jews. Palestine, as a place of Jewish worship, is a sentiment to be respected, and the Jews would have a just cause of complaint against Musulman idealists if they were to prevent Jews from offering worship as freely as themselves.

By no canon of ethics or war, therefore, can Palestine be given to the Jews as a result of the war. Either Zionists must revise their ideal about Palestine, or, if Judaism permits the arbitrament of war, engage in a 'holy war' with the Muslims of the world with the Christians throwing in their influence on their side. But one may hope that the trend of world opinion will make 'holy wars' impossible and religious questions or differences will tend more and more towards a peaceful adjustment based upon the strictest moral considerations. But, whether such a happy time ever comes or not, it is clear as day-light that the Khilafat terms to be just must mean the restitution of Jazirut-ul-Arab to complete Muslim control under the spiritual sovereignty of the Caliph.

[As regards the Zionists' position, the following quotation from *The Nation's* review of Mr. Israel Zangwill's latest book, "The Voice of Jerusalem," will be of interest, as indicating the views of a distinguished Jew:

His mind has the great merit of a certain amount of originality, of refusing to work merely along other people's grooves. Hence on the question of Zionism he has always taken what was, for a Jew, an unconventional attitude, and he saw, earlier than most people, the central difficulty in the problem of making Palestine the national home of the Jews. The difficulty is that

Palestine happens to-day to be the national home of 600,000 Arabs, and that, even if you get rid of the Arabs, it is quite unfit to accomodate even a half of the Jewish population of the world. A real Jewish State was, therefore, possible in Palestine only if you expelled the Arabs, and even then there would be a very large Jewish irredenta. Hence Mr. Zangwill was a Zionist, but his Zion was not in Palestine but in "Canada, Brazil, Asia Minor, or Siberia." When the war altered the whole situation, he gave his support, it is true, to the diplomacy of the Zionist leaders but obviously with considerable hesitation. His doubts have been amply realized. He pours out his scorn upon the mirage of the Jewish State, that shadowy Zion whose twin foundations are the chicanery of the mandate system and a strategic base for the British Empire.—*Asst. Ed. Y. I.*]

29th June, 1921

THE TURKISH QUESTION

(BY M. K. GANDHI)

If we mean really well by our Mussalman brethren, we must sympathise with them over the movement going on in Europe to destroy Turkish nationalism. It is a thousand pities that the British Government is secretly or openly leading the movement. Let Hindus not be frightened by Pan-Islamism. It is not—it need not be —anti-Indian or anti-Hindu. Mussalmans must wish well to every Mussalman state, and even assist any such state, if it is undeservedly in peril. And Hindus, if they are true friends of Mussalmans, cannot but share the latter's feelings. We must, therefore, co-operate with our Mussalman brethren in their attempt to save the Turkish Empire in Europe from extinction.

Hindus may not then be agitated, when Mussalmans become alarmed at the slightest hint that the British Government might openly join the Greeks against the Turkish Government in Angora. If British should go so mad, India cannot possibly help the British Government in any such design upon Turkey. It would be tantamount to a war with Islam.

England has her choice. She can no longer hold the awakened Hindus and Mussalmans as slaves. If India is to remain equal partner with every other member of the Empire, India's voting strength must be infinitely superior to that of any other member. In a free commonwealth, every partner has as much right to retire if the rest go wrong, as it is his duty to remain so long as the rest are faithful to certain common principles. If India votes wrong, England can retire from partnership, as every other partner can. Thus, the centre of equilibrium must shift to India rather than remain in England, when India has come into her own. That is my meaning of Swaraj within the Empire. Brute force must be ruled out of account in all deliberations. Reference must be had always to Reason and never to the sword.

And as with England, so with India. The latter, too, has her choice. To-day, we are striving for Swaraj within the Empire in the hope that England will in the end prove true, and for independence if she fails. But when it is incontestably proved that Britain seeks to destroy Turkey, India's only choice must be independence. For Mussalmans, when Turkey's existence, such as it is, is threatened, there is no looking back. They would draw the sword if they could, and perish or rise victorious with the brave Turks. But if, as is certain, thanks to the policy of the Government of India, they cannot declare war against the British Government, they can at least forswear allegiance to a Government which wickedly goes to war against Turkey. The duty of the Hindus is no less clear. If we still fear and distrust the Mussalmans, we must side with the British and prolong our slavery. If we are brave and religious enough not to fear the Mussalmans, our countrymen, and if we have the wisdom to trust them, we must make common cause with the Mussalmans in every peaceful and truthful method to secure Indian independence. For a Hindu, as I conceive Hinduism to be, whether for independence or for Swaraj within the Empire, there is no road but Non-violent Non-co-operation. India can have dominion or independent status to-day, if India learns and assimilates the secret and the invincible power of Non-violence. When she has learnt that lesson, she is ready to take up all the stages of Non-co-operation including non-payment of taxes. India is not ready to-day, but if we would be prepared to frustrate every plot that may be hatched for the destruction of Turkey or for prolonging our subjection, we must secure an atmosphere of enlightened non-violence as fast as possible, not the non-violence of the weak. but the non-violence of the strong, who would disdain to kill but would gladly die for the vindication of truth.

18*th August*, 1921

THE KHILAFAT

(By M. K. Gandhi)

At Lucknow I found natural impatience on the part of the Musalmans regarding the Khilafat. Moulvi Salamatulla voiced in moderate language the public feeling regarding the position of the Angora Government when he said that the British attitude was becoming unbearable. There is no doubt the growing distrust of the British declarations about friendliness towards the Turks. Nobody believes either that the British declarations are genuine or that the British Government is powerless to afford relief. In their impatient anger, the Mussalmans ask for more energetic and more prompt action by the Congress and Khilafat organisations. To the Mussalmans, Swaraj means, as it must mean, India's ability to deal effectively with the Khilafat question. The Mussalmans therefore decline to wait if the attainment of Swaraj means indefinite delay or a programme that may require the Mussalmans of India to become impotent witnesses of the extinction of Turkey in European waters.

It is impossible not to sympathise with this attitude. I would gladly recommend immediate action if I could think of any effective course. I would gladly ask for postponement of Swaraj activity if thereby we could advance the interest of the Khilafat. I would gladly take up measures outside Non-co-operation, if I could think of any in order to assuage the pain caused to the millions of Musalmans.

But, in my humble opinion, attainment of Swaraj is the quickest method of righting the Khilafat wrong. Hence it is that for me the solution of the Khilafat question is attainment of Swaraj and *vice versa*. The only way to help the afflicted Turks is for India to generate sufficient power to be able to assert herself. If she cannot develop that power in time, there is no way out for India and she must resign herself to the inevitable. What can a paralytic do to stretch forth a helping hand to a neighbour but to try to cure himself of his paralysis? Mere ignorant, thoughtless and angry outburst of violence may give vent to pent-up rage but can bring no relief to Turkey. Nor can it increase the power of India to assert herself. And the measures taken to put down violence may well lessen the speed with which we are marching to our goal.

But there is no cause whatsoever for despair. The whole of the Congress programme has been framed, and measures are being adopted to meet the Khilafat crisis. There is no doubt that two months for finishing the Swadeshi work is a most intensive measure calculated to bring the best out of the nation. And if India completes the boycott by September and comes to her own in October, surely it must satisfy the most sanguine temperament and the most impatient and ardent Khilafatist as I claim myself to be.

The fact is that all the workers are not convinced of the possibility of completing the Swadeshi programme during the time fixed or of its power to effect all that is claimed for it. Such doubters have to stand out, unless they can suggest a better and quicker method and get it accepted by the country. In spite of their doubt, they should faithfully plunge themselves into Swadeshi work and give the experiment a fair trial. And does not this doubting of India's ability to go through the Swadeshi programme show, if the doubt is justified, that India has really no interest in the Khilafat or it has no desire to sacrifice anything for it? Is it a big sacrifice for every Hindu and Musalman to discard all foreign cloth and to use only Khadi? And if India is not to have that ability, will it not also be proof that India is unfit for any higher sacrifice and therefore unfit for helping Turkey? Let us all work for complete boycott of foreign cloth and the manufacture of the required quantity of Khadi and we shall be in sight of the heaven.

A suggestion was seriously put forth at Lucknow that we should boycott Ralli Bros., a Greek firm, and avenge ourselves against the Greeks and should invite the labourers to stop work on the export cargo. The suggestions, it seems to me, are as absurd as they are impossible to carry out. Assume for one moment that we can in a moment extinguish the business of Ralli Bros., how can that affect the Greeks? Ralli Bros., do not send all or a great part of their flour to Greece. Theirs is a world trade. And it is more difficult to deal with their trade than with Swadeshi. Any such attempt, apart from its inherent wrong, can only expose us to well-deserved ridicule. Interference with the labourers working on export cargo is equally fantastic. If we had such absolute control over the masses, we should have won our battle long ago. To stop the export of cargo requires not only a permanent or an indefinitely long stoppage of work by the existing labourers, but it presupposes our ability to stop any replacement of withdrawn labour. I fear we are not organised enough for the work. Any such attempt can only end in failure if not worse.

The only feasible suggestion is the immediate taking up of Civil Disobedience. I am convinced that the country is not ready for its adoption on an extensive scale. It can be safely and successfully adopted, if the country evinces sufficient organising ability, resourcefulness and discipline necessary for bringing the eminently practical Swadeshi enterprise to a successful end. Let us hope and pray that the country will.

8th September, 1921

THE MEANING OF THE KHILAFAT

(BY M. K. GANDHI)

I continue to receive letters from far and near, warning me against my interest in the Khilafat. Here is a typical letter from an old friend from New Zealand:

> Just a few lines to say I do not forget you. Were I in danger of so doing, the cables that often appear in our papers would prevent me forgetting. I see you have a mighty problem you are trying to solve in regard to India. Whether you are facing it in the wisest way I cannot say, for I am not in a position to judge. I would esteem it a favour, if you would hand enclosed post office order for 10/-to the publisher of your paper *Young India.* I think it is called, if it is published in English, or to the publisher of any paper in English representing your side of the case. Perhaps as an old friend, I may be borne with if I speak freely, even although I should be speaking without full knowledge. It always grieved me that you should be an arch-supporter of the Turkish Empire, and that the Khilafat question should be turned to political ends to undermine and cripple and confuse the adminitration of British Government of India. Turkey's crimes afainst Bulgarians, Greeks and Armenians call to heaven for judgment. I wonder how far the Moslems in their All-India Khilafat Congress during recent years protested against those atrocities, and dissociated themselves from the Turkish policy of extermination of a noble, excellent, industrious and gentle race (the Armenians). The blood of those martyrs will cry to heaven for justice, and not one can be forgotton by him who marks the sparrow's fall. If Turkey's history has been one of rapine and massacre, is it not therefore to be shorn of its power as no longer worthy to be trusted with it? If political power is not to be used to maintain justice, freedom and fraternity of tributary races, but is to be used for oppression, persecution, examination, robbery and rapine, is such a nation not to be judged by other powers and deprived of her power to continue a malevolent way? To be shorn of political power need not deprive Islam of its spiritual weapons, if it has such. By its spiritual force let it live, or die if it has not such. Political

power is a curse to any religion, and history shows it has often been used tyrannically, *e.g.*, the Roman Catholic Church.

I do not know what are exactly the aims of the Non-co-operators, but it would appear they have come to object, *in toto*, to any British officials in the country. Rome was not built in a day, and a constitution cannot be framed ahead of the conditions of a country. Suppose all British officials were to leave bag and baggage to-morrow and Natives put in their place, would the administration be as pure as it is, would justice be done everywhere through the courts of your great country? I understand that the Indians fear the native police and their officials (natives) are peculiarly open to bribery and corruption. Before a people can be self-governing, there must be a basis of national *character* on which to build, and with which to build, and has the day come, when there are forces running through your various spheres of social, educational and political life that are regenerative and purifying?

Political propaganda, if revolutionary, may easily attract the basest and most malevolent among men, and if they capture the control of machinery of organisation, the blind and more than blind will lead those who follow their dictum to the pit. I am sure that you personally have not departed from your noble ideals and unselfish spirit of patriotism and justice, and freedom of soul, but there may be great slumbering forces awakened in the state of society around you that may carry you far beyond the points of wisdom and measures that make for true national well-being. Your country has all the elements that might make India a Russia, a Sinn Fein Ireland, a land of civil war, inter-tribal bloodshed. Division may easily spread through a land like India, your independent princes become arrayed on opposing sides, and no strong controlling unifying power be forthcoming to preserve peace, conserve progress and lead the way to *fuller* national life. Your pathway must be surrounded by snares and pitfalls which you can only escape by a clear vision of the will of God and unfaltering adherence thereto. As long as you coincide with the wishes of the popular clamour, there will be many who will cry "Hosanna" and will strew your path with palm leaves, but if you adhere to the high principles of the vision of God, the same people will cry, "crucify him, away with him". You know the parallel. He unfalteringly followed the will of God and they rejected Him. His aims were too pure, His kingdom too spiritual, His methods too divine.

He died, but God raised Him up and made that resurrection the life of the world's thought, made Him meet the need of all the men as Saviour, High Priest to represent, King to rule over.

Courage, brother ; do not stumble,
Though thy path be dark as night ;
There's a star to guide the humble ·
Trust in God and do the right.
Let the Road be rough and dreary
And its end far out of sight,
Foot it bravely, strong or weary,
Trust in God, and do the right.

Perish policy and cunning,
Perish all that fears the light.
Whether losing, whether winning,
Trust in God, and do the right,
Trust no party, sect or faction,
Trust no leaders in the fight ;
But in every word and action
Trust in God and do the right.

Trust no lovely forms of passion,—
Friends may look like angels bright ;
Trust no custom, school or fashion ;
Trust in God and do the right.

Some will hate thee, some will love thee,
Some will flatter, some will slight ;
Cease from man and look above thee,
Trust in God and do the right.

Simple rule, and safest guiding,
Inward peace, and inward might,
Star upon our path abiding,—
Trust in God, and do the right.

Courage, brother, do not stumble,
Though thy path be dark as night ;
There's a star to guide the humble,
Trust in God, and do the right.

The great thing is to have Divine wisdom, the deep insight into principles and far-seeing wisdom of true statesmanship. You are doubtless familiar with the life of Abraham Lincoln, his clear-sighted vision, his aboslute integrity, tender-heartedness, humility humour and humaneness.

I often say to my friends, "If you heard Mr. Gandhi on the great grievances that exist under the present order of things, you would understand his opposition."

The question is, what is the best way for the welfare of India to correct existing abuses. Strikes, violence, arouse passions, and a hundred discontents and ill-feeling, and in most cases defeat their own ends. Reforms must come along constitutional lines, if the gain is to be accompanied by good feeling and unity and peace. Gains by revolutionary means cannot be a natural evolution. From my distant corner I can only earnestly pray, that God may guide and make you an instrument for the true well-being of India.

The warmth and the sincerity are unmistakable. I know the friend to be a devout God-fearing Christian. But it must be evident to any one who knows anything about the Turkish question, that my correspondent is strongly prejudiced against the Turks. His pictures of the Armenians as 'a noble, excellent, industrious and gentle race' betrays the extent of his ignorance about the question. He cannot be blamed for it. The Turkish side has been sedulously kept from the English-reading public. All these good Christians scattered about in different parts of the world have only one class of reading presented to them. The missionary journals are fanatically, I was going to say, criminally, anti-Turkish and anti-Islam. The very word charity about which St. Paul wrote so magnificently is absent from the minds of the writers in the missionary journals, when they write about Islam and Turkey. The Turk is to them the arch-infidel created by God only to be cursed. It is this prejudiced but honest attitude that stands in the way of Truth and Justice.

I have no desire to defend Turkey against the Armenians or the Greeks. I am not prepared to deny Turkish misrule or misdeeds. But the Greeks and the

Armenians have an infinitely worse record. What is more, the defence of the Khilafat is the defence of a pure ideal. It is not necessary to defend the conduct of individual Popes in order to support the institution of Papacy. Oppose all Turkish misrule by all means, but it is wicked to seek to efface the Turk and with him Islam from Europe under the false plea of Turkish misrule.

What is still worse is that the defeat of the Central Powers should be utilised to crush Islam. Was the late War a crusade against Islam, in which the Musalmans of India were invited to join? To say that the Musalmans may have any one they choose as their spiritual head, but that they may not interfere with the disintegration of Turkey, is not to know the Khilafat. The Khalifa must ever be the Defender of the Faith of the Prophet, and therefore nobody can become or remain Khalifa, immediately he is deprived of or loses the power of defending Islam against the whole world. One may dispute the ethics of the doctrine in the abstract, but England is not engaged in a war against Islam because it is unethical. In that case, England has to renounce her association with millions whose faith is divorced from ethics.

As a matter of fact, is there anything immoral in a religion seeking to sustain itself by possession of temporal power? In practice, has not Christianity been sustained by temporal power? And even in Hinduism, have not Rajput Kings been custodians of Hinduism?

What I venture to commend to the many Christians who honestly think like my friend, is to join the defence of the Khilafat as an ideal, and thus recognise that the struggle of Non-co-operation is one of religion against irreligion.

For my part I have the clearest possible conscience in

this matter. The end to me is just. I fight to bolster up no fraud or injustice. The means are equally just. In the prosecution of the fight, Truth and Non-violence are the only weapons. Self-suffering is the truest test of sincerity.

9th June, 1920

THE MAHOMEDAN DECISION

(BY M. K. GANDHI)

The Khilafat meeting at Allahabad has unanimously reaffirmed the principle of Non-co-operation and appointed an executive committee to lay down and enforce a detailed programme *. This meeting was preceded by a

* In the issue of *Young India*, dated 5th May, Mr. Gandhi wrote, under the heading, "How to work Non-co-operation": "Perhaps the best way of answering the tears and criticism as to Non-co-operation is to elaborate more fully the scheme of Non-co-operation. The critics seem to imagine that the organisers propose to give effect to the whole scheme at once. The fact however is that the organisers have fixed definite, progressive four stages. The first is the giving up of titles and resignation of honorary posts. If there is no response or if the response received is not effective, recourse will be had to the second stage. The second stage involves much previous arrangement. Certainly not a single servant will be called out unless he is either capable of supporting himself and his dependents or the Khilafat Committee is able to bear the burden. All the classes of servants will not be called out at once and never will any pressure be put upon a single servant to withdraw himself from the Government service. Nor will a single private employee be touched for the simple reason that the movement is not anti-English. It is not even anti-Government. Co-operation is to be withdrawn because the people must not be party to a wrong—a broken pledge—a violation of deep religious sentiment. Naturally, the movement will receive a check if there is any undue influence brought to bear upon any Government servant or if any violence is used or countenanced by any member of the Khilafat Committee. The second stage must be entirely successful, if the

joint Hindu-Mahomedan meeting at which Hindu leaders

response is at all on an adequate scale. For no Government—much less the Indian Government—can subsist if the people cease to serve it. The withdrawal therefore of the police and the military—the third stage—is a distant goal. The organisers however wanted to be fair, open and above suspicion. They did not want to keep back from the Government or the public a single step they had in contemplation even as a remote contingency. The fourth, *i.e.*, suspension of taxes, is still more remote. The organisers recognise that suspension of general taxation is fraught with the greatest danger. It is likely to bring a sensitive class in conflict with the police. They are therefore not likely to embark upon it, unless they can do so with the assurance that there will be no violence offered by the people." "I admit as I have already done", continued Mr. Gandhi, "that Non-co-operation is not unattended with risk, but the risk of supineness in the face of a grave issue is infinitely greater than the danger of violence ensuing from organizing Non-co-operation. To do nothing is to invite violence for a certainty".

After pointing out that Non-co-operation is the only way to aviod violence, Mr. Gandhi continued: "There is however one formidable argument urged by friends against my joining the Khilafat movement. They say that it ill becomes me, a friend of the English and an admirer of the British constitution, to join hands with those who are to-day filled with nothing but ill-will against the English. I am sorry to have to cofess that the ordinary Mahomedan entertains today no affection for Englishmen. He considers, not without some cause, that they have not played the game. But if I am friendly towards Englishmen, I am no less so towards my countrymen, the Mahomedans. And as such they have a greater claim upon my attention than Englishmen. My personal religion however enables me to serve my countrymen without hurting Englishmen or for that matter anybody else. What I am not prepared to do my blood-brother I would not do to an Englishman. I would withdraw co-operation from him if it became necessary, as I had withdrawn from my own brother (now deceased) when it became necessary. I serve the Empire by refusing to partake in its wrong. William Stead offered public prayers for British reverses at the time of the Boer war because he considered that the nation to which he belonged was engaged in an unrighteous war. The present Prime Minister risked his life in opposing that war and did everything he could to obstruct his own Government in its prosecution.

were invited to give their views. Mrs. Besant*, the Hon'ble Pandit Malaviyaji, the Hon'bles Dr. Sapru†, Motilal Nehru‡, Chintamani§ and others were present at the meeting. It was a wise step on the part of the Khilafat Committee to invite Hindus representing all shades of thought to give them the benefit of their advice. Mrs. Besant and Dr. Sapru strongly dissuaded the Mahomedans present from the policy of Non-co-operation. The

* Mrs. Annie Besant was a leading figure in Indian politics from 1915-1919 as an Extremist leader. She subsequently threw in her lot with the Moderates and became a most determined anti-Non-co-operationist.

† A Moderate leader of Allahabad, subsequently appointed Law Member of the Viceroy's Executive Council.

‡ A rich Advocate enjoying a princely practice in the United Provinces; subsequently became a Non-co-operator.

§ A (Moderate) journalist and editor of the *Leader* of Allahabad; subsequently became a Minister in the United Provinces Government.

And to-day if I have thrown in my lot with the Mahomedans a large number of whom bear no friendly feelings towards the British, I have done so frankly as a friend of the British and with the object of gaining justice and of thereby showing the capacity of the British constitution to respond to every honest determination when it is coupled with suffering. I hope by my 'alliance' with the Mahomedans to achieve a threefold end—to obtain justice in the face of odds with the method of Satyagraha and to show its efficacy over all other methods, to secure Mahomedan friendship for the Hindus and thereby internal peace also, and last but not least to transform ill-will into affection for the British and their constitution which in spite of its imperfections, has weathered many a storm. I may fail in achieving any of the ends. I can but attempt. God alone can grant success. It will not be denied that the ends are all worthy. I invite Hindus and Englishmen to join me in a full hearted manner in shouldering the burden the Mahomedans of India are carrying. Theirs is admittedly a just fight. The Viceroy, the Secretary of State, the Maharaja of Bikaner and Lord Sinha have testified to it. The time has arrived to make good the testimony. People with a just cause are never satisfied with a mere protest. They have been known to die for it. Are a high spirited people like the Mahomedans expected to do less?

other Hindu speakers made non-committal speeches. Whilst the other Hindu speakers approved of the principle of Non-co-operation in theory, they saw many practical difficulties and they feared also complications arising from Mahomedans welcoming an Afghan invasion of India. The Mahomedan speakers gave the fullest and frankest assurances that they would fight to a man any invader who wanted to conquer India, but they were equally frank in asserting that any invasion from without undertaken with a view to uphold the prestige of Islam and to vindicate justice would have their full sympathy if not their actual support. It is easy enough to understand and justify the Hindu caution. It is difficult to resist the Mahomedan position. In my opinion, the best way to prevent India from becoming the battle ground between the forces of Islam and those of the English is for Hindus to make Non-co-operation a complete and immediate success, and I have little doubt that, if the Mahomedans remain true to their declared intention and are able to exercise self-restraint and make sacrifices, the Hindus will "play the game" and join them in the campaign of Non-co-operation. I feel equally certain that Hindus will not assist Mahomedans in promoting or bringing about an armed conflict between the British Government and their allies, and Afghanistan. British forces are too well organised to admit of any successful invasion of the Indian frontier. The only way, therefore, the Mahomedans can carry on an effective struggle on behalf of the honour of Islam is to take up Non-co-operation in real earnest. It will not only be completely effective if it is adopted by the people on an extensive scale, but it will also provide full scope for individual conscience. If I cannot bear an injustice done by an individual or a corporation and

I am directly or indirectly instrumental in upholding that individual or corporation, I must answer for it before my Maker; but I have done all it is humanly possible for me to do consistently with the moral code that refuses to injure even the wrong-doers, if I cease to support the injustice in the manner described above. In applying therefore such a great force, there should be no haste, there should be no temper shown. Non-co-operation must be and remain absolutely a voluntary effort. The whole thing, then, depends upon Mahomedans themselves. If they will but help themselves, Hindu help will come and the Government, great and mighty though it is, will have to bend before this irresistible force. No Government can possibly withstand the bloodless opposition of a whole nation.

23rd June, 1920

THE NON-CO-OPERATION COMMITTEE

(BY M. K. GANDHI)

There seems to be a great deal of misunderstanding and misconception about the Non-co-operation Committee appointed by the Khilafat Committee at Allahabad on the 3rd instant. A friend who was present at the meeting writes to say that the Committee was formed for the purpose of giving full effect to Non-co-operation and to act in all matters in connection with it as if it was representative of the whole Mussalman population of India even in the matter of making representations to the authorities. That this was not the Committee's scope is the purpose of this writing to show.

As I stated its objects when I invited the formation of the Committee, they were to ascertain and enforce the wish of the nation on Non-co-operation. Whilst it is a representative body with full powers to act, it cannot be said—it is not intended—to represent all the best and the most influential Mahomedan opinion. It does not, for instance, represent the titled nobility in Islam. It is no fault in the Committee. It has been purposely restricted to those who are able to give their whole time and attention to the work of organising Non-co-operation and in the process of ensuring obedience to instructions, other discipline and non-violence. It is therefore a Committee of workers. It is not expected that the whole of the Mussalman India will be equally strong in Non-co-operation. Some doubt its efficacy, others consider it to be a milk and water remedy, some dread it as being too strong for India in her present stage, they say she has not developed the measure of sacrifice at present to ensure success. The Committee does not represent or contain such doubting elements, though they may otherwise be much more influential than many Mussalmans who are on the Committee. It contains those only who have the largest faith in Non-co-operation and who, although they swear by it, yet will not force the pace to the breaking point but will endeavour to carry the nation with its programme in so far as it is practicable, and who, whilst doing so, will not themselves be deterred from taking the boldest steps and will seek out those who are prepared to do likewise. This Committee, therefore, starting without any, has to build its reputation upon its work and upon results it may achieve. It will cease to exist if it shows no work or in spite of work shows no results. For outsiders it has the least representative capacity. Shaukat Ali is an amiable man but a rabid fanatic carrying no weight with anybody, Hasrat Mohani a useless man who thinks of nothing but Swadeshi, Dr. Kitchlew a man of yesterday with no experience of the world outside Amritsar. Much the same may he said against the others. I am no doubt a superior person but after all a crank and an interloper at that. Any representation signed by it will carry little weight with the outside world in so far as it depends upon the influence of the signatories. It does not therefore mean that it will never make representations. It certainly will, when swiftness is of the essence or when others for reasons of expediency or otherwise are not prepared to sign representations. Indeed canvassing of signatures to weighty representations will be one of the means of gauging public opinion and testing the spirit of sacrifice among the elite of the land. For the masses and for internal work, however, the Committee is the most representative. It is difficult perhaps to find two men more representative of Mussalman opinion than Shaukat Ali and Hasrat Mohani. The others though less known have been chosen for the qualities of strength, perseverance, patience, calmness, truthfulness, courage under difficulty and sacrifice, believed to be possessed by them.

It has been suggested that I am to lead the movement. The statement is only partially true.* I say this not out

* Mr. Gandhi's connection with the movement is further explained in the famous letter he addressed to the Viceroy regarding the inauguration of Non-co-operation. He wrote:

Your Excellency,—As one who has enjoyed a certain measure of your Excellency's confidence, and as one who claims to be a devoted well-wisher of the British Empire, I owe it to your Excellency, and through your Excellency to His Majesty's Ministers, to explain my connection with and my conduct in the Khilafat Question.

At the very earliest stage of the war, even whilst I was in London organising the Indian Volunteer Ambulance Corps, I began to interest myself in the Khilafat Question. I perceived how deeply moved the little Musslman World in London was when Turkey decided to throw in her lot with Germany. On my arrival in India in the January

of humility merely but it is a literal fact. If the belief gains ground that I am leading the movement, it may prove fatal to it. I am leading the movement in the sense that I am the adviser whose advice is most acceptable to-day and who has the determination not surpassed by anybody to carry out the programme of Non-co-operation. But I do not pretend to represent Mussalman opinion. I can only try to interpret it. I could not stand alone and expect to carry the Mussalman masses with me. I should be very properly hooted out by a

---

of 1915, I found the same anxiousness and earnestness among the Mussalmans, with whom I came in contact. Their anxiety became intense when the information about the Secret Treaties leaked out. Distrust of British intentions filled their minds, and despair took possession of them. Even at that moment I advised my Mussalman friends not to give way to despair, but to express their fear and their hopes in a disciplined manner. It will be admitted that the whole of Mussalman India has behaved in a singularly restrained manner during the past five years, and that the leaders have been able to keep the turbulent sections of their community under complete control.

The peace terms and your Excellency's defence of them have given the Mussalmans of India a shock from which it will be difficult for them to recover. The terms violate ministerial pledges and utterly disregard Mussalman sentiment. I consider that, as a staunch Hindu wishing to live on terms of the closest friendship with my Mussalman countrymen, I should be an unworthy son of India if I did not stand by them in their hour of trial. In my humble opinion, their cause is just. They claim that Turkey must not be *punished* if their sentiment is to be respected. Muslim soldiers did not fight to inflict punishmen on their own Khalifa or to deprive him of his territories. The Mussalman attitude has been consistent throughout these five years.

My duty to the Empire to which I owe my loyalty requires me to resist the cruel violence that has been done to the Mussalman sentiment. So far as I am aware, Mussalmans and Hindus have as a whole lost faith in British justice and honour. The report of the majority of the Hunter Committee, Your Excellency's despatch thereon and Mr. Montagu's reply have only aggravated the distrust.

In these circumstances, the only course open to one like me is either

mixed Mussalman audience if I tried to make a point against the best Mussalman opinion in matters of religion. But if I were a Mussalman, I would not mind contesting issues before a Mussalman meeting in the face of heavy odds against me. I consider myself to be a sagacious worker and my sagacity means no more and no less than a fine perception of my limitations. I hope I never travel beyond my limits. Certainly I have never done so consciously. It is necessary for every intelligent Mussalman to bear in mind my limitations and the scope

---

in despair to sever all connection with British rule, or, if I still retained faith in the inherent superiority of the British constitution to all others at present in vogue, to adopt such means as will rectify the wrong done, and thus restore confidence. I have not lost faith in such superiority and I am not without hope that somehow or other justice will yet be rendered if we show the requisite capacity for suffering. Indeed, my conception of that constitution is that it helps only those who are ready to help themselves. I do not believe that it protects the weak. It gives free scope to the strong to maintain their strength and develop it. The weak under it go to the wall.

It is, then, because I believe in the British constitution that I have advised my Mussalman friends to withdraw their support from Your Excellency's Government, and the Hindus to join them, should the peace terms not be revised in accordance with the solemn pledges of Ministers and the Muslim sentiment.

Three courses were open to the Mahomedans in order to mark their emphatic disapproval of the utter injustice to which His Majesty's Ministers have become party, if they have not actually been the prime perpetrators of it. They are:

(1) To resort to violence.

(2) To advise emigration on a wholesale scale.

(3) Not to be party to the injustice by ceasing to co-operate with the Government.

Your Excellency must be aware that there was a time when the boldest, though the most thoughtless, among the Mussalmans favoured violence, and the *Hijrat* (emigration) has not yet ceased to be the battle-cry. I venture to claim that I have succeeded by patient reasoning in weaning the party of violence from its ways. I confess

of my function. Ignorance is likely to prove fatal to the success of the movement. My connection with it must not stupefy workers into indolence or indifference. My connection should mean, if it is to be productive of good results, greater watchfulness, greater sense of responsibility, greater capacity and willingdess for work and greater efficiency. I can think out plans but execution must ever rest with Mussalman workers. The movement must be worked and led by them with the assistance of friends like me but also without, if need be. I must not be expected to make Non-co-operators;

---

that I did not—I did not attempt to—succeed in weaning them from violence on moral grounds, but purely on utilitarian grounds. The result, for the time being at any rate, has however been to stop violence. The school of "Hijrat" has received a check, if it has not stopped its activity entirely. I hold that no repression could have prevented a violent eruption, if the people had not presented to them a form of direct action involving considerable sacrifice and ensuring success if such direct action was largely taken up by the public. Non-co-operation was the only dignified and constitutional form of such direct action. For it is the right recognised from time immemorial of the subject to refuse to assist a ruler who misrules.

At the same time I admit that Non-co-operation practised by the mass of people is attended with grave risks. But in a crisis such as has overtaken the Mussalman of India, no step that is unattended with large risks can possibly bring about the desired change. Not to run some risks now will be to court much greater risks if not virtual destruction of Law and Order.

But there is yet an escape from Non-co-operation. The Mussalman representation has requested your Excellency to lead the agitation yourself, as did your distinguished predecessor at the time of the South African trouble. But if you cannot see your way to do so, and Non-co-operation becomes a dire necessity, I hope that your Excellency will give those who have accepted my advice and myself the credit for being actuated by nothing less than a stern sense of duty.

Laburnam Road,
Gamdevi, Bombay,
22nd June, 1920.

I have the honour to remain,
Your Excellency's faithful servant,
(Sd.) M. K. Gandhi.

Mussalman leaders alone can make them. No amount of sacrifice on my part will produce in the Mussalman world the spirit of Non-co-operation, *i.e.*, sacrifice in a matter of religion. The Mussalman leaders will have to show it in their own persons before the masses evolve it.

And now the question, why there are no Hindu leaders on the Committee, is easily answered. The supreme Committee can only be purely Mussalman. My presence too, I consider as an evil but it is a necessary evil because of my qualifications. I have specialised in Non-co-operation. I have successfully experimented with it. The resolution about Non-co-operation was conceived by me at the conference at Delhi. I am on the Committee therefore as a specialist and not because I am a Hindu. My function is, therefore, of an adviser merely. That I happen to be a staunch Hindu with the conviction that every Hindu should consider it to be his duty to go with the Mussalmans the full length in Non-co-operation, is no doubt an advantage to the Committee. But that advantage was at its disposal whether I was on it or not.

Whilst I am considering the Hindu connection with the Khilafat movement, even at the risk of repetition, I would like to clear up my own position. As I consider the Muslim claim to be intrinsically (as distinguished from religiously) just, I propose to go with them to the extent of fullest Non-co-operation. And I consider it to be perfectly consistent with my loyalty to the British connection. But I would not go with the Mussalmans in any campaign of violence. I could not help them in promoting, for instance, an invasion of India through Afghanistan or otherwise for the purpose of forcing better peace terms. It is, I hold, the duty of every Hindu to resist any inroad on India even for the purpose specified as it is his duty to help his Mussalman brethren to satisfy their just demands by means of Non-co-operation or other form of suffering, no matter how great, so long as it does not involve loss of India's liberty or inflicting of violence on any person. And I have thrown myself whole-heartedly into the Non-co-operation movement if only because I want to prevent any such armed conflict.

30*th June*, 1920

THE MUSSALMAN REPRESENTATION*

(By M. K. Gandhi)

Slowly but surely the Mussalmans are preparing for the battle before them. They have to fight against odds that are undoubtedly heavy but not half as heavy as the prophet had against him. How often did he not put his life in danger? But his faith in God was unquenchable. He went forward with a light, for God was on his side, for he represented truth. If his followers have half the prophet's faith and half his spirit of sacrifice

*In pursuance of the Allahabad decision, both Mr. Gandhi (*See* p. 197) and the Muslim leaders issued manifestoes declaring that they would resort to Non-co-operation if by the 1st of August 1921 the peace terms were not revised and calling upon the Viceroy to resign his office if the Muslim demands were refused by his Majesty's Government. The following is the representation sent under date Bombay, 22nd June, 1921 to H. E. the Viceroy on be half of the Indian Mussalmans by many prominent leaders including the Hon. Mr. Mazrul Haque, Mr. Yakub Hasan, Moulana Abdul Bari, Mr. Shaukat Ali and Mr. Azad:

"We, the undersigned, claim to represent the largest body of Sunni Muslim opinion. We have most carefully read the Turkish peace terms, and we consider them to be in direct violation of the religious sentiments of Mussalmans. They violate the obligations imposed

the odds will be presently even and will in a little while turn against the despoilers of Turkey. Already the rapacity of the Allies is telling against themselves. France finds her task difficult. Greece cannot stomach her ill-gotten gains. And England finds Mesopotamia a tough job. The oil of Mosul may feed the fire she has so wantonly lighted and burn her fingers badly. The newspapers say the Arabs do not like the presence of the Indian soldiery in their midst. I do not wonder. They are a fierce and a brave people and do not understand why Indian soldiers should find themselves in Mesopotamia. Whatever the fate of Non-co-operation, I wish that not a single Indian will offer his services for Mesopotamia whether for the civil or the military

---

upon Sunnis and wound the susceptibilities of all Mussalmans. They are contrary to the pledges of British Ministers on the strength of which it has been admitted it was possible to draw upon India for Muslim recruits during the war.

We hold that the British Empire which is "the greatest Mahomedan Power" in the world cannot treat the Turkish Empire, which represents the Khilafat, in the same manner that it may treat a defeated enemy. Indeed we contend that in certain respects Turkey has been treated worse than the other Powers. We respectfully submit that in the treatment of Turkey the British Government are bound to respect Indian Muslim sentiment in so far as it is neither unjust or unreasonable. In our opinion, the position taken up by Indian Mussalmans is simple. They cannot bear the thought of the temporal power of the Sultan being adversely affected by way of punishment for his having joined Germany under circumstances which need not be examined here. But we have no desire to ask for anything that would interfere with the principle of self-determination. We have no desire to uphold any misrule such as has been attributed to Turkey. Our delegates in Europe have asked for an independent commission of inquiry to investigate the charge of wanton cruelty said to have been practised by Turkish soldiers in Armenia. We cannot look with indifference upon the partition of Turkey and her Empire for the sake of punishing or humiliating her.

department. We must learn to think for ourselves and before entering upon any employment find out whether thereby we may not make ourselves instruments of injustice. Apart from the question of Khilafat and from the point of abstract justice, the English have no right to hold Mesopotamia. It is no part of our loyalty to help the Imperial Government in what is in plain language daylight robbery. If therefore we seek civil or military employment in Mesopotamia, we do so for the sake of earning a livelihood. It is our duty to see that the source is not tainted.

It surprises me to find so many people shrinking over the very mention of Non-co-operation. There is no instrument so clean, so harmless and yet so effective

---

"We would therefore request your Excellency and your Government to ask His Majesty's Ministers to secure a revision of the peace terms and tell them that on failure to do so, your Excellency will make common cause with the people of India. We make this suggestion as your Excellency has repeatedly declared that your Government has consistently and often pressed upon the attention of His Majesty's Ministers the case of Indian Mussalmans in this matter of vital concern to the vast majority of them. We feel, therefore, that we have a right to ask your Excellency to re-assure the Mussalmans of India that they still retain your active co-operation and powerful advocacy in the prosecution of their claims even to the point of resignation of your high office, should His Majesty's Ministers fail to secure a revision of the terms consistenly with the pledges and the sentiment mentioned above. We venture respectfully to suggest that had India been a Dominion enjoying full self-government, her responsible ministers would have, as a matter of course, resigned as a protest against such a serious breach of pledges and flouting of religious opinion as are involved in the peace terms.

If unfortunately your Excellency will not adopt our humble suggestion, we shall be obliged as from the first August next to withdraw co-operation from the Government and to ask our co-religionists and Hindu brethren to do likewise.

We ask your Excellency not to regard our statement as a threat or

as Non-co-operation. Judiciously hauled it need not produce any evil consequences. And its intensity will depend purely on the capacity of the people for sacrifice.

The chief thing is to prepare the atmosphere of Non-co-operation. "We are not going to co-operate with you in your injustice," is surely the right and the duty of every intelligent subject to say. Were it not for our utter servility, helplessness and want of confidence in ourselves, we would certainly grasp this clean weapon and make the most effective use of it. Even the most despotic government cannot stand except for the consent of the governed which consent is often forcibly procured by the despot. Immediately the subject ceases to fear the despotic force, his power is gone. But the British Government is never and nowhere entirely or even

---

in any way as a mark of disrespect. We claim to be as loyal subjects of the Crown as any in India. But we consider our loyalty to an earthly sovereign to be subservient to our loyalty to Islam. The latter enjoins upon every Mussalman to consider those who wantonly injure the status of the Khalifa to be enemies of Islam and to resist them with arms if necessary. We recognise that even if we had the power we must not resort to arms so long as any other means are at our disposal. We feel that the least that a Mussalman can do in these circumstances is not to assist those who are guilty of trying to reduce the Khilafat practically to nothingness. It would, therefore become our duty to refuse to co-operate with a Government which accepts the peace terms and advise acceptance thereof by us.

"We shall hope that such a serious step as Non-co-operation will not become necessary, but should it unfortunately happen to be otherwise, we assure your Excellency that we shall strive our utmost to avoid violence. We fully recognise our responsibility. We know that any eruption of violence must check and injure the peaceful demonstration contemplated by us and what is more the sacred cause which is dear to us as life. We shall therefore take up Non-co-operation in progressive stages and so as to cause the least necessary dislocation or embarrassment to the Government and so as to enable us to control and discipline popular feeling."

chiefly laid upon force. It does make an honest attempt to secure the goodwill of the governed. But it does not hesitate to adopt unscrupulous means to compel the consent of the governed. It has not gone beyond the 'Honesty is the best policy' idea. It therefore bribes you into consenting to its will by awarding titles, medals and ribbons, by giving you employment, by its superior financial ability to open for its employees avenues for enriching themselves and finally when these fail, it resorts to force. That is what Sir Michael O'Dwyer did and that is almost every British administrator will certainly do if he thought it necessary. If, then, we would not be greedy, if we would not run after titles and medals and honorary posts which do the country no good, half the battle is won.

My advisers are never tired of telling me that, even if the Turkish peace terms are revised, it will not be due to Non-co-operation. I venture to suggest to them that Non-co-operation has a higher purpose than mere revision of the terms. If I cannot compel revision, I must at least cease to support a government that becomes party to the usurpation. And if I succeed in pushing Non-co-operation to the extreme limit, I do compel the Government to choose between India and the usurpation. I have faith enough in England to know that at that moment England will expel her present jaded ministers and put in others who will make a clean sweep of the terms in consultation with an awakening India, draft terms that will be honourable to her, to Turkey and acceptable to India.

But I hear my critics say, "India has not the strength of purpose and the capacity for the sacrifice to achieve such a noble end." They are partly right. India has not these qualities now, because we have not—shall we not evolve them and infect the nation with them? Is not the attempt worth making? Is any sacrifice too great to gain such a great purpose?

14*th July*, 1920

THE LAW OF MAJORITIES

(By M. K. Gandhi)

Mrs. Besant having read a report of my speech at the Punjab Meeting organised by the Home Rule Leagues and the National Union, Bombay, and having therein seen that I had moved the resolution asking for the prosecution of General Dyer and the impeachment of Sir Michael O'Dwyer, asks how I could move a resolution whose terms I had not approved. Mr. Shastriar has also felt uneasy about the same act. I have not seen any report of my speech. I am unable to say therefore whether I am correctly reported. My speech was in Gujerati and may have suffered at the hands of the translating reporter. I shall endeavour to explain my own position independently of the reports of my speech. And I do so gladly because I recognise that the principle raised by the two great leaders is very important.

I have often been charged with having an unyielding nature. I have been told that I would not bow to the decision of the majority. I have been accused of being autocratic. Now on the occasion of the Punjab Meeting, I was pressed to move a resolution which did not commend itself to me. I undertook to do so reserving to myself the right to expressing emphatic opinion to the contrary. And I did so. I have never been able to subscribe to the charge of obstinacy or autocracy. On the conrary, I pride myself on my yielding nature in non-vital matters. I detest autocracy. Valuing my freedom and independence I equally cherish them for others. I have no desire to carry a single soul with me, if I cannot appeal to his or her reason. My unconventionality I carry to the point of rejecting the divinity of the oldest Sastras if they cannot convince my reason. But I have found by experience that, if I wish to live in society and still retain my independence, I must limit the points of utter independence to matters of first rate importance. In all others which do not involve a departure from one's personal religion or moral code, one must yield to the majority. In the case in question, I had an opportunity of illustrating my position. Of my so-called unyielding nature, the country had abundant illustration. It was happy to find a great occasion where I could safely yield. I believe still that the country is wrong in asking for General Dyer's prosecution and Sir Michael O'Dwyer's impeachment. That is purely the business of the British. My purpose is to secure the removal of the wrong-doers from any office under the Crown. Nothing I have seen since has altered my view. And I pressed it before the very meeting at which I moved the resolution in question. Yet I moved it, because there is nothing immoral in asking for General Dyer's prosecution. The country has the right to demand it. The Congress Sub-Committee has advised that waiver of that right can only do good to India. I thought therefore that I had my position quite clear, namely, that I still opposed the idea of prosecution, and yet I had no objection in moving the resolution that involved prosecution because it was not bad or harmful *per se*.

I admit however that, during the crisis we are passing through, my moving the resolution was a dangerous experiment. For, whilst we are evolving new codes of public conduct and trying to instruct, influence or lead the masses, it is not safe to do anything that is likely to confuse the mass mind or to appear to 'be truckling to the multitude.' I believe that at the present moment it is better to be 'dubbed' obstinate and autocratic than even to appear to be influenced by the multitude for the sake of its approbation. Those who claim to lead the masses must resolutely refuse to be led by them, if we want to avoid mob law and desire ordered progress for the country. I believe that mere protestation of one's opinion and surrender to the mass opinion is not only not enough but in matters of vital importance, leaders must *act* contrary to the mass of opinion if it does not commend itself to their reason.

21*st July*, 1920

AT THE CALL OF THE COUNTRY

(By M. K. Gandhi)

Dr. Sapru delivered before the Khilafat Conference* at Allahabad an impassioned address sympathising with the Mussalmans in their trouble but dissuaded them from embarking on Non-co-operation. He was frankly unable to suggest a substitute but was emphatically of opinion that, whether there was a substitute or not, Non-co-operation was a remedy worse than the disease. He said further that Mussalmans will be taking upon their shoulders a serious responsibility, if, whilst they

* A conference of leaders of all communities and parties was held at Allahabad in July, 1920, to consider whether Non-co-operation was the remedy to gain justice for India in regard to the Khilafat wrong. (*See* p. 191).

appealed to the ignorant masses to join them, they could not appeal to the Indian judges to resign and if they did, they would not succeed.

I acknowledge the force of Dr. Sapru's last argument. At the back of Dr. Sapru's mind is the fear that Non-co-operation by the ignorant people would lead to distress and chaos and would do no good. In my opinion, any Non-co-operation is bound to do some good. Even the Viceregal door-keeper saying, 'Please, Sir, I can serve the Government no longer because it has hurt my national honour,' and resigning is a step mightier and more effective than the mightiest speech declaiming against the Government for its injustice.

Nevertheless, it would be wrong to appeal to the door-keeper until one has appealed to the highest in the land. And as I propose, if the necessity arose, to ask the door-keepers of the Government to dissociate themselves from an unjust Government, I propose now to address an appeal to the Judges and the Executive Councillors to join the protest that is rising from all over India against the double wrong done to India, on the Khilfat and the Punjab questions. In both, national honour is involved.

I take it that these gentlemen have entered upon their high offices not for the sake of emolument, nor I hope for the sake of fame, but for the sake of serving their country. It was not for money, for, they were earning more than they do now. It must not be for fame, for, they cannot buy fame at the cost of national honour. The only consideration that can at the present moment keep them in office must be service of the country.

When the people have faith in the government, when it represents the popular will, the judges and the executive officials possibly serve the country. But when that government does not represent the will of the people, when it supports dishonesty and terrorism, the judges and the executive officials by retaining office become instruments of dishonesty and terrorism. And the least therefore that these holders of high offices can do is to cease to become agents of a dishonest and terrorising government.

For the judges the objection will be raised that they are above politics, and so they are and should be. But the doctrine is true only so far as the government is on the whole for the benefit of the people and at least represents the will of the majority. Not to take part in politics means not to take sides. But when a whole country has one mind, one will, when a whole country has been denied justice, it is no longer a question of party politics, it is a matter of life and death. It then becomes the duty of every citizen to refuse to serve a government which misbehaves and flouts national wish. The judges are at that moment bound to follow the nation if they are ultimately its servants.

There remains another argument to be examined. It applies to both the judges and the members of the executive. It will be urged that my appeal could only be meant for the Indians and what good can it do by Indians renouncing offices which have been won for the nation by hard struggle. I wish that I could make an effective appeal to the English as well as the Indians. But I confess that I have written with the mental reservation that the appeal is addressed only to the Indians. I must therefore examine the argument just stated. Whilst it is true that these offices have been secured after a prolonged struggle, they are of use not because of the struggle but because they are intended to serve the nation. The moment they cease to possess that quality, they become useless and as in the present case harmful, no matter how hard-earned and therefore valuable they may have been at the outset.

I would submit too to our distinguished countrymen who occupy high offices that their giving up their offices will bring the struggle to a speedy end and would probably obviate the danger attendant upon the masses being called upon to signify their disapproval by withdrawing co-operation. If the title-holders gave up their titles, if the holders of honorary offices gave up their appointments and if the high officials gave up their posts, and the would be councillors boycott the councils, the Government would quickly come to its senses and give effect to the people's will. For, the alternative before the Government then would be nothing but despotic rule pure and simple. That would probably mean military dictatorship. The world's opinion has advanced so far that Britain dare not contemplate such dictatorship with equanimity. The taking of the steps suggested by me will constitute the peacefullest revolution the world has ever seen. Once the infallibility of Non-co-operation is realised, there is an end to all bloodshed and violence in any shape or form.

Undoubtedly a cause must be grave to warrant the drastic method of national Non-co-operation. I do say that the affront such as has been put upon Islam cannot be repeated for a century. Islam must rise now or 'be fallen' if not for ever, certainly for a century. And I cannot imagine a graver wrong than the massacre of Jallianwalla and the barbarity that followed it, the whitewash by the Hunter Committee, the dispatch of the Government of India, Mr. Montagu's letter upholding the Viceroy and the then Lieutenant-Governor of the Punjab, the refusal to remove officials who made of the lives of the Punjabis 'a hell' during the Martial Law period. These acts constitute a complete series of continuing wrongs against India, which, if India has any sense of honour, she must right at the sacrifice of all the material wealth she possesses. If she does not, she will have bartered her soul for a 'mess of pottage'.

28*th July*, 1920

THE FIRST OF AUGUST

(BY M. K. GANDHI)

It is hardly likely that before the 1st August there will be on the part of His Majesty's Ministers promise of a revision of the peace terms and the consequent suspension of the inauguration of Non-co-operation. The first of August next will be as important an event in the history of India as was the 6th of April last year. The sixth of April marked the beginning of the end of the Rowlatt Act. No one can consider the Rowlatt Act can possibly live in the face of the agitation that has only been suspended—never given up. It must be clear to anyone that the power that wrests justice from an unwilling Government in the matter of the Punjab and the Khilafat will be the power that will secure repeal of the Rowlatt Act. And that power is the power of Satyagraha, whether it is known by the name of Civil Disobedience or Non-co-operation.

Many people dread the advent of Non-co-operation, because of the events of last year. They fear madness from the mob and consequent repetition of last year's reprisals almost unsurpassed in their ferocity in the history of modern times. Personally I do not mind Governmental fury as I mind mob fury. The latter is a sign of national distemper and therefore more difficult to deal with than the former which is confined to a small corporation. It is easier to oust a Government that has rendered itself unfit to govern than it is to cure unknown people in a mob of their madness. But great movements cannot be stopped altogether because a Government or a people or both go wrong. We learn and profit through our mistakes and failures. No general worth the name gives up a battle because he has suffered reverses, or which is the same thing, made mistakes. And so we must approach Non-co-operation with confidence and hope. As in the past, the commencement is to be marked by fasting and prayer— a sign of the religious character of the demonstration. There should also be on that day suspension of business, and meetings to pass resolutions praying for revision of the peace terms and justice for the Punjab and inculcating Non-co-operation until justice has been done.

The giving up of titles and honorary posts should also commence from the first of August. Doubt has been expressed as to the sufficiency of notice regarding surrender of titles and honorary posts. It is however quickly dispelled by bearing in mind that the first of August marks the commencement of the surrender of titles. It is not the only day on which surrender has to take place. Indeed I do not expect a very large response on the first day. A vigorous propaganda will have to be carried on and the message delivered to every title or post holder and the argument presented to him proving the duty of such surrender.

But the greatest thing in this campaign of Non-co-operation is to evolve order, discipline, co-operation among the people, co-ordination among the workers. Effective Non-co-operation depends upon complete organisation. Thousands of men who have filled meetings throughout the Punjab have convinced me that the people want to withdraw co-operation from the Government but they must know how. Most people do not understand the complicated machinery of the Government. They do not realise that every citizen silently but nonetheless certainly sustains the government of the day in ways of which he has no knowledge. Every citizen therefore renders himself responsible for every act of his government. And it is quite proper to support it so long as the actions of the government are bearable. But when they hurt him and his nation, it becomes his duty to withdraw his support.

But as I have said, every citizen does not know how to do so in an orderly manner. Disorderliness comes from anger, orderliness out of intelligent resistance. The first condition therefore of real success is to ensure entire absence of violence. Violence done to persons representing the Government or to persons who don't join our ranks, *i.e.*, the supporters of the Government, means in every case retrogression in our case, cessation of Non-co-operation and useless waste of innocent lives. Those therefore who wish to make Non-co-operation a success in the quickest possible time will consider it their first duty to see that in their neighbourhood complete order is kept.

PART III

THE PRINCIPLES OF NON-CO-OPERATION

PART III

THE PRINCIPLES OF NON-CO-OPERATION

4th August, 1920

ON Ist August, 1920, Mr. Gandhi addressed the following letter to the Viceroy, inaugurating the Non-co-operation Movement:

It is not without a pang that I return the Kaisar-i-Hind gold medal granted to me by your predecessor for my humanitarian work in South Africa, the Zulu war medal granted in South Africa for my services as officer in charge of the Indian volunteer ambulance corps in 1906 and the Boer war medal for my services as assistant superintendent of the Indian volunteer stretcher bearer corps during the Boer war of 1899-1900. I venture to return these medals in pursuance of the scheme of Non-co-operation inaugurated to-day in connection with the Khilafat movement. Valuable as these honours have been to me, I cannot wear them with an easy conscience so long as my Mussalman countrymen have to labour under a wrong done to their religious sentiment. Events that have happened during the past month have confirmed me in the opinion that the Imperial Government have acted in the Khilafat matter in an unscrupulous, immoral and unjust manner and have been moving from wrong to wrong in order to defend their immorality. I can retain neither respect nor affection for such a Government.

The attitude of the Imperial and Your Excellency's Governments on the Punjab question has given me additional cause for grave dissatisfaction. I had the honour, as Your Excellency is aware, as one of the Congress commissioners to investigate the causes of the disorders in the Punjab during the April of 1919. And it is my deliberate conviction that Sir Michael O'Dwyer was totally unfit to hold the office of Lieutenant Governor of Punjab and that his policy was primarily responsible for infuriating the mob at Amritsar. No doubt the mob excesses were unpardonable ; incendiarism, murder of five innocent Englishmen and the cowardly assault on Miss Sherwood were most deplorable and uncalled for. But the punitive measures taken by General Dyer, Col. Frank Johnson, Col. O'Brien Mr. Bosworth Smith, Rai Shri Ram Sud, Mr. Mallik Khan and other officers were out of all proportion to the crime of the people and amounted to wanton cruelty and inhumanity almost unparalleled in modern times. Your Excellency's light-hearted treatment of the official crime, your exoneration of Sir Michael O'Dwyer, Mr. Montagu's dispatch and above all the shameful ignorance of the Punjab events and callous disregard of the feelings of Indians betrayed by the House of Lords, have filled me with the gravest misgivings regarding the future of the Empire, have estranged me completely from the present Government and have disabled me from tendering, as I have hitherto wholeheartedly tendered, my loyal co-operation.

In my humble opinion the ordinary method of agitating by way of petitions, deputations and the like is no remedy for moving to repentance a Government so hopelessly indifferent to the welfare of its charge as the Government of India has proved to be. In European countries, condonation of such grievous wrongs as the Khilafat and the Punjab would have resulted in a bloody revolution by the people. They would have resisted at all cost national emasculation such as the said wrongs imply. But half of India is too weak to offer violent resistance and the other half is unwilling to do so. I have therefore ventured to suggest the remedy of Non-co-operation which enables those who wish, to dissociate themselves from the Government and which, if it is unattended by violence and undertaken in an ordered manner, must compel it to retrace its steps and undo the wrongs committed. But whilst I shall pursue the policy of Non-co-operation in so far as I can carry the people with me, I shall not lose hope that you will yet see your way to do justice. I therefore respectfully ask Your Excellency to summon a conference of the recognised leaders of the people and in consultation with them find a way that would placate the Mussalmans and do reparation to the unhappy Punjab.

23rd February, 1921

NON-CO-OPERATION—ITS THEORY AND PRACTICE *

The following is published not for its originality but as an able contribution by a young Punjabi student who has non-co-operated lately:

There is not denying the truth contained in Thoreau's saying that that government is best which governs least and therefore an ideal government would be one which

* The following appeared in *Young India* further elucidating the idea of Non-co-operation :

Satyagraha, Civil Disobedience Passive Resistance, Non-co-operation.—It is often my lot to answer knotty questions on all sorts of topics arising out of this great movement of national purification. A company of collegiate Non-co-operators asked me to define for them the terms which I have used as heading for this note. And even at this late day, I was seriously asked whether Satyagraha did not at times warrant resistance by violence, as, for instance, in the case of a sister whose virtue might be in danger from a desperado. I ventured to suggest that it was the completest defence without irritation, without being ruffled, to interpose one-self between the victim and the victimizer, and to face death. I added that this (for the assailant) novel method of defence would, in all probability, exhaust his passion and he will no longer want to ravish an innocent woman, but would want to flee from her presence for very shame, and that, if he did not, the act of personal bravery on the part of her brother would steel her heart for putting up an equally brave defence and resisting the lust of man, turned brute for the while. And I thought I clinched my argument by saying that if, in spite of all the defence, the unexpected happened, and the physical force of the tyrant overpowered his victim, the disgrace would not be that of the woman, but of her assailant, and that both she and her brother, who died in the attempt to defend her virtue, would stand well before the Throne of Judgment. I do not warrant that my argument convinced my listenor or that it would convince the reader. The world, I know, will go on as before. But it is well at this moment of self-examination to understand and appreciate the implications of the powerful movement of non-violence. All religions have emphasised the highest ideal, but all have more or less permitted departures as so many concessions to human weaknesses.

governs not at all. In fact, the saying is a self-evident truth, for certainly an ideal state of society would be one in which everybody thought right and did right of

---

I now proceed to summarise the explanations I gave of the various terms. It is beyond my capacity to give accurate and terse definitions.

Satyagraha, then, is literally holding on to Truth and it means. therefore, Truth-force. Truth is soul or spirit. It is, therefore, known as soul-force. It excludes the use of violence because man is not capable of knowing the absolute truth and, therefore, not competent to punish. The word was coined in South Africa to distinguish the non-violent resistance of the Indians of South Africa from the contemporary 'passive resistance' of the suffragettes and others. It is not conceived as a weapon of the weak.

Passive resistance is used in the orthodox English sense and covers the suffragette movement as well as the resistance of the Non-conformists. Passive resistance has been conceived and is regarded as a weapon of the weak. Whilst it avoids violence, being not open to the weak, it does not exclude its use if, in the opinion of the passive resister, the occasion demands it. However, it has always been distinguished from armed resistance, and its application was at one time confined to Christian martyrs.

Civil Disobedience is civil breach of unmoral statutory enactments. The expression was, so far as I am aware, coined by Thoreau to signify his own resistance to the laws of a slave state. He has left a masterly treatise on the duty of Civil Disobedience. But Thoreau was not perhaps an out and out champion of non-violence. Probably, also, Thoreau limited his breach of statutory laws to the revenue law, *i.e.*, payment of taxes, whereas the term Civil Disobedience, as practised in 1919, covered a breach of any statutory and unmoral law. It signified the resister's outlawry in a civil, *i.e.*, non-violent manner. He invoked the sanctions of the law and cheerfuly suffered imprisonment. It is a branch of Satyagraha.

Non-co-operation predominantly implies withdrawing of co-operation from the State that in the Non-co-operator's view has become corrupt and excludes Civil Disobedience of the fierce type described above. By its very nature, Non-co-operation is even open to children of understanding and can be safely practised by the masses. Civil Disobedience presupposes the habit of willing obedience to laws without fear of their sanctions. It can therefore be practised only

his own accord without standing in need of any guidance or interference from outside. But since the state of our society is far from being perfect and some measure of

---

as a last resort and by a select few in the first instance at any rate. Non-co-operation, too, like Civil Disobedience is a branch of Satyagraha which includes all non-violent resistance for the vindication of Truth.—M. K. G. in *Young India* of 21st March, 1921.

Co-operation and Non-co-operation defined—It is no small thing for the country that Dwijendranath Tagore, fondly known as Bada Dada by his friends, follows with keen attention even in his old age and in his seclusion at Shantiniketan all that is going on in the country. Mr. Andrews has circulated a free translation of his latest thoughts on Non-co-operation. Although the whole of it is published in the daily press, I cannot resist reproducing his definitions of Co-operation and Non-co-operation; they are so true and telling. Writing of the former, he says: "Our rulers, in order to hide their despotic measures from the world's eye, dressed up a puppet show in the form of Legislative Councils, in which a few platform orators have been invited to co-operate. Our rulers believe that, by doing so, they have placed us under an eternal debt of gratitude, but in reality they have only added insult to injury. These Councils cling to us now, and threaten to choke us like the old man in the story of Sindbad, the sailor." "If this is the meaning of co-operation," proceeds Bada Dada, "according to our English rulers, then it is no very difficult matter to understand what Non-co-operation means to us. We shall never accept, even if it costs us our lives to refuse it, anything that will bring evil upon our country. That is Non-co-operation."—*Young India* of 14th July, 1920.

Is Non-co-operation Sanyas?—Mr. V. P. Madhavrao is reported to have said that Non-co-operation was impracticable, because it was *Sanyas*, and therefore could be resorted to only by unworldly men. But Non-co-operation cannot be dismissed quite so lightly. The ordinary method of condemning a thing is to give it a bad name. Mr. V. P. Madhavrao has discovered a novel method of condemnation. He gives a very ordinary thing a sacred name in order to pronounce his condemnation upon it. Sinn Feiners are resorting to Non-co-operation in a most acute form, and it would be like what is being preached in India if there was no violence in it. But nobody considers them to be *Sanyasis*. General Botha declined to co-operate with Lord Milner after the Boer War unless the Boers were granted full

evil is almost always present in it, man parts with a fraction of his individual liberty in exchange for the sundry benefits which are expected to accrue from association with the State; and thus the institution called the State comes into existence.

The association of the individual with the state is thus a purely voluntary matter, and it is clear that the sole justification for the existence of the State is the assumption that it promotes the well-being of the people. This alone constitutes its claim to the allegiance of its subjects. Therefore, it goes without saying that, as soon as it begins to fail in its duty or begins to pass measures and frame laws which are contrary to the conscience and the best interests of the people, it loses its right to their allegiance, and it not only becomes necessary but a matter of religious duty for the people to withdraw their support from the State when the dictates of conscience require it.

But although, theoretically speaking, this association of the people with the State is, and ought to be, a purely voluntary affair, the State has everywhere grown to be a most formidable engine of tyranny and repression, of organised violence and plunder, by which a few persons

---

self-government, not in stages as Lord Milner had intended, but all at once. He produced such a tremendous effect upon public opinion that the Boers got more than they wanted. General Smuts was one of the Non-co-operators. There was no violence connected with General Botha's Non-co-operation. Yet he was not by any means an unworldly man. And we know by this time that General Smuts, his right-hand man, is a minister of the Union Cabinet. The fact is that we want self-government, we want justice done in the Punjab and the Khilafat questions without our having to suffer any inconvenience or losses. We submit that it is an impossible fact we are attempting. 'Verily there is no remission of sin without the shedding of (one's) blood'.—*Young India* of 14th July, 1920.

govern and exploit the many. "Man is born free and yet," lamented Rousseau, "he is everywhere in chains," —this is the sad spectacle which to-day meets our sight on whatever side we turn.

All efforts made hitherto to cope with this evil have not only signally failed; they have, on the contrary, simply served to aggravate the evil. Democracy which at one time, it was hoped, would serve as a panacea for all social evils, has proved to be far worse than the lawless, feudal regime of the Middle Ages. It has simply replaced the erratic plundering raids of the "crag-barons" of the mediaeval times, with a silent, universal process of organised robbery of the modern capitalistic State, all the more dangerous because it lulls the people into a false sense of security while vampire-like it sucks their life-blood, all the more deadly because whereas, the "crag-baron" of the past times could only enslave the body, the modern "bag-baron" with the far bitter poison of his purse infects and destroys the soul as well.

Now the methods tried so far to cure this evil might conveniently be described as:

(1) Those based on the principle of Reform.

(2) Those based on the principle of Violence.

They failed, because, either they were half-measures or were unsound measures—that is, no measures at all. Reforms have already failed as they are bound to fail because they imply a compromise and co-operation with the principle of evil. Now a State does not exist by virtue of sheer brute-force but by gaining the moral support of the good people in it. Evil in itself is sterile. It is self-destructive; it exists and flourishes through the implication of good that is in it. Further, the acceptance of partial reforms takes away the ground under the reformer's feet. Science teaches us that a lever cannot move a body unless it has got a resting point outside the body against which it is applied. Similarly, in order to overcome evil one must stand wholly outside it, *i.e.*, on the firm, solid ground of unadulterated good.

The methods of violence, again, have not only failed in their purpose but have produced an effect opposite to what they were intended to produce. Because, when once physical force comes on the scene, it calls forth a superior physical force which subdues it for the time being. Then it puts forth more force and the chain of violence lengthens and strengthens. This method is wrong because it overlooks the fundamental fact that evil can never be overcome with evil, it ceases only through good. We will remember how Lord Krishna in Bhagwad Gita, in the vision of the cosmic form, showed to Arjuna, Duryodhana and the other Kauravas as self-destroyed already by their own evil. "Kalo-smi" says He, "I am *a priori* time seated in *a priori* space." Nor must we forget that in Shelley's 'Prometheus Unbound' Zeus, the principle of evil, is dethroned not by any form of force but topples down by its own weight. It is dethroned by Chronos which is the same thing as "*a priori* time seated in *a priori* space."

Both these methods fail because they deal with the superficial symptoms only and do not touch the root of the evil, the disease itself. Advocates of these methods think that, by partially reforming the various institutions which constitute the State, they would be able to put an end to the sufferings of Society. They overlook the fact that, the State-evil is not the cause but the effect of Social-evil, just as the sea-waves are the effect and not the cause of the storm. The only way of curing disease is to remove the causes thereof. Let people purify themselves, let them cease to indirectly participate in the evil of the State and it will disappear by itself.

Self-purification, then, and not violence, or reform is the real remedy. To purify oneself by withdrawing co-operation from the State: this is the great doctrine of Non-co-operation.

Non-co-operation, however, does not in any way mean anarchy or absence of order. For Non-co-operation with the State means a closer co-operation among the people themselves. Thus Non-co-operation is a process of evolution: it has most aptly been described as Evolutionary Revolution.

Now the question naturally arises: what are the various methods by which a State maintains its hold on the people? To describe briefly, they are four in number:

(1) *Intimidation.*—Representing the State as something sacred and immutable, punishing any attempt to alter it. This it does through the agency of its law-courts and councils—the latter investing the former with the authority which they rigorously use in the interests of the State. And as for the councils, it is clear that no real reform can ever come through them.. For the rulers having the power to sanction or disallow any law they like would never allow any measure to be passed which in any way curtails their power. What they really do is something like this: when any particular individual or section of the community becomes too noisy and troublesome, they say, "Look here, be quiet and we will widen our system of plunder a little, so as to admit you into it and then we will together exploit the masses and have the plunder between us." This they call reform, and so the process of exploitation goes on.

(2) *Corruption.*—Taxing the workers in order to pay salaries to officials who are bound in return to .maintain

the State in the process of exploiting the masses, and also by rewarding its agents by bestowing titles, honours and honorary offices.

(3) *Hypnotism.*—Through the State-aided and State-controlled schools and colleges, where children are taught to regard allegiance to the State as something higher than allegiance to their conscience and are infected with false doctrines regarding patriotism and "duty of obedience to superiors", so that they easily fall under the spell of "the creak of the rotten state-machine".

(4) *Militarism.*—By selecting men who have been enslaved by the foregoing three methods, and by uniforms, drilling, barracks, music, etc., deadening their conscience, till they cease to be men and become submissive machines.

The only way in which people can escape from the clutches of a corrupt state, then, is to cease to participate, directly or indirectly, in its evil by:

(1) Lawyers suspending their practice, and the people boycotting the law-courts and settling disputes among themselves by private arbitration, along with which must go the process of organizing the village communes and Punchayats.

(2) People refusing to accept titles, honours, salaried posts or any other benefits from a government whose hands are shown to be unclean.

(3) By emptying the government schools and colleges and thus saving their children from the deadly effects of intellectual asphyxia to which they are subjected there, such withdrawal being accompained by the establishment of national schools, where the children should receive national and religious training and learn the habit of self-respect and that of following their conscience.

(4) By refusing to serve the military and the police and abjuring all violence so as to remove the necessity of the former.

It is clear that, when all these things are gone through, the necessity of paying taxes will automatically disappear. The people then should refuse to pay taxes, and patiently abide by the consequences.

This, then, is a brief outline of the great doctrine of Non-co-operation. This sacred, fundamental and inalienable right of the people to non-co-operate with a government, when the dictates of conscience require it, has been accepted by all the thinking minds of all the ages. Even an ardent apostle of "Constitutionalism," like Tennyson, has paid homage to it.

"Should banded unions persecute
Opinion and induce a time,
When single thought is civil crime
And individual freedom mute;

"Though power should make from bound to bound
The name of Britain trebly great—
Though every channel of the State
Should fill and choke with golden sand—

"Yet waft me from the harbour mouth,
Wild winds, I seek a warmer sky,
And I will see before I die
The palms and temples of the South."

But the one thing absolutely essential for success is that people should scrupulously shun all violence in word, deed or thought. The slightest attempt at violence would injure the cause. It would take away from the people the power of patient and clean suffering by tainting their conscience and let loose the retaliatory machinery of the government which would be but too glad to find some pretext for its use.

People must bring to the altars of liberty the offerings of pure self-sacrifice and patient suffering. There will be provocations and oppressions which will tax their powers of endurance to the utmost, but, as it has been said, "He alone who endures on to the end shall be saved." Thus alone would they gain real freedom, real Swaraj; thus alone will they get true happiness, thus alone will they gain real victory, for in the immortal lines of Shelley:

> To suffer woes which hope thinks infinite;
> To forgive wrongs darker than death or night,
> To love, to bear, to hope till Hope creates
> From its own wreck the thing it contemplates;
> Neither to change, to falter, nor repent;
> This like the glorious Titan is to be
> Great, good and joyous, beautiful and free;
> This is alone life, joy, Empire and Victory.

16*th June*, 1920

THE LAW OF SUFFERING

(By M. K. Gandhi)

No country has ever risen without being purified through the fire of suffering. Mother suffers so that her child may live. The condition of wheat-growing is that the seed grain should perish. Life comes out of Death. Will India rise out of her slavery without fulfilling this eternal law of purification through suffering?

If my advisers are right, evidently India will realise her destiny without travail. For their chief concern is that the events of April 1919 should not be repeated. They fear Non-co-operation, because it would involve the sufferings of many. If Hampden had argued thus, he would not have withheld payment of ship-money, nor would Wat Tayler have raised the standard of revolt. English and French histories are replete with instances of men continuing their pursuit of the right, irrespective of the amount of suffering involved. The actors did not stop to think whether ignorant people would not have involuntarily to suffer. Why should we expect to write our history differently? It is possible for us, if we would, to learn from the mistakes of our predecessors to do better, but it is impossible to do away with the law of suffering which is the one indispensable condition of our being. The way to do better is to avoid, if we can, violence from our side and thus quicken the rate of progress and to introduce greater purity in the methods of suffering. We can, if we will, refrain, in our impatience, from bending the wrong-doer to our will by physical force as Sinn Feiners are doing to-day, or from coercing our neighbours to follow our methods, as was done last year by some of us in bringing about *hartal*. Progress is to be measured by the amount of suffering undergone by the sufferer. The purer the suffering, the greater is the progress. Hence did the sacrifice of Jesus suffice to free a sorrowing world. In his onward march, he did not count the cost of suffering, entailed upon his neighbours, whether it was undergone by them voluntarily or otherwise. Thus did the sufferings of a Harischandra suffice to re-establish the kingdom of truth. He must have known that his subjects would suffer involuntarily by his abdication. He did not mind, because he could not do otherwise than follow truth.

I have already stated that I do not deplore the massacre of Jallianwala Bagh so much, as I deplore the murders of Englishmen and destruction of property by ourselves. The frightfulness at Amritsar drew away public attention from greater, though slower, frightfulness at Lahore where attempt was made to emasculate the inhabitants by slow processes. But before we rise higher, we shall have to undergo such processes many more times, till they teach us to take up suffering voluntarily and to find joy in it. I am convinced that the Lahorians never deserved the cruel insults that they were subjected to; they never hurt a single Englishman; they never destroyed any property. But a wilful ruler was determined to crush the spirit of a people just trying to throw off his chafing yoke. And if I am told that all this was due to my preaching Satyagraha, my answer is that I would preach Satyagraha all the more forcibly for that, so long as I have breath left in me, and tell the people that next time they would answer O'Dwyerean insolence, not by opening shops by reason of threats of forcible sales, but by allowing the tyrant to do his worst and let him sell their all but their unconquerable souls. Sages of old mortified the flesh, so that the spirit within might be set free, so that their trained bodies might be proof against any injury that might be inflicted on them by tyrants seeking to impose their will on them. And if India wishes to revise her ancient wisdom and to avoid the errors of Europe, if India wishes to see the Kingdom of God established on earth, instead of that of Satan which has enveloped Europe, then I would urge her sons and daughters not to be deceived by fine phrases, the terrible subtleties that hedge us in, the fears of suffering that India may have to undergo, but to see what is happening to-day in Europe, and from it understand that we *must* go through the suffering even as Europe has gone through, but not the process of making others suffer. Germany wanted to dominate Europe and the Allies wanted to do likewise by crushing Germany. Europe is no better for Germany's fall. The Allies have proved themselves to be just as deceitful, cruel, greedy and selfish as Germany was or would have been. Germany would have avoided the sanctimonious humbug that one sees associated with the many dealings of the Allies.

The miscalculation that I deplored last year was not in connection with the sufferings imposed upon the people, but about the mistakes made by them and violence done by them, owing to their not having sufficiently understood the message of Satyagraha. What then is the meaning of Non-co-operation in terms of the Law of Suffering? We must voluntarily put up with the losses and inconveniences that arise from having to withdraw our support from a Government that is ruling against our will. Possession of power and riches is a crime under an unjust government, poverty in that case is a virtue, says Thoreau. It may be that, in the transition state, we may make mistakes; there may be avoidable suffering. These things are preferable to national emasculation.

We must refuse to wait for the wrong to be righted till the wrong-doer has been roused to a sense of his iniquity. We must not, for fear of ourselves or others having to suffer, remain participators in it. But we must combat the wrong by ceasing to assist the wrong-doer directly or indirectly.

If a father does an injustice, it is the duty of his

children to leave the parental roof. If the head-master of a school conducts his institution on an immoral basis, the pupils must leave the school. If the chairman of a corporation is corrupt, the members thereof must wash their hands clean of his corruption by withdrawing from it; even so, if a government does a grave injustice, the subject must withdraw co-operation wholly or partially, sufficiently to wean the ruler from his wickedness. In each of the case conceived by me, there is an element of suffering whether mental or physical. Without such suffering, it is not possible to attain freedom.

8th September, 1920

THE INWARDNESS OF NON-CO-OPERATION

(BY M. K. GANDHI)

I commend to the attention of the readers of "Young India" the thoughtful letter* received from Miss Anne

* The letter is contained in the following extract from *Young India* of 8th September 1920:

A Missionary on Non-co-operation.—The following letter has been received by Mr. Gandhi from Miss Anne Marie Peterson of the Danish Mission in Madras. Most personal references have been omitted:

Dear Mr. Gandhi,—I cannot thank you enough for your kindness and the way in which you received me and I feel that meeting more or less decided my future. I have thrown myself at the feet of India. At the same time I know that in Christ alone is my abode and I have no longing and no desire but to love Him, my crucified Saviour, and reveal Him for those with whom I come in contact. I just cling to His feet and pray with tears that I may not disgrace Him as we Christians have been doing by our behaviour in India. We go on crucifying Christ, while we long proclaim the Power of His resurrection by which He has conquered untruth and unrighteousness. If we who bear His name were true to Him, we would never bow ourselves before the Powers of this world, but we would always be on the side

Marie Peterson. Miss Peterson is a lady who has been in India for some years and has closely followed Indian affairs. She is about to sever her connection with her

---

of the poor, the suffering and the oppressed But we are not, and therefore I feel myself under obligation not only to Christ but to India for His sake at this time of momentous importance for her future.

Truly it matters little what I, a lonely and insignificant person, may say or do What is my protest against the common current the race to which I belong is taking and (what grieves me more) which the missionary societies seem to follow? Even if a respectable number protested, it would not be of any use. Yet were I alone against the whole world, I must follow my conscience and my God.

I therefore cannot but smile when I see people saying you should have awaited the decision of the National Congress before starting the Non-co-operation movement. You have a message for the country, and the Congress is the voice of the nation, its servant, and not its master. A majority has no right simply because it is a majority.

But we must try to win the majority. And it is easy to see that now the Congress is going to be with you. Would it have done so if you had kept quiet and not lent your voice to the feelings of the people? Would the Congress have known its mind? I think not.

I myself was in much doubt before I heard you. But you convinced me. Not that I can feel much on the question of the Khilafat. I cannot. I can see what service you are doing to India, if you can prevent the Mahomedans from using the sword in order to take revenge and get their rights. I can see that, if you unite the Hindus and the Mahomedans, it will be a master stroke. How I wish the Christian would also come forward and unite with you for the sake of their country and the honour not only of their Motherland but of Christ. I may not feel much for Turkey, but I feel for India, and I can see she (India) has no other way to protest against being trampled down and crushed than Non-co-operation.

I also want you to know that many in Denmark and all over the world, yes, I am sure every true Christian, will feel with and be in sympathy with India in the struggle which is now going on. God forbid that in the struggle between might and right, truth and untruth, the spirit and the flesh, there should be a division of races. There is not. The same struggle is going on all over the world. What does it matter then that we are a few? God is on our side.

Mission for the purpose of giving herself to education that is truly national.

I have not given the letter in full. I have omitted all personal references. But her argument has been left entirely untouched. The letter was not meant to be

---

Brute force often seems to get the upper hand but righteousness always has and always shall conquer, be it even through much suffering and what may even appear to be a defeat. Christ conquered, when the world crucified Him. Blessed are the meek; they shall inherit the earth.

When I read your speech given at Madras, it struck me that it should be printed as a pamhlet in English, Tamil, Hindustani and all the most used language and then spread to every nook and corner of India.

The Non-co-operation movement once started must be worked so as to become successful. If it is not, I dread to think of the consequences. But you cannot expect it to win in a day or two. It must take time and you will despair if you do not reach your goal in a hurry. For those who have faith there is no haste.

Now for the withdrawal of the children and students from Government schools, I think it a most important step. Taking the Government help, (even if it be your money they pay you back) we must submit to its scheme, its rules and regulation. India and we who love her have come to the conclusion that the education the foreign Government has given you is not healthy for India and can certainly never make for her real growth. The movement would lead to a spontaneous rise of national schools. Let them be a few but let them spring up through self-sacrifice. Only by indigenous education can India be truly uplifted. Why this appeals so much to me is perhaps because I belong to the part of the Danish people who started their own independent, indigenous national schools. The Danish Free Schools and Folk-High-Schools, of which you may have heard, were started against the opposition and persecution of the State. The organisers won and thus have regenerated the nation. With my truly heart-felt thanks and prayers for you.

I am,
Yours Sincerely,
ANNE MARIE

printed. It was written just after my Vellore speech.* But it being intrinsically important, I asked the writer for her permission, which she gladly gave, for printing it.

I publish it all the more gladly in that it enables me to show that the movement of Non-co-operation is neither anti-Christian nor anti-English nor anti-European. It is a struggle between religion and irreligion, powers of light and powers of darkness.

It is my firm opinion that Europe to-day represents not the spirit of God or Christianity, but the spirit of Satan. And Satan's successes are the greatest, when he appears with the name of God on his lips. Europe is to-day only nominally Christian. In reality, it is worshipping Mammon. 'It is easier for a camel to pass through the eye of a needle than for a rich man to enter the Kingdom.' Thus really spoke Jesus Christ. His so-called followers measure their moral progress by their material possession. The very national anthem of England is anti-Christian. Jesus, who asked his followers to love their enemies even as themselves, could not have sung of his enemies, 'Confound his enemies, frustrate their knavish tricks.' The last book that Dr. Wallace wrote set forth his deliberate conviction that the much vaunted advance of science had added not an inch to the moral stature of Europe. The last war however has shown, as nothing else has, the Satanic nature of the civilization that dominates Europe to-day. Every canon of public morality has been broken by the victors in the name of virtue. No lie has been considered too foul to be uttered. The motive behind every crime is not religious or spiritual, but grossly material. But the Musulmans and the Hindus, who are struggling against the Government, have religion and honour as their motive.

* A speech on Non-co-operation omitted in this collection.

Even the cruel assassination* which has just shocked the country is reported to have a religious motive behind it. It is certainly necessary to purge religion of its excrescences, but it is equally necessary to expose the hollowness of moral pretensions on the part of those who prefer material wealth to moral gain. It is easier to wean an ignorant fanatic from his error than a confirmed scoundrel from his scoundrelism.

This, however, is no indictment against individuals or even nations. Thousands of individual Europeans are rising above their environment. I write of the tendency in Europe, as reflected in her present leaders. England through her leaders is insolently crushing Indian religious and national sentiment under her heels. England, under the false plea of self-determination, is trying to exploit the oil fields of Mesopotamia which she is almost to leave, because she has probably no choice. France through her leaders is lending her name to training Cannibals as soldiers, and is shamelessly betraying her trust as a mandatory power by trying to kill the spirit of the Syrians. President Wilson has thrown on the scrap heap his precious fourteen points.

It is this combination of evil forces, which India is really fighting through non-violent Non-co-operation. And those like Miss Peterson, whether Christian or European, who feel that this error must be dethroned, can exercise the privilege of doing so by joining the Non-co-operation movement. With the honour of Islam is bound up the safety of religion itself and with the honour of India is bound up the honour of every nation known to be weak.

* A Muslim monomaniac assassinated Mr. Willoughby, I.C.S., Deputy Commissioner, United Provinces.

4th August, 1920

CRUSADE AGAINST NON-CO-OPERATION

(By M. K. Gandhi)

I have most carefully read the manifesto* addressed by Sir Narayan Chandavarkar and others dissuading the people from joining the Non-co-operation movement. I had expected to find some solid argument against Non-co-operation, but to my great regret I have found in it nothing but distortion (no doubt unconscious) of the great religions and history. The manifesto says that 'Non-co-operation is deprecated by the religious tenets and traditions of our motherland, nay, of all the religions that have saved and elevated the human race.' I venture to submit that the *Bhagwad Gita* is a gospel of Non-co-operation between the forces of darkness and those of light. If it is to be literally interpreted, Arjun representing a just cause was enjoined to engage in bloody warfare with the unjust Kauravas. Tulsidas advises the *Sant* (the good) to shun the *Asant* (the evil-doers). The Zendavesta represents a perpetual duel between Ormuzd and Ahriman, between whom there is no compromise. To say of the Bible that it taboos Non-co-operation is not to know Jesus, a prince among passive resisters, who uncompromisingly challenged the might of the Sadducees and the Pharisees and for the sake of truth did not hesitate to divide sons from their parents†. And what did the Prophet of Islam do? He non-co-operated in Mecca in a most active manner so long as his life was not in danger and wiped the dust of Mecca off his feet

* Omitted in this collection.

† *Christ and Non-co-operation.—Apropos* it is interesting that Christ himself has suggested Non-co-operation. In the eighteenth chapter of Matthew, we read:

Moreover, if thy brother shall trespass against thee, go, and tell

when he found that he and his followers might have uselessly to perish, and fled to Medina and returned

---

him his fault between thee and him alone; if he shall hear thee, thou has gained thy brother.

But if he will not hear thee, then take with thee one or two more, that in the mouth of two or three witnesses every word may be established.

And if he shall neglect to hear them, tell it up to the Church: but if he neglect to hear the Church, *let him be unto thee as an heathen man and a publican.*—*Young India* of 10th November, 1920.

The following appeared in *Young India* of 19th January, 1921, under the heading, "Did Christ Non-co-operate?":

Dear Mr. Gandhi,—Mr. Lyle has been hear and he told me that you had been enquiring kindly about me. I thank you for your kind inquiries. Of course I have been following your activities with the greatest interest, but it grieves me to have to say that I do not and cannot approve of your Non-co-operation movement. I have been praying that God may show you your mistake and that He may use you—and us all—for the glory of His Holy Name, and for the real enduring welfare of the whole of India. From your many articles and speeches I have gathered that you attempt to justify your movement on the ground that if, in spite of argument and dissuasion, one's nearest and dearest even be seen pursuing a wrong course of action, one is bound to dissociate oneself from him or her lest one be charged with being an accomplice in the wrong-doing.

But surely, one fundamental doctrine of both the Christian and Hindu Scriptures points to quite a different course of conduct. Both tell us of Divine incarnations, and though these differ in some respects yet in each case the underlying idea is that when God, Who is Himself infinitely holy, saw the sin-begotten misery of men, He did not hold aloof from them but graciously stooped down and came to them to render help and to save their sin and its effects. Jesus Christ, the Holy and Undefiled One, did not refuse to work along with sinful men, but, on the contrary, while loathing all evil and scathingly denouncing it even in the great ones of his time, He freely and closely associated with all men, from the Pharisee down to the hated tax-gatherer of an alien government and the notorious sinner and endeavoured, both by

when he was strong enough to give battle to his opponents. The duty of non-co-operation with unjust men

wise precept and loving example, to wean them from their wickedness and to win them to righteousness.

From this I gather that it is the obvious duty of all true patriots at the present time not to hold themselves aloof from a government unfairly denounced as "devilish" and "satanic", but to take every possible step (*e.g.*, the encouraging of the new councils), to keep in touch with it and endeavour to bring it round to what they consider a more righteous course of conduct. I am hoping and praying that as you were led to acknowledge your mistake of last year in the matter of Satyagraha, so God may open your eyes before it is too late and lead you from Non-co-operation to co-operation.

You are at liberty to use these few words in any way you like. With kind regards,

RAJKOT, 20-11-20.

I am, yours sincerely,
S. GILLESPIE.

[I print this letter without a word of alteration. I print it specially because it shows that in spite of ceaseless denunciation by me of the existing system of Government, I have the good fortune to retain the warm friendship of Britishers like the Rev. Gillespie. I know that he honestly believes what he says. He gives me credit for honesty of belief and purpose, yet we differ as poles asunder even in our interpretation of the Christian and the Hindu scriptures. Of the latter I can write with confidence, and I make bold to assert that it is the *duty* of a Hindu to dissociate himself from the evil-doer, *i.e.*, to refrain from participating in or countenancing the evil in him. Prahlad dissociated himself from the evil done by his father. The divine Sita rejected the services tendered to her by Ravan. Bharat denounced the deeds of Kaikeyi, his mother, and rejected the throne wickedly secured for him by her. I can write of the Bible only with diffidence. But my reading of it has clearly confirmed the opinion derived from a reading of the Hindu scriptures. Jesus mixed with the publicans and the sinners neither as a dependent nor as a patron. He mixed with them to serve and to convert them to a life of truthfulness and purity. But he wiped the dust off his feet of those places which did not listen to his word. I hold it to be my duty not to countenance a son who disgraces himself by a life of shame and vice. *Enlightened Non-co-operation is the expression of anguished love.* My esteemed

and kings is as strictly enjoined by all the religions as is the duty of co-operation with just men and kings.

correspondent mixes up dissociation from evil with dissociation from persons for service. Would Jesus have accepted gifts from the money changers, taken from them scholarships for his friends, and advanced loans to them to ply their nefarious traffic? Was His denunciation of hypocrites, Pharisees, and Sadducees merely in word? Or did He not actually invite the people to beware of them and shun them? But Mr Gillespie thinks that I unfairly describe the Government to be satanic. Perhaps that alters our view-points. I consider that I would be less than truthful if I did not describe as satanic a government which has been guilty of fraud, murder, and wanton cruelty: which still remains unrepentant and resorts to untruth to cover its guilt. I really believe I am performing the office of a friend by denouncing in precise language the pretentions of a government which has nothing to commend itself to the people under its charge.—M. K. G.]

The Rev. Mr. Gillespie replied to the above which reply together with Mr. Gandhi's comments thereon appeared in the issue of *Young India* of 23rd February, 1921. They are given below:

Dear Mr. Gandhi,—I see from *Young India* of the 12th instant that you have been kind enough to find time to criticise my last letter to you. In reference to your remarks, please permit me to say that while agreeing for the most part with much of what you write, I wish to make my position absolutely clear. Of course for all Christians the Lord Jesus Christ is the Great Exemplar. But, while He who was perfectly holy and just was in a position to denounce the wicked hypocrisy of the Scribes and Pharisees of his day, after He had with a perfect love done his utmost to convert them to a life of sincerity and purity, yet we mere men, imperfect in wisdom and love and holiness as even the best of us are, can neither afford nor assume the right to denounce finally and absolutely any of our fellows however depraved. While loathing their vice we should try to seek out and save them. While we must not 'countenance a son who disgraces himself by a life of shame and vice' yet we should co-operate with him—and this is true co-operation by waiting for the prodigal in 'anguished love' and with prayerful soul-energy, and when he returns receive him with open arms. Such is my belief and therefore it is that I advocate co-operation as against Non-co-operation even with a Government.

Indeed most of the scriptures of the world seem even to go beyond Non-co-operation and prefer violence to effeminate submission to a wrong. The Hindu religious

---

that issaid to have been "guilty of fraud, murder and wanton cruelty."

While I am at it, may I go on to suggest if the present Government be held to be still unrepentant and desirious of covering up its guilt by untruth, now is the time to draw up explicit memoranda of its sins of omission and commission backed by incontrovertible proofs, with a view to laying the whole matter before the incoming Viceroy. If the present Government be beyond redemption, at least give the new one a fair sporting chance before refusing to co-operate with it. Lastly, may I add that I read with much interest and loving sympathy your article on the 'Sin of untouchability.' As I read it and could not help thinking 'what is the mistake of Non-co-operation with a few Government officials as compared with the sin of untouchability practised by Indians against millions of their own brethren!' Might not one be justified in quoting to any Non-co-operator who tried to defend untouchability the saying of Jesus, "Thou hypocrite, cast out first the beam out of thine own eyes, and then shall thou see clearly to cast out the mote out of thy brother's eye." Please make whatever use you like of this latter.

With kind regards,
I am,
Yours sincerely,
S. GILLESPIE.

[The reader will perhaps agree with me that the Rev. Gillespie has made a bad case worse. Every Non-co-operator will, I am sure, be prepared to co-operate on the same terms that he mentions, in connection with the prodigal son. Let this prodigal Government return like the Biblical son and all Non-co-operators will rejoice exceedingly. The incoming Viceroy will have all the assistance he may expect from the Non-co-operators if he means to do well. As to untouchability Rev. Gillespie is on safe ground. No one who hugs untouchability has any right to denounce this Government. He who seeks equity must come with clean hands is a maxim of universal application. And the Rev. gentleman will find that those who want to retain untouchability are certainly among the co-operators. Non-co-operation is nothing if it is not reformation from within.—M. K. G.]

tradition,* of which the manifesto speaks, clearly proves the duty of Non-co-operation. Prahlad dissociated himself from his father, Meerabai from her husband, Bibhishan from his brutal brother.

The manifesto, speaking of the secular aspect, says, 'The history of nations affords no instance to show that it (meaning Non-co-operation) has, when employed, succeeded and done good.' One most recent instance of brilliant success of Non-co-operation is that of General Botha who boycotted Lord Milner's reformed councils and thereby procured a perfect constitution for his

* The following appeared in *Young India* of 22nd September, 1920 : *The Inner Meaning of Mahatma Gandhi's Non-co-operation.*— Sjt. Dwijendranath Tagore, fondly known as 'Bada Dada' at Shantiniketan, has written down in Bengali his views on Non-co-operation under the above heading. We give below the translation prepared for us by Mr. Banarasidas Chaturvedi and revised by Mr. C. F. Andrews :

There has been a great discussion in the papers over the question of Non-co-operation movement started by Mahatma Gandhi. I have been reading this discussion and I am afraid that the inner meaning of Mahatma Gandhi's movement has been misunderstood by many persons in various ways. The reason why many of our countrymen have not been able to understand the true purpose of Mahatma Gandhi is clear. We know how terrible and deplorable was the result of Ram being deceived by the '*Maya Mriga*'. In our present age, we have been deceived by another '*Maya Mriga*' and we cannot tell what the future has in store for us. As a cow, wishing to drink water at a river bank in perfect happiness, may, being in illusion, remain side by side with a tiger, so we too, being deceived by a mirage, are hoping against hope. If we do not wake up in time, it is clear what fate awaits us. No doubt it will be a second edition of "*Sita Haran*" It will mean the loss of the very essence of our life and manhood.

The inner meaning of Mahatma Gandhi's Non-co-operation, as far as I have been able to understand it with my commonsense, is this. So long as we cannot establish the ideals of our country according to our own purpose so long shall we be unable to stand on an equal footing with the foreigners.

country. The Dukhobours of Russia offered Non-co-operation, and a handful though they were, their grievances so deeply moved the civilized world that Canada offered them a home where they form a prosperous community. In India, instances can be given by the dozen, in which in little principalities the rayats when deeply grieved by their chiefs have cut off all connection with them and bent them to their will. I know of no instance in history where well-managed Non-co-operation has failed.

If both the parties cannot stand on an equal footing, then the co-operation between them is a mere lip expression. This sort of co-operation can mean only two things. Either the weaker party follows the stronger in humilation, or it courts the bitter displeasure of the stronger party by giving vent to its feelings.

In the light of the education that we are receiving now-a-days in our schools and colleges, co-operation can have only one meaning, *viz.*, that the weaker party has slavishly to follow the stronger.

And what does this education mean? It means the forgetting of our national ideas and ideals and appeasing the hunger for knowledge to a slight extent with crumbs cast away by the foreigners.

How is co-operation possible under these circumstances?

Therefore I say that the weaker party should detach itself from the influence of the stronger party till it can give a full expression to the best that is within it. Till it does that, it must occupy the status of a beggar. Therefore till the conditions are equalised, co-operation by the weaker party must be a glaring proof of its worthlessness, inertia and helplessness.

In this extreme crisis of our country, it is incumbent upon the wisest in the land to stand apart from the blood-sucking influence of the authorities, and with their own exertions and in their own way to give a full expression to their own ideal. When we are able to do that, then alone will any talk of co-operation become us, and not till then.

If any proof were required of what I have said, the way in which co-operation with the authorities has been going on in the past and the endless succession of disastrous results that have followed it are in themselves a striking proof. Any other would be redundant.

Hitherto I have given historical instances of bloodless Non-co-operation. I will not insult the intelligence of the reader by citing historical instances of Non-co-operation combined with violence, but I am free to confess that there are on records as many successes as failures in violent Non-co-operation. And it is because I know this fact that I have placed before the country a non-violent scheme in which, if at all worked satisfactorily, success is a certainty and in which non-response means no harm. For, if even one man non-co-operates, say by resigning some office, he has gained, not lost. That is its ethical or religious aspect. For its political result naturally it requires polymerous support. I fear therefore no disastrous result from Non-co-operation save for an outbreak of violence on the part of the people whether under provocation or otherwise. I would risk violence a thousand times than risk the emasculation of a whole race.

25*th August*, 1920

RELIGIOUS AUTHORITY FOR NON-CO-OPERATION

(By. M. K. Gandhi)

It is not without the greatest reluctance that I engage in a controversy with so learned a leader like Sir Narayan Chandavarkar. But in view of the fact that I am the author of the movement of Non-co-operation, it becomes my painful duty to state my views even though they are opposed to those of the leaders whom I look upon with respect. I have just read during my travels in Malabar Sir Narayan's rejoinder to my answer to the Bombay mainfesto against Non-co-operation. I regret to have to say that the rejoinder leaves me unconvinced.

He and I seem to read the teachings of the Bible, the Gita and the Koran from different standpoints, or we put different interpretations on them. We seem to understand the words Ahimsa, politics and religion differently. I shall try my best to make clear my meaning of the common terms and my reading of the different religions.

At the outset, let me assure Sir Narayan that I have not changed my views on Ahimsa. I still believe that man, not having been given the power of creation, does not possess the right of destroying the meanest creature that lives. The prerogative of destruction belongs solely to the creature of all that lives. I accept the interpretation of Ahimsa, namely, that it is not merely a negative state of harmlessness but it is a positive state of love, of doing good even to the evil-doer. But it does not mean helping the evil-doer to continue the wrong or tolerating it by passive acquiescence. On the contrary, love, the active state of Ahimsa, requires you to resist the wrong-doer by dissociating yourself from him even though it may offend him or injure him physically. Thus if my son lives a life of shame, I may not help him to do so by continuing to support him; on the contrary, my love for him requires me to withdraw all support from him although it may mean even his death. And the same love imposes on me the obligation of welcoming him to my bosom when he repents. But I may not by physical force compel my son to become good. That, in my opinion, is the moral of the story of the Prodigal Son.

Non-co-operation is not a passive state, it is an intensely active state—more active than physical resistance or violence. Passive resistance is a misnomer. Non-co-operation in the sense used by me must be non-violent and therefore neither punitive nor vindictive nor based on malice, ill-will or hatred. It follows therefore that it would be sin for me to serve General Dyer and co-operate with him to shoot innocent men. But it will be an exercise of forgiveness or love for me to nurse him back to life, if he was suffering from a physical malady. I cannot use in this context the word co-operation as Sir Narayan would perhaps use it. I would co-operate a thousand times with this Government to wean it from its career of crime, but I will not for a single moment co-operate with it to continue that career. And I would be guilty of wrong-doing if I retained a title from it or "a service under it or supported its law courts or schools." Better for me a beggar's bowl than the richest possession from hands stained with the blood of the innocents of Jallianwala. Better by far a warrant of imprisonment than honeyed words from those who have wantonly wounded the religious sentiment of my seventy million brothers.

My reading of the Gita is diametrically opposed to Sir Narayan's. I do not believe that the Gita teaches violence for doing good. It is pre-eminently a description of the duel that goes on in our own hearts. The divine author has used a historical incident for inculcating the lesson of doing one's duty even at the peril of one's life. It inculcates performance of duty irrespective of the consequences, for, we mortals, limited by our physical frames, are incapable of controlling actions save our own. The Gita distinguishes between the powers of light and darkness and demonstrates their incompatibility.

Jesus, in my humble opinion, was a prince among politicians. He did render unto Cæsar that which was Cæsar's. He gave the devil his due. He ever shunned him and is reported never once to have yielded to his incantations. The politics of his time consisted in securing the welfare of the people by teaching them not to be seduced by the trinkets of the priests and the Pharisees. The latter then controlled and moulded the life of the people. To-day the system of government is so devised as to affect every department of our life. It threatens our very existence. If therefore we want to conserve the welfare of the nation, we must religiously interest ourselves in the doings of the governors and exert a moral influence on them by insisting on their obeying the laws of morality. General Dyer did produce a 'moral effect' by an act of butchery. Those who are engaged in forwarding the movement of Non-co-operation, hope to produce a moral effect by a process of self-denial, self-sacrifice and self-purification. It surprises me that Sir Narayan should speak of General Dyer's massacre in the same breath as acts of Non-co-operation. I have done my best to understand his meaning, but I am sorry to confess that I have failed.

5th January, 1921

"MORAL VALUES"

(BY M. K. GANDHI)

There is an extract from the letter of an English friend. It is a pleasure to me to receive letters from English friends. I know that there are many honest Englishmen who are following the movement of Non-co-operation with sympathetic attention, and would gladly help if they are clear about the moralities of Non-co-operation. This letter is a typical instance :

"I understand that you are striving to establish

Swaraj in India by appealing to moral force to attain which you rely upon selflessness. Permit me to observe that the idea is simply *excellent.* But, is there no fear that the means of Non-co-operation which you are adopting will fail you in the end, if applied before *every* unit acts from a purely selfless motive? When moral success is aimed at, surely the means *must* be of the same trend?

I also earnestly look forward to the day when, not only India, but also, the whole race of man, will enjoy Swaraj on the following lines:

The human species exist at the junction of the animal and the moral kingdoms of creation, blessed with free-will by the Creator, wherewith to adjudicate between the demands of a material frame (the human animal body) and a moral form (character), and thereby to express the image of the first Great Cause in finite form (in the latter). When every unit of the species learns to appreciate moral values in *every* thought, word and deed, by always giving preference to moral demands because they hail from a higher Kingdom of creation and—to do otherwise will be to defy Omnipotence—selflessness must obviously follow. The results will be that every human being will love the other automatically and true Swaraj knit the whole family together.

Does it not seem likely, on the other hand, that, to begin with Non-co-operation, will lead to the subordination of your moral goal to ulterior and inferior material desires; and, therefore, even if you do succeed, that you will have lost the very cream of your efforts unintentionally, by making fellowmen greater animals than they already are? The co-operation of selfless representatives, of a selfless nation, will sooner make a selfless government, than Non-co-operation of a nation, which strives to follow a selfless leader, before waiting *first* to learn how to conquer self ! *

Kindly pause to consider these facts : Whatever you do should be for the good of the whole brotherhood of

* The following appeared in *Young India* of 21st January, 1921, under the heading, "Moral Values of Non-co-operation" :

Revered Mahatmaji,—I have read with interest your English friend's letter on the above subject. His contention seems to be that the desired end, namely *Swarajya*, cannot be peacefully attained by such means as you have adopted, unless every individual has become selfless in thought, word and deed. Selflessness will then automatically produce love for one's neighbour and the goal *Swarajya* will have been reached as a matter of course.

In the first place, the full import of the term 'selflessness' is to be understood. It connotes the highest stage of perfection or freedom, such as would enable a person to forget his self. The self is *not* lost, but only its presence ceases to intrude itself on a man's mind. The ideal man may be compared to the ideal musician, who is no longer encumbered with the deadweight of notes, which nevertheless exist all the time in his mind. His music is a sort of spontaneous flow, but cannot, therefore, be said to be 'automatic'. Even so an ideal man's love for his fellow-beings may better be called spontaneous than automatic. Having made clear the interpretation of the term 'selfless,' it will be easy to see how Non-co-operation is the most natural, and in the present circumstances, the only means of attaining full freedom or perfection. To return once more to the cause of a musician, it is known that before he gains mastery in his art, he usually passes through an arduous period of training. Also, until he has attained perfection, he has to learn his art in solitude or away from all discordant noise that may hamper his efforts or work. This is precisely the attitude of Non-co-operators, for they only wish to withdraw themselves away from all disturbing or harmful influences, before they can hope to attain full freedom or perfection.

I may add that this letter is meant to supplement your own answer, which is at once clear and convincing.

Wishing God-speed to you and to your movement,

I am,
Your very sincerely,
DWIJENDRANATH TAGORE.

SANTINIKETAN,
Jan. 14, 1921.

man; and moral values must *on no account* take a second place, even in an ostensible trivial instance; otherwise, the cure may be worse than the disease."

I have given the letter in full omitting an introductory sentence. I have refrained from publishing the name because I am not sure of the writer's intention regarding the publication of his name. His moral difficulty is entitled to careful consideration. In my opinion, there is confusion of thought in this statement of the case. It ever has been my purpose to show that dishonourable means cannot bring about an honourable end.* What

* The following taken from Tolstoy's "Letter to the Liberals" appeared in *Young India* of 10th November, 1920:

As to the ordinary methods of combating Government.—"There are people who realise that our Government is very bad and who struggle against it, and there have been two ways of carrying on the struggle." And Tolstoy calls the methods, one "the method of the Revolutionaries" which consists in "an attempt to alter the existing regime by violence," and the other "the methods of the Gradualists" which consists in "carrying on the struggle without violence and within the limits of the law, conquering constitutional rights bit by bit," and he says: "Reflection and experience alike show me that both the means of combating Government used hithertofore are not only ineffectual but actually tend to strengthen the power and irresponsibility of the Government."

* * * *

As to co-operation with the Government.—"This method is ineffectual and irrational because Government—holding in its grasp the whole power, and framing what are called the laws on the basis of which the Liberals wish to resist it—this Government knows very well what is really dangerous to it and will never let people, who submit to it and act under its guidance, do anything that will undermine its authority."

* * * *

. . . "But not only is this actually irrational and ineffectual, it is also harmful. It is harmful because enlightened, good, and honest people by entering the ranks of the Government give it a moral authority which, but for them, it would not possess. If the Government

the writer may challenge and in fact does challenge is the motive of the Non-co-operators in general. I confess that the motive of all Non-co-operators is not love

were made up entirely of that coarse element—the men of violence, self-seekers and flatterers—who form its core, it could not continue to exist." "Another evil is that to secure opportunities to carry on their work, these highly enlightened and honest people have to begin to compromise and so, little by little, come to consider that for a good end one may swerve somewhat from truth in word and deed"

* * * *

"*As to withdrawal of children from Government controlled schools.*—"The strength of the Government lies in the people's ignorance, and the Government knows this and will therefore always oppose true enlightenment. It is time we realized that fact. And it is most undesirable to let the Government, while it is spreading darkness, pretend to be busy with the enlightenment of the people. It is doing this now by means of all sorts of pseudo-educational establishments it controls: schools, high schools, and universities. But good is good, and enlightenment is enlightenment: not when it is toned down to meet the requirements of the Government, but only when it is quite good and quite enlightened."

* * * *

As to boycott of Councils.—"What is it to be done? Merely the simple, quiet, truthful carrying on of what you consider good and needful, quite independently of the Government, or of whether it likes it or not. In other words, standing up for one's rights not as a member of Parliament, but standing up for one's rights as a rational and free man, and defending them in the only way in which moral and human dignity can be defended.

* * * *

True, the rights of a member of Parliament are greater than the rights of an ordinary man; and it seems as though we could do much by using those rights. But the hitch is that to obtain the rights of a Member of Parliament, one has to abandon part of one's rights as a man, there is no longer any fixed point of leverage, and one can no longer either conquer or maintain any real right. In order to lift others out of a quagmire, one must oneself stand on firm ground, and if, hoping the better to assist others, you go into the quagmire, you will not pull others out, but yourself will sink in."

but a meaningless hatred. I call it meaningless, for the hatred of so many of the Non-co-operators has no meaning in the plan of Non-co-operation. A man does not sacrifice himself out of hatred. He helplessly tries to inflict an injury on his supposed enemy. In Non-co-operation, the result to be achieved is not infliction of punishment but the attainment of justice. The end of hatred is never justice; it is retaliation: it is blind fury. The hatred of the mob at Amritsar resulted in the cruel murder of innocent men. But the hatred of a Non-co-operator turning upon himself loses its points, purifies him, and makes it possible for the object of his hatred to reform and retrace his steps. Thus a Non-co-operator starting as an enemy ends by becoming a friend. What does it matter with what motive a man does the right thing? A right act is right whether done for policy or for its own sake.* I recognise the danger of a thing done from policy being abandoned, if it does not produce the desired result. But the existence of such danger is not an argument against the morality of the act itself.

The writer has suggested an impossible solution. He wants Non-co-operators to be perfect beings. But he forgets that, if we were perfect, there would be no occasion for Non-co-operation. For there would have been no co-operation with evil. Non-co-operation is an attempt to purify or perfect oneself. And the majority follow the path of purification from faith, not from knowledge. In other words, selfish Non-co-operationists following a selfless leader will have done well at the end, for they will realise the virtue of Non-co-operation as a doctrine of selflessness.

* Mr. Gandhi should not be understood to mean that motive does not matter. See his *Ethical Religion*.

The difficulty of Englishmen lies really in believing that their rule is wholly an evil for India, *i.e.*, it has made India worse for the English rule in everything that counts. India is poorer in wealth, in manliness, in godliness and in her sons' power to defend themselves. It is sinful to coquet with evil—God and Satan. The writer asks me to pause and consider. I have done so for thirty years and have been driven to the final conclusion that English Rule in its present form has proved a curse to India. Let Englishmen pause and consider what is happening before their eyes. Let them turn the searchlight inward. May they ask me to co-operate with a government that has betrayed the Mussalmans of India and stabbed humanity in the Punjab? Let them not call the Massacre of Jallianwala an error of judgment. Let them not believe the Prime Minister if and when he says that he has not committed a breach of solemn promise given to the Mussalmans of India. The cause is just: the means are equally just. The motive is mixed. The struggle is being prolonged, only because the motive is not as unmixed as the means and the end.

24th March, 1920

VIOLENCE *vs.* NON-VIOLENCE

(By M. K. Gandhi)

The Khilafat day has come and gone. It was a great success and a complete triumph of Satyagraha, *i.e.*, not Civil Disobedience but Truth and Non-violence. No *hartal* has been so voluntary as that of the 19th March in that all the canvassing that ever took place was before the 19th. It was an example of wonderful self-restraint on the part of the Committee not to have called out the mill-hands. The Committee deserves the highest praise for its efficient management and for the definite recognition of voluntarism. If the people continue to show the discipline and self-restraint shown on the 19th and add thereto in an equal measure the spirit of self-sacrifice, nothing can prevent the full fruition of our hopes regarding Khilafat. Nobody could have believed a year ago the possibility of peace being observed by the fanatical element among the Mahomedans on a matter of life and death to them and on a day of no business for the idlers. But there can be no idleness when there is prayer. All were enjoined not to quarrel, not to be angry but to pray for the right to be done. It is true that all did not definitely pray, but the spirit of prayer was abroad and it dominated the people rather than the spirit of revenge, anger, excitement and so we had the amazing spectacle of the *hartal* day passing off like an ordinary day when every body expects peace to be observed. The vast meeting of Bombay attended perhaps by thirty thousand men was a sight worth seeing. There was firmness in the faces of those thousands of people who listened to the speeches, yet without applause or any other effusive demonstration. The organisers deserve the warmest praise for having introduced into our meetings the ancient peacefulness, quiet determination and orderliness in the place of modern bluster, excitement and disorderliness. The one develops just the qualities that make for *Satyagraha*, the other inevitably leads to violence. And the message of the great meeting and the very successful *hartal* is not violence but non-violence. I hope that the authorities will not misread the situation. They will not fail to understand the admirable spirit of the whole demonstration or the equally admirable spirit of the resolution—a resolution to which, in my humble opinion, it is impossible for any honest lover of this country or the Empire to take exception. I hope, too, that they will read the spirit of the movement in the manner in which it is developing. I hope that the exemplary patience, self-restraint and orderliness that are evolving in our midst will have their due weight with them and that they will inform the Imperial Government that, whilst there is this admirable peace in the land, there is also a grim determination behind it which will not take "no" for an answer. I hope that Government will not repeat the sin of last April and entertain any false hope of tyranny to the crush unquenchable spirit that has come into being and that will suffer everything but humiliation, dishonour and defeat.

It is a matter of deep regret that so respected a body as the Liberal League should have hastily and in advance condemned the *hartal.** Surely a people so

* On 4th May, 1921, Gandhi wrote in *Young India* under the heading "Abuse of Hartal": A correspondent from Karachi writes to me deploring the frequency of 'hartals' in that city. I have also seen a cutting from the *Indian Social Reformer* dealing with the same subject. I agree with the *I. S. Reformer's* criticism that the 'hartals' have become cheap of late. They are fast losing their value. But for the sacred character of the 16th and the 13th April, I would have refrained from advising 'hartals' for those two days. 'Hartals' are either meant as a protest against something extraordinary or a religious demonstration. There was no meaning in declaring a 'hartal' when H. E. the Governor visited Karachi. If it was meant to be a demonstration against him personally, it was bad taste, for, in my opinion, he is among the wisest officials, and but for the vicious system he is called upon to administer, he would make a popular Governor. 'Hartals' for imprisonments or discharges are equally bad taste. Imprisonments must not inspire fear in us. Under an unjust government, imprisonments of innocent men must be regarded as their ordinary lot even as disease is the ordinary state of persons living in insanitary conditions. The Government will cease to

stricken with grief and with disappointment probably staring them in the face must have an outlet for orderly manifestation. It was because not very long ago we were afraid to speak or write that we thought that our sentiments burrowed under and became foul with stench because of the absence of the fierce sun and the open air of public opinion playing upon them. Hence we had a secret revolutionary movement. To-day, thank God, we seem to have outlived the evil day. We dare to think, speak and write openly, without fear, but under restraint that openness imposes upon mankind. I appeal to the members of the Liberal League and those who think with them to recognise this plain fact and to appreciate the superiority of boldness over timid caution. If they desire to harness all the innumerable forces that are coming daily into being for the uplift of the nation, if they wish to become privileged participators in the throes of the new birth, let them not ignore the signs of the time, let them not reject the advances of the younger generation, let them not chill their ardent hopes and aspirations but let them head this growing party of young, enthusiastic, self-sacrificing, dare-devil men. Sympathise with them, respond to the heart's throb, regulate it, for they are amenable to reason or an appeal to their high-souledness—and you have a disciplined

imprison us when we cease to fear imprisonments. The Government will cease to exist or (which is the same thing) will reform itself, when its most frightful punishments, even Dyerism, fail to strike us with fear. 'Hartals' therefore in regard to imprisonments are a symptom of nervous fear and must therefore be tabooed. I quite agree with *I. S. R.* that local leaders ought not to declare 'hartals' without reference to headquarters. As a rule I would say, save the 6th and 13th April, every other Hartal should be declared by the All India Congress Committee and the Central Khilafat Committee in conjunction. It will be a misfortune to cheapen the 'hartals.'

party, obedient to the call of the country. But if they feel neglected, if they feel that the older heads will not patiently listen to their wants, will not give them a helping hand, they may despair and despair may lead to desperation resulting in a catastrophic destruction. I can recall no time so magnificently suitable for leading India to the method of *Satyagraha*—not necessarily Civil Disobedience, but Truth and Non-violence—in which there is no defeat and in which, if there is any error, it hurts but those who err.

11*th August*, 1920

THE DOCTRINE OF THE SWORD

(BY M. K. GANDHI)

In this age of the rule of brute force, it is almost impossible for any one to believe that any one else could possibly reject the law of the final supremacy of brute force. And so I receive anonymous letters advising me that I must not interfere with the progress of Non-co-operation, even though popular violence may break out. Others come to me and, assuming that secretly I must be plotting violence, inquire when the happy moment for declaring open violence is to arrive. They assure me that the English will never yield to anything but violence secret or open. Yet others, I am informed, believe that I am the most rascally person living in India, because I never give out my real intention and that they have not a shadow of a doubt that I believe in violence just as much as most people do.

Such being the hold that the doctrine of the sword has on the majority of mankind, and as success of Non-co-operation depends principally on absence of violence during its pendency and as my views in this matter affect the conduct of a large number of people, I am anxious to state them as clearly as possible.

I do believe that, where there is only a choice between cowardice and violence, I would advise violence. Thus when my eldest son asked me what he should have done, had he been present when I was almost fatally assaulted in 1908, whether he should have run away and seen me killed or whether he should have used his physical force which he could and wanted to use, and defended me, I told him that it was his duty to defend me even by using violence. Hence it was that I took part in the Boer War, the so-called Zulu rebellion and the late War. Hence also do I advocate training in arms for those who believe in the method of violence. I would rather have India resort to arms in order to defend her honour than that she should in a cowardly manner become or remain a helpless witness to her own dishonour.

But I believe that non-violence is infinitely superior to violence, forgiveness is more manly than punishment. Forgiveness adorns a soldier. But abstinence is forgiveness only when there is the power to punish; it is meaningless when it pretends to proceed from a helpless creature. A mouse hardly forgives a cat when it allows itself to be torn to pieces by her. I therefore appreciate the sentiment of those who cry out for the condign punishment of General Dyer and his ilk. They would tear him to pieces if they could. But I do not believe India to be helpless. I do not believe myself to be a helpless creature. Only I want to use India's and my strength for a better purpose.

Let me not be misunderstood. Strength does not come from physical capacity. It comes from an indomitable will. An average Zulu is any way more than a match for an average Englishman in bodily capacity. But he flees from an English boy, because he fears the boy's revolver or those who who will use it for him. He fears death and is nerveless in spite of his burly figure. We in India may in a moment realise that one hundred thousand Englishmen need not frighten three hundred million human beings. A definite forgiveness would therefore mean a definite recognition of our strength. With enlightened forgiveness must come a mighty wave of strength in us, which would make it impossible for a Dyer and a Frank Johnson to heap affront upon India's devoted head. It matters little to me that for the moment I do not drive my point home. We feel too down-trodden not to be angry and revengeful. But I must not refrain from saying that India can gain more by waiving the right of punishment. We have better work to do, a better mission to deliver to the world.

I am not a visionary. I claim to be a practical idealist. The religion of non-violence is not meant merely for the Rishis and saints. It is meant for the common people as well. Non-violence is the law of our species as violence is the law of the brute. The spirit lies dormant in the brute and he knows no law but that of physical might. The dignity of man requires obedience to a higher law—to the strength of the spirit.

I have therefore ventured to place before India the ancient law of self-sacrifice. For Satyagraha and its off-shoots, Non-co-operation and civil resistance, are nothing but new names for the law of suffering. The Rishis, who discovered the law of non-violence in the midst of violence, were greater geniuses than Newton. They were themselves greater warriors than Wellington. Having themselves known the use of arms, they realised their uselessness and taught a weary world that its salvation lay not through violence but through non-violence.

Non-violence in its dynamic condition means conscious suffering. It does not mean meek submission to the will of the evil-doer, but it means the putting of one's whole soul against the will of the tyrant. Working under this law of our being, it is possible for a single individual to defy the whole might of an unjust empire to save his honour, his religion, his soul and lay the foundation for that empire's fall or its regeneration.

And so I am not pleading for India to practise non-violence, because it is weak. I want her to practise non-violence being conscious of her strength and power. No training in arms is required for realisation of her strength. We seem to need it, because we seem to think that we are but a lump of flesh. I want India to recognise that she has a soul that cannot perish and that can rise triumphant above every physical weakness and defy the physical combination of a whole world. What is the meaning of Rama, a mere human being, with his host of monkeys, pitting himself againt the insolent strength of ten-headed Ravan surrounded in supposed safety by the raging waters on all sides of Lanka? Does it not mean the conquest of physical might by spiritual strength? However, being a practical man, I do not wait till India recognises the practicability of the spiritual life in the political world. India considers herself to be powerless and paralysed before the machine-guns, the tanks and the aeroplanes of the English. And she takes up Non-co-operation out of her weakness. It must still serve the same purpose, namely, bring her delivery from the crushing weight of British injustice, if a sufficient number of people practise it.

I isolate this Non-co-operation from Sinn Feinism, for,

it is so conceived as to be incapable of being offered side by side with violence. But I invite even the school of violence to give this peaceful Non-co-operation a trial. It will not fail through its inherent weakness. It may fail because of poverty of response. Then will be the time for real danger. The high-souled men, who are unable to suffer national humiliation any longer, will want to vent their wrath. They will take to violence. So far as I know, they must perish without delivering themselves or their country from the wrong. If India takes up the doctrine of the sword, she may gain momentary victory. Then India will cease to be the pride of my heart. I am wedded to India, because I owe my all to her. I believe absolutely that she has a mission for the world. She is not to copy Europe blindly. India's acceptance of the doctrine of the sword will be the hour of my trial. I hope I shall not be found wanting. My religion has no geographical limits. If I have a living faith in it, it will transcend my love for India herself. My life is dedicated to service of India through the religion of non-violence which I believe to be the root of Hinduism.

Meanwhile, I urge those who distrust me, not to disturb the even working of the struggle that has just commenced, by inciting to violence in the belief that I want violence.* I detest secrecy as a sin. Let them give Non-violent Non-co-operation a trial and they will find that I had no mental reservation whatsoever.

* In *Young India*, of 9th February, 1921, Mr. Gandhi wrote commenting on Dr. Rajan's letter in connection with the Madras Hartal on the Prince's arrival:

There is a little doubt that there are some among us who do not implicitly believe in non-violence even while they are under the pledge, *i.e.*, they do not mind the assistance of those who would do violence. They seem to believe that violence can run parallel to

3rd November, 1920

LUCKNOW SPEECHES

(By M. K. Gandhi)

The recent meeting in Lucknow, held during the visit of the Ali Brothers and myself, has attracted considerable attention and resulted in the secession of Mr. Douglas, an Indian Christian barrister, from the Non-co-operation movement. Mr. Douglas's reason for his decision is

---

non-violence and the two together accelerate the progress of the country towards its goal. Such an attitude besides being hypocritical is positively against the country's interest. Two opposite forces may run parallel but they cannot both go in the same direction! If non-violence was a camouflage or a preparation for violence, an accidental or intended outbreak of it might be by way of trial a great gain even during the pendency of so-called non-violence. But that is not India's religious battle. God is witness above and He is just enough to chastise every double dealing. Our present belief is that India cannot gain anything by violence and must gain her three ends by non-violence alone unsupported by violence. If therefore we will win, there must be on the part of Non-co-operators an unequivocal and emphatic mental and vocal condemnation of every act of violence done out of sympathy for their cause. Let those who do not believe in non-violence or believe in both running together form a party of their own and fight out the issue. That would make a Non-co-operator's task difficult but not so difficult as when he has to fight an enemy in his own camp. His system must be kept pure. Any impurity from within will be an organic disease and may prove fatal. No attack from without can ever prove fatal. The first and indeed the only condition of success therefore is that we must be true to ourselves.

The confession therefore that Dr. Rajan has made is an invigorating process. It strengthens him and the cause for which he stands. Non-co-operation is a vicious and corrupt doctrine, truly an 'ugly' word, if it does not mean down-right self-purification. Stubborn and implacable resistance against internal corruption is enough resistance against the Government. As soon as the process of self-purification is complete, we shall miss the system we appear to be fighting.

Maulana Abdul Bari's speech on that occasion. Mr. Douglas charges the Maulana with having called Christians *kafirs* and with having practically condoned the late Mr. Willoughby's murder.*

*Commenting on this incident under the heading. "The Assassination of a Deputy Commissioner," Mr. Gandhi wrote in *Young India* of 1st September 1920

The assassination of Mr. Willoughby is a most unfortunate event which has naturally evoked public sympathy and indignation. The murder was a cruel, thoughtless and fanatical act. It has not advanced but retarded the cause of Khilafat. Mr. Willoughby had no hand in the Turkish terms. As is quite probable, he was himself a popular officer. It can only be counted as madness to kill an innocent man for a crime committed by a member of his race. And yet the fact must not be disguised that the murder will be regarded by many Mahomedans as a pious act worthy of a martyr. I have heard Mahomedans calmly arguing that such murders are not only justifiable but meritorious. I have known many Hindus who have argued that it was throwing of bombs which brought about the removal of the Partition of Bengal. I know that many consider Dhingra to have been

Mr. Gandhi does not rule out the adoption of Non-violence as a policy. "Do you hope." a correspondent wrote to him, "that this non-violent war which is based on love and soul-force will succeed with those who take it merely as a matter of policy? Pure non-violence necessitates more courage and love of country. But as a weapon of the weak, it will breed fear in the face of coming repression." In answer, Mr. Gandhi wrote in *Young India* of 25th May, 1921: The questioner has partly answered the question himself. Non-violence may succeed, even if it is adopted as a matter of policy rather than creed, if it is combined with courage and real love for the country or the cause Hatred of the wrong-doer does not necessarily mean love of the country. Our difficulty arises from the fact that many people make a pretence of non-violence without believing in it even as a policy. The Ali Brothers believe in it purely as a policy, but in my opinion there are no two truer believers in non-violence as a policy than they. They do believe that violence can only hurt the cause, and that non-violence if extensively practised can entirely succeed. A man who honestly practises truth as a policy certainly gains its material results, but not the one who feigns truth.

Now I was present at the meeting and had reason to listen to every word that Maulana Abdul Bari said with the greatest attention, and I must confess that the speech could not possibly provide any occasion for Mr. Douglas's secession. I deny that the Maulana Saheb either condoned the murder, or, by calling Mr. Willoughby a *kafar* had any intention of insulting Christians. Mr. Douglas was hardly justified in seceding. He never protested at the meeting, he never complained to me. He knew that I had great regard for the Maulana Saheb, and that

---

a martyr. Sinn Feiners openly practise murder and other forms of violence for the purpose of freeing their country from the English connection. Every assassin or incendiary is considered by them a hero. It is because I feared such a result in our midst that I advised non-violent Non-co-operation regarding the Khilafat. In my opinion, it is the active and open preaching of Non-co-operation which has prevented murder and assassinations in the land. The murder of Mr. Willoughby proves that the propaganda of Non-violence and Non-co-operation has not proved sufficient to control individual fanatics and that it is not an easy thing to do so. It proves further that the Khilafat wrong is a deep-seated grievance which with the passage of time will sink deeper still instead of being forgotten.

I observe that *The Times of India* credits the Khilafat propaganda with the murder and calls it the 'first fruits.' I realise that the language used is cautious. It connects 'certain aspects of the agitation' with the crime. But I venture to suggest that no aspect of the agitation is responsible for the unfortunate murder. It is the grievous wrong done by the British ministers which has evoked the cruel deed.

The Times of India is on safer ground when it says that the tragedy 'is a special call to Islam, for all thoughtful Mahomedans must realise that the honour of their religion is at stake.' I wish to emphasise that warning. It must be the special duty of every Khilafat worker to be more careful than hitherto in insisting on complete freedom from violence as the condition precedent to successful Non-co-operation. I am sure it is possible to cite texts from the Koran in condonation of murder being done to wrong-doers in order to compel justice. It is unfortunately the chosen method of the civilized world. It has scriptural authority. Islam is said openly to preach

I myself would have spoken out if there was any condonation of the offence in his speech, or if there was any insult meant to be offered to Christians as such. I could not associate myself with an insult to any of the great religions of the world. Moreover Mr. Douglas suspended his practice and joined Non-co-operation. not merely for the sake of the Khilafat but equally for the Punjab, and he was a party to the extension of Non-co-operation up to the time of the establishment of Swaraj in India. Does Mr. Douglas now not want Swaraj or redress for the Punjab? And can he abandon the

---

violence to the wrong-doer. The so-called votaries of Christianity justify organised warfare for the removal of wrongs, fancied or real. Thousands of Hindus interpret the Gita to be a certificate for war in the cause of justice. It is only a minority (daily growing in numbers) which religiously believes that violence is wrong in itself and cannot be justified even to vindicate truth. But it cannot (it may be civilised) be religious to murder innocent unarmed men without warning. It is not enough for Khilafat workers to be satisfied with public condemnations (necessary as they are) or for the sake of decorum to join them. It is necessary for us to preach privately, publicly and incessantly the necessity of refraining from violence especially when an active campaign of Non-co-operation full of promise is going on. We must feel in every fibre of our own being that every murder, every deed of violence must retard the progress of the movement.

This is an opportunity for distinguishing the Sinn Fein or the Egyptian Non-co-operation from ours. The former does not and did not depend for success on non-violence. The Sinn Feiners resort to violence in every shape and form. Theirs is a 'frightfulness' not unlike General Dyer's. We may pardon it if we choose, because we sympathise with their cause. But it does not on that account differ in quality from General Dyer's act. The Central Khilafat Committee has openly and deliberately accepted Non-violence for its creed so long as Non-co-operation is being carried on. We must therefore seek to guard English life as our own. We must constitute ourselves as self-appointed volunteers guarding English life from violent hands. And our success depends upon our ability to control all the violent and fanatical forces in our midst.

Khilafat movement because a Moulvi however distinguished gives him offence by his speech? Surely there is something wrong and incomprehensible about Mr. Douglas's attitude. However, I must leave Mr. Douglas to clear up his position and justify his secession on more reasonable grounds.

It is necessary for me to deal with the speeches themselves, and more especially the speech delivered by Maulana Abdul Bari Saheb. The difficulty of a reporter is at any time great, but when he has to take down a report in long hand, and at the same time to translate the speaker's remarks made in a tongue the reporter only half understands, the task becomes still more difficult. Such was the position which my co-worker, Mr. Mahadev Desai, occupied when he took notes of the Maulana's speech. I saw his report after it was published in the *Navajivan* and was grieved about it. I thought that a serious though innocent mistake was made by him. The report does not do justice to the Maulana and makes him say that the murderer of Mr. Willoughby was a martyr, and that he, the Maulana, had accepted my word in preference to that of *Al-Koran*. I consider Mr. Mahadev Desai to be one of the best and most careful of the co-workers I have the good fortune to possess. But the best of us may, in spite of the best of intentions, sometimes make mistakes.

To my recollection, what Maulana Abdul Bari Saheb said was that he disliked the murder of Mr. Willoughby as much as any body. He knew that it had damaged the Khilafat cause. He felt sure that, if he had known anything of the proposed murder, he would have himself intervened to prevent it. That was a position he himself could take, and understand when taken by others. But it was a different thing when he was asked, as he was by some of his friends, to condemn the murderer to *Jahanam*. He, as a religious man, found it impossible to do so. He did not know how the murder was committed, or what were the motives actuating it. The murderer's position after death was therefore clearly a matter between him and his Maker, and it would be presumption on the part of any person to anticipate the verdict of the Deity. Mr. Willoughby belonged to the *kafar* race; and had there been *Jehad* proclaimed, anyone belonging to the enemy race could have been lawfully killed by the sword of Islam. But they (the Mussalmans) had decided not to draw the sword and so it was not lawful for any Mussalman to take the life of any member of the enemy race. They had accepted Mr. Gandhi's advice of Non-co-operation. For there was ample warrant for it in the *Koran* and the Prophet's own life. And so long as Non-co-operation continued, he would be guided entirely by Mr. Gandhi. He was rebuked for making friends with the Hindus who were idolators. It was his conviction that it was perfectly competent for a Mussalman to prefer friendship with the Hindus, and even to refrain from killing cows, to friendship with those *kufars* who had left no stone unturned to put Islam in jeopardy.

This is the gist of the Maulana's speech. The speech was certainly bitter. Who can complain of bitterness of speech in a man of such religious devotion as Maulana Abdul Bari when he finds that his religious honour is at stake? I personally dislike the use of the word *kafar* as applied to anyone, as I dislike the use by a Hindu of the word *Mlechha* or *anarya* to any one. But I refuse to quarrel with the Mussalman or the Hindu for the use of words to which they have been accustomed from their childhood. Time will certainly tend towards the discontinuance of such words as friendship between people of different professions and faiths grows. Must I refuse to acknowledge the learning or the goodness of a man like Bishop Heber for calling Hindus heathens and even pitying them? "Man alone is vile," was said of a whole race of mankind and is even to-day sung in many a Christian church. I can therefore see no warrant for Mr. Douglas's decision in the above speech.

Maulana Shaukat Ali was still more unexceptionable. He said no one could regret more than he did the murder of Mr. Willoughby. Had not Khilafat Committees sedulously tried their best to prevent violence, there would certainly have been not one but many such murders. But it was their duty for the sake of their own religion and honour to prevent them so long as they accepted Non-co-operation. But he declined to identify himself with toadying resolutions regarding the murder.

I observe too that I have been misreported. I never said that we would give notice when we intended to draw the sword. I condemned the murder with the emphasis I could command and said that the honour of Islam would be injured if there was any condonation of the murder of an innocent man when an assurance of safety was issued by authoritative religious bodies in Islam. I said further that my own personal religion forbade me to take the life of my enemy in any case whatsoever. But I added that I recognised that Islam, and for that matter lacs of Hindus, believed that killing one's enemy was considered lawful under certain circumstances. And I said that, when the Mussalmans of India wanted to draw the sword, they would as honourable men declare themselves in no equivocal terms and give due notice.

And I repeat what I have often said that the noblest

and the most fearless among the Mussalmans (and I count Maulana Bari Saheb and the Ali Brothers as such) are trying their utmost to prevent violence. I verily believe that but for strenuous efforts of such men, violence would have done no good to Islam or to India. It would only have provided occasion for ruthless repression without doing any honour to Islam or India.

17th November, 1920.

A TRIUMPH OF NON-VIOLENCE

(BY M. K. GANDHI).

The *communique* issued by the Government of India* on the Non-co-operation movement may be regarded as its first triumph of a striking order. For the Government have decided *in view of its non-violent character* to refrain, for the time being at any rate, from repressing by violence what they consider to be an unconstitutional movement. The Government, as well as the people, may be congratulated upon this wise decision; and I have not the slightest doubt that, if the movement continues to be purged of all violence, whether in deed or in word, it would not only be impossible for the Government to resort to repression, but also to resist the ever growing volume of public opinion against it, when that opinion is backed by well-directed acts of renunciation of Government patronage or support, on a national scale.

But the *communique* is careful to hold out the mailed first, if the leaders of " moderate " opinion fail to check the onward march of Non-co-operation. It is interesting

* Omitted in this collection.

to recall the exact wording of the threat. "How long," the *communique* ends, "with due regard to their ultimate responsibility for the public safety, the Government will be able to maintain that policy" (*i.e.* non-repression) "will depend largely on the success, which attends the efforts of the moderate citizens to check the extension of the movement and keep its dangers within bounds."

Thus repression is to replace reason and argument if Non-co-operation becomes effective to the extent or making it impossible for the Government to exist whilst refusing to retrace its steps and repent of its crimes against India. For it must be noticed that the danger here feared is evidently not of violence but of the loss of the existence of this Government. If my analysis is correct, the Government are wickedly playing with the 'moderates' and with India. If they mean well, let them make an irrevocable announcement in the clearest possible terms that, so long as the movement remains non-violent, they will not interfere with it, even though it demands, and may result in, complete independence. That they will have to make that announcement sometime or other I have no doubt, if we, the Non-co-operators, are able to keep the movement free from violence. But the announcement made when they are driven to it by irresistible public opinion will have lost all its grace.

The rest of the *communique* is quite in keeping with the traditional policy of the Government. It is full of the usual self-adulation and misrepresentations about Non-co-operators. It is wrong, for instance, to say that those who have been repressed have been so dealt with for their departure from the principle of non-violence. I challenge the Government to produce from the speeches or writings of those who have been imprisoned any instance of incitement to violence. The language of the defendants has sometimes been reckless, even exaggerated, but the records available to me of the trials of some of them show that there has been no violence preached by the speakers concerned. There is very little that the speakers have said which I would not have said myself. It is equally untrue to say that those who have been punished have been so dealt with for "tampering with the loyalty of the army or of the police," unless a public appeal to recruits, not to sell themselves as mercenary levies for robbing other countries of their independence, amounts to such incitement. The Seditious Meetings Proclamation in the Punjab and the action taken against some Non-co-operation papers is an eloquent repudiation of the statement that the Government "have been reluctant to interfere with the liberty of speech and the freedom of the press at a time when India is on the threshold of a great advance towards the realization of the principle of self-government."

The misrepresentation about the leaders of the movement and the cheap sneer at their supposed desire to seek martyrdom is beneath notice. The Government ought to know what a relief it is to the Ali Brothers and myself to learn that, at least for the present, they do not propose to imprison us. Everybody knows that the danger of an outbreak of violence is the greatest if we are imprisoned. I am aware that this is a humiliating confession. If the people were truly strong and self-reliant, they would remain unperturbed by our or any leaders' imprisonment. So long, however, as the blighting influence of the awe of the Government lasts, so long must there be this fear of an insensate outbreak of violence on the part of the people of this unhappy land, when they are deprived of the assistance and service of those in whom they believe.

The Government's third argument, in favour of the exercise of their self-restraint, is the most specious, and calculated to entrap the unwary. They describe Non-co-operation as "a visionary and chimerical scheme, which, if successful, could only result in wide-spread disorder, political chaos, and the ruin of all those who have any real stake in the country." In this one sentence we have the satanic character of the Government. They must know that successful Non-co-operation means orderly and peaceful destruction of the present system of the Government, and *its replacement not* by disorder and chaos but by political order of the first magnitude, and protection of every legitimate interest in the country—not excluding that of the European merchant who desires to earn an honest living in India. Mention of the 'real stake' is a wilful insult to the masses of India, and a mischievous incitement to the monied classes to range themselves against the masses. Have the masses no stake in India? Are they not the only people with any real stake in the country? The monied classes, if the worst happened, could even migrate from the country. The masses know no other home save the few yards of each space which they possess in this land of sorrow and tears.

It lies ill in the mouth of the framers of the resolution to say "that the appeal of Non-co-operation is to prejudice and ignorance", when they are aware that from every platform the appeal is made for self-sacrifice, self-purification, and discipline. The misrepresentation of Satyagraha is no less wicked. The experience was indeed bitter during that eventful month of April, but the recollection in the minds of the people of official misdeeds during those days will remain an evergreen. India will never forget how a wicked administrator in the Punjab sought to crush an innocent and pure movement by every means, fair or foul. The wonderful awakening of the people of India to a sense of the wrong then done. and to a sense of their duty, gives the lie direct to the implications of the sentence on Satyagraha.

The resolution in question is an appeal not merely to our ignorance and avarice. but it is an appeal also to our helplessness. For this document proceeds: "The full consummation of their hopes would leave India defenceless alike against foreign aggression and internal chaos, all the benefits of a stable Government and undisturbed peace, the results that have been obtained by the orderly progress of India for more than a century and the still greater results which, it is hoped. will attend her advance under the Reform scheme; her material prosperity and her political progress are all to be sacrificed to the irresponsible caprice of a few misguided men." In my humble opinion, this paragraph is, indeed, the most mischievous, the most misleading, and, to borrow the phraseology of the Government, "the most immoral." If the argument advanced is sound, India must ever remain in a defenceless condition without the British bayonet. I cannot imagine for India a prospect more gloomy, more immoral and more unworthy of a nation, that only a century ago was capable of putting in the field more sturdy warriors than all the soldiers that can be mustered together today by any three powers of Europe, barring Russia. What severer condemnation can be pronounced upon the British Government than that, for the commercial greed of the British Nation, it has emasculated a whole people? The framers must be aware that the full consummation of our hopes means an India with the whole of her population having one mind, one purpose, self-contained and self-reliant, producing enough for all her daily wants, and therefore well able to stand a blockade by all the naval powers of the world combined. This may all be a day-dream, but that is the exact meaning of 'the full consummation of our hopes'; and I should very much like the Gods to witness a duel between the powers of all the world pouring into India not to punish her for any offence given by her, but in order to trade with her at the point of the bayonet; and the Sikhs, the Gurkhas, the Poorbhias, the Mussalmans, the Rajputs, and all the other military races of India voluntarily fighting for their hearth and home. If I am told that there never will be in India such unity of purpose and mind, I must say that there never will be Swaraj for India, and therefore true freedom and true progress, moral and material. It was Canning who wrote that under the Indian sky a cloud no bigger than a man's thumb any moment gathers such dimensions as to flood a whole country if it burst. I have implicit faith in the ability of my countrymen to hope that all the bitter experiences of the British Rule, at present lying sub-conscious in the minds of the nation, may any moment take definite shape in the nation recognizing the necessity of unity and self-sacrifice, such as to compel either repentance and a real change of heart, or withdrawal, on the part of the British Government.

I must refrain from burdening this article with any refutation of the charges of immorality, etc., regarding my advice to the student-world. The pages of this journal have made clear to its readers the ethics of the fundamental position taken upon this question. I must close this lengthy article with noticing the absence of the only thing that can stop the inevitable progress of

Non-co-operation, *viz.*, a full and satisfactory revision of the Khilafat terms and complete satisfaction about the Punjab. When, and if, the British nation respects the wishes of India on these two points, co-operation will replace Non-co-operation, and Swaraj within the Empire will be the most natural consequence.

But till that clear repentance comes, in spite of all the resolution and all the repression that may be resorted to by the Government, so far as I can read the national mind, Non-violent Non-co-operation will and must remain the creed of the nation that has grown weary of camouflage, humbug, and honeyed words.

12th January, 1921

THE NEED FOR HUMILITY

(BY M. K. GANDHI)

The spirit of non-violence necessarily leads to humility. Non-violence means reliance on God, the Rock of ages. If we would seek His aid, we must approach Him with a humble and a contrite heart. Non-co-operationists may not trade upon their amazing success at the Congress. We must act, even as the mango tree which droops as it bears fruit. Its grandeur lies in its majestic lowliness. But one hears of Non-co-operationists being insolent and intolerant in their behaviour towards those who differ from them. I know that they will lose all their majesty and glory, if they betray any inflation. Whilst we may not be dissatisfied with the progress made so far, we have little to our credit to make us feel proud. We have to sacrifice much more than we have done to justify pride, much less elation. Thousands, who flocked to the Congress pandal, have undoubtedly given their intellectual assent to the doctrine, but few have followed it out in practice. Leaving aside the pleaders, how many parents have withdrawn their children from schools? How many of those who registered their vote in favour of Non-co-operation have taken to hand-spinning or discarded the use of all foreign cloth?

Non-co-operation is not a movement of brag, bluster, or bluff. It is a test of our sincerity. It requires solid and silent self-sacrifice. It challenges our honesty and our capacity for national work. It is a movement that aims at translating ideas into action. And the more we do, the more we find that much more must be *done* than we had expected. And this thought of our imperfection must make us humble.

A Non-co-operationist strives to compel attention and to set an example not by his violence, but by his unobtrusive humility. He allows his solid action to speak for his creed. His strength lies in his reliance upon the correctness of his position. And the conviction of it grows most in his opponent when he least interposes his speech between his action and his opponent. Speech, especially when it is haughty, betrays want of confidence and it makes one's opponent sceptical about the reality of the act itself. Humility therefore is the key to quick success. I hope that every Non-co-operationist will recognise the necessity of being humble and self-restrained. It is because so little is really required to be done and because all of that little depends entirely upon ourselves that I have ventured the belief that Swaraj is attainable in less than one year.

24th November, 1921

THE MORAL ISSUE

(BY M. K. GANDHI)

As soon as we lose the moral basis, we cease to be religious. There is no such thing as religion overriding morality. Man, for instance, cannot be untruthful, cruel or incontinent and claim to have God on his side. In Bombay, the sympathisers of Non-co-operation lost the moral balance. They were enraged against the Parsis and the Christians who took part in the welcome to the Prince and sought to 'teach them a lesson'. They invited reprisals and got them. It became after the 17th a game of seesaw in which no one really gained and everybody lost.*

Swaraj does not lie that way. India does not want Bolshevism. The people are too peaceful to stand anarchy. They will bow the knee to any one who restores so called order. Let us recognise the Indian psychology. We need not stop to inquire whether such hankering after peace is a virtue or a vice. The average Mussalman of India is quite different from the average Mussalman of the other parts of the world. His Indian associations have made him more docile than his co-religionists outside India, He will not stand tangible insecurity of life and property for any length of time. The Hindu is proverbially, almost contemptibly, mild. The Parsi and the Christian love peace more than strife. Indeed we have almost made religion subservient to peace. This mentality is at once our weakness and our strength.

Let us nurse the better, the religious, part of this

* For further details of the riots in Bombay referred to above, see appendix.

mentality of ours. 'Let there be no compulsion in religion'. Is it not religion with us to observe Swadeshi and therefore *Khadi*? But if the religion of others does not require them to adopt Swadeshi, we may not compel them. We broke the universal law re-stated in the *Quran*. And the law does not mean that there may be compulsion in other matters. The verse means that, if it is bad to use compulsion in religion about which we have definite convictions, it is worse to resort to it in matters of less moment.

We can only therefore argue and reason with our opponents. The extreme to which we may go is Non-violent Non-co-operation with them in private life, for we do not non-co-operate with the men composing the Government, we are non-co-operating with the system they administer. We decline to render official service to Sir George Lloyd the Governor, we dare not withhold social service from Sir George Lloyd the Englishman.*

* The following appeared in "Young India" of 4th August, 1921:

Bad of Karachi—Though I have not read the papers regarding the stoning of Europeans in Karachi by a crowd that was incensed against the imprisonment of Swami Krishnanand, from what I have heard through friends from Sindh I must confess that those who threw stones have done a disservice to the sacred cause they had at heart. They have also shown little honour to the Swami by breaking the pledge of Non-violence. The Swami is undoubtedly a popular and fearless worker. He had been producing by organised picketing a marked impression on the receipts of the liquor-dealers. I hear too that he was falsely charged with having assaulted some one. Granting all this, it was the clear duty of the populace to observe perfect self-restraint. It is a most thoughtless thing to assault innocent Europeans, because the police have wrongly prosecuted and a magistrate has wrongly convicted. Incidents such as these make civil disobedience difficult, if not impossible. Let the crowd that so misbehaved in Karachi honour the Swami by boycotting foreign cloth, and by spinning or weaving.

The mischief, I am sorry to say, began among the Hindus and the Mussalmans themselves. There was social persecution, there was coercion. I must confess that I did not always condemn it as strongly as I might have. I might have dissociated myself from the movement when it became at all general. We soon mended our ways, we became more tolerant but the subtle coercion was there. I passed it by as I thought it would die a natural death. I saw in Bombay that it had not. It assumed a virulent from on the 17th.

We damaged the Khilafat cause and with it that of the Punjab and Swaraj. We must retrace our steps and scrupulously insure minorities against the least molestation. If the Christian wishes to wear the European hat and unmentionables, he must be free to do so. If a Parsi wishes to stick to his *Fenta*, he has every right to do so. If they both see their safety in associating themselves with the Government, we may only wean them from their error by appealing to their reason, not by breaking their heads. The greater the coercion we use, the greater the security we give to the Government, if only because the latter has more effective weapons of coercion than we have. For us to resort to greater coercion than the Government will be to make India more slave than she is now.

Swaraj is freedom for every one, the smallest among us, to do as he likes without any physical interference with his liberty. Non-violent Non-co-operation is the method whereby we cultivate the freest public opinion and get it enforced. When there is complete freedom of opinion, that of the majority must prevail. If we are in a minority, we can prove worthy of our religion by remaining true to it in the face of coercion. The Prophet submitted to the coercion of the majority and remained true to his faith. And when he found himself in a majority, he declared to his followers that there should be no compulsion in religion. Let us not again either by verbal or physical violence depart from the injunction, and by our own folly further put back the hands of the clock of progress.

2nd March, 1922

NEEDLESS NERVOUSNESS

(By M. K. Gandhi)

I am sorry that I find a nervous fear among some Hindus and Mahomedans that I am undermining their faith and that I am even doing irreparable harm to India by my uncompromising preaching of non-violence. They seem almost to imply that violence is their creed. I touch a tender spot if I talk about extreme non-violence in their presence. They confound me with texts from the Mahabharata and the Koran eulogising or permitting violence. Of the Mahabharata I can write without restraint, but the most devout Mahomedan will not, I hope, deny me the privilege of understanding the message of the Prophet. I make bold to say that violence is the creed of no religion and that, whereas non-violence in most cases is obligatory in all, violence is merely permissible in some cases. But I have not put before India the final form of non-violence. The non-violence that I have preached from Congress platforms is non-violence as a policy. But even policies require honest adherence in thought, word and deed. If I believe, that honesty is the best policy, surely whilst I so believe, I must be honest in thought, word and deed; otherwise I become an imposter. Non-violence being a policy means that it can upon due notice be given up when it proves unsuccessful or ineffective. But simple morality demands that, whilst a particular policy is pursued, it must be pursued with all one's heart. It is simple policy to march along a certain route, but the soldier who marches with an unsteady step along that route is liable to be summarily dismissed. I become therefore incredulous when people talk to me sceptically about non-violence or are seized with fright at the very mention of the word non-violence. If they do not believe in the expedient of non-violence, they must denounce it but not claim to believe in the expedient when their heart resists it. How disastrous it would be, if, not believing in violence even as an expedient, I joined, say a violence party and approached a gun with a perturbed heart! The reader will believe me when I say that I have the capacity for killing a fly. But I do not believe in killing even flies. Now suppose I joined an expedition for fly killing as an expedient. Will I not be expected, before being permitted to join the expedition, to use all the available engines of destruction, whilst I remained in the army of fly killers? If those who are in the Congress and the Khilafat Committees will perceive this simple truth, we shall certainly either finish the struggle this year to a successful end, or be so sick of non-violence as to give up the pretention and set about devising some other programme.

I hold that Swami Shraddhanandji has been needlessly criticised for the proposition he intended to move. His argument is absolutely honest. He thinks that we, as a body, do not really believe in non-violence even as a policy. Therefore, we shall never fulfil the programme of Non-violence. Therefore, he says, let us go to the Councils and get what crumbs we may. He was trying to show the unreality of the position of those who believe in the policy with their lips, whereas they are looking forward to violence for final deliverance. I do say that, if Congressmen do not fully *believe* in the policy, they are doing an injury to the country by pretending to follow it. If violence is to be the basis of future government, the Councillors are undoubtedly the wisest. For it is through the Councils that, by the same devices by which the present administrators rule us, the Councillors hope to seize power from the former's hands. I have little doubt that those who nurse violence in their bosoms will find no benefit from the lip-profession of Non-violence. I urge, therefore, with all the vehemence at my command, that those who do not believe in non-violence should secede from the Congress and from Non-co-operation and prepare to seek election or re-join law courts or Government colleges as the case may be. Let there be no manner of doubt that Swaraj established by non-violent means will be different in kind from the Swaraj that can be established by armed rebellion. Police and punishments there will be, even under such Swaraj. But there would be no room for brutalities such as we witness to-day both on the part of the people and the Government. And those, whether they call themselves Hindus or Mussalmans, who do not fully believe in the policy of Non-violence, should abandon both Non-co-operation and Non-violence.

For me, I am positive that neither in the Koran nor in the Mahabharata there is any sanction for and approval of the triumph of violence. Though there is repulsion enough in Nature, she *lives* by attraction. Mutual love enables Nature to persist. Man does not live by destruction. Self-love compels regard for others. Nations cohere, because there is mutual regard among the individuals composing them. Some day we must extend the national law to the universe, even as we have extended the family law to form nations—a larger family. God has ordained that India should be such a nation. For so far as reason can perceive, India cannot become free by armed rebellion for generations. India can become free by refraining form national violence. India has now become tired of rule based upon violence. That to me is the message of the plains. The people of the plains do not know what it is to put up an organised armed fight. And they must become free, for they want freedom. They have realised that power seized by violence will only result in their greater grinding.

Such, at any rate, is the reasoning that has given birth to the *policy*, not the *dharma*, of Non-violence. And even as a Mussalman or a Hindu, believing in violence, applies the creed of Non-violence in his family, so are both called upon without question to apply the policy of Non-violence in their mutual relations and in their relation to other races and classes, not excluding Englishmen. Those who do not believe in this policy and do not wish to live up to it in full, retard the movement by remaining in it.

9th March, 1920

NON-VIOLENCE

(BY M. K. GANDHI)

When a person claims to be non-violent, he is expected not to be angry with one who has injured him. He will not wish him harm; he will wish him well; he will not swear at him; he will not cause him any physical hurt. He will put up with all the injury to which he is subjected by the wrong doer. Thus Non-violence is complete innocence. Complete non-violence is complete absence of ill-will against all that lives. It therefore embraces even sub-human life, not excluding noxious insects or beasts. They have not been created to feed our destructive propensities. If we only knew the mind of the Creator, we should find their proper place in His creation. Non-violence is therefore in its active form good-will towards all life. It is pure Love. I read it in the Hindu Scriptures, in the Bible, in the Koran.

Non-violence is a perfect state. It is a goal towards which all mankind moves naturally though unconsciously. Man does not become divine when he personifies innocence in himself. Only then does he become truly man. In our present state, we are partly men and partly beasts and in our ignorance and even arrogance say that we truly fulfil the purpose of our species, when we deliver blow for blow and develop the measure of anger required for the purpose. We pretend to believe that retaliation is the law of our being, whereas in every scripture we find that retaliation is nowhere obligatory but only permissible. It is restraint that is obligatory. Retaliation is indulgence requiring elaborate regulating. Restraint is the law of our being. For highest perfection is unattainable without highest restraint. Suffering is thus the badge of the human tribe.

The goal ever recedes from us. The greater the progress, the greater the recognition of our unworthiness. Satisfaction lies in the effort, not in the attainment. Full effort is full victory.

Therefore though I realise more than ever how far I am from that goal, for me the Law of complete Love is the law of my being. Each time I fail, my effort shall be all the more determined for my failure.

But I am *not* preaching this final law through the Congress or the Khilafat organisation. I know my own limitations only too well. I know that any such attempt is foredoomed to failure. To expect a whole mass of men and women to obey that law all at once is not to know its working. But I do preach from the Congress platform the deductions of the law. What the Congress and the Khilafat organisations have accepted is but a fragment of the implications of that Law. Given true workers, the limited measure of its application can be realised in respect of vast masses of people within a short time. But the little measure of it to be true must satisfy the same test as the whole. A drop of water must yield to the analyst the same results as a lakeful. The nature of my non-violence towards my brother cannot be diffierent from that of my non-violence to the universe. When I extend the love for my brother to the whole universe, it must still satisfy the same test.

A particular practice is a policy when its application is limited to time or space. Highest policy is therefore fullest practice. But honesty, as policy while it lasts is not anything different from honesty as a creed. A merchant believing in honesty as a policy will sell the same measure and quality of cloth to the yard as a merchant with honesty as a creed. The difference between the two is that, while the political merchant will leave his honesty when it does not pay, the believing one will continue it, even though he should lose his all.

The political non-violence of the Non-co-operator does not stand this test in the vast majority of cases. Hence the prolongation of the struggle. Let no one blame the unbending English nature. The hardest fibre must melt in the fire of love. I cannot be dislodged from that position because I know it. When British or other nature does not respond, the fire is not strong enough, if it is there at all.

Our non-violence need not be of the strong, but it *has* to be of the truthful. We must not intend harm to the English or to our co-operating countrymen, if and whilst we claim to be non-violent. But the majority of us *have* intended harm, and we have refrained from doing it because of our weakness or under the ignorant belief that mere refraining from physical hurt amounted to a due fulfilment of our pledge. Our pledge of non-violence excludes the possibility of future retaliation. Some of us seem unfortunately to have merely postponed the date of revenge.

Let me not be misunderstood. I do not say that the policy of non-violence excludes the possibility of revenge when the policy is abandoned. But it does most emphatically exclude the possibility of future revenge after a successful termination of the struggle. Therefore, whilst we are pursuing the policy of non-violence, we are bound to be actively friendly to English administrators and their co-operators. I felt ashamed when I was told that in some parts of India it was not safe for Englishmen or well-known co-operators to move about safely. The disgraceful scenes that took place at a recent Madras meeting were a complete denial of non-violence. Those who howled down the Chairman because he was supposed to have insulted me, disgraced themselves and their policy. They wounded the heart of their friend and helper, Mr. Andrews. They injured their own cause. If the Chairman believed that I was a scoundrel, he had a perfect right to say so. Ignorance is no provocation. But a Non-co-operator is pledged to put up with the gravest provocation. Provocation there would be, when I act scoundrel-like. I grant that it will be enough to absolve every Non-co-operator from the pledge of Non-violence and that any Non-co-operator will be fully justified in taking my life for misleading him.

It may be that even cultivation of such limited non-violence is impossible in the majority of cases. It may be that we must not expect people even out of self-interest not to *intend* harm to the opponent whilst they are *doing* none. We must then, to be honest, clearly give up the use of the word 'non-violence' in connection with our struggle. The alternative need not be immediate resort to violence. But the people will not then be called upon to subject themselves to any discipline in non-violence. A person like me will not then feel called upon to shoulder the responsibility for Chauri Chaura.* The school of limited non-violence will then still flourish in its obscurity, but without the terrible burden of responsibility it carries to-day.†

* Riots broke out at Chauri Chaura in the United Provinces earlier in the year which necessitated the suspension of the Civil Disobedience campaign. For details, *see* appendix.

† Mr. Gandhi amplified his views in the following notes in *Young India* of 9th March, 1922 :

Perplexed.—A correspondent from Lahore writes under date 3rd March :

" So far as the facts about ' Bardoli decision' have come to light, it appears the decision was arrived at either under the influence of Pundit Malaviya or under some far-fetched notions of non-violence. In the former case the act is most unworthy, and in the latter it is most unwise. Is not the ideal of the Congress Swaraj and not non-violence ? People have imbibed non-violence generally, which surely must do for the Congress purpose. How the breaches like those at Bombay and Gorakhpur can make the engine come to a standstill, I cannot understand. And if M. Paul Richard (as to M. Richard's views, see *infra*) is true as to your aspirations of a World Leader through non-violence even at the cost of Indian interest, it is surely unbecoming and, excuse me to say, dishonest.

" And have you realised the effects of this sudden stand still ? Mr.

But if Non-violence is to remain the policy of the nation, for its fair name and that of humanity, we are bound to carry it out to the letter and in the spirit.

Montagu's threat comes for that. Lord Reading and his Government are harder to us than ever before. It had almost yielded. As to the public, there is a general distrust prevailing among the classes and the masses. Surely it is difficult to make men play-things of the hour and their disgust and disappointment show how the fight was carried on in right earnest. Dont't you perceive that it is a shock and that two such shocks must enervate the combatants altogether ?

"Besides, I have heard the responsible Mussalmans talk of withdrawing co-operation even from the Hindus. The fight is religious with them. It is the 'Jehad', I should say God's Command and the Prophet's is no joke to start and to stop the 'Jehad' at will. If the Hindus should retire, they say they must devise their own course. Will you take care to ease one's heart that feels uneasy on this account ?"

It is impossible to withhold sympathy from the writer. His letter is typical of the attitude I saw reflected in Delhi. I have already given the assurance that Pundit Malaviyaji had nothing to do with the Bardoli decision. Nor have any 'far-fetched notions of non-violence' anything to do with it. The correspondent's letter is the best justification for it. To me the Bardoli decision is the logical outcome of the national pledge of limited non-violence. I entirely endorse the opinion that Swaraj is the nation's goal, not non-violence. It is true that my goal is as much Swaraj as non-violence, because I hold Swaraj for the masses to be unattainable save through non-violence. But have I not repeatedly said in these columns that I would have India to become free even by violence rather than that she should remain in bondage ? In slavery she is a helpless partner in the violence of the slave-holder. It is however true that I could not take part in a violent attempt at deliverance if only because I do not believe in the possibility of success by violence. I cannot pull the trigger against my worst enemy. If I succeed in convincing the world of the supremacy of the law of non-violence and the futility of violence for the progress of mankind, the correspondent will find that India will have automatically gained her end. But I freely confess my utter inability to do so without first convincing India that she can be free only by non-violent and truthful means and no other.

And if we intend to follow out the policy, if we believe in it, we must then quickly make up with the Englishmen and the co-operators. We must get their

---

I must further confess that what Mr. Montagu and Lord Reading would think of the decision did not concern me and therefore their threats do not perturb or affect me. Nor should they affect any non-co-operator. He burnt his boats when he embarked upon his mission. But this I know that if India becomes non-violent in intent, word and deed, even the hearts of Mr. Montagu and Lord Reading will be changed. As it is, marvellous though our progress has been in non-violent action, our hearts and our speech have not become non-violent. Mr. Montagu and Lord Reading do not believe in the sincerity of our profession or in the possibility of sincere workers succeeding in creating a truly non-violent atmosphere. What is therefore required is more and yet more non-violence 'in intent', word and deed.

As for the people, I have little doubt that they will survive the purifying shock. I regard the present depression as a prelude to steady progress. But should it prove otherwise, the truth of the Bardoli decision cannot be denied. It stands independent of public approval. God *is*, even though the whole world deny Him. Truth *stands*, even if there be no public support. It is self-sustained.

I should be sorry, indeed, if responsible Mussalmans will not see the obvious corollaries of non-violence. In my opinion, the fight is as religious with Hindus as with Mussalmans. I agree that ours is a spiritual 'Jehad'. But 'Jehad' has, like all other wars, its strict restrictions and limitations. The Hindus and Mussalmans sail in the same boat. The dissatisfaction is common to both and it is open to both to dissolve partnership with each other. Either or both may also depose me from generalship. It is purely a partnership at will. Finally I assure the correspondent that, when I find that I cannot carry conviction home to the people, I shall withdraw from the command myself.

Other Implications.—I invite the reader to study the leading article (given above) of the week on non-violence. The article became fairly long even with a discussion of the main principles. I did not therefore discuss the important side issues in it but reserved them for the Notes.

Such for instance are the questions:

(1) When can even individual Civil Disobedience be resumed?

certificate that they feel absolutely safe in our midst and that they may regard us as friends, although we belong to a radically different school of thought and politics. We must welcome them to our political platforms as honoured guests. We must meet them on neutral

---

(2) What kind of violence will stop Civil Disobedience ?

(3) Is there room for self-defence in the limited conception of Non-violence ?

(4) Supposing the Mussalmans or the Hindus secede, can a non-violent campaign be carried on by one communty alone ?

(5) Supposing Hindus and Mussalmans both reject me, what would become of my preaching ?

I shall take the questions seriatim. Civil Disobedience—even individual civil disobedience—requires a tranquil atmosphere. It must not be commenced till the workers have assimilated the spirit of Non-violence and have procured a certificate of merit from the co-operators whether English or Indian, *i.e.*, till they have really ceased to think ill of them. The surest test will be when our meetings are purged of intolerance and our writings of bitterness. Another necessary test will be our serious handling of the constructive programme. If we cannot settle down to it, to me it will be proof positive of our disbelief in the capacity of Non-violence to achieve the purpose.

Non-violent Atmosphere—It is not every kind of violence that will stop Civil Disobedience. I should not be dismayed by family feuds even though they may be sanguinary. Nor will the violence of robbers baffle me though they would be to me an indication of the absence of general purification. It is political violence which *must* stop Civil Disobedience. Chauri Chaura was an instance of political violence. It arose from a political demonstration which we should have avoided if we were not capable of conducting it absolutely peacefully. I did not allow Malabar and Malegaon to interrupt our course, because the Moplahs were a special people and they had not come under the influence of non-violence to any appreciable extent. Malegaon is more difficult, but there is clear evidence that the chief Non-co-operators had tried their best to prevent the murders. Nor was mass Civil Disobedience imminent at the time. It could not interrupt individual civil disobedience elsewhere.

platforms as comrades. We must devise methods of such meeting. Our non-violence must not breed violence, hatred and ill-will. We stand like the rest of fellow mortals to be judged by our works. A programme of Non-violence for the attainment of Swaraj necessarily means ability to conduct our affairs on non-violent lines. That means inculcation of a spirit of obedience. Mr. Churchill, who understands only the gospel of force, is quite right in saying that the Irish problem is different in character from the Indian. He means in effect that the Irish having fought their way to their Swaraj through violence will be well able to maintain it by violence, if need be. India, on the other hand, if she wins Swaraj in reality by Non-violence, must be able to maintain it chiefly by non-violent means. This Mr. Churchill can hardly believe to be possible unless India proves her ability by an ocular demonstration of the principle. Such a demonstration is impossible, unless Non-violence has permeated society so that people in their *corporate, i.e.,* political, life respond to non-violence; in other words civil instead of military authority, as at present, gains predominance.

Swaraj by non-violent means can therefore never mean an interval of chaos and anarchy. Swaraj by non-violence must be a progressively peaceful revolution such that the transference of power from a close corporation to the people's representatives will be as natural as the dropping of a fully ripe fruit from a well-nurtured tree. I say again that such a thing may be quite impossible of attainment. But I know that nothing less is the implication of Non-violence. And if the present workers do not believe in the probability of achieving such comparatively non-violent atmosphere, they should drop the non-violent programme and frame another which is wholly different in character. If we approach our programme with the mental reservation that after all we shall wrest the power from the British by force of arms, then we are untrue to our profession of Non-violence.* If

* Mr. Gandhi was never tired of emphasising that no provocation would justify resort to violence. The following appeared in *Young India* of 1st December, 1921 :

Beware of Rumours.—One of the many lessons to be learnt from the events is that we must never believe rumours and that we must have Congress and Khilafat officers in every ward or large street where people can verify rumours. If we are acting as one man with one mind, and we must if we are to succeed—we must learn never to act without thinking and on mere rumours. Three-fourths of the panic was caused by mischievous rumours. What does it matter if the people hear of temples destroyed or some big leader killed or injured ? They may not act without advice. Does an individual soldier act on his own behalf on hearing of a general's death or of a desecration of his mosque or temple ? If he were to act so, he would harm the cause and be liable even to be shot. It is much more necessary for us to act in concert when we are willing soldiers of peace and more capable of restraint than armed soldiers and when we have to win not a single battle but the freedom of our country and religions.

In Young India of 13th July, 1921, the following note appeared :

Difficulties in the Way—I am note however blind to the difficulties that bestrew our path. The news from Aligarh is disquieting. I have seen the official version and the other in the *Independent* I shall apologise to the people of Aligadh if I find that I am in the wrong, but the *Independent* correspondent's version is evasive and attempts to prove too much. It does not deny incendiarism on the part of the mob, and seeks entirely to exculpate the latter. I shall require overwhelmingly strong evidence to prove that the authorities in Aligarh acted wantonly and maliciously without the slightest provocation. I am quite prepared to find that the police wanted to prevent an aggressive demonstration on the part of the mob, and that in so doing they lost self-restraint and opened fire. My point, however, is that there should be no aggressiveness on our part at all. Non-co-operators must not bully or threaten. We are developing quite an irresistible courage which comes only from waiting upon God, in other words, from absolute faith in the righteousness of our

we believe in our programme, we are bound to believe that the British people are not unamenable to the force of affection, as they are undoubtedly amenable to force

cause. If we want to finish our programme successfully and during this year, we have no time for bluster or a show of force. We must be scrupulously truthful to our pledge. We can succeed beyond all expectation, only if we remain non-violent in thought, word and deed. It need not be our final creed, but it must be our present creed for the attainment of our goal. There need be no difficulty in our not thinking or speaking ill of our adversary, as we have found it easy enough on the whole to restrain ourselves from doing ill to him. We must not use the pledge of non-violence and truth to cover violence and exaggeration, if not untruth. Nor must we be afraid to let our best comrades go to jail. I adhere to the belief so often expressed by me, that Pandit Sundarlal and now Pandit Makhanlal are serving the community better by being in jail for the sake of conscience, than they would have being free. Those who think otherwise, in my opinion, do not understand the dynamics of Non-co-operation. The dynamic force behind this great movement is not vocal propaganda, but the silent propaganda carried on by the sufferings of the innocent victims of a mad Government.

Mr. Gandhi wrote in *Young India* of 6th October, 1921, under the heading, *an Apt Anecdote*: Maulana Azad Sobani, who has been doing wonderful work for Swadeshi, was telling me a thrilling story of Egyptian coolness and bravery. He told me that once the soldiers surrounded an Egyptian mosque and wanted to prevent nationalist propaganda inside it. The congregation was listening to a young man speaking to it. He would not desist and was shot. The congregation remained unmoved. Another young man took up the discourse and was shot whilst he was going on, and thus seven young men were shot till the discourse was finished, the congregation remaining unmoved all the while the glorious sacrifice was going on. The Egyptains do not believe in non-violence. But they are fine soldiers. They did not want the mosque to be blown to pieces nor the whole congregation in a vain attempt to retaliate. They wanted to show that they would not be cowed down, and no orders could bend their spirit. And so, as if nothing had happened, the discourse was finished. Death and life became with the congregation synonymous terms. The moral of the story is unmistakable. We who are pledged to

of arms. For the unbelievers, the Councils are undoubtedly the school of learning with their heavy programme of humiliations spread over a few generations or a rapid but bloody revolution probably never witnessed before in the world. I have no desire to take part in such a revolution. I will not be a willing instrument for promoting it. The choice, in my opinion, lies between honest Non-violence

---

non-violence are endeavouring to cultivate the bravery of the seven young Egyptians and the congregation. We must acquire the courage to face death in the pursuit of our goal without even wishing to kill, and victory during the remaining three months is a certainty.

On the use of arms, Mr. Gandhi wrote in *Young India* of 21st July, 1921:

The Kirpan.—The Kirpan, the Shikh scimitar, is for the Shikh, 'what', says the Secretary of the Shikh Young Man's Association, 'the sacred thread is to the Brahman.' And now the Punjab Government is trying to divest the Shikhs of their 'sacred thread' by restricting its length and breadth. Much as I abhor the possession or the use of arms, I cannot reconcile myself to forcible prohibition. As I said three years ago, this forcible disarmament of a people will be regarded by history as one of the blackest sins committed by the British Government against India. If people want to possess arms, they ought to have them without ado. But in the case of the Shikhs who have held Kirpans without let or hindrance all these years, the crime is worse. The Secretary has no difficulty in proving, that this war against the kirpan has synchronised with repressive measures adopted against this brave community. The reason too is obvious. The Shikhs have attained political consciousness. They are not content merely to kill at the bidding of their officers. They want to weigh the pros and cons of a cause in which they are called upon to fight. Above all, they want to know where they come in! They want to become equal partners. This is intolerable, and they must be put down. The bravest among them have, as the Government imagine, been silenced. I can only hope, that rather than surrender their sacred weapon, the Shikhs will court imprisonment. We cannot learn discipline by compulsion. We must learn not to use arms or to use them with responsibility and self-restraint, notwithstanding the right to possess them.

with Non-co-operation as its necessary corollary, or reversion to responsive co-operation, *i.e.*, co-operation *cum* obstruction.

8th December, 1920

SOCIAL BOYCOTT

(BY M. K. GANDHI)

A correspondent writes from Hyderabad (Sind) a letter* regarding boycott which I gladly publish. He refers to what is alleged to have happened to Mr. Khaparde. Hyderabad (Sind) is a far cry from Amraoti. I do not know that Mr. Khaparde has been put to all the inconveniences that the correspondent relates. Mr. Khaparde is well able to take care of himself. I hope, however, that there is much exaggeration in the information supplied to the correspondent about the treatment.

Nevertheless, the issue raised by the correspondent is important and serious. It would be a dangerous thing if, for differences of opinion, we were to proclaim social boycott.

It would be totally opposed to the doctrine of Non-violence to stop the supply of water and food. This battle of Non-co-operation is a programme of propaganda by reducing profession to practice, not one of compelling others to yield obedience by violence direct or indirect. We must try patiently to convert our opponents. If we wish to evolve the spirit of democracy out of slavery, we must be scrupulously exact in our dealings with opponents. We may not replace the slavery of the Government by that of the Non-co-operationists. We must concede to our opponents the freedom we claim for

* Omitted in this collection

ourselves and for which we are fighting. The stoutest co-operationist will bend to the stern realities of practice if there is real response from the people.

But there is a non-violent boycott which we shall be bound to practise, if we are to make any impression. We must not compromise with what we believe to be an untruth, whether it resides in a white skin or a brown. Such boycott is political boycott. We may not receive favours from the new Councillors. The voters, if they are true to their pledge, will be bound to refrain from making use of the services of those whom they have declined to regard as their representatives. They must ratify their verdict by complete abstention from any encouragement of the so-called representatives.

The public will be bound, if they are Non-co-operationists, to refrain from giving these representatives any prestige by attending their political functions or parties.

I can conceive the possibility of non-violent social ostracism under certain extreme conditions, when a defiant minority refuses to bend to the majority, not out of any regard for principle, but from sheer defiance or worse. But that time has certainly not arrived. Ostracism of a violent character, such as the denial of the use of public wells is a species of barbarism, which I hope will never be practised by any body of men having any desire for national self-respect and national uplift. We will free neither Islam nor India by processes of coercion,* whether among ourselves or against Englishmen.

* *Young India* of 2nd February 1922, contained the following :

Sitting Dhurna—Some students of Calcutta have revived the ancient form of barbarity in the form of 'sitting dhurna'. Fortunately, the practice was stopped as soon as it was revived. They blocked the passage of their fellow students who wanted to go to the University for paying their fees or to see some officials of the educational department. I call it 'barbarity', for it is a crude way of

16*th February*, 1921

SOCIAL BOYCOTT

(BY M. K. GANDHI)

Non-co-operation being a movement of purification is bringing to the surface all our weaknesses as also excesses of even our strong points. Social boycott is an age-old institution. It is coeval with caste. It is the one terrible sanction exercised with great effect. It is based upon the notion that a community is not bound to extend its hospitality or service to an excommunicate. It answered when every village was a self-contained unit, and the occasions of recalcitrancy were rare. But when opinion is divided, as it is to-day, on the merits of Non-co-operation, when its new application is having a trial, a summary use of social boycott in order to bend a minority to the will of the majority is a species of unpardonable violence. If persisted in, such boycott is

---

using coercion, It is also cowardly because one who sits 'dhurna' knows that he is not going to be trampled over. It is difficult to call the practice violent, but it is certainly worse. If we fight our opponent, we at least enable him to return the blow. But when we challenge him to walk over us, *knowing* that he will not, we place him in a most awkward and humiliating position. I know that the over-zealous students who sat *dhurna* never thought of the barbarity of the deed. But one, who is expected to follow the voice of conscience and stand even singlehanded in the face of odds, cannot afford to be thoughtless. Non-co-operation, if it fails, will fail only through internal weakness. There is no such thing as defeat in Non-co-operation. It never fails. Its so-called representatives may so badly represent their cause that it may appear to the spectators to have failed. Let Non-co-operationists therefore beware of everything they do. There must be no impatience, no barbarity, no insolence, no undue pressure. If we want to cultivate a true spirit of democracy, we cannot afford to be intolerant. Intolerance betrays want of faith in one's cause.—M. K. G.

bound to destroy the movement. Social boycott is applicable and effective when it is not felt as a punishment and accepted by the object of boycott as a measure of discipline. Moreover, social boycott to be admissible in a campaign of Non-violence must never savour of inhumanity. It must be civilised. It must cause pain to the party using it, if it causes inconvenience to its object. Thus, depriving a man of the services of a medical man, as is reported to have been done in Jhansi, is an act of inhumanity tantamount in the moral code to an attempt to murder. I see no difference in murdering a man and withdrawing medical aid from a man who is on the point of dying. Even the laws of war, I apprehend, require the giving of medical relief to the enemy in need of it. To deprive a man of the use of an only village well is notice to him to quit that village. Surely, Non-co-operators have acquired no right to use that extreme pressure against those who do not see eye to eye with them. Impatience and intolerance will surely kill this great religious movement. We may not make people pure by compulsion. Much less may we compel them by violence to respect our opinion.* It is utterly against the spirit of democracy we want to cultivate.

* *In Young India* of 9th March, 1922, commenting on a letter received by him from a well-known resident of Feni in the Noakhali Dt. Bengal alleging that the Congress Volunteer corps had become an organisation for bad characters, that the whole country thereabout was under it and that these were guilty of extortion, terrorism and humiliating rowdyism, Mr. Gandhi wrote asking the Congress Committee to enquire :

An inquiry therefore is a simple matter. Meanwhile, as I know that publication is also half the remedy, I gladly place the columns of *Young India* at the disposal of those who can send authentic instances of intimidation, coercion, assaults, social boycott by or on behalf of Non-co-operators whether Congressmen or Khilafatists. Indeed every Congressman is a Khilafatist, and every Khilafatist is a Congressman,

There are no doubt serious difficulties in our way. The temptation to resort to social boycott is irresistible when a defendant, who submits to private arbitration, refuses to abide by its award. Yet it is easy to see that the application of social boycott is more than likely to arrest the splendid movement to settle disputes by arbitration which, apart from its use as a weapon in the armoury of Non-co-operation, is a movement fraught with great good to the country. People will take time before they accommodate themselves to private arbitration. Its very simplicity and inexpensiveness will repel many people even as palates jaded by spicy foods are repelled by simple combinations. All awards will not always be above suspicion. We must therefore rely upon the intrinsic merits of the movement and the correctness of awards to make itself felt.

It is much to be desired if we can bring about a complete *voluntary* boycott of law courts. That one event can bring about Swaraj. But it was never expected that we would reach completion in any single item of Non-co-operation. Public opinion has been so far

---

but since we have two organisations in the country I appeal to both to be merciless in exposing our own wrong-doing. I could find a thousand excuses for the wrong-doing of the administrators if only because we impute to them nothing better, whereas we claim to be immaculate so far as Non-violence and honesty are concerned. We shall bring the struggle to a successful issue far more quickly by being strict with ourselves. There is no excuse whatsoever for intimidation, coercion, assault or social boycott on our part. I would urge the correspondents, who may send me letters of complaints, to be brief, strictly accurate and to write in a clear hand on one side of the paper only. It is not an easy matter to go through the heavy correspondence pouring in from day to day. Compliance with this simple request will ensure quicker attention. Correspondents will take care to avoid vague generalisations. Specific details as in the Noakhali letter are absolutely necessary to inspire belief and to assist inquiry.

developed as to recognise the Courts as signs not of our liberty but of our slavery. It has made it practically impossible for lawyers to practise their profession and be called popular leaders.

Non-co-operation has greatly demolished the prestige of law courts and to that extent of the Government. The disintegrating process is slowly but surely going on. Its velocity will suffer diminution if violent methods are adopted to hasten it. This Government of ours is armed to the teeth to meet and check forces of Non-violence. How can a handful of Englishmen resist a voluntary expression of opinion accompanied by the voluntary self-denial of thirty crores of people ?

I hope, therefore, that Non-co-operation workers will beware of the snares of social boycott. But the alternative to social boycott is certainly not social intercourse.* A man who defies strong clear public opinion on vital matters is not entitled to social amenities and privileges. We may not take part in his social functions such as marriage feasts, we may not receive gifts from him. But we dare not deny social service. The latter is a duty. Attendance at dinner parties and the like is a privilege which it is optional to withhold or extend. But it would be wisdom to err on the right side and to exercise the weapon even in the limited sense described by me on rare and well-defined occasions. And in every case the user of the weapon will use it at his own risk. The use of it is not as yet in any form a duty. No one is entitled to its use, if there is any danger of hurting the movement.

* Further commenting on social ostracism Mr. Gandhi wrote in *Young India* of 28th April, 1920 :

A writer in the *Times of India*, the Editor of that wonderful daily and Mrs. Besant have all in their own manner condemned Non-

18*th December*, 1920

(BY M. K. GANDHI)

The columns of "Young India" are open to all who have any grievance against Non-co-operators. 'One who knows' has sent to the Editor a letter which I gladly publish.* He has in a covering letter given his name and pleaded for the publication of his letter. Such pleading was unnecessary in connection with a matter

* Omitted in this collection.

---

co-operation conceived in connection with the Khilafat movement. All the three writings naturally discuss many side-issues which I shall omit for the time being. I propose to answer two serious objections raised by the writers. The sobriety with which they are stated entitles them to a greater consideration than if they had been given in violent language. In Non-co-operation, the writers think, it would be difficult, if not impossible, to avoid violence. Indeed violence, the *Times of India* editorial says, has already commenced in that ostracism has been resorted to in Calcutta and Delhi. Now I fear that ostracism to a certain extent is impossible to avoid. I remember, in South Africa, in the initial stages of passive resistance campaign those who had fallen away were ostracised. Ostracism is violent or peaceful according to the manner in which it is practised. A congregation may well refuse to recite prayers after a priest who prizes his title above his honour. But the ostracism will become violent if the individual life of a person is made unbearable by insults, innuendoes or abuse. The real danger of violence lies in the people resorting to Non co-operation, becoming impatient and revengeful. This may happen, if, for instance, payment of taxes is suddenly withdrawn or if pressure is put upon soldiers to lay down their arms. I, however, do not fear any evil consequences, for the simple reason that every responsible Mahomedan understands that Non-co-operation to be successful must be totally unattended with violence. The other objection raised is that those who may give up their service may have to starve. That is just a possibility but a remote one, for the committee will certainly make due provision for those who may suddenly find themselves out of employment.

of public importance. If the facts related by the correspondent are true, they reflect no credit on the young men of Dharwad. The correspondent has connected the incident with Non-co-operation. It is the fashion nowadays to connect every incident of indecent behaviour with Non-co-operation. I wish that the incident had been brought to my notice when I was at Dharwad. I would then have been able to investigate the matter and dealt with it then. I may state that stones were thrown at a meeting of Dharwad students that was held by me in the open. One boy narrowly escaped being seriously hurt. And it was a pleasure to watch the audience remaining unmoved in spite of the stone-throwing. I was told too that stone-throwing at meetings was not an unusual occurrence at Dharwad in connection with the non-Brahmin movement. I state this fact only to show that Dharwad enjoys the unenviable reputation for stone-throwing in a special manner. I must therefore decline to connect the incident either with Non-co-operation or with any anti-European movement. Though the correspondent's letter is obscure on the point, it is evident from what he says that resentment was felt at the idea of girls taking part in a drama. The correspondent says that the drama was dropped 'in the nick of time at the desire of the guardians.' There must have been persistence to provoke resentment.

But my position is clear. No amount of provocation could possibly justify the hooliganism of the 'mob of young men'. They had no right to prevent the performance that was at last determind upon, if the guardians of the girls did not mind it. The truest test of democracy is in the ability of anyone to act as he likes, so long as he does not injure the life or property of anyone else. It is impossible to control public morals by hooliganism. Public opinion alone can keep a society pure and healthy. If the young men of Dharwad did not like a public exhibition of Dharwad girls on the stage, they should have held public meetings and otherwise enlisted public opinion in their favour. The movement of Non-co-operation is intended to check all such abuses. Non-co-operationists are undoubtedly expected, not only to refrain from taking part in such violent scenes as are represented to have taken place at Dharwad, but they are expected also to prevent them on the part of others. The success of Non-co-operation depends upon the ability of Non-co-operationists to control all forces of violence. All may not take part in the programme of self-sacrifice but all must recognise the necessity of non-violence in word or deed.

I am surprised that the correspondent in his covering letter speaks of the hooliganism at Dharwad in the same breath as the massacre of Jallianwala Bagh. He loses all sense of proportion when he compares the cold-blooded and calculated butchery of innocent men, who had given no provocation, with the undisciplined and thoughtless demonstration of a 'mob of young men,' who were labouring under a fancied or real wrong. Both acts are worthy of condemnation. But there is as much difference between the programme of the Dharwad boys and the Dyerism at Amritsar as there is between an attempt at simple hurt and a completed murder.

10th November, 1919

DIFFICULTIES IN OUR WAY

(By M. K. Gandhi)

Our difficulties are of two kinds; those that are imposed from without and those that are of our own creation. The latter are far more dangerous, because we often hug them and are therefore reluctant to remove them. Thus, for instance, the disturbance created at Mrs. Besant's recent meetings at Bombay was of our own making. * And it is easier to deal with a seditious meetings proclamation than the disturbance at Mrs. Besant's meetings. A prohibition of 'seditious' meetings gives

* Mr. Gandhi condemned hooliganism wherever found. He wrote in *Young India* of 23rd February, 1921:

Certainly, Non-co-operation has received a rude shock by disgraceful behaviour at the Bombay and Poona meetings towards Messrs. Shastri and Paranjpye. I have seen the explanation that the hooliganism was resorted to, not by Non-co-operation students but by those who wanted to discredit the movement itself, and to rouse prejudice against Non-co-operation students. The explanation is likely to be partly true, for there are undoubtedly men who would for the sake of killing the movement even create violence. For Non-co-operation to be speedily successful, we must be able to provide even against such contingencies. A soldier cannot plead difficulties in defence of his defeat. When General Buller failed to relieve Lady Smith, he was superseded. When Lord Roberts failed to finish the South African War, Lord Kitchener took over command. This Government will live on only so long as it can circumvent Non-co-operation. If Non-co-operation students did not want to be discredited, why did they attend the meeting either in Bombay or in Poona? The notices clearly stated that only those who wished to hear the other side of the question were to attend. There was, therefore, no excuse for the scenes that were enacted in Bombay and Poona. Moreover, it is often forgotten that Messrs. Shastri and Paranjpye are among the ablest and the most public-spirited men we have in the country. They are as much lovers of their country as Non-co-operators themselves. We may consider them to be mistaken in their view as they consider us to

us strength. Disturbances created by us undoubtedly weaken our cause. The verbal rowdyism at Mrs. Besant's meeting was a type of violence. It was a distinct departure from the creed of non-violent Non-co-operation. It may easily result in physical violence.

Those who created the disturbance ought to realise its seriousness for the sacred cause they have at heart. It is the very worst training we can give ourselves in Swaraj. Swaraj presupposes mutual toleration of views, no matter how distasteful they may be to us. If the Non-co-operationists refuse to listen to the other party's views, they lay themselves open to the same charge as the Government, which, they complain, comes to decisions without considering their view point. Non-co-operation against the Government, is based on, and is possible with, co-operation among ourselves. We must bring about, as far as possible and consistently with our creed, harmony among ourselves. Rowdyism is hardly the way to do so. By their action at the meetings in question, Non-co-operationists have still further estranged from themselves Mrs. Besant and her friends and followers. The loss is patent enough. They have certainly gained no new adherents by their rowdyism. In so far as the students were concerned in the insult offered to Mrs. Besant, they have discredited themselves at a critical period in their

be mistaken. But we shall grievously err if we refuse to listen to the arguments of our opponents.

Nor need we seek to justify rowdyism on the strength of English precedents. We may not call the movement religious and continue still to copy the bluster and violence of English meetings. Our strength lies in not copying foreign or other precedents without discrimination. This movement, if it is to be non-violent in essence, as it must be, to be successful, has to retain its distinctive character at every step and at all times—M. K. G.

evolution. They are called upon, in the name of religion and country, to disregard the wishes even of their parents, should they dissuade them from leaving schools tainted with Government grant or affiliation. Such disregard is permissible only to sons and daughters who have cultivated the sense of scrupulous respect and obedience towards their parents and elders: That disobedience is a virtue only when it is resorted to in response to a higher call and has not a trace of bitterness, hostility, or resentment in it. It is a positive vice when it becomes thoughtless, insolent, and rowdy. The one ennobles, the other degrades. And after all, do we not owe anything to Mrs. Besant's years, her past brilliant services, and her sex? The rising generation will commit suicide if it becomes ungrateful. India's gratefulness ought to ensure for Mrs. Besant a respectful hearing even when she opposes Indian sentiment. She does so from pure motives. She thinks that we are in error, she is of opinion that we are retarding India's progress. Surely it is her duty to wean us from what she considers is our error. And it is our duty respectfully to consider what she says.

But I have been told that unless, at her meetings, an emphatic dissent is expressed, she would make capital of our supposed silence, and claim that there is a larger body of Indian opinion at her back than is really the case. Surely rowdyism is not the only way of expressing dissent. The best and the chosen way would be not to attend her meetings, unless we wish to go in order to be convinced. We need not swell her audience when we know that we do not approve of her views. The other way, if we must attend, is to enter our respectful dissent at the end of the meeting, or if we consider her remarks to be offensive, to express our dissent by courteously walking out. A noisy demonstration is a sign of our weakness. A dignified withdrawal is a proof of our strength. Rowdyism is, as a rule, intended to cover a minority that wishes to break up a meeting. A majority conscious of its strength produces an eloquent and electrical effect both on the speaker, and his, or, her, minority of followers.

It is true that this rowdyism is not a result of the movement of Non-co-operation. It is a legacy of our past. We have been, to our harm, nurtured in the baneful traditions of the West in the manner of conducting our meetings. Applause and shouts of dissent are essentially a Western institution. With the new method of *non-violent* Non-co-operation, the old must go. The two cannot co-exist. If we are engaged in a duel between religion and irreligion, and if we truly represent the forces of religion, we shall have to give up even verbal violence and learn dignified ways of dealing with our opponents. It is through training in cool courage and self-sacrifice, discipline and faith in God, and therefore humility to the uttermost, that we shall conserve the honour of Islam and our country, and turn our opponents into admirers and fellow-workers.

24th May, 1920

LALA LAJPAT RAI AND THE MODERATES

Let me take the *Indian Social Reformer* into the secret of my methods.* My assistant drew my attention to the hostile criticism of Lalaji's speech and asked me whether I wished to say anything upon it. I had not

* Written in reply to a suggestion that Mr. Gandhi was condoning if not conniving at the violence of words of his followers.

the text of his speech before me, nor had seen any criticism. I therefore wrote to Lalaji, asking him to enlighten me on the matter, and suggesting that he should apologise, if a single hasty word was uttered. It has been my privilege on close acquaintance to find him generous, forgiving and frank. He said in his letter that his Bombay speech was a specially considered utterance, and that he had not attacked any person in it. He had only dealt with the action of the Moderates as a party. He sent me the cutting for my opinion. This was whilst I was in Sindh. I was unable to read it and had forgotten all about it, till the *Reformer's* rebuke reminded me of it. I have now read Lalaji's speech and have much pleasure in stating that I find nothing offensive or discourteous in it. It is undoubtedly in Lalaji's fighting style. It is a party speech. He has adopted, by long residence in the West, the Western form of criticism. But it is best Western form. There is nothing vulgar in it. His charges are not unjustified by the conduct of the Moderate Ministers. His worst charge is that they have merged themselves in the bureaucracy. It is a serious charge to make, but the instances adduced by him surely prove it. The Moderates may retort, if they choose, that outsiders cannot appreciate the difficulties of the Ministers. But that is just what proves the error of the great leaders who find themselves allied with the Government. They should have known that such would be their lot, or they should now know by experience that it is no use being Ministers, until they have an effective control over the Government policy. All the repression that is now going on, is almost as bad as before. It makes little difference that now there is the farce of a trial. The fact is that most of the politicial sections of the Penal

Code are such as to bring almost every Non-co-operation speech under them. I believe that, if I was charged, I should have to plead guilty to the charge of sedition. It is the duty of a Non-co-operator to preach disaffection towards the existing order of things. Non-co-operators are but giving disciplined expression to a nation's outraged feelings. I should like to see a considered reply to Lala Lajpat Rai's strong indictment. In my humble opinion, the speech of Lala Lajpat Rai does not betray any loss of temper, and is quite in keeping with the advice he tendered the youth of the country in his concluding paragraphs.

17th November, 1921

WHAT IS ABUSE ?

(BY M. K. GANDHI)

A correspondent from the United Provinces writes

"Now-a-days the atmosphere is surcharged with clamorous denunciations against the Government. Almost all have on their lips an inexhaustible fund of abuse for it. Everyone calls it wicked, uncivilised, and what not. Every one, as it were, makes it his special study how to outdo the rest in abusing the Government. Practically every speech is a mere list of invectives and imprecations. Not a single lecture but is replete with effusions and fulminations, and the fun of it is that only such a lecture is called soul-stirring. In short, the thing has come to a head. It has become a fashion as it were.

"I for my part heartily abhor this evil. Fuming and fretting, in my view, is indicative of weakness. It shows the total dearth of energy in doing real work on the part of the speaker, who wants to draw a veil on it by thundering forth before his audience his abusive eloquence. In my strict view of the matter, no angry word, not even against the Government, should be uttered. True, we are an injured nation, and our anger is a righteous one. But should we give vent to that anger by abuse ? Should we direct our energy in this channel? On the contrary, should we not profitably utilise whatever amount of energy we waste in abuse in doing substantial work? Surely abusing is not doing real work, nor is it a service to the motherland.

"Violence, to me, does not mean actually assaulting and killing others, but covers also bad language. If so, I cannot see how to justify your own use of the epithets, "satanic," "devilish" and "barbarous" for the Government. There is not the least shadow of doubt that these words come under violence, but that you being the apostle of non-violence utter violence is even in dream unimaginable.

So much for abusive language. Now I take up another question. You always say that you and your followers have arrayed yourselves against the English Government, and not against Englishmen. While you hate the system and want either to mend it or end it, you have absolutely no ill-feeling towards Englishmen themselves. Clearly therefore, though you want to do away with the system, you do not desire to expel the English. If so, even those who claim to be your true followers have not imbibed this high principle. I may substantiate this with a typical instance. in the U. P. Political Conference recently held at Agra Pt. Jawahirlal Nehru, while advocating the boycott of foreign cloth, said that if there were any who earnestly desired to expel the English from India, he was one of them, and the means he had found for achieving this was only Swadeshi. This has appeared in the press, and I think you might have read it. Now, can Pt. Jawahirlal Nehru be said to have understood your doctrine which makes us differentiate between a man and his action, so as to make it quite possible for us to condemn the man's action without bearing any ill-will towards him? Here at least, I can emphatically say that Nehruji's words can be justified in no case, but still I want to know whether you approve or disapprove of them."

In so far as Non-co-operators indulge in *abuse*, it is undoubtedly violence, and a breach of the pledge of Non-violence. But I must dissent from the opinion that 'practically every speech is a mere list of invectives and imprecations.' I assure the writer that the speeches are as full of invectives against ourselves as against the Government, and they are more full of argument in favour of Non-violence, Hindu-Muslim unity and Swadeshi than of invectives. The best proof of my statement perhaps is, that the people have made such wonderful response in all these three matters. Surely the people have not made the progress without having been effectively appealed to.

But after all, what is abuse? I find that the dictionary meaning is 'misuse, perversion, bad use.' When therefore we call a thief a thief or a rogue a rogue, we do not abuse him. A leper takes no offence, being described as such. Only the man using a particular adjective must mean it and be prepared to prove it. I am therefore unable to condemn the use of adjectives in every case and on every occasion, nor is the use of condemnatory adjectives always a sign of violence. I am fully aware that the use of even deserved adjectives may be a sign of violence, as it would be when it is used to excite violence against the person condemned. Condemnation is legitimately used when it is employed to wean the person from his bad habit or the audience from association with him. The Hindu Shastras are full of condemnation of evil-doers. They have pronounced curses upon them. Tulasidas who was the quality of mercy personified has filled the Ramayana with adjectives against the enemies of Rama, which it would be difficult to excel. Indeed the names themselves chosen for the evil-doers are significant of their qualities. Jesus did not hesitate to draw down divine wrath upon those whom he called 'a generation of vipers, hypocrites, whited sepulchres.' Buddha did not spare those who killed the innocent goats in the name of religion. Nor are the Koran or the Zend Avesta free from such use. Only all these seers and prophets had no evil intention in them. They had to describe persons and things as they were, and resort to language so as to enable us to make our choice between good and evil. Having said this much, I am at one with the writer that the more sparing we are in describing the Government or the Governors, the better it is for us. There is too much passion and too much evil in ourselves to warrant the constant use of offensive language. The best use we can make of this Government is to ignore its existence and to isolate it as much as possible from our life, believing that contact with it is corrupting and degrading.

I have said repeatedly that this movement is not intended to drive out the English; it is intended to end or mend the system they have forced upon us. I have not read Pandit Jawahirlal Nehru's speech* referred to by the correspondent, but I know him too well to believe that he could have said what is imputed to him. I know that he does not desire their withdrawal from wanton delight and that he will be the first man to harbour as a bosom friend every Englishman who is a lover of India and who wishes to remain as her servant indeed. Nor, even in an independent India, do we contemplate prohibition against the residence of Englishmen in our midst on terms settled by the future state of our hope.

8th September, 1920

DEMOCRACY *vs.* MOBOCRACY

(By M. K. Gandhi)

Looking at the surface there is but a thin dividing line between mob-law and the people's law. And yet the division is complete and will persist for all time.

* Pandit Jawahirlal subsequently wrote to *Young India* clearing himself of the charges against him.

India is to-day quickly passing through the mob-law stage. The use of the adverb signifies my hope. It may be our misfortune to have to pass through that process even in slow stages. But it is wisdom to adopt every means at our disposal to have done with that stage as quickly as possible.

There is much tendency on our part to yield to the rule of the mob. There was mob rule at Amristar on the 10th April, 1919. There was mob rule at Ahmedabad on the same fateful day. It represented undisciplined destruction and therefore it was thoughtless, profitless, wicked and harmful. War is disciplined destruction, much more bloody than any yet committed by mobs. And yet war has been apostrophised, because we have been deceived by the temporary but brilliant results achieved by some wars. So, if India has to achieve her freedom by violence, it will have to be by disciplined and honourable (in so far as it is possible to associate honour with violence) violence, named war. It will then be an act not of mobocracy, but democracy.

But my purpose to-day is not to write of mobocracy of the Ahmedabad type. I intend to deal with the type with which I am more familiar. The Congress is a demonstration for the mob and in that sense and that only. Though organised by thoughtful men and women, it may be called a mob-demonstration. Our popular demonstrations are unquestionably mob-demonstrations. During the memorable tour of the Khilafat mission through the Punjab, Sindh and Madras, I have had a surfeit of such demonstrations.* I have been

* Mr. Gandhi wrote in *Young India* of 27th October, 1920, under the heading, "Our late tour":

My experiences are becoming so much enriched by every tour that it is difficult for me to cope with them and give the results to the

ashamed to witness, at railway stations, thoughtless though unwitting destruction of passengers' luggage by demonstrators who, in their adoration of their heroes, have ignored everything else and everybody

---

reader. I must therefore content myself with adding to the stock on the necessity of discipline and organisation. I have dealt with our experiences up to the journey to Cawnpore. I was dreading our approach to Cawnpore—the Cawnpore of Maulana Hasrat Mohani and Dr. Murarilal. They are both great workers. The arrangements at the station were perfect. A large crowd awaited us at the station. But the discipline observed was so good that we were able to make our way through two solid rows of men without a single member moving before we had taken our seats in the cars. What might have meant a waste of thirty minutes was finished within five. The procession was happily abandoned. The programme was as business-like as the reception at the station. We reached at about 8 o'clock. We had only a day at our disposal, but during that time there was a meeting with the workers, a private interview with Mr. Frazier Hunt of the "Chicago Tribune", a visit to the Widows' Home, opening of a national Gujarati School, a meeting of the Gujarati ladies (a crowded ladies meeting), opening of a national arbitration court, an open-air meeting, and finally private chats with visitors. All this was finished without any undue rush and strain. There was at first a little confusion at the open-air meeting. It was discovered that no previous instructions were given to the volunteers. But after a little effort, there too perfect silence reigned, and the audience listened to three heavy speeches amid perfect silence. It is my conviction that as soon as we have organised and disciplined ourselves, *Swaraj* will be established. An organised refusal to be ruled by any foreign power is all that is needed in a country like ours. Lucknow was a contrast. . . . The night journey to Bhiwani was perfectly restless. Crowds insisted on *darshan*. One man suggested that Mahatmas needed no rest and that it was their duty to give *darshan*. Some were really angry that we all stolidly refused to move out of our beds. Another remarked that we must be highly inconsiderate not to respect the wishes of the people and get up to give *darshan*. At length tired and sleepless we reached Bhiwani. Probably fifty thousand people had gathered from surrounding villages. I was therefore afraid that we would be crushed to atoms. But to my agreeable surprise, I found

else. They have made, much to the discomfort of their heroes, unmusical and harsh noises. They have trampled upon one another. They have elbowed out one another. All have shouted, all at the same time, in the

---

perfect order there. There was no rush or noisy bustle at the station. All kept their respective places. The procession was comfortably managed in spite of a dense throng. Order observed at the Pandal was still more striking. It was a huge artistic but non-pretentious structure. There was not a single chair—not even for the President. Distinguished visitors were seated on a substantial and commodious platform erected in the midst of the Pandal. Although there was accommodation for 12,000 people, the Pandal appeared to be roomy. The approaches were wide. The ground was excavated to slope towards the centre. All therefore had a perfect view of the centre. The only suggestion I have to make is that a semi-circle is a better arrangement. There should be no seats at the back of the platform. The Sindh arrangement, referred to in these columns, of T inverted as T. is therefore better from an accoustic standpoint.

Let Bhiwani and Hyderabad (Sindh) present a lesson to the approaching Congress. The Reception Committee will save a few thousand rupees and much space if they will dispense with chairs whether on the platform or below. We must cater more and more for the masses and their leaders. We, the educated few, hope to control them only through the leaders of the masses who are as simple as the masses themselves. It is cruel to impose chairs on the many, because the few seem to want them.

Upon inquiry I found that this time people had come from neighbouring villages just for 'darshan.' This 'darshan' has become a most embarrassing process and consumes valuable time. It puts an undue strain upon my nerves and deprives me of the peace I need for writing during the odd moments I get during my travels. The difficulty is largely due to want of forethought and organisation. Workers must either organise these demonstrations in a methodical manner or not have them at all. Happily these are friendly demonstrations and therefore never cause trouble. But imagine the chaos that must ensue if we undertook hostile demonstrations. What would happen if we had to manage such crowds under fire or under angry excitement? I could see in Tundla that mass civil disobedience was an impossibility with a crowd like the one there. We can do no effective

holy name of order and peace. Ten volunteers have been heard to give the same order at the same time. Volunteers often become demonstrators instead of remaining people's policemen. It is a task often dangerous, always uncomfortable, for the heroes to be escorted through a broken chain of volunteers from the platform to the coach intended for them. Often it is a process which, although it should occupy no more than five minutes, has occupied one hour. The crowd, instead of pressing back, presses towards the heroes and who therefore require to be protected, The coach is taken possession of by anybody who dares, volunteers being the greatest sinners. The heroes and other lawful occupants have to reason with the intruders that they may not mount the footboards in that summary fashion. The hood of the coach is roughly handled by the processionists. It is not often that I have seen hoods of motors left undamaged by crowds. On the route instead of crowds lining the streets, they follow the coach. The result is confusion worse confounded. Every moment there is danger of accidents. That there is rarely any accident at such demonstrations is not due to the skill of the organisers, but the crowd is determined to put up with all jostling and retain its perfect good humour. In spite of everyone jostling everyone else, one has the slightest *wish* to inconvenience one's neighbour. To finish the picture, there is the meeting, an ever-growing cause of anxiety. You face nothing but disorder, din, pressing, yelling and shouting there.

---

work unless we can pass instructions to the crowd and expect implicit obedience. Volunteers must therefore undergo training in handling crowds. An Indian crowd is easily the most manageable and docile in the world. But it needs previous preparation. And when we have not had it, it is the wisest thing not to bring together crowds.

A good speaker arrests the attention of the audience. and there is order such that you can hear a pin drop.

All the same this is mobocracy. You are at the mercy of the mob. So long as there is sympathy between you and the mob, everything goes well. Immediately that cord is broken, there is horror. An Ahmedabad episode now and then gives you the mob psychology.

We must then evolve order out of chaos. And I have no doubt that the best and the speediest method is to introduce the people's law instead of mob-law.

One great stumbling block is that we have neglected music. Music means rhythm, order. Its effect is electrical. It immediately soothes. I have seen, in European countries, a resourceful superintendent of police by starting a popular song controlling the mischievous tendencies of mobs. Unfortunately, like our Shastras. music has been the prerogative of the few, either the banter of prostitutes or high class religious devotees. It has never become nationalised in the modern sense. If I had any influence with volunteers, boy scouts and Seva Samiti organisations, I would make compulsory a proper singing in company of national songs. And to that end I should have great musicians attending every Congress or Conference and teaching mass music.

Much greater discipline, method and knowledge must be exacted from volunteers and no chance comer should be accepted as a full-pledged volunteer. He only hinders rather than helping. Imagine the consequence of the introduction of one untrained soldier finding his way into an army at war. He can disorganise it in a second. My greatest anxiety about Non-co-operation is not the slow response of the leaders, certainly not the well-meant and even ill-meant criticism, never unadulterated repression. The movement will overcome these obstacles.

It will go in even strength from them. But the greatest obstacle is that we have not yet emerged from the mobocratic stage. But my consolation lies in the fact that nothing is so easy as to train mobs, for the simple reason that they have no mind, no premeditation. They act in a frenzy.

They repent quickly. Our organised Government does not repent of its fiendish crimes at Jallianwala, Lahore, Kasur, Akalgarh, Ramnagar, etc. But I have drawn tears from repentant mobs at Gujaranwalla and everywhere a frank acknowledgment of repentance from those who formed the mob during that eventful month of April. Non-co-operation I am therefore now using in order to evolve democracy. And I respectfully invite all the doubting leaders to help by refusing to condemn, in anticipation, a process of national purification, training and sacrifice.

Next week I hope to give some illustrations of how in a moment order was evolved out of mob disorder. My faith in the people is boundless. Theirs is an amazingly responsive nature. Let not the leaders distrust them. This chorus of condemnation of Non-co-operation when properly analysed means nothing less than distrust of the people's ability to control themselves. For the present I conclude this somewhat lengthy article by suggesting some rules for guidance and immediate execution.

1. There should be no raw volunteers accepted for big demonstrations. Therefore, none but the most experienced should be at the head.

2. Volunteers should have a general instructions book on their persons.

3. At the time of demonstrations, there must be a review of volunteers at which special instructions should be given.

4. At stations, volunteers should not all be centred at one point, namely, where the reception committee should be. But they should be posted at different points in the crowd.

5. Large crowds should never enter the station. They cannot but inconvenience traffic. There is as much honour in staying out as in entering the station.

6. The first duty of the volunteers should be to see that other passengers' luggage is not trampled upon.

7. Demonstrators ought not to enter the station long before the notified time for arrival.

8. There should be a clear passage left in front of the train for the passengers.

9. There should be another passage, if possible, half way through the demonstrators for the heroes to pass.

10. There should be no chain formed. It is humiliating.

11. The demonstrators must not move till the heroes have reached their coach or till they receive a pre-arranged signal from an authorised volunteer.

12. National cries must be fixed and must be raised not any how, at any time or all the time, but just on the arrival of the train, on the heroes reaching the coach and on the route at fair intervals. No objections need be raised to this on the score of the demonstration becoming mechanical and not spontaneous. The spontaneity will depend upon numbers, the response to the cries, above all the general look of the demonstrators, not in the greatest number of noises or the loudest. It is the training that a nation receives which characterises the nature of its demonstrations. A Mahomedan silently worshipping in his mosque is no less demonstrative than a Hindu temple-goer making a noise either through his voice or his gong or both.

13. On the route the crowd must line and not follow the carriages. If pedestrians form part of the moving procession, they must noiselessly and in an orderly manner take their places and not at their own will join or abstain.

14. A crowd should never press towards the heroes but should move away from them.

15. Those on the last line or the circumference should never press forward but give way when pressure is directed towards them.

16. If there are women in the crowd, they should be specially protected.

17. Little children should never be brought out in the midst of crowds.

18. At meetings volunteers should be dispersed among the crowd. They should learn flag and whistle signalling in order to pass instructions from one to another when it is impossible for the voice to carry.

19. It is no part of the audience to preserve order. They do so by keeping motionless and silent.

20. Above all, everyone should obey volunteers' instructions without question.

This list does not pretend to be exhaustive. It is merely illustrative and designed to stimulate thought and discussion. I hope that all the vernacular papers will translate this article.

24th September, 1920

SOME ILLUSTRATIONS

(BY M. K. GANDHI)

I promised in my article on Democracy *vs.* Mobocracy to give some illustrations of my meaning out of my own experiences. I was however unable, owing to the protracted Congress proceedings, to give those illustrations last week. I do so now. When we reached Madras, a huge crowd awaited us at the station. Our compartment was detached and fortunately drawn up in front of a reserved platform. What would have happened, if we had to alight together with the other passengers, can be better imagined than described. But even on the reserved platform, we were not able to get out for some time. The volunteers were in the way. Instead of dispersing themselves among the crowd and keeping it back, they clustered together to do us honour as they thought. The result was that the pressure was all directed towards where they and we were standing. And 'form a ring' has become the usual word of command. This forming a ring is a humiliating spectacle, and yet it has become such an institution that even when there is no one else but volunteers 'a ring' is formed round the leader to be 'honoured'.

To proceed with my description, the crowd was large, the noises they made were so terrific that the directions given by the volunteers could not be heard at all. All was chaos. My poor toes were every moment in danger of being crushed to a pulp. I often very nearly lost my balance through the jostling of the very volunteers who were trying to protect me. And but for the very great care with which they guarded me and the assistance rendered to them by the stalwart Maulana Shaukat Ali, I would have fared much worse than I did. The atmosphere was suffocating. Thus struggling it took us nearly three-quarters of an hour to reach the motor car, whereas ordinarily it need not have taken three minutes to walk out of the station to the porch. Having reached the car, it was no easy job to get into it. I had to be shoved into it in the best manner possible. I certainly heaved a sigh of relief when I found myself in the car, and I thought that both the Maulana and I deserved the ovation we received from the crowd after the dangerous exercise we had gone through. With a little forethought this mobocracy, for such it was, could have been changed into a splendidly organised and educative demonstration. And it could have been rendered free of all risk to life. The experience of Madras was typical of many. We had an extraordinary experience at Erode on our way to Salem. I was fairly fagged out. My voice had become hoarse with speaking. As at many stations, there was, here too, a surging crowd. It was thoroughly disorganised, though like everywhere else perfectly good humoured and respectful. I appealed to them not to make all kinds of unmusical noises, told them to disperse in an orderly manner as they had already seen us. I told them too that, if they intended to take their share in the Khilafat and the Punjab struggle, they were expected to undergo discipline. I was able to reach my voice to the most intelligent amongst them. I suggested that they should quietly rise, turn towards the station entrance and noiselessly retire. They listened, the rest followed and the station was cleared in two minutes' time. If the friends, who heard me, had haggled, argued, objected and insisted on shouting and remaining, the whole crowd would have done likewise and there would have been a pandemonium throughout the long time that the train stopped there.

I shall finish this description by giving the reverse of our experience at Jolarpet. We were travelling to Madras by the night train leaving Bangalore. We had been taking meetings at Salem during the day, motoring to Bangalore, a distant of 125 miles from Salem, taking there a meeting in drenching rain and thereafter we had to entrain. We needed night's rest but there was none to be had. At almost every station of importance, large crowds had gathered to greet us. About midnight we reached Jolarpet junction. The train had to stop there nearly forty minutes or stopped that night all those terrible minutes. Maulana Shaukat Ali requested the crowd to disperse. But the more he argued, the more they shouted 'Maulana Shaukat Ali-ki-Jai.' evidently thinking that the Maulana could not mean what he said. They had come from twenty miles' distance, they were waiting there for hours, they must have their satisfaction. The Maulana gave up the struggle, he pretended to sleep. The adorers thereupon mounted the foot-boards to have a peep at the Maulana. As the light in our compartment was put out, they brought in lanterns. At last I thought I would try, I rose, went to the door. It was a signal for a great shout of joy. The noise tore me to pieces. I was so tired. All my appeals proved fruitless in the end. They would stop for a while to renew the noise again. I shut the windows but the crowd was not to be baffled. They tried to open the windows from outside. They must see us both. And so the tussle went on till my son took it up. He harangued them, appealed to them for the sake of the other passengers. He produced some effect and there was a little less noise. Peeping however went on to the last minute. It was all well-meant, it was all an exhibition of boundless love, yet how cruel, how unreasonable! It was a mob without a mind. There were no intelligent men of influence among them and so nobody listened to any body.

Before we can make real headway, we must train these masses of men who have a heart of gold, who feel for the country, who want to be taught and led. But a few intelligent, sincere, local workers are needed, and the whole nation can be organised to act intelligently, and democracy can be evolved out of mobocracy. This evolution is really the first step to successful, national Non-co-operation.

20th October, 1920

NECESSITY OF DISCIPLINE

(By M. K. Gandhi)

I have already remarked upon my experiences of want of method and discipline in Madras. The same want is being noticed during the tour in the Rohilkhund. Everywhere there is chaos and disorder not for want of men but because of volunteers without training. They are called upon to handle a situation and crowds that are unprecedented. There is more noise and bustle than work.

Maulana Shaukat Ali is the indefatigable organiser. He wants to satisfy all parties and therefore packs too many events in any programme he arranges. To take only one instance. He accepted for one single day a motor ride from Aligarh to Hathras, thence to Etah and from Etah to Kasgunj with the prospect of a slow night journey from Kasgunj to Cawnpore. The motor ride covered a distance of 90 miles. After a trying meeting of workers at Aligarh early in the morning, we got into our motors at 9-45 a.m. and reached Hathras at about 11 a.m. The sun was burning hot and fierce. The inevitable noisy procession was there. It was followed by a huge meeting involving an intolerable strain on the voice of the strongest speaker. We however got for our pains resignations of three honorary magistracies. We motored thence to Etah. There was a little more order there than at Hathras. Soon after finishing Etah we motored to Kasgunj. We had accidents during the journey, the cars refusing to move. With difficulty we reached Kasgunj, Maulana Shaukat Ali and his companions not reaching in time for the train. We had several resignations at Etah. The meeting at Kasgunj for its enormous size was well managed but not without difficulty. Touching the feet has become an uncontrollable performance causing much waste of time and involving danger when it is resorted to in the midst of a large crowd.

But the most wretched experience was the night journey from Kasgunj to Cawnpore. It was made most uncomfortable by crowds attending at every station. They were everywhere insistent and assertive. The noises they made in order to wake me up were piercing and heart-rending. I was tired. My head was reeling and was badly in want of rest. In vain did Mrs. Gandhi and others plead with the crowds for self-control and silence. The more they implored, the more aggressive the crowds became. It was a tug of war between her and the crowds. The latter would put on the light as often as she put it off. If she put up the shutters, the crowd immediately put them down. I was resting, did they want me to die a premature death? The answer was they had come many miles to have *darshan* and *darshan* they must have.* I had hardened my heart and refused to move

*In *Young India* of 11th August, 1921, Mr. Gandhi wrote under the heading "Discipline":

It is high time that we disciplined ourselves. The demonstrations at railway stations are becoming a menace to the comfort of the travelling public. I am told that some railway passengers who, only a short time before a station demonstration, were

till it was daybreak. But there was not a wink of sleep for any of us during the whole of that night. It was a unique demonstration of love run mad. An expectant and believing people groaning under misery and insult believe that I have a message of hope for them. They come from all quarters within walking reach to meet me.

I do believe that I have a message of hope and certain deliverance, but—?

Yes. It is a big B U T. There is no deliverance and

---

praising me, were, after one or two demonstrations at intermediate stations, heard to curse me. I sympathise with them. I had a fellow-passenger with me during the Allahabad journey. Owing to the pressure of the crowds that besieged the station, he was unable to get a cup of tea or go out for his refreshments. I should not at all be surprised if he considered me to be a plague. On my way back from Allahabad, there was an unmanageable crowd on the Cawnpore platform, yelling the national cries, pressing towards my compartment and making every body uncomfortable. The noise continued the whole time. The leaders were with difficulty able to make the crowd sit, but it could not be made to stop shouting and yelling. I was asked to stand near the door to give *Darshan.* Much to the disappointment of the friends who urged me, I resolutely refused to stir out of my seat, unless there was perfect silence.

This din, noise, and bustle was due purely to want of forethought, management and organisation. It is best now to avoid all demonstrations at stations. We must consult the convenience of the passengers. If there must be a demonstration, national cries must be regulated, every facility must be provided for the easy movement of passengers. The nation must be disciplined to handle mass movements in a sober and methodical manner. This means previous training of volunteers and previous discipline of the masses. It is not impossible to give an elementary training in a few days. Wherever the people have been previously instructed, they have responded wonderfully well. Without this training, we never know when there might be an accident. It is the innate good nature of the people that has saved us hitherto from mishaps. But under proper training, we should be able to feel absolutely safe and comfortable in the midst of the biggest demonstrations. We cannot afford to be hysterical or mad.

no hope without sacrifice, discipline and self-control. Mere sacrifice without discipline will be unavailing. How to evolve discipline out of this habitual indiscipline? Not certainly by the British bayonet or the British hypocrisy. The British officials have no affection for this loving and phenomenal demonstration of a peaceful and peace-loving people. They would put it down, if they could, by barbarous exhibition of force even as Sir Michael O'Dwyer tried and ingloriously failed.

But if this demonstration cannot be put down by force, it cannot also procure *Swaraj* for India unless regulated and harnessed for national good. There are in it all the elements of success as well as of self-destruction. It cannot lead to the promised goal if the nation in extravagant affection wastes its servants by encroaching upon their hours of needed rest. We must therefore cease to hold nocturnal demonstrations. We must have consideration for the feelings of the lowest of our fellow beings. We must not disturb the rest of a train load of passengers. We must learn to transmute our love for our heroes into unquenchable energy and useful action. Love that is satisfied with touching the feet of its hero and making noise at him is likely to become parasitical. Such love ceases to be a virtue and after a time becomes a positive indulgence and therefore a vice. The greatest task before the nation to-day is to discipline its demonstrations if they are to serve any useful purpose. Non-co-operation is not designed to create hatred but to purify the nation to the point of rendering it proof against injurious aggression whether from within or from without. Non-co-operation to be effective must be preceded by co-operation between all the units composing this great and ancient people. Let us begin by co-operating with our loved ones.

PART IV

THE PROGRAMME OF NON-CO-OPERATION

PART IV

THE PROGRAMME OF NON-CO-OPERATION*

9*th June*, 1920

WHAT SHOULD THE VOTERS DO?

MR. GANDHI has devoted an article on the forthcoming elections to the choice of the voters in the columns of *Navajivan*. We give below the substance:

Many who had hitherto no concern with Council elections will be shortly called upon to vote for the reformed Councils. The powers too of elected members will be

* In *Young India* of 7th July, under the heading "How and when to act—details of the 1st stage," appeared the following statement issued by the Non-co-operation Committee for public information and guidance:

"Many questions have been asked of the Non-co-operation Committee as to its expectation and the methods to be adopted for beginning Non-co-operation.

The Committee wish it to be understood that, whilst they expect every one to respond to their recommendation to the full, they are desirous of carrying the weakest members also with them. The Committee want to enlist the passive sympathy, if not the active co-operation, of the whole of the country in the method of Non-co-operation.

Those, therefore, who cannot undergo physical sacrifice will help by contributing funds or labour to the movement.

found to have increased. This adds to the voters' responsibility. In all our cities, the citizens have been exercising the municipal franchise. And of these elections it cannot be said that the electors have always

---

Should Non-co-operation become necessary, the Committee has decided upon the following as part of the first stage:

(1) Surrender of all titles of honour and honorary offices.

(2) Non-participation in Government loans.

(3) Suspension by lawyers of practice and settlement of civil disputes by private arbitration.

(4) Boycott of Government schools by parents.

(5) Boycott of the Reformed Councils.

(6) Non-participation in Government parties, and such other functions.

(7) Refusal to accept any civil or military post, in Mesopotamia or to offer as Units for the army, especially for service in the Turkish territories now being administered in violation of pledges.

(8) Vigorous prosecution of "Swadeshi", inducing the people at the time of this national and religious awakening, to appreciate their primary duty to their country by being satisfied with its own productions and manufactures.

Swadeshi must be pushed forward without waiting for the 1st of August, for it is an eternal rule of conduct not to be interrupted even when the settlement arrives.

In order not to commit themselves, people will refrain now from taking service either civil or military. They will also suspend taking Government loans, new or old.

For the rest, it should be remembered that Non-co-operation does not commence before 1st August next.

Every effort is being, and will still be, made to avoid resort to such a serious breach with the Government, by urging His Majesty's Ministers to secure the revision of a Treaty which has been so universally condemned.

Those who realise their responsibility and gravity of the cause will not act independently, but in concert with the Committee. Success depends entirely upon disciplined and concerted Non-co-operation, and the latter is dependent upon strict obedience to instructions, calmness and absolute freedom from violence.

acquitted themselves in a wise manner. Electors' private relations with the candidates have often weighed with them more than the candidates' qualifications. It would be well if we set up a better standard for the elections

---

In the issue of *Young India* of 11th August 1920, Mahatma Gandhi, wrote ;

The Non-co-operation Committee has included, in the first stage, boycott of law-courts by lawyers and of Government schools and colleges by parents or scholars as the case may be. I know that, it is only my reputation as a worker and fighter, which has saved me from an open charge of lunacy for having given the advice about boycott of courts and schools.

I venture however to claim some method about my madness. It does not require much reflection to see that it is through courts that a government establishes its authority and it is through schools that it manufactures clerks and other employees. They are both healthy institutions when the government in charge of them is on the whole just. They are death traps when the government is unjust.

First as to lawyers—No newspaper has combated my views on Non-co-operation with so much pertinacity and ability as the Allahabad *Leader*. It has ridiculed my views on lawyers expressed in my booklet, 'Indian Home Rule,' written by me in 1908. I adhere to the views then expressed. And if I find time I hope to elaborate them in these columns. But I refrain from so doing for the time being as my special views have nothing to do with my advice on the necessity of lawyers suspending practice. I submit that national Non-co-operation requires suspension of their practice by lawyers. Perhaps no one co-operates with a government more than lawyers through its law courts. Lawyers interpret laws to the people and thus support authority. It is for that reason that they are styled officers of the court. They may be called honorary office-holders. It is said that it is the lawyers who have put up the most stubborn fight against the Government. This is no doubt partly true. But that does not undo the mischief that is inherent in the profession. So when the nation wishes to paralyse the Government, that profession, if it wishes to help the nation to bend the Government to its will, must suspend practice. But, say the critics, the Government will be too pleased, if the pleaders and barristers fell into the trap laid by me. I do not believe it. What is

to the legislative Councils. Only thus shall we be able to make the best use of the Councils. I suggest also that voters should not identify themselves with any party or its quarrels. They should consider candidates' views

---

true in ordinary times is not true in extraordinary times. In normal times the Government may resent fierce criticism of their manners and methods by lawyers, but in the face of fierce action they would be loath to part with a single lawyer's support through his practice in the courts.

Moreover, in my scheme, suspension does not mean stagnation. The lawyers are not to suspend practice and enjoy rest. They will be expected to induce their clients to boycott courts. They will improvise arbitration-boards in order to settle disputes. A nation, that is bent on forcing justice from an unwilling government, has little time for engaging in mutual quarrels. This truth the lawyers will be expected to bring home to their clients. The readers may not know that many of the most noted lawyers of England suspended their work during the late war. The lawyers, then, upon temporarily leaving their profession, became whole-time workers instead of being workers only during their recreation hours. Real politics are not a game. The late Mr. Gokhale used to deplore that we had not gone beyond treating politics as a pastime. We have no notion as to how much the country has lost by reason of amateurs having managed its battles with the serious-minded, trained and whole-time-working bureaucracy.

The critics then argue that the lawyers will starve, if they leave their profession. This cannot be said of the Sinhas of the profession. They do at times suspend work for visiting Europe or otherwise. Of those who live from hand to mouth, if they are honest men, each local Khilafat Committee can pay them an honorarium against full time service.

Lastly, for Mahomedan lawyers, it has been suggested that if they stop their practice, Hindus will take it up. I am hoping Hindus will at least show the negative courage of not touching their Muslim brethren's clients, even if they do not suspend their own practice. But I am sure no religiously minded Mussalman will be found to say that they can carry on the fight only if the Hindus stand side by side with them in sacrifice. If the Hindus do as they must, it will be to their honour and for the common good of both. But the Mussalmans

and not their party. Their character should weigh more even than their views. A man of character will make himself worthy of any position he is given. Even his mistakes will not much matter. I consider it impossible

---

must go forward whether the Hindus join them or not. If it is a matter of life and death with them, they must not count the cost. No cost is too heavy for the preservation of one's honour, especially religious honour. Only they will sacrifice who cannot abstain. Forced sacrifice is no sacrifice. It will not last. A movement lacks sincerity when it is supported by unwilling workers under pressure. The Khilafat movement will become an irresistible force when every Mussalman treats the peace terms as an individual wrong. No man waits for others' help or sacrifice in matters of private personal wrong. He seeks help, no doubt, but his battle against the wrong goes on whether he gains help or not. If he has justice on his side, the divine law is that he does get help. God is the help of the helpless. When the Pandava brothers were unable to help Draupadi, God came to the rescue and saved her honour. The Prophet was helped by God when he seemed to be forsaken by men.

Now for the Schools.—I feel that if we have not the courage to suspend the education of our children, we do not deserve to win the battle.

The first stage includes renunciation of honours or favours. As a matter of fact, no Government bestows favours without taking more than the favours are worth. It would be a bad and extravagant government which threw away its favours. In a government broad-based upon a people's will, we give our lives to secure a trinket which is a symbol of service. Under an unjust government which defies a people's will, rich *Jagirs* become a sign of servitude and dishonour. Thus considered, the schools must be given up without a moment's thought.

For me the whole scheme of Non-co-operation is among other things a test of the intensity and extent of our feeling. Are we prepared to suffer? It has been said that we may not expect much response from title-holders, for they have never taken part in national affairs and have bought their honours at too great a price easily to sacrifice them. I make a present of the argument to the objectors, and ask what about the parents of school-children and the grown-up

for a man without character to do higher national service, so that, if I were a voter from among the list, I would first select men of character and then I would understand their views. My questions to them would be :

(1) Do you approve of the present Swadeshi Movement? If so, are you prepared to levy heavy import duties on foreign cloth? Will you favour legislation for cheapening the materials and machinery required to produce Swadeshi articles?

(2) Do you hold that all the affairs of a province should be conducted in its own vernacular and that the

---

college-students? They have no such intimate connection with the Government as the title-holders. Do they or do they not feel enough to enable them to sacrifice the schooling?

But I contend that there is no sacrifice involved in emptying the schools. We must be specially unfit for Non-co-operation if we are so helpless as to be unable to manage our own education to total independence of the Government. Every village should manage the education of its own children. I would not depend upon Government aid. If there is a real awakening, the schooling need not be interrupted for a single day. The very school-masters who are now conducting Government schools, if they are good enough to resign their office, could take charge of national schools and teach our children the things they need, and not make of the majority of them indifferent clerks. I do look to the Aligarh College to give the lead in this matter. The moral effect created by the emptying of our Madrasas will be tremendous. I doubt not that the Hindu parents and scholars would not fail to copy their Mussalman brethren.

Indeed what could be grander education than that the parents and scholars should put religious sentiment before a knowledge of letters? If therefore no arrangement could be immediately made for the literary instruction of youths who might be withdrawn, it would be most profitable training for them to be able to work as volunteers for the cause which may necessitate their withdrawal from Government schools. For, as in the case of the lawyers, so in the case of boys, my notion of withdrawal does not mean an indolent life. The withdrawing boys will, each according to his worth, be expected to take their share in the agitation.

affairs of the Nation should be conducted in Hindustani —a combination of Hindi and Urdu? If you do, will you endeavour incessantly to introduce the use of the vernaculars in administration of the respective provinces, and the national language in the Imperial administration?

(3) Do you hold that the present division of the provinces of India was made for administrative and political purposes and that no regard was paid to the peoples' wishes? And do you hold that this division has done much harm to the national growth? If you think so. will you try to bring out a redistribution on a linguistic basis as early as possible?

(4) Do you hold that there is not the remotest likelihood of India's regeneration without Hindu-Moslem unity? And if you think so, are you, if a Hindu, willing to help the Mussalmans in all legitimate ways in their trouble?

A satisfactory answer to them alone will entitle the candidates to my vote if I had one. I suggest these questions because I regard them as of great importance. If the electors do not see any significance in these questions, they may put others which they consider to be of greater importance for the upliftment of the Nation. It is not the particular questions that matter but the knowing of candidates' views on national questions. My attempt is to point out that we need an electorate which is impartial, independent and intelligent. If the electors do not interest themselves in national affairs and remain unconcerned with what goes on in their midst, and if they elect men with whom they have private relations or whose aid they need for themselves, this state of things can do no good to the country; on the contrary, it will be harmful.

Now it remains to be considered what the electors

should do if they do not receive satisfactory answer to their questions or if they cannot find men of character. It is an established custom with regard to elections that electors, if they do not find any candidate to their liking, need not register their votes. In such a case, abstention amounts to an exercise of one's votes. Exception was taken to this procedure that, if good electors refuse to make their choice, bad electors would make the worst choice. This is to a certain extent true. But suppose in a certain place all candidates being drunkards the better portion of the electorate abstain from voting and the candidates manage to secure votes from their kind, can they exercise any influence in the Councils? No doubt their vote has its numerical value, but their views and speeches cannot influence the Council. Moreover, an intelligent abstention has its own effect. The electors having once failed to find a proper candidate will next time take steps to find out a suitable man and elect him, and by so doing they will raise the level of their own place. In a growing nation, people are able to understand the national affairs and they are expected to purify the political atmosphere they live in and to maintain its purity. All enlightened and thoughtful voters will find that occasionally situations must arise when they will have to purposely refuse to register their votes.* I earnestly hope that on such occasions our electors will have courage to do so. I hope that, when they do exercise the vote, they will give it to the best man, no matter to which party he belongs.

* The reference presumably is to the possible need for adopting Non-co-operation.

7th July, 1920

NON-CO-OPERATION

Mr. Gandhi writes to the press :

"Needles to say that I am in entire accord with Lala Lajpat Rai on the question of the boycott of the reformed councils.* For me it is but one step in the campaign of Non-co-operation and as I feel equally keenly on the Punjab question as on the Khilafat. Lala Lajpat Rai's suggestion is doubly welcome. I have seen the suggestion made in more quarters than one that Non-co-operation on the reforms should commence after the process of election has been through. I cannot help saying that it is a mistake to go through the election farce and the expense of it when we clearly do not intend to take part in the proceedings of these Legislative Councils. Moreover, a great deal of educative work has to be done among the people. And if I could, I would

* Under the heading, "I shall not stand for election." Lala Lajpat Rai wrote an article in his Urdu paper, *Bande Mataram*. in the course of which, after pointing out how the Punjab wrong was condoned by Government, he concluded :

These new Councils can only prove beneficial to us when and if the Indian and official members work in amity and concord and together solve problems of state by mutual consultation. Yet in the present circumstaces of the Punjab there is no prospect of the fruition of this hope. If the *Civil and Military Gazette* correctly represents the views of Punjab officials (European). then I have no hesitation in saying that the time has not come for Indians and Europeans to work together for the good of the country. I heartily desire that the time should soon come. but to say that the time has come is to shut our eyes to facts. Until now they are the rulers and we are the ruled. The Punjab Publicity Committee which is a confidant of the Government also says the same thing. As long as that relation continues, it is very difficult for us to work together. They suspect us and we suspect them. In my view, therefore, I cannot be useful to my country from inside the Council, and it is better therefore that I should not go into it.

not have the best attention of the country frittered away in electioneering. The populace will not understand the beauty of Non-co-operation if we seek election and then resign. But it would be a fine education for them if the electors are not to elect anybody and unanimously to tell whosoever man seek their suffrage that he would not represent them if he so sought election so long as the Punjab and Khilafat questions were not satisfactorily settled. I hope, however, that Lala Lajpat Rai does not mean to end with the boycott of the reformed councils. We must take, if necessary, every one of the four stages of Non-co-operation if we are to be regarded as a self-respecting nation. The issue is clear. Both the Khilafat terms and the Punjab affairs show that Indian opinion counts for little in the Councils of the Empire. It is a humiliating position, and we shall make nothing of the reforms if we quietly swallow the humiliation. In my humble opinion, therefore, the first condition of real progress is the removal of these difficulties in our path. And unless some better course of action is devised *nolens volens* Non-co-operation must hold the field."

14*th July*, 1920

BOYCOTT OF COUNCILS

(BY M. K. GANDHI).

Pundit Rambhuji Dutt Chaudhry has ranged himself against Lala Lajpat Rai in the matter of the proposed boycott of the Councils. Madras is divided, most of the Nationalist leaders seem disinclined to boycott the Councils. The *Mahratta* has pronounced against it in a well-reasoned article. The reasons for disapproval of boycott are mainly two. (1) If the Nationalists refrain, the Moderates will get all the seats; (2) since through the Legislative Councils we have made some progress, we are likely to make greater progress by reason of larger powers having been granted to popular representatives.

Now the first reason hardly does credit to a great popular party. If it is harmful to enter the Councils, why should Nationalists be jealous of the Moderates entering the Councils? Must they participate in the harm because Moderates will not refrain? Or, is it contended that the harm can be avoided only if all join the boycott? If the last is the contention, it betrays ingorance of the principles of boycott. We boycott an institution, because we do not like it or because we do not wish to co-operate with its conductors. In the matter of the Councils, the latter is the deciding reason. And I submit that in a sense we co-operate by joining, even though the object is obstruction. Most institutions, and a British Legislative Council most of all, thrive upon obstruction. The disciplined obstruction of the Irish members made practically no impression upon the House of Commons. The Irishmen have not got the Home Rule they wanted. The *Mahratta* argues that obstruction would be active and aggressive Non-co-operation. I venture to deny it. In my opinion, it shows want of faith in yourself, *i.e.*, in your doctrine. You doubt and you perish. I do not believe that either the English or the Moderate leaders can possibly contemplate with equanimity a Nationalist boycott of the Councils. We are now face to face with the reality.* Will a single Moderate leader care to enter any Council if more than half his electorate

* In connection with this, Mr. Gandhi wrote in *Navjivan* as follows: The 16th of November is somewhat of a day of trial for the people, because on that day members for the Legislative Councils will be

disapproved of his offering himself as a candidate at all? I hold that it would be unconstitutional for him to do so, because he will not represent his constituency.

---

elected throughout the Bombay presidency. What will the voters do on that day? What is their duty?

(1) I hope that no voter will go to the polling booth to record his vote.

(2) That all the voters will remain indoors.

(3) In case a meeting is held away from the polling booth, voters will attend it and express themselves against being represented on the Council.

(4) The work of canvassing signatures and of asking voters not to vote will cease for 24 hours from the night of the 15th instant.

(5) Volunteers too will not do anything on the 16th instant to dissuade voters from voting.

(6) In short, those who choose to vote should have the day wholly at their disposal..

How can we hope to convert voters whom we have not been able to persuade till the 15th? Surely, we do not want to prevent anybody from voting by physical force. There can therefore be no persuasion on the 16th.

Our campaign is one of educating public opinion. When we have succeeded in doing that, then, and only then is Swaraj within easy reach.—*Young India* of 10th November, 1920.

In *Young India* of 10th November, 1920, the following notes by Mr. C. Rajagopalachariar written to some Madras papers were also reproduced:

An acid test—England and the whole 'civilised' world is now committed irrevocably to the theory of self-determination. But it is said that India has not yet 'self-determined in favour of true Swaraj, because Congress does not represent the Nation: because the educated classes do not represent the national will. Grant all this. But Government has now created an electorate. This electorate cannot but be accepted by Government and the civilised world as adequately representing the Nation. If the majority of this electorate votes now for the Punjab, Khilafat, and Swaraj, the nation will have clearly 'self-determined.'

* * * *

The Choice.—India stands to-day on the parting of ways On

Boycott contemplated by me presupposes a most active discipline and watchful propaganda and it is based on the assumption that the electors themselves will prefer

---

16th November. she will have shown whether she is going the way of immediate and real Swaraj or the way of bureaucratic machinations. Every voter must decide whether he is going to stand by those who are fighting for immediate and true Swaraj—for our national honour and dignity, or stand by the Government that has insulted our national honour through the Punjab crime and our religion through the Khilafat wrong.

* * * *

Do not vote: Why?—The Government wants a fresh lease. under the cloak of the people's consent. to continue its irresponsible career of crime and injustice ; in effect. it wants to delude the people to perpetuate a system that perpetrated the massacre of Jallianwalla Bagh. Think twice before you voté for this system. The new Councils are like gilded pills. They have been decked for the occasion to deceive the voters.

* * * *

What the New Councils cannot do.—The new Councils cannot prevent :

(1) A repetition of the Khilafat injustice and the Punjab crime.
(2) Indian troops from being used to keep in subjugation other nations, and,
(3) Indian moneys from being spent in aiding British Imperialism and foreign wars of aggression.

What the New Councils can do.—The new Councils can prevent

(1) a real and immediate Swaraj. No power has been given to the Councils to vote for increase of responsibility for full Swaraj,
(2) our economic freedom.
(3) our moral and material uplift. and
(4) our inherent-right to be a free people.

* * * *

What is the use. then, of voting ?

What it means not to vote.—Every vote not given to the Councils, means a vote for Swaraj, a vote in favour of the nation's determination for full power and responsibility. a vote for the political and

complete boycott in the form of obstruction. If it is assumed that the people themselves do not want a complete boycott, it would be the duty of those who believe in it to educate the electorates to appreciate the superiority of boycott over obstruction. To enter the Councils is to submit to the vote of the majority, *i.e.*, to co-operate. If then we want to stop the machinery of Government, as we want to, until we get justice in the Khilafat and the Punjab matters, we must put our whole weight against the Government and refuse to accept the vote of the majority in the Council, because it will neither represent the wish of the country nor our own which is more to the point on a matter of principle. A minister who refuses to serve is better than one who serves under protest. Service under protest shows that the situation is not intolerable. I contend that the situation created by the Government has become intolerable and therefore the only course left open to a self-respecting person is Non-co-operation, *i.e.*, complete abstention. General Botha refused to enter Lord Milner's Council, because he utterly disapproved of the principle that governed Lord Milner in dealing with the Boers. And General Botha succeeded, because he had practically the whole of the Transvaal behind him. Politically considered, success depends upon the country accepting the boycott movement. Religiously considered, success is there for the individual as soon as he has *acted* upon the principle he holds and his action has ensured national success because he has laid the foundation by showing the straightest way to it.

The other argument is that we shall succeed by entering the new Councils, because we have after all not done

---

economic emancipation of India, a vote for national Honour, Liberty and Freedom.

quite so badly in having entered less popular bodies before. The answer to the objection is that the dividing line had not then been reached, we had not lost confidence in British honesty and justice or we had not confidence in ourselves then to carry boycott to the successful end or we had not thought of the method in the way we are doing to-day. Probably all the three reasons operate to-day. After all, manners and methods change with the times. We must grow with our years. What was good enough food for our babyhood cannot be good enough for manhood.

24th November, 1920

COUNCIL ELECTIONS

(BY M. K. GANDHI)

The elections in the Bombay Presidency and elsewhere have demonstrated the success of Non-co-operation about Councils, in so far as the voters are concerned. In some cases, not a single voter seems to have registered his vote. What will the so-called representatives do? They know that the voters have refrained from going to the polls not out of laziness, but out of deliberation. They know too that thousands of voters have declared in writing their intention not to be represented. The members had ample opportunity of acting on the electors and convincing them of the desirability of voting. They cannot complain of intimidation or even picketing. For, the instructions were not to picket, and as far as I am aware, the instructions were implicitly followed. In the face of these facts, is it not the clear duty of the members declared to have been elected, not to have anything to do with the Council? The electors have shown in no uncertain terms that they do not want to have anything to do with the reformed Councils. The members will reduce representative institutions to an absurdity, if they persist in going to the Council when they have the clearest possible mandate to the contrary.

If the so-called representatives do not obey the mandate of their electors, the course of the latter is quite clear. They must form voters' associations, and through these bodies pass votes of no confidence ; they must address their respective members notifying their disapproval of their conduct in allowing themselves to be declared elected. It follows too that the electors must not on any account whatsoever take any work from these members. For them the Council does not exist. They must not seek any relief through it.* The next trial of the voters

* The relief was sought in vain in the view of many. The following appeared in *Young India* on 9th March, 1922 :

An M.L.C. Resigns.—Sjt. Sita Ram, a pleader of Kheri, sends me a copy of his resignation as a member of the Legislative Council of the United Provinces. The following is the text :

"It is with feelings of great regret that I beg to announce the resignation of my seat in the U. P. Legislative Council. It was after the announcement of the Reforms that I sought my election to the Council for the first time, and I had faith that the Reformed Government would be different from what it was in pre-Reform days, and that the reign of terror and Dyerism would be a thing of the past, and that there would be no more undue and undeserved repression in the country, and that only guilty persons would be punished and that people would be able to do real service to the country by being returned to the Councils. The experience of one year has, however, belied all my hopes. I have seen that arrogance and haughtiness are much more in evidence in Council than respect and good-will for others. Class and communal interests are still there. The experience of my own district has convinced me that there is still a place for Dyerism in the machinary of the Government. Mr. Young, Special Manager of the—Estate, committed acts tending to lead to breach of peace and tyrannized the entire population of—and the Government will commence when the Council is opened, if at all, in the face of this verdict. The temptation to air grievances by having questions put in the Council will be very great. The electors will have to resist the temptation.

But let us hope for the good of our country that the members themselves will bow to the verdict so emphatically declared by the electors.

6th October, 1920

THE HALLUCINATION OF LAW COURTS

(By M. K. Gandhi)

If we were not under the spell of lawyers and law-courts and if there were no touts to tempt us into the quagmire of the courts and to appeal to our basest

---

has not seen its way of doing any justice in the matter. Pundit Harkaran Nath Misra, who preached non-voilence to the people and directed the tenants to pay up their rent to their landlords and asked them not to resort to Civil Disobedience under the present circumstances, has been sentenced to three years' imprisonment. The recent arrests throughout the whole of India and particularly in these Provinces have led me to believe that the government is determined on the policy of shutting up every person who believes in the real self-government of India. Unfortunately my temperament is not such that I can remain a part and parcel of such a Government and hence I beg to tender the resignation of my seat."

He informs me that there are five candidates for the post. I do not envy the five candidates. Both Sjt. Sita Ram and they are right. Sjt. Sita Ram needed personal experience to show him the true nature of the reforms. The elected candidate, let me hope, will also learn by experience; but even at the end of the chapter there certainly will be some men who will honestly hold the opinion that, whether good or bad, it is only through the Councils that the British administrators give us, that we shall make any progress. For Non-co-operators the proceedings of the Councils and the Assembly ought to be a standing proof of the wisdom of their abstention.

passions, we would be leading a much happier life than we do to-day. Let those who frequent the law-courts—the best of them—bear witness to the fact that the atmosphere about them is fœtid. Perjured witnesses are ranged on either side, ready to sell their very souls for money or for friendship's sake. But that is not the worst of these courts. The worst is that they support the authority of a government. They are supposed to dispense justice and are therefore called the palladile of a nation's liberty. But when they support the authority of an unrighteous Government, they are no longer palladile of liberty, they are crushing houses to crush a nation's spirit. Such were the martial law tribunals and the summary courts in the Punjab. We had them in their nakedness. Such they are even in normal times when it is a matter of dispensing justice between a superior race and its helots. This is so all the world over. Look at the trial of an English officer and the farcical punishment he received for having deliberately tortured inoffensive negroes at Nairobi. Has a single Englishman suffered the extreme penalty of the law or anything like it for brutal murders in India? Let no one suppose that these things would be changed when Indian judges and Indian prosecutors take the place of Englishmen. Englishmen are not by nature corrupt. Indians are not necessarily angels. Both succumb to their environment. There were Indian judges and Indian prosecutors during the martial law regime, who were generally guilty of just as bad practices as the English men. Those, who tortured the innocent women in Amritsar, were Indians, if it was a Bosworth Smith in Manianwala who insulted its women.

What I am attacking, is the system. I have no quarrel with the Englishmen as such. I honour individuals among them to-day as I did before my discovery of the unimprovableness of the existing system. If anything, Mr. Andrews and other Englishmen I could name, are nearer to me to-day than before. But I could not tender my homage even to him who is more than a brother to me, if he became the Viceroy of India. I would distrust his ability to remain pure if he accepted the office. He would have to administer a system that is inherently corrupt and based on the assumption of our inferiority. Satan mostly employs comparatively moral instruments and the language of ethics to give his aims an air of respectability.

I have digressed a little for the purpose of showing that this Government, if it was wholly manned by Indians but worked as it now is, would be as intolerable to us as it is now. Hence it is that the knowledge of Lord Sinha's appointment to a high office fails to fill me with a glow of satisfaction. We must have absolute equality in theory and in practice, and ability to do away with the British connection if we so wish.

But to revert to the lawyers and the law-courts, we cannot gain this desirable status so long as we regard with superstitious awe and wonder the so-called palaces of justice. Let no individuals who get satisfaction of their greed or revenge or their just claims, be blind to the ultimate aim of these courts—the permanence of the authority of the Government which they represent. Without its law-courts, the Government must perish in a day. I admit that under my plan this power of subjugating the people through the courts will still remain even when every Indian lawyer has withdrawn and there are no civil suits in the law-courts. But then they will cease to deceive us. They will have lost their moral prestige and therefore the air of respectability. It is strange but it is true that, so long as we believed in the gradual transference of the power of the English to the people, appointments to high posts in the law-courts were hailed as a blessing. Now that we believe that the system is incapable of being gradually mended, every such appointment by reason of its deceptiveness must be regarded as an evil. Therefore every lawyer suspending his practice to that extent undermines the prestige of the law-courts and to that extent every suspension is a gain for the individual as for the nation.

The economic drain that the law-courts cause, has at no time been considered. And yet it is not a trifle. Every institution founded under the present system is run on a most extravagant scale. Law-courts are probably the most extravagantly run. I have some knowledge of the scale in England, a fair knowledge of the Indian, and an intimate knowledge of the South African. I have no hesitation in saying that the Indian is comparatively the most extravagant and bears no relation to the general economic condition of the people. The best South African lawyers—and they are lawyers of great ability—dare not charge the fees the lawyers in India do. Fifteen guineas is almost a top fee for legal opinion. Several thousand rupees have been known to have been charged in India. There is something sinful in a system under which it is possible for a lawyer to earn from fifty thousand to one lac rupees per month. Legal practice is not—ought not to be—a speculative business. The best legal talent must be available to the poorest at reasonable rates. But we have copied and improved upon the practice of the English lawyers. Englishmen find the climate of India trying. The habits imbued under a cold and severe climate are retained in India, ample margin is kept for frequent migrations to the Hills and to their island home and an equally ample margin is kept for the education of an exclusive and aristocratic type for their children. The scale of their fees is naturally therefore pitched very high. But India cannot bear the heavy drain. We fancy that, in order to feel the equals of these English lawyers, we must charge the same killing fees that the English do. It would be a sad day for India if it has to inherit the English scale and the English tastes so utterly unsuitable to the Indian environment. Any lawyer looking at the law-courts and the profession of law from the view points I have ventured to suggest cannot keep coming to the conclusion that if he wants to serve the nation to the best of his ability, the first condition of service is suspension of his practice. He can come to a different conclusion only if he successfully changes the statement of facts I have made.

6th October, 1920

THE PROFESSION OF LAW AND WHAT IT MEANS

[We are obliged for this article to Babu Rajendra Prasad, M. A., M. L., one of the leading members of the Patna Bar, and a member of the Senate and Syndicate of the Patna University. He presided at this year's session of the Behar Provincial Conference. Needless to say, he has decided to resign the membership of the Senate and Syndicate and to withdraw from practice. His dispassionate article is a result of his own experience at the bar.—Ed. Y. I.]

Litigation in India is a very expensive affair. The whole system of Law Courts and the method whereby one is enabled to obtain justice require enormous expenditure—often by the time one gets the fruit of the decree, one had to spend more than the property in suit is worth.

To begin with, the so-called legal charges come to a high figure. The litigant has to pay a pretty heavy court fee for getting justice, and surprising though it may seem, it is a fact that, in some provinces at any rate, judicial stamp is a profitable source of revenue to the Government. In the next place, every law court is infested with a number of *amalas*, subordinate officers, peons, etc., each one of whom has to be paid a certain fee, not authorised by law, but not for that reason any the less rigorously exacted, as the litigant knows that a refusal to pay these perquisites of the myrmidons of the law is sure to cost him more than those perquisites, besides entailing on him a lot of worry, trouble and perhaps insult.

It must be said to the credit of the judiciary that as a body they are not open to corruption in the sense that they may be bribed, although there are exceptions. But the highest judiciary is not altogether free from other kinds of influences. The anxiety to clear the file, to show quick disposal of cases, and to stick to the technicalities of the law as distinct from what the justice of the case demands, are responsible for many a wrong decision. In arguing a case before a Bench of two Judges of a High Court, a Vakil happened to make the unfortunate remark, " My Lords, the justice of the case demands, and after all you have to do justice," when he was sharply interrupted by one of the judges: "Mr.—,you are entirely mistaken. We do nothing of the sort. We decide cases on the record before us."

The Vakil could only retort: "My Lords—I am distressed to hear that." That gives the keynote to the attitude of most judges. The subordinate judiciary depend also for their promotion and preferment upon showing speedy disposal and a clear file. They are also not free from the other kind of corruption, namely, that of consulting or considering the whims or what they fancy to be the wishes of other authorities. This happens especially when you have the Government taking a keen interest in the result of litigation either as a party or otherwise.

The law's delays and the uncertainties of litigation are proverbial. Some cases have been fought for years. A case which comes to be decided in the normal course takes at least a year before it is taken up for hearing; the appeal to the High Court normally takes two years and if it goes to the Privy Council, it takes another 3 to 4 years. But this is so in short cases. Big cases are heard for months and some cases are known to have been heard from day to day for 12 months or more. Apart from the strain on the purse of the litigant, the strain on the nerves is simply unbearable. One cannot be sure if even in 25 p. c. of the cases that come before a Court, real substantial justice is done. Litigation has come to be regarded, and rightly so, as a sort of gambling. However just your cause and however true your case, you cannot be sure of winning it. The lawyer is mostly responsible for this uncertainty. Many a bad cause is won by a so-called good advocate and many a true cause has been lost on account of the folly or incapacity of the lawyer engaged or the inability of the party to engage an expensive lawyer. In fact, the greater a lawyer's ability to confound and confuse the judge and the true issues in the case, the higher is the fee that he commands. And what has the country to pay for this ability to make the "worse appear the better reason?"

The fee which lawyers charge is out of all proportion to the amount of work done as also to their ability, with that of men as compared in other professions. Some lawyers have been known to charge as much as fifty thousand rupees as perusal fee, that is, fee for reading the papers of the case which they have to argue. A perusal of Rs. 2 to 5 per page of the paper is not an unusual charge for first-rate practitioners. In some cases, the services of practitioners who have occupied seats in the High Court Benches have been regularly put to auction for contending litigants to bid for. Over and above the perusal fee some lawyers also charge what is called a consultation fee, *i.e.*, the fee which the lawyer in question gets for consulting with other lawyers engaged with him on the same side and for enabling him to clear his own ideas and saving his own time by taking notes of cases and precedents collected by the juniors. The usual fee is Rs. 85 per hour of consulation and in some cases even more.

All this is before the case is actually taken up for argument. For the argument a daily fee is usually charged by those who have attained a high standing in the profession. A fee of Rs. 510 per day of 4½ to 5 hours' work in court is now the usual fee. It is also the common practice to charge a full day's fee even when the case is part-heard for only an hour or less. It very often happens that a lawyer is engaged on behalf of an appellant in the High Court, and having argued the case for the appellant, he does not sit in the Court to listen to the argument of the other side but goes to another Court to argue another case for another fee.

And if the party insists upon his attending the Court while the adversary is arguing, he is required to pay Rs. 1,020/-per day. It is not an uncommon occurrence that a lawyer engaged by a party is unable to attend the case, as he is engaged in some other court at the time when it is taken up. Some lawyers in such a case refund the fee, but there are others who would tell the client that what he (the client) engaged for the money he paid, was not their service but their *chance* of appearing, which means, in other words, the chance of their not appearing on the other side. But the fees become really fabulous when a High Court lawyer is taken to a mofussil station. The usual charge with some lawyers is Rs. 5,000 for the first day and Rs. 1,530 for each subsequent day. In particular cases, even this figure has been exceeded. Even in cases when a lawyer has been engaged by the month, the fee has been Rs. 50,000 or Rs. 90,000.

It should not be supposed that the fee charged is at all commensurate with the ability or the labour of the man who is fortunate enough to command it. The difference in ability between one lawyer and another is not so great as to entitle the one to Rs. 1,500 and the other to Rs. 150 or less. Even in case of junior practitioners, the disparity between the fee of one man and another is too great to be justified by any standard of comparison of their abilities.

But the worst feature of the system of administration of justice now prevalent is the wholesale demoralisation of the people. The Law Courts are largely responsible for the constantly diminishing respect for truth. The law of evidence insists on a standard of proof which can very seldom be satisfied unless recourse is had to perjury. The habits of the people are not business-like, and what they do not take care to perfect in the beginning has to be remedied when the matter goes to a court of law by suborning false evidence. In some parts of the country, every village has its tout whose sole business and means of livelihood is setting people by the ears of one another. His ability consists in getting up false cases. His title to position in society lies in his capacity to work mischief The law courts are full of this class of people. If you go to an out of the way village and try to settle a dispute between two parties, you are usually told by witnesses whom you may examine that they will tell the truth, as they are not appearing before a court but before a *punch*. It may be that respectable lawyers do not actually coach witnesses or forge documents, but there can be no doubt that advice on evidence amounts to nothing less than advice to the client—"Get this particular class of witnesses, true if you can, but anyhow get them to prove this and this." There is no denying the fact that by suggestion, insinuation, and innuendo the lawyer indicates what he wants to enable him to plead the case successfully, and the client with the help of the tout procures what the lawyer wants. In arguing a case, the only limit to which even a respectable lawyer puts, which under professional etiquitte he is required to put to himself, is abstention from false or untrue statement of facts. He is free to put the most absurd interpretation on documents or law, provided he can do so with impunity on account of the weakness of the judge or his adversary. And the higher the status of the lawyer, the greater the impunity with which he can bamboozle the judge.

Then again, the lawyer and the judge are not free to deal with a case on its merits. The judge can decide the facts as he likes, but for the law he has to depend not on the acts of the legislature alone but on a large mass of decisions which are not always illuminating or reconcilable. And the greater the number of decisions.

which a lawyer can skifully fling in the face of the judge, the greater is his appreciation by the litigant public and the greater are the chances of his confounding the judge.

To add to all this, there are appeals. second appeals, appeals to the Privy Council and so forth, and not infrequently the decisions of trial-courts are reversed by the High Courts and again resorted by the Privy Council. The frequency of reversals, the want of ability in judges, the presence of ability in lawyers, never leave a litigant without a chance of success and 'hope eternal springs in human breast.' He sometimes wins no doubt, but he wins when he has lost all, his money, his honor and his character.

RAJENDRA PRASAD.

13th October, 1920

PANDIT MOTILAL ON LAW COURTS

[Last week we published, from the able pen of Babu Rajendra Prasad who till lately enjoyed a leading position on the Patna Bar, a thoughtful article on the state of litigation and legal profession in India. Pandit Motilal Nehru, our respected President of the Amritsar Congress and one of the leading lawyers in the country —unquestionably *the* leading lawyer in his province— has now issued an appeal to the members of his profession wherein, besides exhorting them to make the boycott of law-courts a complete success and organise Panchayats for arbitration, he has described the evils of litigation, from his long experience of 37 years at the Bar. We publish the appeal in extenso from the *Independent*—Ed. Y. I.]

There can be no difference of opinion as to the desirability of avoiding litigation in courts and settling all disputes by mutual compromise or private arbitration. You may be in favour of or against the policy of Non-co-operation laid down by the Calcutta Special Congress, you may or may not belong to any of the current schools of political thought, you may not even be interested at all in politics; you cannot, whatever your position or occupation in life, deny that the nature of the litigation introduced by British laws and encouraged by the machinery of British Courts in this country is responsible for some of the greatest evils we suffer from.

I have had the honour of belonging to the legal profession for the last 37 years and whatever its detractors might say, I maintain that it is second to none in the world in its high traditions and its brilliant record of public service. At the same time, I cannot conceal from myself the fact that the moral tone of the profession has steadily declined during my own experience, and that, from top to bottom. The leaders have in succeeding years yielded more and more to the prevailing commercial spirit of the age and have gone on raising their fees from time to time, till they have now reached enormous figures out of all proportion to the nature, quality or quantity of the work required to be done.

The employment of counsel at present partakes of the nature of a contract of hiring which it was never intended to be, and the good old principle that counsel's fees were mere honorariums can only excite laughter in these advanced days. A keen competition to break all previous records in the matter of high fees is proceeding between eminent lawyers with annual income already running into six figures, and it is impossible to say where it will lead to. The effect of this on the unfortunate litigants is thus crisply put in the popular saying: "*Adalat men jojita, so hara, jo hara, so mara.*" (Success in Court is defeat, defeat is death.)

I am free to confess that I have taken no small part in this competition and, indeed, was in the thick of it till some four weeks ago. What contribution I have made to the disastrous results so graphically described in the Hindi saying I cannot tell: but in the very nature of things, the total output during the last 37 years could not have been insignificant. It is perhaps possible in view of modern conditions of life to defend high fees and cite precedents associated with honoured names, but I am concerned here with the consequences to the country at large and these in all honesty can only be described as ruinous.

Much the greater evil of the present system, however, is the creation of a class of lawyers and litigants who, but for the excuse afforded by the existing machinery of the courts, would find no place in any decent society. Their methods are well known and their agents infest the precincts of almost every court. There can be no greater condemnation of the ordinary law court morality than what one often hears when litigants of this class approach each other for an amicable settlement. "We are not in the court, why don't you tell the truth?" is not an uncommon form in which a fact alleged by one party is challenged by the other.

Coming to the courts themselves, we all know what kind of justice is to be expected in criminal matters under the special procedure prescribed for the trial of Europeans. During the last 150 years, every Indian who has met with his death at the hands of a European has either had an enlarged spleen or his death has turned out to be the result of a pure accident. There has not been a single case, so far as I am aware, of murder pure and simple. The climax was reached in the Punjab the other day. After the travesty of justice we have experienced in that unfortunate province, I feel that it is to drag the noble profession in the mire to practise it before courts which are the outcome of an unrighteous and oppressive system. The disreputable class of practitioners I have just referred to are but the black sheep you find in every fold, and under normal conditions it would be the business of the profession to drive them out. But when law courts are made subservient to the ends of the executive and such functions as they exercise can be suspended at the sweet will and pleasure of a legal or a provincial despot, when the enormities committed in the name of law and order are condemned by the British Parliament from which the courts derive their jurisdiction, it is time that we ceased to have anything to do with these effete creations of autocratic power.

We hold widely divergent views on certain public questions. It is idle to waste valuable time in trying to bring about a consensus of opinion on these. The best course is to agree to differ till time and experience show us the wisdom or unwisdom of the course we have decided to follow. Meanwhile, let us combine our energies and make a united and determined endeavour to achieve what we are all agreed is worth achieving.

The increase of litigation is one of those evils which we are all interested in combating against. I earnestly appeal to my countrymen of all shades of political opinion to join in a holy war against this evil. More specially I appeal to legal practitioners of all grades to take their right and proper place at the head of the movement and lead the campaign within their respective spheres of influence. By doing so, they would be upholding the best traditions of the honourable profession to which they belong. Let them organise panchayats and divert to them the ceaseless stream of litigation which flows into the courts.* They are now in the midst of the Dasara vacation and can well afford the time to approach their friends appearing on the opposite side and advise the parties to approach each other. Open the campaign on the reopening day of your court after the vacation by seeing that the number of fresh litigation is cut down within the narrowest limits and that a

* The following appeared in *Young India* of 16th March. 1921 :

A Jullundar Circular—The instructions of the Dy. Commissioner of Jullunder on the Panchayats are innocent to look at. He has laid down the law in an unexceptionable manner but he has missed the point of attack. No doubt the decisions of private Panchayats are not binding in law. But only those will seek the protection of the Panchayats who wish voluntarily to abide by their decisions and therefore need no process of enforcement of Panchayat decrees. No doubt, compounding of a felony is wrong. But no court in the world can compel a man whose property is stolen to lodge a complaint. Even in my capacity as a lawyer. I have had the privilege of advising clients not to prosecute thieves they had known and have rescued some of them from the police. Neither the police nor I. much less did the client. compound a felony in such cases. Why should not a Panchayat excommunicate a habitual thief? Society does not deprive itself of social protection when law-courts are established for the punishment of offenders. The Government have their own remedy when they wish to punish thieves and other offenders. I would therefore strongly advise the Panchayats of Jullunder to continue their very useful work of giving people cheap, speedy. and efficient justice. Care must of course be exercised that they resort to no punitive measures. The only penalty that is at our disposal is the force of public opinion. There is not much danger of parties who voluntarily seek the protection of the Panchayat disobeying the latter's verdicts. We must run the risk of some disobedience ; we must not, in impatience, resort to force or intimidation for the purpose either of securing reference to Panchayats or execution of their decrees.

large number of applications withdrawing pending cases is filed on that day and continues to be filed day after day. Let these cases and others which have not yet gone to court be disposed of by the panchayats which you will have organised by that time. Within the next few days, I hope to submit for your approval a scheme for the organisation of panchayats and the disposal of business before them. The work of educating the clients* and the public should however begin at once.

To those who believe in Non-co-operation—and their number is legion—I say: take your courage in both hands and boycott the courts completely regardless of any loss or inconvenience you may have to suffer. What you now look upon as a loss will undoubtedly be the greatest gain of your life—gain to yourself and to the Motherland. A few of you are rich, some are well off, but the vast majority can hardly make the two ends meet. To the rich and the well-off, I say it is criminal to be either the one or the other with the wrongs inflicted on the Motherland remaining unredressed and the possiblity of similar wrongs being repeated at any time and time after time continuing undiminished. Those who can merely eke out a bare subsistence need only to be reminded of the ineffaceable truth contained in the

* In answer to an enquiry by a friend as to what a man falsely sued was to do, Mr. Gandhi wrote in *Young India* of 25th May, 1921, under the heading, "A defendant's plight": Those who have been falsely charged by the Government have gone to gaol. Those who are falsely sued may, if the plaintiff will not go to private arbitration, make a statement and produce even witnesses without engaging a lawyer. He is likely to have judgment in his favour. But at the worst he runs the risk of having to pay a blackguard. Surely wrong judgments have been given before now in spite of the assistance of the ablest lawyers.

well-known Persian couplet which means, whatever is your lot you shall have it, if you refuse you will be forced to take it.

You may be sure that your country will not forsake you in the hour of your need. As you are aware, the All-India Congress Committee has started a national fund for this and other purposes connected with the Non-co-operation movement. It is your duty to help in collecting this fund for which detailed instructions will soon be issued. Meanwhile remember:

"The Giver of daily bread gives to you His wings to fly"—MOTILAL NEHRU.

30th March, 1921

PRACTISING LAWYERS

The *Patrika* devotes a leading article to an examination of the position taken up by me regarding lawyers,*

* The following appeared in *Young India* of 20th April, 1921:

A Protest.—The Editor, *Young India*, Ahmedabad,—Sir,—The other day when you left Jubbulpore for Cuttack, you had an interview with Gunada Babu at Calcutta. I have seen that interview in the "Independent" of the 2nd instant, which appears to have borrowed it from the "Servant." I refer you to a statement in that article attributed to you.

It runs thus:

"At Jubbulpore, from where he (Mahatma Gandhi) was coming, two young men (sons of rich merchants) were leading the movement very successfully against a whole host of lawyers. Being businessmen, they were carrying on the work of organisation most effectively."

This statement is incorrect.

The facts are:

These young men are not merchants, They are foundation stones of the British Government in India. They are Malguzars. Their trade is to realize Rs. 100 from the poor tenants, give the Government

and strongly dissents from it. The *Patrika* thinks that practising lawyers may continue to lead public opinion on Congress platform. I respectfully suggest that any such deviation from the Non-co-operation resolution will be a serious mistake. I am aware that the *Patrika* thinks that the Congress has not called upon *all* lawyers to suspend practice. I venture to differ from the interpretation. The resolution calls upon all lawyers to make greater effort to suspend practice. And, in my opinion, those lawyers who have not yet

---

Rs. 55 and keep Rs. 45 with themselves as commission and guarantee to recover the money even in the worst times. What a Non-co-operation with the Government! If these Malguzars are not co-operators, no one else is a co-operator. The Malguzari system was an invention of Todermal by which means people could be systematically dominated by the rulers through their mercenaries. These mercenaries are the Malguzars, who. you have said, are leading the movement.

If a lawyer who has not suspended his practice is not a proper person to be an office-bearer, certainly a Malguzar too should not be an office-bearer. A Malguzar is more attached to the Government than a lawyer.

In Jubbulpore these young men, Malguzars, are not leading the movement.

The movement in Jubbulpore is being led by the lawyers and the whole host of them are supporting it.

You did not give sufficient time to Jubbulpore, else the members of the Bar would have gladly seen you and discussed the matter with you. I fully believe that it will never be wealth which will lead the movement. It will always be the intellect and I hope you will correct the wrong impression created by the interview.

I suspended my practice in November last.

I am, etc.,
G. C. VARMA,
Barrister-at-law.

JUBBULPORE,
10-4-21.

[I am glad of Mr. Varma's energetic protest. And I hope that the lawyers of Jubbulpore are leading the N. C. O. Movement. I must however adhere to my statement that the lawyers were conspicuous

succeeded in suspending their practice, cannot expect to hold office in any Congress organisation or lead opinion on Congress platforms. Will titled men be elected as office bearers, although they may not have given up their titles? If we do not face the issues boldly, we stand in danger of corrupting the movement. We must exact correspondence between precept and practice. I hold that a lawyer president of a Provincial Committee cannot lead his province to victory, if he does not suspend his practice. He simply will not carry weight. I have noticed this again and again during my tours. Lawyers, who have hitherto led public opinion, have either renounced practice or public life.

The *Patrika* errs in comparing practising lawyers to merchants. Not many merchants have yet led public opinion, but where they have come forward, they have certainly renounced dealing in foreign cloth. The public will not, I am glad to be able to say, tolerate divorce between profession and practice. But not to seek, or give up public position is one thing, and to help the movement as a weak but humble follower is another.

---

by their absence on the day I visited Jubbulpore, and that the two young men referred to by me, were in charge of the whole management. That they are sons of land-holders is true enough. Theirs to-day is co-operation of necessity. The Congress has not yet called upon land-holders to surrender their lands to the Government, nor is it every likely to. These young men, like some land-holders' sons elsewhere, are taking an honorable part in the national uplift and they deserve every encouragement from lawyers. There are no two opinions about the fact that intellect rather than riches will lead. It might equally be admitted by the correspondent that the heart rather than the intellect will eventually lead. Character, not brains, will count at the crucial moment. And I fancied that these young men showed character. I should be sorry to find otherwise.—M. K.G.]

Thousands are unable to carry out the full advice of the Congress and are yet eagerly helping as silent camp-followers. That is the position that practising lawyers should take up. It will be honourable, dignified, and consistent. We may not, in our progress towards Swaraj, consider the lead of any class or individual as essential to success.

The *Patrika* goes beyond the scope of the Paragraph of "Young India" when it presents as an alternative to suspension, derision and insult. He would be an unworthy Non-co-operator who would deride or insult a lawyer, or any one else who is too weak or otherwise unable to respond to the Congress call. Because we may not elect such persons as office-bearers, we may not be intolerant and insulting to them. On the contrary, those, who are honestly unable to follow the Congress resolution are in every way worthy of sympathy.

Nor is the *Patrika* right in thinking that, before practising lawyers cease to be leaders, there should be a complete boycott of law courts; and as that is impossible without a rebel government, and as we do not contemplate rebellion, practising lawyers may safely lead opinion as hitherto. There is an obvious fallacy underlying this suggestion. Carried to its logical extent, it would mean that no leader need practise what he preaches. The fact is that, although law courts may not be completely boycotted by the sacrifice of Messrs. Nehru and Das, and by our refusal to give any public status to practising lawyers and others who have not carried out the Congress resolution, we have successfully demolished the prestige of these institutions, and, therefore, to that extent, of the Government. If we restore titled men, lawyers, and others, to their status even though they have not responded, we commit national suicide. Lastly, the *Patrika* is wrong in arguing that the Congress has called for suspension in order to secure the lawyer's services. The motive, as the preamble of the original resolution clearly states, is to undermine the Government's prestige by the Non-co-operation of parties to the institutions on which the prestige is built.

—M. K. G.

29th September, 1921

COBBLERS *vs.* LAWYERS

Babu Motilal Ghosh,* whose mind is fresh like that of a youth though he is too frail even to move, summoned Maulana Mahomed Ali and me chiefly to urge us to invite the lawyers to the Congress fold and in effect to restore them to their original status of unquestioned leadership of public opinion. Both the Maulana and I told him that we did want the lawyers to work for the Congress, but that those who would not suspend practice could not and should not become leaders. Moti Babu said that my mention of cobblers in the same breath as lawyers had offended some of them.† I felt sorry to hear this. I remember the note in

* Well-known, old Indian Nationalist; for years Editor of the *Amrita Bazaar Patrika* of Calcutta.

†The following appeared in *Young India* of 25th August, 1921 :

Practising Lawyers—Letters continue to pour in regarding practising lawyers holding offices in Congress Committees. Ever since my arrival in Bengal, the question has been still more pressingly put to me. An ex-student from Dhubri writes to ask whether I expect the movement to succeed under the leadership of practising lawyers. I cannot conceive the possibility of the movement, which is one of self-sacrifice, succeeding if it is led by lawyers who do not believe in self-sacrifice. I have not hesitated to advise that electors rather than be ably led by such lawyers should be content to be more humbly guided. I can certainly imagine a brave and believing weaver or cobbler more,

these pages, and it was certainly not written to offend. I have said many hard things about lawyers, but I have never considered them to be guilty of caste prejudices. I am sure that the lawyers have appreciated the spirit of my remark. I hope I am never guilty of putting a sting in any of my writings. But I certainly meant no offence in the paragraph referred to by Moti Babu. Having been myself a lawyer, I could not so far forget myself as wantonly to offend members of the same profession. Nor can I forget the brilliant and unique services rendered to the country by lawyers such as Pherozeshah Mehta, Ranade, Taiyebjee, Telang, Manomohan Ghose, Krishnaswami Iyer, not to speak of the living ones.

When no one else had the courage to speak, they were the voice of the people and guardians of their country's liberty. And, if to-day the majority of them are no longer accepted as leaders of the people, it is because different qualities are required for leadership from what they have exhibited hitherto. Courage, endurance, fearlessness and above all self-sacrifice are the qualities required of our leaders. A person belonging to the suppressed classes exhibiting these qualities in their fulness would certainly be able to lead the nation; whereas the most finished orator, if he has not these qualities, must fail.

And it has been a matter of keen satisfaction to me to find the lawyers all over India, who have not been able to suspend practice, readily assenting to the proposition and being content to work as humble camp-followers. A general will find his occupation gone, if there were no camp-followers in his army.

---

effectively leading than a timid and sceptical lawyer. Success depends upon bravery, sacrifice, truth, love and faith; not on legal acumen, calculation, diplomacy, hate and unbelief.

"But," said Moti Babu, "there is a great deal of intolerance that has crept into our movement. Non-co-operators insult those lawyers who have not suspended practice." I fear that the charge is true to a certain extent. Intolerance is itself a form of violence and an obstacle to the growth of a true democratic spirit. Arrogant assumption of superiority on the part of a Non-co-operator who has undergone a little bit of sacrifice or put on *Khadi* is the greatest danger to the movement. A Non-co-operator is nothing if he is not humble. When self-satisfaction creeps over a man, he has ceased to grow and therefore has become unfit for freedom. He who offers a little sacrifice from a lowly and religious spirit quickly realises the miserable littleness of it. Once on the path of sacrifice, we find out the measure of our selfishness, and must continually wish to give more and not be satisfied till there is a complete self-surrender.

And this knowledge of so little attempted and still less done must keep us humble and tolerant. It is our exclusiveness and the easy self-satisfaction that have certainly kept many a waverer away from us. Our motto must ever be conversion by gentle persuasion and a constant appeal to the head and the heart. We must therefore be ever courteous and patient with those who do not see eye to eye with us. We must resolutely refuse to consider our opponents as enemies of the country.

Lawyers and others who believe in Non-co-operation but have not, from any cause, been able to non-co-operate in matters applicable to them, can certainly do silent work as lieutenants in the matter of Swadeshi. It requires the largest number of earnest workers. There is no reason why a practising lawyer should not make *Khadi* fashionable by wearing it even in courts. There is no reason why he and his family should not spin during leisure hours. I have mentioned one out of a variety of things that can be done by practising lawyers for the attainment of Swaraj.* I hope, therefore, that no practising lawyer and for that matter no

*The following appeared in *Young India*, 12th January, 1922:

About Lawyers—The Jamnalal Bajaj fund of one lac of Rupees that was given last year for the support of lawyers who had suspended practice as a result of the Nagpur resolution is nearly, as it was intended to be, exhausted. The lawyers cannot go back to practise with any show of decency, and I am sure that many will not countenance even the idea of a return when the country is showing such wonderful example of self-sacrifice. But it would not be proper to leave the lawyers to their own resources. I would therefore certainly suggest to the Provincial Committees that they should take up the burden subject to assistance from the Central fund, if it was at all found necessary. The arrangement should be quickly made so as to avoid suspense and delay in the even tenor of national work.

This, however, is the least among the difficulties that surround the lawyer class at the present moment. They are eager to take part in the national awakening. The spirit is willing, the flesh is weak. I still feel that practising lawyers cannot lead. They cannot but weaken a movement which demands complete, almost reckless, sacrifice. The whole cause can be lost if top-men weaken at a supreme crisis. But the Congress has purposely opened an honourable door for them. The original draft was perhaps uncertain as to any but full Non-co-operators being entitled to sign the volunteer pledge. The conditions for them are easy of fulfilment, being mostly matters of belief. The use of *Khadi* may cause some little inconvenience at first, but I feel sure that they will not mind it, if otherwise they believe in the requirements of the pledge. And, as among Non-co-operators imprisonment covers a multitude of defects, practising lawyers who go through the fire of imprisonment will by that one fact come to occupy the position of honour which once was theirs. There is also the general resolution appealing to and inviting all including full co-operators to take up such activities as do not admit of any sacrifice or any difference of opinion. I hope therefore that lawyers will, to the best of their ability and opportunity, respond to the country's call in many of the

co-operating student will keep himself from serving the movement in every way open to him. All cannot become leaders, but all can be bearers. And Non-co-operators, I hope, will always make it easy for such countrymen to offer and render service.

29th September, 1920

THE HALLUCINATION OF SCHOOLS AND COLLEGES

(By M. K. Gandhi)

Much is being said and written against the proposed boycott of Government-controlled schools and colleges. The proposal has been described as 'mischievous', 'harmful,' 'opposed to the best interest of the country,' etc. Pundit Madan Mohan Malaviyaji is among its most uncompromising opponents.

I have been taxing myself to the best of my capacity in order to discover my error. But the effort has resulted in deepening my conviction that it is sinful to receive any education under the control of the present Government, no matter how high its quality may be, even as it would be to take the richest milk when it is tainted with poison.

---

various ways open to them. Where all are expected to help none should be found wanting or indifferent. Non-co-operators on their part instead of priding themselves upon their achievements should be humble enough to receive all the aid that might be rendered to the country's cause. The spirit of toleration should take the place of intoleration and exclusiveness. It can do no credit to the movement or good to the cause if a man, who has nothing or little to sacrifice, claims, by reason of his putting on *Khadi*, the right of slighting practising lawyers or others who may be honestly and according to their lights serving the country in various ways. Whatever is offered upon the altar of service to the motherland with a willing heart must be thankfully received.

I ask myself why some see the truth of the proposition quite clearly whilst others, the accepted leaders, condemn it as an error. The answer I have been able to find is that the latter do not consider the present system of Government as an unmixed evil as the former do. In other words, the opponents do not sufficiently realise the significance of the Punjab and the Khilafat wrongs. They do not feel as the others do that these wrongs show conclusively that the sum total of the activity of the present Government is injurious to national growth. I know that this is a serious statement to make. It is unthinkable that Malaviyaji and Shastriar cannot feel the wrongs even as I do. And yet that is precisely my meaning. I am positive that they will not put their children in a school where there was any likelihood of their becoming degraded instead of being elevated. I am equally positive that they would not send their children to a school managed, controlled or even influenced by a robber who had robbed them of their possessions. I feel that the nation's children suffer degradation in the Government schools. I feel that these schools and colleges are under the influence of a Government that has deliberately robbed the nation of its honour, and therefore the nation must withdraw its children from such schools. It may be that some learning even in such schools may be able to resist the progress of degradation. But it cannot be right to countenance national humiliation going on in the schools, because some have risen above their environment. In my opinion it is self-evident that the honoured leaders of the nation to-day do not realise that the Government-controlled schools are tainted in the manner described by me.

It may be urged that the schools are no worse to-day

than they were before the Punjab wrong or the Khilafat breach, and that we tolerated them before these events. I admit that the schools are not much worse now than before. But so far as I am concerned, the knowledge of the Punjab and the Khilafat betrayal has revolutionized my view of the existing system of Government. My ignorance of its inherent wickedness made the system tolerable to the extent of. my not rising against the schools. And that is just the reason why I fear that those who oppose the proposed boycott of the schools on the ground of its harmfulness, do not put the same valuation on the Punjab and the Khilafat wrongs that I do.

And so I congratulate Messrs. S. B. Tilak, Patel, Tripathi and others on their having given up their colleges even as they were on the point of finishing their education. That is also why I congratulate Misses Desai and Patel for their having left their high school. It is perhaps not generally known that these high-spirited girls left the schools of their own accord as have the young men.

I have no hesitation in wishing that the youth of India, both boys and girls, will, if they have felt personally the deep humiliation of atrocities of the Punjab, or understood the meaning of the violation of the Khilafat pledge, without any further reflection, empty the Government-controlled schools and colleges. The moral education that they will gain in a moment when they take that step will more than make up for the temporary loss of literary education. For the day that the boys and the girls empty the Government-controlled schools will be the day that will mark a very definite advance towards the goal. It will mark a revolution in the national thought. It will mark our freedom from the hallucination of schools and colleges. Is not the nation able to take charge of its own education without any Government intervention, protection, advice or grant?* Abandonment of the present schools means consciousness of our

* *Young India* of 17th November, 1920, contained the following: *Hallucination of Schools & Colleges*:—Though we would advocate and preach the Boycott of Schools and Colleges, with as much vigour and earnestness as we do now, even if the whole cost of education were borne by Government, we state some facts and figures which will disillusion those who believe it is not possible to nationalise education without Government aid.

The total expenditure on Primary, Secondary and Higher Education, including all educational departments, for the year 1918-19 was Rs. 1,129 lacs or 11.29 crores. It was met as follows:

			Lacs
Government Treasury	...	...	392
Local Funds	...	...	174
Municipal Funds	...	...	49
Fees	...	...	319
Public Funds	...	...	195
			1,129

Thus it will be seen that, while the Government spent 3.92 crores and the Municipalities and Local Boards Rs. 2. 23 crores, the people spent from their own purse directly Rs. 5. 16 crores. It may be noted that a good part of Government contribution was spent towards the upkeep of their own costly Educational Services.

* * *

If we take Secondary education only, which is the chief item of expenditure and of usefulness, we shall have a further revelation. The total amount spent on this branch was Rs. 3.67 crores. It was met as follows:

		Lacs
Government Treasury	...	94.75
Municipal and Local Boards	...	26.36
Fees	...	1.66
Public and Charitable Trusts	...	80
		367.11

ability to educate ourselves in spite of Himalayan difficulties.*

27th October, 1920

ALIGARH

(BY M. K. GANDHI)

Aligarh is an old institution—forty-five years old. It has unique traditions. It has a great record behind it. It may claim to have given to India the Ali Brothers. It is the best known centre of Islamic culture in India.

Why do I seek to destroy it? Some Mussalmans really think that I mean ill under the pretence of wishing well to Aligarh. Little do they know that I am

* The relation between destructive work and construction is discussed in the following which appeared in *Young India* of 3rd November, 1920:

Non-co-operation in Education.—Revered Mahatmaji,—One serious circumstance that impedes the advancement of your cause in this part of the country is the belief, shared by a section of the educated community, that your efforts being avowedly destructive cannot be deemed worthy of promotion. My own faith in your work as a great leaven of good, actual and potential, remains unshaken as before, for I consider it unsound to argue that ' negative agitation, ' as it comes to be called, *ipso facto* forfeits all claim to rational support. When an

---

Thus less than ⅐th was spent by Government, little more than ¼ by Government and Municipalities combined, while the rest was borne by the people directly.

Do these figures not show that practically we ourselves finance the Governmental education system, while all along we entertain the hallucination that the Government does everything, and that we can, with out Government aid, do nothing for ourselves. If we get rid of this hallucination and further decide upon curtailing the useless and costly paraphernalia, we can very easily make education, independent of Government control, stand on its own legs and make improvements, necessary to suit it to the needs of the country.

imploring Punditji to do to the Hindu University what I am asking the Trustees to do to Aligarh.* And I am certainly going to plead with the Benares students as

* The following is from *Young India* of 27th October, 1920:

To The Trustees of the Aligarh College.—Gentlemen,—I know you are about to meet in order to give your decision on a most momentous issue for Islam and India. I hear that you are calling in the aid of the Government and the police for the occasion of your meeting. If the rumour is true you would be making a grievous mistake. In a matter which is purely domestic you need neither the intervention of the Government, nor the protection of its police. Neither the Ali Brothers nor I are engaged in brute war. We are engaged in a war in which our only weapon is force of public opinion and we shall reckon ourselves beaten in the battle, if we do not carry the public with us. In the present dispute the test of public opinion will be in the first instance your majority. Therefore, if you after a full and free discussion decide by a majority, that the college and school students may not remain in the college ground either as students or even as boarders, if they persist in their demand of disaffiliation and

---

individual becomes enslaved, body and soul, to a pernicious habit like drink, the way to wean him is ever double-edged, or to use the opponents' phraseology, at once 'negative and positive.' If the physician wishes to succeed in his cure he must primarily employ all his energy in enabling the patient to resist the temptation and overcome the evil, ere he prescribes to him some substitute in place of the poison. The new recipe must needs fail to produce an effect, if concomitantly, the patient persists in his old habit; from which the lesson may be deduced that the initial 'negative' stage of destruction is as essential for cure as the later 'positive' stage of recuperation. Even so our country should first shake itself free from the shackles of emasculating institutions, in advance of any constructive programme of work that may be undertaken for its regeneration. I appeal to my countrymen not to be oblivious of this important truth, and earnestly trust that it may be driven home in their minds by yourself, with due emphasis and frequency.

Wishing you every success,

Believe me,
Very sincerely yours,

Shantiniketan,
November 10, 1920.

DWIJENDRANATH TAGORE.

earnestly as I have with the Aligarh boys. I have done the same with the Khalsa College. The latter is the only centre of Sikh culture.

---

the rejection of the Government grant, they will be peacefully withdrawn. We propose in that event to carry on their education if at all possible in Aligarh itself, or elsewhere. The desire is not to suspend their secular education for one moment longer than is absolutely necessary. But it is our sincere desire that it should be given in consistence with the Law of Islam and the honour of India. I understand that in the opinion of the recognized Ulemas it is not lawful for a believing Muslim to receive the assistance of a Government that has directly or indirectly sought to cause the destruction of the holy Khilafat and to tamper with the exclusive Muslim control of Jazirat-ul-Arab. You know as well as I do, how this Government has wilfully trampled under foot Indian honour. Consistently, therefore, with the control of the passions by the people, all voluntary association with the Government is being withdrawn by the people. The least that you, in my humble opinion, can do is to decline any further Government grant, disaffiliate the great institution of which you are the trustees and reject the charter of the Muslim University. The least that the Aligarh boys can do, if you fail to respond to the call of Islam and India, is to wash their hands clean of an institution acknowledging the aegis of Government that has forfeited all title to the allegiance of Islam and India and to bring into being a larger, nobler and purer Aligarh that would carry out the inmost wishes of its great founder. I cannot imagine the late illustrious Sir Syed Ahmed keeping his noble creation under the control or influence of the present Government.

As I have been the originator of the idea of disaffiliation of Aligarh and rejection of the Government grant, I feel that I might be able to assist you in your discussions, and therefore, offer my humble services to you, and will gladly attend your meeting if you will allow me to do so. I am proceeding to Bombay and shall await your answer there.

But whether you wish me to attend or not, I hope that you will not summon Government intervention in this purely domestic matter.

And let me say to the Government, through you, that one hears all sorts of rumours of their intentions about the Ali Brothers and myself. I hope, for the peaceful evolution of the struggle, they will not restrict our liberty. We are endeavouring in a most constitutional

I do desire passionately to destroy all these three institutions as they are, and would strive to raise purer and truer ones instead.

I deny that these institutions are in any way true representatives of their respective cultures. Inasmuch as Islam is in peril at English hands, Hinduism and Sikhism are also in peril. I asked an Aligarh professor whether he could preach complete independence for India as her goal if necessary, or if the institution as such could refuse to receive a Governor in his official capacity. He frankly admitted that it was not possible. And yet I make bold to say that to-day the vast majority of the students of India have no regard or respect for British rule. They are disgusted with it. They have certainly no genuine affection for it. I venture to submit that to keep our boys in this false atmosphere is to teach them to deny their faith and for us to do

---

manner to conduct our propaganda. We are seeking to bend the Government to the people's will, or if it will not, to overthrow it, not by brute-force but by creating real public opinion. We hold it to be perfectly constitutional, legitimate and honourable to expose the satanic nature of the Government, and to ask the people by appealing to their heads and their hearts, never to their animal passions, to express their will, not in words but in action, *i.e.*, by withdrawing all possible association with the Government. But if the Government wish even to suppress the liberty of opinion and peaceful action, I hope they will issue no internment orders against us, but will imprison us. For, in spite of our sincere desire not to offer Civil Disobedience even in our own persons, it will not be possible for us to respect any internment orders. So long as our movement is not physically restrained we must use it in such a manner as we consider to be the best in the interests of our mission.

With humble apology,
Your faithful Servant,
M. K. GANDHI.

violence to our respective cultures. We will not make a nation out of hypocrites.

With the knowledge we have of British intentions, it is unmanly, un-Indian, for us to accept even a portion of our own money through hands, stained with the blood of the innocents at Jallianwalla. We may as well accept gifts from a robber who has robbed us of our property. This Government has robbed us of our honour and put one of our religions in peril. In my humble opinion, it is a sin for the nation to receive education in schools financed by or under the influence or control of the Government.

I have therefore no hesitation in advising immediate destruction of these institutions at all cost. But if the trustees, the teachers, and the parents or the boys will act in unison, there is no cost to be paid and everything to be gained.

I am asking for the form to be changed, I do not seek to destroy the soul. Even as we leave bodies which we have outgrown, so must we leave the institutions which we have outgrown, and bring into being others, more in accord with our needs. How can scholastic institutions which represent the youth of a nation, lag behind when the nation is marching forward*? Several High Schools,

* The following appeared in *Young India* of 3rd November, 1920:

To the Parents of Aligarh Boys.—Gentlemen,—I know that the best of my friends are bewildered at many of my doings at the present moment, not the least among which is my advice to the youth of the country. I do not wonder at their bewilderment. I have undergone a complete transformation in my attitude towards the system of Government under which we are labouring. To me it is satanic even as was the system under *Ravan's* rule according to the scriptures of my religion. But my friends are not so convinced as I am of the supreme necessity of ending this rule, unless the system undergoes a radical change and there is definite repentance on the part of the rulers.

I share too your concern about your boys who are learning at

having a more or less distinguished record, have thrown off the yoke of grant and affiliation in Gujarat. They are none the worse for it. They are all the purer for it.

Aligarh. You will believe me when I tell you that I do not wish to hurt your feelings. I am myself the father of four boys whom I have brought up to the best of my lights. I have been an extremely obedient son to my parents, and an equally obedient pupil to my teachers. I know the value of filial duty. But I count duty to God above all these. And in my opinion, the time has come for every young man and young woman in this country to make their choice between duty to God and duty to others. I claim to know the youth of our country in a fairly intimate manner. I know that in the majority of cases the youth of our country have the determining of their higher education in their own hands. I know cases in which parents find it difficult to wean their children from what to them (the parents) appears to be the infatuation of their children, about higher education. I am convinced that I am doing no violence to the feelings of parents when I address our young men and ask them to leave their schools or colleges even in spite of their parents. You will not be astonished to learn that, of the parents of hundreds of boys who have left schools or colleges, I have received only one protest and that from a Government servant, whose boys have left their college. The protest is based on the ground that they were not even consulted before their boys decided to leave their college. In fact my advice to the boys was even to discuss with their parents the question of leaving before arriving at a decision.

I have myself appealed to thousands of parents at scores of meetings at which hardly a parent has objected to the proposition of leaving Government-controlled schools. Indeed they have with wonderful unanimity passed resolutions on Non-co-operation including the item on schools. I therefore take leave to think that the parents of the Aligarh boys are no less convinced than the others of the necessity of withdrawing their children from schools and colleges supported or controlled by a government that has participated in betraying the Mussulmans of India and has wantonly humiliated the nation through its barbarous treatment of the Punjab.

I hope you know that I am as eager as any that our boys' education should not be neglected. But I am certainly more eager that their education is received through clean hands. I hold it to be unmanly

The principals and the trustees can train the youth under their charge in a freer atmosphere.

Financial considerations deter those who do not want to work. Our institutions will collapse if the teachers or the trustees are false to their trust, or the nation really does not want them. The programme of Non-co-operation is based on the belief that the nation is tired of the present Government and wants to change it without resorting to methods of violence. The experience so far gained shows that the nation does definitely desire the change. If there is failure or delay, it will be due to want of workers.

for us to continue to receive grants for our education from a government which we heartily dislike. In my humble opinion that would be even dishonourable and disloyal.

Is it not better that our children should receive their education in a free atmosphere, even though it may be given in humble cottages or in the shade of trees and under teachers who, being themselves free, would breathe into our children the spirit of freedom? I wish you could realise that the destiny of our beloved land lies not in us, the parents, but in our children. Shall we not free them from the curse of slavery which has made us crawl on our bellies? Being weak, we may not have the strength or the will even to throw off the yoke. But shall we not have the wisdom not to leave the cursed inheritance to our children?

They can lose nothing by pursuing their studies as free lads and lasses. Surely they do not need Government university degrees. And if we could but get rid of the love of Government degrees for our boys the question of finding money for their education is in reality simple. For a week's self-denial by the nation will provide for the education of its school-going children for one year. Our existing religious and charitable Hindu and Muslim funds can support our education without even a week of self-denial. The present effort is no more than an attempt to take a referendum of our capacity to govern ourselves and to protect our religions and our honour.

I remain,

Well-wisher of the youth of India,

M. K. Gandhi.

17*th November*, 1920

THE NATIONAL UNIVERSITY OF GUJARAT

By establishing a university and starting a college, at Ahmedabad, Gujarat has shown that Non-co-operation has a constructive side as well.* Only, being a purifying process, Non-co-operation has to destroy before it can construct. The National University stands to-day as a protest against British injustice, and as a vindication of National honour. But it has come to stay. It draws its inspiration from the national ideals of a united India. It stands for a religion which is the Dharma of the Hindus and Islam of Mahomedans. It wants to rescue the Indian vernaculars from unmerited oblivion and make them the fountains of national regeneration and Indian culture. It holds that a systematic study of Asiatic cultures is

*The following also appeared in *Young India* of 17th November, 1920:

The Gujarat National College.—Never have I felt my position as embarrassing as I felt it at the time of inaugurating the Gujarat National College. I knew that it marked a silent and peaceful revolution which my audience might not understand or appreciate. I felt too that the National College would suffer in comparison, if brick and mortar or academic distinction were to be the test. It was hardly possible to have a *national* building, when a government, which claimed to be the ultimate proprietor of all our earthly possessions, had ceased to be the mouth-piece of the nation, and had even forfeited its confidence—yet the new college has in it possibilities which it is impossible to forecast. May it be the seed of national freedom! Its success will depend upon the combined efforts of the teachers and the scholars. Without any literary merit, I have accepted the office of Chancellor, and performed the inauguration ceremony, because I believe in Non-co-operation being the only remedy for national regeneration, and because I believe that the staff of the College and members of the Senate are truly imbued with the same belief. I have approached my task in prayerful humility. May God protect the new University and the College!

no less essential than the study of western sciences for a complete education for life. The vast treasures of Sanskrit and Arabic, Persian and Pali, and Magadhi have to be ransacked in order to discover wherein lies the source of strength for the nation. It does not propose merely to feed on, or repeat, the ancient cultures. It rather hopes to build a new culture based on the traditions of the past enriched by the experience of later times. It stands for the synthesis of the different cultures that have come to stay in India, that have influenced Indian life, and that, in their turn, have themselves been influenced by the spirit of the soil. This synthesis will naturally be of the Swadesi type where each culture is assured its legitimate place, and not of American pattern, where one dominant culture absorbs the rest, and where the aim is not towards harmony, but towards an artificial and forced unity. That is why the University has desired a study of all the Indian religions by its students. The Hindus may thus have an opportunity of studying the Koran and the Muslims of knowing what the Hindu Shastras contain. If the University has excluded anything, it is the Spirit of Exclusion that regards any section of humanity as permanently untouchable. The study of Hindustani, which is a national blend of Sanskrit, Hindi and Persianised Urdu, has been made compulsory. The spirit of independence will be fostered not only through Religion, Politics, and History, but through vocational training also, which alone can give the youths of the country economic independence and a back-bone that comes out of a sense of self-respect. The university hopes to organise higher schools throughout the mofussil towns, so that education may be spread broad-cast and filtered down to the masses as early as possible. The use of Gujrati as the medium of education will facilitate this process and, ere long, the suicidal cleavage between the educated and the non-educated will be bridged. And, as an effect of industrial education to the genteel folks, and literary education for the industrial classes, the unequal distribution of wealth and the consequent social discontent will be considerably checked. The greatest defect of the Government Universities has been their alien control and the false values they have created as regards 'careers.' The Gujarat University by non-co-operating with the Government has automatically eradicated both these evils from its own system. If the founders and promoters stick to this resolve till the Government becomes nationalised, it will help them to cultivate a clear perception of national ideals and national needs. Let us pray to God that the workers get the necessary faith and strength to uphold the banner they have unfurled.

1st September, 1921

NATIONAL EDUCATION

(BY M. K. GANDHI)

So many strange things have been said about my views on national education, that it would perhaps not be out of place to formulate them before the public.

In my opinion, the existing system of education is defective, apart from its association with an utterly unjust Government, in three most important matters :

(1) It is based upon foreign culture to the almost entire exclusion of indigenous culture.

(2) It ignores the culture of the heart and the hand and confines itself simply to the head.

(3) Real education is impossible through a foreign medium.

Let us examine the three defects. Almost from the commencement, the text-books deal, not with things the boys and the girls have always to deal with in their homes, but things to which they are perfect strangers. It is not through the text-books, that a lad learns what is right and what is wrong in the home life. He is never taught to have any pride in his surroundings. The higher he goes, the farther he is removed from his home, so that at the end of his education he becomes estranged from his surroundings. He feels no poetry about the home life. The village scenes are all a sealed book to him. His own civilization is presented to him as imbecile, barbarous, superstitious and useless for all practical purposes. His education is calculated to wean him from his traditional culture. And if the mass of educated youths are not entirely denationalised, it is because the ancient culture is too deeply embedded in them to be altogether uprooted even by an education adverse to its growth. If I had my way, I would certainly destroy the majority of the present text-books and cause to be written text-books which have a bearing on and correspondence with the home life, so that a boy as he learns may react upon his immediate surroundings.

Secondly, whatever may be true of other countries, in India at any rate where more than eighty per cent of the population is agricultural and another ten per cent industrial, it is a crime to make education merely literary and to unfit boys and girls for manual work in after-life. Indeed I hold that, as the larger part of our time is devoted to labour for earning our bread, our children must from their infancy be taught the dignity of such labour. Our children should not be so taught as to despise labour. There is no reason why a peasants's son, after having gone to a school, should become useless, as he does become, as agricultural labourer. It is a sad thing that our schoolboys look upon manual labour with disfavour, if not contempt. Moreover, in India, if we expect, as we must, every boy and girl of school-going age to attend public schools, we have not the means to finance education in accordance with the existing style, nor are millions of parents able to pay the fees that are at present imposed. Education to be universal must therefore be free. I fancy that, even under an ideal system of government, we shall not be able to devote two thousand million rupees which we should require for finding education for all the children of school-going age. It follows, therefore, that our children must be made to pay in *labour* partly or wholly for all the education they receïve. Such universal labour to be profitable can only be (to my thinking) hand-spinning and hand-weaving. But for the purposes of my proposition, it is immaterial whether we have spinning or any other form of labour, so long as it can be turned to account. Only, it will be found upon examination, that on a practical, profitable and extensive scale, there is no occupation other than the processes connected with cloth-production which can be introduced in our schools throughout India.

The introduction of manual training will serve a double purpose in a poor country like ours. It will pay for the education of our children and teach them an occupation on which they can fall back in after-life, if they choose, for earning a living. Such a system must make our children self-reliant. Nothing will demoralise the nation so much as that we should learn to despise labour.

One word only as to the education of the heart. I do

not believe that this can be imparted through books. It can only be done through the living touch of the teacher. And, who are the teachers in the primary and even secondary schools? Are they men and women of faith and character? Have they themselves received the training of the heart? Are they even expected to take care of the permanent element in the boys and girls placed under their charge? Is not the method of engaging teachers for lower schools an effective bar against character? Do the teachers get even a living wage? And we know that the teachers of primary schools are not selected for their patriotism. They only come who cannot find any other employment.

Finally, the medium of instruction. My views on this point are too well known to need re-stating. The foreign medium has caused brain-fag, put an undue strain upon the nerves of our children, made them crammers and imitators, unfitted them for original work and thought, and disabled them for filtrating their learning to the family or the masses. The foreign medium has made our children practically foreigners in their own land. It is the greatest tragedy of the existing system. The foreign medium has prevented the growth of our vernaculars. If I had the powers of a despot, I would to-day stop the tuition of our boys and girls through a foreign medium, and require all the teachers and professors on pain of dismissal to introduce the change forthwith. I would not wait for the preparation of text-books. They will follow the change. It is an evil that needs a summary remedy.

My uncompromising opposition to the foreign medium has resulted in an unwarranted charge being levelled against me of being hostile to foreign culture or the learning of the English language. No reader of "Young

India" could have missed the statement often made by me in these pages, that I regard English as the language of international commerce and diplomacy, and therefore consider its knowledge on the part of some of us as essential. As it contains some of the richest treasures of thought and literature, I would certainly encourage its careful study among those who have linguistic talents and expect them to translate those treasures for the nation in its vernaculars.

Nothing can be farther from my thought than that we should become exclusive or erect barriers. But I do respectfuly contend that an appreciation of other cultures can fitly follow, never precede, an appreciation and assimilation of our own. It is my firm opinion that no culture has treasures so rich as ours has. We have not known it, we have been made even to deprecate its study and depreciate its value. We have almost ceased to live it. An academic grasp without practice behind it is like an embalmed corpse, perhaps lovely to look at but nothing to inspire or ennoble. My religion forbids me to belittle or disregard other cultures, as it insists under pain of civil suicide upon imbibing and living my own.

23rd February, 1921

HOW MAY LAWYERS AND STUDENTS HELP

(BY M. K. GANDHI)

Everywhere I have been asked whether lawyers and students who do not carry out the Congress resolution affecting them can help the movement in any other way.* The question is rather strange, for it assumes

*Students who non-co-operated should not however return to their studies. The following appeared in *Young India* of 19th January, 1920:

that, if a lawyer or a student cannot non-co-operate as such, he cannot help at all.

There are undoubtedly hundreds of students and

To Young Bengal.—Dear Young Friends,—I have just read an account of your response to the nation's call. It does credit to you and to Bengal. I had expected no less: I certainly expect still more. Bengal has great intelligence, it has a greater heart, it has more than its share of the spiritual heritage for which our country is specially noted. You have more imagination, more faith, and more emotion than the rest of India. You have falsified the calumny of cowardice on more occasions than one. There is, therefore, no reason why Bengal should not lead now as it has done before.

You have taken the step: you will not recede. You had ample time to think. You have paused, you have considered. You held the Congress that delivered to the nation the message of Non-co-operation, *i.e.*, of self-purification, self-sacrifice, courage, and hope. The Nagpur Congress ratified, clarified, and amplified the first declaration. It was delivered in the midst of strife, doubt, and disunion. It was open to you to refuse, or to hesitate to respond. You have chosen the better, though, from a worldly-wise standpoint, less cautious way. You dare not go back without hurting yourselves and the cause.

But for the evil spell that the existing systems of government and, most of all, this western education has cast upon us, the question will not be considered as open to argument. Can the brave Arabs retain their independence and yet be schooled under the aegis of those who would hold them under bondage? They will laugh at a person who dare to ask them to go to schools that may be established by their invaders. Is the case different, or if it is different, is it not stronger in our case when we are called upon to give up schools conducted under the aegis of Government which, rightly or wrongly, we seek to bend to our will or destroy?

We cannot get *Swaraj*, if not one class in the country is prepared to work and sacrifice for it. The Government will yield not to the logic of words. It knows no logic but that of brave and true deeds.

Bravery of the sword they know. And they have made themselves proof against its use by us. Many of them will welcome violence on our part. They are unconquerable in the art of meeting and suppressing violence. We propose, therefore, to sterilize their power of inflicting violence by our Non-violence. Violence dies when it ceases

scores of lawyers who are not suspending their normal studies or their practice, as the case may be, only out of weakness. A lawyer who cannot suspend practice,

---

to evoke response from its object. Non-violence is the corner-stone of the edifice of Non-co-operation. You will, therefore, not be hasty or over-zealous in your dealings with those who may not see eye to eye with you. Intolerance is a species of violence and therefore against our creed. Non-violent Non-co-operation is an object lesson in democracy. The moment we are able to ensure non-violence, even under circumstances the most provoking, that moment we have achieved our end because that is the moment when we can offer complete Non-co-operation.

I ask you not to be frightened at the proposition just stated. People do not move in arithmetical progression, not even in geometrical progression. They have been known to perish in a day: they have been known to rise in a day. Is it such a difficult thing for India to realise that thirty crores of human beings have but to feel their strength and they can be free without having to use it? As we had not regained national consciousness, the rulers have hitherto played us against one another. We have to refuse to do so, and we are masters: not they.

Non-co-operation deals first with those sensitive classes upon whom the Government has acted so successfully and who have been lured into the trap consciously or unconsciously as the school-going youths have been.

When we come to think about it, the sacrifice required is infinitesimal for individuals, because the whole is distributed among so many of us. For what is your sacrifice? To suspend your literary studies for one year or till Swaraj is established. If I could infect the whole of the student world with my faith, I know that the suspension of studies need not extend even to a year.

And in the place of your suspended studies, I would urge you to study the methods of bringing about Swaraj as quietly as possible even within the year of grace. I present you with the SPINNING WHEEL and suggest to you that on it depends India's economic salvation.

But you are at liberty to reject it if you wish and go to the College that has been promised to you by Mr. Das. Most of your fellow-students in the National College at Gujarat have undertaken to give at least four hours to spinning every day. It is no sacrifice to learn a beautiful art and to be able to clothe the naked at the same time.

can certainly help with money, he can give his spare hours to public service, he can introduce honesty and fair dealings in his profession, he can cease to consider clients as fit prey for his pecuniary ambition, he can cease to have anything to do with touts, he can promote settlement of cases by private arbitration, he can at least do spinning himself for one or two hours per day, he can simplify the life of his family, he can induce the members of the family to do spinning religiously for a certain time daily, he can adopt for himself and his family the use of Khaddar. These are only some of the things that can be done by every lawyer. Because a man cannot or will not carry out a particular part of the Non-co-operation programme, he need not be shy about the other items. One thing a practising lawyer may not do: he may no longer figure as a leader on public platforms. He must be content to be a silent worker. What I have said about practising lawyers applies to students also who cannot or will not withdraw from schools. Most of our volunteers are drawn from the student world. Volunteering is a privilege and a student who has not been able to withdraw from Government schools cannot receive privileges from the nation. They too must be content to be unambitious servants of the nation. Even if we cannot completely boycott schools and colleges, we must destroy their prestige. That prestige has almost gone and is daily

---

You have done your duty by withdrawing from Government colleges. I have only showed you the easiest and the most profitable way of devoting the time at your disposal.

May God give you strength and courage to sustain you in your determination.

Your well-wisher,
M. K. Gandhi.

decreasing. And we must do nothing that would restore their prestige till they are nationalised and answer the requirements of the nation.

15*th June*, 1921

A PARENT'S DUTY

(BY M. K. GANDHI)

"This year, my third son aged 21 years has passed his B. A. with honours at an enormous expense. He does not wish to enter Government service. He wants to take up national service only. My family consists of twelve members. I have still to educate five boys. I had an estate, which has been sold to pay a debt of Rs. 2,000. In educating my three sons, I have spent all my earnings and all this in the hope, that my third son would secure the highest degree in the University, and then try to retrieve the position I have almost lost. I had expected him to be able to take up the whole burden of my family. But now I am almost led to think that I must give my family up to ruin. There is a conflict of duties on the one hand and motives on the other. I seek your careful consideration and advice."

This is a typical letter. And it is the universality, almost of the attitude, that set me against the present system of education years ago, and made me change the course of the education of all my boys and others with (in my opinion) excellent results.* The hunt after position

* The following appeared in *Young India* of 3rd November, 1921 ; *Education and Non-co-operation*,—To the Editor, *Young India*, Sir,—In the Karti issue of the *Pravasi*, a Bengali monthly edited by the reputed journalist Mr. Ramananda Chatterjee, appears an article, over the initials S. C., on the present educational activities of Russia. In this article occurs a passage to which I wish to draw your attention. I am translating it below :

and status has ruined many a family, and has made many depart from the path of rectitude. Who does not know, what questionable things fathers of families in

"But even under the stress of the present upheavals, Russia has kept burning her torch of learning, faint though it is. None has advised her, like the wise patriots of our country (India), to let education wait. Russia knows that no vital antagonism (incompatibility) exists between war and education, as exists between water and oil."

I apologise for the bad rendering but this is the idea contained in the few Bengali lines I refer to.

I do not exactly understand what the writer means by these lines and as Mr. Gandhi is one of the "wise patriots who have advised us to let education wait." I would respectfully request him to express his views on the above passage, as such a view is held by a section of the community which declares itself to be "sane" and "rational."

Yours, etc.,

Purulia. PHANINDRANATH DASGUPTA.

[I am not surprised at the view expressed in the *Pravasi*. In my humble opinion, it betrays at once ignorance of the position of the wise patriots' and a distorted view of education. The Russians are not non-co-operating with their existing institutions. And yet in a state of war there too, the torch of learning is burning faint even as in Non-co-operation schools. But what happened in England when it was at war with Germany? How many schools were then going on in England? I know that the Inns of Court and many colleges were practically closed. I know that during the Boer war not a Boer child had literary education. The Boer children's education consisted in suffering for the sake of their country.

The fact is that the present peaceful movement is so silent and gentle on the whole, that it is possible for those who do not believe in the doctrine to continue the education of their children under a system against which the country is 'waging war.' That the movement is the more effective for its gentleness will, I prophesy, be recorded by the future historian with grateful appreciation. Lastly we have little reason to be proud of our educational institutions which by their very nature are accessible to a mere fringe of our population. In our state of intoxication, we do not perceive the disastrous effect of the present system of education on the country. I have taxed myself to find something to the credit of the system in

need of money for their children's education have considered it their duty to do. I am convinced that we are in far worse times, unless we change the whole system of our education. We have only touched the fringe of an ocean of children. The vast mass of them remain without education, not for want of will but of ability and knowledge on the part of the parents. There is something radically wrong, especially for a nation so poor as ours, when parents have to support so many grown-up children, and give them a highly expensive education without the children making any immediate return.

I can see nothing wrong in the children, from the very threshold of their education, paying for it in work. The simplest handicraft suitable for all, required for the whole of India, is undoubtedly spinning along with the previous processes. If we introduced this in our educational institutions, we should fulfil three purposes, make education self-supporting, train the bodies of the children as well as their minds, and pave the way for a complete boycott of foreign yarn and cloth. Moreover, the children thus equipped will become self-reliant and independent. I would suggest to the correspondent that he should invite all the members of his family to contribute to its upkeep by spinning or weaving. Under my scheme, no child is entitled to education, who does not spin a minimum quantity of yarn.

---

the way of a solution of the various problems affecting the country: I have failed to find a single thing of that character. There are to-day 7, 851, 946 children receiving instruction in our schools. I claim that it is impossible under the present system even to double the number of learners during the next fifty years. If education is to be universal, the system will have to be revised out of all recognition. This is possible only by Non-co-operation. Public conscience cannot be stung into quickness with a milder remedy.—M. K. G.]

Such families will acquire a prestige for self-respect and independence not hitherto dreamt of. This scheme does not exclude a liberal education, but on the contrary brings it within the easy reach of every boy or girl, and restores literary training to its original dignity by making it primarily a means of mental and moral culture, and only secondarily and indirectly a means of livelihood.

—M. K. G.

25th February, 1920.

HINDU-MAHOMEDAN UNITY

(By M. K. Gandhi)

Mr. Candler * some time ago asked me in an imaginary interview whether, if I was sincere in my professions of Hindu-Mahomedan Unity, I would eat and drink with a Mahomedan and give my daughter in marriage to a Mahomedan. This question has been asked again by some friends in another form. Is it necessary for Hindu-Mahomedan Unity that there should be interdining and intermarrying? The questioners say that if the two are necessary, real unity can never take place because crores of *Sanatanis* would never reconcile themselves to interdining, much less to intermarriage.

I am one of those who do not consider caste to be a harmful institution. In its origin, caste was a wholesome custom and promoted national well-being. In my opinion, the idea that interdining or intermarrying is necessary for national growth, is a superstition borrowed from the West. Eating is a process just as vital as the other sanitary necessities of life. And if mankind had not, much to its harm, made of eating a fetish and indulgence, we would have performed the operation of

* *See* page 162.

eating in private even as one performs the other necessary functions of life in private. Indeed the highest culture in Hinduism regards eating in that light and there are thousands of Hindus still living who will not eat their food in the presence of anybody. I can recall the names of several cultured men and women who ate their food in entire privacy but who never had any ill will against anybody and who lived on the friendliest terms with all.

Intermarriage is a still more difficult question. If brothers and sisters can live on the friendliest footing without ever thinking of marrying each other, I can see no difficulty in my daughter regarding every Mahomedan brother and *vice versa.* I hold strong views on religion and on marriage. The greater the restraint we exercise with regard to our appetites whether about eating or marrying, the better we become from a religious standpoint. I should despair of ever cultivating amicable relations with the world, if I had to recognise the right or the propriety of any young man offering his hand in marriage to my daughter or to regard it as necessary for me to dine with anybody and everybody. I claim that I am living on terms of friendliness with the whole world. I have never quarrelled with a single Mahomedan or Christian, but for years I have taken nothing but fruits in Mahomedan or Christian households. I would most certainly decline to eat cooked food from the same plate with my son or to drink water out of a cup which his lips have touched and which has not been washed. But the restraint or the exclusiveness exercised in these matters by me has never affected the closest companionship with the Mahomedan or the Christian friends or my sons.

But interdining and intermarriage have never been a bar to disunion, quarrels and worse. The Pandavas and the Kauravas flew at one another's throats without compunction although they interdined and intermarried. The bitterness between the English and the Germans has not yet died out.

The fact is that intermarriage and interdining are not necessary factors in friendship and unity though they are often emblems thereof. But insistence on either the one or the other can easily become and is to-day a bar to Hindu-Mahomedan Unity. If we make ourselves believe that Hindus and Mahomedans cannot be one unless they interdine or intermarry, we would be creating an artificial barrier between us which it might be almost impossible to remove. And it would seriously interfere with the growing unity between Hindus and Mahomedans if, for example, Mahomedan youths consider it lawful to court Hindu girls. The Hindu parents will not, even if they suspected any such thing, freely admit Mahomedans to their homes as they have begun to do now. In my opinion, it is necessary for Hindu and Mahomedan young men to recognise this limitation.

I hold it to be utterly impossible for Hindus and Mahomedans to intermarry and yet retain in tact each other's religion. And the true beauty of Hindu-Mahomedan Unity lies in each remaining true to his own religion and yet being true to each other. For, we are thinking of Hindus and Mahomedans even of the most orthodox type being able to regard one another as natural enemies as they have done hitherto.

What then does the Hindu-Mahomedan Unity consist in and how can it be best promoted? The answer is simple. It consists in our having a common purpose, a common goal and common sorrows. It is best promoted by co-operating to reach the common goal, by sharing one another's sorrows and by mutual toleration. A common goal we have. We wish this great country of ours to be greater and self-governing. We have enough sorrows to share. And to-day seeing that the Mahomedans are deeply touched on the question of Khilafat and their case is just, nothing can be so powerful for winning Mahomedan friendship for the Hindu as to give his whole-hearted support to the Mahomedan claim. No amount of drinking out of the same cup or dining out of the same bowl can bind the two as this help in the Khilafat question.

And mutual toleration is a necessity for all time and for all races. We cannot live in peace if the Hindu will not tolerate the Mahomedan form of worship of God and his manners and customs or if the Mahomedan will be impatient of Hindu idolatory or cow-worship. It is not necessary for toleration that I must approve of what I tolerate. I heartily dislike drinking, meat-eating and smoking, but I tolerate all these in Hindus, Mahomedans and Christians even as I expect them to tolerate my abstinence from all these although they may dislike it. All the quarrels between the Hindus and the Mahomedans have arisen from each wanting to *force* the other to his view.

6th October, 1920

HINDU-MUSLIM UNITY

(By M. K. Gandhi)

There can be no doubt that successful Non-co-operation depends as much on Hindu-Muslim Unity as on non-violence. The greatest strain will be put upon both in the course of the struggle, and if it survivs that strain, victory is a certainty.

A severe strain was put upon it in Agra,* and it has been stated that, when either party went to the authorities, they were referred to Maulana Shaukat Ali and me. Fortunately there was a far better man at hand. Hakimji Ajmal Khan is a devout Muslim who commands the confidence and the respect of both the parties. He with his band of workers hastened to Agra, settled the dispute and the parties became friends as they were never before. An incident occurred nearer Delhi, and the same influence worked successfully to avoid what might have become an explosion.

But Hakimji Ajmal Khan cannot be everywhere appearing at the exact hour as an angel of peace. Nor can Maulana Shaukat Ali or I go everywhere. And yet perfect peace must be observed between the two communities in spite of attempts to divide them.†

* About this time Hindu-Muslim relations were strained at Agra over the cow question.

† The following note written by Mr. Satish C. Guha appeared in *Young India* of 10th November, 1920:

Dr. Taylor's "Topography of Dacca" was written in the early part of the nineteenth century and published in 1839 A. C. The book relates that the relation between the two religions was amicable in general. In Chap. 9 (P. 257) of Dr. Taylor's book, we read:

"Religious quarrels between the Hindus and Mahomedans are of rare occurrence. These two classes live in perfect peace and concord, and a majority of individuals belonging to them have even overcome their prejudices so far as to smoke from the same *Hooka*".

Although, both from the sanitary and religious points of view, it may not be an ideal practice for any two smokers to use the same *Hooka* without properly washing it after each use, the practice as observed amongst friends belonging to different religions in those days clearly shows how amicable the relations between the two peoples were in those days.

Another book, a rather earlier publication, 'The East India Gazetteer' by Walter Hamilton (published in 2 Vols. in 1828 A.C.) notices a similar state of things existing all over India and even the

Why was there any appeal made to the authorities at all at Agra? If we are to work out Non-co-operation with any degree of success, we must be able to dispense with the protection of the Government when we quarrel among ourselves. The whole scheme of Non-co-operation must break to pieces, if our final reliance is to be

---

border of India where Hindus and Mahomedans live side by side. The book particularly refers to the following places, (1) Hindustan (Northern India), (2) Rangpur, (3) Malabar and (4) the Deccan within the borders of India, and such places, outside the borders as (5) Khelat, the capital of Baluchistan, (6) Afghanistan with its capital Kabul and Kandahar. The materials from which the above work was compiled were either printed documents or manuscript records deposited at the India Board. The following extracts from the book are given in support of our statement that there was no Hindu-Muslim problem in those days:

(1) "*Hindustan*:—Open violence produced little effect on so patient a people, and although the Mahomedans subsequently lived for centuries, intermixed with the Hindus, no radical change was produced in the manners or tenets of the latter; on the contrary, for almost a century past, the Mahomedans have evinced much deference to the prejudices of their Hindu neighbours, and a strong predilection towards many of their ceremonies." (Vol. I, p. 648).

"*Rangpur*:—The two religions, however, are on most friendly terms, and mutually apply to the deities or saints of the other when they imagine that application to their own will prove ineffectual."
(Vol, II., p. 478).

"*Malabar*:—When the Portuguese discovered India, the dominions of the Zamorin, although ruled by a superstitious Hindu prince, swarmed with Mahomedans, and this class ot population is now considered greatly to exceed in numbers all other descriptions of people in the British District of S. Malabar. This extraordinary progress of the Arabian religion does not appear (with the exception of Hyder and Tipoo) to have been either assisted by the countenance of the Government or obstructed by the jealousy of Hindus, and its rapid progress under a series of Hindu princes demonstrates the toleration or rather the indifference, manifested by the Hindus to the peaceable diffusion of religious practices and opinions at variance with their own.

"*Deccan*:—There is a considerable Mahomedan population in the

upon British intervention for the adjustment of our quarrels or the punishment of the guilty ones. In every village and hamlet, there must be at least one Hindu and one Muslim whose primary business must be to prevent quarrels between the two. Sometimes, however, even blood-brothers come to blows. In the initial stages, we are bound to do so here and there. Unfortunately we who are public workers have made little attempt to understand and influence the masses and least of all the most turbulent among them. During the process of insinuating ourselves in the estimation of the masses

---

countries subject to the Nizam, but those of the lower classes, who are cultivators, have nearly adopted all the manners and customs of the Hindus." (Vol. II, p. 81).

"*Khelat* :—The Hindus are principally mercantile speculators from Multan and Shikarpur, who occupy about 400 of the best houses and are not only tolerated in their religion, but allowed to levy a duty on goods entering the city for the support of their pagoda." (Vol. II p. 81) .

"*Afghanistan* :—Brahmanical Hindus are found all over Kabul, especially in the towns, where they carry on the trade of brokers, merchants, bankers, goldsmiths and grain-sellers." (Vol. I, p. 81).

"*Kabul* :—Many Hindus frequent Kabul, mostly from Peshawar; and as by their industry they contribute greatly to its prosperity, they are carefully cherished by the Afghan Government." (Vol. I, p. 307).

"*Kandahar* :—Among the inhabitants he (Syed Mustafa) receives a considerable number of Hindus (partly Kanoje Brahmans), both settled in the town as traffickers and cultivating the fields and gardens in the vicinity. With respect to religion, a great majority of inhabitants are Mahomedans of Sooni persuasion, the country abounds with Mosques, in which Syed Mustafa asserts both Hindu and Mahomedan worship and in other respects merely assimilate." (Vol. I, d. 341).

May we not infer that the policy of 'Divide and rule' adopted by the foreign Government, especially during the latter half of the 19th Century and after, was the root cause of so many discords between the two religious peoples inhabiting the country ?

and until we have gained control over the unruly, there are bound to be exhibitions of hasty temper now and then. We must learn at such times to do without an appeal to the Government. Hakimji Ajmal Khan has shown us how to do it.

The union that we want is not a patched up thing but a union of hearts based upon a definite recognition of the indubitable proposition that Swaraj for India must be an impossible dream without an indissoluble union between the Hindus and the Muslims of India. It must not be a mere truce. It cannot be based upon mutual fear. It must be a partnership between equals each respecting the religion of the other.

I would frankly despair of reaching such union, if there was anything in the holy Quran enjoining upon the followers of Islam to treat Hindus as their natural enemies or if there was anything in Hinduism to warrant a belief in the eternal enmity between the two.

We would ill learn our history if we conclude that because we have quarrelled in the past, we are destined so to continue unless some such strong power like the British keep us by force of arms from flying at each other's throats. But I am convinced that there is no warrant in Islam or Hinduism for any such belief. True it is that interested or fanatical priests in both religions have set the one against the other. It is equally true that Muslim rulers like Christian rulers have used the sword for the propagation of their respective faiths. But in spite of many dark things of the modern times, the world's opinion to-day will as little tolerate forcible conversions as it will tolerate forcible slavery. That probably is the most effective contribution of the scientific spirit of the age. That spirit has revolutionised many a false notion about Christianity as it has about Islam.

I do not know a single writer on Islam who defends the use of force in the proselytising process. The influences exerted in our times are far more subtle than that of the sword.

I believe that, in the midst of all the bloodshed, chicane and fraud being resorted to on a colossal scale in the West, the whole of humanity is silently but surely making progress towards a better age. And India by finding true independence and self-expression through an imperishable Hindu-Muslim unity and through non-violent means, *i.e.*, unadulterated self-sacrifice, can point a way out of the prevailing darkness.

11th May, 1921

HINDU-MUSLIM UNITY

(BY M. K. GANDHI)

That unity is strength is not merely a copybook maxim but a rule of life, is in no case so clearly illustrated as in the problem of Hindu-Muslim Unity. Divided we must fall. Any third power may easily enslave India so long as we Hindus and Mussalmans are ready to cut each other's throats. Hindu-Muslim Unity means not unity only between Hindus and Mussalmans but between all those who believe India to be their home, no matter to what faith they belong.*

I am fully aware that we have not yet attained that unity to such an extent as to bear any strain. It is a daily growing plant, as yet in delicate infancy, requiring special care and attention. The thing became clear in

*This point was further emphasised in articles on Sikhs, etc. See *Infra*.

Nellore when the problem confronted me in a concrete shape. The relations between the two were none too happy. They fought only about two years ago over what appeared to me to be a small matter. It was the eternal question of playing music whilst passing mosques. I hold that we may not dignify every trifle into a matter of deep religious importance. Therefore a Hindu may not insist on playing music whilst passing a mosque. He may not even quote precedents in his own or any other place for the sake of playing music. It is not a matter of vital importance for him to play music whilst passing a mosque. One can easily appreciate the Mussalman sentiment of having solemn silence near a mosque the whole of the twenty four hours. What is a non-essential to a Hindu may be an essential to a Mussalman. And in all non-essential matters, a Hindu must yield for the asking. It is criminal folly to quarrel over trivialities. The Unity we desire will last only if we cultivate a yielding and a charitable disposition towards one another. The cow is as dear as life to a Hindu; the Mussalman should therefore voluntarily accommodate his Hindu brother. Silence at his prayer is a precious thing for a Mussalman. Every Hindu should voluntarily respect his Mussalman brother's sentiment. This however is a counsel of perfection. There are nasty Hindus as there are nasty Mussalmans who would pick a quarrel for nothing. For these we must provide Panchayats of unimpeachable probity and imperturbability whose decisions must be binding on both parties. Public opinion should be cultivated in favour of the decisions of such panchayats so that no one would question them.

I know that there is much, too much, distrust of one another as yet. Many Hindus distrust Mussalman honesty. They believe that Swaraj means Mussalman Raj, for they argue that without the British, Mussalmans of India will aid Mussalman powers to build up a Mussalman empire in India. Mussalmans, on the other hand, fear that the Hindus being in an overwhelming majority will smother them. Such an attitude of mind betokens impotence on either's part. If not their nobility, their desire to live in peace would dictate a policy of mutual trust and mutual forbearance. There is nothing in either religion to keep the two apart. The days of forcible conversion are gone. Save for the cow, Hindus can have no ground for quarrel with Massalmans. The latter are under no religious obligation to slaughter a cow*. The fact is we have never before now endea-

* *Young India* of 7th January, 1920, contained the following: *Qurbani and Hindu-Muslim Unity.—Apropos* of the question of *Qurbani*, dealt at once from a religious and practical point of view, by Haziq-ul-Mulk Hakim Ajmal Khan in his remarkable address as President of the Muslim League, the following quotation from an article by Dr. Leitner in the *Asiatic Review*, published as far back as 1893, will be of striking interest (Dr. Leitner explains that the Koran only speaks of the offering of the Qurbani, meaning a 'noble sacrifice' which the earliest commentators explained to mean a "ram," and goes on to say):

The Hindustani name for goat is 'bakra,' but the 'k' is a 'kef.' whereas the 'k' in the Arabic word 'Baqr' or 'Bakr' is a 'qaf.' but it makes all the difference to the peace of India if the 'Bakra-Id' is with a 'kef' or a 'qaf.' If it be, as the vulgar call it, and it is in general practise, 'a sacrifice of goats,' or 'bakri-ka-Id' or' even bakra-Id' the contention between Hindus and Muhammadans is at an end, but as mischief makers have invented, 'baqr-Id' is a festival of the sacrifice of a cow, then the Pax Britannica may at any moment give way to a universal rising among Hindus throughout India. *It is therefore the most elementary commonsense and good feeling which would point out to the Muhammadans that the sacrifice of a cow is not* enjoined by the text or tradition regarding the festival, but that on the contrary it is universal as it most certainly is seditious in India. In Turkey,

voured to come together, to adjust our differences and to live as friends bound to one another as children of the same sacred soil. We have both now an opportunity of a lifetime. The Khilafat question will not recur for another hundred years. If the Hindus wish to cultivate eternal friendship with the Mussalmans, they must perish with them in the attempt to vindicate the honour of Islam.

18*th May*, 1921

LET HINDUS BEWARE

(By M. K. Gandhi)

Bihar is the land of promise for Non-co-operation. For the Hindu-Muslim Unity of Bihar is proverbial. I was therefore distressed to find that the unity was suffering a strain which might almost prove unbearable.

Egypt, Syria and Persia, where a cow *might* be sacrificed without the least offence to any one, a sheep is preferred; why then should a cow be killed in India, where it is a most heinous crime in the eyes of the vast majority of the population, and when neither scripture nor practice requires it throughout the Muhammadan world?"

Dr. Leitner even urges that British soldiers and officials should receive as little encouragement as possible in the consumption of beef. Haziq ul-Mulk Hakim Ajmal Khan's address shows that, in declaring that neither the text nor tradition enjoined the slaughter of a cow, he was actuated as much by true patriotism as by commonsense and good feeling. It was a truly noble thing on the Hakim Saheb's part and we hope that our Mussalman countrymen will as nobly respond to his appeal and his practical suggestions,—which, as he rightly emphasised, "were springing from the depth of honesty and sincerity"—and claim the 'proud privilege of being regarded the first to take the initial step towards ensuring the internal peace of the country." We need not say the Hakim Saheb has laid the Hindu community under a debt of gratitude by his bold and noble solution of a most vital issue.

I was told by all responsible leaders—both Hindu and Mahomedan—who are not given to be panicky—that it was taxing their resources to the utmost to avoid a Hindu-Mussalman disturbance. They informed me that certain Hindus, by name Gangaram Sharma. Bhutanath and Vidyanand for instance, had told the people that I had prohibited the use of meat to any Hindus or Mussalmans and that meat and fish were even forcibly taken away from people by overzealous vegetarians. I know that unlawful use is being made of my name in many places, but this is the most novel method of misusing it. It is generally known that I am a staunch vegetarian and food reformer. But it is not equally generally known that *Ahimsa* extends as much to human beings as to lower animals and that I freely associate with meat-eaters.

I would not kill a human being for protecting a cow, as I will not kill a cow for saving a human life, be it ever so precious.* Needless to say I have authorised no

* More than one note appeared in *Young India* regarding this question.

Mr. Gandhi wrote in *Young India* of 4th August. 1920, under the heading. "Cow Protection": Cow protection is an article of faith in Hinduism. Apart from its religious sanctity, it is an ennobling creed. But we, Hindus, have to-day little regard for the cow and her progeny. In no country in the world are cattle so ill fed and ill kept as in India. In beef-eating England, it would be difficult to find cattle with bones sticking out of their flesh. Most of our *panjarapoles* are ill managed and ill kept. Instead of being a real blessing to the animal world, they are perhaps simply receiving-depots for dying animals. We say nothing to the English in India for whose sake hundreds of cows are slaughtered daily. Our Rajas do not hesitate to provide beef for their English guests. Our protection of the cow, therefore, extends to rescuing her from Mussalman hands. This reverse method of cow protection has led to endless feuds and bad blood between Hindus and Mussalmans. It had probably caused greater slaughter of cows than otherwise would have been the case if we had begun the propaganda

one to preach vegetarianism as part of Non-co-operation. I do not know the persons named above. I am sure that our purpose will be defeated if propaganda of any kind is accompanied by violence. Hindus may not compel

---

in the right order. We should have commenced, as we ought now to commence, with ourselves and cover the land with useful propaganda leading to kindness in the treatment of cattle and scientific knowledge in the management of cattle farms, dairies and *panjarapoles*. We should devote our attention of propaganda among Englishmen in the shape of inducing them voluntarily to abandon beef, or, if they will not do so, at least be satisfied with imported beef. We should secure prohibition of export of cattle from India and we should adopt means of increasing and purifying our milk supply. I have not a shadow of doubt that if we proceed along these sane lines, we would secure voluntary Mussalman support, and when we have ceased to compel them to stop killing cows on their festival days, we would find that they have no occasion for insisting on killing them. Any show of force on our part must lead to retaliation and acerbation of feeling. We may not make Mussalmans or anybody respect our feelings religious or otherwise by force. We can really do so only by exciting their fellow-feeling.

My advice to my Hindu brethren is, 'simply help the Mussalmans in their sorrow in a generous and self-sacrificing spirit without counting the cost and you will automatically save the cow.' Islam is a noble faith. Trust it and its followers. We must hold it a crime for any Hindu to talk to them about cow-protection or any other help in our religious matters, whilst the Khilafat struggle is going on.

Mr. Gandhi wrote more than once on this topic. In *Young India* of 16th March, 1920, he opposed attempts made to pass a bye-law prohibiting slaughter of calves by the Lahore Municipality. Writing under the heading, "Impatient Cow Protectors", he declared himself against securing legislative protection for the cow. He returned to the subject in *Young India* of 8th June and deprecated the attempts of the Shikarpur Municipality to pass bye-laws regarding cow protection. Under the heading, "Save the Cow," he wrote:

The Mussalmans are striving their utmost to respect Hindu susceptibilities in this matter of life and death to the Hindu. The Muslim League, under Hakimji Ajmal Khan's presidentship, carried a cow

Mussalmans to abstain from meat or even beef-eating. Vegetarian Hindus may not compel other Hindus to abstain from fish, flesh or fowl. I would not make India sober at the point of the sword. Nothing has lowered

---

protection resolution at Amritsar. two years ago. Maulana Abdul Bari has written upon it. The Ali Brothers, for the sake of their Hindu countrymen. have given up the use of beef in their house Mian Chhotani saved hundreds of cows in Bombay alone during the last Bakr-Id. We could not accuse our Mussalman countrymen of apathy in the matter.

Let us recognise that there is an interest actively working to keep us—Hindus and Mussalmans—divided. That very interest is quite capable of developing regard for Hindu susceptibilities in this respect I should beware of it. and distrust it. I strongly advise the Shikarpur friends to wait for their Mussalman brethren.

Let them by all means abstain from all meat, so that their Mussalman brethren may have other meat cheaper than beef. Let them consider it a shame to have a single cow or her progeny in distress, or undergoing ill-treatment at the hands of Hindus themselves. Let them develop their *Goshala* : so as to make it a model dairy farm as well as a home for aged and infirm cattle. Let them breed the finest cattle in their *Goshala*. They will do real service to *Gomata*. Let the Shikarpuris one and all become true non-co-operators. and hasten the redress of the Khilafat wrong. I promise, they will save the Cow when they have done their utmost to save the Khilafat.

It must be an article of faith for every Hindu. that the cow can only be saved by Mussalman friendship. Let us recognise frankly, that complete protection of the cow depends purely upon Mussalman goodwill. It is as impossible to bend the Mussalmans to our will. as it would be for them to bend us to theirs. We are evolving the doctrine of equal and free partnership. We are fighting Dyerism—the doctrine of frightfulness.

Cow protection is the dearest possession of the Hindu heart. It is the one concrete belief common to all Hindus. No one who does not believe in cow protection, can possibly be a Hindu. It is a noble belief. Cow protection means brotherhood between man and beast. It is a noble sentiment that must grow by patient toil and *tapasya*. It cannot be imposed upon any one. To carry cow protection at the point of the sword, is a contradiction in terms. Rishis of old are said

the morale of the nation so much as violence. Fear has become part of the national character. Non-co-operators will make a serious mistake, if they seek to convert people to their creed by violence. They will play into the hands of the Government, if they use the slightest coercion towards anybody in the course of their propaganda.

The cow question is a big question, the greatest for a Hindu. I yield to no one in my regard for the cow. Hindus do not fulfil their trust so long as they do not possess the ability to protect the cow. That ablity can be derived either from body-force or soul-force. To attempt cow protection by violence is to reduce Hinduism to Satanism and to prostitute to a base end the grand significance of cow protection. As a Mussalman friend writes, beef-eating which is merely permissible in Islam will become a duty, if compulsion is resorted to by Hindus. The latter can protect the cow only by developing the faculty for dying, for suffering. The only chance Hindus have of saving the cow in India from the butcher's knife, is by trying to save Islam from the impending peril and trusting their Mussalman countrymen to return nobility, *i.e.*, voluntarily to protect the cow out of regard for their Hindu countrymen. The Hindus must scrupulously refrain from using any violence against Mussalmans. Suffering and trust are attributes of soul

---

to have performed penance for the sake of the cow. Let us follow in the foot-steps of the Rishis, and ourselves do penance, so that we may be pure enough to protect the cow and all that the doctrine means and implies.

In *Young India* of 19th June, he added:

Nor must the Hindu of Behar mix up vegetarianism with cow-killing. The two stand on a different footing. Cow protection is the creed of twenty million Hindus, vegetarianism is confined to a small minority. The latter cannot be permitted to force its views upon others.

force. I have heard that at big fairs if a Mussalman is found in possession of cows or even goats, he is at times forcibly dispossessed. Those who, claiming to be Hindus, thus resort to violence, are enemies of the cow and of Hinduism. The best and the only way to save the cow is to save the Khilafat. I hope therefore that every Non-co-operator will strain himself to the utmost to prevent the slightest tendency to violence in any shape or form, whether to protect the cow or any other animal or to effect any other purpose.

28th July, 1921

HINDU-MUSLIM UNITY

(By M. K. Gandhi)

Everybody knows that, without unity between Hindus and Mussalmans, no certain progress can be made by the nation. There is no doubt that the cement binding the two is yet loose and wet. There is still mutual distrust. The leaders have come to recognise that India can make no advance without both feeling the need of trust and common action. But though there is a vast change among the masses, it is still not a permanent quantity. The Mussalman masses do not still recognise the same necessity for Swaraj as the Hindus do.* The Mussalmans do not flock to public meetings

* The following appeared in *Young India* of 25th August, 1921 :

Hindu Muslim Unity—Mr. Saiyad Mahammad, President, Khilafat Committee, Unao, writes as follows to the editor :

"I have read with pain and anxiety occasional remarks in your paper about the Mussalmans not joining the Congress. It is a matter for regret that the Hindu leaders in districts generally feel a sort of estrangement from their Mussalman neighbours and both the Hindu

in the same numbers as the Hindus. This process cannot be forced. Sufficient time has not passed for the national interest to be awakened among the Mussalmans. Indeed it is a marvel that, whereas but a year ago the Mussalmans as a body hardly took any interest in Congress affairs, all over India thousands have registered themselves as members. This in itself is an immense gain.

But much more yet remains to be done. It is essentially the work of the Hindus. Wherever the Mussalmans are still found to be apathetic, they should be invited to come in. One often hears from Hindu quarters the complaint that Mussalmans do not join the Congress organisations or do not pay to the Swaraj Fund. The natural question is, have they been invited? In every district, Hindus must make special effort to draw out their Mussalman neighbours. There will never be real

---

and Mussalman workers in small districts are fired with the ambition of personal advertisement and claim a superiority which is the most dangerous poison to real unity. The result is that the Hindu workers hardly take any active part in the Khilafat movement, and the gulf thus gets wider. The Congress Committees are doing nothing so far as the propaganda work is concerned, and they think that their work is quite different from that of the Khilafat Committees. This evil in *small districts* is most deplorable and in spite of my most earnest endeavours to bring about a complete union, matters have not gone beyond a surface unity. Once the Hindus understand and realize this power of unity, I can confidently say that the cow sacrifice in this district will be reduced to almost nothing. Our great impediment is their aloofness."

I should be very sorry, indeed, if the Hindus of Unao are apathetic to the Khilafat cause. I have no doubt that the more interest the Hindus take in the Khilafat, the nearer comes Swaraj. Let us not ignore the fact that it is not yet possible to induce Mussalmans to take interest in Swaraj except in terms of the Khilafat. It is sad but it is true. The two communities have remained so long estranged that the

equality so long as one feels inferior or superior to the other. There is no room for patronage among equals. Mussalmans must not feel the lack of education or numbers where they are in a minority. Deficiency in education must be corrected by taking education. To be in a minority is often a blessing. Superiority in numbers has frequently proved a hindrance. It is character that counts in the end.

A PERTINENT QUESTION

(By M. K. Gandhi)

I paraphrase below what a friend writes regarding the influence of the Moplah outbreak on Hindu-Muslim unity:

> I am a staunch believer in Hindu-Muslim unity. But this Moplah outbreak has raised doubts in me. Success in the Khilafat means strength to Islam. Strength to Islam means attempts at conversion. Have we not often been given the choice between Islam and the sword? Can people such as Moplahs learn the beauty of non-violence? And even if they appreciate non-violence for the sake of their faith, will they not use violence for the sake of spreading their faith? My belief in the necessity of Hindu-Muslim unity is there. But do you not think that the questions I have raised are relevant?

The questions are indeed relevant, if only because they have occurred to one so sane as the writer is. But in my opinion, there is a misunderstanding about the whole question. Our advocacy of the Khilafat would be wrong if Islam were based on force. There is no-

---

Mussalmans had unconsciously almost come to think that India was not their home. The peril to the Khilafat has opened their eyes. The Hindus can take note of the fact, help their Mussalman countrymen and help themselves, and thus for all time cement Hindu-Muslim union. Happily for both, whatever may be true of Unao is most certainly not true of many other places where the Hindus are doing all they can to help the Khilafat movement. There can be no real progress, if the awakening is not general among both the communities.

thing in the Koran to warrant the use of force for conversion. The holy book says in the clearest language possible, 'There is no compulsion in religion'. The Prophet's whole life is a repudiation of compulsion in religion. No Mussalman, to my knowledge, has ever approved of compulsion. Islam would cease to be a world religion if it were to rely upon force for its propagation.

Secondly, historically speaking, the charge of conversion to Islam by force cannot be proved against its followers as a body. And whenever attempts have been made to convert by force, responsible Mussalmans have repudiated such conversions.

Thirdly, the conception of Hindu-Muslim unity does not presuppose a total absence for all time of wrong by any of the parties. On the contrary, it assumes that our loyalty to the unity will survive shocks such as forcible conversions by Moplahs, that in every such case we shall not blame the whole body of the followers but seek relief against individuals by way of arbitration and not by way of reprisals.

Fourthly, acceptance of non-violence for organising India's freedom involves acceptance of non-violence for Hindu-Muslim solidarity. The Moplahs have certainly broken the rule. But they were prevented from having access to the new manifestation. Whilst they had heard something about the Khilafat vaguely, they knew nothing of non-violence.

Fifthly, we need not suspect any evil befalling India under Swaraj; for it is tolerably certain that, had the Congress and the Khilafat workers been permitted to penetrate the Moplah territories, they would have been able to nip the evil in the bud. As it was, it is a matter capable of proof that the Khilafat workers, wherever they could go. were able to exercise great restraining influence. To me the Moplah madness is proof of the Hindu-Muslim solidarity, because we kept calm. As members of a family, we shall sometimes fight, but we shall always have leaders who will compose our differences and keep us under check.

Sixthly, in the face of possibilities of such madness in future, what is the alternative to Hindu-Muslim unity? A perpetuation of slavery? If we regard one another as natural enemies, is there any escape from eternal foreign domination for either of us? Is not the present domination worse than the possibility of forcible conversions or worse? Is Hinduism worth anything, if it cannot survive force? Cannot the Mussalmans too ask the same question as the friend has asked? Is there no possibility of a repetition of pillage and murder on the part of Hindus as happened in Shahabad three years ago? Is not the remedy therefore clearly Hindu-Muslim unity at all hazards? The Hindus as also the Mussalmans, whenever one of them goes mad, have two courses left open. Either to die valiantly without retaliation, that will at once arrest the progress of mischief; or to retaliate and live or die. For individuals both the courses will abide as long as the world lasts. All questionings arise, because we have become helpless. We have forgotten the divine art of dying for our faiths without retaliation, and we have equally forgotten the art of using force in self-defence at the peril of our lives. And Hindu-Muslim unity is nothing, if it is not a partnership between brave men and women. We must trust each other always, but in the last resort we must trust ourselves and our God.

20*th October*, 1921

HINDU-MUSLIM UNITY A CAMOUFLAGE?

(By M. K. Gandhi)

The editorial notes in the current number of the *Modern Review* contain reflections on Hindu-Muslim unity, which deserve a reply. The talented editor has headed them with the word 'camouflage,' and has evidently come to the conclusion that the unity is only so-called. In my opinion, however, it is not only not a camouflage but is fast becoming a permanent reality. I have made the admission in these pages, that it is a sapling requiring delicate handling. But it is certainly not a pretension or make believe if only because both realise the truth of the common danger.

It is unfortunately still true that the communal or the sectarian spirit is predominant. Mutual distrust is still there. Old memories are still alive. It is still true that at elections considerations not of fitness but of religion prevail. But to recognise these facts is to recognise the difficulty of union. When both parties know them and are honestly trying to achieve unity in spite of them, it is hardly just to call the attempt or the limited achievement a camouflage.

It is not correct to say that the appeal of the Khilafat associations against cow-killing leaves the Mussalmans cold and unresponsive. In the first place, is it not a cheering phenomenon that Khilafat workers, themselves Mussalmans, are working to prevent cow-killing? In the second place, I venture to assure the editor that the appeal has had wonderful success in almost all the parts of India. Is it a small matter that the burden of cow protection has been taken over almost entirely by the Mussalman workers? Was it not a soul-stirring thing for Hindus to witness Messrs. Chhotani and Khatri of Bombay rescuing hundreds of cows from their co-religionists and presenting them to the grateful Hindus?

It is certainly true that both Maulana Mahomed Ali and I are careful enough 'not to tread on each other's corns.' But, for frankness of treatment, it would be difficult to beat us. For us the unity is not 'a house of cards' as the writer cruelly suggests, but it is such a substantial fact that we would die to keep it intact. Let me inform the reader that throughout all our journeyings there has never been a jar between us, never any mental reservations. The cruellest cut however is given in the following sentence: 'Reading between the lines of their speeches, it is not difficult to see that with one of them the sad plight of the Khilafat in distant Turkey is the central fact, while with the other the attainment of Swaraj here in India is the primary object in view.' I claim that with us both the Khilafat is the central fact, with Maulana Mahomed Ali because it is his religion, with me because, in laying down my life for the Khilafat, I ensure the safety of the cow, that is, my religion, from the Mussalman knife. Both hold Swaraj equally dear, because only by Swaraj is the safety of our respective faiths possible. This may seem a lower ideal. But there is no concealment in it. For me the attainment of the Khilafat through India's power is the attainment of Swaraj. Love is the basis of our friendship as it is of religion. I ask to join Mussalman friendship by right of love. And if love persists even on the part of one community, unity will become a settled fact in our national life. It is unjust to suggest of Maulana Mahomed Ali that he speaks in elegant Urdu ununderstandable to the majority of Bengali Mussalmans. I know that he has been trying his best to introduce into his Urdu speech as much simplicity as possible.

It is unfortunately true that there are still Hindus and Mussalmans who out of fear of one another consider foreign domination a necessity. And that has not a little to do with the delay in the attainment of our goal. We do not yet clearly perceive that the possibility of a free fight between the two communities is a lesser evil than the existence of foreign domination. And if it is the interposition of the British Government which keeps us from fighting one another, the sooner we are left free to fight, the better for our manhood, our respective religions and our country. It will not be a new phenomenon if we fought ourselves into sanity.

The English carried on internecine warfare for twenty-one years before they settled down to peaceful work. The French fought among themselves with a savage ferocity hardly excelled during recent times. The Americans did nothing better before they evolved their commonwealth. Let us not hug our unmanliness for fear of fighting amongst ourselves. The able writer of the notes loves unity as much as any of us and suggests that there must be 'a root and branch change, a radical transformation and reconstruction from the foundation.' But he leaves the reader to guess the remedy. It would have been better if he had made concrete suggestions. He would evidently have us intermarry and interdine if only by way of a beginning. If that is the radical transformation desired by him and if it is a condition precedent to the attainment of Swaraj, I very much fear that we would have to wait at least for a century. It is tantamount to asking Hindus to give up their religion. I do not say that it is wrong to do so, but I do suggest that it is reformation outside practical politics. And when that transformation comes, if it is ever to come, it will not be Hindu-Muslim unity. And what the present movement is aiming at is to achieve unity even whilst a devout Mussalman retains his faith intact and devout Hindu his. I have therefore often said to my audiences that the Ali Brothers and I serve as an object lesson to all Hindus and Mussalmans in Hindu-Muslim unity. We both claim to be devoted to our respective faiths. In spite of the greatest regard for the Brothers, I would not give my daughter in marriage to one of their sons, and I know that they would not give theirs to my son, assuming that, in spite of his being a Hindu, he so far reformed himself as to covet the hand of their daughter. I do not partake of their meat foods, and they scrupulously respect my bigotry, if my self-denial may be so named. And yet I do not know three persons whose hearts are more united than those of the Ali Brothers and myself. And I wish to assure the reader that the unity is not a camouflage but it is a lasting friendship based upon exquisitely delicate regard and toleration of one another's views and habits.

And I have no manner of fear that, when the protecting hand of the British is withdrawn from me, either the Brothers or their friends would violate my freedom or attack my religion. And I base this security from fear first upon God and His promise of safety to every creature of His who endeavours to walk in His fear, and then upon the honourable conduct of the Brothers and their friends, although I am aware that physically any one of them is more than a match for twelve like me taken together. And so from the particular instance, I have generalised for the whole of India, and shown that Hindu-Muslim unity is possible, if only we have mutual toleration and faith in ourselves and therefore in the ultimate goodness of human nature.

17*th November*, 1920

THE SIKH LEAGUE

(By M. K. Gandhi)

Babu Kalinath Roy, the talented Editor of the *Tribune*, has kindly sent me an extract from a press letter received by him from a Sikh correspondent, for my comments. The extract runs as follows: "Mahatma Gandhi told some of the Sikh gentlemen who went to remonstrate with him on the 21st October last on the pernicious effects of his propaganda on Sikh masses, that his propaganda of Non-co-operation was non-violent, that there were no doubt visible signs that the movement was likely to become violent among the Sikhs, that he would strongly urge the Sikhs to remain non-violent both in word and deed; but that if despite his warning the Sikhs become violent, he shall not regret if the British authorities crushed them by force. He shall then let them be annihilated without letting either Hindus or Mahomedans come to their help, for it shall be by the sacrifice (*ahuti*) and total extinction of an element which is likely to become violent that the propaganda of Non-violent Non-co-operation will succeed." Babu Kalinath Roy, after quoting the foregoing, says: "The writer adds that at a meeting of the Sikh League these words were duly repeated as having been used by you and that you, who was present, did not contradict the report." The letter has, I am further informed, been published by the *Civil and Military Gazette* of Lahore.

The above remarks are, I suppose, intended to discredit me. Now the conversation referred to was long, lasting nearly an hour. Some of the remarks made by me during the conversation have been torn from their setting and put together as though I had made them in the manner and the order given. The fact is that the conversation was carried on partly in Hindustani and partly in English. My remarks were addressed to several members of the deputation. The latter had come to urge me not to put the idea of Non-co-operation before the Sikhs, especially as I had myself witnessed the violent attitude of some members of the League. I told them in the course of my replies to several questioners that I did not like the attitude of some of the Sikhs present at the meeting, and that it filled me with grief. I told them also that, if I was permitted to speak, I would warn the audience against the danger of violence, that it would be suicidal to do violence to co-operators and seek to make them Non-co-operators by compulsion. I told them too that the Non-co-operators would be courting destruction if they committed violence, for the British would in that event have an opportunity of destroying the whole of the community. I certainly told my hearers that, so far as I could, I would dissuade both Hindus and Mahomedans from helping any campaign of violence, and that I would not. in this struggle against the Government, be deterred by the fear of such a calamity as has been described to me.

The summary of my remarks given by the writer thus hardly does justice to me. I may state that I do not know the writer nor have I seen the letter from which Babu Kalinath Roy has taken the extract. I do recollect a speaker at the Sikh League reproducing this conversation. His speech was in Gurumukhi, and in so far as I understood him, I think he correctly represented the gist of my remarks.

17th *November*, 1920

BRAHMINS AND NON-BRAHMINS

(By M. K. Gandhi)

When I wrote in "Young India" on the Non-Brahmin question in Maharashtra,* I little realised that the Non-Brahmin case was largely, if not entirely, a political matter, and that the complaint was not so much against the Brahmins as a class by the Non-Brahmins as a class, as by some educated Non-Brahmins, against the Nationalists who were mostly Brahmins. Non-Brahmins include the Lingayats, the Marathas, the Jains and the "untouchables." The latter, however, have a separate grievance against the other Non-Brahmins in that they are isolated as much by the Non-Brahmins. The case for the educated Non-Brahmins is again not common to all. It may however be stated in the following terms:

(1) Educated Non-Brahmins do not possess the same political power that the Brahmins possess.

The latter have the largest number of Government posts and seats on representative bodies, although the former are, numerically, by far the strongest.

(2) Some Brahmins debar the Lingayats from the inner sanctuary of Temples, which the latter claim as their own; and this false (in their estimation) claim is supported by the Brahmins in general.

(3) The Brahmins treat all Non-Brahmins as Shudras, and treat them precisely as the British treat all Indians.†

In my opinion, the Non-Brahmin case is exceedingly

* Omitted in this collection.

†In South India, there is sought to be made a further difference in that, while the Brahmins cherish Aryan culture, the Non-Brahmins cherish the Dravidian culture.

weak and is certain to disappear from the public life of Maharashtra, if the Brahmins of the Nationalist Party carry out the Congress Non-Co-operation programme in its entirety.

The following is from *Young India* of 27th April, 1920 :

A Non-Brahmin's complaint.—To the editor, *Young India.* Sir,—Mr. Gandhi made some remarks regarding Brahmins and Non-Brahmins in the course of his lecture at the Beach in Madras last Friday. His speech has caused great pain to the Non-Brahmin Nationalists of Madras. It would have been highly preferable if Mr. Gandhi had not at all touched on this point ; for from his speech it was evident that he was completely ignorant of Dravidian civilization, religion, culture, and the inner meaning and causes of the present Non-Brahmin movement. He does not seem to have recognized the special features of Dravidian civilization which marks off South India from the rest of India. In praising the Brahmins for their contribution to the religion and civilization of India (probably he means North India), he has involuntarily cast a slur on the Non-Brahmins whose ancestors have also contributed as much as, if not more than, the Brahmins to the glory of South India as seen in their literature, religion, and philosophy.

It need hardly be pointed out that nothing can offend a whole community like a slur of the above kind, even though it may be done unwittingly by one whose heart is overflowing with love, and for whom the community has the highest regard. Further, the object of Mr. Gandhi's recent visit and proposed long tour in the South in the middle of the next month is, we may take, to strengthen the cause, and propagate the movement of Non-co-operation.

Surely, making hasty and flippant remarks about a highly vexed question, is likely to weaken the cause he advocates and estrange the sympathies of a vast majority of the masses who feel strongly on the matter.

If he really wants to bridge the gulf unhappily widening between the Brahmins and Non-Brahmins of South India, let Mr. Gandhi take up the question in right earnest with an entirely blank and open mind, and then he may in all probability be in a position, after careful study to find out a solution for the problem. Otherwise he will do well in the interest of the great Non-co-operation movement, to leave

The movement owes its vitality, not to the religious or the social disability, but to the political ascendancy of the Brahmins, which the latter undoubtedly enjoy by right of merit. That grievance must vanish if the Nationalist Brahmins, having evolved larger views about Swaraj, taboo all Government posts and boycott the Councils and nominated seats on municipalities. It is clear to me that the Government, in accordance with its confirmed policy, will play the Non-Brahmins against the Brahmins, even without the knowledge of the former, and endeavour to prolong its lease of life by fostering quarrels between the two, and holding out political inducements to the Non-Brahmins.

It is clear too, that the Brahmins will take the wind out of the Non-Brahmin sail, and make that opposition innocuous by a right renunciation of every form of Government patronage. The reason why the question has assumed a more acute form is that Non-Brahmin leaders are trying to influence the electorate in their favour and are telling the electors that, Non-Brahmins being weak, they must seek the British alliance. Brahmin leaders are naturally trying to influence the same electors and dissuade them from using their vote. This

---

severely alone the Brahmin and Non-Brahmin controversy, in the course of his forthcoming long tour in South India.

Madras, 11th April, 1921. C. KANDASWAMY.

[I have received more letters in a similar strain. The correspondents have clearly misunderstood me. I have not seen the report of my speech. I do not therefore know whether it lends itself to misinterpretation. But I claim that the Brahmins' service to Hinduism or humanity is unaffected and undiminished by the achievements of the Dravidian civilisation which nobody denies or disputes. I warn the correspondents against segregating the Dravidian South from the Aryan North. The India of to-day is a blend not only of two, but of many other cultures. M. K. G.]

gives rise to bad blood but not more than when the Moderates and the Nationalists are fighting. The most painful part of the situation, however, is that the Non-Brahmin leaders, who claim to represent the masses and to feel for them. will, by their co-operation with the Government, or by seeking to better their condition by Government aid, actually tighten the hold of the Government on the masses. And by their countenancing the Government aid they will make more difficult the remedy of the Punjab and the Khilafat wrongs. The Non-Brahmin policy is thus demonstrably suicidal.

Whatever their grievance against the Brahmins or the Nationalists, their remedy certainly does not lie through alliance with a Government, whose creed is economic exploitation of the masses and to that end also their emasculation. For, this refusal to right the Punjab, and partly even the Khilafat wrong, is based upon the policy of keeping up the British prestige at any cost. One lac of Englishmen cannot keep under subjection thirty crores of human beings merely by brute force.

But it can, and does, consolidate its power, by making them progressively helpless, in a most subtle manner. I venture, therefore, to warn the Non-Brahmin leaders against the danger of co-operation with the Government which is bound to hurt the very cause which they seek to espouse. They will not better the economic condition of the masses by gaining a few Government posts, or by being elected legislative councillors.

Judged by the economic standard, thirty-five years of our political activity have resulted in disaster. The masses of India to-day are less able to stand the ravages of famine and disease than they were fifty years ago. They are less manly than they were at any period in the history of the nation.

The impending calamity of Non-Brahmin leaders running into the arms of the Government for the supposed betterment of their political condition can easily be averted by the great Brahmin party. It is intelligent, it is strong, it has the traditional prestige of authority. It can afford to stoop to conquer. A whole-hearted acceptance of the Non-co-operation programme does provide an automatic solution. But it is not enough. Bitterness will still remain, unless the Brahmins extend the hand of fellowship to those who feel weak and injured. Complaints were made about nationalist papers in the Karnatak using offensive and haughty language towards Non-Brahmins; of Nationalist Brahmins otherwise also belittling them and treating them with contempt. Their ignorant Non-Brahmin countrymen have a right to expect courtesy and considerateness from comparatively more enlightened Brahmins. The mass of Non-Brahmins are still untouched by the anti-Brahmin prejudice. I have faith enough in the Maharashtra Brahmin to know that he will solve the Non-Brahmin question in a manner befitting the traditions of Hinduism of which he is trustee.

23rd *March*, 1921

TO THE PARSIS

DEAR FRIENDS,—

I know that you are following with considerable interest the present Non-co-operation movement. You may know, too, that all thoughtful Non-co-operators are anxiously waiting to see what part you are going to play in the process of purification through which the whole country is passing. I, personally, have every reason to have full faith in your doing the right thing when the moment for making the final choice comes to you. And I address these few words to you because I feel that, probably, that moment has now arrived.

Apart from your being fellow-countrymen, I am bound to you by many sacred ties. Dadabhai was the first patriot to inspire me. He was my guide and helper when I did not know any other leader. It was to him that I bore, when yet a boy, a letter of introduction. It was the late uncrowned king of Bombay who led me in 1896 and showed me the way to work. It was he who, when I wanted to give battle to a Political Agent as far back as 1892, restrained my youthful ardour and taught me the first practical lesson in Ahimsa in public life. He taught me not to resent personal wrongs if I would serve India. A Parsee merchant in Durban, Rustamjee Ghorkhodoo, was among my most valued clients and friends in South Africa. He gave freely to the public cause, and he and his brave son were the first among my fellow-prisoners.

He gave me shelter when I was lynched, and now, too, he is following the Swaraj movement with considerable interest and has just donated Rs. 40,000 to it.* In my

* The following appeared in *Young India* of 29th June, 1921:

Parsi Generosity.—Mr. Godrej of the "safe" fame has eclipsed all donations to the Tilak Swaraj Fund with his announcement of three lacs of rupees. His donations to public purposes have been hitherto quite unknown. But he was induced to appreciate the necessity this time of a public announcement. I tender my congratulations to Mr. Godrej and the whole Parsi Community. I wish also to testify that, during the collection week in Bombay, not a day has passed without Parsi donations. Parsi ladies and gentlemen are also making door to door collections. Parsis are also working as pickets. Among the newspapers, too, not all the Parsi papers are hostile to the Movement. But Mr. Godrej's generosity puts the Parsis easily first in all India. Parsi Rustamji's 52,000 would in any case have put the Parsis in a espectable position. Mr. Godrej has secured the first place.

humble opinion, probably the first woman in India to-day is a Parsi woman—gentle as a lamb, with a heart that holds the whole humanity. To have her friendship is the rarest privilege of life. I would love to multiply these sacred memories, but I have given you enough of them to enable you to understand and to appreciate the motive of this letter.

You are a very cautious community. You are compact, and you rightly insist on abundant proof of the stability and the morality of any movement before you would take to it. But there is now danger of your becoming over-cautious, and your success in trade may make you oblivious of the wants and aspirations of the multitude of your countrymen.

I dread the Rockfeller spirit that seems to be overtaking the great House of the Tatas. I dread to think of the consequences of their appropriating poor people's properties for the doubtful benefit of making India industrial. But I do believe that this is a passing phase. Your shrewdness will show you the suicidal nature of such enterprises. Your quick wit will tell you that what India needs is not concentration of capital in a few hands, but its distribution so as to be within easy reach of the 7½ lakhs of villages that make this continent 1,900 miles long and 1,500 miles broad. I know, therefore, it is a question of time when you will throw in your lot as a community with the reformers who are hungering to free India from the curse of an Imperialism which is bleeding her to death.

But there is one thing for which it will be criminal to wait. A temperance wave is passing over India. The people want voluntarily to become teetotallers. Society is fast developing a public opinion that would consider drinking an unpardonable vice. Many Parsis make a living by running liquor shops.* Your whole-hearted co-operation can sweep out of existence many of these plague-spots in the Bombay Presidency. The Local Governments almost all over India are making a discreditable attempt to thwart the movement which bids fair to succeed even to the point of destroying the whole of the Abkari reveuue. Will you help the Government or the people? The Bombay Government has not yet been seized by panic. But I can hardly imagine that it will have the courage and wisdom to sacrifice the drink-revenue. You have to make your immediate choice. I do not know what your Scriptures say about drink. I can guess what the Prophet, who separated good from evil and sang the victory of the former over the latter, is likely to have said. But apart from your own religious belief, you have to make up your mind as to whether you will forward the cause of temperance in a whole-hearted manner or whether you will supinely and philosophically watch developments. I shall hope that you as a practical community of India will actively and thoroughly associate yourselves with the great

* The following appeared in *Young India* of 29th June, 1921:

Danger ahead.—The liquor-shop picketing has an intimate relation to Parsis. We will have to exercise great forbearance towards our Parsi countrymen. While we cannot stop picketing altogether, we must meet the liquor-dealers in conference, understand their difficulties and explain our own. Mr. Godrej has earmarked his donation for liquor prohibition and the uplift of the suppressed classes. Let us not, therefore, think that all Parsis are necessarily hostile to the great temperance movement. At the present movement, an outbreak of violence is the most to be feared from the temperance campaign, unless the Moderate ministers take their courage in both hands, refund all auction bids and close liquor-shops. I assure them that the movement can only be regulated, it cannot be checked. The people are bent on ending liquor-shops, and treating as a crime all liquor-selling except as a medicine by chemists. It is a matter that brooks no delay.

temperance movement which bids fair to outshine every such movement in the world.

I am,
Your faithful friend,
M. K. GANDHI.

8th June, 1921

TO THE MODERATES

DEAR FRIENDS,

It is a matter of no small grief to me, that I find myself estranged from you in ideas, although by training and association I have been brought up in the company of those who have been regarded as Moderates. Partly owing to circumstances, and partly owing to temperament, I have never belonged to any of the great parties in India. Nevertheless, my life has been influenced much more by men belonging to the Moderate party than the Extremist. Dadabhai Naoroji, Gokhale, Badruddin Tyabji, Pherozeshah Mehta are all names to conjure with. Their services to the country can never be forgotten. They have inspired the lives of many like myself throughout our country. I have enjoyed the pleasantest associations with many of the living amongst you. What is it that has flung me away from you and into the lap of the Nationalist party? Why do I find more in common with the Nationalists than with you? I am unable to see that you love your country less than the Nationalists. I refuse to believe that you are less willing to sacrifice yourselves for the country's good, than the Nationalists. Certainly, the Moderate party can claim as much intelligence, integrity and ability as the Nationalists, if not more. The difference, therefore, lies in the ideals.

I will not weary you with a discussion of the different ideals. For the moment, I will simply invite your attention to some of the items in the constructive programme in the movement of Non-co-operation. You may not like the word itself. You may intensely dislike, as I know you do, many items in the programme. But if you concede to the Non-co-operators the same credit for love of the land that you will claim for yourselves, will you not view with favour those parts of the programme on which there cannot be two opinions? I refer to the drink evil. I ask you to accept my evidence that the country as a whole is sick of the drink curse. Those unfortunate men, who have become slaves to the habit, require to be helped against themselves. Some of them even ask to be helped. I invite you to take advantage of the wave of feeling that has been roused against the drink traffic. The agitation arose spontaneously. Believe me, the deprivation to the Government of the drink revenue is of the least importance in the campaign. The country is simply impatient of the evil itself. In no country in the world, will it be possible to carry on this traffic in the face of the united and the enlightened opposition of a people, such as is now to be witnessed in India. Whatever the errors or excesses that were committed by the mob in Nagpur, the cause was just. The people were determined to do away with the drink curse that was sapping their vitality. You will not be deceived by the specious argument that India must not be made sober by compulsion, and that those who wish to drink must have facilities provided for them. The State does not cater for the vices of its people. We do not regulate or license houses of ill fame. We do not provide facilities for thieves to indulge their propensity for thieving. I hold drink to be more damnable than thieving and perhaps even prostitution. Is it not often the parent of both? I ask you to join the country in sweeping out of existence the drink revenue and abolishing the liquor-shops. Many liquor-sellers would gladly close their shops, if the money paid by them were refunded.

'What about the education of the children?' may be the question asked. I venture to suggest to you that it is a matter of deep humiliation for the country to find its children educated from the drink revenue. We shall deserve the curse of posterity, if we do not wisely decide to stop the drink evil, even though we may have to sacrifice the education of our children. But we need not. I know many of you have laughed at the idea of making education self-supporting by introducing spinning in our schools and colleges. I assure you that it solves the problem of education as nothing else can. The country cannot bear fresh taxation. Even the existing taxation is unbearable. Not only must we do away with the opium and the drink revenue, but the other revenue has also to be very considerably reduced, if the ever-growing poverty of the masses is to be combated in the near future.

And that brings me to the existing system of government. The country is the poorer for the Reforms. The annual expenditure has grown. A deeper study of the system has convinced me that no tinkering with it will do. A complete revolution is the greatest need of the time. The word revolution displeases you. What I plead for, however, is not a bloody revolution, but a revolution in the thought-world, such as would compel a radical revision of the standard of life in the higher services of the country. I must frankly confess to you that the ever increasing rate of salaries paid to the higher branches of the Civil Service fairly frightens me, as I hope it would frighten you. Is there any correspondence between the life of the governors and of the governed millions who are groaning under their heels? The bruised bodies of the latter are a standing testimony to the truth of my statement. You now belong to the governing class. Let it not be said that your heels are no softer than your predecessors 'or your associates'. Must you also rule from Simla? Must you also follow the policy that, only a year ago, you criticised adversely? It is under your *regime* that a man has been sentenced to transportation for life for holding certain opinions. You may not plead that he was inciting to violence, for not very long ago you dismissed such pleas. The Ali Brothers have apologised for even a suspicion of violence in their speeches.* You will be doing a cruel injustice to the country, if you allow yourselves to believe that any fear of prosecution has prompted the apology. A new spirit has been born in the country. The fear of the judge within is more terrible than that of the one without.

Do you know that, during the past six months several high-souled youths, your countrymen, have gone to gaol, because they will not condescend to give security, which in their opinion was dishonourable for them to do? It is under your *regime* that the patience of utterly innocent Moplas has been put to a severe test, and has as yet not been found wanting. I would gladly think as I really believe that you are not responsible for the atrocities, that are at present being perpetrated in the name of peace and justice. But you will not let the public or me say that you are helpless where you are not hoodwinked. That, however, would bring me to a discussion of our ideals, which I must not enter upon at the present moment. If the country can only get your assistance in stopping the

*Sec *infra.*

drink traffic, you will certainly add to the many services that you have rendered it in the past, and, may be, that one step will open your eyes to many another possibility.

I remain,

Yours, as ever,

M. K. GANDHI.

13*th April*, 1921

THE NATIONAL FLAG

(BY M. K. GANDHI)

A flag is a necessity for all nations. Millions have died for it. It is no doubt a kind of idolatry which it would be a sin to destroy. For a flag represents an ideal. The unfurling of the Union Jack evokes in the English breast sentiments whose strength it is difficult to measure. The Stars and Stripes mean a world to the Americans. The Star and the Crescent will call forth the best bravery in Islam.

It will be necessary for us Indians—Hindus, Mahomedans, Christians, Jews, Parsis, and all others to whom India is their home*—to recognise a common flag to live and to die for.

*The following is from *Young India* of 18th May 1921:

Sikh Colour.—A friend has just drawn my attention to a resolution passed by the Sikh League inviting me to include the Sikh black colour in the national flag. This friend forgets that all other colours are represented on the white strip. We must not be parochial, provincial or clannish. Hindu and Mussalman colours are specially represented, not so much for the numbers they represent, as for the fact that they have remained apart for so long and that their mutual distrust has been an effectual bar against the realization of national aspirations. The Sikhs have never had any quarrel with Hindus. And if one has the Sikh colour separately represented, why not the Parsee, the Christian and the Jewish? I hope the Sikh Leaguers will see the unpractical nature of their suggestion.

Mr. P. Venkayya of the National College, Masulipatam, has for some years placed before the public a suggestive booklet describing the flags of the other nations and

---

I have been flooded with letters suggesting changes in the proposed national flag. I am unable to publish the voluminous correspondence. There is nothing striking in any of the letters. Some deplore the want of artistic beauty about the flag, others would make additions representing Hindu and Mahomedan symbols. The critics have missed the central idea. We must not have any religious symbols and we must find a clear and permanent rallying object. That is the spinning wheel, according to the vast majority who believe with me that we lost our liberty with the loss of the spinning wheel, and we can only regain it when we have revived the spinning-wheel and rejected foreign cloth.

The following is from *Young India* of 4th August, 1921:

The Sikh Colour—The Sikh friends are needlessly agitated over the colours in the proposed national flag. They want the black colour also to be inserted on the ground of their military importance. Apart from the merits. their agitation has no point, as the flag has not even come before the All-India Congress Committee for discussion or decision. And in view of their objection, I do not propose to bring it up before the Committee at all, so long as I have failed to convince them of the unreasonableness of the demand. On the merits, I have not the shadow of a doubt that they should withdraw the objection. The white includes all other colours. To ask for special prominence is tantamount to a refusal to merge in the two numerically great communities. I would have had only one colour if there had been no quarrel between Hindus and Mussalmans. The Sikhs never had any difference with the Hindus. And their quarrel with the Mussalmans was of the same type as the Hindus. It is a dangerous thing to emphasise our differences or distinctions. We must seek for points of contact. Distinguished Mussalman friends on hearing of the Sikh claim advised me to adopt a single colour, either white or red. But that too would be inadvisable. The two colours red and green should be there to perpetuate the growing unity. I am aware of the difficulty of Sikh Nationalists. The Government agents in the Sikh Camp are making all kinds of mischievous suggestions to breed dissensions. And they are naturally afraid. The best thing is not to worry. If they attempt to set right every grievance manufactured

offering designs for an Indian National Flag. But, whilst I have always admired the persistent zeal with which Mr. Venkayya has prosecuted the cause of a national flag at every session of the Congress for the past four years, he was never able to enthuse me; and in his designs I saw nothing to stir the nation to its depths. It was reserved for a Punjabee to make a suggestion that at once arrested attention. It was Lala Hansraj of Jullunder who, in discussing the possibilities of the spinning wheel, suggested that it should find a place on our Swaraj Flag. I could not help admiring the originality of the suggestion. At Bezwada I asked Mr. Venkayya to give me a design containing a spinning wheel on a red (Hindu colour) and green (Muslim colour) back ground. His enthusiastic spirit enabled me to possess a flag in three hours. It was just a little late for presentation to the All-India Congress Committee. I am glad it was so. On maturer consideration, I saw that the background should represent the other religions also. Hindu-Muslim unity is not an exclusive term; it is an inclusive term, symbolic of the unity of all faiths domiciled in India.* If Hindus and Muslims can

* When Mr. Gandhi talks of Hindu-Muslim unity, he should be understood in a broad sense, implying unity among all creeds. Thus he wrote in *Young India* of 15th August, 1921, under the heading, *Christians and Non-co-operation*: An Indian Christian from Basrah North writes:

"I am sorry to say that you do not take us Indian Christians as the people of India, as I have seen many times *Young India* mentioning Mussalmans, Hindus, Sikhs, etc., but omitting the Christians.

---

against Hindus or Mussalmans or against the Non-co-operation movement in general, they will find that they will have no platform to stand upon. Whether they are few or many, Sikh Nationalists must know their own mind and stand unmoved by anything said by their detractors.

tolerate each other, they are together bound to tolerate all other faiths. The unity is not a menace to the other faiths represented in India or to the world. So I suggest

---

I should like you to believe that we Indian Christians are also the people of India, and take much interest in India's own affairs.

I am sure, there are very few who have followed N. C. O. as Indian Christians have. I have much sympathy for my motherland's affairs. I am also a follower of N. C. O.

I promise to give some news about the state of Indians in Mespot now and then."

I assure the correspondent and other Indian Christians that Non-co-operation is no respecter of creeds or races. It invites and admits all to its fold. Many Indian Christians have contributed to the Tilak Swaraj Fund. There are some noted Indian Christains as Non-co-operators in the front rank. There is constant mention of Mussalmans and Hindus. as they have hitherto regarded one another as enemies. Similarly, there always has been some cause when any race has been specially mentioned in these columns.

The above was followed by the following note in *Young India* of 22nd September, 1921: *Christian Non-co-operators*—A Christian student writes: 'Though we are Christian students, you are our national leader, and we feel that we ought to learn from you what India stands for and what is her spiritual heritage. Will you therefore send me your criticism of Western Christianity with constructive suggestions regarding organisation, worship and ministry ?'

My inquirer did not know that he was taking me beyond my depth. It is a pleasure to me, however, that Indian Christians are taking growing interest in the national movement. I know that hundreds of poor Christians in Bombay paid what they could to the Tilak Memorial Swaraj Fund. I know that several educated Christians are devoting their splendid talents to national work. I propose, therefore, to satisfy my inquirer,—not in the way he would have me to—but in the only way I can.

India of the near future stands for perfect toleration of all religions. Her spiritual heritage is simple living and high thinking. I consider Western Christianity in its practical working a negation of Christ's Christianity. I cannot conceive Jesus, if he was living in the flesh in our midst, approving of modern Christian organisations, public worship or modern ministry. If Indian Christians will simply cling

that the background should be white and green and red. The white portion is intended to represent all other faiths. The weakest numerically occupy the first place,

---

to the Sermon on the Mount, which was delivered not merely to the peaceful disciples but a groaning world, they would not go wrong, and they would find that no religion is false, and that if all live according to their lights and in the fear of God, they would not need to worry about organisations, forms of worship and ministry. The Pharisees had all that, but Jesus would have none of it, for they were using their office as a cloak for hypocrisy and worse. Co-operation with forces of Good and Non-co-operation with forces of Evil are the two things we need for a good and pure life, whether it is called Hindu, Muslim or Christian.

The following is from *Young India* of 19th January, 1922:

Christian awakening.—Mr. Andrews writes as follows:

"When I was in Lahore a short time ago in order to see Mr. Stokes in the Central Jail, a group of some fifteen to twenty Indian Christian students came to see me. We sat down and talked very earnestly together. The conversation was chiefly about Mr. Stokes himself, and afterwards they asked me particularly concerning my recent visit to East Africa and Uganda. I tried to point out to them how beautiful a thing it would be, if some of them could go out to Central Africa, not to make money, but simply to help the Africans in love. The talk went on till college time drew near and they said good-bye. But a short time after, two of them came back and said to me: ' "We wanted to come back on behalf of every one of us to tell you that we had a short informal meeting outside, after we had left you and we passed a unanimous resolution asking you to give to Mahatma Gandhi our love and to tell him that our hearts were with him."

The following is from *Young India* of 4th August, 1921:

Sikh Representation.—I regard the Sikh fear about representation at the present stage to be justified. They have been assured by the Congress communal representation if the Mussalmans insist upon the Lucknow compact. The Working Committee issued only advisory instructions because of attempts to divide Mussalmans. The Sikhs therefore are entitled to similar assurances. There should be no difficulty about issuing them. It is largely a question for the three communities in the Punjab to settle among themselves. The Committee can only issue helpful instruction.

the Islamic colour comes next, the Hindu colour red comes last, the idea being that the strongest should act as a shield to the weakest. The white colour, moreover, represents purity and peace. Our national flag must mean that or nothing. And to represent the equality of the least of us with the best, an equal part is assigned to all the three colours in the design.

But India as a nation can live and die only for the spinning wheel. Every woman will tell the curious that with the disappearance of the spinning wheel, vanished India's happiness and prosperity. The womanhood and the masses of India have been awakened as never before at the call of the spinning wheel. The masses recognise in it the giver of life. The women regard it as the protector of their chastity.* Every widow I have met has recognised in the wheel a dear forgotten friend. Its restoration alone can fill the millions of hungry mouths. No industrial development schemes can solve the problem of the growing poverty of the peasantry of India covering a vast surface, 1900 miles long and 1500 broad. India is not a small island, it is a big continent which cannot be converted like England into an industrial country. And we must resolutely set our face against any scheme of exploitation of the world. Our only hope must centre upon utilising the wasted hours of the nation, for adding to the wealth of the country, by converting cotton into cloth in our cottages. The spinning wheel is, therefore, as much a necessity of Indian life as air and water.

Moreover, the Muslims swear by it just as much as the Hindus. As a matter of fact, the former are taking to it more readily than the Hindus. For the Muslim woman is *purdanashin* and she can now add a few

*See *infra* articles on spinning.

paisas to the poor resources that her husband brings to the family. The spinning wheel, therefore, is the most natural, as it is the most important, common factor of national life. Through it we inform the whole world that we are determined, so far as our food and clothing are concerned, to be totally independent of the rest of it. Those who believe with me will make haste to introduce the spinning wheel in their home and possess a national flag of the design suggested by me.

It follows that the flag must be made of *khaddar*, for it is through course cloth alone that we can make India independent of foreign markets for her cloth. I would advise all religious organisations, if they agree with my argument, to weave into their religious flags, as for instance the Khilafat, a miniature National Flag in the upper left hand corner. The regulation size of the Flag should contain the drawing of a full-sized spinning wheel.

8*th September*, 1920

THREE NATIONAL CRIES

(By M. K. Gandhi)

During the Madras tour, at Bezwada I had occasion to remark upon the national cries and I suggested that it would be better to have cries about ideals than men. I asked the audience to replace *Mahatma Gandhi-ki-Jai* and *Mahomed Ali-Shaukat Ali-ki-Jai* by *Hindu-Mussalman-ki-Jai*. Brother Shaukat Ali, who followed, positively laid down the law. In spite of the Hindu-Muslim unity, he had observed that, if Hindus shouted *Bande Mataram*, the Muslims rang out with *Allaho Akbar* and vice versa. This, he rightly said, jarred on the ear and still showed that the people did not act with one mind.

There should be therefore only three cries recognised. *Allaho Akbar* to be joyously sung out by Hindus and Muslims showing that God alone was great and no other. The second should be *Bande Mataram* (Hail Motherland) or *Bharat Mata-ki-Jai* (Victory to Mother Hind). The third should be *Hindu-Mussalman-ki-Jai*, without which there was no victory for India, and no true demonstration of the greatness of God. I do wish that the newspapers and public men would take up the Maulana's suggestion and lead the people only to use the three cries. They are full of meaning. The first is a prayer and a confession of our littleness and therefore a sign of humility. It is a cry in which all Hindus and Muslims should join in reverence and prayerfulness. Hindus may not fight shy of Arabic words, when their meaning is not only totally inoffensive but even ennobling. God is no respector of any particular tongue. *Bande Mataram*, apart from its wonderful associations, expresses the one national wish—the raise of India to her full height. And I should prefer *Bande Mataram* to *Bharat Mata-ki-Jai*, as it would be a graceful recognition of the intellectual and emotional superiority of Bengal. Since India can be nothing without the union of the Hindu and the Muslim heart, *Hindu-Mussalman-ki-Jai* is a cry which we may never forget.

There should be no discordance in these cries. Immediately some one has taken up any of the three cries, the rest should take it up and not attempt to yell out their favourite. Those who do not wish to join may refrain, but they should consider it a breach of etiquette to interpolate their own when a cry has already been raised. It would be better too, always to follow out the three cries in the order given above. Nor should cries be incessantly shouted. One often hears an incessant yell when a popular leader is passing through a station. I doubt if this incessant noise does the slightest good to the nation except to provide an indifferent exercise for one's lungs. Moreover, it is necessary to think of our hero's nerves and time. It is a national waste to keep him occupied in gazing at a crowd and hearing a cry in his praise or any other for full thirty minutes. We must cultivate the sense of proportion.

21*st January*, 1920

AN APPEAL TO MADRAS

(By. M. K. Gandhi)

I use the word Madras here in its popular sense, meaning the people of the whole of the Madras Presidency, speaking all the Dravidian languages.

I observe that Mrs. Besant was disappointed that the proceedings of the Congress were conducted mainly in Hindustani, and she has therefore come to the amazing conclusion that it became a Provincial rather than a National assembly. I entertain a very high regard for Mrs. Besant and her services to India. No one has popularised the idea of Home Rule for India with so much success as she. The best of us, much younger in age, are unable to approach her in her industry, zeal and organising ability, all devoted to the service of India. She has devoted the best part of her mature life to the service of India and she has deservedly attained to popularity in India, second perhaps only to that of Lokamanya Tilak. But, for the present moment, her views being unacceptable to a large body of educated Indians, she has become somewhat unpopular, and it grieves me to have to dissent publicly from her view about

Hindustani making the Congress provincial. In my humble opinion, it is a grave error of judgment, and duty compels me to draw attention to it. I have attended all the Congress Sessions, but one, since 1915. I have studied them specially in order to study the utility of Hindustani compared to English for the conduct of its proceedings. I have spoken to hundreds of delegates and thousands of visitors and I have perhaps covered a larger area and seen a much larger number of people. literate and illiterate, than any public man not excluding Mrs. Besant and Lokamanya Tilak, and I have come to the deliberate conclusion that no language except Hindustani—a resultant of Hindi and Urdu—can possibly become a national medium for exchange of ideas or for the conduct of national proceedings. It is also my deliberate opinion based upon extensive experience that the nation has very materially suffered by reason of the proceedings of the Congress having been conducted almost entirely in English except during the last two years. I further wish to state as a fact that, barring the presidency of Madras, everywhere else the majority of the visitors and delegates to the National Congress have always been able to understand more Hindustani than English. The astounding result therefore has been that the Congress has been national throughout all these long years only as a spectacle but never for its real educative value. In any other country in the world an assembly of this character that has become progressively popular from year to year would have, during thirty-four years of life, given a political education that would have had various questions threshed out before them in their own language. Whatever therefore the shortcomings of the last Congress, it has certainly been more fully national than any of its predecessors, by reason of the majority of the delegates and visitors having understood the proceedings. If the audience was weary of Mrs. Besant, it was not because it was indifferent or disrespectful to her, but because it could not follow her speech, interesting and able though it was. And as national consciousness develops and as the appetite for political knowledge and education grows, as it must, it will become more and more difficult, and rightly so, for a speaker, no matter how able and popular, to command the attention of a popular audience if he spoke in English. I therefore appeal to the people of Madras presidency to recognise the national necessity for public men to learn Hindustani. Audiences outside Madras can more or less understand Hindustani without difficulty. Dayananda Saraswati enthralled audiences outside Northern India with his Hindustani eloquence, and could be understood by even the common people without difficulty. The nation has very materially suffered by reason of the proceedings of the Congress having been conducted in English. That means that, out of a population of three hundred and fifteen millions, only over thirty-eight millions composing the Madras presidency cannot follow a Hindustani speaker. I have deducted the Mahomedan population, for it is common knowledge that the majority of the Mahomedans of Madras presidency understand Hindustani. The question therefore is: what is the duty of the thirty-eight million inhabitants of that Presidency? Should India for their sake learn English? Or should they for the sake of two hundred and seventy-seven million inhabitants of India learn Hindustani? The late Justice Krishnaswami, with his unerring instinct, recognised Hindustani as the only possible medium of expression between the different parts of India. I am not aware that the proposition is seriously challenged by anybody at the present moment. It is not possible for thousands of people to make English their common tongue, and it would be highly undesirable, even if it were possible, for the simple reason that the higher and technical knowledge being acquired through English cannot percolate to the masses, as it would if it became current among the upper classes through any of the vernaculars. It is easier, for instance, to translate the writings of Sir J. C. Bose from Bengalee into Gujarati than it is to translate Huxley from English into Gujarati. And what does the proposition that the Madrasi should learn Hindustani for the sake of the rest of India amount to? It simply means that those public workers in Madras who want to work outside India and who want to take part in national assemblies outside the Madras Presidency should devote an hour a day for one year to learning Hindustani. Such an effort would enable several thousand Madrasis to pick up sufficient Hindustani to enable them to follow at least the drift of the Congress proceedings at the end of a year's study. They have got in several parts of the Presidency Hindi Prachar Offices where Hindustani is taught free of charge to all who wish to learn.*

* The following is from *Young India* of 16th June, 1920:

I have the greatest faith in the Dravidians some day taking up Hindi study seriously. If an eighth of the industry that they put in mastering English were to be devoted to learning Hindi, instead of the rest of India remaining a sealed book to them, they will be one with us as never before. I know that some would say the argument cuts both ways. The Dravidians being in a minority, national economy suggests that they should learn the common language of the rest of India than that the rest should learn Tamil, Telugu, Canarese and Malayalam in order to be able to converse with Dravidian India. It is for that reason that Hindi propaganda work of an intense type has been going on in the Madras Presidency for the past eighteen months under the aegis of the Hindi Sahitya Sammelan of Allahabad.

I appeal to Mrs. Besant, who is already devoting "New India" from time to time to the cause of Hindustani learning, to support my appeal.

In response to an appeal by me to the Agraval Marwadi Sammelan held in Bombay last week, the wealthy Marwadis of Bombay and Calcutta present there subscribed on the spot Rs. 50,000 for five years' Hindi-propaganda in Madras Presidency. They have once more demonstrated that Hindi work is a speciality of this princely merchant class of India. This generous response increases the responsibility of the Sammelan of Allahabad and of those Dravidians who share with me the belief that Madras must take up Hindi for the sake of full national expansion. Let no Dravidian think that learning Hindi is at all difficult. A little time taken from the recreation hour daily and in a systematic manner will enable an average man to learn Hindi in one year. I would venture to suggest too that large Municipalities might now introduce Hindi as an optional language to be learnt in the municipal schools. I can say from experience that Dravidian children take to Hindi in a remarkably easy manner. Little does any one know that almost all the Tamils and the Telugus living in South Africa can carry on an intelligent conversation in Hindi. I venture to hope, therefore, that the young men of Madras will show their appreciation of Marwadi generosity by availing themselves of the facility afforded to them of learning Hindi without payment.

In *Young India* of 2nd February, 1921 Mr. Gandhi wrote under the heading, *The need for Hindustani*: I have ventured to advise every student to devote this year of our trial to the manufacture of yarn and learning Hindustani. I am thankful to the Calcutta students that they have taken kindly to the suggestion. Bengal and Madras are the two provinces that are cut off from the rest of India for want of a knowledge of Hindustani on their part—Bengal, because of its prejudice against learning any other language of India. and Madras, because of the difficulty of the Dravidians about picking up Hindustani. An average Bengali can really learn Hindustani in two months if he gave it three hours a day and a Dravidian in six months at the same rate. Neither a Bengali nor a Dravidian can hope to achieve the same result with English in the same time. A knowledge of English opens up intercourse only with the comparatively few English knowing Indians, whereas a passable knowledge of Hindustani enables us to hold intercourse with the largest number of our country-

21*st April*, 1920

THE CAUSE OF THE VERNACULARS

To anyone who watched the proceedings of the recent Sahitya Sammelans it must be clear that our national awakening is not confined to politics alone. The enthusiasm displayed at these gatherings indicated a happy change. We are giving in thought their proper place to the vernaculars in our national life. Raja Ram Mohan Roy's prophecy that India will one day be an English-speaking country, has not to-day many stars in its favour. The great reformer's spirit, however, still haunts some. A number of our eminent men hastily generalise in favour of English as the national medium. The present status of English as a court language weighs with them unduly. They fail to see that the present status of English is no credit to us and that it is not conducive to the growth of a true democratic spirit. That crores of men should learn a foreign tongue for the convenience of a few hundreds of officials is the height of absurdity. An instance is often cited from our past history to prove the necessity of a *lingua franca* to strengthen the central Government of the country. Nobody disputes the necessity of a common medium. But it cannot be English. The officials have to recognise the vernaculars. The second consideration that appeals to the Anglicists is India's position in the Empire. The argument, put in plain words, amounts to asking

men. I do hope the Bengalis and the Dravidians will come to the next Congress with a workable knowledge of Hindustani. Our greatest assembly cannot be a real object lesson to the masses unless it speaks to them in a language which the largest number can understand. I appreciate the difficulty with the Dravidians, but nothing is difficult before their industrious love for the Motherland.

31 crores of Indians to accept English as their common language, for the sake of the other parts of the Empire whose population is not more than 12 crores.

The first fact that ought to receive consideration from every student of this problem, is that after a century and a half of British Rule English has failed to take the place of a *lingua franca* of India. A kind of broken English, no doubt, does seem to have succeeded in this respect in our cities. But this fact can only dazzle those who profess to study our national problems, in big cities like Bombay and Calcutta. And what is their population after all? It is only 2.2 per cent. of the total population of India. The second fact that the Anglicists ignore is that a very large majority of our vernaculars are akin to one another, and as a result of this, Hindi as a *lingua franca* suits all the provinces except the Madras Presidency. In view of this advantage in favour of Hindi and in view of our present national consciousness, how can we accept English as our *lingua franca*?

The solution of this problem will decide the fate of the vernaculars. In our educational system, English is suffered to have an unnatural dominance over vernaculars. The extreme Anglicists hold that English should be used as the medium of instruction 'at the earliest age possible.' This argument is based on the fact that children in a foreign country pick up the language of the country without difficulty at an early age. Refuting this argument, the Calcutta University Commission say: "Whereas in a foreign country a child is surrounded by others who speak the language of the country, in a class room, he is surrounded by others who, with the exception of the teacher, are as ignorant as himself of the new medium; it is a class of one person teaching many, not of many teaching one; and it is only by experiment that class room methods can be worked out successfully." The 'educational economy,' as an advantage of vernacularising our educational system, has received recognition at the hands of the Commission. We have pointed out, in our issue of Feb. 11,* that the recommendations of the Calcutta University Commission in this connection are a further step. The next logical step after this is recommending the use of vernaculars as the medium in our universities also. The Sadler Commission have made the matricular stage as a halting place between the use of vernaculars as the medium of instruction in secondary schools and their use in the college department. They have suggested as their own opinion a bilingual system for the future. But they also say: "We do not wish to prejudge the future. It is not for us to predict whether the natural desire to use Bengali to the utmost will eventually outweigh the immense advantages of being able to use a medium common not only to the educated classes throughout India, but to more peoples than any other, and giving access in effect to the literature and the scientific records of the world." Though, in view of the evidence submitted to them, the Commissioners could not be persuaded to lay down a policy for the future in favour of vernacularising university education also, it is equally true that they could not find anything in the evidence which supported the Anglicists or the Bilinguists. Thus, though the replies to the Commissioners' question do not in themselves decide the future, they do "reveal a strong movement in favour of the immediate introduction of Bengali for some university purposes, and of its ultimate introduction for others, a movement of which there was little sign in the debate in the Imperial Legislative Council of 1915."

* Omitted in this collection.

If we study the Commissioners' analysis of the replies, we can more fully appreciate their remark. The question put to the witnesses was: "Do you hold English should be used as the medium of instuuction and examination at every stage above matriculation in the university course?"

The replies are analysed as follows:—

(i) 129 are positively in the affirmative;

(ii) 29 are in the affirmative, with slight reservations;

(iii) 68 are in favour of a joint use of English and the vernacular either side by side in the same institution, or in parallel institution;

(iv) 33 replies suggest the gradual replacement of English by the vernacular as the object to be aimed at;

(v) 37 are in the negative; and

(vi) 9 are insusceptible of classification.

So 155 replies are in favour of the English-medium and nearly 138 are not against using the vernacular-medium sooner or later. This proportion is certainly encouraging to the vernacularists. Besides, even among those that favour the English-medium there is not an inconsiderable section of witnesses who advise the foreign medium, because there is no provision for proper and sufficient text-books for different subjects. This school of educationists is not against the vernacular-medium on principle. They do not like us to get into water till we have learnt swimming. Of a similar sort but more decisive is the evidence of the remaining witnesses that stand for the English-medium. This latter evidence has stamped the vernaculars as unfit even to serve the purpose of the medium of instruction. These witnesses betray an ignorance of the history of our vernaculars. There was a time when Sanskrit was the sole medium for Hindu philosophy. But a few enuthsiastic scholars enriched their vernaculars with a decent store of philosophic literature and brought Hindu philosophy within the reach of the masses. Can we not with our present ideas of organisation do for our vernaculars in the sphere of science what once those vernacular scholars did in the sphere of philosophy? As against the diffidence of these witnesses, the vernacularists can cite the example of Japan. The Rev. W. E. S. Holland, Principal of St. Paul's Cathedral College, Calcutta, in his evidence, writes: "Japan, by the use of the vernacular, has built up an educational system that commands the respect of the West." The evidence o Babu Ramananda Chatterjee, the editor of the *Modern Review*, is even more convincing. He says: "The use of the vernaculars in all grades of university education is indispensably necessary. All objections have force only temporarily; for the most highly developed modern languages and literatures were at first no better than Bengali. In their case development was obtained by use: and it will be obtained in our case, too, in the same way." Thus we find that, that though the evidence before Dr. Sadler's Commission is not to-day in favour of vernacularising university education, it does hold high hopes for the future of the cause of the vernacular-meduim. Time was when the vernacularist's cause was looked upon with distrust. There is now not only no distrust but confidence has taken its place. Two important institutions have recently joined the cause. The Women's University of Poona and the Osmania University of Hyderabad are using the vernaculars as the sole medium. Their progress is being keenly watched by many Their success will, as Justice Sir Abdur Rahim says, make the solution of the problem of the vernaculars easier. At the last convocation of the Hindu

University, the Hon. Pandit Madan Mohan Malaviya invited all the eminent vernacularists to meet in a conference. We hope that such an organised effort will hasten full recognition of the vernaculars as media of instruction.

The present distribution of provinces is another factor which has done no less an injury than any other to the cause of the vernaculars. The redistribution of provinces on a linguistic basis will be followed by a re-arrangement of universities.

We have shown above the three allied spheres of work for the cause of vernaculars. And it is evident that, unless we advance this cause, we shall not be able to remove the growing intellectual and cultural gulf between our men and women and between the classes and the masses. It is also equally certain that the vernacular-medium alone can stimulate originality in thought in the largest number of persons.

13*th April*, 1921

'AN UNMITIGATED EVIL'

In reply to a question put to him in a public meeting at Orissa, whether English education was not a mixed evil,* inasmuch as Lok. Tilak, Babu Ram Mohan Rai,

* In *Young India* of 2nd February, 1921, Mr. Gandhi wrote as follows:

The place of English—Alongside of my suggestion about Hindustani has been the advice that the students should, during the transition period from inferiority to equality—from foreign domination to Swaraj, from helplessness to self-help—suspend their study of English. If we wish to attain Swaraj before the next Congress, we must believe in the possibility, we must do all that we are capable of doing for its advancement, and one must do

and Mr. Gandhi were products of English education, Mr. Gandhi replied as follows :

This is a representative view being expressed by several people. We must conquer the battle of Swaraj by conquering this sort of willful ignorance and prejudice of our countrymen and of Englishmen. The system of education is an unmitigated evil. I put my best energy to destroy that system. I don't say that we have got as yet any advantage from the system. The advantages, we have so far got, are in spite of the system, not because of the system. Supposing the English were not here, India would have marched with other parts of the world, and even if it continued to be under Moghul rule, many people would learn English as a language with a literature. The present system enslaves us, without allowing a discriminating use of English literatue. My friend had cited the case of Tilak, Ram Mohan, and myself. Leave aside my case, I am a miserable pigmy.

---

nothing that would not advance it or would actually retard it. Now, adding to our knowledge of English cannot accelerate our progress towards our goal and it can conceivably retard it. The latter calamity is a reality in many cases, for there are many who believe that we cannot acquire the spirit of freedom without the music of the English words ringing in our ears and sounding through our lips. This is an infatuation. If it were the truth, Swaraj would be as distant as the Greek Kalends. English is a language of international commerce, it is the language of diplomacy, and it contains many a rich literary treasure, it gives us an introduction to Western thought and culture. For a few of us, therefore, a knowledge of Engligh is necessary. They can carry on the departments of national commerce and international diplomacy, and for giving to the nation the best of Western literature, thought, and science. That would be the legitimate use of English. Whereas to-day English has usurped the dearest place in our hearts and dethroned our mother-tongues. It is an unnatural place due to our unequal relations with Englishmen. The highest development of the Indian mind must be possible without a knowledge of English. It is doing violence to the manhood and specially the womanhood of India to encourage our boys and girls to think that an entry into the best society is impossible without a knowledge of English. It is too humiliating a thought to be bearable To get rid of the infatuation for English is one of the essentials of Swaraj.

Tilak and Ram Mohan would have been far greater men if they had not had the contagion of English learning (clapping). I don't want your verbal approval by clapping but I want the approval of your intellect and reasoning. I am opposed to make a fetish of English education. I don't hate English education. When I want to destroy the Government, I don't want to destroy the English language but read English as an Indian Nationalist would do. Ram Mohan and Tilak (leave aside my case) were so many pigmies who had no hold upon the people compared with Chaitanya, Shanker, Kabir, and Nanak. Ram Mohan, Tilak, were pigmies before these giants. What Shanker alone was able to do, the whole army of English-knowing men can't do. I can multiply instances. Was Guru Govind a product of English education?

Is there a single English-knowing Indian who is a match for Nanak, the founder of a sect second to none in point of valour and sacrifice? Has Ram Mohan produced a single martyr of the type of Dulip Singh? I highly revere Tilak and Mohan. It is my conviction that, if Ram Mohan and Tilak had not received this education but had their natural training, they would have done greater things like Chaitanya. If that race has even to be revived, it is to be revived not by English education. I know what treasures I have lost in not knowing Hindustani and Sanskrit. I ask you to consider and value the glamour of education at its true worth. English education has emasculated us, constrained our intellect, and the manner of imparting this education has rendered us effeminate. We want to bask in the sunshine of freedom, but the enslaving system emasculates our nation. Pre-British period was not a period of slavery. We had some sort of Swaraj under Moghul rule. In Akbar's time the birth of a Pratap was possible, and in Aurangzeb's time a Sivaji could flourish. Has 150 years of British rule produced any Pratap and Sivaji?

You have got several Feudatory Native Chiefs, every one of whom bends the knee before the Political Agent and admits his slavery. When I find young men complaining against Native Chiefs, my sympathy goes to them. They are doubly oppressed. When the Native Chiefs do so, I ascribe it to the British conqueror, not to the Chiefs. They are victims to the slave-owning system. So my appeal to you all is, "Fly from this monster." Never mind if you beg from door to door. Rather die begging than live in bondage. We must be able to hold the country. Who holds the country now in bondage? It is not the English, it is we the Indian people who have accepted bondage. I refuse to shed a single tear if the English retire at this moment. I ask them to help us as our servants, equals, and friends. I shall not allow them to lord it over us with our consent. They may use aeroplanes, army, navy, but not our consent. Realise your own dignity even though India was infested with robbers. You must do your duty. What can be nobler than to die as free men of India? It is a satanic system. I have dedicated my life to destroy the system.

In "Young India" of 27th April, 1921, Mr. Gandhi further elucidated his point under the heading, '*English Education*. He wrote :

A friend asks me to give my considered view on the value of English education and explain my talk on the sands at Cuttack. I have not read the report of the talk. But I gladly respond to the friend's wish. It is my considered opinion that English education in the manner it has been given has emasculated the English-educated Indian, it has put a severe strain upon the Indian students' nervous energy, and has made of us imitators. The process of displacing the vernacular has been one of the saddest chapters in the British connection. Ram Mohan Rai would have been a greater reformer, and Lokmanya Tilak would have been a greater scholar, if they had not to start with the handicap of having to think in English and transmit their thoughts chiefly in English. Their effect on their own people, marvellous as it was, would have been greater if they had been brought up under a less unnatural system. No doubt they both gained from their knowledge of the rich treasures of English literature. But these should have been accessible to them through their own vernaculars. No country can become a nation by producing a race of translators. Think of what would have happened to the English if they had not an authorised version of the Bible. I do believe that Chaitanya, Kabir, Nanak, Guru Govindsing, Sivaji, and Pratap were greater men than Ram Mohan Rai and Tilak. I know that comparisons are odious. All are equally great in their own way.

But judged by the results, the effect of Ram Mohan and Tilak on the masses is not so permanent or far-reaching as that of the others more fortunately born. Judged by the obstacles they had to surmount, they were giants, and both would have been greater in achieving results, if they had not been handicapped by the system under which they received their training. I refuse to believe that the Raja and the Lokmanya could not have thought the thoughts they did without a knowledge of the English language. Of all the superstitions that affect India, none is so great as that a knowledge of the English language is necessary for imbibing ideas of liberty, and developing accuracy of thought. It should be remembered that there has been only one system of education before the country for the past fifty years, and only one medium of expression forced on the country. We have, therefore, no data before us as to what we would have been but for the education in the existing schools and colleges. This, however, we do know that India to-day is poorer than fifty years ago, less able to defend herself, and her children have less stamina. I need not be told that that is due to the defect in the system of government. The system of education is its most defective part. It was conceived and born in error, for the English rulers honestly believed the indigenous system to be worse than useless. It has been nurtured in sin, for the tendency has been to dwarf the Indian body, mind, and soul.

1st *June*, 1921

ENGLISH LEARNING

Elsewhere * the reader will see my humble endeavour in reply to Dr. Tagore's criticism of Non-co-operation. I have since read his letter to the Manager of Shantiniketan. † I am sorry to observe that the letter is written in anger and in ignorance of facts. The Poet was naturally incensed to find that certain students in London would not give a hearing to Mr. Pearson, one of the truest of Englishmen, and he became equally incensed to learn that I had told our women to stop English studies. The reasons for my advice, the Poet evidently inferred for himself.

How much better it would have been, if he had not imputed the rudeness of the students to Non-co-operation, and had remembered that Non-co-operators worship Andrews, honour Stokes, and gave a most respectful hearing to Messrs. Wedgwood, Ben Spoor and Holford Knight at Nagpur, that Maulana Mahomed Ali accepted the invitation to tea of an English official when he invited him as a friend, that Hakim Ajmalkhan, a staunch Non-co-operator, had the portraits of Lord and Lady Hardinge unveiled in his Tibbi College and had invited his many English friends to witness the ceremony. How much better it would have been, if he had refused to allow the demon doubt to possess him for one moment, as to the real and religious character of the present movement, and had believed that the movement was altering the meaning of old terms, nationalism and patriotism, and extending their scope.

If he, with a poet's imagination, had seen that I was

* See *infra* under Non-co-operation campaign

† Omitted in this collection.

incapable of wishing to cramp the mind of the Indian women, and I could not object to English learning as such, and recalled the fact that throughout my life I had fought for the fullest liberty for women, he would have been saved the injustice which he has done me, and which, I know, he would never knowingly do to an avowed enemy. The Poet does not know perhaps that English is to-day studied because of its commercial and so-called political value. Our boys think, and rightly in the present circumstances, that without English they cannot get Government service. Girls are taught English as a passport to marriage. I know several instances of women wanting to learn English so that they may be able to talk to Englishmen in English. I know husbands who are sorry that their wives cannot talk to them and their friends in English. I know families in which English is being *made* the mother tongue. Hundreds of youths believe that without a knowledge of English freedom for India is practically impossible. The canker has so eaten into the society that, in many cases, the only meaning of Education is a knowledge of English. All these are for me signs of our slavery and degradation. It is unbearable to me that the vernaculars should be crushed and starved as they have been. I cannot tolerate the idea of parents writing to their children, or husbands writing to their wives, not in the own vernaculars, but in English. I hope I am as great a believer in free air as the great Poet. I do not want my house to be walled in on all sides and my windows to be stuffed. I want the cultures of all the lands to be blown about my house as freely as possible. But I refuse to be blown off my feet by any. I refuse to live in other people's houses as an interloper, a beggar or a slave. I refuse to put the unnecesssry strain of learning English upon my sisters for the sake of false pride or questionable social advantage. I would have our young men and young women with literary tastes to learn as much of English and other world-languages as they like, and then expect them to give the benefits of their learning to India and to the world, like a Bose, a Roy or the Poet himself. But I would not have a single Indian to forget, neglect or be ashamed of his mother-tongue, or to feel that he or she cannot think or express the best thoughts in his or her own vernacular. Mine is not a religion of the prison-house. It has room for the least among God's creation. But it is proof against insolence, pride of race, religion or colour. I am extremely sorry for the Poet's misreading of this great movement of reformation, purification and patriotism spelt humanity. If he will be patient, he will find no cause for sorrow or shame for his countrymen. I respectfully warn him against mistaking its excrescences for the movement itself. It is as wrong to judge Non-co-operation by the students' misconduct in London or Malegaon's in India, as it would be to judge Englishmen by the Dyers or the O'Dwyers.

Mr. Gandhi's views on the relations between English culture and Indian are further elucidated in the following which appeared in "Young India" of 9th June, 1920:—

"*Seed of Race.*"—Sir John Woodroffe wrote: Dear Sir, I have just received a criticism of my book "Seed of Race" contained in your issue of the 11th February. (Omitted in this collection). Your reviewer approves of my standpoint, but, dealing with my statement that Indian culture should *also* be given a place together with English studies, says that the tone of this and other remarks sounds apologetic, which seems unfortunate and hardly consistent with the note which I submitted to the Calcutta University Commission. It is certainly unfortunate that I used language which has apparently ill expressed what I wanted to say. To correct this misunderstanding I now write. I am the last person to apologise for Indian culture, the fostering of which I have consistently urged, not as a matter of concession or expediency, but of right—the right of every individual and racial soul to fully and freely express itself in accordance with Svadharma. I have done so also because I believe in its beneficial influence on the world at large.

As your reviewer admirably says, Indian culture is no cripple, and when it borrows from elsewhere it must do so in its fulness and strength and not out of a sense of its own impotency or deficiency, by which I understand incapacity. Indian culture should, he says, be at once the basis, superstructure, and crown of the educational edifice. With this general proposition I agree. But what do we mean by fostering Indian culture? Some merely understand thereby the teaching of what has been thought and done in the past, and then its mere reproduction to-day. I do not.

I understand by this phrase primarily the liberation of the general Indian Sangskara from all alien incrustation, and then its nourishment, so that it may become in its turn a living cause of culture forms to-day. These may or may not be the same as the forms of the past, but whatever they be, they are vitally produced as fresh creations and not merely taken over into the present because they have lingered over, often with spent force, from the past. These past cultural forms are the useful and indeed indispensable subject of our study—indispensable because they recall and strengthen the Sangskara which has produced the Arya Dharma. We steep ourselves in tradition, not merely to automatically reproduce it, but to make ourselves worthy of our forefathers, capable of being as vitally creative as they were. But since they laid the foundations, much has happened. Other cultures have elsewhere grown up and become known to India. Are we not to study these and appropriate from them what is suitable to us? Or are we to build a cultural hot-house, forcing plants which will not live in the rude movements of the airs of Heaven? Certainly not. We enrich the Sangskara by every widening of our knowledge; therefore English and other cultures should "also" be studied. As my remarks were addressed to those interested in the furtherance of English studies, I put it in the form that Indian culture must also have its place. Those who have not fallen into the path of error have scarcely need of counsel.

It is in this way that the so-called "universal" as opposed to "regional" culture will (if at all) come about. As each race and man acts according to his own Dharma, that is according to natural law, he and they perfect their form, for Dharma is the Law of Form.

In perfecting our forms, we approach to others who have perfected theirs. The highly intellectual, moral, and spiritual are everywhere akin, and this is as a Russian friend of mine calls it, "the International of Culture." It is not to be obtained by neglect of one's own Dharma and by taking a bit here and a bit there to make up some combination which is neither "fish, flesh, fowl, nor even good red herring." But in practice the following case arises—the case of those whose intellect, capacity, general development, and opportunities do not permit of this both intensive and extensive culture. Take for instance the ordinary Indian peasant—what of him? If it be the fact that education both in his own and other cultures cannot be given, then, naturally, his own racial culture must be given the first place. Great care must be taken in dealing with the question of primary education in India, for here the mischief may occur. If we sever the people from their past tradition, it is difficult to recall them. Whereas if they are preserved, they can be added to or improved later on. All this is becoming increasingly recognized now-a-days, when the people are getting away from what Henry James called "a superstitious valuation of Europe." If there is in other parts of the world a "rebarbarization," as Herbert Spencer feared, it may be that in such case the True, the Good, and the Beautiful will be upheld by a cultivated and aristocratic India which with its roots deep in the past bears exemplary flower in the present. Certainly it is necessary, as your reviewer does, to feel all this passionately. Those who think it necessary to apologise for their Race and its traditions have ceased to belong to the former and to be worthy to carry on the latter. The late George Tyrrell, in one of his recently published letters, says: "I begin to think the only real sin is suicide or not being oneself." Just so. But if so, we certainly should not apologise for being what we ought to be.

I am, dear Sir.

Bath, Yours truly,

May 8th, 1920. (Sd.) JOHN WOODROFFE.

[We are glad Sir John has explained himself as regards his view of the place of Indian culture in the education of Indian youths. We hope he has not misunderstood us. We are not for reproducing old forms without considering whether they are good or bad. Nor do we want a cultural hot-house; what we maintain is, how much soever important a knowledge of English culture may be to the Indians of to-day, it need not form the *sine qua non* of all Indian education. What we would wish is that, when the Indian Educational System is fully developed and organised, a study of English and other foreign cultures should form part of a post graduate course. We admit that a knowledge of different cultures will enable us to perfect our own by assimilating the best of the others. Perhaps in the God's world differences will persist, but they must not represent divisions; they must be like facets of one beautiful gem. Has not the Lord said "Nastyanto Vistarasya Me"?—Ed. Y. I.]

27th October, 1920

'DEPRESSED' CLASSES

(By M. K. Gandhi)

Vivekananda used to call the Panchamas 'suppressed classes.' There is no doubt that Vivekananda's is a more accurate adjective. We have suppressed them and have consequently become ourselves depressed. That we have become the 'Pariahs of the Empire' is, in Gokhale's language, the retributive justice meted out to us by a just God. A correspondent indignantly asks me in a pathetic letter reproduced elsewhere,* what I am doing for them. I have given the letter with the correspondent's own heading, 'Should not we the Hindus wash our bloodstained hands before we ask the English to wash theirs'? This is a proper question reasonably put. And if a member of a slave nation could deliver the suppressed classes from their slavery without freeing myself from my own, I would do so to-day. But it is an impossible task. A slave has not the freedom even to do the right thing. It is right for me to prohibit the importation of foreign goods, but I have no power to bring it about. It was right for Maulana Mahomed Ali to go to Turkey and to tell the Turks personally that India was with them in their righteous struggle. He was not free

* Omitted in this collection.

to do so. If I had a truly national legislature, I would answer Hindu insolence by erecting special and better wells for the exclusive use of suppressed classes and by erecting better and more numerous schools for them, so that there would be not a single member of the suppressed classes left without a school to teach their children. But I must wait for that better day.

Meanwhile, are the depressed classes to be left to their own resources? Nothing of the sort. In my own humble manner, I have done and am doing all I can for my Panchama brother.

There are three courses open to these down-trodden members of the nation. For their impatience they may call in the assistance of the slave-owning Government. They will get it, but they will fall from the frying pan into the fire. To-day they are slaves of slaves. By seeking Government aid, they will be used for suppressing their kith and kin. Instead of being sinned against, they will themselves be the sinners. The Mussalmans tried it and failed. They found that they were worse off than before. The Sikhs did it unwittingly and failed. To-day there is no more discontented community in India than the Sikhs. Government aid is, therefore, no solution.

The second is rejection of Hinduism and wholesale conversion to Islam or Christianity. And if a change of religion could be justified for worldly betterment, I would advise it without hesitation. But religion is a matter of the heart. No physical inconvenience can warrant abandonment of one's own religion. If the inhuman treatment of the Panchamas were a part of Hinduism, its rejection would be a paramount duty both for them and for those like me who would not make a fetish even of religion and condone every evil in its sacred name. But I believe that untouchability is no part of Hinduism.* It is rather its excrescence to be removed by every effort. And there is quite an army of Hindu reformers who have set their heart upon ridding Hinduism of this blot. Conversion therefore, I hold, is no remedy whatsoever.

Then there remains, finally, self-help and self-dependence, with such aid as the non-Panchama Hindus will render of their own motion, not as a matter of patronage but as a matter of duty. And herein comes the use of Non-co-operation. My correspondent was correctly informed by Mr. Rajagopalachari and Mr. Hanumantrao that I would favour well-regulated Non-co-operation for this acknowledged evil. But Non-co-operation means independence of outside help, it means effort from within. It would not be Non-co-operation to insist on visiting prohibited areas. That may be Civil Disobedience if it is peacefully carried out. But I have found to my cost that Civil Disobedience requires for greater preliminary training and self-control. All can non-co-operate, but few only can offer Civil Disobedience. Therefore, by way of protest against Hinduism, the Panchamas can certainly stop all contact and connection with the other Hindus so long as the special grievances are maintained. But this means organised intelligent effort. And so far as I can see, there is no leader among the Panchamas who can lead them to victory through Non-co-operation.

The better way therefore, perhaps, is for the Panchamas heartily to join the great national movement that is now going on for throwing off the slavery of the present Government.† It is easy enough for the Panchama

*For the detailed views of Mr. Gandhi on Hinduism, See *infra*.

†Commenting on the above, Mr. R. G. Pradhan, a well-known writer and pleader, wrote in *Young India* of 29th December, pointing

friends to see that Non-co-operation against this evil Government pre-supposes co-operation between the different sections forming the Indian nation. The Hindus must realise that, if they wish to offer successful Non-co-operation against the Government, they must make common cause with the Panchamas, even as they have made common cause with the Mussalmans. Non-co-operation when it is free from violence is essentially a movement of intensive self-purification. That process has commenced and whether the Panchamas deliberately take part in it or not, the rest of the Hindus dare not

---

out that he was voicing the view of some leaders of the depressed classes when he said that the Congress politicians and Swarajists were, most of them, social reactionaries, that, while they talked of the Non-co-operation resolution of the Congress as mandatory on the country, they totally ignored the resolution regarding untouchability, that the depressed classes were not and could not be anti-Nationalists and did not desire to play into the hands of the Government because the latter upheld orthodoxy and that if the campaign against untouchability went on simultaneously with the political campaign, the depressed classes would join the Non-co-operation movement.

The following was Mr. Gandhi's note on the letter: "Mr. Pradhan forgets that Non-co-operation against the Government means co-operation among the governed, and if Hindus do not remove the sin of untouchability, there will be no Swaraj whether in one year or in one hundred years. If I invite the depressed classes to join the movement of Non-co-operation, I do so because I want them to realise their strength. Swaraj is as unattainable without the removal of the sin of untouchability as it is without Hindu-Muslim unity.—M.K.G."

In *Young India* of 3rd November, 1921, in reply to a correspondent, Mr. Gandhi wrote:

Untouchability cannot be given a secondary place on the programme. Without the removal of the taint Swaraj is a meaningless term. Workers should welcome social boycott and even public execration in the prosecution of their work. I consider the removal of untouchability as a most powerful factor in the process of attainment of Swaraj and for that matter also the Khilafat. Impure Hinduism cannot help the process of Islamic purification.

neglect them without hampering their own progress. Hence though the Panchama problem is as dear to me as life itself, I rest satisfied with the exclusive attention to national Non-co-operation. I feel sure that the greater includes the less.

Closely allied to this question is the Non-Brahmin question. I wish I had studied it more closely than I have been able to. A quotation from my speech delivered at a private meeting in Madras has been torn from its context and misused to further the antagonism between the so-called Brahmins and the so-called Non-Brahmins. I do not wish to retract a word of what I said at that meeting. I was appealing to those who are accepted as Brahmins. I told them that, in my opinion, the treatment of Non-Brahmins was as satanic as the treatment of us by the British. I added that the Non-Brahmins should be placated without any ado or bargaining. But my remarks were never intended to encourage the powerful Non-Brahmins of Maharashtra or Madras, or the mischievous element among them, to overawe the so-called Brahmins. I use the word 'so-called' advisedly. For the Brahmins who have freed themselves from the thraldom of superstitious orthodoxy have not only no quarrel with Non-Brahmins as such, but are in every way eager to advance Non-Brahmins wherever they are weak. No lover of his country can possibly achieve its general advance if he dared to neglect the least of his countrymen. Those Non-Brahmins therefore who are coqueting with the Government are selling themselves and the nation to which they belong. By all means let those who have faith in the Government help to sustain it, but let no Indian worthy of his birth cut off his nose to spite the face.

19th January, 1921

THE SIN OF UNTOUCHABILITY

(BY M. K. GANDHI)

It is worthy of note that the Subjects Committee and the Committee of the Nagpur Congress held in December, 1920, accepted without any opposition the clause regarding the sin of untouchability. It is well that the National assembly passed the resolution stating that the removal of this blot on Hinduism was necessary for the attainment of Swaraj. The Devil succeeds only by receiving help from his fellows. He always takes advantage of the weakest spots in our natures in order to gain mastery over us. Even so does the Government retain its control over us through our weaknesses or vices. And if we would render ourselves proof against its machinations, we must remove our weaknesses. It is for that reason that I have called Non-co-operation a process of purification. As soon as that process is completed, this government must fall to pieces for want of the necessary environment, just as mosquitos cease to haunt a place whose cesspools are filled up and dried.

Has not a just Nemesis overtaken us for the crime of untouchability? Have we not reaped as we have sown? Have we not practised Dyerism and O'Dwyerism on our own kith and kin? We have segregated the 'pariah' and we are in turn segregated in the British Colonies. We deny him the use of public wells; we throw the leavings of our plates at him. His very shadow pollutes us. Indeed there is no charge that the 'pariah,' cannot fling in our faces and which we do not fling in the faces of Englishmen.

How is this blot on Hinduism to be removed? 'Do

unto others as you would that others should do unto you.' I have often told English officials that, if they are friends and servants of India, they should come down from their pedestal, cease to be patrons, demonstrate by their loving deeds that they are in every respect our friends, and believe us to be equals in the same sense they believe fellow Englishmen to be their equals. After the experiences of the Punjab and the Khilafat, I have gone a step further and asked them to repent and to change their hearts. Even so is it necessary for us Hindus to repent of the wrong we have done, to alter our behaviour towards those whom we have 'suppressed' by a system as devilish as we believe the English system of the government of India to be. We must not throw a few miserable schools at them: we must not adopt the air of superiority towards them. We must treat them as our blood brothers as they are in fact. We must return to them the inheritance of which we have robbed them. And this must not be the act of a few English-knowing reformers merely, but it must be a conscious voluntary effort on the part of the masses. We may not wait till eternity for this much belated reformation. We must aim at bringing it about within this year of grace, probation, preparation, and *tapasya*. It is a reform not to follow *Swaraj* but to precede it.

Untouchability is not a sanction of religion, it is a device of Satan. The devil has always quoted scriptures. But scriptures cannot transcend Reason and Truth. They are intended to purify Reason and illuminate Truth. I am not going to burn a spotless horse, because the Vedas are reported to have advised, tolerated, or sanctioned the sacrifice. For me the Vedas are divine and unwritten. 'The letter killeth.' It is the spirit that giveth the light. And the spirit of the Vedas is purity, truth, innocence, chastity, simplicity, forgiveness, godliness, and all that makes a man or woman noble and brave. There is neither nobility nor bravery in treating the great and uncomplaining scavengers of the nation as worse than dogs to be despised and spat upon. Would that God gave us the strength and the wisdom to become voluntary scavengers of the nation as the 'suppressed' classes are forced to be. There are Augean stables enough and to spare for us to clean.

27th April, 1921

Mr. GANDHI AND THE SUPPRESSED CLASSES

Mr. Gandhi presided at the Suppressed Classes Conference held at Ahmedabad on the 13th and 14th instant. There was a large attendance of ladies and gentlemen from the town, though the number of the untouchables was much less than expected, a rumour having spread in the town that Government would arrest those of them who attended.

Mr. Gandhi regretted in the beginning this small attendance, and said that incidents as the present took away what little faith he had in conferences as an effective agency of social reform. If therefore he occupied the audience shorter than they expected, it would be because his remarks would not reach all he meant to address and not because his enthusiasm for the work was in any way damped.

Coming to the subject, he said:

I do not know how I am to convince those who oppose the reform, of the wrong position they have taken. How am I to plead with those who regard any contact with the members of the suppressed community as entailing defilement and of which they cannot be cleansed without necessary ablutions, and who thus regard omission to perform the ablutions a sin? I can only place before them my innermost convi tions.

I regard untouchability as the greatest blot on Hinduism. This idea was not brought home to me by my bitter experiences during the S. African struggle. It is not due to the fact that I was once an agnostic. It is equally wrong to think, as some people do, that I have taken my views from my study of Christian religious literature. These views date as far back as the time when I was neither enamoured of, nor was acquainted with, the Bible or the followers of the Bible.

I was hardly yet twelve when this idea had dawned on me. A scavenger named Uka, an untouchable, used to attend our house for cleaning latrines. Often I would ask my mother why it was wrong to touch him, why I was forbidden to touch him. If I accidentally touched Uka, I was asked to perform the ablutions, and though I naturally obeyed, it was not without smilingly protesting that untouchability was not sanctioned by religion, that it was impossible that it should be so. I was a very dutiful and obedient child and so far as it was consistent with respect for parents, I often had tussles with them on this matter. I told my mother that she was entirely wrong in considering physical contact with Uka as sinful.

While at school I would often happen to touch the "untouchables", and as I never would conceal the fact from my parents, my mother would tell me that the shortest cut to purification after the unholy touch was to cancel the touch by touching any Mussalman passing by. And simply out of reverence and regard for my mother I often did so, but never did so believing it to be a religious obligation. After some time we shifted to Porebander, where I made my first acquaintance with Sanskrit. I was not yet put to an English school, and my brother and I were placed in charge of a Brahman, who taught us *Ramraksha* and *Vishnu Punjar*. The texts "*jale Vishnuh*" "*sthale Vishnuh*" (there is the Lord (present) in water, there is the Lord (present) in earth) have never gone out of my memory. A motherly old dame used to live close by. Now it happened that I was very timid then, and would conjure up ghosts and goblins whenever the lights went out, and it was dark. The old mother, to disabuse me of fears, suggested that I should mutter the *Ramraksha* texts whenever I was afraid, and all evil spirits would fly away. This I did and, as I thought, with good effect. I could never believe then that there was any text in the *Ramraksha* pointing to the contact of the 'untouchables' as a sin. I did not understand its meaning then, or understood it very imperfectly. But I was confident that *Ram-*

raksha, which could destroy all fear of ghosts, could not be countenancing any such thing as fear of contact with the 'untouchables.'

The *Ramayana* used to be regularly read in our family. A Brahmin called Ladha Maharaj used to read it. He was stricken with leprosy, and he was confident that a regular reading of the *Ramayana* would cure him of leprosy, and, indeed, he was cured of it. 'How can the Ramayana,' I thought to myself, 'in which one who is regarded now-a-days as an untouchable took Rama across the Ganges in his boat, countenance the idea of any human beings being untouchable on the ground that they were polluted souls?' The fact that we addressed God as the 'purifier of the polluted' and by similar appellations, shows that it is a sin to regard any one born in Hinduism as polluted or untouchable—that it is satanic to do so. I have hence been never tired of repeating that it is a great sin. I do not pretend that this thing had crystallised as a conviction in me at the age of twelve, but I do say that I did then regard untouchability as a sin. I narrate this story for the information of the Vaishnavas and Orthodox Hindus.

I have always claimed to be a Sanatani Hindu. It is not that I am quite innocent of the scriptures. I am not a profound scholar of Sanskrit. I have read the Vedas and the Upanishads only in translations. Naturally therefore, mine is not a scholarly study of them. My knowledge of them is in no way profound, but I have studied them as I should do as a Hindu and I claim to have grasped their true spirit. By the time I had reached the age of 21, I had studied other religions also.

There was a time when I was wavering between Hinduism and Christianity. When I recovered my balance of mind, I felt that to me salvation was possible only through the Hindu religion and my faith in Hinduism grew deeper and more enlightened.

But even then I believed that untouchability was no part of Hinduism; and that, if it was, such Hinduism was not for me.

True, Hinduism does not regard untouchability as a sin. I do not want to enter into any controversy regarding the interpretation of the shastras. It might be difficult for me to establish my point by quoting authorities from the Bhagwat or Manusmriti. But I claim to have understood the spirit of Hinduism. Hinduism has sinned in giving sanction to untouchability. It has degraded us, made us the pariahs of the Empire. Even the Mussalmans caught the sinful contagion from us; and in S. Africa, in E. Africa and in Canada, the Mussalmans no less than Hindus came to be regarded as pariahs. All this evil has resulted from the sin of untouchability.

I may here recall my proposition, which is this: So long as the Hindus wilfully regard untouchability as part of their religion, so long as the mass of Hindus consider it a sin to touch a section of their brethren, Swaraj is impossible of attainment. Yudhishthira would not enter heaven without his dog. How can, then, the descendants of that Yudhishthira expect to obtain Swaraj without the untouchables? What crimes, for which we condemn the Government as satanic, have not we been guilty of towards our untouchable brethren?

We are guilty of having suppressed our brethren; we make them crawl on their bellies; we have made them rub their noses on the ground; with eyes red with rage, we push them out of railway compartments—what more than this has British Rule done? What charge, that we bring against Dyer and O'Dwyer, may not others, and even our own people, lay at our doors? We ought to purge ourselves of this pollution. It is idle to talk of Swaraj so long as we do not protect the weak and the helpless, or so long as it is possible for a single Swarajist to injure the feelings of any individual. Swaraj means that not a single Hindu or Muslim shall for a moment arrogantly think that he can crush with impunity meek Hindus or Muslims. Unless this condition is fulfilled, we will gain Swaraj only to lose it the next moment. We are no better than the brutes until we have purged ourselves of the sins we have committed, against our weaker brethren.

But I have faith in me still. In the course of my peregrinations in India, I have realised that the spirit of kindness of which the Poet Tulsidas sings so eloquently, which forms the corner-stone of the Jain and Vaishnava religions, which is the quintessence of the *Bhagavat* and which every verse of the Gita is saturated with—this kindness, this love, this charity, is slowly but steadily gaining ground in the hearts of the masses of this country.

Many a fracas between Hindus and Mussalmans is still heard of. There are still many of these who do not scruple to wrong one another. But as to the net result, I feel that kindness and charity have increased. The Hindus and Mahomedans have become God-fearing. We have shaken ourselves free from the hypnotism of law-courts and Government schools, and no longer labour under many another hallucination. I have also realized that those whom we regard as illiterate and ignorant are the very people who deserve to be called educated. They are more cultured than we, their lives are more righteous than ours. A little study of the present-day mentality of the people will show that according to the popular conception Swaraj is synonymous with *Ram Raj*—the establishment of the Kingdom of Righteousness on earth.

If it can bring any comfort to you, my untouchable brethren, I would say that your question does not cause so much stir as it used to do formerly. That does not mean that I expect you to cease to have misgivings about the Hindus. How can they deserve to be not mistrusted having wronged you so much ? Swami Vivekananda used to say that the untouchables were not depressed, they were suppressed by the Hindus who in turn had suppressed themselves by suppressing them.

I suppose I was at Nellore on the 6th of April. I met the untouchables there and I prayed that day as I have done to-day. I do want to attain Moksha. I do not want to be reborn. But if I have to be reborn. I should be born an untouchable, so that I may share their sorrows, sufferings, and the affronts levelled at them, in order that I may endeavour to free myself and them from that miserable condition. I, therefore, prayed that, if I should be born again, I should do so not as a Brahmin, Kshatriya, Vaishya, or Shudra, but as an Atishudra.

To-day is much more solemn than the sixth. It is hallowed by the memory of the massacre of thousands of innocents. And I prayed, therefore, also to-day that if I should die with any of my desires unfructified, with my service of the untouchables unfinished, with my Hinduism unfulfilled, I may be born again amongst the untouchables to bring my Hinduism to its fulfilment.

I love scavengering. In my Ashram, an eighteen years old Brahmin lad is doing the scavenger's work in order to teach the Ashram scavenger cleanliness. The lad is no reformer. He was born and bred in orthodoxy. He is a regular reader of the Gita and faithfully performs Sandhyavandana. His pronunciation of Sanskrit verses is more faultless than mine. When he conducts the prayer, his soft sweet melodies melt one into love. But he felt that his accomplishments were incomplete until he had become also a perfect sweeper, and that if he wanted the Ashram sweeper to do his work well, he must do it himself and set an example.

You should realize that you are cleaning Hindu society. You have therefore to purify your lives. You should cultivate the habits of cleanliness, so that no one may point his finger at you. Use alkali-ash or earth, if you cannot afford to use soap, to keep yourselves clean. Some of you are given to drinking and gambling which you must get rid of. You will point your finger at the Brahmins and say even they are given to these vices. But they are not looked upon as polluted; and you are. You must not ask the Hindus to emancipate you as a matter of favour. Hindus must do so, if they want, in their own interest. You should, therefore, make them feel ashamed by your own purity and cleanliness. I believe that we shall have purified ourselves within the next five months. If my expectations are not fulfilled, I will think that, although my proposition was fundamentally correct, yet I was wrong in my calculation; and I will again say that I had erred in my calculation.

You claim to be Hindus; you read the Bhagavat; if, therefore, the Hindus oppress you, then you should understand that the fault does not lie in the Hindu Religion but in those who profess it. In order to emancipate yourselves, you shall have to purify yourselves. You shall have to get rid of evil habits like drinking.

If you want to ameliorate your condition, if you want to obtain Swaraj, you should be self-reliant. I was told in Bombay that some of you are opposed to N. C. O. and believe that salvation is only possible through the British Government. Let me tell you that you will never be able to obtain redress by discarding Hindu Religion and courting the favour of a third party. Your emancipation lies in your own hands.

I have come in contact with the untouchables all over the country, and I have observed that immense possibilities lie latent in them of which neither they nor the rest of the Hindus seem to be aware. Their intellect is of virginal purity. I ask you to learn spinning and weaving, and if you take them up as a profession, you will keep poverty from your doors. As regards your attitude towards the Bhangis, I will repeat what I said at Godhra. I cannot understand why you should yourselves countenance the distinction between Dheds and Bhangis. There is no difference between them. Even in normal times their occupation is as honourable as that of lawyers or Government servants.

You should now cease to accept leavings from plates however clean they may be represented to be. Receive grain only—good, sound grain, not rotten grain, and that too only if it is courteously offered. If you are able to do all I have asked you to do, you will secure your emancipation, not in four or five months, but in so many days.

The Hindus are not sinful by nature; they are sunk in ignorance. Untouchability must be extinct in this very year. Two of the strongest desires that keep me in flesh and bone are the emancipation of the untouchables and the protection of the cow. When these two desires are fulfilled, there is Swaraj, and therein lies my own *Moksha*. May God give you strength to work out your salvation.

The following appeared in *Young India* of 27th April, 1921, under the heading, "*Disappearing untouchability*":

Of all the sweet experiences during my Gujarat tour,* none was sweeter than the sympathetic manner in which the 'suppressed' were received by the other Hindus. Everywhere the audience has received my remarks on

* The position in Madras, however, was different. Mr. Gandhi wrote in *Young India* of 29th September, 1921, under the heading, "The Panchamas":

Nowhere is the "untouchable" so cruelly treated as in the Madras presidency. His very shadow defiles the Brahman. He may not even pass through Brahman streets. Non-Brahmans treat him no better. And between the two, the Panchama, as he is called in these parts, is ground to atoms. And yet Madras is a land of mighty temples and religious devotion. The people with their big *tilak* marks, their long locks and their bare clean bodies look like rishis. But their religion seems almost to be exhausted in these outward observances. It is difficult to understand this Dyerism towards the most industrious and useful citizens in a land that has produced Shankara and Ramanuja. And in spite of the satanic treatment of our own kith and kin in this part of India, I retain my faith in these Southern people. I have told them at all their huge meetings in no uncertain terms that there can be no Swaraj without the removal of the curse from our midst.

I have told them, that our being treated as social lepers in practically the whole world is due to our having treated a fifth of our own race as such. Non-co-operation is a plea for a change of heart, not merely in the English but equally in ourselves. Indeed, I expect the change first in us and then as a matter of course in the English. A nation that can throw away an age-long curse in a year, a nation that can shed the drink-habit as we shed our garments, a nation that can return to its original industry and suddenly utilise its spare hours to manufacture sixty crores worth of cloth during a single year, is a transformed nation. Its transformation must react upon the world.

the matter without resentment. At Kalol there was to be a meeting of 'untouchables' to be addressed by me. I pleaded with the Mahajans that they should permit me to address them in the pandal erected for the general meeting. After some hesitation, they agreed. I was to have gone to fetch these 'outcastes' from their quarters. Their abode was too far from the pandal to enable them to come. I therefore addressed them near the hospital. But I was glad to note that many orthodox Hindus, who accompanied me, freely mixed with the men and women who had flocked round me from the pariah quarters. But the height of satisfaction was reached when in Shisodra, a big village near Navsari, there were know-

---

It must constitute even for the scoffer a convincing demonstration of God's existence and grace, and so I say that, if India can become transformed in this wise, no power on earth can deny India's right to establish Swaraj. In spite of all the clouds that are thickening on the Indian horizon, I make bold to prophesy that the moment India has repented of her treatment of the 'untouchables,' and has boycotted foreign cloth that moment India will be hailed, by the very English officials who seem to have hardened their hearts, as a free and a brave nation. And because I believe that, if Hindus will, it is possible for them to enfranchise the so-called Panchamas and extend to them the rights that they claim for themselves, and it is possible for India, if she wills, to manufacture all the cloth she needs even as she cooks all the food she eats, I therefore also believe that Swaraj is attainable their year. This transformation cannot take place by any elaborately planned mechanical action. But it can take place if God's grace is with us. Who can deny that God is working a wonderful change in the hearts of every one of us? Any way it is the duty of every Congress worker everywhere to befriend the untouchable brother, and to plead with the un-Hindu Hindus, that Hinduism of the Vedas, the Upanishads, Hinduism of the Bhagavadgita and of Shankara and Ramanuja contains no warrant for treating a single human being, no matter how fallen, as an untouchable. Let every Congressman plead in the gentlest manner possible with orthodoxy, that the bar sinister is the very negation of Ahimsa.

ingly admitted to the place reserved for the elite of the village, all the many Dheds who were standing at a distance from the great meeting which I was addressing. As they were admitted, not a man or woman moved or protested. Almost every one in the village was present at the meeting. People from surrounding villages too had attended. This deliberate and solemn admission of several hundred men and women of the untouchable class to the centre of a great gathering like the above is to me a sure sign of the pure religious character of the movement. Mr. Vallavabhai Patel in order to make assurance doubly sure asked those who approved of the step to raise their hands, and quite a forest of hands went up. The experiment was repeated in Bardoli before an equally large audience and with equally satisfactory results. Untouchability is surely disappearing, and with its disappearance the way to Swaraj is becoming safe and easy.

8th December, 1920

THE CASTE SYSTEM

(By M. K. Gandhi)

I have received several angry letters about my remarks* during my Deccan tour on the caste system. I am not publishing these letters, because there is nothing but vituperation in them, and when there is no vituperation, there is little argument about them. I am anxious to open the columns of "Young India" to opinions expressing dissent from its views, but the writers must be brief and interesting. Acrimony is no argument. I am obliged to make these remarks, because two writers at

* Omitted in this collection.

least would have gained publicity for their letters, if they had not been prolix and unintelligible in their expression. The question, however, that my correspondents have raised, commands attention and deserves an answer. They argue that the retention of the caste system spells ruin for India and that it is caste which has reduced India to slavery. In my opinion, it is not caste that has made us what we are. It was our greed and disregard of essential virtues which enslaved us. I believe that caste has saved Hinduism from disintegration.

But like every other institution, it has suffered from excrescences. I consider the four divisions alone to be fundamental, natural, and essential. The innumerable sub-castes are sometimes a convenience, often a hindrance. The sooner there is fusion the better. The silent destruction and reconstruction to sub-castes have ever gone on and are bound to continue. Social pressure and public opinion can be trusted to deal with the problem. But I am certainly against any attempt at destroying the fundamental divisions. The caste system is not based on inequality, there is no question of inferiority, and so far as there is any such question arising, as in Madras, Maharashtra, or elsewhere, the tendency should undoubtedly be checked. But there appears to be no valid reason for ending the system because of its abuse. It lends itself easily to reformation. The spirit of democracy, which is fast spreading throughout India and the rest of the world, will, without a shadow of doubt, purge the institution of the idea of predominance and subordination.

The spirit of democracy is not a mechanical thing to be adjusted by abolition of forms. It requires change of the heart. If caste is a bar to the spread of the spirit, the existence of five religions in India—Hinduism, Islam, Christianity, Zorastrianism, and Judaism—is equally a bar. The spirit of democracy requires the inculcation of the spirit of brotherhood, and I can find no difficulty in considering a Christian or a Mahomedan to be my brother in absolutely the same sense as a blood brother, and Hinduism that is responsible for the doctrine of the caste is also responsible for the inculcation of the essential brotherhood, not merely of man but even of all that lives.

One of my correspondents suggests that we should abolish the caste but adopt the class system of Europe —meaning thereby I suppose that the idea of heredity in caste should be rejected. I am inclined to think that the law of heredity is an eternal law and any attempt to alter that law must lead, as it has before led, to utter confusion. I can see very great use in considering a Brahmin to be always a Brahmin throughout his life. If he does not behave himself like a Brahmin, he will naturally cease to command the respect that is due to the real Brahmin. It is easy to imagine the innumerable difficulties if one were to set up a court of punishments and rewards, degradation and promotion. If Hindus believe, as they must believe in reincarnation, transmigration, they must know that nature will, without any possibility of mistake, adjust the balance by degrading a Brahmin, if he misbehaves himself, by reincarnating him in a lower division, and translating one who lives the life of a Brahmin in his present incarnation to Brahminhood in his next.

Interdrinking, interdining, intermarrying, I hold, are not essential for the promotion of the spirit of democracy.* I do not contemplate under a most democratic

* *See* p. 397.

constitution a universality of manners and customs about eating, drinking and marrying. We shall ever have to seek unity in diversity, and I decline to consider it a sin for a man not to drink or eat with any and everybody. In Hinduism, children of brothers may not intermarry. The prohibition does not interfere with cordiality of relations, probably it promotes healthiness of relationships. In Vaishnava households, I have known mothers not dining in the common kitchen, nor drinking from the same pot, without their becoming exclusive, arrogant, or less loving. These are disciplinary restraints which are not in themselves bad. Carried to ridiculous extremes, they may become harmful, and if the motive is one of arrogation of superiority the restraint becomes an indulgence, therefore hurtful. But as time goes forward, and new necessities and occasions arise, the custom regarding interdrinking, interdining and intermarrying, will require cautious modifications or rearrangement.

Thus, whilst I am prepared to defend, as I have always done, the division of Hindus into four castes, as I have so often said in these columns, I consider untouchability to be a heinous crime against humanity. It is not a sign of self-restraint but an arrogant assumption of superiority. It has served no useful purpose and it has suppressed, as nothing else in Hinduism has, vast numbers of the human race who are not only every bit as good as ourselves, but are rendering in many walks of life an essential service to the country. It is a sin of which the sooner Hinduism purges itself the better it is for itself, if it is to be recognised as an honourable and elevating religion. I know no argument in favour of its retention and I have no hesitation in rejecting scriptural authority of a doubtful character in order to support a sinful institution.* Indeed I would reject all authority if it is in conflict with sober reason or the dictates of the heart. Authority sustains and ennobles the weak when it is the hand-work of reason, but it degrades them when it supplants reason, sanctified by the still small voice within.

* Occupation is no test of superiority or otherwise with Mr. Gandhi. The following appeared in *Young India* of 17th November, 1921 :

Prejudice and Insolence.—A correspondent from the Tanjore District writes, saying that he and his brother though Brahmans felt that rather than lead a lazy life, they should do some work and they 'turned their hands to the plough.' So they began agriculture. Thereupon their fellow villagers became disgusted and excommunicated them. They however remained firm in their resolve. When the Shankaracharya of Kumbakonam visited their part of the district they went with their offering which was rejected, because they had committed the sin of labouring for their livelihood. My correspondent tells me he is not at all put out by the Shankaracharya's action. I congratulate the brothers on their public spirit. Excommunication from a tyrannical society is indeed a reward of merit and should be welcomed. To say that a Brahman should not touch the plough is a parody of Varnashrama and a prostitution of the meaning of the Bhagavadgita. Surely the qualities predominantly ascribed to the different divisions are not denied to the others. Is bravery to be the prerogative only of the Kshatriya and restraint only of the Brahman ? Are Brahmans, Kshatriyas and Shudras not to protect the Cow ? Can any one remain a Hindu without readiness to die for the Cow ? Yet strangely enough, I have a letter from the Madras Presidency seriously telling me, that Cow protection has nothing to do with any but the Vaishyas. When there is so much ignorance combined with insolence, the best thing to do is to incur all risks and pursue the path of reform expecting time to prove the truth of one's position. If we combine love with firmness, we shall disarm all opposition in the end. Reformers may neither relent nor become angry.

10*th December*, 1919

SWARAJ IN SWADESHI

(BY M. K. GANDHI)

The real reform that India needs is Swadeshi in its true sense. The immediate problem before us is not how to run the government of the country, but how to feed and clothe ourselves. In 1918, we sent sixty crores of rupees out of India for buying cloth. If we continue to purchase foreign cloth at that rate, we deprive the Indian weaver and spinner of that amount from year to year *without practically giving him or her any other work in exchange*. No wonder a tenth at least of the population is cruelly half-starved and the majority of the rest underfed. He who has eyes may see for himself that *the middle class people are already being underfed and our babies are not getting enough milk for themselves*. The Reform Scheme, no matter how liberal it is, will not help to solve the problem in the immediate future. But Swadeshi can solve it *now*.

The Punjab has made the solution still clearer to me. God be thanked that the beautiful women of the Punjab have not yet lost the cunning of their fingers. High or low, they still know the art of spinning. They have not yet burnt their spinning wheels as many Gujarati women have done. It is to me a perfect delight to find them throwing balls of yarn into my lap. They admit they have time at their disposal for spinning. They admit that the *Khaddar* woven from their hand-spun yarn is superior to the machine-spun yarn. Our forefathers were well able to clothe themselves with little effort and with perfect comfort without having to buy from the foreign markets.

This beautiful art—and yet so simple—is in danger of

being lost if we do not wake up betimes. The Punjab gives proof of its possibilities. But the Punjab too is fast losing her hold of it. Every year witnesses a decrease in the output of hand-spun yarn. It means greater poverty in our homes and greater idleness. The women who have ceased to spin are not utilizing their time in any other or better manner than gossiping.

But one thing is needful to undo the mischief. If every educated Indian will realise his clear primary duty, he will straightway present the women of his household with a spinning wheel and provide the facilities for learning the art of spinning. Millions of yards of yarn can be produced from day to day. And if every educated Indian will condescend to wear the cloth produced from such yarn, he will support and assist in rebuilding the only possible cottage industry of India.

Without a cottage industry the Indian peasant is doomed. He cannot maintain himself from the produce of the land. He needs a supplementary industry. Spinning is the easiest, the cheapest and the best.

I know this means a revolution in our mental outlook. And it is because it is a revolution that I claim that the way to Swaraj lies through Swadeshi. A nation that can save sixty crores of rupees per year and distribute that large sum amongst its spinners and weavers in their own homes will have acquired powers of organisation and industry that must enable it to do everything else necessary for its organic growth.

The dreamy reformer whispers, 'Wait till I get responsible government and I will protect India's industry without our women having to spin and our weaver having to weave.' This has been actually said by thinking men. I venture to suggest that there is a double fallacy underlying the proposition. India cannot wait for a protective tariff and protection will not reduce the cost of clothing. Secondly, mere protection will not benefit the starving millions. They can only be helped by being enabled to supplement their earnings by having a spinning industry restored to them. So whether we have a protective tariff or not, we shall still have to revive the hand-spinning industry and stimulate hand-weaving.

When the war was raging, all available hands in America and England were utilized in the naval yards for building ships and they built them too at an amazing pace. If I would have my way, I would make every available Indian learn spinning or weaving and make him or her do that work for a certain fixed portion of every day. I would start with schools and colleges, presenting as they do ready-made organised units.

Multiplication of mills cannot solve the problem. They will take too long to overtake the drain and they *cannot distribute* the sixty crores in our homes. They can only cause concentration of money and labour and thus make confusion worse confounded.

21*st April*, 1920

SWADESHI

The National week closed on Tuesday the 13th. It was in every way a remarkable demonstration of Hindu-Muslim unity, the determination to secure repeal of the Rowlatt Act and the Satyagrah spirit. The speeches delivered were sober and more to the point than before. There was no disorderliness at any of the meetings of which we have received reports.

What however about Swadeshi? Was Swadeshi too

not a product of Satyagrah spirit and activity? It undoubtedly was.* But Swadeshi work is the most constructive of all. It does not lend itself to speeches

* Mr.Gandhi sharply distinguishes Boycott from Swadeshi, *see* p.147.

In *Young India* of 14th January, 1921, replying to Mr. Baptista, Mr. Gandhi pointed out among other things that Boycott was not constructive like Swadeshi but "operates like an undue influence brought in to secure one's purposes." Further, "one can make Boycott successful only by an appeal to angry passions. It may therefore result in unintended consequences and may even lead to a permanent estrangement between parties. Mr. Baptista, however, denies that appeal to angry passions is a necessary consequence of Boycott especially if some one like me were to manage the movement. I venture to challenge the position. A man suffering from an injustice is exposed to the temptations of having his worst passions roused on the slightest pretext. By asking him to boycott British goods, you inculcate the idea of punishing the wrong-door. And punishment necessarily evokes anger."

In *Young India* of 25th August, 1920, in the course of an article, headed "Boycott of Goods *vs.* Non-co-operation programme," Mr. Gandhi further wrote:

I must deal with the question of boycott which has now received the imprimatur of so able a publicist as Mr. Kasturi Ranga Aiyengar. . . . Boycott of British goods is thoroughly unpractical, for it involves sacrifice of their millions by millionaires. It is in my opinion infinitely more difficult for a merchant to sacrifice his millions than for a lawyer to suspend his practice or for a titleholder to give up his title or for a parent to sacrifice, if need be, the literary instruction of his children. Add to this the important fact that merchants have only lately begun to interest themselves in politics. They are therefore yet timid and cautious. But the class, to which the first stage of Non-co-operation is intended to appeal, is the political class which has devoted years to politics and is not mentally unprepared for communal sacrifice.

Boycott of British goods to be effective must be taken up by the whole country at once or not at all. It is like a siege. You can carry out a siege only when you have the requisite men and instruments of destruction. One man scratching a wall with his finger nails may hurt his fingers but will produce no effect upon the walls.

so much as to solid action. It is not possible to save fifty crores of rupees annually by speeches or demonstrations. It involves much more than the saving of this annual drain. It involves the honour of Indian womanhood. Everyone who has any connection with the mill industry knows that the women working in the mills are exposed to temptations and risks to which they ought not to be exposed. Many women for want of home employment accept road repair labour. And only those who know what this labour is, understand the risks the women run. Give them the spinning wheel and no woman need ever seek any other employment than sitting at the spinning wheel. Swadeshi means even distribution of wealth from an occupation next in importance only to agriculture. It supplements agriculture and therefore automatically assists materially to solve the problem of our growing poverty. Thus Swadeshi is our veritable Kamadhenu* supplying all our wants and solving many of our difficult problems. And

* The divine cow in Hindu Mythology which gives everything that is desired of it.

One title-holder giving up his title has the supreme satisfaction of having washed his hands clean of the guilt of the donor and is unaffected by the refusal of his fellows to give up theirs. The motive of boycott being punitive lacks the inherent practicability of Non-co-operation. The spirit of punishment is a sign of weakness. A strengthening of that spirit will retard the process of regeneration. The spirit of sacrifice is a determination to rid ourselves of our weakness. It is therefore an invigorating and purifying process and is therefore also calculated to do good both to us and to those who evoke the spirit of sacrifice in us. Above all, if India has a mission of her own, she will not fulfill it by copying the doubtful example of the West and making even her sacrifice materialistically utilitarian instead of offering a sacrifice spotless and pleasing even in the sight of God.

an occupation which saves our honour and provides our livelihood, becomes a religious duty.

How can the great consummation be achieved? The answer is simple. Those who realise the importance of the problem must set about working in one or all of the following directions:

(1) Learn spinning yourself whether man or woman. Charge for the labour if you need money, or make a gift of at least one hour's labour to the nation daily.

(2) Learn weaving yourself whether for recreation or for maintenance.

(3) Make improvements in the present handlooms and the spinning wheels, and if you are rich, pay for them to those who would make them.

(4) Take the Swadeshi vow and patronise the cloth that is both hand-spun and hand-woven.

(5) Introduce such cloth among your friends and believe that there is more art and humanity in Khadi whose yarn has been prepared by your poor sisters.

(6) If you are a mother, you will give a clean and national culture to your children and make them wear clothes made out of beautiful Khadi which is available to millions and which can be most easily produced.

Swadeshi then means the creation of a most perfect organisation in which every part works in perfect harmony with every other. If we succeed in bringing into being such an organisation, not only is the success of Swadeshi assured, but real Swaraj comes to us as a matter of course.*

* For a fuller exposition of this point, *see infra*

28th April, 1920

THE USES OF KHADDAR

(BY M. K. GANDHI)

While the Swadeshi movement is going forward by leaps and bounds and Mahomedans are taking it up as enthusiastically as Hindus, it is well to consider the best method of promoting Swadeshi. The veriest tyro in Swadeshi knows that we do not manufacture enough cloth to supply our wants. If therefore we merely use mill-made cloth, we simply deprive the poor of what they need, or at least increase the price of mill-made cloth. The only way therefore to encourage Swadeshi is to manufacture more cloth. Mills cannot grow like mushrooms.* We must, therefore, fall back upon hand-

*The following is from *Young India* of 28th April, 1920 :

The Problem of the Unclothed.—Sir Charles Macara of the Empire Cotton-growing Association has recently published that, out of the world's population, 750 million people are well clothed, 500 million are half clothed and 250 million unclothed. We have no such figures in regard to India : still it is undeniable that the proportion between clothed and unclothed people is highly discreditable to the Indian Nation, especially so in view of the fact that it ranks only second to America among the cotton-growing countries. It is proved by the Cotton Committee that we can grow more and better cotton. We are indefinitely waiting for new mills to be erected to utilise our cotton. We look to others to provide us with machinery. But, the situation regarding mill machinery is very serious even in England which has been one of our largest importing countries. The "Manchester Guardian," in its quarterly review of the cotton industry, tells us "that new mills would be so costly, that hardly anybody contemplates erecting them, and consequently, there is a prospect of the demand for goods exceeding the supply, for quite a considerable period." This makes it evident that, unless we revive our old spinning wheels and handlooms, we cannot solve the problem of the unclothed. Nature has given us enough and it promises more ; we must work to deserve it.

woven and handspun yarn. Yarn has never perhaps been so dear as it is to-day, and mills are making fabulous profits out of yarn. Hand-spinning helps its production and cheapens its price.

How to spin yarn and weave cloth is then the question. I know from personal experience that it is possible to flood the market with handspun yarn and handwoven cloth, if the standard cloth comes to be recognised as fit for wear. This cloth is called Khaddar in Upper India. It is called Khadi in the Bombay Presidency. Thanks to Sarala Devi, she has shown that it is possible to make even Saris out of Khaddar. She thought that she could best express herself during the National Week by wearing Khaddar Sari and Khaddar blouse. And she did it.* She attended parties in her Khaddar Sari. Friends thought it was impossible. They thought a woman who had never worn anything but the finest silk or the finest Dacca Muslin could not possibly bear the weight of heavy Khaddar. She falsified all fears and was no less active or less elegant in her Khaddar Sari than in her finished silk Saris. "If you do not feel awkward in that Sari of yours, you may go anywhere and to any party and you will find it would be well with you." It was with some such words that her great uncle, Sir Rabindranath Tagore, blessed her when he saw her in her Khaddar Sari. I relate this sacred incident in order to show that two of the most artistic people of India found nothing inartistic in Khaddar. This is the cloth I venture to introduce to the cultured families of India, for on its use hangs the immediate success of the Swadeshi movement during this its infant stage.

To me Khaddar is any day more artistic than the

* *See* p. 494.

finest Dacca Muslin, for its associations. Khaddar supports to-day those who were starving. It supports women who have been reclaimed from a life of shame or women who, because they would not go out for work, remained idle and quarrelled among themselves for want of occupation. Khaddar therefore has a soul about it. It has an individuality about it. The wearer is able to trace all the processes of its manufacture to the respective manufacturers. If our tastes were not debased, we would prefer Khaddar to sticky calico even during the summer season. Let those who are now using it certify, if they will, to the truth of my statement.

This Khaddar is now being stocked at the Satyagrah Ashram. And I have accumulated a stock which is beyond the capacity of the space at my disposal. I therefore ask the readers of "Young India" to come to the rescue by introducing Khaddar in their own homes.

Needless to say, the Ashram makes no profits from it. Any margin left is devoted to recouping the loss incurred in the initial stages or in reducing the price of Khaddar received from districts where the cost is heavier than elsewhere, for the cost is not the same all over. In inducing weavers to take to their original occupation, I am obliged to pay enough to support them and for the present.

Khaddar can be used for making underwear, even if one is disinclined to use it for the outer costume. But even if one is not inclined to use it for personal wear, it can be used for making caps, towels, wipers, tea-cloths, satchels, bedsheets, beddings, holdalls, carpet pieces, cushions, covers for furniture, &c. I am having it dyed turkey-red in Swadeshi dye. It then becomes more durable and looks less dirty when it is used for carpets or mattress-making or upholstering. I would advise those who wish to support this industry of the poor and the neglected to send for the Khaddar by corresponding with the Manager, Khaddar Department, Satyagrah Ashram, Sabarmati.

RATES

Mill Yarn Warp and Weft Khadi

Double warp and double weft				RS.	AS.	P.
Width	25	Inches	per yd.	0	9	0
"	27	"	"	0	9	6
"	30	"	"	0	10	0

Mill Yarn Warp and Hand Spun Weft Khadi

				RS.	AS.	P.
Width	25" 20—Counts'warp		per yd.	0	9	6
	8	"	"	0	8	0
"	24" 20	"	"	0	8	0
Lined Khadi			"	0	8	6
Red Coloured			"	0	8	6

Hand Spun Warp and Weft

		RS.	AS.	P.
Khadi 24"	per yd.	0	8	0
" 27"	"	0	8	6

For washed Khadi add 0-0-6 to the above rates.

19*th May*, 1920

SWADESHI DAY-BY-DAY

Readers of "Young India" will be agreebly surprised to learn that the article about Khaddar has not only resulted in complete disposal of the stock that had accumulated at the Ashram, but it has evoked orders from Baluchistan, the Nilgiris, and even Aden. This is as it should be. The revival of the ancient cottage industry of India—hand-spinning during leisure hours in their own homes by the millions of women, and hand-weaving in similar circumstances by men—cannot but produce a silent yet effective revolution in this country and prevent an annual drain of crores of rupees which need never have left India and distribute the savings among the poor millions instead of concentrating them in the hands of a few capitalists.* This is not to say

*The following appeared in *Young India* of 6th July, 1921:

The Potency of the Spinning-wheel.—No amount of human ingenuity can manage to distribute water over the whole land, as a shower of rain can. No irrigation department, no rules of precedence, no inspection and no water-cess. Every thing is done with an ease and a gentleness that by their very perfection evade notice. The spinning-wheel, too, has got the same power of distributing work and wealth in millions of houses in the simplest way imaginable. Those of us who do not know what it is to earn a livelihood by the sweat of one's brow, may consider the three annas a day as a pittance beneath the consideration of any man. They do not know that, even in these days of high prices, there are districts in India where even three annas a day would be a boon to the poor. But we must not consider the question of the spinning-wheel merely from the point of individual earnings. The spinning-wheel is a force in national regeneration. If we wish for real Swaraj, we must achieve economic independence. Boycott of foreign cloth is its negative aspect. For this we must produce cloth sufficient to clothe the country. This can only be done by hand-spinning All the mills that we have got, will not be able together to cope with the situation. If all rush for the thin mill-made cloth, it will rise in price beyond the capacity of the poor, and the experience of 1907-08 will be repeated.

Moreover, the cloth best suited for the three seasons of India is *Khadi*. Those who have used *Khadi* during this summer, have come to realise that, after the soft clean touch of *Khadi*, it is impossible to use sticky Malmal or twills. *Khadi* can enable its wearer to withstand the cold of an average winter as even wool cannot. The climate of India demands that clothes be washed as often as possible. Only *Khadi* can stand this constant wash. *Khadi* was once the dress of the nation at large. One must see to believe how venerable the old Patels and Deshmukhs looked when dressed in home-spun *Khadi*. There are instances of whole villages taking a legitimate pride in the fact that, they had to import nothing but salt in the whole round of

that we do not want capitalists in India. They are there already. They are able to take care of themselves. It is the poor millions who need to be lifted up from grinding poverty and consequent degradation. Nothing but a full revival of the hand-spinning and the hand-weaving industry can raise them effectively and speedily. It is to be hoped therefore that the demand for Khaddar being proved, its production will be stimulated, in every nook and corner of India.

The most wonderful experience, however, of the popularity of Swadeshi has been that of Shrimati Sarladevi Chaudhrani and Mrs. Mohani, the wife of that sincere and indefatigable worker, Maulana Hazrat Mohani. Writing from Lahore whilst preparing to go to Barreilly where she had gone to attend the Khilafat Conference, the former says: "I have done my packing racked with conflicts as to what to take and what not to take with me— whether to wear Khaddar dress there while addressing the audience or Swadeshi silk the point of which will not be so well understood—whether to take up the trunk or to wrap up the hold-all with cloths inside the bedding—whether to be smart and fashionable as of old or to be simple and common only. I have at last chosen to be the latter. But it is taking time and trouble to assimilate the new method." Writing after her experiences of Barreilly, she says: "Just coming back from visits to Mahomedan families. There were two ladies—wife and sister in one place. They took the vow for Charkha and Swadeshi. In another place,

the six seasons. With such conditions, there could be no drain, no exploitation and therefore no Para-raj (Other's Rule). A little village could make terms with the rulers of the land consistent with its self-respect, dignity and independence. Is our love of luxury so inveterate, that we cannot control it even for the sake of Swaraj?

there were six ladies who all took the same vow. It was a family of Cutch Borahs very rich and cultured, settled down here since the days of the Mutiny. I find I can do the Swadeshi and Charka propaganda to perfection in these provinces. My Swadeshi dress is having its effect. At a meeting called in Barreilly by Mrs. Mohani, fifteen Mahomedan ladies took the Swadeshi vow."

Speaking to the Barreilly divisional conference in Hindustani on a resolution on Swadeshi, she laid stress upon the deep poverty of India and her two chief wants—food and raiment—and she said that, if we did not know how to manage our own homes and could not make the two ends meet, we would be ill fitted to undertake the management of the national affairs. It was remarkable, she added, that, whilst the people were ready to listen to speeches, which required from them no action and no sacrifice, they were chary of attending meetings where they were told home-truths and which drew their attention to their primary duty of attending to Swadeshi at all costs. She asked them to work in the spirit of the late Vidyasagar, who was not only not ashamed of but took pride in wearing throughout his life Khaddar cloth. She admitted that return to Khaddar was difficult, but all upward movements were so. India would never be able to produce the beautiful cloth she did before, until she resolutely refused to use silks from China, Japan, France and elsewhere, and was content in the interval to wear cloth made out of coarse yarn that daughters of India were able to produce to-day. Her poverty and her nakedness too left no option to those who realised the actual condition of the country. She appealed to those on the platform to lead the way.

The Chaudhries had not much time left to them to test

the truth of the above remarks in their own home, for they had to prepare dresses for their eldest son whose marriage was to take place on the 14th instant. Pandit Rambhuj Datta Chaudhry writes: "All marriage clothes have been made of Swadeshi silk made in Benares. It is somewhat costly but excellent stuff. We have rigidly excluded all foreign silk."*

21st *July*, 1920

THE MUSIC OF THE SPINNING-WHEEL

(By M. K. Gandhi)

Slowly but surely the music † of perhaps the most

* The following is from *Young India* of 15th June, 1921:

Khadi in Temples—Foreign cloth has made such encroachments upon our life, that we use it even for sacred purposes. Thus I noticed the use of foreign cloth for the decoration of idols in Puri and Ayodhya, and indeed in almost all the temples I have visited. Even the sacred thread is not always hand-made. It refreshes me, therefore, to find a correspondent from Sindh sending the news, that Acharya Gidwani of the Gujarat Vidyapitha was the first, when he recently visited Sindh, to present a *khadi* cover for the Granth Saheb instead of foreign silk which is usually presented. I hope the good example will be followed by all devotees, and foreign cloth replaced in all temples by *Khadi*.

† The following is from *Young India* of 29th June, 1921:

In Praise of the Charkha—A Christian lady writes: "I shall do my very best in working for winning Swaraj by the spinning-wheel. Just before I left, I succeeded in getting good wheels made. *Ratnums* we call them in Tamil. And poor women came, and asked me to give them a wheel and to teach them to spin so as to earn a little for their living. I then remembered the word of Christ, 'I was naked and you clothed me not', 'I was hungry and you gave me not to eat.' I hope that my Master will not say that hard word to me on the Day of Judgment. India is naked and starving. Her poor women whose children are crying for bread, have been tempted to sell their honour

ancient machine of India * is once more permeating society. Pandit Malaviyaji has stated that he is not going to be satisfied until the Ranis and the Maharanis

* The following is from *Young India* of 6th July, 1921 :

The Charkha in Islam.—These notes have been sent by a Mussalman friend :

The following is related in Da-em-ul-Islam, Vol. II, by Kazi Noman ben. Mahomed, the Chief Justice of Cairo during the time of the Fatamide Khalifs of Egypt in about the third quarter of the 10th century A. D. He was one of the greatest scholars of the time, and has left a number of books on religion, laws, history, philosophy, etc.:

" The holy prophet, divine peace be on him, said that *the best occupation for a believing woman is the Charkha.* "

The following commentary on the above occurs in Kitabun Najah by Shaikh Ebrahim Saifee, who lived nearly 250 years ago :

This shows that the prophet has praised the woman who keeps herself engaged with the Charkha, and similarly he has spoken highly of the occupation of spinning. because there are two excellences in the Charkha. One is, that it is an indoor occupation, and the second is, that it is a means of earning something. How excellent is the

---

in order to feed them. And the more is the pity, as India has enough of natural riches within her own borders. She is like a naked starving woman sitting by the roadside in the midst of cotton, rice and wheat fields. Why are the women of India sitting idle, while foreigners grow fat on her produce ? Because they take away the work the women of India ought to be doing. The spinning wheel will give India work, and give the little ones the morsel of food they are crying for And to the music of the spinning-wheel the women will sing their beautiful songs, tell their stories of old, and the beauty and the contentment of simple home-life will be renewed. If I had the gift of a poet, I would sing the song of the spinning-wheel, of its beauty and its usefulness, of its poetry and its religious value. I would sing a song of praise to God for helping us in our hour of need. I should ask all my sisters in India to take to the spinning-wheels keeping the wolf of hunger and starvation and dishonour from their door. But I am not gifted. The song is singing only in my own soul. What can I do then, but let the spinning-wheel sing its own song, while I am working it and teaching others to do likewise. "

of India spin yarn for the nation, and the Ranas and the Maharanas sit behind the handlooms and weave cloth for the nation. They have the example of Aurangzeb

---

occupation, which combines both livelihood in this world and merit in the next ?

It is said that the inventor of the Charkha has made the instrument a replica of the physical world. It represents the world in miniature. It consists of two parts, one higher and the other lower, showing heaven and earth. The rotundity of the wheel represents that of the heavens. Its revolutions indicate the revolutions of the planets. It consists of 12 spokes representing 12 constellations. It has two legs upon which it is supported ; these represent the two 'poles north and south. It has a handle, which indicates the responsive quality of the heavens to man's work. It has got an axis, which represents the relations between the powers of the poles and their support of each other. It has a spindle on which the yarn is wound. This represents the earth, which produces all things. There is a thread which connects the spokes with the spindle and rotates it, whereby the cotton is spun. That thread represents the medium, through which pass the influences of the heavenly bodies over the earth. Cotton represents the four elements, out of which all things are produced, and the yarn represents the three products. *i.e.*, mineral, plant and animal. The two hands of the spinner represent the angels who arrange the creation of the creatures. The right hand indicates the angels of heaven, and the left hand those of the earth. Lastly the spinner represents God the Creator. There is no God but He."

[The foregoing description may be too fanciful for the modern reader. It is reproduced to show, if the dates given are right, what value was attached to the spinning-wheel by Mussalman writers two-hundred-and-fifty years ago.—Ed. *Y. I.*]

* *Young India* of 20th October, 1921, contained the following :

The Charkha in the Gita.—In the last issue, I have endeavoured to answer the objections raised by the Poet against spinning as a sacrament to be performed by all. I have done so in all humility and with the desire to convince the Poet and those who think like them. The reader will be interested in knowing that my belief is derived largely from the "Bhagavadgita." I have quoted the relevant verses in the article itself. I give below Edwin Arnold's rendering of the verses from his Song Celestial for the benefit of those who do not read Sanskrit:

who made his own caps. A greater emperor—Kabir—was himself a weaver and has immortalised the art in his poems. The queens of Europe, before Europe was

---

Work is more excellent than idleness:
The body's life proceeds not, lacking work.
There is a task of holiness to do,
Unlike world-binding toil, which bindeth not
The faithful soul; such earthly duty do
Free from desire, and thou shalt well perform
Thy heavenly purpose. Spake Prajapati
In the beginning, when all men were made,
And, with mankind, the sacrifice—"Do this!
Work! Sacrifice! Increase and multiply
With sacrifice! This shall be Kamadhuk,
Your 'Cow of Plenty', giving back her milk
Of all abundance. Worship the gods thereby;
The gods shall yield ye grace. Those meats ye crave
The gods will grant to Labour, when it pays
Tithes in the alter-flame. But if one eats
Fruits of the earth, rendering to kindly heaven,
No gift of toil, that thief steals from his world."
Who eat of food after their sacrifice
Are quit of fault, but they that spread a feast
All for themselves, eat sin and drink of sin.
By food the living live; food comes of rain.
And rain comes by the pious sacrifice,
And sacrifice is paid with tithes of toil;
Thus action is of Brahman, who is One,
The Only, All-pervading; at all times
Present in sacrifice. He that abstains
To help the rolling wheels of this great world
Glutting his idle sense, lives a lost life,
Shameful and vain.

Work here undoubtedly refers to physical labour, and work by way of sacrifice can only be work to be done by all for the common benefit. Such work—such sacrifice can only be spinning. I do not wish to suggest that the author of the Divine Song had the spinning wheel in mind. He merely laid down a fundamental principle of

caught in Satan's trap, spun yarn and considered it a noble calling. The very words, spinster and wife, prove the ancient dignity of the art of spinning and weaving. 'When Adam delved and Eve span, who was then a gentleman', also reminds one of the same fact. Well may Panditji hope to persuade the royalty of India to the ancient calling of this sacred land of ours. Not on the clatter of arms depends the revival of her prosperity and true independence. It depends most largely upon reintroduction, in every home, of the music of the spinning wheel. It gives sweeter music and is more profitable than the execrable harmonium, concertina and the accordian.

Whilst Panditji is endeavouring in his inimitably suave manner to persuade the Indian royalty to take up the spinning wheel, Shrimati Sarala Devi Choudhrani, who is herself a member of the Indian nobility, has learnt the art and has thrown herself heart and soul into the movement. From all the accounts received from her and others, Swadeshi has become a passion with her. She says she feels uncomfortable in her muslin saris and is content to wear the Khaddar saris even in the hot weather. Her Khaddar saris continue to preach true Swadeshi more eloquently than her tongue. She has spoken to audiences in Amritsar, Ludhiana and elsewhere and has succeeded in enlisting the services, for

---

conduct. And reading in and applying it to India, I can only think of spinning as the fittest and most acceptable sacrificial body labour. I cannot imagine anything nobler or more national than that, for, we should all do the labour that the poor must do and thus identify ourselves with them and through them with all mankind. I cannot imagine better worship of God than that in His name I should labour for the poor even as they do. The spinning-wheel spells a more equitable distribution of the riches of the earth.

her spinning committee at Amritsar, of Mrs. Ratanchand and Bugga Chowdhry and the famous Ratan Devi who, during the frightful night of the 30th April, despite the Curfew Order of General Dyer, sat all alone in the midst of the hundreds of the dead and dying, with her dead husband's cold head in her lap. I venture to tender my congratulations to these ladies. May they find solace in the music of the spinning wheel and in the thought that they are doing national work. I hope that the other ladies of Amritsar will help Sarala Devi in her efforts and that the men of Amritsar will realise their own duty in the matter.

In Bombay, the readers are aware that ladies of noted families have already taken up spinning. Their ranks have been joined by Dr. Mrs. Manekbai Bahadurji who has already learnt the art and who is now trying to introduce it in the Sevasadan. Her Highness the Begum Saheba of Janjira and her sister Mrs. Atia Begum Rahiman have also undertaken to learn the art. I trust that these good ladies will, having learnt spinning, religiously contribute to the nation their daily quota of yarn.

I know that there are friends who laugh at this attempt to revive this great art.* They remind me that, in these days of mills, sewing-machines or typewriters, only a

* The following appeared in *Young India* of 15th September, 1921 : *Hand Spinning and hand-weaving.*—Some people spurn the idea of making in this age of mechanism hand-spinning and hand-weaving a national industry, but they forget there are millions of their countrymen in this age who for want of suitable occupation are eking out a most miserable existence, and thousands who die of starvation and underfeeding every year, whereas only a hundred years ago hand-spinning and hand-weaving proved an insurance against a pauper's death. The extent to which relief was provided by this industry is recorded by Mr. Dutt in his "History of India : Victorian age" from

lunatic can hope to succeed in reviving the rusticated spinning wheel. These friends forget that the needle has not yet given place to the sewing machine nor has the hand lost its cunning in spite of the typewriter. There is not the slightest reason why the spinning wheel may not co-exist with the spinning mill even as the domestic kitchen coexists with the hotels. Indeed typewriters and sewing machines may go, but the needle and the reed pen will survive. The mills may suffer destruction. The spinning wheel is a national necessity. I would ask sceptics to go to the many poor homes where the spinning wheel is again supplementing their slender resources and ask the inmates whether the spinning wheel has not brought joy to their homes.

Thank God, the reward issued by Mr. Rewashanker Jagjiwan bids fare to bear fruit. In a short time, India will possess a renovated spinning wheel—a wonderful invention of a patient Deccan artisan. It is made out of simple materials. There is no great complication about it. It will be cheap and capable of being easily mended. It will give more yarn than the ordinary wheel and is capable of being worked by a five-years old boy or girl.

---

the investigations conducted by Dr. Buchanan for seven years, 1813-1820.

It will be seen from the details published in this book that crores of rupees were earned by these spinners and weavers by following their noble and honest calling. The decentralisation of the industry —every village, town and district having always at its command as much supply as it needed—automatically facilitated its distribution and saved the consumer from Railway, Excise and all sorts of tariffs and middlemen's profits that he is a victim to-day. If we cannot return to these days—though there is no reason, except our own bias and doubt why we should not—can we not at least so organise our industries as to do away without much delay with the foreign cloth with which our markets are being dumped to-day ?

But whether the new machine proves what it claims to be or it does not, I feel convinced that the revival of hand-spinning and hand-weaving will make the largest contribution to the economic and the moral regeneration of India. The millions must have a simple industry to supplement agriculture. Spinning was the cottage industry years ago, and if the millions are to be saved from starvation, they must be enabled to reintroduce spinning in their homes, and every village must repossess its own weaver.

18*th August*, 1920

SWADESHI

(BY M. K. GANDHI)

In criticising my article entitled 'The Music of the Spinning Wheel,'* the *Leader* the other day attributed to me ideas that I have never entertained. And it is necessary, for the purpose of understanding the true value of Swadeshi, to correct some of the current fallacies. The *Leader* considers that I am putting back the hands of the clock of progress by attempting to replace mill-made cloth and mill-spun yarn by hand-woven and hand-spun yarn. Now, I am making no such attempt at all. I have no quarrel with the mills. My views are incredibly simple. India requires nearly 13 yards of cloth per head per year. She produces, I believe, less than half the amount. India grows all the cotton she needs. She exports several million bales of cotton to Japan and Lancashire and receives much of it back in manufactured calico, although she is capable of producing all the cloth and all the yarn necessary for supplying her wants by hand-weaving and hand-spinning. India needs

* *See* p. 497.

to supplement her main occupation, agriculture, with some other employment. Hand-spinning is the only such employment for millions. It was the national employment a century ago. It is not true to say that economic pressure and modern machinery destroyed hand-spinning and hand-weaving. This great industry was destroyed or almost destroyed by extraordinary and immoral means adopted by the East India Company. This national industry is capable of being revived by exertion and a change in the national taste without damaging the mill industry. Increase of mills is no present remedy for supplying the deficiency. The difficulty can be easily supplied only by hand-spinning and hand-weaving. If this employment were revived, it would prevent sixty million rupees from being annually drained from the country and distribute the amount among lacs of poor women in their own cottages. I therefore consider Swadeshi as an automatic, though partial, solution of the problem of India's grinding poverty. It also constitutes a ready-made insurance policy in times of scarcity of rain.

But two things are needful to bring about the needed revival—to create a taste for Khaddar and to provide an organisation for the distribution of carded cotton and collection of yarn against payment.

In one year, by the silent labour of a few men, several thousand rupees have been distributed in Gujarat among several thousand poor women who are glad enough to earn a few pice per day to buy milk for their children, etc.

The argument does not apply to the sugar industry as the "Leader" has attempted. There is not sufficient cane grown in India to supply India's wants. Sugar was never a national and supplementary industry.

Foreign sugar has not supplanted Indian sugar. India's wants of sugar have grown and she therefore imports more sugar. But this importation does not institute a drain in the sense in which importation of foreign cloth does. Production of more sugar means more scientific agriculture, more and better machinery for crushing and refining. The sugar industry therefore stands on a different platform. Swadeshi in sugar is desirable. Swadeshi in cloth is an urgent necessity.

25th August, 1920

KHILAFAT AND SWADESHI

(BY M. K. GANDHI)

It was not without much misgiving that I consented to include Swadeshi as a plank in Non-co-operation. But Maulana Hasrat Mohani by his sheer earnestness bore me down. I fear however that his reasons for including Swadeshi are different from mine. He is a protagonist of boycott of British goods. I cannot reconcile myself to the doctrine as I have explained elsewhere.* But having failed to popularise boycott, Mohani Saheb accepted Swadeshi as the lesser good. It is however necessary for me to explain how I have come to include Swadeshi in the programme of Non-co-operation.

Non-co-operation is nothing but discipline in self-sacrifice. And I believe that a nation that is capable of limitless sacrifice is capable of rising to limitless heights. The purer the sacrifice, the quicker the progress. Swadeshi offers every man, woman and child an occasion to make a beginning in self-sacrifice of a pure type. It therefore presents an opportunity for testing our capacity

*See pp. 487, 488.

for sacrifice. It is the measure for gauging the depth of national feeling on the Khilafat wrong. Does the nation feel sufficiently to move it to go through even the preliminary process of sacrifice? Will the nation revise its taste for the Japanese silk, the Manchester calico or the French lace and find all its decoration out of hand-spun and hand-woven cloth, *i.e.*, Khadi? If crores of people will refuse to wear or use foreign cloth and be satisfied with the simple cloth that we can produce in our homes, it will be proof of our organising ability, energy, co-operation and self-sacrifice that will enable us to secure all we need. It will be a striking demonstration of national solidarity.

Such a consummation cannot be achieved for the mere wish. It cannot be achieved by one man, no matter how capable and sincere he may be. It cannot be achieved by dotting India with Swadeshi stores. It can only be achieved by new production and judicious distribution. Production means lacs of women spinning in their own homes. This requires earnest men to be engaged in honestly distributing carded cotton and collecting yarn and paying for it. It means manufacture of thousands of spinning wheels. It means inducing the hereditary weavers to return to their noble calling and distributing home-spun yarn amongst them and selling their manufactures. It is thus only as an energising agent that I can think of Swadeshi as a plank in Non-co-operation. But it is not to be despised in that capacity. And I hope that every worker for the cause, even if he can do nothing else, will have done something if he can advance Swadeshi first by increasing production and then distribution. He would be simply moving in a circle if he is satisfied with distributing cloth that is already being manufactured in India.

8th September, 1920

SWADESHI

(By M. K. Gandhi)

The Swadeshi propaganda has been going on in a more or less organised manner now for the past eighteen months. Some of its results are surprising and gratifying. It has taken a fairly firm hold in the Punjab,*

* Under the heading, "Swadeshi in the Punjab," Mr. Gandhi wrote in *Young India* of 7th July, 1920 :

The Joint Secretaries of the Bharat Stri Maha Pandal, Punjab Branch, send a report of the Swadeshi activities of Shrimati Saraladevi Chaudhrani ever since her return to Lahore from Bombay. Miss Roy and Mrs. Roshanlal, the Secretaries, state that meetings of women were held respectively on the 23rd, 24th and 25th June, at three different places in Lahore. All the meetings were attended by hundreds of women who were deeply interested in what Shrimati Saraladevi had to say. The burden of her discourses was India's deep poverty. She traced the causes and proved that our proverty was primarily due to the abandonment of Swadeshi by the people. The remedy therefore lay in reverting to Swadeshi.

Saraladevi herself writes to say that her Khaddar Sari impressed her audiences more than her speeches, and her songs came next, her speeches last. The good ladies of Lahore flocked round her and felt her coarse but beautifully white Sari and admired it. Some took pity on her that she who only the other day was dressed in costly thin silk Saris now decked herself in hand-woven Swadeshi Khaddar. Saraladevi wanted no pity and retorted that their thin foreign scarves lay heavier on their shoulders with the weight of their helpless dependence on foreign manufacture, whereas her coarse Khaddar lay light as a feather on her body with the joy of the knowledge that she was free, because she wore garments in the manufacture of which her sisters and her brothers had laboured. This statement so pleased her audience that most of the women present resolved to discard foreign clothes. Saraladevi has now been charged by these ladies to open a shop where they could buy Swadeshi goods. She has since addressed more audiences. She spoke at the District Conference at Sialkot and to a meeting exclusively devoted to ladies numbering over one

Madras and the Bombay Bresidency. Hand-spinning and hand-weaving are steadily increasing in these parts. Several thousand rupees have been distributed in homes where women never did any work before. And if more work of this kind has not been done, it is due to want of workers.

This is however written more to note the mistakes of the past than to sum up the bright side. My observations lead me to the conclusion that, whilst the inauguration of the three vows * and Swadeshi stores have greatly stimulated the Swadeshi spirit, it is no longer possible to advocate the taking of any of the three vows or the opening of new Swadeshi stores for the sale of mill-made cloth. The result of the propaganda has been to send up the prices of yarn and cloth rather than increase production. It is clear that the purpose of Swadeshi is not served until the quantity of yarn and cloth produced is increased. The gain therefore is merely moral and not material. The people have begun to perceive the desirability of wearing only Swadeshi cloth if the real interest of the country is to be advanced. But it is clear that we must take practical steps for

* *See* Appendix.

---

thousand. I hope that the men of Punjab will help Saraladevi in her self-imposed mission. They may harness her talents and her willingness in founding Swadeshi Sabha and organising Swadeshi propaganda on a sound basis. My Swadeshi spirit makes me impatient of garments that denude India of her wealth and equally impatient of the Smiths, the O'Briens, the Shri Rams and the Maliks who denude her of her self-respect and insolently touch women's veils with their sticks, chain innocent men as if they were beasts, or shoot them from armoured cars or otherwise terrorise people into subjection.

meeting the growing demand for Swadeshi cloth. One way, no doubt, is to increase the mills. But it is obvious that capitalists do not need popular encouragement. They know that India needs much more cloth than is manufactured by our mills. But mills do not spring up like mushrooms. It is a matter of getting machinery from outside, let alone the difficulty of getting labour. And after all, India cannot become truly and economically independent so long as she must rely on the supply of machinery from outside for the manufacture of her cloth.

The cleanest and the most popular form of Swadeshi, therefore, is to stimulate hand-spinning and hand-weaving and to arrange for a judicious distribution of yarn and cloth so manufactured. With a little talent and a little industry this thing is easy. Even as each home cooks its own food without difficulty, so may each home weave its own yarn. And just as, in spite of every home having its own kitchen, restaurants continue to flourish, so will mills continue to supply our additional wants. But even as because of our private kitchens we would not starve if every restaurant was through some accident closed, so would we, by reason of domestic spinning, not have to go naked even if every mill, by a blockade from the West, had to stop work. Not long ago, we knew this secret of our own economic independence, and it is possible for us to regain that independence by a little effort, a little organising agency and a little sacrifice.

Therefore true Swadeshi consists in introducing the spinning wheel in every household and every household spinning its own yarn. Many a Punjabi woman does it to-day. And though we may not supply our own cloth entirely, we shall be saving yearly crores of rupees. In any event, there is no other Swadeshi than increased manufacture by hand-spinning and hand-weaving. Whether we take up hand-spinning and hand-weaving or we do not, it is at least necessary to understand what true Swadeshi is.

22nd September, 1920

SWADESHI STORES

(BY M. K. GANDHI)

In a previous issue I endeavoured to show how stores for the sake of selling mill-manufactures did not advance Swadeshi in any way whatsoever, but, on the contrary, tended to send up the price of cloth. I propose to show in this article how, with a small capital, it is possible to advance true Swadeshi and earn a modest livelihood.*

Suppose that there is a family consisting of husband, wife and two children one of whom is ten years old and the other five. If they have a capital of Rs. 500, they can manage a Khaddar Bhandar in a small way.† They can hire, say in a place with a population of 20,000 inhabitants, a shop with dwelling rooms for Rs. 10 per month. If they sell the whole of the stock at 10 p. c. profit, they can have Rs. 50 per month. They have no servants. The wife and the children in their spare time would be expected to help in keeping the shop tidy and looking after it when the husband is out. The wife and children can also devote their spare time to spinning.

*The way in which weaving suffered for lack of organisation and the remedy thereof are detailed at length in Mr. Havell's *Artistic and Industrial Revival in India.* The "Swadeshi Department of the Satyagraha Ashram," says *Young India* of 15th September, 1920 "is being run almost on the same lines as the scheme (Havell's) suggests."

† *See* page 512.

In the initial stages, the Khaddar may not sell at the shop. In that case, the husband is expected to hawk the Khaddar from door to door and popularise it. He will soon find a custom for it.

The reader must not be surprised at my suggesting 10 p.c. profits. The Khaddar Bhandars are not designed for the poorest. The use of Khaddar saves at least half the cost not necessarily because the Khaddar is more durable (though that it certainly is) but because its use revolutionises our tastes. I know what saving of money its use has meant to me. Those, who buy Khaddar from patriotic motives merely, can easily afford to pay 10 p. c. profits on Khaddar. Lastly, the popularising of Khaddar means much care, devotion and labour. And the owner of a Khaddar Bhandar does not buy it at a wholesale shop, but he must wander to get the best Khaddar, he must meet the local weavers and induce them to weave hand-spun yarn. He must stimulate in his own district hand-spinning among its women. He must come in touch with the carders and get them to card cotton. All this means intelligence, organisation and great ability. A man who can exhibit these qualities has a right to take 10 p. c. profits. And a Swadeshi Bhander conducted on these lines becomes a true centre of Swadeshi activity. I commend my remarks to the attention of the managers of Swadeshi stores that are already in existence. They may not revolutionise their method at once, but I have no doubt that they will advance Swadeshi only to the extent that they sell Khaddar.

19*th January*, 1921

THE SECRET OF SWARAJ

(BY M. K. GANDHI)

The Congress* resolution has rightly emphasised the importance of Swadeshi and there anent of greater sacrifice by merchants.

India cannot be free so long as India voluntarily encourages or tolerates the economic drain which has been going on for the past century and a half. Boycott of foreign goods means no more and no less than boycott of foreign cloth. Foreign cloth constitutes the largest drain voluntarily permitted by us. It means sixty crores of rupees annually paid by us for piecegoods. If India could make a successful effort to stop that drain, she can gain Swaraj by that one act.

India was enslaved for satisfying the greed of the foreign cloth manufacturer. When the East India Company came in, we were able to manufacture all the cloth we needed, and more for export. By processes that need not be described here, India has become practically wholly dependent upon foreign manufacture for her clothing.

But we ought not to be dependent. India has the ability to manufacture all her cloth if her children will work for it. Fortunately India has yet enough weavers to supplement the out-turn of her mills. The mills do not and cannot immediately manufacture all the cloth we want. The reader may not know that, even at the present moment, the weavers weave more cloth than the mills. But the latter weave five crore yards of fine foreign counts, equal to forty crore yards of coarser counts. The way to carry out a successful boycott of

* Held at Nagpur in December, 1920.

foreign cloth is to increase the out-put of yarn. And this can only be done by hand-spinning.

To bring about such a boycott, it is necessary for our merchants * to stop all foreign importation, and to sell

* The following is from *Young India* of 16th February, 1921:

The Duty of Merchants.—In the course of his speech, at the merchants' meeting held in Calcutta on January 27, Mr. Gandhi spoke strongly against the waste of time, by thousands of people who gather just to see him and do nothing but shout. "Shouting was of no avail unless they voiced forth their true feeling. There was no necessity for shouting Bande Mataram, Hindu-Mussalman-ki-Jai, and Allah-ho-Akbar. If Swaraj was to be attained in nine months, they must all combine and lend a helping hand. Men must translate into action what they utter.

"If the merchants wished to do the work of 30 crores of men, they must come out with their money. If they did not help with the money, Swaraj will be difficult, but not impossible, to attain. If the students did not help, if the pleaders did not help, if monied men did not help, even then the attainment of Swaraj was not impossible, because it so very much more depended on the labourers and the agriculturists. If the merchants wanted Swaraj, in the shortest possible time, they would have to make sacrifices. They would have to sacrifice themselves, their children, their parents, everything. They had prospered in trade, but did they know that it was a sin to deal in foreign cloth? They must neither buy, nor sell, nor wear foreign cloth. Let them send their stocks of foreign cloth to South Africa, or better burn them. Let them give up their Mulmul pugarees. They ought to be proud to wear Khaddar pugarees. The mill-owners were profiteering and people in Orissa, in Champaran—everywhere—were dying of starvation. There was only one remedy and that was the Charka. If all the women and girls spun yarn, they would be able to feed themselves. But the merchants must henceforth only sell Khaddar. The Marwaris had been dealing in foreign cloth; it was irreligion, they had given up their religion."

Concluding, Mr. Gandhi said that they must be pure, patriotic, and devoted to Swaraj and Khilafat. They must use only Swadeshi things in their households and sell only Swadeshi cloth in their shops. That would save 60 crores and feed the hungry and win Swaraj in nine months.

out, even at a loss, all foreign cloth already stocked in India, preferably to foreign buyers. They must cease to speculate in cotton, and keep all the cotton required for home use. They must stop purchasing all foreign cotton.

The mill-owners should work their mills not for their profits but as a national trust and therefore cease to spin finer counts, and weave only for the home market.

The householder has to revise his or her ideas of fashion and, at least for the time being, suspend the use of fine garments which are not always worn to cover the body. He should train himself to see art and beauty in the spotlessly white *khaddar* and to appreciate its soft unevenness. The householder must learn to use cloth as a miser uses his hoard.

And even when the householders have revised their tastes about dress, somebody will have to spin yarn for the weavers. This can only be done by every one spinning during spare hours either for love or money.

We are engaged in a spiritual war. We are not living in normal times. Normal activities are always suspended in abnormal times. And if we are out to gain *Swaraj* in a year's time, it means that we must concentrate upon our goal to the exclusion of every thing else. I therefore venture to suggest to the students all over India to suspend their normal studies for one year and devote their time to the manufacture of yarn by hand-spinning. It will be their greatest act of service to the motherland, and their most natural contribution to the attainment of *Swaraj*. During the late war, our rulers attempted to turn every factory into an arsenal for turning out bullets of lead. During this war of ours, I suggest every national school and college being turned into a factory for preparing cones of yarns for the nation. The students will lose nothing by the occupation: they will gain a kingdom here and hereafter. There is a famine of cloth in India. To assist in removing this dearth is surely an act of merit. If it is sinful to use foreign yarn, it is a virtue to manufacture more Swadeshi yarn in order to enable us to cope with the want that would be created by the disuse of foreign yarn.

The obvious question asked would be, if it is so necessary to manufacture yarn, why not pay every poor person to do so? The answer is that hand-spinning is not, and never was, a calling like weaving, carpentry, etc. Under the pre-British economy of India, spinning was an honourable and leisurely occupation for the women of India. It is difficult to revive the art among the women in the time at our disposal. But it is incredibly simple and easy for the school-goers to respond to the nation's call. Let no one decry the work as being derogatory to the dignity of man or students. It was an art confined to the women of India, because the latter had more leisure. And being graceful, musical, and as it did not involve any great exertion, it had become the monopoly of women. But it is certainly as graceful for either sex as is music for instance. In hand-spinning is hidden the protection of women's virtue, the insurance against famine, and the cheapening of prices. In it is hidden the secret of *Swaraj*. The revival of hand-spinning is the least penance we must do for the sin of our forefathers in having succumbed to the satanic influences of the foreign manufacturer.

The school-goers will restore hand-spinning to its respectable status. They will hasten the process of making *khaddar* fashionable. For no mother, or father, worth the name will refuse to wear cloth made out of yarn spun by their children. And the scholars' practical recognition of art will compel the attention of the weavers of India. If we are to wean the Panjabi from the calling not of a solider but of the murderer of innocent and free people of other lands, we must give back to him the occupation of weaving. The race of the peaceful Julahis of the Punjab is all but extinct. It is for the scholars of the Punjab to make it possible for the Punjabi weaver to return to his innocent calling.

I hope to show in a future issue* how easy it is to introduce this change in the schools and how quickly, on these terms, we can nationalise our schools and colleges. Everywhere the students have asked me what new things I would introduce into our nationalised schools. I have invariably told them I would certainly introduce spinning. I feel, so much more clearly than ever before that, during the transition period, we must devote exclusive attention to spinning and certain other things of immediate national use, so as to make up for past neglect. And the students will be better able and equipped to enter upon the new course of studies.

Do I want to put back the hand of the clock of progress ? Do I want to replace the mills by hand-spinning and hand-weaving? Do I want to replace the railway by the country cart? Do I want to destroy machinery altogether? These questions have been asked by some journalists and public men. My answer is: I would not weep over the disappearance of machinery or consider it a calamity. But I have no design upon machinery as such. What I want to do at the present moment is to supplement the production of yarn and cloth through our mills, save the millions we send out of India, and distribute them in our cottages. This I

**See* p. 518.

cannot do unless and until the nation is prepared to devote its leisure hours to hand-spinning. To that end we must adopt the methods I have ventured to suggest for popularising spinning as a duty rather than as a means of livelihood.

2nd February, 1921

THE DUTY OF SPINNING

(BY M. K. GANDHI)

In "The Secret of Swaraj,"* I have endeavoured to show what home-spinning means for our country. In any curriculum of the future, spinning must be a compulsory subject. Just as we cannot live without breathing and without eating, so is it impossible for us to attain economic independence and banish pauperism from this ancient land without reviving home-spinning. I hold the spinning wheel to be as much a necessity in every household as the hearth. No other scheme that can be devised will ever solve the problem of the deepening poverty of the people.

How then can spinning be introduced in every home? I have already suggested the introduction of spinning and systematic production of yarn in every national school. Once our boys and girls have learnt the art, they can easily carry it to their homes.

But this requires organisation. A spinning wheel must be worked for twelve hours per day. A practised spinner can spin two tolas and a half per hour. The price that is being paid at present is on an average four annas per forty tolas or one pound of yarn, *i.e.*, one pice per hour. Each wheel therefore should give three annas

* *See* p. 513.

per day. A strong one costs seven rupees. Working, therefore, at the rate of twelve hours per day, it can pay for itself in less than 38 days. I have given enough figures to work upon. Anyone working at them will find the results to be startling.

If every school introduced spinning, it would revolutionize our ideas of financing education. We can work a school for six hours per day and give free education to the pupils. Supposing a boy works at the wheel for four hours daily, he will produce every day 10 tolas of yarn and thus earn for his school one anna per day. Suppose further that he manufactures very little during the first month, and that the school works only twenty-six days in the month. He can earn after the first month Rs. 1-10 per month. A class of thirty boys would yield, after the first month, an income of Rs. 48-12 per month.

I have said nothing about literary training. It can be given during the two hours out of the six. It is easy to see that every school can be made self-supporting without much effort and the nation can engage experienced teachers for its schools.

The chief difficulty in working out the scheme is the spinning wheel. We require thousands of wheels if the art becomes popular. Fortunately, every village carpenter can easily construct the machine. It is a serious mistake to order them from the Ashram or any other place. The beauty of spinning is that it is incredibly simple, easily learnt, and can be cheaply introduced in every village.

The course suggested by me is intended only for this year of purification and probation. When normal times are reached and Swaraj is established, one hour only may be given to spinning and the rest to literary training.

9th February, 1921

ABUSING THE KHADDAR

A friend draws attention to the fact that many who have adopted the Khaddar costume are using it as a passport for arrogance, insolence, and what is worse, fraud. He says that they have neither the spirit of Non-co-operation in them nor the spirit of truth. They simply use the Khaddar dress as a cloak for their deceit. All this is likely, especially during the transition stage, *i.e.*, whilst Khaddar is beginning to become fashionable. I would only suggest to my correspondent that such abuse of Khaddar must not even unconsciously be allowed to be used as an argument against its use. Its use to-day is obligatory on those who believe that there is not sufficient Indian mill-made cloth to supply the wants of the nation, that the wants must be supplied in the quickest way possible by increasing home manufacture, and that such manufacture is possible only by making home-spinning universal. The use of Khaddar represents nothing more than a most practical recognition of the greatest economic necessity of the country. Even a scoundrel may recognise this necessity, and has therefore a perfect right to wear it. And if a Government spy wore it to deceive people, I would welcome his use of Khaddar as so much economic gain to the country. Only I would not give the wearer of the Khaddar more than his due. And I would therefore not ascribe to him any piety or special virtue. It follows, therefore, that Co-operationists or government servants may wear Khaddar without incurring the danger of being mistaken for Non-co-operationists. We may no more shun Khaddar, than a devout church-goer may renounce his church, because bad characters go to it for duping gullible people. I recall the name of an M. P. who successfully cloaked many of his vices by pretending to be a staunch temperance man. Not very long ago, a bold and unscrupulous speculator found entry into most respectable circles by becoming a temperance advocate. Well has a poet said that 'hypocrisy is an ode to virtue.'

16*th February*, 1921

HAND-SPINNING AGAIN

(BY M. K. GANDHI)

The Servant of India has a fling too at spinning and that is based, as I shall presently show, on ignorance of the facts. Spinning does protect a woman's virtue, because it enables women, who are to-day working on public roads and are often in danger of having their modesty outraged, to protect themselves, and I know no other occupation that lacs of women can follow save spinning. Let me inform the jesting writer that several women have already returned to the sanctity of their homes and taken to spinning which they say is the one occupation which means so much *barket* (blessing).

Yes, it does solve the problem of India's chronic poverty and is an insurance against famine. The writer of the jests may not know the scandals that I know about irrigation and relief works. These works are largely a fraud.

The fact is that, in spite of the manufacture of 62.7 crores pounds of yarn in 1917-18, India imported several crore yards of foreign yarn which were woven by the mills as well as the weavers. The writer does not also seem to know that more cloth is to-day woven by our weavers than by mills, but the bulk of it is foreign yarn, and therefore our weavers are supporting foreign spinners. I would not mind it much, if we were doing something else instead. When spinning was almost compulsorily stopped, nothing replaced it save slavery and idleness. Our mills cannot to-day spin enough for our wants, and if they did, they will not keep down prices unless they were compelled. They are frankly money-makers and will not therefore regulate prices according to the needs of the nations.

And now a few figures. One boy could, if he worked say four hours daily, spin ¼ lb. of yarn. 64,000 students would, therefore, spin 16,000 lbs. per day, and therefore feed 8,000 weavers if a weaver wove two lbs. of hand-spun yarn. But the students and others are required to spin during this year of purification by way of penance in order to popularise spinning and to add to the manufacture of hand-spun yarn so as to overtake full manufacture during the current year. The nation may be too lazy to do it. But if all put their hands to this work, it is incredibly easy, it involves very little sacrifice and saves an annual drain of sixty crores, even if it does nothing else. I have discussed the matter with many mill-owners, several economists, men of business and no one has yet been able to challenge the position herein set forth.

What is profitable?—In its issue of the 10th, The *Servant of India* again ridicules the revival of hand-spinning. The writer of the comments has not obviously yet made any attempt to know the precise nature of the revival advocated by Mr. Gandhi. If the income from the spinning wheel is low it can, he says, "only deepen the country's poverty instead of remedying it, firstly, because the wage is not sufficient for the worker's maintenance and secondly, because it prevents him from following a more profitable occupation." His assumption is gratuitous. No one suggests that hand-spinning should replace any wage-earning occupation.* It was never made to do that even in pre-British days. It has always been regarded as a supplementary occupation. Assuming that it was to be a wage-earning occupation—two annas being the daily wage earned by an average spinner,—it promises a better yearly income than the average income at present. The latter income has never yet been estimated over 27 rupees per head per year! If the *Servant of India* is prepared to provide work, at the rate of two annas per day, for every worker, we would entrust thousands of workers to its care. But the fact is that the average income per day is not two annas and that hand-spinning need not prevent anyone from following "more

*The point that spinning was only to be a subsidiary and not a supplanting industry was emphasised by Mr. Gandhi more than once. In *Young India* of 4th August 1921, in reply to the *Leader*, he wrote:

No one has ever said that spinning can be a means of livelihood except to the very poor. It is intended to restore spinning to its ancient position as a universal industry auxiliary to agriculture and resorted to by agriculturists during those months of the year when agricultural operations are suspended as a matter of course and cultivators have otherwise little to do. For the present all people alike are invited to devote their leisure to spinning, with a view to bringing about a complete boycott of foreign cloth in course of the present year. No one asks an able-bodied labourer who can earn twelve annas a day to give up his work in order to take to spinning. However, people are so poor in many parts of the country that a daily wage of even 3 annas a day would be a veritable boon to them and enable them to tide over bad seasons. The spinning wheel is capable of being applied as a complete insurance against famines and droughts. 3 annas again is only a most cautious and conservative estimate. If the reader turns to the second article on the weaving-school which commences to-day, he will find that the daily wage might easily be 4 or 5 annas.

profitable occupations." A vast population of the country remain, part of the year, practically without any occupation. Many of the women of the upper classes have ample leisure. It is for them that hand-spinning is recommended as a profitable occupation for idle hours. And does the *Servant of India* seriously contend that the vast mass of students, who spend their days and nights in cramming, indiscriminately, Shakespeare and Milton, are engaged in a "more profitable occupation" than hand-spinning?

But to come to figures. The *Servant of India* argues that "the combined production of all the students of the arts and professional colleges—about 64,000—would not be equal to the output of a single spinning mill." According to it, 235 mills, were able to produce only 65 *crores* of yarn in one year. Let us now see how much the nation can produce if it determines religiously to dedicate its *spare* hours to spinning. Taking the population of India as consisting of five crore families, let us assume that a fourth of them are either families of co-operators or of those not convinced of the virtues of hand-spinning. If only two members of the remaining four crore families give *two hours* per day to spinning, they would spin a crore lbs. of yarn everyday, *i.e.*, 365 crore lbs. of yarn in the year, which means nearly six times as much as the yarn produced by our mills.

But the only proper way of comparing between the economic value of the spinning wheel and a spinning mill is to consider in each case the cost of production. Every mill-manager knows that the cost of one spindle which can produce a pound of coarse yarn (of six counts) per day is not less than Rs. 100. For a mill producing 20,000 lbs. of coarse yarn, we have got to invest for the full supply of 20,000 lbs. no less than 20 lacs of rupees.

Let us see how much the same capital invested on spinning-wheels would yield. Twenty lacs of rupees would give us four lacs of spinning wheels producing on an average half a pound of yarn daily, *i.e.*, two-hundred thousand pounds of yarn. This is enough to show the extent of the wastefulness of the spinning mill. But economic wastefulness is not the only, or the principal, factor to be considered. Think of the huge moral wastefulness involved, of strikes and similar evils under which the industrial world in Europe is reeling. One shudders to think of perpetuating the inhuman slums that form an universal feature of modern industrial towns. We do not speak here of the utter impracticability of erecting spinning mills in a year or even in the course of a score of years, sufficient to clothe the country. The *Servant of India* by quoting the import figures tries to make out that, as we cannot turn out fine counts either in our spinning mills or on the spinning wheel, we must remain dependent on the foreigner for a large part of the yarn we import. Not being a Non-co-operator, the paper evidently forgets that the enforcement of the Congress Resolution regarding abolition of foreign goods presupposes abolition of all finer fabrics. The figures of exports of yarn only strengthen our case. It is contemplated that, not only should even one out of the 123 millions pounds of yarn not go to foreign countries but, that not a pound of raw cotton should be exported. In the year 1919-20, 8,558,747 cwts. of raw cotton of the value of Rs. 58,60,40,510 was exported to foreign countries. Under the proposed scheme, where every adult will devote some spare hours to spinning, there will be room enough for every pound of cotton that is at present exported and work enough for every weaver in the land. Under this scheme, therefore, and under no other, it is possible to win our economic freedom.

It is strange that, whilst the country's efforts to bring about a complete boycott of foreign cloth are jeered at by a section of publicists in this country, their magnitude has been completely realised by men like Sir Michael O'Dwyer and Mr. Shorrock. The latter in the course of a very long article in the *Evening Standard* writes:

Look for a moment at some hard facts and figures. Our annual trade with India based on the most recent figures available, must be worth at least £ 80,000,000. If "Non-co-operation" succeeds, we should at one stroke lose to that extent in work and wages, and this at a time when the cry of unemployment, due mainly to the tardy revival of our export industries, is daily growing in strength. Factories which cater for this Eastern market could never survive such a blow.

From the Lancashire cotton mills alone we export annually about £ 34,458,000 worth of goods to India, and from the industrial centres of the Midlands and the North, iron and steel worth £ 21,139,000. . . . .

Nor would the £ 80,000,000 represent our total loss. So intimately is one trade interlocked with another that any blow to the chief industries immediately reacts on every other industry. . . . .

It will be seen, then, that, if Mr. Gandhi's programme is actually carried through, the position of this country will be very different from that represented by the latest Board of Trade return headed "Indian Imports and Exports." Great Britain would be poorer by many millions a year. It would be poorer in actual earnings moreover. As every producing country pays for its imported food by manufactured goods, the closure of any big market for such goods means inevitably a new addition to the high cost of living.

It is not necessary now to point out that the scheme of Non-co-operation does not aim at starving any labourer outside the country, it is meant to stop him from starving and keeping naked the people of India.—M. D. "Young India," 2nd March, 1921.

18*th May*, 1921

SPINNING AS FAMINE RELIEF

(By M. K. Gandhi)

Mrs. Jaiji Petit has sent the following notes of an experiment being conducted in spinning among the famine-stricken people at Miri near Ahmednagar. I gladly publish the notes as the experiment is being conducted under the supervision of an Englishwoman. The reader will not fail to observe the methodical manner in which the work is being done. All the difficulties have been met and provided for. Even the very small experiment shows what a potent instrument, the spinning-wheel is for famine relief. Properly organised, it cannot but yield startling results:

In the month of August 1920, when the severity of the famine was being felt, the idea of introducing spinning as a famine relief to respectable middle class people was started and Miss Latham kindly gave a spinning wheel to introduce the work. Attempts were made to introduce the work especially among the Dhangars who were used to spinning-wheel but they proved futile. Spinning a thin thread of cotton was thought an impossibility in a village which did not know anything about it. Doubts were also entertained as to whether the work if taken up would be paying or at least helpful. In such different difficulties and objections, the wheel remained idle for nearly three months, and in spite of vigorous efforts no body seemed willing to take up the work. In December 1920, Miss Latham again sent four more wheels through the kindness of Mrs. J. Petit and some cotton. They were given for trial to different persons. Signs now seemed a little hopeful, and at last one Ramoshi woman was prevailed upon to take up the work seriously. This was about the 20th of January 1921, since when the work has assumed a different shape. The example of this woman was copied by two more who undertook to take up the work. Through great perseverance 4 lbs. of yarn were prepared by these three spinners, and it was sent for sale. In the meantime, many women began to make inquiries and expressed a desire to take it up, if it helped them financially in some way. A rate of spinning, 6 as. a lb., was therefore fixed and it helped other spinners to join the work.

Here another difficutly, *viz.*, that of funds, came in the way. All the five wheels were engaged and five more prepared locally were also engaged. The stock of cotton was also exhausted. It seemed that the work would suffer for want of funds to prepare wheels, purchase cotton, and pay the workers. Rao Bahadur Chitale personally saw this difficulty and helped the work with a grant of Rs. 100. Miss Latham, when she knew of this difficulty, kindly sent another hundred. These two grants came at the right time and gave a stimulus to the work. Local gentlemen helped with their own cotton.

The demand for wheels went on increasing day by day. People being too poor to pay for the wheels, it became necessary to get the wheels prepared locally and lend them to the workers. Twenty-seven more wheels were prepared which also gave work to local carpenters who had no work on account of famine. One carpenter improved the wheel by making it more light and useful for finer yarn. The prices of the wheel were paid at Rs. 3, Rs. 3-8, and Rs. 4 per wheel according to the quality. Three of these wheels have been sold for Rs. 9-8 as. The total sum spent on these wheels is Rs. 103-8-0 which includes the sum for the wheels kindly sent by Mrs. Petit.

Though local cotton was secured for the work, it proved too bad for beginners. A new method therefore was introduced to improve the local cotton, which not only helped the work but also provided work for a few more persons. Raw cotton was secured and the dirt and the dry leaves in it were carefully removed before it was ginned. The rate for this work was fixed at one pice per lb. Any old man who did this work got an opportunity of earning one anna a day, by cleaning 4 lbs. of raw cotton. After it was thus cleaned, it was ginned with a hand-gin which gave work to some women who ginned, at the rate of one anna per 10 lbs. One woman could thus earn 2 as.

and 6 pies each day. This ginned cotton was then cleaned by a *pinjari* who charged at the rate of one anna per pound and earned about 8 as. per day. It would have been better and easier too, if cotton had been purchased from the mills, but as this cleaning process of the local cotton provided work for a few workers, it was thought the more desirable in these days. A major portion of these cleaning charges is, however, made up by the sale of cotton seed secured after ginning. The following statement will show the expenses incurred for this and the price of raw cotton for every 60 lbs.

	Rs.	A.	P.
Price of 60 lbs. of raw cotton at 20 Rs. a patia (240 lbs.)	5	0	0
Removal of dirt waste and dry leaves at 1 pice per pound	0	15	0
Ginning of 52 lbs. of raw clean cotton at 1 anna per 10 lbs.	0	5	3
Cleaning the Lint (17 lbs.) by a pinjari at 1 anna per pound	1	1	0
Total	7	5	3
Deduct price of cotton seed 35 lbs. at 20 lbs. per rupee.	1	12	0
Net charges for 17 lbs. of clean cotton ...	5	9	3

Thus the cost of one pound of cotton comes to 5 as. and 3 pies only. The proportion of waste, *viz.* 8 lbs. in 60 lbs. of raw cotton is too high and could be avoided by securing better and cleaner cotton.

There are at present 29 wheels going and there is still a great demand for wheels. But the funds being limited, more wheels could not be prepared and provided. Spinning is done by those who absolutely know nothing about it previously. Consequently the yarn is still of an inferior sort. It is improving day by day, but if a competent teacher could be secured, it would improve rapidly. Amongst the spinners, some are full-time workers and others are leisure-time workers.

About two lbs. of yarn are now prepared every day and the quantity will increase as the spinners get used to the work. The rate for spinning is fixed at 6 as. a lb., though many workers complain that it is not enough. As the yarn sent for sale realised a price of 12 as. a lb., the spinning charges could not be increased without a loss.

Every lb. of yarn requires Annas 11, pies 3 for expenses, as. 0-5-3 for cotton & 0-6-0 for spinning. Thus every lb. leaves a profit of 9 pies only. The establishment and other charges are not calculated. With the present rate of spinning at 6 as. a lb., one spinner earns 3 as. per day by spinning 20 to 24 tolas, others earn 2 as. a day by spinning 15 tolas and the rest 1½ as. a day for 10 tolas, the beginners excluded. The more the spinner is used to the work, the more he will earn.

An attempt was made to prepare cloth out of the yarn and three and a half lbs. of yarn were given to a weaver for weaving. He, however, charged an exorbitant rate for weaving. He prepared nine and a half yards of cloth and charged Rs. 3-9 for it, practically 1 rupee a lb. The cloth cost Rs. 6-0-6 and was sold at Rs. 6-3-0, with a profit of as. 2, pies 6 only. To obviate the difficulty about weaving, a separate loom with one teacher to teach weaving to local persons is urgently required. Many local people wish to learn this art. A separate loom will reduce the cost of the cloth prepared on it below the prevailing market rate. About 6 lbs. of yarn are given to different weavers to ascertain the exact charges, but all this difficulty can only be removed by having a special loom.

When there was a shortage of cotton and the workers had no work, wool was introduced for spinning till cotton was ready. This work was willingly taken up by the Dhangars. They were however required to spin finer thread of wool than they usually prepared. They took some time to pick up the work, and now there are 10 wool spinners working fine thread. They are also paid at 6 as. a lb. for spinning. Wool worth Rs. 31 at 2 lbs. a rupee was purchased, and though the cotton was ready, the wool spinning was continued by starting a separate department, as the Dhangars readily took up the work. The whole process of cleaning the wool is also done by the Dhangar women, who get an extra anna per lb. for it. The sorting of wool is carefully looked to. The majority of wool spinners use their own spinning wheels but a few are now asking for the improved wheel for preparing finer threads.

Dhangar weavers being locally available, blankets of the Pandharpur and Dawangiri pattern are being prepared from this finer thread and different designs have been suggested to them. The Dhangars being a stubborn race do not readily adopt the new improvement, but this work has set them to work up new designs of blankets which will permanently help them in their own profession. They now require a broader and improved loom and instruction in colouring wool. Efforts are made to secure a clever full-time weaver who will introduce a better method of weaving. Two blankets were prepared and sold at cost price, one for Rs. 5-13-6 and the other for Rs. 6-6 0. Orders are being received for more blankets now, but to continue the work would require some funds.

To keep so many persons working is not only an ideal form of famine relief, but a means to promote village industries, and remove the demoralising effects of successive famines. Thus stands the work of about one month. It now requires an improved handloom, a good teacher, a special loom for wool, more spinning wheels (which the neighbouring villagers are also demanding) and many other things. The work is going on vigorously, and, it is hoped, will not be allowed to suffer for want of funds.

Mr. Gandhi wrote the following in *Young India* of 26th March, 1921, in the course of an article entitled "Famine Insurance:"

A spinning wheel costs, say, six rupees. If we supply a family of three with two wheels and all the members work at it together for eight hours each, they will, between them, earn at least six annas per day. I claim that six annas per day for a family will keep it going during a season of distress. I can conceive it to be possible for them to work at the rate of twelve hours each, when the work has to be done in their homes at their own leisure. They add fifty per cent. to the daily earning making it nine annas per day. Thus at an outlay of Rs. 12,000, we can support for four months one thousand families, or three thousand souls, and get from them a return of

$$\frac{1{,}000 \text{ families} \times 6 \text{ annas} \times 120 \text{ days}}{16} = \text{Rs. } 45{,}000$$

worth of labour. No doubt, forty-five thousand rupees will have to be found in the first instance for organising famine relief, in addition to carded cotton and the spinning wheels. The whole of the yarn that may be produced by the famine-stricken people would be used by the nation. There will be some little waste during the first month of earning. I use the adjectives 'some little' advisedly, because cotton will not be absolutely wasted.

The only requisites, Mr. Gandhi wrote, are (1) the spinning wheel; (2) a supply of cotton; and (3) a ready sale of yarn. Of course, it is assumed that the famine is one of money and that corn is available.

Writing in *Young India* of 6th October, 1921, regarding famine in the Ceded districts which he visited, Mr. Gandhi remarked:

It is not possible to give doles of charity to hundreds of thousands of men. And men who live on charity lose all sense of self-respect. It is not as if there is no corn to be had in the affected area. People have no work and no money. The Government's relief works consist in breaking and carrying stones. A friend remarked that the Government had roads torn down and repaired in order to find work for the men and women in distress. Whether roads are torn down or not, road repair is the only relief work the Government provides. I understood that the actual wage that found its way into a woman's hands was an anna or five pice, and not more than ten pice into a man's hands. I saw, on the other hand, that a Congress Committee was paying three annas per day to Panchama women working at the spinning wheel for eight hours a day. And what is being done for the Panchama women can be done for thousands of famine-stricken women and, for that matter, men. In these districts 3 annas a day, even for men, is a veritable boon. But the spinning wheel has possibilities which no other occupation has. For it involves the preliminary processes of ginning and carding and the subsequent process of weaving. In the Ceded Districts, it is possible without much difficulty to teach weaving. And if the whole of cloth manufacture can be organised, thousands of men can find permanent occupation in their own homes.

SOME FACTS AND COMMENTS

The following additional facts are summarised from *Young India*:

The Loom vs. *the Wheel*.—Dr. S. B. Mitra wrote to *Young India* under date, Calcutta, 12th April, 1921, a letter on the need for "greater use of hand-looms" which was published on 11th May, 1921. Dr. Mitra pointed out that about 143 million pounds of twist and yarn made in India were exported every year from India and that if this stuff was converted into cloth, the Indian cloth problem was solved. Dr. Mitra added that if the present number of hand-looms was doubled, which could be easily done, the necessary cloth could be woven in the country itself. He therefore appealed to the readers of *Young India* to increase the number of hand-looms. Mr. Gandhi, commenting on the letter, stated that "hand spinning includes all that the correspondent suggests and it includes much more." The mill-owners cared for profit and therefore exported yarn. Then, the agriculturists wanted a supplementary industry. After all, hand-weaving was progressing.

Mr. A. V. Thakkar of the Servants of India Society, continuing the above controversy pointed out, in a letter to *Young India* of 3rd June, 1921, that for every ten new wheels introduced there must be one additional hand-loom, but that while thousands of wheels were set to work, not even a few dozen new looms were being made. Women were turned back, as in scores of *Khadi*-producing centres spinning operations were restricted for want of weavers. "The loom is not less important than the wheel for clothing India, as for providing a supplementary industry for our semi-starved peasantry." Mr. Gandhi, commenting on this, said that the existing looms should be fed with hand-spun yarn instead of with foreign yarn, and that for this the weavers must be trained and the quality of yarn improved. The weaver's wages had risen and there was no danger of hand-weaving not keeping pace with hand-spinning.

In *Young India* of 29th June, Mr. Gandhi wrote, under the heading, "The Message of the Charka":

There are *enough weavers and enough looms in India to replace the whole of the foreign import of cloth*. It should be understood that our looms—thousands of them in Madras, Maharashtra and Bengal—are engaged in weaving the fine yarn imported from Japan and

Manchester. We *must* utilize these for weaving hand-spun yarn. And for that purpose, the nation has to revise its taste for the thin tawdry and useless muslins. I see no art in weaving muslins, that do not cover but only expose the body.

Organisation for Khaddar Production.—In *Young India* of 11th August, 1921, Mr. Gandhi stated that while all should spin, weavers, carders and clothiers should also be organised.

The ideal no doubt is for every village to spin and weave for itself, just as to-day most villages grow corn for themselves. It is easier for every village to spin and weave for itself than to grow all its corn. Every village cannot grow wheat or rice, but every village can stock enough cotton and spin and weave without any difficulty. But it must be some time before we can arrive at that happy state. Meanwhile, those provinces that are at all organised for the work, for instance, the Punjab, must not only immediately exclude all foreign cloth from their own markets but must send out to the parts of India that need their superfluous stock of Khadi. Punjab, Andhra, Bihar* and Gujarat seem to be the best organised provinces for the manufacture of Khadi. And they must busy themselves with the work so as to anticipate a famine of Khadi.

Fraudulent Imitations.—The decentralisation of production will prevent fraud which undoubtedly existed and to tackle which Mr. Gandhi wrote in *Young India* of 18th August, 1921: How to detect and check these frauds is the question. The golden rule of course is that we must spin our own yarn and get a weaver to

* *See* pp. 508, 540.

weave it under our superintendence. That time is undoubtedly coming. When we cannot spin for ourselves, we must get the spinning done by the thousands of spinners coming into being all over the country. Where we cannot do it, we must, in choosing our Khadi, reject every piece of cloth that looks at all like mill-made. For coarser counts it will be most difficult to distinguish between imported cloth and that manufactured by our mills. Hand-spun Khadi lacks the dead polish of the mills but is rougher to look at, porous, light to handle, and pleasant to the touch. It is never glossy. Another safeguard I suggest is that the cloth should be unbleached. The third alternative which is not free from danger is that in every Congress district there should be Swadeshi shops licensed by the Congress and there should be expert inspectors who should constantly inspect the stock in licensed shops. If possible, every article should be stamped. I know that we are not organised and trained enough for undertaking this work on a universal scale. But till every district has begun to manufacture all Khadi for itself, some such inspection is undoubtedly necessary, and whatever can be honestly improvised should be done.

Spinning Wheels and Education.—In the course of an article entitled, "A Confession of Error", in *Young India* of 18th August, 1921, Mr. Gandhi wrote:

It would have been better to have insisted on hand-spinning as a necessary part of the educational item in Non-co-operation. I invite those who share my belief to hasten to repair the mistake and earnestly take up the work of production of yarn and Khadi in all national institutions which they influence. They will not ask me to supply them with teachers. I have far too few. But

I jot down for them the processes that bale cotton which is what we usually have to-day has to go through. It must be first carded. There is no district in India which has no carders, *i.e.*, *pinjaras* or *dhunias*. They can card and a mere watching them for a day or two enables one to understand the process. A week's practice at the rate of six hours per day will enable one to card moderately well.

The carded cotton has to be turned into slivers or *punis*, an incredibly simple and easy process.

The cotton is now ready for hand-spinning, which can be learnt from any spinner. Yarn to be yarn must be free from dirt, even and well-twisted. If it is not well-twisted or even, it cannot be woven.

The next process is sizing. It is rather difficult to practice. I have no scientific formula giving the quantity of ingredients. It must be learnt from an experienced weaver.

Joining the thread is also a process to be separately learnt. It requires like cycling a little knack which is easily acquired.

Lastly comes weaving which is purely a matter of practice. One learns the principle in a day. The reader must not be surprised at the ease with which I claim processes can be learnt. All natural and necessary work is easy. Only it requires constant practice to become perfect, and it needs plodding. Ability to plod is Swaraj. It is Yoga. Nor need the reader be frightened of the monotony. Monotony is the law of nature. Look at the monotonous manner in which the sun rises. And imagine the catastrophe that would befall the universe, if the sun became capricious and went in for a variety of pastime. But there is a monotony that sustains and a monotony that kills. The monotony of necessary occupations is exhilarating and life-giving. An artist never tires of his art. A spinner who has mastered his art, will certainly be able to do sustained work without fatigue. There is a music about the spindle which the practised spinner catches without fail. And when India has monotonously worked away at turning out Swaraj, she will have produced a thing of beauty which will be a joy for ever. But it cannot be without the spinning wheel. Therefore, the best National Education for India is undoubtedly intelligent handling of the spinning wheel.

How to deal with shortage of cloth.—Mr. Gandhi issued an appeal to the public, headed, "The Poor Man's Way," which was published in "Young India" of 29th September, 1921, in the course of which he stated: I know that many will find it difficult to replace their foreign cloth all at once. Millions are too poor to buy enough *Khadi* to replace the discarded cloth.* To them I repeat my advice given on the Madras beach. Let them be satisfied with a mere loin cloth. In our climate, we hardly need more to protect our bodies during the warm months of the year. Let there be no prudery about dress. India has never insisted on full covering of the body for the males as a test of culture.

I gave the advice under a full sense of my responsibility. In order, therefore, to set the example, I propose to discard at least up to the 31st of October my *topi* and vest, and to content myself with only a loin cloth and a *chaddar* whenever found necessary for the protection of the body. I adopt the change, because I have always

* The Jamiat-ul-Ulema volunteer pledge did not insist on *Khaddar* on the ground that it was not available.

hesitated to advise anything I may not myself be prepared to follow, also because I am anxious by leading the way to make it easy for those who cannot afford a change on discarding their foreign garments. I consider the renunciation to be also necessary for me as a sign of mourning, and a bare head and a bare body is such a sign in my part of the country. That we are in mourning is more and more being borne home to me, as the end of the year is approaching and we are still without Swaraj. I wish to state clearly that I do not expect co-workers to renounce the use of the vest and *topi* unless they find it necessary to do so for their own work.

Ten Precious Reasons.—"Young India" of 3rd November, 1921, contained the following:

The Behar Government Publicity Bureau has issued leaflets in Hindustani giving ten reasons why foreign cloth should not be boycotted. The reader should know how the reforms are working and the public is being misled at its own expense. Here are the reasons:

1. Cloth manufactured in India is not sufficient for our needs.

2. People being used to wearing fine cloth for a long time find it heavy to wear garments made from Indian yarn.

3. Even Indian mills use foreign yarn for the fine cloth they weave.

4. If we give up foreign cloth, we shall be in the same plight we were in 1905, when, owing to Swadeshi agitation, Indian mills sent up prices and drained our wealth. Thus mill-owners will fatten themselves on our ruin.

5. So long as foreign cloth is imported, there is competition between Indian cloth and foreign cloth, and thus the mill-owners cannot raise prices very high.

6. There are not enough mills and handlooms in India for the cloth required.

7. Hand-spinning is not profitable because it yields no more than two annas per day.

8. Hand-looms produce very little: therefore much cannot be produced from them.

9. By such boycott there will be great unrest and commotion, and India's progress will be greatly arrested.

10. By the rise in the price of cloth the poor will suffer much and discontent will spread all over.

The most natural thing that a national Government will do will be to multiply handlooms and spinning wheels and flood the market with plenty of handspun. A national Government will prevent the mill-owners from unduly raising prices, a national Government would take advantage of the glorious upheaval to stabilize a great cottage industry. It did not strike the author of the precious reasons, that the millions do not even now wear fine cloth, that spinning is intended for leisure hours, that millions will do need to pay anything for spinning, that they will do it themselves and that therefore handspun will always be comparatively cheap for them as home-cooked food is cheaper than hotel-cooked.

Export of Indian yarn—a fallacy.—Writing in "Young India" of 23rd March, 1921, under the heading, "More fallacies," in reply to the Bihar Director of Industries' suggestion that, since India exported in 1919 nearly 12 times as much yarn as she imported, therefore it was ridiculous to suggest that India was helpless, Mr, Gandhi wrote: The revivalists not only insist that more yarn should be manufactured in India, but that no yarn should be exported from India till the whole nation is clothed in Indian spun and Indian woven yarn. Whilst the export of yarn and twist was 10 times the import, the import of piecegoods in the same year was nearly *six times* as much, and the import of handkerchiefs, etc., was *twenty-three* times as much as the export, and there was absolutely no export of hosiery to balance the import of hosiery worth Rs. 1,45,04,692. It is from the bondage of the sixty crore Rupees worth of these imports that the country is sought to be freed by means of a revival of the spinning wheel. India does not need to import finer goods to-day, as the problem, we repeat, is to clothe India and not to decorate her.

Progress of Khaddar Production.—"Ramanuj" was deputed by Mr. Gandhi to Chicacole in Ganjam district (Andhradesa) for conductiug a personal investigation. In his report published in "Young India" of 18th May, 1921, he said he was convinced of the existence in Ganjam, Vizagapatam and Nellore of both home-spinning and home weaving in great prefection. In the village of Umpolu, he saw an old lady spinning yarn of 80 to 100 counts with great dexterity. The processes of carding, cleaning. etc., also she demonstrated which were done to perfection. The same was the case with weaving. The dhoties were silk like and, it was claimed, four times more durable than the mill-made stuff. Unfortunately, the weavers were yielding to the temptation of using cheap Japanese yarn: and the art of weaving hand-spun was near dying out.

Progress of Khaddar in Bihar.—"Young India" of 9th March, 1922, contained the following: The "Bihar Herald" is responsible for the following:

In "the Land Revenue Administration Report of the Bihar and Orissa Government, it is recorded that in Patna, Bhagalpur and Tirhut the levying of 'ahwabs' has materially decreased with the growing knowledge among the tenantry of their rights, and that in Bhagalpur the opposition to such exactions has been stiffened by the Non-co-operation movement."

"The contribution of Non-co-operation to the revival of the *Charka* and the weaving industry is noteworthy. In Bihar, according to official figures, three-eighths of the cloth worn is woven on the hand-loom. The *Charka* gave a further impetus to the weaving trade. In Patna, Tirhut, Orissa and Chota-Nagpur divisions 'Motia' cloth is being spun and woven with success. . . . An extended use of coarse cloth manufactured in country looms is evident . . . the weaving industry of Tasar in Navadah and Daris, etc., in Aurangabad continued."

The extract shows the steady progress made in constructive work in Bihar, a place where 3 years ago it would have been difficult to see a spinning wheel anywhere or a yard of home-spun *khaddar*. Only the poor people of Bihar know what a blessing the *Charka* has been to them.

Some 'ifs'—If you are a *weaver* feeling for the country, the Khilafat and the Punjab—

(1) You should weave only hand-spun yarn, and charge so as to give you a living. You should overcome all the difficulties of sizing and adjusting your loom to the requirements of coarse yarn.

(2) If you cannot possibly tackle hand-spun yarn for warp, you must use Indian mill-spun yarn for it and use hand-spun for woof.

(3) Where even the second alternative is not possible, you should use mill-spun yarn for both warp and woof.

But you should henceforth cease to use any foreign yarn, whether it is silk or cotton.

If you are a *Congress official or worker*, you should get hold of the weavers within your jurisdiction, and place the foregoing propositions before them for acceptance and help them to the best of your ability.

If you are a *buyer*, insist upon the first class of cloth, but if you have not the sense or the courage to do so, take up the second or the third, but on no account purchase foreign cloth or cloth woven in India but made of foreign yarn.

If you are a *householder*,

(1) You should make a fixed determination henceforth not to buy any foreign cloth.

(2) You should interview the weaver in your neighbourhood, and get him to weave for you enough Khadi out of home-spun and failing that to weave out of Indian mill-spun yarn.

(3) You should deliver to the Congress Committee all your foreign cloth for destruction or sending to Smyrna or elsewhere outside India.

(4) If you have not the courage to give up your foreign cloth, you may wear it out at home for all dirty work, but never go out in foreign cloth.

(5) If you have any leisure, you should devote it to learning the art of spinning even and properly-twisted yarn for the sake of the nation.

If you are a *schoolboy or schoolgirl*, you should consider it a sin to receive literary training, before you have spun, carded or woven for the nation for at least four hours per day till the establishment of Swaraj.

22nd September, 1921

WANTED EXPERTS

(By. M. K. Gandhi)

Attacks on hand-spinning notwithstanding, I cling to the belief that Swaraj is unattainable without the beautiful art becoming universal in India. The reasoning applied to the proposition is incredibly simple. India cannot live unless her homes become self-supporting. They cannot become so, unless they have a supplementary occupation. It will, therefore, not avail if all our cloth was manufactured in our mills. If hand-spinning became universal, every home would get a share óf the crores and without any complicated machinery being necessary. And India is able to manufacture all her own cloth. It is understood that, when spinning becomes universal, the millions of weavers and lacs of carders will revert to their original occupation.

This is the economic aspect of hand-spinning.

It will save our women from forced violation of their purity. It will, as it must, do away with beginning as a means of livelihood. It will remove our enforced idleness. It will steady the mind. And I verily believe that, when millions take to it as a sacrament, it will turn our faces Godward.

This is the moral aspect of spinning.

And when it has become universal and traffic in foreign cloth has become a thing of the past, it is the surest sign that India is earnest, sober, and believes in the non-violent and religious character of her struggle.

At present, outsiders do not believe in our ability to boycott foreign cloth and to manufacture enough for our requirements by hand-spinning and hand-weaving.

But when it becomes an established fact, India's opinion too, will become an irresistible force, and if necessary, she can then, but not till then, resort to Civil Disobedience in order to bend a recalcitrant Government to its will.

This is the political aspect.

Therefore, I was sad to see that, in all Bengal, I found no one who was a spinning-expert and who devoted his whole time and attention to nothing but spreading the gospel of hand-spinning, teaching, organising and advising. I found that the masses were ready to take it up, but they did not know how to go about it. What is true of Bengal is perhaps true of most provinces. We should have in each province a standard *charkha** and a body of experts to whom one can refer for advice and guidance. Much splendid talent could be utilised, if there was expert knowledge available. Who is to decide upon the utility or otherwise of over fifteen inventions that were exhibited in the National College Hall at Calcutta? I saw everywhere different kinds of *charkas* in use. But I saw no attempt to test the capacity of these wheels. Thousands are spinning to-day in Bengal, but there is nobody to measure their work. I therefore advise all Congress Committees to set apart at least six men and six women with faith in their mission in this direction.

* See *infra* for tests of a good charka.

3rd November, 1921

CO-OPERATION

(BY M. K. GANDHI)

Probably very few workers have noticed that progress of hand-spinning means the greatest voluntary co-operation the world has ever seen. It means co-operation among millions of human beings scattered over a very wide area and working for their daily bread. No doubt agriculture has required much co-operative effort, but hand-spinning requires still greater and more honest co-operation. Wheat grows more by nature's honesty than by man's. Manufacture of yarn in our cottages is dependent solely on human honesty. Hand-spinning is impossible without the willing and intelligent co-operation of millions of human beings. We have to arrive at a stage when the spinner like the grain-seller is assured of a steady market for his yarn as well as the supply of cotton sliver, if he or she does not know the process of carding. Is it any wonder if I claim that hand-spinning can drive away as if by magic the growing pauperism of the masses? An English friend sends me a newspaper cutting showing the progress of machinery in China. He has evidently imagined that in advocating hand-spinning I am propagating my ideal about machinery. I am doing nothing of the kind. I would favour the use of the most elaborate machinery if thereby India's pauperism and resulting idleness be avoided. I have suggested hand-spinning as the only ready means of driving away penury and making famine of work and wealth impossible. The spinning wheel itself is a piece of valuable machinery, and in my own humble way I have tried to secure improvements in it in keeping with the special conditions of

India. The only question therefore that a lover of India and humanity has to address himself to is how best to devise practical means of alleviating India's wretchedness and misery. No scheme of irrigation or other agricultural improvement that human ingenuity can conceive can deal with the vastly scattered population of India or provide work for masses of mankind who are constantly thrown out of employment. Imagine a nation working only five hours per day on an average, and this not by choice but by force of circumstances, and you have a realistic picture of India.

If the reader would visualise the picture, he must dismiss from his mind the busy fuss of the city life or the grinding fatigue of the factory life or the slavery of the plantations. These are but drops in the ocean of Indian humanity. If he would visualise the picture of the Indian skeleton, he must think of the eighty per cent. of the population which is working its own fields and which has practically no occupation for at least four months in the year and which therefore lives on the borderland of starvation. This is the normal condition. The ever recurring famines make a large addition to this enforced idleness. What is the work that these men and women can easily do in their own cottages so as to supplement their very slender resources? Does anyone still doubt that it is only hand-spinning and nothing else? And I repeat that this can be made universal in a few months' time, if only the workers will. Indeed it is on a fair way to becoming universal. Experts only are needed to organise it. People are ready, and what is most in favour of hand-spinning is that it is not a new and untried method, but people have up to recently been using it. Its successful reintroduction does need skilful endeavour, honesty and co-operation on the largest scale known to the world. And if India can achieve this co-operation, who shall deny that India has by that one act achieved Swaraj?

8th December, 1921

INDIAN ECONOMICS

(By M. K. Gandhi)

A friend has placed in my hands a bulletin on Indian Piece Goods Trade prepared by Mr. A. C. Coubrough, C. B. E., by order of the Government of India. It contains the following prefatory note: 'The Government of India desire it to be understood that the statements made and the views expressed in this bulletin are those of the author himself'. If so, why has the Government of India burdened the tax-payer with the expense of such bulletins? The one before me is 16th in the series. Do they publish both the sides of the question?

The bulletin under review is intended to be an answer to the Swadeshi movement. It is an elaborate note containing a number of charts showing the condition of imports and home manufacture of piece goods, including hand-woven. But it does not assist the reader in studying the movement. The painstaking author has bestowed no pains upon a study of the present movement or its scope. That the Government of India treats the greatest constructive and co-operative movement in the country with supreme contempt and devotes people's money to a vain refutation instead of a sympathetic study and treatment is perhaps the best condemnation that can be pronounced upon the system under which it is carried.

The author's argument is:

(1) The movement if successful will act not as a protective but a prohibitive tariff.

(2) This must result in merely enriching the Indian capitalist and punishing the consumer.

(3) The imports are non-competitive in that the bulk of the kind of piece goods imported are not manufactured in India.

(4) The result of boycotting such piece goods must be high prices without corresponding benefit.

(5) The boycott therefore being against the law of supply and demand and against the consumer must fail in the end.

(6) The destruction of hand-spinning which I have deplored is due to natural causes, *viz.*, the invention of time-saving appliances and was therefore inevitable.

(7) The Indian farmer is responsible for his own ruin in that he has indolently neglected cotton culture which was once so good.

(8) The best service I can render is therefore to induce the agriculturist to improve the quality of cotton.

(9) The author concludes: 'If, instead of filling homes with useless *Charkhas*, he were to start a propaganda for the more intensive cultivation of cotton and particularly for the production of longer staple cotton,' his influence would be felt not only at the present day but for many generations to come.'

The reader will thus see that what I regard as the supreme necessity for the economic salvation of India, the author considers to be rank folly. There is therefore no meeting ground here. And, in spite of the prefatory note of the Government of India reproduced by me, the author does represent the Government attitude. I have invited them and the co-operators definitely to make common cause with the people in this movement at any rate. They may not mind its political implications because they do not believe in them. And surely they need not feel sorry, if, contrary to their expectation, the rise of the *Charkha* results in an increase in the political power of the people. Instead of waging war against *Khadi*, they might have popularised its use and disarmed the terrible suspicion they labour under of wishing to benefit the foreign manufacturer at the expense of the Indian cultivator. My invitation is open for all time. I prophesy that, whatever happens to the other parts of the national programme, Swadeshi in its present shape will bide for ever and must, if India's pauperism is to be banished.

Even though I am a layman, I make bold to say that the so called laws laid down in books on economics are not immutable like the laws of Medes and Persians, nor are they universal. The economics of England are different from those of Germany. Germany enriched herself by bounty-fed beet sugar. England enriched herself by exploiting foreign markets. What was possible for a compact area is not possible for an area 1,900 miles long and 1,500 broad. The economics of a nation are determined by its climatic, geological and temperamental conditions. The Indian conditions are different from the English in all these essentials. What is meat for England is in many cases poison for India. Beef tea in the English climate may be good, it is poison for the hot climate of religious India. Fiery whisky in the north of the British Isles may be a necessity, it renders an Indian unfit for work or society. Fur coats in Scotland are indispensable, they will be an intolerable burden in India. Free trade for a country which has become industrial, whose population can and does live in cities, whose people do not mind preying upon other nations and therefore sustain the biggest navy to protect their unnatural commerce, may be economically sound (though, as the reader perceives, I question its morality). Free trade for India has proved her curse and held her in bondage.

And now for Mr. Coubrough's propositions.

(1) The movement is intended to serve the purpose of a voluntary prohibitive tariff.

(2) But it is so conceived as neither unduly to benefit the capitalist nor to injure the consumer. During the very brief transition stage, the prices of home manufactures may be, as they are, inflated. But the rise can only be temporary as the vast majority of consumers must become their own manufacturers. This cottage manufacture of yarn and cloth cannot be expensive even as domestic cookery is not expensive and cannot be replaced by hotel cookery. Over twenty-five crores of the population will be doing their own hand-spinning and having yarn thus manufactured woven in neighbouring localities. This population is rooted to the soil and has at least four months in the year to remain idle.

If they spin during those hours and have the yarn woven and wear it, no mill-made cloth can compete with their *Khadi*. The cloth thus manufactured will be the cheapest possible for them. If the rest of the population did not take part in the process, it could easily be supplied out of the surplus manufactured by the twenty-five crores.

(3) It is true that non-competitive imports are larger than those that compete with the manufactures of Indian mills. In the scheme proposed by me, this

question does not arise, because the central idea is not so much to carry on a commercial war against foreign countries as to utilise the idle hours of the nation and thus by natural processes to help it to get rid of her growing pauperism.

(4) I have already shown that the result of boycott cannot in the end be a rise in the price of cloth.

(5) The proposed boycott is not against the law of supply and demand, because it does away with the law by manufacturing enough for the supply. The movement does require a change of taste on the part of those who have adopted finer variety and who patronise fantastic combinations of colours and designs.

(6) I have shown, in these pages, that the destruction of hand-spinning was designed and carried out in a most inhuman manner by the agents of the East India Company. No amount of appliances would ever have displaced this national art and industry but for this artificial and systematically cruel manner of carrying out the destruction.

(7) I am unable to hold the Indian farmer responsible for the deterioration in cotton culture. The whole incentive was taken away when hand-spinning was destroyed. The state never cared for the cultivator.

(8) My activity, I am proud to think, has already turned the cultivator's attention to the improvement of cotton. The artistic sense of the nation will insist on fine counts for which long staple is a necessity. Cotton culture by itself cannot solve the problem of India's poverty. For it will still leave the question of enforced idleness untouched.

(9) I therefore claim for the *Charkha* the honour of being able to solve the problem of economic distress in a most natural, simple, inexpensive and businesslike

manner.* The *Charkha* therefore is not only not useless as the writer ignorantly suggests, but it is a useful and indispensable article for every home. It is the symbol of the nation's prosperity and therefore freedom. It is a symbol not of commercial war but of commercial peace. It bears not a message of ill-will towards the nations of the earth but of good-will and self-help. It will not need the protection of a navy threatening world's peace and exploiting its resources, but it needs the religious determination of millions to spin their yarn in their own homes as to-day they cook their food in their own homes. I may deserve the curses of posterity for many mistakes of omission and commission, but I am confident of earning its blessings for suggesting a revival of the *Charkha.* I stake my all on it. For, every revolution of the wheel spins peace, good-will and love. And with all that, inasmuch as the loss of it brought about India's slavery, its voluntary revival with all its implications must mean India's freedom.

*Besides Mr. Gandhi, Mr. A. V. Thakkar and others, Sir P.C. Ray, the eminent Bengali chemist, is also convinced of the need for Charkha. In an introduction to a pamphlet (republished in *Young India* of 2nd February, 1922), Sir P. C. Ray urged that it was absurd for an Indian earning one anna per day to employ a Manchester spinner earning Rs. 3/5 a day, that it was useless to depend on Indian Mills in Bombay and elsewhere which profiteered at the expense of Bengal, that the 93 per cent. of the rural population should have subsidiary employment, that khadi could be spun with greater ease than fine yarn and that therefore all Bengalees should take a vow to use hand-spun and hand-woven coarse cloth only.

6th July, 1921

HOW TO BOYCOTT FOREIGN CLOTH

(BY M. K. GANDHI)

It is needless to say, at this time of the day, that the proposed boycott of foreign cloth is not a vindictive measure, but is as necessary for national existence as breath is for life. The quicker, therefore, it can be brought about, the better for the country. Without it, Swaraj cannot be established or retained after establishment. It is of the highest importance to know how it can be brought about even before the first day of August next.

To arrive at the boycott quickly, it is necessary (1) for the mill-owners to regulate their profits and to manufacture principally for the Indian market, (2) for importers to cease to buy foreign goods, (A beginning has already been made by three principal merchants), (3) for the consumers to refuse to buy any foreign cloth and to buy *Khadi* wherever possible, (4) for the consumers to wear only *Khadi* cloth, mill cloth being retained for the poor who do not know the distinction between Swadeshi and Pardeshi, (5) for the consumers to use, till Swaraj is established and *Khadi* manufacture increased, *Khadi* just enough for covering the body, (6) for the consumers to destroy Pardeshi cloth,* as they

* Under the heading, "Why Burn," Mr. Gandhi gave, in *Young India* of 28th July, 1921, the following reasons as to why foreign cloth should be burned; (1) It revives black memories and is a mark of shame, the East India Company having forced it on us and is an emblem of slavery; (2) the poor should not be given these for they ought not to be dead to patriotism, dignity and respect. And it is after all making a convenience of an act of renunciation to send cloth thus discarded even to Smyrna or elsewhere abroad. But the moral objection to the despatch abroad is certainly not so strong as to its use at home.

would destroy intoxicating liquors on taking the vow of abstinence, or to sell it for use abroad, or to wear it out for all dirty work or during private hours.

In reply to Mr. N. V. Thadani who, *apropos* the Bombay Congress Committee's decision, argued that if foreign cloth be destroyed, all foreign things should be dealt with likewise, that, if the East India Company's policy is the reason for burning them, English cloth alone should be burned and that if foreign cloth was poison to India, it was mean to foist it on the poor Turks, Mr. Gandhi wrote in *Young India* of 15th September, 1921:

I have already admitted the weakness of the argument in favour of sending foreign cloth to Smyrna. But it is a concession to Mussalman opinion. Nevertheless, the use of foreign cloth is poison in India, certainly not in Smyrna, for the cloth industry has never been Smyrna's lung, as it has been India's. In burning foreign clothes, we are burning our taste for foreign fineries. The effect upon India would have been equally disastrous, if Japan instead of England had tempted us in the first instance. The motive was to punish ourselves and not the foreigner. We are boycotting not British but all foreign cloth. The one would be meaningless as the other is a sacred duty. The idea of burning springs not from hate but from repentance of our past sins. A moment's reflection must show the writer that burning must make us earnest and thus stimulate, as it has stimulated, fresh manufacture. The disease had gone so deep, that a surgical operation was a necessity. The ill-clad or the naked millions of India need no charity but work that they can easily do in their cottages. Have not the poor any feeling of self-respect or patriotism? Is the gospel of Swadeshi only for the well-to-do?—M.K.G.

The following appeared in *Young India* of 11th August, 1921:

Burning in Bombay.—If anybody had any doubt as to the necessity and the practical value of burning foreign clothes, those who witnessed the ceremony at Mr. Sobani's yard in Parel must have had their doubts set at rest. It was a most inspiring sight witnessed by thousands of spectators. And as the flame leapt up and enveloped the whole pyramid, there was a shout of joy resounding through the air. It was as if our shackles had been broken asunder. A glow of freedom passed through that vast concourse. It was a noble act nobly performed. It has, I am sure, struck the imagination of the

It is to be hoped that all the parties referred to in the foregoing clauses will respond well and simulataneously. But in the end, success depends upon the persistant determination of the consumer. He has simply to decline to wear the badge of his slavery.

1*st September*, 1921

ETHICS OF DESTRUCTION*

(BY M. K. GANDHI)

The reader, I am sure, will appreciate my sharing

* Dwijendranath Tagore wrote a letter headed. "A dilemma," under date Shantiniketan, 7th September, 1921, to *Young India* (15th September):

On reading the article headed, "Ethics of Destruction" in your paper, the following dilemma has occurred to me:

1. If we consent to wear cheaper foreign clothes, our people will be ruined. This is hard to bear.

---

people as nothing else could have so far as Swadeshi is concerned. And it was as well that it was not rags that were burned, but some of the finest saris, shirts and jackets were consigned to the flames. I know that in some cases choisest silks kept by mothers for their daughters' wedding were given up for burning. The value consisted in destroying such costly things. Not less than one lac and a half pieces were burnt including articles worth several hundred rupees each. I am sure it was all for the good of the country. It would have been a crime to have given such things to the poor. Just imagine the poor people wearing the richest silks. To say the least it would have been highly inartistic and incongruous. The fact is that the majority of the articles burnt had no correspondence with the life of the poor. The dress of the middle classes had undergone such a transformation that it was not fit to be given to the poor people. It would have been like giving discarded costly toilet brushes to them. I hope therefore that the burning process will continue and spread from one end of India to the other and not stop till every article of foreign clothing has been reduced to ashes or sent out of India.

with him the following pathetic and beautiful letter from Mr. Andrews:

"I know that your burning of foreign cloth is with the idea of helping the poor, but I feel that there you have gone wrong. If

---

2. If we consent to wear dearer Swadeshi clothes, we shall have to submit to other hardships.

In both cases, it will be said with equal force by the contending parties, that we must submit to Providence.

My opinion is, that this so called submission to providence would be in the former case submission to the wrong side, and in the latter case submission to the right side.

Bada Dada Dwijendranarh Tagore (Shantiniketan) sent Mr. Gandhi the following letter also upon reading the article headed 'Ethics of Destruction.' "It is naturally a source of joy to me," wrote Mr. Gandhi in publishing it in *Young India* of 6th October, 1921, "that one so venerable and learned should agree with the ethical position taken up by me in opposition even to those whose opinion I value and respect. The reader will be glad to find that in Bada Dada we have a Rishi who in his quiet seclusion follows the national movement with the avidity of a young man of five and twenty, and is constantly thinking of it and praying for its success." Here is the letter:

There was a merchant, who suddenly became bankrupt, and was reduced to utter poverty; at the same time his wife was bed-ridden, suffering from accute rheumatic pain. There was an apothecary who dealt in patent medicine and always wanted cash payment from his customers. A doctor friend came to see the lady, and at the same time her daughter also came from her father-in-law's house to see her sick mother and brought with her a ten-rupee note, so that she might buy the patent medicine which could cure her pain immediately. She handed over the note to the doctor, and told him to get the medicine from the apothecary's shop which was near at hand, and went back. The doctor said that the medicine, no doubt, would give her instant relief, but at the same time it would injure her health to such a degree that she would remain decrepit throughout her life. However, the doctor said that he knew an electrician who was a next door neighbour and could cure rheumatism by electric treatment, his charge being Rs. 10. per day. In a month, he would perfectly cure the disease for good without in the least injuring her general health.

But the patient insisted that she wanted immediate relief, and

you succeed in boycotting all, or a greater part, of foreign cloth, it seems to me self evident that the price of mill-made cloth will rise and it will hit the poor. But there is besides a subtle appeal to racial feeling in that word 'foreign' which day by day seems to me to need checking and not fomenting. The picture of your lighting that great pile, including beautiful fabrics, shocked me intensely. We seem to be losing sight of the great beautiful world to which we belong and concentrating selfishly on India, and this must (I fear) lead back to the old bad selfish nationalism. If so, we get into the vicious circle from which Europe is now trying so desperately to escape. But I cannot argue it out. I can only say again, that it shocked me and seemed to me a form almost of violence; and yet I know how violence is abhorrent to you. I do not at all like this question of foreign cloth being made into a religion.

I was supremely happy when you were dealing great giant blows at the great fundamental moral evils, drunkenness, drug-taking, untouchability, race arrogance, etc., and when you were, with such wonderful and beautiful tenderness, dealing with the hideous

---

repeatedly asked the doctor for the banknote, so that she might send for the medicine at once. But the doctor repeatedly said that he could not conscientiously give her the note for the purpose, and he considered it to be a sin to do so. But the lady implored and beseeched him to give her the note. The doctor then took the match box from his pocket and burnt the note to ashes, and said that she need not be afraid, for he was going to bring the electrician immediately at his own expense, which her husband would pay back as soon as he repaired his fortune. When the hope of obtaining instant relief was thus frustrated in a moment, the patient said to the doctor, "do as you think fit." So the doctor immediately brought the electrician who assured her that she would be permanently cured within a month, if she allowed him to treat her. Then the doctor did what he had promised to the satisfaction of all parties.

Was the burning of the note a virtuous or a sinful act?

The above is exactly analogous with Mr. Gandhi's cloth burning. Mr. Gandhi refuses to give to the poor the relief that could have been given by distributing the foreign cloth among them. In order to avoid making them permanently miserable creatures, he promised to make them permanently happy by providing them with clothes made by their own hands.—M. K. G.

vice of prostitution. But lighting bonfires of foreign cloth and telling people it is a religious *sin* to wear it, destroying in the fire the noble handiwork of one's fellow men and women, one's brothers and sisters abroad, saying it would be 'defiling' to wear it—I cannot tell you how different all this appears to me. Do you know I almost fear now to wear the Khaddar that you have given me, lest I should appear to be judging other people as a Pharisee would, saying, "I am holier than thou!" I never felt like this before.

"You know how, when anything that you do hurts me, I must cry out to you and this has hurt me.

"I wrote the *Modern Review* articles which I have enclosed with such eager joy, because I felt certain that I had found your own life's meaning. But now my mind cries out to you that you are doing something violent, distorted, unnatural. You know that my love is stronger than ever, just as your love for your brother was when you felt he was doing something wrong. Do tell me what you mean. What you said in *Young India* about burning did not convince me a bit.

It is so like him. Whenever he feels hurt over anything I have done (and this is by no means the first such occasion), he deluges me with letters without waiting for an answer. For it is love speaking to love, not arguing. It is the outpouring of an anguished heart. And so it has been over the burning of foreign clothes.

What Mr. Andrews has put in loving language, correspondents already out of tune with me have written in coarse, angry and even vulgar words. Mr. Andrews', being words of love and sorrow have gone deep down in me and command a full answer, whereas the angry ones I was obliged to lay aside save for a passing reference. Mr. Andrews', being non-violent, charged with love, have told. The others being violent, charged with malice, took no effect and would have evoked angry retorts, if I was capable of or disposed to such retorts. Mr. Andrews' letter is a type of non-violence we need in order to win Swaraj quickly.

This is however by the way. I remain just as convinced as ever of the necessity of burning. There is no emphasis in the process on race feeling. I would have done precisely the same thing in the sacred and select family or friendly circles. In all I do or advise, the infallible test I apply is, whether the particular action will hold good in regard to the dearest and the nearest. The teaching of the faith I hold dear is unmistakable and unequivocal in the matter. I must be the same to friend and foe. And it is this conviction which makes me so sure of so many of my acts which often puzzle friends.

I remember having thrown into the sea a pair of beautiful field-glasses, because they were a constant bone of contention between a dear friend and myself. He felt the hesitation at first, but he saw the right of the destruction of a beautiful and costly thing, a present withal from a friend. Experience shows that the richest gifts must be destroyed without compensation and hesitation if they hinder one's moral progress. Will it not be held a sacred duty to consign to the flames most precious heirlooms, if they are plague infected? I can remember having broken to bits when a young man the loved bangles of my own dear wife, because they were a matter of difference between us. And if I remember right, they were a gift from her mother. I did it, not out of hate but out of love—ignorant, I now see in my ripe age. The destruction helped us and brought us nearer.

If the emphasis were on all foreign things, it would be racial, parochial and wicked. The emphasis is on all foreign cloth. The restriction makes all the difference in the world. I do not want to shut out English lever watches or the beautiful Japanese lacquer work.

But I must destroy all the choicest wines of Europe, even though they might have been prepared and preserved with all the most exquisite care and attention. Satan's snares are most subtly laid and they are the most tempting, when the dividing line between right and wrong is so thin as to be imperceptible. But the line is there all the same, rigid and inflexible. Any crossing of it may mean certain death.

India is racial to-day. It is with the utmost effort that I find it possible to keep under check the evil passions of the people. The general body of the people are filled with ill-will, because they are weak and hopelessly ignorant of the way to shed their weakness. I am transferring the ill-will from men to things.

Love of foreign cloth has brought foreign domination, pauperism and what is worst, shame to many a home. The reader may not know that not long ago hundreds of 'untouchable' weavers of Kathiawad having found their calling gone, became sweepers for the Bombay municipality. And the life of these men has become so difficult that many lose their children and become physical and moral wrecks ; some are helpless witnesses of the shame of their daughters and even their wives. The reader may not know that many women of this class in Gujarat for want of domestic occupation have taken to work on public roads, where, under pressure of one sort or another, they are obliged to sell their honour. The reader may not know that the proud weavers of the Punjab, for want of occupation, not many years ago, took to the sword, and were instrumental in killing the proud and innocent Arabs at the bidding of their officers, and not for the sake of their country but for the sake of their livelihood: It is difficult to make a successful appeal to these deluded hirelings and wean them from their murderous profession. What was once an honourable and artistic calling is now held by them to be disreputable. The weavers of Dacca, when they wove the world-famous *subnum*, could not have been considered disreputable.

Is it now any wonder, if I consider it a sin to touch foreign cloth? Will it not be a sin for a man with a very delicate digestive apparatus to eat rich foods? Must he not destroy them or give them away? I know what I would do with rich foods, if I had a son lying in bed who must not eat them but would still gladly have them. In order to wean him from the hankering, I would, though able to digest them myself, refrain from eating them and destroy them in his presence, so that the sin of eating may be borne home to him.

If destruction of foreign cloth be a sound proposition from the highest moral standpoint, the possibility of a rise in the price of Swadeshi cloth need not frighten us. Destruction is the quickest method of stimulating production. By one supreme effort and swift destruction, India has to be awakened from her torpor and enforced idleness. Here is what Mr. Allen, the author of the *Assam Gazetteer*, wrote in 1905 of Kamrup:

"Of recent years, the use of imported clothing has been coming into favour,—an innovation which has little to recommend it, as the time formerly spent at the loom is not as a rule assigned to any other useful occupation."

The Assamese, to whom I have spoken, realise the truth of these words to their cost. Foreign cloth to India is like foreign matter to the body. The destruction of the former is as necessary for the health of India as of the latter for the health of the body. Once grant the immediate necessity of Swadeshi, and there is no half-way house to destruction.

Nor need we be afraid, by evolving the fullest Swadeshi spirit, of developing a spirit of narrowness and exclusiveness. We must protect our own bodies from disruption through indulgence, before we would protect the sanctity of others. India is to-day nothing but a dead mass moveable at the will of another. Let her become alive by self-purification, *i.e.*, self-restraint and self-denial, and she will be a boon to herself and mankind. Let her be carelessly self-indulgent, aggressive, grasping; and if she rises, she will do so like Kumbhakarna only to destroy and be a curse to herself and mankind.

And for a firm believer in Swadeshi, there need be no pharisaical self-satisfaction in wearing *Khadi*. A Pharisee is a patron of virtue. The wearer of *Khadi* from a Swadeshi standpoint is like a man making use of his lungs. A natural and obligatory act has got to be performed, whether others do it out of impure motives or refrain altogether, as they do not believe in its necessity or utility.

PART V

THE NON-CO-OPERATION CAMPAIGN

PART V

THE NON-CO-OPERATION CAMPAIGN

12th May, 1920

NEITHER A SAINT NOR A POLITICIAN

(BY M. K. GANDHI)

A kind friend has sent me the following cutting from the April number of the *East and West*:

"Mr. Gandhi has the reputation of a saint, but it seems that the politician in him often dominates his decisions. He has been making great use of *hartals*, and there can be no gainsaying that under his direction *hartal* is becoming a powerful political weapon for uniting the educated and the uneducated on a single question of the day. The *hartal* is not without its disadvantages. It is teaching direct action, and direct action, however potent, does not work for unity. Is Mr. Gandhi quite sure that he is serving the highest behests of ahimsa, harmlessness? His proposal to commemorate the shooting at Jallianwalla Bagh is not likely to promote concord. It is a tragic incident into which our Government was betrayed, but is the memory of its bitterness worth retaining? Can we not commemorate the event by raising a temple of peace, to help the widows and orphans, to bless the souls of those who died without knowing why? The world is full of politicians and pettifoggers who, in the name of patriotism, poison the inner sweetness of man and, as a result, we have wars and feuds and such shameless slaughter as turned Jallianwalla Bagh into a shambles. Shall we not now try for a larger symbiosis such as Buddha and Christ preached, and bring the world to

> breathe and prosper together? Mr. Gandhi seemed destined to be the apostle of such a movement, but circumstances are forcing him to seek the way of raising resistances and group unities. He may yet take up the larger mission of uniting the world."

I have given the whole of the quotation. As a rule, I do not notice criticism of me or my methods except when thereby I acknowledge a mistake or enforce still further the principles criticised. I have a double reason for noticing the extract. For, not only do I hope further to elucidate the principles I hold dear, but I want to show my regard for the author of the criticism whom I know and whom I have admired for many years for the singular beauty of his character. The critic regrets to see in me a politician, whereas he expected me to be a saint. Now I think that the word "saint" should be ruled out of present life.* It is too sacred a word to be

*The following notes from *Young India* further explain Mr. Gandhi's position:

'*A Messenger of God*'—I have received a cutting, in which I am reported to be credited with being a messenger of God, and I am asked whether I claim to have any special revelation from God. I have already dealt with the miracles attributed to me. As to this the latest charge. I must disown it. I pray like every good Hindu. I believe that we can all become messengers of God, if we cease to fear man and seek only God's Truth. I do believe I am seeking only God's Truth and have lost all fear of man. I therefore do *feel* that God is with the movement of Non-co-operation. I have no special revelation of God's will. My firm belief is that He reveals Himself daily to every human being but we shut our ears to the 'still small voice.' We shut our eyes to the Pillar of Fire in front of us. I *realise* His omnipresence. And it is open to the writer to do likewise.—*Young India* of 25th May, 1921.

Blasphemy—A correspondent writes:—"I regret very much to inform you that one constantly sees pictures in which you and other leaders have been represented as Shri Krishna and Pandavas respectively. Will you not use your influence to stop this, as it must hurt the religious feelings of many like myself, who consider Shri Krishna to have been not merely a great man but God incarnate?"

lightly applied to anybody, much less to one like myself who claims only to be a humble searcher after Truth, knows his limitations, makes mistakes, never hesitates to admit them when he makes them and frankly confesses that he, like a scientist, is making experiments about some 'of the eternal verities' of life, but cannot even claim to be a scientist because he can show no tangible proof of scientific accuracy in his methods or such tangible results of his experiments as modern science demands. But though by disclaiming sainthood I disappoint the critic's expectations, I would have him to give up his regrets by answering him that

---

The correspondent has my fullest sympathy. I have not seen the pictures, but I hold it to be a blasphemy to represent me as Shri Krishna. I claim to be a humble worker and no more among many in a great cause, which can only be injured rather than advanced by glorification of its leaders. A cause has the best chance of success, when it is examined and followed on its own merits. Measures must always in a progressive society be held superior to men, who are after all imperfect instruments, working for their fulfilment. I would therefore urge, with all the strength at my command, enthusiasts or enterprising businessmen to observe some sense of proportion and withdraw all such pictures, which, like the one under notice, are undoubtedly calculated to wound deep religious susceptibilities.—*Young India* of 13th July, 1921.

My Ambition.—A persistent correspondent from Simla asks me whether I intend to found a sect or claim divinity. I have answered him by a private letter. But he would have me make a public declaration for the sake of posterity. I should have thought that I had in the strongest terms repudiated all claim to divinity. I claim to be a humble servant of India and humanity, and would like to die in the discharge of such service. I have no desire to found a sect. I am really too ambitious to be satisfied with a sect for a following. For I represent no new truths. I endeavour to follow and represent Truth as I know it. I do claim to throw a new light on many an old truth. I hope that this declaration will satisfy my inquirer and others like him.—*Young India* of 25th August, 1921.

the politician in me has never dominated a single decision of mine, and if I seem to take part in politics, it is only because politics encircle us to-day like the coil of a snake from which one cannot get out, no matter how much one tries. I wish therefore to wrestle with the snake, as I have been doing with more or less success consciously since 1894, unconsciously, as I have now discovered, ever since reaching years of discretion. Quite selfishly, as I wish to live in peace in the midst of a bellowing storm howling round me, I have been experimenting with myself and my friends by introducing religion into politics. Let me explain what I mean by religion. It is not the Hindu religion which I certainly prize above all other religions, but the religion which transcends Hinduism, which changes one's very nature, which binds one indissolubly to the truth within and which ever purifies. It is the permanent element in human nature which counts no cost too great in order to find full expression and which leaves the soul utterly restless until it has found itself, known its Maker and appreciated the true correspondence between the Maker and itself.

It was in that religious spirit that I came upon *hartal*. I wanted to show that it is not a knowledge of letters that would give India consciousness of herself, or that would find the educated together. The *hartal* illuminated the whole of India as if by magic on the 6th of April 1919. And had it not been for the interruption on the 10th of April, brought about by Satan whispering fear into the ears of a government conscious of its own wrong and inciting to anger a people that were prepared for it by utter distrust of the Government, India would have risen to an unimaginable height. The *hartal* had not only been taken up by the great masses of people in a truly religious spirit, but it was intended to be a prelude to a series of direct actions.

But my critic deplores direct action. For, he says, "it does not work for unity." I join issue with him. Never has anything been done on this earth without direct action. I rejected the word "passive resistance," because of its insufficiency and its being interpreted as a weapon of the weak. It was direct action in South Africa which told and told so effectively that it converted General Smuts to sanity. He was in 1906 the most relentless opponent of Indian aspirations. In 1914, he took pride in doing tardy justice by removing from the Statute Book of the Union a disgraceful measure which, in 1909, he had told Lord Morley would be never removed, for he then said South Africa would never tolerate repeal of a measure which was twice passed by the Transvaal Legislature. But what is more, direct action sustained for eight years left behind it not only no bitterness, but the very Indians, who put up such a stubborn fight against General Smuts, ranged themselves round his banner in 1915, and fought under him in East Africa. It was direct action in Champaran which removed an age-long grievance. A meek submission when one is chafing under a disability or a grievance which one would gladly see removed, not only does not make for unity, but makes the weak party acid, angry and prepares him for an opportunity to explode. By allying myself with the weak party, by teaching him direct, firm, but harmless action, I make him feel strong and capable of defying the physical might. He feels braced for the struggle, regains confidence in himself, and, knowing that the remedy lies with himself, ceases to harbour the spirit of revenge and learns to be satisfied with a redress of the wrong he is seeking to remedy.

It is working along the same line that I have ventured to suggest a memorial about Jallianwalla Bagh. The writer in *East and West* has ascribed to me a proposal which has never once crossed my mind. He thinks that I want "to commemorate the shooting at Jallianwalla Bagh." Nothing can be farther from my thought than to perpetuate the memory of a black deed. I daresay that, before we have come to our own, we shall have a repetition of the tragedy, and I will prepare the nation for it by treasuring the memory of the innocent dead. The widows and the orphans have been and are being helped, but we cannot "bless the souls of those who died without knowing why", if we will not acquire the ground which has been hallowed by innocent blood and there erect a suitable memorial for them. It is not to serve, if I can help it, as a reminder of a foul deed, but it shall serve as an encouragement to the nation that it is better to die helpless and unarmed and as victims rather than as tyrants. I would have the future generations remember that we who witnessed the innocent dying did not ungratefully refuse to cherish their memory. As Mrs. Jinnah truly remarked when she gave her mite to the fund; the memorial would at least give us an excuse for living. After all, it will be the spirit in which the memorial is erected that will decide its character.

What was the larger 'symbiosis' that Buddha and Christ preached? Buddha fearlessly carried the war into the enemy's camp and brought down on its knees an arrogant priesthood. Christ drove out the money-changers from the temple of Jerusalem and drew down curses from Heaven upon the hypocrites and the pharisees. Both were for intensely direct action. But even as Buddha and Christ chastised, they showed unmistakable gentleness and love behind every act of theirs. They would not raise a finger against their enemies, but would gladly surrender themselves rather than the truth for which they lived. Buddha would have died resisting the priesthood, if the majesty of his love had not proved to be equal to the task of bending the priesthood. Christ died on the cross with a crown of thorns on his head defying the might of a whole empire. And if I raise resistances of a non-violent character, I simply and humbly follow in the footsteps of the great teachers named by my critic.

Lastly, the writer of the paragraph quarrels with my 'grouping unities' and would have me to take up 'the larger mission of uniting the world.' I once told him under a common roof that I was probably more cosmopolitan than he. I abide by that expression. Unless I group unities, I shall never be able to unite the whole world. Tolstoy once said that, if we would but left off the backs of our neighbours, the world would be quite all right without any further help from us. And if we can only serve our immediate neighbours by ceasing to prey upon them, the circle of unities thus grouped in the right fashion will ever grow in circumference till at last it is conterminous with that of the whole world. More than that it is not given to any man to try or achieve. *Yatthaa pinde thatthaa brahmande** is as true to-day as ages ago when it was first uttered by an unknown Rishi.

* The Sanskrit expression means: "As with a ball of earth, so with the whole universe." What is meant to convey is that the characteristics of any combination of units will be those of the units themselves taken individually.

1st *September*, 1920

RIDICULE REPLACING REPRESSION

(By M. K. Gandhi)

Had His Excellency the Viceroy* not made it impossible by his defiant attitude on the Punjab and the Khilafat, I would have tendered him hearty congratulations for substituting ridicule for repression in order to kill a movement distasteful to him. For, torn from its context and read by itself, His Excellency's discourse on Non-co-operation is unexceptionable. It is a symptom of translation from savagery to civilization. Pouring ridicule on one's opponent is an approved method in civilised politics. And if the method is consistently continued, it will mark an important improvement upon the official barbarity of the Punjab. His interpretation of Mr. Montagu's statement about the movement is also not open to any objection whatsoever. Without doubt, a government has the right to use sufficient force to put down an actual outbreak of violence.

But I regret to have to confess that this attempt to pour ridicule on the movement, read in conjunction with the sentiments on the Punjab and the Khilafat preceding the ridicule, seems to show that His Excellency has made it a virtue of necessity. He has not finally abandoned the method of terrorism and frightfulness, but he finds the movement being conducted in such an open and truthful manner that any attempt to kill it by violent repression would not expose him only to ridicule but contempt of all right-thinking men.

Let us however examine the adjectives used by His Excellency to kill the movement by laughing at it. It is 'futile,' 'ill advised,' 'intrinsically inane,' 'un-

* Written in reply to a speech of Lord Chelmsford.

practical,' 'visionary.' He has rounded off the adjectives by describing the movement as the 'most foolish of all foolish schemes.' His Excellency has become so impatient of it that he has used all his vocabulary for showing the magnitude of the ridiculous nature of Non-co-operation.

Unfortunately for His Excellency, the movement is likely to grow with ridicule as it is certain to flourish on repression. No vital movement can be killed except by the impatience, ignorance or laziness of its authors. A movement cannot be 'inane' that is conducted by men of action as I claim the members of the Non-co-operation Committee are. It is hardly 'unpractical,' seeing that if the people respond, every one admits that it will achieve the end. At the same time, it is perfectly true that, if there is no response from the people, the movement will be popularly described as 'visionary'. It is for the nation to return an effective answer by organized Non-co-operation and change ridicule into respect. Ridicule is like repression. Both give place to respect when they fail to produce the intended effect.

27th October, 1920

FROM RIDICULE TO——

(BY M. K. GANDHI)

It will be admitted that Non-co-operation has passed the stage of ridicule. Whether it will now be met by repression or respect remains to be seen. Opinion has already been expressed in these columns that ridicule is an approved and civilized method of opposition. The viceregal ridicule, though expressed in unnecessarily impolite terms, was not open to exception.

But the testing time has now arrived. In a civilized country where ridicule fails to kill a movement, it begins to command respect. Opponents meet it by respectful and cogent argument and the mutual behaviour of rival parties never becomes violent. Each party seeks to convert the other or draw the uncertain element towards its side by pure argument and reasoning.

There is little doubt now that the boycott of the councils will be extensive, if it is not complete. The students have become disturbed. Important institutions may any day become truly national. Pandit Motilal Nehru's great renunciation of a legal practice which was probably second to nobody's is by itself an event calculated to change ridicule into respect. It ought to set people thinking seriously about their own attitude. There must be something very wrong about our Government to warrant the step Pundit Motital Nehru has taken. Post-graduate students have given up their fellowships. Medical students have refused to appear for their final examination. Non-co-operation in these circumstances cannot be called an 'inane' movement.

Either the Government must bend to the will of the people which is being expressed in no unmistakable terms through Non-co-operation, or it must attempt to crush the movement by repression.

Any force used by a government under any circumstance is not repression. An open trial of a person accused of having advocated methods of violence is not repression. Every State has the right to put down violence by force. But the trial of Mr. Zafar Ali Khan and two Moulvis of Panipat shows that the Government is seeking not to put down or prevent violence, but to suppress expression of opinion, to prevent spread of disaffection. This is repression. The trials are the beginning of it. It has not still assumed a virulent form but if these trials do not result in stifling the propaganda, it is highly likely that severe repression will be resorted to by the government.

The only other way to prevent the spread of disaffection is to remove the causes thereof. And that would be to respect the growing response of the country to the programme of Non-co-operation. It is too much to expect repentance and humility from a groverment intoxicated with success and power.

We must therefore assume that the second stage in the Government programme will be repression growing in violence in the same ratio as the progress of Non-co-operation. And if the movement survives repression, the day of victory of truth is near. We must then be prepared for prosecutions, punishments, even up to deportations. We must evolve the capacity for going on with our programme without the leaders. That means capacity for self-government. And as no government in the world can possibly put a whole nation in prison, it must yield to its demand or abdicate in favour of a government suited to that nation.

It is clear that abstention from violence and persistence in the programme are our only and surest chance of attaining our end.

The Government has its choice, either to respect the movement or to try to repress it by barbarous methods. Our choice is either to succumb to repression or to continue in spite of repression.

27th October, 1920

TO EVERY ENGLISHMAN IN INDIA *

Dear Friend,

I wish that every Englishman will see this appeal and give thoughtful attention to it.

Let me introduce myself to you. In my humble

* Messrs. H. A. Popley and G. E. Phillips replied to the above letter stating that, so far as the Empire promoted selfish exploitation of other races, traffic in intoxicating liquors, repressive legislation, conduct such as that led to Amritsar incident, they desired the end of it. They resented racial arrogance on the part of Anglo-Indians and stood for government on democratic principles for which they welcomed a national Assembly. Faith in a better ideal—in a commonwealth of free nations—was however working as a leaven among their countrymen. They question however the wisdom of boycott of schools and Mr. Gandhi's alliance with men who believed in the sword.

Mr. Gandhi replied in *Young India* of 15th December, 1920, under the heading, "Rejoinder," appreciating the friendly spirit of the letter. He, however, added :

The British nation has endorsed the Punjab and the Khilafat crimes. There is no doubt a dissenting minority. But a dissenting minority that satisfies itself with a mere expression of its opinion and continues to help the wrong-doer partakes in the wrong-doing. And when the sum total of his energy represents a minus quantity, one may not pick out the plus quantities, hold them up for admiration, and ask an admiring public to help regarding them. It is a favourite design of Satan to temper evil with a show of good and thus lure the unwary into the trap. The only way the world has known of defeating Satan is by shunning him. I invite Englishmen, who could work out the ideal they believe in, to join the ranks of Non-co-operationists. W.T. Stead prayed for the reverse of the British arms during the Boer war. Miss Hobhouse invited the Boers to keep up the fight. The betrayal of India is much worse than the injustice done to the Boers. The Boers fought and bled for their rights. When, therefore, we are prepared to bleed, the right will have become embodied, and the idolatrous world will perceive it and do homage to it.

Mr. Gandhi concluded with justifying his position *Re*: Khilafat, education, etc., on the grounds explained in the previous articles.

opinion, no Indian has co-operated with the British Government more than I have for an unbroken period of twenty-nine years of public life in the face of circumstances that might well have turned any other man into a rebel. I ask you to believe me when I tell you that my co-operation was not based on the fear of the punishments provided by your laws or any other selfish motives. It was free and voluntary co-operation based on the belief that the sum total of the activity of the British Government was for the benefit of India. I put my life in peril four times for the sake of the Empire,—at the time of the Boer war when I was in charge of the Ambulance corps whose work was mentioned in General Buller's dispatches; at the time of the Zulu revolt in Natal when I was in charge of a similar corps; at the time of the commencement of the late war when I raised an Ambulance corps and as a result of the strenuous training had a severe attack of pleurisy; and lastly, in fulfilment of my promise to Lord Chelmsford at the War Conference in Delhi, I threw myself in such an active recruiting campaign in Kaira District involving long and trying marches, that I had an attack of dysentry which proved almost fatal. I did all this in the full belief that acts such as mine must gain for my country an equal status in the Empire. So late as last December I pleaded hard for a trustful co-operation. I fully believed that Mr. Lloyd George would redeem his promise to the Mussalmans and that the revelations of the official atrocities in the Punjab would secure full reparation for the Punjabis. But the treachery of Mr. Lloyd George and its appreciation by you, and the condonation of the Punjab atrocities have completely shattered my faith in the good intentions of the Govern-

But though my faith in your good intentions is gone, I recognise your bravery : and I know that what you will not yield to justice and reason, you will gladly yield to bravery.

See what this Empire means to India:

Exploitation of India's resources for the benefit of Great Britain.

An ever-increasing military expenditure, and a civil service the most expensive in the world.

Extravagant working of every department in utter disregard of India's poverty.

Disarmament and consequent emasculation of a whole nation lest an armed nation might imperil the lives of a handful of you in our midst.

Traffic in intoxicating liquors and drugs for the purpose of sustaining a top heavy administration.

Progressively repressive legislation in order to suppress an ever-growing agitation seeking to give expression to a nation's agony.

Degrading treatment of Indians residing in your dominions;

And you have shown total disregard of our feelings by glorifying the Punjab administration and flouting the Mussalman sentiment.

I know you would not mind if we could fight and wrest the sceptre from your hands. You know that we are powerless to do that, for you have ensured our incapacity to fight in open and honourable battle. Bravery on the battle-field is thus impossible for us. Bravery of the soul still remains open to us. I know you will respond to that also. I am engaged in evoking that bravery. Non-co-operation means nothing less than training in self-sacrifice. Why should we co-operate with you when we know that by your administration of this great country we are being daily enslaved in an increasing degree? This response of the people to my appeal is not due to my personality. I would like you to dismiss me, and for that matter the Ali Brothers too, from your consideration. My personality will fail to evoke any response to anti-Muslim cry if I were foolish enough to raise it, as the magic name of the Ali Brothers would fail to inspire the Mussalmans with enthusiasm if they were madly to raise an anti-Hindu cry. People flock in their thousands to listen to us, because we to-day represent the voice of a nation groaning under iron heels. The Ali Brothers were your friends as I was, and still am. My religion forbids me to bear any ill-will towards you. I would not raise my hand against you even if I had the power. I expect to conquer you only by my suffering. The Ali Brothers will certainly draw the sword, if they could, in defence of their religion and their country. But they and I have made common cause with the people of India in their attempt to voice their feelings and to find a remedy for their distress.

You are in search of a remedy to suppress this rising ebullition of national feeling. I venture to suggest to you that the only way to suppress it is to remove the causes. You have yet the power. You can compel Mr. Lloyd George to redeem his promises. I assure you he has kept many escape doors. You can compel the Viceroy to retire in favour of a better one, you can revise your ideas about Sir Michael O'Dwyer and General Dyer. You can compel the Government to summon a conference of the recognised leaders of the people, duly elected by them and representing all shades of opinion so as to devise means for granting *Swaraj* in accordance with the wishes of the people of India.

But this you cannot do unless you consider every Indian to be in reality your equal and brother. I ask for no patronage, I merely point out to you, as a friend, an honourable solution of a grave problem. The other solution, namely repression, is open to you. I prophesy that it will fail. It has begun already. The Government has already imprisoned two brave men of Panipat for holding and expressing their opinions freely. Another is on his trial in Lahore for having expressed similar opinions. One in the Oudh District is already imprisoned. Another awaits judgment. You should know what is going on in your midst. Our propaganda is being carried on in anticipation of repression. I invite you respectfully to choose the better way and make common cause with the people of India whose salt you are eating. To seek to thwart their aspirations is disloyalty to the country.

I am,
Your faithful friend,
M. K. GANDHI.

1st *December*, 1920

AN ADVICE

(BY M. K. GANDHI)

The following anonymous advice has been received by me:

"Mahatma,"

"Listen to a woman's advice. Reject it, but ponder over it well before you reject, and pray to the All-Wise fervently for wisdom and inspiration. Concentration is strength, diversion is weakness. Limit your scope of Non-co-operation to only three things: foreign goods, the police service, and the army. Thereby you will remove all internal differences and strengthen our cause and speed Swaraj. Confine your efforts chiefly, not wholly, to the border tribes, the Sikhs, the Punjabis, the Dogras, and especially the Gurkhas. Work through secret societies as history teaches. and not by flourish of trumpets. Do not threaten but strike, and strike at the root and not at the branches. May God speed you and our cause to success.—Mrs. F."

The letter is undated. It is evidently not a woman's letter. It is too unwomanly to be a woman's letter. The women of India are infinitely braver than the letter would make them out to be. The writer writes about God but is possessed with the fear of the British bayonet, and would therefore gladly make use of the Sikh and the Gurkha steel. He has ill-digested the gospel of Non-co-operation. In his fearsomeness, he does not see that to exchange British brute force for any other brute force is no real remedy for the ills of India. And if it is the steel that is to decide the issue, it must be not Sikh or Gurkha steel, it must be all-India steel. That is the one supreme lesson that Europe teaches. If it is brute force that is to rule, then the millions of India must learn the art of war, or must for ever remain prostrate at the feet of him who wields the sword, whether he is *pardesi* or *swadeshi*. The millions must remain 'dumb driven cattle.' Non-co-operation is an attempt to awaken the masses to a sense of their dignity and power. This can only be by enabling them to realise that they need not fear brute force, if they would but know the soul within.

The Dogras, the Sikhs, the Gurkhas, and the other martial races of India, we do want, not for the purpose of giving battle to the British soldier, but for the purpose of refraining from helping the British soldier to subjugate us. We want our military classes to realise that they only perpetuate their own and our slavery by wielding the sword at the dictation of a British officer.

And that time will come when the school the writer represents has become defunct, and when the military classes have also understood the necessity of non-violence.

The writer makes me suspicious about himself when he asks us to concentrate our attention on foreign goods, the police and the army. He would thus secure internal unity by waiving all sacrifice, *i.e.*, purification by the very classes who have hitherto led public opinion—whereas the whole battle of Non-co-operation rages round these very classes. It may, for the time being, appear to have struck a discordant note, but, in fact, it will achieve real unity after the process of purification is over.

The writer has moreover missed the grand result already achieved by the absolute openness of our battle. In my opinion, the public has never expressed itself so fearlessly and openly as at present. It has almost lost the fear of the highly artificial law of sedition. When the writer talks of secret societies, he seems to talk of a bygone age. You cannot raise this great nation to its full height by the unclean methods of secrecy. We must, by boldly carrying on our campaign in the light of the blazing sun of openness, disarm the secret and demoralising police department. Non-co-operation is nothing if it does not strike at the root. And you strike at the root when you cease to water this deadly tree of the British Government by means of open and honorable Non-co-operation. The writer takes the name of God in vain, when he advocates in the same breath the secret ways of Satan.

6th April, 1921

A TAXING EXAMINER

(By M. K. Gandhi)

I would love to feel that I was an M.A. of the University of Non-co-operation. But my examiners show me that, whilst I have matriculated in that University, I have yet to fill many a term in the college course. Of all my many correspondents, the Sindhi friends are the most searching and even provoking.* What I present

* The following also appeared in *Young India* of 6th April, 1921:

Some tests.—Mr. T. B Purohit asks several pertinent questions about Non-co-operation. Before answering, it will be, perhaps, better to lay down some general tests. The primary motive of Non-co-operation is self-purification by withdrawing co-operation from an unrighteous and unrepentant Government. The secondary object is to rid ourselves of the feeling of helplessness by being independent of all Government control or supervision, *i.e.*, to govern ourselves in all possible affairs; and, in fulfilling both the objects, to refrain from doing or promoting injury, or any violence, to individual or property.

Let us apply the tests to Mr. Purohit's questions which are as follows:

(1) Whether a Non-co-operator can remain a member of a registered library or reading room?

If I were a member, I would first move my fellow members to disregister the library, and if I cannot, I would resign my membership and agitate for its disregistration, so as to make the people feel self-reliant and independent.

(2) Whether a Non-co-operator can remain a member of existing registered co-operative credit societies or banks which are solely managed by the public for the general public interest?

I have some experience of these societies. And I have no hesitation in saying that registration interferes with their free growth and increases people's dependence upon the Government. The idea of such societies is excellent and should be nursed, but we need not think that we cannot promote such societies without Government aid or inspection. I know the usual arguments in favour of registration. But on an analysis, they will all be found to betray want of faith in ourselves.

to the readers of "Young India" is but a sample of examination papers set to me. Here is one such from Sindh:

(1) Do you expect that violence will ensue from your movement of Non-co-operatiom?

If I did, I would not have advised it.

(2) Explain fully the doctrine of non-violence.

Non-violence is not doing, voluntarily, any injury to person or property. Thus, I would not punish or procure punishment even of General Dyer for his massacre, but I would not call it voluntarily doing injury to him to refuse to give him pension, or to condemn his action in fitting language. It is no part of my duty to protect a murderer even though he may be my son or father. I hold it to be my duty to withdraw my support from him. I will not kill a snake, neither may I harbour it.

(3) If violence ensues from your movement, will you retire to the mountains?

If violence results *from* Non-co-operation, or if Non-co-operators resort to violence, *i.e.*, if India makes violence her creed, and I have survived, I would not care to live in India. She will cease to evoke any pride in me. My patriotism is subservient to my religion. I cling to India like a child to its mother's breast, because I feel that she gives me the spiritual nourishment I need. She has the environment that responds to my highest aspiration. When that faith is gone, I shall feel like an

---

I would, therefore, in this instance, too, first try to convince my fellow-members of inutility of registration, and, on failure, secede from the society or bank, and educate the public to boycott such societies or banks. I know that, at least in one instance, registration has been removed, and everyone knows that India has thousands of unregistered flourishing banks whose honesty and business like methods are still among the wonders of the world.—M.K.G.

orphan without hope of ever finding a guardian. Then the snowy solitude of the Himalaya must give what rest it can to my bleeding soul. Needless to say, the violence that would drive me to the Himalayas is not this violence of language or rowdyism which my critics often fling in my face whilst reminding me of Himalayas. It is violence not due to Non-co-operation, nor is it violence of the real Non-co-operators. These outbursts are a legacy of our undisciplined past. It is being brought under check day by day. It is so insignificant as to be itself a mighty demonstration of the peace that reigns supreme in India to-day. This peace, in the face of provocation attempted by officials knowingly or unknowingly, in the shape of their vexatious and often illegal notices, must, if continued, in itself ensure Swaraj within the year. For it shows unity of purpose and determination among the people.

(4) What should other non-co-operators do, if such violence breaks out? Should they stop the preaching of Non-co-operation?

When (if ever) that tempestuous violence breaks out, true Non-co-operators would have died in the attempt to prevent violence. Question 3 presupposes my sole survivorship. But assume that I have scuttled to the Himalayas, (as it would then be to escape death), the remaining Non-co-operators would certainly be expected to remain true to their faith in spite of my cowardly retreat and be living witnesses to their faith till the flames overwhelm them. The voice of the preacher will then be drowned in the onrushing torrent of blood.

(5) If you retire to the mountains, what will be the fate of the poor students who have boycotted aided or Government institutions?

The questioner forgets that, when violence reigns

supreme in India, there will be no school, aided or unaided, for students to attend. Only those students are called upon to leave Government schools who consider it to be sinful to remain in them. The question of returning to such schools does not arise in their case. And what has my retirement to the mountains to do with the students' withdrawal? Every student is expected to judge for himself what is best for him and his country. The movement of self-government cannot—must not—be made to depend upon one man. I have but presented India with a new and matchless weapon, or rather an extended application of an ancient and tried weapon. She must reject or accept it for her own use. I cannot use it for her. I can use, have used it, for myself and feel free. Others have done, and feel likewise. If the nation uses the weapon, she becomes free.

(9) How far has your movement of Non-co-operation progressed?

So far that I feel Swaraj running to us. If we keep up the same velocity, we shall be a free nation within this year.

(7) Are you aware that most of the Non-co-operating workers are irresponsible? Have you ever condemned them?

I am not. On the contrary, I am aware that most of them are responsible, sober, honest and brave workers. I hope I have condemned irresponsibility wherever I have found it.

(8) Under what circumstances do you expect to get Swaraj in October?

I have often mentioned the conditions in these columns. The correspondent must look up the back numbers.

(9) Will the spinning-wheel solve the problem of India's poverty? If it will, how?

I am more than ever convinced that, without the spinning wheel, the problem of India's poverty cannot be solved. Millions of India's peasants starve for want of supplementary occupation. If they have spinning to add to their slender resources, they can fight successfully against pauperism and famine. Mills cannot solve the problem. Only hand-spinning—and nothing else—can. When India was forced to give up hand-spinning, she had no other occupation in return. Imagine what would happen to a man who found himself suddenly deprived of a quarter of his bare livelihood. Over eighty-five per cent. of her population have more than a quarter of their time lying idle. And, therefore, even apart from the terrible drain rightly pointed out by the G. O. M. of India, she has steadily grown poorer because of this enforced idleness. The problem is now to utilise these billions of hours of the nation without disturbing the rest. Restoration of the spinning wheel is the only possible answer. This has nothing to do with my special views on machinery or with the boycott of foreign goods in general. India is likely to accept the answer in full during this year. It is madness to tinker with the problem. I am writing this in Puri in front of the murmuring waves. The picture of the crowd of men, women, and children with their fleshless ribs under the very shadow of Jagannath, haunts me. If I had the power, I would suspend every other activity in schools, and colleges, and every where else, and popularise spinning; prepare out of these lads and lasses spinning teachers; inspire every carpenter to prepare spinning wheels; and ask the teachers to take these life-giving machines to every home, and teach them spinning. If I had the power, I would stop an ounce of cotton from being exported and would have it turned into yarn in these homes. I would not India with depots for receiving this yarn and distributing it among weavers. Given sufficient steady and trained workers, I would undertake to drive pauperism out of India during this year. This undoubtedly requires a change in the angle of vision and in the national taste. I regard the Reforms and everything else in the nature of opiates to deaden our conscience. We must refuse to wait for generations to furnish us with a patient solution of a problem which is ever-growing in seriousness. Nature knows no mercy in dealing stern justice. If we do not wake up before long, we shall be wiped out of existence. I invite the sceptics to visit Orissa, penetrate its villages, and find out for themselves where India stands. They will then believe with me that to possess, or to wear, an ounce of foreign cloth is a crime against India and humanity. I am able to restrain myself from committing suicide by starvation, only because I have faith in India's awakening, and her ability to put herself on the way to freedom from this desolating pauperism. Without faith in such a possibility, I should cease to take interest in living. I invite the questioner, and every other intelligent lover of his country, to take part in this privileged national service in making spinning universal by introducing it in every home, and make it profitable for the nation by helping to bring about a complete boycott of foreign cloth during this year. I have finished the questions and endeavoured to answer them. The most important from the practical stand-point was the one regarding spinning. I hope I have demonstrated the necessity of home-spinning as the only means of dealing with India's poverty. I know, however, that innumerable difficulties face a worker in putting the doctrine into execution. The most difficult, perhaps, is that of getting a proper wheel. Save in the Punjab where the art is still alive. the difficulty is very real. The carpenters have forgotten the construction and the innocent workers are at their wit's end. The chief thing undoubtedly, therefore, is for the worker to make himself acquainted with the art and the handling of spinning wheels. I lay down some simple tests for testing them. No machine that fails to satisfy the tests should be accepted or distributed.

(1) The wheel must turn easily, freely, and noiselessly.

(2) The turning handle must be rigidly fixed to the axle.

(3) The posts must be properly driven home and joints well fixed.

(4) The spindle must turn noiselessly and without a throb in its holders. Jarring sound cannot be avoided unless the holders are made of knit straw as in the Punjab, or of tough leather.

(5) No machine is properly made unless it manufactures in the hands of a practised spinner at least 2½ tolas of even and properly twisted yarn of six counts in an hour. I know a youngster, who has not had more than perhaps three months' practice, having been able to spin 2½ tolas of the above quality of yarn in 35 minutes. No machine should be given out until it has been worked for at least full one hour in the manner suggested and found satisfactory.

13*th April*, 1921

SUSPEND NON-CO-OPERATION

(By M. K. Gandhi)

Mr. Syed Riza Ali has addressed a public letter advising me to suspend Non-co-operation, so as to give Lord Reading* a chance of studying the situation in a calm atmosphere. In the first place, I see there is nothing in the atmosphere to prevent a study of the situation. In the second place, what disturbance there is, is either fomented by the authorities, or the situation is so mishandled as to give rise to bloodshed. In the Central Provinces, the Government are foisting the drink traffic on a public that is enraged against it. Of Rae Bareily, not having read newspapers, I have not sufficient data to be able to say anything. In any case, Mr. Riza Ali should address his appeal to the permanent officials who are provoking the people and creating alarm in the country. Thirdly, it is not within the power of any one man, even if he wished it, to suspend a movement adopted by the nation through its representative assemblies. Fourthly, what does Mr. Riza Ali mean by suspension of Non-co-operation? Should the title-holders temporarily recall their titles, the lawyers resume practice, the school-boys return to Government schools, the spinners put away their spinning wheels, carpenters cease making new wheels, and tipplers renew their acquaintance with the publicans? Does Mr. Riza Ali desire that national schools should for the time

* Lord Reading had just been appointed Viceroy. Mr. Gandhi, while firm that Non-co-operation should not be suspended, observed that so able and justice-loving a man as Reading should not be prejudged, His appointment kindled hopes which subsequently turned into bitter disappointment.

being close their doors? Unthinkable as it may seem, it is evident that Mr. Riza Ali does not understand the scope of Non-co-operation,* he does not realise that it is like a virtue whose practice cannot be suspended at

---

*The following appeared in *Young India* of 13th April, 1921:

The Times of India—Somewhat similar to the misconceptions I have alluded to is that of the *Times of India* to whose two recent articles a friend has drawn my attention. Not being able to read newspapers regularly, I do not know how much more I must be misrepresented by other journals. when the *Times of India*, which, supposed to know one better, I hope, innocently misunderstands me. One article credits me with having suspended Non-co-operation in that I advised the All-India Congress Committee to concentrate on men, money and the spinning wheel. I fear I cannot take the credit for I have not advised suspension; and I have already shown in answer to Mr. Riza Ali how it cannot be suspended. In the other article brought to my notice, I am not now 'the Mr. Gandhi of old' and, therefore, the reader is told, I will not admit defeat which Non-co-operators are said to have suffered in the first stage.

I see not only no defeat so far but I am amazed at the awakening among the people. I hold that it is a great thing to have created a strong public opinion against the institutions on which a Government builds its credit. *The Times of India* considers Non-co-operation 'to be an easy descent to hell.' I respectfully urge that it is a difficult ascent to heaven If it was a movement to produce anarchy, surely it could be precipitated any moment. *The Times of India* and other critics, who. I believe, are anxious to understand the inwardness of the struggle. will do well to appreciate the fact that not only I but all the leaders are doing their utmost to prevent anarchy. It is no use isolating me from the rest. The critics, who continue to suspect the Ali Brothers, do themselves and the cause a great injustice. The Brothers' position is perfectly clear and intelligible. To them violence is lawful under given circumstances. As Maulana Mahomed Ali often puts it, war is bad but there are worse things than war. The British Government has no two opponents more honourable than the Brothers. They mean no ill in a spirit of wantonness. They are honestly and industriously endeavouring to secure a peaceful settlement. But should their effort prove vain, either for want of response from the Government or the people, as lovers of their faith, they will

will. If Englishmen mean well by India, if Englishmen, who are dependent upon India for their maintenance, will be true to their salt, they must be reconciled to the abolition of the drink traffic and the total destruction of the traffic in foreign cloth and, therefore, also Lancashire cloth. Even when the Khilafat is fully protected, and the Punjab wound healed, the drink revenue cannot be revived nor the use of foreign cloth resumed. What surprises one is that there are intelligent and educated public workers in the country who do not see that this Government must proceed from wrong to wrong, so long as it does not cleanse itself of the original sins. No doubt it can, if it will, even without redressing the two wrongs, co-operate with the people in the two great dynamic movements—the battle against the drink evil and reinstatement of the spinning wheel in all its ancient dignity and purity. It will then break the edge of the two wrongs. Such a co-operation by the Government with the people will, however, increase the capacity of the people to ensure rectification of the two

---

not hesitate to precipitate war if they could. I refuse to be considered so simple as to be readily taken in by my companions. I believe my companions to be incapable of deceiving me. I believe them to be God-fearing, brave, and honourable men, whose association I prize as a privilege. As for my own attitude, whilst my faith would not permit me to invite or encourage a war of violence, I do contemplate with equanimity a state of war in preference to the present state of effeminate peace imposed by force of arms. And it is for that reason that I am taking part in this movement of Non-violent Non-co-operation even at the risk of anarchy being the ultimate result. The critics of Non-co-operation might, if they will, see in every one an intense desire to prevent anarchy and bloodshed. In any case, whether Non-co-operators are understood or not, they cannot afford to lose patience. They must continue to walk along the chosen and narrow path.

wrongs, and for that very reason the Government will not allow the peaceful progress of the drink campaign and boycott of foreign cloth by increased home-manufacture through the spinning wheel.

20th April, 1921

THE MISTS*

(By M. K. Gandhi)

Whenever I find my friends misunderstanding the movement, I mutter to myself the words of a celebrated

*Further, elucidating the idea in this article, in a reply to *The Times of India*, Mr. Gandhi wrote in *Young India* of 4th May, 1921, under the heading, "Gandhi Old and New":

The Times of India has returned to the charge of insincerity which was to be inferred from its previous article which I dealt with recently in these columns. It is a sober article to which no exception could be taken. I am certainly anxious to retain the reputation for sincerity which has been credited to me and which I certainly claim. My article, "The Mists," should generally be regarded as my last word to my critics. I must rely upon my actions for final explanation. No man can be called just, sincere, or good before his death. But I would like to correct some of the misstatements of *The Times of India* writer. Even when I declared Satyagraha, I was charged with having fallen from my original non-political state and the state of isolation. Even in South Africa, I was referred by my critics to the past. Every campaign that I have been connected with had its critics who praised my past at the expense of the then present. I state this fact not to disprove the present charge but to steel my heart against believing in the charge of unconscious insincerity and self-deception. I never suspended Satyagraha, I certainly never retired into private life. I suspended Civil Disobedience, and it remains still suspended, because I believed, as I still believe, the country not to be ripe for it. My Himalayan mistake was my miscalculation of the preparedness of the country. Non-co-operation of the type undertaken is not attended with any danger such as is attendant on Civil Disobedience. The latter is not

hymn: "We shall know each other better when the mists have rolled away." A friend has just sent me the

---

always a duty as Non-co-operation is. Hence it is that I have said that I must continue to advise Non-co-operation even though it may result in anarchy. Am I to recall my medals, or advise friends to recall theirs, or advise lawyers to resume practice because, supposing, anarchists have gained the upperhand? Am I to associate myself for fear of anarchy with a dishonest government which believes in Dyerism as a faith? I know that anarchy as a creed is devilish, but Dyerism is still more so, for it is anarchy wearing the mask of constituted authority. Ordered anarchy is infinitely worse than avowed anarchy. Only, in the latter event, I should dissociate myself from the anarchy of the mob as I have dissociated myself from the anarchy of the Government. For me both are evils to be shunned. I have not asked for reprisals against the author of the Jallianwala Massacre. I have asked for nothing more than the stopping of the pensions to the culprits and the dismissal of those who are yet holding office. I have not advised the Sikhs to give any pension to Mahant Naraindas or to keep him in office. I have ventured to advise the Sikhs to waive the prosecution of the murderers as I have advised the nation to waive the prosecution of the official murderers in the Punjab. I claim consistency of conduct about Amritsar and Nankhana. I have said repeatedly that I am acting towards the Government as I have acted towards my own dearest relatives. Non-co-operation on the political field is an extension of the doctrine as it is practised on the domestic field. The reference to my association with lawyers, etc., is hardly becoming. As a matter of fact, there are very few practising lawyers now holding office in Congress organisations.

I adhere to my opinion that, where Non-co-operators are in a majority, none who has not fully non-co-operated should hold office. The Congress Committee has not rejected the proposal. I do not know that practising lawyers presented me with any address in Surat. But I would not hesitate to receive one even from them so long as I was free to wean them from the error of their ways. So far as my association with the Ali Brothers is concerned, I consider it a proud privilege. But in South Africa, I had as my associates murderers and thieves, men who had certainly suffered imprisonment for attempts to murder or steal. Only they carried out their compact as to Non-violence as honourably as any other Satyagrahi. I see no difference

paragraphs on Non-co-operation* in the 'Servant of India' of the 14th inst. It is such a fruitless task explaining resolutions and motives. The year will soon pass away, and our actions, more than words, will demonstrate the meanning of Non-co-operation.

For me Non-co-operation is not suspended, and never will be, so long as the Government has not purged itself of the crimes against India, the Mussalmans and the Punjabees, and so long as the system is not changed to respond to the will of the nation. Surely it was necessary to remove the hallucination about titles, law-courts, schools and councils. I venture to think that on the whole the Nationalists have responded nobly in regard to these items. There are no titled men among them, no Nationalist lawyer who has not suspended practice has any public status among Non-co-operators, schools and colleges have furnished boys and girls who are now giving a good account of themselves by their sacrifice when the time of their trial has arrived. Those who have refrained from entering the Councils are rendering, as all who care may see, a service which they could not have rendered in the Council halls. The few who have given up their titles have shown the way to the others. All these are acting as leaven in the community. Now, there is little need for verbal propaganda among these special classes. The action and character of those who have renounced titles, schools, courts or councils, constitute a propaganda more telling and effective than speeches.

* Omitted in this collection.

---

between the old Gandhi and the New, except that the new has a clearer conception of Satyagraha and prizes the doctrine of Ahimsa more than ever. Nor, I promise *The Times of India* writer, is there any self-deception in this belief. But time must show who is right Precedent is on my side.

National schools are multipying themselves, boys are still leaving schools aud colleges. The Government statistics are hopelessly wrong. I remember having seen a councillor quoting that less than 3000 students had left educational institutions. This takes no count of thousands who are studying in nationalised schools. The number of suspensions of practice is steadily growing—see the list of suspensions in Dharwar and Guntur given in another column.* Even titles are still being surrendered. And as the timid or the cautious realise that the movement is a serious and a religious effort, that it has taken permanent hold of the people, they too will renounce.

I shall not be surprised if the history of the South African movement repeats itself in India. I should be surprised if it proves otherwise. The movement in South Africa started with a unanimous resolution. When the first part began, the majority weakened. Only 150 were found willing to court imprisonment. Then there was a settlement and a breach and a revival. Nobody even believed, save a few of us, that the response would come in time. Well, the last stage commenced with sixteen men and women who sought imprisonment. This was followed by a perfect storm. The whole community rose like a surging wave. Without organisation, without propaganda, all—nearly 40,000—courted imprisonment. Nearly ten thousand were actually imprisoned. The sequel is known. The community gained all it had fought for at the time. A bloodless revolution was effected after strenuous discipline in self-suffering.

I refuse to believe that India will do less. To recall Lord Canning's words, under the blue and serene Indian sky, a cloud no bigger than a man's thumb may appear

* Omitted here.

on the horizon, but it may any moment assume dimensions unexpected by any, and no man can tell when it may burst. When India as a whole will responed by action, I cannot say. But this I do say that the educated classes to whom the Congress has appealed will one day—and probably during this year,—respond in a manner worthy of the nation.

But whether they do or not, the progress of the nation cannot be arrested by any person or class. The uneducated artisans, the women, the men in the street, are taking their share in the movement. The appeal to the educated classes paved the way for them. The goats had to be sifted from the sheep. The educated classes had to be put upon their trial. The beginning had to be made by and through them. Non-co-operation has hitherto, thank God, followed its natural course.

Swadeshi propaganda in its intensive and exclusive form had to come and it has come in its order. It was, and is, part of the Non-co-operation programme. It is, I claim, the biggest, the safest, and the surest part. It could not be taken up earlier in its present form. The country had to see its way clear to the spinning wheel. It had to be purged of the old superstitions and prejudices. The country had to appreciate the futility of the boycott of British goods merely, and equally of *all* foreign goods. It had to see that it lost its liberty by giving up Swadeshi in cloth and that it could regain it by reverting to hand-spun and hand-woven cloth. It had to see that it lost its artistic taste and talent, when it innocently ceased to spin and weave by the hand. It had to see that it was not even so much the military drain, as the loss of this supplementary industry that sapped India's vitality and made famines an ever-recurring event in Indian life. Men with faith in the spinning wheel had to rise in every province, and people had to appreciate the beauty and the use of *khaddar*.

All these things have now happened. The crore men and women and the crore rupees are required to resuscitate this national *dharma*. The problem is not that of a few *charkhas* but of putting *charkhas* in every one of the six crore homes. The problem is that of manufacturing and distributing the whole of the cloth required by India. It cannot be done by one crore rupees. But if India gives one crore rupees, one crore men and women, and introduces two million *charkhas* in working order in as many homes before the 30th June, she is nearly ready for Swaraj, because the effort will have created, in the nation as a whole, all the qualities that make a nation good, great, self-reliant and self-contained. When the nation has, by a voluntary effort, completed its boycott of foreign cloth, it will be ready for Swaraj. Then I promise that the various forts in the Indian cities will, instead of being an insolent menace to the freedom of India, become play-grounds for her children. Then the relations between Englishmen and ourselves will have been purified.

Then the Lancashire vote will have been sterilised. And Englishmen will, if they choose, remain in India as friends and equals, with one sole aim—truly of benefiting and helping India. Non-co-operation is a movement intended to invite Englishmen to co-operate with us on honourable terms or retire from our land. It is a movement to place our relations on a pure basis, to define them in a manner consistent with our self-respect and dignity.

But call the movement by any other name.. Call it 'Swadeshi and temperance.' Assume that all these previous months have been a waste of effort. I invite the

Government and the Moderate friends to co-operate with the nation in making hand-spinning universal and in making drinking a crime. Neither party need speculate as to the result of these two movements. The tree will be judged by its fruit.

20th April, 1920

DIVIDE AND RULE

(BY M. K. GANDHI)

Sir William Vincent's speech * before the Legislative Assembly makes painful reading. I shall hope that he has been kept in utter darkness by his informants and that the speech is ignorant, not unscrupulous.

It is a plausible defence of the Government's policy of repression. It is a distortion or concoction of facts. It is an appeal to our cupidity and a mis-interpretation of the motives of Non-co-operationists.

He says that the declared object of Non-co-operationists is paralysis of the Government and that "in their effort to achieve the object there is no source of discontent which they have not used." Now both these statements are half-truths. The primary object of Non-co-operation is nowhere stated to be paralysis of the Government. The primary object is self-purification. Its direct result must be paralysis of a Government which lives on our vices and weaknesses. Similarly it is a dangerous half-truth to say that we have left no source of discontent unused. We could not help using sources of legitimate discontent. But Non-co-operationists have rigidly refrained from using any and every discontent, if only because we would weaken our cause if we did.

* Omitted in this collection.

The illustration of what I mean will be best seen from the refutation of the very next sentence which Sir William has spoken in support of the contention: "wherever they find discord between employer and employee, there some agent or emissary of Non-co-operation party proceeds at once to foster discontent and promote ill-feeling." This is not only untrue, but it is an incitement to the two to oppose Non-co-operation. The avowed policy of Non-co-operation has been not to make political use of disputes between labour and capital. They have endeavoured to hold the balance evenly between the two—we would be fools if we wantonly set labour against capital. It would be just the way to play into the hands of a Government which would greatly strengthen its hold on the country by setting capitalists againt labourers and *vice versa*. In Jharia, for instance, it was a Non-co-operator who prevented an extending strike. The moderating influence in Calcutta was that of Non-co-operators. The latter will not hesitate to advance the cause of strikers where they have a just grievance. They have ever refused to lend their assistance to unjust strikes. "Where there is a racial ill-feeling", declares Sir William Vincent, "these emissaries hurry on their evil errand." He must know that this is a false statement. There is a racial feeling between Englishmen and Indians. There is the memory of Jallianwala—an evergreen. But "these emissaries" have been veritable messengers of peace. They have every where restrained the fury of the unthinking. And I make bold to say that, but for the existence of the spirit of Non-violence, there would have been more innocent blood spilt in spite of the threat of Dyerism and O'Dwyerism. Our fault has lain in refusing to lick the boot that has kicked, in withdrawing co-operation until there was frank repentance. Non-co-operators are to be blessed for turning the fury of an outraged people from Englishmen to the system they are called upon to administer.

But Sir William is nothing if he is not thorough in his attempt to divide and rule. He declaims: " where there are quarrels between landlord and tenant—have we not seen this in the United Provinces?—there again proceed these emissaries of evil to propagate unrest, and stir up disorder." Sir William should know that the tenant movement is under the control of Pandit Jawaharlal Nehru whose one purpose regarding the tenants has been to educate them to be patient and calm. Sir William has simply attempted to set the landlords against the Non-co-operation movement. Fortunately, the landlords know as well as the tenants that, so long as they are just, they have nothing to fear from Non-co-operators.

'The movement,' says Sir William, 'is purely destructive, and, so far as I have been able to ascertain, contains no element of constructive ability.' It is undobtedly destructive in the sense that a surgeon who applies the knife to a diseased part may be said to make a destructive movement. This destructive movement bears in it the surest seed of construction as the surgeon's knife contains the seed of health. Is temperance destructive? Are national schools springing up everywhere destructive? Are the thousands of spinning wheels destructive of a nation's prosperity? They will destory foreign domination whether it hails from Lancashire or is threatened from Japan.

Having attempted to set classes against masses, Sir William proceeds to paralyse both, with the feeling of helplessness and the fear to internal strife and aggression from without. Is Hindu-Muslim Unity such flimsy stuff that we shall begin to quarrel as soon as the British guns are withdrawn from our shores? Were we sixty years ago less able to protect ourselves than we are now? Or is it not a fact that, judged by the western standard, we were never so helpless as we now are? 'Self-government, as I have said before, connotes the power of self-protection, and a country which cannot protect itself is not prepared for immediate and complete self-government.' In this one sentence, Sir William has unwittingly condemned British rule and proved the necessity of immediate mending or ending of that rule. According to my method—the method of suffering or soul-force,—the country is to-day prepared for self-protection. According to Sir William's standard, the reforms have nothing in them to enable India even in a hundred years to arm herself for defence against a combination of world powers. Judged by that standard, the reforms do forge stronger the chains that bind India and make her feel helpless. The speaker talks glibly of impending destruction of every vested interest. He needs to be reminded that the greatest vested interest of India—her self-sufficiency—was destroyed by this foreign domination and the speaker's plan will still further deepen India's poverty.

Even as Sir William has misrepresented Non-co-operators' motives, so has he misconstrued their methods. We have not failed in our effort regarding the educated classes. I admit that the response in practice might have been greater from them. But I make bold to say that the vast majority of them are with us in spirit, though the flesh being weak, they are not able to make what from their point of view is a sacrifice. We have been trying to act on the masses from the commencement. We regard them as our main-stay, for it is they who have to attain Swaraj. It is neither the sole concern of the monied men or that of the educated class. Both must subserve their interest in any scheme of Swaraj, and as soon as the masses have attained sufficient self-control and learnt mass discipline, we shall not hesitate, if necessary, to advise them to suspend payment of taxes to a Government that has never truly looked after their welfare and that has exploited and terrorised them every time they have shown the least symptom of rising against their exploitation.

Sir William has been extremely disingenuous in describing the Government's methods of dealing with Non-co-operation. Defence of India Act he will not use against men who have hurt nobody and who are restraining people from committing violence. But he is using ordinary statutes against them in an extraordinary manner under a licence given to him by Non-co-operators who will not challenge orders in a court of law. He will not conciliate the malcontents by granting Swaraj, for that would lead to anarchy. He does not bother his head about the two things which have caused all the unrest and which have acted like two active and corroding poisons in the Indian body—the Khilafat and the Punjab wrongs. He does not tell us what catastrophe is likely to befall India if the Khilafat promises were redeemed and the Punjab wound healed.

He has ornamented his extraordinary speech with an ungentlemanly and insinuating attack upon the Ali Brothers who are putting up a noble fight for Islam and India, and a still more ungentlemanly attack on a 'gentleman of the name of Yakub Hasan', and an ungracious reference to his Turkish wife.

As I have said, it was painful for me to read the speech, still more painful to have to criticise it. I assure the reader that, self-restrained as I am in language, the speech has been a severe strain upon my capacity for restraint. I have scored out many an adjective which I believe would accurately describe Sir William's performance. I am sorry.

25th May, 1921

THE SIMLA VISIT

(By M. K. Gandhi)

Many are asking why I waited upon His Excellency the Viceroy.* Some inquire why the author of Non-co-operation should seek to see the Viceroy. All want to know the result of the interview. I like the rigorous scrutiny of the Non-co-operators, who, more than Caesar's wife, must be above suspicion. Non-co-operation is self-reliance. We want to establish Swaraj, not obtain it from others. Then why approach a Viceroy? This is all good, so far as it goes. And I should be a bad representative of our cause, if I went to anybody to ask for Swaraj. I have had the hardihood to say that Swaraj could not be granted even by God. We would have to earn it ourselves. Swaraj from its very nature is not in the giving of anybody.

But we want the world with us in our battle for freedom, we want the good-will of everybody. Our cause, we claim, is based upon pure justice. There are certain things we want Englishmen to surrender. All these things need mutual discussion and mutual understanding. Non-co-operation is the most potent instrument for creating world opinion in our favour. So long as we protested and co-operated, the world did not

*Not long after Lord Reading arrived, Mr. Gandhi had an interview with the Viceroy.

understand us. The erst while lion of Bengal in his early days used to relate the story of Englishmen, who asked him how many broken heads there were in India, if things were really so bad as he represented them to be. That was the way John Bull understood best. The other question the world has undoubtedly been asking is if things are really so bad, why do we co-operate with the Government in so pauperising and humiliating us? Now the world understands our attitude, no matter how weakly we may enforce it in practice. The world is now curious to know what ails us. The Viceroy represents a big world. His Excellency wanted to know why I, with whom co-operation was an article of faith, had non-co-operated. There must be something wrong with the Government or me.

And so His excellency mentioned to Pandit Malaviyaji and to Mr. Andrews that he would like to see me and hear my views. I went to see the Panditji, because he was anxious to meet me. I hold him in such high regard that I would not think, even if he was well and I could help it, of letting him come to me. As it was, he was too weak to travel to me. It was my duty to go to him. And when I heard the purport of his conversation with His Excellency, I did not require any persuasion to prompt me to ask for an appointment, if His Excellency wished to hear my views. I have devoted so much space to the reason for my seeking an appointment, for I wanted to make clear the limits and the meaning of Non-co-operation.

It is directed not against men but against measures.*

* Commenting on one of Lord Reading's speeches, Mr. Gandhi wrote in *Young India* of 13th July, 1921, under the heading, 'A Running sore':

We admit that we did wrong in Amritsar, in Kasur, in Jallianwala

It is not directed against the Governors, but against the system they administer. The roofs of Non-co-operation lie not in hatred but in justice, if not in love. Gladstone used to draw a sharp distinction between bad actions and bad men. He was accused of discourtesy for using some very strong expressions about the arts of his

---

and in Gujranwala. We have been made to pay for it heavily. We have been humiliated, kicked. Both the innocent and the guilty have been hanged. We have ourselves made a frank, free and open confession from many a platform. We ask for no humiliation of official wrong-doers. All we ask is, that they may not be imposed upon us as masters. An English official once frankly told me that, rather than be party, by remaining in the service, to the removal from the pension list of Sir Michael O'Dwyer or General Dyer, he would resign. I told him that, whilst I could see my way to sympathise with such an attitude, he must not expect me to agree with him. Nor did he. Hundreds, if not thousands, of Englishmen and Englishwomen consider Sir Michael O'Dwyer and General Dyer as saviours of the Empire and the honour of their kind. It is highly likely that, if I were an Englishman intent upon holding India at any cost, I would feel even as they. But I hold that, so long as that attitude is retained, so long must co-operation between the Government and the people be impossible.

The plain fact is, that, Englishmen are not prepared to remain in India on the sufferance of the millions of Hindus and Mussalmans. The latter are not prepared to give the former any advantageous position by reason of their controlling all the most destructive appliances that human ingenuity has ever invented. There is no choice before the latter but that of making a supreme effort to neutralise the effect of all those appliances by ceasing to fear them, *i.e.*, by non-resistance. This may all appear to be arrogant or visionary. I hope, however, that Lord Reading at any rate will soon find that I have spoken the real mind of India. And the sooner this fundamental truth is realised, the sooner will there be real hearty co-operation between Englishmen and Indians. I am longing for such co-operation, and it is this very longing which deters me from accepting any apology, no matter how tempting, for co-operation. Non-co-operation is not born of ignorance and ill-will, but it is the only effective step towards co-operation, and therefore it rises from knowledge and love.

opponents. He put up the defence that he would have failed in his duty if he had not characterised their actions as they deserved to be, but he did not therefore mean to convey that his opponents deserved the epithets he had used about their acts. As a youth, when I heard this defence, I could not appreciate it. Now with years of experience and use, I understand how true it was. I have found some of the truest of my friends capable of indefensible acts. For me there are few truer men than V. S. Srinivasa Shastriar, but his actions confound me. I do not think he loves me less, because he believes that I am leading India down to the abyss.

And so I hope this great movement of Non-co-operation has made it clear to thousands, as it has to me, that, whilst we may attack measures and systems, we may not, must not, attack men. Imperfect ourselves, we must be tender towards others and be slow to impute motives.

I therefore gladly seized the opportunity of waiting upon His Excellency and of assuring him that ours was a religious movement designed to purge Indian political life of corruption, deceit, terrorism and the incubus of white superiority.

The reader must not be too curious. He must not believe the so-called 'reports' in the press. The veil must remain drawn over the details of the conversation between the Viceroy and myself.* But I may assure him that I explained, as fully as I knew, the three claims—the Khilafat, the Punjab, and Swaraj,—and gave him the genesis of Non-co-operation. His Excellency heard me patiently, courteously and attentively. He appeared to me to be anxious to do only the right thing.

* An agreed statement giving an account of the interview was subsequently published by Government. *See* Appendix.

We had a full discussion of the burning topics as between man and man. We discussed the question of non-violence, and it appeared to me to be common cause between us. Of that I may have to write more fully later.

But beyond saying that we were able to understand each other, I am unable to say that there was more in the interview. Some may think with me that a mutual understanding is in itself no small gain. Then, in that sense, the interview was a distinct success.

But at the end of all the long discussions, I am more than ever convinced that our salvation rests solely upon our own effort. His Excellency can only help or hinder. I am sanguine enough to think that he will help.

We must redouble our efforts to go through our programme. It is clearly as follows: (1) removal of untouchability, (2) removal of the drink curse, (3) ceaseless introduction of the spinning wheel, and the ceaseless production of *Khaddar* leading to an almost complete boycott of foreign cloth, (4) registration of Congress members, and (5) collection of Tilak Swaraj Fund.

1st *June*, 1921

THE POET'S ANXIETY

(By M. K. Gandhi)

The Poet of Asia, as Lord Hardinge called Dr. Tagore, is fast becoming, if he has not already become, the Poet of the world. Increasing prestige has brought to him increasing responsibility. His greatest service to India must be his poetic interpretation of India's message to the world. The Poet is therefore sincerely anxious that

India should deliver no false or feeble message in her name. He is naturally jealous of his country's reputation. He says he has striven hard to find himself in tune with the present movement. He confesses that he is baffled. He can find nothing for his lyre in the din and the bustle of Non-co-operation. In three forceful letters,* he has endeavoured to give expression to his misgivings, and he has come to the conclusion that Non-co-operation is not dignified enough for the India of his vision, that it is a doctrine of negation and despair. He fears that it is a doctrine of separation, exclusiveness, narrowness and negation.

No Indian can feel anything but pride in the poet's exquisite jealousy of India's honour. It is good that he should have sent to us his misgivings in language at once beautiful and clear.

In all humility, I shall endeavour to answer the Poet's doubts. I may fail to convince him or the reader who may have been touched by his eloquence, but I would like to assure him and India that Non-co-operation in conception is not any of the things he fears, and he need have no cause to be ashamed of his country for having adopted Non-co-operation. If, in actual application, it appears in the end to have failed, it will be no more the fault of the doctrine, than it would be of Truth, if those who claim to apply it in practice do not appear to succeed. Non-co-operation may have come in advance of its time. India and the world must then wait, but there is no choice for India save between violence and Non-co-operation.

Nor need the Poet fear that Non-co-operation is intended to erect a Chinese wall between India and the West. On the contrary, Non-co-operation is intended

*Omitted in this collection.

to pave the way to real, honourable and voluntary co-operation based on mutual respect and trust. The present struggle is being waged against compulsory co-operation, against one-sided combination, against the armed imposition of modern methods of exploitation masquerading under the name of civilisation.

Non-co-operation is a protest against an unwitting and unwilling participation in evil.

The Poet's concern is largely about the students. He is of opinion that they should not have been called upon to give up Government schools before they had other schools to go to. Here I must differ from him. I have never been able to make a fetish of literary training. My experience has proved to my satisfaction that literary training by itself adds not an inch to one's moral height and that character-building is independent of literary training. I am firmly of opinion that the Government schools have unmanned us, rendered us helpless and God-less. They have filled us with discontent, and providing no remedy for the discontent, have made us despondent. They have made us what we were intended to become—clerks and interpreters. A Government builds its prestige upon the apparently voluntary association of the governed. And if it was wrong to co-operate with the Government in keeping us slaves, we were bound to begin with those institutions in which our asssociation appeared to be most voluntary. The youth of a nation are its hope. I hold that, as soon as we discovered that the system of Government was wholly, or mainly evil, it became sinful for us to associate our children with it.

It is no argument against the soundness of the proposition laid down by me that the vast majority of the students went back after the first flush of enthusiasm. Their recantation is proof rather of the extent of our degradation than of the wrongness of the step. Experience has shown that the establishment of national schools has not resulted in drawing many more students. The strongest and the truest of them came out without any national schools to fall back upon, and I am convinced that these first withdrawals are rendering service of the highest order.

But the Poet's protest against the calling out of the boys is really a corollary to his objection to the very doctrine of Non-co-operation. He has a horror of everything negative. His whole soul seems to rebel against the negative commandments of religion. I must give his objection in his own inimitable language. "R, in support of the present movement has often said to me that passion for rejection is a stronger power in the beginning than the acceptance of an ideal. Though I know it to be a fact, I cannot take it as a truth . . . Brahmavidya in India has for its object *Mukti* (emancipation), while Buddhism has *Nirvana* (extinction). *Mukti* draws our attention to the positive and *Nirvana* to the negative side of truth. Therefore, he emphasised the fact of *dukha* (misery) which had to be avoided and the Brahmavidya emphasised the fact of *Ananda* (joy) which had to be attained." In these and kindred passages, the reader will find the key to the Poet's mentality. In my humble opinion, rejection is as much an ideal as the acceptance of a thing. It is as necessary to reject untruth as it is to accept truth. All religions teach that two opposite forces act upon us and that the human endeavour consists in a series of eternal rejections and acceptances. Non-co-operation with evil is as much a duty as co-operation with good. I venture to suggest that the Poet has done an unconscious injustice to Buddhism in describing *Nirvana* as merely a negative state. I make bold to say that *Mukti* (emancipation) is as much a negative state as *Nirvana*. Emancipation from or extinction of the bondage of the flesh leads to *Ananda* (eternal bliss). Let me close this part of my argument by drawing attention to the fact that the final word of the Upanishads (Brahmavidya) is *Not*. *Neti** was the best description the authors of the Upanishads were able to find for *Brahman*.

I therefore think that the Poet has been unnecessarily alarmed at the negative aspect of Non-co-operation. We had lost the power of saying 'no'. It had become disloyal, almost sacrilegious to say 'no' to the Government. This deliberate refusal to co-operate is like the necessary weeding process that a cultivator has to resort before he sows. Weeding is as necessary to agriculture as sowing. Indeed, even whilst the crops are growing, the weeding fork, as every husbandman knows, is an instrument almost of daily use. The nation's Non-co-operation is an invitation to the Government to co-operate with it on its own terms as is every nation's right and every good government's duty. Non-co-operation is the nation's notice that it is no longer satisfied to be in tutelage. The nation had taken to the harmless (for it), natural and religious doctrine of Non-co-operation in the place of the unnatural and irreligious doctrine of violence. And if India is ever to attain the Swaraj of the Poet's dream, she will do so only by Non-violent Non-co-operation. Let him deliver his message of peace to the world, and feel confident that India, through her Non-co-operation, if she remains true to her pledge, will have exemplified his message. Non-co-operation is intended to give the very meaning to patriotism that the Poet is yearning after. An India prostrate at the feet of

* Not this.

Europe can give no hope to humanity. An India awakened and free has a message of peace and goodwill to a groaning world. Non-co-operation is designed to supply her with a platform from which she will preach the message.*

8th June, 1921

THE VICEROY SPEAKS

(BY M. K. GANDHI)

What the Viceroy said † with reference to Mr. Shafi's speech, is perhaps equally true of his own. For His Excellency described Mr. Shafi's speech as post-prandial oratory. I have been, in my early days, a student more or less accurate of the so-called historic speeches delivered by various Prime Ministers at the Mansion House. They seemed to me to have always an air of unreality about them. And it grieves me, after having studied the speech of His Excellency the Viceroy, to have to say that this one also has the same air of unreality about it. Not that Lord Reading had intended to clothe his speech with any such air. On the contrary, there are in it evident traces of his having laboured to deliver a true message to an expectant India. But the speech has failed, in my humble opinion, in doing so, because of the many limitations that the office of a Viceroy carries with it. He could not, for instance, override the tradition of claiming infallibility for British rule. He laid it down as a proposition, "beyond the possibility of a doubt," that "here in India there can be no trace, and

* For further criticism of Dr. Tagore's views, see *infra*.
† Omitted in this collection.

must be no trace of racial inequality." There is no more unreal proposition to the ear of the Indian than this, because his experience, be he ever so tall, belies it. Superiority of race is a passion, has become almost a religion, with the average Englishman. Nor does he strive to conceal it from view. It obtrudes itself upon you in India as it does in the Colonies. It is written in the Statute Book. One misses in the Viceregal speech a frank recognition of the many failures of the past, and therefore a sincere desire for opening a new page.

If His Excellency, in my humble opinion, was hardly happy in his statement of the 'fundamental principle of British rule,' he was, I fear, even less so in his reference to Maulanas Shaukat Ali and Mahomed Ali. I recognise that he has been exceedingly cautious in his speech. He has attempted not to wound susceptibilities. As a matter of fact, there was no question of wounding susceptibilities. He need not have spared the Maulanas where they might have erred. The statement made by the brothers was instigated by me and me alone. It is an apology tendered to friends, and not to the Government. It is made not to evade prosecution, but to put themselves right with their own conscience and with their friends. The assurance to them, therefore, that there would be no prosecution so long as they abided by their undertaking was gratuitous, if not offensive. Lord Reading's Government is free to take up prosecution against the brothers at any moment they choose.

This campaign of Non-co-operation has no reference to diplomacy, secret or open. The only diplomacy it admits of is the statement and pursuance of truth at any cost. The Viceroy showed me the speeches. I realised that some passages in them did not read well. They were capable of being interpreted as an incitement to violence, and I realised that, prosecution or no prosecution, there was no doubt in my mind as to the advice I should tender to the brothers. I venture to suggest to His Excellency that, if he is anxious to disarm Non-co operators, he will do so only by becoming undiplomatic and absolutely frank. The latter seek and need no shelter or protection, and I invite His Excellency to reciprocate by not shielding the offenders amongst the governing class.

Indeed, there is no room in the India of to-day and of to-morrow, for a governing class. His Excellency will therefore find out his mistake, if he clings to the belief that "Indians will respond whole-heartedly to the just rule which we [British] intend to carry on." I venture to prophesy that it is not what the British intend that will count for the future destiny of India, but what the Indians themselves intend. And they are claiming more and more insistingly to govern themselves, anyhow. Good government, they are coming to see, is no substitute for self-government.

The fear, then, is not about His Excellency's intentions, which I am convinced are good, but the fear is as to the ideal he is working for. He thinks of a high destiny which is in store for India at some indefinable period, whereas Non-co-operators at any rate are of opinion that India's high destiny is even now being frustrated by the existing system, which appears to them to be devised for her prolonged, if not perpetual, subjection. Sometimes a difference of degree itself constitutes a difference of ideals. And I hold it to be an ideal totally different from India's, when anybody considers that, whilst the distant goal must be one of freedom for India, its present state must be that of tutelage. Swaraj is India's birthright, as the late Lokamanya Tilak truly said. And India throughout these long, long years, has been baulked of her birthright. No wonder that she has become impatient.

Lord Reading will, perhaps, now better appreciate the truth of the proposition he has read and heard; *viz.*, that any action of the Government that falls short of the fullest reparation, however good it may appear in itself, will, by non-co-operators at least, be charged with a bad motive, that of prolonging India's agony in her slave-state. British rule, to-day, lies under a shadow. It is tainted with the blood of the innocent victims of Jallianwala, and with treachery towards Islam. And even as the purest milk poured into a poison bowl will be counted by every sane man as poison, so will every act of the British Government be judged in the light of its immediate past. The unrest of India can only be cured by dealing with the causes which have brought it about, never by covering the bitterness thereof by sweets of office or other privileges, no matter how tempting they may be, if they are not capable of dealing effectively with the causes themselves.

29th June, 1921

OFFICERS AND OFFICIALS

The Viceroy's reply to the Ahmadiyya community* shows that he has passed into the hands of a bureaucracy that is clever, united and utterly unscrupulous. His defence of officers and officials supplies the meaning of racial equality. The Viceroy sees no inequality in the impunity with which Europeans may commit crimes against Indian humanity. I recall the extraordinary

*Omitted in this collection.

judgment of a Punjab magistrate, who considers that justice is satisfied, when he draws upon his imagination for extenuating causes, and fines a young Irish soldier fifty rupees for interfering with the liberty of an innocent Indian woman.

His Excellency does not care to study the daily press, which is replete with instances of insults hurled against Indians by Europeans. He seems to be unaware of the fact that British officers will not tolerate the presence of Indian judges in their railway compartment. The Viceroy says, 'there is no foundation, I verily believe, for any suggestion that the British official is anxious to assert racial superiority over the Indian with whom he comes in contact.' I assure Lord Reading that his observation is so contrary to the everyday experience of the average Indian that it must prejudice the people against the soundness of his judgment or even the honesty of his purpose. They will see in his certificates of character to officials and officers, a studied refusal to see the truth and do justice. They will not give him the benefit of the doubt, and think, as I do, that the Viceroy is not wilfully blind but is not permitted to see things, except so much as the bureaucracy is prepared to let him see.

The fact is that it is impossible for any Viceroy to see the truth, living as he does on the mountain tops seven months in the year, and in complete isolation even when he lives on the plains. Imagine a businessman in Bombay, conducting his business from topfloor, with only lifts and phones between him and his clerks and salesmen. The people of Bombay are hardly satisfied with the condition, wherein at least there is an unbroken chain of inhabited floors between the top and the ground floors. But with the big business house in Simla and the groaning millions on the plains, there is solid dead rock, and even the piercing cry of the feeble millions is broken into nothingness, as it heaves up to the mountain-top from the plains. Prince Siddhartha was kept in such isolation that he did not know what misery, want and death were. He was an honest lad. But for an accident, he would have been lost to the world. Well, he was living not much above his people. He had the same coloured pigment as his father's subjects. Whilst Siddhartha was living hardly thirty feet above the people, the Viceroy lives seven thousand five hundred feet above them. It would be no fault in him, if he did not willingly cut himself from the people that he could not understand the people's hopes and fears. So long as he lives both physically and mentally in Simla, so long will he be kept in ignorance of the truth, even as Siddharta was. But there is an accident in store for him, as there was for the renowned young prince, whom the world worships as Buddha, the Enlightened. Non-co-operation is the accident. And if Lord Reading has open eyes and open ears, it will not be long before he sees and hears the truth.

6th October, 1921

NOT GOOD ENOUGH

(By M. K. Gandhi)

The Report of the Repressive Laws Committee* would

*A Committee appointed by Government under the Presidentship of Dr. Sapru, the Law Member, recommended the repeal of the Rowlatt Act, the Press Act, etc., and a modification of the existing laws so as to enable Government to possess adequate punitive powers.

have excited thrilling interest fifteen months ago. No one now cares whether these laws are repealed or retained. They have ceased to frighten us, because we have ceased to fear arrests and imprisonments. We are now seeking not repeal of particular laws or regulations but a total repeal of the system that has made them possible. We know now that the Government could have done (under ordinary law) all the things (with slight variations) that they have hitherto done under the laws that are to be repealed. Under pressure of necessity, the law advisers of the Government have discovered a potency in sections 144, 107 and 108 of the Criminal Procedure Code, of which they were before unaware. The fact is that, even if the ordinary law were to be changed without a change of spirit, the people of India will not be benefitted by it.

Though therefore the report has no interest for the people, it is a document of abiding interest to the student of the political situation in the country. The report could have been written in identical language ten years ago by the most reactionary of the civilians. The Committee concludes :—"Their retention (of Prevention of Seditious Meetings Act and Part II of the Indian Criminal Law Amendment Act, 1908) is necessary in view of recent occurrences and possible developments which we cannot but regard with the greatest apprehension." I have no doubt that every repressive measure that has ever been undertaken has been passed under the same 'stern sense of duty' under which the laws mentioned are being retained.

I refuse to think that the officials who passed all the repressive laws took wanton delight in repression. Lord Curzon certainly considered the Partition of Bengal a matter of public necessity, and the opponents of the measure as enemies of progress. Sir Michael O'Dwyer honestly believed that the educated classes were idiots who did not know their own welfare, meddled in things they never knew, and were no benefactors of the masses in whose name they professed to speak. General Dyer undoubtedly thought that, unless he could teach us a lesson, every Englishwoman's life was in jeopardy. Only in all these three cases, we (including the majority of the members of the Committee) considered the officials to have perverted minds incapable of understanding the proud spirit of Bengal, of understanding the agony of educated India which knew by instinct the wants of the masses more truly than the officials in spite of their winter picnics amongst them, and of knowing that Indians would not be guilty of such diabolical unmanliness as General Dyer in his unsoldierlike manner thought us to be. We then used to think the officials were wrong in overriding the people's wishes even though the latter might be in error. We argued to our complete satisfaction that we were the best judges of our own condition. But now a change has come over some of us. Some of us occupy the position analogous to that of the officials. These consider themselves to be 'trustees' for the ignorant masses who are being misled by visionaries, if not also by unscrupulous agitators, and therefore in the teeth of their stubborn opposition (ignorant it may be), they carry on 'reformed' legislatures, suppress a revolt in Malabar by sacrificing precious blood although we have offered men ready to go to Malabar unarmed and persuade the Moplahs to stop their mad career of pillage and plunder. They sincerely believe that by so doing they are serving the country.

Thus we are no better than before: probably, if not

certainly, we are much worse off. For now there is not only a foreign bureaucracy to cope with, but we have also a national bureaucracy to contend against. Well has Lala Lajpat Rai remarked in his forceful analysis of the report that what we want is not a change of masters but a change of the system, a change in the relations between the people and the state. The latter must represent the people or be ended. The reason for the strange phenomenon disclosed in the report is to be found in the fact that the non-official members are irresponsible, but they sincerely feel that they know our interests better than we. How can any tinkering, therefore, answer the aspirations of a people that are awakened and are prepared to suffer for what they understand to be their rights ?

15th December, 1921

IRELAND AND INDIA

(By. M. K. Gandhi)

Lord Reading has flung Ireland in our faces. Let us contemplate for a moment that romantic nation. I would like the reader to believe with me that it is not the blood that the Irishmen have taken which has given them what appears to be their liberty. But it is the gallons of blood that they have willingly given themselves. It is not the fear of losing more lives that has compelled a reluctant offer from England, but it is the shame of any further imposition of agony upon a people that loves its liberty above everything else. It is the magnitude of the Irish sacrifice which has been the deciding factor. The late President Kruger, when he, with a handful of his undisciplined countrymen hurled his ultimatum against the British Empire, said he would stagger humanity. He meant that he would sacrifice every Boer man, woman and child and leave not a single Boer heart to subdue, but he would gladly let Englishmen roam about the desert soil of South Africa dyed with the blood of the Boer martyrs. And England yielded when she was tired of concentration camps in which Boer women and children died like flies, and when she was choked with the bloody feast that the Boers had provided for her. And even so has Ireland been staggering humanity for many a long year. And England has yielded when she is able no longer to bear the sight of blood pouring out of thousands of Irish arteries. I know for certain that it is not legal subtleties, discussions on academic justice or resolutions of Councils and Assemblies that will give us what we want. We shall have to stagger humanity even as South Africa and Ireland have been obliged to. Only instead of repeating South African and Irish histories, Non-co-operators are learning from the living examples of these two nations the art of spilling their own blood without spilling that of their opponents. If they could do that, they could attain Swaraj within a few days or a few months. But if they want slavishly to follow South Africa and Ireland, Heaven help India. Then there is no Swaraj during the present generation. And I know that the Swaraj promised by Mr. Montagu, no matter how well-intentioned he may be, will turn out to be a delusion and a snare. Councils are no factories for making stout hearts. And freedom is miasma without stout hearts to defend it.

2nd March, 1922

A LYING PLACARD

(By M. K. Gandhi)

The following was handed to me in Delhi:

"Mahatma Gandhi's Message to Non-co-operators—'Stop Hartals'—'Suspend all Non-co-operation Activities'—*O ye people of Delhi!—Come in your hundreds!! Come in your thousands!!!*—Welcome H. R. H. The Prince of Wales."

I can only conclude that it was issued by or on behalf of the Government. I wish, indeed, I could have sent such a message. As it was, my misfortune was to send quite the opposite. *Hartals* were specifically retained in the Bardoli resolutions. Non-co-operation activities were not suspended. Aggressive Civil Disobedience and aggressive activities, preparatory thereto, were suspended. Apart from the untruthfulness of the placard, the organisers did not even see that such lies could only strengthen the movement. But as a Non-co-operator, I do not want even co-operators to resort to lies. I need not be told that Non-co-operators too have been found lying. It is known by this time that I spare neither friend nor foe when it is a question of departing from the code of honour.

22nd June, 1921

OUR SHORTCOMINGS

(By M. K. Gandhi)

Whilst Dr. Pollen's criticism,* by reason of its

* Dr. Pollen, I.C.S. (retired), wrote a letter to Mr. Gandhi. Its 'ignorant' preface was followed by an unsupported denial of all the propositions that Mr. Gandhi believes in common with the rest of India, viz.: (1) The Indian administration is the most expensive in the world. (2) India is poorer to-day than it ever has been (3) The

ignorance and arrogant assumptions, irritates without helping, an Englishman in Madras, who signs himself 'John Bull', sends the following very helpful and candid criticism :

"Permit an Englishman to send you a few words of appreciation of your work and career, and a few words of explanation. I am moved to do this by your remarks in 'Young India' on Lord Reading's speech. You have, it seems to me, the most valuable capacity of seeing and stating the simple truth, in greater measure than any other living politician. You see the root of the trouble in India in the fact that the European in India looks down upon the Indian as an inferior. So do I. But what I want you to consider is, first, 'Whose fault is that ?' And second, 'How can it be mended ?'

"Can the Engliseman in India help regarding Indians in the mass as inferior to his own people ? Those of us who try to see things as they are, what do we see ? We

---

drink evil has been never so bad as it is to-day. (Nobody has contended that there was no drink evil in India before the advent of the British.) (4) India is held in the last resort by a system of terrorism." Mr. Gandhi continued : "Not only does Dr. Pollen deny these truths known to us all, but he asserts that the administration is cheaper than elsewhere. and forgets that the Indian Civil Service is the most highly paid service in the world, and that more than a third of the revenue is absorbed by the military service. Imagine the state of a family. which has to devote a third of its income for paying its doorkeepers. Dr. Pollen asserts that India is 'really a marvellously rich country inhabited for the most part by a comparatively poor and reckless peasantry.' He then asks me to multiply the average annual income of Rs. 27 by five, and argues that Rs. 135 a year for a family of five will suffice for its support. I suggest to him that Rs. 2-4 0 per head per month will not feed, clothe and house the poorest among the poor, and that I should still further reduce the average for the masses of poor men, because it is reached by including the millions of millionaires. The average income of the poor, therefore, is an incontestible proof, not only of the poverty, but of the semi starvation of India.'

find that the Indian is inferior to the Englishman as a servant or employee. He is less conscientious, he takes more holidays, he requires to be watched. We find he is inferor to the Englishman as a master or employer, he has less justice and less generosity. We find him inferior as an animal, he succumbs to disease, he (if of higher class) usually shirks exercise, and is very frequently a worn out old man, when he ought to be in his prime. His children die in swarms. Here, in Madras, the deaths of children under five frequently are half as numerous as the births. He is inferior as a citizen, very seldom does he resist any pressure towards bribe-giving. He boasts of his humanity, because he will not kill animals, but he lets even cows starve to death, and nowhere in any civilised land are horses and oxen so ill-treated as in India. In order to maintain purity of married life, he has built up the institutions of pre-puberty marriage and perpetual widowhood, and yet venereal disease is even more rampant in India than in England, and in the name of religion little girls are trained up to prostitution. What record can India show of lives devoted to non-Indian humanity like all those British men and women who (to take one example only) are at work now in what were enemy countries in the war? If India had obtained complete Swaraj, and were in danger, would five million men out of every forty-five millions of population voluntarily enlist in her armies?

"Out of her vast population, how few are the great men India has produced—three living, Tagore, Bose and Gandhi—an extraordinarily rich crop for India! The population of England in the time of Queen Elizabeth was no greater than that of Mysore to-day.

"All this may seem a very one-sided and mistaken

view to you. Probably it is. But how can an Englishman help seeing the comparison between English and Indian in some such light as that?

"If so, the remedy is in Indian hands, and not in ours. You are already pointing the way. I do not like your term 'Non-co-operation,' and it does not seem to me to express your meaning. I should prefer 'Independent action.' Let Indians abolish untouchability; let them exercise restraint in marital relations, and not procreate millions of children doomed to early death, let Brahmins learn at school to spin and weave and cease to despise manual labour, let India have one common language spoken and understood from Kashmir to Comerin, whatever local vernaculars are permitted to survive. When there is something to be done, let Indians put their hands to the plough and not merely say, 'The Government must. . . ' These things you have preached, and if all the people who shout 'Gandhiji-ki-Jai' will do them, Englishmen will speedily entertain much more respect for Indians than they feel at present. When these things are done, there are plenty more to do. Most important of all, perhaps, is to rebel against the tyranny of ancient custom, when it is no longer felt to be right or necessary. You will no doubt be able to point out one task after another. Meanwhile, we wait and see. Will that crore of rupees be paid up? Will the twenty lakhs of *charkhas* be obtained, and if so, will they be used? Will Non-co-operators learn to maintain self-discipline and abstain from riot? Will Gandhi cease calling a Government consisting of men who, on the average, are more ready to make sacrifices for the service of India than the average Indian is—satanic? Will the temperance crusade lead to any better result than unbridled illicit drinking?

"If we find these questions answered in the affirmative —if—But shall we?

"The English are ready to give respect, when it is earned Do not complain that English do not respect Indians: complain instead that Indians have not commanded respect.

"For my own part, I believe you are accomplishing and will accomplish great things. 'Man lives by admiration, hope and love.' On these. great nations are built up. May India be one."

John Bull's letter shows that the writer has attempted to understand the movement. Much of his criticism is not wholly undeserved. 'John Bull' has given the experience of the average Englishman. His generalisations in my opinion cannot be sustained. His experience is confined to a microscopic minority of Indians, drawn to the cantonments from ambitious motives, and by no means representing the mass of the people. In my opinion, based upon an extensive experience of both the races, man for man, the Indian is, in no way, inferior, in all that matters, to any other race in the world. That as animals we are inferior to Englishmen, must be admitted. But that is due more largely to the climate than to anything else. The charge of indifference to the welfare of our animals can also, I think, be easily sustained. I do not believe that, except in large towns, we suffer more from venereal diseases than the other races. Dedication of girls to prostitution is certainly a serious blot on our culture. If Indians were trained in the same manner as Englishmen, and if India was similarly situated as England, she would give quite a good account of herself. But we have a different culture, which, I hope, we will retain to the end of time. India's temperament is not warlike. She would refuse to see any greatness in sending her millions to the trenches for the purpose of killing fellowmen, even though the latter might be in error. India, including her Mussalman population, is in my opinion, more fitted for self-suffering than for inflicting suffering upon others. It is in this belief that I have ventured to offer to her Non-co-operation as a remedy for her many ills. Whether she will really respond or not, remains to be seen. If it has been taken up purely from revengeful motives, it will fail. If it has been taken up, as I believe it has been, for the purpose of self-purification and self-sacrifice, it is bound to succeed.

That Indians are not a nation of cowards, is proved by the personal bravery and daring of her martial races, whether Hindu, Mussalman, Sikh or Gurkha. My point is that the spirit of fighting is foreign to India's soil, and that probably she has a higher part to play in the evolution of the world. Time alone can show what is to be her destiny.

But 'John Bull' is entitled to treat all I have said in answer as so much special pleading. I would, far rather, that we took such criticism as a friendly warning, and that we began to rid ourselves of all our impurities. I agree with 'John Bull' that it is better to command respect than to grumble about the want of it. And that is exactly the reason why India has taken up Non-co-operation. The writer does not like the word. I would reject it to-day, if I could find a better. But it is the only word that meets the case. We have co-operated long enough in our own degradation. It is our duty to refuse to do so any longer, One need not even apportion the blame. The fact stands, as 'John Bull' has properly admitted, that the average Englishman has little respect for us. We must therefore stand aside, till we and they *feel* as equals.

But there is the other side to 'John Bull's argument. His attitude betrays race-repugnance. Assuming the shortcomings to exist, just as they are described by the writer, is that a reason for looking down upon Indians as inferior beings? Or, does not the doctrine of equality require mutual regard, irrespective of the possession of the same qualities? Does not 'John Bull' commit the same error that many Hindus do regarding the "untouchables'? If I am right in calling the spirit of untouchability satanic, am I less right in calling the cult of English superiority also by the same name? Do Englishmen behave towards their less fortunate brethren, in the same way as they behave towards Indians? Do they not consider themselves to be born to rule, and Indians born to obey, even as Hinduism is said to have consigned the 'untouchables' to perpetual subjection? My whole soul has risen against the existing system of Government, because I believe that there is no real freedom for India under the British connection, if Englishmen cannot give up the fetish of their predestined superiority. This attitude of Englishmen has deprived the tallest Indian of any chance of rising to his full height, and therefore, in spite of all the good intentions of individual English administrators, we have really lost in our own estimation, so much so that many of us have come to believe that we require a long course of training under the English, whereas it is my conviction that we are to-day quite fit to govern ourselves, and therefore we must resolutely refuse to co-operate with them in the administration of reforms that fall short of full self-government. We will no doubt make mistakes, more perhaps than now. We shall learn through our mistakes, never by being forcibly prevented from making them.

29*th June*, 1921

A PLANTER'S LETTER

The following appeared in *Young India* of 29th June, 1921:

To Mr. Gandhi and others connected with the Non-co-operation movement.

Gentlemen,—Have you ever stopped to consider where your Non-co-operation movement is going to lead India to? I speak if permitted to do so, for Assam. Non-co-operation is not the remedy or I might say, is not the cure for the evident evils you are trying to remedy, but Legislation. Legislation and compulsory Education are the things required in the order named. Coolies in Assam are very well looked after by the Europeans on European-controlled tea gardens, but even on such gardens, I regret to say that the desire on the part of your own countrymen to extort money by unfair means from the poor coolie, is more prevalent than it should be. The wages on tea gardens are distinctly good. My coolies earn on an average for men Rs. 10-3-8, for women Rs. 6-12-8, for children Rs. 4-15-9. (Sept. 1920, Government Return.) In addition to these wages, free fuel, free medicine, free medical attendance, free housing accommodation, free grazing ground, free khet-land, rice supplied at much below bazaar rates, when there is a famine on,—these are the comforts bestowed on all the tea garden coolies of Assam, and I feel sure you will agree with me, that "you can take a horse to the water, but you cannot make him drink," and you can take a coolie to the work, but you cannot make him work, and in every trade in the world a man must work. Piece-work is given on tea gardens, and a coolie can easily earn 8 to 10 annas daily, and a women 4 to 6 annas, *i.e.*, in the busy season. If they work with all the comforts above named, can you, Non-co-operators, truthfully say the tea planter is not doing his duty towards the coolie? No. Your countrymen are beginning to realize that the poor coolie is not quite such a fool as he used to be, and not quite so much can be extorted out of him now-a-days, and as money must come from somewhere, you are endeavouring to take it through the coolie by telling him that he is under-paid, sweated labour, ill-treated and a host of other lies. Where are your reformed councils and where is your legislating? At the rate you people are travelling, you will be looking for your rest shortly.

What then is required? In Assam, the pay of the Indian staff should be increased 100 per cent. This would stop the present dissatisfaction amongst the Baboo clerks, who in most cases have to support huge families on salaries which are inadequate, and to live they are compelled to get the money from somewhere; hence they extort from the weak, being unable to from the strong. My staff consists of one head and two junior clerks, all disgracefully paid. They do not steal; they can't because I am too cute for them. I am exceedingly sorry for them, but as I am struggling to live, I cannot help them from my salary. Why should I? My employers do not permit me to pay them more, but it is bound to come sooner or later by agitation and co-operation, not by Non-co-operation. The present methods of your followers have a Bolshevik tendency by turning a land now flowing with milk and honey into a chaos, and causing complete disorganization Agitate, agitate. Co-operate, co-operate, co-operate. Legislate, legislate, legislate. I ask you to banish Non-co-operate from your mind, it is useless.

I want to see in Assam:

1. Free Labour. Liberty is wealth.

2. That every Indian can travel to any part of India from famine area to plenty without any restriction.

3. Legislation, the same for the poor and the rich, the same for the Indian and the European.

4. Legislation for the protection of Indian women and their Eurasian children.

5. The Panchayat as a legal power on every tea garden, of which the manager must be president and if the Indian can be tried by Panchayat, so can the European. (My coolies have permission to try me.)

6. Payment of sick allowance to coolies compulsory.

7. Restriction of coolie marriages abolished.

8. Confinement allowance to pregnant women compulsory for six months.

You will admit all these suggestions are for legislators, not for Non-co-operators: therefore agitate, co-operate, legislate, and *Love.* "*Mobut*" *Dayal* "*Mia*" *Beechar.*

What are your members of Council doing? Make them work, make them pass suitable laws, make them listen to the voice of the people. My strength is the love of my people (coolies); their strength is the love of their people, Indians, Non-co-operators, co-operators, agitators, Legislators, or it should be a house that is divided against itself and cannot stand; therefore co-operate. I co-operate with all Indians that I meet or have dealing with, from the Chamar to the Brahman, from the coolie to the Rajah. All are God's own, all are human, all I regard as my brothers. Where I can help I help, where I can alleviate trouble I do so, where I can teach I teach. Let brotherly love continue, it is not obtained by Non-co-operation, but brotherly love is co-operation.

I am glad to be able to tell you that I am the manager of the most contented and the best paid labour force in tea, and I can truthfully say that I have always, ever since I have been in India, made a point of alleviating the sufferings of my coolies, though of course one cannot please all. This has been done by co-operation and no strike has or will take place on the garden under my control. I speak with confidence. So I ask you, Mr. Gandhi, to stay your hand and the hand of your sympathisers, and stop this mad exodus from Assam. Think of the thousands of deaths being caused by this stampede. Two wrongs will never make one right.

I personally am very much against the methods employed in every tea garden except my own and a few others. They are, I admit, a disgrace to the tea industry, *i.e.*, gardens worked through the Baboos. But what is required is co-operation, agitation, legislation, and not your methods, namely, Bolshevism with a Non-co-operation tendency. The truth hurts no one.

Apologizing for the tone of my letter, which only speaks my mind.

I remain,
"Chi tace confessa."
"He, who keeps silent confesses."

Mr. Gandhi replied to the above as follow: I publish this letter without an alteration. The writer has sent me his name, but wishes to remain anonymous. I have seen, both in Natal and Champaran, the writer's prototypes. He means well, but does not know that he is no more than a fine cattle-keeper. Once admit that men may be treated like cattle, many a European manager would earn a certificate of merit from a Prevention of Cruelty to Animals Society. I know from experience, that free medicine, free medical attendance, free housing acommodation and free grazing-ground are so many tricks of the trade, designed to keep the 'coolie' a serf for ever. He would be a freer man for being paid full wages and charged for housing and medicine. Free grazing ground is to him, almost like breathing, indispensable. Eurasian children tell on every estate the story of man's and woman's shame. If I had the power, I would stop all the estates, where the crime against Indian womanhood is proved by the presence of Eurasian children. I know the problem is difficult. But, if the European learnt to respect the chastity of the Indian woman as his sister's there would be no Eurasian children born out of wedlock. I am no believer in 'free' intercourse. The subject is too painful, the chastity of man and woman too sacred for me, to enable me to write with restraint on what I have seen on such estates, and heard. I do not for one moment wish to suggest that Indian managers would not commit the same crimes that European managers do. I know that their colour hides the shame in the faces of their crimes' creation. But I do maintain that the European manager does with impunity what the Indian dare not. But I must close this chapter here. The disingenous suggestion that the manager should be the President of Panchayats, gives away the planters' case. The correspondent's advice regarding Non-co-operation proceeds from ignorance. I can assure him that I never advised a single coolie in Assam to strike. I do not profess to know the problem of labour there. He should, moreover, know that there is no Non-co-operation going on with capital or capitalists, Non-co-operation is going on with the existing Government as a system. But there is bound to be Non-co-operation, wherever there is evil, oppression and injustice, whether anybody wishes it or not. The people, having found the remedy, will resort to it. If they do so stupidly or unjustifiably, they alone will be the real losers. I do not believe that legislation or debates in the Councils can do much good. Not until employers begin to look upon labourers as members of their own family, or until the latter are educated to understand their own rights and know the method of securing them, will labourers be able to better their position. Legislation in advance of public opinion is often worse than useless. Non-co-operation is the quickest method of creating public opinion, in the present case a change of manners, or, as I have often put it, of heart.

13*th July*, 1921

TO EVERY ENGLISHMAN IN INDIA

DEAR FRIEND,

This is the second time I venture to address you. I know that most of you detest Non-co-operation. But I would invite you to isolate two of my activities from the rest, if you can give me credit for honesty.

I cannot prove my honesty, if you do not feel it. Some of my Indian friends charge me with camouflage, when I say we need not hate Englishmen, whilst we may hate the system they have established. I am trying to show them that one may detest the wickedness of a brother without hating him. Jesus denounced the wickedness of the Scribes and the Pharisees, but he did not hate them. He did not enunciate this law of love for the man and hate for the evil in him for himself only, but he taught the doctrine for universal practice. Indeed, I find it in all the scriptures of the world.

I claim to be a fairly accurate student of human nature and vivisector of my own failings. I have discovered that man is superior to the system he propounds. And so I feel that you as an individual are infinitely better than the system you have evolved as a corporation. Each one of my countrymen in Amritsar on that fateful 10th of April, was better than the crowd of which he was a member. He, as a man, would have declined to kill those innocent English bank managers. But in that crowd, many a man forgot himself. Hence it is that an Englishman in office is different from an Englishman outside. Similarly an Englishman in India is different from an Englishman in England. Here in India, you belong to a system that is vile beyond description. It is possible, therefore, for me to condemn the system in the strongest terms, without considering you to be bad and without imputing bad motives to every Englishman. You are as much slaves of the system as we are. I want you, therefore, to reciprocate, and not impute to me motives which you cannot read in the written word. I give you the whole of my motive when I tell you that I am impatient to end or mend a system, which has made India subservient to a handful of you and which has made Englishmen feel secure only in the shadow of the forts and the guns that obtrude themselves on one's notice in India. It is a degrading spectacle for you and for us. Our corporate life is based on mutual distrust and fear. This, you will admit, is unmanly. A system that is responsible for such a state of thing, is necessarily satanic. You should be able to live in India as an integral part of its people and not always as foreign exploiters. One thousand Indian lives against one English life is a doctrine of dark despair, and yet, believe me, it was enunciated in 1919 by the highest of you in the land.

I almost feel tempted to invite you to join me in destroying a system that has dragged both you and us down. But I feel I cannot as yet do so. We have not shown ourselves earnest, self-sacrificing and self-restrained enough for that consummation.

But I do ask you to help us in the boycott of foreign cloth and in the anti-drink campaign.

The Lancashire cloth, as English historians have shown, was forced upon India, and her own world-famed manufactures were deliberately and systematically ruined. India is, therefore, at the mercy not only of Lancashire but also of Japan, France and America. Just see what this has meant to India. We send out of India every year sixty crores (more or less) of rupees for cloth. We grow enough cotton for our own cloth. Is it not madness to send cotton outside India, and have it manufactured into cloth there and shipped to us? Was it right to reduce India to such a helpess state?

A hundred and fifty years ago, we manufactured all our cloth. Our women spun fine yarn in their own cottages, and supplemented the earnings of their husbands. The village weavers wove that yarn. It was an indispensable part of national economy in a vast agricultural country like ours. It enabled us in a most natural manner to utilise our leisure. To-day our women have lost the cunning of their hands, and the enforced idleness of millions has impoverished the land. Many weavers have become sweepers. Some have taken to the profession of hired soldiers. Half the race of artistic weavers has died out, and the other half is weaving imported foreign yarn for want of finer hand-spun yarn.

You will perhaps now understand what boycott of foreign cloth means to India. It is not devised as a punishment. If the Government were to-day to redress the Khilafat and the Punjab wrongs and consent to India attaining immediate Swaraj, the boycott movement must still continue. Swaraj means at least the power to conserve Indian industries that are vital to the economic existence of the nation, and to prohibit such imports as may interfere with such existence. Agriculture and hand-spinning are two lungs of the national body. They must be protected against consumption at any cost.

This matter does not admit of any waiting. The interests of the foreign manufacturers and the Indian importers cannot be considered, when the whole nation is starving for want of a large productive occupation auxiliary to agriculture.

You will not mistake this for a movement of general boycott of foreign goods. India does not wish to shut herself out of international commerce. Things other than cloth which can be better made outside India, she must gratefully receive upon terms advantageous to the contracting parties. Nothing can be forced upon her. But I do not wish to peep into the future. I am certainly hoping that before long it would be possible for India to co-operate with England on equal terms. Then will be the time for examining trade relations. For the time being, I bespeak your help in bringing about a boycott of foreign cloth.

Of similar and equal importance is the campaign against drink. The liquor-shops are an insufferable curse imposed upon society. There never was so much awakening among the people as now upon this question. I admit that here it is the Indian ministers who can help more than you can. But I would like you to speak out your mind clearly on the question. Under every system of government, total prohibition, so far as I can see, will be insisted upon by the nation. You can assist the growth of the ever-rising agitation by throwing in the weight of your influence on the side of the nation.

9th *May*, 1921

SOME QUESTIONS ANSWERED

From time to time, Mr. Gandhi was asked to answer questions and clear difficulties. The following are from *Young India* :

Carping Criticism.—Often do young men criticise the conduct of leaders without just cause. The latest instance that has come to my notice is rather striking. A special train was arranged for a visit to Sindh. This was too much for a correspondent. He thought that the leaders had indulged in a waste of national funds. I had not stopped to inquire the reason why the special was arranged. He advised me to cancel the special and give a day more to Sindh and save the money. If he had inquired into the matter, the friend would have discovered that without the special it was impossible to take me to Mirpur Khas; that I could not have given a day more to Sindh without disturbing the rest of the programme, that it was necessary for me to go to Mirpur Khas and that the expense was comparatively small. Criticism of public men is a welcome sign of public awakening. It keeps workers on the alert. Those who pay have a right to ensure economy. There is undoubtedly an extravagance often noticed about popular demonstrations, much money is spent in tinsel splendour. The expense is often thoughtless. And we are likely to gain by fearless criticism of public expenditure or general conduct of public men. But all such criticism must be well informed and thoughtful. All carping criticism must be avoided.*

Whilst on the question of railway travelling, I must remark that there is still noticeable a desire to avoid 3rd class travelling. I am sorry to say that, being no longer

* The following appeared in *Young India* of 18th August, 1921:

Some Questions and Answers—An English friend sent me five questions for answer. As they were interesting, I reproduce from memory both the questions and the answers.

(1) Do you think time will increase or decrease the divergence of views between you and Lord Reading.

Answer—The divergence is as likely to decrease as it is to increase

(2) When do you expect to establish Swaraj?

Ans—I am trying to establish government over myself as rapidly as possible. I cannot establish Swaraj for India. But I do certainly expect her to establish it during this very year.

(3) Do you now think the Prime Minister to be more satanic or evil than ever?

Ans.—I must confess that the Prime Minister is an enigma to me. He certainly still owes to Indian Mussalmans a debt which he has failed to discharge.

(4) Why do you not encourage the ministers born and bred in your own country who are trying to establish through the reformed councils full responsible government for India?

Ans.—I most respectfully refuse to encourage the ministers until they wash their hands clean of a system which uses them as tools for debasing India.

(5) Do you think a sense of humour is necessary in life?

Ans.—If I had no sense of humour, I should long ago have committed suicide.—M. K. G.

physically able to travel 3rd class, I am deprived of the inestimable experiences of third class railway travelling. It affords an opportunity of contact with the national mind which nothing else does. It enables one to render service which cannot be otherwise rendered. I would therefore urge all workers to avoid 2nd class travelling save in rare cases. No one perhaps knows better than I do the discomfort of 3rd class railway travelling. I put it down partly to callous railway management and partly to bad national habits that ignore the convenience of the neighbours. Observant workers travelling 3rd class would efficiently deal with the disregard both of the management and the passengers. There is no doubt that 2nd class travelling is not within the reach of the masses. And national servants may claim no privileges not enjoyed by the latter.—"M. K. G." in *Young India* of 11th May, 1921.

Is Non-co-operation anti-Government?—In the course of an article in "Young India" of 19th May, 1920, under the heading, "Some objections answered," Mr. Gandhi wrote in reply to a friend:

My friend objects to my statement that Non-co-operation is not anti-Government, because he considers that refusal to serve it and pay its taxes is actually anti-Government. I respectfully dissent from the view. If a brother has fundamental differences with his brother, and association with the latter involves his partaking of what in his opinion is an injustice, I hold that it is his brotherly duty to refrain from serving his brother and sharing his earnings with him. This happens in everyday life. Prahlad did not act against his father when he declined to associate himself with the latter's blasphemies. Nor was Jesus anti-Jewish when he declaimed against the Pharisees and the hypocrites, and would have none of them. In such matters, is it not the intention that determines the character of a particular act? It is hardly correct as the friend suggests that withdrawal of association under general circumstances would make all government impossible. But it is true that such withdrawal would make all injustice impossible.

Non-co-operation Programme.—In "Young India" of 18th August, 1920, replying to *Swadesamitran*, defending the Non-co-operation programme, Mr. Gandhi stated *inter alia*:

I agree with the Editor that the quickest and the largest response is to be expected in the matter of suspension of payment of taxes, but as I have said, so long as the masses are not educated to appreciate the value of non-violence even whilst their holdings are being sold, so long must it be difficult to take up the last stage to any appreciable extent.

I agree too that a sudden withdrawal of the military and the police will be a disaster if we have not acquired the ability to protect ourselves against robbers and thieves. But I suggest that when we are ready to call out the military and the police on an extensive scale, we would find ourselves in a position to defend ourselves. If the police and the military resign from patriotis motives, I would certainly expect them to perform the same duty as national volunteers, not as hirelings but as willing protectors of the life and liberty of their countrymen. The movement of Non-co-operation is one of automatic adjustment. If the Government schools are emptied, I would certainly expect national schools to come into being, If the lawyers as a whole suspended practice, they would devise arbitration courts and the nation ,will have expeditious and cheaper method of setting private disputes and awarding punishment to the wrong-doer.

Regarding the leaving of civil employment, no danger is feared, because no one will leave his employment, unless he is in a position to find support for himself and family either through friends or otherwise.

Disapproval of the proposed withdrawal of students betrays, in my humble opinion, lack of appreciation of the true nature of Non-co-operation. It is true enough that we pay the money wherewith our children are educated. But when the agency imparting the education has become corrupt, we may not employ it without partaking of the agent's corruption. When students leave schools or colleges I hardly imagine that the teachers will fail to perceive the advisability of themselves resigning. But even if they do not, money can hardly be allowed to count where honour or religion are at stake.

As to the boycott of the councils, it is not the entry of the Moderates or any other persons that matters so much as the entry of those who believe in Non-co-operation. You may not co-operate at the bottom. A councillor cannot remain in the council and ask the *gumasta* who cleans the council table to resign.

The Depressed Classes and Education.—In "Young India" of 24th November, 1920, under the heading, "More difficulties," Mr. Gandhi wrote with reference to criticisms about the Gujarat National University:

The simple reason why there is no Mussalman representative on the Senate is that no higher educated Mussalman, able to give his time, has been found to take sufficient interest in the national education movement. I merely refer to this matter to show that we must reckon with attempts to discredit the movement even by misinterpretation of motives. That is a difficulty from without and easier to deal with.

The 'depressed' classes difficulty is internal and therefore far more serious, because it may give rise to a split and weaken the cause—no cause can survive internal difficulties if they are indefinitely multiplied. Yet there can be no surrender in the matter of principles for the avoidance of splits. You cannot promote a cause when you are undermining it by surrendering its vital parts. The 'depressed' classes problem is a vital part of the cause. *Swaraj* is as inconceivable without full reparation to the 'depressed' classes as it is impossible without real Hindu-Muslim unity. In my opinion we have become 'pariahs of the Empire' because we have created 'pariahs' in our midst. The slave owner is always more hurt than the slave. We shall be unfit to gain *Swaraj* so long as we would keep in bondage a fifth of the population of Hindustan. Have we not made the 'pariah' crawl on his belly? Have we not segregated him? And if it is religion so to treat the 'pariah,' it is the religion of the white race to segregate us. And if it is no argument for the white races to say that we are satisfied with the badge of our inferiority, it is less for us to say that the 'pariah' is satisfied with his. Our slavery is complete when we begin to hug it.

The Gujarat Senate therefore counted the cost when it refused to bend before the storm. This Non-co-operation is a process of self purification. We may not cling to putrid customs and claim the pure boon of *Swaraj*.

Government and Non-co-operation.—In *Young India* of 9th March, 1921, in reply to the Viceroy's two speeches stating the Government had done all it could towards Khilafat and that Non-co-operation led only to anarchy, Gandhi said:

One who sincerely sympathises with a starving man is presumed to share such sufferings, and is not expected to shoot him when the latter shows symptoms of becoming mad through the pangs of hunger. The responsibility for anarchy, if it does overtake India, will therefore rest with the Indian Government and with those who support it in spite of its wrongs, not upon those who refuse to perform its wrongs, not upon those who refuse to perform the impossible task of making people forget vital wrongs and try to direct their anger in a proper channel.

His Excellency wonders at the description of the Government as satanic. He is wrong in adopting the description for himself. For nobody has accused individuals of being satanic. His Excellency's adroitly taking in that category his Indian colleagues, is too artless to deceive anyone. But the system that the Viceroy and his colleagues, whether Indian or English, administer, possesses all the attributes of Satan—deceitfulness, hypocrisy, unscrupulousness, and unmitigated tyranny on occasion and its justification tempered by half-hearted confessions. His Excellency may rest assured that there is no partiality in Non-co-operation. There is always a place of honour for an Englishman in the ranks of Non-co-operationists. And no Indian co-operator will be spared the criticism that may be deserved by him for his complicity in the crimes of an evil government.

His Excellency is on safest ground when he enunciates the doctrine of meeting Non-co-operation by propaganda—by the counter propaganda of co-operation. He is entitled to take all the comfort he can from the fact that both the title-holders and the students have made a poor response in point of numbers and that sufficient Indians have been found to act as members of the reformed legislatures. Non-co-operationists, whilst admitting that the numerical response might have been greater, manage, however, to take pleasure in the titles and the schools and the law-courts having fallen into disrepute. These institutions no longer remain the objects of idolatry than they once were. Non-co-operationists are satisfied that practising lawyers and title-holders can no longer be popular leaders. They know that even those, who have not given up titles, practice, or schools, are at heart non-co-operators and confess their weakness.

His Excellency has been misled by his advisers in believing that non-co-operationists have only now turned their attention to the masses. Indeed, they are our sheet-anchor. But we are not going to tamper with them. We shall continue patiently to educate them politically till they are ready for safe action. There need be no mistake about our goal. As soon as we feel reasonably confident of non-violence, continuing among them in spite of provoking executions, we shall certainly call upon the sepoy to lay down his arms and the peasantry to suspend payment of taxes. We are hoping that that time may never have to be reached. We shall leave no stone unturned to avoid such a serious step. But we will not flinch when the movement has come and the need has arisen.

Humanity v. Patriotism—Gandhi wrote in *Young India* of 16th March, 1921:

A dear friend has drawn my attention to what he considers is an unfortunate appeal to patriotism rather than humanity in my letter to the Sikhs.* The portion objected to is this: "The purest way of seeking justice against the murders is not to seek it. The perpetrators whether they are Sikhs, Pathans or Hindus, are our countrymen. Their punishment cannot recall the dead to life. I would ask those whose hearts are lacerated to forgive them, not out of their weakness—for they are able in every way to have them punished,—but out of their immeasurable strength. Only the strong can forgive." I have read the foregoing again and again. I feel that if I had to rewrite the letter, I should not alter a single word in it. My appeal in that letter is to the Sikhs as Indians. And it was enough for me to confine my appeal to the point that could be easily appreciated and reached by those whom I was addressing. The main reasoning would be the same for all, and at all times. My letter as addressed to the Sikhs would have lost its force somewhat if I had broadened the appeal as from patriotism to humanity. A Sikh who will want to punish a non-Sikh criminal but would forgive a Sikh may be told that to him Sikh and Indian must mean the same thing in matters such as the incident covers. The appeal to an Indian as against an Englishman will be to his humanity rather than to his patriotism.

But I am free to confess that in the present state of feeling, an Englishman may easily misinterpret the motive of the letter. For me patriotism is the same as humanity. I am patriotic because I am human and humane. It is not exclusive. I will not hurt England

* Omitted in this collection

or Germany to serve India. Imperialism has no place in my scheme of life. The law of a patriot is not different from that of the patriarch. And a patriot is so much the less a patriot if he is a lukewarm humanitarian. There is no conflict between private and political law. A Non-co-operator, for instance, would act exactly in the same manner towards his father or brother as he is to-day acting towards the Government.

The Destructive Part—Replying to the *Leader* which suggested, with reference to the Bezwada Programme, that he had suspended Non-co-operation, Mr. Gandhi wrote in *Young India* of 8th June, 1921:

The vocal propaganda of the destructive part in the first step in Non-co-operation is over. We know exactly where we are, regarding the titles, the law courts, the schools and the councils. I believe Non-co-operators are satisfied that these institutions have lost their former prestige. The opponents are entitled to comfort in the knowledge that the numerical response has not been large enough to be striking. Those that have responded to the call, constitute the most effective though silent propaganda in the direction. But one thing is clear. There can be no resumption of co-operation, till the three conditions laid down by the Congress are satisfied. The Bezwada programme,* I admit, is not in itself

*Under the heading, "The Need of the Hour," Mr. Gandhi wrote in *Young India* of 8th June, 1921:

The following may serve as a working basis:—

(1) Salaried men to pay one-tenth of their monthly pay.

(2) Lawyers, doctors, merchants and such others to pay one-twelfth of their nett annual income as at the end of May last.

(3) Propertied men to pay 2½ p. c. of the valuation of their property.

(4) All the others to pay not less than four annas each.

enough to establish Swaraj. But I do hold that it is a very substantial step towards it. The fulfilment of the programme will inspire the nation with self-confidence, and enable it to take the other steps, if necessary. One crore electors—for, to become Congress members is to become electors for national representatives for various bodies—is to find the nucleus for a real electorate under Swaraj. To have twenty lacs of spinning-wheels in working order, is to know that India is determined to drive out poverty, to become self-reliant and to achieve her economic independence. The collection of one crore of rupees is a tangible token of the nation's determination to achieve her destiny.

We have so fed ourselves with the history of other nations, that we find it impossible to believe that we can attain our end without a repetition of thirty years' or a hundred years' war, and therefore without military training and huge armament. We do not care to read our own history and remember, that whilst kings have come and kings have gone, whilst dynasties have been formed and destroyed, India has remained unmoved and unaffected. We will not read the lesson of the late war that it is not so much military preparation we want, as a change of our own outlook upon India's future. Habit has forced the conviction upon us that we, the countless millions, are nothing before one hundred thousand Englishmen, not all of whom are even administrators. As soon as we have discarded the awe of the British rule, and ceased to consider ourselves as cheap as dirt, we shall be free. I know that it is possible to perform

If all were to pay according to this scale, there would be several crores of rupees. But one is aware that Non-co-operators and sympathisers are drawn from all classes. No single class is so wholly Non-co-operationist as to feel the personal responsibility for payment.

this revolution of thought during the year, and it is my hope that India will be ready for it during the time. Hitherto, we have promised ourselves many things and fulfilled little. If we were to turn up even two years old resolutions of the Congress, we shall find that we have failed even to send petitions we had resolved upon. Hitherto we have looked up to the Government to do everything for us, and we have found it almost wholly irresponsive in everything that matters. We have therefore been filled with blank despair. We have ceased to believe in ourselves or the Government. The present movement is an attempt to change this winter of our despair into the summer of hope and confidence. When we begin to believe in ourselves, Englishmen will, I promise, begin to believe in us. Then, and not till then, is there any hope of co-operation between the Government and us. The existing system of government, it will be found upon analysis, is based upon a scientific study of our weaknesses, which have rather been promoted by it than reduced. Non-co-operation is, therefore, as much a protest against our own weakness, as against the inherent corruption of the existing system. British and Indian, we become impure by belonging to it. The withdrawal from it of one party purifies both. I invite even the sceptics to follow the programme of Non-co-operation as a trial, and I promise that there will be Swaraj in India during the year, if the programme is carried out in its fulness.

Conscience or Expedience—A correspondent wrote to *Young India* of 19th January, 1921:

> "Our conduct would be quite consistent if we did not take our stand on religion or conscience but simply declared that we

wanted to render this Government impotent and would employ such means (provided they are peaceful and not immoral) as would help us to achieve our object. Then there would be no question of the money coming from the Government being tainted or otherwise, though withdrawal of students from Government or aided institutions may even then be undertaken if we thought we would thus help to render the Government impotent. Such withdrawal will then be based not on any principle of religion or conscience but simply on the principle of expediency.'

Mr. Gandhi replied to the above as follows:

I have a horror of the word 'expediency' because of its bad odour. As a rule, expediency is often opposed to morality and does not exclude the use of violence. But the writer has removed the sting from the word by using it in its root meaning. For he insists upon being moral and peaceful. I would therefore not quarrel with the admirable presentation of the argument. I have presented Non-co-operation in terms of religion because I enter politics only in so far as it develops the religious faculty in me. My correspondent has presented the case in terms of politics. I submit that my presentation is freer from pitfalls than his. There certainly is room for stages in a religious as in a political programme. The fundamental distinction is that a programme conceived in a religious spirit admits of no tactics or compromise with things that matter. Our present Non-co-operation refers not so much to the paralysis of a wicked government as to our being proof against wickedness. It aims therefore not at destriction but at construction. It deals with causes rather than with symptoms.

In answer to questions by a Muslim correspondent, Mr. Gandhi wrote *inter alia* in *Young India* of 4th May, 1921: I think that only God-fearing people can become true Non-co-operators. But the programme of

Non-co-operation does not require a man to declare his faith. Any person believing in non-violence and accepting the Non-co-operation programme can certainly become a Non-co-operator. . . The correspondent misapprehends the position. The nation has not embarked on complete Non-co-operation, not for want of faith or will, but for want of abitity. It has, therefore, not called upon Government servants as yet to give up their posts. But any such servant is free to throw up his office whenever he likes. But there cannot be such a call until all reasonable precautions are taken against an outbreak of violence. Not until the nation is in a position to find occupation for such men, can the call therefore be made. Thus, here, there is no question of expediency as it is generally understood. But purest religion is highest expediency. Many things are lawful but they are not all expedient. The law, the Ideal of Non-co-operation, is before the country.

27th October, 1921

THE SECRET OF IT

A correspondent sent Mr. Gandhi a formidable list of questions about the struggle which deserve public notice. He commenced thus: "You will admit that both your followers and non-followers are in a state of suspense as regards the aims of your political activities. Can you therefore be charitable enough to enlighten them by answering the following questions?" The following are the questions and answers:

I. Are you really a Mahatma?

I do not feel like being one. But I do know that I am among the humblest of God's creatures.

2. If so, will you define the word Mahatma ?

Not being acquainted with one, I cannot give any definition.

3. If not, did you ever tell your followers that you are not one ?

The more I repudiate, the more it is used.

4. Is your 'soul force' attainable by the ignorant masses ?

They have it already in abundance. Once upon a time an expedition of French scientists set out in search of knowledge and in due course reached India. They tried hard to find it, as they had expected, among the learned ones but failed. Unexpectedly they found it in a pariah home.

5. You say machinery has been the bane of civilization. Then why do you allow yourself to travel in railway trains and motor cars ?

There are certain things which you cannot escape all at once, even whilst you are avoiding them. This earthy case in which I am locked up is the bane of my life, but I am obliged to put up with it and even indulge it as this friend knows. But does he seriously doubt that the machine age was responsible for the organised murders during the late war ? Asphyxiating gas and such other abominations have not advanced us by an inch.

6. Is it a fact that formerly you travelled third class in railway trains and now you travel in special trains and first class carriages ?

Alas ! the correspondent is correctly informed. The Mahatma-ship is responsible for the special trains, and the earthy case for the degradation to the second class.

7. In what relation do you stand to Count Tolstoy ?

As a devoted admirer who owes much in life to him.

8. Why do you not define Swaraj? Do you not feel that you are in duty bound to define the word at least to your followers.

In the first place the word is indefinable; in the second place, if the correspondent will turn to the file of *Young India* he will find a workable definition there. I will try another here. It means complete freedom of opinion and action without interference with another's right to equal freedom of opinion and action. Therefore it means India's complete control of sources of revenue and expenditure without interference from or with any other country.

9. What will be your own position when Swaraj is obtained?

I would certainly like a prolonged and perhaps well-deserved holiday.

10. When Swaraj is attained, how are the political and religious interests of Mussalmans to be safeguarded?

They will not need any safeguarding, because every Indian will be as free as very other Indian, and because there will then be mutual toleration, respect and love, and therefore mutual trust.

11. Do you honestly believe that Government will pack up and beat a hasty retreat from India on the 31st of October, 1921 or at any other time within this year that you will be pleased fix?

The Government is the system, and I do believe that it can be destroyed even before the 31st October, if the Hindus, the Mussalmans, the Sikhs, the Parsis, the Christians and the Jews of India *will*. I am still hoping that they will destroy it before the end of the year. But under the new system not a single Englishman who wishes to remain in India as her faithful servant need leave the country.

12. Do you not think that the Government is too weak to check your propaganda?

I certainly do, and it is becoming daily weaker.

13. Would you leave your own son undefended if (which God forbid) he was being prosecuted for murder, not for sedition?

I really believe that I have the courage to do so. I certainly had the hardihood to give that advice to many a dear friend. And I have already advised a dear friend of the Andhra district to sake the whole of his valuable property by not defending a civil suit which has been brought against him from pure political malice.

14. What should your son (for example) do if some one defrauded him of some money and has made himself scarce.

My son if he is a good Non-sc-operator would certainly let the thief keep the money. Maulana Shaukat Ali was robbed of Rs. 600 nine months ago. He knew the person who has robbed him. He thought no more about it.

15. What was the effect of your Satyagraha on the Punjab?

Sir Michael O'Dwyer would not let the message of Satyagraha reach the Punjab. Some Punjabis therefore got excited, a few went mad. Sir Michael O'Dwyer became madder still and butchered innocent men by deputy. But Satyagraha is a powerful tonic, and now the Punjab is as lively as any other province of India, and is showing in spite of her mercurial population a degree of self-restraint that is worthy of emulation by the rest of the provinces.

16. Do you really believe that Non-co-operation can remain non-violent.

Certainly. The wonderful restraint shown by the

people over the arrests in Sindh, Karnatak and East Bengal is proof of it.

17. How do the forcible conversions of Hindus and pillage of Hindu homes reflect upon the unity of Hindus and Mahomedans in India?

They have put a severe strain upon Hindu patience, but it has stood the strain and its survival proves that the unity is based on knowledge. No Mussalman approves of the Moplah fanaticism.

18. What is the actual cause of this rupture of Hindu-Muslim unity in Malabar?

There is no rupture of the unity in the disturbed area. The Moplahs could not at any time have considered Hindus as their brethern. The causes of the violence are that as in the Punjab in 1919, so in Malabar now the message of Non-co-operation was only vaguely delivered when its progress was arrested by the authorities. The Moplahs were never particularly friendly to the Malabar Hindus. They had looted them before. Their notions of Islam were of a very crude type. They were kept in utter darkness by the Government and neglected both by Mussalmans and Hindus. Being wild and brave but ignorant, they have mistaken the mission of the Khilafat and acted in a savage, inhuman and irreligious manner. It is quite improper to judge Islam or the Mussalmans of the rest of India by the present conduct of the Moplahs.

19. Can you say what made you to couple the Khilafat with the Punjab wrongs?

The Khilafat wrong was born before the Punjab wrong and I made it my own in the year 1918 at the Delhi War Conference (*vide* my open letter to the Viceroy). Non-co-operation was conceived at Delhi in 1919 before the Punjab wrong had taken definite shape.

The latter was tacked to the Khilafat, when it became clear that it required as drastic a remedy as the Khilafat.

20. Can you say why the Mahomedans of India are so demonstrative for the Khilafat, when the Mahomedans of other Islamic countries do not seem to care for it?

I do not know that non-Indian Mussulmans do not care for the Khilafat, but if they do not and the Indian Mussalmans do, for me it is proof enough that the latter have developed greater religious consciousness than the former.

21. Since the Sultan of Turkey has failed to defend the Muslim holy places, has he any right now to be considered a Khalifa?

This is hardly a question for a Hindu to answer. But if I may venture a reply, the Khilafat rests in the Turks by right of valiant defence for hundreds of years. The Sultan may have failed, the Turks have not. The Khilafat agitation does not centre round an individual but round an idea, which is at once temporal, spiritual and political. If the Turks cannot defend, if the Mussalmans of the world do not by their power of opinion and active sympathy stand by the Turks, both they and the latter will suffer irretrievably. Such an event will be a calamity for the world, for I believe that Islam has its place in the world as much as Christianity and every other religion. Chivalry demands the support of the Turks in the hour of their need.

22. Is the economic law that man must buy in the best and the cheapest market wrong?

It is one of the most inhuman among the maxims laid down by modern economists. Nor do we always regulate human relations by any such sordid considerations. An Englishman pays more (and rightly) for the English collier in preference to cheap (say) Italian labour. Any attempt to introduce cheap labour into England will lead to a revolution. It would be sinful for me to dismiss a highly paid faithful servant because I can get a more efficient and cheaper servant although the latter may be equally faithful. The economics that disregard moral and sentimental considerations are like wax works that being life-like still lack the life of the living flesh. At every crucial moment, these new-fangled economic laws have broken down in practice. And nations or individuals who accept them as guiding maxims must perish. There is something noble in the self-denial of the Mussalman who will pay more for food religiously prepared or a Hindu who will decline to take food unless it is ceremonially clean. We lost when we began to by our clothing in the cheap markets of England and Japan. We will live again, when we appreciate the religious necessity of buying our clothes prepared by our own neighbours in their cottages.

23. Is picketing non-violent?

It certainly has been non-violent in the vast majority of cases. It was the easiest thing to resort to violence in picketing, but the volunteers all over, have exercised great restraint.

24. Do you explain the beauty (spiritual or otherwise) of bonfires, when many people are going half-naked in the country and are shivering at the thought of the coming winter?

I do; for I know that their half-nakedness is due to our criminal neglect of the fundamental law of life in India that she should wear only handspun just as she must eat only home-cooked food. My giving my discarded foreign clothes to them will only prolong the agony. But if the warmth generated by the bonfires are kept up till the last piece is burnt, the warmth will last for ever, and each successive winter will see the nation more and more invigorated.

17*th November*, 1921

MY INCONSISTENCY

(By M. K. Gandhi)

A correspondent asks some pertinent questions in the following pungent fashion:

"When the Zulus broke out for liberty against the British usurpers, you helped the British in suppressing the so-called rebellion. Is it a rebellion to try to shake off the foreign yoke? Was Jean D'arc a rebel? Was George Washington a rebel? Is De Valera one? You may say that the Zulus had recourse to violence. I then ask, was the end bad or the means? The latter may have been so but certainly not the former; so you will be kind enough to explain the riddle. In the last war, when the gallant Germans and Austrians were fighting so bravely against a world combination, you raised recruits for the British to fight against the nations that had done India no harm. Whenever there is a war between two races, one has to hear both parties before coming to a decision either for or against any of them. In the last war, we had a one-sided version only and that from a nation certainly not renowned for truthfulness or honesty. You have all along been an advocate of passive resistance and non-violence. Why then did you induce people to take part in a war the merits of which they knew not, and for the aggrandisement of a race so miserably wallowing in the mire of imperialism? You may say you had faith in the British bureaucracy.

Is it possible for any person to have faith in an alien people at all whose acts have run so glaringly counter to their promises? It cannot have been so with a person of such high attainments as yourself. So you will please answer the second riddle.

"There is another point to which I should like to refer. You are an advocate of non-violence. Under the present circumstances, we should be strictly non-violent. But when India will be free, should we strictly eschew arms even if a foreign nation invaded us? Would you also boycott railways and telegraphs and steamers even when they will have ceased to promote exports of the products of our soil?"

I hear and read many charges of inconsistency about myself. But I do not answer them as they do not affect any one but myself. The questions however raised by the correspondent are of general importance and deserve notice. They are by no means new to me. But I do not remember having answered them in the columns of *Young India*.

Not only did I offer my services at the time of the Zulu revolt, but before that, at the time of the Boer war, and not only did I raise recruits in India during the late war, but I raised an ambulance corps in 1914, in London. If therefore I have sinned, the cup of my sins is full to the brim. I lost no occasion of serving the Government at all times. Two questions presented themselves to me during all those crises. What was my duty as a citizen of the empire as I then believed myself to be, and what was my duty as an out and out believer in the religion of *Ahimsa*—Non-violence?

I know now that I was wrong in thinking that I was a citizen of the empire. But on those four occasions, I did honestly believe that, in spite of the many disabilities that my country was labouring under, it was making its way towards freedom, and that on the whole the Government from the popular stand-point was not wholly bad and that the British administrators were honest though insular and dense. Holding that view, I set about doing what an ordinary Englishman would do in the circumstances. I was not wise or important enough to take independent action. I had no business to judge or scrutinise ministerial decisions with the solemnity of a tribunal. I did not impute malice to the ministers either at the time of the Boer war, the Zulu revolt or the late war. I did not consider Englishmen nor do I now consider them as particularly bad or worse than other human beings. I considered and still consider them to be as capable of high motives and actions as any other body of men and equally capable of making mistakes. I therefore felt that I sufficiently discharged my duty as a man and a citizen by offering my humble services to the empire in the hour of its need, whether local or general. That is how I would expect every Indian to act by his country under Swaraj. I would be deeply distressed, if on every conceivable occasion every one of us were to be a law unto oneself and to scrutinise in golden scales every action of our future National Assembly. I would surrender my judgment in most matters to national representatives, taking particular care in making my choice of such representatives. I know that in no other manner would a democratic government be possible for one single day.

The whole situation is now changed for me. My eyes, I fancy, are opened. Experience has made me wiser. I consider the existing system of government to be wholly bad and requiring special national effort to end or mend it. It does not possess within itself any capacity for self-improvement. That I still believe many English administrators to be honest does not assist me, because I consider them to be as blind and deluded as I was myself. Therefore I can take no pride in calling the empire mine or describing myself as a citizen. On the contrary, I fully realise that I am a pariah untouchable of the empire. I must therefore constantly pray for its radical reconstruction or total destruction, even as a Hindu pariah would be fully justified in so praying about Hinduism or Hindu society.

The next point, that of *Ahimsa*, is more abstruse. My conception of *Ahimsa* impels me always to dissociate myself from almost every one of the activities I am engaged in. My soul refuses to be satisfied so long as it is a helpless witness of a single wrong or a single misery. But it is not possible for me a weak, frail, miserable being, to mend every wrong or to hold myself free of blame for all the wrong I see. The spirit in me pulls one way, the flesh in me pulls in the opposite direction. There is freedom from the action of these two forces, but that freedom is attainable only by slow and painful stages. I cannot attain freedom by a mechanical refusal to act, but only by intelligent action in a detached manner. This struggle resolves itself into an incessant crucifixion of the flesh so that the spirit may become entirely free.

I was again an ordinary citizen no wiser than my fellows, myself believing in *Ahimsa* and the rest not believing in it at all but refusing to do their duty of assisting the Government because they were actuated by anger and malice. They were refusing out of their ignorance and weakness. As a fellow worker, it became my duty to guide them aright. I therefore placed before them their clear duty, explained the doctrine of *Ahimsa* to them and let them make their choice which they did. I do not repent of my action in terms of *Ahimsa*. For under Swaraj too, I would not hesitate to advise those who would bear arms to do so and fight for the country.

23rd February, 1921

A CIVILIAN REPLIES

We reproduce below the correspondence that recently took place between Mr. Fremantle of the Indian Civil Service and Mr. Gandhi, with reference to the latter's letter "To every Englishman in India" published in these columns:

MR. FREMANTLE'S LETTER

To Mahatma Gandhi Sahib,

Sir,—I have not had the pleasure of perusing in full the open letter to Europeans in India which I understand you indited last year, and am acquainted with its contents merely through a Hindi translation which I have partly read.

You began, I believe, by some detail of the services you had rendered to the British Empire. Have you ever asked yourself, and if you have not, I would request you to do so now, how far you can hope to impress us with them, having in regard the circumstances. Between August 4, 1914 and November 11, 1920, thousands of Englishmen, I am not including those thousands who fought because they were already in the services, or for country's sake or for adventure, or who were conscribed, thousands of Englishmen joined the colours merely for justice's sake. All of these lost men who had no lust for conquest, who would never have fought in the Boer War or any other war of which they in their consciences did not approve, cheerfully faced, not death merely,—that was nothing,—but the exquisite torture of lying wounded for hours in "No man's Land," and the foul ignominy of a German prisoner's camp. Many were wounded again and again. Many more who have escaped unscathed were six years ago starting hopefully on their careers and now see themselves, by their own voluntary act in joining up cheerfully at the call of right, reduced to indigence. And all this not for a particular motive, but, I repeat, to establish a universal principle. Compared with these what have you suffered ? What have you lost that you should presume to place yourself upon an eminence on the strength of any losses or sufferings, and to lecture others ?

An eminence ! Yes, you are upon one, I will not deny it, but of what elevation ? Do you know the delightful story of Alphonse Daudet about the Alpine Club, at Tarscon ? You may have seen the low hills he speaks of, from the train between Marseilles and Paris. They had zeal and "selflessness"—these members ; their arrangements were perfect ; they had axes to their zeal and ropes and alpen stocks and all the paraphernalia of mountaineers ; they climbed zealously and with reckless courage to the very topmost point which they from their provincial boulevards could descry ; but it was not Mount Blanc. Scarcely one-tenth as high ! Just similarly you have merely reached just the highest pinnacle within your own orbit of vision and cannot get higher without first going down, which you are not likely to do. There is another thing which distinguishes you, your "idealism." I do not myself think great things of that shallow quality, that miscalled idealism which turns from history and experience to evolve a misty Utopia out of the inner consciousness. To me it seems more like cynicism. To suppose, for example, that the history of the dealings of the West with India, a history of the determintion of British and French traders, soldiers and administrators to settle among people who believed that the West had something valuable to give, of the relinquishment—often voluntary—of large territories in their sway, the eventual secure establishment of a pax Britannica, to supposethat this was all merely a sort of Beelzebub's progress ending in the aggrandisement of a power with Satanic attributes—is not this to take a cynic's view of human nature ?

But though you have not that higher idealism which looks hard at the facts and perceives the ideal in them, which finds in the great march of history a continual progress towards good, you have yet idealism of a kind, low, you are yet high above the depths, above those revolutionaries whose weapons are lies, the dagger, and the bomb. Violence you will not have within the orbit of your personal influence ;—we have much to be thankful for. On truth you appear to set a peculiar value. One would suppose that you were in possession of some special Ithuriel's spear, the touch of whose celestial temper "no falsehood can sustain." It would be a mistake however were we to be so dazzled by the high idea you set before yourselves as not to realise that practice toils painfully behind. Not only—to take a recent example—does your unnecessary letter to H.R.H. the Duke of Connaught* contain two blatantly false statements, but truthful yourself in the main, you are not—if newspaper reports are correct—scrupulous about lies uttered in your presence. Witness the disgusting aspersion on a British officer now recognised as the Kachgarhi fable, about his brutally slashing the face or neck of the helpless dying Pathan. It is said that when these edifying details had been recounted before you by the Khilafat lecturer you, far from rebuking what the most elementary knowledge of Englishmen and their ways would have revealed as an absurd concoction—got up at the close and made a feeling allusion to the story, treating it as accepted truth. The "Tribune" apology is published; we await yours and are likely still to await it For what is your responsibility? Merely that of getting the seal of your approval on a lie. And what is the seal for your approval worth ? Little evidently in your own estimation.

But a public expression of regret for publicly countenancing a gross libel is a sacrifice to truth too great for you to make. It would be too much, too, to expect you to realize what we mean by ingenuousness ; to comprehend that a plain man does not—as you do—postpone the issue of orders counteracting the excessive zeal of subordinates till it is too late. But you are not a plain man. If you were, you would condemn a rule permitting direct pressure to be brought on school boys of over sixteen to leave school, but not upon those under sixteen, as the most transparent humbug. But we cannot expect you to see this. You cannot perceive Mont Blanc from where you sit, even although it is upon a pinnacle of veracity far above the Serbonism morass of that riff-raff of followers of yours which undertook to explain to Punjab peasants what the Rowlatt Bills were about.

If you have had patience to follow me so far, you will have been enabled dimly to perceive why I am far indeed from accepting your claims to a sort of spiritual ascendancy, claims which, I am afraid, strike me as profane. Neither they nor anything else that I know of entitled you to write an "Open Letter to Europeans in India." But as you have done so, I consider myself equally entitled to reply.

* See *infra*.

I do not ask you to retrace your steps. Not only because it would be useless to do so—not only because I would not for the credit of human nature and the good of India have you reveal yourself what I suspect you of being at heart—a co-operator waiting only for a suitable time to come to terms with this Satanic Government. No, the reason is because you are already on the right path, if you would only pursue it further, even though you yourself hardly know why it is the right path. You have right ideas, however, if you have come by them. But it is necessary to strip off unworthy motives. Cease even to recognize Government by struggling against it. Take a step further and ignore it. Those of us who love learning for its own sake and have been shocked time and again to see it pursued for the sake of degree,—and the degree itself valued only as a stepping stone to Government service,—would be glad indeed to see educational institutions which are really independent of Government. Then again there is ligitation. You appear to have recently recognized the evil,—an evil grossly apparent to myself from the day,—twenty years ago,—when I first landed in this country. But it is well that you have done so. Only in the last few months in my district I have had to deplore two distressing cases of homicide arising directly out of litigation. Empty our law courts, not because you are under the fond impression that Government likes them full, but simply because litiguousness is bad Another idea is that of home industries. It is puerile to connect the spinning-wheel with Swaraj, as if it were any more likely to introduce Swaraj than the American Constitution or the Great Moghal. But you are on the right road if you teach your fellow countrymen to love and beautify their homes more than they do, to esteem the dignity of manual labour, and to discard shoddy machine-made goods. If the Spanish saying is true that fine words butter no parsnips it is equally true that harsh words do not either. The work that lies before you needs no admixture of racial hate. If you can carry it through, it will be a hard task enough, and yet an easier, as well as a more useful, one than the subversion of the British Government.

I am, dear Sir,
Yours faithfully,
(Sd.) A. F. FREMANTLE,
Indian Civil Service.

12TH FEBRUARY, 1921.

MR. GANDHI'S REPLY

Dear Sir,—I have just received your letter of the 12th inst. You will please excuse me if I do not reply to your letter in detail.

You have hardly done justice to yourself, in criticising a letter you have never seen and whose translation you have only partly read. If you had read the letter, you would have seen that I did not mention my services to demonstrate my sufferings, much less to show that they were selfless. I mentioned them merely to show how consistently loyal I was to the British connection even in the midst of adverse conditions. My services were not selfless, because I believe that I would by those services be assisting my country's progress towards freedom. Your mention of British bravery and selflessness is therefore irrelevant. British bravery and capacity for suffering are beyond question. The claim to national selflessness, you will permit me to deny in toto. I did not believe then, the world does not believe to-day, that the late war was one for justice or was selfless. You wanted to crush the Germans, and for the movement you have succeeded. I do not believe that the Germans are the fiends the English Press has made them out to be, nor do I believe that the world would have come to an end if they had won.

You think that I am on an eminence. I assure you that I am unaware of that. I am however on the top of a valcano which I am trying to turn into hard incombustible rock. It may erupt any moment before I have succeeded. That unfortunately has always been a possible fate for a reformer.

My idealism worries you. If you had taken pains to read my writings, you would have known that it is intensely practical.

You have rightly guessed that I am at bottom a co-operator. How would I be otherwise having been that for nearly thirty years? I am certainly waiting for the first opportunity to co-operate, but believe my co-operation will not be tendered until Englishmen have realised the necessity of settling the Khilafat terms in accordance with the Moslem sentiment, until they have repented of the calculated torture of the Punjab, and until they have ceased to consider themselves as our patrons and rulers. India will gladly have Englishmen as friends, fellow-workers and equal partners in India, but if they desire to exploit the country for their own gain, they must do so if they can without our co-operation.

You have seen fit to accuse me of deviation from truth. Here again your amazing ignorance is to blame. You were rightly informed that I believed the statement about the Kachagari incident, made to me upon oath by persons whom I had no reason for doubting. I published over my signature a denial* as soon as I received it. I refer you to the file of *Young India*. Lastly, may I ask you to try to study and understand the movement of Non-co-operation? You will find that it is not anti-English in spirit. It is a religious movement, it is a purifying movement. It is a movement intended to resist injustice, untruth, terrorism and to establish Swaraj in India. You will admit that it is better to replace mutual distrust and fear by trust and fearlessness.

This movement is an attempt to end that unhappy state. And I seek your co-operation in the effort.

I am,
Yours Faithfully,
(Sd). M. K. GANDHI.

*Omitted in this collection.

13*th October*, 1921

THE GREAT SENTINEL

(By M. K. Gandhi)

The Bard of Shantiniketan has contributed to the *Modern Review* a brilliant essay* on the present movement. It is a series of word pictures which he alone can paint. It is an eloquent protest against authority, slave mentality or whatever description one gives of blind acceptance of a passing mania whether out of fear or hope. It is a welcome and wholesome reminder to all workers that we must not be impatient, we must not impose authority no matter how great. The poet tells us summarily to reject anything and everything that does not appeal to our reason or heart. If we would gain Swaraj, we must stand for Truth as we know it at any cost. A reformer who is enraged because his message is not accepted must retire to the forest to learn how to watch, wait and pray. With all this one must heartily agree, and the Poet deserves the thanks of his countrymen for standing up for Truth and Reason. There is no doubt that our last state will be worse than our first, if we surrender our reason into somebody's keeping. And I would feel extremely sorry to discover that the country had unthinkingly and blindly followed all I had said or done. I am quite conscious of the fact that blind surrender to love is often more mischievous than a forced surrender to the lash of the tyrant. There is hope for the slave of the brute, none for that of love. Love is needed to strengthen the weak, love becemes tyrannical when it exacts obedience from an unbeliever. To mutter a *mantra* without knowing its value is unmanly. It is good, therefore, that the Poet has invited all who are

*Not included in this collection.

slavishly *mimicking* the call of the *charkha* boldly to declare their revolt. His essay serves as a warning to us all who in our impatience are betrayed into intolerance or even violence against those who differ from us. I regard the Poet as a sentinel warning us against the approach of enemies called Bigotry, Lethargy, Intolerance, Ignorance, Inertia and other members of that brood.

But whilst I agree with all that the Poet has said as to the necessity of watchfulness lest we cease to think, I must not be understood to endorse the proposition that there is any such blind obedience on a large scale in the country to-day. I have again and again appealed to reason, and let me assure him that if happily the country has come to believe in the spinning wheel as the giver of plenty, it has done so after laborious thinking, after great hesitation. I am not sure that even now educated India has assimilated the truth underlying the *Charkha*. He must not mistake the surface dirt for the substance underneath. Let him go deeper and see for himself, whether the *charkha* has been accepted from blind faith or from reasoned necessity.

I do indeed ask the poet and the sage to spin the wheel as a sacrament. When there is war, the poet lays down the lyre, the lawyer his law reports, the schoolboy his books. The poet will sing the true note after the war is over, the lawyer will have occasion to go to his law books when people have time to fight among themselves. When a house is on fire, *all* the inmates go out, and each one takes up a bucket to quench the fire. When all about me are dying for want of food, the only occupation permissible to me is to feed the hungry. It is my conviction that India is a house on fire because its manhood is being daily scorched, it is dying of hunger because it has no work to buy food with. Khulna is starving not because the people cannot work, but because they have no work. The Ceded Districts are passing successively through a fourth famine. Orissa is a land suffering from chronic famines. Our cities are *not* India. India lives in her seven and a half lacs of villages, and the cities live upon the villages. They do not bring their wealth from other countries. The city people are brokers and commission agents for the big houses of Europe, America and Japan. The cities have co-operated with the latter in the bleeding process that has gone on for the past two hundred years. It is my belief based on experience, that India is daily growing poorer. The circulation about her feet and legs has almost stopped. And if we do not take care, she will collapse altogether.

To a people famishing and idle, the only acceptable form in which God can dare appear is work and promise of food as wages. God created man to work for his food, and said that those who ate without work were thieves. Eighty per cent. of India are compulsorily thieves half the year. Is it any wonder if India has become one vast prison? Hunger is the argument that is driving India to the spinning wheel. The call of the spinning wheel is the noblest of all. Because it is the call of love. And love is Swaraj. The spinning wheel will 'curb the mind' when the time is spent on necessary physical labour can be said to do so. We must think of millions who are to-day less than animals, who are almost in a dying state. The spinning wheel is the reviving draught for the millions of our dying countrymen and countrywomen. 'Why should I who have no need to work for food, spin?' may be the question asked. Because I am eating what does not belong to me. I am living on the spoliation of my countrymen. Trace the course of every pice that finds its way into your pocket, and you will realise the truth of what I write. Swaraj has no meaning for the millions if they do not know how to employ their enforced idleness. The attainment of this Swaraj is possible within a short time and it is so possible only by the revival of the spinning wheel.

I do want growth, I do want self-determination, I do want freedom, but I want all these for the soul. I doubt if the steel age is an advance upon the flint age. I am indifferent. It is the evolution of the soul to which the intellect and all our faculties have to be devoted. I have no difficulty in imagining the possibility of a man armoured after the modern style making some lasting and new discovery for mankind, but I have less difficulty in imagining the possibility of a man having nothing but a bit of flint and a dail for lighting his path or his matchlock ever singing new hymns of praise and delivering to an aching world a message of peace and good will upon earth. A plea for the spinning wheel is a plea for recognising the dignity of labour.

I claim that in losing the spinning wheel we lost our left lung. We are therefore suffering from galloping consumption. The restoration of the wheel arrests the progress of the fell disease. There are certain things which all must do in all climes. There are certain things which all must do in certain climes. The spinning wheel is the thing which all must turn in the Indian clime for the transition stage at any rate and the vast majority must for all time.

It was our love of foreign cloth that ousted the wheel from its position of dignity. Therefore I consider it a sin to wear foreign cloth. I must confess that I do not draw a sharp or any distinction between economics and ethics. Economics that hurt the moral well-being of an individual or a nation are immoral and therefore sinful. Thus the economics that permit one country to prey upon another are immoral. It is sinful to buy and use articles made by sweated labour. It is sinful to eat American wheat and let my neighbour the grain dealer starve for want of custom. Similarly it is sinful for me to wear the latest finery of Regent Street, when I know that if I had but worn the things woven by the neighbouring spinners and weavers, that would have clothed me, and fed and clothed them. On the knowledge of my sin bursting upon me, I must consign the foreign garments to the flames and thus purify myself, and thenceforth rest content with the rough *Khadi* made by my neighbours. On knowing that my neighbours may not, having given up the occupation, take kindly to the spinning wheel, I must take it up myself and thus make it popular.

I venture to suggest to the Poet that the clothes I ask him to burn must be and are his. If they had to his knowledge belonged to the poor or the ill-clad, he would long ago have restored to the poor what was theirs. In burning *my* foreign clothes I burn my shame. I must refuse to insult the naked by giving them clothes they do not need, instead of giving them work which they sorely need. I will not commit the sin of becoming their patron, but on learning that I had assisted in impoverishing them, I would give them a privileged position and give them neither crumbs nor cast off clothing, but the best of my food and clothes and associate myself with them in work.

Nor is the scheme of Non-co-operation or Swadeshi an

exclusive doctrine. My modesty has prevented me from declaring from the house top that the message of Non-co-operation, Non-violence and Swadeshi, is a message to the world. It must fall flat, if it does not bear fruit in the soil where it has been delivered. At the present moment India has nothing to share with the world save her degradation, pauperism and plagues. Is it her ancient Shastras that we should send to the world? Well they are printed in many editions, and an incredulous and idolatrous world refuses to look at them, because we, the heirs and custodians, do not live them. Before, therefore, I can think of sharing with the world, I must possess. Our Non-co-operation is neither with the English nor with the West. Our Non-co-operation is with the system the English have established, with the material civilisation and its attendant greed and exploitation of the weak. Our Non-co-operation is a retirement within ourselves. Our Non-co-operation is a refusal to co-operate with the English administrators on their own terms. We say to them, 'Come and co-operate with us on our terms, and it will be well for us, for you and the world.' We must refuse to be lifted off our feet. A drowning man cannot save others. In order to be fit to save others, we must try to save ourselves. Indian nationalism is not exclusive, nor aggressive, nor destructive. It is health-giving, religious and therefore humanitarian. India must learn to live before she can aspire to die for humanity. The mice which helplessly find themselves between the cat's teeth acquire no merit from their enforced sacrifice.

True to his poetical instinct the Poet lives for the morrow and would have us do likewise. He presents to our admiring gaze the beautiful picture of the birds early in the morning singing hymns of praise as they soar into the sky. These birds had their day's food and soared with rested wings in whose veins new blood had flown during the previous night. But I have had the pain of watching birds who for want of strength could not be coaxed even into a flutter of their wings. The human bird under the Indian sky gets up weaker than when he pretended to retire. For millions it is an eternal vigil or an eternal trance. It is an indescribably painful state which has to be experienced to be realised. I have found it impossible to sooth suffering patients with a song from Kabir. The hungry millions ask for one poem—invigorating food. They cannot be given it. They must earn it. And they can earn only by the sweat of their brow.

Niyatham kuru karmathvam karmajyaayohyakarmanah :
. . . . (8)

Yagnyaarthaath karmanonyathra lokoyam karmabandhanah :
Thadarttham karma Kountheya mukthasanga : samachara (9)

Saha yagnaah : prajaah srishtva purovaacha prajaapathihi :
Anena prasavishyaddvamesha Voasthishtakaamaddhuk (10)

Devaanbhaavayathaanena the devaabhaavayanthu vah :
Parasparam bhaavayanthah : sreyah : paramavaapsyattha (11)

Ishtaanbhogaanhivodevaa daasyanthe yagnyabhaavithaah .
Thairdattaanapradaayaibhyo yo bhungthe sthena eva sah : (12)

Yagnasishtaasinah : santho mutchyamte sarvakilbishaii :
Bhujamthe the thvagham paapaa ye pachanthyaathmakaranaath (13)

Annaathbhavanthi dhuthaani parjanyaadannasambhavah :
Yagnyaathbhavathi parjanyo yagnah : karmasamudbhavah : (14)

Karma brahmoobhavam viddhi brahmaaksharasamudbhavam
Thasmaathsarvagatham brahma nithyam yagne prathishtitham (15)

Evam pravarthitham chakram naanuvarthayathiiha yah :
Aghaayurindriyaaraamo mogham paarttha sa jiivathi (16)

Gita—CHAPTER III.

In these verses* is contained for me the whole truth of the spinning wheel as an indispensable sacrament for the India of to-day. If we will take care of to-day, God will take care of the morrow.

20th October, 1921

THE MEANING OF THE MOPLAH RISING

(By M. K. Gandhi)

A correspondent from Scotland takes me to task for not dealing sufficiently with the Moplah rising † in these columns. The result, he says, has been that those in Great Britain who are in the habit of studying Indian affairs have been induced to believe that an Islamic kingdom is established in India. The reproof is not wholly undeserved, but I have not shirked duty in the matter. I have been simply helpless. I wanted to go to Calicut and reach the bottom of the trouble as I believed I could have. But the Government had willed it otherwise. I am sorry to believe, but it is my belief, that the men on the spot do not wish to give Non-co-operators the credit for peacefully ending the trouble. They are desirous of showing once more that it is only the British soldier who can maintain peace in India. And I could not then give battle to the Government by disregarding the instructions not to enter the disturbed area.

* The general sense of the verses is "perform right action, for action is supreme to inaction, and, inactive, even the maintenance of the body would not be possible." The verses summarise the whole philosophy of the *Gita* "free from attachment, perform right action" regardless of the fruits thereof. For Edwin Arnold's translation of these verses, *See* p. 500.

† *See* Appendix.

I should like to think better of the men on the spot. It is contrary to my nature to believe in the depravity of human beings. But there is so much evidence about me of the depravity of the bureaucratic mind that it will stop at nothing to gain its end. It is the literal truth I tell, when I say that before I went to Champaran, I did not believe the stories I was told of atrocities committed against the peasantry of Champaran. When I went there, I found the state much worse than was described to me. I had refused to believe that innocent people could have been murdered in cold blood without warning as they were in Jallianwala Bagh. I had refused to believe that human beings could be made to crawl upon their bellies. But on reaching the Punjab, I found to my horror that much more than what I was told had happened. And all this was done in the name of peace and order so called, but in reality for the purpose of sustaining a false prestige, a false system and an unnatural commerce. It is true that a strong Lieutenant-Governor was able to attain justice in Champaran in the face of overwhelming opposition. But that was really an exception due to exceptional causes. And so I feel the Moplah revolt has come as a blessing to a system that is crumbling to pieces by the weight of its own enormity.

The Moplah revolt is a test for Hindus and Mussalmans. Can Hindu friendship survive the strain put upon it? Can Mussalmans in the deepest recesses of their hearts approve of the conduct of the Moplahs? Time alone can show the reality. A verbal and forced philosophic acceptance of the inevitable is no test of Hindu friendship. The Hindus must have the courage and the faith to feel that they can protect their religion in spite of such fanatical eruptions. A verbal disapproval by the Mussalmans of Moplah madness is no test of Mussalman friendship. The Mussalmans must naturally feel the shame and humiliation of the Moplah conduct about forcible conversions and looting, and they must work away so silently and effectively that such things might become impossible even on the part of the most fanatical among them. My belief is that the Hindus as a body have received the Moplah madness with equanimity and that the cultured Mussalmans are sincerely sorry of the Moplah's perversion of the teachings of the Prophet.

The Moplah revolt teaches another lesson, *viz.*, that each individual must be taught the art of self-defence. It is more a mental state that has to be inculcated than that our bodies should be trained for retaliation. Our mental training has been one of feeling helpless. Bravery is not a quality of the body, it is of the soul. I have seen cowards encased in tough muscle, and rare courage in the frailest body. I have seen big bulky and muscular Zulus cowering before an English lad and turning tail if they saw a loaded revolver pointed at them. I have seen Emily Hobhouse with a paralytic body exhibiting courage of the highest order. She was the one noble woman who kept up the drooping spirits of brave Boer generals and equally brave Boer women. The weakest of us physically must be taught the art of facing dangers and giving a good account of ourselves. What was more detestable, the ignorant fanaticism of the Moplah brother, or the cowardliness of the Hindu brother who helplessly muttered the Islamic formula or allowed his tuft of hair to be cut or his vest to be changed? Let me not be misunderstood. I want both the Hindus and Mussalmans to cultivate the cool courge to die without killing. But if one has not that courage, I want him to cultivate the art of killing and being killed, rather than in a cowardly manner flee from danger. For the latter, in spite of his flight, does commit mental *himsa*. He flees because he has not the courage to be killed in the act of killing.

There is yet another lesson the Moplah outbreak teaches us. We dare not leave any section of our countrymen in utter darkness and expect not to be overtaken by it ourselves. Our English 'masters' were uninterested in the Moplahs becoming orderly citizens and learning the virtue of toleration and the truth of Islam. But we too have neglected our ignorant countrymen all these long centuries. We have not felt the call of love to see that no one was left ignorant of the necessity of humaneness or remained in want of food or clothing for no fault of his own. If we do not wake up betimes, we shall find a similar tragedy enacted by all the submerged classes. The present awakening is affecting all classes. The "untouchables" and all the so-called semi-savage tribes will presently bear witness to our wrongs against them if we do not do penance and render tardy justice to them.

23rd February, 1922

NO END TO MY SORROWS

(By M. K. Gandhi)

The Manager of the *Lokamanya* has forwarded to me the following interview between the representative of that paper and Mr. Paul Richard. He asks me to publish it and to offer my remarks upon it. I do so not without great hesitation and reluctance, but often a public worker has no choice. He has to overcome reluctance as also hesitation. It was sorrowful for me to have to correct what was an honest but gross misrepresentation of my views about Shantiniketan.* There are some things which one holds sacred and which one does not care to discuss in public. The interview that I am now asked to publish adds to my many sorrows. Here is it:

"*Question*:—After the last postponement of civil disobedience at Bardoli, the number is increasing among the Non-co-operationists who do not understand the mind of the Mahatma. What do you think about it?

"*Answer*:—Everything is easy to understand in the attitude of Mahatma Gandhi if one remembers that his true aim is not what people generally think, but what he has expressed to me a few days ago, saying "I do not work for freedom of India, I work for non-violence in the world and that is the difference between me and Mr. Tilak. Mr. Tilak was telling me, 'I would sacrifice even truth for freedom of my country,' but I am ready to sacrifice even freedom for the sake of truth." In the light of these words you can understand the reason of the actual postponement of national programme, until the spirit of violence has been shaken everywhere in India; that means probably until the end of the world!

"The mind of Mahatmaji can be expressed in a word—'Non-violence at any cost'; just as the mind of Mrs. Besant and of the moderate party can be expressed by the motto "Law and Order at any cost": and such is also the will of the Government. But the will of the national soul behind and above all is 'At any cost a new Law and a new Order.'

"This will of the new spirit in India, Asia and all over the world, is the only one which by any way is sure to triumph."

I had a rare time with Mr. Paul Richard. We had many happy hours together. I could see at once that our views of life were fundamentally different in some respects, but that did not matter in the slightest degree to me. We met each other as distant acquaintances. We parted as the best of friends. Though it is now my lot to criticise what Mr. Paul Richard has said, my

* See *infra*.

regard for his learning, for his humanity and his philosophy remains undiminished. But I cannot help expressing my deep regret that he should have related what was sacred conversation between him and me and that in an attenuated form. He makes me cut a sorry figure in that interview. It is not possible to deny the substance of it, and yet torn from its context and put in the language of Mr. Paul Richard, it makes me look so utterly ridiculous. The Maharashtra party and I are endeavouring to understand each other. We are coming daily nearer. That party would rightly resent any reflection on my part upon the career or the character of one of the greatest of Indians and one who rules that party's hearts as no other man rules the hearts of any other set of men. Mr. Paul Richard and I were engaged in a deeply religious discourse. I was trying to give to him the fundamentals of my own faith. I was arguing upon the sharp difference that both he and I observed between us, and whilst I was elucidating my point I came upon the differences between the Lokamanya and myself in a reverent spirit. After many a frank chat with the Lokamanya I had come to see that on some vital matters we would never agree. Drawing illustrations from his inexhaustible store of Sanskrit learning, he used to challenge my interpretation of life and frankly and bluntly would say, truth and untruth were only relative terms, but at bottom there was no such thing as truth and untruth just as there was no such thing as life and death. Whilst I could not resist the abstract presentation, I detected a flaw in its application to actual life and I put it before him in all reverence. In my opinion, we never misunderstood each other. At Sinhagad where both he and I were trying to take rest we came closer together. I noticed that he was fearless and sincere in the enunciation of his views and he tried to live up to them. I could discover also the reasons for the marvellous hold he had on millions of his countrymen. I have claimed no superiority for myself. I only know that we fundamentally differed, but my respect for him grew with greater contact, and I believe that his affection for me also grew as time went on. The remarks, therefore, that were made to Mr. Paul Richard were made, I assure the reader, in no disparagement of the character of the illustrious deceased and I hope that the bald presentation of that difference in the interviews will not in any way acerbate the members of the great Maharashtra party whose hearty co-operation in the national struggle I value so highly and in order to conciliate whom I go many a mile so long as I have not to sacrifice my principle.

Mr. Paul Richard's presentation of my views about non-violence is really a caricature. I have no doubt that he understands me in the manner in which he has represented me. There is undoubtedly a sense in which the statement is true when I say that I hold my religion dearer than my country and that therefore I am a Hindu first and nationalist after. I do not become on that score a less nationalist than the best of them. I simply thereby imply that the interests of my country are identical with those of my religion. Similarly when I say that I prize my own salvation above everything else, above the salvation of India, it does not mean that my personal salvation requires a sacrifice of India's political or any other salvation. But it implies necessarily that the two go together. Just in the same sense I would decline to gain India's freedom at the cost of non-violence, meaning that India will never gain her freedom without non-violence or through violence. That I may be hopelessly wrong in holding the view is another matter, but such is my view and it is daily growing on me. I have so often remarked that whatever may be true of other countries, India's salvation lies only through the path of non-violence. If Mr. Paul Richard had understood me correctly he would have pacified his interviewer by saying that I believed that India could gain her liberty quickly only through non-violence and that therefore so long as the country accepted my guidance the country would have to be satisfied with my limitations and therefore permit me to guide her so long as the country believed that, as it is circumstanced, it had no means open to her for gaining her end, except by non-violence and truth. Mr. Paul Richard had made the position worse by remarking that if India's freedom depends upon non-violence, it will never be attained. It passes comprehension how he could have omitted to take notice of the phenomenal progress made by the country in the direction of freedom. Indeed, I claim that India is substantially free to-day, she has found the way, she is asserting herself, she has thousands of her children—men and women—who have learnt the sovereign virtue of sacrifice without retaliation, and it is my certain conviction that if only workers will work out the constructive programme placed before them with industry and honesty, I have not a shadow of a doubt that we shall gain all the three ends in no time. I do not for one moment believe that the Congress workers cannot control forces of hooliganism that exist in the country. Only we have not tried whole-heartedly to gain that control.

15*th March*, 1922

HIS SORROW IS MY SORROW

[The following reply by Mr. Paul Richard to Mr. Gandhi's article, "No End to my Sorrows" in *Young India* of February '23, was received some time ago. As it appears from subsequent correspondence that Mr. Richard wanted it to be published, Mr. Gandhi handed it over to me about half-an-hour before his arrest on the night of the 10th instant.—K.]

A few lines of an interview have brought sorrow to the Mahatmaji. I am pained at it: his sorrow is my sorrow. He is for me more than a friend. I was a stranger and a vagabond, and he welcomed me. I am bad, and he has been good to me. For him I have reverence and love. The last thing I would do is to grieve him and make his burden heavier. I am surprised that he has attached such importance to this interview. My opinion is of very little value in public affairs. I would gladly and thankfully accept his reproaches and remain silent; but I can also comment on my own words in perfect accordance with his views and wishes. Though I believe, for men such as we are, nothing sacred need remain secret. I should deeply repent if I had really repeated what was "a sacred conversation between us." But in this interview I have quoted only two words out of a conversation of two hours; and one of these is itself a quotation of a well-known utterance, discussed many a time in many a paper, and attributed to the great Tilak, the Karmadeva, "who died in order to conquer."

My poor mind fully accepts the charge of misunderstanding, for it fails even to understand in what way it has misunderstood. I fail to understand also how any intelligent and benevolent mind can misunderstand the obvious meaning of the few words that I have quoted. It is plain that when Mr. Tilak, expressing in a forcible manner his wonderful patriotism, said: "I will sacrifice even Truth for the freedom of my country," he meant by these words, "for the freedom of my country I am ready to sacrifice everything, including myself, my own soul, and the Truth which is the soul of my soul, and my salvation, to the salvation of my people " For the Saviour is he who does not care to save himself, who loses himself in saving others." I fail to understand how the followers and the admirers of the master-patriot could in any way be "acerbated" by the quotation of one of his masterful sayings, and how they can be otherwise than proud of him, if he has really pronounced such a noble, grand and selfless utterance.

In the same way when the Mahatmaji said, "I am ready to sacrifice even freedom for the sake of Truth and Non-violence, " it is obvious that he does not mean that this sacrifice has in any way to be done. Everyone knows that the two things are closely associated in his mind and action. But it is obvious also that if for any reason he has to choose between these two things, he means that he will choose the Truth and Non-violence rather than the freedom of India. And in saying this, he also expresses in a forcible manner this beautiful fact that for him personal or even national interests are of less importance than moral principles and human progress. And thus he reveals himself as greater than the greatest patriot, as a prophet of humanity, a messenger, an incarnation of the god of Non-violence in this world.

I fail to understand in what way this presentation can be a misrepresentation, this magnification "a caricature," and how my language can make the Mahatmaji "so utterly ridiculous." I accept again this epithet "ridiculous", but only for my bad language. Each one fights the English as he can, and this is my way of Non-co-operation,—linguistic Non-co-operation and speech disobedience.

One thing, however, I have not said, and I could also complain to have been misquoted. I never remarked that "if India's freedom depends upon non-violence it will never be attained." I simply said that if the national programme has to be postponed "until the spirit of non-violence has been shaken everywhere in India, it means, probably, until the end of the world."

As for freedom of India, I have full faith in it. I have unceasingly said that it will come, that it is coming; but perhaps by other ways. It may come neither by violence nor by non-violence. It may come from England itself, even as it came to her at the fall of the Roman Empire. For, great changes are impending in England, in Europe, in the whole world. The ways of God are most often the most unexpected ones. It is this way that I expect. What I have always said is that if the national movement does not bring freedom to India, it prepares India for freedom.

It leads to the awakening of the masses; this awakening of the masses to social chaos, this chaos to new creation, this new creation to greatness—and this greatness will make India ready for and worthy of the freedom which comes to her.

Is there any room for any "Sorrow"?

EFFECTS OF NON-CO-OPERATION

From time to time, Mr. Gandhi examined the effects of Non-co-operation on individuals and on the country. The following from *Young India* relate to them:

How it purifies.—Every one knows Mr. Abbas Tyabji, Retired Chief Justice of Baroda, a son of the patriot Badraddin Tyabji. Ever since his labours on the Congress Committee's Punjab Report, Mr. Abbas has been doing some service or other to the country, but Non-co-operation has revolutionised his life, as it has many other lives. Mr. Abbas, though old, is now working night and day in Kheda, in order to finish its part of the Bezwada programme. He is not used to the strenuous life of the peasant. And yet he is at the present moment engaged in mixing with the simple farmers of Kheda on their own terms. Young friends working with him tell me that he is beating every one of them in energy and application. I am sure the reader will appreciate the following from a letter, which he wrote to me in reply to mine betraying anxiety about his health. This is what he says:

> "I assure you, you need have not the slightest anxiety about my health. I have not been healthier for many years. In fact, the *Khaddar* adopted at Bezwada has simply made me twenty years younger. What an experience I am having? Everywhere I am received most cordially and affectionately even by the women of the villages. Most of the places visited by me have subscribed twice or thrice their quota. It is only the big towns like Anand and Nadiad that lag behind. But Nadiad, where I have already spent four days, is coming up, and I feel that it will make up its

quota, if indeed it does not even go beyond it. To-day I am going to Kapadvanj, and I shall continue to pass my nights at Nadiad; otherwise the good friends will go to sleep!

* * * *

"Some of our workers are lacking in 'go'. I suppose they represent the very respectable class to which I have ceased to belong. God! what an experience? I have so much love and affection from the common folk to whom it is now an honour to belong! It is this fakir's dress that has broken down all barriers. And now men and women meet me as I would have them meet. If one had only known years ago, how the 'fenta,' the 'saya,' the 'angarakha,' boots and stockings separated one from one's poorer brethren! How, so dressed, it was impossible to get them to confide in one, is what I realise only now. How much I have missed in life, is just dawning on me.

* * * *

"How much the movement has affected the course of my life, is only dimly perceptible to me. Still I do perceive it, which is what counts. To realise what pleasure there is in giving is also a fresh experience."—*29th June*, 1921.

The Beauty of it.—By the kind permission of the Pandit Motilal Nehru, I reproduce the following instructive and entertaining description, word for word, of his life at Ramgadh where he was recently recuperating:

The climate and the surroundings of the little hill top on which I am perched all by myself save for one servant has agreed with me remarkably. There is a trace of asthma and cough still left but it is bound to disappear with returning health and strength. The only pity is that I am not allowed sufficient time for the after cure, and this is due to the past sins of professional life which are still following me. Out of the hundreds of briefs on my hands when I suspended practice, there were two which I could not give up. One of these cases came on immediately before Sarp's marriage, and was to a certain extent responsible for the break-down of my health, and the other is now interfering with my rest cure. It is a long original trial and begins on the 5th of July, requiring three or four days' previous study. I am trying to have it shunted off after the All-India meeting in Lucknow, but have provisionally fixed the 30th June, as the date of my departure from Ramgadh. If I am only allowed a couple of weeks more. I can promise you that I would be as strong as a bull, but perhaps it is not safe for a Non-violent Non-co-operator to be so strong in body.

You will be interested to know the kind of life I am leading here. In the good(?) old days, two kitchen establishments—one English and the other Indian—accompanied me in the hills. After Chhota-Hazri in camp. we would start off for the jungle with a full equipment of rifles, short guns and ammunition, and on occasions with quite a little army of beaters and killed such innocent creatures as came on our way till late in the afternoon—lunch and tea being served in the jungle with as much punctilious care as at home. A hearty dinner awaited our return to camp, and after doing full justice to it we slept the sleep of the just! There was nothing to disturb the even tenor of life except occasional annoyance at a stupid miss which saved the life of some poor beast. And now—the brass cooker (purchased in Delhi when we were all there for the opening of the Tibbi college) has taken the place of the two kitchens, a solitary servant not over-intelligent that of the old retinue—three small bags containing rice, dal and masala that of the mule loads of provisions (I shall never excuse Kamla for making these bags of Bideshi cloth instead of Khadi)—one square meal of rice, dal, vegetables, sometimes khir (milk and rice cooked together) in the middle of the day. that of breakfast, lunch and dinner *a la' Anglaiser*—lots of fruit with morning and afternoon tea and an occasional egg or two when available. The Shikar has given place to long walks and the rifles and guns to books, magazines and newspapers (the favourite book being Edwin Arnold's *Song Celestial* which is now undergoing a third reading). When it rains hard as it is doing now, there is nothing but to write silly letters like this. "What a fall, my countrymen!" But really I have never enjoyed life better. Only the rice has given out, and I have applied Brahman-like for a dole from the ministerial stores of Jagatnarayan who happens to be near.—*21st July*, 1921.

Two Students.—Messrs. Mahomed Husain and Shafique Rahman Kidwai are students of the National Muslim University. They were posted in the Andhra District by Maulana Mahomed Ali. They were there doing great work in a most unassuming manner. They have already gone to gaol whilst their chief is still on his trial. The circumstances in which they went to gaol are graphically described in their letter written on their way to prison, which I give below in full :

After seeing you off at Guntakal, we went to Adoni where we received a wire from Mr. Harisarvottama Rao calling us to Cuddapah because three Congress workers had been arrested there. We went there on the eleventh October, and were working with some of our Guntur friends. We held serveral meetings and formed Congress and Khilafat committees. On the 21st October., in a monster meeting of over six thousand people, we distributed the *Fatwa* and the audience reiterated the Karachi resolution standing. We also procured 1,400 signatures on the spot and collected two thousand and five hundred rupees for Angora. On the evening of the 24th. all the workers were served with an order under Sec. 144, gagging us for two months. Yesterday early in the morning, we were served with summons to appear before the court and furnish securities for good behaviour. Accordingly, we went to the court and had an informal talk with the Superintendent of Police (a European) for two hours, with the permission of the Collector. The case then began and we were charged under Sec. 108 for seditious speeches and under Sec. 124-A for seducing the soldiery by distributing the *Fatwa* and explaining it. After two prosecuting witnesses were examined, we gave our statement and the court adjourned till four in the afternoon. Every one was amazed to see that we were allowed to go to our place in the city without any sort of police custody. We returned to the court at four and the Magistrate asked us to furnish securities which we refused to do. The Magistrate then sentenced us to 6 months' simple imprisonment and said: "Gentlemen, it is a painful duty to sentence men of your stamp." He then shook hands with us. The Superintendent then embraced us and said, "I wish to work hand in hand with you for the good of the country." Even then they did not take us in custody. We went to the mosque, said our prayers and walked to the station with the people of the town and there we found a sub-inspector and two constables waiting to take us to Central Jail, Vellore. This sort of behaviour was never expected from the police as they behaved with Mr. Ramamurti and others very roughly.

> We are glad that we have followed in the footsteps of our loving and respected Principal Maulana Mahomed Ali and congratulate ourselves that we are the first to be imprisoned for the so-called seducing the military by distributing the *Fatwa* and reiterating the Karachi resolution. We have done our duty and request you to bless us with your prayers. We are cheerful at heart and pray to God to endow us with courage and strength to undergo all rigours and hardships.

I do not know whom to congratulate most, the brave youngmen, the Magistrate and the police, or the Principal who has moulded the character of these young men. As for the Government which sends such innocent men to prison, I can only say it is digging its own grave in a way no Non-co-operator can.—*3rd November*, 1921.

Language of the Heart.—The fire of suffering has brought forth some fine thoughts clothed in beautiful language. I must confess that I have seen nothing like it before in all the ponderous speeches and addresses which have tickled our ears or delighted our intellect. Whether one looks at Lalaji's manifesto, Pandit Motilalji's message, or Maulana Abul Kalam Azad's, one cannot fail to be struck with their beauty. But no one has been more touching, more fervent, more prolific than the President-elect. He has poured forth short crisp messages that have come straight from the heart. I wish some enterprising publisher will collect all these messages and publish them in book form. But I cannot resist the temptation of culling two passages from his message to the students given after hearing of two years' rigorous imprisonment awarded to Professor Jitendralal Banerji. The first is a striking quotation from Jiten Babu's own vigorous statement before the court. Here it is:

> "If it is a sin to have demanded liberty for my countrymen with full and passionate intensity of soul, then I have sinned grievously,

sinned beyond pardon or penitence and I rejoice that I have so sinned. If it is an offence to have asked my people to shake off the fetters of foreign servitude that degrades and dwarfs our humanity, then I am one of the most offending souls alive, and I rejoice that God gave me the courage and hardihood to commit such an offence. And as the All-merciful gave me courage and strength in the past to speak out the truth that is within me, so I hope that He will give me endurance in the future to go through the agony of man's unrighteous persecution."

And here are the closing paragraphs of Deshabandu's appeal:

"What is Jitendralal Banerjee? I ask the students of Calcutta to realise the truth of his life. Words cannot convey it. The work that he did, the life which he lived, the qualities of his head and heart, all culminating in the grand sacrifice which he had the courage to make—these are more eloquent than any words that I can employ.

"I ask again, what is Jitendralal Banerjee? I wish with all the craving of my heart the students of Calcutta knew how to answer this question. He had given his life for the well-being of his dear devoted students. Are there none now to tell us the meaning of his sacrifice not by speaking angry words, nor by shedding idle tears but by taking up the cause he loved so well and by strengthening that cause by their own sacrifice?

"Merely existing is not living. I wish I could say students of Calcutta were living as men should live, as Jitendralal Banerjee lived. Now that his body is imprisoned, is there no one amongst the students of Calcutta who has the heart to hear the call of his soul?"

Let no one underrate the importance of these appeals as mere emotion. Let no one belittle or scoff henceforth at Bengal's emotion. Bengal has moved out to the call of the country in a manner not expected even by me with all my staunch faith in Bengal. All the response that is being made is not confined to Calcutta merely nor to Chittagong but to every place in Bengal where repression has gone. It is not froth. One does not undergo suffering by empty appeals or empty emotionalism. Bengal has proved the solidity of her emotion.—*22nd December*, 1921.

15*th December*, 1921

A CROP OF DIFFICULTIES

A Bihar corespondent who gives his name writes as follows:

"I was to some extent considered to be a zealous worker in the cause of our country's welfare. I had sided with non-co-operation with full belief that it was religiously compulsory upon every Moslem. I never deceived myself with any hope of India's regeneration through Non-co-operation nor have I yet been persuaded to hope so. On the contrary, I believed that we were to Non-co-operate with the British Government at the sacrifice of our best interests. By this I do mean that I consider Non-co-operation to be less effective but I do most strongly say that our countrymen are not capable of adhering to it with perfect non-violence. I have had opportunities enough to see that your lieutenants are more anxious to make a name than do any good to the cause they stand for. I think the morale of the country has so far deteriorated that it is beyond possibility that our present generation can effectively practise Non-co-operation with non-violence. Is it not strange that a responsible leader like yourself could shut his eyes to this apparent and abject condition of things?

"I have taxed my brain to the last degree to find the reason why we are in such a hurry about Swaraj. Of course to delay would be sinful if Swaraj was within our grip, but after so much evidence of failures, why do you still stick to dating the advent of Swaraj by months? If it was only to rouse the teeming masses, I am afraid the idea was not well conceived as clear from recent happenings. To give out absurd hopes is nothing but playing with people's passion.

"I make bold to beseech you in the interest of India and Indians to make a halt. Let us first train the countrymen and then march them to do battle. We have begun the fight with bad soldiers. It is better to accept defeat for next offensive than defend with such conditions. I am sure God's laws are just, and therefore Islam makes it conditional to see the capacity before taking up any thing. The pilgrimage to Mecca is one of the five Fundaments or Islam but not for all and sundry. To work for Swaraj, *i.e.*, freedom of one's country, ought to be one of our foremost duties, but is it not cruelty to try us far beyond our capacity? I am afraid this hurry is at the root of most of the mischief done.

"I should like to hear through *Young India* your views."

He is a well known Bihari. There is no doubt about his honesty. I therefore gladly respond to his suggestion to give a public reply to his letter. Though Non-co-operation was in the first instance conceived in connection with the Khilafat, neither I nor my first associates ever thought that Non-co-operation with the British Government involved any sacrifice whatsoever of the country's interests. On the contrary, we believed that, if we could compel surrender to the just demands of the Mussalmans of India regarding the Khilafat. we could also compel surrender in the matter of the Punjab and consequently in the matter of Swaraj. Non-violence was believed from the very commencement to be an integral part of Non-co-operation, and if the former failed the latter failed *ipso facto*. Indeed, the recent happenings have furnished abundant proof of the progress of non-violence. They show, I hope conclusively, that Bombay's aberration was an isolated instance in no way symptomatic of the general condition of the country. A year ago it would have been impossible for the Government to arrest so many leaders of the front rank in so many parts of the country leaving the people absolutely self-controlled. It would be a mistake to suppose that it is the machine gun which has kept all the people under restraint. No doubt it has its share, but he who runs may see that there are hundreds, if not thousands, of people in India to-day to whom machine guns have ceased to be a terror. Nor can I subscribe to the doctrine that the country has suffered deterioration. On the contrary, every province can demonstrate the marvellous revolution brought about by this movement of purification in the lives of people. A distinguished Mussalman friend was telling me only the other day how the younger generation of Mussalmans was reclaimed from a life of indolent and atheistical luxury to one of religious simplicity and industry.

We are certainly in a hurry to get Swaraj. Who can help it? Were the Moplahs in the death-wagon in a hurry when in their asphyxiated state they were crying out for a breath of fresh air and a drink of water? The death-wagon of foreign domination in which we are suffering from moral asphyxiation is infinitely worse than the Moplah death-wagon. And the wonder is that all these long years we have not felt the want of the oxygen of liberty. But having known our state, is it not most natural for us to cry out for the fresh air of Swaraj? I am unable to accept any blame for having set the time limit. I would have been wrong not to do so, knowing as I did that, if the people fulfilled the conditions which were capable of easy fulfilment, Swaraj was a certainty inside of twelve months. If the atmosphere of non-violence is truly established, I make bold to say that we shall achieve the substance even during the remaining days of this year, though we might have to wait for the form yet a while. The time limit was not fixed in order to rouse the teeming millions, but it was fixed in order to rivet the attention of Congressmen and Congresswomen on their sense of immediate duty and on the grand consequence of its fulfilment. Without the time limit we would not have collected the crore nor would we have introduced so many spinning wheels, nor manufactured thousands of rupees worth of handspun *Khadi* and distributed lakhs amongst the poorest workers in the country. It is not a sign of bad soldiery to find Bengal, the United Provinces, and the Punjab supplying prisoners as fast as Government can take them. And when the word passes round the other provinces for repression of a violent type, I doubt not that they will shine just as brilliantly as the three fortunate ones I have mentioned.

PART VI

MISCELLANEOUS

PART VI

MISCELLANEOUS

7th July, 1921

THE PRINCE

(By M. K. Gandhi)

Mr. Baptista has written to the *Bombay Chronicle* on the forthcoming visit of His Royal Highness, the Prince of Wales and has combated views he imputes to me. Much as I should like for the present to observe silence on this delicate subject I cannot allow it to be said of me that I would 'visit the sins of ministers on the Prince.' I entirely agree with Mr. Baptista that the Prince has no voice in the government and that he is not concerned with the acts of the ministers of the Crown, much less with their blunders. I am just as keen as any one could be to give a royal reception to the Prince and it is because I appreciate the constitution and its working that I would boycott the visit under present conditions. It is because I know that the Royalty is above politics that I would not allow the ministers or the Government of India, if I can help it, to use the Prince for their own political purposes. If I can do nothing else, at least I must not become a tool in the hands of the ministers and the Government of India and allow them, under cover of the Prince's visit, to make their hold of India tighter and to demonstrate to the world that under their benign administration the whole of India is happy and contented. For let there be no mistake that such will be the result if we remained silent and, under a mistaken sense of loyalty or of the constitution, gave any reception to the Prince. On the contrary, I hope that our loyalty requires us to make it clear to His Majesty's ministers that if they send the Prince to India, we shall be in no mood to join any receptions they might arrange. I would tell them in no veiled language that we are sick at heart over the Khilafat and the Punjab questions and that whilst we are fighting them for very life, we must not be expected to co-operate with them in giving receptions to His Royal Highness. We would be doing a wrong to the public, if we neglected our clear duty of educating them to a truer perception of the meaning of the proposed Royal visit. Let it be known that the Prince will arrive by and with the advice of the ministers, and consent and approval of the Government of India. The visit therefore will be not an act of the Prince but that of the ministers and in boycotting the visit at this juncture, we would be visiting their sins upon themselves and not on the Prince. In other words, we would not be playing into their hands. Supposing the ministers sent Sir Michael O'Dwyer to replace Lord Chelmsford and he arranged the reception, would Mr. Baptista have us to fall into Sir Michael's trap? Suppose further that he insulted the Punjab under the Prince's nose by ignoring the Punjab leaders, should the Punjab pocket the insult and join the reception because Royalty is above politics! To say so would be to betray a woeful display of ignorance of the meaning of loyalty and politics.

I venture to suggest that if the Australian people were intensely dissatisfied with the acts or the blunders of the the ministers in the sense we are, they would boycott the visit without the slightest hesitation. The ministers want to make political capital out of the proposed visit. It is our duty to refuse to let them do so.

Mr. Baptista says and I agree that we are in mourning. He therefore hopes that the Prince would not be sent but if he is, Mr. Baptista says, we should give him a welcome in spite of the mourning. I want the prince to come and therefore I would try to remove the cause of mourning and not take it as a settled fact. I would tell the ministers that as we want to give the Prince an enthusiastic welcome, they should remove the Khilafat and the Punjab grievances. I should further tell them that if they did not do so and still persisted in sending the Prince to India, they would be responsible for placing the people in the awkward position of having to boycott the visit or the reception.

4th August, 1920

WHO IS DISLOYAL?

Mr. Montagu has discovered a new definition of disloyality.* He considers my suggestion to boycott the visit of the Prince of Wales to be disloyal and some newspapers taking the cue from him have called persons who have made the suggestion 'unmannerly.' They have even attributed to these 'unmannerly' persons the suggestion of 'boycotting the Prince.' I draw a sharp and fundamental distinction between boycotting the

*In the course of a speech in the Commons, Mr. Montagu stated that the movement to boycott the Prince's visit was a disloyal one.

Prince and boycotting any welcome arranged for him. Personally I would extend the heartiest welcome to His Royal Highness if he came or could come without official patronage and the protecting wings of the Government of the day. Being the heir to a constitutional monarch, the Prince's movements are regulated and dictated by the ministers no matter how much the dictation may be concealed beneath diplomatically polite language. In suggesting the boycott, therefore, the promoters have suggested boycott of an insolent bureaucracy and dishonest ministers of His Majesty.

You cannot have it both ways. It is true that under a constitutional monarchy, the royalty is above politics. But you cannot send the Prince on a political visit for the purpose of making political capital out of him, and then complain that those, who will not play your game and, in order to checkmate you, proclaim a boycott of the Royal visit, do not know constitutional usage. For the Prince's visit is not for pleasure. His Royal Highness is to come, in Mr. Lloyd George's words, as the "Ambassador of the British nation," in other words, his own ambassador in order to issue a certificate of merit to him and possibly to give the ministers a new lease of life. The wish is designed to consolidate and strengthen a power that spells mischief for India. Even as it is, Mr. Montagu has foreseen that the welcome will probably be excelled by any hitherto extended to Royalty, meaning that the people are not really and deeply affected and stirred by the official atrocities in the Punjab and the manifestly dishonest breach of official declarations on the Khilafat. With the knowledge that India was bleeding at heart, the Government of India should have told His Majesty's ministers that the moment was inopportune for sending the Prince.

I venture to submit that it is adding insult to injury to bring the Prince and through his visit to steal honours and further prestige for a Government that deserves to be dismissed with disgrace. I claim that I prove my loyalty * by saying that India is in no mood, is too deeply in mourning, to take part in and to welcome His Royal Highness, and that the ministers and the Indian Government show their disloyalty by making the Prince a cat's paw of their deep political game. If they persist, it is the clear duty of India to have nothing to do with the visit.

1*st December*, 1920

ROYAL VISITS: THEIR 'USE' AND ABUSE

(BY C. F. ANDREWS)

With the visit of the Duke of Connaught to this country still pending, it is of the greatest importance for the people of India clearly to understand how these royal visits are often unscrupulously used by Government for political purposes. The idea is, first of all, sedulously propagated that the royal visit has nothing to do with politics; that the Royal Family are above politics —that they are strictly neutral in their political attitude. Then, afterwards, the news is placarded on all sides that a great political success has been obtained. The late King Edward VII was rightly called the greatest

* In *Young India* of 17th November, 1921, Mr. Gandhi wrote in reply to a correspondent, Mr. A. H. Jayasinhani: (1) As a Non-co-operator, I neither own nor disown George as my King. I have dissociated myself from the system administered under the King's name. I keep myself free to give my allegiance to him, if I can attain my full growth in his kingdom and can secure full redress of the Khilafat and the Punjab wrongs.

diplomatist in the British empire. The present Prince of Wales has now earned the title of 'Our Greatest Ambassador."

If it were merely the spreading of messages of goodwill and peace to all nations that could be accomplished by such diplomatic and ambassadorial tours, the world might be all the better for them. But the danger always lurks at the back, that some distinctly political objects may be aimed at behind the scenes; that evil systems, which have power and authority behind them, may receive from them an added power and an added authority for oppression of the poor and subjection of the weak. Even to-day, the greater proportion of Europeans on the continent of Europe believe that the visits of King Edward were used by English politicians for the encirclement of Germany by a ring of hostile powers. Whether that opinion is right or wrong, need not be discussed here. I only wish to point out, how from a bitter past experience, these royal visits are surely feared in Europe. Europe has had her hard lesson to learn; and the proverb is true,—"Once bit, twice shy."

I wish now to tell the story of what happened, behind the scenes, in the Prince of Wales' recent visit of Fiji. The facts have just come to light, and they are most instructive.

The Indian community were suffering, at the time, from a most painful injustice. They had been charged with the offence of stirring up racial hatred against the Europeans and breaking out into 'open rebellion'; yet the truth was simply this, that the Indian labourers were nearly starving and had struck work in order to obtain from the plutocratic Colonial Sugar Refining Company a more just and equitable share of the enormous profits from sugar. The Colonial Sugar Refining Company had reaped these successive profits out of Indian labour, year after year, during the War. After the war also these had gone on still further increasing. Yet the Company continually refused to share what they had gained with the Indian labourers.

When I was in Fiji in 1917, there was an attempted suicide of an Indian. In open Court the Indian declared that he could not bear to see his young children crying for bread and to have nothing to give them to eat. The judge dismissed him with a warning. That was cold comfort indeed! And what can be said strong enough about the oppression of the poor by this wealthy Sugar Company with its many crores of capital? Yet it held out to the last, against a mere rise in wages of *3d.* per day when I tried to negotiate this for the Indian labourers in the Colony in 1917.

The Indian community, when freed at last from indenture, demanded a decent living wage—the wage of a free man and a free woman. I know for certain that the C. S. R. Company could easily have afforded to give this out of its surplus profits. But it would not budge from its hard and fast position; and when at last the strike began, the news was everywhere spread abroad that the Indians were in 'open rebellion' and were proposing to massacre the Europeans. Troops with machine guns were hurried in a warship of the New Zealand Navy, from Auckland, and the Indian labourers were terrorised back into their work, without getting their rise in wages.

Soon after these troubles, the Indian Community wished to present an address to the Prince of Wales who came to Fiji. They asked permission from the Governor to state their position in the following terms: "We do not think it proper to pain your Royal Highness by describing our secular difficulties and grievances, which will not remain hidden to your Royal Highness. One thing, however, we are compelled to bring to your notice. It is the fact that we have been misrepresented to the effect that our recent agitation for better rights and economical improvement was based on racial feelings. This has wounded our hearts. This surmise, on the part of the authorities, is not only without any foundation, but is a great slur and an irreparable stain on our character, which should be removed at once."

These were the proposed words. But the Governor cut them out of the address altogether, and substituted others, which, while seemingly a mere abbreviation, were actually a perversion of the meaning. The Indians wished to say that the accusation of racial hatred, levelled against *themselves*, were unjust and unbearable. What they were made to say was that there was no racial feeling on the part of any one at all,—either European or Indian. Now this was the opposite of the truth; because the European racial feeling had been excessive. I wish my readers to notice how subtly and cleverly this was done. The Governor of Fiji struck out the words of the address of welcome, which I have stated above, and substituted the following:

"We do not think it proper to refer to political matters. It is inevitable, however, that your Royal Highness should have heard of the recent Indian troubles in Fiji; and we desire to assure you that they were due solely to economic causes and not to any racial feeling."

The Indian Community protested against this perversion of their own meaning. But the Governor of Fiji insisted, and the Indians weakly gave way. The result was that the Prince of Wales was prompted to pick out those very words declaring that there was no racial feeling, which would camouflage the whole matter. They were telegraphed all over the world by Reuter. We received them here in India. London, and New York, and Capetown, and Tokio, and Melbourne received them also. The Prince stated that "*he was glad to hear that the recent Indian troubles had not been due to any racial feelings.*" Thus the impression was spread abroad, that the Europeans were very good friends of the Indians and were living in social friendliness with them. The truth all the while was this, that the Europeans, as I have said, had brought troops from New Zealand and, by sheer military power, crushed Indians back into accepting the harshest terms of settlement. They had even passed racial laws against the Indians, marking them out from all other races in Fiji.

This incident in Fiji affected the honour of a few thousands of Indians in that colony. The Duke of Connaught's visit will affect the honour of nearly thirty-two crores in India itself. Let us take warning from this weak surrender of our poorer Indian brethren in Fiji. We cannot blame them for that surrender, for their manhood has been crushed by servile labour.

But let *us* not weakly surrender ourselves, or put trust in Governments, which can use such weapons of compulsion as these. The only course, which is dignified and self-respecting, during the coming royal visit of the Duke of Connaught is to refrain altogether from offering addresses of welcome. Such a royal visit at this crisis is *not* welcome to us. It cannot possibly be welcome. Silence therefore is golden.

9th February, 1921

TO H. R. H. THE DUKE OF CONNAUGHT

The following letter, which has appeared in the Press, was sent by Mr. Gandhi to H. R. H. The Duke of Connaught last week:

Sir,—Your Royal Highness must have heard a great deal about Non-co-operation, Non-co-operationists, and their methods, and, incidentally, of me, its humble author. I fear that the information given your Royal Highness must have been in its nature one-sided. I owe it to you, to my friends and myself, that I should place before you what I conceive to be the scope of Non-co-operation, as followed not only by me, but my closest associates, such as Messrs. Shaukat Ali and Mahomed Ali.

For me it is no joy and pleasure to be actively associated in the boycott of Your Royal Highness's visit. I have tendered loyal, voluntary assistance to the Government for an unbroken period of nearly 30 years in the full belief that through that lay the path of freedom for my country. It was, therefore, no slight thing for me to suggest to my countrymen that we should take no part in welcoming Your Royal Highness. Not one amongst us has anything against you as an English gentleman. We hold your person as sacred as that of a dearest friend.* I do not know any of my friends who would not guard it with his life if he found it in danger.

* *Young India* of 1st December, 1920, contained the following:

The Duke's Visit.—His Royal Highness the Duke of Connaught will be soon in our midst. It is a matter of great sorrow to me that I should have to advise a complete boycott of all public functions held in his honour. He is personally an amiable English gentleman. But, in my humble opinion, public interest demands that this official visit should be strictly ignored. His Royal Highness comes to sustain

We are not at war with individual Englishmen. We seek not to destroy English life. We do desire to destroy the system that has emasculated our country in body, mind and soul. We are determined to battle with all our might against that in English nature which has made O'Dwyerism and Dyerism possible in the Punjab and has resulted in a wanton affront upon Islam, a faith professed by seven crores of our countrymen. We consider it inconsistent with our self-respect any longer to brook the spirit of superiority and dominance which has systematically ignored and disregarded the sentiments of thirty crores of innocent people of India on many a vital matter. It is humiliating to us. It cannot be a matter of pride to you that thirty crores of Indians should live day in and day out in fear of their lives from one hundred thousand Englishmen and, therefore, be under subjection to them.

Your Royal Highness has come, not to end the system I described, but to sustain it by upholding its prestige. Your first pronouncement was a laudation of Lord Willingdon. I have the privilege of knowing him. I believe him to be an honest, amiable gentleman, who will not willingly hurt even a fly, but he certainly failed as a ruler. He allowed himself to be guided by those whose interest it was to support their power. He is not reading the mind of the Dravidian province. Here, in

a corrupt system of government, he comes to whitewash an irresponsible bureaucracy, he comes to make us forget the unforgettable, he comes not to heal the wounds inflicted upon us, but to mock us by flinging deceptive reforms at us. To welcome His Royal Highness is to associate with him in promoting our own dishonour. No government official, whether he be European or Indian, has a right to claim any welcome or honour from us so long as the government, whose power he represents, remains unrepentant and unresponsive to the one thing needful.

Bengal, you are issuing a certificate of merit to a Governor who is again, from all I have heard, an estimable gentleman, but who knows nothing of the heart of Bengal and its yearnings. Bengal is not Calcutta. Fort William and the palaces of Calcutta respresent an insolent exploitation of the unmurmuring and highly cultured peasantry of this fair province.

The Non-co-operators have come to the conclusion that they must not be deceived by the reforms that tinker with the problem of India's distress and humiliation, nor must they be impatient and angry. We must not in our impatient anger resort to stupid violence. We freely admit that we must take our due share of blame for the existing state. It is not so much British guns that are responsible for our subjection as our voluntary co-operation.

Our non-participation in a hearty welcome to Your Royal Highness is thus, in no sense, a demonstration against your high personage, but it is against the system you come to uphold. I know individual Englishmen cannot, even if they will, alter the English nature all of a sudden. If we would be the equals of Englishmen, we must cast off fear. We must learn to be self-reliant and independent of schools, courts, protection, and patronage of a Government we seek to end, if it will not mend.

Hence this non-violent non-co-operation. I know we have not all yet become non-violent in speech and deed, but the results so far achieved have, I assure Your Royal Highness, been amazing. The people have understood the secret and value of non-violence as they have never done before. He, who will, may see that this is a religious, purifying movement. We are leaving off drink. We are trying to rid India of the curse of untouchability

We are trying to throw off foreign tinsel splendour, and by reverting to the spinning wheel, revive the ancient and poetic simplicity of life. We hope thereby to sterilize the existing harmful institutions.

I ask Your Royal Highness as an Englishman to study this movement and its possibilities for the Empire and the world. We are at war with nothing that is good in the world. In protecting Islam in the manner we are, we are protecting all religions; in protecting the honour of India, we are protecting the honour of humanity. For our means are hurtful to none. We desire to live on terms of friendship with Englishmen, but that friendship must be friendship of equals both in theory and in practice, and we must continue to non-co-operate, *i.e.*, to purify ourselves till the goal is achieved. I ask Your Royal Highness, and through you every Englishman, to appreciate the view-point of Non-co-operation.

I beg to remain,
Your Royal Highness's faithful servant,
(Sd.) · M. K. GANDHI.

27th October, 1921

HONOUR THE PRINCE

(By M. K. Gandhi)

The reader must not be surprised at the title of this writing. Supposing that the Prince was a blood brother in a high place, supposing that he was to be exploited by neighbours for their own base ends, supposing further that he was in the hands of my neighbours, that my voice could not effectively reach him and that he was being brought to my village by the said neighbours, would I not honour him best by dissociating myself from all the ceremonial that might be arranged in his 'honour' in the process of exploitation and by letting him know by every means at my disposal that he was being exploited?* Would I not be a traitor to him if I did not warn him against entering the trap prepared for him by my neighbours?

I have no manner of doubt that the Prince's visit is being exploited for advertising the 'benign' British rule in India. It is a crime against us if His Royal Highness is being brought for personal pleasure and sport when India is seething with discontent, when the masses are saturated with disaffection towards the system under which they are governed, when famine is raging in

*The following appeared in *Young India* of 10th July, 1921:

The Prince's Proposed Visit.—It is a great pity that the talk of the prince's visit has been revived and a provisional date fixed. India will refuse to welcome a representaive of a system of which she is sick unto death. And if his visit is forced upon an unwilling India there must be the same effective *Hartal* on the day of His Royal Highness's visit that there was on the Duke's visit. I repeat once more that Non-co-operators have nothing against the Prince as a man. But he cannot be divested of the office he holds. Whilst it is true that the King and his heirs do not actively meddle in the affairs of state (which is a convenience for the state), he is as effective a representative of the existing system of Government as the most meddlesome Prime Minister or Viceroy. I am disposed to think that as a supporter of the institution, he is more effective by reason of his isolation. If the Prince comes, he will not come to bless the Non-co-operators or the cause, but to sing the song of praise for a Government which is responsible for the dishonour of the Punjab, for breach of faith with the Mussalmans, for forcing the drink traffic on India, for impoverishing her and for so emasculating her that she almost thinks she must remain in slavery for an unthinkable time. In my humble opinion, the projected visit will be an insult added to injury. And it will be the duty of every Non-co-operator, respectfully but firmly and in no unmistakable manner, to express his strong disapproval of all such efforts to bolster up a system which is tottering to its fall.—M. K. G.

Khulna and the Ceded Districts and when an armed conflict is raging in Malabar: it is a crime against India to spend millions of rupees on a mere show when millions of men are living in a state of chronic starvation. Eight lacs of rupees have been voted away by the Bombay Council alone for the pageant.

The visit is being heralded by repression in the land. In Sindh, over fifty-six Non-co-operators are in gaol. Some of the bravest of Mussalmans are being tried for holding certain opinions.* Nineteen Bengal workers have been just imprisoned, including Mr. Sen Gupta, the leading Barrister of the place. A Mussalman Pir and three other selfless workers are already in gaol for a similar 'crime'. Several leaders of Karnatak are also imprisoned, and now its chief man is on trial for saying what I have said repeatedly in these columns and what Congressmen have been saying all over during the past twelve months. Several leaders of the Central Provinces have been similarly deprived of their liberty. A most popular doctor, Dr. Paranjapye, a man universally respected for his selflessness, is suffering rigorous imprisonment like a common felon. I have, by no means, exhausted the list of imprisonments of Non-co-operators. Whether they are a test of real crime or an answer to growing disaffection, the Prince's visit is, to say the least, most inopportune. There is no doubt that the people do not want His Royal Highness to visit India at the present juncture. They have expressed their opinion in no uncertain terms. They have declared that Bombay should observe *Hartal* on the day of his landing at Bombay. It is a clear imposition upon the people to bring the Prince in the teeth of their opposition.

*See *infra*

What are we to do in the circumstances? We must organise a complete boycott of all functions held in the Prince's honour. We must religiously refrain from attending charities fetes or fireworks organised for the purpose. We must refuse to illuminate or to send our children to see the organised illuminations. To this end we must publish leaflets by the million and distribute them amongst the people, telling them what their duty in the matter is, and it would be true honour done to the Prince if Bombay on the day of his landing wears the appearance of a deserted city.

But we must isolate the Prince from the person. We have no ill-will against the Prince as man. He probably knows nothing of the feeling in India, he probably knows nothing about repression. Equally probably he is ignorant of the fact that the Punjab wound is still bleeding, that the treachery towards India in the matter of the Khilafat is still rankling in every Indian breast, and that on the Government's own admission the reformed councils contain members who, though nominally elected, do not in any sense represent even the few lacs who are on the electoral rolls. To do or to attempt to do any harm to the person of the Prince would be not only cruel and inhuman, but it would be on our part a piece of treachery towards ourselves and him, for we have voluntarily pledged ourselves to be and remain non-violent. Any injury or insult to the Prince by us will be a greater wrong done by us to Islam and India than any the English have done. They know no better. We can lay no such claim to ignorance, we have with our eyes open and before God and man promised not to hurt a single individual in any way connected with the system we are straining every nerve to destroy. It must therefore be our duty to take every precaution to protect his person as our own from all harm. In spite of all our effort, we know that there will be some who would want to take part in the various functions from fear or hope or choice. They have as much right to do what they like as we have to do what we like. That is the test of the freedom we wish to have and enjoy. Let us, whilst we are being subjected by an insolent bureaucracy to a severe irritation, exercise the greatest restraint. And if we can exhibit our firm resolve to have nothing to do with it by dissociating ourselves from its pageant and at the same time we show forbearance towards those who differ from us, we would advance our cause in a most effective manner.

29th December, 1921

'ONE STEP ENOUGH FOR ME'

(BY M. K. GANDHI)

Mr. Stokes is a Christian who wants to follow the light that God gives him. He has adopted India as his home. He is watching the Non-co-operation movement from the Kotagiri hills where he is living in isolation from the India of the plains, and serving the hillmen. He has contributed three articles* on Non-co-operation to the columns of the *Servant* of Calcutta and other papers. I had the pleasure of reading them during my Bengal tour. Mr. Stokes approves of Non-co-operation but dreads the consequences that may follow complete success, *i.e.*, evacuation of India by the British. He conjures up before his mind a picture of India invaded by the Afghans from the North-west, plundered by the

*Omitted in this collection. For Mr. Stokes's views, *see* his *National Self-realisation*.

Gurkhas from the Hills. For me I say with Cardinal Newman: 'I do not ask to see the distant scene; one step enough for me.' The business is essentially religious. The business of every God-fearing man is to dissociate himself from evil in total disregard of consequences. He must have faith in a good deed producing only a good result: that in my opinion is the *Gita* doctrine of work without attachment. God does not permit him to peep into the future. He follows truth, although the following of it may endanger his very life. He knows that it is better to die in the way of God than to live in the way of Satan. Therefore whoever is satisfied that this Government represents the activity of Satan has no choice left to him but to dissociate himself from it.

However, let us consider the worst that can happen to India on a sudden evacuation of India by the British. What does it matter that the Gurkhas and the Pathans attack us? Surely we would be better able to deal with their violence than we are with the continued violence, moral and physical, perpetrated by the present government. Mr. Stokes does not seem to eschew the use of physical force. Surely the combined labour of the Rajput, the Sikh and the Mussalman warrior in a united India may be trusted to deal with plunders from any or all the sides. Imagine however the worst: Japan overwhelming us from the Bay of Bengal, the Gurkhas from the Hills, and the Pathans from the North-West. If we do not succeed in driving them out, we make terms with them and drive them out at the first opportunity. This will be a more manly course than a helpless submission to an admittedly wrongful State.

But I refuse to contemplate the dismal outlook. If the movement succeeds through Non-violent Non-co-operation, and that is the supposition Mr. Stokes has started with, the English whether they remain or retire, they will do so as friends and under a well-ordered agreement as between partners. I still believe in the goodness of human nature, whether it is English or any other. I therefore do not believe that the English will leave in 'a night.'

And do I consider the Gurkha and the Afghan being incorrigible thieves and robbers without ability to respond to purifying influences? I do not. If India returns to her spirituality, it will react upon the neighbouring tribes;* she will interest herself in the welfare of these hardy but poor people, and even support them, if necessary, not out of fear but as a matter of neighbourly duty. She will have dealt with Japan simultaneously with the British. Japan will not want to invade India, if India has learnt to consider it a sin to use a single foreign article that she can manufacture within her own borders. She produces enough to eat, and her men and women can without difficulty manufacture enough cloth to cover their nakedness and protect themselves from heat and cold. We become prey to invasion if we excite the greed of foreign nations by dealing with them under a feeling of dependence on them. We must learn to be independent of every one of them.

Whether therefore we finally succeed through violence or non-violence, in my opinion, the prospect is, by no means, so gloomy as Mr. Stokes has imagined. Any conceivable prospect is, in my opinion, less black than the present unmanly and helpless condition. And we

* Mr. Andrews writes that it was the Mahatma's intention to work among the border tribes and make them friends and even die in the attempt, if necessary. *See* his *Terence Mac Swiney and the New World Movement.*

cannot do better than following out fearlessly and with confidence the open and honourable programme of Non-violence and sacrifice that we have mapped for ourselves.*

4th May, 1921

THE AFGHAN BOGEY

(BY M. K. GANDHI)

The reader will find elsewhere a string of questions put by a correspondent.† The most important relates to a speech delivered by Maulana Mahomed Ali on the fear of an Afghan invasion. I have not read Maulana Mahomed Ali's speech referred to by the correspondent. But whether he does or not, I would, in a sense, certainly assist the Amir of Afghanistan, if he waged war against the British Government. That is to say, I would openly tell my countrymen that it would be a crime to help a Government which had lost the confidence of the nation to remain in power. On the other hand, I would not ask Indians to raise levies for the Amir. That would be against the creed of non-violence accepted by both Hindus and Muslims for the purpose of the Khilafat, the Punjab and Swaraj. And I apprehend that Maulana Mahomed Ali could not mean more in his speech than what I have suggested. He could not very well do otherwise, so long as the Hindu-Muslim compact subsists. But it would be found upon an examination of the case, that the compact is indissoluble. Dissolution of the compact

* The Congress Working Committee advocated in October, 1921, a foreign policy for India based on these principles and condemned the use of Indian troops abroad in Mesopotamia, etc., with whose peoples the Indians had no quarrel.

† Some of these questions are answered elsewhere. *See* page 651.

means destruction of India's purpose. I cannot conceive the present possibility of Hindus and Muslims entering upon a joint armed revolt And Muslims can hardly expect to succeed with any plan of an armed revolt.

However, I warn the reader against believing in the bogey of an Afghan invasion. Their own military writers have often let us into the secret that many of the punitive expeditions were manufactured for giving the soldiers a training or keeping idle armed men occupied. A weak, disarmed, helpless, credulous India does not know how this Government has kept her under its hypnotic spell. Even some of the best of us to day really believe that the military budget is being piled up for protecting India against foreign aggression. I suggest that it is being piled up for want of faith in the Sikhs, the Gurkhas, the Pathans, and the Rajputs, *i.e.*, for want of faith in us and for the purpose of keeping us under forced subjection. My belief (I write under correction) is that the anxiety of the Government always to have a treaty with the Amir was based, not so much upon the fear of a Russian invasion as upon the fear of losing the confidence of the Indian soldiery. To-day there is certainly no fear of a Russian invasion. I have never believed in the Bolshevik menace. And why should any Indian Government, to use the favourite phrase of the erstwhile idol of Bengal, 'broad-based upon a people's affection,' fear Russian, Bolshevik or any menace? Surely a contented, and a powerful India (all the more), in alliance with Great Britain, can any day meet any invasion upon her. But this Government has deliberately emasculated us, kept us under the perpetual fear of our neighbours and the whole world, and drained India of her splendid resources, so that she has lost faith in herself either for defence or for dealing with the simple problem of the growing poverty. I, therefore, do certainly hope that the Amir will not enter into any treaty with this Government. Any such treaty can only mean unholy bargain against Islam and India. This Government being unwilling to part with O'Dwyerism as an 'emergency' measure, being unwilling to keep its faith with the Muslims, (I must decline to treat the Government of India separately from the Imperial Government) and being unwilling to let India rise to her full height, wants Afghanistan to enter into a treaty of offence against India.* I hope that there is but one opinion so far as

*On Mr. Andrews asking Mr. Gandhi whether the above-article was not an invitation to the Afghans to invade India and whether thereby he did not become a party to violence, Mr. Gandhi wrote in *Young India* of 18th May, 1921, denying that he invited Afghans, expressing his anxiety that they should not go to India's assistance and affirming that India was quite capable of settling with the Government without extraneous aid. He added :

What however I would do is totally different from what I can do. I am sorry to have to confess that the movement has not yet acquired such hold on the soldier class as to enbolden them to refuse assistance to the Government in time of need. When the soldier class has realised that they live for the nation, and that it is a travesty of a soldier's calling when he undertakes to kill to order, the battle of India's worldly freedom is won without more. As it is, the Indian soldier is as much subject to fear as the layman. He fills the recruiting ranks, because he believes that there is no other means of livelihood. The Government has made the profession of killing attractive by a system of special rewards, and by a system of skilfully devised punishments has made it well nigh impossible for the soldier once he is in, to get out without difficulty. In these circumstances I do not delude myself with the belief that the British Government will be without Indian help in the event of an immediate Afghan invasion. But it was my duty, especially when challenged, to put before the nation the position logically arising from non-co-operation. It was necessary, too, to warn the nation against being frightened by the Afghan bogey.

The second part of the question contains, in my opinion, a miscon-

Non-co-operators are concerned. Whilst unwilling ourselves, we cannot wish others to co-operate with the Government.

25th May, 1921

THE FRONTIER FRIENDS

(By. M. K. Gandhi)

The Punjabees living on the Frontier deserve the sympathy of the whole of India. They are exposed to attacks from the neighbouring tribes, they are defenceless, and from all the accounts received by me, the Government seem to give them little or no protection, and now-a-days the rule for the officers, if any one complains, is to refer the complainant to the Ali Brothers and to me. If we had charge of the Frontier, I know what we would have done. We would certainly have died in the attempt to defend the unarmed population of the districts. We would have, if necessary, armed the population for self-defence. But what is more, we would have won over the tribesmen and turned them from marauding bands into trustworthy neighbours. But we have to take things as they are. I assume that the Hindus and the Mussalmans are

---

ception of Non-violence. It is no part of the duty of a Non-violent Non-co-operator to assist the Government against war made upon it by others. A Non-violent Non-co-operator may not secretly or openly encourage or assist any such war. He may not take part directly or indirectly in it. But it is no part of his duty to help the Government to end the war. On the contrary, his prayer would be, as it must be, for the defeat of a power which he seeks to destroy. I therefore, so far as my creed of Non-violence is concerned, can contemplate an Afghan invasion with perfect equanimity, and equally so far as India's safety is concerned.

friendly to one another, and that no Mussalman traitorously helps the tribesmen against his Hindu brothers. The Mussalman population on this side of the Frontier is in an exceptionally strong position to help.

We must not despair of the tribesmen. We have too often considered them to be hopeless. In my opinion, they are amenable to reason. They are God-fearing. They do not loot merely for pleasure. I believe that they are themselves coming under the influence of the wave of self-purification that is spreading.

I know that the process of reforming the tribesmen is slow and tedious. It provides poor comfort to those that are robbed of their possessions or their dear ones.

The difficulty is to be traced to the same cause we fear Englishmen, and we have become slaves. We fear the tribesmen and we are satisfied with our slavery, we are thankful that we are protected by the former against the latter. I cannot imagine a greater humiliation for the self-respecting man to be dependent, for the safety of himself or his family, on those who he thinks prey upon him. I would prefer total destruction of myself and my all to purchasing safety at the cost of my manhood. This feeling of helplessness in us has really arisen from our deliberate dismissal of God from our common affairs. We have become atheists for all practical purposes. And therefore we believe that in the long run we must rely upon physical force for our protection. In the face of physical danger, we cast all our philosophy to the winds. Our daily life is a negation of God. If then we would but have a little trust in God, *i.e.*, ourselves, we shall find no difficulty with the tribesmen. Only in that case, we will have to be prepared at times to surrender our possessions and under certain circumstances our lives rather than our honour. We must refuse to believe that our neighbours are savages incapable of responding to the finer instincts in man.

Thus consistently with our self-respect there are but two courses open to us, to prepare in so far as we wish to defend ourselves, however weakly, against robbery and plunder, or to believe in the capacity of our neighbours to respond to the nobler instinct in man and to endeavour to reform the tribesmen. I apprehend that the two processes will go hand in hand. We must avoid the third at any cost, that is, reliance on the British bullet to protect us from harm. It is the surest way to national suicide.

If my writings can reach the tribesmen, I would certainly urge them to leave their predatory habits.* Inas much as they loot a single man or woman, they believe the teaching of the Prophet whose name they prize above all others and whom they believe to be the messenger of the God of mercy and justice. It is the duty of every Mussalman and Ulema who has any influence with these simple men to tell them that if they will play

* The following appeared in *Young India* of 5th May, 1921, under the heading, "Kidnapping at the Border:"

The recent instance of kidnapping a European girl by tribesmen on the North-west Border shows that they are no respecters of persons.

The Abhyodaya of Allahabad has however published from its correspondent harrowing details of kidnapping of Hindus. Several Hindus from the N.-W. Border have also been coming to Mr. Gandhi, complaining of members of their families having been kidnapped and ransomed after heavy payments. One man from Bannu told him that his people were obliged to pay Rs. 14,000 as ransom. The Hindu complainants have even been questioning the utility of Hindu-Muslim Unity, if such things could happen at the Border. With all our desire to secure relief from the depredations complained of, we fail to see how Hindu-Muslim unity can be blamed for the continuance of the mischief. The Mahomedans of India have, as a rule as much, or as little influence as the Hindus over these free booting tribes who have been known to

their part in defending Islam from impending danger, the least they can do is to refrain from molesting their neighbours, who have done not only no harm to them but who, whether they are Hindus or Mussalmans, are doing their best to safeguard the honour of Islam.

The following appeared in *Young India* of 13th July, 1921:

Frontier Friends.—Mr. Mahomed Nawezkhan, B.A., LL.B., of Bannu, writes a long letter on my appeal to the Frontier Friends. I propose to give a brief summary of it instead of reproducing the whole letter, which is too discursive for the columns of *Young India*. He thinks that the tribesmen who learn the message will gladly respond. He traces the history of the annexation of the territory of the tribesmen, and proves that before these territories were annexed, there were practically no raids. Moreover, all were equally armed, and therefore the raided parties were well able to take care of themselves. But after annexation, the tribesmen who were wantonly robbed of their lands treated both the Hindu

---

carry away Mahomedans almost as frequently as Hindus. In the first instance, it is the office of the Government to protect the Border villages from the free booters. Secondly, it is for the Hindus themselves to be resourceful enough, to combine together, for resisting the attacks of desperadoes. Thirdly, both the Hindus and the Mahomedans living in these Border villages should open communications with the tribesmen and induce them to behave better, promising them pecuniary help for a temporary period if they are likely to starve, having been used for generations to live simply on depredations. And lastly, it is certainly expected of those Mahomedans who have any influence over or connection with the tribesmen to wean them from their unneighbourly habits. If all the remedies are simultaneously adopted, we have no doubt that the evil will be brought under control, if it is not entirely eradicated.

and the Mussalman inhabitants of the annexed territories as their enemies, the more so as the latter helped the Government in subduing the tribesmen. The writer, who claims an intimate acquaintance with the situation, is of opinion that the tribesmen have been no respecters of religions, and have subjected to their depredations the Hindus and the Mussalmans alike, and that Mussalmans have never been known to assist the Hindus against the raiders. In proof of impartiality, the writer instances the cordial treatment meted out to the Hindus in the independent territory of the Frontier tribes. He states that the Hindus living there have greater freedom of worship than even in the British territory. Their social status is any day better than under the British Government, and the Maliks are ever ready with all their might to defend their Hindu friends living within their jurisdiction. The writer gives it as his judgment that the British Government in the Frontier Province has sinfully abdicated its function of protecting the inhabitants, who have unfortunately come under the so-called protecting wings of the British Empire. He winds up his letter by saying that the Frontier regulations are worth studying, the procedure there is most arbitrary, and the life and property of the people are at the mercy of military officers who are incapable of giving judicial decisions. Extra Assistant commissioners, he says, in effect disgrace their commissions and become instruments of injustice and oppression. No man's honour is safe in the hands of these administrators. They have the power to put under lock-up any respectable man upon the slightest suspicion.

1st *June*, 1921

THE AFGHAN ALARM

(BY M. K. GANDHI)

It must be a matter of surprise to many people as it is to me that Mr. Bepin Chandra Pal should be alarmed at the Afghan cry raised in interested quarters. He is a believer in full Swaraj, and I venture to suggest to Mr. Pal that we cannot establish Swaraj in India, till we rid ourselves of the feeling of helplessness. Swaraj means our preparedness to deal with the Afghan and every other menace in our country. The whole scheme of Non-co-operation is based on trusting other people, and if they prove untrustworthy, on our being prepared to meet their deceit by self-suffering. I remind Mr. Pal of what he truly said at Allahabad at the Hindu-Mahomedan Conference in reply to Dr. Sapru that the same power of combination, resourcefulness and suffering that would end the present system of slavery, would enable us to deal with every other system of a similar nature.

Pan-Islamism, which Mr. Pal fears, is an admirable doctrine in so far as a Mussalman wishes the solidarity of all Moslem states. It would be a dangerous doctrine, if it were to mean a combination of Islamic powers for the purpose of exploiting the world or converting it to Islam by force. No sane Mussalman of my acquaintance has ever entertained the latter idea. The world is growing sick of the domination of brute force.

I assure Mr. Pal that I do not believe in flirtation with any sentiment. I reject those that are bad, and hug those that are good. I do not believe that serious Mussalmans will welcome Afghan rule, any more than serious Hindus would. In writing my article on the Afghan Bogey, I was minded only to defend the correct position of a comrade, and to warn India against being frightened by the interested cry.

I totally dissent from Mr. Pal's view that the event of an Afghan invasion, or even the mere circulation of a rumour of such invasion, will incite a very large part of our Muslim population to lawlessness, if not to open "revolt.' On the contrary, it is my firm belief that the Mussalmans have too much at stake to-day—the honour of their religion—to do any such foolish act. As Maulana Shaukat Ali has said so often, the Mussalmans are too shrewd to mix up violence with non-violence. Mr. Pal has done a grave injustice to the Hindus by attributing to 'a very large proportion' of Hindus 'a desire to settle their own account with the Mahomedans.' He has, I venture to assure him, entirely misread the Hindu mind. The Hindus are as much in earnest about the cow, as the Mussalmans about the Khilafat. And the former know that they cannot save the cow—the cherished dream of every Hindu—without the good-will of the latter. I promise that the Hindus will forget every wrong done in the past by every Mussalman, when the latter help them to save the cow, as I know every Mussalman will feel eternally grateful to the Hindus, if he finds that he has retrieved the honour of Islam by their voluntary aid.

I deny *in toto* the truth of the proposition laid down by Mr. Pal that Muslims and Hindus would welcome an Afghan invasion. The protests that have been made against the supposed intentions of Maulana Mahomed Ali are surely enough to convince anybody that India will not tolerate an Afghan invasion.

Mr. Pal suggests that, if the Amir invades and if we do not aid the Government, there can only be a revolution. I venture to suggest another alternative. If India as a Non-co-operating India does not assist, the Government will make terms with the people. I do not consider the British people to be so utterly devoid of commonsense or resourcefulness as to leave India, rather than come to terms with her and heal the Khilafat and the Punjab wounds. That India does not yet possess the power to command attention, I know only too well. I have simply suggested a contingent alternative.

Mr. Pal sees a difference between Lalaji's and my declaration at Simla and our previous declarations. I know none—neither Lalaji nor I—have ever welcomed an Afghan invasion. But I gladly lay down my own position in categorical terms.

(1) I do not believe that the Afghans want to invade India.

(2) I believe that the Government is fully prepared to meet an Afghan invasion.

(3) I am sorry to confess that, if there was an Afghan invasion, every Raja and Maharaja will render unconditional assistance to the Government.

(4) I believe too that we as a people are still so demoralised, diffident and distrustful of Afghan intentions, and Hindus and Mussalmans of one another, that many would in mere panic rush to the help of the Government and thus still further strengthen the chain that binds India.

(5) In theory, it is possible to distinguish between an invasion of India and no invasion of the British Government for the purpose of the Khilafat. In practice, I do not believe in the Afghans invading India to embarrass the Government, and being able in the event of being successful to resist the temptation of establishing a kingdom in India.

(6) In spite of such belief, I hold it to be contrary to

the faith of a Non-co-operator to tender unconditional assistance to a Government which he seeks to end or mend.

(7) A handful of conscientious objectors may make no impression on the then current of events, but they will sow the seed for raising a manly India.

(8) I would rather see India perish at the hands of Afghans, than purchase freedom from Afghan invasion at the cost of her honour. To have India defended by an unrepentant Government that keeps the Khilafat and the Punjab wounds still bleeding is to sell India's honour.

(9) My faith, however, in the British nation is such that when we have shown sufficient strength of purpose, and undergone enough measure of self-sacrifice, the British people will respond fully. My reading of history is that they do not yield to justice pure and simple. It is too abstract for their 'commonsense.' But they are far-seeing enough to respond to justice when it is allied with force. Whether it is brute-force, or soul-force, they do not mind.

(10) It is the duty of every Non-co-operator to let the Afghans know that he believes in the capacity of Non-co-operation to restore the Khilafat to the pre-war status, and that India does not want their armed intervention, that Non-co-operators would appreciate their refusal to enter into any deal with the British Government for holding India in subjection, and that India has none but the friendliest feelings for her neighbours.

CONDITION OF LABOUR

Mr. Gandhi writes in the "Nava Jivan" of the 8th instant:

Two paths are open before India to-day, either to

introduce the western principle of 'Might is right' or to uphold the eastern principle that truth alone conquers, that truth knows no mishap, that the strong and the weak have alike a right to secure justice. The choice is to begin with the labouring class. Should the labourers obtain an increment in their wages by violence? Even if that be possible, they cannot resort to anything like violence, howsoever legitimate may be their claims. To use violence for securing rights may seem an easy path, but it proves to be thorny in the long run. Those who live by sword die also by sword. The swimmer often dies by drowning. Look at Europe. No one seems to be happy there, for, not one is contented. The labourer does not trust the capitalist and the capitalist has no faith in the labourer. Both have a sort of vigour and strength but even the bulls have it. They fight to the very bitter end. All motion is not progress. We have got no reason to believe that the people of Europe are progressing. Their possession of wealth does not argue the possession of any moral or spiritual qualities. King Duryodhan was a master of untold wealth, but with all that he was a pauper in comparison to Vidura and Sudama. To-day the world adores Vidura and Sudama, whereas Duryodhan's name is remembered only as a byword for the evil qualities one should shun.

What shall we do then? The labourers in Bombay made a fine stand. I was not in a position to know all the facts. But this much I could see that they could fight in a better way. The mill-owner may be wholly in the wrong. In the struggle between capital and labour, it may be generally said that more often than not the capitalists are in the wrong box. But when labour comes fully to realise its strength, I know it can become more tyrannical than capital. The mill-owners will have to work on the terms dictated by labour, if the latter could command intelligence of the former. It is clear, however, that labour will never attain to that intelligence. If it does, labour will cease to be labour and become itself the master. The capitalists do not fight on the strength of money alone. They do possess intelligence and tact.

The question before us is this: When the labourers, remaining what they are, develop a certain consciousness, what should be their course? It would be suicidal if the labourers rely upon their numbers or brute-force, *i.e.*, violence. By so doing, they will do harm to industries in the country. If, on the other hand, they take their stand on pure justice and suffer in their person to secure it, not only will they always succeed but they will reform their masters, develop industries and both master and men will be as members of one and the same family. A satisfactory solution of the condition of labour must include the following:

(1) The hours of labour must leave the workmen some hours of leisure.

(2) They must get facilities for their own education.

(3) Provision should be made for an adequate supply of milk, clothing and necessary education for their children.

(4) There should be sanitary dwellings for the workmen.

(5) They should be in a position to save enough to maintain themselves during their old age.

None of these conditions is satisfied to-day. For this both the parties are responsible. The masters care only for the service they get. What becomes of the labourer does not concern them? All their endeavours are generally confined to obtaining maximum service with minimum payment. The labourer, on the other hand, tries to hit upon all tricks whereby he can get maximum pay with minimum work. The result is that although the labourers get an increment there is no improvement in the work turned out. The relations between the two parties are not purified and the labourers do not make proper use of the increment they get.

A third party has sprung up between these two parties. It has become the labourers' friend. There is need for such a party. Only to the extent to which this party has disinterested friendship of the labourers can it befriend them.

A time has come now when attempts will be made to use labour as a pawn in more ways than one. The occasion demands consideration at the hands of those that would take part in politics. What will they choose? Their own interest or the service of labour and the nation? Labour stands in sore need of friends. It cannot proceed without a lead. What sort of men give this lead will decide the condition of labour.

Strikes, cessation of work and Hartal are wonderful things no doubt, but it is not difficult to abuse them. Workmen ought to organise themselves into strong Labour Unions, and on no account shall they strike work without the consent of these Unions. Strikes should not be risked without previous negotiations with the mill-owners. If the mill-owners resort to arbitration, the principle of *Panchayat* should be accepted. And once the *Panch* are appointed, their decision must be accepted by both the parties alike, whether they like it or not.

Readers, if you are interested in ameliorating the condition of labour, if you want to befriend the workman and serve him, you will see from the above that there is only one royal road before you, *viz.*, to elevate the workmen by creating between the two parties family relationship. And to secure this end there is no path like Truth. Mere increase in wages should not satisfy you; you must also watch by what means they get it and how they spend it.

6th October, 1920

WAGES AND VALUES

The following is a free rendering of Mr. Gandhi's address to the mill-hands of Ahmedabad on the occasion of the second anniversary of the struggle that took place between the mill-owner and the mill-hands:

I do not propose to examine the duty of the capitalist. If the labourer alone were to understand his rights and responsibilities and confine himself to the purest means, both must gain. But two things are needful—both the demands and the means adopted to enforce them must be just and clear. It is an unlawful demand which seeks merely to take advantage of the capitalists' position. But it is an altogether lawful demand when the labourer asks for enough wages to enable him to maintain himself and to educate his children decently. To seek justice without resorting to violence and by an appeal to the goodsense of the capitalist by arbitration is lawful means.

In order to achieve the end, you must have Unions. A beginning has already been made. I trust that the mill-hands in every department will form their Unions and every one should scrupulously observe the rules that may be formed for them. You will then approach the mill-owners through your Unions and if, the decisions of the former do not satisfy you, you will appeal to arbitration. It is a matter for satisfaction that both parties have accepted the principle of arbitration. I hope that that principle will be fully developed and that strikes will for ever become an impossibility. I know that strikes are an inherent right of the working men for the purpose of securing justice, but they must be considered a crime immediately the capitalists accept the principle of arbitration. Wages are improving and there is every possibility of a continuous improvement. But there is equal need for reducing hours of labour. The mill-hands seem to be working twelve hours or more.

The mill-owners tell me that the mill-hands are lazy, they do not give full time to their work and they are inattentive. I for one cannot expect attention and application from those who are called upon to work twelve hours per day. But I would certainly hope that when the hours are reduced to ten the labourers will put in better and almost the same amount of work as in twelve hours. Reduction in hours of labour has brought about happy results in England. When mill-hands learn to identify themselves with the interest of the mill-owners, they will rise and with them will rise the industries of our country. I would therefore urge the mill-owners to reduce the hours of labour to ten and urge the mill-hands to give as much work in ten, as they have been doing in twelve.

It is now time to examine the use we should make of the increasing wages and the hours saved. It would be like going into the frying pan out of the fire to use the increase in wages in the grog-shop and the hours saved from the gambling den. The money received, it is clear, should be devoted to education of our children, and the time saved to our education. In both these matters the mill-owners can render much assistance. They can open cheap restaurants for the working men where they can get pure milk and wholesome refreshments. They can open reading-rooms and provide harmless amusements and games for them. Provided such healthy surroundings, the craving for drink and gambling will leave them. The Unions also should attempt similar things. They will be better employed in divising means of improvement from within than fighting the capitalists.

It is a sign of national degradation when little children are removed from schools and are employed in earning wages. No nation worthy of the name can possibly afford so to misuse her children. At least up to the age of sixteen they must be kept in schools. Similarly women also must be gradually weaned from mill-labour. If man and woman are partners in life and complementary each of the other, they become good householders only by dividing their labour, and a wise mother finds her time fully occupied in looking after her household and children. But where both husband and wife have to labour for mere maintenance, the nation must become degraded. It is like a bankrupt living on his capital.

And just as it is necessary for the labourers to develop their minds by receiving education and to educate their children, so it is necessary to develop the moral faculty in them. Development of the moral faculty means that of the religious sense. The world does not quarrel with those who have a true faith in God and who understand the true nature of religion. And if it does, such men turn away the wrath of their adversaries by their gentleness. Religion here does not mean merely offering one's *namaz* or going to the temple. But it means knowledge of one's self and knowledge of God, and just as a person does not become a weaver unless he knows the art of weaving so does he fail to know himself unless he complies with certain rules. Chief amongst these are three that are of universal observance. The first is observance of Truth. He who does not know what it is to speak the truth is like a false coin valueless. The second is not to injure others. He who injures others, is jealous of others, is not fit to live in the world. For the world is at war with him, and he has to live in perpetual fear of the world. We all are bound by the tie of love. There is in everything a centripetal force without which nothing could have existed. Scientists tell us that without the presence of the cohesive force amongst the atoms that comprise this globe of ours, it would crumble to pieces and we would cease to exist, and even as there is cohesive force in blind matter, so much must there be in all things animate and the name for that cohesive force among animate beings is Love. We notice it between father and son, between brother and sister, friend and friend. But we have to learn to use that force among all that lives, and in the use of it consists our knowledge of God. Where there is love there is life; hatred leads to destruction. I hope that Anasuya Bai will help you to learn this great law of Love and I ask you if you recognise her love towards you to reciprocate it by feeling in your own persons that same love towards the whole of humanity. The third rule is that we have to conquer our passions. It is called *Brahmacharya* in Sanskrit. I do not use it here merely in its accepted narrow sense. He is not a *Brahmachari*, who, although he may be a celebate or may be living a chaste life as a married man, otherwise gives himself up to a variety of indulgences. He alone is capable of knowing himself who brings under complete subjection all his passions. He who exercises self-restraint in its widest sense is also a *Brahmachari*—a man of faith, a true Hindu or a true Mahomedan.

It is a breach of *Brahmacharya* to hear questionable language or obscene songs. It is licentiousness of the tongue to utter foul abuse instead of reciting the name of God, and so with the other senses. He alone can be considered the true man who having subjected his passions becomes perfectly self-restrained. We are like a rider who cannot keep his horse under control and is quickly brought down. But one who, drawing in the reins, keep the animal under subjection stands a fair chance of reaching his destination. Even so does a man who can control his passions make for the goal. He alone is fit for *Swarajya.* He alone is a seeker after truth. He alone becomes capable of knowing God. It is my earnest wish that you will not reject these remarks as if they were copybook maxims. I ask you to believe that we shall never go forward until we have learnt the value of observing these truths. What I have told you is a fragment of my own experiences. My service of you is due simply to my love for you and I partake of your sorrows, because I hope thereby to justify myself before my Maker. What though your wages were quadrupled and you had to work only a quarter of the time you are doing now, if, notwithstanding, you did not know the value of true speech, if the Rakshasa in you injured others and gave the reins to your passions. We must have more wages, we must have less work, because we want clean houses, clean bodies, clean minds and a clean soul, and we strive for better wages and less work in the belief that both are essential for this fourfold cleanliness. But if that be not the object to be achieved, it would be a sin to attempt and get better wages and reduce the hours of labour. May God grant you and Ansuyabai the power to achieve the end.

16*th February*, 1921

STRIKES

(By M. K. Gandhi)

Strikes are the order of the day. They are a symptom of the existing unrest. All kinds of vague ideas are floating in the air. A vague hope inspires all, and great will be the disappointment if that vague hope does not take definite shape. The labour world in India, as elsewhere, is at the mercy of those who set up as advisers and guides. The latter are not always scrupulous, and not always wise even when they are scrupulous. The labourers are dissatisfied with their lot. They have every reason for dissatisfaction. They are being taught, and justly, to regard themselves as being chiefly instrumental in enriching their employers. And so it requires little effort to make them lay down their tools. The political situation too is beginning to affect the labourers of India. * And there are not wanting labour leaders who consider that strikes may be engineered for political purposes.

*As a sign of labour's awakening and patriotism the following from *Young India* of 11th August, 1921, may be read with interest:

Labourers' Mite—The public have no idea of the part labourers have played in contributing to the Tilak Swaraj Fund. Twenty-one thousand mill-hands of Ahmedabad have paid nearly Rs .54,000 to the Fund and this at the prescribed rate, *i.e.*, one-tenth of their monthly wages. Seven thousand have become members. Similarly though not so scientifically or largely as the Ahmedabad labourers, the Bombay labourers have also sent their purses unasked. It is a sign of the

In my opinion, it will be a most serious mistake to make use of labour strikes for such a purpose. I don't deny that such strikes can serve political ends. But they do not fall within the plan of non-violent non-co-operation. It does not require much effort of the intellect to perceive that it is a most dangerous thing to make political use of labour until labourers understand the political condition of the country and are prepared to work for the common good.* This

*Regarding sympathetic strikes and the use of strikes as a political weapon, the following from *Young India* of 22nd September, 1921, will be read with interest :

Of Strikes—The Assam Bengal Railway and the steamer strikes were out of the ordinary, the first attempt as I have found, to have strikes out of sympathy for those outside labour unions. The strikes were therefore sympathetic, humanitarian or political. I had the pleasure of meeting the strikers all over the railway line, but specially at Gauhati, Chittagong and Barisal. Having talked to them freely, I have come to the conclusion that the people did not fully realise the cost of their undertaking. But having embarked on the strike, they have endeavoured to suffer the consequence. It is always dangerous and uncharitable for an outsider to say, what he would have done if he had the handling of a situation. But if one may hazard an opinion, I think that the labourers were not ready for a philanthropic strike. In my opinion, the labourers and artisans of India have not yet arrived at that degree of national consciousness, which is necessary for successful sympathetic strikes. The fault is ours. We who have interested ourselves in national service, have not until recently studied the wants and aspirations of these classes, nor taken

---

times. As the labourers become more organised and think of the country as well as themselves, they will fight for a due adjustment of prices of manufactures to the making of which they contribute so much labour. And then there will be no question of mills charging exorbitant prices just to swell the shareholders' dividends irrespective of the interests of the working man or the consumer. A time must come, and the sooner the better, when there would be a respectable proportion between dividends, wages and prices.

is hardly to be expected of them all of a sudden and until they have bettered their own condition so as to enable them to keep body and soul together in a

---

the trouble of informing them of the political situation. We have hitherto believed, that only those who had passed through high schools and colleges were fit to take part in national work. It is hardly therefore proper to expect the labouring and the artisan class all of a sudden to appreciate, and sacrifice themselves for interests outside their own. We may not exploit them for political or any other ends. The best service we can render them and take from them at the present stage is to teach them self-help, to give them an idea of their own duties and rights, and put them in a position to secure redress of their own just grievances. Then and not till then are they ready for political, national or humanitarian service.

Any premature precipitation of sympathetic strikes must therefore result in infinite harm to our cause. In the programme of non-violence, we must rigidly exclude the idea of gaining anything by embarrassing the Government. If our activity is pure and that of the Government impure, the latter is embarrassed by our purity, if it does not itself become pure. Thus, a movement of purification benefits both parties. Whereas a movement of mere destruction leaves the destroyer unpurified, and brings him down to the level of those whom he seeks to destroy.

Even our sympathetic strikes therefore have to be strikes of self-purification, *i.e.*, Non-co-operation. And so, when we declare a strike to redress a wrong, we really cease to take part in the wrong, and thus leave the wrong-doer to his own resources, in other words enable him to see the folly of continuing the wrong. Such a strike can only succeed, when behind it is the fixed determination not to revert to service.

Speaking, therefore, as one having handled large successful strikes, I repeat the following maxims, already stated in these pages, for the guidance of all strike leaders:

(1) There should be no strike without a real grievance.

(2) There should be no strike, if the persons concerned are not able to support themselves out of their own savings or by engaging in some temporary occupation, such as carding, spinning and weaving. Strikers should never depend upon public subscriptions or other charity.

decent manner. The greatest political contribution, therefore, that labourers can make is to improve their own condition, to become better informed, to insist on their rights, and even to demand proper use by their employers of the manufactures in which they have had such an important hand. The proper evolution, therefore, would be for the labourers to raise themselves to the status of part proprietors. Strikes, therefore, for

---

(3) Strikers must fix an unalterable minimum demand, and declare it before embarking upon their strike.

A strike may fail in spite of a just grievance and the ability of strikers to hold out indefinitely, if there are workers to replace them. A wise man, therefore, will not strike for increase of wages or other comforts, if he feels that he can be easily replaced. But a philanthropic or patriotic man will strike in spite of supply being greater than the demand, when he feels for and wishes to associate himself with his neighbour's distress. Needless to say, there is no room in a civil strike of the nature described by me for violence in the shape of intimidation, incendiarism or otherwise. I should therefore be extremely sorry to find, that the recent derailment near Chittagong was due to mischief done by any of the strikers. Judged by the tests suggested by me, it is clear that friends of the strikers should never have advised them to apply for or receive Congress or any other public funds for their support. The value of the strikers' sympathy was diminished to the extent, that they received or accepted financial aid. The merit of a sympathetic strike lies in the inconvenience and the loss suffered by the sympathisers.

As to what should be done now for or by the strikers, who have in spite of threats and temptations manfully held out—and they are more than 50 p.c.—I have already given my opinion to the Bengal Provincial Congress Committee. And by that I wish to abide. If the strikers struck on the sole issue of sympathy for the outraged coolies at Chandpur and without intimidating their brethren, they had every moral right to do so, and they showed an unexpected measure of patriotism and fellow-feeling. I hope that they will refuse to rejoin service, until the Government have fully and frankly apologised, and refunded to the parties concerned the monies paid for the repatriation of the coolies.

the present should only take place for the direct betterment of labourers' lot, and, when they have acquired the spirit of patriotism, for the regulation of prices of their manufactures.

The conditions of a successful strike are simple.* And when they are fulfilled, a strike need never fail.

(1) The cause of the strike must be just.

(2) There should be practical unanimity among the strikers.

(3) There should be no violence used against non-strikers.

(4) Strikers should be able to maintain themselves

*Strikes should not mean absence of discipline or resort to lightning strike. The following appeared in *Young India* of 1st December, 1921:

Strikes—When *Hartal* takes place what should mill hands and other employees do who cannot get leave from their unsympathetic or alien employers? In terms of non-violence there can be but one answer. An employee who gives himself leave uses violence, for he commits a criminal breach of the contract of his service. He cannot absent himself without the permission of his employer. All he can do is to resign, if he is not satisfied with his employer. But this too a body of employees may not do all of a sudden. For they may not in order to enforce their political opinion threaten to leave without due notice. In short, mill hands and such other employees should not be encouraged to co-erce their employers into giving leave. Non-violent action is not quite so simple as one may imagine. I have heard men describing as Non-violent the holding tight of the legs of persons proceeding to drink-shops. Similarly youngsters have classed foul abuse of liquor dealers among Non-violent acts. This is merely playing with language and bore bitter fruit in Bombay. We must be true to ourselves if we wish to give Non-violence a fair trial. Even if we cannot make our thought Non-violent, we must so regulate our speech and action as to make them completely innocuous. If we find it impossible or too difficult to practise, we must give up the attempt but we must not blame one of the greatest doctrines of life for our incapacity. If failure has to be written against us, it won't be failure of Non-violence but of the violent to respond to it.

during the strike period without falling back upon Union funds and should therefore occupy themselves in some useful and productive temporary occupation.

(5) A strike is no remedy when there is enough other labour to replace strikers. In that case, in the event of unjust treatment or inadequate wages or the like, resignation is the remedy.

(6) Successful strikes have taken place even when all the above conditions have not been fulfilled, but that merely proves that the employees were weak and have a guilty conscience. We often make terrible mistakes by copying bad examples. The safest thing is not to copy examples of which we have rarely complete knowledge but to follow the conditions which we know and recognise to be essential for success.

It is the duty of every well wisher of the country, if we are to attain Swaraj during the year, not to precipitate any action that may even by a day retard the fulfilment of the great national purpose.

9th March, 1921

INSTRUCTIONS TO THE PEASANTS OF THE UNITED PROVINCES

We give below a free rendering of the Hindi instuructions addressed by Mr. Gandhi to the peasants of the United Provinces during his visit to Oudh.* Pandit

* The following appeared in *Young India* of 18th May, 1921:

The Zamindars and the Ryots.—Whilst the U. P. Government is crossing the bounds of propriety, and intimidating people, there is little doubt that the Kisans too are not making wise use of their newly found power. In several Zamindaries, they are said to have overstepped the mark, taken the law into their own hands and to have become impatient of anybody who would not do as they wish. They

Motilal Nehru, in his capacity as president of the Kisan Sabha, has distributed them in thousands among the peasantry.

Attainment of Swaraj or redress of grievances is impossible unless the following rules are strictly observed:

1. We may not hurt anybody. We may not use our sticks against anybody. We may not use abusive language or exercise any other undue pressure.

2. We may not loot shops.

3. We should influence our opponents by kindness, not by using physical force nor stopping their water supply nor the services of the barber and the washerman.

4. We may not withhold taxes from the Government or rent from the landlord.

5. Should there be any grievances against Zamin-

---

are abusing social boycott and are turning it into an instrument of violence. They are reported to have stopped the supply of water, barber, and other paid services to their Zamindars in some instances and even suspended payment of the rent due to them. The Kisan movement has received an impetus from Non-co-operation but it is anterior to and independent of it. Whilst we will not hesitate to advise the Kisans when the moment comes, to suspend payment of taxes to the Government, it is not contemplated that at any stage of Non-co-operation we would seek to deprive the Zamindars of their rent. The Kisan movement must be confined to the improvement of status of the Kisans and the betterment of the relations between the Zamindars and them. The Kisans must be advised scrupulously to abide by the terms of their agreement with the Zamindars, whether such is written or inferred from custom. Where a custom or even a written contract is bad, they may not try to uproot it by violence or without previous reference to the Zamindars. In every case there should be a friendly discussion with the Zamindars and an attempt made to arrive at a settlement. Our capacity for Swaraj depends upon our capacity for solving without reference to, or intervention of, the Government, all the varied and complex problems that must arise in the affairs of one of the biggest and the most ancient nations like ours.

dars, they should be reported to Pandit Motilal Nehru and his advice followed.

6. It should be borne in mind that we want to turn Zamindars into friends.

7. We are not at the present moment offering civil disobedience; we should, therefore, carry out all Government orders.

8. We may not stop railway trains not forcibly enter them without tickets.

9. In the event of any of our leaders being arrested, we may not prevent his arrest nor create any disturbance. We shall not lose our cause by the Government arresting our leaders; we shall certainly lose it if we become mad and do violence.

10. We must abolish intoxicating drinks, drugs and other evil habits.

11. We must treat all women as mothers and sisters and respect and protect them.

12. We must promote unity between Hindus and Muslims.

13. As amongst Hindus we may not regard any one as inferior or untouchable. There should be the spirit of equality and brotherhood among all. We should regard all the inhabitants of India as brothers and sisters.

14. We may not indulge in gambling.

15. We may not steal.

16. We may not tell an untruth on any account whatsoever. We should be truthful in all our dealings.

17. We should introduce the spinning wheel in every home and all—male and female—should devote their spare time to spinning. Boys and girls should also be taught and encouraged to spin for four hours daily.

18. We should avoid the use of all foreign cloth

and wear cloth woven by the weavers from yarn spun by ourselves.

19. We should not resort to law courts but should have all disputes settled by private arbitration.

The most important thing to remember is to curb anger, never to do violence and even to suffer violence done to us.

8th June, 1921

THE ASSAM COOLIES

(By M. K. Gandhi)

I have purposely refrained from dealing with this trouble, though I have remained in touch with Mr. Andrews and others, who are on the spot dealing with it. I refer to the trouble only to state that I knew nothing of its coming. I should be sorry, if anybody used my name to lead the men to desert their employers. It is clear enough that it is purely a labour trouble. It is admitted that the employers reduced the wages. Both Mr. Das and Mr. Andrews report that the trouble is purely economic,* and that the coolies have a substantial grievance. It is evident that the reformed Government has failed to cope with it. I observe that the *Times of India* has made the most illegitimate use of the trouble to impute enmity to English commercial interests in India. It has become the fashion to attribute hatred to Non-co-operators. I make bold to say that Non-co-operation has alone prevented racial feuds and disturbances, and directed the anger of the people in the

* Mr. Andrews's detailed survey of the situation appeared in the *Modern Review* wherein he dwells on the oppression of the poor consequent on Assam troubles.

proper channel. The aim of Non-co-operation is to hurt no interest whatsoever, by reason only of its belonging to a race. Its aim is to purge every interest of its injurious or impure character. Every English or Indian interest that is based on injustice or brute force, or is antagonistic to the growth of India as a whole, is undoubtedly in peril. No interest that is supported merely by brute force but not by people's good-will, can possibly survive the fire of Non-co-operation. If the Assam planters are not sustained by the exploitation of Indian labour, they have nothing to fear. A time is certainly coming, when there will be no more unconscionable dividends. The profits of big concerns must bear relation to the wages of the workers. I lay down these categorical propositions, because I know that Non-co-operation is beyond the reach of the bayonet. It has found an abiding place in the Indian heart. Workers like me will go when the hour has struck, but Non-co-operation will remain. I am aware, too, that the labouring class in India has not yet become enlightened enough to have the ability to regulate the relations between capital and labour on a just basis. But that time is coming soon,—faster than we may imagine. I am hoping that the capitalists, be they European or Indian, will appreciate the new awakening, and the new force that has arisen in our midst.

21*t July*, 1921

THE SHADOW OF SIMLA

(By M. K. Gandhi)

If proof were wanted that the movement of Non-co-operation is neither anti-British nor anti-Christian, we have the instance of Mr. Stokes, a nationalised British subject and staunch Christian, devoting his all to the eradication of the evil of Begar. Mr. Stokes is a convinced Non-co-operator and Congressman. I think I am right in saying, that he has come to it by slow degrees. No Indian is giving such battle to the Government as Mr. Stokes. He has veritably become the guide, philosopher and friend of the hillmen. The reader should know that Begar is going on under the shadow of Simla, under the Viceroy's nose as it were. And yet Lord Reading is powerless to remedy the mischief. I have no doubt, that he is willing enough. But he cannot carry the district officers and others with him. And some of the officials are so unscrupulous that, if they cannot have their way in the territories directly administered, they do so through the native states. Now, on the hills near Simla, there are small native states in which the British officer is all-powerful, more so in his own jurisdiction than the Viceroy. He can make the states do as he wills, and yet profess to be unconnected with their doings. There is one such state under the Court of Wards. And it is here, that through the influence of the Deputy Commissioner of Simla, repression is going on in order to suppress the Begar movement. The chosen way, which as a Parsi friend corrected me dates not from British days but from Adam's, is to lop off tall poppies. The axe must be laid at the root. And so the most efficient and cultured of the poor hillmen, named Kapur Singh, has been put under lock and key. Here is a graphic description of the way evidence was collected. 'People were subjected to a reign of terror. The Simla Police were brought, a number of them arrested, all the people scared by threats of machine-guns and Kalapani. . . It was in such an atmosphere, that the evidence for the prosecution was collected.' This reminds one of the Punjab martial law days.

Naturally the hillmen feel sore about this persecution of their trusted leader. I hope that, under Mr. Stokes's inspiration, they will resolutely refuse to do any Begar at all even for full value, until their leader is discharged. They must not weaken, but must invite upon their devoted heads the wrath of the authorities, and face imprisonment even as he did.

Why this persistence in exacting Begar? For the authority, the influence and the comfort of the officials and officers depend upon the continuance of Begar. Without it, they cannot sport and kill wild beasts in the forests of the Himalayas. The Duke could not have been taken for *shikar* to the mountain fastnesses, if Begar had gone out of use. For the doubtful pleasure of shooting tigers and innocent 'game,' a way had to be cut by impressing the labours of thousands of unwilling villagers. If the beasts had intelligent speech at their command, they would state a case against man that would stagger 'humanity.' I can understand the shooting of wild beasts which come to annoy us. But I have found no cogent reasons advanced for wasting treasures upon organising parties for satisfying man's thirst for blood. And yet, if there was no Begar, there would be no 'sport' for the officer or the globetrotter. I need not have the practice of Indian princes and precedents from the Mahabharata flung in my face. I decline to be slave to precedents or practice I cannot understand or defend on a moral basis.

21st July, 1921

POSITION OF WOMEN

(By M. K. Gandhi)

Shrimati Saraladevi of Katak writes:—"Don't you admit that the treatment of women is as bad a disease as untouchability itself? The attitude of the young 'nationalists' I have come in contact with, is beastly in ninety cases out of a hundred. How many of the Non-co-operators in India do not regard women as objects of enjoyment? Is that essential condition of success—self-purification—possible without a change of attitude towards women?"

I am unable to subscribe that the treatment of women is a 'disease as bad as untouchability.' Shrimati Saraladevi has grossly exaggerated the evil. Nor can the charge levelled against the Non-co-operators of mere gratification of lust be sustained. A cause can only lose by exaggeration. At the same time, I have no difficulty about subscribing to the proposition, that in order to fit ourselves for the Swaraj, men must cultivate much greater respect than they have for woman and her purity. Mr. Andrews has struck a much truer note than this lady, when he tells us in burning language that we dare not gloat over the shame of our fallen sisters. That any Non-co-operator could have been found willing to relate with gusto that there were some of these erring sisters who reserved themselves for Non-co-operators, is a degrading thought. There can be no distinction between Co-operators and Non-co-operators in this matter of vital importance for our moral well-being. All of us men must hang our heads in shame, so long as there is a single woman whom we dedicate to our lust. I will far rather see the race of man extinct, than that we should become less than beasts by making the noblest of God's creation the object of our lust. But this is not a problem merely for India. It is a world problem. And if I preach against the modern artificial life of sensual enjoyment, and ask men and women to go back to the simple life epitomised in the charkha, I do so because I know that, without an intelligent return to simplicity, there is no escape from our descent to a state lower than brutality. I passionately desire the utmost freedom for our women. I detest child marriages. I shudder to see a child widow, and shiver with rage when a husband just widowed with brutal indifference contracts another marriage. I deplore the criminal indifference of parents who keep their daughters utterly ignorant and illiterate and bring them up only for the purpose of marrying them off to some young man of means. Notwithstanding all this grief and rage, I realise the difficulty of the problem. Women must have votes and an equal legal status. But the problem does not end there. It only commences at the point where women begin to affect the political deliberations of the nation.

To illustrate what I mean, let me relate the enchanting description a valued Mussalman friend gave me of a talk he had with a noted feminist in London. He was attending a meeting of feminists. A lady friend was surprised to find a Mussalman at such a meeting! She inquired how he found himself there. The friend said he had two major and two minor reasons for so doing. His father died when he was an infant. He owed all he was in life to his mother. Then he was married to a woman who was a real partner in life. And he had no sons but four daughters all minors in whom as a father he was deeply interested. Was it any wonder that he was a feminist? He went on. Mussalmans were accused of indifference to women. There never was a grosser libel uttered. The law of Islam gave equal rights to women. He thought that man for his lust had degraded woman. Instead of adoring the soul within her, he had set about adoring her body, and he had succeeded so well in his design, that woman to-day did not know that she had begun to hug her bodily adornment which was almost a sign of her slavery. He added with his voice almost choked; if it was not so, how could it be, that the fallen sisters delighted most in the embellishment of the body? Had we (men) not crushed the very soul out of them? No, he said regaining self-possession, he wanted not only the mechanical freedom for women, he wanted also to break down the shackles that bound her of her own will. And so he had intended to bring up his daughters to an independent calling.

I need not pursue the ennobling conversation any further. I want my fair correspondent to ponder over the central idea of the Mussalman friend's discourse and tackle the problem. Woman must cease to consider herself the object of man's lust. The remedy is more in her hands than man's. She must refuse to adorn herself for men, including her husband, if she will be an equal partner with man. I cannot imagine Sita ever wasting a single moment on pleasing Rama by physical charms.

15th September, 1921

OUR FALLEN SISTERS

(BY M. K. GANDHI)

The first occasion I had of meeting those women who earn their livelihood out of their shame was at Cocanada in the Andhra province. There it was a few moments' interview with only half a dozen of them. The second occasion was at Barisal. Over one hundred of them met by appointment. They had sent a letter in advance, asking for an interview and telling me that they had become members of the Congress and subscribed to the Tilak Swaraj Fund, but could not understand my advice not to seek office in the various Congress Committees. They wound up by saying that they wished to seek my advice as to their future welfare. The gentleman who handed me the letter did so with great hesitation, not knowing whether I would be offended or pleased with the receipt of the letter. I put him at ease by assuring him, that it was my duty to serve these sisters, if I could in any way.

For me the two hours I passed with these sisters is a treasured memory. They told me that they were over 350 in the midst of a population of about 20,000 men, women and children. They represent the shame of the men of Barisal, and the sooner Barisal gets rid of it, the better for its great name. And what is true of Barisal is true, I fear, of every city. I mention Barisal, therefore, as an illustration. The credit of having thought of serving these sisters belongs to some young men of Barisal. Let me hope that Barisal will soon be able to claim the credit, too, of having eradicated the evil.

Of all the evils for which man has made himself responsible, none is so degrading, so shocking or so brutal as his abuse of the better half of humanity to me, the female sex, not the weaker sex. It is the nobler of the two, for it is even to-day the embodiment of sacrifice, silent suffering, humility, faith and knowledge. A woman's intuition has often proved truer than man's arrogant assumption of superior knowledge. There is method in putting Sita before Rama and Radha before Krishna. Let us not delude ourselves into the belief, that this gambling in vice has a place in our evolution because it is rampant and in some cases even state-regulated in civilized Europe.* Let us not also perpetuate the vice on the strength of Indian precedents.

* The following appeared in *Young India* of 18th August, 1921:

Plague-spots of Lucknow.—An English friend writes to me at Lucknow:

"I am just writing to ask you to write a word before you go to some one in authority among your supporters here in regard to the brothels in Lucknow. I was talking to the military police this morning in Aminabad, and it seems that there are some fifty of these places in that locality frequented by soldiers (some of whom have been court-martialled as it is out of bounds) Europeans and Anglo-Indians. He did not say anything about Indians, but I heard the other day that they also go to these women. A word from you as to this debasing of manhood and lack of self-control would do more than anything else to counteract this evil. I will pledge myself to do all I can to help in the matter."

I wish I could share the English friend's belief that my word has the power he attributes to it. As I write this paragraph, the picture of the dear sisters who visited me at Cocanada after night-fall haunts me. They were dearer to me after I learnt of their shame. It was only by suggestion they could tell me what their life was. As the spokeswoman spoke to me, she had shame and sorrow written in her eyes. I could not bring myself to hold them guilty. I devoted my speech after this meeting to the necessity of personal purity. My heart therefore goes out to the fallen sisters of Lucknow. They are driven to a life of shame. I am satisfied that they do not go to it from choice. And the beast in man has made the detestable crime a lucrative profession. Lucknow is noted for its love of ease. But

We should cease to grow the moment we cease to discriminate between virtue and vice, and slavishly copy the past which we do not fully know. We are proud heirs to all that was noblest and best in the by-gone age. We must not dishonour our heritage by multiplying past errors. In a self-respecting India, is not every woman's virtue as much every man's concern as his own sister's? Swaraj means ability to regard every inhabitant of India as our own brother or sister.

And so, as a man I hung my head in shame before these hundred sisters. Some were elderly, most were between twenty and thirty, and two or three were girls below twelve. Between them all, they told me, they had six girls and four boys, the eldest of whom was married to one of their own class. The girls were to be brought up to the same life as themselves, unless something else was possible. That these women should have considered their lot to be beyond repair, was like a stab in the living flesh. And yet they were intelligent and modest. Their talk was dignified, their answers were clean and straight. And for the moment their determination was as firm as that of any Satyagrahi. Eleven of them promised to give up their present life and take to spinning and weaving from the following day, if they received a

---

Lucknow is also the seat of a Mussalman divine. It has its full share of all that is noble in Islam. For the Hindus Lucknow is the capital of the Province where the spotless Sita and Rama roamed and reigned. It recalls the best days of Hindu purity, nobility, bravery and steadfastness to truth. Non-co-operation is self-purification, and I urge all the non-co-operators and others to deal with this moral plague of Lucknow. I hope no custodian of Lucknow's good name will remind me that Lucknow is no worse than the other cities in India. Lucknow has come in by chance as an illustration. We are responsible throughout India for the purity and the safety of our womanhood. Why should not Lucknow lead?

helping hand. The others said they would take time to think, for they did not wish to deceive me.

Here is work for the citizens of Barisal.* Here is work for all true servants of India, men as well as women. If there are 350 unhappy sisters in a population of 20,000, there may be 52,50,000 in all India. But I flatter myself with the belief that four-fifths of the population of India, which live in the villages and are purely agricultural, are not touched by the vice. The lowest figure for all India would therefore be 10,50,000 women living on the sale of their own honour. Before these unfortunate sisters could be weaned from their degradation, two conditions have to be fulfilled. We men must learn to control our passions, and these women should be found a calling that would enable them to earn

*The following appeared in *Young India* of 17th November 1921:

Fallen Sisters.—The reader will be glad to learn that the work of reclaiming the fallen sisters of Barisal has been taken up in right earnest. Dr. Rai writes saying that many of them have been visited, and spinning is being introduced among them. Jagadish Babu who has been in charge of Babu Ashvinikumar Dutt's school for years has promised to guide the young workers who have undertaken this responsible service. I hope that those who have taken up this much-needed service will not leave it half finished. They must be prepared for disappointments, they must expect slow progress. It is only in such work that is free from excitement or immediate promise of renown that one's love of service for its own sake is tested. I commend the example of Barisal to the other cities also. This purifying work has to be done even after Swaraj. Now every one is qualified for it. Those therefore who feel the call and have the requisite purity should turn their attention to the eradication of this growing vice. The movement naturally has two branches, the reclamation of fallen sisters and the weaning of men from the degrading vice which makes man look upon his sisters with lust and tempts him to make her a prey to it. The qualities required for both the branches of work are the same, and the work should be simultaneously done in both the branches, if it is to bear fruit.

an honourable living. The movement of Non-co-operation is nothing, if it does not purify us and restrain our evil passions. And there is no occupation but spinning and weaving which all can take up without over crowding. These sisters, the vast majority of them, need not think of marriage. They agreed that they could not. They must therefore become the true *Sannyasinis* of India. Having no cares of life but of service, they can spin and weave to their heart's content. One million fifty thousand women diligently weaving every day for eight hours means that number of rupees per day for an impoverished India. These sisters told me they earned as much as two rupees per day. But they they admitted, that they had many things needed to pander to man's lust, which they could discard when they took to spinning and weaving, reverting to a natural life. By the time I had finished with my interviews, they knew without my telling them, why they could not be office-bearers in Congress Committees if they did not give up their sinfulness. None could officiate at the altar of Swaraj, who did not approach it with pure hands and a pure heart.

11th August, 1921

TO THE WOMEN OF INDIA

Dear Sisters,

The All-India Congress Committee has come to a momentous decision in fixing the 30th September next, as the final date for completing the boycott of foreign cloth begun by the sacrificial fire lit on the 31st July in Bombay in memory of Lokamanya Tilak. It was accorded the privilege of setting fire to the huge pile containing costly sadis and other dresses which you have hitherto considered fine and beautiful. I feel that it was right and wise on the part of the sisters who gave their costly clothing. Its destruction was the most economical use you could have made of it, even as destruction of plague-infected articles is their most economical and best use. It was a necessary surgical operation designed to avert more serious complaints in the body politic.

The women of India have during the past twelve months worked wonders on behalf of the motherland.* You have silently worked away as angels of mercy. You have parted with your cash and your fine jewellery.

* The following appeared in *Young India* of 22nd December, 1920:

Behold the Woman.—We may learn much from the women of India. I wish the Englishmen as well as our unbelievers in the efficacy or the necessity of Non-co-operation were to witness the demonstration of the women of India in favour of Non-co-operation. Everywhere they have flocked in their hundreds and thousands. They have even come out of their Pardahs and given Maulana Shaukat Ali and me their blessings. They have instinctively understood the purity of the movement. Their hearts have been touched. They have given up their pearl and diamond bangles, their necklaces and their rings. All have come—both rich and poor—and given us their blessings and accompanied them with rich gifts, rich because of the absolutely voluntary nature thereof. They have understood, too, that the purity of the poor women of India is hidden in the music of the spinning wheel. They do not flock to the standard of Non-co-operation through hatred.

The other side.—But the men are impatient and grievously err as they are reported to have done at Delhi and in Bengal. It was cruel and sinful to deny the rights of burial to the corpse of a man whom the so-called Non-co-operators (if they were Non-co-operators) disliked. It was filthy to throw, at a place in East Bengal, night soil on a candidate who had stood for election as a council member, or to cut the ears of a voter for daring to exercise his vote. These are just the ways of defeating our own purpose. Non-co-operation is non-violent not merely in regard to the Englishmen and Government

You have wandered from house to house to make collections. Some of you have even assisted in picketing. Some of you who were used to fine dresses of variegated colours and had a number of changes during the day, have now adopted the white and spotless, but heavy Khadi sadi reminding one of a woman's innate purity. You have done all this for the sake of India, for the sake of the Khilafat, for the sake of the Punjab. There is no guile about your word or work. Yours is the purest sacrifice untainted by anger or hate. Let me confess to you that your spontaneous and loving response all over India has convinced me that God is with us. No other proof of our struggle being one of self-purification is needed than that lacs of India's women are actively helping it.

Having given much, more is now required of you. Men bore the principal share of the subscriptions to the Tilak Swaraj Fund. But completion of the Swadeshi programme is possible only if you give the largest share. Boycott is impossible, *unless you will surrender the whole of your foreign clothing.** So long as

* *Of Tamil Woman.*—A friend writes from Tirupati:

"The greatest obstacle in the way of success of our movement in Madras are our women. Some of them are very reactionary and a very large number of the high class Brahmin ladies have become addicted to many of the western vices. They drink coffee not less than three times a day and consider it very fashionable to drink more. In dress they are no better, they have given up the homely cheap cloth and are running after costly foreign cloth. In the matter of jewels,

---

officials. It has to be equally so as between ourselves. A co-operator is as much entitled to freedom of action, speech and thought as the tallest among Non-co-operators. Non-co-operation is directed against all slavery. Every Non-co-operator therefore retards the function of his cause by resorting to violence. It is a sure sign of want of faith of his mission.

the taste persists, so long is complete renunciation impossible. And boycott, means complete renunciation, We must be prepared to be satisfied with such cloth as

---

Brahmin ladies excel all others. Among Brahmins, Shri Vaishnava ladies are the worst sinners. When men are trying to return to a purer life, our ladies are becoming extravagant. While going to temples to worship God, they cannot think of a plain, simple dress. They should wear the costliest jewels available and still more costly laces. I know of many honest women who refuse to go to temples because they have not got rich clothes and costly jewels."

I am loth to think that what the friend who is himself a Non-co-operating Vaishnava pleader says is all true. And I am inclined to disbelieve the statement that the Tamil sisters are worse than the rest in the matter of love of gaudiness. All the same, his letter ought to serve as a warning to the Tamil sisters. They must revert to the original simplicity and certainly God will be better pleased with those who wear the spotless Khadi sadi as a symbol of the inner purity than with those who are gaudily dressed. Our temples are not meant for show but for expression of humility and simplicity which are typical of a devotional mood. There should be a continuous propaganda amongst women in the Madras Presidency with reference to the evil complained of.

The following appeared in *Young India* of 25th August, 1921:

Tamil Sisters again.—A South Indian lawyer sends me the following note:

"*Khadi* is not as widely used in the Tamil province as in the other provinces, mainly because the women-folk do not wear it. The spinning-wheel is not much in evidence for the same reason. Plain white cannot be worn by married women here. They can only wear dyed *sadis*. In former times cotton was the only wear of ladies. Now except by the poorest, cotton *sadis* are discarded, and silk *sadis* form the daily wear. Silk *sadis* were at first locally manufactured at Koranadu (near Mayavaram) and later on at Conjeeveram, and dyed with Indian dyes. They cost from Rs. 10 to 30. They were only occasionally used. Lately the market has been exclusively captured by Bangalore *sadis* dyed with German or English dyes, the least of which costs about Rs. 50. This presses on the poor Brahman householder specially as he has to clothe the members of his family only with these; and when it is the daily wear, he has to go in for a number of

India can produce, even as we are thankfully content with such children as God gives us. I have not known a mother throwing away her baby even though it may appear ugly to an outsider. So should it be with the patriotic women of India about Indian manufactures. And for you only hand-spun and hand woven can be

them. On marriage occasions the minimum cost of a *sadi* fit for presentation is above Rs. 100. Many a decent family is ruined by a marriage, mostly on this account. This ruinous habit, which was confined to the Brahmans, has spread among other classes also.

"Besides the question of expense, there is the other aspect of comfort and convenience. Silk is non-absorbing and heavy, and working or cooking in it is martyrdom. It is always hot here except for one or two months of the year. There is also the peculiar insanitary habit of not washing the more costly *sadis* lest they should lose colour and get crimpled. The perspiration and smell emitted are awful.

"Many a householder on the verge of ruin would feel grateful to you if you would bring about a return to economy, simplicity and comfort."

I hope the workers in Madras will deal with the evil complained of in the correspondent's letter. I dread my forthcoming visit to Madras. I share the correspondent's feeling that the Tamil woman is over-fond of her silk *sadi*. There is no more unwholesome garment than silk in a hot climate like that of Madras. And one hundred rupees for a *sadi* is a criminal waste of money in a poor country like India. Men are no better, for they are proud of their handwoven *pugris, dhotis uparnas*, little thinking that the yarn used for these things is all foreign. Strange as it may appear, absorbent *Khadi* is cooler than the fine garments which are so prized by men. I am hoping, however, that my faith in the spirituality of Tamilians will be realised even in that difficult matter of Swadeshi, and that they will perceive the spiritual necessity of complete renunciation of foreign cloth and return to the *Charkha*. In the melting plains of Madras and Andhra I can imagine no industry so helpful as the gentle-moving *Charkha*. Dravida land is responible for sending out the largest number of emigrants to a life of servility and exile. Restoration of the *Charkha* automatically solves that difficult problem of enforced emigration. Land alone cannot support the poor peasantry of India even if there was no assessment to be paid.

regarded as Indian manufatures. During the transition stage you can only get coarse Khadi in abundance. You may add all the art to it that your taste allows or requires. And if you will be satisfied with coarse Khadi for a few months, India need not despair of seeing a revival of the fine rich and coloured garments of old which were once the envy and the despair of the world. I assure you that a six months ' course of self-denial will show you that what we to-day regard as artistic is only falsely so, and that true art takes note not merely of form but also of what lies behind. There is an art that kills and an art that gives life. The fine fabric that we have imported from the West or the far East has literally killed millions of our brothers and sisters, and delivered thousands of our dear sisters to a life of shame. True art must be evidence of happiness, contentment and purity of its authors. And if you will have such art revived in our midst, the use of Khadi is obligatory on the best of you at the present moment.

And not only is the use of Khadi necessary for the success of the Swadeshi programme, but it is imperative for every one of you to spin during your leisure hours. I have suggested to boys and men also that they should spin. Thousands of them, I know, are spinning daily. But the main burden of spinning must, as of old, fall on your shoulders. Two hundred years ago, the women of India spun not only for home demand but also for foreign lands. They spun not merely coarse counts but the finest that the world has ever spun. No machine has yet reached the fineness of the yarn spun by our ancestors. If then we are to cope with the demand for Khadi during the two months and afterwards, you must form spinning-clubs, institute spinning competitions and flood the Indian market with handspun yarn. For this purpose some of you have to become experts in spinning, carding and adjusting the spinning-wheels. This means ceaseless toil. You will not look upon spinning as a means of livelihood. For the middle class it should supplement the income of the family, and for very poor women, it is undoubtedly a means of livelihood. The spinning-wheel should be as it was the widow's loving companion. But for you who will read this appeal, it is presented as a duty, as *Dharma*. If all the well-to-do women of India were to spin a certain quantity daily, they would make yarn cheap and bring about much more quickly than otherwise the required fineness.

The economic and the moral salvation of India thus rests mainly with you. The future of India lies on your knees, for you will nurture the future generation. You can bring up the children of India to become simple, God-fearing and brave men and women, or you can coddle them to be weaklings unfit to brave the storms of life and used to foreign fineries which they would find it difficult in after life to discard. The next few weeks will show of what stuff the women of India are made. I have not the shadow of a doubt as to your choice. The destiny of India is far safer in your hands than in the hands of a Government that has so exploited India's resources that she has lost faith in herself. At every one of women's meetings, I have asked for your blessings for the national effort, and I have done so in the belief that you are pure, simple and godly enough to give them with effect. You can ensure the fruitfulness of your blessings by giving up your foreign cloth and during your spare hours by ceaselessly spinning for the nation.

I remain,

Your devoted brother,

M. K. GANDHI.

15*th December*, 1921

WOMEN'S PART

(BY M. K. GANDHI)

The women of Calcutta have obstructed the gentlemen of Calcutta by trying to sell *Khadi* and a telegram in the newspapers has announced that they have been consequently arrested. The company includes the devoted partner of the President—elect, his widowed sister and his niece. I had hoped that in the initial stages at any rate women would be spared the honour of going to gaol. They were not to become aggressive civil resisters. But the Bengal Government, in their impartial zeal to make no distinction even of sex, have conferred the honour upon three women of Calcutta. I hope that the whole country will welcome this innovation. The women of India should have as much share in winning Swaraj as men. Probably in this peaceful struggle, woman can outdistance man by many a mile. We know that she is any day superior to man in her religious devotion. Silent and dignified suffering is the badge of her sex. And now that the Government of Bengal have dragged the woman into the line of fire, I hope that the women all over India will take up the challenge and organise themselves. In any case they were bound, when a sufficient number of men had been removed, for the honour of their sex to step into their places. But now let it be side by side with men in sharing the hardships of gaol life. God will protect their honour. When as if to mock man her natural protectors became helpless to prevent Draupadi from being denuded of her last piece of cloth, the power of her own virtue preserved her honour. And so will it be to the end of time. Even the weakest physically have been given the ability to protect their own honour. Let it be man's privilege to protect woman, but let no woman of India feel helpless in the absence of man or in the event of his failing to perform the sacred duty of protecting her. One who knows how to die need never fear any harm to her or his honour.

I would suggest to the women of India quietly but without loss of time to collect names of those who are ready to enter the line of fire.* Let them send their offer to the women of Bengal and let the latter feel that their sisters elsewhere are ready to follow their noble example. It is likely that there will not be many forthcoming to brave the risks of a gaol life and all it must mean to

* The following is from *Young India* of 22nd December, 1921:

Selling Khadi.—The lead given by Shrimatis Vasantidevi Das and Urmiladevi in selling *Khadi* from house to house and hawking it in streets has been quickly taken up in the other parts of the country. Shrimati Sarala Devi writes, "I have to go immediately to the city to arrange to send 40 ladies in 20 groups under two volunteers each to sell *Khadi* in 20 lanes." In Madras too they are organising similarly. I cannot conceive any better occupation for ladies especially besides hand spinning that popularising *Khadi* by hawking it themselves. It is fine training in throwing off false pride or false modesty. And it is a most harmless challenge to the police to arrest them, if they dare. But if the practice is to become common, it must be regulated by grown up ladies of position and without any bluster. Needless to say, there should be no undue pressure put upon the public to buy. We must not sicken them. Our business is merely to take this most useful national ware to their doors and give them the choice of buying or rejecting it.

The following appeared in *Young India* of 28th July, 1921.

Women as Pickets.—A Parsi sister writes to say that when picketing is recommenced in Bombay, she is quite prepared to join any party that may be raised and she hopes that many other sisters will come forward. She is of opinion that if women respond in large numbers, their presnece will be an effective check on violence. I entirely endorse her remarks, and hope that many other sisters will send in their names to the Committee at Bombay as candidates.

women. The nation will have no cause to be ashamed, if only a few offer themselves for sacrifice in the first instance.

Men's duty is clear. We must not lose our heads. Excitement will not protect our women or our country. We have asked Government neither to spare women nor children. It certainly did not in the Punjab, during those martial law days. I consider it decidedly more civilized that the officials in Calcutta should on a legal pretence arrest our sisters in Calcutta for what they consider is a crime than that a Bosworth Smith in the Punjab should spit upon, swear at and otherwise humiliate the women of Manianwala. We did not offer our women to be insulted thuswise. But we do offer our women for imprisonment, if they will arrest them in the prosecution of public service. We must not expect the Government to look on with indifference, whilst the women are spreading the gospel of Swadeshi and undermining the very basis of its existence,—its traffic in foreign cloth and the consequent ability to exploit India's resources. If, therefore, we, men, allow our sisters to take part in the Swadeshi agitation, we must concede the right of the Government to imprison them equally with men.

We must therefore control our anger. It will be cowardly to challenge a duel and then swear at the adversary for taking up the challenge. Men must fill the gaols. Men must prove to the Government that the awakening is not confined to a few men, but it has permeated the masses, that the spirit of non-violence possesses not merely a select number, but that it possesses the best part of India. We must show by our conduct that the sudden eruption was an exception and not a symptom of a general disease. And now, when the cause for irritation is almost the greatest, is the time for showing the greatest forbearance and self-restraint. I modify the adjective by using an adverb before it. For I do not think that the greatest irritation has yet been offered. I can conceive occasions which may cause irritation to the straining point. If we are to gain freedom and vindicate the honour of the Khilafat and the Punjab, we must pay a much higher price and not lose equanimity in the midst of the greatest possible irritation. Let us prepare for the worst and give credit to the Government for decency by expecting the least. Let us acknowledge frankly that in most cases they are obeying the laws of war by being courteous. If they handcuffed Pir Badshah Mian and Dr. Suresh Banerjee, they have not done so in the case of the Ali Brothers, Lala Lajpatrai, Maulana Mohiuddin or Pandit Motilal Nehru. Nor would I quarrel with handcuffing, if they imposed it on all. It is a gaol regulation to handcuff a prisoner. I should certainly have loved to travel to Allahabad to see Pandit Motilal Nehru and his son being handcuffed together and made to walk to their destination. I would have loved to watch the radiant smiles on their faces in the consciousness of their handcuffs hastening the advent of Swaraj. But the Government did not provide any such treat. What I do not expect, what I do not want for the sake of man's dignity, is a repetition of petty and degrading insults of the Punjab or the unthinkable inhumanities of the Moplah death wagon. But Non-co-operators have stipulated for no such immunity. We have conceived the possibility of the worst happening, and under a full sense of our responsibility pledged ourselves to remain non-violent. Swaraj is within our grasp: let it not step away from us by self-forgetfulness.

With leaders in gaols, there should be *hartals* wherever the Prince goes. No meetings are necessary to organise them. The people have sufficient training for spontaneous action. Let the Government realise that it was not force, but willing response that brought about *hartals*. There must be nowhere any unauthorised or ill-conceived Civil Disobedience. Every forward step must be taken with the greatest deliberation and calmness. The people can discuss things in their own homes. The merchants meet a thousand times for business. They may easily discuss and decide matters arising out of the situation as it developes hourly. But whilst I would like *hartals* to follow the Prince, I would take no risk of violence and would not countenance the slightest exercise of force or threat of it. Absence of prescribed *hartal* would somewhat discredit us, but an outbreak of violence would retard our progress and may even indefinitely postpone Swaraj.

I hope, too, that every vacancy in the ranks of delegates will be filled, and that there will be a full attendance at the Congress of members who will have made up their minds as to what they want and how they will have it.

Whilst this was being printed, advice was received that the three ladies were discharged after a few hours' detention. Nevertheless, I allow the writing to go to the public, as the argument holds good in the main. I observe, too, that the ladies have been discharged with a caution!

Maulana Abul Kalam Azad.—Begum Abul Kalam Azad sends me the following telegraphic message by letter post:

"Judgment has been delivered to-day in the case

against my husband Maulana Abul Kalam Azad. He has been sentenced to only one year rigorous imprisonment. This is astoundingly less than what I was waiting for. If conviction and imprisonment be the reward of national service, you will admit that great injustice has been done to him in the inadequacy of the sentence. It does not even approximate to the minimum of his deserts. I make bold to inform you that I offer my humble services to fill up the gap caused by his absence in the rank of national workers in Bengal. All those activities which he performed will still continue to be carried on normally. This is a heavy burden for my shoulders, but I have fullest faith in God's help. Undoubtedly, the void created by his absence is not merely in work in Bengal, but also in all-India activities. It is, however, beyond my fragile frame to endeavour to make up for the bigger void. Before this, during his last four years' internment, I have gone through a first test, and I am confident that, in this my second trial, I will with God's grace come off triumphant. For the last six years my health has been very broken down and mental exertion has become a positive torture. That was why the Maulana hitherto insisted on my not taking an active part in his activities and patriotic strivings. I had, however, all along determined to consecrate my whole being completely and unreservedly to national duties after his conviction. From to-day, I will dischage all the duties connected with the Bengal Provincial Khilafat Committees with the assistance of my brother. My husband has asked me to convey to you his loving and reverent greetings and the following message:

'At the present juncture, both the sides—the Government and the country—are wholly unprepared for any compromise. The only duty before us is to prepare ourselves. Bengal will, in the next stage, also retain the lead which it has establised to-day. Kindly add the name of Bengal to that of Bardoli Taluka. And if any time comes for a settlement, do please not give to our release the importance which is unfortunately being attached to it to-day. Have the terms of settlement fixed with the single end in view of our national aspirations, unconcerned with the question of our release.'"

I have not yet received the telegram, although the letter of advice tells me that it was sent both to Ahmedabad and Bardoli. I am able to give the telegram to the public, only because the Secretary of the Bengal Provincial Khilafat Committee has very kindly sent me a copy by letter post at the instance of the Begum Saheba. It is a matter of no small comfort that ladies, occupying the highest station in life, are coming forward, one after another, to step into the breach created by the withdrawal of male national workers. I tender my congratulations to Begum Abul Kalam Azad for her having offered to take her share in the public work. The readers will take to heart the message of the Maulana. It is perfectly true that neither the Government nor the country is to-day prepared for any compromise. The Government will not be; till we have suffered long and suffered more. Bengal has certainly led in the direction. Bardoli has yet done little. Twice has it been baulked of its privilege by cruel Nature, but it is a matter of no consequence whether it is Bengal or Bardoli which leads, so long as we get rid of a system which, as is daily becoming more and more clear, is based upon terrorism. In the present mood of the country, there is little danger of the vital interests being sacrificed, as the Maulana fears, to the momentary pleasure of securing the release of Non-co-operation prisoners.

A Wife's Faith.—Mrs. Stokes in writing to Mr. Andrews, says:

"I know it well that when my husband is in jail with many other sons of India, suffering for the sake of righteousness, he is sure to be happy. I am quite confident that the Almighty God will hear the cry of the oppressed and deliver His judgment."

The reader will be glad to hear that Mr. Stokes is happy and well in his prison. He is occasionally seen by friends in Lahore.

9th February, 1921

A MUNICIPAL ENTERPRISE

(BY M. K. GANDHI)

The reader will find elsewhere* the text of the correspondence between the municipality of Nadiad and the Government of Bombay as represented by the Collector of the District of Kaira in which Nadiad is situated. Nadiad is an important town in Gujarat with a population of about 35,000. Its municipality has an elected chairman and contains a majority of elected members. Nadiad is noted for its educational activity and has the honour of having produced some of the best educated sons of Gujarat. The town has two high schools. Its aided high school has been nationalized. The municipality runs several primary schools which instruct over five thousand children.

The question before the citizens was to nationalize all the primary schools. The rate-payers, instead of withdrawing the children from these schools, passed a resolution calling upon the municipality to nationalize the primary schools. They were in receipt of a yearly grant

* Omitted in this collection.

of Rs. 21,000 and were naturally under the control and supervision of the Education Department. The municipality, therefore, resolved in accordance with the instructions of the electors to nationalize the schools and informed the Government accordingly. It will be noticed that the municipality in its proceedings has directly referred to the Congress resolution on Non-co-operation and has adopted this bold policy in furtherance of the attainment of Swaraj.*

*Mahatma Gandhi seems to be of opinion that municipalities being elected bodies should, wherever possible, carry out the wishes of the electorates. The following notes from *Young India* further elucidate his views;

The faithful few.—All honour to the few Municipalities which have had the courage to come to the right decision of abstention from the Peace celebrations. While it is a sign of our growing civic consciousness, the paucity serves but to bring into high relief the ground we have to cover before we can prove to the world that we are a self-respecting people. The proceedings at the meeting of some of the corporations where the question of participation came to be considered will illustrate our meaning. The Ahmedabad Municipality has 40 councillors. About thirty attended the meeting and, whilst about three-fourth of the number voted against participation, one-fourth voted for it. Now, it is impossible to believe that those who voted against, and they were a very large majority, could have been till the day of the meeting insensible to the public feeling in the matter, but they were surely indifferent in the matter until a letter protesting against the contribution came for consideration. In Allahabad, there was no quorum on the first day the question came to be considered, and on the day it was decided there was a small attendance. That is also an index of our indifference. In Amraoti, whilst the question whether something should be contributed or not was dropped altogether, because the councillors realised that the contribution was against the strong current of public feeling and against law, there were some who even then decided that they should contribute to the Peace celebrations fund privately. The instance of Amraoti suggests a painful reflection. It shows that, though the members there had a full appreciation of the public feeling in the matter, some of them had not the *nerve* to take a decisive action even in a matter in which they

There was the technical point about the municipality's statutory obligation to conduct schools under the direct supervision of the Government. On this the

---

thought the law was clear and adopted the doubtful device of compensating for the displeasure of Government by private contributions. These instances have a distinct moral for both the voting public and the municipal councillors. The fact that many municipalities voted the contribution means not that the members were all in favour of participation and they could not be insensible to the state of public feeling in the matter. but because they either have given no thought to a matter of the most vital importance or because they are cowed down by a superstitious fear of displeasing the authorities. The beginning though small is an unmistakeble index that the rapid growth of public life will bring in councillors with better sense of self-respect and their duties as representatives of the people.—17th December, 1920.

Worthy of Imitation.—Mr. Vithalbhai Patel is never so happy as when he is fighting Municipal or Legislative Councils. He was therefore in his element on the 6th inst., when he moved and carried in the Thana District Board the following resolutions:

1. This Board expresses its sorrow to find that the sale of liquor is on the increase, resulting in the loss of public morals, health and wealth.

2. This Board welcomes the popular movement for removing the evil, and congratulates the organisers upon this exhibition of a spirit of public service.

3. This Board notes with regret the absence of any power of prohibiting the sale of liquor within its jurisdiction. Therefore, the Board is of opinion, that it should take advantage of all the powers it possesses of undertaking picketing on its responsibility, of helping Congress Committees and of compensating those liquor-dealers who may voluntarily undertake to close their shops.

4. For the purposes aforesaid, the Board hereby appoints a Committee consisting of the Chairman, the Vice-chairman, the mover and Mr. Acharya with powers to conduct or control picketing and to bring about total prohibition.

5. The Board authorises the said Committee to incur an expense not exceeding Rs. 3,000 as a beginning, and will be prepared to incur greater expenditure in future, if necessary.

municipality's attitude is thus stated. "It is in complete sympathy with the movement of Non-co-operation designed for the attainment, among other things, of full

---

This is distinctly a courageous step If the Board persists in the enforcement of its resolutions to the bitter end, and brings about a speedy closing of all the liquor-shops within its jurisdiction, it will have covered itself with glory, and will have rendered a signal service to the country. I hope that Mr. Patel's initiative will be copied by other members and councillors throughout India. A simultaneous move on the part of Local Boards and Municipalities all over India will strengthen the hands of reformers all over, will force the hands of the Government and is therefore likely to obviate all danger of violence, which a three-cornered tussle between pickets, the police and the publicans is likely to precipitate.—13th July, 1921.

A Municipal Model.—The Rajpur (C. P.) Municipality has adopted by a majority the following proposals:

That all the boys reading in the Municipal schools should have the national uniform of *Khadi* coat or *Kudta* and *Khadi* cap from the 1st August 1921.

That the 1st August, 1921 should be declared a holiday in all the Municipal schools and offices in honour of the Lokamanya Bal Gangadhar Tilak.

That this Committee expects its servants to use country-made cloth.

That all dresses supplied to Municipal servants should be of *Khadi*.

It is a wise use the Raipur Municipality has made of its powers. Indeed all the municipalities can carry out all the constructive permanent features of Non-co-operation without being wholly Non-co-operationist. There is not one among the foregoing proposals, to which reasonable exception could possibly be taken by anybody. Any municipality which adopts Swadeshi, the vernacular of its province as the medium of its proceedings, the amelioration of the suppressed classes, the abolition of the drink traffic, prostitution and such other things will assist the work of national purification, and thus justify its existence.—11th September, 1921.

Well done Nagpur.—The Municipality of Nagpur certainly deserves congratulations for its public service, in that it has taken a referendum on total prohibition. The result is striking. Two thousand three hundred and forty-three voters registered their votes. Of these two thousand three hundred and thirty-two recorded their votes in favour

Swaraj and, so long as this municipality remains in existence, it will be its bounden duty to help the people of Nadiad in achieving the national purpose. . . So far as the legal difficulty is concerned, it is respectfully suggested that *sec.* 58, if it runs counter to the express wish of the residents of Nadiad, must automatically remain in abeyance because, if the Board correctly understands the temper of the people of Nadiad, they are clearly determined to have nothing to do with Government control over the education of the children, and it need hardly be pointed out that the Board is in full sympathy with the determination of the people."

No one can take exception to the admirable spirit of the people or the correctness of the attitude of the municipality. Of course, the Government may, if it dare, disband the municipality. But any such disbandment

---

of total prohibition. Six voted with reservations, and only *five* voted against prohibition. The reader will be pained to find that of the five voters against prohibition two were graduates. It is possible to look at the revelation in another light, and say that the two graduates had the courage of their conviction to incur popular odium and vote in accordance with their conscience. There is no doubt as to the educative value of such a referendum. I wish the Secretary of the Congress Committee, at whose instance the poll was taken, had given the full strength of the electoral roll. It is to be hoped that other municipalities would follow the example of Nagpur.—29th September, 1921.

Imitate Lahore.—The Municipality of Lahore which contains a majority of Non-co-operators has resolved that all its cab-drivers and such other employees shall wear Khadi caps and that all municipal departments are to use as much Khadi as possible. The lawyers of Amritsar are said to have adopted Khadi for their dresses. I hope that the other municipalities will follow the good example set by Lahore and that the lawyers all over India will follow the Amritsar precedent. This is about the least that they can do for the country and Swadeshi.—11th August, 1921.

must be futile, if the rate-payers are determined not to have Government control over the education of their children. This is a peaceful revolution on a small scale. The success of the movement is due to the cohesion of the people and their ability to manage and finance the education of their children. Violence being eschewed, the people of Nadiad are able to give an education in Swaraj to their children. What is true of the municipality regarding the education of the children is true of the whole of India in every other respect.

When the people have one mind, ability of management, and recognise the necessity of non-violence, if only as a business proposition, Swaraj is won. Finance is a matter of little consideration. For the Government does not bring money from heaven. It receives, to paraphrase an expressive Gujarati saying, an anvil weight of metal and returns a needle weight. And the pity and the disgrace of it is that, even with that niggardly donation, it imprisons and emasculates the tender mind of the nation. Were it not for self-delusion, we would at least refuse to be party to the ruin of our own children. The municipality of Nadiad has shown how easy the whole process of nationalization of education is; Lala Daulat Ram's articles* have shown how easy the question of finance is, and how the ordinary fees are almost enough to conduct all our educational institutions. I hope that the object lesson given by the municipality of Nadiad will not be lost upon other municipalities similarly situated.

* Omitted in this collection.

25th October, 1921

CHIRALA-PERALA

(BY M. K. GANDHI)

Chirala-Perala is in fact one village not far from the sea, with a nice climate and containing a compact population of about 15,000. The place is situated in the Andhra Province, and possesses in Mr. Gopal Krishnayya, a talented and self-sacrificing leader, who has by his perseverance and sacrifice been able to hold the people together without difficulty. Municipal government is a transferred department. The Minister in charge began last year to make his presence felt by these brave people. A vexatious trading license was imposed upon them. They retorted by trading without a license The result was a prosecution and convictions against the resisters, who, including an old woman, went to gaol. The Government has been endeavouring to impose a municipality on the people, who protested against the measure. But what could a minister who had accepted office in the teeth of public opposition do but seek to impose his will upon the people and show that he cared little for it?

Let us see what the municipality meant to the people; certainly not better sanitation, for the place was unusually well kept by the people themselves; certainly not more education, for the people were non-co-operators. It meant more taxation, more interference with their liberty. This was an intolerable evil for the people.

They therefore decided to remove to a bare place of ground near by outside the municipal area. They erected huts there for residence and evacuated Chirala-Perala about May last. Nothing daunted, the Minister has sought and received the assistance of the Revenue

Department which has levied penal cesses in respect of the sheds on the ground that they were erected on Government waste. The rate for each shed is Rs. 10-2-6, whereas the value thereof is only Rs. 25. If this payment is not made, the occupants have to vacate the sheds.

The commencement of repression is thus described in its note by the Andhra Provincial Congress Committee:

> In the repression at Chirala-Perala, the roll of honour is lengthening. Already 12 men and one woman have served out their term of imprisonment for refusing to pay the municipal taxes. Three men are now undergoing rigorous imprisonment in the Central Jail at Rajahmandry, six more are awaiting orders of incarceration. It is extraordinary that these were sentenced to imprisonment nearly a month ago and the sentence held in abeyance. We have not heard of any other instance in which convicted persons are quietly told that they might go home and await orders, not even bail bonds being taken from them. Many more in Chirala-Perala are prepared to fill the prisons. The struggle is being carried on with remarkable vigour and persistence, though the dislocation of business caused by the evacuation and the loss of living in the case of poorer inhabitants have entailed serious hardship.
>
> The property of the convicted persons has been attached and brought to sale a number of times at Bapatla and at Guntur for realising the amount of fine levied on them. But no bidders have come forward in either place. This is an eloquent testimony to the sympathy generally felt for the sufferings of the Chirala-Perala patriots.

Here we have a concrete instance of the meaning of the reforms and responsibility. I doubt not that the Minister believes that what he is doing is good for the people. Did not the English officials, whenever they imposed anything on us even the Rowlatt Act, seek to justify the imposition on the ground of public weal? What Non-co-operation is fighting among other things, is the spirit of patronage. We must have the liberty to do evil before we learn to do good. Even 'liberty' must not be 'forced' upon us. The democratic spirit demands that a most autocratic minister must yield to a people's will, or resign office. He must be patient enough to carry enlightened public opinion with him even in the most perfect measures of amelioration.

The brave people of Chirala-Perala have challenged the Government to do its worst and refused to have a municipality. They need not have done so. They might have waited for Swaraj. But they chose to do otherwise. The responsibility is entirely theirs. They may not now yield in any circumstance whatsoever. Nor must they under provocation lose their heads. They must cheerfully let the Government subject them to any penalty it chooses to inflict upon them. By their meek and unyielding suffering, they will cover themselves and India with glory, and will give an object lesson to the country in non violence.

27th October, 1921

MUNICIPALITIES, BEWARE

The Government of Bombay note* regarding the Ahmedabad, Surat and Nadiad municipalities, shows that it refuses to see the writing on the wall.† Its dictatorial tone is now no longer in keeping with the

* The Note condemned the action of the municipalities in sympathising with and handing over their schools to Non-co-operators and exhorted the rate-payers to safeguard their interests by proceeding against the municipal councillors under the law.

† *Young India* of 16th February, 1922, contained the following:

Ahmedabad and Surat.—Ahmedabad and Surat Municipalities have been superseded—not because they have been found inefficient but because they have been too efficient and too independent. These two

rising spirit of the people. Its incitement to the individual rate-payers to sue the councillors who believe they have performed their duty is hardly dignified. The proper course for the Government was to let the municipalities take their own course and not to invite trouble. As it is, the Government note is calculated to precipitate a crisis. The councillors must take up the challenge and dare the Government to disregard the municipalities, if they choose. The municipalities must have the right to misgovern themselves, if they wish. If a city is misgoverned, it is as much the rate-payers' fault as is the-

municipalities and that of Nadiad have been putting up a brave, dignified and orderly fight against the Government interference and undue control. Their crime consisted in freeing primary education from Government control. They gave up Government assistance and noted that the elected councillors who have commanded a majority have always acted after close consultation with the rate-payers. But that is just what the Government evidently does not want. It makes the public opinion effective.

The duty before the councillors and the electors is quite simple. They must still retain control of primary education. The rate-payers may refuse to pay the rates to the nominated committees that the Government may impose upon the citizens and they must pay for the national education of their children. The councillors must keep together and put up as it were a national municipality in so far as it is practicable. In my opinion, there is hardly a department, for running of which enlightened citizens require Government aid. There is no earthly reason why the Ahmedabadis, the Nadiadis and the Suratis should not be able to sweep and light their own streets educate their own children and look afer their sick and their water-supply without hanging on to the Government. The police control they do not possess. The only thing for which they may need Government assistance is in enforcing payment of rates. Replace Government force by force of public opinion and you have the sanction for collecting rates. More money is raised in Ahmedabad by voluntary contributions than by enforced rates. The public will watch the duel between nominated committees and popularly elected representatives in awakened constituencies.

councillors'. But our wise Government, whilst recognising the independent existence of the municipalities, wants to stick to the letter of the law which killeth and would itself rule instead of letting the municipalities alone, so long as they do not cost the Government anything. The municipalities must now take up the challenge and prepare for action on its part. Government may succeed in getting a few rate-payers to file suits. That will be the least it can do. The most it can do is to disband the municipalities concerned. And the most of the Government should prove most welcome, if only the protestants are a strong body. Assuming that they are, they must simply educate the rate-payers to understand what is happening and to prepare them for battle. I can see Swaraj peeping even through the Government note, if the latter take and the former are ready for action. So long as there is no disbandment, the municipalities have all power; as soon as there is disbandment, the Government is powerless, assuming of course that the rate-payers are strong, intelligent and united. The rate-payers are all that but they require to be organised for action. Hitherto the people have been the football of officials or so-called representatives. Non-co-operation enables the people to become the players in the game. Representatives *must* represent or they perish.

17*th November*, 1921

THE PEN OR THE SWORD

(By M. K. GANDHI)

In Lahore on the Mall there is a statue of John Lawrence with a defiant look in the face, with the pen in the right hand and the sword in the left. The writing underneath is, 'Will you have the pen or the sword?' As a work of art it is said to be very good. But it has always been a matter of offence to the citizens of Lahore. They neither want the pen nor the sword imposed upon them.

The statue is municipal property. It was put up in the early eighties when the sense of self-respect was not so keen as now, though I understand that even when it was put up, some of the citizens keenly felt the indignity. Recently the Lahore Municipality passed a resolution by a majority vote, ordering removal of the statue to the Town Hall building pending final disposal. The resolution was sent in due course to the Government as all resolutions are. Three or four days after, an engineer was sent by the Municipality to see how the statue could be removed. Without any notice to the Municipality, the Deputy Commissioner sent a party of police to turn away the engineer and his men. And when the Municipality wanted to know why and how this undue interference took place, the Commissioner issued the following order:

> "At a general meeting of the Lahore Municipal Committee held on the 8th instant, the following resolution was passed with regard to the Lawrence Statue:
>
> (1) That the statue be removed,
>
> (2) that it may be removed for the present to the Town Hall building,
>
> (3) that a sub-committee be appointed to consider the final disposal of the statue.
>
> I consider at present from a perusal of such records as I have been able to consult, that statue cannot be removed from the present site without the consent of the Punjab Government.
>
> Secondly, I consider from the tone of the debates in the committee on this subject that it is possible that the statue, after removal by the committee, will not be treated with proper respect, with the result that annoyance will be caused to a number of the residents of Lahore.

For these reasons, and pending consideration and decision by the Government of its rights in this matter, I suspend the execution of the two first parts of the above resolution relating to the immediate removal of the statue.

It is clear that the Deputy Commissioner was guilty of assault in having sent the police to turn out the engineer who was doing his legal duty. The Commissioner's order is an illustration of the meaning of the pen. The Commissioner's pen is just as much an outrage as the Deputy Commissioner's sword. The Commissioner, because he has the sword, has arrogated to himself judicial powers which do not belong to him. Whether the Municipality has or has not the power to dispose of its own property is purely for a Court of Law to decide. And what right has the Commissioner to impute malice to the Municipality? The fact is that the Commissioner cannot tolerate the disappearance from a fashionable quarter of Lahore of the spirit that the statue represents. So he has not hesitated to dictate the law to the Municipality.

Thus what was but an ordinary incident in the affairs of a Municipality which has responded to the new awakening has become a matter of the highest public importance. The citizens, the rate-payers of Lahore, must by public meetings support the Councillors who have been instrumental in passing the resolution. The councillors must take prompt action and give notice, if they have not already done so, that unless Government show good reason to the contrary, the Municipality must do its duty and remove the statue.

The Commissioner has unintentionally given a golden opportunity to the civil resisters of Lahore to try civil resistance in the cleanest and the most intensive manner. If the Government defy the Municipality and use its brute force to prevent removal of the statue, the civil resisters can, after due notice to tbe Government, proceed to the site with the intention of removing the statue and offer themselves for arrest or being shot, if the Government so wishes.

But this last step can only be taken by disciplined people. It can only be taken when Lahorians are ready to act as one man. There should be no crowds gathering. Only a few individuals can go at a time, say five, of whom one will become the spokesman. They must not bluster, must not argue but simply court arrest. For the immediate object would be not the removal of the statue but inviting arrest. Removal must be the result, if enough men and women offer themselves as sacrifice. There must be a perfect spirit of non-violence prevailing among the people in order to ensure the success of such civil disobedience. Whilst I point out the drastic remedy of civil disobedience, I must warn the citizens of Lahore against adopting the advice without the greatest deliberation. My own experience of a Lahore crowd is that it does not think. It knows no discipline. The volunteers must work methodically amongst the people to create an atmosohere of peace and discipline. I was grieved to notice that, at the Convocation meeting organised on the 9th instant, by the National Board of Education, several people had entered Bradlaugh Hall without tickets and without permission. This is not merely uncivil but criminal disobedience. For they entered by force where they knew their force would not be resisted by force. Such men are unfit for civil disobedience which presupposes a scrupulous and willing observance of all laws which do not hurt the moral sense. Obedience to laws of voluntary associations as the rule of the managers of the Convocation is only the first step to voluntary and ungrudging obedience to the laws imposed by the state. Thoughtless disobedience means disruption of society. The first thing, therefore, for those who aspire after civil disobedience is to learn the art of willingly obeying laws of voluntary associations such as Congresses, Conferences and other bodies and similarly obeying the state laws whether they like them or not. Civil disobedience is not a state of lawlessness and license, but presupposes a law-abiding spirit combined with self-restraint.

13*th July*, 1921

A CONFESSION OF FAITH

(BY M. K. GANDHI)

A strange anonymous letter has been received by me, admiring me for having taken up a cause that was dearest to Lokamanya's heart, and telling me that his spirit was residing in me and that I must prove a worthy follower of his. The letter, moreover, admonishes me not to lose heart in the prosecution of the Swaraj programme, and finishes off by accusing me of imposture in claiming to be politically a disciple of Gokhale. I wish correspondents will throw off the slavish habit of writing anonymously. We, who are developing the Swaraj spirit, must cultivate the courage of fearlessly speaking out our mind. The subject-matter of the letter, however, being of public importance, demands a reply. I cannot claim the honour of being a follower of the late Lokamanya. I admire him like millions of his countrymen for his indomitable will, his vast learning, his love of country, and above all the purity of his private life and great sacrifice. Of all the men of modern times, he captivated most the imagination of his people. He breathed into us the spirit of Swaraj. No one perhaps realised the evil of the existing system of Government as Mr. Tilak did. And in all humility I claim to deliver his message to the country as truly as the best of his disciples. But I am conscious that my method is not Mr. Tilak's method.*

*The following is from *Young India* of 28th January, 1920:

Lok. Tilak wrote to *Young India* under date Poona city, 28th January, 1920: I am sorry to see that in your article on 'Reform Resolution' in the last issue, you have represented me as holding that I considered 'every thing fair in politics.' I write this to you to say that my view is not correctly represented herein. Politics is a game of worldly people, and not of *Sahdus*, and instead of the maxim "akkhodhenajine kkhodham" as preached by Buddha, I prefer to rely on the maxim of Shri Krishna "ye gatthaa maam prapadyamthe thaamsthatthaiva bhajaamyaham". That explains the whole difference and also the meaning of my phrase 'responsive co-operation'. Both methods are equally honest and righteous but the one is more suited to this world than the other. Any further explanation about the difference will be found in my "Gita-Rahasya."

Mahatma Gandhi replied to the above as follows: I naturally feel the greatest diffidence about joining issue with the Lokamanya in matters involving questions of interpretation of religious works. But there are things in or about which instinct transcends even interpretation. For me there is no conflict between the two texts quoted by the Lokamanya. The Buddhist text lays down an eternal principle. The text from the Bhagvad Gita shows to me how the principle of conquering hate by love, untruth by truth, can and must be applied. If it be true that God metes out the same measure to us that we mete out to others, it follows that, if we would escape condign punishment, we may out-return angerfor anger but gentleness even against anger. And this is the law not for the unworldly but essentially for the worldy. With deference to the Lokamanya, I venture to say that it betrays mental laziness to think that the world is not for *Sahdus*. The epitome of all religious is to promote *Purushartha*, and *Purushartha* is nothing but a desperate attempt to become *Sahdu*, *i.e.*, to become gentleman in every sense of the term.

Finally, when I wrote the sentence about 'everything being fair in

And that is why I have still difficulty with some of the Maharashtra leaders. But I sincerely think that Mr. Tilak did not disbelieve in my method. I enjoyed the privilege of his confidence. And his last word to me in the presence of several friends was, just a fortnight before his death, that mine was an excellent method if the people could be persuaded to take to it. But he said he had doubts. I know no other method; I can only hope that, when the final test comes, the country will be proved to have assimilated the method of Non-violent Non-co-operation. Nor am I unaware of my other limitations. I can lay no claim to scholarship. I have not his powers of organisation, I have no compact disciplined party to lead, and having been an exile for twenty-three years, I cannot claim the experience that the Lokamanya had of India. Two things we had in common to the fullest measure—love of country and the steady pursuit of Swaraj. I can, therefore, assure the anonymous writer that, yielding to none in my reverence for the memory of the deceased, I will march side by side with the foremost of the Lokamanya's disciples in the pursuit of Swaraj. I know that the only offering accepatable to him is the quickest attainment of Swaraj by India. That and nothing else can give his spirit peace.

Discipleship, however, is a sacred personal matter.

politics' according to the Lokamanya's creed, I had in mind his oft-repeated quotation "shaddham prathi shaddhyam." To me it enunciates bad law. And I shall not despair of the Lokamanya with all his acumen agreeably surprising India one day with a philosophical dissertation proving the falsity of the doctrine. In any case, I pit the experience of a third of a century against the doctrine underlying 'shaddham prati shaddhyam." The true law is "shaddham pratyapi satyam."

I fell at Dadabhai's feet in 1888, but he seemed to be too far away from me. I could be as son to him, not disciple. A disciple is more than son. Discipleship is a second birth. It is a voluntary surrender. In 1896, I met almost all the known leaders of India in connection with my South African mission. Justice Ranade awed me. I could hardly talk in his presence. Badruddin Tyabji fathered me and asked me to be guided by Ranade and Pherozeshah. The latter became a patron. His will had to be law. "You must address a public meeting on the 26th September, and you must be punctual." I obeyed. On the 25th evening, I was to wait on him. I did.

"Have you written out your speech?" he inquired.

"No, Sir."

"That won't do, young man. Can you write it out to-night?"

"Munshi, you must go to Mr. Gandhi and receive the manuscript from him. It must be printed over night and you must send me a copy." Turning to me, he added, "Gandhi, you must not write a long speech, you do not know Bombay audiences cannot stand long addresses." I bowed.

The lion of Bombay taught me to take orders. He did not make me his disciple. He did not even try.

I went thence to Poona. I was an utter stranger. My host first took me to Mr. Tilak. I met him surrounded by his companions. He listened, and said, "We must arrange a meeting for you. But perhaps you do not know that we have unfortunately two parties. You must give us a non-party man as chairman. Will you see Dr. Bhandarkar?" I consented and retired. I have no firm impression of Mr. Tilak, except to recall that he shook off my nervousness by his affectionate familiarity.

I went thence, I think, to Gokhale, and then to Dr. Bhandarkar. The latter greeted me, as a teacher his pupil.

"You seem to be an earnest and enthusiastic young man. Many people do not come to see me at this the hottest part of the day. I never now-a-days attend public meetings. But you have recited such a pathetic story that I must make an exception in your favour."

I worshipped the venerable doctor with his wise face. But I could not find for him a place on that little throne. It was still unoccupied. I had many heroes, but no king.

It was different with Gokhale, I cannot say why. I met him at his quarters on the college ground. It was like meeting an old friend, or better still, a mother after a long separation. His gentle face put me at ease in a moment. His minute inquiries about myself and my doings in South Africa at once enshrined him in my heart. And as I parted from him, I said to myself, 'you are my man'. And from that moment, Gokhale never lost sight of me. In 1901, on my second return from South Africa, we came closer still. He simply 'took me in hand', and began to fashion me. He was concerned about how I spoke, dressed, walked and ate. My mother was not more solicitous about me than Gokhale. There was, so far as I am aware, no reserve between us. It was really a case of love at first sight, and it stood the severest strain in 1913. He seemed to me all I wanted as a political worker—pure as crystal, gentle as a lamb, brave as a lion and chivalrous to a fault. It does not matter to me that he may not have been any of these things. It was enough for me that I could discover no fault in him to cavil at. He was and remains for me the most perfect man on the political field. Not, therefore, that we had no differences. We differed even in

1901 in our views on social customs, *e.g.*, widow re-marriage. We discovered differences in our estimate of western civilization. He frankly differed from me in my extreme views on non-violence. But these differences mattered neither to him nor to me. Nothing could put us asunder. It were blasphemous to conjecture what would have happened if he were alive to-day. I know that I would have been working under him. I have made this confession, because the anonymous letter hurt me, when it accused me of imposture about my political discipleship. Had I been remiss in my acknowledgment to him who is now dumb? I thought I must declare my faithfulness to Gokhale, especially when I seemed to be living in a camp which the Indian world calls opposite.

4th August, 1920

LOKAMANYA

(BY M. K. GANDHI)

Lokamanya Bal Gangadhar Tilak is no more. It is difficult to believe of him as dead. He was so much part of the people. No man of our times had the hold on the masses that Mr. Tilak had. The devotion that he commanded from thousands of his countrymen was extraordinary. He was unquestionably the idol of his people. His word was law among thousands. A giant among men has fallen. The voice of the lion is hushed.

What was the reason for his hold upon his countrymen? I think the answer is simple. His patriotism was a passion with him. He knew no religion but love of his country. He was a born democrat. He believed in the rule of majority with an intensity that fairly frightened me But that gave him his hold. He had an iron will which he used for his country. His life was an open book. His tastes were simple.* His private life was

* The following appeared in *Young India* of 4th August, 1921:

Reminiscences of Lokamanya.—When Lhkamanya went to Delhi to interview Mr Montagu, Government prohibited the holding of any procession in his honour. The illiterate people on the street were talking among themselves:—"Aj Poona-ka Raja ane-vala hai. Sarkar us-se bahut darti hai." (The King of Poona is coming to-day. Government are mightily afraid of him.)

* * *

A friend of Tilak once asked him in course of conversation. 'Balvantrao, what portfolio will you select under Swaraj? Will you be Prime Minister or will you be Foreign Member?' Tilak replied 'No, Sir. Under Swaraj I will become Professor of Mathematics in a Swadeshi college and retire from public life. I detest politics. I still wish to write a book on differential calculus. The country is in a very bad way and none of you is doing anything for it. So I am compelled to look into the matter.'

* * *

There was a meeting in Bombay, where many scholars attended. Tilak delivered a learned and original address on Chaldean civilisation and the parallels between Indian and Iranian civilisations. When the meeting was over, the President who was a Parsi said, 'Mr. Tilak, you are making a misuse of your talents. With such a magnificent intellect, you are eminently fitted for historical research, and if you devote yourself to it, you will acquire a world-wide reputation. Leaving this, why do you entangle yourself in the mire of politics?' Tilak replied, 'India is not a sterile woman. When there is Swaraj, there will be thousands of scholars like myself. To-day there is a supreme necessity for every one of us to run to our country's succour, and to devote our abilities, our energy and our all to the attainment of Swaraj.'

* * *

When the "Rashtramata" was started in Bombay, there was a talk about tables, chairs and other requisites for its office. Tilak said, "When we started the 'Kesari' and the 'Maratha', we had no such paraphernalia of editorial dignity. We got not a pie from the papers. We used to roll up our bedding, and that served us as a

spotlessly clean. He had dedicated his wonderful talents to his country. No man preached the gospel of the Swaraj with the consistency and the insistence of Lokamanya. His countrymen, therefore, implicitly believed in him. His courage never failed him. His optimism was irrepressible. He had hoped to see Swaraj fully established during his life-time. If he failed, it was not his fault. He certainly brought it nearer by many a year. It is for us, who remain behind, to put forth redoubled effort to make it a reality in the shortest possible time.

Lokamanya was an implacable foe of the bureaucracy, but this is not to say that he was a hater of Englishmen or English rule. I warn Englishmen against making the mistake of thinking that he was their enemy.

I had the privilege of listening to an impromptu, learned discourse by him, at the time of the last Calcutta Congress on Hindi being the national language. He had just returned from the Congress pandal. It was a

---

table. Our articles, written on such loose yielding stuff, were still powerful and trenchant enough."

* * *

When the New English School was first started, it naturally did not get very bright students. Its boys were either dull or mischievous. When some one was disappointed at this, Tilak said,'there lies our real test. When we make something even of such boys, the people will begin to believe in us.'

* * *

Tilak drew a salary of Rs. 30 from the school. One of his comrades remarked that on such an income they would hardly be able to save enough to purchase funeral requisites in case they died. Tilak replied,'Society must bother about it more than ourselves. They will see to the burning of our corpse for purposes of sanitation, if not of hero-worship.'

D. B. KALELKAR.

(from the Gujarati "Navajivan.")

treat to listen to his calm discourse on Hindi. In the course of his address, he paid a glowing tribute to the English for their care of the Vernaculars. His English visit, in spite of his sad experience of English juries, made him a staunch believer in British democracy and he even seriously made the amazing suggestion that India should instruct it on the Punjab through the cinematograph. I relate this incident not because I share his belief (for I do not), but in order to show that he entertained no hatred for Englishmen. But he could not and would not put up with an inferior status of India and the Empire. He wanted immediate equality which he believed was his country's birthright. And in his struggle for India's freedom, he did not spare the Government. In the battle for freedom, he gave no quarter and asked for none. I hope that Englishmen will recognise the worth of the man whom India has adored.

For us, he will go down to the generations yet unborn as a Maker of Modern India. They will revere his memory as of a man who lived for them and died for them. It is blasphemy to talk of such a man as dead. The permanent essence of him abides with us for ever. Let us erect for the only Lokamanya of India an imperishable monument by weaving into our own lives his bravery, his simplicity, his wonderful industry and his love of his country. May God grant his soul poace.

17th November, 1921

INTROSPECTION

(By M. K. Gandhi)

Correspondents have written to me in pathetic language asking me not to commit suicide in January, should

Swaraj be not attained by then, and should I find myself outside the prison walls. I find that language but inadequately expresses one's thought, especially when the thought itself is confused or incomplete. My writing in the *Navajivan* was, I fancied, clear enough. But I observe that its translation has been misunderstood by many. The original too has not escaped the tragedy that has overtaken the translation.

One great reason for the misunderstanding lies in my being considered almost a perfect man. Friends who know my partiality for the Bhagavad-Gita have thrown relevant verses at me, and shown how my threat to commit sucide contradicts the teachings which I am attempting to live. All these mentors of mine seem to forget that I am but a seeker after Truth. I claim to have found the way to it. I claim to be making a ceaseless effort to find it. But I admit that I have not yet found it. To find Truth completely is to realise oneself and one's destiny, *i.e.*, to become perfect. I am painfully conscious of my imperfections, and therein lies all the strength I possess, because it is a rare thing for a man to know his own limitations.

If I was a perfect man, I own I should not feel the miseries of my neighbours as I do. As a perfect man, I should take note of them, prescribe a remedy and compel adoption by the force of unchallengeable Truth in me. But as yet, I only see as through a glass darkly and, therefore, have to carry conviction by slow and laborious processes, and then too, not always with success. That being so, I would be less than human if, with all my knowledge of avoidable misery pervading the land and of the sight of mere skeletons under the very shadow of the Lord of the Universe, I did not feel with and for all the suffering but dumb millions of India.

The hope of a steady decline in that misery sustains me; but suppose that, with all my sensitiveness to sufferings, to pleasure and pain, cold and heat, and with all my endeavour to carry the healing message of the spinning wheel to the heart, I have reached only the ear and never pierced the heart, suppose further that at the end of the year I find that the people are as sceptical as they are to-day about the present possibility of attainment of Swaraj by means of the peaceful revolution of the wheel. Suppose further, that I find that the excitement during the past twelve months and more has been only an excitement and a stimulation, but no settled belief in the programme, and lastly suppose that the message of peace has not penetrated the hearts of Englishmen, should I not doubt my *tapasya* and feel my unworthiness for leading the struggle? As a true man, what should I do? Should I not kneel down in all humility before my Maker, and ask Him to take away this useless body and make me a fitter instrument of service?

Swaraj does consist in the change of Government and its real control by the people, but that would be merely the form. The substance that I am hankering after is a definite acceptance of the means and, therefore, a real change of heart on the part of the people. I am certain that it does not require ages for Hindus to discard the error of untouchability, for Hindus and Musalmans to shed enmity and accept heart friendship as an eternal factor of national life, for all to adopt the *charkha* as the only universal means of attaining India's economic salvation and finally for all to believe that India's freedom lies only through non-violence, and no other method. Definite, intelligent and free adoption by the nation of this programme, I hold, as the attainment of the substance. The symbol, the transfer of power, is sure to follow, even as the seed truly laid must develop into a tree.

The reader will thus perceive that, what I accidentally stated to friends for the first time in Poona and then repeated to others, was but a confession of my imperfections and an expression of my feeling of unworthiness for the great cause which, for the time being, I seem to be leading. I have enunciated no doctrine of despair. On the contrary, I have felt never so sanguine, as I do at the time of writing, that we will gain the substance during this year. I have stated at the same time as a practical idealist that I should no more feel worthy to lead a cause which I might feel myself diffident of handling. The doctrine of labouring without attachment means as such a relentless pursuit of truth as a retracing after discovery of error and a renunciation of leadership without a pang after discovery of unworthiness. I have but shadowed forth my intense longing to lose myself in the Eternal and become merely a lump of clay in the Potter's divine hands, so that my service may become more certain, because uninterrupted by the baser self in me.

19*th January*, 1921

"INDIA" AND THE BRITISH COMMITTEE

The "Chronicle", I observe, calls the decision to end the British Committee and 'India' an unfortunate decision. The argument advanced in support of the view is that the Constitution Committee had not advised abolition of the British Committee and 'India', and that both were doing good work. It is true that the

Constitution Committee had not recommended abolition. But it should be remembered that the Committee was appointed at the Amritsar Congress, and its report was conceived before the Non-co-operation resolution of the Special Congress. Much has happened since then to revolutionize the country's ideas about foreign propaganda and the British Committee. The abolition was a matter of principle. It was felt that a Non-co-operation Congress could not keep a foreign agency for helping its work. The Congress has deliberately burnt its boats. It has decided to become self-reliant. The question of efficiency of the Committee as constituted becomes irrelevant. It is hardly dignified for the Congress in the altered situation to subsidise a foreign agency for doing propganda work. No amount of misrepresentation about it could possibly blot out effective action by the nation.

Whether you advertise the fact or not, a body not receiving the food it needs dies. Whether we advertise the fact or not the moment we cease to support the Government, it dies a natural death. Personally I dislike even the resolution voting the money to be used at the discretion of the All-India Congress Committee in foreign propaganda. We want all the money we need in this country. I would far rather invest Rs. 45,000 in spinning wheels or establishing primary schools than in wasting it in advertising our work. Every good deed is its own advertisement. And I shall certainly hope that the money will still be saved for a better purpose. So far as the newspaper 'India' is concerned, we are certainly better without it. It raised in us false hopes. The British people are as much on their honour and trial as we are. If they choose to be misinformed by interested or dishonest journals, we cannot help them. Have we not published the Congress Punjab report? Who believes it? Mr. Montagu discredits it and the British public echoes his opinion. In the art of advertising bogus things, the British journalists are to be beaten only by the Americans. I would not enter into the unequal competition and court defeat.

We must adopt new methods for combating the evils of sensational and untruthful journalism and public life. The Congress has given the lead by abolishing the Committee and its organ 'India.'

9th March, 1922

FOREIGN PROPAGANDA

(BY. M. K. GANDHI)

I see that there is a great deal of misunderstanding about the scope of foreign propaganda undertaken by the Working Committee. I see that it was a mistake not to have published the report that was adopted by the Working Committee. Here it is:

Bardoli, 22nd Feb., 1922.

To

The Chairman of the Working Committee
of the All-India Congress Committee, Delhi.

SIR,—At the meeting of the Working Committee held at Surat on 31st January last, the following resolution was passed:

"The Working Committee records its firm conviction that dissemination of correct news about Indian political situation in foreign countries is absolutely essential and refers to Mahatma Gandhi all the correspondence on the subject of foreign propaganda now with the Working Secretary with a request that he should prepare a definite scheme in that behalf at an early date so as to enable the next meeting of the Working Committee to consider it."

Having considered the resolution and the papers forwarded to me by the Secretary, I beg to report as follows:—

In my opinion, it is not only undesirable but it may prove even harmful to establish at the present stage any Agency in any foreign country for the dissemination of correct news in such country about the political situation in India, for the following reasons:

First, because it would distract public attention and instead of making the people feel that they have to rely purely on their own strength, it will make them think of the effect of their actions on foreign countries and the support the latter can render to the national cause. This does not mean that we do not care for the world's support, but the way to gain that support is to insist upon the correctness of every one of our actions and rely upon the automatic capacity of Truth to spread itself.

Secondly, it is my experience that when an Agency is established for any special purpose, independent interest ceases to a certain extent and what is distributed by the Agency is previoulsy discounted as coming from interested quarters.

Thirdly, the Congress will not be able to exercise effective check over such Agencies, and there is great danger of authoritative distribution of wrong information and wrong ideas about the struggle.

Fourthly, it is not possible at the present moment to send out of India any person of importance for the sole purpose of disseminating news in foreign countries, for such men are too few for the internal work.

I am, therefore, of opinion that the work of publishing the Congress Bulletin should be better organised, if necessary, by engaging a special editor for the purpose and by sending the Congress Bulletin regularly to the chief news agencies of the world. The editor should be instructed to enter into correspondence with those newspapers or news agencies which may be found to interest themselves in Indian questions.

It is my firm opinion based upon experience gained through the conduct of the journals I have edited in South Africa and here that the more solid the Congress work and the sufferings of the Congress men and women, the greater the publicity will the cause attain without special effort. From the exchanges of letter and correspondence that I receive day by day from all parts of the world in connection with the conduct of *Young India*, I observe that never was so much interest taken in Indian affairs throughout the world as it is to-day. It follows that the interest will increase in the same proportion as the volume of our sufferings. The very best method of disseminating correct information about the political situation, therefore, is to make the Congress work purer, better organised and to evoke a greater spirit of suffering. Not only is curiosity thereby intensified, but people become more eager to understand the inwardness and the exact truth about the situation.

I remain,
Yours faithfully,
(Sd.) M. K. GANDHI.

After having gone through all the papers that were given to me and after having heard all the arguments for and against, I remain convinced that at least for the present we want no news agency outside India. We want the whole world with us, but we shall not get it by carrying on a foreign agency. We can only send correct information to those who care for it. If a foreign country does not keep its own agency for gathering information from a particular country or about a particular movement, it is proof to me that that country is not interested in it. We have been without our agency in London now for nearly 15 months. I venture to think that we are no worse off to-day than we were 15 months ago. We are certainly better off because and to the extent that we have done substantial work in India itself. There are more people in the world interested to-day in India than they ever were. We, therefore, owe it to them that we place at their disposal correct information, but our duty must end there. I have before me a letter from Italy from an Italian editor telling me how deeply interested people in Italy are in the Indian movement, and the Italian newspapers are therefore busy instructing the Italian public in Indian affairs. This is what I call a natural and organic movement, but if on the strength of this information we were to establish an Indian agency in Italy to awaken further interest, we would not mend matters but would spoil them by overdoing. We shall therefore better consult our own interest by relying upon our own strength to speak for itself.

Moreover, the Non-co-operation movement is one of self-help. Its formula is 'we shall succeed only to the extent of our strength and no further.' No certificate of merit from the world will give us success, if we have not earned it by the sweat of the brow. No condemnation of the movement will kill it, unless we are ourselves so fickle-hearted as to give it up by reason of the condemnation. Let us not therefore turn our attention from our own work. Let us simply mind our work and let sure that the world will mind us without any further effort. I am really jealous of even taking away from their work some of the young men who necessarily have to be engaged in the preparation and distribution of the Congress Bulletin. But we have really no authentic record of the progress of our work from week to week. The Congress Bulletin will therefore be useful as well for workers in India as it undoubtedly will be for our friends in foreign countries.

Being almost impatient to see the work inaugurated, the Working Committee has given me a free hand in organising the Bulletin. I hope to issue the first Bulletin next week and thenceforth it would be issued from week to week. The Bulletin will be sent to all the readers of *Young India* at a nominal charge to cover a part or the whole of the cost of paper and printing. *Young India* has a registered circulation of over 25,000 and it goes to almost all parts of the world. It has a comprehensive exchange list. The price for the subscribers to the Bulletin only will be announced later. The method I have sketched is intended to save the Congress as much expense as possible and to give the widest publicity to the Bulletin. Whereas *Young India* represents my own views and those of my associates in the conduct of the journal, the Bulletin will contain nothing in the shape of individual views. It will be mainly a record of Congress activities all over India in all its multifarious department, and an epitome of newspaper opinions, both pro-Congress and anti-Congress. It will contain a Khilafat section registering all Khilafat activities during the preceding week. Such a Bulletin cannot become a success unless there is co-operation from all Congress and Khilafat workers. I invite therefore all who are interested in the Bulletin to send their suggestions and news addressed to the Editor, "Congress Bulletin" c/o *Young India*. Correspondents will please take care to mark all such correspondence for the "Congress Bulletin" in order to save the *Young India* staff from having to handle correspondence intended for the Bulletin. To start with, I would ask every Provincial Congress Committee to send the number of members on its provincial register, the number of village and district organisations, the names and addresses of nationalist newspapers, the number of national educational institutions with the average attendance during the past 6 months, the number of *Panchayat* and all other information regarding Non-co-operation activities.

6th October, 1921

HINDUISM

(BY M. K. GANDHI)

In dealing with the problem of untouchability during the Madras tour, I have asserted my claim to being a Sanatani Hindu with greater emphasis than hitherto, and yet there are things which are commonly done in the name of Hinduism, which I disregard. I have no desire to be called a Sanatani Hindu or any other, if I am not such. And I have certainly no desire to steal in a reform or an abuse under cover of a great faith.

It is therefore necessary for me once for all distinctly to give my meaning of Sanatana Hinduism. The word Sanatana I use in its natural sense.

I call myself a Sanatani Hindu, because,

(1) I believe in the Vedas, the Upanishads, the Puranas and all that goes by the name of Hindu scriptures, and therefore in *avataras* and rebirth,

(2) I believe in the *Varnashrama dharma* in a sense in my opinson strictly Vedic, but not in its present popular and crude sense.

(3) I believe in the protection of the cow in its much larger sense than the popular.

(4) I do not disbelieve in idol-worship.

The reader will note that I have purposely refrained from using the word divine origin in reference to the Vedas or any other scriptures. For I do not believe in the exclusive divinity of the Vedas. I believe the Bible, the Koran and the Zend Avesta to be as much divinely inspired as the Vedas. My belief in the Hindu scriptures does not require me to accept every word and every verse as divinely inspired. Nor do I claim to have any first-hand knowledge of these wonderful books. But I do claim to know and feel the truths of the essential teaching of the scriptures. I decline to be bound by any interpretation, however learned it may be, if it is repugnant to reason or moral sense. I do most emphatically repudiate the claim, (if they advance any such) of the present Shankaracharyas and Shastris to give a correct interpretation of the Hindu scriptures. On the contrary, I believe that our present knowledge of these books is in a most chaotic state. I believe implicitly in the Hindu aphorism, that no one truly knows the Shastras who has not attained perfection in Innocence (*Ahimsa*), Truth (*Satya*) and Self-control (*Brahmacharya*) and who has not renounced all acquisition or possession of wealth. I believe in the institution of Gurus, but in this age millions must go without a Guru, because it is a rare thing to find a combination of perfect purity and perfect learning. But one need not despair of ever knowing the truth of one's religion, because the fundamentals of Hinduism as of every great religion are unchangeable, and easily understood. Every Hindu believes in God and his Oneness, in rebirth and salvation. But that which distinguishes Hinduism from every other religion is its cow protection, more than its *Varnashrama*.

Varnashrama is, in my opinion, inherent in human nature, and Hinduism has simply reduced it to a science. It does attach to birth. A man cannot change his *varna* by choice. Not to abide by one's *varna* is to disregard the law of heredity. The division, however, into innumerable castes is an unwarranted liberty taken with the doctrine. The four divisions are all-sufficing.

I do not believe that interdining or even intermarriage necessarily deprives a man of his status that his birth has given him. The four divisions define a man's calling, they do not restrict or regulate social intercourse. The divisions define duties, they confer no privileges. It is, I hold, against the genius of Hinduism to arrogate to oneself a higher status or assign to another a lower. All are born to serve God's creation, a Brahman with his knowledge, a Kshatriya with his power of protection, a Vaishya with his commercial ability and a Shudra with bodily labour. This, however, does not mean that a Brahman, for instance, is absolved from bodily labour, or the duty of protecting himself and others. His birth makes a Brahman predominantly a man of knowledge, the fittest by heredity and training to impart it to others. There is nothing, again, to prevent the Shudra from acquiring all the knowledge he wishes. Only, he will best serve with his body and need not envy others their special qualities for service. But a Brahman who claims superiority by right of knowledge falls and has no knowledge. And so with the others who pride themselves upon their special qualities. *Varnashrama* is self-restraint and conservation and economy of energy.

Though therefore *Varnashrama* is not affected by interdining or intermarriage, Hinduism does most emphatically discourage interdining and intermarriage between divisions. Hinduism reached the highest limit of self-restraint. It is undoubtedly a religion of renunciation of the flesh, so that the spirit may be set free. It is no part of a Hindu's duty to dine with his son. And by restricting his choice of a bride to a particular group, he exercises rare self-restraint. Hinduism does not regard a married state as by any means essential for salvation. Marriage is a 'fall' even as birth is a 'fall.' Salvation is freedom from birth and hence death also. Prohibition against intermarriage and interdining is essential for a rapid evolution of the soul. But this self-denial is no test of *varna*. A Brahman may remain a Brahman, though he may dine with his Shudra brother, if he has not left off his duty of service by knowledge. It follows from what I have said above, that restraint in matters of marriage and dining is not based upon notions of superiority. A Hindu who refuses to dine with another from a sense of superiority misrepresents his *Dharma*.

Unfortunately to-day, Hinduism seems to consist merely in eating and not eating. Once I horrified a pious Hindu by taking toast at a Mussalman's house. I saw that he was pained to see me pouring milk into a cup handed by a Mussalman friend, but his anguish knew no bounds when he saw me taking toast at the Mussalman's hands. Hinduism is in danger of losing its substance, if it resolves itself into a matter of elaborate rules as to what and with whom to eat. Abstemiousness from intoxicating drinks and drugs, and from all kinds of foods, especially meat, is undoubtedly a great aid to the evolution of the spirit, but it is by no means an end in itself. Many a man eating meat and with everybody, but living in the fear of God is nearer his freedom than a man religiously abstaining from meat and many other things, but blaspheming God in every one of his acts.

The central fact of Hinduism however is cow protection. Cow protection to me is one of the most wonderful phenomena in human evolution. It takes the human being beyond his species. The cow to me means the entire sub-human world. Man through the cow is enjoined to realise his identity with all that lives. Why the cow was selected for apotheosis is obvious to me. The cow was in India the best companion. She was the giver of plenty. Not only did she give milk, but she also made agriculture possible. The cow is a poem of pity. One reads pity in the gentle animal. She is the mother to millions of Indian mankind. Protection of the cow means protection of the whole dumb creation of God. The ancient seer, whoever he was, began with the cow. The appeal of the lower order of creation is all the more forcible because it is speechless. Cow protection is the gift of Hinduism to the world.

And Hinduism will live so long as there are Hindus to protect the cow.

The way to protect is to die for her. It is a denial of Hinduism and *Ahimsa* to kill a human being to protect a cow. Hindus are enjoined to protect the cow by their *tapasya*, by self-purification, by self-sacrifice. The present-day cow protection has degenerated into a perpetual feud with the Mussalmans, whereas cow protection means conquering the Mussalmans by our love. A Mussalman friend sent me some time ago a book detailing the inhumanities practised by us on the cow and her progeny; how we bleed her to take the last drop of milk from her, how we starve her to emaciation, how we ill-treat the calves, how we deprive them of their portion of milk, how cruelly we treat the oxen; how we castrate them, how we beat them, how we overload them. If they had speech, they would bear witness to our crimes against them which would stagger the world. By every act of cruelty to our cattle, we disown God and Hinduism. I do not know that the condition of the cattle in any other part of the world is so bad as in unhappy India. We may not blame the Englishman for this. We may not plead poverty in our defence. Criminal negligence is the only cause of the miserable condition of our cattle. Our *Panjrapoles*, though they are an answer to our instinct of mercy, are a clumsy demonstration of its execution. Instead of being model dairy farms and great profitable national institutions, they are merely depots for receiving decrepit cattle.

Hindus will be judged not by their *tilaks*, not by the correct chanting of *mantras*, not by their pilgrimages, not by their most punctilious observance of rules but by their ability to protect the cow. Whilst professing the religion of cow protection, we have enslaved the cow and her progeny, and have become slaves ourselves.

It will now be understood why I consider myself a Sanatani Hindu. I yield to none in my regard for the cow. I have made the Khilafat cause my own, because I see that through its preservation full protection can be secured for the cow. I do not ask my Mussalman friends to save the cow in consideration of my service. My prayer ascends daily to God Almighty, that my service of a cause I hold to be just may appear so pleasing to Him, that he may change the hearts of the Mussalmans, and fill them with Pity for their Hindu neighbours and make them save the animal the latter hold dear as life itself.

I can no more describe my feeling for Hinduism than for my own wife. She moves me as no other woman in the world can. Not that she has no faults; I daresay, she has many more than I see myself. But the feeling of an indissoluble bond is there. Even so I feel for and about Hinduism with all its faults and limitations. Nothing elates me so much as the music of the Gita or the Ramayana by Tulasidas, the only two books in Hinduism I may be said to know. When I fancied I was taking my last breath, the Gita was my solace. I know the vice that is going on to-day in all the great Hindu shrines, but I love them in spite of their unspeakable failings. There is an interest which I take in them an which I take in no other. I am a reformer through and through. But my zeal never takes me to the rejection of any of the essential things of Hinduism. I have said I do not disbelieve in idol worship. An idol does not excite any feeling of veneration in me. But I think that idol worship is part of human nature. We hanker afte symbolism. Why should one be more composed in a church than elsewhere? Images are an aid to worship. No Hindu considers an image to be God. I do not consider idol whorship a sin.

It is clear from the foregoing, that Hinduism is not an exclusive religion. In it there is room for the worship of all the prophets of the world. It is not a missionary religion in the ordinary sense of the term. It has no doubt absorbed many tribes in its fold, but this absorption has been of an evolutionary, imperceptible character. Hinduism tells every one to worship God according to his own faith or *Dharma*, and so it lives at peace with all the religions.

That being my conception of Hinduism, I have never been able to reconcile myself to untouchability. I have always regarded it as an excrescence. It is true that it has been handed down to us from generations, but so are many evil practices even to this day. I should be ashamed to think that dedication of girls to virtual prostitution was a part of Hinduism. Yet it is practised by Hindus in many parts of India. I consider it positive irreligion to sacrifice goats to Kali and do not consider it a part of Hinduism. Hinduism is a growth of ages. The very name, Hinduism, was given to the religion of the people of Hindusthan by foreigners. There was no doubt at one time sacrifice of animals offered in the name of religion. But it is not religion, much less is it Hindu religion. And so also it seems to me that when cow protection became an article of faith with our ancestors, those who persisted in eating beef were ex-communicated. The civil strife must have been fierce. Social boycott was applied not only to the recalcitrants, but their sins were visited upon their children also. The practice which had probably its origin in good intentions hardened into usage, and even verses crept in our sacred books giving the practice a permanence wholly undeserved and still less justified. Whether my theory is correct or not, untouchability is repugnant to reason and to the instinct of mercy, pity or love. A religion that establishes the worship of the cow cannot possibly countenance or warrant a cruel and inhuman boycott of human beings. And I should be content to be torn to pieces rather than disown the suppressed classes. Hindus will certainly never deserve freedom, nor get it if they allow their noble religion to be disgraced by the retention of the taint of untouchability. And as I love Hinduism dearer than life itself, the taint has become for me an intolerable burden. Let us not deny God by denying to a fifth of our race the right of association on an equal footing.

29th September, 1920

THE MEANING OF THE EMPIRE

(BY M. K. GANDHI)

The following circular has been issued by the Education Department:

"Teachers and Educational officers of this Presidency should be asked to co-operate in bringing about a right understanding of the meaning of the Empire and in dispelling the idea that the Empire is based on force and militarism, by encouraging the parties concerned to look upon each other as brethren in advancement of the liberal aims and mutual friendship and sympathy particularly in India where a contrary feeling is gaining ground."

It is dated at Poona, the 1st instant.

The circular in my opinion is a triumph of Non-co-operation. We have been often told authoritatively that the Empire is based finally on force. When an attempt is being made to isolate this force, and to show by not meeting it by force that it is utterly useless when it is not backed by the co-operation, conscious or unconscious of the people, we have a circular calling upon the teachers to co-operate in showing that the Empire is based not on force of militarism, but that it is based on mutual friendship. This I consider a triumph of Non-co-operation, because force recedes into the background. Sir Michael O'Dwyer flaunted his brute force in the face of the nation, and terrorism reigned supreme for a time. It did not answer. Now it is to be covered under soft-sounding phrases. It too must fail.

The circular is hypocritical. The talk of friendship and sympathy between terrorists and their victims is to add deception to tyranny. The way out is through Non-co-operation.

It is a vain attempt to expect to secure friendship by false pretentions. The best and only way to secure the real friendship of the people and to prove to them that the Empire is not based on force and militarism, is to withdraw the superfluous military force even at the risk of losing the Empire, to trust the people, and for Englishmen in general to regard us in every way their equals in thought and in deed. This presupposes righting the Khilafat wrong in accordance with the Mussalman sentiment and to give full reparation regarding the Punjab.

But this seems impossible for the general body of Englishmen to do. They have been brought up to work upon us as mere chattels. I invite the attention of the reader to the account of the treatment of our countrymen in New Zealand. I cannot conceive anything more wantonly brutal than the doings of the whitemen of New Zealand. It is not as if the colonists are a depraved people. They are brave, generous, charitable and cultured in their own sphere. But they are thrown off their balance immediately they come in contact with us. We are their natural prey. And culture is no bar to their maltreatment of us, even as culture is no bar to the killing even say of snakes by the majority of mankind. I have not used a far-fetched illustration. Thousands of Englishmen cannot bear the idea of an Indian claiming or living on terms of equality with them. White superiority, as Mr. Andrews has shown, has become a religion. President Kruger used to say that God had ordained Asiatics to be whitemen's slaves. He even introduced the idea in his statute book. He was frank and he avowed it. Others believe it, practise it, but would fain break its force by using euphemistic language or worse.

It is not possible to blame anybody but ourselves for this badge of inferiority, and we alone can remove it by supreme effort.

23rd March, 1921

'FOR GOD, KING AND COUNTRY'

(By M. K. Gandhi)

During my peregrinations I once came across boys in uniform and asked them what their uniform meant. I observed that their uniform was made of foreign cloth or cloth woven out of foreign yarn. They said it was scouts' uniform. They whetted my curiosity by the answer. I was eager to know what they did as scouts. The answer was that they lived for God, King and

Country. 'Who is your King?' I asked. 'King George,' was the reply. 'How about Jallianwala? Supposing you had been in that place on the 13th April 1919, and were asked by General Dyer to shoot your terrified countrymen, what would you have done?'

'Of course I would not have obeyed the command.'

'But General Dyer wore the King's uniform?'

'Yes, but he belongs to the bureaucracy, and I have nothing to do with it.'

I suggested that he could not separate the bureaucracy from the King, that the King was an impersonal ideal existence which meant the British Empire and that no Indian could remain loyal, in the accepted sense, to the Empire as it was at present represented and be loyal to God at the same time. An Empire, which could be responsible for the terrorism of the Martial Law regime, that would not repent of the wrong, that could enter into secret treaties in breach of solemn obligations, could only be reckoned as a godless Empire. Loyalty to such an Empire was disloyalty to God.

The boy was puzzled.

I continued my argument. 'Supposing our country becomes godless in order to enrich itself, exploits other people, trafficks in intoxicants, goes to war for the sake of extending its trade and resorts to fraud in order to sustain its power and prestige, how can we be consistently loyal to God and country? Must we not forsake the country for the sake of God? I suggest, therefore, that you should bind yourself to be faithful and loyal only to God and none else in the same sense and in the same breath.'

There were many of his companions who were deeply interested in the conversation. Their chief too came in. I repeated my argument to him and asked him to tax himself and stimulate the inquiring spirit of the grown up young men whom he was guiding. Hardly was the absorbing topic exhausted, when the train steamed out of the station. I felt sorry for the splendid lads and understood better the deep meaning of the movement of Non-co-operation. There can be but one universal creed for man, that is loyalty to God. It includes, when it is not inconsistent, loyalty to King, country, and humanity. But it equally often excludes all else. I hope that the youth of the country as well as their tutors will revise their creed and set themselves right where they are convinced of their error. It is no small matter for tender minds to have formulas presented to them which cannot bear scrutiny.

27th April, 1921

THE CURSE OF BETTING

(By M. K. Gandhi)

"You will earn the gratitude and thanks of thousands of wives, both European and Indian, if you can succeed in putting a stop to betting at the races. My husband was an ideal husband—until he took to betting at the races. We are now in debt, and, although he draws a good salary and does not drink alcohol, we are hard up, and I am sure this is the experience of very many wives. I have often implored him on my bended knees not to go to the races but to no purpose. And does it not seem very hard that wives and children should suffer because their husbands cannot refrain from going to the races and losing money?

"It is true that alcohol is ruining thousands, but betting at the races is certainly ruining tens of thousands.

"By practically robbing the public, the W. I. T. Club can afford to pay its European employees handsome salaries. If you were only in the know, I am sure you would agree with me that hanky-panky tricks are carried on by the Turf Club, and thus the public are cheated and robbed of a lot of money. Do, for God's sake, try and right matters. Things were certainly better when the book-makers were allowed to take bets on the race-course.

"Sir, I am sure you are acquainted with a number of men on the new Councils, and, with their aid, I do hope you will succeed in putting a stop to betting at the races. If Government would take over and manage the totes, I am sure, things would be more fair and square. The public invariably lose and those who win are the owners of horses and their trainers and jockeys; and is it not a scandalous shame that Government should connive at it, simply because some of their big officials are keenly interested in horse racing?

"I had better not offer my signature to this letter as my husband is in Government service; but I pray that you will interest yourself in what I have written and succeed in stopping betting at the races."

This letter has been travelling with me for some time. The reader will share my feelings that it is a pathetic letter. Anonymous letters are rarely valuable. But this one is certainly an exception, though the writer has chosen not to disclose her name.

I know nothing of horse-racing. I have ever looked upon it with horror for its associations. I know that many men have been ruined on the race course.

But I must confess I have not had the courage to write anything against it. Having seen even an Aga Khan, prelates, viceroys, and those that are considered the best in the land, openly patronising it and spending thousands upon it, I have felt it to be useless to write about it.* As a journalist and reformer, my function is

* The following also appeared in *Young India* :

The Curse of Betting.—Babu Bhagwandas, the learned Chancellor of the National University, Kashi, has sent me extracts from Manusmriti on the sin of betting. I reproduce them below :

"The King should diligently keep gambling (*dyuta*) and betting (*samahvaya*) away from the State ; for these two vices destroy the State and the sovereign themselves. (221)

Gambling and betting are indeed as daylight robbery : and the ruler should endeavour diligently to eradicate them. (222)

That wherein inanimate things are used, that is *dyuta*, gambling ; that, wherein living things are used, that is *samahvaya*, betting. (223)

He who does these himself, or causes them to be done by others, secretly or openly, may be punished by the ruler with punishment up to that of death, at the ruler's discretion, like cheats and impersonators pretending to follow vocations other than their rightful ones. Or gamblers and betters (*kitawah*) may be banished from the land, like those who practise prostitution under cover of dancing and singing and acting, or those who make and sell spirituous liquors and other such cruel deceivers and spreaders of vice and followers of sinful trades. (224-228).—26th May, 1921.

'Satya' wrote under date 25th May, 1921 :

I am glad, *Young India* and its Editor have taken up the question of the evils of betting. I feel, however, that a casual article in *Young India* is not enough to root out this evil, imported from the west. The evil has spread from the idle rich to the commercial communities, the middle classes, the labourers working in factories, and the schoolboys. Over and above thousands of people regularly going to the Races week after week, there are thousands more, to whom temptation to gamble comes in the shape of bucket-shops, openly plying their trade in the heart of the city. The Government have appointed a committee to consider the question of closing down these shops, and they will have some Legislation at the next sessions. But that is not enough. Public opinion must be created, and it must be definitely shown that race-going and betting is as bad as drinking and prostitution. For this, a strong agitation is required, and I hope, readers of *Young India* will respond to it.

to call public attention to these vices about which there is likelihood of public opinion being created. Much as I disapprove of vaccination, I deem it to be waste of effort to draw public attention to the evil. I must own that I had not the courage to bring the drink traffic in the campaign of purification. It has come unsought The people have taken it up of their own accord.

The surest sign that Non-co-operation is a movement of purification is that many abuses are being removed by the people without any guidance or preaching. And it is in such hope about betting that I have published the above letter.

I am aware that the writer would be satisfied merely with some modification. What is required is a total destruction of the pest. Betting at races is a part of the gambling mania. If only the people will Non-co-operate, the evil will die a natural death. Thousands who attend the race course do so merely for fun. They attend either to see horses run breathlessly, or because it is the fashion, but they, nevertheless, aid and abet the ruin of many a gambler.

But betting is, I apprehend, more difficult to deal with than drinking. When vice becomes a fashion and even a virtue, it is a long process to deal with it. Betting is not only fashionable but is hardly regarded as a vice. Not so drinking. Fortunately, it is still the fashion to

---

Mr. Gandhi replied as follows in *Young India* of 22nd June, 1921:

As I have already said, unfortunately the races and gambling in connection therewith are fashionable. They do not excite the same feeling of shame that drinking does. Race-going, therefore, is more difficult to deal with than drinking. 'Satya' knows the evils of race-going in a special manner. I invite him to come out in the open, and personally tackle the vice which is slowly but surely undermining the morals of society.

consider drinking a weakness, if not positively a vice.. Every religion has denounced it with more or less vehemence. But betting has escaped much special attention. Let us hope, however, that the vigilant public will find a more innocent recreation than attending the race course, and thus show its disapproval of gambling at the race course.

PART VII

CONGRESS AND SWARAJ

PART VII

CONGRESS AND SWARAJ

7th January, 1920

THE CONGRESS

(By M. K. Gandhi)

THE Congress this time was for many of us a pilgrimage because of its having been held in Amritsar. Jallianwala Bagh was visited during the Congress * week by the thousands of delegates and visitors with the pilgrim mind. It is said that some touched the blood-stained earth with their foreheads, some took away with them a little of that earth to be preserved as a sacred treasure. Some used it as *vibhuti*, and smeared their foreheads with it. All went to the Bagh as a sacred duty. There is no doubt many went to the Congress only as a mark of their respect for the memory of the innocent dead.

The speeches of Swami Shri Shraddhanandji, the Chairman of the Reception Committee, and of the Hon'ble Pandit Motilal Nehru were models of sobriety and breathed an earnest spirit. Each bore the individuality of its author. The Swami's had a religious ring about it. He was full of good-will towards mankind. "How can we hate Englishmen if we love Andrews,

* The Session of the Congress held at Amritsar in December, 1919.

Wedderburn, Hume, Hardinge and others? We must conquer the English with our love," said the Swami. The Pandit's language, though perfectly courteous and restrained, is bitter. He compels a tear from the eye as he takes you with him through the different acts of the Punjab tragedy. He has examined the events of the Punjab with his legal acumen. Iron has entered his soul. He demands stern justice against the culprits.

The Presidential speech suffers for being in English. It was painful to see him labouring through his speech, spoken in a foreign tongue before an audience of nearly 15,000 people, not one-seventh of which could follow his English. The Congress proceedings have conclusively demonstrated the necessity of their being mainly, if not entirely, conducted in Hindi. That is the only course left open to us, if we would work for the masses and draw upon them for delegates. In the Central Provinces, the United Provinces, Delhi, the Punjab and Behar, only Hindnstani is spoken and in all the other parts of India except the Presidency of Madras, Hindi can be generally understood. For it is a language cognate to the Vernaculars of the other provinces. Madras alone presents any difficulty and for the sake of a few hundred delegates from that Presidency, it would not be proper to do violence to thousands who cannot understand English, but who can more or less understand Hindustani. The only straight, economical and politically sound course is to make the proceedings of the Congrsss predominantly Hindustani, the Dravidian members being free to speak in English, or for that matter, in Tamil or Telugu. I grant that for a few years the Subjects Committee must deliberate in English, but if we are to give a proper political education to the country through the medium of the Congress, it must be clear to every one that it can only be done through Hindi. I trust, therefore, that those in the Madras Presidency who are desirous of doing All-India public work outside their presidency and of aspiring after becoming delegates of the Congress will make haste to learn Hindi. They have got facilities in the Madras Presidency for learning Hindi, and if they will begin now and give at least one hour per day regularly to it, they will, by the end of the year, be able generally to follow the proceedings of the Congress. All must recognise that the insistent demand of the delegates from year to year for Hindustani cannot be resisted for any length of time.

Another absurdity which is becoming more and more grave needs also to be removed. Very few people could follow the President while he was reading his speech. The very best of leaders may not occupy the attention of the audience for longer than an hour. The President's address was necessarily long. It occupied thirty-eight foolscap pages in print. Fortunately Pandit Nehru skipped over many pages whilst he was reading it, but he would have taken no less than three hours, if he had insisted on reading the whole of the thirty-eight pages. It is highly necessary, therefore, that the addresses of the Chairman of the Reception Committee and the President should be printed in Hindustani (both in Devanagri and Urdu scripts), English and the Vernacular of the province in which the Congress is held, and distributed at the entrance either gratis or for the cost price. They ought not to be distributed in the pandal, as is often done much to the inconvenience of everybody. Both the Chairman and the President might read or orally give the summary of their addresses, each occupying no longer than thirty minutes.

The third absurdity is the terrible, evergrowing waste of money in creating a huge pandal. The Indian climate admits of holding meetings in the open air. But I refrain from saying more on this matter as the All-India Congress Committee has appointed a sub-committee consisting of Messrs. Kelkar, I. B. Sen, A. Rangaswami Iyengar, the Hon'ble V. J. Patel and myself to consider the whole constitution of the Congress.

The resolutions of the Congress show that there are very sharp divisions and as time goes forward, parties are inevitable. Hitherto the Congress has represented only one party, but it cannot be kept any longer as one party organisation, if it is not to have seceders from it on an increasing scale from year to year. Measures must be devised whereby all parties can be represented on it and the annual assembly can retain its truly national character.

Let us consider the resolutions. Take the condemnation of the excesses. There is no doubt that without that resolution some of the resolutions would have lost all force and value. We could not with any justification condemn the excesses of the authorities and therefore urge the dismissal of General Dyer or Sir Michael O' Dwyer, or even the Viceroy's recall, if we were not ready to condemn our own. That resolution was the necessary *prayaschitta* for the mob frenzy in April. If we are to make orderly progress, we must unequivocally disapprove of violence being committed by the people in any shape or form. It is true that often in the West mob violence is resorted to, but by creating a strong popular opinion against it, we must make such violence impossible in India. Few can deny that on the sixth of April, India found itself in possession of a new force and a new power—a force that could prove irresistible under almost every conceivable circumstance provided that truth was on our side. It is my firm belief that had the developments of Satyagraha not been interrupted in April, by our own folly, not only would the Rowlatt Act have been removed from the Statute Book but we would have been spared the humiliating and degrading spectacle of a British general running amuck. Indeed we shall find it impossible, when we have full control over our national affairs, to carry on the Government of the country without self-restraint. In a vast country like India where the people are ordinarily peaceful, we shall find it impossible to carry on the Government if mob rule becomes the custom of the land, and in order to check that tendency, popular opinion is a far greater and more potent instrument than the employment of physical force. I would, therefore, give the first place in point of importance to this resolution as a token of the correctness of our conduct and for the sake of a lead to the country. These resolutions of the Congress, especially those that require any action on the part of the people, are valuable for the formation of public opinion, and I hope that workers recognizing the full force of the truth underlying the resolution will on due occasion impress upon the people the necessity of refraining from violence.

Only less in importance than the resolution on condemnation was the resolution on Reforms.* Whilst

* *Young India* of 14th January, contained the following:

The Reforms Resolution in the Congress.—The Reforms Resolution has been the subject of much criticism in the Press and it may be interesting to summarise the criticism here briefly. The "Servant of India" is of opinion that the Congress failed to give the lead to the country mainly because of the "essential weakness of Mr. Gandhi's position" that he did not set out to examine in detail the Reform Act as Mrs. Besant did. Mrs. Besant in a leading article in "New India" charges Mr. Gandhi and Pandit Malaviaji with not having stood firmly

I subscribe entirely to the proposition that India is fit now for responsible Government, I do not for one moment believe that we can get it without working for it. We can work either by adopting obstructive tactics, or by co-operation. Healthy obstruction is a condition of our being. We must ever obstruct untruth, injustice and

---

by their first amendment, and says that had they done so, "they would have carried it, for Mr. Tilak had told his followers to yield at the last moment." She has no doubt that Mr. Tilak is using Mr. Gandhi and Pandit Malaviaji as tools as three years ago she says he was using her in a similar way. The "Leader" is of opinion that the Resolution means practically a victory for the "Super extremists" and that the resolution as it was passed in its final form "does not at all events bring out clearly the sense the extremists would co-operate with the authorities in making the Reforms a success." It complains that after emphatically explaining the plain connotation of the word "disappointing", Mr. Gandhi failed to stick to his amendment and the result was that a compromise clause was at last added, which differed in no wise from Mr. Pal's amendment and of course Mr. Pal made no secret of his attitude in that in moving the amendment he did, he only made light of the idea of co-operation and almost jeered the idea of thanking Mr. Montagu. The "Leader" is clear that "Messrs. Pal, Das, and Satyamurthi had their way and Mr. Gandhi must acnkowledge that he including Pandit Malaviya and Mr. Jinnah were defeated."

In refreshing contrast with these opinions is that of the *Times of India*. It will be remembered that before the Resolution had been passed at the Congress the paper had expressed the opinion that the "doctrine preached at Amritsar is for all practical purposes the doctrine of disunion." After the acceptance of the Resolution, it seems to be satisfied that the party which "desired to use the Reforms whole-heartedly for the advancement of the country, in the confident knowledge that good work will quicker bring the expansion of responsible institution," substantially prevailed in the end. It adds that the exact working of the amendment is immaterial, and that haulting though the final Resolution was, "it was in the right direction" and "the main and important fact is that the Congress pledged itself open to do, what in fact all had made up their minds to do, namely, to co-operate in the Reforms."

The comment on the above appears on page 826 of this volume.

evil. It was because I did not consider, and do not consider, the Reforms to be an evil or unjust and because I consider them to be a progressive step towards responsible Government, that I decline to consider them to be disappointing, however inadequate and unsatisfactory they may be. I endorse Mr. Bepin Chandra Pal's opinion that for me to decline to consider the Reforms disappointing means that I did not expect them. I had certainly much fear that the Reforms might not go through when they did and I was unprepared for material improvements in the measure as it was originally published. The opponents of the amendment admitted that they would co-operate when co-operation was essential for the country's good and not hesitate to obstruct when obstruction advanced it. That no doubt was the only meaning, and no other, of the amendment of which I had the honour to be in charge. But let it be said to the credit of the opponents that they resisted the amendment as long as they could, because they frankly said that they had a faith in the bureaucracy even under the altered conditions. In my humble opinion, it is a wrong attitude. The Royal Proclamation has been framed in a most liberal spirit. It is full of good-will and it would have been wrong on the part of the Congress not to have responded to the King's call for co-operation. My faith in human nature is irrepressible, and even under the circumstances of a most adverse character, I have found Englishmen amenable to reason and persuasion, and as they always wish to appear to be just even when they are in reality unjust, it is easier to shame them than others into doing the right thing. Be that however as it may, it would be a fall from our culture and it would be unwise not to grasp the hand of fellowship extended through the Proclamation. If we are strong, we shall lose nothing by beginning with co-operation. We at once place the bureaucracy in the wrong by our readiness to co-operate for the common purpose.

It was equally important for us to thank Mr. Montagu for his valuable services in connection with the Reforms. The Hon'ble Pandit Madan Mohan Malaviya, Mr. Jinnah and I therefore felt that even at the risk of dividing the house we were bound to press the amendment home. That ultimately there was a compromise shows the good nature of Lokamanya Tilak and Mr. Das. It was a perfect pleasure to see both of them, whilst holding to their views, anxious not to divide the house. And it was equally a pleasure to see so many on the platform working to secure a compromise.

14*th January*, 1920

THE REFORMS RESOLUTION IN THE CONGRESS

The divergence of views on the Reforms Resolution, summarised in one of our notes,* is not to be wondered at. Compromises never give complete satisfaction to all parties. In their very nature they must just fall short of that and yet be acceptable to all. In our opinion, the country did get the lead through the Congress that it was possible to give it. The Congress must, if it is to serve the country, more and more tend to represent not one view but many and, that not merely in the Subjects Committee, but on the open platform. There is no denying the fact there are several parties in the country. Extremist and Moderate do not cover all parties. There are, for instance, in the extremist camp Mr. Kasturiranga Iyengar's, Mr. Das's and Lokamanya Tilak's parties.

**See page* 823

No doubt they sailed under the extremist flag. But as differences become accentuated, as they must be in course of time, each group will begin to assert itself. The Hon. Pandit Malaviaji represents a body of opinion distinct from the Extremist. Similarly in the moderate camp there are undoubtedly divisions, which as time goes on will become sharper, rather than otherwise, and *with a proper consitution* there is no reason why the Congress should not represent a resultant of all these different views *thrashed out with calmness and becoming dignity on* the Congress platform. For the first time in the history of the Congress, an open and reasoned discussion took place before the delegates, on a matter of the greatest importance to the country, and for the first time were those elaborate preparations made in order to ascertain by their votes the decision of the Congress. That in itself in our opnion was something worth attaining. But there was more than this. No doubt it was open to either party to push the matter to a division. We cannot accept Mrs. Besant's view that L. Tilak had told his followers to vote for Mr. Gandhi's amendment if he had held out, and even if Mrs. Besant's information is correct, it would hardly have been proper for Mr. Gandhi to have pushed the matter to such an extreme. His amendment alone brought forth Mr. Pal's. The latter was purely tactical move. Had the audience been called upon merely to decide between the original proposition, *i.e.*, without co-operation and thanks, and Mr. Gandhi's, with thanks, a division would have been a duty. But Mr. Pal's amendment came as a feeler and also was an earnest of the extremist groups to conciliate an opposing amendment, so long as they could consistently do so. Mr. Pal's amendment could not be accepted because of the offensive word 'use' in it. Naturally therefore a third amendment providing a middle course had to be framed and comfort lies not merely in the fact of the compromise but in the fact that all were anxious to avoid an open division. Surely for the country it means that the Congress desires to co-operate with the authorities in so far as that co-operation can hasten the advent of the responsible Government, and to thank Mr. Montagu for his valuable labours on the reforms. We would certainly have liked it better if the graceful language of the original amendment had been accepted, if thanks had been expressed in warmer twrns and extended to Lord Sinha. But it would have been wrong to divide the house after the principle of co-operation and thanks was granted by the three leaders. We are unable to assoc'ate ourselves with the suggestion that L. Tilak in accepting the amendment wanted to use Messrs. Malaviya and Gandhi as his tools, and if they allowed themselves to be so used it would not be the Lokamanya who would be to blame, but Messrs. Malaviya and Gandhi would be clearly held blameworthy for their simplicity. For, as party formation progresses, we suppose it would be considered quite the proper thing for party leaders to use others as tools so long as there are any to be used. Care will therefore have to be taken rather to purify our politics, than for fear of being used as tools to hesitate to take the right course. L. Tilak represents a definite school of thought of which he makes no secret. He considers that everything is fair in politics. We have joined issue with him in that conception of political life. We consider that political life of the country will become thoroughly corrupt, if we import western tactics and methods. We believe that nothing but the strictest adherence to honesty, fairplay and charity can advance the true interests of the country. But we refuse, because of the essential difference just pointed out, to believe that in accepting the amendment L. Tilak was guided by any motive other than that of meeting his opponents' views so far as it was possible. On the whole, therefore, in our opinion, the analysis given by the *Times of India* is the only true analysis of the position ultimately arrived at under the compromise.

15th September, 1920

THE CONGRESS

(By M. K. Gandhi)

Never has the Congress* been called upon to decide an issue so momentous as the one it was called upon to decide at its special session, presided over by Lala Lajpat Rai. Never perhaps has the Congress witnessed such determined opposition as was offered to the Non-co-operation resolution. And yet never, within my experience, has a decisive majority listened with such respect and attention to the opposition argument as it did at the last session. Again never has there been such united opposition shown to a Subjects Committee resolution by the noted leaders of the people.

Mrs. Besant has a fine record of service to India. Pandit Madan Mohan Malaviyaji is a name to conjure with. He has to his credit an unbroken record of many years' brilliant service to the country and an unblemished character. Mr. Das leads a party ever growing in influence and strength. I felt the late Lokamanya Bal Gangadhar Tilak's absence most keenly at such a juncture. Mr. Baptista led the Deccan. Mr. Kasturi Ranga

* Special Congress held at Calcutta.

Aiyengar, the talented editor of the '*Hindu,*' led the Madras Nationalist party. All these and many other leaders strenuously opposed the Non-co-operation resolution. I warned that great audience against accepting my proposal, unless they were prepared to suffer and were convinced that true Non-co-operation was possible only through the programme submitted by me. But the audience wanted action, wanted suffering. The voting was elaborately registered. The Congress pandal was cleared for the purpose of voting. Lala Lajpat Rái personally superintended the operation. It lasted for six hours. All the provinces but the Central Provinces and the Berars voted in favour of my resolution. The Central Provinces gave for my proposition 30 votes as against 33 for Babu Bipin Chandra Pal's. I give the figures below:

		For Res.	For Amendment.
Bombay	...	243	93
Madras	...	161	135
Bengal	...	551	395
U. P.	...	259	28
Punjab	...	254	92
Andhra	...	59	12
Sindh	...	36	16
Delhi	...	59	9
Behar	...	184	28
Burma	...	14	4
C. P.	...	30	33
Berar	...	5	28
		1855	873

My resolution adopted the principle of the whole of the Khilafat Programme, even non-payment of taxes, and advised for immediate adoption, boycott of titles and honorary offices, law courts by litigants, schools and colleges and reformed councils. Babu Bipin Chandra Pal proposed a mission to England to present our demands and meanwhile to establish national schools, formulate arbitration courts and not to boycott the councils. His resolution would have meant in effect seeking election to the councils, and these probably adopting obstructive tactics. This meant a virtual postponement of the real struggle to the next general election. The opposition therefore chiefly centred on the boycott of councils. And the Congress has decided by an overwhelming majority that the councils must be abandoned. I hope that those who do not believe that boycott of councils would postpone the attainment of Swarajya (let alone hastening it) will work with all their might to advance the purpose of the Congress.

An analysis of the votes shows that the country wants Non-co-operation. Mrs. Besant who consistently, fearlessly and frankly opposed it had very few adherents. I do not propose to examine the merits of the case at the present moment. My argument is before the country in favour of boycott of councils, schools and courts. Nothing I heard on the Congress platform has shaken my belief in the necessity or the efficacy of these steps. But I would respectfully address a few words to the majority and to the minority.

To the majority I would say: The hour of the greatest triumph is the hour of the greatest humility. The majority has taken upon its shoulders a tremendous responsibility. Every individual voter in favour of my proposal has certainly bound himself, if he is a parent, to withdraw his children from schools or colleges subject in any way to Government control. Every voter being a lawyer is bound at the earliest opportunity to suspend his practice and promote the cause of settlement of disputes by private arbitration. Every candidate for the Councils, who has voted with the majority, has undertaken to withdraw his candidature, every such voter to refrain from voting at the elections. Every delegate voting with the majority has bound himself to stimulate hand-spinning and hand-weaving and in his own person to use only hand-spun and hand-woven cloth. Everyone of the majority having accepted the principle of non-violence, self-sacrifice and discipline in regard to non-co-operation is bound to treat the minority with respect and fairness. We may not use physical or wordy violence against them. We must endeavour by our intensive practice and by scrupulously honourable methods to convert it to our views. Those who voted with the minority were either weak or not ready. Some few doubted the rightness of withdrawing children from schools for instance. But when they see schools being emptied, national schools springing into being, lawyers suspending practice and yet not starving, and the councils deserted at least by the best of nationalists, they will soon begin to believe in the programme, lose their weakness and be themselves ready to adopt it. We need not therefore be impatient with the minority, because it does not see eye to eye with us.

To the minority, I would say, they have lost in a fair fight. Unless now therefore it is a matter of conscience with them, they must come forward to prosecute the programme of Non-co-operation in a most vigorous manner. Those who think that the majority has grievously erred are no doubt entitled to carry on a campaign of conversion of the majority to their views. By far the largest number in the minority, however, have accepted the principle of establishment of private arbitration-courts and national schools. They wanted only a postponement of the boycott of councils. I venture to suggest to them that now that the majority has decided in favour of quicker pace, the minority should accept the verdict and help to make the programme a success.

Boycott of foreign goods finds a place in my resolution. I am sorry for it. I may not state how it came to find a place there. But as it did not conflict with my conscience, and in order to show my reasonableness, I undertook to move a resolution whose musical harmony was marred by a false note. Boycott of foreign cloth is included in Swadeshi. Boycott of all other foreign goods is a senseless proposition, if only because it is a virtual impossibility. But if the introduction of the addendum stimulates us to sacrifice our luxuries and superfluities, it would have served a good purpose. It is certainly our right and duty to discard everything foreign that is superfluous and even everything foreign that is *necessary*, if we can produce or manufacture it in our country.

3rd November, 1920

THE CONGRESS CONSTITUTION

(BY M. K. GANDHI)

The belated report of the Congress Constitution Committee has now been published for general information, and opinion has been invited from all public bodies in order to assist the deliberations of the All-India Congress Committee. It is a pity that, small though the Constitution Committee was, all the members never met at any one time in spite of efforts to have a meeting of them all.

It is perhaps nobody's fault that all the members could not meet. At the same time, the draft report has passed through the searching examination of all but one member, and the report represents the mature deliberations of four out of the five members. It must be stated at the same time that it does not pretend to be the unanimous opinion of the members. Rather than present a dissenting minute, a workable scheme has been brought out leaving each member free to press his own views on the several matters in which they are not quite unanimous. The most important part of the constitution, however, is the alteration of the creed. So far as I am aware, there is no fundamental difference of opinion between the members. In my opinion, the altered creed represents the exact feeling of the country at present moment.

I knew that the proposed alteration has been subjected to hostile criticism in several newspapers of note. But the extraordinary situation that faces the country is that popular opinion is far in advance of several newspapers which have hitherto commanded influence and have undoubtedly moulded public opinion. The fact is that the formation of opinion to-day is, by no means, confined to the educated classes, but the masses have taken it upon themselves not only to formulate opinion but to enforce it. It would be a mistake to belittle or ignore this opinion, or to ascribe it to a temporary upheaval. It would be equally a mistake to suppose that this awakening amongst the masses is due either to the activity of the Ali Brothers or myself. For the time being we have the ear of the masses because we voice their sentiments. The masses are by no means so foolish, or unintelligent as we sometimes imagine. They often perceive things with their intuition, which we ourselves fail to see with our intellect. But whilst the masses know what they want, they often do not know how to express their wants and, less often, how to get what they want. Herein comes the use of leadership, and disastrous results can easily follow a bad, hasty, or what is worse, selfish lead.

The first part of the proposed creed expresses the present desire of the nation, and the second shows the way that desire can be fulfilled. In my humble opinion, the Congress creed with the proposed alteration is but an extension of the original. And so long as no break with the British connection is attempted. it is strictly within even the existing article that defines the Congress Creed. The extension lies in the contemplated possibility of a break with the British connection. In my humble opinion, if India is to make unhampered progress, we must make it clear to the British people that, whilst we desire to retain the British connection, if we can rise to our full height with it, we are determined to dispense with, and even to get rid of that connection, if that is necessary for full national development. I hold that it is not only derogatory to national dignity, but it actually impedes national progress superstitiously to believe that our progress towards our goal is impossible without British connection. It is this superstition which makes some of the best of us tolerate the Punjab wrong and the Khilafat insult. This blind adherence to that connection makes us feel helpless. The proposed alteration in the creed enables us to rid ourselves of our helpless condition. I personally hold that it is perfectly constitutional, openly to strive after independence, but lest there may be dispute as to the consitutional character of any movement for complete independence, the doubtful and highly technical adjective "constitutional" has been removed from the altered creed in the draft.

Surely it should be enough to ensure that the methods for achieving our end are legitimate, honourable, and peaceful. I believe that this was the reasoning that guided my colleagues in accepting the proposed creed. In any case, such was certainly my view of the whole alteration. There is no desire on my part to adopt any means that are subversive of law and order. I know, however, that I am treading on delicate ground when I write about law and order; for, to some of our distinguished leaders even my present methods appear to be lawless and conducive to disorder. But even they will, perhaps, grant that the retention of the word 'Constitutional' cannot protect the country against methods such as I am employing. It gives rise, no doubt, to a luminous legal discussion, but any such discussion is fruitless when the nation means business. The other important alteration refers to the limitation of the number of delegates. I believe that the advantages of such a limitation are obvious. We are fast reaching a time when without any such limitation the Congress will become an unwieldy body. It is difficult even to have an unlimited number of visitors; it is impossible to transact national business, if we have an unlimited number of delegates.

The next important alteration is about the election of the members of the All-India Congress Committee making that Committee practically the Subject Committee, and the redistribution of India for the purposes of the Congress on a linguistic basis. It is not necessary to comment on these alterations, but I wish to add that, if the Congress accepts the principle of limiting the number of delegates, it would be advisable to introduce the principle of proportional representation. That would enable all parties, who wish to be represented at the Congress.

I observe that the *Servant of India* sees an inconsistency between my implied acceptance of the British Committee so far as the published draft constitution is concerned, and my recent article in *Young India* on that Committee* and the newspaper *India*. But it is well-known

* The following appeared in *Young India* of 20th October, 1920:

I gladly reproduce in another column an open letter sent to me by Miss Normanton.(Here omitted.) I do not know the lady save by her writings in "India" whilst it was being edited by her. Her views on Non-co-operation are refreshingly strong and her unqualified support of the boycott of the reformed Councils ought to prove consoling to the waverers. But I would ask my reader not to overweigh the effect of the boycott on the British public or the League of Nations. It is better for us to rivet our attention on our own duty irrespective of the effect of its performance on outside opinion. We have over-estimated the effect of our action on British public opinion and in doing so have often damaged the true interests of the nation. At the same time, Miss Normanton's argument appears to me to be perfectly sound.

What will however interest the public more are perhaps her views on the British Committee. I do not know the merits of the controversy she discusses. But apart from the merits, her views on the constitution of the Committee would appear to be original. I entirely associate myself with her remark that a British Committee, to be true to the name, should be composed exclusively of the British people and financed by them. It is then more likely to exert influence on British public opinion than now.

In any case, we would then have a real index of the British interest in Indian affairs. I endorse Miss Normanton's views about the newspaper "India" also. The paper costs much more than it is worth. Its influence on English opinion is practically nothing and it is an indifferent vehicle of English opinion for India's enlightenment. Its only value therefore consists in its parliamentary reports which can be received and distributed by the All-India Congress Committee with very little cost. An enterprising newspaper could take over that duty any day and make it a paying venture. And now that we have embarked on Non-co-operation and are determined to become self-reliant, it would be more consistent for us to dis-establish the British Committee and stop "India." It would save a needless waste of public money and turn our attention more towards ourselves.

that for several years I have held my present views about the existence of that body. It would have been irrelevant for me, perhaps, to suggest to my colleagues the extinction of that committee. It was not our function to report on the usefulness or otherwise of the Committee. We were commissioned only for preparing a new constitution. Moreover, I knew that colleagues were not averse to the existence of the British Committee. And the drawing-up of a new constitution enabled me to show that, where there was no question of principle, I was desirous of agreeing quickly with my opponents.

It is not easy for me to reconcile myself to the alternative suggested by Miss Normanton, *viz.*, that we should have a kind of an advisory committee or an advisor or resident in London to help the proposed British Committee with suggestions. I would far rather concentrate all our attention and all our best workers on work in India. The harvest is truly rich and the labourers are few. We can ill-spare a single worker for foreign work. It will be time for us to consider the propriety of sending a representative abroad after we have created a permanent impression in India itself by substantial and solid work.

[We are in possession of further evidence, which we have received from another esteemed correspondent in London, in connection with the very unsatisfactory condition of the newspaper "India." The total circulation of "India," our correspondent informs us, is 500 only (!), 220 in Great Britain, the rest in India. Last year's income was £ 4-17-0 (!!) only, while expenditure for the current year is estimated at £ 3300. This is how our correspondent puts it:

For the maintenance of "India" we pay—that is the poor people in India pay—£ 1800 a year out of which Mr. Syed Hussain as Editor-Secretary gets £ 550 a year with effect from October 1, Mr. Fenner Brockway as co-Editor-Secretary gets £ 550, Mr. G. P. Blizzard as Secretary £ 400, the typist £ 150, clerk £ 150.

The paper has had a chequered career but was never a success from the propagandist point of view. It has never had a constructive policy. To squander £ 1800 on a 3d. weekly with a circulation of 500, and to spend another £ 1500 on establishment charges, £ 3300 in all, looks like reckless extravagance.—Ed. *Y. I.*]

For further views about foreign propaganda *see Supra* page 795.

in opinions. But I propose certainly to press for abolition of the Committee as it is at present constituted. and the stopping of its organ *India*.

5th January, 1921

THE CONGRESS

(BY M K. GANDHI)

The largest and the most important Congress* ever held has come and gone. It was the biggest demonstration ever held against the present system of Government. The President uttered the whole truth when he said that it was a Congress in which, instead of the President and the leaders driving the people, the people drove him and the latter. It was clear to every one on the platform that the people had taken the reins in their own hands. The platform would gladly have moved at a slower pace.

The Congress gave one day to a full discussion of the creed and voted solidly for it with but two dissentients after two night's sleep over the discussion. It gave one day to a discussion of Non-co-operation resolution and voted for it with unparalleled enthusiasm. It gave the last day to listening to the whole of the remaining thirty-two Articles of the Constitution† which were read and translated word for word by Maulana Mahomed Ali in a loud and clear voice. It showed that it was intelligently following the reading of it, for there was dissent when Article Eight was reached. It referred to non-interference by the Congress in the internal affairs of

*The session of the Congress held at Nagpur in December, 1920.

†*See* Appendix.

the Native States.* The Congress would not have passed the proviso if it had meant that it could not even voice the feelings of the people residing in the territories ruled by the princes. Happily a resolution suggesting the advisability of establishing Responsible Government in their territories enabled me to illustrate to the audience that the proviso did not preclude the

* The following appeared in *Young India* of 17th November, 1921: *Feudatory States*—The All-India Congress Committee having defined the Congress policy regarding foreign states, the demand was naturally made to define its policy towards our own states. The broad outlines of Congress policy were formulated by the Congress at the Nagpur session, namely of non-intervention in the internal affairs of these states. The states themselves could not wish for anything better or more unequivocal. And the All-India Congress Committee can only define the policy within the four corners of that resolution. Strictly in accord with that resolution, Congress workers have refrained from taking the message of Non-co-operation to the states, except its permanent, purifying or economic parts which would hold good even without Non-co-operation. These are the drink evil, Swadeshi, Hindu-Muslim unity, non-violence and untouchability. The Congress can have nothing but good-will towards these states, so long as their subjects are well treated. And even when they are ill-treated, the Congress cannot and will not exercise any pressure or force save that of public opinion. And therefore nationalist organs do not hesitate to discuss, when necessary, in strong language the grievances of the subjects in some of these states. The thoughtless and wanton ill-treatment, for instance, of Seth Jamanlalji and his party in the confines of Bikaner state whilst they were prosecuting merely their campaign of Swadeshi has justly evoked hostile criticism. The liberal states may therefore look for every encouragement from the Congress and the reactionary ones at the most fierce criticism of their methods and measures. Moreover, the Congress cannot but sympathise with the states in their humiliating plight. The imperial power has used them as pawns in its game of exploitation. They are least able to resist the illegitimate and insidious pressure that is brought to bear upon them from time to time. They must therefore realise that the increase of people's power means decrease of the humiliating influence described by me.

Congress from ventilating the grievances and aspirations of the subjects of these states, whilst it clearly prevented the Congress from taking any executive action in connection with them ; as for instance holding a hostile demonstration in the Native States against any action of theirs. The Congress claims to dictate to the Government but it cannot do so by the very nature of its constitution in respect of the Native States.

Thus the Congress has taken three important steps after the greatest deliberation. It has expressed its determination in the clearest possible terms to attain complete self-government, if possible still in association with the British people, but even without, if necessary. It proposes to do so only by means that are honourable and non-violent. It has introduced fundamental changes in the constitution regulating its activities and has performed an act of self-denial in voluntarily restricting the number of delegates to one for every fifty thousand of the population of India and has insisted upon the delegates being the real representatives of those who want to take any part in the political life of the country. And with a view to ensuring the representation of all political parties, it has accepted the principle of "single transferable vote." It has reaffirmed the Non-co-operation resolution of the special session and amplified it in every respect. It has emphasised the necessity of non-violence and laid down that the attainment of *Swaraj* is conditional upon the complete harmony between the component parts of India, and has therefore inculcated Hindu-Muslim unity. The Hindu delegates have called upon their leaders to settle disputes between Brahmins and non-Brahmins and have urged upon the religious heads the necessity of getting rid of the poison of untouchability. The Congress has told the parents of school-going children, and the lawyers that they have not responded sufficiently to the call of nation and that they must make greater effort in doing so. It therefore follows that the lawyers who do not respond quickly to the call for suspension and the parents who persist in keeping their children in Government and aided institutions must find themselves dropping out from the public life of the country. The country calls upon every man and woman in India to do their full share. But of the details of the Non-co-operation resolution, I must write later.

30th March, 1921

THE CONGRESS CONSTITUTION

(By M. K. Gandhi)

The last Congress* has given a constitution whose working is in itself calculated to lead to Swaraj. It is intended to secure in every part of India representative committee working in conjunction with, and under willing and voluntary submission to, a central organisation—The All-India Congress Committee. It establishes an adult suffrage open to men and women, subject only to two qualifications, signing of the creed and a nominal payment of four annas. It is intended to secure due representation of all parties and communities. If, then, it is honestly worked, and commands confidence and respect, it can oust the present Government without the slightest difficulty. For, the latter has no power except through the co-operation, willing or forced, of the people. The force it exercises is almost through our own people. One lac of Europeans, without our help, can only hold

*Nagpur Congress held in December, 1920.

less than one-seventh of our villages each, and it would be difficult, for one man, even when physically present to impose his will on, say, four hundred men and women—the average population of an Indian village.

The problem before us, therefore, is one of opposing our will to that of the will of the Government, in other words, to withdraw our co-operation from it. If we are united in purpose, the Government must obey our will or retire. It is the disturbing factors of which the Government avails itself for the consolidation of its power. When we are violent, it resorts to terrorism; when we are disunited, it resorts to bribery; when we are united, it resorts to cajolery and conciliation; when we are clamant, it puts temptations in the way of those who cry out most. All, therefore, we need do is to remain non-violent, united, and unresponsive to bribery and cajolery.

Surely, there is not much education required to accomplish this much among a people who are cultured and intelligent. It is not difficult to present to them a common purpose and a common platform which they can appreciate and understand. But this means not talking, but acting and organising. I suggest that we concentrate on registering before the 30th June, in an accurate manner, at least one crore of members in the Congress organisation. No registration is to be deemed complete without the payment of four annas and the acceptance of the creed. We must aim at enlisting every adult member of every family. It should be our boast to have as many women as men on our registers. We should have all the Mussalmans, all the castes, all the artisans, and all the pariahs, whom we can induce to come to our register. It will then become a most democratic register of voters that the world can show.

If the suggestions made by me are acceptable, we have to concentrate our attention up-to the 30th June, on getting:

(1) One crore Rupees for the Tilak Swaraj Fund,
(2) One crore members on the Congress register,
(3) The spinning wheel introduced in twenty lacs of homes.

In order to register one crore members, I estimate that we shall have canvassed at least twenty lacs of homes, counting five members to a family. Workers can certainly persuade Congress families to take up one wheel per family. Twenty-five lacs of spinning wheels in twenty-one provinces, is not an ambitious scheme.

Let us not waste our resources in thinking of too many national problems and their solutions. A patient, who tries many nostrums at a time, dies. A physician, who experiments on his patient with a combination of remedies, loses his reputation and passes for a quack. Chastity in work is as essential as chastity in life. All dissipation is bad. We have hitherto all pulled our own way, and thus wasted away national strength in a most extravagant manner. To boycott foreign cloth within the year is a practical feasibility. To bring into being a working organisation for the Congress is an easy thing for honest workers. The collection of one crore of rupees in a methodical manner will at once create confidence and will be a tangible token of our earnestness and determination.

This programme does not mean cessation of the other activities of Non-co-operation. They go on. Drink and untouchability must vanish. The education movement is steadily going forward. The national institutions that have sprung up will, if they are efficiently managed, make headway and attract students who are still hesitating. The pleaders, always a cautious and calculating class by training, will, as they see the movement progressing more and more, fall in line with the rest of the country. Boycott of law courts by the public is making fair progress. These things do not now require concentration of universal effort. They apply to special classes. But the three things mentioned by me are the most essential: they must be done now, and without them the movement, as a mass movement, must be pronounced a failure.

5th January, 1921

MR. GANDHI'S SPEECH ON THE CREED

"The object of the Indian National Congress is the attainment of Swarajya by the people of India by all legitimate and peaceful means."

There are only two kinds of objections, so far as I understand, that will be advanced from this platform. One is that we may not to-day think of dissolving the British connection. What I say is that it is derogatory to national dignity to think of permanence of British connection at any cost. We are labouring under a grievous wrong, which it is the personal duty of every Indian to get redressed. This British Government not only refuses to redress the wrong, but it refuses to acknowledge its mistake and so long as it retains its attitude, it is not possible for us to say all that we want to be or all that we want to get, retaining British connection. No matter what difficulties be in our path, we must make the clearest possible declaration to the world and to the whole of India, that we may not possibly have British connection, if the British people will not do this elementary justice. I do not, for one moment, suggest that we want to end the British connection at all costs, unconditionally. If the British connection is for the advancement of India, we do not want to destroy it. But if it is inconsistent with our national self-respect, then it is our bounden duty to destroy it. There is room in this resolution for both—those who believe that, by retaining British connection, we can purify ourselves and purify British people, and those who have no belief. As for instance, take the extreme case of Mr. Andrews. He says all hope for India is gone for keeping the British connection. He says there must be complete severance—complete independence. There is room enough in this creed for a man like Mr. Andrews also. Take another illustration, a man like myself or my brother Shaukat Ali. There is certainly no room for us, if we have eternally to subscribe to the doctrine, whether these wrongs are redressed or not, we shall have to evolve ourselves within the British Empire: there is no room for me in that creed. Therefore, this creed is elastic enough to take in both shades of opinion and the British people will have to beware that, if they do not want to do justice, it will be the bounden duty of every Indian to destroy the Empire.

I want just now to wind up my remarks with a personal appeal, drawing your attention to an object lesson that was presented in the Bengal camp yesterday. If you want Swaraj, you have got a demonstration of how to get Swaraj. There was a little bit of skirmish, a little bit of squabble, and a little bit of difference in the Bengal camp, as there will always be differences so long as the world lasts. I have known differences between husband and wife, because I am still a husband; I have noticed differences between parents and children, because I am still a father of four boys, and they are all strong enough to destroy their father so far as bodily struggle is concerned; I possess that varied experience of husband and parent. I know that we shall always have squabbles, we shall always have differences; but the lesson that I want to draw your attention to is that I had the honour and privilege of addressing both the parties. They gave me their undivided attention and what is more, they showed their attachment, their affection and their fellowship for me by accepting the humble advice that I had the honour of tendering to them, and I told them I am not here to distribute justice that can be awarded only through our worthy president. But I ask you not to go to the president, you need not worry him. If you are strong, if you are brave, if you are intent upon getting Swaraj, and if you really want to revise the creed, then you will bottle up your rage, you will bottle up all the feelings of injustice that may rankle in your hearts and forget these things here under this very roof, and I told them to forget their differences, to forget the wrongs. I don't want to tell you or go into the history of that incident. Probably most of you know. I simply want to invite your attention to the fact.* I don't say they have settled up their differences. I hope they have, but I do know that they undertook to forget the differences. They undertook not to worry the President, they undertook not to make any demonstration here or in the Subjects Committee. All honour to those who listened to that advice.

I only wanted my Bengali friends and all the other friends who have come to this great assembly with a fixed determination to seek nothing but the settlement of their country, to seek nothing but the advancement of their respective rights, to seek nothing but the conservation of the national honour. I appeal to every one

* See *infra*

of you to copy the example set by those who felt aggrieved and who felt that their heads were broken. I know, before we have done with this great battle on which we have embarked at the special sessions of the Congress, we have to go probably, possibly through a sea of blood, but let it not be said of us or any one of us that we are guilty of shedding blood, but let it be said by generations yet to be born that we suffered, that we shed not somebody's blood but our own, and so I have no hesitation in saying that I do not want to show much sympathy for those who had their heads broken or who were said to be even in danger of losing their lives. What does it matter? It is much better to die at the hands, at least, of our own countrymen. What is there to revenge ourselves about or upon? So I ask everyone of you that, if at any time there is blood-boiling within you against some fellow countryman of yours, even though he may be in the employ of Government, even though he may be in the Secret Service, you will take care not to be offended and not to return blow for blow. Understand that the very moment you return the blow from the detective, your cause is lost. This is your non-violent campaign. And so I ask everyone of you not to retaliate but to bottle up all your rage, to dismiss your rage from you and you will rise graver men. I am here to congratulate those who have restrained themselves from going to the President and bringing the dispute before him.

Therefore, I appeal to those who feel aggrieved to feel that they have done the right thing in forgetting it and if they have not forgotten, I ask them to try to forget the thing; and that is the object lesson to which I wanted to draw your attention, if you want to carry this resolution. Do not carry this resolution only by acclamation for this resolution, but I want you to accompany the carrying out of this resolution with a faith and resolve which nothing on earth can move. That you are intent upon getting Swaraj at the earliest possible moment and that you are intent upon getting Swaraj by means that are legitimate, that are honourable and by means that are non-violent, that are peaceful, you have resolved upon, so far you can say to-day. We cannot give battle to this Government by means of steel, but we can give battle by exercising, what I have so often called, "Soul force," and soul force is not the prerogative of one man, of a, Sanyasi or even a so-called saint. Soul force is the prerogative of every human being, female or male, and therefore I ask my countrymen, if they want to accept this resolution, to accept it with that firm determination and to understand that it is inaugurated under such good and favourable auspices as I have described to you.

In my humble opinion, the Congress will have done the rightest thing, if it unanimously adopts this resolution. . . . May God grant that you will pass this resolution unanimously, may God grant that you will also have the courage and the ability to carry out the resolution and that within one year.

29th June, 1921

THE WORKING COMMITTEE AND ITS FUNCTION

(By M. K. Gandhi)

The resolutions of the Working Committee have come in for some hostile criticism. Its ruling questioning the propriety of Non-co-operating lawyers attending law-courts and Non-co-operating defendants entering upon their defence in law-courts, has been seriously called in question, and it has even been suggested that its rulings may be disregarded. It is, therefore, necessary to examine the function of the Working Committee. And before we can understand this, we must understand the Congress Constitution.

The goal of the Congress is attainment of Swaraj by peaceful and legitimate means. The Congress must be worked, so as to hasten India's progress towards her destined goal. The Constitution is so devised as to tax and prove the nation's capacity for self-government. It undoubtedly sets up a system of voluntary Government, in which the only force available is public opinion and the good-will of the people. And seeing that the Congress is to-day engaged in opposing, and if need be, destroying the existing system, if follows that the greater the authority of the Congress, the less must be that of the Government. When the Congress commands complete confidence and *willing obedience* to its instructions, there is full Swaraj. For, then the Government must respect popular opinion expressed through the Congress, or must commit suicide. The Congress must, therefore, become the most united, the strongest in character and the largest organisation in the land. The Congress policy, therefore, must command the readiest acceptance.

The Congress meets in session only once a year. It lays down policies. The All-India Congress Committee is designed to carry out the Congress policy as embodied in its resolutions. It must interpret all resolutions, and attend to all new matters, with the same authority as the Congress. The members may debate upon different propositions and interpretations as much as they choose, but except on matters of vital principle, the dissenters must conform to, and faithfully carry out, the resolutions of the majority. The discussions in the Committee are not open for rediscussion in public. In order to make the All-India Congress Committee an efficient body, the Constitution has provided for a Working Committee of fifteen, which must meet often and must be able to deal with all the matters delegated to it by the All-India Congress Committee. It is designed to exercise all the functions of the All-India Congress Committee, when the latter is not sitting. It must watch and guide public opinion, it must interpret it, it must keep all the subsidiary organisations in working order, it must attend to All-India finance, it must distribute it, and whenever decision on matters of grave importance has to be taken, it must summon a meeting of the All-India Congress Committee for direction. The Working Committee is to the Congress, what a Cabinet is to a Parliament. Its decisions must command respect, if we are to evolve constitutional government during this year. Naturally, therefore, its members must be those, who command the greatest respect of the All-India Congress Committee and of the nation. It dare not take any hasty decisions, and it must be a homogenous body. It cannot have two policies or two parties within itself. Whilst the Congress represents the whole nation, and may therefore have every type and all parties, the Working Committee must consist of men representing the policy and the party, that have the confidence of the majority of the delegates. Its decisions have largely to be unanimous. When a member cannot pull on with the rest, he can resign, but he may not obstruct or affect the deliberations of the Committee by an open discussion of its deliberations in the Press. Whilst, therefore, the decisions of the Working Committee should be carried out by Congressmen, it is not an irresponsible body. It can be dismissed by the All-India Congress Committee by a vote of no confidence. Its decisions are subject to be reviewed by the All-India Congress Committee, and even set aside for grave reasons. In my humble opinion, unless the Working Committee carries weight with people, it is hardly possible to attain Swaraj during this year. Every one of us must, therefore, work to make the Congress an irresistible body by its resolutions being carried out in every little detail. What the Government does in the last resort by force of arms, the Congress expects to do by force of affection. The Government has rendered itself irresistible by striking terror in the hearts of the people; the Congress must make itself felt by securing the free-will acceptance of its doctrines and policies. Non-violence, thus, runs through everything connected with the people's programme. But each organisation expects to succeed by reason of people's co-operation. Loyalty to the Congress decisions is a *sine qua non* of success of the Nagpur determination to achieve Swaraj during the year.

10*th November*, 1921

THE ALL-INDIA CONGRESS COMMITTEE

(By M. K. Gandhi)

The present All-India Congress Committee met for the last time at Delhi on the 4th November. The arrangements were under the control of the renowned Hakimji Ajmal Khan. He is ailing and badly needs rest. But he will not have any. His spacious house and Dr. Ansari's have been turned into *Dharmashalas* for the accommodation of guests, whether Hindu or Mahomedan. The Hindus have their prejudices scrupulously respected. Those who will not take even water at a Muslim house are provided separate quarters. Here in Delhi one certainly finds Hindu-Muslim unity in full working order. The Hindus implicitly and gratefully accept Hakimji's leadership and they do not hesitate to place their religious interests too in his keeping.

The All-India Congress Committee is the People's Parliament elected annually. It has year by year grown in importance and representative character. And to-day it is undoubtedly the mouthpiece of all those adult men and women belonging to any religion or party who can afford to pay four annas, who accept the simple creed of the Congress and who have cared to have their names entered in the Congress register. As a matter of fact, the delegates include Hindus, Mussalmans, Sikhs, Christians almost, perhaps, in their numerical proportion. I do not know whether it has Parsis and Jews. It has a very fair proportion of women delegates. It has also *Panchama* delegates. If any interest is under-represented, the fault lies with that interest. The delegates are all unpaid and attend at their own expense and pay for their own board and lodging. If the healthy practice on the part of the inviting cities of entertaining the delegates as guests has sprung up, it is a sign of the liberality of the citizens, no part of their statutory obligation. The majority of these elected representatives travel third class and are satisfied with mere elementary comforts. The house of this People's Parliament consisted of a temporary canvass pandal with a few shrubs to decorate it. Chairs and tables were provided, I presume, because it would have been difficult to ensure sufficient cleanliness and freedom from dust in the compound where the pandal was erected. Yellow-coloured *Khadi* cloth served as table-cloth for the President's table. The members, both men and women, were dressed mostly in coarse *Khadi*, a few only had what is now known as the Bezwada fineness. The dresses were simple and of Indian style. I have gone into these details, because the All-India Congress Committee to many of us is a model for the future Parliament under Swaraj. It is in keeping with the real state of India. It is somewhat a reflection of the poverty of the country, its simplicity and of its climatic requirements.

Contrast this with the false show, the pomp and the extravagance at Simla and at the new Delhi!

As the outer, so the inner. The most important business of the nation was finished in a most businesslike manner inside of twelve hours. Nothing was done or allowed without the closest scrutiny. The resolution on the dispute between the President and the Working Committee was discussed in the calmest manner possible. Jealous of its own rights, the Committee ratified the decision of the Working Committee that the right of interpretation of substantive law belonged to it rather than the President. It would not however allow anything to appear in the resolution which could by any stretch of imagination be considered discourteous to the President.

The resolution of the session was, however, the one on Civil Disobedience which I give below:

"Whereas there is not much over one month for the fulfilment of the national determination to establish Swaraj before the end of the year, and whereas the nation has demonstrated its capacity for exemplary self-restraint by observing perfect non-violence over the arrest and imprisonment of the Ali Brothers and the other leaders, and whereas it is desirable for the nation to demonstrate its capacity for further suffering and discipline, discipline sufficient for the attainment of Swaraj, the All-India Congress Committee authorises every province, on its own responsibility, to undertake Civil Disobedience, including non-payment of taxes, in the manner that may be considered the most suitable by the respective Provincial Congress Committees, subject to the following conditions:

1. In the event of individual Civil Disobedience, the individual must know hand spinning, and must have completely fulfilled that part of the programme which is applicable to him or her, *e.g.*, he or she must have entirely discarded the use of foreign cloth and adopted only handspun and hand-woven garments, must be a believer in Hindu-Muslim unity and in the unity amongst all the communities professing different religions in India as an article of faith, must believe in non-violence as absolutely essential for the redress of the Khilafat and the Punjab wrongs and the attainment of Swaraj, and if a Hindu, must, by his personal conduct, show that he regards untouchability as a blot upon nationalism.

2. In the event of mass Civil Disobedience, a District or Tahsil should be treated as a unit, and therein a vast majority of the population must have adopted full Swadeshi and must be clothed out of cloth handspun and hand woven in that District or Tahsil, and must believe in and practise all the other items of Non-co-operation.

Provided that no civil resister should expect to be supported out of public funds, and members of the families of civil resisters undergoing sentence will be expected to support themselves by carding, hand-spinning, and hand-weaving or any other means.

Provided further that upon application by any Provincial Congress Committee, it is open to the Working Committee to relax the conditions of Civil Disobedience, if it is satisfied that any conditions should be waived."

Those who were eager to start Civil Disobedience immediately brought forward a series of amendments which they supported with considerable skill, and yet the speeches were models of brevity. Every one of the amendments was rejected after the fullest discussion. The chief debater was Maulana Hasrat Mohani, who being impatient for Civil Disobedience could not understand the imposition of the tests laid down for would-be civil resisters. One and only one addition was accepted at the instance of the Sikh delegates. They are most sensitive about their special rights. If, therefore, Hindu-Moslem unity was maintained, Hindu-Moslem-Sikh unity in the Punjab must also be insisted upon. 'Then why not mention the others?' was the burden of other speeches. The result was, that 'unity among all the communities professing other religions' was added. It is a wise addition, for it shows that Hindu-Moslem unity is not a menace but it is a symbol of unity among all.

Whilst, therefore, there is perfect unanimity in the Committee, it would be wrong to suppose that there is no obstruction or opposition in the Committee. The Maharashtra party is a capable and drilled body. It has adopted the programme more from loyalty to the Congress and the rule of majority than from deep conviction.* It is giving a trial to a programme in which it has not implicit faith. It makes its presence felt by mild obstruction. But it is too patriotic to carry obstruction to the point of destruction. Mr. Abhyankar fortifies it by his sledge-hammer oratory. Mr. Aney

* See *infra*.

supports it by his calm logic. Mr. Jamnadas Mehta is the freelance of the party. He effectively uses the Committee for developing his debating skill and obstructive tactics. The Committee refuses to treat him seriously, and he lets you know that he does not expect to be treated seriously. The house laughs at his expense and he heartily joins in it. He enlivened the proceedings at the outset by proposing himself to the chair if no other member would allow himself to be proposed in the place of a member of the Working Committee. He considers the members of the Working Committee to be all honourable men, and the measure of the honour is, that they are constantly in his opinion arrogating to themselves rights they do not possess. The reader, however, must not think that all this is done with any poison in the performance. I have not known a better-behaved or more good-humoured assembly. And I regard the Maharashtra party to be an acquisition of which any nation would feel proud. Indeed, I refer to the party to emphasise my contention that the Committee is composed of men who know their minds and who are determined to give a good account of themselves in their effort to win India's freedom.

4th August, 1920

THE CONGRESS AND NON-CO-OPERATION

(BY M. K. GANDHI)

The Hon'ble Pundit Malaviyaji, for whom I entertain the highest regard and whom I have so often described as *Dharmatma*, has appealed to me both publicly and privately to suspend Non-co-operation till the Congress has pronounced upon it. The *Mahratta* has also done-likewise. These appeals have made me pause and think, but I regret to say that I have not been able to respond to them. I would do much and give much to please Punditji. I am anxious to receive his approbation and blessing for all my actions. But a higher duty requires me not to turn from the course mapped out by the Non-co-operation Committee. There are moments in your life when you must act, even though you cannot carry your best friends with you. The still small voice within you must always be the final arbiter when there is a conflict of duty.

The reason for asking me to suspend action is that the Congress will presently meet and consider the whole question of Non-co-operation and give its verdict. It would therefore be better, says Punditji, to await the Congress decision. In my humble opinion, it is no Congressman's duty to consult the Congress before taking an action in a matter in which he has no doubts. To do otherwise may mean stagnation.

The Congress is after all the mouth-piece of the nation. And when one has a policy or a programme which one would like to see adopted, but on which one wants to cultivate public opinion, one naturally asks the Congress to discuss it and form an opinion. But when one has an unshakable faith in a particular policy or action, it would be folly to wait for the Congress pronouncement. On the contrary, one must act and demonstrate its efficacy so as to command acceptance by the nation.

My loyalty to the Congress requires me to carry out its policy when it is not contrary to my conscience. If I am in a minority, I may not pursue my policy in the name of the Congress. The decision of the Congress on any given question therefore does not mean that it prevents a Congressman from any action to the contrary, but if he acts, he does so at his own risk and with the knowledge that the Congress is not with him.

Every Congressman, every public body has the right, it is sometimes their duty, to express their own opinion, act upon it even and thus anticipate the verdict of the Congress. Indeed it is the best way of serving the nation. By initiating well-thought-out policies, we furnish data for a great deliberative body like the Congress to enable it to form a well-informed opinion. The Congress cannot express national opinion with any definiteness, unless at least some of us have already firm views about a particular course of conduct. If all suspended their opinion, the Congress must necessarily suspend its own.

There are always three classes of people in an institution. Those who have favourable views on a given policy, those who have fixed but unfavourable views on it and those who hold no fixed views. The Congress decides for this third and large group. I hold fixed views on Non-co-operation. I believe that, if we are to make anything of the reforms, we will have to create a pure, clean and elevating atmosphere instead of the present fœtid, unclean and debasing atmosphere to work them in. I believe that our first duty is to compel justice from the Imperial Government in regard to the Khilafat and the Punjab. In both these matters, injustice is being sustained by untruth and insolence. I therefore consider it to be the duty of the nation to purge the Government of the uncleanness before they can co-operate with each other. Even opposition or obstruction is possible where there is mutual respect and confidence. At the present moment, the governing authority has no respect for us or our feelings. We have no faith in it. In these circumstances, co-operation is a crime. Holding these strong views, I can serve the Congress and the country only by reducing them to practice and thus affording to the Congress material for forming an opinion.

For me to suspend Non-co-operation would be to prove untrue to the Mussalman brethren. They have their own religious duty to perform. Their religious sentiment has been deeply hurt by a total disregard of laws of justice and their own promises by British ministers. The Mussalmans must take action now. They cannot await the Congress decision. They can only expect the Congress to ratify their action and share their sorrows and their burdens. Their action cannot be delayed till the Congress has decided on a policy nor can their course be altered by an adverse decision of the Congress unless their action is otherwise found to be an error. The Khilafat is a matter of conscience with them. And in matters of conscience, the Law of Majority has no place.

8th December, 1921

WHAT TO DO?

(BY M. K. GANDHI)

Mr. Jayakar's address has been followed by a conference of all Maharashtra at Akola. Mr. Jayakar is a thinker, he loves his country. He commands and deserves respectful attention. Those who gathered together at Akola are earnest patriotic seasoned soldiers. They are amongst the boldest and the most disciplined workers in the land. And one has to pause and think when they dissent from a programme.

Mr. Jayakar's address and the proceedings of the Akola conference have made me think furiously. There is no difficulty about understanding and appreciating the suggested modifications. It is a programme, if I may venture to say so, of unbelief. It is based upon the assumption that Swaraj is not attainable within a short time and that we must make such use as we can of the existing machinery with a view to improving it. The programme now being worked is based upon the belief that the existing machinery is worthless and its use only retards our progress and distracts attention.

The corner-stone of the national movement is Non-co-operation with violence whether of the pen or the sword. Education and legislation are the instruments to-day in the hands of the violent. To make use of their law courts or their legislatures or their schools is to take part in their violence. There is a fundamental distinction between the two processes. The one is a septic and the other antiseptic. They are diametrically opposite. In the one you rely upon the inherent purity of the system to destroy all poisonous germs that have entered the body, and in the other you resort to outside applications, stronger poisons to destroy the intruding germs. Both may be effective, but they cannot be used at the same time. We definitely rejected the antiseptic treatment last year. The majority at Maharashtra frankly suggest a return.

We are no longer in the dark. We have the results of fifteen months' working of the new method. Rejection of courts, schools and councils is an integral part of the programme. We may not give up parts because we have not achieved full success, if we are convinced that in themselves they are desirable. Although we have not succeeded in emptying the three institutions, we have demolished their prestige. They neither worry nor dazzle us. That many parents, many lawyers and many law-givers have not responded, shows that we must make a greater attempt to wean them, not now by arguing but by the exemplary conduct of abstainers. For me they are the Government. Just as I may not apply for a paid post because no Government servant resigns, I may not join the ranks of voluntary servants because the latter do not come away. I am convinced that the country has risen because of the abstention even of the few from association with these emblems of the existing Government.

Inadequate response is an eloquent plea if you will for establishing better schools and panchayats, not for confession of incapacity by returning to the fleshpots of Egypt.

But we have passed the stage of argument. When the sun is shining, you do not need to demonstrate its heat giving power by argument. And if anybody shivers in spite of being in the sun, no amount of argument can convince him of the sun's warmth, nor may you quarrel with the shivering one. He must seek other means, if there be any, of warming himself. My plea is for everyone to act according to his belief. The Congress provides the widest platform. Its creed is incredibly simple. A full-fledged co-operator as well as a nationalist who wants a change in the programme can work in it. Let us not push the mandate theory to ridiculous extremes and become slaves to resolutions of majorities. That would be a revival of brute force in a more virulent form. If rights of minorities are to be respected, the majority must tolerate and respect their opinion and action. There is no reason whatsoever why nationalists may not practise as lawyers or send their children to Government schools or seek election to the councils and still belong to the Congress. Only they may not act in the name of the Congress so long as they have not brought round to their view the majority of Congressmen. It will be the duty of the majority to see to it that minorities receive a proper hearing and are not otherwise exposed to insults. Swaraj will be an absurdity if individuals have to surrender their judgment to majority.

I wish to make a personal appeal to all Congressmen. I would ask them to believe me when I say that as leader and orginator of the movement inaugurated at Calcutta, I would feel hampered if I have not the hearty co-operation of those who vote for the programme. I would gladly find myself in a minority and confidently expect to march to victory. This Government cannot stand for one day the determined religious opposition of one district, if only the others will not interfere in the manner Bombay did.

There is room enough in our great country for as many parties as there are honest men. I would welcome an efficient and able organisation containing men, who believe in using Government institutions, and finding what warmth they can give them, even as I would have all organisations to extend toleration to those whole-hoggers who wish to cut of all possible connection with the Government. There is no reason why a province which can carry the people with it should not organise itself even on either basis.

I plead, that is to say, for a truthful programme and truthful parties. Let people only work programmes in which they believe implicitly. Loyalty to human institutions has its well defined limits. To be loyal to an organisation must not mean subordination of one's settled convictions. Parties may fall and parties may rise, but if we are to attain freedom, our deep convictions must remain unaffected by such passing changes.

We are on the eve of a new life. We may not see the image of Swaraj risen before us at the end of the month, but we must feel the warm glow of the coming event in no unmistakable fashion. And we shall feel it only if every one of us will try to be true to himself. To believe in the infallibility of our means is to attain Swaraj. The vote of the Congress this year must not be a leap in the dark. It must not be any more in the nature of an experiment. It should be an emphatic endorsement or rejection of the existing programme.

2nd March, 1922

CONGRESS A FETISH

We must avoid the Congress becoming a fetish. I love the idea of everybody becoming a Congressman and everybody yielding willing and intelligent obedience to the Congress resolutions. But I abhor the idea of anybody becoming a Congressman merely because it is an old or a great institution or yielding obedience to its resolutions whether one likes it or no. The rule of majority has a narrow application, *i.e.*, one should yield to the majority in matters of detail. But it is slavery to be amenable to the majority no matter what its decisions are. Thus notwithstanding Congress resolution, it is wrong, in my opinion, to withdraw from councils or not to covet election thereto, if one believes that councils are even a tolerably good institution. It is similarly wrong for a lawyer to suspend practice merely because the Congress says so. Democracy is not a state in which people act like sheep. Under democracy, individual liberty of opinion and action is jealously guarded. I, therefore, believe that the minority has a perfect right to act differently from the majority so long as it does not act in the name of the Congress. A practising lawyer may become a Congressman, he cannot be called a Non-co-operator. He cannot and should not, therefore, be on the All-India Congress Committee. Similarly one who does not wear hand-spun and hand-woven *Khaddar* or a title-holder or a councillor may not be called "Non-co-operators" though all those may be Congressmen. . . .

But not only do I think that a Congressman is not bound by the resolutions which he does not approve of; he is also entitled always to go beyond the Congress resolutions, provided that he does not violate the creed and if he does not act in the name of the Congress. Supposing that the restrictions put by the Congress do not suit a particular province, that that province has even voted against them, that that province finds that it can look after itself, it has every right to go forward and justify its rebellion by success. The Congress only finds the highest common factor, but it may conceivably be far short of the requirements of a particular province. That province may, if it has confidence and if it is not likely to jeopardise any Congress interest, certainly go on with its own programme on its own responsibility and at the risk of a vote of censure from the Congress. This, in my opinion, is what the spirit of democracy requires. What I have stated is an illustration of domestic Civil Disobedience. Thus and thus only shall we save ourselves from false idolatry.

26th *January*, 1921

'HIND SWARAJ' OR THE INDIAN HOME-RULE

(By M. K. Gandhi)

It is certainly my good fortune that this booklet of mine is receiving wide attention. The original is in Gujarati. It had a chequered career. It was first published in the columns of the 'Indian Opinion' of South Africa. It was written in 1908 during my return voyage from London to South Africa in answer to the Indian school of violence, and its prototype in South Africa. I came in contact with every known Indian anarchist in London. Their bravery impressed me, but I feel that their zeal was misguided. I felt that violence was no remedy for India's ills, and that her civilization required the use of a different and higher weapon for self-protection. The *Satyagraha* of South Africa was still an infant hardly two years old. But it had developed sufficiently to permit me to write of it with some degree of confidence. It was so much appreciated that it was published as a booklet. It attracted some attention in India. The Bombay Government prohibited its circulation. I replied by publishing its translation. I thought that it was due to my English friends that they should know its contents. In my opinion, it is a book which can be put into the hands of a child. It teaches the gospel of love in the place of that of hate. It replaces violence with self-sacrifice. It pits soul-force against brute force. It has gone through several editions and I commend it to those who would care to read it. I withdraw nothing except one word of it, and that in deference to a lady friend. I have given the reason for the alteration in the preface to the Indian edition.

The booklet is a severe condemnation of 'modern

civilization.' It was written in 1908. My conviction is deeper to-day than ever. I feel that, if India would discard 'Modern civilization,' she can only gain by doing so.

But I would warn the reader against thinking that I am to-day aiming at the Swaraj described therein. I know that India is not ripe for it. It may seem an impertinence to say so. But such is my conviction. I am individually working for the self-rule pictured therein. But to-day my corporate activity is undoubtedly devoted to the attainment of Parliamentary Swaraj* in

* The following notes appeared in *Young India* in regard to this term:

What is Swaraj?—"The Times of India" questions whether I have any clear notion of Swaraj. If the writer will go through the back numbers of *Young India*, he will find a complete answer to the question. But I may mention here briefly that the least that Swaraj means is a settlement with the Government in accordance with the wishes of the chosen representatives of the people. Therefore the Congress representatives, if they can make good their claim by providing an inexhaustible supply of prisoners, will have a determining voice in any settlement that may be made. Swaraj therefore means the capacity of the people of India to enforce their demands. I totally dissent from the Viceroy's view that Swaraj must come from the British Parliament unless it comes through the sword. The British Parliament will not ratify the people's wish when the 'sword' had made it irresistible. Non-co-operators are trying to use the sword of self-sacrifice in preference to that of steel. India's soul is pitted against British steel. We shall not have to wait long to know what popular Swaraj is.—15th December, 1921.

The Meaning of Swaraj.—A friend from South Africa writes to say that several Europeans there are prepared to help the struggle for Swaraj, but they want to be assured on certain points. As the points raised are of general importance, I gladly deal with them here.

(1) Does Mr. Gandhi's Swaraj mean sovereign independence, or full responsible Government within the Empire on the Dominion lines?

I should certainly be satisfied with full responsible Government on accordance with the wishes of the people of India. I am not aiming at destroying railways or hospitals, though I would certainly welcome their natural destruction. Neither railways nor hospitals are a test of a high and pure civilization. At best they are a necessary evil. Neither adds one inch to the moral stature of a nation. Nor am I aiming at a permanent destruction of law courts, much as I regard it as a 'consummation devoutly to be wished for.' Still less am I trying to destroy all machinery and mills. It requires a higher simplicity and renunciation than the people are to-day prepared for.

The only part of the programme which is now being carried out in its entirety is that of Non-violence. But I regret to have to confess that even that is not being carried out in the spirit of the book. If it were, India would establish Swaraj in a day. If India adopted the

---

Dominion lines, if the Khilafat and the Punjab wrongs are redressed. India cannot remain within the Empire, if the latter cannot redress the two wrongs, for full responsible Government will have no meaning for India, if she cannot refuse to give pensions to officers who have wronged her, or if she cannot secure a settlement of the Khilafat terms. England then becomes an 'enemy country' for India.

(2) Do the Muslims claim Palestine, or will they restore it to the Jews who are the original owners?

The Muslims claim Palestine as an integral part of Jazirat-ul-Arab. They are bound to retain its custody, as an injunction of the Prophet. But that does not mean that the Jews and the Christians cannot freely go to Palestine, or even reside there and own property. What non-Muslims cannot do is to acquire sovereign jurisdiction. The Jews cannot receive sovereign rights in a place which has been held for centuries by Muslim powers by right of religious conquest. The Muslim soldiers did not shed their blood in the late war for the purpose of surrendering Palestine out of Muslim control. I would like my Jewish friends to impartially consider the position of the seventy million Muslims of India. As a free nation, can they tolerate what they must regard as a treacherous disposal of their sacred possession?
—6th April, 1921.

doctrine of love as an active part of her religion and introduced it in her politics, Swaraj would descend upon India from heaven. But I am painfully aware that that event is far off as yet.

I offer these comments, because I observe that much is being quoted from the booklet to discredit the present movement. I have even seen writings suggesting that I am playing a deep game, that I am using the present turmoil to foist my fads on India, and am making religious experiments at India's expense. I can only answer that *Satyagraha* is made of sterner stuff. There is nothing reserved and nothing secret in it. A portion of the whole theory of life described in 'Hind Swaraj' is undoubtedly being carried into practice. There is no danger attendant upon the whole of it being practised. But it is not right to scare away people by reproducing from my writings passages that are irrelevant to the issue before the country.

23rd February, 1921

THE CONDITIONS OF SWARAJ

(By M. K. Gandhi)

Swaraj is easy of attainment before October next, if certain simple conditions can be fulfilled. I ventured to mention one year in September last, because I knew that conditions were incredibly simple and I felt that the atmosphere in the country was responsive. Past five months' experience has confirmed me in the opinion. I am convinced that the country has never been so ready for establishing Swaraj as now.

But it is necessary for us as accurately as possible to know the conditions. One supreme indispensable condition is the continuance of non-violence. Rowdyism, hooliganism, looting that we have recently witnessed are disturbing elements. They are danger-signals. We must be able to arrest their progress. The spirit of democracy cannot be established in a year in the midst of terrorism whether governmental or popular. In some respects, popular terrorism is more antagonistic to the growth of the democratic spirit than the governmental. For the latter strengthens the spirit of democracy, whereas the former kills it. Dyerism has evoked a yearning after freedom as nothing else has. But internal Dyerism, representing as it will terrorism by a majority, will establish an oligarchy such as stifle the spirit of all free discussion and conduct. Non-violence, therefore, as against the Government and as between ourselves, is absolutely essential to speedy success. And we must be able to devise means of observing it on our part in spite of the gravest provocations.

The next condition is our ability to bring into being the Congress organisation in terms of new constitution, which aims at establishing a Congress agency in every village with a proper electorate. It means both money and ability to give effect to Congress policies. What is really needed is not a large measure of sacrifice but ability to organise and to take simple concerted action. At the present moment we have not even succeeded in carrying the Congress message to every home in the 7½ lacs of villages of India. To do this work means at least 250 honest workers for as many districts, who have influence in their respective districts and who believe in the Congress programme. No village, no circle need wait for instructions from headquarters for founding their respective organisations.

There are certain things that are applicable to all.

The most potent thing is Swadeshi. Every home must have the spinning wheel and every village can organise itself in less than a month and become self-supporting for its cloth. Just imagine what these silent revolution means and there would be no difficulty in sharing my belief that Swadeshi means *Swaraj* and *Swadharma*.

Every man and woman can give some money—be it even a pice—to the Tilak Swaraj Fund. And we need have no anxiety about financing the movement. Every man and woman can deny himself or herself all luxury, all ornamentation, all intoxicants at least for one year. And we shall have not only money but we shall have boycotted many foreign articles. Our civilization, our culture, our Swaraj depend not upon multiplying our wants—self-indulgence, but upon restricting our wants—self-denial.

We can do nothing without Hindu-Muslim unity and without killing the snake of untouchability. Untouchability is a corroding poison that is eating into the vitals of Hindu society. *Varanashram* is not a religion of superiority and inferiority. No man or God can consider another man as inferior to himself. He must consider every man as his blood-brother. It is the cardinal principle of every religion.

If this is a religious battle, no argument is necessary to convince the reader that self-denial must be its supreme test. Khilafat cannot be saved, the Punjab humanity cannot be redressed, without godliness. Godliness means change of heart—in political language, changing the angle of vision. And such a change can come in a moment. My belief is that India is ripe for that change.

Let us then rivet our attention on :

(1) Cultivating the spirit of non-violence.

(2) Setting up Congress organisations in every village.

(3) Introducing the spinning wheel in every home and manufacturing all the cloth, required for our wants, through the village weaver.

(4) Collecting as much money as possible.

(5) Promoting Hindu-Muslim unity and

(6) Ridding Hinduism of the curse of untouchability and otherwise purifying ourselves by avoiding intoxicating drinks and drugs.

Have we honest, earnest, industrious, patriotic workers for this very simple programme? If we have, Swaraj will be established in India before next October.

22nd September, 1920

SWARAJ IN ONE YEAR

(By M. K. Gandhi)

Much laughter has been indulged in at my expense for having told the Congress audience at Calcutta* that if there was sufficient response to my programme of Non-co-operation Swaraj would be attained in one year. Some have ignored my condition and laughed because of the impossibility of getting Swaraj anyhow within one year.† Others have spelt the 'if' in capitals and

*Calcutta Special Congress.

†The following appeared in *Young India* of 29th December, 1920: *Swaraj in nine months.*—Asked by the " Times " representative as to his impressions formed as a result of his activities during the last three months' extensive experience copy is that this movement of Non-co-operation has come to stay, and it is most decidedly a purifying movement, in spite of isolated instances of rowdyism, as for instance at Mrs. Besant's meeting in Bombay, at some places in Delhi, Bengal and even in Gujarat. The people are assimilating day after day the

suggested that if 'ifs' were permissible in argument, any absurdity could be proved to be a possibility. My proposition however is based on a mathematical calculation.

---

spirit of non-violence, not necessarily as a creed, but as an inevitable policy. I expect most startling results, more startling than, say, the discoveries of Sir J. C. Bose, or the acceptance by the people of non-violence. If the Government could be assured beyond any possibility of doubt that no violence would ever be offered by us, the Government would from that moment alter its character, unconsciously and involuntarily, but none the less surely on that account."

"Alter its character,—in what directions?" asked the *Times* representative.

"Certainly in the direction which we ask it should move--that being in the direction of Government becoming responsive to every call of the nation."

"Will you kindly explain further?" asked the representative.

"By that I mean," said Mr. Gandhi, "people will be able by asserting themselves through fixed determination and self-sacrifice to gain the redress of the Khilafat wrong, the Punjab wrong, and attain the Swaraj of their choice."

"But what is your Swaraj, and where does the Government come in there—the Government which you say will alter its character unconsciously?"

"My Swaraj," said Mr. Gandhi, "is the Parliamentary Government of India in the modern sense of the term for the time being and that Government would be secured to us either through the friendly offices of the British people or without them."

"What do you mean by the phrase, 'without them?'" questioned the interviewer.

"This movement," continued Mr. Gandhi, "is an endeavour to purge the present Government of selfishness and greed which determine almost every one of their activities. Suppose that we have made it impossible by dissociation from them to feed their greed. They might not wish to remain in India, as happened in the case of Somaliland, where the moment its administration ceased to be a paying proposition they evacuated it."

"How do you think," asked the representative, "in practice this will work out?"

"What I have sketched before you," said Mr. Gandhi, "is the final

And I venture to say that true Swaraj is a practical impossibility without due fulfilment of my conditions. Swaraj means a state such that we can maintain our separate existence without the presence of the English. If it is to be a partnership, it must be a partnership at will. There can be no Swaraj without our feeling and

---

possibility. What I expect is that nothing of that kind will happen. In so far as I understand the British people, I will recognise the force of public opinion when it has become real and potent. Then, and only then, will they realise the hideous injustice which in their name the Imperial ministers and their representatives in India have perpetrated. They will therefore remedy the two wrongs in accordance with the wishes of the people, and they will also offer a constitution exactly in accordance with the wishes of the people of India, as represented by their chosen leaders."

"Supposing that the British Government wish to retire because India is not a paying concern, what do you think will then be the position of India?"

Mr. Gandhi answered: "At that stage surely it is easy to understand that India will then have evolved either outstanding spiritual height or the ability to offer violence against violence. She will have evolved an organising ability of a high order, and will therefore be in every way able to cope with any emergency that might arise."

"In other words," observed the *Times* representative, "you expect the moment of the British evacuation, if such a contingency arises, will coincide with the moment of India's preparedness and ability and conditions favourable for India to take over the Indian administration as a going concern and work it for the benefit and advancement of the nation?"

Mr. Gandhi answered the question with an emphatic affirmative. "My experience during the last months fills me with the hope," continued Mr. Gandhi, "that within the nine months that remain of the year in which I have expected Swaraj for India we shall redress the two wrongs and we shall see Swaraj established in accordance with the wishes of the people of India."

"Where will the present Government be at the end of the nine months?" Asked the *Times* representative.

Mr. Gandhi, with a significant smile, said: "The lion will then lie with the lamb."

being the equals of Englishmen. To-day we feel that we are dependent upon them for our internal and external security, for an armed peace between the Hindus and the Mussalmans, for our education and for the supply of daily wants, nay, even for the settlement of our religious squabbles. The Rajahs are dependent upon the British for their powers and the millionaires for their millions. The British know our helplessness and Sir Thomas Holland cracks jokes quite legitimately at the expense of Non-co-operationists. To get Swaraj then is to get rid of our helplessness. The problem is no doubt stupendous even as it is for the fabled lion who having been brought up in the company of goats found it impossible to feel that he was a lion. As Tolstoy used to put it, mankind often laboured under hypnotism. Under its spell continously we feel the feeling of helplessness. The British themselves cannot be expected to help us out of it. On the contrary, they din into our ears that we shall be fit to govern ourselves only by slow educative processes. The *Times* suggested that if we boycott the councils we shall lose the opportunity of a training in Swaraj. I have no doubt that there are many who believe what the *Times* says. It even resorts to a falsehood. It audaciously says that Lord Milner's Mission listened to the Egyptians only when they were ready to lift the boycott of the Egyptian Council. For me the only training in Swaraj we need is the ability to defend ourselves against the whole world and to live our natural life in perfect freedom even though it may be full of defects. Good Government is no substitute for self-Government. The Afghans have a bad Government but it is self-Government. I envy them. The Japanese learnt the art through a sea of blood. And if we to-day had the power to drive out the English by superior brute force, we would be counted their superiors, and in spite of our inexperience in debating at the Council table or in holding executive offices, we would be held fit to govern ourselves. For brute force is the only test the west has hitherto recognised. The Germans were defeated not because they were necessarily in the wrong, but because the allied Powers were found to possess greater brute strength. In the end, therefore, India must either learn the art of war which the British will not teach her, or she must follow her own way of discipline and self-sacrifice through Non-co-operation. It is as amazing as it is humiliating that less than one hundred-thousand white men would be able to rule three hundred and fifteen million Indians. They do so somewhat undoubtedly by force but more by securing our co-operation in a thousand ways and making us more and more helpless and dependent on them as time goes forward. Let us not mistake reformed councils, more law-courts and even governorships for real freedom or power. They are but subtler methods of emasculation. The British cannot rule us by mere force. And so they resort to all means, honourable and dishonourable, in order to retain their hold on India. They want India's billions and they want India's man power for their imperialistic greed. If we refuse to supply them with men and money, we achieve our goal, namely, Swaraj, equality, manliness.

The cup of our humiliation was filled during the closing scenes in the Viceregal Council. Mr. Shastri could not move his resolution on the Punjab. The Indian victims of Jallianwala received Rs. 1250, the English victims of mob-frenzy received lacs. The officials who were guilty of crimes against those whose servants they were, were reprimanded. And the councillors were satisfied. If

India were powerful, India would not have stood this addition of insult to her injury.

I do not blame the British. If we were weak in numbers as they are, we too would perhaps have resorted to the same methods as they are now employing. Terrorism and deception are weapons not of the strong but of the weak. The British are weak in numbers, we are weak in spite of our numbers. The result is that each is dragging the other down. It is common experience that Englishmen lose in character after residence in India and that Indians lose in courage and manliness by contact with Englishmen. This process of weakening is good neither for us two nations, nor for the world.

But if we Indians take care of ourselves, the English and the rest of the world would take care of themselves. Our contribution to the world's progress must, therefore, consist in setting our own house in order.

Training in arms for the present is out of the question. I go a step further and believe that India has a better mission for the world. It is within her power to show that she can achieve her destiny by pure self-sacrifice, *i.e.*, self-purification. This can be done only by Non-co-operation. And Non-co-operation is possible only when those who commenced to co-operate begin the process of withdrawal. If we can but free ourselves from the threefold *maya* of Government-controlled schools, Government law-courts and legislative councils, and truly control our own education, regulate our disputes and be indifferent to their legislation, we are ready to govern ourselves and we are only then ready to ask the Government servants, whether civil or military, to resign, and the tax-payers to suspend payment of taxes.

And is it such an impracticable proposition to expect parents to withdraw their children from schools and colleges and establish their own institutions or to ask lawyers to suspend their practice and devote their whole time and attention to national service against payment, where necessary, of their maintenance, or to ask candidates for councils not to enter councils and lead their passive or active assistance to the legislative machinery through which all control is exercised? The movement of Non-co-operation is nothing but an attempt to isolate the brute force of the British from all the trappings under which it is hidden and to show that brute force by itself cannot for one single moment hold India.

But I frankly confess that, until the three conditions mentioned by me are fulfilled, there is no Swaraj. We may not go on taking our college degrees, taking thousands of rupees monthly from clients for cases which can be finished in five minutes and taking the keenest delight in wasting national time on the council floor and still expect to gain national self-respect.

The last, though not the least, important part of the *maya* still remains to be considered. That is Swadeshi. Had we not abandoned Swadeshi, we need not have been in the present fallen state. If we would get rid of the economic slavery, we must manufacture our own cloth and at the present moment only by hand-spinning and hand-weaving.

All this means discipline, self-denial, self-sacrifice, organising ability, confidence and courage. If we show this in one year among the classes that to-day count, and make public opinion, we certainly gain Swaraj within one year. If I am told that even we who lead have not these qualities in us, there certainly will never be Swaraj for India but then we shall have no right to blame the English for what they are doing. Our salvation and its time are solely dependent upon us.

13*th July*, 1921

AN INDIAN REPUBLIC

An esteemed correspondent writes:

"Your attention must have been drawn to statements made by Maulana Mohamed Ali and Shaukat Ali that, 'if no settlement is arrived at before Christmas regarding our campaign, an Indian republic will be declared at the Ahmedabad session of the Congress. Special importance attaches to this statement, as it is not made by any irresponsible person but by responsible leaders like the Maulanas. It is felt, however, that the statement is both unfortunate and premature, and is likely to come in the way of the programme laid down for the country by the Congress. The country as a whole has responded magnificently to the appeal of the Congress, and is prepared, excepting certain sections, to work for the attainment of Swaraj. I would ask you to give your views regarding the Maulanas' statement, and to assure the public that no departure from the policy of Non-violent Non-co-operation accepted by the Congress, will be made."

I am sorry to have to confess, that I have not seen the Maulanas' declaration, but I have no hesitation in giving the assurance, that no stone will be left unturned by me to prevent a departure even by a hair's breadth from the policy of Non-violent Non-co-operation that has been deliberately adopted by the country. Nor do I entertain the slightest fear of any departure from that policy on the part of the Brothers. I have however no difficulty about understanding the Maulanas' mind. They are quite capable of saying, that if India does not get the relief she demands in the matters of the Punjab and the Khilafat, she will at the next session of the Congress make a declaration of independence. Swaraj within the Empire is a possibility, only if England washes her hands clean of the taint of the Khilafat breach and the Jallianwala Bagh massacre. The Congress creed has been purposely made elastic enough to admit of a demand for independence. To go no further, the Maulanas have, after all, if they have, but reiterated the opinion pronounced by Mr. Andrews, who, unlike me, considers that there is no room in the British Empire for a self-respecting and self-governing India, and who expects that some day, I shall myself be driven to that position. I am differently constituted. I never give up hope so long as there is the least chance, and I have faith enough in the British people to feel that, whilst they will test our determination and strength to the uttermost, they will not carry it to the breaking point. They are too self-conscious to part with an India awakened and strong for the sake of shielding Dyerism and O'Dwyerism and of the questionable advantage of Greek friendship. The Non-conformist conscience which is ignorantly hostile to the just aspirations of the brave Turks, will prove yielding under the Indian strain which is daily gathering force. Long before the Congress meets, if India proves true to herself, I look forward not to a Declaration of Independence, but to an honourable settlement that will satisfy the just demand of India *re*: the Punjab and the Khilafat, and that will assure to her full immediate Swaraj in accordance with the wishes of her chosen representatives. Let the reader, however, not run away with the idea, that my forecast is based upon any knowledge of what is going on in Simla or Whitehall. I base it upon my profound belief in the ability of India during the next three months to assert herself, *i.e.*, in the ability of India to carry out an almost complete boycott of foreign cloth, and by still greater self-restraint to prove her ability to adopt Civil Disobedience of a very stern character.

5th January, 1922

INDEPENDENCE

(By M. K. Gandhi)

Maulana Hasrat Mohani put up a plucky fight for Independence on the Congress platform and then as President of the Muslim League and was happily each time defeated. There is no mistake about the meaning of the Maulana. He wants to sever all connections with the British people even as partners and equals and even though the Khilafat question be satisfactorily solved. It will not do to urge that the Khilafat question can never be solved without complete independence. We are discussing merely the theory. It is common cause that if the Khilafat question cannot be solved without complete independence, *i.e.*, if the British people retain hostile attitude towards the aspirations of the Islamic world, there is nothing left for us to do but to insist upon complete independence. India cannot afford to give Britain even her moral support and must do without Britain's support moral and material, if she cannot be induced to be friendly to the Islamic world.

But assuming that Great Britain alters her attitude, as I know she will when India is strong, it will be religiously unlawful for us to insist on independence. For it will be vindictive and petulant. It would amount to a denial of God, for the refusal will then be based upon the assumption that the British people are not capable of response to the God in man. Such a position is untenable for both a believing Mussalman and a believing Hindu.

India's greatest glory will consist not in regarding Englishmen as her implacable enemies fit only to be turned out of India at the first available opportunity but in turning them into friends and partners in a new commonwealth of nations in the place of an Empire based upon exploitation of the weaker or undeveloped nations and races of the earth and therefore finally upon force.

Let us see clearly what Swaraj together with the British connection means. It means undoubtedly India's ability to declare her independence, if she wishes. Swaraj therefore will not be a free gift of the British Parliament. It will be a declaration of India's full self-expression. That it will be expressed through an Act of Parliament is true. But it will be merely a courteous ratification of the declared wish of the people of India even as it was in the case of the Union of South Africa. Not an unnecessary adverb in the Union scheme could be altered by the House of Commons. The ratification in our case will be of a treaty to which Britain will be party.

Such Swaraj may not come this year, may not come within our generation. But I have contemplated nothing less. The British Parliament, when the settlement comes, will ratify the wishes of the people of India as expressed not through the bureaucracy but through her freely chosen representatives.

Swaraj can never be a free gift by one nation to another. It is a treasure to be purchased with a nation's best blood. It will cease to be a gift when we have paid dearly for it. The Viceroy was confused when he said that Swaraj would have to come from the Parliament unless it came by the sword. He paid no compliment to his country when he allowed his audience to infer that England was incapable of listening to the moral pressure of suffering, and he insulted the intelligence of his audience if he wished it to understand that the British Parliament would give Swaraj when it wished, irrespective of India's desires and aspirations. The fact is that Swaraj will be a fruit of incessant labour, suffering beyond measure.

But His Excellency is unused to any substitute for the sword and therefore does probably think that by exercising our debating skill in the legislative councils, some day or other we shall be able to impress the British Parliament with the desirability of granting us Swaraj. He will soon learn that there is better and more effective substitute for the sword and that is Civil Disobedience. It is daily becoming increasingly clear that Civil Disobedience will afford the course of suffering through which India must pass before she comes to her own.

We have not come to our own. There is still mutual distrust between Mussalmans and Hindus. The untouchables have not yet felt the glow of the Hindu touch. The Parsis and the Christians of India do not yet know their future under Swaraj to a certainty. We have not yet learnt the art nor realised the necessity of obeying our own laws. The spinning wheel has not yet found a permanent place in our homes. *Khadi* has not yet become the national garment. In other words, we have not yet understood the art or the conditions of self-protection.

There is still a body of opinion diminishing in volume but not yet negligible which considers that violence alone will bring Swaraj to us and that therefore violence might be permitted to continue side by side with non-violence, *i.e.*, our non-violence should be regarded as merely a prelude to and a preparation for violence. Those who hold these views little know that their attitude constitutes a fraud upon the world. Our pledge requires that whilst we are under it we believe in the efficacy of non-violence for the quickest attainment of our goal. Each one of us is under a sacred obligation to cancel the pledge as soon as he believes that Swaraj is unattainable by non-violenee or except by violence. Non-violence is a creed while it lasts. It is an expedient because it is an experiment. But whilst we are under the pledge, we are not only bound to believe in and observe non-violence but we are equally bound to persuade others to be non-violent and condemn those who do violence. I am more than ever convinced that we have not reached our goal because even we who have subscribed to the Congress creed have not all remained non-violent in word and deed nor endeavoured to be non-violent in thought or intent.

8th December, 1920

ON THE WRONG TRACK

(BY M. K. GANDHI)

Lord Ronaldshay has been doing me the favour of reading my booklet on Indian Home Rule which is a translation of *Hind Swaraj*. His Lordship told his audience that if Swaraj meant what I had described it to be in the booklet, the Bengalis would have none of it. I am sorry that Swaraj of the Congress resolution does not mean the Swaraj depicted in the booklet: Swaraj according to the Congress means Swaraj that the people of India want, not what the British Government may condescend to give. In so far as I can see, Swaraj will be a Parliament chosen by the people with the fullest power over the finance, the police, the military, the navy, the courts and the educational institutions.*

I am free to confess that the Swaraj I expect to gain within one year, if India responds, will be such Swaraj

* In the course of a speech at Calcutta on 13th October, 1920, Mr. Gandhi had something to say on his idea of Swaraj. He said: Lord Ronaldshay who has done me the honour of reading my booklet on Home Rule has warned my countrymen against engaging themselves in a struggle for a Swaraj such as is described in that booklet. Now though I do not want to withdraw a single word of it, I would say to you on this occasion that I do not ask India to follow out to-day the methods prescribed in my booklet. If they could do that, they would have Home Rule not in a year but in a day, and India by realising that ideal wants to acquire an ascendency over the rest of the world. But it must remain a day dream more or less for the time being. What I am doing to-day is that I am giving the country a pardonable programme, not for the abolition of law courts, posts, telegraphs and of railways, but for the attainment of Parliamentary Swaraj.

He added: It was not a joke when I said on the Congress platform that Swaraj would be established in one year if there was sufficient response from the nation. . . .

I have proposed a limited programme workable within one year having especial regard to the educated classes. We seem to be labouring under the illusion that we cannot possibly live without Councils, law courts and schools provided by the Government. The moment we are disillusioned we have Swaraj. It is demoralising both for Government and the governed that a hundred thousand pilgrims should dictate terms to a nation composed of three hundred millions. And how is it they can thus dictate terms? It is because we have been divided and they have ruled. I have never forgotten Hume's frank confession that the British Government was sustained by the policy of "Divide and Rule." Therefore it is that I have laid stress upon Hindu-Moslem Unity as one of the most important essentials for the success of Non-co-operation. But it should be no lip unity, nor *bania* unity, it should be a unity broad-based on a recognition of the heart . . . Light brings light, not darkness, and nobility done with a noble purpose will be twice rewarded.

as will make practically impossible the repetition of the Khilafat and the Punjab wrongs, and will enable the nation to do good or evil as it chooses, and not be 'good' at the dictation of an irresponsible, insolent, and godless bureaucracy. Under that Swaraj, the nation will have the power to impose a heavy protective tariff on such foreign goods as are capable of being manufactured in India, as also the power to refuse to send a single soldier outside India for the purpose of enslaving the surrounding or remote nationalities. The Swaraj that I dream of will be a possibility only when the nation is free to make its choice both of good and evil.

I adhere to all I have said in that booklet and I would certainly recommend it to the reader. Government over self is the truest Swaraj, it is synonymous with *moksha* or salvation, and I have seen nothing to alter the view that doctors, lawyers, and railways are no help, and are often a hindrance, to the one thing worth striving after.

* * *

But it has become the fashion now-a-days to ascribe hatred to Non-co-operationism. And I regret to find that even Col. Wedgwood has fallen into a trap. I make bold to say that the only way to remove hatred is to give it disciplined vent. No man can—I cannot—perform the impossible task of removing hatred so long as contempt and despise for the feelings of India are sedulously nursed. It is a mockery to ask India not to hate when in the same breath India's most sacred feelings are contemptuously brushed aside. India feels weak and helpless and so expresses her helplessness by hating the tyrant who despises her and makes her crawl on the belly, lifts the veils of her innocent women and compels her tender children to acknowledge his power by saluting his flag four times a day. The gospel of

Non-co-operation addresses itself to the task of making the people strong and self-reliant. It is an attempt to transform hatred into pity.

A strong and self-reliant India will cease to hate Bosworth Smiths and Frank Johnsons, for she will have the power to punish them and therefore the power also to pity and forgive them. To-day she can neither punish nor forgive, and therefore helplessly nurses hatred.

16th February, 1921

WHAT WILL KILL NON-CO-OPERATION?

(By M. K. Gandhi)

Certainly violence on the part of Non-co-operators. But that is not what I wanted to answer. What can the Government do to kill Non-co-operation?—Is the question I have been asked. A settlement of the Khilafat in accordance with the Muslim demand, a settlement of the Punjab in accordance with the Indian demand, and the grant of Swaraj in accordance with a scheme to be framed by authorised representatives of the nation.

What is Swaraj? That is the next question. It is partly answered in the foregoing paragraph. No one man can produce a swaraj scheme because it is not one man's swaraj that is wanted nor can a scheme be framed in advance. What may satisfy the nation today may not satisfy it to-morrow. Our evolution is and must be an organic growth. National will is therefore subject to change from day to-day. But some broad outlines can certainly be laid down in advance of Swaraj. The nation's representatives must have full control over education, law, police and military. We must have full financial control. And if we are to be self-governing, not a soldier can leave India without our consent.

What about European interests? They will be as safe in a self-governing India as they are to-day. But there will be no privileges of a superior race, no concessions and no exploitation. Englishmen will live as friends in every sense of the term but not as rulers.

And as to the British connection, nobody, so far as I am aware, wants to end it for the sake of ending it. There must be complete independence if England's policy is in conflict with the Muslim sentiment on the Khilafat question or with the Indian sentiment in the Punjab. In any case, it must be a partnership at will, based upon mutual love and esteem.

Is India ready for this? Time will show. I am convinced that it is. The Swaraj that the Congress demands is not one that is to be granted by England. It must be that which the nation demands, and can enforce, in the same sense that South Africa received it.

PART VIII

TOWARDS CIVIL DISOBEDIENCE

PART VIII

TOWARDS CIVIL DISOBEDIENCE

22nd September, 1921

THE LAST ACT

(By M. K. GANDHI)

THE much talked of arrest* of Maulana Mahomed Ali took place at Waltair, whilst we were on our way to Madras. I am writing this in the train, just after writing out a few telegrams. The train halted at Waltair for over twenty-five minutes. Maulana Mahomed Ali and I were going outside the station to address a meeting. Hardly had we gone a few paces from the entrance, when I heard the Maulana shouting to me and reading the notice given to him. I was a few paces in front of him. Two whitemen and half a dozen Indian police composed the party of arrest. The officer in charge would not let the Maulana finish reading the notice, but grasped his arm and took the Maulana away. With a smile on his lips he waved good-bye. I understood the

*Arrested under Secs. 107 and 108 Cr.P.C. only to be taken to Karachi to be tried under Secs. 121-A and 124-A I. P. C. The arrest inaugurated a campaign of repression against the Non-co-operation movement which was intensified when the Prince of Wales arrived a few days later. *See* appendix.

meaning. I was to keep the flag flying. May God help me to prove worthy of the message of a Comrade with whom it was a privilege to work.

I continued my journey to the meeting place. I asked the people to remain calm, and fulfil the Congress programme. I then retraced my steps, and went where the Maulana was being detained. I asked the officer in charge whether I could see the Maulana. He said he had orders to let his wife and Secretary only meet him. I saw Begum Mahomed Ali and Secretary Mr. Hayat coming out of the detention room.

Waltair is a beauty spot in Andhra. It is a sanatorium. I envied the Maulana his arrest at such a lovely place. He was contemplating staying at Waltair a few days to rest and complete his accounts of the deputation. But the unexpectedly long stay in Bengal and the Moplah outbreak had rendered it impossible.

God had willed it otherwise. He wanted to give the Maulana enforced rest. And I know that he is happy in his detention.

Here is a copy of the warrant of arrest:

"To

F. E. CUNNINGHAM, Esq.,
Deputy Inspector General of Police,
C. I. D. and Railways, Madras.

Whereas Mahomed Ali is to be called on to show cause why he should not be bound over to keep the peace or to be of good behaviour for a period of one year under Secs. 107 and 108 Cr. P. C., you are hereby directed to arrest the said Mahomed Ali and produce him before me. Therein fail not. Dated the 14th day of September, 1921.

(Sd.) J. R. HUGGINS,
Dt. Magistrate, Vizagapatam."

Is it not funny that he, who has not only been himself peaceful, but has endeavoured, and that successfully, to ensure peace among others and who has been a pattern of good behaviour, should be called upon by an insolent power to be 'bound over to keep the peace and be of good behaviour'? A Government that is evil has no room for good men and women except in its prisons.

What has happened to the younger is bound to happen to the elder brother.* They call themselves Siamese twins. They are inseparable. And if the one has misbehaved, the other undoubtedly has. I hope, that by the time this is in print, India would have learnt of the Maulana Shaukat Ali's arrest.

In imprisoning Maulana Mohamed Ali, the Government has imprisoned the Khilafat. For, the two brothers are the truest representatives of the Khilafat. They cannot rest so long as the Khalifat remains practically a prisoner and their holy places virtually under non-Muslim control. The imprisonment of either or both means a flat refusal to recognise the Khilafat claim.

The Government will however find that they have not succeeded in imprisoning the spirit of the Brothers, and that the Khilafat struggle will rage all the fiercer for their imprisonment. The spirit of the Brothers will live in every true Hindu and Mussalman who will keep the Khilafat flame steady and shining.

But the Brothers to-day stand for more than the Khilafat. They want Swaraj and the redress of the Punjab wrong equally with the redress of the Khilafat wrong. They are too honourable to sell themselves even for securing the redress of the Khilafat wrong. To them the three are inextricably mixed up. It cannot well be otherwise, for to grant or to get the one is to grant or to get the other.

For me the imprisonment is a good omen. The

*Shaukat Ali was also subsequently arrested and taken to Karachi.

Government were playing with the thing so long as they were arresting the rank and file. Every Government that does not wish to yield to popular will is bound to arrest popular leaders and attempt to crush the popular spirit. With the Indian Government, it has become the code of honour to arrest and imprison leaders and yield to popular will when there is no grace left in the giving.

This imprisonment therefore may safely be regarded as a preliminary to the establishment of Swaraj. Only the Swaraj Parliament can unlock the gaol gate and relieve the Brothers and their fellow prisoners with becoming honours. For this is a fight to the finish.

The best tribute we can pay the Brothers and their fellow prisoners is to throw away all doubts, fears and lethargy. We have been doubtful as to the value of non-violence and Swadeshi for attainment of our goal, and our ability to finish the programme within the year. We have entertained fear regarding our ability to undergo the necessary sacrifice, and we have been prosecuting our programme lazily. Let us imitate the courage, the faith, the fearlessness, the truthfulness, and the vigilant incessant activity of the Brothers, and we shall certainly attain Swaraj. 'Therein fail not' were the concluding words of the Magistrate's order. Well, the officer in charge 'failed not': Many an English officer, be it said to his credit, has lost his life in trying not to fail. The Congress and the Khilafat command, mandate, advice, whatever it may be called, is 'Therein fail not.' Shall we, during the remaining period of grace, so work as to be able to report to the Congress, 'we have failed not'? The orders are clear:

(1) Be non-voilent even under the greatest provocation.

(2) Preserve Hindu-Muslim unity even under the severest strain.

(3) Boycott the use of foreign cloth, even though you may have to be satisfied with the merest loin-cloth, and take to hand spinning, during every odd moment that can be spared.

When we have carried out these conditions, but not till then, are we ready to offer Civil Disobedience, that will compel obedience from the mightiest Government to a people's wish.

6th October, 1921

FREEDOM OF OPINION

The following Manifesto appeared in "Young India" of 6th October, 1921:

In view of the prosecution of the Ali Brothers and others for the reasons stated in the Government of Bombay Communique* dated the 15th September 1921, we, the undersigned, speaking in our individual capacity, desire to state that it is the inherent right of every one to express his opinion without restraint about the propriety of citizens offering their services to, or remaining in the employ of the Government, whether in the civil or the military department.

We, the undersigned, state it as our opinion, that it is contrary to national dignity for any Indian to serve as a civilian, and more especially as a soldier, under a system of Government, which has brought about India's economic, moral and political degradation and which has used the soldiery and the police for repressing national aspirations, as, for instance, at the time of the Rowlatt Act agitation, and which has used the soldiers for crushing the liberty of the Arabs, the Egyptians, the Turks and other nations who have done no harm to India.

* Omitted in this collection.

We are also of opinion that it is the duty of every Indian soldier and civilian to sever his connection with the Government and find some other means of livelihood.

M.K. Gandhi; Abdul Kalam Azad, (Calcutta); Ajmal Khan, (Delhi); Lajpatrai, (Lahore); Motilal Nehru, (Allahabad); Sarojini Naidu, (Bombay); Abbas Taiyabji; N. C. Kelkar; V. J. Patel; Vallabhbhai J. Patel, (Ahmedabad); M. R. Jayakar, (Bombay); D. V. Gokhale, (Poona); S. G. Banker; Jawahirlal Nehru, (Allahabad); Gangadhar B. Deshpande, (Belgaum); Lakshmidas Tersi; Umar Sobani; Jamnalal Bajaj; M. S. Ane, (Amraoti); S. E. Stokes, (Kotgarh, Simla); M. A. Ansari, (Delhi); Khaliquzzaman, (Delhi); K. M. Abdul Gafur, (Delhi); Abdul Bari, (Lucknow); Krishnaji Nilkanth, (Belgaum); C. Rajagopalachari, (Madras); Konda Venkatappayya, (Guntur); G. Harisarvottam Rao, (Guntur); Anasuya Sarabhai; Jitendralal Banerji; Mushir Husen Kidwai, (Delhi); Shyam Sundara Chakravarthi, (Calcutta); Rajendra Prasad, (Patna); Azad Sobani, (Lucknow); Hazrat Mohani, (Cawnpore); Mahadeo Haribhai Desai; Barjorji Framji Bharucha; Yakub Hasan; B. S. Munje, (Nagpur); Jeramdas Dolatram; M. R. Cholkar, (Nagpur); V. V. Dartane, (Bhusaval); Ahmed Haji Sidick Khatri, (Bombay); Gudar Ramachandra Rao, (Andhra); D. S. Vijayarao, (Lahore); B. L. Subaramayya, (Andhra); Mia Mahomed Haji Jan Mahomed Chhotani.*

6th October, 1921

EXPRESSION OF OPINION

Mahatma Gandhi wrote in "Young India" of the 6th October, under the above heading:

When in any movement violence is religiously eschewed, it becomes a propaganda movement of the purest type. Any attempt to crush it is an attempt to crush public opinion. And such the present repression

*In a subsequent issue of *Young India*, Mr. Gandhi stated that innumerable letters had been received by him requesting that the writer's name also be added to the list of signatories of the manifesto including one from Mr. C. R. Das.

has become. Why should I not express my profound conviction,

(1) that it is sinful to serve the Government in any capacity whatsoever, especially that of a soldier,

(2) that it is sinful to drink intoxicating liquors,

(3) that it is sinful to wear foreign cloth,

(4) that it is sinful to gamble or speculate in foodstuffs or cotton?

The Government may, as it is carrying on a counter-propaganda, successfully draw recruits for civil and military employment, by various methods induce people to drink and wear foreign cloth and speculate in foodstuffs and cotton, and thus continue to govern so long as people intentionally or ignorantly co-operate with it. It will fall the day the people are convinced to the contrary. And just as I carry on my propaganda among the wine-bibbers and the cotton speculators to wean them from their evil ways, I claim the right to tell the soldier face to face what is his duty in accordance with my opinion. Why should the soldier be kept in ignorance of what is going on in the country? Is the Government afraid, that if he comes to know the truth he will no longer serve it? A Government worth the name should be able fully to educate the soldiery and hold its loyalty. But in India everything is armed,—peace, loyalty and opinion. Only the people are disarmed. Our duty therefore is clear. We must claim, even though it be on the gallows, to hold and openly to express any opinion we choose, so long as we do not directly or indirectly cause violence. That is the battle of Non-violent Non-co-operation. It must be fought to the finish. I warn the public that the prosecution for 'tampering with the loyalty of the army' is but the precursor of prosecutions for tampering with the loyalty of the people to foreign cloth. What was the burning of the *Khadi* vests and caps of the young men of Calicut? What is the crusade against the students of the Vizagapatam Medical School, if it is not an insensate crusade against *Khadi*?

13th October, 1921

THE FEAR OF DEATH

(By M. K. Gandhi)

I have been collecting descriptions of Swaraj. One of these would be: Swaraj is the abandonment of the fear of death. A nation which allows itself to be influenced by the fear of death cannot attain Swaraj, and cannot retain it if somehow attained.

English people carry their lives in their pockets. Arabs and Pathans consider death as nothing more than an ordinary ailment; they never weep when a relation dies. Boer women are perfectly innocent of this fear. In the Boer war, thousands of young Boer women became widowed. They never cared. It did not matter in the least if the husband or the son was lost; it was enough and more than enough that the country's honour was safe. What booted the husband if the country was enslaved? It was infinitely better to bury a son's mortal remains and to cherish his immortal memory than to bring him up as a serf. Thus did the Boer women steel their hearts and cheerfully give up their darlings to the angel of Death.

The people I have mentioned kill and get killed. But what of those who do not kill, but are only ready to die themselves? Such people become the objects of a world's adoration. They are the salt of the earth.

The English and Germans fought one another; they

killed and got killed. The result is that animosities have increased. There is no end of unrest, and the present condition of Europe is pitiful. There is more of deceit, and each is anxious to circumvent the rest.

But the fearlessness which we are cultivating is of a nobler and purer order and it is therefore that we hope to achieve a signal victory within a very short time.

When we attain Swaraj, many of us will have given up the fear of death; or else we shall not have attained Swaraj. Till now mostly young boys have died in the cause. Those who died in Aligarh were all below twenty-one. No one knew who they were. If Government resort to firing now, I am hoping that some men of the first rank will have the opportunity of offering up the supreme sacrifice.

Why should we be upset when children or young men or old men die? Not a moment passes when some one is not born or is not dead in this world. We should feel the stupidity of rejoicing in a birth and lamenting a death. Those who believe in the soul—and what Hindu, Musalman or Parsi is there who does not?—know that the soul never dies. The souls of the living as well as of the dead are all one. The eternal processes of creation and destruction are going on ceaselessly. There is nothing in it for which we might give ourselves up to joy or sorrow. Even if we extend the idea of relationship only to our countrymen and take all the births in the country as taking place in our own family, how many births shall we celebrate? If we weep for all the deaths in our country, the tears in our eyes would never dry. This train of thought should help us to get rid of all fear of death.

India, they say, is a nation of philosophers; and we have not been unwilling to appropriate the compliment

Still, hardly any other nation becomes so helpless in the face of death as we do. And in India again, no other community perhaps betrays so much of this helplessness as the Hindus. A single birth is enough for us to be beside ourselves with ludicrous joyfulness. A death makes us indulge in orgies of loud lamentation which condemn the neighbourhood to sleeplessness for the night. If we wish to attain Swaraj, and if having attained it, wish to make it something to be proud of, we must perfectly renounce this unseemly fright.

And what is imprisonment to the man who is fearless of death itself? If the reader will bestow a little thought upon the matter, he will find that if Swaraj is delayed, it is delayed because we are not prepared calmly to meet death and inconveniences less than death.

As larger and larger numbers of innocent men come out to welcome death, their sacrifice will become the potent instrument for the salvation of all others; and there will be a minimum of suffering. Suffering cheerfully endured ceases to be suffering and is transmuted into an ineffable joy. The man who flies from suffering is the victim of endless tribulation before it has come to him, and is half dead when it does come. But one who is cheerfully ready for anything and everything that comes, escapes all pain; his cheerfulness acts as an anæsthetic.

I have been led to write about this subject, because we have got to envisage even death, if we will have Swaraj this very year. One who is previously prepared often escapes accidents; and this may well be the case with us. It is my firm conviction that Swadeshi constitutes this preparation. When once Swadeshi is a success, neither this Government nor any one else will feel the necessity of putting us to any further test.

Still it is best no to neglect any contingency whatever. Possession of power makes men blind and deaf; they cannot see things which are under their very nose, and cannot hear things which invade their ears. There is thus no knowing what this power-intoxicated Government may not do. So it seemed to me that patriotic men ought to be prepared for death, imprisonment and similar eventualities.

The brave meet death with a smile on their lips, but they are circumspect all the same. There is no room for foolhardiness in this non-violent war. We do not propose to go to gaol or to die by an immoral act. We must mount the gallows while resisting the oppressive laws of this Government. (Translated from the Gujarati *Navajivan* by D.)

8th December, 1921

IN EARNEST

(By M. K. Gandhi)

The arrest of Lala Lajpatrai and Messrs. Lalkhan, Santanam and Gopichand in the Punjab, of Messrs. Phooken and Bardolai in Assam, Babu Jitendralal Banerji in Bengal, Maulana Mohiuddin and others in Ajmer and Mr. Harkarannath Mishra and others in Lucknow means business.* It shows not merely that the Government is in earnest but that it is not going to tolerate Non-co-operation any longer; no longer is it a question of putting down violence, it is one of compelling co-operation. And this is as it should be. The Government had to appear in its true colours some day or other. No Prince had such welcome as is being offered to the

*For other measures and methods of repression, *see* appendix.

Prince of Wales. The chosen leaders of the people are being put away so that the latter may accept the lead of the Government and so that there may be no *hartal* on the day of the Prince's entry into the various provinces.

All this the Government of India, constituted as it is, has a right to do, and we non-co-operate because it claims and exercises such right on due occasion. The right consists in its imposing its will upon the people, not recognising that of the people to have their own way except on pain of being imprisoned. The issue is clear, and neatly summed up in the Lawrence statue whose removal the Government will not allow, although it is the property in law of the people. It must govern by the Pen or the Sword. Once more the choice has been offered to the people. Will they accept the honourable imposition of the Sword and reject the degrading dictation of the Pen ?

The people cannot complain if after fifteen months' training they do not know what to do. Indeed the best thing they can do is to do nothing, *i.e.*, to remain as they were and continue as if nothing extraordinary had happened. England did not stop the war because Lord Kitchener died. 'Business as usual was her motto. She was well organised for violence—well enough to do without a general or to find an endless succession of generals. Are we so well organised for Non-violence as to do without leaders, *i.e.*, have an endless succession of them ?

In the person of Lala Lajpatrai the Government have arrested one of the greatest of us. His name is known all over India. His self-sacrifice has enshrined him in the hearts of his countrymen. He has laboured as very few have for non-violence side by side with the freest expression and organisation of public opinion. His arrest typifies, as nothing else can, the attitude of the Government.

The Punjab has lost no time in choosing a successor.* The Punjabis could not have made a better choice than by electing Agha Safdar. He is one of the truest of Mussalmans and one of the bravest of Indians. His services are all rendered in a most unassuming manner. I have no doubt that he will command the same loyal co-operation that Lalaji has. The best honour that the Punjabis can do to Lalaji is to continue his work as if he was in their midst. It is blind, foolish and selfish love which dissolves with the disappearance, permanent or temporary, of the earthy tabernacle which holds the deathless spirit. The Punjabis may not always get an Agha Safdar to guide them in the place of Lalaji. He may be removed from their midst sooner than we may expect. In well ordered organisations leaders are elected for convenience of work, not for extraordinary merit. A leader is only first among equals. Some one must be put first, but he is and should be no stronger than the weakest link in the chain. Having therefore made our selection we must follow him, or the chain is broken and all is loose.

I wish I could impart my faith to the people that nothing much remains to be done in order to take us to the heaven. The way is clear before us. The President-elect has stated it in unquivocal terms: 'My first word and my last word to you is never to forsake the ideal of Non-violent Non-co-operation. I know that sometimes the provocation is so great that it is extremely difficult to remain non-violent in thought, word and deed. The

* About the procedure that people should adopt in case of arrests and of conduct in jail, see *infra*.

success of the movement, however, depends upon this great principle.'

In order to enable us to enforce this great principle in our own lives, we must avoid all occasions for provocation. We therefore need no demonstrations now nor big meetings, we must discipline those who have become awakened to withstand provocation and to do constructive national work which is organisation of carding, hand-spinning and hand-weaving, so as to enable the nation to supplement her slender resources and to find work for the idle hours of the millions. Hindu-Muslim unity is an article of faith with us. It is not to be cultivated or demonstrated except by all working together for national uplift and, therefore, devoting their time exculsively to manufacture of *Khadi*.

As soon as we have attained a complete boycott of foreign cloth and begun to manufacture our own *Khadi* in our respective provinces and villages, we can become free probably without having to resort to mass Civil Disobedience. Therefore aggressive Civil Disobedience should be avoided, at least till after finishing the boycott of foreign cloth and qualifying for the manufacture of of handspun *Khadi*. Defensive Civil Disobedience which is forced on us in the prosecution of our campaign we ought to welcome, whenever it comes.

It will be a distinct sign of weakness and unfitness for Swaraj, if these imprisonments dishearten or demoralize us. He is no soldier who is afraid or unwilling to pay the toll demanded of him. The more he is called upon to pay, the more glad he is to find himself the first to have to pay. Let us believe and know that we must provide the Government gaols with all the work they can take. I am convinced that it is not argument but suffering of the innocent that appeals both to the persecutor and the persecuted. The nation will shed her slothful indifference and the Governors their callousness by the sight of such suffering. But it must be the willing suffering of the strong and not the unwilling suffering of the helpless weak. Those who have gone or are about to go to goal can say, 'It is finished.' We who remain outside have to prove worthy of their finished work by continuing their work till we have set them free or have joined them. He serves best who suffers most.

15th December, 1921

DESHABANDHU DAS

Lord Reading has been as good as his word. The highest in the land has not been immune from arrest. Lord Ronaldshay had perhaps given the public to understand that he would not be arrested till after the Congress and, then too, if he did not behave himself. But Lord Reading's threat was later than, and therefore cancelled, the implied opinion of Lord Ronaldshay. Why should the President-elect be left free, if he enlisted volunteers and issued manifestoes? There was no cessation in the activity for bringing about *hartal* on the day of the Prince's arrival in Calcutta. It was some such reasoning, I suppose, that was applied in effecting the arrest of the President-elect. His arrest was accompanied by that of other prominent workers. Maulana Abul Kalam Azad, one of the most learned among Mussalman divines, Maulvi Akramkhan, the Secretary of the Khilafat Committee, Mr. Sasmal, Secretary of the Provincial Congress Committee and Mr. Padmaraj Jain who exercised influence over the Marwadis were arrested with the President-elect. This must be obviously to prevent *hartal*. These arrests mean that the authorities do not want to tolerate even quiet persuasion and canvassing. They want in fact a forcible opening of shops. They will not adopt the way of Colonel Johnson and threaten to open the shops and put soldiers in charge, but they wish to influence the timid shopkeepers by arresting their leaders. The merchants of Calcutta have now a chance of showing their determination and independence by observing complete *hartal* in spite of the withdrawal of leaders. It is more necessary than ever for the people now to observe *hartal* on the 24th. The idea of making a demonstration has now become a subsidiary object. The honour of their leaders requires the people of Calcutta to observe a complete *hartal.* It will be a proof of their confidence in their leaders and proof also of the exercise of their own free will. I am hoping that the people of Calcutta will not fail to do their obvious duty on the 24th instant. And now that their leaders are withdrawn from them, every non-co-operator will constitute himself a leader for keeping the peace. They cannot do better than simply keep themselves at home on the 24th except volunteers whose duty it will be to protect from harm those who may choose to open their shops. I assume that both the Congress and the Khilafat Committees have elected fresh, office bearers. Our true test is certainly now. The assumption of leadership to-day is like the assumption of Lord Mayorship by the late Mac Swiney. It carries with it the liability for immediate imprisonment. If the nation is truly awakened, there should be a ceaseless flow of leaders and men and women to be led. Our supply must always be equal to the demand made upon us by the Government. We win when we have established sufficient credit for ourselves for being able to cope with the demand.

22nd December, 1921

THINGS THAT SINK

(By M. K. Gandhi)

To imprison those who, whether high or low, break the commandments, to treat them as common felons, to deprive them of their privileges, one can understand. I would not call that foul play. If you incur the wrath of one who is over you or who has you under his power for the time being, to be punished by him for your disobedience is what you expect. But if he humiliates you, if he makes your children, do things you and they do not like and which you are not required in law to do, if he treats you like dirt, it becomes unbearable. One learns that in Coconada a Magistrate had the Swaraj and the Khilafat flags pulled down, that he issued orders prohibiting the use of such flags for one week, that the children of a school were compelled to salute the Union Jack, that a distinguished Professor in Calcutta, going out in his academic costume and, on the strength thereof, going up to an officer to stop a wanton hunt of inoffensive men, was brutally assaulted for his innocent inquiry as to the cause of the hunt, that a party of brave cultured young men were kicked about by those who were their warders for the time being. These are things that sink. These humiliations show that there is little change in the manners of our 'masters'. The O'Dwyerian spirit has not died out. Of what use is it that Lord Ronaldshay sends for the injured Professor, soothes him and assures him that the thing will not happen again? What will not happen again? The Professor will not be assaulted? Of course he will not be during the present crisis. The Professor himself will not again presume upon his academic costume and challenge an officer very soon. But has the officer any respect for the Professor? The Professor did not seek relief for himself. He interceded for injured humanity. Will Indian humanity be protected and respected in future because of his Lordship's assurance? It is the habitual training given to the soldier that matters. He is converted into a vicious animal to be let loose on harmless people on given occasions. The Dases and the Azads have gone to gaol to prevent a repetition of such unmanly and brutal exhibitions. They have welcomed imprisonment, in order that even the worst criminal may be protected against wanton injury, that even he may not have his self-respect wounded. They have not gone to gaol for any mechanical transference of power. The organic change they want, that Lala Lajpatrai has been pining for years, that has become the breath of life for the ease-loving Motilal Nehru and has made of him practically a Fakir, is not to be brought about by Lord Ronaldshay, however well-intentioned he may be in his apologies, nor by Lord Reading's smooth phrases and his personal care that officers and men might not overstep the limits of law. The organic change will be and can only be brought about by the suffering that has come to the people and for which, thank God, they find themselves prepared. A cautious friend in order to restrain my optimism tells me that the suffering has only just begun, that for the end in view we must pay a much higher price still. He really expects that we shall have to invite a repetition of Jallianwalas and that, instead of approaching the triangles of the crawling lane fame tremblingly and reluctantly, we shall have now to walk to them cheerfully and with a steady step and suffer lashes for refusing to crawl. I assure the friend that my optimism has room for all these things and much worse that he can imagine. But I promise, too, that if India remains calm and unperturbed and does not retaliate even mentally—a very difficult process, I admit, and yet not so difficult in India's present exalted mood,—our very preparedness and consequent absence of re-action will exhaust the brute spirit for want nutrition, and Lord Reading, instead of talking big things to us, will himself adopt the human language of penitence and see ample occasion in the Indian atmosphere for a new diplomacy. Whereas if we forget ourselves and our pledge, we must be ready for a thousand Jallianwalas and India being turned into a vast shambles. The President-elect has prepared us for such a consummation. He is sure that we have shed the fear of the prison. He is almost certain probably from the experience of his brave son and his company that we will be prepared to undergo the ordeal of assaults. But he bids us give up the fear of death itself. If that time is in store for us, I hope that there will be non-violent Non-co-operators enough in India, of whom it will be written:

'They suffered bullets without anger and with prayer on their lips, even for the ignorant murderer.'

Well, if the reports are to be credited, two Assamese volunteers have been whipped, the volunteers of Lahore have meekly borne the wanton assaults committed on them. This fight is not a joke. We have disciplined ourselves for the past twelve months and more, and we must now go through it to the end. There is no turning back.

The following appeared in *Young India* of 17th December, 1921:

Viceroy's Share.—I am sorry that I suspect Lord

Reading of complicity in the plot to unman India for eternity. A friend has suggested an alternative. He says that, whilst Lord Reading must be held responsible for the threats used by him in his recent utterance, he might be quite unaware of the lawlessness of the subordinate official or that he must have become helpless, the subordinate officials having simply disregarded his wishes to be strictly within the law. I must reject both the interpretations. Lord Reading, if he is trying legitimately to suppress popular lawlessness, must study and regulate the development of his campaign which he will not even allow to be called repression. If his subordinates being interested parties have gone out of hand, he must forthwith resign, at least publicly disown and condemn such illegalities and assaults and not attempt to excuse them on the flimsy plea of 'trying times.' I have myself suggested a possible explanation. His Excellency sympathises with our aspirations, and knowing his own countrymen, realises that we have got to be severely tried before they think of coming to terms; he is therefore trying and directing repression to see how far we are capable of bearing it and therefore sincere in our desire for freedom, and then having made out a case for us his clients, desires to compel a settlement. I am afraid, however, that I have to state the case only to be rejected. Human nature does not work quite that way. Lord Reading is not so entirely selfess, and if he is, he cannot possibly remain in charge of a Government which under its present constitution can give no relief to the people. It is therefore with the greatest reluctance that I am forced to conclude that Lord Reading is trying to emasculate India by forcibly making free speech and popular organisation impossible. I am prepared to believe that,.in all this, he thinks that he is doing good to us and that we are not yet fit to be called men and women. He will soon have his eyes opened. We must not quarrel with his belief. Nor need we feel anxious about it. Let us acquit ourselves like men and women, and we shall find that everything and everybody become favourable to us.

22nd December, 1921

ROUND TABLE CONFERENCE

The pages of "Young India" are rarely occupied with an examination of what rulers think. It is an idle speculation. But as the papers are discussing, advising and debating upon such a conference, I have considered it appropriate to devote some space to an examination of the mentality of the chief actor in the drama, now being played in India. In my opinion such a conference is bound to prove abortive, till Lord Reading is disabused of the idea that Non-co-operation is confined to a few misguided zealots. If he wants co-operation and contentment, he must placate Non-co-operators. He must see that Non-co-operation is not the disease, it is the chief symptom of a disease. The disease consists in a triple injury to the people of India. And no palliative will soothe the patient so long as the centre of the disease is not tackled. Outside the redress of the Khilafat and the Punjab wrongs and the grant of Swaraj in accordance with a scheme framed by the chosen representatives of the people, repression is the easiest and the shortest way to a settlement. No Viceroy can, I freely confess, possibly allow things to drift. I admit that he must suppress civil disobedience as he would an armed rebellion unless he is prepared to remedy the evil towards which the disobedience is directed. Abstract truth has no value, unless it incarnates in human beings who represented it by proving their readiness to die for it. Our wrongs live because we only pretend to be their living representatives. The only way we can prove our claim is by readiness to suffer in the discharge of our trust. We are on a fair way to proving ourselves worthy of it. But I hardly think we can yet claim to have given conclusive proof. Who knows if we shall not be found wanting when imprisonment means utter discomfort, and even lashes? Who knows how many of us are ready to mount the gallows?

In my opinion, therefore, a conference at which the Government is represented will be useful only when the latter has tried the Non-co-operators to its satisfaction and measured their strength in quantity and quality.

But since Non-co-operation is a method of cultivating public opinion, I would certainly welcome a conference of co-operators and Non-co-operators. I am sure that they want the Khilafat and the Punjab wrongs redressed. I am aware that they want freedom for the country as much as Non-co-operators. It has given me much pleasure to see almost every moderate journal condemning the present repressive policy of the Government. I had expected nothing less. And I know that, if Non-co-operators keep self-restraint, do not become violent, do not abuse their opponents, every liberal will become a Non-co-operator. Indeed even Englishmen will veer round to the Non-co-operators and the Government will, as it then must, capitulate. That is the expected and intended working of the method of Non-co-operation. It reduces friction to a minimum. And, if to-day it seems to have produced a contrary effect, it is because Non-co-operators have only now begun to see that it is not enough to have been fairly Non-violent in deed. It is equally necessary to be Non-violent in word and thought. It is unlawful for a Non-co-operator even to wish ill to his enemies. What our opponents dread most is undisciplined violence breaking out under cover of Non-violence. They do not believe in our sincerity, *i.e.*, of the vast majority of us. They see in it nothing but chaos and perdition. This repression therefore has come as a blessing in disguise. It is showing them and us that we have acquired influence over the populace to keep it under check even under provoking circumstances. Our restraint has not yet been tried long enough to be considered permanent. We are still in a state of uncertainty. The people in Sialkot did stray away from the line, be it ever so slightly. We have had so many such little jerks that we do not possess the sense of security required to inspire an outsider's faith in the movement. I would therefore welcome every opportunity of meeting the co-operators on neutral ground or for showing the *bona fides* of Non-co-operators. The Government has shown itself in true colours by declaring its intention to suppress Non-co-operation as such. It was on safe ground so long as it sought to put down violence or incitement to or approval of it. I have therefore no doubt that the co-operators will rise to a man against the Government madness—this vain attempt to stifle expression of opinion and agitation for redress of grievances. But I warn our friends against entertaining the idea of a conference with the Government till they find that it is truly penitent and means to appreciate the popular side. Let there be no conference on the boycott of welcome or the right of holding public meetings or forming associations of volunteers or others so long as they have no violent purpose. Boycott of the welcome will and must continue so long as the people's wishes are flouted, and public meetings and associations are elementary rights on which there can be no parleying. We must fight for them.

Let it be understood that Non-co-operators are not offering Civil Disobedience that they had intended to. Their insistence on calling and attending public meetings and forming peaceful volunteer associations ought not to be dignified by the name of Civil Disobedience. Non-co-operators are merely on the defensive. They have not taken, as they certainly intend to take, the offensive as soon as they are fairly certain of non-violent atmosphere. The Government has obliged them by anticipating them and providing them with a test of their own capacity.

22nd December, 1921

THE PROPOSED CONFERENCE

Referring to Lord Ronaldshay's speech at the Bengal Legislative Council on Monday last, Mr. Gandhi made the following statement to the correspondent of the Associated Press at his Ashram late in the night: I have read Lord Ronaldshay's speech* in the Bengal Legislative Council. Whilst I appreciate the note of conciliation about it, I cannot help saying that it is most misleading. I do not want to criticise those parts of the speech which lend themselves to criticism. I simply want to say that the present situation is entirely his own and the Viceroy's doing. In spite of my strong desire to avoid suspecting the Government of India and the Local Governments of a wish to precipitate a conflict.

*Omitted in this collection.

with the people, up to now all that I heard and read leads me to the conclusion that my suspicion is justified. Whilst I do not wish to deny the existence of some sort of pressure, even intimidation, on the part of individuals, I do wish emphatically to deny that in connection with the phenomenal *hartal* on the 17th November, in Calcutta, there was any intimidation, organised or initiated by or on behalf of the Local Congress or the Khilafat Committees. On the contrary, I am certain that the influence exerted by both these bodies was in the direction of avoiding all intimidation. Moral pressure there certainly was and will always be in all big movements, but it must be clear to the simplest understanding that a complete *hartal* such as Calcutta witnessed on the 17th November, would be an impossibility by mere imtimidation. But assume that there was intimidation. Was there any reason for disbanding Volunteer Corps, prohibiting public meetings and enforcing laws which are under promise of repeal? Why has no attempt been made to prove a single case of intimidation? It grieves me to have to say that the Governor of Bengal has brought in the discovery of swords or sword-sticks in one place in Calcutta to discredit large public organisations Who intimidated the people into observing a complete *hartal* in Allahabad after all the leaders were arrested and in spite of the reported undue official pressure that was exercised upon shopkeepers and ghariwallas at that place? Again, His Lordship says, "If we are to assume that this development means there is genuine desire to bring about improvement, there must be a favourable atmosphere. In other words, it will be generally agreed that to trust must be an essential preliminary to any possible conference. If responsible leaders of Non-co-operation now come forward with definite assurance that this is the correct interpretation, I should then say we were in sight of such a change of circumstances as would justify Government in reconsidering the position. But words must be backed by deeds. If I were satisfied only that there was general desire for the conference and that responsible Non-co-operation leaders were prepared to take action, then I should be prepared to recommend my Government to take steps in consonance with the altered situation." This is highly misleading. If wherever words "Non-co-operation leaders" occur, the word "Government" were put in, and if the whole of the statement came from a Non-co-operator, it would represent the correct situation. Non-co-operators have really to do nothing, for they have precipitated nothing. They are over-cautious. The disturbance in Bombay was allowed to override their keen desire to take up aggressive Civil Disobedience, but in the present circumstances the phrase "Civil Disobedience" is really a misnomer. What Non-co-operators are doing to-day, I claim, every co-operator would do to-morrow under similar circumstances. When the Government of India or the Local Governments attempt to make our political existence or agitation, no matter how peaceful, an utter impossibility, may we not resist such attempt by every lawful means at our disposal? I cannot imagine anything more lawful or more natural than that we should continue our volunteer organisations purging them of every tendency to become violent and continue also to hold public meetings taking the consequences of such a step. Is it not proof of the law-abiding instinct of hundreds of young men and old men that they have meekly, without offering any defence and without complaining, accepted imprisonment for having dared to exercise their elementary rights in the face of Government persecution? And so it is the Government which is to prove its genuine desire for a conference and an ultimate settlement. It is the Government which has to arrest the fatal course along which repression is taking it. It is the Government that is to prove to Non-co-operators its *bona fides* before it can expect them to take part in any conference. When the Government does that, it will find that there is an absolutely peaceful atmosphere. Non-co-operation, when the Government is not resisting anything except violence, is a most harmless thing. There is really nothing for us to suspend. We cannot be expected, until there is actual settlement or guarantee of settlement, to ask schoolboys to return to Government schools or lawyers to resume practice or public men to become candidates for the Councils or title-holders to ask for return of titles. In the nature of things, it is therefore clear that Non-co-operators have to do nothing. Speaking personally, I can certainly say that if there is a genuine desire for a conference, I would be the last person to advise precipitating aggressive Civil Disobedience, which certainly it is my intention to do immediately I am entirely satisfied that the people have understood the secret of Non-violence; and let me say the last ten days' events have shown that the people seem clearly to understand its inestimable value. If then the Government recognises that Non-co-operators mean business and intend to suffer limitlessly for the attainment of their goal, let the Government unconditionally retrace its steps, cancel the notifications about disbandment of volunteer organisations and prohibitions of public meetings and realease all those men in the different provinces who have been arrested and sentenced for so-called Civil Disobedience or for any other purpose given under the definition of Non-co-operation but excluding acts of violence, actual or intended. Let the Government come down with a heavy hand on every act of violence or incitement to it, but we must claim the right for all time of expressing our opinions freely and educating public opinion by every legitimate and non-violent means. It is therefore the Government who have really to undo the grave wrong they have perpetrated and they can have the conference they wish in a favourable atmosphere. Let me also say that, so far as I am concerned, I want no conference to consider the ways and means of dealing with Non-co-operation. The only conference that can at all avail at this stage is a conference called to deal with the causes of the present discontent, namely, the Khilafat and the Punjab wrongs and Swaraj. Any conference again which can usefully sit at the present stage must be conference that is really representative and not a conference to which only those whom the Government desire are invited.

19th January, 1922

THE VICEROY'S REPLY

Interviewed by Associated Press correspondent, Mr. Gandhi made the following statement regarding Lord Reading's speech at Calcutta in reply to the deputation led by Pandit Madan Mohan Malaviya: I must confess that I have read the Viceregal utterance with deep pain. I was totally unprepared for what I must respectfully call his mischievous misrepresentation of the attitude of the Congress and the Khilafat organisations in connection with the visit of His Royal Highness, the Prince of Wales. Every resolution passed by either organisation and every speaker has laid the greatest stress upon the fact that there was no question of showing the slightest ill-will against the Prince or exposing him to any affront. The boycott was purely a question of principle and directed against what we have held to be the unscrupulous methods of the bureaucracy. I have always held, as I hold even now, that the Prince has been brought to India in order to strengthen the hold of the Civil Service corporation which has brought India into a state of abject paupersim and political serfdom. If I am proved to be wrong in my supposition that the visit has that sinister meaning, I shall gladly apologise.

It is equally unfortunate for the Viceroy to say that the boycott of the welcome means an affront to the British people. His Excellency does not realise what grievous wrong he is doing to his own people by confusing them with the British administrators in India. Does he wish India to infer that the British administrators here represent the British people and that agitation directed against their methods is an agitation against the British people? And if such is the Viceregal contention and if to conduct a vigorous and effective agitation against the methods of bureaucracy and to describe them in their true colours is an affront to the British people, then I am afraid I must plead guilty. But then I must also say in all humility, the Viceroy has entirely misread and misunderstood the great national awakening that is taking place in India. I repeat for the thousandth time that it is not hostile to any nation or any body of men, but it is deliberately aimed at the system under which the Government of India is being to-day conducted, and I promise that no threat and no enforcement of threats by the Viceroy or any body of men will strangle that agitation or send to rest that awakening.

I have said in my reply to Lord Ronaldshay's speech that we have not taken the offensive; we are not the aggressors, we have not got to stop any single activity. It is the Government that is to stop its aggravatingly offensive activity aimed not at violence but a lawful, disciplined, stern but absolutely non-violent agitation. It is for the Government of India and for it alone to bring about a peaceful atmosphere, if it so desires. It has hurled a bomb-shell in the midst of material rendered inflammable by its own action and wonders that the material is still not inflammable enough to explode. The immediate issue is not now the redress of the three wrongs; the immediate issue is the right of holding public meetings and the right of forming associations for peaceful purposes. And in vindicating this right we are fighting the battle not merely on behalf of Non-co-operators, but we are fighting the battle for all schools of politics. It is the condition of any organic growth, and I see in the Viceregal pronouncement an insistence upon submission to a contrary doctrine which an erstwhile exponent of the law of liberty has seen fit to lay down upon finding himself in an atmosphere where there is little regard for law and order on the part of those very men who are supposed to be custodians of law and order. I have only to point to the unprovoked assaults being committed, not in isolated cases, not in one place, but in Bengal, in the Punjab, in Delhi and in the United Provinces. I have no doubt that as repression goes on in its mad career, the reign of terrorism will overtake the whole of this unhappy land. But whether the campaign is conducted on civilised or uncivilised lines, so far as I can see, there is only one way open to Non-co-operators, indeeed I contend, even to the people of India. On this question of the right of holding public meetings and forming associations there can be no yieding. We have burnt our boats and we must sail onward till that primary right of human beings is vindicated.

Let me make my own position clear. I am most anxious for a settlement. I want a Round Table Conference. I want our position to be clearly known by everybody who wants to understand it. I impose no conditions, but when conditions are imposed upon me prior to the holding of the conference. I must be allowed to examine those conditions, and if I find that they are suicidal, I must be excused if I don't accept them. The amount of tension that is created can be regulated solely by the Government of India, for the offensive has been taken by the Government.

19*th January*, 1922

THE MALAVIYA CONFERENCE

(By M. K. Gandhi)

The Conference* was both a success and a failure. It was a success in that it showed an earnest desire on the part of those who attended to secure a peaceful solution of the present trouble, and in that it brought under one roof people possessing divergent views. It was a failure in that, through certain resolutions have been adopted, the Conference did not leave on my mind the impression that those who assembled together as a whole realised the gravity of the real issue. The mind of the Conference

* A conference of leaders of all parties, arranged by Pandit Malaviya, was held in Bombay on 14th January, 1922, at which over a hundred leaders of all parties from all provinces were present. It recommended stopping of repression and the convoking of a round table conference between Government and Non-co-operators and other leaders. Government rejected the proposals. For further details *see* appendix.

seemed to be centred more on a round table conference than upon asserting the popular right of free speech, free association and free press which are more than a round table conference. I had expected on the part of the Independents to declare their firm attitude that no matter how much they might differ regarding the method of Non-co-operation, the freedom of the people was a common heritage and that the assertion of that right was three-fourths of Swaraj; that therefore they would defend that right even with Civil Disobedience, if need be.

However, as the attention of the Conference could not be rivetted on that point, but on a round table conference, the discussion turned upon the essentials of such a conference.

My own position was clear. I would attend any conference as an individual, without any conditions. My purpose as a reformer is to convert people to the view I hold to be right and therefore to see everybody who would care to listen to me. But when I was asked to mention the conditions necessary for an atmosphere favourable for a successful conference, I had to press home certain conditions. And must own that the Resolutions Committee approached my view-point with the greatest sympathy and showed every anxiety to eccommodate me. But side by side with this, I observed an admirable disposition on its part to consider the Government's difficulties. Indeed the Government's case could not have been better presented, if it had been directly and officially represented in the Conference.

The result was a compromise. The withdrawal of notifications and the discharge of prisoners coming under the notifications and of the *futwa* prisoners, *i.e.*, the Ali Brothers and others who have been convicted in respect of the *futwas* regarding military service, was common cause. The Committee saw the force of the suggestions that the distress warrants should be discharged, the fines imposed upon the Press, etc. should be refunded and that the prisoners convicted for non-violent or otherwise innocent activities under cover of the ordinary laws should be discharged upon the proof of their Non-violence. For this purpose, I had suggested the committee appointed by the conference. But on the Resolutions Committee showing that it would be difficult for the Government to accept such an uncontrolled recommendation, I agreed to the principle of arbitration now imported in the resolution. The second compromise is regarding picketing. My suggestion was that in the event of the round table conference being decided upon, Non-co-operation activities of a hostile nature should be suspended and that all picketing except *bona fide* peaceful picketing should also be suspended, pending result of the conference. As the implications of hostile activities appeared to me to be too dangerous to be acceptable, I hastily withdrew my own wording and gladly threw over even *bona fide* peaceful picketing, much though I regretted it. I felt that the friends interested in liquor picketing for the sake of temperance would not mind the temporary sacrifice.

I agreed too to advise the Working Committee to postpone general mass Civil Disobedience comtemplated by the Congress to the 31st instant in order to enable the Committee and the Conference to enter into negotiations with the Government. This, I felt, was essential to show our *bona fides*. We could not take up new offensives, whilst negotiations for a conference were being conducted by responsible men. I further undertook to advise the Committee, in the event of the proposed conference coming off, to stop all *hartals* pending the conference.

This I hold to be inevitable. *Hartals* are a demonstration against bureaucracy. We cannot continue them, if we are conferring with them for peace. Workers will bear in mind that as yet no activity of the Congress stops save general Civil Disobedience. On the contrary, enlistment of volunteers and Swadeshi propaganda must continue without abatement. Liquor shop picketing may continue where it is absolutely peaceful. It should certainly continue where notices unnecessarily prohibiting picketing have been issued. So may picketing continue regarding schools or foreign cloth shops. But whilst all our activities should be zealously continued, there should be the greatest restraint exercised and every trace of violence or discourtesy avoided. When restraint and courtesy are added to strength, the latter becomes irresistible. Civil Disobedience being an indefeasible right, the preparations for it will continue even if the conference comes off. And the preparations for Civil Disobedience consist in:

1. the enlistment of volunteers,
2. the propaganda of Swadeshi,
3. the removal of untouchability,
4. the training in non-violence in word, deed and thought,
5. unity beetween diverse creeds and classes.

I hear that many are enrolled as volunteers in various parts of India, although they do not wear *Khadi*, do not believe in complete non-violence, or, if they are Hindus, do not believe in untouchability as a crime against humanity. I cannot too often warn the people that every deviation from our own rules retards our progress. It is the quality of our work which will please God and not quantity. Not all the lip Mussalmans and the lip Hindus will enter the Kingdom of Heaven. Islam is no stronger than the Kingdom of Heaven. Islam is no stronger than the best Mussalman. Thousands of nominal followers of Hinduism belie their faith and discredit it. One true and perfect follower of Hinduism is enough to protect it for all time and against the whole world. Similarly, one true and perfect Non-co-operator is any day better than a million Non-co-operators so-called. The best preparation for Civil Disobedience is to cultivate civility, that is truth and non-violence, amongst ourselves and our surroundings.

An Unfortunate Incident.—The abrupt withdrawal of Sir Sankaran Nair* was an unfortunate incident. In my opinion, he had nothing to do with my, or later, with Mr. Jinnah's opinions. As Speaker, especially, he was exempt from any implied or express identification with anybody's views. I cannot help feeling that Sir Sankaran erred in the conception of his duty as Speaker. But as we progress towards democracy, we must be prepared even for such erroneous exercise of independence. I congratulate Sir Sankaran Nair upon his boldly exercising his independence, which I have not hesitated to call cussedness in private conversation, and upon the independence of the Committee in not suffering a nervous collapse, but quietly electing Sir Vishveshwarayya and voting thanks to the retiring Speaker for the services rendered.

* Sir Sankaran was the speaker of the Bombay Leaders' Conference on the first day and retired the second day alleging that, in view of Mr. Gandhi's attitude, there was no use for a conference.

19th January, 1922

THE DEMANDS

(BY M. K. GANDHI)

In order that all may approach the round table conference with perfect knowledge of the Congress demands, I laid all our cards on the table and reiterated the claims regarding the Khilafat, the Punjab and Swaraj. Let me repeat them here:

(1) So far as I can write from memory, full restoration to the Turks of Constantinople, Adrianople, Anatolia, including Smyrna and Thrace. Complete withdrawal of non-Muslim influence from Arabia, Mesopotamia, Palestine and therefore Syria and withdrawal of British troops whether English or Indian from these territories.

(2) Full enforcement of the report of the Congress Sub-Committee and therefore the stopping of the pensions of Sir Michael O'Dwyer, General Dyer and other officers named in the report for dismissal.

(3) Swaraj means, in the event of the foregoing demands being granted, full Dominion status. The scheme of such Swaraj should be framed by representatives duly elected in terms of the Congress Constitution. That means four annas franchise. Every Indian adult, male or female, paying four annas and signing the Congress creed, will be entitled to be placed on the electoral roll. These electors would elect delegates who would frame the Swaraj constitution. This shall be given effect to without any change by the British Parliament.

If the Congress programme is so cut and dried, where is the necessity for a conference?—asks the critic. I hold that there is and there always will be.

The method of execution of the demands has to be

considered. The Government may have a reasonable and a convincing answer on the claims. The Congressmen have fixed their minimum, but the fixing of the minimum means no more than confidence in the justice of one's cause. It further means that there is no room for bargaining. There can, therefore, be no appeal to one's weakness or incapacity. The appeal can only be addressed to reason. If the Viceroy summons the conference, it means either that he recognises the justice of the claims or hopes to satisfy the Congressmen, among others, of the injustice thereof. He must be confident of the justice of his proposals for a rejection or reduction of the claim. That is my meaning of a meeting of equals who eliminate the idea of force, and instantly shift their ground as they appreciate the injustice of their position. I assure His Excellency the Viceroy and everybody concerned that the Congressmen or Non-co-operators are as reasonable beings as may be found on earth or in India. They have every incentive to be, so for theirs is the duty of suffering as a result of rejection of any just offer.

I have heard it urged that on the Khilafat the Imperial Government is powerless. I should like to be convinced of this. In that case and if the Imperial Government make common cause with the Mussalmans of India, I should be quite satisfied and take the chance with the Imperial Government's genuine assistance of convincing the other powers of the justice of the Khilafat claim. And even when the claim is admitted, much requires to be discussed regarding the execution.

Similarly regarding the Punjab. The principle being granted, the details have to be settled. Legal difficulties have been urged about stopping the pensions to the dismissed officials. The reader may not know that Maulana Shaukat Ali's pension (I suppose he occupied the same status as Sir Michael O'Dwyer) was stopped without any inquiry or previous notice to him. I believe that service regulations do provide for removing officers and officials from the pensions list on proof of gross neglect of duty or disloyal service. Anyway let the Government prove a case for refusal to grant the Punjab demand save the plea of the past services of these officials. I must refuse to weigh their service to the Empire against their disservice to India, assuming the possibility of two such things co-existing.

Swaraj scheme is undoubtedly a matter on which there will be as many minds as there are men and women. And it is eminently a thing to be debated in a conference. But here again there must be a clean mind and no mental reservations. India's freedom must be the supreme interest in everybody's mind. There should be no obstruction such as the preoccupation of the British elector or the indifference of the House of Commons or the hostility of the House of Lords. No lover of India can possibly take into account these extraneous matters. The only question to consider will be—is India ready for what she wants? Or does she ask like a child for food she has no stomach for? That can be determined not by outsiders but by Indians themselves.

From that standpoint, I do consider the idea of the conference for devising a scheme of full Swaraj premature. India has not yet incontestably proved her strength. Her suffering is great indeed, but nothing and not prolonged enough for the object in view. She has to go through greater discipline. I was punctiliously careful not to make Non-co-operators party to the conference resolutions, because we are still so weak. When India has evolved disciplined strength, I would knock myself at the Viceregal door for a conference, and I know that the

Viceroy will gladly embrace the opportunity whether he be an eminent lawyer or a distinguished militarist. I do not approach directly, because I am conscious of our weakness. But being humble I make it clear through Moderate or other friends that I would miss not a single opportunity of having honest conferences or consultations. And so I have not hesitated to advise Non-co-operators thankfully to meet the Independents and place our services at their disposal to make such use of them as they may deem fit. And if the Viceroy or a party desires a conference it would be foolish for Non-co-operators not to respond. The case of Non-co-operators depends for success on cultivation of public opinion and public support. They have no other force to back them. If they forfeit public opinion, they have lost the voice of God for the time being.

For the manner of preparing the scheme too, I have simply suggested what appears to me to be a most feasible method. The All-India Congress Committee has not considered it nor has the Working Committee. The adoption of the Congress franchise is my own suggestion. But what I have laid down as the guiding principle is really unassailable. The scheme of Swaraj is that scheme which popular representatives frame. What happens then to the experts in administration and others who may not be popularly elected? In my opinion, they also should attend and have the vote even, but they must necessarily be in a minority. They must expect to influence the majority by a constant appeal to the logic of facts. Given mutual trust and mutual respect, a round table conference cannot but result in a satisfactory and honourable peace.

7th July, 1920

PURE CIVIL DISOBEDIENCE

All the readers of "Young India" may not know that Ahmedabad came under a heavy fine for the misdeeds of the April of last year.* The fine was collected from the residents of Ahmedabad but some were exempted at the discretion of the collector. Among those who were called upon to pay the fines were income-tax payers. They had to pay a third of the tax paid by them. Mr. V. J. Patel, a noted barrister, and Dr. Kanuga, a leading medical practitioner, were among those who were unable to pay. They had admittedly helped the authorities to quell the disturbance. No doubt they were Satyagrahis, but they had endeavoured to still the mob fury even at some risk to their own persons. But the authorities would not exempt them. It was a difficult thing for them to use discretion in individual cases. It was equally difficult for these two gentlemen to pay any fine when they were not to blame at all. They did not wish to embarass the authorities and yet they were anxious to preserve their self-respect. They carried on no agitation but simply notified their inability to pay the fines in the circumstances set forth above. Therefore an attachment was issued. Dr. Kanuga is a very busy practitioner and his box is always full. The watchful attaching official attached his cash box and extracted enough money to discharge the writ of execution. A lawyer's business cannot be conducted on those lines. Mr. Patel sported on cash box. A sofa of his sitting room was therefore attached and advertised for sale and duly sold. Both these Satyagrahis have thus completely saved their consciences.

* *See* p. 15

Wiseacres may laugh at the folly of allowing writs of attachment and paying for the collection of fines. Multiply such instances and imagine the consequence to the authorities of executing thousands of writs. Writs are possible when they are confined to a few recalcitrants. They are troublesome when they have to be executed against many high-souled persons who have done no wrong and who refuse payment to vindicate a principle. They may not attract much notice when isolated individuals resort to this method of protest. But clean examples have a curious method of multiplying themselves. They bear publicity and the sufferers instead of incurring odium receive congratulations. Men like Thoreau brought about the abolition of slavery by their personal examples. Says Thoreau: "I know this well, that if one thousand, if one hundred, if ten men whom I could name,—if ten *honest* men only—aye, if *one* honest man, in this state of Massachusettes *ceasing to hold slaves* were actually to withdraw from this co-partnership and be locked up in the country gaol therefor, it would be the abolition of slavery in America. For it matters not how small the beginning may seem to be, what is once well done is done for ever." Again, he says, "I have contemplated the imprisonment of the offender rather then seizure of his goods—though both will serve the same purpose, because they who assert the purest right and consequently are most dangerous to a corrupt State, commonly have not spent much time in accumulating property." We therefore congratulate Mr. Patel and Dr. Kanuga on the excellent example set by them in an excellent spirit and in an excellent cause.

3rd November, 1921

REQUISITE CONDITIONS

Those only can take up Civil Disobedience, who believe in willing obedience even to irksome laws imposed by the State so long as they do not hurt their conscience or religion, and are prepared equally willingly to suffer the penalty of Civil Disobedience. Disobedience to be civil has to be absolutely non-violent, the underlying principle being the winning over of the opponent by suffering, *i.e.*, love.

For the purpose of the Khilafat, the Punjab or Swaraj civil resisters must implicitly believe in the necessity of Hindu-Muslim unity based not upon expediency but upon real affection. Civil resisters must believe in Swadeshi and therefore use only handspun. Humanly speaking, if not even one out of the two hundred and fifty districts of India is thus ready, I consider the attainment of Swaraj during this year nearly impossible. If one district can be found where ninety per cent. of the population have completely boycotted foreign cloth and are manufacturing all the cloth required by them by hand spinning and hand weaving, if the whole of the population of that district, whether Hindu, Mussalman, Parsi, Sikh, Christian or Jew, is living in perfect amity, if the whole of its Hindu population is purged of the sin of untouchability and if at least one in every ten of its inhabitants is capable of suffering imprisonment or even mounting the gallows, and if, while that district is civilly, peacefully and honourably resisting the Government, the rest of India remains non-violent and united and prosecutes the programme of Swadeshi, I hold it to be perfectly possible to establish Swaraj during this year. I shall hope that there are several such districts ready. In any case, the method now to adopt is for workers to concentrate on and develop their own districts without reference to the rest. They must not invite imprisonment till they are ready, nor must they avoid it if it comes to them unsought. They should make no speeches but simply finish the Swadeshi programme in a businesslike manner. Where workers find no response from their districts, they must not get disheartened but should simply become expert carders, spinners and weavers. Their out-turn will be their best and whole work whilst their neighbours are thinking what to do.

10th November, 1921

THE MOMENTOUS ISSUE

(BY M. K. GANDHI)

The next few weeks should see Civil Disobedience in full working order in some part of India. With illustrations of partial and individual Civil Disobedience the country has become familiar. Complete Civil Disobedience is rebellion without the element of violence in it. An out and out civil resister simply ignores the authority of the state. He becomes an outlaw claiming to disregard every unmoral state law. Thus, for instance, he may refuse to pay taxes, he may refuse to recognise the authority of the state in his daily intercourse. He may refuse to obey the law of trespass and claim to enter military barracks in order to speak to the soldiers, he may refuse to submit to limitations upon the manner of picketing and may picket within the prescribed area. In doing all this, he never uses force and never resists force when it is used against him. In fact, he invites imprisonment and other uses of force against himself. This he does, because, and when he finds the bodily freedom, he seemingly enjoys to be an intolerable burden. He argues to himself that a state allows personal freedom only in so far as the citizen submits to its regulations. Submission to the state law is the price a citizen pays for his personal liberty. Submission, therefore, to a state wholly or largely unjust is an immoral barter for liberty. A citizen who thus realises the evil nature of a state is not satisfied to live on its sufference, and therefore appears to the others who do not share his belief to be a nuisance to society, whilst, he is endeavouring to compel, the state without committing a moral breach to arrest him. Thus considered, civil resistance is a most powerful expression of a soul's anguish and an eloquent protest against the continuance of an evil state. Is not this the history of all reform? Have not reformers, much to the disgust of their fellows, discarded even innocent symbols associated with an evil practice?

When a body of men disown the state under which they have hitherto lived, they nearly establish their own government. I say nearly, for they do not go to the point of using force when they are resisted by the state. Their 'business' as of the individual is to be locked up or shot by the state, unless it recognises their separate existence, in other words bows to their will. Thus three thousand Indians in South Africa, after due notice to the Government of the Transvaal, crossed the Transvaal border in 1914 in defiance of the Transvaal immigration law and compelled the Government to arrest them. When it failed to provoke them to violence or to coerce them into submission, it yielded to their demand. A body of civil rssisters is, therefore, like an army subject to all the discipline of a soldier, only harder because of want of excitement of an ordinary soldier's life. And as a civil resistance army is or ought to be free from passion because free from the spirit of retaliation, it requires the fewest number of soldiers. Indeed one *perfect* civil resister is enough to win the battle of Right against Wrong.

Though, therefore, the All-India Congress Committee has authorised Civil Disobedience by Provincial Congress Committees on their own responsibility, I hope they will put due emphasis on the word 'responsibility' and not start Civil Disobedience with a light heart. Every condition must be given its full effect. The mention of Hindu-Muslim unity, non-violence, Swadeshi and removal of untouchability means that they have not yet become an integral part of our national life. If an individual or a mass have still misgiving about Hindu-Muslim unity, if they have still any doubt about the necessity of non-violence for the attainment of our triple goal, if they have not yet enforced Swadeshi in its completeness, if the Hindus among that mass have still the poison of untouchability in them, that mass or that individual are not ready for Civil Disobedience. Indeed it would be best to watch and wait whilst the experiment is being carried on in one area. Reverting to the analogy of the army, those divisions that watch and wait are just as much co-operating actively as the division that is actually fighting. The only time, whilst the experiment is going on, that individual Civil Disobedience may be resorted to simultaneously, is when the Government obstruct even the silent prosecution of Swadeshi. Thus if an order of prohibition is served upon an expert spinner going to teach or organise spinning, that order should be summarily disregarded and the teacher should court imprisonment. But in all other respects, in so far as I can judge at present, it will be best for every other part of India scrupulously to respect all orders and instructions, whilst one part is deliberately taking the offensive and committing a deliberate breach of all the unmoral state laws it possibly can. Needless to add that any outbreak of violence in any other part of India must necessarily injure and may even stop the experiment. The other parts will be expected to remain immovable and unperturbed, even though the people within the area of experiment may be imprisoned, riddled with bullets or otherwise ill-treated by the authorities. We must expect them to give a good account of themselves in every conceivable circumstance.

17th *November*, 1921

CIVIL VERSUS CRIMINAL

(By M. K. Gandhi)

When a man wilfully breaks his own laws, the disobedience becomes criminal. For he commits the breach not against himself but against some one else, and not only escapes punishment for the breach, for there is none provided against himself by the maker of laws, but he avoids also the inconvenience caused by their observance. What is true of the individual is true of the corporation. At the present moment, one observes this criminal breach by the Government of its own laws throughout India. Sections of the Penal Code and the Criminal Procedure Code are being freely abused. And because Non-co-operators refrain from questioning orders issued by officials, bare-faced illegalities are being committed by them with impunity. We have seen this in Bulandshahr, in Chittagong, all over Sindh, and nowhere so systematically and so deliberately as in the Madras Presidency. Mr. Yakub Hassan has pointed out with great justification that his arrest and conviction are contrary to the spirit of the Viceregal pledge. Indeed, it is against not only the spirit of Lord Reading's pledge but it is against the letter even of his predecessor's communique in which it was declared in solemn tones that, so long as Non-co-operation remained non-violent, there would be no repression. No one dare accuse Mr. Yakub Hassan of having incited to violence in his Tanjore address before an audience of picked representatives. Nor was any violence done in the Tanjore district as a result of his speech. The Magistrate in the case of Mr. Iyer of the *Deshabhaktan* actually admitted that there was not a trace of violence in the writing that was impeached and that it actually contained exhortations to Non-violence. Mr. Ramaswami Iyengar, a leading pleader of Coimbatore, has been arrested for a spirited letter to the *Hindu*, though there was no violence in it. And so have Dr. Varadarajulu and Mr. Gopalakrishnayyah been arrested for their speeches and writings, although it is known that they not only do not incite to violence but that theirs is actually a restraining influence in the face of provocation. Is it any wonder if one infers from this campaign of repression an intention on the part of the Government to invite violence? In not one of these cases I have mentioned has there been any outbreak of violence as a result of the speeches and writings concerned. And so we see that the Government is guilty of criminal breach of its own laws. And what legal remedy has the afflicted individual against the Government? There is certainly no sanction provided against the Government in law when it prostitutes the law itself to its own base ends.

When therefore a Government thus becomes lawless in an organised manner, Civil Disobedience becomes a sacred duty and is the only remedy open specially to those who had no hand in the making of the Government or its laws. Another remedy there certainly is, and that is armed revolt. Civil Disobedience is a complete, effective and bloodless substitute. And it is well that by exemplary restraint and discipline in the way of submission to unjust and even illegal orders we have created the necessary atmosphere for Civil Disobedience. For thereby on the one hand the tyrannical nature of the Government has been made more manifest, and on the other by willing obedience we have fitted ourselves for Civil Disobedience.

It is equally as well that Civil Disobedience is being confined even now to the smallest area possible. It must be admitted that it is an abnormal state, even as a corrupt and unpopular Government should be in civilised society, like disease, an abnormal state. Therefore, only when a citizen has disciplined himself in the art of voluntary obedience to the state laws is he justfied on rare occasions deliberately but non-violently to disobey them, and expose himself to the penalty of the breach. If then we are to achieve the maximum result in the minimum of time, whilst fiercest disobedience is going on in a limited area, perfect submission to the laws must be yielded in all the other parts so as to test the nation's capacity for voluntary obedience and for understanding the virtue of Civil Disobedience. Any unauthorised outbreak of disobedience, therefore, in any part of India will most certainly damage the cause and will betray an unpardonable ignorance of the principles of Civil Disobedience.

We must expect the Government to take the strictest

measures to suppress this impending defiance of authority, for on it depends its very existence. Its instinct of self-preservation alone will actuate measures of repression adequate for suppression. And if it fails, the Government of necessity disappears. That is, it either bends to the national will or it is dissolved. The greatest danger lies in violence breaking out anywhere by reason of provocation. But it would be wrong and unmanly to invite the sternest measures and then to be incensed against them, apart from the fact that it will be a breach of our solemn pledge of non-violence. I may be arrested, thousands who take part in the peaceful revolt may also be arrested, imprisoned, even tortured. The rest of India must not lose its head. When the proper time comes, the rest India may respond by undertaking Civil Disobedience and inviting arrests, imprisonments and tortures. It is the sacrifice of the innocent we want to make. That alone will appear pleasing to God. And therefore, on the eve of the great battle the nation is embarking upon, my earnest exhortation to every Non-co-operator is to fit himself for Civil Disobedience by fulfilling to the letter and in the spirit the conditions of Civil Disobedience laid down at Delhi,* and to ensure non-violence everywhere. Let us not be satisfied that we remain non-violent individually. We boast that Non-co-operation has become universal in India. We boast that we have acquired sufficient influence even over the unruly masses to restrain them from violence. Let us prove true to our claim.

* *See* appendix.

8th December, 1921

BARDOLI

I have paid in the company of Maulana Azad Sobhani the much expected visit to Bardoli *taluka*. It has a population of nearly one hundred thousand. It has about 140 villages. It had about sixty-five Government schools. Of these fifty-one have been nationalised. The Government schools are continued in some cases but have an attendance of less than 10 boys. The national schools have charge of over six thousand children, including a few hundred girls. And spinning is compulsory in all these schools, though it is not yet being regularly taught or practised. Most of the schools have been nationalised only during the past three months. In all the villages I found the women taking keen interest in the national movement. We met thousands of people and visited six villages during the two days of our stay. The majority of men were dressed from top to toe in handspun *Khadi* and a large number of women too were so dressed. Those who were not, complained that they could not obtain *Khadi*. This does not however mean that the people, either men or women, have given up the use of their old foreign stock. Many, I am sorry to say, still use it for domestic wear. Much is still left to be done in the shape of manufacture of *Khadi*. There is a good number of wheels but very few looms in the *taluka*. The reader will be pained to hear that its staple crop is cotton which has hitherto been all exported. There is complete harmony between Hindus and Mussalmans. The relations with the co-operators have not been bitter. The untouchables freely attend meetings. I have however suggested that it can hardly be considered satisfactory so long as the managers of national schools do not go out of their way to bring 'untouchable' children to their schools and villagers do not take a personal interest in the welfare of these suppressed countrymen. Many liquor shops are deserted. From all the accounts received by me, there has been little or no intimidation resorted to in order to achieve this very wonderful result. In two or three cases, volunteers visited villagers, and on the parents hesitating to withdraw their children from Government schools, sat *dhurna* and fasted until the bewildered parents had complied with their request. I told the workers that even this kind of pressure bordered on violence, for we had no right to make people conform to our opinion by fasting. One may conceivably fast for enforcing one's right but not for imposing one's opinion on another.

There was too a social boycott of a liquor dealer who had not kept his promise. I have advised even against such a boycott among a people so helpless as ours. Strong public opinion must for the time being be our only remedy for correcting internal abuses. Social boycott such as stopping barbers, washermen, etc., is undoubtedly a punishment which may be good in a free society but it becomes oppressive in a country which has for years been governed by force.

But I was remarkably struck by the almost completely peaceful manner in which the *taluka* of Bardoli has made a radical change for the better in many departments of life. It was an agreeable surprise, too, to find the movement being handled by elderly men who have never taken part in politics. The reader will be pleasingly astonished to find that all the wonderful work in Bardoli has been done by unpaid volunteers. Bardoli happens to be a *taluka* in which there are few paupers and most people have easy means of livelihood. This manifestation of public life is all the more remarkable on that account and is mainly, if not entirely, due to the utterly selfless services of a band of able and enthusiastic workers who only know to do or die. But in spite of all this great work, I was reluctantly obliged to give my verdict in which Maulana Azad Sobhani fully concurred and which was accepted by the noble band of workers, that Bardoli before it challenged the might of a great Empire, must complete its Swadeshi programme to the extent of manufacturing sufficient handspun to clothe itself, must freely admit untouchables into the national schools and must be so far non-violent that solitary unarmed co-operators and English and other officials might feel absolutely secure in their midst. And those conditions, God willing, the good people of Bardoli have undertaken to fulfil in a few months' time. An elderly co-operator put down six months at the outside. An enthusiastic young man who knew what he was talking about put down the period at one month. I close this happy recollection of our visit to Bardoli by informing the reader that several co-operators whom I met testified to the peaceful and zealous manner in which the volunteers had worked in this *taluka* which, let us hope, will still have the privilege, if necessary, of giving battle to the Government.

5th January, 1922

THE IMMEDIATE ISSUE

(BY M. K. GANDHI)

Swaraj, the Khilafat, the Punjab occupy a subordinate place to the issue sprung upon the country by the Government. We must first make good the right of free speech and free association before we can make any further progress towards our goal. The Government would kill us if they could by a flank attack. To accept defeat in the matter of free speech and free association is to court disaster. If the Government is allowed to destroy non-violent activities in the country, however dangerous they may be to its existence, even the moderates' work must come to a stand still. In the general interest, therefore, we must defend these elementary rights with our lives. We cannot be coerced into welcoming the Prince nor can we be coerced into disbanding volunteer association or giving up any other activities which we may deem desirable for our growth.

The safest and the quickest way to defend these rights is to ignore the restriction. We must speak the Truth under a shower of bullets. We must band together in the face of bayonets. No cost is too great for purchasing these foundamental rights. And on these there can be no compromise, no parleying, no conference. Withdrawal of notifications of disbandment and prohibition orders and discharge of all who are imprisoned for non-violent activities must precede any conference or settlement. We must be content to die, if we cannot live as free men and women.

I wish I could persuade everybody that Civil Disobedience is the inherent right of a citizen. He dare not give it up without ceasing to be a man. Civil Disobedience is never followed by anarchy. Criminal Disobedience can lead to it. Every state puts down Criminal Disobedience by force. It perishes, if it does not. But to put down Civil Disobedience is to attempt to imprison conscience. Civil Disobedience can only lead to strength and purity. A civil resister never uses arms and, hence, he is harmless to a state that is at all willing to listen to the voice of public opinion. He is dangerous for an autocratic state, for he brings about its fall by engaging public opinion upon the matter for which he resists the state. Civil Disobedience, therefore, becomes a sacred duty when the state has become lawless, or which is the same thing, corrupt. And a citizen that barters with such a state shares its corruption or lawlessness.

It is, therefore, possible to question the wisdom of applying Civil Desobedience in respect of a particular act or law; it is possible to advise delay and caution. But the right itself cannot be allowed to be questioned. It is a birthright that cannot be surrendered without surrender of one's self-respect.

At the same time that the right of Civil Disobedience is insisted upon, its use must be guarded by all conceivable restrictions. Every possible provision should be made against an outbreak of violence or general lawlessness. Its area as well as its scope should also be limited to the barest necessity of the case. In the present case, therefore, aggressive Civil Disobedience should be confined to a vindication of the right of free speech and free association. In other words, Non-co-operation, so long as it remains non-violent, must be allowed to continue without let or hindrance. When that position is attained, it is time for a representative conference to be summoned for the settlement of Khilafat, the Punjab and Swaraj but not till then.

12th January, 1922

LIBERTY OF THE PRESS

(BY M. K. GANDHI)

One by one the pretensions of the Government that the reforms represent more liberty and more concession to popular feeling are dropping out under the stress of circumstances. The pretensions can be justified, only if they can stand the test under a severe strain. Liberty of speech means that it is unassailed, even when the speech hurts; liberty of the Press can be said to be truly respected only when the Press can comment in the severest terms upon and even misrepresent matters, protection against misrepresentation or violence being secured not by an adminisitrative gagging order, not by closing down the Press but by punishing the real offender, leaving the Press itself unrestricted. Freedom of association is truly respected, when assemblies of people can discuss even revolutionary projects, the State relying upon the force of public opinion and the civil police, not the savage military at its disposal, to crush any actual outbreak of revolution that is designed to confound public opinion and the State representing it.

The Government of India is now seeking to crush the three powerful vehicles of expressing and cultivating public opinion and is thus once more, but happily for the last time, proving its totally arbitrary and despotic character. The fight for Swaraj, the Khilafat, the Punjab means a fight for this threefold freedom before all else.

The *Independent* is no longer a printed sheet. The *Democrat* is no more. And now the sword has descended upon the *Pratap* and the *Kesari* of Lahore. The *Bande Mataram*, Lalaji's child, has warded off the blow by depositing Rs. 2,000 security. The other two have had their first security forfeited and are now given ten days' notice to deposit Rs. 10,000 each or close down. I hope that the security of Rs. 10,000 will be refused.

I presume that what is happening in the United Provinces and the Punjab will happen in the others in due course, unless the infection is prevented from spreading by some action on the part of the public.

In the first place, I would urge the Editors of the papers in question to copy the method of the *Independent* and publish their views in writing. I believe that an Editor who has anything worth saying and who commands a *clientele* cannot be easily hushed so long as his body is left free. He has delivered his finished message as soon as he is put under duress. The Lokamanya spoke more eloquently from the Mandalay fortress than through the columns of the printed *Kesari*. His influence was multiplied a thousandfold by his incarceration and his speech and his pen had acquired much greater power after he was discharged than before his imprisonment. By his death he is editing his paper without pen and speech through the sacred resolution of the people to realise his life's dream. He could not possibly have done more, if he were to-day in the flesh preaching his *Mantra*. Critics like me would perhaps be still finding fault with this expression of his or that. To-day all criticism is hushed and his *Mantra* alone rules millions of hearts which are determined to raise a permanent living memorial by the fulfilment of his *Mantra* in their lives.

Therefore let us first break the idol of machinery and leaden type. The pen is our foundry and the hands of willing copyists our printing machine. Idolatry is permissible in Hinduism when it subserves an ideal. It becomes a sinful fetish when the idol itself becomes the ideal. Let us use the machine and the type, whilst we can, to give unfettered expression to our thoughts. But let us not feel helpless when they are taken away from us by a 'paternal' Government, watching and controlling every combination of types and every movement of the printing machine.

But the handwritten newspaper is, I admit, a heroic remedy meant for heroic times. By being indifferent to the aid of the printing room and the compositor's stick we ensure their free retention or restoration for all time.

We must do something more. We must apply Civil Disobedience for the restoration of that right before we think of what we call larger things. The restoration of free speech, free association and free Press is almost the whole Swaraj. I would therefore respectfully urge the conference that is meeting on Saturday* next at the instance of Pandit Malaviyaji and other distinguished sons of India to concentrate upon the removal of these obstacles on which all can more heartily join than upon the Khilafat, the Punjab and Swaraj. Let us take care of those precious pennies and then the pound will taken care of itself.

25th January, 1922

NON-PAYMENT OF TAXES

(BY M. K. GANDHI)

The idea of non-payment of taxes is in the air. The Andhras have made us more familiar with the cry than any other part of India. Whilst the Congress has given provincial autonomy to every Province, I have ventured to warn the provinces against embarking upon a non-payment campaign till I had tried the experiment myself in some area under my own supervision.† I

* *See* p. 921.

† The following appeared in *Young India* of 19th Jaunary 1921 :

I observe a desire in some places to precipitate mass Civil Disobedience by suspending payment of taxes. But I would urge the

abide by that warning. I must also draw attention to the fact that we are not to start offensive Civil Disobedience till the 31st instant, or if it is sooner, till the Malaviya Conference Committee knows the result of negotiations and knows that the proposed round-table conference is not to come off. Therefore any suspension of taxes at the present moment can only be regarded as temporary holding back, pending the result of the negotiations carried on by that Committee. But 31st January will be soon upon us. And it is necessary to consider the question of non-payment of taxes in all its bearings.

On this subject, a friend who is in deep sympathy with the national movement, and who is a fairly accurate student of it, thus expresses his apprehensions :

"I have often thought to what extent the non-violent Non-co-operation movement transgresses the religious limits, when it embarks on Civil Disobedience in the

---

greatest caution before embarking upon the dangerous adventure. We must not be indifferent about violence, and we must make sure of masses exercising self-control whilst they are witnesses to the confiscation of their crops and cattle or forfeiture of their holdings. I know that withholding of payment of taxes is one of the quickest methods of overthrowing a Government. I am equally sure that we have not yet evolved that degree of strength and discipline which are necessary for conducting a successful campaign of non-payment of taxes. Not a single *tehsil* in India is yet ready, except perhaps Bardoli and to a lesser degree Anand. More than fifty per cent. of the population of such *tehsil* has to rid itself of the curse of untouchability, must be dressed in *Khadi* manufactured in the *tehsil*, must be Non-violent in thought, word and deed, and must be living in perfect friendliness with all, whether co-operators or Non-co-operators. Non-payment of taxes without the necessary discipline will be an act of unpardonable madness. Instead of leading to Swaraj, it is likely to lead to no-Raj. I must therefore repeat the caution I have so often uttered that mass Civil Disobedience ought not to be tried in the first instance, except under my personal supervision, and certainly never without the fulfilment of the conditions laid down at Delhi.

form of non-payment of taxes. I look upon the non-violent Non-co-operation as essentially a spiritual movement. I know Mr. Gandhi does not think it otherwise. Will not the programme of the non-payment of taxes transgress the religious limit and lead to violence and bring into the movement people who are not as yet saturated with the principle of non-violence? Is not Mr. Gandhi holding out, however unconsciously, a material bait for his spiritual movement by which he means to conquer the Government? Recent events have shown that the temper of violence and the belief in violence are not eliminated from our character in the masses. And, therefore, it would be a leap in the dark fraught with disastrous consequences to carry out the programme of Civil Disobedience in the form of non-payment of taxes. I am therefore most anxious that Mr. Gandhi should not begin Civil Disobedience in this form as yet."

The validity of the objection lies in the statement that the non-payment campaign will bring into the movement people who are not as yet saturated with the principle of non-violence. This is very true, and because it is true, non-payment does 'hold out a material bait'. It follows, therefore, we must not resort to non-payment because of the possibility of a ready response. The readiness is a fatal temptation. Such non-payment will not be civil or non-violent, but it will be criminal or fraught with the greatest possibility of violence. Let us remember the experience of Pandit Jawaharlal Nehru when the peasants, after they had taken the pledge of non-violence, told him that if he advised them to do violence, they would be certainly ready to do so. Not until the peasantry is trained to understand the reason and the virtue of *civil* non-payment and is prepared to look with calm resignation upon the confiscation (which can only be temporary) of their holdings and the forced sale of their cattle and other belongings, may they be advised to withhold payment of taxes. They must be told what happened in holy Palestine. Arabs who were fined were surrounded by soldiers. Aeroplanes were hovering over head. And the sturdy men were dispossessed of their cattle. The latter were impounded and left without fodder and even water. When the Arabs, stupefied and rendered helpless, brought the fine and additional penalty, as if to mock them, they had their dead and dying cattle returned to them. Worse things can and certainly will happen in India. Are the Indian peasantry prepared to remain absolutely non-violent, and see their cattle taken away from them to die of hunger and thirst? I know that such things have already happened in Andhra Desh. If the peasantry in general knowingly and deliberately remain peaceful even in such trying circumstances, they are nearly ready for non-payment.

I say 'nearly ready,' for non-payment is intended to transfer the power from the bureaucracy into our hands. It is therefore not enough that the peasantry remain non-violent. Non-violence is certainly nine-tenths of the battle, but it is not all. The peasantry may remain non-violent, but may not treat the untouchables as their brethren; they may not regard Hindus, Mussalmans, Christians, Jews, Parsis, as the case may be, their brethren; they may not have learnt the economic and the moral value of the *charkha* and the *khaddar*. If they have not, they cannot gain Swaraj. They will not do all these things after Swaraj, if they will not do them now. They must be taught to know that the practice of these national virtues means Swaraj.

Thus civil non-payment of taxes is a privilege capable of being exercised only after rigorous training. And even as *Civil* Disobedience is difficult in the case of a habitual offender against the laws of the State, so is *Civil* non-payment difficult for those who have hitherto been in the habit of withholding payment, of taxes on the slightest pretext. Civil non-payment of taxes in indeed the last stage in Non-co-operation. We must not resort to it, till we have tried the other forms of Civil Disobedience. And it will be the height of unwisdom to experiment with non-payment in large or many areas in the beginning stages.

I hear the talk even of refusing payment of rent to Zamindars. It must not be forgotten that we are not Non-co-operating with Zamindars, whether Indian or foreign. We are engaged in a fight with one big Zamindar—the bureaucracy—which has made of us and the Zamindars themselves serfs. We must try to bring round the Zamindars to our side, and isolate the big Zamindar. But if they will not come to us, we must be patient with them. We may not even proclaim a social boycott against them. That is to say, we may not refuse social service such as dhobie, barber, etc., to them. In areas under permanent settlement therefore, there can be no non-payment campaign except in respect of cesses that might be payable directly to the Government. But the mention of Zamindars merely shows the difficulties that beset us in the pursuit of no-tax campaign. All things considered, therefore, it is my deliberate opinion that the no-tax movement for the objects of the Congress should be, for the time being, left to me; meanwhile workers can develop their own districts along constructive lines. They can discover various other methods of offering mass Civil Disobedience, and then, as the people become purified and enlightened, lead them on to non-payment.

As for the Andhras where preparations on an intensive scale have already been made, I do not wish to damp the ardour of the workers. If they are satisfied that the people in the selected areas fulfil all the tests laid down at Delhi,* and that they are capable of endless suffering without retaliation, I have nothing to say but to pronounce 'God bless the brave Andhras.' They must know that the responsibility will be entirely theirs for any mishap that may occur. They will not be blamed by anybody, if they do not take up the no-tax movement.

26th January, 1922

POLES ASUNDER

(By M. K. Gandhi)

The debate in the Assembly and the Council of State affords the clearest possible justification for my distrust of the Government and, therefore, any round table conference at the present moment. The Government supporters consider the Congress demands to be impossible and repression to be the only way possible to put down Non-co-operation. If I believed the Congress demands to be impossible and the use of force to be justifiable for putting down the pursuit of impossible ideals, I should also vote with the Government. I have, therefore, no difficulty about understanding and even appreciating the attitude of the Government and its supporters.

But I oppose the Government and thoroughly distrust it, because I so thoroughly understand its attitude. India can never attain freedom by going along the route the Government will take her.

Let us see.

*See appendix.

Why is the Khilafat demand impossible? All that the Congress asks in effect is that Government of India and the Imperial Government, if they wish to retain the people's co-operation, should work with them in getting the demands fulfilled. They should, therefore, perform that part of the obligation which rests with them, and vigorously prosecute the rest as if it was their own grievance. What will the Imperial Government do if France were to attempt to deprive England of Dover, and India were secretly to help France or openly to show indifference or hostility to England's struggle to retain Dover? Can Indians be expected to sit idle when the Khilafat is vivisected?

What is impossible about the Punjab demand? Why do they talk about the legalities of the case? If they will take care of the moralities, legalities will take care of themselves. As a boy I learnt a legal maxim that where there is a conflict between Law and Equity, the latter should prevail. It is not with me a copy book maxim. But I am told it is immoral to ask for the deprivation of a pension, which is but deferred pay. Why has Sardar Gauharsingh been deprived of his "deferred pay" and why are the other pensioners threatened if they should take part in the present agitation? Does a servant who vilifies his employer receive pay or pension? Have Sir Michael O'Dwyer or General Dyer ever admitted their 'error of judgment'? Why should the children of the murdered men of Jallianwalla Bagh, or the men who were brutally flogged or made to crawl, although they had done no wrong, pay those who were responsible for these barbarities? I do not know a single principle of ethics, save that of might, that can justify the continuation of pensions to servants who are unrepentant. The viewpoints of the two parties are so different that what appears to be just and moral to the one, appears unjust and immoral to the other. I venture to claim that in asking for the stoppage of pensions, the Congress is just, without being vindictive. It waives penalties. It merely refuses still further to participate in the wrong by continuing to give pensions. The truth is that the Government still considers the two offenders to be distinguished servants of the Crown. *That* attitude has to be changed before a repetition of the Punjab becomes impossible.

As with the Punjab so with Swaraj. It appears to the Government impossible to return to India what is hers. Reforms by instalments is the motto. The underlying idea is not to give anything, unless it is absolutely necessary. The differences are so great that I dread to think of Swaraj before the Khilafat and the Punjab wrongs are put away. They seem so simple in the statement. But they are as difficult as Swaraj, because their redress means obedience to India's will.

This is all cold logic. There is nothing impossible about the demands. The impossibility consists in the unwillingness of the power-holders to part with the power that should never have been theirs.

Why should there be repression at all, if only the Government will do their duty? Assume that violence is a certainty if mass Civil Disobedience is precipitated. Are the people to be baulked of their rights for fear of violence? It does not strike the co-operators that they uphold injustice and add insult to it, when they accuse civil resisters of precipitating a crisis. The Government are deliberately inviting a crisis. They are precipitating violence by removing every one who has any influence over the people and who can keep them non-violent. Co-operators do not see that the action of the Government is like that of a man, who refuses to give food to a hungry man and then threatens to shoot him whilst he is attempting to help himself.

In the midst of an enervating atmosphere such as ours, the duty before Non-co-operators is clear. They must keep exemplary patience. They must not be goaded into precipitate action. They must refuse battle where they are not ready. It is no business of the Government to keep us Non-violent or to help us to remain so. Even their method of restraining violence is exasperatingly violent. In one respect, however, we must feel thankful to them, for their protest and criticism amount to nothing but this, that we do not know how to practise our creed and that we are incompetent to inflict successful violence, even if we would. Let us admit both these arguments. We must be true to our creed. Then it is common cause that the Government must lay down arms. And let those who do not believe in the creed at least see that *India is neither ready nor willing to meet violence with violence.* I wish those who believe in the necessity of violence for India's freedom will realise the truth of my position. They must not think that because *they* are ready and willing to do violence, India is likewise ready or willing. I claim that India is unready, *not* because she is helpless *but* because she is unwilling. Therefore Non-violence is unexpectedly succeeding, whereas violence, in spite of the vaunted talk of human nature, would have failed. India's past training for ages, I mean the training of the masses, has been against violence. Human nature in India has advanced so far that the doctrine of Non-violence is more natural for the people at large than that of violence. Let us also remember that the experiences of Bombay and Madras prove my proposition. If the people of India were violent by nature, there was enough in Bombay and

Madras to give rise to an unquenchable conflagration. A little violence like dirt is enough to disturb or soil a peaceful or clean surface, but either being a foreign addition is soon removed. To train India for violence and thus to wrest Swaraj by violence is a work of ages. I verily believe that this wonderful manifestation of energy and national consciousness is purely and simply due to the advent of Non-violence. People have come to their own. Let no hasty action arrest its progress.

26th January, 1922

AN ENGLISH LADY BLESSES

'An English lady' who sends her name and address writing from Calcutta, says:

> "It elevates one to see the admirable way in which Mr. Gandhi shows us the truth and opens our eyes to the atrocious things that our so-called noble Government are doing daily. The letter that an 'English missionary'* has written is admirable. I am afraid, there are many more like her, but are too proud to come forward and acknowledge the noble work that Mr. Gandhi is doing. His patience and work are like the spring that lies hidden far below: No matter what the world may preach, God will give him a harvest greater than he expects. It is only those who work in silence reap the harvest. Millions are watching and judging him. But there is One above all, watching and judging each struggle in his daily life, and when his toil and struggle are over, his work and name will live for ever. His name will be worshipped by millions who have gained freedom by his hard work. God bless and spare him and his dear wife, and give them both health and strength to go on until this struggle is over, which will not be long."

It is not without hesitation that I share this letter with the reader. Although written impersonally, it is so personal. But I hope there is no pride in me. I feel I

*Omitted in this collection.

recognise fully *my* weakness. But my faith in God and His strength and love is unshakable. I am like clay in the Potter's hands. And so in the language of the *Gita*, the compliments are laid at His feet. The blessings such as these, I confess, are strength-giving. But my reason for publishing this letter is to encourage every true Non-co-operator in the non-violent path he is pursuing, and to wean the false ones from their error. This is a terribly true struggle. It is *not* based on hate though men of hate are in it. It is a struggle which is based on love, pure and undefiled. If I felt any hate towards Englishmen or those who in their blindness are associated with the blind administrators, I have the courage to retire from the struggle. A man who has the least faith in God and His mercy, which is his justice, cannot hate men, though, at the same time, he must hate their evil ways. But having abundant evil in himself and ever standing in need of charity, he must not hate those in whom he sees evil. This struggle, therefore, is intended to make friends with Englishmen, and the whole world. It cannot be by false flattery but, by plainly telling Englishmen of India that their ways are evil and that we will not co-operate with them so long as they retain them. If we are wrong in so thinking, God will forgive us, for we mean no ill to them and we are prepared to suffer at their hands. If we are right, as sure as I am writing this, our suffering will open their eyes even as it has opened those of 'an English lady'. Nor is she the only one. I meet Englishmen during my travels. I do not know them, but they greet me cordially and wish me success and pass on. True, as against scores who thus bless me, there are hundreds that curse me. These curses also I am bidden to lay at His feet. They come from ignorance. Many Englishmen and even some Indians consider me and my activity to be mischievous. Non-co-operators must tolerate even these. If they get angry and retaliate, they lose the battle, whereas if they suffer, they win without fail and without delay. *The whole of the delay is due, I am convinced to our shortcomings.* We have not been always non-violent. We have, contrary to our pledge, laboured ill-will. Our opponents, the English administrators, their co-operators, the Taulkdars, the Rajahs, have distrusted us and have felt afraid of us. We are bound by our pledge to clothe them with the fullest protection. Whilst we may not help them in the exploitation of the poor and the weak, we must not harm them. Though they are in a hopeless minority, they must be made to feel safer in our midst than they are behind the bayonets. If we were in a hopeless minority, ours would be an easier position—we would long ago have proved our faith. As it is, our numbers embarass us. The dissatisfaction with the present regime is common to us; but not the burning faith in non-violence. We must not be satisfied till we have rendered impossible the disgraceful scenes that took place in Madras.* We must not, with non-violence on our lips, obstruct court proceedings. Either we seek imprisonment, or we do not. If we do, we must let the Government take us away as fast as they wish. The struggle is prolonged to the extent that we fail to understand the implications of non-violence.

* When the Prince arrived in Madras, there was a hartal, but there was some coercion in some parts of the city.

26th January, 1922

FRAUGHT WITH DANGER

(By M. K. Gandhi)

"Jhajjar is a tehsil town in the Rohtak district with a population of about 11,000. It has got a Municipality with 4 nominated and 8 elected members. The President is elected. Yet the Municipality was not sympathetic towards popular activities. Therefore the local Congress workers, rightly or wrongly issued a notice upon the Municipality without any permission from the District Congress Committee, that if it did not make itself popular within 15th to 22nd January, the Congress Committee will take possession of the Town Hall. The Municipality ignored this notice altogether. On the other hand, the local leading worker, Pandit Sriram, was charged under section 107, and sent to prison for a year by the D. C. on the 15th January, the first day of the allotted period. The Pandit unveiled a portrait of the Lokamanya in the Town Hall on that day, for which the D. C. had given previous permission upon an application from the Municipality. After Pandit Sriram's imprisonment, the President of the local Congress Committee and the volunteers took possession of the Town Hall on the 16th. A regular guard of volunteers was set up. The volunteers took possession also of the four gates of the town and disturbed the octroi arrangement. As soon as this news reached Rohtak, I started for Gajjar, for Lala Shyamlal was not present there, having gone to Ferozepur-Jhirka to attend a Congress Committee meeting. The people are even bent on violence. I advised them at night to remain non-violent, which produced some effect. But an influential preacher of Non-violence is necessary to convert them. On the 18th night at 8 p.m., some respectable citizens of the town called together Congress workers and Municipal Commissioners and tried to settle the matter amicably. All the elected members excepting the President, who was absent, and two nominated members of the Municipality, agreed to resign. And it was decided also that the Town Hall would be under the control of the Congress Committee. However, the matter will be finally settled at noon to-day. The volunteers are still guarding the premises. The people have proclaimed by *Panchayet* a social boycott of the six witnesses who stood against Pt. Sriram, *viz.*, the Tahsildar,

> Thandar, Lambardar, and the President, Vice-President and Secretary of the Municipal Committee. The Town Hall was erected with public subscription in memory of the late Queen Victoria. For some 5 or 6 years it remained uncared for, but now for the last ten years or so the Municipality has taken charge of the building. If the settlement arrived at the conference of the 18th night is not observed, popular excitement will grow which may, I fear, ultimately lead to violence. The local leaders and volunteers are unbending. I am writing this at 10 a. m., on the 19th. Please guide us as to what to do by wire or by letter to the address at Rohtak."

Thus writes (the original is in Hindi) Lala Daulatram Gupta, acting President of Rohtak District Congress Committee. The action of the Congress workers in Jahjjar is audacious and inspiring. But it is fraught with the greatest danger. It has reached the border line of violence and in discipline. I can fully appreciate the noble desire of the people to possess their own property. Municipalities are perhaps the greatest fraud palmed off upon India. The Government has hitherto used them for consolidating its power. But where the citizens are united, they can attain the municipal home-rule in a moment. I have not yet described the quiet, orderly and evolutionary revolution that is going on in three big municipalities in the Bombay Presidency, *viz.*, Ahmedabad, Surat and Nadiad.* Of that, some other time. It is not as yet a completed picture. But Jhajjar will outpace the three municipalities, if it remains steady and absolutely non-violent. Possession of the Town Hall can be retained without any ado, if the citizens of the place are unanimous. It cannot be retained, if there is real opposition. Any outbreak of popular violence will be a crime of the first magnitude, because it would be wanton and unprovoked. India, in the language of Maulana Abdul Kalam, is

* *See* page 769

the greatest Gurdwara; it is the largest Town Hall. And if we have not yet succeeded in possessing it, we may wait for the occupation of the Town Hall of Jhajjar. The Congress officers *must* surrender it, (1) if there is the slightest fear of violence, (2) if the elected members oppose the act of occupation, (3) if the Committee at Rohtak, or failing that, the Committee at Lahore vetoes the occupation, (4) if the Police demand it at the point of the bayonet, unless the occupiers are prepared to die at their post without retaliation or resentment, and if the other citizens are certain not to get excited, impatient and violent.

The occupation appears to me to be a hasty act, but if it can be defended non-violently, the defect can be cured.

There is no harm in surrender. We shall gain strength by retracing every false or hasty step. What may have been taken wrongly, must be given up, and can be retaken by methodical work. In the case of Jhajjar, if the Town Hall has to be surrendered, it can be retaken by the elected members, who are in a majority, passing a resolution giving the use to the Congress Committee. If the elected members will not do so, the electors may, by a requisition, call upon the elected members to give effect to their views.

Social boycott of the witnesses who gave evidence against Pandit Sri Ram is clearly a mistake and will defeat its own end. We must not resort to social boycott of our opponents. It amounts to coercion. Claiming the right of free opinion and free action as we do, we must extend the same to others. The rule of majority, when it becomes coercive, is as intolerable as that of a bureaucratic minority. We must patiently try to bring round the minority to our view by gentle persuasion and argument. Having been trained only to do things by order and under fear of punishment, we are likely, in the consciousness of strength we are daily acquiring, to repeat the mistakes of the rulers in an exaggerated form in our relations with those who may happen to be weaker than we are. That will be a worse state than the first.

I am aware that, by discussing Lala Daulatram Gupta's letter publicly, I am exposing the actors in the little drama in Jhajjar to misrepresentation and risk. The authorities can easily distort and exaggerate the facts related, as they are often prone to do. But as the matter is of great importance, and as the workers have exposed themselves to greater risks than I can possibly expose them to, I have felt it my duty publicly to discuss the pros and cons of the act of occupation which, though fraught with danger, commands one's admiration for its bravery. Non-co-operators have burnt their boats. They have no secrets. But correspondents who wish to write in confidence are welcome to do so. I shall respect their confidence. But as all my work is done in open daylight, and as my post passes through the hands of many helpers, I would like to discountenance confidential correspondence as much as possible. Though the Government, be it said to their credit, have generally not tampered with my correspondence, the correspondents must also note that, like all correspondence, mine is equally at their mercy.

2nd February, 1922

BARDOLI'S DECISION

(By M. K. Gandhi)

Bardoli has come to a momentous decision. It has made its final and irrevocable choice. Vithalbhai Patel, the President, addressed a conference of the representatives of the Taluka in a speech impressive for its warning. He certainly did not mince matters. There was an audience of *khaddar* clad representatives numbering 4.000. There were five hundred women, a large majority of whom were also in *khaddar*. They were interested and interesting listeners. It was an audience of sober, responsible men and women with a stake.

I followed Vithalbhai and went through every one of the conditions of mass Civil Disobedience laid down by the Congress.* I took the sense of the meeting on every one of the conditions separately. They understood the implications of Hindu-Muslim Parsi-Christian unity. They realised the significance and the truth of non-violence. They saw what the removal of untouchability meant; they were prepared, not merely to take into National Schools, but to induce 'untouchable' children to join them; they have had no objection to the 'untouchable' drawing water from the village wells. They knew that they were to nurse the 'untouchable' sick as they would nurse their ailing neighbours. They knew that they could not exercise the privilege of non-payment of revenue and other forms of Civil Disobedience until they had purified themselves in the manner described by me. They knew too, that they had to become industrious and spin their own yarn and weave their own *khaddar*. And lastly, they were ready to face forfeiture of their movables, their cattle and their land. They were ready to face imprisonment and even death, if necessary, and they would do all this without resentment.

There was an old dissentient voice on the question of untouchability. He said, what I said was right in theory

*The conditions laid down by the All-India Congress Committee at its Delhi meeting on 4th November, 1921. *See* appendix.

but it was difficult in practice to break down the custom all of a sudden. I drove the point home that the audience had made up its mind.

Before the larger meeting, I had met the real workers about fifty in number. Before that meeting, Vithalbhai Patel, some workers and I conferred together and felt that we should pass a resolution postponing the decision for about a fortnight, to make the Swadeshi preparation more complete and removal of untouchability more certain, by actually having untouchable children in all the sixty National Schools. The brave and earnest workers of Bardoli will not listen to the postponement. They were certain that more than 50 per cent. of the Hindu population were quite ready about untouchability and they were sure of being able to manufacture enough *khaddar* for their future wants. They were bent on trying conclusions with the Government. They bore down every objection raised by Vithalbhai Patel, and Abbas Tyabji, with his hoary beard and ever smiling face, was there to utter the warning. But they would not budge an inch from their position and so the resolution which I give below was unanimously passed:

"After having fully understood and considered the conditions as essential for the starting of mass Civil Disobedience, this Conference of the inhabitants of the Bardoli Taluka resolves that this Taluka is fit for mass Civil Disobedience.

"This Conference is of opinion:

(*a*) That for the redress of India's grievances, unity among Hindus, Mahomedans, Parsis, Christians and other communities of India is absolutely necessary.

(*b*) That non-violence, patience and endurance are the only remedy for the redress of the said grievances.

(*c*) That the use of the spinning wheel in every home, and the adoption of hand-spun and hand-woven garments to the exclusion of all other cloth by every individual are indispensable for India's freedom.

(*d*) That Swaraj is impossible without complete removal of untouchability by the Hindus.

(*e*) That for the people's progress and for the attainment of freedom, readiness to sacrifice movable and immovable property, to suffer imprisonment and. if necessary, to lay down one's life is indispensable.

"This Conference hopes that the Bardoli Taluka will have the privilege to be the first for the aforesaid sacrifices, and this Conference hereby respectfully informs the Working Committee that unless the Working Committee otherwise decides or unless the proposed Round Table Conference is held, this Taluka will immediately commence mass Civil Disobedience under the advice and guidance of Mr. Gandhi and the President of Conference.

"This Conference recommends those tax-payers of the Taluka who are ready and willing to abide by the conditions laid down by the Congress for mass Civil Disobedience, will refrain, till further instruction, from paying land revenue and other taxes due to the Government."

Who knows the issue? Who knows whether the men and women of Bardoli will stand the repression that the Government may resort to? God only knows. In His name has the battle been undertaken. He must finish it.

The Government have acted hitherto in a most exemplary manner. They might have prohibited the Conference. They did not. They know the workers. They could have removed them long ago. They have not done so. They have not interfered with any of the activities of the people. They have permitted them to make all preparations. I have watched their conduct with wonder and admiration. Both sides have up to the time of writing behaved in a manner worthy of chivalrous warriors of old. In this battle of peace, it ought not to be otherwise. If the battle continues in this fashion, it will end only in one way. Whoever has the ear of 85,000 men and women of Bardoli will gain the day.

The Working Committee has to sit and pass its judgment upon Bardoli's decision. The Viceroy has still choice and will have yet another choice given to him. No charge of hurry, want of preparation or thought, no charge of discourtesy will it be possible to bring against the people of Bardoli.

Therefore,

Lead kindly Light, amid the encircling gloom,
Lead Thou me on;
The night is dark, and I am far from home:
Lead Thou me on.

9th February, 1922

MR. GANDHI'S LETTER TO THE VICEROY

TO

HIS EXCELLENCY

The Viceroy, Delhi.

Sir,—Bardoli is a small *tehsil* in the Surat District in the Bombay Presidency, having a population of about 87,000 all told.

On the 29th ultimo, it decided under the presidency of Mr. Vithalbhai Patel to embark on mass Civil Disobedience, having proved its fitness for it in terms of the resolution of the All-India Congress Committee which met at Delhi during the first week of November last. But as I am perhaps chiefly responsible for Bardoli's decision, I owe it to Your Excellency and the public to explain the situation under which the decision has been taken.

It was intended under the resolution of the All-India Congress Committee, before referred to, to make Bardoli the first unit for mass Civil Disobedience in order to mark the national revolt against the Government for its consistently criminal refusal to appreciate India's resolve regarding the Khilafat, the Punjab and Swaraj.

Then followed the unfortunate and regrettable rioting on the 17th November last in Bombay, resulting in the postponement of the step contemplated by Bardoli.

Meanwhile, repression of a virulent type has taken place, with the concurrence of the Government of India, in Bengal, Assam, the United Provinces, the Punjab, the Province of Delhi and in a way in Bihar and Orissa and elsewhere. I know that you have objected to use of the word "repression" for describing the action of the authorities in these provinces. In my opinion, when action is taken which is in excess of the requirements of a situation, it is undoubtedly repression. The looting of property, assaults on innocent people, the brutal treatment of prisoners in the jails including flogging can in no sense be described as legal, civilized or in any way necessary. This official lawlessness cannot be described by any other term but lawless repression. Intimidation by Non-co-operators or their sympathisers to a certain extent in connection with *hartals* and picketing may be admitted but in no case can it be held to justify the wholesale suppression of peaceful volunteering or equally peaceful public meetings under a distorted use of an extraordinary law which was passed in order to deal with activities which were manifestly violent both in intention and action, nor is it possible to designate as otherwise than repression, action taken against innocent people under what has appeared to many of us an illegal use of the ordinary law, nor again can the administrative interference with the liberty of the Press under a law that is under promise of repeal be regarded as anything but repression.

The immediate task before the country, therefore, is to rescue from paralysis freedom of speech, freedom of association and freedom of the Press. In the present mood of the Government of India and in the present unprepared state of the country in respect of complete control of the forces of violence, Non-co-operators were unwilling to have anything to do with the Malaviya Conference whose object was to induce Your Excellency to convene a Round Table Conference. But as I was anxious to avoid all avoidable suffering, I had no hesitation in advising the Working Committee of the Congress to accept the recommendations of that Conference. Although in my opinion the terms were quite in keeping with your own requirements as I understood them through your Calcutta speech and otherwise, you have summarily rejected the proposal.

In the circumstances, there is nothing before the country but to adopt some non-violent method for the enforcement of its demands including the elementary rights of free speech, free association and free Press. In my humble opinion, the recent events are a clear departure from the civilized policy laid down by Your Excellency at the time of the generous, manly and unconditional apology of the Ali Brothers, *viz.*, that the Government of India should not interfere with the activities of Non-co-operators so long as they remained non-violent in word and deed. Had the Government's policy remained neutral and allowed public opinion to ripen and have its full effect, it would have been possible to advise postponement of the adoption of Civil Disobedience of an aggressive type till the Congress had acquired fuller control over the forces of violence in the country and enforced greater discipline among the millions of its adherents. But this lawless repression (in a way unparalleled in the history of this unfortunate country) has made the immediate adoption of mass Civil Disobedience an imperative duty. The Working Committee of the Congress has restricted it to only certain areas to be selected by me from time to time, and at present it is confined only to Bardoli. I may, under said authority, give my consent at once in respect of a group of 100 villages in Guntur in the Madras Presidency, provided they can strictly conform to the conditions of non-violence, unity among different classes, the adoption and manufacture of handspun *khadi* and untouchability.

But before the people of Bardoli actually commence mass Civil Disobedience, I would respectfully urge you as the head of the Government of India finally to revise your policy and set free all the Non-co-operating prisoners who are convicted or under trial for non-violent activities and to declare in clear terms a policy of absolute non-interference with all non-violent activities in the country, whether they be regarding the redress of the Khilafat or the Punjab wrongs or Swaraj or any other purpose and even though they fall under the repressive sections of the Penal Code or the Criminal Procedure Code or other repressive laws subject always to the condition of non-violence. I would further urge you to free the Press from all administrative control and to restore all the fines and forfeitures recently imposed. In thus urging, I am asking Your Excellency to do what is being done to-day in every country which is deemed to be under civilized Government. If you can see your way to make the necessary declaration within seven days of the date of publication of this manifesto, I shall be prepared to advise postponement of Civil Disobedience of an aggressive character, till the imprisoned workers have, after their discharge, reviewed the whole situation and considered the position *de novo*. If the Government make the requested declaration, I shall regard it as an honest desire on its part to give effect to public opinion and shall therefore have no hesitation in advising the country to be engaged in further moulding public opinion without violent restraint from either side and trust to its working to secure the fulfilment of its unalterable demands. Aggressive Civil Disobedience in that case will be taken up only when the Government departs from its policy of strictest neutrality or refuses to yield to clearly expressed opinion of the vast majority of the people of India.

I remain,
Your Excellency's faithful
servant and friend,
M. K. GANDHI.

9th February, 1922

THE ONLY ISSUE

(BY M. K. GANDHI)

It was not without deep thought and prayer that I wrote the letter to His Excellency the Viceroy.* It is not a threat because every word in it is meant. It is a

* Given above

heartfelt prayer to the tyrant to desist from evil. Lord Reading is not the tyrant. The system of which he is himself an unconscious and helpless victim is the tyrant. But every system becomes embodied in a person. To-day it is personified in Lord Reading, no matter how unconscious he is of it. I have invited him in all humility seriously, to consider the position and ask himself whether the official lawlessness can in any case be justified. Let him turn to the week's summary to which the old heading "In Cold Blood"* is restored. It is all true if the witnesses are not all liars. Should these things be?

But what of defiance of authority? Must defiance (non-violent at least) indeed of authority be met by barbarous and wicked abuse of it?

If the Viceroy cannot or will not see such an incredibly simple issue, must India sit still? Defensive Civil Disobedience *must* continue at any cost. If the whole of India were to say that even peaceful public meetings may not be held without permission, that peaceful volunteer association may not be formed without permission and that newspapers cannot be published without permission, that prohibition cannot be accepted. For a man may not be expected to ask for another's leave to breathe or eat or drink. The three things I have mentioned are the breath, the food and the drink of public life.†

*Omitted in this collection. For the nature of the contents thereof, *see* appendix under Repression.

†For the Government of India's reply and the Mahatmaji's comments thereon, *see* appendix.

2nd February, 1922

AWAKENING IN ANDHRADESHA

(By M. K. Gandhi)

To the date of writing, the following two telegrams have been received at the "Young India" office from the Secretary of the Provincial Congress Committee:

(1) "The Andhra Provincial Congress Working Committee met yesterday at Guntur in Desabhakta's house. Messrs. Bhogaraju, Pattabhi Sitaramayya, Tanguturu Prakasam, Dhanmayya, Ramchandra Rao, Kasindhuni Nageswarrao, Dandu Narayanrao, Desabhakta Konda Venkatappayya and others were present. Several ryots from different parts of the District, including Pedanandipadu, also attended the meeting and made representations of the conditions prevailing in their places. A graphic description was given how many male adults, including very aged men, enlisted themselves as volunteers in each one of the 50 villages in the neighbourhood of Pedanandipadu and how every one fully clad in *khaddar* has been serving and observing strict non-violence in spite of provocation sometimes given by the military drafted there, the attachments of movables and high-handed removal of carts and bulls even without a show of restraint. They have also stated that in almost all villages all the village officers including the *vettians* have resigned their appointments. Accounts of resignations of village officers in other areas also were given. The Working Committee after prolonged deliberation as a measure of special caution adopted the following resolution:

"This Committee is of opinion that the Guntur District Congress Committee should, instead of carrying on the campaign of non-payment of taxes in several talukas simultaneously as previously resolved by them, limit the area and appoint a Committee to investigate as to how far the Delhi conditions are satisfied in the said area and resolve on the question of final refusal of taxes in accordance with the opinion of the said Committee."

(2) "Guntur Congress Committee met day before yesterday in the house of Desabhakta at 1 p. m. for the purpose of considering, amongst other things, the resolution of the Working Committee of the Provincial Congress of the 25th on the question of non-payment of taxes. Mr. Anche Siviah, a leading ryot, and President, District Congress Committee, presided. Mr. Prakasam who came here for the Working Committee meeting of the Provincial Congress Committee was also present. In response to a requisition made to them, leading ryots from different Talukas in the District and some Congress workers also attended the meeting. Having been invited to explain the situation in their respective *talukas* and *fircas*, representative ryots gave accounts of the progress of the movement among the people. Most of them showed their determination to carry on the campaign in spite of all difficulties, while some expressed that some of the conditions of the Delhi resolution had not been fully satisfied in the *fircas* to which they belonged, and that there was need for further preparation in the matter of untouchability, and in one or two even in respect of non-violence. Mr. Prakasam addressed the meeting dealing at some length on the responsiblity of the step taken up by the people of the District. He quoted and explained the letter of Mahatmaji regarding non-payment of taxes published in the *Bombay Chronicle* of the 26th. Mr. Venkatappiah stated that the necessity for conveying this arose out of the letter

addressed to him by Mahatmaji and subsequent correspondence with him. Delhi resolution referred to areas where intensive preparations had been made. Amongst those that spoke on the occasion was Mr. Patri Ananth, arow of Atulur, who, in view of his imminent arrest by the police, came to the meeting, gave an account of the readiness of the people of his village and areas he had visited, and urged upon the necessity of continuing the movement undeterred, and left the meeting saying that he would be arrested forthwith. Hardly had he passed a few paces from the meeting when he was arrested and taken away by the police. Notwithstanding this incident, the meeting continued till 8 p. m. when it was adjourned to yesterday, not one amongst the audience getting out of the meeting. The members of the District Congress Committee reassembled in the house of Desabhakta yesterday morning at 8 a. m. and after prolonged discussion the following resolutions were adopted:

(1) In view of the resolution of the Working Committee of the Andhra Provincial Congress Committee dated the 25th, this meeting appoints the gentlemen named below, as a special committee to enquire in the different areas of Guntur District as to how far conditions of Delhi Resolution have been satisfied and how far they have qualified themselves for Civil Disobedience by way of non-payment of taxes, and send up their report to the District Congress Committee by the 10th February. This Committee further resolves that, soon after the receipt of the report above mentioned, it be placed before the meeting of the District Congress Committee and a final resolution be adopted on the question of non-payment of taxes and until then the people in the areas specified in the resolution passed at Ponur do continue the suspension of non-payment of taxes.

Members of the Special Committee are Sjt T. Prakasam, Dandu Narain Rau and K. Nageshwar Rao.

(2) This meeting tenders its hearty congratulations to all patriots who have been sent to jail from this District since the meeting at Ponur. This meeting expresses its grateful appreciation of the resignations by village officers in different parts of the District, and urges upon other village officers also the necessity of giving up their offices and helping the great national movement.

The following is the Associated Press message about Government preparations:

In regard to the state of affairs in Guntur where Civil Disobedience and non-payment of taxes campaign and resignation of village officers are in operation, Madras Government propose to undertake emergency legislation in direction of amending Madras Revenue Recovery Act (2 of 1864) mainly to do away with intervening period allowed under the present Act between distraint and attachment of property and to bring at once to sale effects of ryot who refuse to pay his dues. Other steps will also be taken by Government on the executive side such as institution of disobeying area subject to such exemptions as may be ordered by the Government in favour of persons who shall, by date to be prescribed, have paid into Government treasury or to officer appointed for the purpose taxes due from them. Where land is bought in by Government owing to combination to prevent bidding, opportunity will be taken to provide land for members of depressed classes. With regard to resignations of village officers the Government say they cannot be accepted under the circumstances and if officers refuse to carry on duties they must be dismissed."

In my opinion, the Government has the right to take

precautionary measures of the kind foreshadowed. It has the right to suspend ordinary legislation when it is threatened with combined suspension of its revenue. That a wise Government would not exasperate public opinion into refusal to pay taxes is of course true. But a Government that rides roughshod over popular opinion, cannot be expected to allow itself to be extinguished without an effort. The least, therefore, it would do is to protect its revenue collection. Nor is it possible to cavil at the proposed transfer of confiscated property to the members of the depressed classes. Such an arrangement should suit both parties. Non-co-operators have undertaken to be non-violent, to risk the loss of their all for the purpose of gaining their end and must therefore, allow their belongings to be sold. The Government, on the other hand, must try, if it can, to break the movement of non-payment and to apply all remedies just enough to secure collection. The proposal to allow the depressed classes to bid for and purchase forfeited lands is ideal. What can be better than that the forfeited lands should be temporarily occupied by the very classes whom we want to see raised from their depressed state?

I use the adverb 'temporarily,' for the present occupiers must have faith in their mission to know that they must get Swaraj and that under Swaraj they must be restored to their original status with honour added thereto. The depressed classes, who are being used as pawns in the game by the Government, cannot be adversely affected by dispossession, for it will be the primary care of the Swaraj Government to see them well-settled, happy and contented.

So much for the necessary Government measure. The panic that has possessed them shows a guilty conscience. They do not rely upon their popularity to secure payment. They have to rely upon the bayonet and persecution to do so. They are arresting popular leaders and goading the people to violence so as to enable them to justify 'bloody' measures.

And therein lies the test of the Andhras. They have hitherto proved their bravery and sacrifice. Their chosen leaders have gone to jail. Their cattle have been taken away from them and they have remained still. The worst, however, is yet to come. When the Government military is opened on them, they are expected to expose their willing breasts, not their unwilling backs, to the bullets and still not harbour revenge or resentment. They must let their utensils and belongings be taken away from them, whilst, like Draupadi or Prahlad, they are praying to God and proving their faith in Him.

Non-payment is a privilege. This is meant not to enrich the resisters, but by their voluntary poverty to enrich the nation. And they can exercise the privilege only if they have purified themselves, only if they are wearing handspun *khaddar* to the exclusion of foreign cloth and, if, being Hindus, they have washed themselves clean of the taint of untouchability and are prepared to treat the untouchable as a privileged brother. They must not grudgingly touch him, but they must lovingly embrace him and serve him. The touch must be a token of true penitence even as we expect the Government to be truly penitent regarding the many wrongs done to us. No niggardly acceptance of the inevitable will appear pleasing to God. It must be a thorough change of heart. We must share our schools with them, we must share our public places with them. We must nurse them in their sickness as we would nurse a brother. We must not be their patrons. We must not twist religious texts against them. We must expunge texts that are of doubtful origin and are capable of interpretation against their human rights. We must gladly give up custom that is against reason, justice, and religion of the heart. We must not ignorantly cling to bad custom and part with it when we must, like a miser parting with his ill-gotten hoard out of pressure and expedience.

I have dwelt at length upon untouchability because I have received wires and letters warning me against accepting assurances of compliance with the Congress condition about untouchability. They tell me that the Andhras are not ready to give up untouchability. I urge the leaders to be strictly on the watch. The slightest deviation from the right path will irreparably injure our cause. God requires the purest sacrifice. Hinduism is on its trial equally with Islam and Christianity. Hindus will be false representatives of their religion of the Upanishads, which recognises no privilege but that of merit and which accepts nothing that does not appeal to the heart and reason.

The Andhras are a virile people proud of their traditions. They are devoutly religious people capable of sacrifice. Much is expected of them by the country and I have every hope that they will not be found wanting. They will lose nothing by waiting if they are not ready for exact fulfilment of all conditions. But they will lose all and ill serve the country if they go to battle without full preparation.

2nd February, 1922

DANGER OF MASS MOVEMENT

Whilst there is every reason for self-gratification over mass awakening, it would be foolish to ignore its undoubted dangers. I have just read a notice in the papers that a girl has been pretending to be my daughter and receiving on that account all kinds of attention. I do not mind owning, I should be proud to own, thousands of good, restrained girls as my daughters. They will do credit to me and the country. The world would recognise them as members of an ever increasing family by adoption. As it is, I have to remark for the tenth time that I do not possess the good fortune to have a daughter. There is a tiny 'untouchable' girl whom I do proudly call my adopted daughter. She has brought happiness to me, and I hope by the time she has grown up she will bring truth and humility to her future field of service. To-day she is a veritable 'devil'. She believes in all play and no work. She finds it hard to work without the ebony ruler which used to keep her straight in her parental home. But I do not mind this charming idler of seven years claiming me as father. There are also some grown up girls who permit me the pleasure of claiming them as my daughters, but then they make it difficult for me to live up to the standard they exact from me. They are ever in danger of my being a discreditable father to them. But I must inform all the girls of India that I decline to run the risk of being discredited by their forcible adoption. I want certainly to adopt all the exacting girls like the ones whose names too I dare not give to the world.

But the reported forcible adoption of me by a girl is a comparatively harmless pastime. I hear that a gentleman by name Motilal Puncholi hailing from Udepur claims to be my disciple and to preach temperance and what not among the rustics of the Rajputana States. He is reported to be surrounded by an armed crowd of admirers and establishing his kingdom or some otherdom wherever he goes. He claims too miraculous power. He or his admirers are reported also to have done some destructive work. I wish that people will once for all understand that I have no disciples. I have for the time being at any rate no existence apart from the Congress and the Khilafat Committee. All my activity is referable to these two organisations. None works in my name: none has authority to use my name save under my own writing. No one has any work save the Congress or the Khilafat work. And nobody has any authority from me to use any arms, even sticks, against any person.

I understand that these brave but simple rustics have been induced to refuse payment of taxes due to the State to which they belong. They are even told that I have asked the tax-payers belonging to the Sirohi State not to pay more than Rs. 1¼ each. Now I know nothing of all this. No one consulted me about the matter. Pandit Ramakant Malaviya, Chief Minister of the State, has kindly brought the matter to my notice and he tells me that great mischief is being done in my name. If my writing reaches these countrymen at all, I would like to tell them that they should lay all their grievances before the State authorities and never resort to arms. If they wish to withhold payment of tax which they consider excessive, it is their right. But it is a right never to be exercised lightly. They must cultivate public opinion and let their case see the light of day. If they do not take these precautions, they will find everything and eveybody arrayed against them and they will find themselves heavy losers in the end.

2nd February, 1922

A WARNING VOICE FROM BENGAL

There is a friend, an old and tried servant of the nation, who never fails to inform me of threatening clouds that appear in time and again on the horizon in Bengal. This time he warns me against countenancing a general non-payment movement. He thinks that precipitate action is quite likely in Bengal as most of the leaders are in jail. I cannot complain, but I cannot help noting that the imprisonment of leaders is due to the criminal folly of the Government which has treated the real peace-makers as if they were peace-breakers. The Government are inviting violence. They are, as if of a set purpose, preparing the country for violence. But here again I must not complain. I admit that most of us had expected all this and more, and yet we came to the conclusion that we had to take our courage in both our hands and move forward without faltering. Our trust then was, as it to-day is, in God.

But I know that we must take every possible precaution to avert every unexpected crisis. I have therefore strongly advised and advise again that wisdom requires that all parts of India should wait for the experiment which I have undertaken personally to supervise. Bengal has done much. She has worked wonders, she has suffered much, is still suffering and is still keeping herself under great restraint. I would appeal to all the Bengal leaders to rest on their oars and not to take a single new step. Let them by all means assert the right of free speech and free association. But there is no occasion for embarking on mass Civil Disobedience, or non-payment, which is one phase of it. The workers will have taken the masses through a richer discipline by advising them to pay the rents due for the current period.

The following appeared in "Young India" of 9th March 1922:

Calcutta's Unreadiness:—A correspondent in the course of a letter from Calcutta writes:

"My mind compels me to say that Bengal is doing nothing about Swadeshi in comparison to the neighbouring Province of Bihar. It is lagging far behind. Even those who boast themselves of being volunteers are not clad in *khaddar*. I have travelled through almost all the important quarters of this great town, but have not found a single person clad in *khaddar*. In Bihar, on the other hand, you will rarely find a man wearing foreign cloth. In the villages they have not yet begun to wear *khaddar dhoties*, but the attempt is being made to replace mill-made *dhoties* with *khaddar* ones."

I have merely given a few extracts from the correspondent's letter. He goes on to say that, if Calcutta's unpreparedness is reflected in the villages of Bengal also, the battle of Satyagraha cannot be won. This letter is supported by several others, but I am not prepared to admit that even in Calcutta no progress has been done in the *khaddar* movement. At the same time, I fear that the charge against Calcutta is mainly true. *khaddar* wear in Calcutta is rather an exception than the rule, and there is no denying the fact that full Satyagraha is impossible without full compliance with the conditions precedent. If we are to usher in peaceful Swaraj—and Swaraj attained by peaceful means must be peaceful Swaraj—we must be as ready for construction as we seem to be for destruction. Boycott and manufacture, evacuation and occupation, disobedience and obedience must go hand in hand, if we are to avoid an interval of confusion, anarchy and civil strife. The *khaddar* movement is the largest part of construction. We dare not neglect it if the struggle is to remain non-violent to the end.

9th February, 1922

AGGRESSIVE *vs.* DEFENSIVE

It is now necessary to understand the exact distinction between aggressive Civil Disobedience and defensive. Aggressive, assertive or offensive Civil Disobedience is non-violent, wilful disobedience of laws of the state whose breach does not involve moral turpitude and which is undertaken as a symbol of revolt against the state. Thus disregard of laws relating to revenue or regulation of personal conduct for the convenience of the state, although such laws in themselves inflict no hardship and do not require to be altered, would be assertive, aggressive or offensive Civil Disobedience.

Defensive Civil Disobedience, on the other hand, is involuntary or reluctant non-violent disobedience of such laws as are in themselves bad and obedience to which would be inconsistent with one's self-respect or human dignity. Thus formation of volunteer corps for peaceful purposes, holding of public meetings for like purposes, publication of articles not contemplating or inciting to violence in spite of prohibitory orders, is defensive Civil Disobedience. And so is conducting of peaceful picketing undertaken with a view to wean people from things or institutions picketed in spite of orders to the contrary. The fulfilment of the conditions mentioned above is as necessary for defensive Civil Disobedience as for offensive Civil Disobedience.

9th February, 1922

AMONG CHRISTIAN CIRCLES

The talk, I hear, is going the round among Christian circles that I have said in private conversation that had India been equipped for the use of arms, I would certainly have resorted to and advised the use of arms. I had fondly hoped that such a thing could never have been said and believed of me in India. I assure my Christian and other readers that I have never made any such statement to any person whatsoever. On the contrary, it has been my belief and practice for over forty years deliberately to practise the doctrine of Non-resistance to evil, not to retaliate. There are more instances than one in my public life when, with the ability to retaliate, I have refrained from doing so and advised friends to do likewise. My life is dedicated to the spread of that doctrine. I read it in the teaching of all the greatest teachers of the world, Zoroaster, Mahavir, Daniel, Jesus, Mahomed, Nanak and a host of others. Indeed, I am not sure that we do justice to Moses when we impute to him the doctrine of retaliation in the sense that he made it obligatory on his followers to exact an eye for an eye and a tooth for a tooth. It may be my wish that is father to the thought. But I do think that in an age when people were unrestrained in their appetite for the enemy's blood, Moses restricted retaliation to equal measure and no more. But I must not lead the reader into religious discussion. Whilst, however, non-violence is now, has ever been and I pray to God it ever may be, my final creed for all occasions, it is true that there are thousands in the ranks of Non-co-operation, with whom non-violence is an expedient or a policy to which they are not committed for all time and all circumstances. They believe that for India and she is constituted, there is no method but that of non-violence for regaining her freedom. And this they believe, not merely because she has no arms or training in them, but also because with her diverse creeds and races there is nothing for her but constant internecine strife, if her children began the habit of invoking the God of war for every occasion. The best of us are beginning to see more in the doctrine of non-violence than when we first approached it.

In this connection, my attention has also been drawn to a paragraph in the *Dnyanodaya*; Sadhu Sundarsingh. it is there stated, 'made quite plain his profound disapproval of Mr. Gandhi's methods, telling him in so many words that they can lead India to nothing but ruin and useless suffering.' I am sorry that the Sadhu's name has been thus dragged into the controversy. But now that it has been, in justice to the Sadhu and the cause, I must say that, so far as my recollection goes, not only did he not disapprove of my methods in 'so many words', but he entirely approved of them and agreed that India had no other choice. We had the closest communion. The Sadhu came purposely to understand some things about which he had no first-hand knowledge. He did not know, for instance, what the implications of the Hindu-Muslim friendship were and where the minorities stood and whether the movement could remain non-violent to the end. We had long discussions over all these and other matters, and he certainly left on me the impression that for a religious man there was no course left open. The greatest difficulty undoubtedly is about the masses keeping non-violent to the end. With men nothing may be possible, for God nothing is impossible. I would fain have avoided any reference whatsoever to our conversation. But the friends who have brought the matter to my notice tell me that Sadhu Sundersingh is on the waters, and that the paragraph in question is being exploited to wean Indian Christians from the movement. It has to stand or fall on its own merits. No certificate can save it, if its professors betray their trust; no condemnation can injure it permanently if the professors remain true to it to the end. But I felt that I could not withhold from the public what I knew about Sadhu Sundersingh's views.

9th February, 1922

CAUTION ABOUT CIVIL DISOBEDIENCE

Writing of his own District, Lala Shyamlal of Maltra says: "The District Magistrate here does not believe in making arrests, unless there is apprehension of a breach of the peace. The result is that our volunteers are having their own way. No foreign cloth is being imported. No liquor contract has been sold." Lala Shyamlal then inquires whether in the districts where no arrests are made people should go out of their way to court arrest. I thought that I had made the position absolutely clear in previous issues. Whilst we may do nothing to avoid arrest in the ordinary course of our duty, we must not go outside our beat in order to compel arrest. That would be either aggressive Civil Disobedience or criminal disobedience. The latter is out of question. The former *i.e.*, aggressive Civil Disobedience is a right to be exercised when necessary and when we are thoroughly ready, and is also a duty we must discharge if we are ready and circumstances require the performance of it. But aggressive Civil Disobedience, whether mass or individual, is a most dangerous weapon though also most effective among all the peaceful weapons at our disposal. I am myself satisfied that the country as a whole is not ready for this form of self-assertion. We have to go through much greater and stricter discipline. We have to understand the exact, I was almost going to say, the spiritual value of obedience to laws and discipline which may be irksome and even repugnant to us. Assertive Civil Disobedience is a right that accrues to us only after severe *tapasya* through which we have not yet gone. Any premature resort to assertive Civil Disobedience therefore may precipitate a crisis we neither anticipate nor want, and which we must avoid by every means we can think of. The least, therefore, that we must do is to await the result of the experiment I personally wish to conduct. It is a new thing and surely, simple prudence requires us to watch that experiment. Indeed, if aggressive Civil Disobedience, whether mass or individual, is attempted in other parts of India, it is likely to embarrass me and damage the country's cause. I invite the attention of all Non-co-operators to the resolution of the Working Committee* which now makes it incumbent upon all the Congress organisations to refrain from aggressive Civil Disobedience except with my express consent and, so far as I can see, the only exception I am likely to make will be in favour of a group of 100 villages in Andhradesha. But even there I have informed Sjt. Konda Venkatapayya that, if it is at all possible for him to avoid taking the offensive, I would appreciate it, and that he would resort to it, only if he found that retracing would be demoralising and if, humanly speaking, he was certain of non-violence being

* *See* appendix.

observed throughout Andhradesha, and also certain that the other conditions laid down by the Congress were strictly fulfilled. I have a suspicion that in many parts of India the condition about the hand-spun *khadi* is not being strictly carried out and that we are not yet everywhere cured of the disease of untouchability. In my opinion, the ability to go to jail is of far less consequence than ability and the readiness to observe in their fulness the conditions about Hindu-Muslim-Sikh-Parsi-Christian unity, about untouchability and hand-spun *khadi*. Without a due fulfilment of these conditions, we shall find that all our going to jail is bravado and so much wasted effort. Self-purification is the main consideration in seeking the prison. Embarrassment of the Government is a secondary consideration. It is my unalterable conviction that, even though the Government may not feel embarrassed in any way whatsoever by the incarceration or even execution of an innocent, unknown but a purified person, such incarceration will be the end of that Government. Even a single lamp dispels the deepest darkness. Non-co-operation is not allopathic treatment, it is homeopathic. The patient does not taste the drops given to him. He is sometimes even incredulous, but if the homeopaths are to be trusted, the tasteless drops or the tiny pills of homeopathy are far more potent than ounce dozes or choking pills of allopathy. I assure the reader that the effect of purifying Non-co-operation is more certain than the effect of homeopathic medicine. I do wish, therefore, that everywhere non-co-operators will insist upon due fulfilment of all the conditions of civil disobedience. One may be a lawyer, title-holder, even a councillor and yet properly eligible for Civil Disobedience, if he is sincerely non-violent in thought, word and deed, wears hand-spun *khadi* as a sacred duty, shuns untouchability as an intolerable evil and believes in the unity of all races and classes of India as for all times essential for the well-being and the attainment, as also retention, of Swaraj.

23rd February, 1922

ESSENCE OF CIVIL DISOBEDIENCE

A friend, a Congress official, writes from Simla:

" In the present mood of my countrymen, I find certain members belonging to different Congress organisations, in order to comply with your behests regarding the practising of Civil Disobedience, have found out certain novel methods of disobeying law by staging certain plays which have been prescribed by the Government, for instance, *Zakhmi-i-Punjab* which was staged sometime ago in Multan and very recently in Simla, resulting in arrests in both the cases. Now, may I ask your opinion about this form of disobedience which was practised before the date fixed as laid down in the resolution of the All-India Congress Committee, viz., 15th January, 1922? Further, were the actors in these plays justified in informing the Government in a spirit of defiance beforehand that they were going to stage a proscribed play and by such action inviting arrests?

" Furthermore, I will draw your attention to the stormy literature which is issuing forth from Delhi and other places in the shape of cheap poetical booklets and is being recited by small boys and by certain irresponsible volunteers (for I must call them irresponsible) containing matter which is obviously inconsistent with the principle of non-violent Non-co-operation, inasmuch as it contains words and phrases which are calculated to spread hatred and create contempt against every individual Englishman in this country and may result in violence. I bring this fact to your notice because, methinks, that the authors pose to be Non-co-operators and to be with you in this struggle for the salvation of our dear motherland. May I ask if this kind of propaganda, instead of proving helpful, will not bring about mischievous results ?"

The staging of the play was certainly not justified if it was done before the 15th January. It was also not justified if it was done without the consent of the Provincial Congress Committee. Every form of Civil Disobedience was subject to the previous sanction of the local Congress Committee. The staging of the play was also unjustified if the play itself was calculated needlessly to excite passions and to induce hatred. Assuming that all the conditions I have named were fulfilled, the managers were quite right in giving previous information to the Government in a dignified manner, because the essence of Civil Disobedience is that it is public and made specially known to those interested in arresting.

As to the "stormy literature," it is a sad thing that pamphlets such as the writer alludes to are being published and so largely patronised. The writer has mentioned two such booklets. I am, however, not printing the names. Some other correspondent sends me one of the booklets also for my edification and advice. The title as well as the contents are objectionable and breathe nothing but hatred. It is our duty to bring every wrong to public notice, but there are ways and ways of doing the things.* No point is gained by

* The following is from *Young India*: I gladly publish though not without sorrow, a letter (omitted in this collection) from a Madras correspondent on the recent occurrences in that city. Evidently the

putting things offensively. The offence contains in the fact itself. To embellish such facts is to detract from the demerit, and at the present moment when people are

---

hooliganism was far more serious than described in the first impressions given by Dr. Rajan. Mr. Rajagopalan is justified in blaming the Non-co-operators.

It is difficult to distinguish between hooligans and Non-co-operators when hundreds or thousands take part in smashing cars, swearing at innocent passengers or threatening a cinema-keeper. Non-co-operators cannot 'have the cake and eat it too. They claim to be millions. They claim to have almost the whole of India at their back. We must either regulate our procedure in accordance with our creed or dissociate ourselves entirely from all mass acitivity, even if it involves self-ostracism. We have still many *hartals* to go through. Let Delhi, Nagpur and other places beware. I would advise them not to have any *hartals* at all, if they cannot with certainty, avoid the disgraceful scenes enacted in Bombay, and unfortunately repeated in Madras. I hope that the Madras Congress Committee will sift the matter thoroughly and take all the blame that attaches to it. After the frightful experience of Bombay, Madras should have been fully insured against all risk of mob violence. Mr. Rajagopalan's letter is fortified with another from an active Non-co-operator. As he makes detailed charges, giving names, I simply content myself with giving a few extracts. The writer says :

"An eye-witness to the mad excesses of that day, I shall be false to my creed of non-violence, if I do not deplore the *hartal* as a miserable failure. The racial bitterness of the Pulianthope days has revived. You have probably read the bitter speeches of the 'non-Brahmin' leaders in their confederation. At a time when you are straining your every nerve to bring the moderates round to your point of view, we, in Madras, have succeeded in widening the gulf between us and the non-Brahmins on the one hand, and the Adi-Dravidas on the other. The least that we can do by way of reparation is a frank confession of our weakness, and a religious endeavour from now to promote inter-communal unity, especially between the Panchamas and others."

I do not hesitate to criticise the Government for sparing neither man, woman nor child. But the Government have no creed of non-violence to fetter their discretion. Their creed is terrorism in the last resort. But non-co-operators have to be above suspicion.

under the pledge of non-violence, publication of such literature is highly reprehensible. It spreads anger and

---

Madras leaves much to be desired if the two letters referred to by me at all tell a true story. I have little doubt that it is in the main true. Then non-co-operators and their friends have certainly not left man, woman or child free from their unholy attention. It was a bad augury of Swaraj to have interfered with women, to have molested the poor scout boys, and otherwise played havoc with the liberty of the people, no matter how provoking their participation in the welcome to the Prince was.

We have more to fear from ourselves than from the violence or mistakes of the Government. The latter, if we use them aright, do us good, as they have already.

Our own violence or untruth will be veritable death for us. If we are not able to set our own house in order we shall cartainly destroy ourselves. Non-co-operation will be a byword of execration and reproach.

In this connection I cannot help noticing a cutting given to me from the *Rangoon Daily News*. It runs :

" We are credibly informed that the wife of Nizamuddin, hackney carriage owner, East Rangoon, got a divorce from her husband on Thursday last, on the ground that he disobeyed the Fatwa in taking his gharries and persuading others to ply at the time of the Prince's visit. "

I make bold to say that whoever granted the divorce (assuming the truth of the statement) grievously erred against the law of Islam and decency. Divorces are not so lightly granted in Islam. If *hartals* can be brought about by means such as the foregoing statement suggests, they can do no good whatsoever. They are no free expression of public opinion. But I am less concerned with the expedience of *hartals* than with the good name of Islam and Non-co-operation. The law of Non-co-operation demands perfect toleration and respect for the opposite opinion and action. The law of Islam, in so far as a non-Muslim can speak of it, requires equally strict toleration. Nothing could have so deeply hurt the Prophet as the intoleration of the people of Mecca during the early period of his ministry towards the new Faith he was preaching. He could not possibly therefore at any time have been party to intolerance. 'There shall be no compulsion in religion' must have descended to

makes the task of offering Civil Disobedience more and more difficult.

16th February, 1922

THE CRIME OF CHAURI CHAURA

(By M. K. Gandhi)

God has been abundantly kind to me. He has warned me the third time that there is not as yet in India that truthful and non-violent atmosphere which, and which alone, can justify mass disobedience, which can be at all described as civil which means gentle, truthful, humble, knowing, wilful yet loving, never criminal and hateful.

He warned me in 1919 when the Rowlatt Act agitation was started. Ahmedabad, Viramgam, and Kheda erred; Amritsar and Kasur erred. I retraced my steps, called it a Himalayan miscalculation, humbled myself before God and man, and stopped not merely mass Civil Disobedience, but even my own which I know was intended to be civil and non-violent.

The next time it was through the events of Bombay that God gave a terrific warning. He made me eye-witness of the deeds of the Bombay mob on the 17th November. The mob acted in the interest of Non-co-operation. I announced my intention to stop the mass Civil Disobedience which was to be immediately started

---

him, when some of his new converts were more zealous than wise in the preaching of the new faith.

Whether we are Hindus or Mussalmans or what, does not matter. The spirit of democracy which we want to spread throughout India cannot be spread by violence whether verbal or physical, whether direct, indirect or threatened.

in Bardoli. The humiliation was greater than in 1919. But it did me good. I am sure that the nation gained by the stopping. India stood for truth and non-violence by the suspension.

But the bitterest humiliation was still to come. Madras did give the warning, but I heeded it not. But God spoke clearly through Chauri Chaura. I understand that constables who were so brutally hacked to death had given much provocation. They had even gone back upon the word, just given by the Inspector, that they would not be molested, but when the procession had passed, the stragglers were interfered with and abused by the constables. The former cried out for help. The mob returned. The constables opened fire. The little ammunition they had was exhausted and they retired to the Thana for safety. The mob, my informant tells me, therefore set fire to the Thana. The self-imprisoned constables had to come out for dear life, and as they did so, they were hacked to pieces and the mangled remains were thrown into the raging flames.

It is claimed that no Non-co-operation volunteer had a hand in the brutality and that the mob had not only the immediate provocation, but they had also general knowledge of the high-handed tyranny of the police in that district. No provocation can possibly justify the brutal murder of men who had been rendered defenceless and had virtually thrown themselves on the mercy of the mob. And when India claims to be non-violent and hopes to mount the throne of Liberty through non-violent means, mob-violence even in answer to grave provocation is a bad augury. Suppose the 'non-violent' disobedience of Bardoli was permitted by God to succeed, the Government had abdicated in favour of the victors of Bardoli, who would control the unruly element that must be expected to perpetrate inhumanity upon due provocation? Non-violent attainment of self-government presupposes a non-violent control over the violent elements in the country. Non-violent Non-co-operators can only succeed, when they have succeeded in attaining control over the hooligans of India, in other words, when the latter also have learnt patriotically or religiously to refrain from their violent activities, at least whilst the campaign of Non-co-operation is going on. The tragedy at Chauri Chaura, therefore, roused me thoroughly.

'But what about your manifesto to the Viceroy and your rejoinder to his reply?' spoke the voice of Satan. It was the bitterest cup of humiliation to drink. 'Surely it is cowardly to withdraw the next day after pompous threats to the Government and promises to the people of Bardoli.' Thus Satan's invitation was to deny Truth and therefore Religion, to deny God Himself. I put my doubts and troubles before the Working Committee and other associates whom I found near me. They did not all agree with me at first. Some of them probably do not even now agree with me. But never has a man been blessed, perhaps, with colleagues and associates so considerate and forgiving as I have. They understood my difficulty and patiently followed my argument. The result is before the public in the shape of the resolutions of the Working Committee.* The drastic reversal of practically the whole of the aggressive programme may be politically unsound and unwise, but there is no doubt that it is religiously sound, and I venture to assure the doubters that the country will have gained by my humiliation and confession of error.

The only virtue I want to claim is Truth and Non-violence. I lay no claim to superhuman powers. I want

*See *infra*.

none. I wear the same corruptible flesh that the weakest of my fellow beings wears, and am therefore as liable to err as any. My services have many limitations, but God has up to now blessed them in spite of the imperfections.

For, confession of error is like a broom that sweeps away dirt and leaves the surface cleaner than before. I feel stronger for my confession. And the cause must prosper for the retracing. Never has man reached his destination by persistence in deviation from the straight path.

It has been urged that Chauri Chaura cannot affect Bardoli. There is danger, it is argued, only if Bardoli is weak enough to be swayed by Chauri Chaura and is betrayed into violence. I have no doubt whatsoever no that account. The people of Bardoli are, in my opinion, the most peaceful in India. But Bardoli is but a speck no the map of India. 'Its effort cannot succeed unless there is perfect co-operation from the other parts. Bardoli's disobedience will be civil only when the other parts of India remain non-violent, just as the addition of a grain of arsenic to a pot of milk renders it unfit as food so will the civility of Bardoli prove unacceptable by the addition of the deadly poison from Chauri Chaura. The latter represents India as much as Bardoli.

Chauri Chaura is after all an aggravated symptom. I have never imagined that there has been no violence, mental or physical, in the places where repression is going on. Only I have believed, I still believe and the pages of *Young India* amply prove, that the repression is out of all proportion to the insignificant popular violence in the areas of repression. The determined holding of meetings in prohibited area I do not call violence. The violence I am referring to is the throwing of brickbats or intimidation and coercion practised in stray cases. As a matter of fact, in Civil Disobedience there should be no excitement. Civil Disobedience is a preparation for mute suffering. Its effect is marvellous though unperceived and gentle. But I regarded a certain amount of excitement as inevitable, a certain amount of unintended violence even pardonable, *i.e.*, I did not consider Civil Disobedience impossible in somewhat imperfect conditions. Under perfect conditions, disobedience when civil is hardly felt. But the present movement is admittedly a dangerous experiment under fairly adverse conditions.

The tadgedy of Chauri Chaura is really the index finger. It shows the way India may easily go, if drastic precautions be not taken. If we are not to evolve violence out of non-violence, it is quite clear that we must hastily retrace our steps and re-establish an atmosphere of peace, re-arrange our programme and not think of starting mass Civil Disobedience until we are sure of peace being retained in spite of mass Civil Disobedience being started and in spite of Government provocation. We must be sure of unauthorised portions not starting mass Civil Disobedience.

As it is, the Congress organisation is still imperfect and its instructions are still perfunctorily carried out. We have not established Congress Committees in every one of the villages. Where we have, they are not perfectly amenable to our instructions. We have not probably more than one crore of members on the roll. We are in the middle of February, yet not many have paid the annual four annas subscription for the current year. Volunteers are indifferently enrolled. They do not conform to all the conditions of their pledge. They do not even wear hand-spun and hand-woven *khaddar*.

All the Hindu volunteers have not yet purged themselves of the sin of untouchability. All are not free from the taint of violence. Not by their imprisonment are we going to win Swaraj or serve the holy cause of the Khilafat or attain the ability to stop payment to faithless servants. Some of us err in spite of ourselves. But some others among us sin wilfully. They join volunteer corps well knowing that they are not and do not intend to remain non-violent. We are thus untruthful even as we hold the Government to be untruthful. We dare not enter the kingdom of Liberty with mere lip homage to Truth and Non-violence.

Suspension of mass Civil Disobedience and subsidence of excitement are necessary for further progress, indeed indispensable to prevent further retrogression. I hope, therefore, that by suspension every Congressman or woman will not only not feel disappointed but he or she will feel relieved of the burden of unreality and of national sin.

Let the opponent glory in our humiliation or so called defeat. It is better to be charged with cowardice and weakness than to be guilty of denial of our oath and sin against God. It is million times better to *appear* untrue before the world than to *be* untrue to ourselves.

And so, for me the suspension of mass Civil Disobedience and other minor activities that were calculated to keep up excitement is not enough penance for my having been the instrument, howsoever involuntary, of the brutal violence by the people at Chauri Chaura.

I must undergo personal cleansing. I must become a fitter instrument able to register the slightest variation in the moral atmosphere about me. My prayers must have much deeper truth and humility about them than their evidence. And for me there is nothing so helpful and cleansing as a fast accompanied by the necessary mental co-operation.

I know that the mental attitude is everything. Just as a prayer may be merely a mechanical intonation as of a bird, so may a fast be a mere mechanical torture of the flesh. Such mechanical contrivances are valueless for the purpose intended. Again, just as a mechanical chant may result in the modulation of voice, a mechanical fast may result in purifying the body. Neither will touch the soul within.

But a fast undertaken for fuller self-expression, for attainment of the spirit's supremacy over the flesh, is a most powerful factor in one's evolution. After deep consideration, therefore, I am imposing on myself a five day's continuous fast permitting myself water. It commenced on Sunday evening, it ends on Friday evening. This is the least I must do.

I have taken into consideration the All-India Congress Committee meeting in front of me. I have in mind the anxious pain even the five days' fast will cause many friends; but I can no longer postpone the penance nor lessen it.

I urge co-workers not to copy my example. The motive in their case will be lacking. They are not the orginators of Civil Disobedience. I am in the unhappy position of a surgeon proved skilless to deal with an admittedly dangerous case. I must either abdicate or acquire greater skill. Whilst the personal penance is not only necessary but obligatory on me, the exemplary self-restraint prescribed by the Working Committee is surely sufficient penance for every one else. It is no small penance and if sincerely carried out, it can become infinitely more fruitful than a greater fulfilment of the vow of non-violence in thought, word and deed or the spread of that sprit. It will be more than food for me during the week to observe that comrades are all silently and without idle discussion, engaged in fulfilling the constructive programme sketched by the Working Committee, in enlisting Congress members after making sure that they understand the Congress creed of truth and non-violence for the attainment of Swaraj, in daily life and religiously.spinning for a fixed time, in introducing the wheel of prosperity and freedom in every home, in visiting 'untouchable' homes and finding out their wants, in inducing national schools to receive 'untouchable' children, in organising social service specially designed to find a common platform for every variety of man and woman, and in visiting the homes which the drink curse is desolating, in establishing real *Panchayats* and in organising national schools on a proper footing. The workers will be better engaged in these activities than in fasting. I hope, therefore, that no one will join me in fasting, either through false sympathy or in ignorant conception of the spiritual value of fasting.

All fasting and all penance must as far as possible be secret. But my fasting is both a penance and a punishment, and a punishment has to be public. It is penance for me and punishment for those whom I try to serve, for whom I love to live and would equally love to die. They have unintentionally sinned against the laws of the Congress, though they were sympathisers if not actually connected with it. Probably they hacked the constables—their countrymen and fellow beings—with my name on their lips. The only way love punishes is by suffering. I cannot even wish them to be arrested. But I would let them know that I would suffer for their breach of the Congress creed. I would advise those who feel guilty and repentant to hand themselves voluntarily to the

Government for punishment and make a clean confession. I hope that the workers in the Gorakhpur district will leave no stone unturned to find out the evil-doers and urge them to deliver themselves into custody. But whether the murderers accept my advice or not, I would like them to know that they have seriously interfered with Swaraj operations, that, in being the cause of the postponement of the movement in Bardoli, they have injured the very cause they probably intended to serve. I would like them to know, too, that this movement is not a cloak or a preparation for violence. I would, at any rate, suffer every humiliation, every torture, absolute ostracism and death itself to prevent the movement from becoming violent or a precursor of violence. I make my penance public also, because I am now denying myself the opportunity of sharing their lot with the prisoners. The immediate issue has again shifted. We can no longer press for the withdrawal of notifications or discharge of prisoners. They and we must suffer for the crime of Chauri Chaura. The incident proves, whether we wish it or no, the unity of life. All, including even the administrators, must suffer. Chauri Chaura must stiffen the Government, must still further corrupt the police, and the reprisals that will follow must further demoralise the people. The suspension and the penance will take us back to the position we occupied before the tragedy. By strict discipline and purification we regain the moral confidence required for demanding the withdrawal of notifications and the discharge of prisoners.

If we learn the full lesson of the tragedy, we can turn the curse into a blessing. By becoming truthful and non-violent, both in spirit and deed, and by making the swadeshi, *i.e.*, the *khaddar* programme complete, we can establish full Swaraj and redress the Khilafat and the Punjab wrongs without a single person having to offer Civil Disobedience.

23rd February, 1922

BARDOLI AND AFTER

Mahatma Gandhi wrote the following notes in *Young India* in justification of the Bardoli Decision.:

Only '6 Months' Simple' for the President.—If Begum Abul Kalam Azad and the Maulana* himself complain about the inadequacy of the sentence pronounced upon the Maulana Saheb,* what must be the feeling of the President of the Congress and his devoted partner on having heard that he together with Mr. Sasmal was to have only 6 months' simple imprisonment? Why on earth the trial should have been dragged and judgment postponed it such an untheatrical sentence was to be pronounced, only the Government can tell. The gossip that was sent to me along the rails was that the Government were seeking a suitable opportunity for discharging both the Maulana and the Deshabandhu. The latest gossip which is supposed to be authentic, I dare not disclose. Nor is it of importance for the reader to know. We must take, not even excluding the President, our lot as it comes to us. I am receiving biting letters from corrsepondents accusing me of simplicity, of hard-heartedness, of faint-heartedness and all such kindred weaknesses. Some correspondents tell me that I have sold the cause of the prisoners. Others tell me that I have thrown all my Non-co-operation views to the winds and I have been faithless to the President of the Congress. Fortunately, many years of service have given me a

*For being a member of an unlawful assembly under the Cr. L. A.

fairly tough hide and these shafts do not pierce it, but I do assure all these impatient critics that not a particle of the principle of Non-co-operation has been surrendered by the resolutions. On the contrary, refusal to suspend mass Civil Disobedience in the face of grave warnings from Nature would have meant a complete surrender of the fundamental principle of Non-co-operation. The discharge of prisioners I purposely brought to the surface when it became a point of national honour, because with the change of issue from the immediate attainment of the triple goal to the immediate attainment of the three-fold freedom, the demand for the discharge of prisioners became a natural consequence. But Chauri Chaura has raised another immediate issue, *viz.*, terrible penance and a fierce process of purification and this penitential purification requires the sacrifice of the imprisioned workers and the temporary sacrifice of many of our activities which have revivified the nation. But such things happen in all wars, much more frequently in spiritual warfare such as ours is claimed to be. I call it spiritual in the sense that we have resolutely declined to make use of physical force for the attainment of our end. We were in danger of being drifted away from our moorings, and it was necessary for us to return, but the return is merely meant to give us greater purity, greater perception and therefore greater strength, and if Non-co-operators have to become seasoned soldiers for the nation's battle, they will doubtless understand the value of waiting and preparing. He who waits for preparation or otherwise, advances the cause as much as the warrior who stands three feet deep in the trenches. All our sufferings will have been lost upon us if we do not realise these elements of the science of war, whether it is spiritual or physical.

Constructive Programme.—Hence it is that the constructive programme has been framed. It will steady and calm us. It will wake our organising spirit, it will make us industrious, it will render us fit for Swaraj, it will cool our blood. We shall be spat upon, laughed at, sworn at, may be even kicked and cursed. We must put up with it all in as much as we have harboured anger in our breasts even though we have been under the pledge of non-violence. I must frankly state that unless we can retrieve our steps deliberately, cultivate non-violence and manufacture *Khaddar*, we cannot render effective help to the Khilafat, we cannot get redness of the Punjab wrong, nor can we attain Swaraj. My leadership is perfectly useless if I cannot convince co-workers and the public of the absolute and immediate necessity of vigorously prosecuting the constructive programme.

We must know whether we can get a crore men and women in all India who believe in the attainment of Swaraj by peaceful, *i.e.*, Non-violent and legitimate, *i.e.*. truthful means.

We must get money for the prosecution of Swadeshi and we will know how many people there are in India who are willing honestly to pay one rupee out of every hundred of their past year's income to the Tilak Memorial Swaraj Fund. This subscription the Committee expects from Congressmen and sympathisers.

We must spend money like water in introducing the spinning wheel in every home, in the manufacture and the distribution of *khaddar* wherever required.

Surely we have long neglected the 'untouchable' brother. He has slaved for us too long. We must now serve him.

Our liquor picketing has done some good but not

substantial. Not till we pierce the home of the drunkard shall we make any real advance. We must know why he drinks; what we can substitute for it. We must have a census of all the drunkards of India.

Social Service Department has been looked at with the utmost contempt. If the Non-co-operation movement is not malicious, that department is a necessity. We want to render alike to friend and foe service in times of distress. We are thereby able to keep our relations sweet with all in spite of our political aloofness.

Laughing at it.—Social service and temperance reform were laughed at as part of the struggle of Swaraj. It was a painful exhibition of ignorance of the essentials of Swaraj. I claim that human mind or human society is not divided into water-tight compartments called social, political and religious. All act and react upon one another. What is more, the vast majority of Hindus and Mussalmans have joined the struggle believing it to be religious. The masses have come in, because they want to save the Khilafat and the Cow. Deprive the Mussalman of the hope of helping the Khilafat and he will shun the Congress; tell the Hindu he cannot save the Cow if he joins the Congress, he will to a man leave it. To laugh at moral reform and social service is to laugh at Swaraj, the Khilafat and the Punjab.

Even the organisation of schools was laughed at. Let us see what it means. We have demolished the prestige of Government schools. It was perhaps necessary in 1920 to do the picketing and certainly not to mind the boys being neglected, but it would be criminal any longer to picket Government schools or to neglect National institutions. We can now only draw more boys and girls by putting existing National schools on a better footing. They have the advantage of being institutions where they breathe free air and where they are not shadowed. But the advantage of scientific training in carding, hand-spinning and hand-weaving and of having intellectual training in keeping with the requirements of the country must be added. We shall show by successful experiment the superiority of training in National schools and colleges.

Even the *Panchayats* come in for ridicule. Little did the critics realise that the masses in many parts of India had ceased to resort to law courts. If we do not organise honest *Panchayats*, they will certainly go back to the existing lawcourts.

Political Results.—Nor is a single step devoid of vast political results. Adequate manufacture and universal use of *khaddar* means a permanent boycott of foreign cloth and automatic distribution of sixty crores of rupees annually among the poor people. Permanent disappearance of the drink and the opium evils means an annual saving of seventeen crores to the people and a diminution of that revenue for the Government. Constructive effort for the untouchables means the addition to the Congress ranks of six crores of men and women who will for ever be bound to the Congress. Social Service Department, if it becomes a live thing, will restore the strained relations that exist to-day among co-operators (whether Indian or English) and Non-co-operators. To work the full constructive programme therefore is to achieve all we want. To fail in fulfilling the programme is to postpone all possibility of effective Civil Disobedience.

Need of Excitement!—Some friends argue that in order to continue the struggle the people need some stimulant.

No person or nation can be kept alive merely upon stimulants. We have had much too much of it latterly. And the antidote now is a depressant. If therefore depression follows the cessation of all aggressive activities and people forsake us, it would not only not hinder our cause but help it. Then we shall not have to shoulder the responsibility for the Chauri Chaura. Then we could go forward with a steady step without any danger of having to look back. If however we can survive the depression and keep the people with us, we shall have positive proof that the people have caught the message of non-violence and that the people are as capable of doing constructive work as they have shown themselves capable of doing destructive work. Whatever the result, the present excitement must be abated at any cost.

What of the Khilafat?—Several Mussalman friends have said: "Your programme is good for Swaraj but it is too slow to be good enough for saving the Khilafat. The Khilafat question will be solved in a few months and whatever can be done must be done now." Let us examine the question. The cause of the Khilafat, thank God, is safe in the hands of Gazi Mustafa Kamal Pasha. He has retrieved the prestige of the Khilafat as no Mussalman of modern times has done. India has in my opinion helped not much by her money though that has meant something, but by Hindu-Muslim unity and by telling the Government in the plainest terms possible that India will have nothing to do with the Government and will declare complete independence if England persists in her anti-Turk policy and exploits India's resources against the Turks. The greater the strength in that declaration, the greater becomes the prestige of

Islam and the greater the power of Mustafa Kemal Pasha. Some people think that mere temporary embarrassment of the Government by a few thousand men, irrespective of qualification, going to jail will make the Government yield to our wishes. Let us not underrate the power of the Government. I am sure that the Government does possess as yet the power to crush the spirit of violence. And it is nothing but violence to go to jail anyhow. It is the suffering of the pure and God-fearing which will tell, not the bluster of the rabble. The purer India becomes, the stronger she becomes. Purity is the only weapon of the weak in body. The strong in body in their insolence often mobilise their 'hard fibre' and seek to usurp the very function of the Almighty. But when that 'hard fibre' comes in contact, not with its like, but with the exact opposite, it has nothing to work against. A solid body can only move on and against another solid body. You cannot build castles in the air. Therefore, the impatient Mussalmans must see the obvious truth that the little disorganised bluster of the rabble, whether it expresses itself by going to jail or by burning buildings or by making noisy demonstrations, will be no match for the organised insolence of the 'hard fibre' of the 'most determined people in the world.' This terrific insolence can only be met by the utter humility of the pure and the meek. God helps the helpless, not those who believe they can do something. Every page of the Koran teaches me, a non-Muslim, this supreme lesson. Every *sura* of the Koran begins in the name of God, the Compassionate and the Merciful. Let us therefore be strong in soul, though weak in body.

If the Mussalmans believe in the policy of non-violence, they must give it a fair trial and they will not have given it any trial at all, if they harbour anger, *i.e.*, violence in their breasts.

As it is, by our bluster, by show of force, by violent picketing we shall estrange more than intimidate men into co-operation with us. And how can we dare seek co-operation by compulsion when we have refused to be coerced into co-operation with the Government? Must we not observe the same law that we expect others to observe towards us?

If the Treaty of Sevres is not revised to our satisfaction, it is not finished. The virtue lies in India's determination, not to be satisfied with anything less than her demands. After all, Mustafa Kemal may not insist upon the settlement of the Jazurut-ul-Arab. We must continue the fight, so long as it is not returned in tact to the Mussalmans. If the Mussalmans consider that they can gain their end by force of arms, let them secede from the non-violent alliance by all means. But if they know that they cannot, let them carry it out in thought, word and deed, ane they will find that there is no surer or quicker remedy for assuaging their grief and redressing the Khilafat wrong.

'*Somersaults*'.—I have carefully read Mr. Kelkar's article in the *Mahratta* criticising the Bardoli resolutions. I acknowledge the gentle and considerate manner with which he has handled me. I wish I could persuade him and many who think like Mr. Kelkar that what he calls a somersalt was an inevitable operation. Consistency is a desirable quality, but it becomes a 'hobgoblin' when it refuses to see facts. I have known dispositions of armies changed from hour to hour. Once during the Zulu revolt, we were all asleep. We had definite orders for the morrow. But suddenly at about midnight, we were awakened and ordered to retire behind bags of grain which served as protecting walls, because the enemy was reported to be creeping up the hill on which we had encamped. In another hour it was understood that it was a false alarm and we were permitted to retire to our tents. All the 'Somersaults' were necessary changes. Remedies vary with the variation in diagnosis. The same physician one day detects malaria and gives a large dose of quinine, detects typhoid the next and stops all medicine and orders careful nursing and fasting, later detects consumption and orders change and solid food. Is the physician capricious or cautious and honest?

Without being untruthful and indifferent, if not stupid, I could not do what Mr. Kelkar suggests I should have done at the time of the Bombay Conference. It would have been untruthful to have yielded to the Moderate friends beyond what was conceded, as the Indian sky appeared to me to be clear blue and promised to remain so. My diagnosis may be blamed but not my decision based on the then diagnosis, nor could I possibly conceal the demands especially in the teeth of the Viceregal declaration at Calcutta that nothing was to be expected in the matters of the Khilafat and the Punjab, and that, as the reforms had only just been granted, no advance was to be expected. I would have been unfair to the Viceroy as also to the Moderate friends if I had not said that our demands were emphatic and clear-cut. To have then suspended mass Civil Disobedience would have been a weakness. But Chauri Chaura darkened the horizon and I discovered a new diagnosis. It would have been idiotic on my part not to have declared in the clearest possible language that the patient required a drastic change of treatment. Not to have suspended after

Chauri Chaura would have been unpardonable weakness. I assure the reader that Bardoli's unpreparedness had nothing to do with the decision. For Bardoli, in my opinion, was quite able to give battle. I have stated several times in the columns of *Young India* and *Nava Jivan* that I considered Bardoli to be quite ready for the fray.

The fact is that the critics do not realise the implications of Civil Disobedience. They seem unconsciously to ignore the potent adjective 'Civil.'

The more I think of the Bardoli decision and the more I rehearse the debates and the talks at Delhi, the more convinced I am of the correctness of the decision and of the necessity of Provinces stopping all offensive activities for the time being, even at the risk of being considered weak, and forfeiting popular applause and support.

2nd March, 1922

THE ALL-INDIA CONGRESS COMMITTEE

(By M. K. Gandhi)

The session, just past, of the All-India Congress Committee was in some respects more memorable than the Congress. There is so much under-current of violence, both conscious and unconscious, that I was actually and literally praying for a disastrous defeat. I have always been in a minority. The reader does not know that in South Africa I started with practical unanimity, reached a minority of sixty-four and even sixteen, and went up again to a huge majority. The best and the most solid work was done in the wilderness of minority.

I know that the only thing that the Government dread is the huge majority I seem to command. They little know that I dread it even more than they, I have become literally sick of the adoration of the unthinking multitude. I would feel certain of my ground if I was spat upon by them. Then there would be no need for confession of Himalayan and other miscalculations, no retracing, no re-arranging.

But it was not to be.

A friend warned me against exploiting my dictatorship. He little knew that I had never once used it, if only because the legal occasion had not yet arisen for its use. The 'dictatorship' accrues to me only when the ordinary Congress machinery is rendered unworkable by the Government.

Far from my consciously or unconsciously exploiting my 'dictatorship', I have begun to wonder if I am not unconsciously allowing myself to be 'exploited.' I confess that I have a dread of it such as I never had before. My only safety lies in my shamelessness. I have warned my friends of the Committee that I am incorrigible. I shall continue to confess blunders each time the people commit them. The only tyrant I accept in this world is the 'still small voice' within. And even though I have to face the prospect of a minority of one, I humbly believe I have the courage to be in such a hopeless minority. That to me is the only truthful position.

But I am a sadder, and I hope, a wiser man to-day. I see that our non-violence is skin-deep. We are burning with indignation. The Government is feeding it by its insensate acts. It seems almost as if the Government wants to see this land covered with murder, arson and rapine, in order to be able once more to claim exclusive ability to put them down.

This non-violence therefore seems to be due merely to our helplessness. It almost appears as if we are nursing in our bosoms the desire to take revenge the first time we get the opportunity.

Can true voluntary non-violence come out of this seeming forced non-violence of the weak? It is not a futile experiment I am conducting? What if, when the fury bursts, not a man, woman or child is safe and every man's hand is raised against his fellow being? Of what avail is it then, if I fast myself to death in the event of such a catastrophe coming to pass.

What is the alternative? To lie and say that what I know to be evil, is good? To say that true and voluntary co-operation will come out of false and forced co-operation is to say that light will result from darkness.

Co-operation with the Government is as much a weakness and a sin, as alliance with suspended violence.

The difficulty is almost insurmountable. Hence with the growing knowledge of the fact that this non-violence is merely superficial, I must continually make mistakes and retrace, even as a man wading his way through a tractless forest must continually stop, retrace, stumble, be hurt and even bleed.

I was prepared for a certain amount of depression' disappointment and resentment, but I confess I was totally unprepared for the hurricane of opposition. It became clear to me that the workers were in no mood to do any serious work of construction. The constructive programme lent no enchantment. They were not a social reform association. They could not wrest power from the Government by such humdrum reform work. They wanted to deliver 'non-violent' blows! All this appeared so thoroughly unreal. They would not stop think that even if they could defeat the Government by a childish display of rage, they could not conduct the

Government of the country for a single day without serious and laborious organisation and construction.

We must not go to gaol, as Mahomed Ali would say, 'on a false issue.' It is not *any* imprisonment that will lead to Swaraj. It is not *every* disobedience that will fire us with the sprit of obedience and discipline. Jails are no gate-way to liberty for the confirmed criminal. They are temples of liberty only for those who are innocence personified. The execution of Socrates made immortality a living reality for us,—not so the execution of countless murderers. There is no warrant for supposing that we can steal Swaraj by the imprisonment of thousands of nominally non-violent men with hatred, ill-will and violence raging in their breasts.

It would be otherwise, if we were fighting with arms, giving and receiving blow for blow. The imprisonment of those who may be caught intimidating, assaulting and murdering will certainly embarrass the Government and when they are tired, they would as elsewhere yield. But such is not our fight to-day. Let us be truthful. If it is through 'show of force' that we wish to gain Swaraj, let us drop non-violence and offer such violence as we may. It would be a manly, honest and sober attitude—an attitude the world has been used to for ages past. No one can then accuse us of the terrible charge of hypocrisy.

But the majority will not listen to me. In spite of all my warnings and passionate plea for rejecting my resolution, if they did not believe in non-violence as indispensdble for the attainment of our gaol, they accepted it without a single material change. I would ask them therefore to realise their responsibility. They are now bound not to rush to Civil Disobedience, but to settle down to the quiet work of construction. I would urge them to be indifferent to the clamour for immediate action. The immediate action is not courting imprisonment, nor even free speech and free association or free pen, but self-purification, introspection, quiet organisation. We have lost our foothold. If we do not take care, we are likely to be drowned in the waters whose depth we do not know.

It is no use thinking of the prisoners. When I heard of Chauri Chaura, I sacrificed them as the first penitential act. They have gone to jail to be released only by the strength of the people, indeed the hope was the Swaraj Parliament's first act would be to open the prison gates. God had decreed otherwise. We who are outside have tried and failed. The prisoners can now only gain by serving the full term of their imprisonment. Those who went under false pretences, or under any misapprehension or under a mistaken understanding of the movement can come out by apologising and by petitioning. The movement will be all the stronger for the purging. The stoutest hearts will rejoice in the opportunity of unexpectedly greater suffering. Though thousands of Russians have 'rotted' in the Russian prisons for years and years, those unhappy people are not yet free. Liberty is a jilt most difficult to woo and please. We have shown the power of suffering. But we have not suffered enough. If the people in general keep passively non-violent and if only a few are actively, honestly and knowingly non-violent in intent, word and deed, we can reach the gaol in quickest time with the least suffering. But we shall indefinitely postpone the attainment, if we send to prison men who harbour violence in their breasts.

Therefore, the duty of the majority in their respective provinces is to face taunts, insults, and if need be depletion in their ranks, but determinedly to pursue their goal without swerving an inch. The authorities mistaking our suspension for weakness may resort to still greater oppression. We should submit to it. We should even abandon defensive Civil Disobedience and concentrate all our energy on the tasteless but health-giving economic and social reform. We should bend down on our knees and assure the Moderates that they need fear no harm from us. We should assure the Zamindars that we have no ill-will against them.

The average Englishman is haughty, he does not understand us, he considers himself to be a superior being. He thinks that he is born to rule us. He relies upon his forts or his gun to protect himself. He despises us. He wants to compel co-operation, *i.e.*, slavery. Even him we have to conquer, not by bending the knee, but remaining aloof from him, but at the same time not hating him nor hurting him. It is cowardly to molest him. If we simply refuse to regard ourselves as his slaves and pay homage to him, we have done our duty. A mouse can only shun the cat. He cannot treat with her till she has filled the points of her claws and teeth. At the same time, we must show every attention to those few Englishmen who are trying to cure themselves and fellow Englishmen of the disease of race superiority.

The minority has different ideals. It does not believe in the programme. Is it not right and patriotic for them to form a new party and a new organisation? They will then truly educate the country. Those who do not believe in the creed should surely retire from the Congress. Even a national organisation must have a creed. One, for instance, who does not believe in Swaraj has no place in the Congress. I submit that even so has one who does not believe in 'peaceful and legitimate means' no place in the Congress. A Congressman may not believe in Non-co-operation and still remain in it, but he cannot believe in violence and untruth and still be a Congressman. I was therefore deeply hurt when I found opposition to the note in the resolution about the creed and still more when I found opposition to my paraphrase of the two adjectives 'peaceful' and 'legitimate' into 'non-violent' and 'truthful' respectively. I had reasons for the paraphrase. I was seriously told that the creed did not insist upon non-violence and truth as the indispensable means for the attainment of Swaraj. I agreed to remove the paraphrase in order to avoid a painful discussion, but I felt that truth was stabbed.

I am sure that those who raised this opposition are as patriotic as I claim to be, they are as eager for Swaraj as every other Congressman. But I do say that the patriotic spirit demands their loyal and strict adherence to non-violence and truth and if they do not believe in them, they should retire from the Congress organisation.

It is not national economy to let all the ideals be sharply defined and to work independently of one another? That then which is most popular will win the day. If we are going to evolve the real spirit of democracy, we shall not do so by obstruction but by abstention.

The session of the All-India Congress Committee was a forcible demonstration of the fact that we are retarding the country's progress towards Swaraj, and not the Government. Every mistake of the Government helps. Every neglect of duty on our part hinders.

2nd March, 1922

THE BARDOLI RESOLUTIONS

The following resolution was passed on the 25th ultimo at the session of the All-India Congress Committee held at Delhi:

The All-India Congress Committee having carefully considered the resolutions passed by the Working Committee at its meeting held at Bardoli on the 11th and 12th instant, confirms the said resolutions noted therein and further resolves that individual Civil Disobedience whether of a defensive or aggressive character may be commenced in respect of particular places or particular laws at the instance of and upon permission being granted therefor by the respective Provincial Committee; provided that such Civil Disobedience shall not be permitted unless all the conditions laid down by the Congress or the All-India Congress Committee or the Working Committee are stictly fulfilled.

Reports having been received from various quarters that picketing regarding foreign cloth is as necessary as liquor picketing, the All-India Congress Committee authorises such picketing of a *bona fide* character on the same terms as liquor-picketing mentioned in the Bardoli resolutions*. The All-India Congress Committee wishes it to be understood that the resolutions of the Working Committee do not mean any abandonment of the original Congress programme of Non-co-operation or permanent abandonment of mass Civil Disobedience, but considers that an atmosphere of necessary mass non-violence can be established by the workers concentrating upon the constructive programme framed by the Working Committee at Bardoli.

* Given below

The All-India Congress Committee holds Civil Disobedience to be the right and duty of the people to be exercised and performed, whenever the State opposes the declared will of the people.

Note :—Individual Civil Disobedience is disobedience of orders or laws by a single individual or an ascertained number of group of individuals. Therefore a prohibited public meeting where admission is regulated by tickets and to which no unauthorised admission is allowed, is an instance of Individual Civil Disobedience, whereas a prohibited meeting to which the general public is admitted without any restriction is an instance of Mass Civil Disobedience. Such Civil Disobedience is defensive when a prohibited public meeting is held for conducting a normal activity, although it may result in arrest. It would be aggressive if it is held not for any normal activity, but merely for the purpose of courting arrest and imprisonment.

The following appeared in *Young India* of 2nd March, 1922 :

The Bardoli Resolutions : (As revised and confirmed by the A. I. C. C., 11th February, 1922) :

1. The Working Committee deplores the inhuman conduct of the mob at Chauri Chaura, in having brutally murdered constables and wantonly burnt the police *thana* and tenders its sympathy to the families of the bereaved.

In view of Nature's repeated warnings every time mass Civil Disobedience has been imminent and some popular violent outburst has taken place indicating that the atmosphere in the country is not non-violent enough for mass Civil Disobedience, the latest instance being the tragic and terrible events at Chauri Chaura near Gorakhpur, the Working Committee of the Congress resolves that mass Civil Disobedience contemplated at Bardoli and elsewhere be suspended, and instructs the local Congress Committees forthwith to advise the cultivators to pay the land revenue and other taxes due to the Government and whose payment might have been suspended in anticipation of mass Civil Disobedience, and instructs them to suspend every other preparatory activity of an offensive nature.

The suspension of mass Civil Disobedience shall be continued till the atmosphere is so non-violent as to ensure the non-repetition of popular atrocities such as at Gorakhpur or hooliganism such as at Bombay and Madras respectively on the 17th November 1921 and 13th January last.

In order to promote a peaceful atmosphere, the Working Committee advises till further instruction all Congress organisations to stop activities specially designed to court arrest and imprisonment save normal Congress activities including voluntary *hartals* wherever an absolutely peaceful atmosphere can be assured and for that end all picketing shall be stopped save for the *bonafide* and peaceful purpose of warning the visitors to liquor-shops against the evils of drinking, such picketing to be controlled by Persons of known good character and specially selected by the Congress Committees concerned.

The Working Committee advises till further instructions the stoppage of all volunteer processions and public meetings merely for the purpose of defiance of the notification regarding such meetings; this, however, shall not interfere with the private meetings of Congress and other Committees or public meetings which are required for the conduct of the normal activities of the Congress.

Complaints having been brought to the notice of the Working Committee that ryots are not paying rents to the Zemindars, the Working Committee advises Congress workers and organisations to inform the ryots that such witholding of rents is contrary to the resolutions of the Congress and that it is injurious to the best interests of the country.

The Working Committee assures the Zemindars that the Congress movement is in no way intended to attack their legal rights and that even where the ryots have grievances, the Committee's desire is that redress should be sought by mutual consultations and by the usual recourse to arbitration.

Complaints having been brought to the notice of the Working Committee that in the formation of Volunteer Corps great laxity prevails in the selection and that insistence is not had on the full use of hand-spun and hand-woven *khaddar* and on the full observance by Hindus of the rule as to the removal of untouchability nor is care being taken to ascertain that the candidates believe fully in the observance of non-violence in intent, word and deed in terms of the Congress resolution, the Working Committee calls upon all Congress organisations to revise their lists and remove from them the names of all such volunteers as do not strictly conform to the requirements of the pledge.

The Working Committee is of opinion that unless Congressmen carry out to the full the Congress constitution and the resolutions from time to time issued by the Working Committee, it is not possible to achieve its objects expeditiously or at all.

The foregoing resolution will have effect only pending the meeting to be specially convened of the All-India Congress Committee and thereafter subject to confirmation by it, the Secretary to call such meeting as early as possible after consultation with Hakim Ajmal Khan.

II. In the opinion of the Working Committee a project is necessary for the purpose of finding employment for those who may give up Government service and to that end the Committee appoints Messrs. Mian Mahomed Haji Jan Mahomed Chhotani, Jamnalal Bajaj and V. J. Patel to draw up a scheme for consideration by the special meeting of the All-India Congress Committee.

III. 12th February: Whereas the Gorakhpur tragedy is a powerful proof of the fact that the mass-mind has not yet fully realised the necessity of non-violence as an integral, active and chief part of Mass Civil Disobedience, and whereas the reported indiscriminate acceptance of persons as volunteers in contravention of the Congress instructions betrays want of appreciation of the vital part of Satyagraha and whereas in the opinion of the Working Committee the delay in the attainment of the national aim is solely due to the weak and incomplete execution in practice of the constitution of the Congress and with a view to perfecting the internal organisation:

The Working Committee advises all Congress organisations to be engaged in the following activities:

(1) To enlist at least one crore of members of the Congress,

Note (i):—Since *peaceful* * and *legitimate means*† are the essence of the Congress creed, no person should be enlisted who does not believe in such means as indispensable for the attainment of Swaraj. The creed of the

* Replaced for *peace* (*non-violence*).

† " " *legitimateness* (*truth*).

This is a fresh addition.

Congress must therefore be carefully explained to each person who is appealed to join the Congress.

Note (ii) :—The workers should note that no one who does not pay the annual subscription can be regarded as a qualified Congressman; all the old members are therefore to be advised to re-register their names.

(2) To popularise the Spinning Wheel and to organise the manufacture of hand-spun and hand-woven khaddar *and popularise its use by house to house visit.**

Note:—To this end all workers and office-bearers should be dressed in *khaddar* and it is recommended that, with a view to encourage others, they should themselves learn hand-spinning.

(3) To organise national schools.

Note :—No picketing of Governmet schools should be resorted to, but reliance should be placed upon the superiority of national schools in all vital matters to *draw students from Government and aided schools.*†

(4) To organise the Depressed Classes for a better life, to improve their social, mental and moral condition, to induce them to send their children to national schools and to provide for them the ordinary facilities which the other citizens enjoy.

Note :—Whilst therefore where the prejudice against the untouchables is still strong in places, separate schools and separate wells must be maintained out of Congress funds, every effort should be made to draw such children to national schools and to persuade the people to allow the untouchables to use the common wells.

(5) To organise the temperance campaign amongst the people addicted to the drink habit by house to house

*Replaced by the A. I. C. C. for *said.*

† Replaced for *command attendance.*

visits and to rely more upon appeal to the drinker in his home than upon picketing.

(6) To organise village and town *panchayats* for the private settlement of all disputes, reliance being placed solely upon the force of public opinion and the truthfulness of *panchayat* decisions to ensure obedience to them.

Note:—In order to avoid even the appearance of coercion, no social boycott should be resorted to against those who will not obey *panchayat's* decisions.

(7) In order to promote and emphasize unity among all classes and races and mutual good-will, the establishment of which is the aim of the movement of Non-co-operation, to organise a social service department that will render help to all irrespective of differences in times of illness or accident.

Note:—A non-co-operator, whilst firmly adhering to his creed, will deem it a privilege to render personal service in case of illness or accident to every person whether English or Indian.

(8) To continue the Tilak Memorial Swaraj Fund and to call upon every Congressman or Congress sympathiser to pay at least one hundredth part of his *annual income* for the year 1921, every Province to send every month 25 per cent of its income from the Tilak Memorial Swaraj Fund to the All-India Congress Committee.

The above resolutions shall be brought before the forthcoming session of the All-India Congress Committee for revision if necessary.*

*Revised as above stated.

9th March, 1922

INTERESTING INFORMATION

Though now stale, the report issued by Messrs. Prakasam, Nageshwara Row and Narayan Rao about the preparedness for mass Civil Disobedience of the areas selected by the Guntur District Congress Committee makes interesting reading. The Commissioners divide the area into two parts: Peddanandipadu Firka and all the neighbouring villages forming 'one' contiguous whole, and the second the rest of the Firkas consisting of Palnad, Vinukonda, Settanapalle and portions of Ongole, Narasaraopet, Tenali and Repalle. The Commissioners found that the second part of the selected area fully satisfied the conditions about *khaddar* but not so about untouchability, although there was a great advance in the mentality of the people. As to non-violence, whilst the Commissioners admit that the people are non-violent by temperament, they say: "Still we doubt whether they could withstand a provocation or insult if it is of an extreme nature." They found that the condition about Hindu-Muslim unity was largely fulfilled.

Of the first part of the area, the Commissioners are much more enthusiastic. They estimate the total number of volunteers at about 4,000. "They are clad in *khaddar* uniform with badges. Men of all ages have enlisted themselves. We found even men of 60 to 65 years doing active work. In some villages there were Panchama volunteers doing active work and freely mixing with others. The excellence of the organisation among these ryots consists in their devotion to duty and observance of non-violence as part of their religion."

As to *khaddar* the Commissioners remark: "Most of the villages are self-contained. In some villages almost every house has one or more *charkas* actually working. The yarn made in each village is woven generally by the village Panchamas. Even orthodox Brahmins have been getting their clothes made by their Panchama brethren. In most of the villages more than 50 per cent. wear *khaddar* made by themselves. In some the percentage is as high as 95."

Remarking upon untouchability, they say: "We were surprised at the extraordinary progress made by some of the villages in this area in their attempt to remove untouchability within so short a time. We could not believe that it was humanly possible to effect such a revolution in the minds of these countrymen of ours. We found the so-called untouchables admitted into the *panchayat* Board. In some places orthodox Brahmins took the Panchamas by hand and seated them in their midst, and in some places they are admitted into the premises of Brahmins to do the same services which other castes have been doing. One rich Brahmin gentleman told us that he and some of his friends in the neighbouring villages would spend all their income to make provision for their needy Panchama brethren." Their final opinion, however, is: "In some villages untouchability has ceased to exist and in several it is likely to disappear soon. We consider the progress not uniform and not sufficient." Their final summing-up is: "No doubt all this is a good record, but it is difficult to see how far the masses can remain absolutely peaceful if more drastic and inhuman measures are employed. The time at their disposal for discipline has been too short. They have been just at the beginning of the fight. We consider it more advisable to postpone the campaign until the people have sufficient time to steel their hearts against all engines of oppression."

I have given relevant extracts from this valuable report to show: (1) the utter impartiality with which the Commissioners approach their mission, (2) the marvellous progress made in the selected area in fulfilling the conditions laid down by the Congress, (3) the necessity for much greater work before the idea of Civil Disobedience could be approached with any confidence. I am aware that extraordinary efforts were being put forth in many parts of India for the fulfilment of the Congress conditions in order that the people might be able to exercise the privilege of Civil Disobedience. That in itself is certainly a matter for congratulation, but the work of construction ought not to have to depend upon stimulation. It must go on irrespective of the excitement of Civil Disobedience. Removal of untouchability, manufacture of *khaddar*, Hindu-Muslim unity, cultivation of non-violence are not measures of a temporary character. They are the four pillars on which the structure of Swaraj must for ever rest. Take away any one of them and it must topple down. The greater, therefore, the progress in these four matters, the nearer we are to Swaraj, and the nearer also to capacity for Civil Disobedience. Indeed, even disobedience, if it is truly civil, excludes the idea of excitement. When Daniel threw open his doors in defiance of the laws of Medes and Persians, when John Bunyan became a non-conformist, when Latimer thrust his hand into the fire, when Prahlad embraced the red-hot iron pillar, not one of these civil resisters of old resisted under excitement. On the contrary they were, if possible, more collected and deliberate than on ordinary occasions. Absence of excitement is an infallible test of Civil Disobedience. I therefore hope that the good people of the selected area will not go to sleep now that mass Civil Disobedience has been suspended but that they will go on with the programme of construction with greater zeal and devotion.

10th November, 1920

IF I AM ARRESTED—

(TRANSLATED FROM MR. GANDHI'S ARTICLE IN *Navajivan*).

I have been constantly thinking of what the people would do in case I am arrested. My co-workers also have been putting this question to me. What would be the plight of India, if the people took to the wrong path through love run mad? What would be my own plight in such a case?

Rivers of blood shed by the Government cannot frighten me; but I would be deeply pained even, if the people did so much as abuse the Government for my sake or in my name. It would be disgracing me if the people lost their equilibrium on my arrest. The nation can achieve no progress merely by depending upon me. Progress is possible only by their understanding and following the path suggested by me. For this reason I desire that the people should maintain perfect self-control and consider the day of my arrest as a day of rejoicing. I desire that even the weaknesses existing to-day should disappear at that time.

What can be the motive of the Government in arresting me? The Government are not my enemy, for I have not a grain of enmity towards them. But they believe that I am the soul of all this agitation, that, if I am removed, the ruled and the rulers would be left in peace, that the people are blindly following me. Not only the Government, but some of our leaders also share this belief. How, then, can the Government put the people to the test? How can the Government ascertain whether the people understand my advice or are simply dazzled by my utterances? The only way left to them is to arrest me. Of course, there still remains an alternative for them and that lies in the removal of the causes which have led me to offer this advice. But intoxicated as they are with power, the Government will not see their own fault and even if they do, they will not admit it. The only way then that remains for them is to measure the strength of the people. They can do this by arresting me. If the people are thus terrorised into submission, they can be said to deserve the Punjab and the Khilafat wrongs.

If, on the other hand, the people resort to violence, they will merely be playing into the hands of the Government. Their aeroplanes will then bomb the people, their Dyers will shoot into them, and their Smiths will uncover the veils of our women. There will be other officers to make the people rub their noses against the ground, crawl on their bellies, and undergo the scourge of whipping. Both those results will be equally bad and unfortunate. They will not lead to *Swaraj*. In other countries governments have been overthrown by sheer brute-force, but I have often shown that India cannot attain *Swaraj* by that force. What, then, should the people do if I am arrested? The answer now is simple. The people

(1) should preserve peace and calmness,

(2) should not observe *Hartals*,

(3) should not hold meetings,

but

(4) should be fully awake.

I should certainly expect—

(5) all the Government schools to be vacated and shut down.

(6) Lawyers to withdraw from practice, in greater numbers.

(7) Settlement by private arbitration of cases pending before the Law Courts.

(8) Opening of numerous national schools and colleges.

(9) Renunciation of all foreign cloth in favour of the exclusive use of hand spun and hand woven garments by lacs of men and women, and selling or burning of any foreign cloth in stock.

(10) None to enlist in the army or in any other Government Service.

(11) Those able to earn their livelihood by other means to give up Government Services, civil and even military.

(12) Contribution of as much as is wanted towards national funds.

(13) Title holders to surrender titles in greater numbers.

(14) Candidates to withdraw from elections, or if already elected to resign their seats.

(15) Voters, who have not yet made up their minds, to resolve that it is sin to send any representative to the Councils.

If the people resolve and carry this out, they would not have to wait for *Swaraj* even for a year. If they can exhibit this much strength, we shall have attained *Swaraj*.

I shall then be set free under the nation's seal. That will please me. My freedom to-day is like a prison to me.

It will only prove the people's incompetence, if they use violence to release me, and then depend upon my help to attain *Swaraj* for them. Neither I nor anyone else can get *Swaraj* for the nation. It will be got on the nation proving its own fitness.

In conclusion, it is useless to find fault with the Government. We get what Government we deserve. When we improve, the Government also is bound to improve. Only when we improve can we attain Swaraj. Non-co-operation is the nation's determination to improve. Will the nation abandon the resolve and begin to co-operate after my arrest? If the people become mad and take to violence and as a result of it crawl on their bellies, rub their noses on the ground, salute the Union Jack and walk eighteen miles to do it, what else is that but co-operation? It is better to die than to submit to crawling, &c. In fine, consider it from any point of view, the course suggested by me is the right one for the people to take.

9th March, 1922

IF I AM ARRESTED——

(By M. K. Gandhi)

The rumour has been revived that my arrest is imminent. It is said to be regarded as a mistake by some officials that I was not arrested when I was to be, *i.e.*, on the 11th or 12th of February, and that the Bardoli decision ought not to have been allowed to affect the Government's programme. It is said, too, that it is now no longer possible for the Government to withstand the ever rising agitation in London for my arrest and deportation. I myself cannot see how the Government can avoid arresting me, if they want a permanent abandonment of Civil Disobedience, whether individual or mass.

I advised the Working Committee to suspend mass

Civil Disobedience at Bardoli, because that disobedience would not have been civil, and if I am now advising all provincial workers to suspend even individual Civil Disobedience, it is because I know that any disobedience at the present stage will be not civil but criminal. A tranquil atmosphere is an indispensable condition of Civil Disobedience. It is humiliating for me to discover that there is a spirit of violence abroad and that the Government of the United Provinces has been obliged to enlist additional police for avoiding a repetition of Chauri Chaura. I do not say that all that is claimed to have happened has happened, but it is impossible to ignore all the testimony that is given in proof of the growing spirit of violence in some parts of those provinces. In spite of my political differences with Pundit Hridayanath Kunzru, I regard him to be above wilful perversion of truth. I consider him to be one of the most capable among public workers. He is not a man to be easily carried away. When, therefore, he gives an opinion upon anything, it immediately arrests my attention. Making due allowance for the colouring of his judgment by reason of his pro-Government attitude, I am unable to dismiss his report of the Chauri Chaura tragedy as unworthy of consideration. Nor is it possible to ignore letters received from zemindars and others informing me of the violent temperament and ignorant lawlessness in the United Provinces. I have before me the Bareilly report signed by the Congress Secretary. Whilst the authorities behaved like madmen and forgot themselves in their fit of anger, we are not, if that report is to be believed, without fault. The volunteer procession was not a civil demonstration. It was insisted upon in spite of a sharp division of opinion in our own ranks. Though the crowds that gathered were not violent, the spirit of the demonstrations was undoubtedly violent. It was an impotent show of force wholly unnecessary for our purpose and hardly a prelude to Civil Disobedience. That the authorities could have handled the procession in a better spirit, that they ought not to have interfered with the Swaraj flag, that they ought not to have objected to the use of the Town Hall which was town property as Congress offices in view of the fact that it had been so used for some months with the permission of the Town Council, is all very true. But we have ceased to give credit to the authorities for common or reasonable sense. On the contrary, we have set ourselves against them because we expect nothing but unreason and violence from them, and knowing that the authorities would act no better than they did, we should have refrained from all the previous irritating demonstrations. That the U. P. Government are making a mountain out of a mole-hill, that they are discounting their own provocation given by the murdered men at Chauri Chaura is nothing new. All that I am concerned with is that it is not possible for us to claim that we have given them no handle whatsoever. It is therefore as a penance that Civil Disobedience has been suspended. But if the atmosphere clears up, the people realise the full value of the adjective 'civil' and become in reality non-violent both in spirit and in deed, and if I find that the Government still do not yield to the people's will, I shall certainly be the first person to advocate individual or mass Civil Disobedience as the case may be. There is no escape from that duty without the people wishing to surrender their birthright.

I doubt the sincerity of Englishmen who are born fighters, when they declaim against Civil Disobedience as if it was a diabolical crime to be punished with exemplary severity. If they have glorified armed rebellions and resorted to them on due occasions, why are many of them up in arms against the very idea of civil resistance? I can understand their saying that the attainment of a non-violent atmosphere is a virtual impossibility in India. I do not believe it, but I can appreciate such an objection. What, however, is beyond my comprehension is the deadset made against the very theory of Civil Disobedience, as if it was something immoral. To expect me to give up the preaching of Civil Disobedience is to ask me to give up preaching peace, which would be tantamount to asking me to commit suicide.

I have now been told that the Government are compassing the destruction of the three weeklies which I am conducting, viz., *Young India*, *Gujarati Nava Jivan* and *Hindi NavaJivan*. I hope that the rumour has no foundation. I claim that these three journals are insistently preaching nothing but peace and good will. Extraordinary care is taken to give nothing but truth as I find it, to the readers. Every inadvertent inaccuracy is admitted and corrected. The circulation of all the weeklies is daily growing. The conductors are voluntary workers, in some cases taking no salary whatsoever and in the others receiving mere maintenance money. Profits are all returned to the subscribers in some shape or other, or are utilised for some constructive public activity or other. I cannot say that I shall not feel a pang, if these journals cease to exist. But it is the easiest thing for the Government to put them out. The publishers and printers are all friends and co-workers. My compact with them is that the moment Government asks for security, that moment the newspapers must stop. I am conducting them upon the assumption that whatever view the Government may take of my activities, they at least give me credit for preaching through these newspapers nothing but the purest non-violence and truth, according to my lights.

I hope, however, that whether the Government arrest me or whether they stop by direct or indirect means the publication of the three journals, the public will remain unmoved. It is a matter of no pride or pleasure to me but one of humiliation that the Government refrain from arresting me for fear of an outbreak of universal violence and awful slaughter that any such outbreak must involve. It would be a sad commentary upon my preaching of, and upon the Congress and Khilafat pledge of, non-violence, if my incarceration was to be a signal for a storm all over the country. Surely, it would be a demonstration of India's unreadiness for a peaceful rebellion. It would be a triumph for the bureaucracy, and it would be almost a final proof of the correctness of the position taken up by the Moderate friends, *viz.*, that India can never be prepared for non-violent disobedience. I hope therefore that the Congress and Khilafat workers will strain every nerve and show that all the fears entertained by the Government and their supporters were totally wrong. I promise that such act of self-restraint will take us many a mile towards our triple goal.

There should therefore be *hartals*, no noisy demonstrations, no processions. I would regard the observance of perfect peace on my arrest as a mark of high honour paid to me by my countrymen. What I would love to see, however, is the constructive work of the Congress going on with clock-work regularity and the speed of the Punjab Express. I would love to see people who have hitherto kept back, voluntarily discarding all their foreign cloth and making a bonfire of it. Let them fulfil the whole of the constructive programme framed at Bardoli, and they will not only release me and other prisoners, but they will also inaugurate Swaraj and secure redress of the Khilafat and the Punjab wrongs. Let them remember the four pillars of Swaraj: Non-violence, Hindu-Moslem-Sikh-Parsi-Christain-Jew unity, total removal of untouchability and manufacture of hand-spun and hand-woven *khaddar* completely displacing foreign cloth.

I do not know that my removal from their midst will not be a benefit to the people. In the first instance, the superstition about the possession of supernatural powers by me will be demolished. Secondly, the belief that people have accepted the Non-co-operation programme only under my influence and that they have no independent faith in it will be disproved. Thirdly, our capacity for Swaraj will be proved by our ability to conduct our activities in spite of the withdrawal even of the orginator of the current programme. Fourthly and selfishly, it will give me a quiet and physical rest, which perhaps I deserve.

PART IX

ARREST AND TRIAL.

PART IX

ARREST AND TRIAL

15*th March*, 1922

ARREST AND AFTER

THE long expected has happened at last. The wished for, longed for consummation has been reached. Mr. Gandhi pined for his arrest and imprisonment by the Government under which it became intolerable for him to live. His heart's desire has been fulfilled. He now feels himself free, though imprisoned.

Even from the 8th instant the rumour of his arrest began to thicken. He left for Ajmere that day on an urgent invitation from Mr. Chhotani by an afternoon train, and it was even whispered that he might be arrested on the way. Nothing however happened then. In the meantime, the rumour was growing from hour to hour. A suspicious telegram from Ajmere made Mrs. Gandhi and some others to run up to the Sabarmati Station to see him safely return. He reached the *Ashram* in the afternoon of the 10th as free as ever and as if bursting under the weight of his simple and child-like joy.

At the *Ashram* the rumour of the last two days was being received with calm and stolid indifference. For there have been so many final partings since he had decided to start Civil Disobedience in November last that the ideas of arrest, imprisonment or even worse became quite common and familiar. So the daily routine of work of the *Ashram* was not disturbed in the least by these rumours. Only when the day wore on, the evening came and the bell rang out the hour of prayer, there was a sudden hush all around as all the *Ashramites* proceeded with anxious and hasty steps to join their *Bapu* in his last prayer, perhaps for a long time to come.

He was unusually light and happy and played with the children like one of their own spreading the contagion of his lightness and happiness all round.

After the prayer he returned to his work as usual and dictated replies to some correspondence. During this time, friends continued to come to see him from the city, bringing tit-bits of news all of which went to confirm the prevailing rumour.

Mr. Gandhi arose at about quarter to ten* for his last ablutions before retiring and the small assembly that had all this time surrounded him began to disperse. Mr. Banker who had come with Mr. Shvaib and Anasuyabai to confirm the strength of the rumour also departed at that time. A few minutes after, Mr. Shvaib returned with Anasuyabai and brought the news that Mr. Banker was arrested and that the S. P. was waiting on the road for Mr. Gandhi's arrest. The news spread in a minute thoughout the *Ashram* quarters, and almost all the inmates, men, women and children, hastened to Mr. Gandhi to bid him farewell and have his blessings. At his desire, his favourite Gujarati hymn which describes the qualities of a true *vaishnava* was sung in chorus. After this, he accosted each one of the *Ashramites* in suitable terms, encouraged them all by his sprightliness and abundant joy and then prepared to surrender himself. While proceeding from his residence to the Police Officer on the road, he expressed himself several times that he felt very happy and gratified over the arrest.

* Mr. Gandhi was arrested at 10-30 P.M. by Mr. Healey, the Superintendent of Police, Ahmedabad on a complaint in respect of four articles in *Young India*, namely, "Disaffection a Virtue," of 15th June 1921 and three others referred to elsewhere. Mr. Shvaib took up the editorship till Mr. C. Rajagopalachari who was appointed editor took charge.

Maulana Hasrat Mohani who travelled with Mr. Gandhi from Ajmere by the same train and stopped at Ahmedabad came to the *Ashram* just before the arrival of the Police Commissioner and when Mr. Gandhi had retired for his ablutions. Mr. Gandhi was supremely happy when he met the Maulana just before his arrest. They embraced each other with feelings of mutual esteem and regard. The Maulana seem to have been deeply moved by this and assured Mr. Gandhi that he would give his whole-hearted support to the cause of non-violent Non-co-operation.

Both Mr. Gandhi and Mr. Banker were taken to the Sabarmati Jail. Mrs. Gandhi with a small company of four or five was allowed to accompany them and see them lodged in their quarters, which consists of a row of eight rooms with an open verandah about 10 feet wide and a fairly large courtyard with a line of small trees in the middle. The two rooms given to them are furnished each with an iron cot, a matress, two sheets, a pillow, a blanket and a carpet. Light is provided in the evening. The doors of the rooms are made of wooden frames, the planks about six inches wide with thick iron bars fixed in them, the distance between two bars being a little over an inch. The whole place was scrupulously clean.

The next day they were produced before the trying Magistrate, Mr. Allan Brown, I.C.S., who held his court at the Commissioner's office, outside the city proper and under the shelter of the cantonment and easily accessible by rail from Sabarmati. The news was kept a secret. Yet a good many spectators who were permitted by the Magistrate attended the trial. Five witnesses consisting of the D. S. P. Mr. Healey, the Registrar of the Bombay High Court, Mr. Dinshaw Gharda, Mr. Chatfield, the District Magistrate of Ahmedabad, a Sub-

Inspector and a C. I. D. subordinate of police were examined by the prosecutor on the Government side. There were two issues on which these evidences were taken and articles from *Young India* were read before the Court, *viz*., (1) proving the editorship and (2) proving the intention of the articles. These were simple issues upon which several precious hours of the day were uselessly spent simply to keep up the forms of law. But it appeared to be unreasonable that so much time should be taken to prove a self-evident fact. There was also an air of artificiality or theatricality about the whole business. The dignity and aloofness maintained by the trying Magistrate even while taking down statement from his friends, colleagues and superiors had an element of acting which was admirably done; similarly the deference shown to the chair of justice, irrespective of the person who may occupy it for the time being. Perhaps these are matters of traditions which grow upon those whose daily duty is to practise them. But to a new observer they appear incongruous, out of place and unnatural, although dignified and invested with gravity and splendour.

What struck one most during the whole affair of Mr. Gandhi's arrest and trial was the perfect peace and goodwill that was maintained between the two parties. Mr. Gandhi seems to have infected with his gentleness of spirit the whole atmosphere of the court-room and even the men and officers of the police who came into contact with him. Ahmedabad seems also to be specially fortunate in having a pair of very nice gentlemen in its District Magistrate Mr. Chatfield, and the D. S. P. Mr. Healey. On the night of the 10th, when Mr. Healey came to arrest Mr. Gandhi, he never entered the precincts of the *Ashram* but kept on waiting on the public road till

Mr. Gandhi himself felt that he should not tarry any longer. There was no show of force at all. Mr. Healey came with only one associate. His martial uniform was thoroughly out of harmony with his courteous manners and his gentle face and bearing. When he drove away with Mr. Gandhi and Mr. Banker amidst the subdued shouts of joy of th e*Ashram* people, it did not appear that there had been any arrest at all. He was as if one of the friends of the company. Similarly, Mr. Chatfield's graceful way of parting after his deposition, touched every heart in the court room. All this experience taught one how to differentiate a man from as ystem and gave practical illustration of the possibility of waging an implacable war against a system without bearing any ill-will or hatred against the persons who may form part of it. They taught also how there could be mutual appreciation of heart between Indians and Englishmen, and increased one's longing to see that appreciation properly and soundly based after the demolition of the present unrighteous system of Government and the establishment of Swaraj in India.

When Mr. Gandhi was asked about his occupation, he uttered the three words : "Farmer and Weaver" with a slow, clear and emphatic accent. The magistrate was as if startled, because the answer was, so out of the ordinary. He paused a little before noting them down, perhaps to ascertain whether Mr. Gandhi was really serious in making that declaration. Little did he know that Mr. Gandhi's whole philosophy of work and existence was summed up in those three words, and that they are the shibboleth of India's revolt against western exploitation of her resources and the domination of western culture and life.

23rd March, 1922

THE GREAT TRIAL

At the Circuit House at Shahi Bag, the trial of Mr. Gandhi and Mr. Banker commenced on Saturday noon, the 18th of March, before Mr. C. N. Broomsfield, I. C. S., District and Sessions Judge of Ahmedabad.

Sir J. T. Strangman with Rao Bahadur Girdharlal conducted the prosecution, while the accused were undefended. The Judge took his seat at 12 noon, and said there was a slight mistake in the charges framed. which he corrected. The charges were then read out by the Régistrar, the offence being in three articles published in the *Young India* of September 29, December 15, of 1921 and February 23, 1922. The offending articles were then read out: first of them was, "Tampering with Loyalty"; the second, "The Puzzle and Its Solution"; and the last was "Shaking the Manes."

The Judge said the law required that the charge should not only be read out but explained. In this case, it would not be necessary for him to say much by way of explanation. The charge in each case was that of bringing or attempting to bring into hatred or contempt or exciting or attempting to excite disaffection towards His Majesty's Government, established by law in British India. Both the accused were charged with the three offences under section 124 A, contained in the articles read out, written by Mr. Gandhi and printed by Mr. Banker. The words 'hatred and contempt' were words the meaning of which was sufficiently obvious. The word 'disaffection' was defined under the section, where

* The complaint in respect of the earlier article, "Disaffection, a Virtue," seems to have been dropped subsequently after enquiry by the Magistrate.

they were told that disaffection included disloyalty and feelings of enmity, and the word used in the section had also been interpreted by the High Court of Bombay in a reported case as meaning political alienation or discontent, a spirit of disloyalty to Government or existing authority. The charges having been read out, the Judge called upon the accused to plead to the charges. He asked Mr. Gandhi, whether he pleaded guilty or claimed to be tried.

Mr. Gandhi: I plead guilty to all the charges. I observe that the King's name has been omitted from the charge, and it has been properly omitted.

The Judge: Mr. Banker, do you plead guilty, or do you claim to be tried?

Mr. Banker: I plead guilty.

Sir J. Strangman then wanted the Judge to proceed with the trial fully; but the Judge said he did not agree with what had been said by the Counsel. The Judge said that from the time he knew he was going to try the case, he had thought over the question of sentence, and he was prepared to hear anything that the Counsel might have to say, or Mr. Gandhi wished to say, on the sentence. He honestly did not believe that the mere recording of evidence in the trial which Counsel had called for would make no (sic) difference to them, one way or the other. He, therefore, proposed to accept the pleas.

Mr. Gandhi smiled at this decision.

The Judge said nothing further remained but to pass sentence, and before doing so, he liked to hear Sir J. T. Strangman. He was entitled to base his general remarks on the charges against the accused and on their pleas.

Sir J. T. Strangman: It will be difficult to do so. I

ask the Court that the whole matter may be properly considered. If I stated what has happened before the Committing Magistrate, then I can show that there are many things which are material to the question of the sentence.

The first point, he said he wanted to make out, was that the matter which formed the subject of the present charges formed a part of the campaign to spread disaffection openly and systematically to render Government impossible and to overthrow it. The earliest article that was put in from "Young India". was dated 25th May, 1921, which said that it was the duty of a Non-co-operator to create disaffection towards the Government. The counsel then read out portions of articles written by Mr. Gandhi in the *Young India.*

Court said, nevertheless, it seemed to it that the Court could accept plea, on the materials of which the sentence had to be based.

Sir J. Strangman said the question of sentence was entirely for the Court to decide. The Court was always entitled to deal in a more general manner in regard to the question of the sentence, than the particular matter resulting in the conviction. He asked leave to refer to articles before the court, and what result might have been produced, if the trial had proceeded in order to ascertain what the facts were. He was not going into any matter which involved dispute.

The Judge said there was not the least objection.

Sir J. Strangman said he wanted to show that these articles were not isolated. They formed part of an organised compaign, but so far as "Young India" was concerned, they would show that from the year 1921. The Counsel then read out extracts from the paper, dated June 8, on the duty of a non-co-operator, which was to preach disaffection towards the existing government and preparing the country for Civil Disobedience. Then in the same number, there was an article on disobedience. Then in the same number there was an article on "Disaffection—a virtue" or something to that effect. Then there was an article on the 28th of July 1921, in which it was stated that "we have to destroy the system". Again, on September 30, 1921, there was an article headed, "Punjab Prosecutions", where it was stated that a non-co-operator worth his name should preach disaffection. That was all so far as "Young India" was concerned. They were earlier in date than the article, "Tampering with Loyalty", and it was referred to the Governor of Bombay. Continuing, he said the accused was a man of high educational qualifications and evidently from his writings a recognised leader. The harm that was likely to be caused was considerable. They were the writings of an educated man, and not the writings of an obscure man, and the Court must consider to what the results of a campaign of the nature disclosed in the writings must inevitably lead. They had examples before them in the last few months. He referred to the occurrences in Bombay last November and Chauri Chaura leading to murder and destruction of property, involving many people in misery and misfortune. It was true that in the course of those articles they would find Non-violence was insisted upon as an item of the campaign and as an item of the creed. But what was the use of preaching Non-violence when he preached disaffection towards Government or openly instigated others to overthrow it? The answer to that question appeared to him to come from Chauri Chaura, Madras and Bombay. These were circumstances which he asked the Court to take into account in sentencing the accused, and it would be for the Court to consider those circumstances which involve sentences of severity.

As regards the second accused, his offence was lesser. He did the publication and he did not write. His offence nevertheless was a serious one. His instructions were that he was a man of means and he asked the Court to impose a substantial fine in addition to such term of imprisonment as might be inflicted upon. He quoted Section 10 of the Press Act as bearing on the question of fine. When making a fresh declaration, he said a deposit of Rs. 1,000 to Rs. 10,000 was asked in many cases.

Court: Mr. Gandhi, do you wish to make a statement on the question of sentence?

Mr. Gandhi: I would like to make a statement.

Court: Could you give me in writing to put it on record?

Mr. Gandhi: I shall give it as soon as I finish it reading.

Before reading his written statement, Mr. Gandhi spoke a few words as introductory remarks to the whole statement. He said:

Before I read this statement, I would like to state that I entirely endorse the learned Advocate-General's remarks in connection with my humble self. I think that he was entirely fair to me in all the statements that he has made, because it is very true and I have no desire whatsoever to conceal from this Court the fact that to preach disaffection towards the existing system of Government has become almost a passion with me, and the learned Advocate-General is also entirely in the right when he says that my preaching of disaffection did not commence with my connection with *Young India*, but that it commenced much earlier;

and in the statement that I am about to read, it will be my painful duty to admit before this Court that it commenced much earlier than the period stated by the Advocate-General. It is the most painful duty with me, but I have to discharge that duty knowing the responsibility that rests upon my shoulders, and I wish to endorse all the blame that the learned Advocate-General has thrown on my shoulders in connection with the Bombay occurrences, Madras occurrences and the Chauri Chaura occurrences. Thinking over these deeply and sleeping over them night after night, it is impossible for me to dissociate myself from the diabolical crimes of Chauri Chaura or the mad outrages of Bombay. He is quite right when he says that as a man of responsibility, a man having received a fair share of education, having had a fair share of experience of this world, I should have known the consequences of every one of my acts. I knew that I was playing with fire, I ran the risk, and if I was set free, I would still do the same. I have felt it this morning that I would have failed in my duty, if I did not say what I said here just now.

I wanted to avoid violence, I want to avoid violence. Non-violence is the first article of my faith. It is also the last article of my creed. But I had to make my choice. I had either to submit to a system which I considered had done an irreparable harm to my country, or incur the risk of the mad fury of my people bursting forth, when they understood the truth from my lips. I know that my people have sometimes gone mad. I am deeply sorry for it and I am therefore here to submit not to a light penalty but to the highest penalty. I do not ask for mercy. I do not plead any extenuating act. I am here, therefore, to invite and cheerfully submit to the highest penalty that can be inflicted upon me for what in law is a deliberate crime and what appears to me to be the highest duty of a citizen. The only course open to you, the Judge, is, as I am just going to say in my statement, either to resign your post, or inflict on me the severest penalty, if you believe that the system and law you are assisting to administer are good for the people. I do not expect that kind of conversion, but by the time I have finished with my statement, you will perhaps have a glimpse of what is raging within my breast to run this maddest risk which a sane man can run.

The Statement was then read out.

Statement

"I owe it perhaps to the Indian public and to the public in England to placate which this prosecution is mainly taken up, that I should explain why from a staunch loyalist and co-operator I have become an uncompromising disaffectionist and Non-co-operator. To the Court too I should say why I plead guilty to the charge of promoting disaffection towards the Government established by law in India.

My public life began in 1893 in South Africa in troubled weather. My first contact with British authority in that country was not of a happy character. I discovered that as a man and an Indian I had no rights. More correctly, I discovered that I had no right as a man, because I was an Indian.

But I was not baffled. I thought that this treatment of Indians was an excrescence upon a system that was intrinsically and mainly good. I gave the Government my voluntary and hearty co-operation, criticising it freely where I felt it was faulty but never wishing its destruction.

Consequently when the existence of the Empire was

threatened in 1899 by the Boer challenge, I offered my services to it, raised a volunteer ambulance corps and served at several actions that took place for the relief of Ladysmith. Similarly in 1906, at the time of the Zulu revolt, I raised a stretcher-bearer party and served till the end of the 'rebellion'. On both these occasions I received medals and was even mentioned in despatches. For my work in South Africa I was given by Lord Hardinge a Kaiser-i-Hind Gold Medal. When the war broke out in 1914 between England and Germany, I raised a volunteer ambulance corps in London consisting of the then resident Indians in London, chiefly students. Its work was acknowledged by the authorities to be valuable. Lastly, in India, when a special appeal was made at the War Conference in Delhi in 1918 by Lord Chelmsford for recruits, I struggled at the cost of my health to raise a corps in Kheda and the response was being made when the hostilities ceased and orders were received that no more recruits were wanted. In all these efforts at service I was actuated by the belief that it was possible by such services to gain a status of full equality in the Empire for my countrymen.

The first shock came in the shape of the Rowlatt Act, a law designed to rob the people of all real freedom. I felt called upon to lead an intensive agitation against it. Then followed the Punjab horrors beginning with the massacre at Jallianwala Bagh and culminating in crawling orders, public flogging and other indescribable humiliations. I discovered too that the plighted word of the Prime Minister to the Mussalmans of India regarding the integrity of Turkey and the holy places of Islam was not likely to be fulfilled. But in spite of the forebodings and the grave warnings of friends, at the Amritsar Congress in 1919, I fought for co-operation and working the

Montagu-Chelmsford reforms, hoping that the Prime Minister would redeem his promise to the Indian Mussalmans, that the Punjab wound would be healed and that the reforms, inadequate and unsatisfactory though they were, marked a new era of hope in the life of India.

But all that hope was shattered. The Khilafat promise was not to be redeemed. The Punjab crime was white-washed and most culprits went not only unpunished but remained in service and in some continued to draw pensions from the Indian revenue, and in some cases were even rewarded. I saw too that not only did the reforms not mark a change of heart, but they were only a method of further draining India of her wealth and of prolonging her servitude.

I came reluctantly to the conclusion that the British connection had made India more helpless than she ever was before, politically and economically. A disarmed India has no power of resistance against any aggressor if she wanted to engage in an armed conflict with him. So much is this the case that some of our best men consider that India must take generations before she can achieve the Dominion status. She has become so poor that she has little power of resisting famines. Before the British advent, India spun and wove in her millions of cottages just the supplement she needed for adding to her meagre agricultural resources. This cottage industry, so vital for India's existence, has been ruined by incredibly heartless and inhuman processes as described by English witnesses. Little do town-dwellers know how the semi-starved masses of India are slowly sinking to lifelessness. Little do they know that their miserable comfort represents the brokerage they get for the work they do for the foreign exploiter, that the profits and the brokerage are sucked from the masses. Little do they realise that the Government established by law in British India is carried on for this exploitation of the masses. No sophistry, no jugglery in figures can explain away the evidence that the skeletons in many villages present to the naked eye. I have no doubt whatsoever that both England and the town-dwellers of India will have to answer, if there is a God above, for this crime against humanity which is perhaps unequalled in history. The law itself in this country has been used to serve the foreign exploiter. My unbiassed examination of the Punjab Martial Law cases has led me to believe that at least ninety five per cent. of convictions were wholly bad. My experience of political cases in India leads me to the conclusion that in nine out of every ten the condemned men were totally innocent. Their crime consisted in the love of their country. In ninety-nine cases out of hundred justice has been denied to Indians as against Europeans in the Courts of India. This is not an exaggerated picture. It is the experience of almost every Indian who has had anything to do with such cases. In my opinion, the administration of the law is thus prostituted consciously or unconsciously for the benefit of the exploiter.

The greatest misfortune is that Englishmen and their Indian associates in the administration of the country do not know that they are engaged in the crime I have attempted to describe. I am satisfied that many Englishmen and Indian officials honestly believe that they are administering one of the best systems devised in the world and that India is making steady though slow pregress. They do not know that a subtle but effective system of terrorism and an organised display of force on the one hand, and the deprivation of all powers of retaliation or self-defence on the other, have emasculated the people and induced in them the habit of simulation. This awful habit has added to the ignorance and the self-deception of the administrators. Section 124-A under which I am happily charged is perhaps the prince among the political sections of the Indian Penal Code designed to suppress the liberty of the citizen. Affection cannot be manufactured or regulated by law. If one has no affection for a person or system, one should be free to give the fullest expression to his disaffection, so long as he does not contemplate, promote or incite to violence. But the section under which Mr. Banker and I are charged is one under which mere promotion of disaffection is a crime. I have studied some of the cases tried under it, and I know that some of the most loved of India's patriots have been convicted under it. I consider it a privilege, therefore, to be charged under that section. I have endeavoured to give in their briefest outline the reasons for my disaffection. I have no personal ill-will against any single administrator, much less can I have any disaffection towards the King's person. But I hold it to be a virtue to be disaffected towards a Government which in its totality has done more harm to India than any previous system. India is less manly under the British rule then she ever was before. Holding such a belief, I consider it to be a sin to have affection for the system. And it has been a precious privilege for me to be able to write what I have in the various articles, tendered in evidence against me.

In fact, I believe that I have rendered a service to India and England by showing in Non-co-operation the way out of the unnatural state in which both are living. In my humble opinion, Non-co-operation with evil is as much a duty as is co-operation with good. But in the past, Non-co-operation has been deliberately expressed in violence to the evil doer. I am endeavouring to show to my countrymen that violent Non-co-operation only multiplies evil and that as evil can only be sustained by violence, withdrawal of support of evil requires complete abstention from violence. Non-violence implies voluntary submission to the penalty for Non-co-operation with evil. I am here, therefore, to invite and submit cheerfully to the highest penalty that can be inflicted upon me for what in law is a deliberate crime and what appears to me to be the highest duty of a citizen. The only course open to you, the Judge, is either to resign your post and thus dissociate yourself from evil, if you feel that the law you are called upon to administer is an evil and that in reality I am innocent; or to inflict on me the severest penalty if you believe that the system and the law you are assisting to administer are good for the people of this country and that my activity is therefore injurious to the public weal."

Mr. Banker: I only want to say that I had the privilege of printing these articles and I plead guilty to the charge. I have nothing to say as regards the sentence.

THE JUDGMENT

The following is the full text of the judgment:

Mr. Gandhi, you have made my task easy in one way by pleading guilty to the charge. Nevertheless, what remains, namely, the determination of a just sentence, is perhaps as difficult a proposition as a judge in this country could have to face. The law is no respector of persons. Nevertheless, it will be impossible to ignore the fact that you are in a different category from any person I have ever tried or am likely to have to try. It would be impossible to ignore the fact that, in the eyes of millions of your countrymen, you are a great patriot and a great leader. Even those who differ from you in politics look upon you as a man of high ideals and of noble and of even saintly life. I have to deal with you in one character only. It is not my duty and I do not presume to judge or criticise you in any other character. It is my duty to judge you as a man subject to the law, who by his own admission has broken the law and committed what to an ordinary man must appear to be grave offence against the State. I do not forget that you have consistently preached against violence and that you have on many occasions, as I am willing to believe, done much to prevent violence. But having regard to the nature of your political teaching and the nature of many of those to whom it was addressed, how you could have continued to believe that violence would not be the inevitable consequence, it passes my capacity to understand.

There are probably few people in India, who do not sincerely regret that you should have made it impossible for any Government to leave you at liberty. But it is so. I am trying to balance what is due to you against what appears to me to be necessary in the interest of the public, and I propose in passing sentence to follow the precedent of a case in many respects similar to this case that was decided some twelve years ago, I mean the case against Bal Gangadhar Tilak under the same section. The sentence that was passed upon him as it finally stood was a sentence of simple imprisonment for six years. You will not consider it unreasonable, I think, that you should be classed with Mr. Tilak, *i.e.*, a sentence of two years simple imprisonment on each count of the charge; six years in all, which I feel it my duty to pass upon you, and I should like to say in doing so that, if the course of events in India should make it possible for the Government to reduce the period and release you, no one will be better pleased than I.

The Judge to Mr. Banker: I assume you have been to a large extent under the influence of your chief. The sentence that I propose to pass upon you is simple imprisonment for six months on each of the first two counts, that is to say, simple imprisonment for one year and a fine of a thousand rupees on the third count, with six months simple imprisonment in default.

MR. GANDHI ON THE JUDGMENT

Mr. Gandhi said: I would say one word. Since you have done me the honour of recalling the trial of the late Lokamanya Bal Gangadhar Tilak, I just want to say that I consider it to be the proudest privilege and honour to be associated with his name. So far as the sentence itself is concerned, I certainly consider that it is as light as any judge would inflict on me, and so far as the whole proceedings are concerned, I must say that I could not have expected greater courtesy.

Then the friends of Mr. Gandhi crowded round him as the Judge left the Court and fell at his feet. There was much sobbing on the part of both men and women. But all the while, Mr. Gandhi was smiling and cool and giving encouragement to everybody who came to him. Mr. Banker also was smiling and taking this in a light-hearted way. After all his friends had taken leave of him, Mr. Gandhi was taken out of the Court to the Sabarmati Jail.

And thus the great trial finished.

16*th March*, 1922

TO HAKIMJI

The following letter has been addressed by Mr. Gandhi to Hakim Ajmal Khan:

SABARMATI JAIL, 12*th March*, 1922.

My dear Hakimji,

Since my arrest this is the first letter I have commenced to write after having ascertained that under the Jail Rules I am entitled to write as many letters as I like as an under-trial prisoner. Of course you know that Mr. Shankerlal Banker is with me. I am happy that he is with me. Every one knows how near he has come to me—naturally, therefore, both of us are glad that we have been arrested together.

I write this to you in your capacity as Chairman of the Working Committee and, therefore, leader of both Hindus and Mussalmans or better still of all India.

I write to you also as one of the foremost leaders of Mussalmans, but above all I write this to you as an esteemed friend. I have had the privilege of knowing you since 1915. Our daily growing association has enabled me to prize your friendship as a treasure. A staunch Mussalman, you have shown in your own life what Hindu-Muslim unity means.

We all now realise, as we have never before realised, that without that unity we cannot attain our freedom, and I make bold to say that without that unity the Mussalmans of India cannot render Khilafat all the aid they wish. Divided, we must ever remain slaves. This unity, therefore, cannot be a mere policy to be discarded when it does not suit us. We can discard it only when we are tired of Swaraj. Hindu-Muslim unity must be our creed to last for all time and under all circumstances.

Nor must that unity be a menace to the minorities—the Parsees, the Christians, the Jews or the powerful Sikhs. If we seek to crush any of them, we shall some day want to fight each other.

I have been drawn so close to you chiefly because I know that you believe in Hindu-Muslim unity in the full sense of the term.

This unity in my opinion is unattainable without our adopting Non-violence as a firm policy. I call it a policy because it is limited to the preservation of that unity. But it follows that thirty crores of Hindus and Mussalmans, united not for a time but for all time, can defy all the powers of the world and should consider it a cowardly act to resort to violence in their dealings with the English administrators. We have hitherto feared them and their guns in our simplicity. The moment we realise our combined strength, we shall consider it unmanly to fear them and, therefore, ever to think of striking them. Hence am I anxious and impatient to persuade my countrymen to feel non-violent, not out of our weakness, but out of our strength. But you and I know that we have not yet evolved the non-violence of the strong. And we have not done so, because the Hindu-Muslim union has not gone much beyond the stage of policy. There is still too much mutual distrust and consequent fear. I am not disappointed. The progress we have made in that direction is indeed phenomenal. We seem to have covered in eighteen months' time the work of a generation. But infinitely more is necessary. Neither the classes nor the masses feel instinctively that our union is necessary as the breath of our nostrils.

For this consummation we must, it seems to me, rely

more upon quality than quantity. Given a sufficient number of Hindus and Mussalmans with almost a fanatical faith in everlasting friendship between the Hindns and the Mussalmans of India, we shall not be long before the unity permeates the masses. A few of us must first clearly understand that we can make no headway without accepting non-violence in thought, word and deed for the full realisation of our political ambition. I would, therefore, beseech you and the members of the Working Committee and the All-India Congress Committee to see that our ranks contain no workers who do not fully realise the essential truth I have endeavoured to place before you. A living faith cannot be manufactured by the rule of majority.

To me the visible symbol of all-India unity and, therefore, of the acceptance of Non-violence as an indispensable means for the realisation of our political ambition is undoubtedly the *charkha*, *i.e.*, *khaddar*. Only those who believe in *cultivating* a non-violent spirit and eternal friendship between Hindus and Mussalmans will daily and religiously spin. Universal hand-spinning and the universal manufacture and use of hand-spun hand-woven *khaddar* will be a substantial, if not absolute proof of the real unity and non-violence. And it will be a recognition of a living kinship with the dumb masses. Nothing can possibly unify and revivify India as the acceptance by all India of the spinning wheel as a daily sacrament and the *khaddar* wear as a privilege and a duty.

Whilst, therefore, I am anxious that more title-holders should give up their titles, lawyers law-courts, scholars the Government schools or colleges, the Councillors the Councils and the soldiers and the civilians their posts, I would urge the nation to restrict its activity in this direction only to the consolidation of the results already achieved and to trust its strength to command further abstentions from association with a system we are seeking to mend or end.

Moreover, the workers are too few. I would not waste a single worker to-day on destructive work, when we have such an enormous amount of constructive work. But perhaps, the most conclusive argument against devoting further time to destructive propaganda is the fact that the spirit of intolerance which is a form of violence has never been so rampant as now. Co-operators are estranged from us; they fear us. They say that we are establishing a worse bureaucracy than the existing one. We must remove every cause for such anxiety. We must go out of our way to win them to our side. We must make Englishmen safe from all harm from our side. I should not have to labour the point, if it was clear to every one as it is to you and to me that our pledge of Non-violence implies utter humility and good-will, even towards our bitterest opponent. This necessary spirit will be automatically realised, if only India will devote her sole attention to the work of construction suggested by me.

I flatter myself with the belief that my imprisonment is quite enough for a long time to come. I believe in all humility that I have no ill-will against any one. Some of my friends would not have to be as non-violent as I am. But we contemplated the imprisonment of the most innocent. If I may be allowed that claim, it is clear that I should not be followed to prison by anybody at all. We do want to paralyse the Government considered as a system—not, however, by intimidation, but by the irresistible pressure of our innocence. In my opinion, it would be intimidation to fill the jails anyhow. And why should more innocent men seek imprisonment till one considered to be the most innocent has been found inadequate for the purpose.

My caution against further courting of imprisonment does not mean that we are now to shirk imprisonment. If the Government will take away every *non-violent* non-co-operator, I should welcome it, but it should not be because of our Civil Disobedience, defensive or aggressive. Nor, I hope, will the country fret over those who are in jail. It will do them and the country good to serve the full term of their imprisonment. They can be fitly discharged before their time only by an act of the Swaraj Parliament. And I entertain an absolute conviction that universal adoption of *khaddar* is Swaraj.

I have refrained from mentioning untouchability. I am sure every good Hindu believes that it has got to go. Its removal is as necessary as the realisation of Hindu-Muslim unity.

I have placed before you a programme which is in my opinion the quickest and the best. No impatient Khilafatist can devise a better. May God give you health and wisdom to guide the country to her destined goal.

I am,
Yours sincerely,
(Sd.) M. K. GANDHI.

23rd March, 1922

HAKIMJI'S REPLY

The following is the reply sent by Hakim Ajmal Khan to Mahatma Gandhi's letter which was u b lished in the "Young India" of 16th March, 1922.

Ahmedabad, 17th March 1922

My Dear Mahatmaji,

I have received the letter which you wrote to me from Sabarmati Jail and thank you very sincerely for the kind sentiments that you have expressed towards me. Whether I really deserve them is another question into which I do not propose to enter.

I am glad that Mr. Shankerlal Banker is with you in the jail. He has great affection for you and possesses qualities which have endeared him to you. I feel sure that his company in jail will be a source of extra pleasure and satisfaction to you.

I can, however, feel happy at your arrest only when I find that, as a mark of the profound respect that it has for you, the country takes still greater interest in the national movement than it did when you were free. But it gives me infinite pleasure to see that the country observed perfect peace on your arrest. This is a clear sign of the spread of the spirit of Non-violence in the country, which is as essential for our success as pure air is for life.

I have no doubt that the secret of the progress of our country lies in the unity of the Hindus, the Mussalmans and other races of India. Such a unity should not be based on policy, for that, in my opinion, will only be a kind of armistice which might with difficulty be sufficient for present requirements. But I clearly see that the two great communities are coming closer to each other every day. And although the number of men whose hearts are absolutely free from any sectarian prejudices may not be very great in the two communities, I feel convinced that the country has found the road to real unity and will advance on it with steady steps towards its goal. So highly do I prize the unity of races inhabiting our country that, if the country gave up all other activities and achieved that alone, I would consider the Khilafat and the Swaraj questions automatically solved to our satisfaction. For the achievement of our objects is so intimatety connected with this unity that to me the two appear identical.

The question naturally arises, how are we to achieve this living and lasting unity ? I can find only one answer to that. We can only achieve it by the sincerity and purity of our hearts. Not until every one of us has driven selfishness out of his mind, will our country succeed in achieving its object. I know that the differences which have been created by a century of this system of Government cannot very soon be eradicated and, therefore, we cannot expect our efforts to bear fruit immediately. But there can be no doubt that we have accomplished the work of generations in months and have actually achieved what the pessimists among us considered impossible of achievement.

I do not consider the question of the Khilafat in other words, the question of the evolution of Islamic policy, a passing phase. Just as in centuries past, it presented itself in one form or another, so will it in centuries to come. God alone knows how and when it will finally be solved. Therefore, even those who do not believe in Hindu-Muslim unity in the true sense of the term must understand that even as a policy it carries centuries under its arms. It is an admitted fact that looking to the present condition of India, next to Hindu-Muslim unity in importance is the question of Non-violence. How far have our efforts, or rather your efforts, been successful in that direction is shown by the progress of events. But the most striking proof of all of our success in that direction is afforded by our North-West Frontier Province where Non-violence had the least chance of success. When we find our brethern in that corner of India generally opposing the shield of Non-violence to the violent attacks of their opponents, we feel convinced that the spirit of Non-violence has spread and is spreading satisfactorily in the country.

Doubts are entertained with regard to the United Provinces in this matter; but my own opinion is that in consequence of the dearth of national workers, the Congress creed has not been sufficiently explained to the people. I feel sure, however, the United Provinces will very soon come up to the level of other Provinces.

If some extraordinary or special causes have occasionally led to violence in some parts of the country, they should afford no ground for despair. We should not be unprepared for such stray cases, when we remember that we have been working with a limited number of workers in the midst of a population of 33 crores and working for eighteen months only. At the same time we should not minimise the significance of such occurrences and concentrate all our efforts on preventing their recurrence. Unity of the races inhabiting India and Non-violence are the two essential conditions for the success of the present movement.

Khaddar, too, no doubt is of invaluable help to us in the achievement of our objects. It will demonstrate our unity and show us how far we have advanced towards Swaraj. I do not think that picketing is so necessary for popularising *khaddar* as the country considers it to be. The country considers it a short cut and spends its limited time over it, although as you yourself have observed, the real work lies in creating in the minds of our people love for home-made things. But so far, I think, our Congress Committees have not sufficiently devoted their time and attention to it. This is the reason why they want to make up for this neglect by adopting the comparatively easier method of picketing. I, however, hope that in future the various Congress Committees would adopt as their ideal to persuade people to use hand-spun and hand-woven *khaddar* and prefer it to picketing.

You have also touched upon the question of untouchability in your letter. On the face of it, it might appear to be a communal question. It is really a national question, for, the country as a whole cannot progress until and unless its component parts progress too. It is the duty of every person who has the interest of the country at heart to interest himself in all such question as affect our national growth. Consequently, everything which comes in the way of the material or moral progress of the country must engage our attention. It is, therefore, as much a Muslim question as Hindu. Similarly, if the Mussalmans are backward in education, every good Hindu should think of their educational advancement, for every step in that direction is a step towards the educational advancement of the country as a whole, even though it may superficially appear to be to the advantage of one community only. I hope, therefore, the country will pay to the question of untouchability the attention that it deserves.

Bordoli and Delhi resolutions invite the country to concentrate its efforts on the constructive programme laid down by you. I hold that if we were to start Civil Disobedience, we would not have the necessary atmosphere required for the success of the constructive programme. It is very difficult to find a *via media*. I trust the Working Committee will fully consider the question and adopt a proper and suitable course.

Now that we are starting constructive work, we should re-organise the Congress office to suit our requirements. We should divide the work and create seperate departments for different works, each under a member of the Working Committee selected for the purpose.

In the end, I join you in your prayers and wish to assure you that, though my failing health will not enable me to be of very great service to my country, it will be my earnst endeavour to discharge my duties, until Mr. C. R. Das is once more amongst us. May God help us in the sacred work which you and the country have undertaken for truth and justice, and may your going to jail lead to the achievement of our triple goal.

Yours sincerely,
MOHAMAD AJMAL KHAN.

MRS. GANDHI'S MESSAGE

My dear Countrymen and Countrywomen,

My dear husband has been sentenced to-day to six years simple imprisonment. While I cannot deny that this heavy sentence has to some extent told upon me, I have consoled myself with the thought that it is not beyond our powers to reduce that sentence and release him by our own exertions long before his term of imprisonment is over.

I have no doubt that, if India wakes up and seriously undertakes to carry out the constructive programme of the Congress, we shall succeed not only in releasing him, but also in solving to our satisfaction all the three issues for which we have been fighting and suffering for the last eighteen months or more.

The remedy, therefore, lies with us. If we fail, the fault will be ours. I, therefore, appeal to all men and women who feel for me and have regard for my husband to wholeheartedly concentrate on the constructive programme and make it a success.

Among all the items of the programme, he laid the greatest emphasis on the spinning wheel and *khaddar*. Our success in these will not only solve the economic problem of India in relation to the masses, but also free us from our political bondage. India's first answer, then, to Mr. Gandhi's conviction should be that:

(*a*) All men and women give up their foreign cloth and adopt *khaddar* and persuade others to do so.

(*b*) All women make it a religious duty to spin and produce yarn every day and persuade others to do so.

(*c*) All merchants cease trading in foreign piece-goods.

KASTURIBAI GANDHI.

PART X

APPENDICES.

PART X

APPENDICES

[A]

SOME OBITER DICTA

THE following notes appeared in "Young India" on the dates specified against them:

Gandhi Cigarettes.—Of all the abuses to which my name has been put, I know nothing so humiliating to me as the deliberate association of my name with cigarettes. A friend has sent me a label purporting to bear my portrait. The cigarettes are called 'Mahatma Gandhi' cigarettes. Now I have a horror of smoking as I have of wines. Smoking I consider to be a vice. It deadens one's conscience and is often worse than drink, in that it acts imperceptibly. It is a habit which is difficult to get rid of when once it seizes hold of a person It is an expensive vice. It fouls the breath, discolours the teeth and sometimes even causes cancer. It is an unclean habit. No man has received my permission to associate my name with cigarettes. I should feel thankful, if the unknown firm were to withdraw the labels from the market, or if the public would refuse to buy packets bearing such labels.—*13th January*, 1921.

Lokamanya and Non-co-operation.—The up-country

English papers in giving obituary notices about the late Lokamanya Tilak have attributed to him views against Non-co-operation. So far as we are aware Mr. Tilak held very strong views on Non-co-operation. We know that he assured Maulana Shaukat Ali that, if the Mussalmans offered Non-co-operation, his party and the Hindus in general would certainly follow them. The deceased had no final views on the details of Non-co-operation including boycott of councils, but when Maulana Shaukat Ali with Mr. Gandhi visited him at Sirdar Graha before going to the Punjab, he said that, if the Mussalmans boycotted the Councils, he and his party would follow suit. It is therefore strange that views should be attributed to the deceased which he never held.—*11th August*, 1920.

Government Non-co-operation.—Mr. Gandhi wrote in reply to a correspondent regarding railways and telegraphs:

I am not myself banishing the personal use of these conveniences myself. I certainly do not expect the nation to discard their use, nor do I expect their disuse under Swaraj. But I do expect the nation under Swaraj not to believe, that these agencies necessarily advance our moral growth or are indispensable for our material progress. I would advise the nation to make a limited use of these agencies and not to be feverishly anxious to connect seven hundred and fifty thousand villages of India by telegraph and railway. The nation, when it feels the glow of freedom, will realise that they were needed by our rulers more for our enslavement than for enlightenment. Progress is a lame woman. It can only come hopping. You cannot send it by wire or rail.

Therefore, if we believe in our programme, we must not

mind if the Government non-co-operate with us in every particular. I hear from Mr. Rajagopalachari and Agha Safdar that they are not permitted to send full telegrams. It is a surprise to me that they permit the transmission of any telegrams at all or let us travel or meet each other. Having made up my mind to expect the worst, nothing that the Government does in the shape of curbing our activity surprises or irritates me. It is struggling for its very existence, and I feel that I would have done much the same that this Government is doing if I was in its place. Probably I should do much worse. Why should we expect it to refrain from using the powers it has? Only we must find the means of living and carrying on our Non-co-operation without its aid. We must keep our heads, even if inter-provincial communication is denied to us. Having got our programme, each province must be able to carry on its own activity. Indeed it may even be an advantage, for in the event of communication being cut off, we should be unaffected by reverses in other provinces.—*17th November*, 1921.

Slow but Sure.—If the luxury of wires be denied to us, we must manage with the post. If the postal communication be also stopped, we must use messengers. Friends travelling to and fro will oblige us. When the use of the railways is denied, we must use other methods of conveyance. No amount of slowness imposed from without can checkmate us if we are sure within. 'Rock of ages cleft for me, let me hide myself in thee' is a prayer common to all religions. If we can but throw ourselves into His lap as our only Help, we shall come out scatheless through every ordeal that the Government may subject us to. If nothing happens without His permitting, where is the difficulty in believing that he is trying us even through this Government? I would take our complaints to Him and be angry with Him for so cruelly trying us. And He will soothe us and forgive us, if we will but trust Him. The way to stand erect before the tyrant is not to hate him, not to strike him, but to humble ourselves before God and cry out to Him in the hour of our agony.—*15th December*, 1921.

Is it a Breach?—Friends have suspected me of having committed a breach of the Congress resolution, in that I have appealed to the Moderates to co-operate with us in the liquor campaign and, especially, in that I have actually invited them to legislate for prohibition. A friend asks, "Why should we seek the help of the councils which we have boycotted? Does it not mean a modification of your previous attitude?" I venture to say that it does not. There is all the difference between a challenge and a petition. If I had appealed out of our helplessness, it would have been a breach of the Congress resolution and a modification of my own attitude. But, in my opinion, I strengthen our position, when I invite the Moderates in gentle language to do their duty, and prove their claim to be popular representatives. I see nothing wrong in inviting the Moderates and the Government to co-operate with us in all we are doing. I see nothing wrong in appealing to the Moderates or even to the Government through their authorised channels, to help us in the Khilafat and the Punjab matters. or to shut up all the liquor-shops, or to dot every one of their schools with spinning-wheels or to recognise the force of public opinion and to prohibit by legislation the import of foreign cloth. For, if they succeed in doing these things, I would cease to think evil of the institution they adore or administer. In making my appeal, I have shown them a way to partial reinstatement in public estimation, and have furnished myself and the country with a further effective cause, in the event of the failure of the appeal, to demonstrate the wooden nature of the system. I have appealed, not as myself a part of the system, but as an outsider.—*6th July*, 1921.

If Mussalmans or Hindus Secede.—If one of the big communities secede from the compact of Non-violence, I admit that it is most difficult, though certainly not impossible, for one party only to carry on the struggle. That party will need to have an invulnerable faith in the policy of Non-violence. But if one community does realise that India cannot gain Swaraj for generations through violent means, it can by its consistently non-violent, *i.e.*, loving, conduct bring round all the opposing parties to its side.

If both the parties reject me, I should keep my peace just as ever and most decidedly carry on my propaganda of Non-violence. I should then not be restricted as I am now. Then I should be enforcing my creed, as to-day I seem to be enforcing only the policy.—*9th March*, 1922.

Self-defence.—The Non-co-operators' pledge does not exclude the right of private self-defence. Non-co-operators are under prohibition as to political violence. Those, therefore, with whom Non-co-operation is not their final creed, are certainly free to defend themselves or their dependents and wards against their assailants. But they may not defend themselves against the police acting in discharge of their duties, whether assumed or authorised. Thus there was no right of self-defence under the pledge against Collectors who have, I hold, —*9th March*, 1922.

Party Organisations.—Replying to a letter in August, 1919, of Mr. G. S. Arundale, Mr. Gandhi wrote:

"You suggest the desirability of unity. I think unity of goal we have. But parties we shall have—we may not find a common denominator for improvements. For some will want to go further than others. I see no harm in a wholesome variety. What I would rid ourselves of, is distrust of one another and imputation of motives. Our besetting sin is not our differences, but our littleness. We wrangle over words, we fight often for shadow and lose the substance. . . . It is not our differences that really matter. It is the meanness behind that is ugly."—*5th February*, 1920.

Freedom of Minorities.—Mahatma Gandhi incessantly emphasised the importance of safe-guarding the rights of the minorities. He wrote *inter alia* on 9th February, 1921, under the heading, "The Greatest Thing":

Shall we copy Dyerism and O'Dwyerism, even whilst we are condemning it? Let not our rock be violence and devilry. Our rock must be non-violence and godliness. Let us, workers, be clear as to what we are about. *Swaraj depends upon our ability to control all the forces of violence on our side.* Therefore, there is no Swaraj within one year, if there is violence on the part of the people.

We must then refrain from sitting *dhurna*, we must refrain from crying 'shame, shame' to any body, we must not use any coercion to persuade our people to adopt our way. We must guarantee to them the same freedom we claim for ourselves. We must not tamper with the masses. It is dangerous to make political use of factory labourers or the peasantry—not that we are not entitled to do so, but we are not ready for it. We have neglected their political (as distinguished from literary) education all these long years. We have not got enough honest, intelligent, reliable, and brave workers to enable us to act upon these countrymen of ours.

Communal Representation.—We have absurdities enough in India in communal representation being demanded by other small groups, because the principle has been conceded in the case of Mahomedans. But when the cry for communal representation comes from Indians in Burma, the absurdity becomes criminal. We understand some Indians of Rangoon have pleaded for communal representation in the Burmese Council to be formed under the reforms. We do hope that the demand will be withdrawn before mischief is done. The Burman will have every right to resent any such separate treatment of Indian settlers there. We are in Burma as guests of the Burmese for their and our mutual good, not for the exploitation of the former. Their welfare should be our first consideration. As a friend correctly points out the Indian demand would be like Gujaratis or Marwaris claiming communal representation for themselves in the Bengal Council. Surely, Indians of Burma would have a right to enter the Burmese Council, only if they, by force of ability and service, can command the Burmese vote. We, who desire that nobody should set up claims in India which are against our interests, are bound to guard against desiring rights in Burma in conflict with the interests of the Burmans. And yet that is precisely what lies at the bottom of this demand for communal representation by Indian settlers. We, therefore, trust that wiser counsel will prevail and that we shall hear no more of communal representation for Indians in Burma.—*21st April*, 1920.

Lawyers and Volunteering.—In reply to Mr. Ramadas Chhokra, Bar-at-Law of Lyallpur, Mahatma Gandhi wrote:

Lawyers cannot become office-bearers. They could not become members of executive committees. But the Volunteer's pledge is for the purpose, among others, of nullifying the effect of the disbandment notices of the Government. In my opinion, a lawyer who conscientiously signs the pledge is sufficiently pure for the purpose of going to jail. And the very fact of his readiness to go to jail ensures suspension of practice for the period of imprisonment. Suspension contemplated by the Non-co-operation resolution is meant to last till Swaraj is attained, which a lawyer may not be able to brave, though he may not mind, by signing the pledge, the risk of loss of practice, should he have to go to jail. In the one case suspension is a certainty, in the other a possibility—very remote, if a large number took the pledge. The gain in lawyers signing the pledge is great. They show their open sympathy with the cause in a limited sense perhaps, and they definitely and in their own persons advance the cause of Swadeshi. I would give much to see the lawyers having the courage of discarding their totally unnecessary foreign cloth and foreign cut, and taking up the *khaddar* dress and thus identifying themselves with the wonderful manifestation of the mass spirit. All the cloth that is handspun and handwoven, whether wool, silk or cotton, is *khaddar*. But it is expected that no one will take to silk or wollen *khaddar*, except when it is required by climatic or other urgent considerations. The fashion certainly should be, as Dr. Ray says, to wear the coarse *khaddar*. Let me repeat what I have said before, the *khaddar* that is coarse to look at is like tussor silk soft to the touch, and protects the skin much better than the soft-looking *khadi.—2nd February, 1922.*

A Threatened Infliction.—I have just heard that Mr. Painter, who has distinguished himself by his wanton provocation of the people of Dharwad, is to be promoted and inflicted upon Gujarat as Commissioner. An official, who in the public estimation has disgraced himself, earns rewards from the Government for meritorious service. I hope that Gujarat will mark in a suitable and special manner its disapproval of the insult sought to be offered by the Dharwad Collector being imposed upon it. Gujarat will have, if the rumoured appointment is actually made, a unique opportunity of showing how such insult can be dealt with in a Non-co-operation spirit. We must distinguish between the man and the Commissioner. We must boycott the latter and render social service to the former. We must therefore permit him to receive all he may reasonably need as man for creature comforts, but if we have the people with us, the Commissioner Mr. Painter may not get a blade of grass for the upkeep of the dignity of his office. We must therefore inculcate among the people the habit of refusing *salaam* to him in virtue of office. They must not send any applications to him. They must not, whilst he is touring in the country, supply him with any convenience whatsoever. He must be made, in every dignified and peaceful manner, to feel that he is not wanted as an official in Gujarat. The municipalities containing Non-co-operators should refuse to recognise him as Commissioner in every way possible. If we have developed the spirit of real independence and manliness, we would refuse to put up with an official who has forfeited public opinion as Mr. Painter has.

What, for instance, would be said of us, if Col. Frank Johnson or Gen. Dyer were imposed upon us? We have to pass through certain rigid tests as proof of our capacity for self-Government. One of them is refusal to submit to national insults. Indeed, if we had evolved that capacity sufficiently, I would expect even the employees, who would come under Mr. Painter's direct control, to resign by way of protest. We have such mortal fear of loss of livelihood, that the employees are the last to be expected to develop that sense of self-respect which is so necessary for national existence. But their reluctance will not materially interfere with attainment of Swaraj this year, if the general public is responsive enough. It is time for them to assert themselves individually as well as collectively. We must begin our battle with a disciplined and complete *hartal*. when the gentleman enters Ahmedabad if he does. And to the end at seeing that there is ample time, the Provincial Congress Committee should secure permission from the Working Committee for declaring a *hartal* all over Gujarat in the event of Mr. Painter being sent to Gujarat in any official capacity. If a *hartal* becomes necessary, I need hardly say that it must be completely voluntary. The labourers should participate after due notice and permission.—*8th September*, 1921.

Distress Warrants.—Inquiries are being made in several places as to what should be done in cases where fines are imposed and distress warrants issued for recovery. One finds a readiness to suffer imprisonment and assaults, but not loss of goods. The anomaly is at first sight difficult to understand, but it is really easy to appreciate. We are so much tied down to our goods and other possessions that, when no disgrace attaches to imprisonment, we prefer the inconvenience to loss of property. But we must perceive that we will lose a winning game, if we are not prepared to sacrifice our earthly possessions as well as bodily ease for the sake of it. In an ill-managed state, a man with conscience pawns to it his goods, all other wealth, and his body and sets his conscience free. This struggle, therefore, can give us victory, only if we become indifferent to everything through which the state can press us into subjection to its will. We must be prepared, therefore, to let our goods and our land be taken away from us and rejoice over the dispossession even as we rejoice to-day over imprisonments. We must rest assured that the Government will be more quickly tired of selling our chattels than it is already of taking charge of our bodies. And if we are sure, as we must be of winning full Swaraj before long, we must have faith enough to know that all the land that can be taken away will return to us intact and the best part even of money. When Belgium was overrun by the Germans, the Belgians knew that they would return to their own lands so long as they retained the will to suffer for the restoration of their property. The late General Botha was a fugitive from his own rich possessions including hundreds of acres of land and finest cattle in South Africa. He did not count the cost, put up a fine fight and become virtually the crowned king of South Africa and had all his property returned to him with honour. We may not do less than the Boers and the Belgians, especially as ours is a struggle in which we are pledged to make all sacrifice and exact none. We must voluntarily, though temporarily, embrace poverty, if we will banish pauperism and pariahdom from the land. The sacrifice of the ease by a few of us is nothing compared to the reward which is in store for us, *viz.*, the restoration of the honour and prosperity of this holy land.—*12th January, 1922.*

The Malaviyas.—The most remarkable feature in the remarkable Non-co-operation struggle is the fact that it has divided families. And of all such instances, none is so striking as the division in the Malaviya family. It furnishes, in my opinion, an object-lesson to India in toleration and Civil Disobedience. Pandit Malaviyaji's toleration is really beyond compare. I know that he is against seeking imprisonment. I know too, that if he believed in it, he is not the person to shirk it. I should not be surprised to find him, when the agony has reached white heat and when his faith in British justice is completely gone like mine, to be the foremost in seeking imprisonment. But whilst he is himself against the course of Civil Disobedience for the present, he has never interfered with the choice of even those who are nearest to him and over whom he has unquestioned authority by right of love and eldership. On the contrary, he has left even his own sons absolutely free to do as they please. To me the instance of Govind's Civil Disobedience is one to treasure. Panditji tried hard to wean that brave boy in his own gentle and sweet manner. Govind tried his very best to carry out what he knew to be his father's wish up to the last moment. He prayed for light. He was torn by conflict of duties. The arrests of the Nehrus proved too strong for the young man. And invoking the blessings of his great and great-hearted father, he decided to throw himself into the struggle, and the jails of India probably hold no more joyous heart than Govind Malaviya's. I make bold to say that he has by his act of Civil Disobedience proved as dutiful to his father as he has been dutiful to his country. Govind's act is a pattern for our time in dutiful Civil Disobedience of children. There is, I am sure, no gulf between father and son. Probably Malaviyaji is prouder of his son Govind now than he was before the latter's decision to seek imprisonment. It is truthful acts like these which prove to me the religious nature of the struggle.—*12th January*, 1922.

The Police Conference.—The address delivered by Babu Purna Chandra Bishwas, Deputy Superintendent of Police, as President of the All-India Police Conference, held some time back in Calcutta, has not drawn the same amount of public attention as its importance deserves. Purna Babu has lucidly stated the whole case for the police. There is no doubt about the unpopularity of the police in India, and the present outrageous acts of repression have probably added to it. But we must not forget that the police are mere instruments wielded by the Government. The President says:

"Here in India, the laws are made by Government and the people are of opinion that the laws are made to rule them, to control their natural aspirations and not for their benefit. We maintain the dignity of these laws and enforce them. That is one reason why we are so very unpopular." Again—"With the inauguration of the Reforms Scheme, the people have begun to realise that it is the laws that are unpopular and not the police, and that our only fault is that we are to carry out these unpopular laws."

The idea of ruling the people, of dominating them, of controlling their natural aspirations, as the President says, runs through the whole system of bureaucratic organisation in India. And as that work is done more directly through the agency of the police, it is interesting to read the confession of a distinguished member of that service on the matter:

"When I speak of our unpopularity, I cannot refrain from uttering, though unpleasant it may be, that our conduct rules and the attitude of our superiors rather accentuate our estrangement from the public. We cannot freely mix with them, independently invoke their hearty co-operation and sympathy, for which there is the greatest need for our duties: if we do so, we are, on flimsiest pretexts, looked upon with suspicion by superiors, even penalised and our promotions are stopped. I ask, comrades, who are responsible for this? I can at once say, we have absolutely no fault except that we belong to this unpopular department, and it is our superiors and conduct rules that widen this gulf."

But though the Government utilises the Indian police in this way, does it treat them any the better on that account? The ban of racial inferiority sits upon them as tightly as upon the general mass of the people, as the long list of their grievances will show. It is producing restlessness in the service, indications of which are not wanting. The President thus cautiously expresses it:

"What will be the effect, if the subordinate police refuse to obey the command of their superior officer for dispersing or firing on a riotous mob? You may laugh at the idea, I too know that such a thing is impossible or at least undesirable. But no one knows how things change. You must not forget that the people of the country are no longer afraid of jail, and this spirit has also been imbibed by the subordinate police."

Purna Babu had to pay for all this out-spokenness. He was summoned before Sir Henry Wheeler and ordered abruptly to join duty. But the delegetes mildly remonstrated against the order, and Purna Babu was triumphantly brought back from his train and taken in a procession to the conference to finish the proceedings.—*26th January*, 1922.

The Appeal to Nature and History.—In reply to the Rev. G. H. Macfarlane who wrote a sarcastic letter to the

Mahatma about his achievement, Mr. Gandhi replied as follows :

The writer asks to know the accomplishment of the movement. It has brought about a tremendous awakening among the people. Whereas they had given up hand-spinning entirely, to-day thousands of homes are spinning hundreds of thousands of yards of yarn. Whereas handspun garments had gone out of use, to-day thoususnds of men and women are wearing *khaddar* which has resulted in driving away hunger from thousands of homes. The people know that Swaraj means their power over the purse, the law, the police, and the military. They know that there can be no peace till the Punjab wound is healed and the Khilafat wrong is redressed.

The nations have progressed both by evolution and revolution. The one is as necessary as the other. Death, which is an eternal verity, is revolution, as birth and after is slow and steady evolution. Death is as necessary for man's growth as life itself. God is the great Revolutionist the world has ever known or will know. He sends deluges. He sends storms where a moment ago there was calm. He levels down mountains which He builds with exquisite care and infinite patience. I do watch the sky and it fills me with awe and wonder. In the serene blue sky, both of India and England, I have seen clouds gathering and bursting with a fury which has struck me dumb. History is more a record of wonderful revolution than of so-called ordered progress—no history more so than the English. And I beg to inform the correspondent that I have seen people trudging slowly up mountains and have also seen men shooting up the air through great heights.

Swaraj is India's birthright. The British system has

balked her of it. India is struggling to regain her lost liberty, and in doing so she is trying not to repeat but to make new history. In the process she betrays a woeful desire to repeat it as in Bombay, Madras and Malegaon. Malabar is not to be mixed up with the movement. Independence necessarily means freedom to err. Lastly, I assure the writer and others who think like him that the movement is not one of ill-will, but of good will towards all. Time alone can prove the truth of it. The agony does not permit us to see the new birth concealed beneath it. Let us watch, wait, and pray.—*2nd February*, 1922.

Force vs. *Non-violence*.—Mr. Zacharias argues in the *Servant of India* that the Khilafat is based on force. The Khilafat is the earthly representative of Islam pledged to defend it even with the sword. And how can I, a believer in non-violence, fight to sustain an institution that is permitted to resort to physical force for its defence?

Mr. Zacharias is right in his description of the Khilafat. He is wrong in his estimate of the function of a votary of non-violence. A believer in non-violence is pledged not to resort to violence of physical force either directly or indirectly in defence of anything, but he is not precluded from helping men or institutions that are themselves not based on non-violence. If the reverse were the case, I would, for instance, be precluded from helping India to attain Swaraj, because the future Parliament of India under Swaraj, I know for certain, will be having some military and police forces, or to take a domestic illustration, I may not help a son to secure justice, because forsooth he is not a believer in non-violence.

Mr. Zacharias' proposition will reduce, all commerce by a believer in non-violence to an impossibility. And there are not wanting men, who do believe that complete non-violence means complete cessation of all activity.

Not such, however, is my doctrine of non-violence. My business is to refrain from doing any violence myself, and to induce by persuasion and service as many of God's creatures as I can, to join me in the belief and practice. But I would be untrue to my faith, if I refused to assist in a just cause any men or measures that did not entirely coincide with the principle of non-violence. I would be promoting violence, if, finding the Mussalmans to be in the right, I did not assist them by means strictly non-violent against those who had treacherously plotted the destruction of the dignity of Islam. Even when both parties believe in violence, there is often such a thing as justice on one side or the other. A robbed man has justice on his side, even though he may lie preparing to regain the lost property by force. And it would be accounted as a triumph of non-violence, if the injured party could be persuaded to regain his property by methods of Satyagrah, *i.e.*, love or soul-force rather than a free fight.

Of course it is open to Mr. Zacharies to reject my claim as a devotee of non-violence, in view of all the limitations I have mentioned. I can only suggest to him that life is a very complex thing, and truth and non-violence present problems, which often defy analysis and judgment. One discovers truth and the method of applying the only legitimate means of vindicating it, *i.e.*, Satyagraha or soul-force, by patient endeavour and silent prayer. I can only assure friends that I spare no pains to grope my way to the right, and that humble but constant endeavour and silent prayer are always my two trusty companions along the weary but beautiful path that all seekers must tread.—*1st June*, 1921.

British vs. *Other Governments*.—'Observer' in the *Times of India* asks me whether the British 'is not a better Government than the Mogul and the Maratha. I must dare to say, that the Mogul and the Maratha Government were better than the British, in that the nation as a whole was not so emasculate or so impoverished as it is to-day. We were not the Pariahs of the Mogul or the Maratha Emire. We *are* Pariahs of the British Empire.—*22nd June*, 1921.

Cause of India's Decay.—A correspondent asks, 'Is it not true that the loss of Hindu Kingdoms is on account of the people having attained to the highest order of spirituality?' I do not think so. We know, as a matter of fact, that the Hindus have lost each time for want of spirituality, in other words, moral stamina. The Rajputs fought amongst themselves for trifles and lost India. Of personal bravery there was a great deal, but of real spirituality there was a great dearth at the time. Why did Ravana lose and Rama with his monkeys win if it was not for the latter's spirituality? Did not the Pandavas win bacause of their superior spirituality? We often confuse spiritual knowledge with spiritual attainment. Spirituality is not a matter of knowing scriptures and engaging in philosphical discussions. It is a matter of heart culture, of immeasurable strength. Fearlessness is the first requisite of spirituality. Cowards can never be moral.

The Root Cause.—The same correspondent further asks, 'Don't you think that the success of the present foreign Government is due to the oppression of the poor, the weak, of the so-called untouchables by the higher classes?' This oppression by us of our own kith and kin is certainly the root cause. It is a fall from spirituality. The curse of foreign domination and the attendant exploitation is the justest retribution meted out by God to us for our exploitation of a sixth of our own race and their studied degradation in the sacred name of religion. Hence it is that I have put the removal of untouchability as an indispensable condition of attainment of Swaraj. Slave-holders ourselves, we have no business to quarrel with our own slavery if we are not prepared unconditionally to enfranchise our own slaves. We must first cast out the beam of untouchability from our own eyes before we attempt to remove the mote from that of our 'masters'.—*13th October*, 1921.

An Essential Condition of Swaraj.—The following appeared *inter alia* in an article entitled *Thefts on Railways*:

Swaraj can be maintained, only where there is a majority of loyal and patriotic people to whom the good of the nation is paramount above all other considerations whatever including their personal profit. Swaraj means Government by the many. Where the many are immoral or selfish, their Government can spell anarchy and nothing else. I am in this movement, only as I believe that the many are good and true at the bottom but being cowardly and careless are ignorant of their inherent qualities, and that when once they have realised the power of goodness, they will begin to practise it and succeed in the attempt.—*28th July*, 1921.

Need for Simplicity.—In an article entitled, "The Distress in Puri," Mahatma Gandhi wrote *inter alia*:

In India, it must be held to be a crime to spend money on dinner and marriage parties, *tamashas* and other luxuries so long as millions of people are starving. We would not have a feast in a family if a member was about to die of starvation. If India is one family, we should have the same feeling as we would have in a private family.—*22nd December*, 1920.

How to Kill Swadeshi.—We are familiar with the official ban put upon the *Khadi* cap in various parts of India. In Bihar, I heard that a magistrate actually sent hawkers to sell foreign cloth. Mr. Painter of Dharwad fame has gone one better, and has issued an official circular in which he says :

'All officers subordinate to the Collector and District Magistrate are desired to take steps to make people realise, that in as much as India produces less than her population requires, a boycott of foreign cloth and its destruction or export must inevitably lead to a serious rise in prices, which may lead to a serious disorder and looting, and that these consequences will be the result, not of any action on the part of Government, but of Mr. Gandhi's campaign.'*

In two other paragraphs, means are indicated of combating the Swadeshi propaganda, *i.e.*, by holding meetings, and by dealers who are opposed to boycott attending the Collector's office at stated hours. The Madras Government have issued a still more pedantic circular. The meaning of these circulars is obvious. Pressure is to be put upon the dealers and others not to countenance boycott. The subordinate officials will

* It subsequently transpired that similar circulars had been issued throughout the country in pursuance of the Government of India's instructions in the matter.

take liberties which the authors of ciculars may not even have contemplated. . . . The people have been purposely or ignorantly kept in the dark hitherto. They have been wrongly taught to believe that all the cloth needed cannot be manufactured in India's homes as of yore. They have been figuratively amputated, and then made to rely upon foreign or mill-made cloth. I wish the people concerned will give the only dignified answer possible to these circulars. They will forthwith burn or send out all their foreign cloth, and courageously make up their minds to spin and weave for their own requirements. It is incredibly easy for every one who is not an idler.—*15th September*, 1921.

For Employees.—A correspondent inquires, "Would you advise the servants of railway companies, European firms and others who do not want their servants to subscribe to national funds or wear *Khadi*, to resign in obedience to the Congress call?" I should have thought that such a question could not require solution at this almost the last stage in the struggle. The surprise to me is, that any person can still remain in an office where he cannot follow his religion or maintain self-respect. That hundreds of clerks find it impossible to leave their offices although they are prevented from wearing the life-giving *Khadi* or subscribing openly to national fund, shows the depth to which we have sunk. It did not require the stern lesson of Non-co-operation to learn the elements of self-respect. And yet, that is just what Non-co-operation has been doing all these months. I commend to every employee the example of the brave Vizagapatam medical students who would not leave their *Khadi* dress for the sake of being able to remain in their school.—*3rd November*, 1921.

Deferred Pay.—The Government have found no difficulty in stopping the deferred pay as pensions are now-a-days called, of Mr. Vinayakrao, Joshi of Dharwar for no other reason than that he has tried to serve his country. Whereas, Sir Michael O'Dwyer who never loses an opportunity of vilifying educated Indians and of insolently patronising the masses, as if they were little children always needing the attention and care of an elder, and General Dyer, who still believes that he performed a simple duty when he massacred the innocent men in Jallianwalla Bagh, continue to draw pensions. We are told that there are legal difficulties in stopping their pensions and that if the legal obstacle can be surmounted, it would be immoral to take away their pensions. Verily there is one law for an Indian, another for an Englishman; one law for a patriot, another for a persecutor. What is moral in the case of one is immoral in the case of the other! I congratulate Mr. Joshi on his spirited reply to the Government and on his patriotic courage in foregoing his pension, when it became a matter of choice between service of his country and retention of his pension. Mr. Joshi's sacrifice strengthens India's cause. His material loss is India's moral gain.

13*th October*, 1920

IN CONFIDENCE

I receive so many letters questioning me regarding celibacy and I hold such strong views upon it, that I may no longer, especially at this the most critical period of national life, withhold my views and results of my experience from the readers of *Young India*.

The word in Sanskrit corresponding to celibacy is

Brahmacharya* and the latter means much more than celibacy. Brahmacharya means perfect control over all the senses and organs. For the perfect Brahmachari nothing is impossible. But it is an ideal state which is rarely realised. It is almost like Euclid's line which exists only in imagination, never capable of being physically drawn. It is nevertheless an important definition in Geometry yielding great result. So may a perfect Brahmachari exist only in imagination. But if we did not keep him constantly before our mind's eye, we should be like a rudderless ship. The nearer the approach to the imaginary state, the greater the perfection.

But for the time being, I propose to confine myself to Brahmacharya as in the sense of celibacy. I hold that a life of perfect continence in thought, speech and action is necessary for reaching spiritual perfection. And the nation that does not possess such men is the poorer for the worst. But my purpose is to plead for Brahmacharya as a temporary necessity in the present stage of national evolution.

We have more than an ordinary share of disease, famines and pauperism—even starvation among millions. We are being ground down under slavery in such a subtle manner that many of us refuse even to recognise it as such, and mistake our state as one of progressive freedom in spite of the triple curse of economic, mental and moral drain. The evergrowing military expenditure, and the injurious fiscal policy purposely designed to benefit Lancashire and other British interests, and the extravagant manner of running the various departments of the state constitute a tax on India which has deepened her poverty and reduced her capacity for withstanding

* For further details on the subject, see the Mahatma's *Guide to Health* and *Indian Home Rule*.

diseases. The manner of administration has, in Gokhale's words, 'stunted' national growth so much that the tallest of us have to bend. India was even made to crawl on her belly in Amritsar. The studied insult of the Punjab and the refusal to apologise for the insolent breach of the pledged word to Indian Mussalmans are the most recent examples of the moral drain. They hurt the very soul within us. The process of emasculation would be complete, if we submit to those two wrongs.

Is it right for us who know the situation to bring forth children in an atmosphere so debasing as I have described? We only multiply slaves and weaklings, if we continue the process of procreation whilst we feel and remain helpless, diseased and famine-stricken. Not till India has become a free nation, able to withstand avoidable starvation, well able to feed herself in times of famine, possessing the knowledge to deal with malaria, cholera, influenza and other epidemics, have we the right to bring forth progeny. I must not conceal from the reader the sorrow I feel, when I hear of births in this land. I must express that for years I have contemplated with satisfaction the prospect of suspending procreation by voluntary self-denial. India is to-day ill-equipped for taking care even of her present population, not because she is over-populated, but because she is forced to foreign domination whose creed is progressive exploitation of her resources.

How is the suspension of procreation to be brought about? Not by immoral and artificial checks that are resorted to in Europe, but by a life of discipline and self-control. Parents must teach their children the practice of Brahmacharya. According to the Hindu Shastras the lowest age at which boys may marry is 25. If the mothers of India could be inclined to believe that it is sinful to train boys and girls for a married life, half the marriages of India will automatically stop. Nor need we believe the fetish of early puberty among girls, because of our hot climate. I have never known a grosser superstition than this of early puberty. I make bold to say that the climate has absolutely nothing to do with puberty. What does bring about untimely puberty is the mental and moral atmosphere surrounding our family life. Mothers and other relations make it a religious duty to teach innocent children that they are to be married when they reach a particular age. They are betrothed, when the are infants, are even babes in arms. The dress and the food of the children are also aids to stimulating passions. We dress our children like dolls, not for their but for our pleasure and vanity. I have brought up children by the score. And they have without difficulty taken to and delighted in any dress given to them. We provide them with all kinds of heating and stimulating foods. Our blind love takes no note of their capacity. The result undoubtedly is an early adolescence, and unmature progeny and an early grave. Parents furnish an object lesson which the children easily grasp. By reckless indulgence in their passions they serve for their children as models of unrestrained licence. Every untimely addition to the family is amid trumpets of joy and feasting. The wonder is that we are not less restrained than we are, notwithstanding our surroundings. I have not a shadow of doubt that married people, if they wish well to the country and want to see India become a nation of strong and handsome, full-formed men and women, they would practise perfect self-restraint and cease to procreate for the time being. I tender this advice even to the newly married. It is easier not to do a thing at all than to cease doing it, even as it is easier for a life-abstainer to remain teetotaller than for a drunkard or even a temperate man to abstain. To remain erect is infinitely easier than to rise from a fall. It is wrong to say that continence can be safely preached only to the satiated. There is hardly any meaning, either, in preaching continence to an enfeebled person. And my point is that whether we are young or old, satiated or not, it is our duty at the present moment to suspend bringing forth heirs to our slavery.

May I point out to parents that they ought not to fall into the argumentative trap of the rights of partners. Consent is required for indulgence, never for restraint, this is an obvious truth.

When we are engaged in a death grip with a powerful government, we shall need all the strength physical, material and moral and spiritual. We cannot gain it unless we husband the one thing which we must prize above everything else. Without this personal purity of life, we must remain a nation of slaves. Let us not deceive ourselves by imagining that, because we consider the system of government to be corrupt, Englishmen are to be despised as competitioners in a race for personal virtue. Without making any spiritual parade of the fundamental virtues, they practise them at least physically in an abundant measure. Among those who are engaged in the political life of the country, there are more celibates and spinsters than among us. Spinsters among us are practically unknown, except the nuns who leave no impression on the political life of the country. Whereas in Europe, thousands claim celibacy as a common virtue.

I now place before the readers a few simple rules

which are based on the experience not only of myself, but of many of my associates.

(1) Boys and girls should be brought up simply and naturally in the full belief that they are and can remain innocent.

(2) All should abstain from heating and stimulating foods, condiments such as chillies, fatty and concentrated foods such as fritters, sweets and fried substances.

(3) Husband and wife should occupy seperate rooms and avoid privacy.

(4) Both body and mind should be constantly and healthily occupied.

(5) Early to bed and early to rise should be strictly observed.

(6) All unclean literature should be avoided. The antidote for unclean thoughts is clean thoughts.

(7) Theatres, cinemas, etc., which tend to stimulate passion should be shunned.

(8) Nocturnal dreams need not cause any anxiety. A cold bath every time for a fairly strong person is the finest preventive in such cases. It is wrong to say that an occasional indulgence is a safeguard against involuntary dreams.

(9) Above all, one must not consider continence even as between husband and wife to be so difficult as to be practically impossible. On the contrary, self-restraint must be considered to be the ordinary and natural practice of life.

(10) A heart-felt prayer everyday for purity makes one progressively pure.

22nd December, 1920

THE SIN OF SECRECY

One of the curses of India is often the sin of secrecy. For fear of an unknown consequence we talk in whispers. Nowhere has this secrecy oppressed me more than in Bengal. Everybody wishes to speak to you 'in private.' The spectacle of innocent youngmen looking around, before opening their lips, to see that no third party overhears their conversation has given me the greatest grief. Every stranger is suspected of belonging to the secret service. I have been warned to beware of strangers. The cup of my misery was filled, when I was told that the unknown student who presided at the students' meeting belonged to the secret service department. I could recall the names of at least two prominent leaders who are suspected in high Indian circles of being spies of the Government.

I feel thankful to God that for years past I have come to regard secrecy as a sin, more especially in politics. If we realised the presence of God as witness to all we say and do, we would not have anything to conceal from anybody on earth. For, we would not think unclean thoughts before our Maker, much less speak them. It is uscleanness that seeks secrecy and darkness. The tendency of human nature is to hide dirt, we do not want to see or touch dirty things: we want to put them out of sight. And so must it be with our speech. I would suggest that we should avoid even thinking thoughts we would hide from the world.

This desire for secrecy has bred cowardice amongst us and had made us dissemble our speech. The best and the quickest way of getting rid of this corroding and degrading Secret Service is for us to make a final effort to think everything aloud, have no privileged conversation with any soul on earth and to cease to fear the spy. We must ignore his presence and treat everyone as a friend entitled to know all our thoughts and plans. I know that I have achieved most satisfactory results from evolving the boldest of my plans in broad daylight. I have never lost a minute's peace for having detectives by my side. The public may not know that I have been shadowed throughout my stay in India. That has not only not worried me, but I have even taken friendly services from these gentlemen: many have apologised for having to shadow me. As a rule what I have spoken in their presence has already been published to the world. The result is that now I do not even notice the presence of these men and I do not know that the Government is much the wiser for having watched my movements through its secret agency. My opinion is that these agents accompany me as a matter of form or routine. They certainly never bother me. I venture to make a present of my experience to every young man in Bengal and for that matter in India. No one need think that my public position, and not my openness, saves me from offensive attention. It is the simplest thing to see that moment you cease to dread the presence of the spy and therefore refuse to treat him as such, that moment his presence ceases to offend you. Soon the Government will feel ashamed to have its secret service department or, if it does not, the secret police will be sick of an occupation which serves no use.

Non-co-operation is essentially a cleansing process. It deals with causes rather than symptoms. The detective department is a symptom of the secrecy which is the cause. Removal of secrecy brings about the full disappearance of the secret service without further effort.

The Press Act is a symptom of the disease of cowardice. If we would boldly declare our intentions, the Press Act will die of inanition. The beginners will have to suffer for their so-called daring. I hear that the *Servant* of Calcutta has been served with a warning for its tenacity to take over an article from *Young India* condensing Mr. Rajgopalachari's admirable instructions to voters. I notice too that the most telling passages of my speech in Calcutta have been omitted by the Press, evidently for fear of the censor. I would far rather see a complete stoppage of a newspaper, if the editor cannot without fear of the consequence freely express his sentiments or publish those which he approves.

Non-co-operation, while it gladly avails itself of the assistance that may be rendered by the Press, is,—has to be—by its very nature independent of the Press. There can be no doubt that every thought we print is being printed on sufferance. As soon as its circulation takes effect, the Government, for the sake of its existence, will try to prohibit it. We may not expect this or any government to commit suicide. It must either reform or repress.

In the ordinary course, repression must precede reform under a despotic government such as ours. The stoppage of the circulation of potent ideas that may destroy the Government or compel repentance, will be the least among the weapons in its repressive armoury. We must, therefore, devise methods of circulating our ideas unless and until the whole Press becomes fearless, defies consequences and publishes ideas, even when it is in disagreement with them, just for the purpose of securing its freedom. An editor with an original idea or an effective prescription for India's ills can easily write them out, a hundred hands can copy them, many more can read them out to thousands of listeners. I do hope, therefore, that Non-co-operation editors, at any rate, will not refrain from expressing their thoughts for fear of the Press Act. They should regard it as sinful to keep their thoughts secret—a waste of energy to conduct a newspaper that cramps their thoughts. It is negation of one's calling for an editor to have to suppress his best thoughts.

[B]

15*th June*, 1921

THAT APOLOGY

The Ali Brothers' apology* still continues to tax people's minds. I continue to receive letters expostulating with me for having gone to the Viceroy at all. Some consider that I have bungled the whole affair, others blame the Brothers for having for once weakened, and that in deference to me. I know, that in a short while, the storm will blow over. For, in spite of all I have heard and read, I feel that I did the right thing in responding to the Viceroy's wish to know my views. It would have been wrong on my part to have waited for a formal written invitation from His Excellency. I feel, too, that I gave the best advice possible in the interests of Islam and India, when I asked the Brothers to make the statement issued by them. The Ali Brothe have showed humility and courage of a high order in making the statement. They have shown that they are capable of sacrificing their pride and their all for the sake of their faith and country. They have served the cause by

*The Ali Brothers, at the instance of Mahatma Gandhi, issued a statement repudiating any intention to incite people to violence in the speeches. *See infra* "Agreed Statement."

making the statements, as they would have injured it by declining to make it.

In spite of all that conviction in me, I am not surprised at the remonstrances I am receiving. They but show that the methods now being pursued are new, that the country will not surrender a tittle of its just demands, and for their satisfaction, it wishes to rely purely upon its own strength.

I give below the relevant parts of the strongest argument in condemnation of my advice and its acceptance by the Brothers. The letter, moreover, is written by one of the greatest among the Non-co-operators. It is not written for publication at all. But I know the writer will not mind my sharing it with the reader. For I have no doubt that he represents the sentiments of several thoughtful Non-co-operators. It is my humble duty to discuss the issues arising from the incident, and the implications of Non-co-operation. It is only by patient reasoning, that I hope to be able to demonstrate the truth, the beauty and the reasonableness of Non-co-operation. Here then are the extracts :

"The statement of the Brothers, taken by itself and read without reference to what has preceded and followed it, is a manly enough document. If in the heat of the moment they have said things which, they now find, may reasonably be taken to have a tendency to incite to violence, they have, in publishing their regret, taken the only honourable course open to public men of their position. I should also have been prepared to justify the undertaking they have given for the future, had that undertaking been addressed to those of their co-workers, who unlike themselves, do not believe in the cult of violence in any circumstances whatever. But the general words, public assurance and promise to all who may require it, cannot in the circumstances leave any one in doubt as to the particular party who did require such 'assurance and promise', and at whose bidding it was given. The Viceroy's speech has now made it perfectly clear and we have the indisputable fact that the leader of the Non-co-operation movement has been treating with the Government, and has secured the suspension of the prosecution of the Brothers, by inducing them to give a public apology and an undertaking.

"In this view of the case,—and I fail to see what other view is possible—very serious questions affecting the whole movement arise for consideration. Indeed, it seems to me that the whole principle of Non-co-operation has been given away.

"I am not one of those who fight shy of the very name of Government, nor of those who look upon an eventual settlement with the Government as the only means of obtaining redress of our wrongs and establishing Swaraj. I believe in what you have constantly taught, viz., that the achievement of Swaraj rests entirely and solely with us. At the same time, I do not, nor so far as I am aware, do you exclude the possibility of a settlement with the Government under proper conditions. Such settlement, however, can only relate to principles, and can have nothing to do with the convenience or safety of individuals. In a body of co-workers, you cannot make distinctions between man and man, and the humblest of them is entitled to the same protection at the hands of the leaders as the most prominent. Scores, if not hundreds, of our men have willingly gone to gaol for using language far less strong than that indulged in by the Brothers. Some at least of these could easily have been saved by giving a similar apology and undertaking, and yet it never occured to any one to advise them to do so. On the contrary, their action was applauded by the leaders and the whole of the Non-co-operationist press. The case, which more forcibly than any other comes to my mind at the moment. is that of Hamid Ahmad, who has recently been sentenced at Allahabad to transportation for life and forfeiture of property. Is there any reason why this man should not be saved? I find Maulana Mahomed Ali pays him a high tribute in his Bombay speech of the 30th May. What consolation this tribute will bring to Hamid Ahmad from a man, similarly situated, who has saved himself by an apology and an undertaking, I cannot say. Then there are so many others rotting in gaol who have committed no offence, and a great many more already picked out for the same fate. Is it enough for us to send them our good wishes from the safe positions we ourselves enjoy?

"The Viceroy in his speech has made it clear, that the only definite result of the several interviews you had with him, is the apology and the undertaking from the Brothers. You have also made it quite clear in your subsequent speeches, that our campaign is to go on unabated. It seems that no point involving any principle has been settled, except what needed no negotiating on either side, viz., that there is to be no incitement to violence. I do not say that in this state of things there should have been no treating with the Government though much can be said in support of the view. When it was found that the game had to be played out, it would have been quite legitimate for two such honourable adversaries as yourself and Lord Reading to agree to the rules of the game, so as to avoid foul play on either. These rules would, of course, apply to all who took part in the game, and not to certain favoured individuals only. The most essential thing was to agree upon the weapons to be used. While certain local Governments profess to meet propaganda by propaganda, they are really using repression of the worst type. Many other similar points would, in my opinion, be proper subjects of discussion, even when no agreement could be arrived at on the main issue.

"I hope you will not misunderstand me. I yield to none in my admiration of the sacrifices made by the Brothers, and consider it a high privilege to have their personal friendship. What has been preying upon my mind for some time past is, that we, who are directly responsible for many of our workers going to goal and suffering other hardships, are ourselves practically immune. For example, the Government could not possibly have devised any form of punishment which would cause some of us more pain and mental suffering, than sending innocent boys to goal for distributing leaflets, while the author remained free. I think the time has come, when the leaders should welcome the opportunity to suffer, and stoutly decline all offers of escape. It is in this view of the case that I have taken exception to the action of the Ali Brothers. Personally I love them."

The letter breathes nobility and courage. And those very qualities have led to a misapprehension of the situation. The unfortunate utterance of the Viceroy is responsible for the misunderstanding.

The apology of the Brothers is not made to the Government. It is addressed and tendered to friends, who drew their attention to their speeches. It was certainly not given 'at the bidding of the Viceroy.' I betray no confidence, when I say that it was not even suggested by him. As soon as I saw the speeches, I stated, in order to prove *bona fides* of the Brothers and the entirely non-violent character of the Movement, that I would invite them to make a statement. There was no question of bargaining for their freedom. Having had my attention drawn to their speeches, I could not possibly allow them to go to gaol (if I could prevent it) *on the ground of proved incitement to violence.* I have given the same advice to all the accused, and told them that if their speeches were violent, they should certainly express regret. A non-co-operator could not do otherwise. Had the Brothers been charged before a Court of Law, I would have advised them to apologise to the Court for some of the passages in their speeches, which, in my opinion, were capable of being interpreted to mean incitement to violence. It is not enough for a non-co-operator not to mean violence; it is necessary that this speech must not be capable of a contrary interpretation by reasonable men. We must be above suspicion. The success of the Movement depends upon its retaining its absolute purity. I therefore suggest to the writer and to those who may think like him, that the whole principle of Non-co-operation has not only not been 'given away' as the writer contends, but its non-violent character has been completely vindicated by the Brothers' apology, and the case therefore greatly strengthened.

What, however, is galling to the writer, is that whilst the Brothers have remained free, the lesser lights are in prison for having spoken less strongly than they.

That very fact shows the real character of Non-co-operation. A Non-co-operator may not bargain for personal safety. It was open to me to bargain for the liberty of the others. *Then* I would have given away the whole case for Non-co-operation. I did not bargain even for the Brothers' liberty. I stated in the clearest terms, that no matter what the Government did, it would be my duty on meeting the Brothers to advise them to make the statement to save their honour.

We must 'play the game,' whether the Government reciprocate or not. Indeed, I for one do not *expect* the Government to play the game. It was when I came to the conclusion that there was no honour about the Government that I non-co-operated. Lord Reading may wish, does wish to do right and justice. But he will not be permitted to. If the Government were honourable, they would have set free all the prisoners, as soon as they decided not to prosecute the Ali Brothers. If the Government were honourable, they would not have caught youths and put them in prison, whilst they left Pandit Motilal Nehru, the arch-offender, free. If the Government were honourable, they would not countenance bogus Leagues of Peace.* If the Government were honourable, they would have long ago repented for their heinous deeds, even as we have for every crime committed by our people in Amritsar, Kasur, Viramgam, Ahmedabad, and recently in Malegaon. I entertain no false hopes or misgivings about the Government. If the Government were to-morrow to arrest the Ali Brothers, I would still justify the apology. They have acted in the square, and we must all do likewise. Indeed, inasmuch as the Government are still arresting people for disaffection, they are arresting the Ali Brothers.

The writer is, again, not taking a correct view of Non-co-operation in thinking that Non-co-operators, who are in gaol, are less fortunate than we who are outside. For me, solitary confinement in a prison cell,

* *Amansabhas* or Leagues of Peace were established in the province under official pressure and influence to combat Non-co-operation, especially in the U. P.

without any breach on my part of the code of Non-co-operation, or private or public morals, will be freedom. For me, the whole of India is a prison, even as the master's house is to his slave. A slave, to be free, must continuously rise against his slavery, and be locked up in his master's cell for his rebellion. The cell-door is the door to freedom. I feel no pity for those who are suffering hardships in the goals of the Government. Innocence under an evil Government must ever rejoice on the scaffold. It was the easiest thing for the Brothers to have rejected my advice, and embraced the opportunity of joining their comrades in the gaols. I may inform the reader that when during the last stage of the South African struggle I was arrested, my wife and all friends heaved a sigh of relief. It was in the prisons of South Africa that I had leisure and peace from strife and struggle.

It is perhaps now clear why the Non-co-operation prisoners may not make any statement to *gain their freedom.*

THE AGREED STATEMENT

The following appeared in "Young India" of 4th August 1921:

His Excellency's attention has been directed, and notably by Mr. Gandhi, to various statements that have appeared, and to inferences that have been drawn in the public Press, relating to the conversations between His Excellency and Mr. Gandhi, concerning Mr. Shaukat Ali and Mr. Mahomed Ali, which in some respects do not correctly represent the purport of those communications.

The interviews between the Viceroy and Mr. Gandhi resulted from a conversation between the Viceroy and Pandit Malaviya, relating to the conditions generally prevailing in India. His Excellency informed Pandit Malaviya of the Government's decision to commence criminal proceedings against Mr. Shaukat Ali for having made speeches inciting to violence and the discussion turned upon the disturbances that might possibly ensue. Pandit Malaviya expressed the opinion that it would be of advantage for His Excellency to meet Mr. Gandhi. His Excellency replied that he would be glad to meet Mr. Gandhi and hear his views, if he applied for an interview. On the next day, Mr. Andrews saw His Excellency and suggested that he should see Mr. Gandhi. It should be observed that various important matters were discussed during these conversations and that the proposed interview between His Excellency and Mr. Gandhi was intended to have reference to the situation generally. His Excellency is, however, aware that Pandit Malaviya, in inviting Mr. Gandhi to Simla, did not refer to the contemplated proceedings against Mr. Shaukat Ali and Mr. Mahomed Ali.

In due course Mr. Gandhi came to Simla, at the request of Pandit Malaviya and Mr. Andrews, and asked for an interview, with His Excellency, which was immediately arranged. At the first interview, no mention was made of the proposed prosecutions. The conversation related to the causes of discontent in India. Upon the next occasion His Excellency stated that according to the Government reports, responsible Non-co-operators had made speeches inciting to violence, contrary to the doctrine advocated by Mr. Gandhi. Mr. Gandhi repudiated incitement to violence on the part of any of the responsible Non-co-operators and said that, if he was satisfied that any of them had incited to violence, he would publicly repudiate them and their teachings, unless they withdrew their statements that amounted to incitement to violence. His Excellency mentioned the names of the Ali brothers and promised to show Mr. Gandhi passage in their speeches which, in his opinion, were calculated to incite to violence, and when the passages were actually read to Mr. Gandhi he admitted that they were capable of bearing the interpretation His Excellency put upon them. He, however, asserted that he was convinced that it was not intended by Mr. Shaukat Ali and Mr. Mahomed Ali to incite the audience to violence. Mr. Gandhi added that he would see them as soon as he left Simla and advise them to express publicly their regret for the unintentional incitement, contained in the passages. His Excellency, thereupon, asked whether, in view of the importance of the document, Mr. Gandhi would show him the draft of the statement he intended to advise Mr. Shaukat Ali and Mr. Mahomed Ali to publish.

It was at this stage the Viceroy said that it was proposed to institute criminal proceedings against Mr. Shaukat Ali and Mr.

Mahomed Ali in respect of these passages and that, if Mr. Gandhi showed him the statement and it satisfied him from the standpoint of his Government, he would use his influence to prevent the institution of prosecution, for, the Viceroy said, the object of the Government would be attained if the making of speeches of a violent character was in future prevented. Mr. Gandhi readily agreed to show the statement. The draft statement was duly shown by Mr. Gandhi to His Excellency, who pointed out that the introduction of certain paragraphs gave the statement the appearance of a manifesto, including that of the religious creed of Mr. Shaukat Ali and Mr. Mahomed Ali. The Viceroy observed further that the statement was incomplete so far as it did not contain a promise to refrain in the future from speeches inciting to violence and added that after publication of the statement Mr. Shaukat Ali and Mr. Mahomed Ali could give any explanation by means of speeches, provided they did not infringe the law. Mr. Gandhi agreed to delete the paragraphs in question and to add a passage to cover promises of future conduct. His Excellency then informed Mr. Gandhi that if Mr. Shaukat Ali and Mahomed Ali signed the statement as then altered by Mr. Gandhi, with the addition of the promise as to the future conduct, steps would be taken to suspend the institution of proceedings and that no prosecution would take place so long as the promises given in the published statement were observed. The Government remained free to take up prosecutions for the past speeches. The Viceroy added that, in the event of the publication of the statement by Mr. Shaukat Ali and Mr. Mahomed Ali and of the Government refraining in consequence from the prosecutions, it would be necessary to issue a *communique* explaining the attitude of the Government. There was, however, no desire to bargain. Mr. Gandhi even said that, whether the prosecutions took place or not, he would be bound, after having shown the extracts to his friends for their own honour and that of the cause, to advise them to express publicly their regret.

During the whole discussion, His Excellency and Mr. Gandhi were actuated by the desire to prevent any untoward events that might result from the prosecutions, as also to prevent speeches inciting to violence. The Viceroy informed Mr. Gandhi that he might not be able to prevent the commencement of proceedings, if the statement was not published with the least possible delay. There was already much discussion of the speeches not only in India but also in the United Kingdom. Mr. Gandhi agreed that the statement should be published without delay. Mr. Gandhi then left Simla and some days afterwards telegraphed to His Excellency that Mr. Shaukat Ali and Mr. Mahomed Ali had signed the statement with immaterial alteration and sent it to the Press for publication. The alteration was as follows: For the passage in Mr. Gandhi's draft statement, "We desire to state that we never intended to incite to violence, but we recognise that certain passages in our speeches are capable of bearing the interpretation put upon them," Mr. Shaukat Ali and Mr. Mahomed Ali put, "We desire to state that we never intended to incite to violence, and we never imagined that any passages in our speeches were capable of bearing the interpretation put upon them, but we recognise the force of our friends' argument and interpretation."

After the publication of the statement, an official *communique* was issued by the Government. The terms of the *communique* were not actually settled until just before its issue and Mr. Gandhi never saw it although the substance of it, as already indicated, had been communicated to him. The main part of the interviews between His Excellency and Mr. Gandhi consisted of conversations which ranged over the various causes of discontent in India, including the Punjab disturbances, the Khilafat agitation, the Treaty of Sevres and the general condition of the people. Mr. Gandhi did not submit any scheme of Swaraj to His Excellency, nor was a scheme of Swaraj discussed at the interviews.

Commenting on the above "Agreed statement," Mahatma Gandhi wrote:

His Excellency, the Viceroy, has now issued a statement agreed between him and me regarding the interviews, I had the honour of having with him. The statement sets forth all the details that the public need know. I do not propose to discuss it. In my opinion it makes it clear that the apology, as I have called the statement of regrets, initiated with me, that it was conceived before I ever knew of the impending prosecution for the speeches that were shown to me and that it was neither suggested nor made for fear of the prosecution of the Brothers, certainly not to avoid imprisonment.* It is my

* The Ali Brothers were arrested and prosecuted in the second week of September, 1921. The following appeared in *Young India* of 29th September, *inter alia* in an appeal to the Muslims:

firm belief that the Brothers have rendered a great service to the cause by making the statement. I do not regret having given them the advice. I wish also to

---

Whilst the arrest of Maulanas Shaukat Ali and Mahomed Ali has touched every Indian heart, I know what it has meant to you. The brave brothers are staunch lovers of their country, but they are Mussalmans first and everything else afterwards. It must be so with every religiously-minded man. The brothers have for years past represented all that is best and noblest in Islam. No two Mussalmans have done more than they to raise the status of Islam in India. They have promoted the cause of the Khilafat as no two other Mussalmans of India have. For they have been true, and they dared to tell what they felt. even in their internment in Chindwara. Their long internment did not demoralise or weaken them. They came out just as brave as they went in.

And since their release from internment, they have shown themselves true nationalists, and you have taken pride in their being so.

The Brothers have by their simplicity, humility and inexhastible energy fired the imagination of the masses as no other Mussalman has.

All these qualities have endeared them to you. You regard them as your ideal men You are, therefore, sorry of their separation from you. Many besides you miss their genial presence. For me, they had become inseparable. I seem to be without arms. For anything connected with Mussalmans, Shaukat Ali was my guide and friend. He never once misled me. His judgment was sound and unerring in most cases. With the Brothers among us, I felt safe about Hindu-Muslim unity, the value of which they understood as few of us have.

But whilst we all miss them we must not give way to grief or dejection. We must learn, each one of us, to stand alone. God only is our infallible and eternal guide.

To be dejected is not only not to have known the Brothers, but it is, if I may venture to say so, not to know what religion is.

For do we not learn in all religions, that the spirit of the dear ones abides with us even when they physically leave us? Not only is the spirit of the Brothers with us, but they are serving better by their suffering, than if they were in our midst giving us some of their own courage, hope and energy. The secret of Non-violence and Non-cooperation lies in our realising that it is through suffering that we are to attain our goal. What is the renunciation of titles, councils, law

place on record my appreciation of the willingness with which Lord Reading approached my request for the publication of an agreed statement. In the lengthy

---

courts and schools but a measure (very slight indeed) of suffering? That preliminary renunciation is a prelude to the larger suffering—the hardships of a gaol life and even the final consummation on the gallows, if need be. The more we suffer and the more of us suffer, the nearer we are to our cherished goal.

The earlier and the more clearly we recognise that it is not big meetings and demonstrations that would give us victtory, but quiet suffering, the earlier and more certain will our victory be.

I have made your cause my own, because I believe it to be just. Khilafat, I have understood from your best men, is an ideal. You are not fighting to sustain any wrong or even misrule. You are backing the Turks, because they represent the gentlemen of Europe, and because the European and especially the English prejudice against them is due, not to the Turks being worse than others as men, but to their being Mussalmans and not assimilating the modern spirit of exploitation of weaker people and their lands. In fighting for the Turks, you are fighting to raise the dignity and the purity of your own faith.

You have naturally, therefore, chosen pure methods to attain your end. It cannot be denied, that both Mussalmans and Hindus have lost much in moral stamina. Both of us have become poor representatives of our respective faiths. Instead of each one of us becoming a true child ofGod, we expect others to live our religion and even to die for us. But we have now chosen a method that compels us to turn, each one of us, our face towards God. Non-co-operation presumes that our opponent with whom we non-co-operate resorts to methods which are as questionable as the purpose he seeks to fulfil by such methods. We shall therefore find favour in the sight of God only by choosing methods which are different in kind from those of our opponents. This is a big claim we have made for ourselves, and we can attain success with in the short time appointed by us, only if our methods are in reality radically different from those of the Government.

Hence the foundation of our movement rests on complete non-violence, whereas violence is the final refuge of the Government. And as no energy can be created without resistance, our non-resistance to Government violence must bring the latter to a standstill. But our

correspondence that ensued between us for setting the form and the language of the statement, I did not observe on His Excellency's part any inclination to

---

non-violence to be true must be in word, thought and deed. It makes no difference that with you non-violence is an expedient. Whilst it lasts, you cannot consistently with your pledge harbour designs of violence. On the contrary we must have implicit faith in our programme of non-violence, which presupposes perfect accord between thought, word and deed. I would like every Mussalman to realise, while the occasion for anger is the greatest, that by non-violence alone can we gain complete victory even during this year.

Nor is non-violence a visionary programme. Just imagine what the united resolve of seven crores of Mussalmans (not to count the Hindus) must mean. Should we not have succeeded already, if all the titled men had given up their titles, all the lawyers had suspended their practice and all the students had left their schools and all had boycotted councils? But we must recognise, that with many of us the flesh has proved too weak. Seven crores are called Mussalmans and twenty two crores are called Hindus, but only a few are true Mussalmans or true Hindus. Therefore, if we have not gained our objective, the cause lies within us. And if ours is, as we claim it is, a religious struggle, we dare not become impatient save with yourselves, not even with another.

The brothers, I am satisfied, are as innocent as I claim I am, of incitement to violence. Theirs, therefore, is a spotless offering. They have done all in their power for Islam and their country. Now, if the Khilafat and the Punjab wrongs are not redressed and Swaraj is not established during this year, the fault will be yours and mine.

We must remain non-violent, but we must not be passive. We must repeat the formula of the Brothers regarding the duty of soldiers and invite imprisonment. We need not think that the struggle cannot go on without even the best of us. If it cannot we are neither fit for Swaraj nor for redressing the Khilafat or the Punjab wrong. We must declare from a thousand platforms that it is sinful for any Mussalman or Hindu to serve the existing Government, whether as soldier or in any other capacity whatsoever.

Above all, we must concentrate on complete boycott of foreign cloth, whether British, Japanese, American, French or any other, and begin, if we have not already done so, to introduce spinning wheels

avoid mention of any relevant detail. On my part, I had informed him that I had no intention to hide anything whatsoever. The public, therefore, have a full statement from both sides.

The suffering must not be accompanied by any resentment against Government. On Pandit Motilal Nehru being arrested, Mr. Gandhi wrote *inter alia* in "Young India" of 8th December, under the heading, "Love, not Hate":

In the moment of our trial and our triumph let me declare my faith. I believe in loving my enemies. I believe in non-violence as the only remedy open to the Hindus, Mussalmans, Sikhs, Parsis, Christians and Jews of India. I believe in the power of suffering to melt the stoniest heart. The brunt of the battle must fall on the first three. The last named three are afraid of the combination of the first three. We must by our honest conduct demonstrate to them that they are our kinsmen. We must by our conduct demonstrate to every Englishman that he is as safe in the remotest corner of India, as he professes to feel behind the machine gun.

---

and handlooms in our homes and manufacture all the cloth we need. This will be at once a test of our belief in non-violence for our country's freedom and for saving the Khilafat. It will be a test also of Hindu-Muslim unity, and it will be a universal test of our faith in our own programme. I repeat my conviction that we can achieve our full purpose within one month of a complete boycott of foreign cloth. For we are then in a position, having confidence in our ability to control forces of violence, to offer Civil Disobedience, if it is at all found necessary.

I can, therefore, find no balm for the deep wounds inflicted upon you by the Government other than non-violence, translated into action by boycott of foreign cloth and manufacture of cloth in our own homes.

Islam, Hiduism, Sikhism, Christianity, Zoroastrianism and Judasim—in fact, religion is on its trail. Either we believe in God and His righteousness, or we do not. My association with the noblest of Mussalmans has taught me to see that Islam has spread not by the power of the sword, by the prayerful love of an unbroken line of its saints and fakirs. Warrant there is in Islam for drawing the sword; but the conditions laid down are so strict that they are not capable of being fulfilled by everybody. Where is the unerring general to order Jehad? Where is the suffering, the love and the purification that must precede the very idea of drawing the sword? Hindus are at least as much bound by similar restrictions as the Mussalmans of India. The Sikhs have their recent proud history to warm them against the use of force. We are too imperfect, too impure and too selfish, as yet, to resort to an armed conflict in the cause of God as Shaukat Ali would say. Will a purified India ever need to draw the sword? And it was the definite process of purification we commenced last year at Calcutta.*

Whilst we must not avoid arrest, we must not provoke it by giving unnecessary offence.

We must hold the Congress at any cost in spite of the arrest of every one of the leaders, unless the Government dissolve it by force. And if we are neither cowed down nor provoked to violence but are able to continue national work, we have certainly attained Swaraj. For no power on earth can stop the onward march of a peaceful, determined and godly people.

* Non-co-operation was first accepted by the Congress at Calcutta in September, 1920.

[C]

CONDUCT IN PRISON

Why Suffer?—Imprisonments are not courted with the object of embarrassing the Government, though as a matter of fact they do. They are courted for the sake of discipline and suffering. They are courted because we consider it to be wrong to be free under a government we hold to be wholly bad. No stone should be left unturned by us to make the Government realise that we are in no way amenable to its control. And no Government has yet tolerated such upon defiance, however respectful it may be. It might safely therefore be said that, if we are yet outside the prison walls, the cause lies as much with us as with the Government. We are moving cautiously in our corporate capacity. We are still voluntarily obeying many of its laws. There was, for instance, nothing to prevent me from disregarding the Madras Government's order and courting arrest, but I avoided it. There is nothing to prevent me save my prudence or weakness from going without permission into the barracks and being arrested for trespass. I certainly believe the barracks to be the nation's property and not that of a Government which I no longer recognise as representative of the people. Thus there is an apparent inconsistency between the statement on the one hand that it is painful to remain outside the prison walls under a bad Government and this deliberate avoidance, on the other hand, of arrest upon grounds which are not strictly moral, but largely expedient. We thus avoid imprisonment, because first we think that the nation is not ready for complete civil revolt, secondly we think that the atmosphere of voluntary obedience and non-violence has not been firmly established, and thirdly we have not done any constructive, corporate work to inspire self-confidence. We, therefore, refrain from offering Civil Disobedience amounting to peaceful rebellion, but court imprisonment merely in the ordinary pursuit of programme and in defence of complete freedom of opinion and action, short of revolt.

Thus it is clear that our remaining outside the gaols of a bad Government has to be justified upon very exceptional grounds, and that our Swaraj is attained when we are in gaol or when we have bent the Government to our will. Whether, therefore, the Government feel embarrassed or happy over our incarceration, the only safe and honourable place for us is the prison. And if this position be accepted, it follows that when imprisonment comes to us in the ordinary discharge of our duty, we must feel happy because we feel stronger, because we pay the price of due performance of duty. And if exhibition of real strength is the best propaganda, we must believe that every imprisonment strengthens the people and thus brings Swaraj nearer.—*3rd November*, 1921.

15th December, 1921

WORK IN GAOLS

An esteemed friend asks me whether now that the Government have provided an opportunity for hundreds to find themselves imprisoned and as thousands are responding, will it not be better for the prisoners to refuse to do any work * in the gaols at all? I am

*Mahatma Gandhi wrote in *Young India* of 17th November, 1921:
As Non-co-operators we *must* work in the gaols, for we do not non-co-operate with gaols as such. We submit to the courts' discipline

afraid that the suggestion comes from a misapprehension of the moral position, We are not out to abolish gaols as an institution. Even under Swaraj, we would have our gaols. Pure Civil Disobedience, therefore, must not be carried beyond the point of breaking the unmoral laws of the country. Breach of the laws to be civil assumes the strictest and willing obedience to the gaol discipline, because disobedience of a particular rule assumes a willing acceptance of the sanction provided for its breach. And immediately a person quarrels both with the rule and the sanction for its breach, he ceases to be civil and lends himself to the precipitation of chaos and anarchy. A civil resister is, if one may be permitted such a claim for him, a philanthropist and a friend of the state. An anarchist is an enemy of the state and is, therefore, misanthrope. I have permitted myself to use the language of war, because the so-called constitutional method has become so utterly ineffective. But I hold the opinion firmly that Civil Disobedience is the purest type of constitutional agitation. Of course, it becomes degrading and despicable, if its civil, *i.e.*, non-violent character is a mere camouflage. If the honesty of non-violence be admitted, there is no warrant for condemnation even of the fiercest disobedience, because of the likelihood of its leading to violence. No big or

---

when we are dragged to the courts. Civil Disobedience by its very nature requires us to yield complete obedience to gaol regulations, for as civil resisters *invite* imprisonment and, therefore, are bound to suffer the rigours of its discipline. But we can civilly resist such regulations as are not only irksome, or hard to bear but are humiliating or specially designed to degrade Non-co-operators. Our self-respect demands willing obedience to gaol discipline. The same self-respect may require resistence to misbehaviour, euphemistically called discipline. For instance, we would refuse to draw lines with our noses, whether within or without gaols.

swift movement can be carried on without bold risks, and life will not be worth living, if it is not attended with large risks. Does not the history of the world show that there would have been no romance in life, if there had been no risks? It is the clearest proof of a degenerate atmosphere that one finds respectable people, leaders of society, raising their hands in horror and indignation at the slighest approach of danger or upon an outbreak of any violent commotion. We do want to drive out the beast in man, but we do not want on that account to emasculate him. And in the process of finding his own status, the beast in him is bound, now and again, to put up his ugly appearance. As I have often stated in these pages, what strikes me down is not the sight of blood under every conceivable circumstance. It is blood spilt by the Non-co-operator or his supporters in breach of his declared pledge, which paralyses me as I know it ought to paralyse every honest Non-co-operator.

Therefore, to revert to the original argument, as civil resisters, we are bound to guard against universal indiscipline. Gaol discipline must be submitted to, until gaol government itself becomes or is felt to be corrupt and immoral. But deprivation of comfort, imposition of restriction and such other inconveniences do not make gaol government corrupt. It becomes that, when prisoners are humiliated or treated with inhumanity as when they are kept in filthy dens or are given food unfit for human consumption. Indeed, I hope that the conduct of Non-co-operators in the gaol will be strictly correct, dignified and yet submissive. We must not regard gaolers and warders as our enemies, but as fellow human beings, not utterly devoid of the human touch. Our gentlemanly behaviour is bound to disarm all suspicion or bitterness. I know that this path of discipline, on the one hand, and fierce defiance, on the other, is a very difficult path, but there is no royal road to Swaraj. The country has deliberately chosen the narrow and the straight path. Like a straight line, it is the shortest distance. But even as you require a steady and experienced hand to draw a straight line, so are steadiness of discipline and firmness of purpose absolutely necessary, if we are to walk along the chosen path with an unerring step.

I am painfully conscious of the fact that it is not going to be a bed of roses for any of the civil resisters. And my head reels and the heart throbs, when I recall the lives of Motilal Nehru and C. R. Das in their palatial rooms, surrounded by numerous willing attendants and by every comfort and convenience that money can buy, and when I think of what is in store for them inside the cold unattractive prison walls where they will have to listen to the clanking of the prisoner's chains in the place of the sweet music of their drawing rooms. But I steel my heart with the thought that it is the sacrifice of just such heroes that will usher in Swaraj. The noblest of South Africans, Canadians, Englishmen, Frenchmen, Germans have had to undergo much greater sacrifices than we have mapped out for ourselves.

29th December, 1921

A MODEL PRISONER

"Should Non-co-operators shout Bande Mataram inside jails against jail discipline which may excite ordinary prisoners to violence, should Non-co-operators go on hunger strike for the improvement of food or other conveniences, should they strike work inside jails on *hartal* days and other days? Are Non-co-operators entitled to break rules of jail discipline unless they affect their conscience?" Such is the text of a telegram I received from a Non-co-operator friend in Calcutta. From another part of India when a friend, again a Non-co-operator, heard of the indiscipline of Non-co-operator prisoners, he asked me to write on the necessity of observing jail discipline. As against this, I know prisoners who are scrupulously observing in a becoming spirit all the discipline imposed upon them.

It is necessary, when thousands are going to jail, to understand exactly the position a Non-co-operator prisoner can take up consistenly with his pledge of non-violence. Non-co-operation, when its limitations are not recognised, becomes a licence instead of being a duty and therefore becomes a crime. The dividing line between right and wrong is often so thin as to become indistinguishable. But it is line that is breakable and unmistakable.

What is then the difference between those who find themselves in jails for being in the right and those who are there for being in the wrong? Both wear often the same dress, eat the same food and are subject outwardly to the same discipline. But whilst the latter submit to discipline most unwillingly and would commit a breach of it secretly, and even openly if they could, the former will willingly and to the best of their ability conform to the jail discipline and prove worthier and more serviceable to their cause than when they are outside. We have observed that the most distinguished among the prisoners are of greater service inside the jails than outside. The co-efficient of service is raised to the extent of the strictness with which jail discipline is observed.

Let it be remembered that we are not seeking to destroy jails as such. I fear that we shall have to maintain jails even under Swaraj. It will go hard with us, if we let the real criminals understand that they will be set free or be very much better treated when Swaraj is established. Even in reformatories by which I would like to replace every jail under Swaraj, discipline will be exacted. Therefore we really retard the advent of Swaraj, if we encourage indiscipline. Indeed the swift programme of Swaraj has been conceived on the supposition that we being a cultured people are capable of evolving right discipline within a short time.

Indeed whilst on the one hand Civil Disobedience authorises disobedience of unjust laws or unmoral laws of a state which one seeks to overthrow, it requires meek and willing submission to the penalty of disobedience and therefore cheerful acceptance of the jail discipline and its attendant hardships.

It is now therefore clear that a civil resister's resistance ceases and his obedience is resumed as soon as he is under confinement. In confinement he claims no privileges because of the civility of his disobedience. Inside the jail by his exemplary conduct he reforms even the criminals surrounding him, he softens the hearts of jailors and others in authority. Such meek behaviour springing from strength and knowledge ultimately dissolves the tyranny of the tyrant. It is for this reason that I claim that voluntary suffering is the quickest and the best remedy for the removal of abuses and injustices.

It is now manifest that shouts of Bande Mataram or any other in breach of jail discipline are unlawful for a Non-co-operator to indulge in. It is equally unlawful for him to commit a stealthy breach of jail regulations.

Non-co-operator will do nothing to demoralise his

fellow prisoners. The only occasion when he can openly disobey jail regulations or hunger-strike is when an attempt is made to humiliate him or when the warders themselves break, as they often do, the rules for the comfort of prisoners or when food that is unfit for human consumption is issued as it often is.* A case for Civil Disobedience also arises when there is interference with any obligatory religious practice.

* *The Ali Brothers.*—I reproduce the following telegram received from Karachi by post, because it would not be sent by the authorities :

"Moulana Mohammad Ali reduced 25 lbs. in jail. Light at night not permitted to him though recommended by Magistrate and Medical Officer. Superintendent opposed to allowing this.

"Medical Officer recommended groundnuts or extract of cheese by way of food for Moulana Mohammad Ali on account of diabetes. Superintendent not disposed but after all provided groundnuts worth one anna per day and on Moulana's insistence raised it to two annas. This serves as his morning meal.

"Deviating from usual treatment Moulana Shaukat Ali, Doctor Kitchlew, Moulvi Nisar Ahmad, Pir Gulam Majdid all convicted at Karachi trial for conspiring to seduce Indian troops from their allegiance were asked on Saturday the 28th, to submit to search of their person, a practice commonly followed in case of convicts. This consists in making the prisoners absolutely naked with the exception of a *langoti* made loose. The prisoners in this condition are asked to raise hands and open their mouths as though to show if there was anything hidden anywhere. This humiliation Moulana Shaukat Ali and his companions were saved so far. On Saturday 28th, on being asked to submit to this they refused. On Monday the 30th, their person was forcibly searched and as punishment for refusing voluntarily to submit to this indignity and humiliation the forenamed leaders have been confined to solitary cells for one month. In solitary cells prisoners are allowed insufficient bedding and that at night alone. Moulana Shaukat Ali and his companions thus forced to say their prayers on uncleaned ground contrary to their religious susceptibilities. Moulvi Nisar Ahmad was searched while offering his prayers.

"Moulana Mohammad Ali protests and demands like treatment.

"The leaders in jail ready to obey all Jail Rules except those that

[D]

ON PICKETING

The Indian Social Reformer contests the utility of picketing in its own vigorous style. Without entering upon any examination of its argument, I would perhaps

---

offend against their Religion or against their sense of honour and dignity as Indians or human beings.

"The jail authorities were up to the last moment asked by the leaders to refer the matter to Government but they refused to wait."

It is evident that instructions have gone forth that the policy of wise discretion is to give place to the policy of cast iron rigidity of enforcement of prison rules. Imagine Maulana Shaukat Ali or any of the high-spirited prisoners standing almost naked before the Jailor and in the presence of one another and submitting to what to them must be a most humiliating examination. I can understand the necessity and utility of such examination of confirmed criminals for whom alone the ordinary prison regulations are framed, but it is nothing short of lunacy to enforce obedience to such regulations on the part of men who apart from their political agitation have been regarded as orderly citizens and in some cases even as distinguished public men. To enforce some of the present regulations in respect of such prisoners is hopelessly to ignore the reality and to court trouble. Ordinary discipline must be exacted from the best of men when they happen to be in prison, more so when they court imprisonment. Discomfort of jail life they must expect and cannot grumble at. Respect for the jail officials must be exacted from them if they will not give it voluntarily and gracefully. Our discipline must not take the form of humiliation. Discomfort must not be torture, and respect must not take the form of crawling on one's belly. And therefore, on pain of being put in irons in solitary confinement or of being shot, Non-co-operating prisoners must decline even in the name of discipline to stand naked before the jailor, must decline in the name of discomfort to wear stinking clothes or to eat food that is unclean or indigestible and must similarly decline even in the name of respect to open out their palms or to sit in a crouching position or to shout '*Sarkar Ek Hai*' or '*Sarkar Salam*' when a jail official is passing. And if the Government is now intent upon putting us through the fire in the jails and subject us to physical

take up less space if I simply state my view and experience. Picketing in its nature must be temporary, but it is like what a stimulant is in medicine. Drink is more

---

pains in order to bend us, we must respectfully decline to be humiliated and must fall back upon God to give us strength to withstand studied humiliation and to suffer physical tortures instead. Let the proud Brothers and their comrades purify the Karachi Jail.

But be the treatment what it may, the course before those who are put in prison is clear. We must not be irritated into taking a false or a hasty step. Our final salvation lies in the strictest adherence to our pledge. If we feel keenly, let us be still more non-violent, not less so; let us further concentrate on Civil Disobedience, let us lose no time in fulfilling the conditions necessary for Civil Disobedience. Let Hindus, Mussalmans and other races come still closer, let us rid ourselves of the remnants of foreign cloth still in our possession, let us bestir ourselves to manufacture more handspun *khadi*. Our progress depends upon calmly fulfilling the programme mapped out by ourselves, and not wasting a single minute in idle fretting and fuming. Let us not worry about the ill-treatment of those who are in jail. The Government have made no terms with us as to treatment. We have unconditionally surrendered our bodies to them even to be hacked to pieces without a quiver, if God will give us the strength. We must not lose temper on any account.

Moulana Shaukat Ali's suggestions.—In the course of a letter, dated 21st January, 1922, to his son, on the subject which was published in *Young India* of 22nd February, 1922, Moulana Shaukat Ali suggested the following instructions to prisoners:

(1) They must be courteous to all especially to their fellow prisoners and Indian warders who are weak and helpless and made to do dirty work. We must lift them up and give them real courage and teach them partiotism and discipline. Along with this, we must have full confidence in ourselves and in our capacity for suffering.

(3) We must ask for clean food, clothing and bedding. But this is the least important thing in my opinion. The more important things come later.

(3) We must do as much work as we can easily accomplish, without detriment to our health. If forced to do more than our strength or circumstances permit, we can readily retaliate by refusing to work, the

a disease than a vice. I know scores of men who would gladly leave off drink if they could. I know some who have asked that the temptation might be put away from

---

only weapon in our hands. It is a strong weapon and so as to be used carefully. This weapon can always bring the jail people to their senses, but it is not easy to wield it. We must cheerfully face the penalties and through suffering defeat them. Hunger-strike is another weapon; it is here weak and Muslims cannot use it. It only weakens our health while we must really get strong here, both physically and spiritually. *We must teach this Government both outside the jail and inside of it that it cannot coerce or force us to do things against our wishes.* At the same time we must not shirk work or show that we are not capable of bearing hardships. There are some very humiliating practices which we *must* refuse to perform:

(*a*) Every evening all cloths are taken off and only in a little flin we show that we have not concealed anything in our loins.

(*b*) Jail parade, where you are made to do things which kill self-respect and in the name of discipline, humiliates you.

(*c*) Paying the call of nature with many people round about you and a warder watching you and so forth.

(*d*) *Azan* must be openly said by each 5 times daily at prayer time. They objected to my calling *Azan* but I smiled and told the Superintendent that he should never expect such a thing from me and should not even mention them. He kept quiet. The result is that now nearly four times more people say their prayers than before, and *Azan* the beautiful is heard in four places daily. Of course we must see that no violence is used. Tell our great chief that non-violence is maintained by prisoners also. They love and respect us and I think will obey us cheerfully. The Superintendent thinks that if all political prisoners were like me his life would be happy, I never complain, never ask for anything, and I am always laughing and singing."

Mahatma Gandhi commented on the above as follows:

I do not think that I need add anything to the letter by way of supplementary instructions. Besides laying down the instructions, it serves another useful purpose. It sets at rest all doubts as to the Brothers' attitude. I know that they are not implacable. They are most reasonable but, thank God, they are also firm. They will yield not an inch out of *their* weakness. They will yield everything by

them. In spite of the temptation having been put away at their instance, I have known them to steal drink. I do not, therefore, think that it was wrong to have removed the temptation. Diseased persons have got to be helped against themselves.* If I have a son who is

*Mr. S. N. Ray of Benares wrote to *Young India* of 15th September, asking Mr. Gandhi to explain why, while he disapproved of sitting *Dhurna* he approved of picketting. He wrote with reference to Calcutta boys picketing the examination hall:

When the picketing party laid themselves before the gateway, they did so on the very argument that "diseased persons have got to be helped against themselves." As brothers who deemed themselves blessed in truly understanding your advice about modern education and in possessing boldness enough to leave their colleges, they thought it a duty incumbent upon them to dissuade their brothers from appearing at the examination. Lying flat on the ground is indisputably an oriental way of moral persuasion. It was nothing but humility preached in its real aspect. If I am truly inspired with the feeling that drinking is a dire vice and every one has to be saved from its clutches, shall I be deemed using physical force if I lie down in front of the drinking den and ask the intending drinker to trample over my body and get his drink? Here in this case I appeal to his heart. And by moral persuasion I understand appealing to the heart. By laying themselves in front of the Senate House, the Bengal pickets appealed to the heart of the examinees and certainly that was moral persuasion,

Mr. Gandhi replied as follows:

The writer assumes, without warrant, that I would countenance liquor-shop picketing of the type discribed in his letter. If the unseemly obstruction of the passage had been persisted in there would have been a revulsion of feeling in the country, such as would have thoroughly discredited Non-co-operation. Moreover it is a far-fetched analogy to compare the drink habit with education. In the matter of education, it is a conflict of ideals, and Non-co-operation is for this generation a new ideal. Whereas of drink the conflict is between

---

reason. Being God-fearing they are capable of entering into their opponents' real difficulties. Given perfect sincerity in the opponent and readiness to do right and acknowledge the wrong, no opponent need fear or distrust them. But to think of placating Musalmans without placating the Brothers is to attempt to ignore Islam in India.

addicted (say) to gambling, and a gambling company imposes itself on me to tempt my boy, I have either violently to knock the company down or to post watches at its offices, in order, if possible, to shame my son into not going there. It is true that there are other gambling companies some distance for my place. Still I take it, I would be held in the right in having posted a watch at the company's door. I must make it difficult for my son to gamble. If the *Reformer* accepts the doctrine of state prohibition, it must accept the corollary of picketing, so long as the state is a tyranny being perpetrated in the face of public opinion. What, for instance, should the public do, if the state were to build palaces in every street for women of ill fame, and issue to them licences to play their trade ? Will it not be its duty, unless it destroys these palaces inhabited by vice, to quarantine them and warn the public of the danger of falling an easy prey to the temptation forced on it ? I recognise the necessity of using only men and women of character as pickets and of guarding against violence being offered to those who insist on drinking in the face of public opinion. Picketing is a duty a citizen must discharge, when he is not helped by the state. What is a police patrol, if it is not picketing against thieves ? The police use the gun, when the thief betrays an incli-

---

abstinence and a recognised vice. A young lad considers it a virtue to go to a Government college, a drinker knows drinking to be an evil habit. The educated youth reads newspapers, knows all the argument for and against. Visitors to liquor-shops read nothing and not being in the habit of attending meetings, hear nothing. Picketing therefore, in the case of colleges and schools was not only superfluous, but in the manner it was carried out, constituted a sort of violence utterly unjustified in any event and for a Non-co-operator a breach of his pledge. I am glad, therefore, that the picketing stopped, if it did, as a result of my severe criticism.

nation to break into another's house. A picket uses the pressure of shame, *i.e.*, love, when he warns a weak brother against the dangers or the drink evil. The *Reformer* has attributed to picketing claims never put forth on its behalf.

22nd December, 1921

THE RIGHT OF PICKETING

The Government must have thought that Bombay having stopped picketing of liquor-shops, all other places would necessarily follow suit. But Poona has shown that it is a right that cannot be abandoned without good cause. As soon as orders were issued to prohibit picketing, "we decided to break the orders," says Mr. Kelkar, "and this morning notice has been sent to the District Magistrate that we shall even to-day proceed to break the order, at a place and time specified. Myself, my son and Messrs. Bhopatkar, Gokhale, Paranjpye and about 16 others will form the first batch. Succession will, I am sure, be provided for by those who are left behind. Let us see how far Poona gives an account of itself in this matter." The party went, they were arrested, their names taken, and they were let off. Fresh parties have since been regularly going with the same result. Of course, Maharashtra wil never lag behind in suffering. It possesses the hardes body of workers in India. It is remarkable how in every province the front rank leaders have run the boldest risks. But whilst Mr. Kelkar and his party had not the good fortune to be imprisoned, the Ajmer people fared better. On prohibition notices being issued, the workers regarding picketing as a 'religious right' took up the challenge. "Swaraj Seva volunteers were posted," says Pandit Chand Karan Sarda, "on all liquor shops. The Government also posted its police force and mounted Sewars on each shop with orders to arrest the pickets, As soon as one batch was arrested, the reserve volunteers took their place. The police arrested only 17 volunteers who were summarily tried and sentenced to 4 months and 3 weeks rigorous imprisonment." They offered no defence. No more arrests seem to have been made at Ajmer. Where picketing can be practised without violence and ill-will against the liquor dealer or the drinker, it is a moral duty. That it has advanced the cause of temperance as nothing else has, no one can deny. Only the other day, at Karamsad, the Christian and Hindu Dhedhs gratefully informed me that as a result of picketing they had banished drink from their midst. Bombay has forfeited the right for the time being at any rate, because of its wanton and malicious destruction of Parsi liquor shops and its disgraceful behaviour towards Parsis and Christians on the fateful 17th November, and the two following days. I hope, however, that wherever picketing is practised, it will be entrusted to men or women of unimpeachable character, and carried on in the friendliest spirit. We do not want to make people virtuous by force.

23rd February, 1922

OUR LAXITY

A reliable correspondent writes to me saying that in Allahabad and Benares, the volunteers have been enlisted without regard te their qualifications.* Hardly

*The following appeared in *Young India* of 23rd February, 1922, under the heading " rather free, than sober":

50 could be found dressed in handspun *khaddar* from top to toe. Some more could be found wearing *khaddar* for outer covering, all the rest being foreign cloth. The same correspondent says that some of the volunteers do not mind an occasional drink and that they are not tested as to their belief in non-violence and that in many instances the local Congress officials have lost control over them. It has been officially reported that there are 96,000 volunteers enlisted in the United Provinces. If it is a fact that there are so many volunteers on the roll and that the vast majority of them do not conform to the Congress conditions, they are worse than useless. The complaints mentioned by me are formidable, yet as a matter of fact, I have not exhausted them all. The same news comes from Calcutta, again from a reliable source. My informant tells me that

Just as I am writing these notes, my assistant puts into my hand a cutting from the *Leader*, containing the text of Pandit Gopinath Kunzru's letter, describing in the calmest manner possible what befell him and his friend when they were purchasing in Agra brandy from a liquor shop for outward application for a patient. The volunteers would not allow them to take the brandy in spite of all the assurance of *bona fides* given by Pandit Kunzru. This is not only not non-violence but is unadulterated violence. Peaceful picketing does not mean that so long as no physical violence is used, any kind of pressure could be exercised. The volunteers, if they had remained true to their pledge, would have allowed safe passage to Pandit Gopinath and his friend. The picketers' duty is merely to warn drinkers against the vice of drink, not molest them or otherwise prevent them if they will not listen. If we may force temperance upon the people believing it to be good for them, the English administrators and their Indian supporters are certainly performing an analogous operation. They too force the present system on us well believing that it is good for us. If the Swaraj volunteers may, therefore, take such liberties as they have undoubtedly taken in respect of Pandit Gopinath Kunzru, they are seeking not to change the *system*, but the *masters*. I would rather have India to be free than sober if freedom has to be sold to buy sobriety.

hundreds who have gone to jail know nothing about the pledge,* are not dressed in *khaddar*, are not dressed even in Indian mill cloth but have gone to jail wearing foreign cloth, and that they have had no training in non-violence. A correspondent from Rohtak writes bitterly complaining that in many parts of that district the volunteers do not obey instruction and make the position of Congress officials most difficult and embarrassing.

If one-tenth of these complaints is true, I fear that we have not been able to cope with the wonderful awakening and to bring under control all the new additions to the Congress organisation. It is possible that it is nobody's fault that this is so. The Government precipitated a crisis by hurling the notifications about public meetings and volunteers at us. The challenge had to be and was taken up. New and inexperienced men

* The following about volunteer pledge, on the lines of which the Ahmedabad Congress also adopted a pledge, appeared in *Young India* of 22nd December, 1921 :

To show the thorough nature of the work of ensuring peace that is being done in Delhi, I extract the following remarkable pledge from Mr. Asaf Ali's letter which he wrote when he offered himself and fifty-two others for arrest :

" With full consciousness of the omnipresence and omniscience of God I declare that it shall be my solemn duty (1) to attain Swaraj by peaceful means, (2) to preserve and foster unity between the members and followers of the various communities and religions of India, (3) to regard no class or community as contemptible or untouchable, (4) to sacrifice life and property for the honour and interest of my country, (5) to wear clothes made of cloth handspun and hand-woven in the country, (6) to obey without demur the orders of the officers, (7) so long as I am not discharged from the Corps, to observe myself and persuade others to observe non-violence (or as long as the Congress continues to follow this policy) and finally I will cheerfully bear privations and troubles which may confront me during my connection with the National Volunteer Corps and neither I nor any of my dependents and relations expect any compensation. "

found themselves clothed with office and they were called upon to deal with a crisis which would have taxed to its utmost the capacity even of the experienced leaders withdrawn from public guidance.

There is much to be said in favour of this argument. No one need therefore be blamed, but we must not blink the facts. On the contrary, we must face them sternly, boldly and set our own house in order. No army in the world has yet marched to victory, which has not consisted of soldiers possessing the qualities of them. An army of peace has greater need to exhibit the qualities laid down for its soldiers. It would not do to retort that the standard is too high. A recruiting officer who takes recruits below the standard renders himself guilty of dishonesty, if he takes such recruits knowingly. All he can do is to report to the head-quarters that he cannot get recruits on the conditions prescribed, but on no account will he be justified in departing from them.

The conditions laid down by the Congress were read by myself in detail to the whole audience last December in the Congress pandal. They were exhaustively discussed by the All-India Congress Committee and the Working Committee, and then they were explained by me to the delegates and visitors from the different provinces at numerous informal discussions. The plea of impossibility of fulfilment cannot therefore be accepted. The delegates knew what they were about. They were nearly 6,000. They came to represent their respective constituencies and there should have been no difficulty about the fulfilment of the conditions.

I should personally be satisfied with 300 volunteers thoroughly understanding and complying with the conditions, but I should not care to lead a struggle with 30,000 volunteers who know nothing of and care less about the conditions. The reason is obvious. In the one case I have at least 300 stalwarts to support me, in the other case I have to carry a burden of 30,000 men, not volunteers, who are a drag upon me. The 300 would help me, would obey instructions, but 30,000 will certainly not carry out instructions and may throttle me. We must therefore once for all make up our minds that all the resolutions which are passed by the Congress Working Committee have to be fulfilled literally. They are part of a swift and practical programme upon whose due fulfilment rests the future of India, the redress of the Khilafat and the Punjab wrongs and the attainment of Swaraj. Resolutions by themselves mean nothing if they are not to be carried out in full. We used to complain when our resolutions, which were in days gone by addressed to the Government, were not carried out by it. Who is to complain when the resolutions voluntarily and deliberately passed by us are not carried out by ourselves? I, therefore, strongly advise all Congress and Khilafat organisations to see that they are strictly enforced in their respective jurisdictions. If they do not, it is they who will endanger the movement and no one else. It is for us to make or mar the future.

[E]

2nd February, 1922

POLITICAL AGENCIES

Repression is slowly spreading its net in all directions, and now-a-days precedes the Prince's visit as if to prove to the people the might His Royal Higheess represents. As he is expected in Indore, Babus Badrilal Aryadutta and Chhotelal have been deported from Indore Camp by the Agent to the Governor-General. Orders have also been issued prohibiting public meetings within the Residency area. It may be that public life is not so well organised in these Residencies as in British India proper. But if it is, I have no doubt about the duty of the residents of the camp. If they can retain the non-violent spirit and if they are at all well organised, they should hold meetings notwithstanding the orders, and risk deportation or imprisonment. In my opinion, those who are deported should return to be arrested.

A similar story comes from Kathiawad. It seems that the Princes of Kathiawad have arranged Shikar parties and other non-political but expensive amusements for H. E. the Governor. The subjects of the States are angry, not over the Governor's visit, but over the expensive amusements arranged in his honour. Probably the Governor does not even appreciate them. Why should these functionaries always want amusements? It is not as if they are without any, whilst they are working at headquarters. Indeed these amusements themselves must become a task for at least some of them. Neither party can be natural at these shows. They must put on their best behaviour and observe their respective distances. They must always act both officially and correctly even when they are meeting unofficially. In the circumstances, it would certainly save a great deal of time and expense if these amusements were cut down and the visits limited to State business only. Moreover, the Shikar parties offend vegetarian of Kathiawad. The people of Kathiawad cannot but resent, even when they say nothing, the waste of animal life for no purpose whatsoever. I am told that, in order to draw the beasts of prey, goats have to be sacrificed for days in advance. Such Shikar, over which so much innocent blood is spilt and is without any risk of life or limb on the part of the Shikari, is robbed of all charm and becomes a mild copy of the law that prevails between the Government and the people in India, whereby the public are always the sport of the Government which never runs any risk. It is not the Mosaic law of tooth for tooth, but it is the law of bullets against brickbats, life for a scratch. When the hunter runs no risk, it is not good sport but is downright cruelty. But the Agent to the Governor in Kathiawad evidently could not tolerate protest meetings even against the extravagance of the Princes and has therefore, it appears, prohibited public meetings and arrested Messrs. Munilal Kothari and Mansukhlal Ravjibhai Metha.

All this activity in the Agencies is a new development. I congratulate those we are arrested. The law of non-violence is just as imperative in the Agencies and the States as it is in the pure British area. What is more, the residents in the States must not embarrass the latter in respect of or in the interest of the movement of Non-co-operation with the Government. They may fight against their local grievances but even then not in the intensive Non-co-operation manner except under very grave circumstances and except when public opinion is with them. In the States, the subjects cannot claim to have exhausted all their resources with the Princes themselves. They must form public opinion, carry on agitation and otherwise organise themselves. I often hear the talk that the Congress became useful only when Non-co-operation came in. This is an utterly wrong view of the situation. The Congress agitation paved the way for Non-co-operation. The latter was the fitting corollary to the previous Congress activities. The Congress has always been in India the greatest demonstrative and effective agency for ventilating people's grievances. It has always been a true register of popular strength and weakness. The States subjects, too, must have their Congress and Conferences quite apart from the British Indian prototype and probably differently managed. They may learn from the mistakes of the parent body but they have to go through that preliminary discipline. A mere unexaggerated exposure of a wrong is by no means a small matter. Wrong like vice flourishes in secrecy. It dies of sunlight. Therefore let the subjects of States organise themselves quickly and in a methodical manner without mixing up and spoiling their local matters with the National Congress. The States subjects can work as so many are doing on the Congress and for the Congress outside the States area.

TOO SACRED FOR PUBLICATION

9th February, 1922

There are things one does not like to see published, not because there is anything secret about them but because they are too sacred for publication. Sometimes the published version gives an impression totally different from the spoken sword, even though the reporting may be ever so accurate. When I call a little child a fiend in perfect good humour or with a frown, it would not do to report me as having called some one a fiend without giving long explanations as to the why and the how. Some such disservice has been done by the manifestly friendly reporter of a conversation and a discourse at Satyagraha Ashram as reported in the *Bombay Chronicle* of the 2nd instant. I dislike such things being reported. In a swift conversation there are many things understood. An accurate report of such a conversation is impossible without copious footnotes. I am, for instance, reported as having said that Shantiniketan is for material progress and Satyagraha Ashram exists solely for spiritual progress. When the Poet sees this, he will either laugh at it if he remembers that I could not possibly say or mean any such thing about Shantiniketan, or he will be angry and despondent that even I should be so hopelessly ignorant and inartistic as not to see the spirituality of Shantiniketan. The Poet, I feel sure, is not likely to do me the injustice of thinking me capable of holding the belief imputed to me. I could say to the Poet, as indeed I have done, that Shantiniketan lacks discipline. He had laughed over it and even endorsed my criticism and justified it, saying he was a Poet and Shantiniketan was for his amusement. He could only sing and make others sing. I was free to introduce all the discipline I liked but he was only a Poet. The reader must know that I have lived at Shantiniketan for more than once. I am permitted to regard it as a home of retreat. My boys have had shelter there and at the Gurukula when I was away in England. My conversation with the Hindi teacher was on the basis that both he and I were lovers of Shantiniketan. How can Shantiniketan be otherwise than spiritual when the author of pure spiritual poetry is the dominating spirit there? I am not so dull as to think that a place where Devendranath Tagore lived could be devoid of spirituality. The readers of *Young India* are aware that I receive spiritual draughts from Shantiniketan from time to time sent by Badadada* who is incessantly watching over me and praying for the success of my mission. I

*Dwijendranath Tagore.

hasten to inform the reader that I regard many professors and teachers of Shantiniketan as highly spiritual and good men whose association I have valued as a privilege. I must further inform the reader that I consider Bengal to be the most spiritual among our provinces. The whole of my conversation which is unfortunately reported was carried on in a humorous strain. I have often claimed among lovers of Shantiniketan greater spirituality for Satyagraha Ashram than Shantiniketan. But such competition and claim must not be interpreted into an assumption of superiority. I am most desirous to keep Satyagraha Ashram veiled from the public. We are there a band of humble unlettered workers knowing our own failings, trying to understand them still further and undoubtedly intent upon finding the truth and wanting to live and die for it. Comparisons between kindred, but not identical, institutions must never be made. But if a comparison must be made, in spite of the early rising and the discipline of Satyagraha Ashram, I would vote really and sincerely for Shantiniketan as an elder brother. It is older by far in age and I know it is so also in wisdom. But there is that 'but'. The inmates of Shantiniketan must beware of the race that the little place in Gujerat is running.

Having said so much of Shantiniketan by way of reparation, I have no time or space left for giving my version of the morning course nor must I attempt it. It came from the very pith of my soul. I could not report it myself with the same force. I heard a sister give it in one sentence. It was so true. I wish the unknown friend had never thought of reporting it. The report does not convey the central truth of it.

I HAVE LOST ALL CREDIT

23rd February, 1922

A friend from Lahore without giving his name sends me the following thundering note:

"On Tuesday the 14th, I read the *Tribune* and the resolutions therein, passed at the emergency meeting of the All-India Congress Working Committee.* On Monday when I came from my office, I heard a flying rumour that Mahatmaji had postponed the date of the mass Civil Disobedience, but at that time I thought the news devoid of foundation. After a short time, a friend of mine hawked me at my house and we went to bazaar. His face was somewhat sadder than usual. I enquired of him the reason of his sadness. He said he was utterly disgusted and so gave up the idea of following this movement. Mahatmaji was going to give up the lead of this movement and at the same time he had advised all the Provincial Congress Committees not to enrol any more volunteers. No picketing propaganda should be undertaken as long as the special session of the All-India Congress Committee had not confirmed what to do further.

"The people are of this opinion that you have turned your face and become fickle-minded. They will co-operate with the Government without any hesitation and join the ceremony of His Royal Highness the Prince of Wales. Some say that they will not observe *hartal* and will accord a hearty reception at Lahore.

"Some merchants are under the impression that you have removed all the restrictions from all liquor shops and *videshi* cloth.

"Truly speaking, each and every one in Lahore city is holding meeting in the bazaar as well as in the house, and you will forgive me if I will say boldly that they are condemning the action of the All-India Congress Committee.

'I now for my sake ask you these questions.

"(1) Will you now give up the lead of this movement? If so, why?

"Will you be good enough to let me know why you have given such instructions to all Provincial Congress Committees? Have you given an opportunity to Pandit Malaviya for a Round Table Conference for a settlement, or has Pandit Malaviya agreed to embrace your movement in case the Government has not turned true to its words?

* Where the "Bardoli decision" suspending Civil Disobedience was arrived at.

"(3) Grant a compromise is arranged and the Khilafat and the Punjab wrongs are redressed and in the case of Swaraj the Government may only extend the reforms, will you be satisfied with that or continue your activities till you have got the full dominion status?

"(4) Suppose no decision is arrived at. Will Pandit Malaviya and all others who are connected with this conference come to your side, or will their fate remain in the balance just as now?

"(5) In case no decision is arrived at, will you give up the idea of Civil Disobedience, if there is danger of violence?

"(6) Is your intention now to disband the present volunteer corps and enlist those who know spinning and wear handspun and handwoven *khaddar*?

"(7) Suppose violence has made appearance when you have started your mass Civil Disobedience, what will you do at that time? Will you stop your activities at the very moment?"

There is much more criticism in this letter than I have reproduced. The writer tells me that the people are so disgusted that they now threaten to become co-operators and are of opinion that I have sold Lala Lajpat Rai, Deshabandhu Chitta Ranjan Das, Pandit Motilal Nehru, the Ali Brothers and others, and tell me that if I give up the leadership, there are thousands who will leave this world by committing suicide. I may assure the citizens of Lahore, in particular and the Punjabis in general, that I do not believe what is said of them. I used to receive such letters even during the Martial Law days, because of the suspension of Civil Disobedience, but I discounted all the news and on my reaching the Punjab in October, I found that I was right in my analysis of the Punjab mind and I discovered that there was no one to challenge the propriety of my act. I feel still more confident of the correctness of the decision of the Working Committee, but if it is found that the country repudiates my action, I shall not mind it. I can but do my duty. A leader is useless when he acts against the promptings of his own conscience, surrounded as he must be by people holding all kinds of views. He will drift like an anchorless ship if he has not the inner voice to hold him firm and guide him. Above all, I can easily put up with the denial of the world, but any denial by me of my God is unthinkable, and if I did not give at this critical period of the struggle the advice that I have, I would be denying both God and Truth. The telegrams and letters I am receiving from all parts of the country thanking me for my decision—telegrams from both non-co-operators and co-operators—confirm my belief that the country appreciates the decision and that the Lahore writer has given undue prominence to some heated bazaar talk which was bound to take place after the Bardoli decision which, all of a sudden, disturbed all previous calculations. I can understand the effect of the first shock, but I am also sure that when the people begin to analyse the implications of non-violence, they will come to no other conclusion than that of the Working Committee.

And now for the questions of the correspondent:

(1) I am not likely to give up the lead of the movement unless I have a clear indication that the people want me to. One method of giving that indication is an adverse vote of the Working Committee or the All-India Congress Committee.

(2) I assure the public that Pandit Malaviyaji had absolutely no hand in shaping my decision. I have often yielded to Panditji, and it is always a pleasure for me to yield to him whenever I can and always painful to differ from one who has an unrivalled record of public service and who is sacrifice personified. But so far as the decision of suspension is concerned, I arrived at it on my reading the detailed report of the Chauri Chaura

tragedy in the *Chronicle*. It was in Bardoli that telegrams were sent convening the Working Committee meeting and it was in Bardoli that I sent a letter to the members of the Working Committee advising them of my desire to suspend Civil Disobedience. I went thereafter to Bombay at the instance of Panditji, who, together with the other friends of the Malaviya Conference, undoubtedly wished to plead with me for a suspension and who were agreeably surprised when I told them that, so far as I was concerned, my mind was made up, but that I had kept it open so that I could discuss the point thoroughly with the members of the Working Committee. The suspension has no reference to a round table conference or to any settlement. In my opinion, a round table conference is bound to prove fruitless. It requires a much stronger Viceroy than Lord Reading has proved to be to perceive the situation in the country and then to describe it correctly. I certainly feel that Pandit Malaviyaji has already come into the movement. It is not possible for him to keep away from the Congress or from danger, but the Bardoli decision was arrived at purely on its merits, and I could not have shaken from the original purpose, had I not been unnerved by the Chauri Chaura tragedy which was the last straw.

(3) Nothing short of a full Dominion status is likely to satisfy me personally, and nothing short of complete severance will satisfy me, if the Khilafat and the Punjab wrongs remain unredressed, but the exact form does not depend upon me. I have no clear-cut scheme. It has to be evolved by the people's representatives.

(4) At the present moment there is no question of a settlement. Therefore, the question as to what Panditji and all others will do is premature, if not irrelevant.

But assuming that Panditji holds any conference and that its resolutions are ignored by the Government, Panditji and others will act as all self-respecting men do in such circumstances.

(5) I can never give up the *idea* of Civil Disobedience, no matter what danger there is of violence, but I shall certainly give up the idea of *starting* mass Civil Disobedience, so long as there is a certain danger of violence. Individual Civil Disobedience stands on a different footing.

(6) There is no question of disbanding any Volunteer Corps, but the names of those who do not conform to the Congress pledge have certainly to be removed from the list, if we are to be honest.

(7) If we have understood the essential parts of non-violence, we can but come to one conclusion that any eruption of widespread violence—and I call the Chauri Chaura tragedy widespread for the purpose—automatically stops mass Civil Disobedience. That many other parts of the country have nobly responded to the spirit of non-violence is good, but it is not good enough to continue mass Civil Disobedience even as a most *peaceful* meeting is disturbed if one man obstructs or commits violence. Mass Civil Disobedience for becoming successful requires a non-violent environment. The reason for restricting it to one single small area is to prevent violence elsewhere. It, therefore, means that mass Civil Disobedience in a particular area is possible when the other areas passively co-operate by remaining non-violent.

REPLY TO THE GOVERNMENT OF INDIA

The Government of India in a Communique published on the

6th February replied to Mr. Gandhi's Bardoli letter, repudiating his statements and urging that the issue before the country was no longer between this or that programme of political advance, but between lawlessness with all its consequences on the one hand and the maintenance of those principles which lie at the root of all civilised Governments. Mr. Gandhi issued the following rejoinder :

I have very carefully read the Government's reply to my letter. I confess that I was totally unprepared for such an evasion of the realities of the case as the reply betrays.

I will take the very first repudiation. The reply says they (the Government) emphatically repudiate the statement that they have embarked on a policy of lawless repression and also the suggestion that the present campaign of Civil Disobedience has been forced on the Non-co-operation party in order to secure the elementary rights of free association, free speech and free press. Even a cursory glance at my letter would show that, whilst Civil Disobedience was authorised by the All-India Congress Committee meeting held on the 4th November, at Delhi, it had not commenced. I have made it clear in my letter that the contemplated mass Civil Disobedience was indefinitely postponed on account of the regrettable events of the 17th November, in Bombay. That decision was duly published and it is within the knowledge of the Government as also the public that herculean efforts were being made to combat the still lingering violent tendency amongst the people. It is also within the knowledge of the Government and the public that a special form of pledge was devised to be signed by volunteers with the deliberate purpose of keeping out all but men of proved character. The primary object of these volunteers' associations was to inculcate amongst the masses the lessons of non-violence and to keep the peace at all Non-co-operation functions. Unfortunately, the Government of India lost its head completely over the Bombay events and, perhaps, still more over the very complete hartal on the same date at Calcutta. I do not wish to deny that there might have been some intimidation practised in Calcutta, but it was not, I venture to submit, the fact of intimidation, but the irritation caused by the completeness of the hartal that maddened the Government of India as also the Government of Bengal. Repression there was even before that time, but nothing was said or done in connection with it. But the repression that came in the wake of the notifications proclaiming the Criminal Law Amendment Act for the purpose of dealing with volunteers' associations and the Seditious Meeting Act for the purpose of dealing with public meetings held by Non-co-operators, came upon the Non-co-operation community as a bombshell.

I repeat, then, that these notifications and the arrests of Deshbandu Chittaranjan Das and Moulana Adul Kalam Azad in Bengal, the arrest of Pandit Motilal Nehru and his co-workers in the U. P. and of Lala Lajput Rai and his party in the Punjab made it absolutely necessary to take up, not yet aggressive Civil Disobedience, but only defensive Civil Disobedience, otherwise described as passive resistance. Even Sir Hormusji Wadia was obliged to declare that, if the Bombay Government followed the precedents set by the Governments of Bengal, U. P. and the Punjab, he would be bound to resist such notifications, that is, to enrol himself as a volunseer or to attend public meetings in defiance of Government order to the contrary. It is thus clear that a case has been completely made out for Civil Disobedience, unless the Government revised its policy which has resulted in the stopping of public meetings.

public associations and the Non-co-operation press in many parts of India.

Now for the statement that the Government have embarked on a policy of lawless repression instead of an ample expression of regret and apology for the barbarous deeds that have been committed by officers in the name of law and order. I regret to find in the Government reply a categorical denial of any lawless repression. In this connection, I urge the public and Government carefully to consider the following facts whose substance is beyond challenge: (1) Official shooting at Entally in Calcutta and the callous treatment even of a corpse, (2) The admitted brutality of the civil guards, (3) The forcible dispersal of a meeting at Dacca and the dragging of innocent men by their legs although they had given no offence or cause whatsoever, (4) Similar treatment of volunteers in Aligarh, (5) The conclusive (in my opinion) finding of the committee presided over by Dr. Gokhul Chand about the brutal and uncalled for assaults upon volunteers and the public in Lahore, (6) The wicked and inhuman treatment of volunteers and the public at Jullundur, (7) The shooting of a boy at Dehra Dun and the cruelly forcible dispersal of a public meeting of that place, (8) The looting admitted by the Bihar Government of villages by an officer and his company without any permission whatsoever, from any one, but as stated by Non-co-operators, at the invitation of a planter, assaults upon volunteers and the burning of Khaddar and papers belonging to the Congress at Sonepur, (9) the midnight searches and arrests in the Congress and Khilafat offices.

I have merely given a sample of the many infallible proofs of official lawlessness and barbarism.* I have

* *Young India* published from week to week detailed accounts of these cases of alleged lawless repression.

mentioned not even a tithe of what is happening all over the country. I wish to state, without fear of successful contradiction, that the scale on which this lawlessness had gone on in so many provinces of India puts into shade the inhumanities that were practised in the Punjab, if we except the crawling order and the massacre at Jallianwalabagh. It is my certain conviction that the massacre at Jallianwallabagh was a clean transaction compared to the unclean transactions described above, and the pity of it is that, because people are not shot or butchered, the tortures through which hundreds of inoffensive men have gone through do not produce a sufficient effect to turn everybody's face against this Government.

But as if this warfare against innocence was not enough, the reins are being tightened in the jails. We know nothing of what is happening to-day in Karachi jail, to a solitary prisoner in the Sabarmati jail and to a batch in the Benares jail, all of whom are as innocent as I claim to be myself. Their crime consists in their constituting themselves the trustees of national honour and dignity. I am hoping that these proud and defiant spirits will not be sent into submission masquerading in the official garb. I deny the right of the authorities to insist on high-souled men appearing before them almost naked or paying any obsequious respect to them by way of salaming with open palms brought together, or reciting to the intonation of "Sarkar-ike-hai." No God-fearing man will do the latter even if he has to be kept standing in his stock for days and nights, as a Bengal schoolmaster is reported to have been for the sake of the dignity of human nature.

I trust that Lord Reading and his draftsmen do not know the facts that I have adduced or are being carried away by their belief in the infallibility of their employees. I refuse to believe in the statements which the public regards as God's truth. If there is the slightest exaggeration in the statements that I have made, I shall as publicly withdraw them and apologise for them as I am making them now, but, as it is, I undertake to prove the substance of every one of these charges if not the very letter and much more of them, before any impartial tribunal of men or women unconnected with the Government. I invite Pandit Malaviyaji and those who are performing the thankless task of securing a round table conference to form an impartial commission to investigate these charges by which I stand or fall.

It is the physical and brutal ill-treatment of humanity which has made many of my co-workers and myself impatient of life itself, and, in the face of these things, I don't wish to take public time by dealing in detail what I mean by abuse of the common law of the country but I cannot help correcting the mis-impression which is likely to be created in connection with the Bombay disorders, disgraceful and deplorable as they were. Let it be remembered that, of the persons who lost their lives, over 45 were Non-co-operators or their sympathisers, the hooligans, and of the 400 wounded, to be absolutely on the safe side, over 350 were also derived from the same class. I do not complain; the co-operators, the Non-co-operators and the friendly hooligans got what they deserved: they began the violence and they reaped the reward. Let it also not be forgotten that, with all deference to the Bombay Government, it was Non-co-operators, ably assisted by Independents and co-operators, who brought peace out of that chaos of the two days following the fateful 17th.

I must totally deny the imputation that the application

of the Criminal Law Amendment Act was confined to associations the majority of the members of which had habitually indulged in violence and intimidation. The prisons of India to-day hold some of the most inoffensive men and hardly any who are convicted under the law. Abundant proof can be produced in support of this statement as also of the statement of the fact that almost wherever meetings have been broken up, there was actually no risk of violence.

The Government of India deny that the Viceroy has laid down upon the apology of the Ali Brothers the civilised policy of non-interference with the non-violent activities of Non-co-operators. I am extremely sorry for this repudiation. The very part of the communique reproduced in the reply is in my opinion sufficient proof that the Government did not intend to interfere with such activities. The Government did not wish to be inferred that speeches promoting disaffection of a less violent character were not an offence against the law. I have never stated that breach of any law was not to be an offence against it, but I have stated, as I repeat now, that it was not the intention of the Government then to prosecute for non-violent activities, although they might amount to a technical breach of the law.

As to the conditions of the conference, the Government reply evidently omits to mention the two words "and otherwise" after the words "Calcutta speech" in my letter. I repeat that the terms "I would gather from the Calcutta speech and otherwise" were nearly the same that were mentioned in the resolutions of the Malaviya Conference. What are called the unlawful activities of the N. C. O. party, being a reply to the notifications of the Government, would have ceased automatically with the withdrawal of these notifications, because the formation of volunteer corps and public meetings would not be unlawful activities after the withdrawal of the offending notification. Even while the negotiations were going on in Calcutta, the discharge of Fatwa prisoners was asked for, and I can only repeat what I have said elsewhere that, if it is disloyal to say that military service under the existing system of Government is a sin against God and humanity, I fear that such disloyalty must continue.

The Government communique does me a cruel wrong imputing to me a desire that the proposed round table conference should be called merely to register my decrees. I did state, in order to avoid any misunderstanding the Congress demands, as I felt I was in duty bound, in as clear terms as possible. No Congressman could approach any conference without making his position clear. I accepted the ordinary courtesy of not considering me or any Congressmen to be impervious to reason or argument. It is open to anybody to convince me that the demands of the Congress regarding the Khilafat, the Punjab and Swaraj are wrong or unreasonable and I would certainly retrace my steps and, so far as I am concerned, rectify the wrong. The Government of India know that such has been always my attitude.

The communique, strangely enough, says that the demands set forth in my manifesto are even larger than those of the Working Committee. I claim that they fall far below the demands of the Working Committee, for what I now ask against the total suspension of Civil Disobedience of an aggressive character is merely the stoppage of ruthless repression, the release of prisoners convicted under it and a clear declaration of policy. The demands of the Working Committee included a Round Table Conference. In my manifesto, I have not asked for a Round Table Conference at all. It is true that this wanting of a Round Table Conference does not proceed from any expediency, but it is a confession of present weakness. I freely recognise that, unless India becomes satuarated with the spirit of non-violence and generates disciplined strength that can only come from non-violence, she cannot enforce her demads, and it is for that reason that I now consider that the first thing for the people to do is to secure a reversal of this mad repression and then to concentrate upon more complete organisation and more construction. And here again the Communique does me an injustice by merely stating the Civil Disobedience of an aggressive character will be postponed until the opportunity is given to the imprisoned leaders of reviewing the whole situation after their discharge and by conveniently omitting to mention the following conclusion of my letter. "If the Government make the requested declaration, I shall regard it as an honest desire on its part to give effect to public opinion and shall therefore have no hesitation in advising the country to be engaged in further moulding public opinion without violent restraint from either side and trust to its working to secure the fulfilment of its unalterable demands. Aggressive Civil Disobedience in that case will be taken up only when the Government departs from its policy of strictest neutrality or refuse to yield to the clearly expressed opinion of the vast majority of the people of India."

I venture to claim extreme reasonableness and moderation for the above presentation of the case. The alternative before the people, therefore, is not, as the communique concludes, between "lawlessness with all its disastrous consequences on the one hand and on the other the maintenance of those principles which lie at the root of all civilised Government." Mass Civil Disobedience, it adds, is fraught with such danger to the State that it must be met with "sterness and severity." The choice befere the people is mass Civil Disobedience with all its undoubted dangers and lawless repression of the lawful activities of the people. I hold that it is impossible for any body of the self-respecting men for fear of unknown dangers to sit still and do nothing effective when looting of property and assaulting of innocent men are going on all over the country in the name of law and order.

24th November, 1921

THE BOMBAY RIOTS

A Deep Stain.—Under the foregoing heading, Mr. Gandhi published the following note after having witnessed the unfortunate disturbances in Bombay:

The reputation of Bombay, the hope of my dreams, was being stained yesterday even whilst in my simplicity I was congratulating the citizens upon their non-violence in the face of provocation. For the volunteers with their captain were arrested during the previous night for pasting posters under authority on private property. The posters advised the people to byocott the welcome to the Prince. They were destroyed. The Swaraj Sabha's office was mysteriously entered and the unused posters, so far as I am aware not declared unlawful, were also removed. The Prince's visit itself and the circumstances attending the cermonials arranged and public money wasted for the manufacture of a welcome to His Royal Highness constituted an unbearable provocation. And yet Bombay had remained self-restrained. This, I thought, was a matter for congratulation. The burning of the pile of foreign cloth was an eloquent counter-demonstration to the interested official demonstration.

Little did I know that at the very time that the Prince was passing through the decorated route and the pile of foreign cloth was burning, in another part of the city the mill hands were in criminal disobedience of the wishes of their masters emptying them, first one and then the others, by force, that a swelling mob was molesting peaceful passengers in the tramcars and holding up the tram traffic, that it was forcibly depriving those that were wearing foreign caps of their head-dresses and pelting inoffensive Europeans. As the day went up, the fury of the mob now intoxicated with its initial success rose also. They burnt tramcars and a motor, smashed liquor shops and burnt two.

I heard of the outbreak at about 1 o'clock. I motored with some friends to the area of disturbance and heard the most painful and the most humiliating story of molestation of Parsi sisters. Some few were assaulted, and even had their *sadis* torn from them. No one from among a crowd of over fifteen hundred who had surrounded my car denied the charge, as a Parsi with hot rage and quivering lips was with the greatest deliberation relating the story. An elderly Parsi gentleman said, "Please save us from this mob rule." This news of the rough handling of Parsi sisters pierced me like a dart. I felt that my sisters or daughters had been hurt by a violent mob! Yes, some Parsis had joined the welcome. They had a right to hold their own view free of molestation. There can be no coercion in Swaraj. The Moplah fanatic who forcibly converts a Hindu believes that he is acquiring religious merit. A non-co-operator or his associate who uses coercion has no apology whatsoever for his criminality.

As I reached the Two Tanks, I found a liquor shop smashed, two policemen badly wounded and lying unconscious on cots without anybody caring for them. I alighted. Immediately the crowd surrounded me and yelled "Mahatma Gandhiki jai." That sound usually grates on my ears, but it has grated never so much as it did yesterday when the crowd unmindful of the two sick brethren choked me with the shout at the top of their voices. I rebuked them and they were silent. Water was brought for the two wounded men. I requested two of my companions and some from the crowd to take the dying policemen to the hospital. I proceeded then to the scene a little further up where I saw a fire rising. There were two tramcars which were burnt by the crowd. On returning, I witnessed a burning motor car. I appealed to the crowd to disperse, told them that they had damaged the cause of the Khilafat, the Punjab and Swaraj. I returned sick at heart and in a chastened mood.

At about five, a few brave Sindhi young men came to report that in Bhindi Bazaar the crowd was molesting every passer-by who had a foreign cap on and even seriously beating him, if he refused to give up his cap. A brave old Parsi who defied the crowd and would not give up his *Pugree* was badly handled. Maulana Azad Sobhani and I went to Bhindi Bazaar and reasoned with the crowd, told them that they were denying their religion by hurting innocent men. The crowd made a show of dispersing. The Police were there but they were exceedingly restrained. We went further and, on retracing our steps, found to our horror a liquor shop on fire. Even the fire brigade was obstructed in its work. Thanks to the efforts of Pandit Nekiram Sharma and others the inmates of the shop were able to come out.

The crowd did not consist of hooligans only or boys. It was not an unintelligent crowd. They were not all mill hands. It was essentially a mixed crowd unprepared and unwilling to listen to anybody. For the moment it had lost its head. And it was not a crowd but several crowds numbering in all not less than twenty thousand. It was bent upon mischief and destruction.

I heard that there was firing resulting in deaths and that in the Anglo-Indian quarters every one came in for hard beating, if he did not put off his *Khadi* cap or shirt. I heard that many were seriously injured. I am writing this in the midst of six Hindu and Mussalman workers who have just come in with broken heads and bleeding and one with a broken nasal bone and other lacerated wounds and in danger of losing his life. They went to Parel led by Maulanas Azad Sobani and Mozzam Ali to pacify the mill hands, who, it was reported, were holding up tramcars there. The workers, however, were unable to proceed to their destination. They returned with their bleeding wounds to speak for themselves.

Thus the hope of reviving mass Civil Disobedience has once more in my opinion been dashed to pieces. The atmosphere for mass Civil Disobedience is absent. It is not enough to say that such an atmosphere is to be found in Bardoli, and, therefore, it may go on side by side with the violence in Bombay. This is impossible. Neither Bardoli nor Bombay can be treated as separate, unconnected units. They are parts of one great indivisible whole. It was possible to isolate Malabar. It was also possible to disregard Malegaon. But it is not possible to ignore Bombay.

Non-co-operators cannot escape liability. It is true that Non-co-operators were ceaselessly remonstrating everywhere with the people at considerable risk to themselves, to arrest or stop the mischief and that they are responsible for saving many precious lives. But that is not enough for launching out on Civil Disobedience or to discharge us from liability for the violence that has taken place. We claim to have established a peaceful atmosphere, *i.e.*, to have attained by our non-violence sufficient control over the people to keep their violence under check. We have failed when we ought to have succeeded. For yesterday was a day of our trial. We were under our pledge bound to protect the person of the Prince from any harm or insult. And we broke that pledge inasmuch as any one of us insulted or injured a single European or any other who took part in the welcome to the Prince. They were as much entitled to take part in the welcome as we were to refrain. Nor can I shirk my own personal responsibility. I am more instrumental than any other in bringing into being the spirit of revolt. I find myself not fully capable of controlling and disciplining that spirit. I must do penance for it. For me the struggle is essentially religious. I believe in fasting and prayer, and I propose henceforth to observe evey Monday a twenty-four hours' fast till Swaraj is attained.

The working Committee will have to devote its attention to the situation and consider in the light there of whether mass Civil Disobedience can be at all encourged until we have obtained complete control over the masses. I have personally come deliberately to the conclusion that mass Civil Disobedience cannot be started for the present. I confess my inability to conduct a campaign of Civil Disobedience to a successful issue unless a completely non-violent spirit is generated among the people. I am sorry for the conclusion. It is a humiliating confession of my incapacity, but I know that I shall appear more pleasing to my Maker by being what I am instead of appearing to be what I am not. If I can have nothing to do with the organised violence of the Government, I can have less to do with the unorganised violence of the people. I would prefer to be crushed between the two

---

APPEALS ON THE SITUATION

As soon as riots broke out in Bombay on November 17th, Mahatma Gandhi engaged himself wholly in re-establishing peace by visiting the disturbed areas and issuing appeals to his co-workers as well as to the breakers of peace. These were published in "Young India" of 24th November and 1st December as well as in the Press. We give below a summary of these appeals :

Mr. Gandhi's Appeal to Bombay Citizens.—This appeal Mr. Gandhi wrote at 3 30 A.M. on the 19th November. "I must refuse," he said in it, "to eat or drink anything but water till the Hindus and Mussalmans of Bombay have made peace with the Parsis, the Christians and the Jews, and till the Non-co-operators have made peace with the co-operators." "The Swaraj that I have witnessed during the last two days has stunk in my nostrils." "I invite my fellow-workers," he added, "not to waste a single word of sympathy for me. I need or deserve none. But I invite them to make a ceaseless effort to regain control over the turbulent elements." "The Mussalmans have to my knowledge," concluded the Mahatmaji, "played the leading part during the two days of carnage. It has deeply hurt me. I ask every Mussalman worker to rise to his full height, to realise his duty to his faith and see that the carnage stops."

An Appeal to the Mavalis (Hooligans) of Bombay.—In this appeal which Mr. Gandhi issued on the 21st November, he wrote *inter alia* : "Whether you call yourself a Hindu, Mussalman, Parsi, Christian or Jew, you have certainly failed to consider even your own religious interests. . . . You have used the mass awakening for your own lust for plunder, rapine, and even indulging in your worst animal appetite. Some of my friends would, I know, accuse me of ignorance of human nature. If I believed the charge, I would plead guilty and retire from human assemblies and return only after acquiring knowledge of human nature." Mr. Gandhi went on to state that he had no difficulty in controlling the Indian Mavalis of S. Africa and concluded by asking them to stop retaliation and give him and his workers a chance to work among them.

To Co-workers.—In his appeal to co-workers dated 22nd November, Mahatma Gandhi stated that the majority being weak enough to do violence, the minority, Jews, Parsis and Christians, sought Government aid and indulged in retaliatory madness with that aid against the white cap-wearing innocent men without the police or the military raising a finger to stop it. "So the task before the workers," he said, "is to take the blows from the Government and our erring countrymen." "We must secure the co-operation of the rowdies of Bombay . . . They must either be amenable to our love or helplessly submit to the bayonet. They may not seek shelter under the banner of non-violence for the purpose of doing violence. . . . We must reach the rowdy element, befriend them and help them to understand the religious character of the struggle. We must neither neglect them nor pander to them. We must become their servants." Continuing Mr. Gandhi emphasised that the workers must respect the freedom of others to co-operate, to use foreign cloth or whatever they like to do. "Our struggle," he concluded, "consists in winning opponents, including Englishmen to our side. We can only do so by being free from ill-will against the weakest or the strongest of them. And this we can only do by being prepared to die for the faith within us and not by killing those who do not see the truth we enunciate."

Fast Broken.—Peace was restored the next day and, at the instance of the leaders of all the communities of all political parties, Mahatma Gandhi publicly broke his fast at a public breakfast. Speaking on the occasion, he said he found peace only in an empty stomach as a result of the disturbances and exhorted all not to resort to violence in the future but each community and party to respect the freedom of the other.

MOPLAH OUTBREAK

On August 19th, the Moplahs of Malabar broke out in open revolt. The immediate cause for the outbreak was the attempted arrest by the District Magistrate of some Khilafat workers at Tirurangadi. The Moplahs, however, seem to plead grave provocation in the shape of ruthless repression of all legitimate activities. The Moplahs not only resisted the arrests, but broke out in open rebellion at first against Government, but subsequently against the Hindu population as well. There were innumerable cases of looting Hindu houses, forced conversions and unmentionable atrocities on the Hindu population as a result of Moplah ignorance and fanaticism. The Muslim public were naturally unwilling to believe these and at least one or two Muslim public men almost condoned these. Moulana Hasrat Mohani, for instance, was one such and he said that Moplahs simply fought for their religion. The Congress workers in Malabar naturally resented this. Mahatma Gandhi, writing under the heading "Hindus and Moplahs" in *Young India* of 26th January, 1922, while sympathising with the Hindus, pointed out that Non-co-operation was self-realisation and that the Hindus must develop sufficient strength of will to withstand brute force and die in the act, if necessary.

Under the heading, "The two incompatibles," Mr. Gandhi wrote in

Young India of 6th September, 1921, condemning Moplah violence and pointing out that violence is the obstacle to success.

CONGRESS RESOLUTIONS

Amritsar, Calcutta, Nagpur and Ahmedabad resolutions are summarised in the History of Non-co-operation given in the beginning of the book.

DELHI CONDITIONS

See the "History of Non-co-operation" given in the beginning of the book.

CHAURI CHAURA RIOTS

See the "History of Non-co-operation" in the beginning of the book.

SWADESHI VOW

The following is the Swadeshi vow suggested for adoption by all:

" With God as my witness, I solemnly declare that from to-day I shall confine myself for my personal requirements, to the use of cloth manufactured in India from Indian cotton, silk and wool; and I shall altogether abstain from using foreign cloth in my possession."

It will be noticed that the above permits the use of Indian mill-made cloth. The two other vows were more difficult of fulfilment.

THE SATYAGRAHA PLEDGE

The following is the text of the Satyagraha Pledge:

Being conscientiously of opinion that the Bills known as the Indian Criminal Law (Amendment) Bill No. I of 1919, and the Criminal Law (Emergency Powers) Bill No. II of 1919, are unjust, subversive of the principle of liberty and justice, and destructive of the elementary rights of individuals on which the safety of the community as a whole and the State itself is based, we solemnly affirm that in the event of these Bills becoming law until they are withdrawn, we shall refuse civilly to obey these laws and such other laws as a committee to be hereafter appointed may think fit and further affirm that in this struggle we will faithfully follow truth and refrain from violence to life, person or property.

[F]

CONSTITUTION OF THE INDIAN NATIONAL CONGRESS ORGANISATION

As adopted by the Congress of 1908, *and amended by the Congresses of* 1911, 1912, 1915, 1916, 1917, 1918 *and* 1920

THE OBJECT

ARTICLE I.—The object of the Indian National Congress is the attainment of Swaraj by the people of India by all legitimate and peaceful means.

ARTICLE II.—*The Sessions of the Congress.*—(*a*) The Indian National Congress shall ordinarily meet once every year during Christmas holidays at such a place as may have been decided upon at its previous session or such other place as may have been determined by the All-India Congress Committee hereinafter referred to.

(*b*) An extraordinary session of the Congress may be summoned by the All-India Congress Committee either of its own motion or on the requisition of a majority of the Provincial Congress Committees, wherever it may deem it advisable to hold such a session; and the Articles of this Constitution shall apply with such modifications as the All-India Congress Committee may consider necessary in respect of each session.

Component Parts of the Congress Organisation

ARTICLE III.—The Indian National Congress Organisation shall consist of the following:

(*a*) The Indian National Congress. (*b*) Provincial Congress Committees. (*c*) District Congress Committees. (*d*) Sub-Divisional, Taluqa or Tehasil, Firka or other Local Congress Committees. (*e*) The All-India Congress Committee. (*f*) Such other committees outside India as may, from time to time, be recognised by the Congress in this behalf. (*g*) Bodies formed or organised periodically by the Provincial, District, Taluqa or Tehasil, Firka or other Local Congress Committees such as the Reception Committee of the Congress and the Provincial, District, Taluqa or Tehasil or other Local Conferences.

ARTICLE IV.—*Membership*—No person shall be eligible to be a member of any of the organisations, referred to in the foregoing Article, unless he or she has attained the age of 21 and expresses in writing his or her acceptance of the object and the methods as laid down in Article I of this Constitution and of the Rules of the Congress.

Provincial Congress Committees

ARTICLE V.—The following shall be the Provinces with headquarters mentioned against them and, where no headquarters are mentioned or in every other case, the respective Provincial Congress Committees shall have the power to fix or alter them from time to time.

	PROVINCE	LANGUAGE	HEAD-QUARTER
1	Madras	... (Tamil)	Madras
2	Andhra	... (Telugu)	
3	Karnatak	... (Canarese)	Gadag
4	Kerala	.. (Malayalam)	Calicut
5	City of Bombay	... (Marathi & Gujrati)	Bombay
6	Maharashtra	... (Marathi)	Poona
7	Gujrat	... (Gujrati)	Ahmedabad
8	Sindh	... (Sindhi)	
9	United Provinces	... (Hindustani)	Allahabad
10	Punjab	... (Punjabi)	Lahore
11	Frontier Prov.	... (Hindustani)	Peshawar
12	Delhi	... (Hindustani)	Delhi
13	Ajmer, Merwar, & Br. Rajputana	... (Hindustani)	Ajmer
14	Central Prov.	... (Hindustani)	Jubbulpore
15	Central Prov.	... (Marathi)	Nagpur
16	Behar	... (Marathi)	Amraoti
17	Behar	... (Hindustani)	Patna
18	Utkal Orissa	... (Oriya)	
19	Bengal & Surma Valley	... (Bengali)	Calcutta
20	Assam	... (Assamese)	Gauhati
21	Burma	... (Burmese)	Rangoon

Provided that the All-India Congress Committee may from time to time assign particular Indian States to particular Provinces and a Provincial Congress Committee may in its turn allot particular Indian States assigned to it by the All-India Congress Committee to particular Districts within its jurisdiction.

The existing Provincial Congress Committees shall forthwith proceed to reorganise themselves in terms of this Constitution. Such reorganisation shall be final, until it is revised by the All-India Con-

ARTICLE VI.—(*a*) There shall be a Provincial Congress Committee in and for each of the Provinces named in the foregoing article.

(*b*) Each Provincial Congress Committee shall organise district and other commitees referred to in article III and shall have the power to frame rules for laying down conditions of membership and for the conduct of business, not inconsistent with his constitution or any rules made by the All India Congress Committee.

(*c*) Each Provincial Congress Committee shall consist of representative elected annually by the members of the district and other Commitees in accordance with the rules made by the Provincial Congress Committees.

ARTICLE VII.—*Member ship of local Congress Organisation*—Every person not diaqualified under article IV and paying a subscription of 4 as. per year shall be entitled to become a member of any organisation controlled by Provincial Congress Committees.

ARTICLE VIII.—*Election of Delegrates*—Each Provincial Congress Committee shall be responsible for the election of delegates to the Congress creed.

No one shall be qualified for election who is not of the age of 21 years and who does not subscribe to the Congress creed.

The number of delegates shall be not more than one for every 50 thousand of the inhabitants of the Province in its jurisdiction, including the Native States therein, in accordance with the last census: provided, however, that the inclusion of Native States in the electorate shall not be taken to include any interference by the Congress with the internal affairs of such States.

Each Provincial Congress Committee shall frame rules for the election of delegates and representation of minorities, special interests of classes needing special protection.

The rules shall provide for the organisation of electorates and shall prescribe the procedure to be adopted for securing the proportional representation (by a single transferable vote) of every variety of political opinion.

The rules framed by each Provincial Congress Committee shall be sent to the General Secretaries of the Congress not latter than the 30th April 1921, which rules shall be published for general information by the Secretaries as soon as possible after the reciept thereof.

Each Provincial Congress Committee shall send to the Reception Committee of the ensuing Session of the Congress, an alphabetical list of the delegates so elected containing the full name, occupation age, sex, religion and address of each of them to reach the Committee not latter than the 15th day of December every year, and in the case of an Extraordinary Session, not latter than ten days before the date advertised for the holding of such Session.

ARTICLE IX.—*Subscription*—(*a*) Each provincial 'Congress Committee shall pay annually such subscription to the All-India Congress Committee as may be fixed by the latter from time to time.

(*b*) No Member of the Congress Committee shall vote at the election of representatives or delegates or be elected as such, unless and untill he has paid the subscription due by him.

ARTICLE X.—*Delegation Certificates*—Each committee referred to in the Article VIII shall issue certificates to the delegates duly elected in accordance with the form hereto attached, marked appendix A, and signed by the Secretary of the Committee.

ARTICLE XI.—*Delegation fees*—Every delegate on presenting such a certificate and paying a fee of Rs. 10 at the Congress office shall receive a ticket entitling him to admission to the Congress Pandal.

ARTICLE XII.—*Right to vote*—Delegates shall alone have the power of voting that the Congress sittings or otherwise taking part in its deliberations.

ARTICLE VIII.—*Reception Committee*—The Reception Committee shall be formed by the Provincial Congress Commitee, at least six months before the meeting of the annual session and may include persons who are not members of the Provincial Congress Committee. The Members of the Reception Committee shall pay not less than Rs. 25 each.

ARTICLE XIV.—The Reception Committee shall elect its Chairman and other office bearers from among its own members.

ARTICLE XV.—It shall be the duty of the Reception Committee to collect funds for the expenses of the Congress Session, to elect President of the Congress in the manner set forth in the following article, and to make all necessary arrangements for the reception and accommodation of delegates and guests, and as far as practicable, of visitors, and for the printing and publication of the report of the proceedings, and to submit a statement of receipt and expenditure to the Provincial Congress Committee within 4 months of the Congress Session.

ARTICLE XVI.—*Election of President.*—The several Provincial Congress Committees shall, as far as possible, by the end of June, suggest to the Reception Committee the names of persons who are, in their opinion, eligible for the Presidentship of the Congress as the Reception Committee shall, as far as possible, in the first week of July, submit to all the Provincial Committees the names as suggested for their final recommendations, provided that such final recommendation will be of any one, but not more, of such names, and the Reception Committee shall as far as possible meet on the month of August to consider such recommendations. If the person recommended by a majority of the Provincial Congress Committees is accepted by a majority of the members of the Reception Committee, present at a special meeting called for the purpose, that person shall be the President of the next Congress. If, however, the Reception Committee is unable to accept the president recommended by the Provincial Congress Committees, or in the case of emergency by resignation, death or otherwise of the President elected in this manner, the matter shall forthwith be referred by it to the All-India Congress Committee whose decision shall be arrived at, as far as possible, before the end of September: in either case the election shall be final provided that in no case shall the person so elected as President belong to the provinces in which the Congress is to be held.

The President of a special or extraordinary session shall be elected by the All-India Congress Committee, subject to the same Provision.

ARTICLE XVII.—*Disposal of Funds.*—(a) The Reception Committee shall, through, the Provincial Congress Committee of the Province, remit to the All-India Congress Committee not later than two weeks after the termination of the Congress Session, ordinary or extraordinary, half the deligation fees from the Congress Fund.

(*b*) If the Reception Committee has a balance after defraying all the expenses of the session, it shall hand over the same to the Provincial Congress Committee in the Province in which the session was held to from the Provincial Congress Fund for that province.

ARTICLE XVIII.—*Audit.*—The receipts and expenditure of the Reception Committee shall be audited by an auditor or auditors, appointed by the Provincial Congress Committee concerned, and the statement of accounts together with the Auditor's report shall be sent by the Provincial Congress Committee not later than six months from the termination of the Congress to the All-India Congress Committee.

The All-India Congress Committee

ARTICLE XIX.—The All-India Congress Committee shall consist of 350 members, exclusive of Ex-Officio members. The Ex-Officio members shall be all past president of the Congress and the General Secretaries and treasurers of the Congress.

Each Provincial Congress Committee shall elect the alloted number of members of the All-India Congress Committee from among the members of the Congress Committee within their jurisdiction.

The allotment shall be on the basis of the population according to the linguistic redistribution of Provinces or in such other manner as may appear more equitable to the All-India Congress Committee, and shall be published by the All-India Congress Committee before the 31st day of January, 1921.

The method of election shall be the same as already prescribed for the election of delegates.

Election to the All-India Congress Committee shall ordinarily be in the month of November.

The first All-India Congress Committee under this Constitution shall be elected on or before the 30th June 1921. Until then the members of the All-India Congress Committee recently elected shall continue in office.

ARTICLE XX.—The Secretaries of the respective Provincial Congress Committees shall issue certificates of membership of the All-India Committee to the persons so elected.

ARTICLE XXI.—The All-India Congress Committee shall be the Committee of the Congress from year to year and deal with all the new matters that may arise during the year and may not be provided for by the Congress itself. For this purpose, the All-India Congress Committee shall have the power to frame its own rules not inconsistent with this Constitution.

ARTICLE XXII—(a) The President of the Congress shall be the Chairman of the All-India Congress Committee for the year following.

ARTICLE XXIII.—*The General Secretaries*—The Indian National Congress shall have three General Secretaries who shall be annually elected by the Congress. They shall prepare the report of the work of the All-India Congress Committee during the year and submit it with a full account of the funds which may come into their hands to the All-India Congress Committee at a meeting to be held at the place and about the time of the session of the Congress for the year; and copies of such account and report shall then be presented to the Congress and sent to the Congress Committees.

ARTICLE XXIV.—*Working Committee.*—The All-India Congress Committee shall at its first meeting appoint a Working Committee consisting of the President, the General Secretaries, the Treasurers and nine other members which shall perform such functions as may be delegated to it from time to time by the All-India Congress Committee.

ARTICLE XXV.—*Meetings of the All-India Congress Committee*—The All-India Congress Committee shall meet as often as may be necessary for the discharge of its obligations, and every time upon requisition by 15 members thereof, who shall state in their requisition the definite purpose for which they desire a meeting of the All-India Congress Committee.

The Subjects Committee

ARTICLE XXVI.—*Subjects Committee*—The members of the All-India Congress Committee shall constitute the Subjects Committee for the ordinary or the extraordinary session following.

ARTICLE XXVIII.—The SubjectsCommittee shall meet at least two days before the meeting of the Congress in open session. At this meeting, the President-elect shall preside and the outgoing Secretaries shall submit the draft programme of the work for the ensuing session of the Congress, including resolutions recommended by the different Provincial Congress Committees for adoption.

ARTICLE XXIX.—The Subjects Committee shall proceed to discuss the said programme and shall frame resolutions to be submitted to the open session.

ARTICLE XXX.—The Subjects Committee shall also meet from time to time, as the occasion may require, during the pendency of the Congress Session.

Contentious subjects, and Interests of Minorities.—(*a*) No subject shall be passed for discussion by the Subjects Committee or allowed to be discussed at any Congress by the President thereof, to the introduction of which the Hindu or Mahomedan Delegates as a body object by a majority of ¾ths of their number; and if, after the discussion of any subject, which has been admitted for discussion, it shall appear that the Hindu or Mahomedan Delegates, as a body, are by majority of ¾ths of their number, opposed to the resolution which it is proposed to pass thereon, such resolution shall be dropped.

ARTICLE XXXI.—*Rules.*—The All-India Congress Committee shall have the power to frame rules in respect of all matter not covered by the constitution and not inconsistent with its articles.

ARTICLE XXXII.—*Repeal.*—The article and the creed of the constitution now in force are hereby repealed without prejudice to all acts done thereunder.

DRAFT MODEL RULES FOR PROVINCIAL CONGRESS COMMITTEES

The following draft rules were suggested in *Young India*:

1. The old Provincial Congress Committee or the old District Congress Committee of a newly created Province shall from the Provincial Congress Committee under the new Constitution.

2. The existing members who accept the new creed shall forthwith proceed to divide the Province into districts, the existing political districts being retained wherever possible.

3. Each such district shall divide itself into Talukas or Tahsils, the existing divisions being retained as far as possible.

4. Each Taluka shall divide itself into firkas or circles.

5. Each existing District Committee shall enrol, from among the villagers within its jurisdiction, as many members as are eligible under the constitution and these members shall form the electoral roll for the election of delegates to the Congress and representatives for the various district Congress Committees.

6. An alphabetical list of members with the full name and address and occupation of each shall be forwarded to the Provincial Congress Committee every Monday.

7. Each District Committee shall be responsible for the collection of subscription of the members and shall remit half of the proceeds to the Provincial Congress Committee at the same time as the list referred to in rule 6.

8. Each village containing more than five members of a Congress organisation formed for it shall elect its secretary, treasurer, chairman and two other members who shall form the Village Panchayat or Mahajan.

9. Each such Panchayat shall be responsible for the primary education of every child, male or female, residing in the village, for the introduction of spinning wheels in every home, for the organisation of hygiene and sanitation therein, and for carrying out all the other items of the Non-co-operation Resolution of the Congress, in so far as it is applicable to such villlage.

10. It shall be the duty of every District Committee to supervise and regulate the work of village and other organisations within its jurisdiction.

11. Each District Committee shall consist of ten members elected by the members belonging to the different organisations and shall as far as possible contain Mussalmans in proportion to the Mussalman

population of the District and shall contain so far as possible at least one member belonging to the female sex and one belonging to the depressed classes.

12. The representatives of a District Committee so elected shall from among themselves elect their chairman, treasurer, and secretary.

13. The representatives elected to the District Committees shall elect representatives to the Provincial Congress Committees subject to the same provisions as in rule II. The number to be ten more than the number attached for the A. I. C. C.

14. The representatives so elected shall elect from among themselves chairman, secretary, treasurer and four other members who shall conduct the affairs of the province and shall be responsible to the Provincial Committee for the due carrying out of the Congress resolutions from time to time

15. The election of representatives to the District Congress Committees shall take place on the 21st February 1921 and shall be on the basis of the roll of members as on the 15th day of February, at 5 p.m.

16. Elections shall take place at a convenient place to be appointed by each District Congress Committee in an open manner and at a meeting of the electors convened for the purpose, the secretary of the committee shall be the convener and the election officer.

17. The election of representatives of the Provincial Congress Committee shall take place on the 4th March 1921 at the head-quarters of the Province. The Secretary of the outgoing Provincial Congress Committee shall be the convener and the election officer.

18. Electors of the Provincial Congress Committee may register their vote by post.

19 Results of all elections shall be sent to the press for publication by the Secretary.

20. The Secretaries of the Provincial Congress Committees and the District Congress Committee should, so far as possible, be whole-time workers and may if necessary be paid out of the Provincial or District funds.

21. Election of delegates to the Congress shall take place on the 15th November 1921.

22. The Provincial Congress Committee shall assign as far as possible in proportion of the population of each Taluka of delegates to be elected by it. And the elections shall take place in such Taluka at a central place to be selected by the District Committee and shall be supervised by agents affiliated by the District Committees.

23. The result of elections shall be forwarded by the respective District Committee not latter than the 1st December 1921.

24. The Provincial Congress Committee shall meet at least once every month and consider reports from District organizations and adopt measnres for the furtherance of the resolutions passed by the Congress.

25. These rules shall be in force for one year ending 31st December 1921 and till such time as they are recevied by the new Provincial Congress Committee or altered or amended from time to time.

Commenting on the above, Mahatma Gandhi wrote :

For the purpose of faciliating the work of the Provincial Congress Committees, I have ventured to frame the foregoing draft rules which they will naturally alter as they please or reject in toto. They are merely designed to serve for guidance. There is no time to lose if we are to set the whole of the new machinery in motion by the end of June, as we are bound to, under the new constitution. If we can bring into being the new organisation in an orderly and efficient manner and succeed in enrolling hundreds of thousands of men and women as active workers, determind to carry out the Non-co-operation resolution, he who runs may see that we shall have accomplished a peaceful and bloodless revolution within one year. The whole of the scheme of Non-co-operation is based upon the supposition that the British control is independent upon the voluntary association with it of the people. It is true that it is unconscious ; it is true, too true, that is due to fear ; it is true that it is due to a variety of tempting iinducements held out to a few of us. The present movement then is an attempt to show that the moment we cease to give our voluntary association, to fear and be tempted, that moment we become a free people. I hold that this process is not so difficult as many imagine. The current year will show whether my opinion is justified. The thousands who gathered under Congress pandal have shared my belief. It is now for them to translate their belief into action.

AN INSTRUCTIVE TABLE

The following appeared in *Young India* of January 1921:

By the courtesy of the Secretary of the Reception Committee, I am able to give the following table, showing the number of delegates who attended the Congress and their composition :--

NUMBER OF DELEGATES

No.	Name of Province			No. of Delegates under the constitution	Actual arrivals
1	Andhra	...	...	360	383
2	Kerala	...	...	260	33
3	Maharashtra	...	...	192	263
4	Karnataka	...	...	320	304
5	Gujarat	..	...	185	185
6	Bombay	..	...	18	17
7	Burma	...	...	100	56
8	Punjab and N.W.F.		...	540	518
9	Sindh	...	...	71	63
10	Delhi	...	...	100	92
11	Rajputana	...	...	400	399
12	Utkal	...	...	300	108
13	C. P. (Marathi)	...	...	50	44
14	Assam	...	...	63	17
15	Berar	...	...	61	58
16	Madras	...	...	410	162
17	Bengal	...	...	986	373
18	United Provinces	...	...	960	888
19	C P. (Hindusthani)		...	209	205
20	Bihar	...	...	588	558
				6,173	4,726

ANALYSIS OF THE ATTENDANCE

No.	Ladies	Musal.	Parsis	Sikhs	Autyajas	The rest
1	8	10	...	...	...	365
2	...	1	...	...	...	32
3	1	9	...	...	...	253
4	9	29	...	..	...	266
5	11	22	5	...	2	145
6	3	2	...	...	...	15
7		2	...	...	...	51
8	17	67	...	54	...	380
9	1	11	...	...	...	61

No.	Ladies	Musal.	Parsis	Sikhs	Antyajas	The rest
10	7	13	...	4	...	68
1	11	13	...	..	...	375
12	...	3	...	...	...	105
13	1	5	...	...	...	38
14	...	2	...	...	...	15
15	2	5	...	...	...	5
16	2	13	...	...	...	147
17	10	36	..	4	...	323
18	10	114	...	3		761
19	6	29	...	...	..	170
21	7	83	...	...	...	468
	106	469	5	65	2	4079

It will be noticed that out of the total permissible (6,175) as many as 4,726 attended the Congress. Hitherto the number has been swelled by local delegates who could under the old constitution become delegates for the asking by simply paying Rs. 10. This time not even Pandit Malaviyaji could be regarded as a delegate because he was not elected. The actual attendance of 4,726 was therefore a fine record. That the United Provinces and Bengal, in spite of so many arrests, could have sent 888 and 373 respectively, and the far off Assam should have sent 17 and Utkal 108, shows the keen interest that is being taken in the National Assembly. No less remarkable is the attendance of 106 lady delegates representing almost all the provinces. The attendance of 65 Sikhs delegates must also be regarded as altogether remarkable. Hardly few Sikhs attended two years ago. But not that community is everywhere pushing itself forward in all national movements. The number of 469 Mussalman delegates is a good number, but we must not be satisfied till we have got the full quota which must be more than 1200. I am sure that there were more than 2 'untouchable' delegates. I cannot imagine the Punjab and the Andhra provinces not sending any such delegates. The presence of 5 Parsi delegates is of course beyond their numerical proportion which is 2. The Parsis, as I have so often remarked, have in proportion to their numbers occupied the foremost place whether in point of sacrifice, attendance, ability or generosity. I know as a matter of fact that there were at least two Christians. And of course, if Messrs. Stokes and George Joseph had been free, they would have attended. But it is up to the Hindus and the Mussalmans to go out of their way to induce a more general interest in the movement on the part of the Christian community.

THE RULES AND REGULATIONS OF SATYAGRAH ASHRAM

OBJECT

The object of this home is to learn how to serve the motherland and to serve it.

DIVISIONS

This home is divided into three classes :—Managers, Candidates and Students.

(1) MANAGERS

Managers believe that, in order to learn how to serve the country, the following observances should be enforced in their own lives, and they have been doing so for some time.

I. THE VOW OF TRUTH

It is not enough that one ordinarily does not resort to untruth : one ought to know that no deception may be practised even for the good of the country, that Truth may require opposition to one's parents and elders. Consider the example of Prahlad.

2. THE VOW OF AHIMSA (NON-KILLING)

It is not enough not to take the life of any living being. The follower of this Vow many not hurt even those whom he believes to be unjust : he may not be angry with them, he must love them : thus he would oppose the tyranny whether of parents, Governments or others but will never hurt the tyrant. The follower of Truth and Ahimsa will conquer the tyrant by love, he will not carry out the tyrant's will but he will suffer punishment even unto death for disobeying his will until the tyrant himself is conquered.

3. THE VOW OF CELIBACY

It is well nigh impossible to observe the foregoing two Vows unless celibacy is also observed: for this vow it is not enough that one does not look upon another woman with a lustful eye, he has so to control his animal passions that they will not be moved even in thought : if he is married, he will not have a carnal mind regarding his wife but considering her as his life-long friend, will establish with her the relationship of perfect purity.

4. Control of the Palate

Until one has overcome the pleasures of the palate, it is difficult to observe the foregoing Vows, more especially that of celibacy. Control of the Palate is therefore treated as a separate observance. One desirous of serving the country will believe that eating is necessary only for sustaining the body, he will, therefore, daily regulate and purify his diet and will either gradually or immediately in accordance with his ability leave off such foods as may tend to stimulate animal passions or are otherwise unnecessary.

5. The Vow of Non-stealing

It is not enough not to steal what is commonly considered as other men's property. It is theft if we use articles which we do not really need. Nature provides from day to day just enough and no more for our daily needs.

6. The Vow of Non-possession

It is not enough not to possess and keep much, but it is necessary not to keep anything which may not be absolutely necessary for our bodily wants: thus if one can do without chairs, one should do so. The follower of this vow will, therefore, by constantly thinking thereover simplify his life.

Subsidiary Observances

Two observances are reduced from the foreging.

I. Swadeshi

It is inconsistent with Truth to use articles about which or about whose makers there is a possibility of deception. Therefore, for instance, a votary of Truth will not use articles manufactured in the mills of Manchester, Germany or India, for he does not know that there is no deception about them. Moreover, labourers suffer much in the mills. Use of fire in the mills causes enormous destruction of life besides killing labourers before their time. Foreign goods and goods made by means of complicated machinery are, therefore tabooed to a votary of Ahimsa. Further reflection will show that use of such goods will involve a breach of the vows of non-stealing and non-possession. We wear foreign goods in preference to simple goods made in our own hand looms because custom attributes greater beauty to them. Artificial beautifying of the body is a hindrance to a Brahmachari; he will, therefore, avoid the use of any but the simplest goods. Therefore, the vow of Swadeshi requires the use of simple and simply made clothing to the exclusion of even buttons, foreign cuts, etc., and so will Swadeshi be applied to every department of life.

2. Fearlessness

He who is acted upon by fear can hardly follow Truth or Ahimsa. Managers will, therefore, endeavour to be free from the fear of kings, people, caste, families, thieves, robbers, ferocious animals such as tigers and even death. A truly fearless man will defend himself against others by truth-force or soul-force.

Vernaculars

It is the belief of the managers that no nation can make real progress by abandoning its own languages; they will, therefore, train themselves through the medium of their respective vernacular and as they desire to be on terms of intimacy with their brethren from all parts of India, they will learn the chief Indian language, they will learn that also.

Hand Labour

Managers believe that bodily labour is a duty imposed by nature upon mankind. We may, therefore, resort to bodily labour alone for our sustenance and use our mental and spiritual powers for the common good only, and as the largest percentage in the world lives upon agriculture, managers will devote some part of their time to working on the land: and when such is not possible, perform some other bodily labour.

Hand Looms

Managers believe that one of the chief causes of poverty in the land is the virtual disappearance of cotton-spinning wheels and hand looms. They will, therefore, make a great effort to revive this industry by working upon hand looms themselves.

Politics

Politics, economic progress, etc., are not considered to be independent branches of learning but that they are all rooted in religion.

An effort will, therefore, be made to learn Politics, Economics, Social Reform, etc., in a religious spirit, and work in connection with these matters will be taken up by the managers with energy and devotion.

CANDIDATES

Those who are desirous of following out the foregoing programme but they are not able immediately to take the necessary vows may be admitted as candidates. It is obligatory upon them to conform to the observances referred to above, though they do not take the vows, whilst they are in the Ashram and they will occupy the status of managers, when they are able to take the necessary vows.

(3) STUDENTS

1. Any children whether boys or girls from four years and upwards may be admitted.

2. Parents will have to surrender all control over their children.

3. Children may not be permitted to visit their parents until the whole course of study is finished.

4. Students will be taught to observe all the vows observable by the managers.

5. They will be taught principles of religion, agriculture, hand loom weaving and literature.

6. Literary knowledge will be imparted through the respective vernaculars of the students and will include History, Geography. Mathematics, Economics, etc., learning of Sanskrit, Hindi and at least one Dravidian Vernacular is obligatory.

7. English will be taught as a second language.

8. They will be taught Urdu, Bengali, Tamil, Telugu and Devanagiri characters.

9. Managers believe that the whole course will be completed in ten years. Upon reaching the age of majority, students will be given the option of taking the vows referred to in section I or retire from the Ashram, if its programme has not commended itself to them.

10. This option they will exercise when no longer they will require the assistance of their parents or other guardians.

11. Every endeavour will be made to teach the students from the very beginning not to have the fear, "what shall I do for my maintenance if and when I become an independent man."

12. Grown up persons also may be admitted as students.

13. As a rule the simplest and the same style of clothing will by worn by all.

14. Food will be simple. Chillies will be excluded altogether and no condiments will be used generally except salt, pepper and turmeric Milk and its products being a hindrance to a celebate life and milk being often a cause of tuberculosis, and having the same stimulating qualities as meat will be most sparingly used if at all. Food will be served thrice. In it dried and fresh fruits will be liberally used. All in the Ashram will be taught principles of Hygiene.

15. There will be no vacation in this Ashram and no holidays as a rule, but during 1½ days per week the ordinary routine will be altered and students will have leisure to attend to their private personal work.

16. During 3 months in the year those whose health permits will be enabled to travel mostly on foot in the different parts of India.

17. No fees will be charged either against students or candidates, but parents or members themselves will be expected to contribute as much as they can towards the expenses of the Ashram.

MISCELLANEOUS

The management will be controlled solely by the managers. The chief manager will control all admissions. The expenses of conducting the Ashram are being met from moneys already received by the chief manager and being received from friends who are more or less believers in this Ashram. The Ashram is situated in a house on the banks of the Sabarmati, Ahmedabad. It is expected that in a few months about 100 acres of ground will be acquired for locating the Ashram thereon.

Visitors are requested during their stay at the Ashram to observe as nearly as possible the rules of the Ashram. Every endeavour will be made to make them comfortable; but they will confer upon the management a favour if they will bring with them their bedding and eating utensils. Those parents who intend sending their children to the Ashram are advised to visit the Ashram. No children will be admitted without being thoroughly examined as to their mental and moral condition.

The B. N. Press, Printers, Madras.

[G]

The following are the three articles published in "Young India" which formed the subject matter of the charge against Mahatma Gandhi and Mr. Banker:—

19th September 1921

TAMPERING WITH LOYALTY

His Excellency the Governor of Bombay had warned the public sometime ago, that he 'meant business', that he was not going to tolerate the speeches that were being made. In his note on the Ali Brothers and others he has made clear his meaning. The Ali Brothers are to be charged with having tampered with the loyalty of the sepoy and with having uttered sedition. I must confess that I was not prepared for the revelation of such hopeless ignorance on the part of the Governor of Bombay. It is evident that he has not followed the course of Indian History during the past twelve months. He evidently does not know that the National Congress began to tamper with the loyalty of the sepoy in september last year, that the Central Khilafat Committee began it earlier still, for I must be permitted to take the credit or the odium of suggesting that India had a right openly to tell the sepoy and everyone who served the Government in any capacity whatsoever, that he participated in the wrongs done by the Government. The Conference at Karachi merely repeated the Congress declaration in terms of Islam, but speaking for Hinduism and speaking for nationalism I have no hesitation in saying that it is sinful for anyone, either as soldier or civilian, to serve this Government which has proved treacherous to the Mussalmans of India and which had been guilty of the inhumanities of the Punjab. I have said this from many a platform in the presence of sepoys. And if I have not asked individual sepoys to come out, it has not been due to want of will but of ability to support them. I have not hesitated to tell the sepoy that, if he could leave the service and support himself without the Congress or the Khilafat aid, he should leave at once. And I promise that, as soon as the spinning wheel finds an abiding place in every home and Indians begin to feel that weaving gives anybody any day an honourable livelihood, I shall not hesitate, at the peril of being shot, to ask the Indian sepoy individually to leave his service and become a weaver. For, has not the sepoy been used to hold India under subjection, has he not been used to murder innocent people at Jallianwala Bagh, has he not been used to drive away innocent men, women and children during that dreadful night at Chandpur, has he not been used to subjugate the proud Arab of Mesopotamia, has he not been utilised to crush the Egyptians? How can any Indian having a spark of humanity in him and any Mussalman having any pride in his religion feel otherwise than as the Ali Brothers have done? The sepoy has been used more often as a hired assassin than as a soldier defending the liberty or the honour of the weak and the helpless. The Governor has pandered to the basest in us by telling us what would have happened in Malabar but for the British soldier or sepoy. venture to inform His Excellency that Malabar Hindus would have fared better without the British bayonets, that Hindus and Mussalmans would have jointly appeased the Moplas, that possibly there being no Khilafat question there would have been no Moplah riot at all, that at the worst supposing that Mussalmans had common cause with the Moplas, Hinduism would have relied upon its creed of non-violence and turned every Mussalman into a friend, or Hindu valour would have been tested and tried. The Governor of Bombay has done a disservice to himself and his cause (whatever it might be) by fomenting Hindu-Mussalman disunion, and has insulted the Hindu as, by letting them infer from his note, that Hindus are helpless creatures unable to die for or defend their hearth, home or religion. If however the Governor is right in his assumptions, the sooner the Hindus die out the better for humanity. But let me remind His Excellency that he has pronounced the greatest condemnation upon British rule, in that it finds Indians to-day devoid of enough manliness to defend themselves against looters, whether they are Mopla, Mussalmans or infuriated Hindus of Arrah.

His Excellency's reference to the sedition of Ali Brothers is only less pardonable than his reference to the tampering. For he must know that sedition has become the creed of the Congress. Every Non-co-operator is pledged to preach disaffection towards the Government established by law. Non-co-operation, though a religious and strictly moral movement, deliberately aims at the overthrow of the Government, and it is therefore legally seditious in terms of the Indian Penal Code. But this is no new discovery. Lord Chelmsford knew it. Lord Reading knows it. It is unthinkable that the Governor of Bombay does not know it. It was common cause that so long as the movement remained non-violent nothing would be done to interfere with it.

But it may be urged that the Government has a right to change its policy when it finds that the movement is really threatening its very existence as a system. I do not deny its right. I object to the Governor's note, because it is so worded as to let the unknowing public think that tampering with the loyalty of the sepoy and sedition were fresh crimes committed by the Ali Brothers and brought for the first time to His Excellency's notice.

However, the duty of the Congress and Khilafat workers is clear. We ask for no quarter; we expect none from the Government. We did not solicit the promise of immunity from prison so long as we remained non-violent. We may not now complain, if we are imprisoned for sedition. Therefore our self-respect and our pledge require us to remain calm, unperturbed and non-violent. We have our appointed course to follow. We must reiterate from a thousand platforms the formula of the Ali Brothers regarding the sepoys, and we must spread disaffection openly and systematically till it pleases the Government to arrest us. And this we do, not by way of angry retaliation, but because it is our *Dharma.* We must wear *Khadi* even as the Brothers have worn it, and spread the Gospel of Swadeshi. The Mussalmans must collect for Smyrna Relief and the Angora Government. We must spread like the Ali Brothers the Gospel of Hindu-Muslim Unity and of non-violence for the purpose of attaining Swaraj and the redress of the Khilafat and the Punjab wrongs.

We have almost reached the crisis. It is well with a patient who survives a crisis. If on the one hand we remain firm as a rock in the presence of danger, and on the other observe the greatest self-restraint, we shall certainly attain our end this very year. —M.K.G.

15th December 1921

A PUZZLE AND ITS SOLUTION

Lord Reading is puzzled and perplexed. Speaking in reply to the addresses from the British Indian Association and the Bengal National Chamber of Commerce at Calcutta, His Excellency said: "I confess that when I contemplate the activities of a section of the community, I find myself still, notwithstanding persistent study ever since I have been in India, puzzled and perplexed. I ask myself what purpose is served by flagrant breaches of the law for the purpose of challenging the Government in order to compel arrest?" The answer was partly given by Pandit Motilal Nehru when he said on being arrested that he was being taken to the house of freedom. We seek arrest because the so-called freedom is slavery. We are challenging the might of this Government because we consider its activity to be wholly evil. We want to overthrow the Government. We want to *compel* its submission to the people's will. We desire to show that the Government exists to serve the people, not the people the Government. Free life under the Government has become intolerable, for the price exacted for the retention of freedom is unconscionably great. Whether we are one or many, we must refuse to purchase freedom at the cost of our self-respect or our cherished convictions. I have known even little children become unbending when an attempt has been made to cross their declared purpose, be it ever so flimsy in the estimation of their parents.

Lord Reading must clearly understand that the Non-co-operators are at war with the Government. They have declared rebellion against it in as much as it has committed a breach of faith with the Mussalmans, it has humiliated the Punjab and it insists upon imposing its will upon the people and refuses to repair the breach and repent for the wrong done in the Punjab.

There were two ways open to the people, the way of armed rebellion and the way of peaceful revolt. Non-co-operators have chosen, some out of weakness, some out of strength, the way of peace, *i. e.*, voluntary suffering.

If the people are behind the sufferers, the Government

must yield or be overthrown. If the people are not with them, they have at least the satisfaction of not having sold their freedom. In an armed conflict the more violent is generally the victor. The way of peace and suffering is the quickest method of cultivating public opinion, and therefore when victory is attained it is for what the world regards as Truth. Bred in the atmosphere of law Courts, Lord Reading finds it difficult to appreciate the peaceful resistance to authority. His Excellency will learn by the time the conflict is over that there is a higher court than courts of justice and that is the court of conscience. It supersedes all other courts.

Lord Reading is welcome to treat all the sufferers as lunatics, who do not know their own interest. He is entitled therefore to put them out of harm's way. It is an arrangement that entirely suits the lunatics and it is an ideal situation if it also suits the Government. He will have cause to complain if having courted imprisonment, Non-co-operators fret and fume or 'whine for favours' as Lalaji puts it. The strength of a Non-co-operator lies in his going to goal uncomplainingly. He loses his case if having courted imprisonment he begins to grumble immediately his courtship is rewarded.

The threats used by His Excellency are unbecoming. This is a fight to the finish. It is a conflict between the reign of violence and of public opinion. Those who are fighting for the latter are determined to submit to any violence rather than surrender their opinion.—M.K.G.

23th February 1922

SHAKING THE MANES

How can there be any compromise whilst the British Lion continues to shake his gory claws in our faces?

Lord Birkenhead reminds us that Britain has lost none of her hard fibre. Mr. Montagu tells us in the plainest language that the British are the most determined nation in the world, who will brook no interference with their purpose. Let me quote the exact words telegraphed by Reuter :—

"If the existence of our Empire were challenged, the discharge of responsibilities of the British Government to India prevented and demands were made in the very mistaken belief that we contemplated retreat from India, then India would not challenge with success the most determined people in the world, who would once again answer the challenge with all the vigour and determination at its command."

Both Lord Birkenhead and Mr. Montagu little know that India is prepared for all the hard fibre that can be transported across the seas and that her challenge was issued in the September of 1920 at Calcutta that India would be satisfied with nothing less than Swaraj and full redress of the Khilafat and the Punjab wrongs. This does involve the existence of the 'Empire, and if the present custodians of the British Empire are not satisfied with its quiet transformation into a true Commonwealth of free nations, each with equal rights and each having the power to secede at will from an honourable and friendly partnership, all the determination and vigour of 'the most determined people in the world' and the 'hard fibre' will have to be spent in India in a vain effort to crush the spirit that has risen and that will neither bend nor break. It is true that we have no 'hard fibre'. The rice-eating puny millions of India seem to have resolved upon achieving their own destiny without any further tutelage and without arms. In the Lokamanya's language it is their 'birthright', and they will have it in spite of the 'hard fibre' and in spite of the vigour and determination with which it may be administered. India cannot and will not answer this insolence with insolence, but if she remains true to her pledge, her prayer to God to be delivered from such a scourge will certainly not go in vain. No empire intoxicated with red wine of power and plunder of weaker races has yet lived long in this world, and this British Empire, which is based upon organised exploitation of physically weaker races of the earth and upon a continuous exhibition of brute force, cannot live if there is a just God ruling the universe. Little do these so-called representatives of the British nation realise that India has already given many of her best men to be dealt with by the British 'hard fibre'. Had Chauri Chaura not interrupted the even course of the national sacrifice, there would have been still greater and more delectable offerings placed before the Lion, but God had willed it otherwise. There is nothing, however, to prevent all those representatives in Downing Street and Whitehall from doing their worst. I am aware that I have written strongly about the insolent threat that has come from across the seas, but it is high time that the British people were made to realise that the fight that was commenced in 1920 is a fight to the finish, whether it lasts one month or one year or many months or many years, and whether the representatives of Britain re-enact all the indescribable orgies of the Mutiny days with redoubled force or whether they do not. I shall only hope and pray that God will give India sufficient humility and sufficient strength to remain non-violent to the end. Submission to the insolent challenges that are cabled out on due occasions is now an utter impossibility.—M.K.G.

[H]

SATYAGRAHA MANIFESTOES

[About March and April 1919, Mahatma Gandhi issued a number of manifestoes, messages and leaflets expounding and popularising the doctrine of Satyagraha. The Satyagraha leaflets particularly are not now available anywhere. We give in this section a collection of these which have been secured with greatest difficulty.]

FIRST STATEMENT TO THE PRESS

Mr. M. K. Gandhi sent the following to the Press under date 2nd March 1919:—

I enclose herewith the Satyagraha pledge regarding the Rowlatt Bills. The step taken is probably the most momentous in the history of India. I give my assurance that it has not been hastily taken. Personally, I have passed many a sleepless night over it. I have endeavoured duly to appreciate Government's position, but I have been unable to find any justification for the extraordinary Bills. I have read the Rowlatt Committee's report. I have gone through its narrative with admiration. Its reading has driven me to conclusions just the opposite of the Committee's. I should conclude from the report that secret violence is confined to isolated and very small parts of India, and to a microscopic body of people. The existence of such men is truly a danger to society. But the passing of the Bills, designed to affect the whole of India and its people and arming the Government with powers out of all proportion to the situation sought to be dealt with, is a greater danger.

The Committee utterly ignore the historical fact that the millions in India are by nature the gentlest on earth.

Now, look at the setting of the Bills. Their introduction is accompanied by certain assurances, given by the Viceroy regarding the Civil Service and the British commercial interests. Many of us are filled with the greatest misgivings about the viceregal utterance. I frankly confess I do not understand its full scope and intention. If it means that the Civil Service and the British commercial interests are to be held superior to those of India and its political and commercial requirements, no Indian can accept the doctrine. It can but end in a fratricidal struggle within the Empire. Reforms may or may not come. The need of the moment is a proper and just understanding upon this vital issue. No tinkering with it will produce real satisfaction. Let the great Civil Service corporation understand that it can remain in India only as its trustee and servant, not in name, but in deed, and let the British commercial house understand that they can remain in India only to supplement her requirements, and not to destroy indigenous art, trade and manufacture, and you have two measures to replace the Rowlatt Bills. They, I promise, will successfully deal with any conspiracy against the State.

Sir George Lowndes* simply added fuel to the fire when he flouted public opinion. He has forgotten his Indian history or he would have known that the Government he represents has, before now, surrendered its own considered opinion to the farce of public opinion.

It will be now easy to see why I consider the Bills to be an unmistakable symptom of a deep seated disease in the governing body. It needs, therefore, to be drasti-

* The then Law Member of the Government of India.

cally treated. Subterranean violence will be the remedy applied by impetuous and hot-headed youths who will have grown impatient of the spirit underlying the Bills and the circumstances attending their introduction. The Bills must intensify the hatred and ill-will against the state, of which the deeds of violence are undoubtedly an evidence. The Indian Covenanters, by their determination to undergo every form of suffering, make an irresistible appeal to the Government, towards which they bear no ill-will, and provide, to the believers in the efficacy of violence as a means of securing redress of grievances, with an infallible remedy and withal a remedy that blesses those that use it and also those against whom it is used. If the covenanters know the use of this remedy, I fear no ill from it. I have no business to doubt their ability. They must ascertain whether the disease is sufficiently great to justify the strong remedy and whether all milder ones have been tried. They have convinced themselves that the disease is serious enough, and that milder measures have utterly failed. The rest lies in the lap of the gods.

THE PLEDGE

Being conscientiously of opinion that the Bills, known as the Indian Criminal Law (Amendment) Bill No. I of 1919, and the Criminal Law (Emergency Powers) Bill No. II of 1919, are unjust, subversive of the principle of liberty and justice, and destructive of the elementary rights of individuals on which the safety of the community as a whole and the state itself is based, we solemnly affirm that, in the event of these Bills becoming law and until they are withdrawn, we shall refuse civilly to obey these laws and such other laws as a Committee to be hereafter appointed may think fit and we further affirm that in this struggle we will faithfully follow truth and refrain from violence to life, person or property.

MESSAGE TO MADRAS

On 30th March 1919, at a meeting at the Madras Triplicane Beach the following message of Mahatma Gandhi who could not attend the meeting, as he had left for Bezwada that day, was read :—

I am sorry that I shall not be with you for this evening's meeting, as I must take the train for Bezwada in order to keep my engagement with our Andhra friends. But before my departure, I would like to reduce to writing my impressions of the tour through the Southern part of the Presidency, which I have just completed, and to answer some criticisms and some doubts that have been offered by friends.

I have visited Tanjore, Trichinopoly, Madura, Tuticorin and Negapatam; and taking the lowest estimate, the people addressed must have been not less than thirty thousand. Those who have a right to give us warnings, to express misgivings and who have just as great a love of the motherland as we claim to have, have feared that however well-meaning we may be, and however anxious we may be to avoid violence, the people who may join the movement under an enthusiastic impulse may not be able to exercise sufficient self-control and may break out into violence, resulting in needless loss of life, and what is more, injury to the national causes. After embarking upon the movement, I began addressing meetings at Delhi. I passed then through Lucknow, Allahabad and Bombay to Madras. My experience of all these meetings shows that the advent of Satyagraha has already altered the spirit of those who attend the Satyagraha meetings. In Lucknow, upon an innocent remark by the Chairman as to the manifesto signed by some of the members of the Imperial Legislative Council disapproving of our movement, the audience cried out "Shame, Shame!" I drew their attention to the fact that Satyagrahis and those who attended Satyagraha meetings should not use such expressions and that the speeches at our meetings ought not to be punctuated with either marks of disapproval or of approval. The audience immediately understood the spirit of my remarks and never afterwards made any demonstration of their opinion. In the towns of this Presidency as elsewhere, whilst it is true that the large crowds have refrained from any noisy demonstration out of regard for my health, they have fully understood the necessity of refraining from it on the higher ground. The leaders in the movement have also fully understood the necessity for self-restraint. These experiences of mine fill me with the greatest hope for the future. I never had any apprehensions of the danger our friends fear; and the various meetings I have described, confirm my optimism. But I would venture further to state that every precaution that is humanly possible is being and will be taken to avert any such danger. It is for that reason that our pledge commits the signatories to the breach of those laws that may be selected for the purpose by a Committee of Satyagrahis; and I am glad that our Sindh friends have understood their pledge and obeyed the prohibition of the Hyderabad Commissioner of Police to hold their inoffensive procession, for it is no part of the present movement to break all the laws of the land, the breach of which is not inconsistent with the pledge. A Satyagrahi is nothing if not instinctively law-abiding, and it is his law-abiding nature which exacts from him implicit obedience of the highest law, i.e., the voice of conscience, which over-rides all other laws. His Civil Disobedience even of certain laws is only seeming disobedience. Every law gives the subject an option, either to obey the primary sanction or the secondary; and I venture to suggest that the Satyagrahi by inviting the secondary sanction obeys the law. He does not act like the ordinary offender who not only commits a breach of the laws of the land whether good or bad, but wishes to avoid the consequences of that breach. It will seem, therefore, that everything that prudence may dictate has been done to avoid any untoward results.

Some friends have said, 'We understand your breach of the Rowlatt legislation, but as a Satyagrahi there is nothing for you in it to break. How can you however break the other laws which you have hitherto obeyed, and which may also be good?' So far as the good laws are concerned, i.e., laws which lay down moral principles, the Satyagrahi may not break them, and their breach is not contemplated, under the pledge. But the other laws are neither good nor bad, moral or immoral. They may be useful, or may even be harmful. These laws one obeys for the supposed good government of the country. Such laws are laws framed for purposes of revenue, or political laws creating statutory offences. These laws enable the Government to continue its power. When, therefore, a Government goes wrong to the extent of hurting the national fibre itself, as does the Rowlatt legislation, it becomes the right of the subject, indeed it is his duty, to withdraw his obedience to such laws, to the extent it may be required to bend the Government to the national will.

A doubt has been expressed during my tour, and by friends who have written to me, as to the validity in terms of Satyagraha of the entrustment of the selection of the laws for breach to a committee. For, it is argued that it amounts to a surrender of one's conscience to others. This doubt betrays a misunderstanding of the pledge. A signatory to the pledge undertakes, so far as he is concerned, to break if necessary all the laws which it would be lawful for a Satyagrahi to break. It is not, however, obligatory on him to break all such laws. He can, therefore, perfectly conscientiously leave the selection of the laws to be broken, to the judgment of those who are experts in the matter and who in their turn are necessarily subject to the limitations imposed by the pledge. The worst that can happen to any signatory is that the selection may not be exhaustive enough for him.

I have been told that I am diverting the attention of the country from the one and only thing that matters, viz., the forthcoming Reforms. In my opinion the Rowlatt legislation, in spite of the amendments which, as the Select Committee very properly says, does not affect its principle, blocks the way to progress, and therefore to the attainment of substantial reforms. To my mind, the first thing needful is to secure a frank and full recognition of the principle that public opinion properly expressed shall be respected by the Government. I am no believer in the doctrine that the same power can at the same time trust and distrust, grant liberty and repress it. I have a right to interpret the coming reforms by the light that the Rowlatt legislation throws upon them; and I make bold to promise that, if we do not gather sufficient force to remove from our path this great obstacle in the shape of the Rowlatt legislation, we shall find the Reforms to be a whited sepulchre.

Yet another objection to answer. Some friends have argued, "Your Satyagraha movement only accentuates the fear we have of the onrush of Bolshevism." The fact, however, is that if anything can possibly prevent this calamity descending upon our country, it is Satyagraha. Bolshevism is the necessary result of modern materialistic civilization. Its insensate worship of matter has given rise to a school which has been brought up to look upon material advancement as the goal, and which has lost all touch with the finer things of life. Self-indulgence is the Bolshevik creed, self-restraint is the Satyagraha creed. If I can but induce the nation to accept Satyagraha, if only as a predominant factor in life, whether social or political, we need have no fear of the Bolshevik propaganda. In asking the nation to accept Satyagraha, I am asking for the introduction in reality of nothing new. I have coined a new word for an ancient law that has hitherto mainly governed our lives, and I do prophesy that, if we disobey the law of the final supremacy of the spirit over matter, of truth and love over brute-forces, in a few years' time we shall have Bolshevism rampant in this India which was once so holy.

DUTY OF SATYAGRAHIS

Mr. Gandhi wrote the following letter to the *Bombay Chronicle* under date 3rd April 1919.

I venture to seek the hospitality of your columns to make a few remarks on the Delhi tragedy. It is alleged against the Delhi people who were assembled at the Delhi Railway Station,

(1) that some of them were trying to coerce the sweetmeat sellers into closing their stalls;

(2) that some of them were forcibly preventing people from boarding tramcars and other vehicles;

(3) that some of them threw brickbats;

(4) that the whole crowd that marched to the station demanded the release of the men who are said to be the coercers and who were for that reason arrested at the instance of the Railway authorities;

(5) that the crowd declined to disperse, when the Magistrate gave the order to disperse.

I have read Sanyasi Swami Shraddanandji's account of the tragedy. I am bound to accept it as true, unless it is authoritatively proved to be otherwise, and his account seems to me to deny allegations 1, 2, and 3. But assuming the truth of all the allegations, it does appear to me that the local authorities in Delhi have made use of a Nasmyth hammer to crush a fly. On their action, however, in firing on the crowd, I shall seek another opportunity of saying more.

My purpose in writing this letter is merely to issue a note of warning to all Satyagrahis. I would, therefore, like to observe that the conduct, described in allegations 1 to 4, if true, would be inconsistent with the Satyagraha pledge. The conduct, described in allegation 5, can be consistent with the pledge, but if the allegation is true, the conduct was premature, because the committee contemplated in the pledge has not decided upon the disobedience of orders that may be issued by Magistrates under the Riot Act. I am anxious to make it as clear as I can that in this movement, no pressure can be put upon people who do not wish to accept our suggestions and advice. The movement being essentially one to secure the greatest freedom for all, Satyagrahis cannot forcibly demand the release of those who might be arrested, whether justly or unjustly. The essence of the pledge is to invite imprisonment. And until the committee decides upon the breach of the Riot Act, it is the duty of Satyagrahis to obey without making the slightest ado magisterial orders to disperse, etc., and thus to demonstrate their law-abiding nature. I hope that next Sunday at Satyagraha meetings, all speeches will be free from passion, anger or resentment. The movement depends for its success entirely upon perfect self-possession, self-restraint, absolute adherence to Truth and an unlimited capacity for self-suffering.

Before closing this letter, I would add that in opposing the Rowlatt legislation, the Satyagrahis are resisting the spirit of terrorism which lies behind it and of which it is a most glaring symptom. The Delhi tragedy imposes an added responsibility upon Satyagrahis of stealing their hearts and going on with their struggle until the Rowlatt legislation is withdrawn.

TO MY COUNTRYMEN

Mr. Mahadev Desai wired as follows to the Press under date 10th April 1919:

Mahatma Gandhi, on his way to Delhi, was at Kosi served with an order not to enter the Punjab, and not to enter Delhi, and restrict himself to Bombay. The officer, serving the order, treated him most politely, assuring him it would be his most painful duty to arrest him if he elected to disobey, but that there would be no ill-will between them. Mr. Gandhi smilingly said, he must elect to disobey, as it was his duty and that the officer ought also to do what was his duty.

In the few minutes that were left to us, he dictated the following message, laying special emphasis in his oral messages to me as in the written message, that none shall resent this arrest or do anything tainted with untruth or violence which were sure to damn the sacred cause.

The message reads :

It is a matter of the highest satisfaction to me, as I hope to you, that I have received an order from the Punjab Government not to enter that province, and another from the Delhi Government not to enter Delhi, while an order of the Government of India served on me immediately later, restricts me to Bombay. I had no hesitation in saying to the officer who served the order on me that I was bound in virtue of my pledge to disregard it which I have done, and I shall presently find myself a free man, my body being taken by them in their custody.

It was galling to me to remain free whilst the Rowlatt legislation disfigured the statute Book.

My arrest makes me free. It now remains for you to do your duty which is clearly stated in the Satyagraha pledge. Follow it and you will find it will be your *Kumadhenu.*

I hope there will be no resentment about my arrest. I have received what I was seeking, either withdrawal of the Rowlatt Legislation or imprisonment. The departure from truth by a hair's breadth or violence committed against anybody, whether Englishmen or Indian, will surely damn the great cause the Satyagrahis are handling.

I hope the Hindu-Muslim unity which seems now to have taken a firm hold of the people will become a reality and I feel convinced that it will only be a reality if the suggestions I have ventured to make in my communication to the press are carried out. The responsibility of the Hindus in the matter is greater than that of the Mahomedans, they being in a minority, and I hope they will discharge their responsibility in a manner worthy of their country.

I have also made certain suggestions regarding the proposal of Swadeshi. Now, I commend them to your serious attention and you will find that as your ideas of Satyagraha become matured, the Hindu-Muslim unity are but parts of Satyagraha.

Finally, it is my firm belief that we shall obtain salvation only through suffering and not by reforms dropping on us from England, no matter how unstintingly they might be granted. The English are a great nation, but the weaker also go to the wall if they come in contact with them. When they are themselves courageous, they have borne untold sufferings and they only respond to courage and sufferings, and partnership with them is only possible after we have developed indomitable courage and the faculty for unlimited suffering. There is a fundamental difference between their civilization and ours. They believe in the doctrine of violence or brute force as the final arbiter. My reading of our civilization is that we are expected to believe in soul force or moral force as the final arbiter, and this is Satyagraha. We are groaning under the sufferings which we would avoid if we could, because we have swerved from the path laid down for us by ancient civilization.

I hope that Hindus, Mohamedans, Sikhs, Parsees, Christians, Jews and all who are born in India or who made India their land of adoption will fully participate in these national observances, and I hope too that women will take therein as full a share as men.

SATYAGRAHA AND DURAGRAHA

Mr. Gandhi returned to Bombay on the 11th April having been prevented from entering the Provinces of Punjab and Delhi. An order was soon after served on him requiring him to confine his activities within the limits of the Bombay Presidency. On arrival, he issued the following message:

I have not been able to understand the cause of so much excitement and disturbance that followed my detention. It is not Satyagraha. It is worse than Duragraha. Those who join Satyagraha demonstrations were bound one and all to refrain at all hazard from violence, not to throw stones or in any way whatever to injure anybody.

But in Bombay we have been throwing stones. We have obstructed tramcars by putting obstacles in the way. This is not Satyagraha. We have demanded the release of about 50 men who had been arrested for deeds of violence. Our duty is chiefly to get ourselves arrested. It is breach of religious duty to endeavour to secure the release of those who have committed deeds of violence. We are not therefore justified on any grounds whatever in demanding the release of those who have been arrested. I have been asked whether a Satyagrahi is responsible for the results that follow from that movement. I have replied that they are. I therefore suggest that if we cannot conduct this movement without the slightest violence from our side the movement might have to be abandoned or it may be necessary to give it a different and still more restricted shape. It may be necessary to go even further. The time may come for me to offer Satyagraha against ourselves. I would not deem it a disgrace that we die. I shall be pained to hear of the death of a Satyagrahi, but I shall consider it to be the proper sacrifice given for the sake of struggle. But if those who are not Satyagrahis, who shall not have joined the movement, who are even against the movement, received any injury at all, every Satyagrahi will be responsible for that sinful injury. My responsibility will be a million times heavier. I have embarked upon the struggle with a due sense of responsibility.

I have just heard that some English gentlemen have been injured. Some may even have died from such injuries. If so, it would be a great blot on Satyagraha. For me, Englishmen too are our brethren. We can have nothing against them, and for me since such as I have described are simply unbearable, but I know how to offer Satyagraha against ourselves. As against ourselves what kind of Satyagraha can I offer? I do not see what penance I can offer, excepting that it is for me to fast and if need be, by so doing, to give up this body and thus prove the truth of Satyagraha. I appeal to you to peacefully disperse and to refrain from acts that may in any way bring disgrace upon the people of Bombay.

RULES OF CONDUCT AT MEETINGS

On 14th April 1919, Mr. Gandhi has issued the following advice to the public:

In order that Satyagraha may have full play and a chance of permeating the masses, in my humble opinion the following instructions should be strictly obeyed:

Some of the items may require change later, the rest are inviolable principles of Satyagraha. No procession, no organised demonstration, no hartal on any account whatsoever without instructions of the Committee.

All police orders to be implicitly obeyed.

No violence, no stone-throwing, no obstructions to tramcars and other traffic, no pressure to be exercised against any one.

At public meetings no clapping hands, no demonstrations of approval or disapproval, no cries of shame, no cheers, perfect stillness, perfect obedience to instructions of volunteers or management.

SUSPENSION OF THE FIRST CIVIL DISOBEDIENCE CAMPAIGN

On 18th April 1919, Mr. Gandhi, who arrived in Bombay that day from Ahmedabad, addressed the following letter to the Secretaries of the Satyagraha Sabha:

'It is not without sorrow that I feel compelled to advice temporary suspension of Civil Disobedience. I give this advice, not because I have less faith in its efficacy, but because I have, if possible, greater faith than before. It is my perception of the law of Satyagraha which impels to suggest suspension. I am sorry that when I embarked upon a mass movement I underrated the forces of evil, and I must now pause and consider how best to meet the situation. But whilst doing so, I wish to say that from a careful examination of the tragedy at Ahmedabad and Viramgam, I am convinced that Satyagraha had nothing to do with the violence of the mob and that many swarmed round the banner of mischief raised by the mob largely because of their affection for Ansuya Ben and myself. Had Government in an unwise manner not prevented me from entering Delhi and so compelled me to disobey their orders, I feel certain that Ahmedabad and Viramgam would have remained free from the horrors of the last week. In other words, Satyagraha has neither been the cause nor the occasion of the upheaval. If anything the presence of Satyagraha has acted as a check, howsoever slight, upon previously existing lawless elements.

As regards the events in the Punjab, it is admitted that they are unconnected with the Satyagraha movement. In the course of the Satyagraha struggle in South Africa several thousand indentured Indians had struck work. This was a Satyagraha strike and therefore, entirely peaceful and voluntary. Whilst the strike was going on, a strike of European miners, railway employees, etc. was declared. Overtures were made to me to make common cause with the European strikers. As a Satyagrahi, I did not require a moment's consideration to decide not to do so. I went further and for fear of our strike being classed with the strike of Europeans, in which methods of violence and the use of arms found prominent place, ours was suspended and Satyagraha from that moment came to be recognized by the Europeans of South Africa as a humble and honest movement and, in the words of General Smuts, a "constitutional movement."

I can do no less at the present critical moment. I would be untrue to Satyagraha if I allowed it, by any action of mine to be used as an occasion for feeding violence, for embittering relations between the English and the Indians. Our Satyagraha must, therefore, now consist in ceaselessly helping the authorities in all the ways available to us as Satyagrahis to restore order and to curb lawlessness. We can turn the tragedies going on before us to good account if we could but succeed in gaining the adherence of the masses to the fundamental principles of Satyagraha. Satyagraha is like a banian tree with innumerable branches. Civil Disobedience is one such branch. Satya (truth) and Ahimsa (non-violence) together make the parent trunk from which all innumerable branches shoot out. We have found, by bitter experience, that whilst in an atmosphere of lawlessness, Civil Disobedience found ready acceptance, Satya (truth) and Ahimsa (non-violence) from which alone Civil Disobedience can worthily spring, have commanded little or no respect. Ours then is a Herculian task, but we may not shirk it. We must fearlessly spread the doctrine of Satya and Ahimsa and then and not till then, shall we be able to undertake mass Satyagraha.

My attitude towards the Rowlatt legislation remains unchanged. Indeed I do feel that the Rowlatt legislation is one of many causes of the present unrest, but in a surcharged atmosphere I must refrain from examining these causes.

The main and only purpose of this letter is to advise all Satyagrahis to temporarily suspend Civil Disobedience, to give Government effective co-operation in restoring order and by preaching and practice to gain adherence to the fundamental principles mentioned above.

MR. HORNIMAN'S DEPORTATION

On 27th April Mr. Gandhi issued the following manifesto on receipt of the news of Mr. Horniman's deportation :

To brothers and sisters,—With great sorrow and equal pleasure I have inform you that Government have to-day removed Mr. Horniman from Bombay and he has been placed on board a steamer bound for England. Mr. Horniman is a very brave and generous Englishman,

He has given us the *mantram, liberty*. He has fearlessly exposed the wrong wherever he has seen it and thus has been an ornament to the race to which he belongs and rendered it a great service. Every Indian knows his services to India. I am sorry for the event because a brave Satyagrahi has been deported while I retain my physical liberty. I am glad because Mr. Horniman has been given the occasion of fulfilling his pledge. The publication of the *Chronicle* will, for the time being, be discontinued because the directors have wisely decided not to accede to the improper demands of Government. In reality, however, the continuance of the *Chronicle* without Mr. Horniman would be like an attempt to sustain a body when the soul has departed. The condition I have described is truly serious. Satyagraha is on the anvil. At the same time this is a fine opportunity for demonstrating its purity and its invincibility. It will rest with Saryagrahis and other inhabitants of India to take advantage of the opportunity. I can fully appreciate the deep wound that will be caused to every Satyagrahi by the separation of a brave comrade. The National cause will certainly feel hurt to find that the one who presented it with a daily draught of liberty is no more in its midst. At a time like this Satyagrahis and others will in my opinion demonstrate their true affection for Mr. Horniman by only remaining perfectly calm. It will be sheer thoughtlessness to break the peace. Modern civilisation challenges the ancient. The Satyagraha now going on is based upon the teachings of the ancient civilisation, and if India accepts Satyagraha, the superiority of the ancient civilisation will be indicated. The world will see modern civilisation in its nakedness and there is no doubt that its votaries will retrace their steps. The following are the practical suggestions I venture to place before you.

There should be no stoppage of business anywhere in Hindustan; there should be no large public meetings of protests, no processions; no violence of any kind whatsoever; every effort should be made to stop any tendency thereto. I ask Satyagrahis and the sympathisers not to lose faith in the efficacy of Satyagraha and firmly to believe that the Satyagraha pledge will be carried out in its entirety.—M. K. G.

SATYAGRAHA LEAFLETS

DISTRIBUTION OF PROHIBITED LITERATURE

The following was issued on 7th April, 1919, on behalf of the Bombay Satyagraha Sabha:

Satyagrahis should receive copies of prohibited literature for distribution. A limited number of copies can be had from the Secretaries of the Satyagraha Sabha. Satyagrahis should, as far as possible, write their names and addresses as sellers so that they may be traced when wanted by the Government for prosecution.

Naturally, there can be no question of secret sale of this literature. At the same time, there should be no forwardness either, in distributing it. It is open to Satyagrahis to form small groups of men and women to whom they may read this class of literature. The object in selecting prohibited literature is not merely to commit a civil breach of the law regarding it, but it is also to supply people with clean literature of a high moral value. It is expected that the Government will confiscate such. Satyagrahis have to be as independent of finance as possible. When, therefore, copies are confiscated, Satyagrahis are requested to make copies of prohibited literature themselves or by securing the assistance of willing friends and to make use of it until it is confiscated by giving readings to the people from it. It is stated that such readings would amount to dissemination of prohibited literature. When whole copies are exhausted by dissemination or confiscation, Satyagrahis may continue Civil Disobedience by writing out and distributing extracts from accessible books.

THE "SATYAGRAHI"

On 7th April 1919, Mr. Gandhi issued as Editor the first number of the "Satyagrahi," an unregistered single sheet newspaper, in contravention of the Press Act. It was issued for sale at one pice per copy.

It thus referred to the risks it underwent: "The editor is liable at any moment to be arrested, and it is impossible to ensure the continuity of publication until India is in a happy position of supplying editors enough to take the place of those who are arrested. It is not our intention to break for all time the laws governing the publication of newspapers. This paper will, therefore, exist so long only as the Rowlatt Legislation is not withdrawn."

The article went on to give the following advice to Satyagrahis: "We are now in a position to expect to be arrested at any moment. It is, therefore, necessary to bear in mind that if any one is arrested, he should, without causing any difficulty, allow himself to be arrested, and, if summoned to appear before a Court, he should do so. No defence should be offered and no pleaders engaged in the matter. If a fine is imposed with the alternative of imprisonment, the imprisonment should be accepted. If only fine is imposed, it ought not to be paid; but his property, if he has any, should be allowed to be sold. There should be no demonstration of grief or otherwise made by the remaining Satyagrahis by reason of the arrest and imprisonment of their comrade. It cannot be too often repeated that we court imprisonment, and we may not complain of it when we actually receive it. When once imprisoned, it is our duty to conform to all prison regulations, as prison reform is no part of our campaign at the present moment. A Satyagrahi may not resort to surreptitious practices. All that the Satyagrahis do can only and must be done openly.

Regarding the civil breach of the law governing the publication of newspapers, the idea is to publish in every Satyagraha centre a written newspaper without registering it. It need not occupy more than one side of half a foolscap. When such a newspaper is edited, it will be found how difficult it is to fill up half a sheet. It is a well known fact that a vast majority of newspapers contain much padding. Further, it cannot be denied that newspaper articles written under the terror of the very strict newspaper law have a double meaning. A Satyagrahi for whom punishments provided by law have lost all terror can give only in an unregistered newspaper his thoughts and opinion unhampered by any other consideration than that of his own conscience. His newspaper, therefore, if otherwise well edited, can become a most powerful vehicle for transmitting pure ideas in a concise manner and there need be no fear of inability to circulate a hand-written newspaper, for it will be the duty of those who may receive the first copies to re-copy till at last the process of multiplication is made to cover if necessary the whole of the masses of India and it must not be forgotton that we have in India the tradition of imparting instruction by oral teaching.

SELF-EXAMINATION

Satyagraha has made unexpectedly rapid progress in the course of one short week. But it is necessary to consider whether the movement is progressing in the right direction or not. Several very regrettable and untoward incidents have occurred.

It has been brought home to Satyagrahis that Satyagraha is not an easy weapon to handle. Satyagrahis have been often asked if they are not responsible for the varied consequences of this struggle. We have always answered this inquiry in the affirmative. Satyagrahis will always follow truth, and will not by thought, word, or deed, hurt anybody. They will carry on the struggle with such self-restraint and discipline as will enable them to acquire firm control over the people whose sympathy and co-operation they desire and have already been successful in winning in such an appreciable degree. The experience of the last week has clearly shown that Satyagrahis are not yet in a position to control the masses. The true spirit of Satyagraha has not yet permeated the people with the result that they are not yet able to express their feelings in a manner worthy of Satyagraha. This undoubtedly casts a slur upon Satyagraha.

All the same, the Satyagrahi will not be discouraged. It is only when the Rowlatt legislation is withdrawn or when he has sacrificed himself at the altar of truth that he will rest. He will learn from his daily experiences during the struggle, educate the people, explain to them in public and in private the secret of Satyagraha. He will make it clear to them what priceless happiness can be found in suffering, in refraining from returning evil for evil, in adhering to truth, in sacrificing himself. He will capture their hearts with love and will show them how to conquer our enemies by love. The path of a Satyagrahi is beset with insurmountable difficulties. But in true Satyagraha there is neither disappointment nor defeat. As truth is all powerful, Satyagraha can never be defeated. India is a vast country and the ancient law of Satyagraha appears new to our countrymen, but this cannot deter us. Satyagrahis will work day and night to educate the people and will show to them that true Satyagraha can be our "Kamadhenu." If he is not heeded, he will plead with the people, will offer Satyagraha even to them, by fasting unto death and so will induce his countrymen to join in the crusade, which must end in victory.—*16th April 1919.*

"TO MY SISTERS AND BROTHERS"

I could not speak to you at length in my address at the Satyagrahashram on Monday last; but I wish to place my thoughts before the public through a few leaflets. Let me first render accounts. I had received till yesterday Rs. 770 towards the Fund suggested by me. I request that there should be no delay with regard to this fund, and that none in Ahmedabad should be found wanting in his duty. This fund has had its origin in the idea of penance, but its public utility is no less than its penitential value. I visited the Civil Hospital yesterday in company with Ben Anasuya and Mr. Krishnalal Desai, and spoke to all the patients there. I see that we shall have to get pecuniary help to the families of the many of the wounded. I learnt on the spot that 22 of the men brought there had died of the wounds. There is no doubt, there have been many more deaths. A clear duty, therefore, lies upon us, as citizens, to find out the families of the deceased and to give them what help we can. I have been asked as to who will be the beneficiaries of these moneys? I am afraid that we could not compensate those, who have sustained loss of property; we can render some little help only to the families of the dead and wounded. These include two or three Englishmen; (now ascertained to be one); our first duty is to render help to their families, since we are responsible for their deaths. We had no excuse whatsoever for killing them. They have been killed simply out of animosity. If we do really repent for what we have done, it is our duty to aid their families. That is the least penance we can do. I have been able to see that most of our brethren, too, who have died, were altogether innocent. I saw amongst the wounded several boys of 10 or 11. Our next duty is to help all these. A man from Viramgam came to me complaining that he had lost two of his brothers. Very likely many more such cases will be forthcoming. If Viramgam also pays its quota to the Fund, we might be able to extend our help to them. If it fails, I am afraid, we shall not be able to render that assistance.

Some of us believe that we can obtain our rights by such acts of terrorisation, violence and arson. Satyagraha, on the contrary, holds that the rights so obtained should be rejected. I admit that, of the two parties using brute force, the one possessing more of it than the other apparently gains its end. My 40 years' experience tells me that objects so attained do not permanently benefit the winner. There may well be two opinions on this point. But there can be no difference of opinion on the fact that, so far as brute force is concerned, we are no match for the Government. Our physical force is as nought before theirs. I would dare say, therefore, that those who advise us to use physical force are sadly mistaken, and we should never listen to their advice. Expediency tells us that there is one and only one recourse for us and that is Satyagraha or Dharmabala (*i.e.* spirit force). Now Dharmabala can spring only from suffering. Oppressing, harrasing, or assaulting others cannot add to our spiritual strength. The events in Ahmedabad would have been impossible, had we but a true sense of Dharma. It is one of our duties to prevent mischief. If the men and women of Ahmedabad could be brave, all mischief would cease. It is obviously a far greater thing to overcome mischief by Spirit Force, than to do so by Brute Force. We have seen that violent outbreaks have not benefited us at all. I have already said that they had nothing to do with my release. The outbreaks commenced on the 10th. The decision to release me in Bombay was arrived at on the 9th. It cannot therefore have been in any way the result of those outbreaks. Moreover, those who have faith in Satyagraha should be the last men to resort to violence to secure my release.

Let us now consider what further loss we have sustained. I reminded you on Monday that the Offices which were burnt down belonged to ourselves. But we have an indirect ownership therein, and the fact that the expenses of rebuilding them may perhaps not fall directly on us may make us indifferent to the mischief done. The loss to our commerce by closing of the Telegraph Office may also fail to affect us. But consider the consequence of burning down the University Examination Pandal. I understand that it was erected by a contractor, it was his property and was worth about Rs. 18,000. Who will compensate the contractor? Can we imagine the soreness of his feelings? Surely the incendiaries must never have thought of making up for the loss. I am informed that there were many ornaments deposited in the District Court Treasury as being matter of dispute in Civil cases and otherwise. Some estimate their value at Rs. 50,000, while others value them at a higher figure still. We know nothing about the owners of these ornaments. They have lost them for good. Government may not compensate them; and even if they do, it will be from our money. The poor innocent people, who have thus lost their ornaments, will not perhaps so much as approach the Government to demand them. Where was the justice of our ferreting out from Rao Bahadur Bulakhidas' house, all the things therein and making a bonfire of them? I have been told the Rao Bahadur's career has been far from good; that he harasses the people. Granting that this is so, may we, therefore, burn the property of such officers? If people were thus to take the law into their own hands, there would be an end to peace and public safety and a perpetual reign of terror would prevail. If any and every person, aggrieved by an officer's conduct, were to be regarded as within his rights to violate the person and property of that officer, no officer would be safe. A country, where such a state of affairs prevails, is not considered to be civilised, and the people there live in constant fear. Consider the hideous barbarity of burning alive the Aval Karkun of Viramgam. What offence had he committed? Or if he had committed any, why had we not the courage to obtain his dismissal? Sergeant Fraser, an innocent Englishman who had sought refuge in an Indian house, was marched out of the house and hacked to pieces. What can India gain out of such a piece of brutality? One direct result we have already had and that is, the bitterness of feeling between the English and ourselves has been augmented, and several innocent lives have been lost. The only result to obtain rights through association and co-operation with such hooligans can be that if such attempts succeed, the rights so obtained could be enjoyed only on conditions imposed by the hooligans. Rights so obtained are not rights at all, they are rather the signs of our enslavement. The events of Ahmedabad and Viramgam are no indication of our heroism; they do not in any way prove our manliness; they have simply disgraced us; our movement has received a set-back; Satyagraha has had to be restricted. In giving you this bare picture, my purpose is to show how thousands of people, who disliked such violence, put up with it as helpless and powerless creatures. It indicates that at this moment, we do not possess the true force of Dharma and Truth. It is therefore that I have said that there is no salvation for India except through Satyagraha. I shall endeavour as best as I can, to explain what this Satyagraha is in later leaflets, which I entreat my sisters and brothers to carefully read and understand and ponder upon and carry out the suggestions made therein.

M. K. G.

CHARACTERISTICS OF MAHATMA GANDHI'S WRITINGS

There are two poems published and being distributed, entitled "Mahatma Gandhino Satyagraha" and "Mahatma Gandhina Udgar." They bear the signature of Labhshanker Harjiwandas Dihorkar. The ideas expressed in these verses are not mine. Some of them are poisonous, calculated to promote ill-will and excite passions. They are, therefore, opposed to Satyagraha. I therefore advise all brothers and sisters not to accept anything as written by me unless it is signed by me. The present times are so critical that one cannot be too cautious about anything lest he might be led astray.

My writings cannot be poisonous, they must be free from anger, for it is my special religious conviction that we cannot truly attain our goal by promoting ill-will against the rulers or any one else. There can be no room for untruth in my writings, because it is my unshakable belief that there is no religion other than truth and because I am capable of rejecting aught obtained at the cost of truth. My writings cannot but be free from hatred towards any individual because it is my firm belief that it is love that sustains the earth. There only is life where there is love. Life without love is death. Love is the reverse of the coin of which the obverse is truth. It is my firm faith and it is my experience of forty years that we can conquer the world by truth and love. I believe that we can remedy the mistakes of our rulers by means of truth and love, and my writings can therefore have no incitement to violence to person or property. It is obviously not possible for me to read everything that is written or printed in my name and I would therefore ask everyone to apply the above-mentioned test to all that purports to be published in my name and I further wish and pray that every one should reject anything that has the slightest trace of untruth, disaffection, hatred, violence and the like. I do not know the author of the poems mentioned above, but should he see this leaflet, I advise him that it is necessary for him before attributing any words or statements to any one to show them to him and obtain his permission to publish them as his. This is the least that prudence and self-restraint demands. M. K. G.

WHAT THEN OUGHT WE TO DO?

It is a good omen for Satyagraha that Bombay has preserved peace in spite of the unendurable separation of Mr. Horniman from us. I hope that it will be preserved whenever our other friends are arrested and even if I am arrested. The Government are entitled to arrest those whom they suspect. Moreover, in our movement we consider it the proper thing to be arrested and imprisoned, when before our conscience we are found guiltless. How can we, therefore, be angry when any Satyagrahi is arrested? We ought to know that the sooner innocent men are arrested the sooner will this struggle end. I have heard some people say that in Satyagraha also the end is achieved by violence. They argue that when Satyagrahis are arrested, people become excited, resort to violence and thus get their demands acceded to. I held this to be a dreadful superstition. The reverse is the truth. By the arrest of a Satyagrahi, violence ensued in Ahmedabad and we have experienced the results of that violence. The people there are cowed down. Gujerat which never had the military in its midst has had an experience of it. It is my firm conviction that the victory of Satyagraha is attainable only by adherence to truth, avoidance of violence and by suffering. My experience in South Africa, Champaran, Kaira and other places fully bear out the truth of my statement. So long as we do not appreciate this truth, we are in no way fitted for Satyagraha. The question arises—"What then ought we to do? Are we to sit with folded hands in spite of Mr. Horniman's deportation?" I reply that the observance of perfect calm is itself a demonstration of our grief over the separation, and of our intense activity along Satyagraha lines, and by maintaining the same calmness of spirit we shall be better able to reach our goal and to welcome back our friend. When Hindustan accustomed in the course of this struggle to rely only upon truth and non-violence, we shall be able to begin Civil Disobedience. Some say that it will take years before India recognises the supremacy of Truth and Non-violence and therefore it must take years to bring this struggle to a successful end. I would content myself with saying that when once the forces of Truth and *Ahimsa* are set in motion, the speed as they move becomes so accelerated that they take no time in permeating millions. For, what is needful is to produce an impression of Truth and Non-Violence upon their hearts and to infect them with faith in the efficacy of these two forces. If the Satyagrahis are true it need not take longer than a month or two to bring about this result.

I venture to tender the following advice in order that, as suggested above, Truth and Non-Violence may permeate the masses with an ever-increasing velocity. Great movements all the world over depend for their success largely upon the mercantile class. Bombay is a great emporium of trade in Hindustan, indeed in the world. With what rapidity will the force of truth move if the merchants of Bombay were to avoid untruth and all the faults flowing from it, even though introduction of truth in their business may mean smaller profits or even loss. What greater honour can we pay to Mr. Horniman than by adopting honesty as our watch-word in our mercantile transactions? The foundations of our success rests in Truth and, if it pervades mercantile affairs, it will be a play-thing to pull down the other citadels of untruth? I feel convinced that it is not difficult for those merchants of Bombay who have regard for Mr. Horniman to act according to the advice tendered by me that, if we can impress the Government with the truth in us and by strictly observing the principle of non-violence assure them of their harmlessness, it may not be necessary for us to resume Civil Disobedience.—

28th April 1919. M. K. G.

BE PATIENT AND HAVE FULL FAITH

Brothers and Sisters,

Friends have been incessantly telling me, a strong feeling prevails that some way ought to be found to give expression to popular feeling in the matter of Mr. Horniman's deportation. The desire is quite natural. But as I have already observed, the fact that we have preserved peace is itself an eloquent demonstration of our feelings. It is my special opinion that such preservation of peace is only possible where Satyagraha is going on. I believe that the authorities have also been amazed at the profound peace prevailing throughout the city. And no wonder. The Government know that popular feeling regarding Mr. Horniman runs high. In order that a demonstration of this feeling may not run in undesirable channels, the Government have made elaborate military dispositions. But it is highly creditable to Bombay that the Military have had to remain idle. It is a worthy achievement for Satyagraha. I have no doubt that if people could thus restrain themselves on all occasions, the nation would occupy a much higher status. No one need assume that we have not been taking or that we shall no longer take measures for getting Mr. Horniman back in our midst. Of all measures the present calmness is the greatest. Yet I suggest that those who are keen on suspension of business may devote a day's profits to some public activity. But the chief thing I am desirous of in this leaflet is the following: The agitation, hitherto, adopted in this country is as different from Satyagraha as the North Pole is from the South. An appreciation of this fact will of itself remove many of our perplexities. We have seen that there is a difference between Satyagraha meetings and others. Satyagraha is based upon Religion. In it only truth, calmness, serenity, patience, fearlessness, etc., should alone be seen. A Satyagraha strike must differ from the others. I have already quoted an occasion when a Satyagraha strike had to be suspended when a different strike was declared. What we expect to attain by acclamations in ordinary movements we often gain by silence, in Satyagraha. The human voice can never reach the distance that is covered by the still small voice of conscience. Instances to show the unique character of Satyagraha can easily be multiplied and we ought not to be surprised to see things not going in the orthodox fashion. And I, therefore, beseech all not to be agitated because they see no outward demonstration over Mr. Horniman's deportation. I ask them to be patient and to have full faith that by going along the path of Satyagraha we shall meet our brother all the sooner for it.—*28th April 1919.*

M. K. G.

OBSERVE SELF-RESTRAINT

Sisters and Brothers,

I have two letters from Mr. Horniman which I expect you must all be anxious to read. The one addressed to me reads :—

My Dear Mahatmaji,

They are taking me away at last. I have been rushed off without notice. This is only to say 'Au revoir' and to ask your blessing. God speed you in your work for the Indian people.

I shall do what I can wherever I am.

Ever Yours affectionately,
(Sd.) B. G. HORNIMAN

That to Mr. Jamnadas is as follows: —

My dear Jamnadas,

I hope whatever happens Bombay will remain quiet.

I don't know whether this letter will reach you, but if it does, give my love to every body. In the meanwhile, I shall work for India wherever I may be.

Ever yours,
(Sd.) B. G. HORNIMAN.

Both these letters were written by him from S. S. "Takada." Further news is that his health is alright, that he is being well looked after and that the officers have treated him with all courtesy. The order of deportation means that Mr. Horniman will be absolutely free on reaching England, that there will be no restriction whatsoever on his liberty, and as he is resolved to work for India wherever he is, it is likely that he will render great service to India while in England. This, however, is but a poor consolation for the people. They would be satisfied only if the order of deportation is withdrawn and we cannot sit still till we find him back in our midst. We know how we can get him back in our midst. The first and the foremost thing is to observe self-restraint and to learn to keep peace. If we break the peace we shall only be delaying Mr. Horniman's return and paining him.—*30th April 1919.*

M. K. G.

SATYAGRAHA AND CIVIL OBEDIENCE

Brothers and Sisters,

Letters continue to pour in containing complaints about the so-called inactivity regarding Mr. Horniman's deportation. Most of these letters are anonymous. One of them states that it does not matter even if violence be the result of our holding large meetings etc. It adds that we shall gain nothing without violence and that without it we shall not be able to bring Mr. Horniman back to India.

It is simple enough to give a reply to the foregoing along the lines of Satyagraha. If violence be the condition of Mr. Horniman's return to India, then Satyagrahis have to be content with separation. But there is absolutely no fear of any such result from non-violence. We can certainly bring about his return by Satyagraha. Indeed we can hasten it by Satyagraha alone—Satyagraha consists at times in Civil Disobedience and other times in civil obedience. It consists at times in declaring *hartal*, or holding large public meetings or arranging processions and other times in refraining from any one or all of these things. Satyagrahis may not do a single thing that would bring about or encourage violence. At the present moment people are in a ferment, they are angry and it is likely that large meetings, processions, *hartals* may increase excitements and even end in violence. Both the people and the Police are liable to err and both may have to suffer for the mistake of either. It is therefore clear that Satyagrahis ought to prevent such untoward results by every means at their disposal. Therein lies their Satyagraha. The nation can only rise higher by reason of the effort to be put forth, the discipline to be undergone and the soul-force to be exerted for the attainment of such an end. When the people have disciplined themselves to remain calm, to curb anger, to handle processions with self-restraint, to bring about *hartals* without threat or violence, when volunteers are so trained that the people listen to and act according to their instructions, we are in a position to hold meetings, declare *hartals* and arrange processions. It is enough to see that the just demands of a people so trained become irresistible. The present activity is directed towards the attainment of that end and I urge all to read this leaflet and those who are able to help, to go to the Satyagraha Sabha offices and have their names registered as helpers.

Now let us for a moment examine, not from the Satyagraha but from the ordinary standpoint, the proposition that we can by violence bring about Mr. Horniman's early return or accomplish our other objects. I believe that what is true and possible in other countries is not necessarily true and possible in Hindustan. India has from times immemorial received a different training. In India one cannot recall a time when the whole people were engaged in the use of brute-force. It is my belief that India deliberately abandoned universal use of brute force. We have noted the results of violence in the Punjab. Ahmedabad is still suffering. We shall hereafter be able to measure the full dreadful effect of violence. One such effect is the suspension of Civil Disobedience. We ought, therefore, to consider as erroneous the belief that by violence we can hasten Mr. Horniman's return or gain other objects.

In one of the letters received by me, it is argued that Satyagrahis have no right to advise others to refrain from demonstrations etc., even if they choose to do so. But we observe at the present moment in Hindustan a vast number of people are desirous of taking part in all Satyagraha activities, other than Civil Disobedience. This state of things causes as much anxiety as pleasure. It throws a tremendous responsibility upon Satyagrahis. One of them is this: if the people are interested in Satyagraha and are desirous of experiencing its wonderful results, Satyagrahis have to so act that the people may become trained to participate in the movement in strict accordance with its principles and its fundamental principle is adherence to truth and non-violence to person or property, and when the people have accepted this principle the whole work will have a demonstration of the efficacy of Satyagraha.—*1st May 1919.*

M. K. G.

WHEN IS SATYAGRAHA GOING TO BE RESUMED?

When is Satyagraha going to be resumed? is the question many have been asking me. There are two answers. One is that Satyagraha has not at all ceased. As long as we practise truth, and ask others to do so, so long Satyagraha can never be said to have ceased. And if all practise truth, and refrain from violence to person and property, we would immediately get what we want. But when all are not prepared to do so, when Satyagrahis are only a handful, then we have to devise other methods deducible from Satyagraha. One such method is *Civil Disobedience.* I have already explained the reason why this Civil Disobedience has been for the time being suspended. As long as we know that there is every likelihood, bordering on certainty, of rioting and violence following Civil Disobedience, so long disobedience of laws cannot be regarded as Civil Disobedience, but it is disobedience that is thoughtless, uncivil, and devoid of truth. Satyagrahis may never commit such disobedience. The resumption of Civil Disobedience can however be hastened by the Satyagrahis completely fulfilling their duty. My confidence in Satyagrahis has led me to assume that we shall be fitted for resuming Civil

Disobedience in about two months *i. e.* if the Rowlatt legislation is not withdrawn in the meantime, we may resume Civil Disobedience by the beginning of July next. In provisionally fixing this period, I am guided by the following considerations: One of them is that we shall have by that time spread our message throughout the country, *viz.*, that during the pendency of Civil Disobedience no one, under cover of Satyagraha, or the pretence of helping it, should resort to rioting or violence. It may be hoped that the people being convinced that the true interest of the country will be served by acting in accordance with the message will preserve peace. And peace thus voluntarily sustained will materially contribute towards India's progress. But it is possible that India may not understand Satyagraha to this extent. In that case there is one more hope of the non-recurrence of violence, though the condition upon which the hope is based is humiliating for us. It is open to the Satyagrahis however to avail of this condition. Indeed it becomes their duty to resume Satyagraha under such conditions. The military dispositions that are now going on will naturally ensure non-recurrence of violence that is so detrimental to the country. The recent outbreaks were all so sudden that the Government were not prepared to cope with them there and then. But the Government arrangements are quite likely to be completed in two months' time and breach of public peace will then be well nigh impossible, and therefore also conscious or unconscious abuse of Satyagraha. Under such a state of things the Satyagrahis may, without any fear of disturbance, commit Civil Disobedience and thereby demonstrate that not violence but Satyagraha alone can help us to secure justice.—*2nd May 1919.*

M. K. G.

DUTY OF SATYAGRAHIS

Brothers and Sisters,

A proper understanding of two things in Satyagraha enables one to solve without effort many doubts. One of them is that a Satyagrahi never does anything out of fear from without. He should fear only God. By bearing this thing in mind we shall clearly see why we have suspended Civil Disobedience, why over Mr. Horniman's deportation we have not declared hartal, not held large meetings and not arranged processions. In so refraining we have not been actuated, if we are true Satyagrahis, by fear, but purely by a sense of duty. The more a Satyagrahi fulfils his duty as such the nearer he brings victory. The other thing to be remembered and which is at the present moment perhaps of greater importance than the first is that a Satyagrahi never desires to reach the goal by harbouring or increasing ill-will or hatred against his opponent. He will look upon him even as a friend and yet ever resist the wrong done by him without bearing malice towards him. By such conduct worthy of a Satyagrahi causes conducing to enmity will decrease and both parties will acknowledge and avoid mistakes. We know the Rowlatt legislation to be altogether bad, but that is no reason for harbouring ill-will against the Government. The harbouring of ill-will in no way enables us the better to assess the evil in that legislation or to advance the movement against it. On the contrary, such ill-will can only damage the movement. For obsessed by it we refuse to understand or weigh the opponents' argument. We thus disable ourselves producing the necessary impression upon the opponent and to that extent retard victory if we do not make it impossible. We are aware that the question regarding Turkey etc., have caused greater hurt to our Mahomedan brethren than has been caused to Hindus, Mahomedans and others by the Rowlatt legislation. But they cannot solve their difficulties by ill-will. These difficulties can only be solved by proper deliberation, by properly framing and publishing their demands and by firm adherence thereto. So doing, they can enlist the help of Hindus, Parsis, Christians: in fact the whole world and thus make their demands irresistible. If we harbour ill-will or anger against the Government on account of the Rowlatt legislation or Islamic or other questions and therefore resort to violence, we shall be powerless even to consolidate Indian opinion. The gulf between the English and ourselves will widen and we shall be no nearer the goal. Victory attained by violence is tantamount to a defeat, for it is momentary. Then there is increase of ill-will between both the parties and each prepares to give battle to the other. There is no such untoward end to Satyagraha. A Satyagrahi, by reason of suffering for his principle, draws towards himself universal sympathy and even melts the heart of the so-called enemy. Had we not erred in Ahmedabad and Viramgaum the history of the movement would have been written differently. There would have been no increase of ill-will between the English and ourselves, no military dispositions such as we see about us and yet our determination to get rid of the Rowlatt legislation would have remained just as firm. The movement against it would have gone much further forward; probably by this time it might have been crowned with success resulting at the same time in a bridging of the gulf between the English and ourselves. It is however never too late to mend: we can retrace our steps. The retracing consists in curbing anger and ill-will against the English and therefore refraining from violence. As a matter of fact, the mistake in passing the Rowlatt legislation is not of the English nation nor of the English in India. It is purely of those in authority. Nations are often ignorant of what is done in their names. The powers that be do not make deliberate mistakes, they act as they think fit. That fact however does not cause the people any the less harm and therefore whilst we harbour no ill-will against those in authority, we spare no pains in taking effective steps for mending the mistake but regarding it only such and no more we refrain from violence and secure its reversal by self-suffering.—*3rd May 1919.*

M. K. G.

SATYAGRAHA IS IMPOSSIBLE SO LONG AS THERE IS ILL-WILL

Brothers and Sisters,

We have seen in our last leaflet that the actions of a Satyagrahi should not be prompted by fear from without but by the voice from within and that a Satyagrahi should not think of attaining his objects by harbouring ill-will towards his opponents but should win him over by his friendliness. I see that many hesitate to accept the second proposition. They argue: 'How can we help being angry with wrong doers? It is against human nature to do otherwise. How can we separate the wrong from the wrong doer? How is it possible to direct our anger against the wrong without directing it against the wrong-doer?' A father, far from getting angry with his son, often expresses his disapproval of wrong action by taking suffering on his own person. Only on such mutual conduct is continuance of friendly relations between father and son possible. These relations cease with the ceasing of such conduct. It is our daily lot to go through these experiences and hence the proverb 'Let quarrels perish.' We can live in peace and be free from our fearful position only if we apply the domestic law to our relations with the Government. The doubt need not be raised whether the domestic law can at all be extended to our relations with the Government and whether the law of love does not for its operation require reciprocity. In Satyagraha both the parties need not be Satyagrahis. Where both the parties are Satyagrahis there is no play for Satyagraha, no opportunity for the test of love. Insistence on truth can come into play only when one party practises untruth or injustice. Only then can love be tested. True friendship is put to the test only when one party disregards the obligation of friendship. We stand to love everything when we are angry against the Government. Mutual distrust and mutual ill-will are thereby augmented. But if we act without in the least being angry with the Government, but also without being cowed down by their armed force, and without submitting to what we believe to be injustice, injustice would of itself be removed and we would easily attain the equality which is our goal. This equality does not depend on our power to answer their brute-force with brute-force, but on our ability to stand our ground without fear of brute-force, and real fearlessness is not possible without love. A clear victory for Satyagraha is impossible so long as there is ill-will. But those who believe themselves to be weak, are incapable of loving. Let then our first act every morning be to make the following resolve for the day: 'I shall not fear anyone on earth. I shall fear only God; I shall not bear ill-will towards anyone. I shall not submit to injustice from any one. I shall conquer untruth by truth and in resisting untruth I shall put up with all suffering'—*4th May 1919.*

M. K. G.

HARTAL

Brothers and Sisters,

Bombay has borne with great calmness the separation of Mr. Horniman. The long-sustained calmness observed by Bombay even under unendurable circumstances has demonstrated its capacity for self-restraint. But the discussions at the meetings of the Satyagraha Sabha and reports of popular discussions show that the minds of the people are by no means appeased. They are desirous of publicly expressing their grief and feelings in some way or other. The desire is and must be irrepressible. The people will never forget what Mr. Horniman has done for them. He has given them a new life, a new hope and there is no doubt that they have remained calm in the hope that an occasion would be provided for them to mark their pure affection for Mr. Horniman. The Satyagraha Sabha last night decided after mature deliberation that next Sunday, 11th instant, should be the day of observance of *hartal,* fasting for 24 hours reckoning from previous evening, and private religious devotion in every home.

The first suggestion *i. e. hartal* is applicable to the City of Bombay. In times of unrest such as we are passing through, it does not seem proper to declare *hartal* in other places. Not to observe it in other places is for the people thereof an act of self-restraint and in the

City of Bombay, too, it is to be confined to independent business men. Those who are employed in public or private offices are in no way to suspend business unless they obtain leave. There should be no pressure exerted upon anybody, no force used against any one with a view to induce suspension. For suspension brought about by force is no suspension, for a mind acted upon by force continues to contemplate the act from which it is restrained by force. We are bound not only not to interfere with a man who wants to open a shop or a *Ghariwalla* who wishes to ply for hire, but to afford him every protection. I hope that both men and women in Bombay and elsewhere who have no religious or medical objection will observe the fast and devote the day to religious contemplation and try to understand the true nature of Satyagraha by recalling the illustrations of Satyagraha from their own scriptures. We shall consider hereafter the efficacy of fasting as an aid to national progress, to the development of national ideals and to the attainment of restraint over our passions such as hunger etc. For the time being it is enough that we observe an absolutely voluntary Satyagraha *hartal* next Sunday in the city of Bombay, we observe a fast everywhere and engage in private religious devotion in a spirit of calmness and love. We shall thereby add to our honour and speed Mr. Horniman's return.—*5th May 1919.*

M. K. G.

HARTAL: ITS RELIGIOUS SPIRIT

Brothers and Sisters,

To declare a *hartal* is no small matter. It requires strong reasons to support it. Let us therefore examine the justification for it. The citizens of Bombay are impatient to give some outward evidence of their deep affection for Mr. Horniman. They can provide it in a striking manner by means of *hartal*. Everybody's feelings will be tested thereby. Moreover, *hartal* is an ancient Indian institution for expressing national sorrow and we can therefore demonstrate through *hartal* our grief over the deportation, and *hartal* is the best method of marking our strong disapproval of the action of the Government. It is a means, more powerful than monster meetings, of expressing national opinion. Thus we serve three purposes by *hartal* and all of them are so great that we do not expose ourselves to the charge of exaggeration in declaring *hartal*.

This much is clear that none of the purposes above-named will be served if suspension of business is brought about through fear of public opprobrium or physical pressure. If suspension were to be brought about by terrorism and if Mr. Horniman came to know it, he could not but be displeased and grieved by the knowledge, and such artificial *hartal* would fail to produce any effect upon the Government. *Hartal* forcibly brought about cannot be considered Satyagrahi *hartal*. In any thing Satyagrahi there should be purity of motive, means and end. I therefore hope that no man or woman who is unwilling to suspend business will in any way be interfered with, but that he or she will be guaranteed protection from any harm whatsoever. *I would far rather wish that people did not suspend business on Sunday in the city of Bombay and that the organisers were exposed to ridicule than that force was used upon a single person in order to make him suspend business.* In order to avoid all risk of commotion in Bombay on Sunday, the idea of holding public meetings has been discountenanced and all have been advised to remain indoors. As all Satyagraha activity should be guided by the religious spirit, I have suggested that we should fast for twenty four hours and devote the day to religious contemplation, and it is to be hoped that all the members of families including children and servants will take part in the religious observance. Hindus may have Bhagwad Gita read to them. It takes four hours to read through it with clear pronunciation and other Hindu religious books might be read in addition or in place of it. The Mahomedans and others may have their own scriptures read to them. It will be a proper way of spending the day to read the stories of great Satyagrahis such as Prahlad, Harishchandra, Mirabai, Imams Hasan and Hoosein, Socrates and others. It will be opportune also to explain to family gatherings Mr. Horniman's title to our affection. The chief thing to be remembered is that we may not fritter away next Sunday in playing cards, *Chowpat,* gambling or in sheer laziness, but that it should be so spent as to make us better men and women for national service. Better placed and well-to-do families will, I hope, invite such of their neighbours as may be poor, solitary or ignorant, to participate in the religious devotion. A brotherly spirit is cultivated not by words but only by deeds.

Mr. Motilal Dahyabhas Zaveri of Kalbadevi Road has just dropped in and informed me that before the news of the declaration of *hartal* next Sunday, he had issued invitations for a wedding party on that day. He also said there were many such parties to be given on the same day. Mr. Motilal was most anxious that he and his friends should take part in the observance. I venture to advise that so far as the religious part of the wedding ceremonial was concerned, it should be gone through without disturbance, but that dinner parties and other rejoicings might be postponed to Monday. His patriotic affection for Mr. Horniman was such that he immediately accepted the advice and I tender it for the acceptance of those who may be similarly situated.—*6th May 1919.*

M. K. G.

HARTAL AND FASTING

Brothers and Sisters,

By *hartal,* fasting and religious devotion on Sunday next the people propose to demonstrate to the Government in terms of Satyagraha that it is not possible for them to bring about true contentment by force of arms. So long as the Rowlatt legislation is not withdrawn, so long as the Government continue to suppress men like Mr. Horniman who carry on innocent agitations against such acts of the Government, not only is true contentment impossible, but discontent must increase. All the world over a true peace depends not upon gunpowder but upon pure justice. When Government perpetrate injustice and fortify it by the use of arms, such acts are a sign of anger and they add injustice to injustice. If people also become angry by reason of such acts on the part of Government, they resort to violence and the result is bad for both, mutual ill-will increases. But whenever people regard particular acts of Government as unjust and express their strong disapproval by self-suffering, Government cannot help granting redress. This is the way of Satyagraha and the people of Bombay will have an opportunity on Sunday next of giving expression in a clean manner to such disapproval.

A *hartal* brought about voluntarily and without

pressure is a powerful means of showing popular disapproval, but fasting is even more so. When people fast in a religious spirit and thus demonstrate their grief before God, it receives a certain response. Hardest hearts are impressed by it. Fasting is regarded by all religions as a great discipline. Those who voluntarily fast become gentle and purified by it. A pure fast is a very powerful prayer. It is no small thing for lakhs of people voluntarily to abstain from food and such a fast is a Satyagrahi fast. It ennobles individuals and nations. In it there should be no intention of exercising undue pressure upon the Government. But we do observe that like so many other good acts this one of fasting too is sometimes abused. In India we often see beggars threatening of fast, fasting, or pretending to fast, until they receive what they ask for. This is *duragrahi* fasting and the person so fasting degrades himself and it will be the proper thing to let such people fast. It is false kindness to give anything under pressure of such fasting. If it were to be otherwise, fasting may be resorted to even for securing unlawful demands. Where it is a question of determining the justice or otherwise of a particular act there is no room for any other force but that of a reason regulated by the voice of conscience. The coming fast is thus in no way to be interpreted as designed to put pressure upon the Government.—*7th May 1919.*

M. K. G.

BOMBAY'S TEST

Brothers and Sisters,

Bombay will be tested on Sunday. To observe *hartal*, fast, religious contemplation are easy enough for sensible people. Bombay will prove her sensibility on Sunday. In England, more especially in Scotland, business is suspended every Sunday for religious reasons. Trains too are running most sparingly. Even in India public offices are closed on Sundays. There would therefore, generally, be no occasion for anxiety over *hartal*. There is just a little anxiety about our *hartal* because of the present unrest and because ours is intended to be an expression of our grief and respect. From the news received from different quarters and from the impression gathered from meetings that have been held to explain the reasons for the Sunday observance, there is every reason to hope that Bombay will do credit to herself and India by observing perfect calm on Sunday.

It is to be wished that in every mosque, church and temple and in every assembly visitors will be told to suspend business and advised to fast, and devote the day in religious contemplation and observe peace.

I have stated in the first leaflet on the *hartal* that employees may only suspend work on receiving permission from their employers. But those who are working in hospitals, or in connection with the sanitation of the town, dock-labourers handling the grain to be despatched to famine areas ought not to suspend work at all. In a Satyagrahi *hartal* we are bound to give the first place to public weal, more especially the requirements of the poor. And when we use the sense of discrimination fully in all our activities, our difficulties will disappear even as the mist before the morning sun.—*9th May 1919.*

M. K. G.

HATRED EVER KILLS—LOVE NEVER DIES

Brothers and Sisters,

My one request to Hindus, Mahomedans, Parsis, Christians and Jews is that by our conduct to-morrow we may demonstrate to the Government our absolutely harmless intention and show that nobody in Bombay wishes to commit a breach of the peace, and further show that Bombay is capable of discharging heavy responsibilities with patient calmness. We should at the same time demonstrate that we are capable of acting in perfect unity and determined to secure a fulfilment of our cherished will. But we do not desire to obtain justice by harbouring ill-will against the Government but by good-will. Hatred ever kills, Love never dies. Such is the vast difference between the two. What is obtained by Love is retained for all time. What is obtained by Hatred proves a burden in reality; for, it increases Hatred. The duty of human being is to diminish Hatred and to promote Love. I pray that Bombay will observe full hartal, fast and pray and do all this in a loving spirit.—*10th May 1919.*

M. K. G.

PEACEFUL HARTAL

Brothers and Sisters,

Bombay covered itself with glory by preserving perfect calm, and the citizens have shown by their peaceful *hartal* they have understood a portion of *Satyagraha.* They have done true honour to Mr. Horniman and demonstrated to Government that they disapprove of his deportation. Bombay has set a worthy example to the whole of India. It is a matter of pride for Bombay from the Satyagraha standpoint, that some shops were open. This fact proved the voluntary character of the *hartal.* Many causes contributed to the success of this remarkable demonstration, but the chief among them was the performance of their duty by volunteers under Mr. Vithaldas Jerajani. They had commenced operations from the commencement of the talk of *hartal*, and we had the results of their efforts yesterday. Our thanks are due also to the police. If aggressive military dispositions had been made, the people would have become excited and the task of preserving peace would have been much more difficult.

A nation enjoying or desiring to enjoy *Swaraj* must possess the following four attributes: —

(1) The police should be the least needed for self-protection and there should be concord between them and the people :—

(2) Jails should be the least patronised;

(3) The hospitals should have few cases; and

(4) The law courts should have the least work.

Where people do violence, commit crimes, and not exercising control over their senses and committing a breach of nature's laws become diseased and engage in perpetual quarrels resulting in law-suits, they are not free but in bondage. We shall learn the first chapter of Swaraj and Liberty when India adopts the example of Bombay as a permanent way of life.—*12th May 1919.*

M. K. G.

[I]

MAHATMAJI'S EARLIER WRITINGS

[On 27th April, 1919 when Mr. B. G. Horniman, Editor of The "Bombay Chronicle," was deported, Mahatma Gandhi was requested to supervise the editing of "Young India" which was then under the control of a Bombay Syndicate. Between this date and the October following when Mahatmaji secured full control and ownership of the journal and removed to Ahmedabad, many contributions from his pen appeared in the journal. Some of these which were typical of his writings in those days are given below.]

14th June 1919

THE BOMBAY MANIFESTO.*

We are grieved to have to criticise the manifesto of loyalty issued by a number of well-known citizens of Bombay. With deference to the signatories, we feel constrained to observe that it is not a document that reflects any credit on Bombay, the first city of India. Our loyalty must be a very indifferent virtue if it requires periodical protestations. Englishmen, for instance, never protest their loyalty. They show it in their deeds. We hold that it should be above suspicion. Every Indian who asks for, agitates for reforms is loyal to the British connection because he seeks not to destroy it, but to alter its nature. He wishes to rise from the status of a serf to that of an equal partner in the Empire—by no means a mean or an unworthy ambition. We believe that the King's representatives will be

* Omitted in this Collection.

better advised if they will not foster the spirit of protesting loyalty. This constant protestation debases both parties—those who desire protestation and those who indulge in it. Action is the only true test. And we submit to all concerned that our atmosphere will be all the purer for being cleared of the cant of loyalty. We remember Lord Milner having once told a Boer deputation that was effusive in its loyal declarations that it would be monstrous if they were not loyal. He asked for deeds. We would appreciate a similar rebuke from a ruler against effusive demonstrations of loyalty which often mean nothing. We venture to suggest to the signatories that thousands of men and women throughout the length and breadth of India who stemmed the tide of violence in April were more truly loyal than they, and yet no declaration of loyalty, is needed of them. They are the silent and most efficient police of the Empire of law and order. But for the Herculean efforts of hundreds of men who worked for peace in Bombay—and we would gladly add the forbearance of the authorities--the tale in Bombay would have been differently told. And yet they are not signatories to the document.

Let us examine the Manifesto. The citizens of Bombay who have signed the document "view with horror and detestation the atrocious deeds of lawlessness recently committed in certain parts of the Presidency and elsewhere in India." Every sane man must share the view. But of what use can its expression be nearly two months after the outburst? It can only be justified on the assumption that the unfortunate disorder represented not a sporadic and unintentional outburst, but deliberate and continuing acts of a body of people bent on mischief directed against the Government. The fact that serious disorder was confined only to the Punjab and certain parts of Gujarat only shows that it was a sudden outburst, due to local causes. Of the causes in Gujarat, we have enough evidence to prove that the outburst was sudden and not deliberately planned. That some evilly disposed persons took advantage of the temper of the mob and organised and directed it, is patent enough. But no academic pronouncement upon it by the citizens of Bombay at the present moment can affect what has passed. Many who took part in the events are probably much more sorry then the signatories for the disorders to which they were unwittingly drawn. Of the Punjab the true causes have yet to be known. Evidence is daily coming in to show that probably the provocation given at the time to the mob was so great that it would form an extenuating circumstance of no mean importance. Any way, the unreserved condemnation of the Punjab disorders at this time of the day is as uncalled for as it is ungracious. And it is not a necessary ingredient in the support tendered to the Government of Bombay, which is what the signatories have set out to do.

We submit further that this one-sided condemnation represents but a partial truth. What was the cause of the sudden fury of people who have rarely, if ever before, been known to have taken part in such organised disorder? Have not Governmental acts and measures contributed to the resentment of the mob that found expression in deplorable lawlessness? We hold that a loyal citizen only half performs his function when he corrects the people and is silent about the mistakes of the rulers. For, the mere putting down of lawlessness, without removing the causes therefor, will be a remedy worse than the disease. It was the duty of the signatories to help the authorities by tracing the causes of the disorders.

The second paragraph of the Manifesto ignores the lessons of History. English history is replete with instances of criminal disobedience, for, armed rebellions are no less resorted to for the purpose of bringing about reforms. Satyagraha being our creed, we would associate ourselves with condemnation of criminal disobedience in every case, for we would fain have India unlearn the lessons of English history and replace criminal by Civil Disobedience. But the illustrious authors of the Manifesto have condemned both civil and criminal disobedience. We wish that the doctrine of Civil Disobedience had been so "sedulously promulgated amongst ignorant people" as to make its promulgation successful. In that case, there would have been no disorders to deplore or condemn. By "binding" themselves "to combat these doctrines as far as possible by every means in our power", the signatories have, we firmly believe, actually, though ever so unknowingly, encouraged criminal disobedience. Disobedience of some sort is implanted in the human breast. An undisciplined man, impatient of what he believes to be wrong, resists it by force of arms, *i. e.*, by criminal disobedience. A disciplined man, knowing himself to be an imperfect being and likely to err, resists wrong by suffering in his own person, *i.e.*, by Civil Disobedience. A reformer, whether political or social, does some time or other resist authority which he ever obeys for the common well-being, never for its own sake.

A part of the last paragraph of the Manifesto is a repetition of the first, and the remainder gives the reason for issuing it which, to say the least, puts His Excellency, Sir George Lloyd, in a bad light before the public. For they say, "we make this declaration in response to the address made to us by His Excellency, Sir George Lloyd in his speech of April 16th last, wherein he appealed to all leading citizens to make clear their determination to uphold the cause of law and order and to trample underfoot the twin Demons of Lawlessness and Disorder." We should be sorry to think that His Excellency could ever have approved of the wording of the Manifesto, as the quotation would lead one to suppose. His Excellency appealed for help whilst the fire had hardly died out. He would be a bad helper who, when hailed to bring a bucketful of water to quench a fire, brought it after even the ashes had been removed. *Then* they could have responded by prompt action in the shape of condemnation and going amongst the people to appease them and to understand their grievances. The response *now* can best be made by suggesting preventive methods such as the removal of known causes of discontent, *e. g.*, the Rowlatt legislation and the Moslem grievance. An additional method would be to suggest the appointment of a committee of enquiry for investigating the other causes of discontent referred to by Mr. Montagu, as also the immediate cause of mob-violence. We regret to say that the authors of the Manifesto have failed either to act promptly, as they might have, on the outbreak of violence, or now to suggest, as they ought to have, preventive methods.

9th July 1919

THE DUTY OF SATYAGRAHIS

The above was the title given by Mr. Gandhi to the address which he delivered before a Nadiad audience on Sunday last. Mr. Gokuldas D. Talati, President of the

Nadiad Municipality, presided. Between two to three thousand people were present. The following is the substance of Mr. Gandhi's speech as edited by himself:—

Mr. Gandhi speaking on the subject said that he had a special claim on the people of Nadiad in particular and the population of Kaira in general, as he had lived for so long in their midst and was surrounded with so much affection from them. His largest experiments were carried on in Kaira. It was no small matter for law-abiding people to suspend the payment of revenue. It was a very serious responsibility he had taken upon his shoulders in advising them to do so. The actual working of that experiment showed that there was no cause for regret. It was acknowledged by officers concerned that this was a most peaceful, orderly and becoming demonstration of their grievance. It was this exemplary and successful act of Civil Disobedience which betrayed him into the miscalculation of April last and, if he then considered his mistake to be as big as the Vindhya Range, now after longer experience he felt that it was a Himalayan miscalculation. Not only, however, was his claim upon the Kaira people based upon the revenue struggle but also upon the recruiting campaign.

Mr. Gandhi further said:—The first was to the people's liking: recruiting by reason of long disuse in the training of arms and of absence of real affection was unattractive and unpleasant, and yet I know that you had begun to respond nobly and I feel confident that had the war been prolonged, Kaira would have quite voluntarily contributed from the middle classes probably not less than 1,000 recruits. I had therefore hoped as I still hope that Kaira would play no mean part in the work of national regeneration and that my service to the motherland will be rendered largely through you or perhaps more correctly speaking, Gujarat. And so as I may have to offer Civil Disobedience at a very early date, I thought I would speak to you to-day about the duty of Satyagrahis. It is hardly possible to understand this duty without a correct appreciation of the meaning of Satyagraha. I have already given its definition, but the mere definition often fails to convey the true meaning. Unfortunately, popular imagination has pictured Satyagraha as purely and simply Civil Disobedience, if not in some cases even Criminal Disobedience. The latter, as you all know, is the very opposite of Satyagraha. The former *i.e.*, Civil Disobedience, is undoubtedly an important branch, but by no means always the main part of Satyagraha. To-day, for instance, on the question of Rowlatt legislation Civil Disobedience has gone into the background. As Satyagraha is being brought into play on a large scale on the political field for the first time, it is in an experimental stage. I am therefore ever making new discoveries. And my error in trying to let Civil Disobedience take the people by storm, appears to me to be Himalayan because of the discovery I have made, namely, that he only is able and attains the right to offer Civil Disobedience who has known how to offer voluntary and deliberate obedience to the laws of the state, in which he is living. It is only after one has voluntarily obeyed such laws a thousand times that an occasion rightly comes to him civilly to disobey certain laws. Nor is it necessary for voluntary obedience that the laws to be obeyed must be good. There are many unjust laws which a good citizen obeys so long as they do not hurt his self-respect or the moral being, and when I look back upon my life, I cannot recall a single occasion when I have obeyed a law whether of Society or the State because of the fear of punishment. I have obeyed bad laws of the Society as well as of the State, believing that it was good for me and the State or the Society to which I belonged to do so, and I feel that having regularly and in a disciplined manner done so, the call for disobedience to a law of Society came when I went to England in 1888, and to a law of the State in South Africa when the Asiatic Registration Act was passed by the Transvaal Government. I have therefore come to the conclusion that Civil Disobedience, if it has to be renewed, shall be offered in the first instance only by me as being the fittest to do so, and the duty of fellow Satyagrahis will be to assimilate for the time being the first essential just mentioned of Civil Disobedience. In the instructions I have drawn up, I have suggested that Civil Disobedience by the others should not be taken up for at least one month after I have been taken charge of by the Government. And then too by one or two chosen Satyagrahis, chosen in the sense above mentioned, and only if it is found that no violence has been offered after my incarceration by the Satyagrahis so-called or others acting in co-operation with them. The next duty then is for the remaining Satyagrahis themselves to observe perfect calm and quiet and to see that others do likewise. You will, therefore, see to it that after I have offered Civil Disobedience, if I do, there is no *hartal,* no public meetings, and no demonstrations of any kind whatsoever so as to give excitement. And I feel sure that if perfect peace is observed after my incarceration, Rowlatt legislation will go, by reason of that very fact. But it is quite likely that the Government may remain perfectly obstinate. In that event, under the conditions I have already mentioned, it will be open to the Satyagrahis to offer further Civil Disobedience and continue to do so till every Satyagrahi has rendered a good account of himself.

For the intervening period, I have drawn up constructive work in the instructions. I have suggested the Swadeshi Movement as an item—Swadeshi in a religious and true spirit without even a suspicion of boycott, Swadeshi which would enable the Viceroy down to the humblest ryot to take part in. At the lowest estimate 80% of the population of India is agricultural. This makes over 24 crores. It is well-known that during half the year this population remains practically idle or has at least many hours at its disposal for useful work. If this population is given an easy substantial and profitable work to do, one of the highest economic problems will have been solved. In my humble opinion, such an occupation is hand-spinning. It can be easily learned by everybody and it is the most perfect way in my opinion of utilising the idle hours of the nation. Swadeshi is mainly a matter of production and manufacture. The more goods we manufacture, more Swadeshi there is in the country. The vows have been framed in order to serve as an incentive to manufacture and production. This work requires a large number of volunteers whose sole qualification needs to be perfect honesty and love of the country. I would like every man and woman in India to devote themselves heart and soul to this work. And I doubt not that, in an incredibly short time, we would have restored to its original vigour the lost art of weaving the finest cloth of the most effective design.

There is one more subject I have to touch upon. Painful as were, in their consequences, the tragic events of the mad mob in Ahmedabad and Viramgam in April last, some of the doings in Kaira were, if possible, still more tragic, if you contemplate what might have happened. I refer to the cutting down of the telegraph wires and the tearing down of the railway. The acts of the mob in Ahmedabad betoken mad frenzy. The acts in Kaira betoken deliberation. They were also done in anger, but even in anger there can be thoughtlessness or thoughtfulness. The Kaira crimes, though far less disastrous in consequences than those of Ahmedabad, were from a Satyagraha standpoint more inexcusable, if there can be any excuse for any crime whatsoever. I understand that those who were responsible for the misdeeds of April, have not at all come forward to boldly confess the crime. It was a pity that Kaira which behaved so nobly during the revenue struggle should have forgotten itself during April, but it is a greater pity that the guilty ones should now try to hide themselves. It is therefore the plain duty of Satyagrahis to make an open confession if any of them is in any shape or form responsible for the crime and to persuade, if they have the knowledge, those who have committed the crimes to make the confession. It is cowardly enough to tear down the railway and thus endanger the lives of soldiers who were proceeding to restore peace and order. It is still more cowardly not to come forward boldly and admit the wrong. A hidden sin is like poison corrupting the whole body. The sooner the poison is thrown off, the better it is for society. And just as a bit of arsenic mixed with milk renders it none the less vitiating for the addition of pure milk, so also do good deeds in a society fail to cover unexpiated sins. I hope that you will strain every nerve to find out those whose mad grief betrayed them into unpardonable crimes and appeal to them to own up like men and thus purify the social, moral and political atmosphere of this district.

[I have considerably abridged the speech, but added one or two sentences to complete or amplify my meaning.—M. K. G.]

23rd July 1919

THE CIVIL RESISTANCE PART OF SATYAGRAHA

The Government of India have given me, through His Excellency the Governor of Bombay, a grave warning that resumption of Civil Disobedience is likely to be attended with serious consequences to the public security. This warning has been enforced by His Excellency the Governor himself at interviews to which I was summoned. In response to this warning and to the urgent desire, publicly expressed by Dewan Bahadur Govindaraghava Iyer, Sir Narayan Chandavarkar and several editors, I have, after deep consideration, decided not to resume Civil Resistance for the time being. I may add that several prominent friends belonging to what is called the Extremist Party have given me the same advice on the sole ground of their fear of recrudescence of violence on the part of those who might not have understood the doctrine of Civil Resistance. When, in common with most other Satyagrahis, I came to the conclusion that time was ripe for the resumption of the Civil Resistance part of Satyagraha, I sent a respectful letter to His Excellency the Viceroy advising him of my intention so to do and urging that Rowlatt Legislation should be withdrawn, that an early declaration be made as to the appointment of a strong and impartial committee to investigate the Punjab disturbances with power to revise the sentences passed, and that Babu Kalinath Roy who was, as could be proved from the record of the case, unjustly convicted, should be released. The Government of India deserve thanks for the decision in Mr. Roy's case. Though it does not do full justice to Mr. Roy, the very material reduction in the sentence is a substantial measure of justice. I have been assured that the Committee of Inquiry, such as I have urged for, is in the process of being appointed. With these indications of good-will, it would be unwise on my part not to listen to the warning given by the Government. Indeed my acceptance of the Government's advice is a further demonstration of the true nature of Civil Resistance. A Civil Resister never seeks to embarrass Government. He often co-operates and does not hesitate civilly to resist where resistance becomes a duty. He attains the goal by creating good-will, believing as he does that unfailing exercise of good-will even in the face of unjust acts of a Government can only result in good-will being ultimately returned by the Government. Further suspension of Civil Resistance is, therefore, nothing but a practical application of Satyagraha.

Yet it is no small matter for me to suspend Civil Resistance even for a day while Rowlatt Legislation continues to disfigure our statute book. The Lahore and Amritsar judgments make suspension still more difficult. Those judgments, read by me with an unbiassed mind, have left an indelible impression that most of the Punjab leaders have been convicted without sufficient proof and that the punishments inflicted on them are inhuman and outrageous. The judgments go to show that they have been convicted for no other reason than that they were connected with stubborn agitation against Rowlatt Legislation. I would, if I had my way, have therefore preferred to court imprisonment to retaining the restricted liberty vouchsafed to me by the Government of India. But a Satyagrahi has to swallow many a bitter pill and the present suspension is one such. I feel that I shall better serve the country and the Government and those Punjabi leaders who, in my opinion, have been so unjustly convicted and so cruelly sentenced, by suspension of Civil Resistance for the time being.

But this suspension, while it lightens my responsibility by reason of the feared out-break of violence, makes it incumbent upon the Government and the eminent public men who have advised suspension to see that the Rowlatt Legislation is removed without delay.

I have been accused of throwing lighted matches. If my occasional Civil Resistance be a lighted match, Rowlatt Legislation and persistence in retaining it on the statute book is a thousand matches scattered throughout India, and the only way to avoid Civil Resistance altogether is to withdraw that legislation. Nothing that the Government have published in justification of that legislation has moved the Indian public from the attitude of opposition to it.

I have thus suspended Civil Resistance to hasten the end of that legislation. But Satyagrahis will pay for its removal by their lives if it cannot be removed by lesser means. The period of suspension is for Satyagrahis an opportunity for further discipline in an enlightened and willing obedience to the laws of the State. The right of Civil Resistance is derived from the duty of obedience voluntarily performed. And Satyagraha consists not merely, or even chiefly, in civilly resisting laws, but mainly in promoting national welfare by strict adherence to Truth. I would respectfully advise fellow-Satyagrahis and seek the co-operation of all great and small in the propagation of pure Swadeshi and promotion of Hindu-Moslem unity. Swadeshi is, I hold, a necessity of national existence. No Englishman or Indian can view with equanimity the huge enforced waste of the labour of twenty crore peasants during half the year. That labour can be quickly and immediately utilised only by restoring to the women their spinning wheels and to the men their handlooms. This means the elimination of the unnatural Lancashire interest and the Japanese menace. The elimination of the unnatural Lancashire interest purifies the British connection and makes the position of equality possible. The elimination of the Japanese menace will avert a national and Imperial disaster. Extension of Japan's hold upon India through her commerce can end only in India's degradation or a bloody war.

The Hindu-Moslem unity is equally a national and Imperial necessity. A voluntary League between Hindus, Mahomedans and Englishmen is a league in my conception infinitely superior to, and purer than, the League of Nations just formed. Permanent union between Hindus and Mahomedans is the preliminary to such Triple Union. That unity can be materially advanced by the Hindus whole-heartedly associating themselves with the Mahomedans in their very just aspirations regarding the Caliphate, the holy Mecca and the other holy places of Islam.

The Swadeshi propaganda and work for Hindu-Moslem unity require powers of organisation, honesty of purpose, integrity in trade, and immense self-sacrifice and self-restraint. It is, therefore, easy enough to perceive that Swadeshi propaganda on the purest lines and promotion of Hindu-Moslim unity cannot but have an indirect, though none the less effective, bearing on the movement for securing withdrawal of Rowlatt Legislation for which the Government can claim no justification—little as they can claim even now—when we give an unexampled demonstration of the qualities named above.—*21st July, 1919.*

M. K. G.

23rd August 1919

SATYAGRAHA—A MORAL REVOLUTION

The following letter from Mr. Gandhi was published in the "Times of India," in reply to an open letter published in the same paper, some days ago, over the signature of "Pennsylvanian." The open letter was not so much a criticism of the doctrine of Civil Resistance, as an appeal to Mr. Gandhi to devote his energies to improve the Society by an active, ceaseless propaganda of social, educational and economic reform, or as the writer put it, by 'evil resistance' and 'civil assistance.'

TO THE EDITOR "THE TIMES OF INDIA"

Sir,—You will perhaps permit me to reply to 'Pennsylvanian's' well-meant advice to me. I am aware that many Englishmen honestly hold the opinion 'Pennsylvanian' does, and I thank him for providing me with an opportunity for removing some of the misunderstanding that exists about Satyagraha.

'Pennsylvanian' has commended to me the example of his illustrious countryman, Abraham Lincoln. I have endeavoured to the best of my ability to translate into my life one of his sayings, namely, "Let us have faith that right makes might, and in that faith let us to the end dare to do our duty as we understand it."

'Pennsylvanian' rightly insists on a "moral revolution." Now, Satyagraha is that and nothing else. Civil Resistance is but a part, though a necessary part, of it.

Its root meaning is "Insistence on truth at all cost." Life-Satyagrahis are under the pledge of absolute adherence to truth, non-violence, poverty and chastity. An institution is at present in existence at which practically the whole of the programme sketched by 'Pennsylvanian' is being carried out. English and American friends have visited it. I invite 'Pennsylvanian' to visit it and report upon it to the public. He will find there that men and women belonging to all station in life are living on terms of perfect equality, that the unlettered receive literary education in so far as the daily toil permits it, and that the lettered members do not hesitate to take up the pickaxe and the shovel. He will find there that, besides agriculture, the inmates are under the obligation to learn the art of spinning and weaving. By exploring the records of its past, he will discover that its members helped with medicine the people of the surrounding villages during the Influenza epidemic, that they helped the famine committee to distribute grain among the poor, that they distributed again for the same agency several thousand rupees against manufacture by the needy weaver and thus added to the production in the country, that through their labour several women who were but the other day earning nothing, are able by spinning cotton during their leisure hours, to earn a few coppers daily. In short, he will find that most of the items in the comprehensive programme sketched by 'Pennsylvanian' are being worked there to the utmost extent of the capacity of the Satyagrahis. This is the silent moral revolution going on in our midst. It suffers by advertisement and it is not without some hesitation that I have placed before the public the constructive work that is being done by Life-Satyagrahis.

Let me add further that the advent of Satyagraha has, to my knowledge, weaned many an anarchist from his blood-thirsty doctrine. He has found that secret societies and methods of secret murder have brought nothing but a military and economic burden on this unhappy land, that it has tightened the coil of the Criminal Investigation Department, and that it has demoralised and wrecked the lives of hundreds of youths who have been led astray by it. Satyagraha has presented the rising generation with a new hope, an open road and an infallible remedy for most ills of life. It has armed that generation with an indestructible and matchless force which any one may wield with impunity. Satyagraha tells the youth of India, self-suffering is the only sure road to salvation,—economic, political and spiritual.

For the most part Satyagraha *is* "evil resistance" and "civil assistance". But sometimes it *has* to be "civil resistance". Here I must call to my assistance another illustrious countryman of 'Pennsylvanian', Henry Thoreau. He asks: "Must the citizen ever for a moment or in the least degree resign his conscience to the legislator?" He answers: "I think that we should be men first and subjects afterwards. It is not desirable to cultivate a respect for the law so much as for the right." I think that the position taken up by Thoreau is unassailable. The only question is that of the remedy to be applied for vindicating the rights of conscience. The remedy in vogue is that of inflicting violence on those who wish to wound your conscience. Thoreau in his immortal essay shows that Civil Disobedience, not violence, is the true remedy. In Civil Disobedience the resister suffers the consequences of disobedience. This was what Daniel did when he disobeyed the law of the

Medes and Persians. That is what John Bunyan did and that is what the raiyats have done in India from times immemorial. It is the law of our being. Violence is the law of the beast in us. Self-suffering, i.e., civil resistance, is the law of the man in us. It is rarely that the occasion for civil resistance arises in a well-ordered state. But when it does, it becomes a duty that cannot be shirked by one who counts his honour, i.e. conscience, above everything. Rowlatt Act is legislation that affects the conscience of thousands of us, and I respectfully suggest that an appeal should be addressed by Englishmen to the Government that they withdraw an act that hurts the self-respect of the nation and that has roused such unanimous opposition, rather than that I should be asked to refrain from civil resistance in respect of it.—*20th August, 1919.*

M. K. G.

13th September 1919

"NAVA JIVAN"

In a leading article Mr. Gandhi gives the *raison d'etre* of "Nava Jivan." We give a substance of the principal part of it.

Though his sense of his own limitations is overwhelming, Mr. Gandhi thinks that he has something to give to India which others do not possess in an equal degree. "With very great effort I have framed certain principles of life and have practised them and the pleasure and happiness I have derived therefrom has not seemed to me to be the privilege of others to enjoy. Many of my friends have borne testimony to this. I propose to lay my principles at the feet of India and to let her share my joy and happiness. One of the media of doing this is a newspaper.

"Satyagraha, to me, is not a mere shibboleth. It is the rule of life. Everything appears to me to be lifeless without truth. I am convinced that untruth will never benefit the country, and even if untruth seem to bring immediate benefit, I firmly believe that truth ought never to be abandoned. I have grasped this truth ever since I learnt to think for myself, and I have been trying to put it into practice for the last 40 years. And still I feel that I have not been uniformly successful in preserving unity in thought, word and deed. But what matters it? Ideals seem to recede from us as we approach them. Manliness lies in accelerating our motion towards them all the more. 'We fall to rise, are baffled to fight better.' It will suffice simply if we never turn our backs.

"I have come across many gems in my search for the life-truth, and I think of placing them before the public by means of 'Nava Jivan.' I have found that it is our first duty to render voluntary obedience to law, but whilst doing that duty I have also seen that when law fosters untruth it becomes a duty to disobey it. How may this be done? We can do so by never swerving from truth and suffering the consequences of our disobedience. That is Civil Disobedience. No rules can tell us how this disobedience may be done and by whom, when and where, nor can they tell us which laws foster untruth. It is only experience that can guide us, and it requires time and knowledge of facts. 'Nava Jivan' will address itself to supplying this last thing.

'Nava Jivan' will try to demonstrate how though we may be fighting with the authorities in matters where we differ from them, we may still co-operate with them in matters where we do not differ.

" But the relations between the rulers and the ruled do not exhaust the application of Satyagraha. Social and Religious reform, Hindu-Moslem Unity and many other allied questions can be solved by this sovereign remedy. All such questions will therefore be discussed in 'Nava Jivan.'

" The agitation against the Rowlatt Legislation is an object-lesson in Satyagraha. 'Nava Jivan' will keep the agitation alive before the people. I have no doubt that the Act will be repealed before its time, because I am confident of the power of truth and the capacity of Satyagrahis.

" I firmly believe that India's economic salvation lies in Swadeshi. Swadeshi is firmly founded on religion and no nation that has forsaken religion has risen. 'Nava Jivan' will therefore carry on a vigorous Swadeshi propaganda.

" I am by birth and action a Gujarati and believe that unless I become one with the people in Gujarat through their, *i.e.*, my mother tongue, I cannot truly serve my country. Gujarat should be my principal and first field of activities and it is through Gujarat and Gujarati that I can serve India. To how many can I teach my message through the medium of English? And the enthusiasm and energetic effort for English is after all misdirected. 'Nava Jivan' will demonstrate that also.

" India lives in the cottages of her peasants. The art of weaving reminds us of the ancient stories of our land. It is hence that I take pride in calling myself farmer and weaver. I want to send 'Nava Jivan' to the cottages of our farmers and weavers and I must approach them in their language. 'Nava Jivan' will deal with the stories of their weal and woe in their own tongue.

In a fear-stricken, indebted and diseased peasantry I see the ruin of India.

"It is my earnest desire that women in every home should read 'Nava Jivan.' Who else but women will protect our religion? If they remain ignorant and stupid, if they know nothing about the condition of their country, what would be in store for the future generation? 'Nava Jivan' will therefore try to keep women alive to their duties and well-informed, and it will also keep men awake to their duties towards women.

"This is a most ambitious programme, but no steady effort in the directions outlined can go in vain. In the present state of the Press law, how can messages be effectively given to illiterate India, someone will ask. That is, however, the question of the pessimist who does not know the great moral that love can break the chains of ignorance. And need love and truth fear the Press Act? 'Nava Jivan' will speak out what it must, without the fear of the Press Act. The manager and the editing staff of the 'Nava Jivan' have pledged themselves to do so."

13th September 1919

SATYAGRAHA

The following is a translation of Mr. Gandhi's article in the Pateti number of the "Sanj Vartman":—

I see so much misapprehension about Satyagraha amongst us as well as Englishmen that though I have said and written much about it, I think it proper to say something even at the risk of repetition.

Satyagraha was a word coined in South Africa to

name a certain movement. First even the Gujarati word for the great movement our countrymen in South Africa were carrying on was 'passive resistance.' Once I happened to address a meeting of Europeans in connection with the movement and on that occasion the European President of the meeting said that there was nothing active in the power of Indians who were voteless and unarmed, to offer passive resistance, which could only be a weapon of the weak. He was my friend. He expressed these views without meaning any insult to us, but I felt humiliated. I was conscious that the nature of the fight that the Indians were offering in South Africa was not the result of their weakness. They had purposely decided on that sort of agitation. I took the next earliest opportunity to correct my friend's views and demonstrated to him that it was beyond the power of weak men to put up a fight of the nature the Indians in South Africa were doing. They were exhibiting a greater courage than that required of a soldier.

Whilst in connection with the same movement I was in England, I saw that the suffragist women were burning buildings and whipping officers, and were calling their own agitation by the name of 'passive resistance,' and people also called it so. In the agitation of the Indians in South Africa there was no room for these violent acts. I thus saw that to let our movement be known by the name of 'passive resistance' was fraught with dangers. I could not find an English word that could correctly express our movement. In the meeting of Europeans above referred to I called our movement one of 'soul force'. But I could not dare to make the word current as expressive of our movement. Some capable Englishmen could see the imperfectness of the word 'passive resistance', but they could not suggest a better word. I now see that 'Civil Resistance' is the word which can correctly express our movement. Only sometime ago I somehow hit upon this word, and so I have now been using that word in English. 'Civil Resistance' expresses much more than is conveyed by the word 'Civil Disobedience,' though it expresses much less than Satyagraha.

I also saw that in South Africa truth and justice were our only weapons, that the force we were putting forth was not brute-force but was soul-force, be it ever so little. This force is not found to be within the power of the brutes and as truth ever contains soul-force, the South African agitation began to be known in our vernaculars by the name of 'Satyagraha.'

That Satyagraha is thus based on purity is no exaggeration. We can now understand that Satyagraha is not merely Civil Disobedience. At times it may be Satyagraha not to offer Civil Disobedience. When it appears to us to be our duty to offer Civil Disobedience, when not to offer it seems to us derogatory to our manliness, and to our soul, then only Civil Disobedience can be Satyagraha.

This Satyagraha can be offered not only against Government, but against family and society. In short, Satyagraha may be used as between a husband and wife, father and son and between friends. We may use this weapon in any sphere of life and to get redress of any grievance. The weapon purifies one who uses it as one against whom it is used. A good use of the weapon can never be undesirable, and it is ever infallible. If Satyagraha is converted into *Duragraha* and thus becomes fruitful of evil results, Satyagraha cannot be blamed.

This sort of Satyagraha consciously or unconsciously

appears to be used mostly in families. That is to say, if a son finds that his father is unjust to him, he does not put up with the injustice and pays the penalty with pleasure, and in the end he succeeds in winning over his callous father and in having justice from him. But a deadening inertia prevents us from carrying Satyagraha beyond the family sphere. And I have therefore thought the use of Satyagraha in the political and social sphere to be a new experiment. Tolstoy in one of his letters drew attention to the fact that this was a new experiment.

There are some who believe that Satyagraha may be used only in the religious sphere. My wide experience points to a contrary conclusion. We may use it in other spheres and spiritualise them and by so doing hasten the victory and are saved many a false thing. I am firmly of opinion that Satyagraha contains the observance of the manifest laws of economics, and therefore I believe Satyagraha to be a practical affair. Satyagraha being, as I have shown above, a new-fangled weapon may take time to be understood and accepted by the people—and things pregnant with results great and good do take time—but when it pervades the land, political and social reforms which to-day take very long time to be achieved will be obtained in comparatively less time, the gulf that separates rulers and the ruled will be bridged over, and trust and love will take the place of distrust and estrangement.

There is only one thing needful for a wide propagation of Satyagraha. If the leaders understand it correctly, and put it before the people, I am sure the people are ready to welcome it. To understand its true beauty, one should have unflinching faith in Truth and Non-violence. Truth does not require to be explained. I do not mean to enter here into a minute explanation of Non-violence. It means in short that we should not be actuated by spite against those from whom we seek to obtain justice, that we should never think of obtaining anything from him by any violence to his person, but by pure civility. If we can trust overselves to be equal to only this much non-violence, the required reforms can be easily achieved.

When the whole nation adopts Satyagraha as an eternal weapon, all our movements will take a new form. We shall be spared much of the hubbub and stump oratory, much of petition-making and passing of resolutions and much of our mean selfishnesses. I see nothing in which lies the social, economic and political advancement of the nation so much as in Satyagraha.

THREE LETTERS TO MAHATMA GANDHI

TOLSTOY ON SATYAGRAHA

The following is a translation of the letter by Count Tolstoy to Mr. M. K. Gandhi, written in 1910 just at a time when Mr. Gandhi's efforts in the famous South African Passive Resistance campaign were about to be crowned with success. The letter shows how fully its writer had understood the position of Governments. He says: "The Governments know where their chief danger lies and they vigilantly guard in this question, not only their interests, but question: "To be or not to be?"

Kotchety-Russia. September 7, 1910.

I received your journal, and was pleased to learn all contained therein concerning the passive resisters. And I felt like telling you all the thoughts which that reading called up in me.

The longer I live and especially now, when I vividly

feel the nearness of death, I want to tell others what I feel so particularly, clearly and what to my mind is of great importance—namely, that which is called passive resistance, but which is in reality nothing else than the teaching of love, uncorrupted by false interpretations. That love—i.e., the striving for the union of human souls and the activity derived from this striving—is the highest and only law of human life, and in the depth of his soul every human being (as we most clearly see in children) feels and knows this; he knows this until he is entangled by the false teachings of the world. This law was proclaimed by all—by the Indian as by the Chinese, Hebrew, Greek and Roman sages of the world. I think this law was most clearly expressed by Christ, who plainly said that "in this only is all the law and the prophets." But besides this, foreseeing the corruption to which this law is and may be subject, he straightway pointed out the danger of its corruption, which is natural to people who live in worldly interests, the danger, namely, which justifies the defence of these interests, by the use of force, or, as he said, "with blows to answer blows, by force to take back things usurped," etc. He knew, as every sensible man must know, that the use of force is incompatible with love as the fundamental law of life, that as soon as violence is permitted, in whichever case it may be, the insufficiency of the law of love is acknowledged, and by this the very law is denied. The whole Christian civilisation, so brilliant outwardly, grew upon this self-evident and strange misunderstanding and contradiction, sometimes conscious, but mostly unconscious.

In reality, as soon as force was admitted into love there was no more, and there could be no love as the law of life, and as there was no law of life, there was no law at all except violence—i.e., the power of the strongest. So lived Christian humanity for nineteen centuries. It is true that in all times people were guided by violence in arranging their lives. The difference between the Christian nations and all other nations is only that in the Christian world the law of love was expressed clearly and definitely, whereas it was so expressed in the religious teaching, and that the people of the Christian world have solemnly accepted this law, whilst at the same time they have permitted violence, and built their lives on violence and that is why the whole life of the Christian peoples is a continuous contradiction between that which they profess and the principles on which they order the lives—a contradiction between love accepted as the law of life and violence which is recognised and praised, acknowledged even as a necessity in different phases of life, such as the power of the rulers, courts and armies. This contradiction always grew with the development of the people of the Christian world, and lately it reached the highest stage. The question now evidently stands thus: either to admit that we do not recognise any religio-moral teaching, and we guide ourselves in arranging our lives only by power of the stronger, or that all our compulsory taxes, court and police establishments, but mainly our armies, must be abolished.

This year, in spring, at a Scripture examination in a Girls' High School at Moscow, the teacher and the bishop present asked the girls questions on the Commandments, and especially on the sixth. After a correct answer the bishop generally put another question, whether murder was always in all cases forbidden by God's law and the unhappy young ladies were forced by previous instruction to answer, "Not always"—that murder was permitted in war and in execution of criminals. Still, when one of those unfortunate young ladies (what I am telling is not an invention, but a fact told me by an eye-witness) after her first answer, was asked the usual question, if killing were always sinful, she agitated and blushing, decisively answered, "Always" and to all the usual sophisms of the bishop, she answered with decided conviction, that killing always was forbidden in the old testament and forbidden by Christ, not only killing, but even every wrong against a brother. Notwithstanding all his grandeur and art of speech, the bishop became silent and the girl remained victorious.

Yes, we can talk in our newspapers of the progress of aviation, of complicated diplomatic relations, of different clubs and conventions, of unions of different kinds, of so-called productions of art, and keep silent about what that young lady said. But it cannot be passed over in silence, because it is felt, more or less dimly, but always felt by every man in the Christian world. Socialism, Communism, Anarchism, Salvation Army, increasing crime, unemployment, the growing insane luxury of the rich and misery of the poor, the alarmingly increasing number of suicides—all these are the signs of that "internal contradiction which must be solved and cannot remain unsolved." And of course solved in the sense of acknowledging the law of love and denying violence. And so your activity in the Transvaal, as it seems to us, at the end of the world, is the most essential work, the most important of all the work now being done in the world, and in which not only the nations of the Christian, but of all the world, will unavoidably take part.

I think that you will be pleased to know that here, in

Russia, this activity is also fast developing in the way of refusals to serve in the Army, the number of which increases from year to year. However insignificant is the number of our people who are passive resisters in Russia, who refuse to serve in the Army, these and the others can boldly say that God is more powerful than man.

In acknowledging Christianity, even in the corrupt form in which it is professed amongst the Christian nations and at the same time in acknowledging the necessity of armies and armament for killing on the greatest scale in wars, there is such a clear clamouring contradiction, that it must sooner or later, possibly very soon, inevitably reveal itself and annihilate either the professing of the Christian religion, which is indispensable in keeping up these forces or the existence of armies and all the violence kept up by them, which is not less necessary for power. This contradiction is felt by all governments, by your British as well as by our Russian Government, and out of a general feeling of self-preservation the persecution by them (as seen in Russia and in the journal sent by you) against such anti-government activity as those above-mentioned, is carried on with more energy than against any other form of opposition. The governments know where their chief danger lies, and they vigilantly guard in this question, not only their interests, but the question: "To be or not to be?

Yours very faithfully
Leo Tolstoy

[Translated from the original Russian by Pauline Padlashuk.—Johannesburg, November 15th 1910. *Indian Opinion.*]

The following letter has been sent to Mr. M. K. Gandhi by (Sir) Rabindranath Tagore and also communicated to the Press :—

Shantiniketan, 12th April 1919

Dear Mahatmaji,

Power in all its forms is irrational, it is like the horse that drags the carriage blindfolded. The moral element in it is only represented in the man who drives the horse. Passive resistance is a force which is not necessarily moral in itself; it can be used against truth as well as for it. The danger inherent in all force grows stronger when it is likely to gain success, for then it becomes temptation.

I know your teaching is to fight against evil by the help of the good. But such a fight is for heroes and not for men, led by impulses of the moment. Evil on one side naturally begets evil on the other, injustice leading to violence and insult to vengefulness. Unfortunately such a force has already been started and either through panic or through wrath. Our authorities have shown us their claws whose sure effect is to drive some of us into the secret path of resentment and others into utter demoralisation.

In this crisis you, as a great leader of men, have stood among us to proclaim your faith in the ideal which you know to be that of India, the ideal which is both against the cowardliness of hidden revenge and the cowed submissiveness of the terror-stricken. You have said, as Lord Buddha has done in his time and for all time to come.

'*Akkedhena jine, kodham asadhum jine*

'Conquer anger by the power of non-anger and evil by the power of good.'

This power of good must prove its truth and strength

by its fearlessness, by its refusal to accept any imposition which depends for its success upon its power to produce frightfulness and is not ashamed to use its machines of destruction to terrorise a people completely disarmed. We must know that moral conquest does not consist in successes, that failure does not deprive it of its dignity and worth. Those who believe in spiritual life know that to stand against wrong which has overwhelming material power behind it is victory itself: it is the victory of the active faith in the ideal in the teeth of evident defeat.

I have always felt, and said accordingly, that the great gift of freedom can never come to a people through charity. We must win it before we can own it. And India's opportunity for winning it will come to her when she can prove that she is morally superior to the people who rule her by their right of conquest. She must willingly accept her penance of suffering, the suffering which is the crown of the great. Armed with her utter faith in goodness, she must stand unabashed before the arrogance that scoffs at the power of spirit.

And you have come to your motherland in the time of her need to remind her of her mission, to lead her in the true path of conquest, to purge her present-day politics of its feebleness which imagines that it has gained its purpose when it struts in the borrowed feathers of diplomatic dishonesty.

This is why I pray most fervently that nothing that tends to weaken our spiritual freedom may intrude into our marching line, that martyrdom for the cause of truth may never degenerate into fanaticism for more verbal forms, descending into the self-deception that hides itself behind sacred names.

With these few words for an introduction, allow me to

offer the following as poet's contribution to your noble work :—

I

Let me hold my head high in this faith that thou art our shelter, that all fear is mean distrust of those.

Fear of man? But what man is there in this world, what king, O King of Kings, who is thy rival, who has hold of me for all time and in all truth?

What power is there in this world to rob me of freedom? For, do not thy arms reach the captive through the dungeon-walls bringing unfettered release to the soul?

And must I cling to this body in fear of death, as a miser to his barren treasure? Has not this spirit of mine the eternal call to the feast of everlasting life?

Let me know that all pain and death are shadows of the moment; that the dark force which sweeps between me and thy truth is but the mist before the sunrise; that thou alone art mine for ever and greater than all pride of strength that dares to make my manhood with its menace.

II

Give me the supreme courage of love, this is my prayer, the courage to speak, to do, to suffer at thy will, to leave all or be left alone.

Give me the supreme faith of love, this is my prayer, the faith of the life in death, of the victory in defeat, of the power hidden in the frailness of beauty, of the dignity of pain that accepts hurt, but disdains to return it.

Very sincerely yours,
(Sd) Rabindranath Tagore.

(Sir) Rabindranath Tagore's eldest brother Babu Dwijendra Nath Tagore who is eighty years old, and who leads the life of a recluse at his peaceful hermitage at Shantiniketan has addressed the following letter to Mahatma Gandhi, supporting his passive resistance movement:—

Shantiniketan, April 11, 1919

My most revered friend Mr. Gandhi,

I wish with all my heart that you will go on unflinchingly with your work of helping our misguided people to overcome evil by good. At times it seems to me that the penance and fastings etc., which you enjoin are not quite the things that are necessary and therefore may be dispensed with. But on the second thought I find that we are not competent to judge the matter aright from our stand-point. You are deriving your inspiration from such a high source that instead of calling in question, the appropriateness of your sayings and doings, we ought to thankfully recognise in them the fatherly call of Providence full of divine wisdom and power.

May the Almighty and All-merciful God be your shield and strength in this awful crisis.

Your affectionate old friend,
Dwijendranath Tagore.

17th May 1919

THE SWADESHI VOW

The idea of Swadeshi was first broached on the 6th of April meeting at Chowpati when thousands of men and some women met together, but the Swadeshi Vow was not taken on that day. It has now been fully threshed out and the way is clear. It is our duty to take Swadeshi Vow; in it lies the prosperity of India. To use foreign articles rejecting those that are manufactured in India is to be untrue to India, it is an unwarranted indulgence. To use foreign articles because we do not like indigenous ones is to be a foreigner. It is obvious that we cannot reject indigenous articles, even as we cannot reject the native air and the native soil because they are inferior to foreign air and soil. Cotton imports amounted to about Rs. 570,000,000 and silk imports to Rs. 4,00,00,000 in the year 1917-18. India has a population of three hundred millions and so it means that we sent out in that year about Rs. 2 per head, with starvation as the result. More than thirty million men in India hardly get more than one meal a day. Such a starvation must have been unknown when every house in India had its spinning wheel and when thousands of people were busy with their handlooms. No wonder that starvation and other ills arise whenever people depart from the path of duty. One of the remedies for these ills is Swadeshi. The Swadeshi Vow of which the text is given at the foot of this article has therefore been proposed and it has been divided into two classes. The first represents purer Swadeshi Vow, but the purest is that under which those taking it restrict themselves to the use of hand-woven clothes made out of hand-spun yarn. The ruin of the handloom industry makes such a vow for the time being impossible. But if those who take the first vow keep the ideal Swadeshi as their goal, we shall ere long be able to obtain sufficient hand-woven cloth.

I have already pointed out the great difference between Swadeshi and Boycott. I for one am sure that boycott cannot benefit India in the least. Resorting to boycott amounts to cutting off the nose to spite the face. Shall we open our door wider for Japan by boycotting British goods in order to rid ourselves of the evil of the Rowlatt Bill? The fact is that Swadeshi has nothing to do with the agitation against the Rowlatt Bills. A great movement like Satyagraha sets the people a-thinking about the duties and it is thus that the idea of the Swadeshi has possessed the people. We shall continue to observe the vow even after the repeal of the Rowlatt legislation and after India becomes an honoured partner in the British Empire. And our vow will then not be the limited Swadeshi Vow to-day, it will be a far wider one as we shall then have been capable of meeting in India itself many of our requirements. We shall appeal to our English brethren also to join us in this Swadeshi Vow.

In order to enable lacs of men and women to take and observe the Swadeshi Vow, commercial honesty will be a "sine qua non." The millowners will have to fix their rates in a patriotic spirit. Merchants, great and small will also likewise have to keep honest dealings. I have no doubt that Swadeshi cannot advance unless thousands of petty shopkeepers from whom the poor millions buy introduce honesty into their dealings. The organisers of Swadeshi have ventured to place before the nation the Swadeshi pledge for its acceptance upon the belief that our merchants possess the patriotic spirit and that for the sake of the country they will be kind to the poor and be truthful towards them.

Those who have foreign clothing seem to hesitate to take the pledge. Though this is natural, it is also painful. We want Swadeshi to produce big results. These cannot be attained without sacrifice. Moreover, it is hoped that the spirit of Swadeshi will bring in that of simplicity, and those who take to simple, though more durable clothing, will be able to recoup themselves for any loss sustained by reason of the giving up of foreign articles.

It is necessary to give the warning that none should lay by a large stock of Swadeshi clothing. There is not enough cloth in Hindustan to enable many of us to have a stock to last four or five years. When there are many Swadeshists, there is no doubt that we will have many Swadeshi shops and that day by day we shall have more cloth woven in India. Those who take the pledge should have faith in the possibility of their being able to buy Swadeshi cloth whenever they need it. As a matter of fact, every one should learn to weave his own cloth and those who cannot should engage their own weavers. So doing they would avoid all cause for deceipt and they would be able to have durable and pure cloth for their use. This is what we used to do in days gone by.

Swadeshi depends upon women adopting it. I hope that thousands of them will give up foreign cloth in their possession and take the Swadeshi pledge. It behoves us to suffer some inconvenience if only by way of penance for our past mistakes. Moreover, it is possible to put foreign cloth to other uses. It can even be sold for despatch out of India. Further the nation has a right to expect its women to cloth their children in Swadeshi garments.—*13th May, 1919.*

M. K. G.

PURE SWADESHI VOW

I solemnly declare that, henceforth, in Hindustan I shall not wear clothing except such as is made in India out of Indian cotton, silk or wool spun in India.

This vow shall be binding on me for life-years.

MIXED SWADESHI VOW

I solemnly declare that, henceforth, in Hindustan I shall not wear any clothing except such as is woven in India whether made out of foreign or Indian yarn, silk and wool.

This vow shall be binding on me for life-years.

Explanation.—The true Swadeshi ideal consists in the use of hand-woven cloth only made out of hand-spun yarn, but it is physically impossible to-day to secure a supply of such cloth for any large number of people. It is expected, however, that true lovers of Swadeshi and real art will not only themselves, even at some inconvenience, wear hand-woven cloth made out of hand-spun yarn, but will also endeavour to set going as many handlooms and spinning wheels as possible.

Note 1.—It should be remembered that this movement has nothing to do with the agitation for securing repeal of Rowlatt legislation. Repeal of that legislation or the granting of other concessions or reforms will make no alteration whatsoever in the Swadeshi vow or the movement for the spread of Swadeshi.

Note 2.—The suggestion for destruction of foreign cloth in the possession of the signatories to the pledge has been totally abandoned lest a mistaken interpretation of the suggestion may lead to the growth or the promotion of ill-will against Europeans, the idea of ill-will being entirely foreign to the originators of the present Swadeshi movement. But the pledge precludes the use of any personal clothing of foreign make that the signatory may possess at the time of taking the vow.

Note 3.—Mahomadans, Parsis, Christians and Jews taking the Swadeshi pledge are not precluded from using and wearing foreign cloths, having a religious significance.

The following are among the signatories to the first vow:—

Mohandas Karamchand Gandhi, Mrs. Kasturibai Gandhi, Mahadeo Haribhai Desai, Mrs. Sarojini Naidu, Jamnadas Dwarkadas, Umar Sobhani, Shankerlal G. Banker, Devji Damoder, Behan Ansuya Sarabhai, Lakhamidas Rawji Tersi, Jamnadas Madhawji Mehta, and Vaikunthray Ambalal Desai.

ECONOMIC SALVATION OF INDIA

(BY M. K. GANDHI)

The following is the text of the Swadeshi vow:—

"With God as my witness, I, solemnly, declare that from to-day I shall confine myself, for my personal requirements, to the use of cloth, manufactured in India from Indian cotton, silk or wool and I shall altogether abstain from using foreign cloth, and I shall destroy all foreign cloth in my possession."

For a proper observance of this pledge, it is really necessary to use only handwoven cloth made out of handspun yarn. Imported yarn, even though spun out of Indian cotton and woven in India, is not Swadeshi cloth. We shall reach perfection only when our cotton is spun in India on indigenous spinning wheels and the yarn so spun is woven on similarly made handlooms. But requirements of the foregoing pledge are met if we all only use cloth woven by means of imported machinery from yarn spun from Indian cotton by means of similar machinery.

I may add that covenanters to the restricted Swadeshi referred to here, will not rest satisfied with Swadeshi clothing only. They will extend the vow to all other things as far as possible.

I am told that there are in India English-owned mills which do not admit Indian shareholders. If this information be true, I would consider cloth manufactured in such mills to be foreign cloth. Moreover, such cloth bears the taint of ill-will. However well-made such cloth may be, it should be avoided. The majority do not give thought to such matters. All cannot be expected to consider whether their actions promote or retard the welfare of their country. But it behoves those who are learned, those who are thoughtful, whose intellects are trained or who are desirous of serving their country, to test every action of theirs, whether public or private in the manner aforesaid, and when ideas which appear to be of national importance and which have been tested by practical experience should be placed before the people and, as has been said in the Divine Song, "the multitude will copy the actions of the enlightened." Even thoughtful men and women have not hitherto generally carried on the above-mentioned self-examination. The nation has therefore suffered by reason of this neglect. In my opinion such self-examination is only possible where there is religious perception.

Thousands of men believe that by using cloth woven in Indian mills, they comply with the requirements of the Swadeshi vow. The fact is that most fine cloth is made out of foreign cotton, spun outside India. Therefore the only satisfaction to be derived from the use of such cloth is that it is woven in India. Even on hand-looms for very fine cloth only foreign yarn is used. The use of such cloth does not amount to an observance of Swadeshi. To say so is simple self-deception. Satyagraha *i. e.*, insistence on truth is necessary even in Swadeshi. When men will say, "we shall confine ourselves to pure Swadeshi cloth even though we may have to remain satisfied with a mere loin cloth, and when women will resolutely say, 'we shall observe pure Swadeshi even though we may have to restrict ourselves to clothing just enough to satisfy the sense of modesty," then shall we be successful in the observance of the great Swadeshi vow. If a few thousand men and women were to take the Swadeshi vow in this spirit, others will try to imitate them as far as possible. They will then begin to examine their wardrobes in the light of Swadeshi. Those who are not attached to pleasures and personal adornment, I venture to say, can give a great impetus to Swadeshi.

Generally speaking, there are very few villages in India without weavers. From times immemorial, we have had village farmers and village weavers, as we have village carpenters, shoemakers, blacksmiths, etc. But our farmers have become poverty-stricken and our weavers have patronage only from the poor classes. By supplying them with Indian cotton, spun in India, we can obtain the cloth we may need. For the time being it may be coarse, but by constant endeavours we can get our weavers to weave out of fine yarn and so doing we shall raise our weavers to a better status, and if we would go a step still further, we can easily cross the sea of difficulties lying in our path. We can easily teach our women and our children to spin and weave cotton, and what can be purer than cloth woven in our own home? I tell it from my experience that acting in this way, we shall be saved from many a hardship, we shall be ridding ourselves of many an unnecessary need, and our life will be one song of joy and beauty. I always hear divine voices telling me in my ears that such life was a matter of fact once in India. But even if such an India be the idle dream of the poet, it does not matter.

Is it not necessary to create such an India now, does not our 'Purushartha' lie therein? I have been travelling throughout India. I cannot bear the heart-rending cry of the poor. The young and old all tell me, 'we cannot get cheap cloth, we have not the means wherewith to purchase dear cloth. Everything is dear, provision, cloth and all. What are we to do?" and they heave a sigh of despair. It is my duty to give these men a satisfactory reply. It is the duty of every servant of the country, but I am unable to give a satisfactory reply. It should be intolerable for all thinking Indians that our raw materials should be exported to Europe and that we have to pay heavy prices therefore. The first and the last remedy for this is Swadeshi. We are not bound to sell our cotton to anybody and when Hindustan rings with the echoes of Swadeshi, no producer of cotton will sell it for its being manufactured in foreign countries. When Swadeshi pervades the country, every one will be set a-thinking why cotton should not be refined and spun and woven in the place where it is produced. And when the Swadeshi mantra resounds in every ear, millions of men will have in their hands the key to the economic salvation of India. Training for this does not require hundreds of years. When the religious sense is awakened, people's thoughts undergo a revolution in a single moment. Only selfless sacrifice is the *sine qua non*. The spirit of sacrifice pervades the Indian atmosphere at the present moment. If we fail to preach Swadeshi at this supreme moment, we shall have to wring our hands in despair. I beseech every Hindu, Mussalman, Sikh, Parsi, Christian and Jew who believes that he belongs to this country to take the Swadeshi vow and to ask others also to do likewise. It is my humble belief that if we cannot do even this little for our country, we are born in it in vain. Those who think deep will see that such Swadeshi contains pure economics. I hope that every man and woman will give serious thought to my humble suggestion. Imitation of English economics will spell our ruin.

21st June 1919

SWADESHI

The following address on Swadeshi delivered by Mr. Gandhi before the Missionary Conference of 1916 at Madras, being seasonable, is reprinted here for the benefit of those who are interested in the Swadeshi :—

It was not without great diffidence that I undertook to speak to you at all. And I was hard put to it in the selection of my subject. I have chosen a very delicate and difficult subject. It is delicate because of the peculiar views I hold upon Swadeshi, and it is difficult because I have not that command of language which is necessary for giving adequate expression to my thoughts. I know that I may rely upon your indulgence for the many short-comings you will no doubt find in my address, the more so when I tell you that there is nothing, in what I am about to say, that I am not either already practising or am preparing to practice to the best of my ability. It encourages me to observe that last month you devoted a week to prayer in the place of an address. I have earnestly prayed that what I am about to say may bear fruit and I know you will bless my word with a similar prayer.

After much thinking, I have arrived at a definition of Swadeshi that perhaps best illustrates my meaning. Swadeshi is that spirit in us which restricts us to the use and service of our immediate surroundings to the exclusion of the more remote. Thus, as for religion, in order to satisfy the requirements of the definition, I must restrict myself to my ancestral religion. That is the use of my immediate religious surrounding. If I find it defective, I should serve it by purging it of its defects. In the domain of politics I should make use of the indigenous institutions and serve them by curing them of their proved defects. In that of economics I should use only things that are produced by my immediate neighbours and serve those industries by making them efficient and complete where they might be found wanting. It is suggested that such Swadeshi, if reduced to practice, will lead to the millenium. And as we do not abandon our pursuit after the millenium, because we do not expect quite to reach it within our times, so may we not abandon Swadeshi, even though it may not be fully attained for generations to come.

Let us briefly examine the three branches of Swadeshi as sketched above. Hinduism has become a conservative religion and therefore a mighty force, because of the Swadeshi spirit underlying it. It is the most tolerant because it is non-proselytising, and it is as capable of expansion to-day as it has been found to be in the past. It has succeeded, not in driving out as I think it has been erroneously held, but in absorbing Buddhism. By reason of the Swadeshi spirit, a Hindu refuses to change his religion, not necessarily because he considers it to be the best, but because he knows that he can complement it by introducing reforms. And what I have said about Hinduism is, I suppose, true of other great faiths of the world, only it is held that it is specially so in the case of Hinduism. But here comes the point I am labouring to reach. If there is any substance in what I have said, will not the great missionary bodies of India, to whom we owe a deep debt of gratitude for what they have done and are doing, do still better and serve the spirit of Christianity better by dropping the goal of proselytising, while continuing their philanthropic work? I hope you will not consider this to be an impertinence on my part. I make the suggestion in all sincerity and with due humility. Moreover I have some claim upon your attention. I have endeavoured to study the Bible. I consider it as part of my scriptures. The spirit of the Sermon on the Mount competes almost on equal terms with the Bhagwad Gita for the domination of my heart. I yield to no Christian in the strength of devotion with which I sing "Lead kindly Light" and several other inspired hymns of a similiar nature. I have come under the influence of noted Christian missionaries belonging to different denominations, and I enjoy to this day the privilege of friendship with some of them. You will perhaps, therefore, allow that I have offered the above suggestion not as a biased Hindu, but as a humble and impartial student of religion with great leanings towards Christianity. May it not be that "Go ye unto all the world" message has been somewhat narrowly interpreted and the spirit of it missed? It will not be denied, I speak from experience, that many of the conversions are only so-called. In some cases the appeal has gone not to the heart but to the stomach. And in every case a conversion leaves a sore behind it which, I venture to think, is avoidable. Quoting again from experience, a new birth, a change of heart, is perfectly possible in every one of the great faiths. I know I am now treading upon thin ice. But I do not apologise, in closing this part of my subject, for saying that the frightful outrage that is just going on in Europe, perhaps shows that the message of Jesus of Nazareth the Son of Peace, has been little understood in Europe and that light upon it may have to be thrown from the East.

I have sought your help in religious matters, which it is yours to give in a special sense. But I make bold to seek it even in political matters. I do not believe that religion has nothing to do with politics. The latter divorced from religion is like a corpse only fit to be buried. As a matter of fact, in your own silent manner you influence politics not a little. And I feel that if the attempt to separate politics from religion had not been made as it is even now made, they would not have degenerated as they often appear to have done. No one considers that the political life of the country is in a happy state. Following out the Swadeshi spirit, I observe the indigenous institutions and the village panchayat hold me. India is really a republican country, and it is because it is that that it has survived every shock hitherto delivered. Princes and potentates whether they were Indian born or foreigners have hardly touched the vast masses except for collecting revenue. The latter in their turn seem to have rendered unto Cæsar what was Cæsar's and for the rest have done much as they have liked. The vast organisation of caste answered not only the religious wants of the community, but it answered to its political needs. The villagers managed their internal affairs through the caste system, and through it they dealt with any oppression from the ruling power or powers. It is not possible to deny of a nation that was capable of producing the caste system its wonderful power of organisation. One had but to attend the great Kumbha Mela at Hardwar last year to know how skillful that organisation must have been, which without any seeming effort was able effectively to cater for more than a million pilgrims. Yet it is the fashion to say that we lack organising ability. This is true, I fear, to a certain extent, of those who have been nurtured in the new traditions. We have laboured under a terrible handicap owing to an almost fatal departure from the Swadeshi spirit. We, the educated classes, have received our education through a foreign tongue. We have therefore not reacted upon the masses. We want to represent the masses, but we fail. They recognize us not much more than they recognize the English officers. Their hearts are an open book to neither. Their aspirations are not ours. Hence there is a break. And you witness, not in reality, failure to organise but want of correspondence between the representatives and represented. If during the last fifty years had we been educated through the vernaculars, our elders and our servants and our neighbours would have partaken of our knowledge; the discoveries of a Bose or a Ray would have been household treasures as are the Ramayan and Mahabharat. As it is, so far as the masses are concerned, those great discoveries might as well have been made by foreigners. Had instruction in all the branches of learning been given through the vernaculars, I make bold to say that they would have been enriched wonderfully. The question of village sanitation, etc., would have been solved long ago. The village panchayats would be now a living force in a special way, and India would almost be enjoying self-government suited to its requirements and would have been spared the humiliating spectacle of organised assassination on its sacred soil. It is not too late to mend. And you can help if you will, as no other body or bodies can.

And now for the last division of Swadeshi. Much of the deep poverty of the masses is due to the ruinous departure from Swadeshi in the economic and industrial life. If not an article of commerce had been brought from outside India, she would be to-day a land flowing with milk and honey. But that was not to be. We were greedy and so was England. The connection between England and India was based clearly upon an error. But she (England) does not remain in India in error. It is her declared policy that India is to be held in trust for her people. If this be true, Lancashire must stand aside. And if the Swadeshi doctrine is a sound doctrine, Lancashire can stand aside without hurt, though it may sustain a shock for the time being. I think of Swadeshi not as a boycott movement undertaken by way of revenge. I conceive it as a religious principle to be followed by all. I am no economist, but I have read some treatises which show that England could easily become a self-sustained country, growing all the produce she needs. This may be an utterly ridiculous proposition, and perhaps the best proof that it cannot be true is, that England is one of the largest importers in the world. But India cannot live for Lancashire or any other country before she is able to live for herself. And she can live for herself only if she produces and is helped to produce everything for her requirements, within her own borders. She need not be, she ought not to be drawn into the vortex of mad and ruinous competition which breeds fratricide, jealousy and many other evils. But who is to stop her great millionaires from entering into the world competition ? Certainly not legislation. Force of public opinion, proper education, however, can do a great deal in the desired direction. The handloom industry is in a dying condition. I took special care during my wanderings last year to see as many weavers as possible, and my heart ached to find how they had lost, how families had retired from this once flourishing and honourable occupation. If we follow the Swadeshi doctrine, it would be your duty and mine to find out neighbours who can supply our wants and to teach them to supply them where they do not know how to proceed, assuming that there are neighbours who are in want of healthy occupation. Then every village of India will almost be a self-supporting and self-contained unit, exchanging only such necessary commodities with other villages where they are not locally producible. This may all sound nonsensical. Well, India is a country of nonsense. It is nonsensical to parch one's throat with thirst when a kindly Mahomedan is ready to offer pure water to drink. And yet thousands of Hindus would rather die of thirst than drink water from a Mahomedan household. These nonsensical men can also, once they are convinced that their religion demands that they should wear garments manufactured in India only and eat food only grown in India, decline to wear any other clothing or eat any other food. Lord Curzon set the fashion of tea-drinking. And that pernicious drug now bids fair to overwhelm the nation. It has already undermined the digestive apparatus of hundreds of thousands of men and women and constitutes an additional tax upon their slender purses. Lord Hardinge can set the fashion for Swadeshi, and almost the whole of India will forswear foreign goods. There is a verse in the Bhagwadgita, which, freely rendered, means masses follow the classes. It is easy to undo the evil if the thinking portion of the community were to take the Swadeshi vow, even though it may for a time cause considerable inconvenience. I hate legislative interference in any department of life. At best, it is the lesser evil. But I would tolerate, welcome, indeed plead for a stiff protective duty upon foreign goods. Natal, a British Colony, protected its sugar by taxing the sugar that came from another British colony, Mauritius. England has sinned against India by forcing free trade upon her. It may have been food for her, but it has been poison for this country.

It has often been urged that India cannot adopt Swadeshi in the economic life at any rate. Those who advance this objection do not look upon Swadeshi as a rule of life. With them it is a mere patriotic effort, not to be made if it involved any self-denial. Swadeshi, as defined here, is a religious discipline to be undergone in utter disregard of the physical discomfort it may cause to individuals. Under its spell the deprivation of a pin or a needle, because these are not manufactured in India, need cause no terror. A Swadeshist will learn to do without hundreds of things which to-day he considers necessary. Moreover, those who dismiss Swadeshi from their minds by arguing the impossible forget that Swadeshi after all is a goal to be reached by steady effort. And we would be making for the goal, even if we confined Swadeshi to a given set of articles; allowing ourselves as a temporary measure to use such things as might not be procurable in the country.

There now remains for me to consider one more objection that has been raised against Swadeshi. The objectors consider it to be a most selfish doctrine without any warrant in the civilized code of morality. With them, to practise Swadeshi is to revert to barbarism. I cannot enter into a detailed analysis of the proposition. But I would urge the Swadeshi is the only doctrine consistent with the law of humility and love. It is arrogance to think of launching out to serve the whole of India, when I am hardly able to serve even my own family. It were better to concentrate my effort upon the family, and consider that through them I was serving the whole nation, and if you will, the whole of humanity. This is humility and it is love. The motive will determine the quality of the act. I may serve my family, regardless of the sufferings I may cause to others, as for instance I may accept an employment which enables me to extort the money from people; I enrich myself thereby and then satisfy many unlawful demands of the family. Here I am neither serving the family nor the state. Or I may recognize that God has given me hands and feet only to work with for my sustenance and for that of those who may be dependent upon me. I would then at once simplify my life and that of those whom I can directly reach. In this instance I would have served the family without causing injury to anyone else. Supposing that everyone followed this mode of life, we should have at once an ideal state. All will not reach that state at the same time. But those of us who, realising its truth, enforce it in practice will clearly anticipate and accelerate the coming of that happy day. Under this plan of life, in seeming to serve India to the exclusion of every other country, I do not harm any other country. My patriotism is both exclusive and inclusive. It is exclusive in the sense that in all humility I confine my attention to the land of my birth. But it is inclusive in the sense that my service is not of a competitive or antagonistic nature. *Sic utere tuo ut alienum non laedas.* It is not merely a legal maxim, but it is a grand doctrine of life. It is the way to a proper practice of *Ahimsa* or love. It is for you, the custodians of a great faith, to set the fashion and show by your preaching, sanctitied by practice, that patriotism based on hatred "killeth," and that patriotism based on love "giveth life."

28th June 1919

THE NECESSITY OF VOWS

The "Leader" has fallen foul of the Swadeshi vow and incidentally of all vows. Its remarks deserve attention. We, therefore, reproduce elsewhere* the whole of the criticism. It is certainly better not to take a vow than having taken it to break it. One cannot be too cautious about taking vows. But we hold that the vast mass of mankind need the binding force of pledges. They build up a man's character. They are, on the one hand, a recognition of the fickleness of the human nature and, on the other, an additional help to strong minds. Every one recognises the excellent effect produced by temperance pledges. With the support derived from such pledges, many have succumbed to the temptation to drink. A vow is a fixed and unalterable determination to do a thing, when such a determination is related to something noble which can only uplift the man who makes the resolve. A vow is to all other indifferent resolves what a right angle is to all other angles. And just as a right angle gives an invariable and correct measure, so does a man of vows, rightly followed, gives of himself an invariable and correct measure. It is therefore hardly correct to say that Swadeshi based on a vow is Swadeshi based on a formula. No one takes or should take a vow blindly. It is and can be taken only when one is fully

* Omitted in this collection.

convinced of the necessity and the rightness of a particular step. It is a question of strengthening the flesh when the spirit is willing. Without the binding effect of a vow, one may easily succumb to the temptation of buying a fine looking foreign garment. With the binding power of a vow, a man recognising the necessity of supporting home industries would prefer the less attractive indigenous garment. It can only do good to a man to be able to say "I shall never tell a lie" in the place of saying "So far as possible, I shall never tell a lie." Whilst therefore we regard the institution of vows as a necessity in national evolution, we entirely agree with our contemporary in its remark that "no amount of Swadeshi vows will avail so long as the daily necessities of life are not produced in the country or are produced in very small quantities or of inferior quality. Swadeshi is a question of capital, organization, skill, enterprise and determination."

20th August 1919

SWADESHI AND SUPPRESSED CLASSES

Godhra, last week, showed what could be done by co-operation between the officials and the leaders. The occasion was Mr. Gandhi's visit to Godhra on the 14th instant to open the Swadeshi Bhandar. The organisers had decided to secure the co-operation of the officials in the non-political part of the heavy programme arranged by them. The chief items in it were two Swadeshi meetings, one specially for the women of Godhra and the other for the public in general. Mrs. Clayton had gracefully accepted the invitation to be present at the ladies' meeting and Mr. Clayton, the Collector, to preside at the public meeting. He had naturally stipulated that the meeting should be purely non-political. There was also a conference arranged between the leaders and Mr. Clayton on the question of forced labour. Mr. Gandhi was present at the conference. Mr. Clayton was very conciliatory and courteous to the deputation and said that he was desirous of removing this and all difficulties by mutual discussion and co-operation, and wished the leaders to approach him whenever they found that there was a grievance, and assured them that though he might not always agree, they could always rely upon his giving every matter his best attention.

Before the interview, was performed the opening ceremony of the store. A silver lock and key locally made were presented to Mr. Gandhi. The owners who have taken up the enterprise purely from a public standpoint asked Mr. Gandhi to announce that they would not charge more than 7½ per cent on the cost price of the goods in Godhra, *i.e.*, the price in Bombay and the railage and packing. This applies only to the articles required for the Swadeshi vows. The store was opened before a large audience. Mr. Gandhi said the enterprise depended for its success on the integrity of the managers and the patriotism of the Godhra public.

WOMEN AND SWADESHI

The women's meeting came off at 4 p.m. Over one thousand women must have been present at the meeting. Mrs. Jerbanu Merwanji Kothawala, the accomplished wife of Khan Saheb Kothawala, presided. The following is the precis of Mr. Gandhi's address to the ladies :

Mr. Gandhi said he was grateful to Mrs. Clayton for her presence at the gathering and he was sure he had his audience with him in expressing the sentiment. After briefly introducing Mrs. Clayton to the ladies present, the speaker said Swadeshi was that spirit in us which required us to serve our immediate neighbours before others and to use things produced in our neighbourhood in preference to those more remote. So doing we served humanity to the best of our capacity. We could not serve humanity by neglecting our neighbours. Similarly with our wants. We were bound to supply them through the agency of our neighbours and therefore prefer their labour and wares to those of others. India abandoned Swadeshi, a hundred years ago, and had consequently become comparatively poor and helpless. We were well able to supply all our cloth and to supply the world's market to a certain extent when we were observing the law of Swadeshi. During that period, the majority of the women of India spun yarn as a national duty and the men wove the yarn so spun. Now the 21 crore peasants of India had at least four months out of the year thrown on their hands. They did not shirk work. They had none to occupy their time and to supplement their earnings from cultivation. Swadeshi therefore was a question of finding a subsidiary industry for our farmers. No country in the world could prosper that had one third of time of the vast majority of its inhabitants lying unutilised. Moreover, there were other men and women who had many hours in the day at their disposal. If these idle hours of the nation were fully occupied in producing yarn and weaving it, we could manufacture the whole of our cloth and thus save crores of rupees going out of the country every year. The condition of success was that cultured men and women took up spinning and weaving. The poorer people would follow their example. Lady Dorab Tata, Lady Petit and Mrs.

Jayji Petit had promised to learn the art of spinning and introduce it to their sisters. Mrs. Ramabai Ranade proposed to introduce the music of the spinning wheel in her Seva Sadan. Mrs. Banker worked six hours a day and produced fine yarns and made of it a gift to the nation. We could expect no less from the sisters of Godhra. Mr. Gandhi did not hesitate to recommend it to his European friends. One such sister had already undertaken the work. He hoped that those who did not need pecuniary assistance would make it a point of honour to give at least one hour a day to the nation for producing yarn. As an encouragement in this direction he called upon his hearers to pledge themselves henceforth not to buy foreign cloth. Every village of India would thus become self-supporting and self-producing so far as the two main wants of life—food and clothing—were concerned.

The Chairwoman exhorted the ladies present to help the movement in the direction Mr. Gandhi indicated. Mrs. Clayton said she was glad she was able to be present at the meeting. She always was in favour of home industries.

THE PUBLIC MEETING ON SWADESHI

The women's meeting was followed by a brief recess. The Vanita Vishram was visited at 6-30 p.m. The public meeting came off at 9-15 p.m. There was a very large audience. It was held in the open air. Mr. Gandhi's address dealt with the religious and the economic aspect. At the outset he said he was deeply grateful to Mr. Clayton for presiding at the meeting. He knew and appreciated the condition under which he had accepted the invitation of the organisers. And he would endeavour faithfully to carry out the compact. To him the economic and the religious aspects of Swadeshi were far more attractive than the political, and as it was his dream that all, from the Viceroy down to the sweeper, should accept the Swadeshi, he was desirous of conducting the Swadeshi propaganda from the economic and the religious standpoints. He was thankful too that Mr. Clayton had permitted the officials to be present at the meeting. To him the religious aspect was all sufficient. That elementary religion which was common to mankind taught us to be kind and attentive to our neighbours. An individual's service to his country and humanity consisted in serving his neighbours. If that was true, it was our religious duty to support our farmers, our artisans such as weavers, carpenters, &c. And so long as the Godhra farmers and weavers could supply the wants of the Godhra citizens, the later had no right to go outside Godhra and support even 'say' the Bombay farmers and weavers. He could not starve his neighbour and claim to serve his distant cousin in the North Pole. This was the basic principle of all religions and they would find it was also of true and humane economics. India was suffering from a triple curse, the curse of disease—disease, not of a normal but of an abnormal kind, the curse of want of food and lastly that of want of clothing. All proceeded largely from the same cause, poverty, and poverty was due largely to the economic drain. We gave to the producers outside India, in 1917-18, the enormous sum of sixty crores of rupees. And we had not, in any measure worthy of consideration, provided the millions of our spinners and weavers with any other occupation. The whole of the labour thus unwillingly set free was running to waste like a mighty torrent of water. The evil could only be corrected by our reversion to Swadeshi and by rehabilitating our spinners and weavers in their former honourable occupation. He sought, in this gigantic task, the help of the officials, the millionaries and the other leaders of society. It was the most urgent need of the country. We had twenty-one crore farmers. His own experience and the experience of authoritative writers showed that they had nearly four months of the year lying idle on their hands. This was a huge economic waste. No wonder that we were poor. Swadeshi therefore was the problem of inducing and enabling the farmers to take up the supplementary industry of spinning and weaving. Our Shastras and the history of spinning and weaving throughout the world showed that the queens down to their maids considered it an honour to spin cotton. Weaving was largely specialised. In those halcyon days when our mothers spun for the nation, we were able to produce the finest muslin. We could still regain the lost art and with it the lost prosperity. But one thing was needful for the people, to insist on getting only Swadeshi cloth and on producing it themselves as far as possible. In the Punjab, thousands of women of high birth spun their own yarn and got it woven by professional weavers. The Swadeshi vows were designed to create a taste for Swadeshi. They must not be ashamed of coarse cloth. As a matter of fact, there was more art about hand-spun and hand-woven cloth, however coarse, than about machine-made cloth however fine. But art apart, they were bound by every tie of honour, every consideration of prudence and economics to wear what cloth every village could produce and be satisfied with it, till our skill, industry and enterprise could produce a better quality.

At the close of the proceedings, the chairman said he was glad to be able to preside at the meeting. He thanked Mr. Gandhi for his instructive address and exhorted the audience to support home manufacture. A vote of thanks to the chair brought the meeting to a close.

7th May 1919

THE VOW OF HINDU-MOSLEM UNITY

The following is a free translation, approved by Mr. Gandhi, of his leaflet on Hindu-Moslem Unity:

In the huge mass meeting of Hindus and Mahomedans held in the Sonapur Masjid compound, on Sunday the 6th April, the day of humiliation and prayer, a vow of Hindu-Moslem Unity was proposed to be taken as in the case of Swadeshi, proposed at the Chowpaty meeting, and I had to utter a note of warning on both the occasions. At times, in a fit of joyous passion, we are spurred on to certain courses of action for which we have afterwards to repent. A vow is a purely religious act which cannot be taken in a fit of passion. It can be taken only with a mind purified and composed and with God as witness. Most of what I have said whilst writing about the Swadeshi vow applies here. Acts which are not possible by ordinary self-denial, become possible with the aid of vows which require extraordinary self-denial. It is hence believed that vows can only uplift us. If the Hindu and Moslem communities could be united in one bond of mutual friendship, and if each could act towards the other even as children of the same mother, it would be a consummation devoutly to be wished. But before this unity becomes a reality, both the communities will have to give up a good deal, and will have to make radical changes in ideas held heretofore. Member of one community, when talking about those of the other, at times indulge in terms so vulgar that they but accentuate the relations between the two. In Hindu society, we do not hesitate to indulge in unbecoming language when talking of the Mahomedans and *vice versa.* Many believe that an ingrained and ineradicable animosity exists between the Hindus and Mahomedans. In many places we see that each community harbours distrust against the other. Each fears the other. It is an undoubted fact that this anomalous and wretched state of things is improving day by day. The Time-Spirit is ceaselessly working on unchecked, and willy-nilly we have to live together. But the object of taking a vow is speedily to bring about, by the power of self-denial, a state of things which can only be expected to come in the fulness of time. How is this possible? Meetings should be called of Hindus—I mean the orthodox Hindus—where this question should be seriously considered. The standing complaint of the Hindus against the Mussalmans is that the latter are beef-eaters and that they purposely sacrifice cows on the Bakr-i-Id day. Now it is impossible to unite the Hindus and Mahomedans so long as the Hindus do not hesitate to kill their Mahomedan brethren in order to protect a cow. For I think it is futile to expect that our violence will ever compel the Mahomedans to refrain from cowslaughter. I do not believe the efforts of our cow-protection societies have availed in the least to lessen the number of cows killed every day. I have had no reason to believe so. I believe myself to be an orthodox Hindu and it is my conviction that no one who scrupulously practises the Hindu religion may kill a cow-killer to protect a cow. There is one and only one means open to a Hindu to protect a cow and that is that he should offer himself a sacrifice, if he cannot stand its slaughter. Even if a very few enlightened Hindus thus sacrificed themselves, I have no doubt that our Mussalman brethren would abandon cowslaughter. But this is Satyagraha; this is equity; even as, if I want my brother to redress a grievance, I must do so by taking upon my head a certain amount of sacrifice and not by inflicting injury on him. I may not demand it as of right. My only right against my brother is that I can offer myself as sacrifice.

It is only when the Hindus are inspired with a feeling of pure love of this type that Hindu-Moslem Unity can be expected. As with the Hindus, so with the Mussalmans. The leaders among the latter should meet together and consider their duty towards the Hindus. When both are inspired by a spirit of sacrifice, when both try to do their duty towards one another, instead of pressing their rights, then and then only would the long standing differences between the two communities cease. Each must respect the other's religion, must refrain from even secretly thinking ill of the other. We must politely dissuade members of both the communities from indulging in bad language against one another. Only a serious endeavour in this direction can remove the estrangement between us. Our vow would have value only when masses of Hindus and Mussalmans join in the endeavour. I think I have now made sufficiently clear the seriousness and magnitude of this vow. I hope that on this auspicious occasion—and surely the occasion must be auspicious when a wave of Satyagraha is sweeping over the whole country—we could all take this vow of unity. For this it is further necessary that leading Hindus and Mahomedans should meet together and seriously consider the question and then pass a unanimous resolution at a public meeting. This consummation will certainly be reached if our present efforts are vigorously continued. I think the vow may be taken individually even now and I expect that numerous people will do so every day. My warnings have reference to the taking of the vow publicly by masses of men. If it is taken by the masses it should, in my humble opinion, be as follows:

"With God as witness, we Hindus and Mahomedans declare that we shall behave towards one another as children of the same parents, that we shall have no differences, that the sorrows of each shall be the sorrows of the other and that each shall help the other in removing them. We shall respect each other's religion and religious feelings and shall not stand in the way of our respective religious practices. We shall always refrain from violence to each other in the name of religion."

11th June 1919

BABU KALINATH ROY

(By M. K. Gandhi)

By the courtesy of the "Young India" syndicate, composed as it is largely of Satyagrahis, since the deportation of Mr. Horniman I have been permitted to supervise the editing of this journal. I asked for such supervision because I was anxious that nothing should appear in it that was in any way inconsistent with the general principles of Satyagraha, *i.e.*, of truth and non-violence to person or property. In pursuance of the plan I have hitherto also written some leading articles in the usual editorial style. But, for this issue I wish to take the sole responsibility, if there be any, of writing on the case of Babu Kalinath Roy, the Editor of the now defunct "Tribune".* Personally, I consider that even from the point of view of the authorities there is nothing wrong or out of the way in what I am about to say. But lest they may think otherwise, it is due to the public and to the "Young India" syndicate that the authorship of this writing should be known.

With reference to the Punjab disturbances, by my complete silence over them I have allowed myself to be misunderstood by many friends and, as is now well-known, I have been deprived of the co-operation, though never the friendship, of so respected and renowned a leader and co-worker as Sanyasi Swami Shri Shraddhanandji. But I still believe that I have done well in persisting in my silence, for I had no conclusive data to go upon. No public declaration of mine could have in any way affected for the better the action of the authorities. But Babu Kalinath Roy's case materially alters the situation. In my humble opinion the case represents a manifest and cruel wrong. I have not the honour of knowing him personally. When I took up the Judgment in the case, I approached it with a feeling that there would be at least a *prima facie* case made out against the accused on some isolated passages in his writings. But as I proceeded with it, the impression grew on me that it was a kind of special pleading in order to justify a conviction and a heavy sentence. In order to check myself I took up the numbers of the "Tribune," referred to in the Judgment, and on which the serious charge against Babu Kalinath Roy under Section 124 A of the Indian Penal Code was based, and a careful reading of every one of the writings in the "Tribune" more than confirmed the impression produced by a perusal of the

* Resumed publication a few days later.

Judgment and led me to think that the Martial Law Court had allowed its judgment to be warped and clouded by the atmosphere of suspicion and distrust surrounding it. The best proof of my statement must be the Judgment and the writings on which it is based. They are, therefore, reproduced* in this issue in full. I have prefaced the Judgment and the offending articles in the "Tribune" with extracts from the other numbers showing the whole tendency and tone of the writings from the beginning of April just after the Delhi affairs. They are not extracts torn from their context, but they are representative of the issue of the "Tribune" published after the 30th March last. The dominant note pervading all the issues is that the agitation against the Rowlatt legislation should be conducted with sobriety, truth and non-violence. I could nowhere trace in them ill-will, either against Englishmen in general, or against the English Government in particular. Indeed, it would be difficult to surpass the "Tribune" in calmness and self-restraint in the face of circumstances brought about by the Delhi affairs.

This is the test that the Special Tribunal put before itself for its guidance:

"You will have to consider whether this publication was or was not a calm and temperate discussion of the events that had occurred. The people have a right to discuss any grievances that they may have to complain of, but they must not do it in a way to excite tumult." "You may point out to the Government their errors. . . . . The question is always as to the manner. A question is made whether they (writings) shew an intention to instruct by appealing to the judgment or to irritate and excite to sedition. In other

* Omitted in this collection.

words, whether they appeal to the sense or the passions."

Judged by the standard set before the Court, the articles complained against do not warrant a conviction. They cannot excite tumult, when daily during a period of exceeding stress the writer asks his readers to refrain all violence, telling them in unmistakable terms that disturbance can only damage their cause. The Editor has continuously appealed to the judgment of the readers, by asking them not to prejudge, but to await the results of an inquiry which he persistently asked for. The Court's discussion of the passages and articles fails to convince one of the propriety of its decision. The Court has resented the use of the term "Delhi Martyrs" in the issues of the 6th and the 8th April. When you read the contents under the headings, the one has reference to prayer at the Jumma Musjid and the other to a Relief and Memorial Fund. The crime in the language of the Court was that "the accused chose to emphasise the memorial for martyrs and not the relief," and the Court proceeds, "inference from this is plain." The plain inference from this is that who ever put the heading felt that those who were shot down at Delhi were so dealt with, without sufficient cause. Why this should be considered seditious passes comprehension. And if such an inference shows, as it undoubtedly does, that the action of the Magistrate who gave the order for firing was wrong, is the drawing of such a deduction to be punished? We are told by the Court that one may point out to Government their errors. I submit that Mr. Roy justly pointed out the error of one of the local authorities. (Incidentally, I may mention that there is no such Editorial heading as "Memorial to Delhi Martyrs," referred to in the Judgment) The next indictment consists in the Editor having used the word "dupe" in connection with the action of some honorary magistrates and Municipal Commissioners who tried to dissuade shop-keepers from closing their shops. This is what the article describing the demonstration of the 6th April says: "The masses of India are no fools. . . . That they cannot be successfully duped ought to be clear from the very ignominious failure in this very case of certain Municipal Commissioners and honorary magistrates and several others who went round the city trying to persuade shop-keepers to keep their shops open." This is a bare statement of fact as the accused knew it. Then follows in examination of the other articles as to which the gravamen of the charge is the assertion of the Editor that the action of the Punjab Government was both "unjust and unwarranted," and that it had "exposed itself to the severest criticism at the bar of public opinion." Here, too, the Editor has, after having reasoned to the reader, led him to the conclusion to which he himself has arrived—a procedure held to be entirely justifiable under the test accepted by the Court itself. The wrong would undoubtedly be if the Editor had misstated facts. But in every case, as would appear from the articles reproduced herewith the writer has fortified himself with what he belived to be facts, and which so far as the Judgment allows us to see, have not been controverted. The other two articles referred to by the Court are 'Delhi Tragedy' in the issue of the 9th and 'Blazing Indiscretion' in the issue of the 10th April. The "Delhi Tragedy" is a dispassionate review of the tragedy of the 30th March, and ends with an exhortation to the Government of India to appoint a public inquiry.

'Blazing Indiscretion' is undoubtedly an indictment against Sir Michael O'Dwyer about his speech before the Punjab Legislative Council. The speech analysed in the article in question certainly contains more than one "blazing indiscretion." The truth of the matter is that the wrong man was in the wrong box, the right man to have been in the box of the accused should certainly have been Sir Michael O'Dwyer. Had he not made inflammatory and irritating speeches, had he not belittled leaders, had he not in a most cruel manner flouted public opinion and had he not arrested Drs. Kitchlew and Satyapal, the history of the last two months would have been differently written. My purpose, now is not to prove Sir Michael O'Dwyer's guilt, but it is to prove Babu Kalinath Roy's complete innocence, and to show that he has suffered a grievous wrong in the name of British justice, and I do not hesitate to ask Englishmen as I ask my countrymen to join me in the prayer for Babu Kalinath Roy's immediate release. As Mr. Norton has shown, and quite recently Sir P. S. Sivaswami Aiyer, a Martial Law Tribunal was never contemplated to be one for the trial of cases involving delicate interpretations of difficult sections of ordinary enactments. Such tribunals are properly designed only for summary justice being meted out to men who are caught red-handed in acts of rebellion or crimes which mean, if left unchecked, complete disruption of society.

One thing more remains to be considered. Why should this case be singled out for special treatment when it is highly likely that an independent and impartial committee is likely to be appointed to overhaul the Martial Law administration in the Punjab and so revise the sentences passed by the Martial Law Court? My answer is that Mr. Roy's case does not admit of any doubt about it. It is capable of being immediately considered by the Government and if the articles on which the charge against Mr. Roy was based do not amount to sedition—as I hold it does not—he should be immediately set free. Moreover time is an important consideration in this case, for Mr. Roy, as Mr. Andrews has pointed out, has a very delicate constitution.

7th June 1919

MR. TILAK'S SERVICES: MR. GANDHI'S TRIBUTE

A public meeting was held on Saturday evening at Shantaram's Chawl, Girgaum, Bombay, under the presidency of Mr. Gandhi, for the purpose of expressing appreciation of the services rendered by Mr. Tilak to India, and calling upon his countrymen to contribute to the expenses incurred by him in his case against Sir Valentine Chirol. The following is a full translation of his speech in Gujarati:

I am thankful to the organizers of the meeting for asking me to preside. The goal of every thinking Indian must be the same, though the methods for its attainment may be different and it is a matter known to all that my ways differ from Mr. Tilak's. And yet I would wish to heartily associate myself with every occasion to pay a tribute to his great services to the country, his self-sacrifice, and his learning—and with the present occasion in especial. The nation does not honour him any the less for his defeat in his case against Sir Valentine Chirol. It honours him, if that were possible, all the more and this meeting is but a token of it. I have come to offer hearty support to it.

Truly speaking I am in no love with fighting in law courts. Victory there does not depend on the truth of your case. Any experienced vakil will bear me out that it depends more on the judge, the counsel, and the venue of the court. In English there is a proverb that it is always the man with the longest purse that wins. And there is a good deal of truth in this, as there is exaggeration in it. The Lokamanya's defeat therefore made me only wish he was a Satyagrahi like me, so that he would have saved himself the bother of victory or defeat. And when I saw that far from losing heart at the result of his case, far from being disappointed, he faced the English public with cool resignation and expressed his views to them with equal fearlessness, I was proud of him. He has been in his life acting to the very letter up to what he has believed to be the essential teaching of the Gita. He devotes himself entirely to what he believes to be his *karma*, and leaves the result thereof to God. Who could withhold admiration from one so great?

I think it our duty to contribute to the expenses of his suit. He surely did not fight for his personal ends, he fought in the public interests. I am sure, therefore, that you will accept the resolution that is going to be proposed this evening to find for Mr. Tilak the expenses of his suit, and to express our gratefulness for his services to the country.

19th July 1919

MANY HAPPY RETURNS

According to the Hindu year, Lokmanya Tilak enters upon his sixty-fourth year to-day. India is to celebrate the event on the 23rd instant. Among the living Indians there are few to-day who have braved as many storms as Mr. Tilak has, there are few who occupy the place in the public estimation that Mr. Tilak does. One may differ from his views and his methods but none can doubt his intense patriotism and burning love for his country, his great intellectual gifts and his vast learning. It has often been said by his opponents that he is anti-English. We have good reasons to know to the contrary. He is undoubtedly an uncompromising opponent of bureaucracy but not of English connection or of the English people. Hot from the Congress work at Calcutta in 1917, the writer remembers his having appeared before a purely Indian audience before which he delivered a panegyric on British rule such as would have delighted the heart of any Anglophile. He paid an unstinted tribute to the British effort in the early fifties on behalf of the vernaculars. Indeed his very work in England is an eloquent demonstration of his faith in the desire of the British people to do well by India. We wish that the English officials in India could appreciate Mr. Tilak's worth and seek the assistance of nationalists like him in the difficult task of administration. They and the country lose by constant and mutual vilification and distrust. A little charity, a little trust and it is possible to remove the growing estrangement between the two classes. In wishing Lokmanya Tilak many happy returns of the day, we would commend the thought we have expressed, to the earnest attention of Englishmen who, we would wish, could share the national rejoicings that would take place on Wednesday next over the fact that the great Indian has been spared so long for the service of India. We would plead with the organisers of the demonstration that they would make the day not one for reminding us of the many grievances which Mr. Tilak may be long spared to fight against, but that they would mark it as one on which we shall pray that we may fit ourselves by sacrifice and righteousness for the task before us of regeneration, and that Englishmen may be blessed with the needful wisdom to see that the fulfilment of their professed mission is to be sought not in distrusting but in fully trusting the leaders of the people.

27th September 1919

HOW NOT TO DO IT

(BY M. K. GANDHI)

At the very earnest request of Mayadevi, 16 years' old wife of Kesar Mal, I reproduce elsewhere * her picturesque petition praying for the release of her young husband, 21 years old. The case presented seems to me to be unanswerable but a good cause has been spoiled, by a bad advocate. Though the petition is that of Mayadevi, it is quite clear that it is the handiwork of a draughtsman who has written in a fit of rage against what he has, undoubtedly and with good cause, believed to be a monstrous injustice. But anger is short of madness and noblest eauses have been damaged by advocates affected with temporary lunacy. The petition is overlaid with useless adjectives and declamation. Whilst it has been a pleasure to me to dissect the many business-like petitions that have come from that land of sorrow, in the present instance I have been obliged to labour through violent language to what I consider to be a right conclusion. I do not happen to know the draughts-

* Omitted in this collection.

man of the petition. Mayadevi, who has sent a covering letter equally violently worded, gives me no information about the draughtsman. But I do wish as a practised draughtsman to warn writers of petition, whether they be pleaders or otherwise, to think of the cause they may be espousing for the time being. I assure them that a bare statement of facts unembellished with adjectives is far more eloquent and effective than a narrative glowing with exuberent language. Petition writers must understand that they address busy men, not necessarily sympathetic, sometimes prejudiced, and almost invariably prone to sustain the decisions of their subordinates. In the case of the Punjab they approach a Viceroy and a Lieutenant Governor who have preconceived ideas. Petitions have to be read and analysed by public workers and journalists who have none too much time at their disposal. I know to my cost how difficult it is for me to do full justice to the value of the papers that pour in upon me week to week from the Punjab. I make a present of my valuable experience to young patriots who wish to try the art of advocating public cause by writing petitions or otherwise. I had the privilege of serving under the late Mr. Gokhale and for a time under the G. O. M. of India. Both told me that if I wanted to be heard I must be brief, I must write to the point and adhere to facts, and never travel beyond the cause under notice, and I must be most sparing in my adjectives. And if some success has attended my effort it is due to my acceptance of the golden advice given to me by the two illustrious deceased.

4th October 1919

MR. GANDHI'S THANKS FOR BRITHDAY GREETINGS

The following is the translation from Gujarati of the letter written by Mr. Gandhi in the "Nava Jivan" of the 28th September and addressed to those who celebrated his birthday :—

Dear Brothers and Sisters,

I have received numerous telegrams, letters and post cards congratulating me upon my 51st birthday. How shall I requite all this love? In what words should I express my gratefulness? There is no doubt that I appreciate discriminating and wise affection and that I shun blind affection. It has, therefore, given me much pleasure to find that the affection has in many places taken a practical and beneficent form. I have such a vivid experience of India's deep proverty that whenever money is uselessly spent it seems to me that so much has been taken away from the poor. If all the money that has been spent over sending me telegrams had been devoted towards purchasing Swadeshi *khadi* and therewith clothing the deserving naked or towards feeding the helpless, would not they have blessed the donors? The curse of the poor has destroyed nations, has deprived kings of their crowns and the rich of their riches. Retributive justice is inexorable. The blessings of the poor have made kingdoms flourish.

The true method of bestowing affection on me is to copy such actions of mine as may seem to be worthy of imitation. No higher compliment can be paid to a man than to follow him. Many took the Swadeshi vow on my birthday. Many sisters have sent me parcels containing yarn spun by themselves. Many took the vow of serving the suppressed classes. The Ahmedabad

Swadeshi Store managers broke through the many difficulties that faced them and decided that day to lower their prices. The managers of the Swadeshi Bhandar in Surat have done likewise. Such methods of celebrating birthdays are a sign of enlightened affection and one would welcome such birthdays for ever so as to enable men and women to take forward steps from day to day.

Bhagini Samaj has decided to present me with a purse. This places a heavy responsibility upon me. It requires me to solve the difficulty of making the best use of it. But this I am able to say without much forethought that I shall make use of it for some of the women of India. I shall feel grateful to those sisters and brothers —who will give me benefit of their advice as to the best way of utilising the funds.

All have wished me long life. My desire is to close this life searching for truth, acting truth and thinking truth and that alone and I request the blessings of the nation that that desire of mine may be fulfilled.

I hope that those who have sent me telegrams and letters will excuse me for my inability to send them separate acknowledgments.

M. K. G.

[J]

12th January 1922

NEXT IS GUNPOWDER

(BY M. K. GANDHI)

The reader will peruse with careful attention the informing *resume* * by K. of the new type of repression that is fast coming into vogue. It is possible that there is exaggeration in the details but almost all the reports hitherto received from non-co-operation quarters have proved so accurate and the denials so false that I am not disposed to discount the graphic details collected by K. from the correspondence received by me and from the newspapers.

The police are mostly our own countrymen but it is evident that they are being incited to become lawless by the example and the precept of their superior officers. When a mob becomes unruly, it knows no better; when the police become unruly, their action is deliberate and unpardonable. The mob frenzy can be controlled, the police frenzy spells disaster for an unprepared people. We have groaned under it all these long years. Thank God, India is to-day prepared to meet the ordered frenzy of the Government.

We must tear down the mask of the so-called enforcement of the ordinary law against so-called intimidators and we must invite and welcome honest martial law. O'Dwyerism and Dyerism are honest ideals, be they ever so indefensible. But what is going on in India to-day is indescribable hypocrisy.

* See p. 1312

If it is true that under the cover of distress warrants the police have entered our homes in Benares and taken away ornaments even from the inmates, if it is true that in Bulandshaher under the pretence of preserving order they have entered people's homes in order to assualt them if it is true that they have stripped prisoners almost naked in order to execute distress warrants, the case is complete for the fiercest Civil Disobedience of the most aggressive type consistently with the preservation of non-violence on our side. We must not wait for gun-powder to be used upon helpless people nor can we afford to put an undue strain upon the people's patience by merely remaining on the defensive and letting the Government agents pillage and plunder our homes. We must draw the gunpowder on our own heads and that too at the earliest possible opportunity. We the principal workers cannot afford to watch with philosophic calmness these exasperating criminal assaults upon inoffensive people although they are volunteers and have therefore undertaken to suffer.

The shooting of a Mussalman youth by a European "youth" (are European youths armed?) for the crime of wearing or selling (whichever it was) a *Khadi* cap, cannot be passed by in silence. We must avenge the wrong if necessary by inviting the shooting on our own heads.

The Government want to goad us into violence or abject submission. We must do neither. We must retort by such Civil Disobedience as would compel shooting.

They want civil war. We must not play into their hands. Here is what I call open canvassing for civil war. The Magistrate of Aligadh is responsible for the following circular to the Raises of the Aligadh District:—

"As you are doubtless aware the Khilafat and Congress Volunteers have been declared by the Local Government to be illegal associations and orders have been received for their suppression. They are becoming very active in Aligadh and may at any time give trouble in Hathras also by picketing shops, intimidation and by causing loss and annoyance to private persons as well as to Government.

"The number of police at my disposal is limited and I am very reluctant to ask for military assistance in dealing with a matter of this kind unless it leads to actual and violent disorder.

"I am therefore writing to a number of the leading Raises and gentlemen of the District to ask for their assistance in case the present trouble proves to be too widespread for the police to deal without undue fatigue and harassment. If you are willing to help me in this matter, I would ask you kindly to slect 50 of your retainers and tenants, stout able-bodied men, whom you could send in, on receiving a message that they are required for enrolment as special police.

"At present it is only necessary that selection of the men should be made and list prepared of their names and residence so that they can be readily collected when called for.

"I shall be glad to hear from you in due course."

(Sd) J. C. Smith.

We must refuse the bait by letting the gullible Raises do as they like. We must seek only such forms of Civil Disobedience as would prevent any clash with our own people, whether turned into civil guard or still laymen. Given unflinching courage and preservation of complete non-violence, the fight can be brought to a victorious end inside of a month. May God grant India light and courage.

I had hoped that the pledge to face death was a distant event. Evidently God wills that we must be tested thoroughly and well. In His name was the battle begun. He must give us the strength to go through it.

12th January 1922

WHAT NEXT?

If arrests and imprisonments have become the order of the day, they are now being followed by frequent cases of assault and calculated brutality of which we have already given the reader some illustrations. Government censorship is preventing many cases from coming to light in proper time, but no veil of darkness can ever cover up truth from view for all time. And reports are pouring in from Assam, from Amritsar, from Bulandshaher and other parts of the country, of what the Government are doing to strike terror into the heart of the people, the only method which a Government, that is based on tyranny and finds its sap in the weakness of the governed, can by the very nature of things adopt to save itself from ruin.

And so from Assam the Secretary of the District Congress Committee of Gauhati writes, that the Government has given a *carte blanche* to the Gurkhas who have been posted there to behave themselves in any way they like. At Nálbari, Kamrup, after the order of processions under section 144 Cr. P. C. the police seized all the drums and other musical instruments in that little town. But after a day they were pleased to summon the owners of those instruments to return to them their things. But when the people got back their things, a party of Gurkhas fell upon them, broke all the instruments, and assaulted with lathis indiscriminately. Seven volunteers whom the Gurkhas met on the road on another occasion were similarly assaulted. Many innocent passers by were also beaten by them at will. At Boka, some 50 miles away from Gauhati, which is a very strong centre of non-co-operation activities, Mr. Bentinck, the D, C. of Kamrup, went with a number of Gurkhas and constables and stayed for several days during which he flogged two men and threatened a third with shooting for refusing to work as '*Begar.*' But the latter, nothing daunted, exposed his breast to be fired at. The D. C. got a blank fire to be shot, but that did not shake the determination of the brave man.

From Assam let the reader turn his attention to Amritsar. A correspondent writes:—"On the 14th December, 38 volunteers were arrested. They are awaiting their trial as yet. On this occasion, as on a previous occasion, some three days back, the behaviour of the police and the officers over them was very mischievous and brutal. I call it mischievous because it was not an ordinary provocation. You have perhaps read some meagre account of the fact that the police even pulled the beard of a Mussalman volunteer. On the 14th, the assault was directed more on the surrounding spectators than the volunteers. The whip and the cane were mercilessly used on them. But thanks to the emphasis on non-violence and the discipline to which the country has been subjected under the Congress programme, there was no counter-madness, no counter-demonstration of violence. People bore this all boldly and many offered themselves for arrest."

After this, the correspondent relates the incident of the 19th, which has called forth a letter of strong and emphatic protest from the Municipal Commissioners of

Amritsar. Let us follow the narrative of the correspondent:—"A band of volunteers under their captain was out to be arrested and passed through many streets singing national songs. Near the Clock Tower Chauk, they were confronted with the mounted police and some fifty to sixty Gurkhas armed with big lathis mounted with brass-nobs. These lathis have replaced the rifles and bayonets. The *Sowars* had rifles, a belt of cartridges and a slim cane. The volunteers were at once surrounded. Upon this, they fell to their prayers, each according to the custom of his religion. A crowd of some fifteen to twenty thousands gathered to see the arrest of the volunteers. At the bidding of the Akalis or the volunteers all the people sat down. The Superintendent of Police who accompanied the force asked the people to move away, but they did not. Then began the beating and caning of the crowd. The Gurkhas charged as if they were thrusting in their bayonets. The cane was applied as furiously. The blows from lathis were thicky laid. The Superintendent not only superintended all this, but himself played the hero. My nephew saw some three or four small boys of say eight or nine years receiving the lashes of a short riding whip. They were mercilessly lashed. I have it on good authority that the Kotwal remonstrated with the officer that they could arrest the people, but not beat them in that fashion, whereupon some hot words were exchanged between the two. Then the madness stopped. The beauty of all this was that the volunteers were not arrested at all."

But all these atrocious deeds seem to be overshadowed by what has been done in Bulandshaher where the Sub-Divisional Magistrate, with the knowledge of the District Magistrate, and perhaps also with his consent, descended to the level of a lawless marauder with all the weapons of law at his command. The situation developed in this way. Volunteers began to be enrolled from the 16th December. On the 17th, two batches of volunteers reached the Kotwali, of whom 14 from the first batch and 8 from the second were arrested by the Joint Magistrate. Then from the 18th to the 21st, the volunteers went on with their work unmolested. On the 22nd, the District was proclaimed, section 30 of the Police Act was promulgated and Indian and European military with four machine guns paraded through the town. On the 23rd, when some of the volunteers were returning from duty, they were caught up on the way by the police and mercilessly beaten with batons, canes, lathis and even shoes. But this did not demoralise the volunteers. They were again out on the 24th. When they reached the Chowk Bazaar, they met the civil and armed police under the command of a Sub-Inspector, who was accompanied by other Sub-Inspectors. On account of the previous day's happenings the public had crowded in very large numbers to see what was going to be done by the police who appeared to have come with a determined policy. As anticipated, the police at once began to belabour the public and the volunteers with thick canes, lathis and batons, quite indiscriminately and very severely. All remained firm and quite non-violent. One Shivlal was very mercilessly beaten and was left by the police in an unconscious state. He was quite unconscious till last night (December 27th). Owing to the exemplary attitude of the volunteers and the people, the hearts of the police began to fail and they called Mr. Niaz Mohd. Sub-Divisional Magistrate, for help. The strength of the crowd had by this time risen to several thousands. Soon after his arrival, Mr. M. Niaz

Mohd. allowed the volunteers to proceed and kept back the police. He also called the European military from their camping ground. The bazaar began to be closed mostly out of fear of military excesses and partly through the pressure of the police. The S.D.M. began to terrorise the people in many ways. He arrested B. Shiam Nath B.A., student of L.L.B. Class, B. Atar Singh, B.A., LL.B., Vakil practising at Bulandshaher, for reasons best known to him. Ch. Amar Singh and M. Syed Ali were also arrested under the same circumstances. None of the four were enrolled as volunteers. The police began to chase people and beat them even in their interior streets and in their shops and houses, wherever they could overtake them. Efforts were made to create a panic in the whole town. All the four gentlemen were handcuffed in pairs and marched at their running speed, accompanied by the S.D.M., Police Sub-Inspectors and the rest of armed paraphernalia, consisting of civil and military police and European military, equipped with the machine gun, to the District Jail.

But the story does not end here. Again on 25th December 1921, a batch of Bugrasi volunteers, many of whom were sturdy Pathans, was out on its usual rounds. M. Niaz Mohd. with his police force went to meet them half way. There was no public with the volunteers as the latter had warned them on account of the anticipated action of the police. The S.D.M. first called the few volunteers, one by one. They were individually and consecutively belaboured by the S.D.M. and many a constable all at a time. Some of them received 25 to 50 cuts of batons, canes and lathis. They suffered all that without the least murmur or complaint. They then fell on the ground and fainted. The constables were then ordered to carry them one by one in different directions. The rest of the volunteers were all standing in a dignified mood to await their share of sacrifice. They were then attacked all in a body by the entire police force and were most cruelly belaboured. Many of them had no strength left to cover even a few paces of distance and were consequently found lying on the ground in streets close by.

The S. D. M. with his other companions then turned towards the bazaar. He offered gratuitous insults and injuries to individual shopkeepers and peaceful people who were busy marketing or doing other business. Such men were indiscriminately beaten by the S. D. M. and by the police at his command and were forcibly made to go to pointed directions on pain of punishment which was still more severely inflicted, if there was the least deviation in the way of obeying it. Normal pace also invited punishment, because it suited the fancy of the S. D. M. to see men running before him quite irrespective of any consideration of age or position. A prominent physician, while returning from a patient's house after a visit, happened to pass the same street. He was directed to move in a different direction than the one in which his house was. He was severely beaten in spite of his repeatedly telling the S. D. M. that he was going to his house which was quite close by. He was mercilessly belaboured by the S. D. M. and constables and the Sub-Inspectors and was ultimately left with the remark that he appeared to have gone mad. He is up till now in bed, unable to move and passes urine with difficulty and has had no motions. Men who had run upstairs to save themselves from such treatment were forcibly taken down and beaten. A Vakil of the High Court, standing alone in his residential quarters in the second story, abutting the said road was ordered to move back and go into his interior rooms as such actions did not suit the fancy of the S. D. M. Three men, including a Doctor, were abusively addressed and compelled to salute him on pain of being beaten. A Mukhtiar, sitting on the same Doctor's dispensary, was ordered to go away to his house and while he was coming down from the shop was given a stroke of cane on his back for not going away as quickly as suited the fancy of the S.D.M. A compounder in the same place was also made to run away, but was spared the cane because he was pointed out to be in Government service. A shopkeeper with some of his friends was confined in a shop and bolted from outside by the Superintendent of Police for reasons best known to him. A police constable who has recently resigned on account of non-co-operation was beaten with a *danda* on his head which broke and began to bleed. The Congress Committee office was entered by the S. D. M. and some of the police force. Some volunteers were present there. The room was ordered to be vacated within a few minutes, otherwise opening of fire was threatened. Papers lying in the outer portion of the building were either torn to pieces and thrown outside or were taken away without preparation of any list of them or any other property. Drinking water vessels were broken and the lantern was smashed to pieces. Some beddings and blankets with some other property were taken away. The owner of the building was ordered to get the rooms vacated at once, which he did by locking the door of the office with his own lock. The room was left in a topsyturvy condition. The officer went into an interior *mohalla* and ascending the roofs of some of the houses uttered most indecent and foul abuse in the presence and within the hearing of *Pardanashin* ladies.

Judgment against the arrested volunteers has been passed and they have been sentenced to various terms of rigorous imprisonment. But what is new and takes away even the forms of legality from the imposition of lawless laws of the Government is that the relatives of the accused volunteers have been penalised, and their movable property consisting of cooking utensils, lamps, and ornaments from the persons of the ladies of their families have been forcibly attached by the police, while in two cases, even the neighbours were made to pay fine in cash on behalf of the accused volunteers.

Another instance of unprovoked attack on harmless people comes from a place in the Rangpur District of Bengal, where on the 30th December last, a band of Gurkhas, numbering 30, fully armed, suddenly appeared at the *Hat* (bi-weekly bazaar) with a Sub-Inspector at their head. The *Hat* was attended by thousands of unarmed, inoffensive people of all ages to buy or sell things. The Gurkhas, without any cause or provocation, quite suddenly fell upon the unsuspecting assembly and charged with their weapons. Many people have been wounded, although the exact number has not yet been ascertained. Six are in local hospital, the condition of two of whom is regarded as serious.

Lawlessness of the worst kind is being adopted by the police in Benares to stifle the volunteer movement, instances of which are coming out from day to day in the columns of the local paper *Aj* as statements of volunteers and letters from other sufferers. In a note, the *Aj* writes that they do not hesitate to enter the Zenana, and attach anything they came across including things of immediate use, blankets, utensils &c., without even enquiring whether they belong to the accused persons or not. It is also alleged that ornaments were taken off the person of women and that *Stridhan* was not respected. One volunteer states that, after the conclusion of their case, the volunteers were then and there denuded of their clothes after which it was announced that the things would be put up for auction sale. Things that were not saleable and especially the white caps were to be burnt. Another volunteer says that before their release at midnight from the *hajat*, they were stripped of all clothing. One correspondent writes under heading,--"Is it attachment or dacoity?"—that the police came when he was not at home and forcibly entering the house took away cash, ornaments and other things. Two other correspondents write that in their absence the police broke open the lock of the doors of their houses, and while the one was lucky enough to save his things on payment of fifty rupees cash, the other found everything taken away in payment, as he heard from his neighbours on his return, of a fine of ten rupees imposed on one of his relatives who is a volunteer.

K.

19th January 1922

FLOGGING IN PRISONS

[The following is the translation of a letter received from Mr. Mahadev Desai on his way to the Agra jail. It is possible that the posting of the letter is a breach of jail discipline. I hate any breach of discipline, but in this instance I have no choice. Duty compels me to publish the letter as it has compelled Mr. Desai to post the letter. I do not mind Mahadev Desai being rewarded with flogging for the indiscipline which is certainly more mischievous than the refusal to wear lousy clothes or the innocent shouts of *jais*—M. K. G.]

Near Etawa,
En route to Agra,
Dated 10th morning.

I feel like one who has long been pent up in a dark and ill-ventilated cell and who all at once finds himself inhaling deep draughts of the fresh air of heaven. You can easily imagine what longing I must have had to write to you, I who was in the habit of writing to you almost daily and of thus easing the many troubles of my mind. We are permitted to write one letter in a fortnight; the letter again must be in English and must be forwarded through the Superintendent. How then could I hope to tell you everything that was happening behind the prison walls? But yesternight, we were set free, at least till we reached Agra. And this morning we are on our way thereto.

Yesternight, 39 of us started from Naini in a prison van comprising four barred compartments, each being 3 cubits long and 5 broad. The bars were apparently not considered to be an adequate safeguard; for the prison van has no doors and no windows. Only there are crooked holes, one inch broad by the side of the carriage for the passage of air. I asked the Sergeant who escorts us whether there was any intention of repeating the Moplah tragedy. The poor fellow naively replied that there was no fear, as it was winter and that it would have been intolerable, had it been summer. Besides the four prisoners' compartments, there was a fifth which was like ordinary third class and was meant for our friends, the guard. Should they not have sufficient light and air to be able to keep us in a suffocated condition?

Devdas and Durga (Mrs. Desai) were at Allahabad Station to see us. They could not have a view of our faces, but they stood outside, near the place where I was, and we could have a hearty talk. From this prison van I could inform Devdas of the many horrors about which I had been unable to tell him anything in the jail; for, the police who escort us do not act as jailors. So some of the things in this letter will have already appeared in Devdas' *Independent* before this reaches you.

We had had hardly a wink of sleep from about one or two o'clock, when at four we were roused at Cawnpore. The sergeant said, 'Desai, Govind and Krishnakant Malaviya, Shahsaheb and two others, follow me. We shall seat you elsewhere, so that there might be more room here.' I could not understand how this selection was made, but it looked like segregation, and so I said that any seven of us would come, but not the seven that were named. The sergeant replied that only those whom he named must come as he did not know the rest and therefore could not take the risk of seating any of them in an ordinary compartment. As 'political' prisoners, some of us had our own clothes on; with the exception of these three or four, the rest were in jail dress and in irons, so that our shame (even as it was) was boundless. To it was now added the insult of being considered more 'trustworthy' than the rest. I thought the three out of the seven would be ordinary prisoners, and that with the aid of light, I would have an opportunity of writing to you, an opportunity not lightly to be allowed to slip as I could not hope to have it anywhere else; and so we came out. I am writing this in an ordinary third class compartment. Seven policemen are mounting guard over us seven!

But I must cut this story short, as there is little time and much to write. How can I give you an idea of the perplexities we have suffered on account of your injunction, that we should obey all orders in jail? Every moment we are troubled by doubts as to what to obey and what not to obey, as always the sun sets on novel experiences and on various oppressions. So I am not at all certain as to the propriety of my conduct on every occasion when I have been anxious to obey.

I am not going to detail here all the experiences in jail. That would take many letters like this, and this is hardly the time for it. I am going to give such select information as I think ought to be placed before the public.

I was taken to Naini jail on the 24th and was at once taken in the presence of the Superintendent, who said angrily, 'Look here. you may be a non-co-operator or anything you please, but here you are a prisoner like all others and will be treated accordingly. You will tire of your life out here, but I can't help it. We will not trouble you so long as you do not trouble us.'

This homily over, I was soon taken to my own cell. I had previously resolved that I should accept everything cheerfully including jail dress and irons. So I put on jail dress as soon as it was given to me. Fifteen members of the Provincial Committee had arrived here a week before me, and their cell was adjoining mine. I got the news, after I had changed my dress, that one of them had refused to put on jail dress and had consequently received a flogging. The jail authorities were somewhat surprised to find that I had accepted the change in dress without demur. I was given a rough woollen coat, worn almost threadbare by long use, a shirt worn out by some prisoner of twice my size and emitting horrible stink, an equally dirty pair of shirts and loincloth, along with two blankets as bedding. In a few minutes I felt an itching sensation, and an inspection at one or two places resulted in the find of a pretty big louse. It was difficult to say whether the vermin lived in the blanket or the shirt, but as there was fairly bitter cold, I had to choose between lice and offensive smell. I elected against the smell, placed the coat as a pillow, put away the shirt, and decided to pass the night under the sole protection of the blanket. I had thought that as I was dead tired, I would sleep soundly. But the lice in the blanket never ceased troubling me. My friends in the adjoining cell gave me from their place an account of the misbehaviour of the jailor and the superintendent. One of them was flogged for the grave offence of not standing up and pushing his hand out through the bars, when the jailor arrived! Another suffered the same punishment for refusing to wear dirty clothes! Add to the stings of lice the noisy cries, rending the heavens, with which prisoners were counted every quarter of an hour from 6 p. m. to 6 a. m. and you can understand that I got hardly any sleep. But I knew that sheer physical necessity would induce sleep on the following days, no matter if I was unable to sleep on the first.

I took no food in the evening, as I did not feel inclined. I was given a large iron bowl for eating and drinking. In spite of all the scrubbing I could give it, I found in the morning that the water in it had turned blood-red with rust. We were taken out thrice in the day for drinking water and for natural purposes. There was a paved reservoir from which all of us were to have our water by putting our bowls into it. Filtering the water was out of the question, as we were not provided with any extra piece of cloth.

[At this point, the Sergeant sees me writing and gives me notice that I should not pass any of my writing to my friends. So I must be brief.]

For bathing purposes, there was a long paved channel

joining with the reservoir mentioned above. We were all to sit in it and bathe. As for food, we were given *Dalia* (a porridge of pounded wheat) in the morning, wheat bread and *dal* at noon, and the same bread and a vegetable in the evening. What shall I say as to how I liked this appetising *menu*? The other prisoners were taking it all right, and so I can hardly describe it as falling within your definition of food, unfit for human consumption.

But let me now come to other matters. There is a rule that a newly arrived prisoner is only confined and not given any work for the first ten days of his term. So my friends of the Provincial Committee and myself, having no work, were given books which we read, heard the bitter language of the jailor and the superintendent in the mornings and saw prisoners striking and abusing one another. The second day, I requested the superintendent to give us spinning wheels or let us have them from our homes. He replied that wheels were given to women and that Government who spent 10 rupees on each prisoner had somehow to manage to raise a like amount out of his labour, and that therefore grinding was given to him. I said that, if the Government had commonsense, they could earn 500 rupees out of our work. He angrily asked, if he was to get us to write articles.

In answer to my companions, the superintendent said, Owing to you, disloyal people having arrived, I could not get my leave for ten days sanctioned. We have to suffer much on account of you. You must behave properly. Do not think I am alone. I have fifty millions of people behind me (referring to the population of England).

This went on for a few days. The ten days' period

of the Provincial Committee people was soon over, and they were made to wear an iron neckring and a wooden tablet, showing the Section against which they had offended and the term of the sentence of imprisonment. They already had irons on their feet. The same day they lost their lousy clothes and got new ones. My clothes were still the same, but I had remained bare-bodied for two days, and washed them thoroughly with earth. Thus the stink had disappeared and my friends had combined for one or two days to pick out the lice from my blankets in the sunshine.

When the friends left, I felt somewhat lonely and so gradually grew very friendly with the other prisoners, some of them dacoits. An old man with a term of seven years' imprisonment came near my cell and sat near the door. I read the Ramayana to him and he expounded it. He was a man of much common sense and knowledge. He had the Ramayana by heart. Then we recited *bhajans* and many prisoners began to sit near my cell. Prisoners here are finely divided into two classes, national and Government prisoners, *i. e.*, ordinary prisoners and politicals. The politicals are gratefully admired and served by the others.

While my new friendships were thus flourishing, I had heard that the Provincial friends had been given hard labour. Eleven had to grind fifteen seers of corn every day, and the deputy jailor had ordered the convict warder to harass them in all possible ways, in order that they might weaken and apologise. One or two of these poor men fell ill in two days. All had warts on their palms, but had in three or four days progressed up to about nine seers, when I received the news that the Government had directed that I should be treated as a political prisoner. I was sorry for this. While my friends were given hard labour, I was denied the privilege of spiritual elevation through physical suffering. My own clothes, in which I had arrived in jail and in which I was furbished up for the day when Devdas and Durga were to see me in order that she might not take fright at the convict's dress, were returned to me, but the 'Gandhi cap' was withheld. I asked the superintendent what it was. He could not explain anything beyond saying that it was like the one I wore and that I would not be allowed to wear it. I might change the shape, he added, or wear a *Fez* like Sherwani's. I laughed and said that I would do neither. 'Then you must go bareheaded,' he said. I agreed. I had thought of refusing to take the other ordinary clothes, but then I remembered your 'Model Prisoner'* and quietly submitted.

I passed my first day as a political prisoner in great trouble. But the next day I was at ease, as I realised that even so there was an opportunity of suffering. Some of my friends described their personal experience. There is a young man, named Kailasnath, still in his teens, the son of a well-known pleader of Cawnpore and a political prisoner. Being religiously minded, he takes food after bath, worship and the application of sandal paint etc. to the forehead. The jailor had admitted sandal and other things for him, but when one day, he saw the sandal mark, he ordered Kailasnath to rub it out. The young man obeyed but refused to take food. And so the jailor arrived on the scene and threatened punishment, but Kailasnath persisted in his refusal all the same. For this, he received filthy abuse, was severely flogged with a wooden cudgel and kicked with boots. His utensils were dashed to the ground. The hero responsible for this is Hamilton, an Englishman who has been promo-

* See p. 1120.

ted to jailorship for his services during the war. This incident got into the newspapers, though not in detail, and there was an inquiry. The Inspector-General visited the prison and told Kailasnath that he must obey all orders. Apparently he took the jailer also to task, as the latter came to Kailasnath and abused the Inspector-General before him!

On hearing this, I could see that life even as a political prisoner need not be uneventful. Meanwhile the attitude of the jailor and the superintendent towards me had changed and I had friendly conversations with them about non-co-operation and other topics. I did not quite relish this development, as I was afraid that these officers might be trying to win me over as a prelude to oppressing the rest.

The same evening, I heard successive cries of 'Gandhijiki Jai.' In the morning, I had read your observations in *Young India* and wished I could communicate them to the friends who had been given hard labour. Here was no means of doing so. The cry started from one block and received a response from other blocks, one after another. To the superintendent and the jailor it looked like a mutiny. They ran up. One of those fifteen friends was seized, and the warder fell upon him like a wolf. The poor man was greeted with foul abuse and flogged with lathis along with an ironical order to repeat 'Gandhijiki Jai.' After he had received ten blows of a lathi, one inch and a half in diameter, his magnificent frame tottered to the ground and then he was beaten with fists etc.

The friend who thus suffered is Lakshminarayan Sharma, a pious and inoffensive young man of twenty-two, who used to be Secretary, Aligarh Congress Committee. The other prisoners could not bear the sight of this suffering and offered to retaliate upon the warder. But Lakshminarayan prevented them all and said it was their duty to suffer. The others, however, were greatly enraged and continued the cries of 'Gandhijiki Jai' for which about fifty or sixty of them were cruelly flogged. As if this were not enough, the next morning all the prisoners were taken outside, including the Provincial Committee men, and in the presence of all of them, two prisoners who were suspects had their hands fastened with a stick and then caned. The caning was so severe that the cries of the sufferers could be heard in my cell at a distance of two or three furlongs. When a prisoner swooned after some blows, he was given rest; and as he revived, the caning was continued. In this way, two of them received 23 cuts. It is worthy of remark that at each cut the sufferer and his fellow prisoners sent up a joint cry of 'Gandhijiki Jai' in spite of the jailer and the superintendent, and these cries stopped only when the authorities were tired of inflicting any more punishment. After this, three or four were flogged with sticks and fists. One of them suffered so severely that there was an involuntary discharge of excreta and urine. Two or three are in hospital. I was told that prisoners had died in this jail before, in consequence of such oppression.

Having performed his 'dirty job' (Dyer's phrase) in this way, the jailer came to see me. I asked him for an explanation of the trouble. He replied that there might have been a big mutiny and that severe punishment was necessary to prevent it. I told him that, be that as it might, I would fast and pray for the day. He asked me why. I said I would pray not only for my brethren who were no doubt in error, but for those who despitefully used them. The jailer asked me what was the value of prayer. The talk then turned upon the Bible. I explained to him that Jesus and the Bible were not the sole property of Christians like himself, but the joint estate of humanity at large. He then appeared to melt somewhat. I said how good it would be, if I was permitted to read to the prisoners Mr. Gandhi's observations pertinent to their case, and I offered to meet all of them and talk to them about our duty. But this was not at all acceptable to the jailer. Only last evening, he was saying to the prisoners, 'There is no victory to Gandhi here, the victory is to Government. So you must cry victory to Government.' He was however abashed a little, said it was no use crying over spilt milk and then left me.

After the jailer came the superintendent. He also tried to tease me, saying ironically how obedient my non-co-operator friends were. I was quiet and only said that he at least was amused by the whole affair. Then he told me I did not know the utility of punishment. I replied I did not care to, as there was a world of difference between his mentality and mine, and that he on his part had no appreciation of our methods. He then expatiated upon the value of 'force' and said, 'You Indians, are unpractical visionaries. We are practical. You only talk big.' I was listening quietly and contented myself with asking whether it was I or he that was talking big. He said nothing more and left me. Meanwhile I had obtained permission to see Lakshminarayan, that friend who had been so cruelly dealt with. I saw him. He showed me terrible marks of the flogging upon his body. I told him we were forbidden to cry 'Gandhijiki Jai' and that I read about it in the papers only the other day. On hearing this the young man burst into tears and said at once he must then tell the superintendent that he had done wrong. Thus he evidenced the incomparable tenderness of his soul. But what does the enemy know or care about our tenderness? So that we can only learn to send forth like sandal-wood greater fragrance, the more roughly we are handled. I assure you, after the experiences that I have had, that our people are mastering this lesson in some miraculous manner.

But now I must close. There is much to say, but I shall rest content if this much reaches you by post for the present. We are not permitted to post letters, but how long should these facts be kept from the public? It is also a question to be considered how far we should obey the order not to give out anything.

I have had no sleep last night, am thoroughly fatigued and must seize an early opportunity of posting this. I will write in English if possible, but perhaps there may be no time.

We are all on our way to Agra, 39 in all including the members of the Provincial Committee and some Allahabad volunteers. Since he received the orders of removal, the superintendent was kindness itself to us. He must have heaved a sigh of relief at our departure as of some great trouble. On the last day he said, 'You are an awful nuisance. I should get an allowance of Rs. fifty for each one of you.' We are being removed, for the fear that we might influence the prison population and bring them to a knowledge of their slavery and ignorance.

19th January 1922

MR. GANDHI'S TWO SPEECHES

The following is the text, as revised by him, of Mr

Gandhi's speech at the Congress Sessions, introducing the central resolution :—

It has taken me exactly 35 minutes to read the resolution in English and in Hindustani. I shall hope if I can at all avoid it not to take even the 30 minutes that Hakimji Saheb has allotted to me. And I do not propose if I can help it to take all that time because I feel that the resolution explains itself. If, at the end of fifteen months' incessant activity, you, the delegates, assembled in this Congress, do not know your own minds, I am positive that I cannot possibly carry conviction to you even in a two hours' speech; and what is more, if I could carry conviction to you to-day because of my speech, I am afraid I would lose all faith in my countrymen, because it would demonstrate their incapacity to observe things and events; it would demonstrate their incapacity to think coherently; because, I submit, there is absolutely nothing new in this resolution that we have not been doing all this time, that we have not been thinking all this time. There is absolutely nothing new in this resolution which is at all startling. Those of you who have followed the proceeding from month to month of the Working Committee, of the All-India Congress Committee every three months and have studied their resolutions, can but come to one conclusion, that this resolution is absolutely the natural result of the national activities, during the past fifteen months; and if you have at all followed the course, the downward course, that the repressive policy of the Government has been taking, you can only come to the conclusion that the Subjects Committee has rightly come to this resolution; and that the only answer that a self-respecting nation can return to the Viceregal pronouncements and to the repression that is overtaking this land, is the course mapped out in this resolution.

I am not going to take the time of the English knowing friends over the religious subtleties of the pledge that the volunteers have to take. I wish to confine my remarks in Hindustani to that subject. But I want this assembly to understand the bearing of this resolution. This resolution means that we have outgrown the stage of helplessness and dependence upon anybody; this resolution means that the nation through its representatives is determined to have its own way without the assistance of any single human being on earth and with the help of only God above.

This resolution, whilst it shows the indomitable courage and the determination of the nation to vindicate its rights and to be able to stare the world in the face, also says in all humility to the Government: 'No matter what you do, no matter how you repress us, we shall one day wring reluctant repentance from you; and we ask you to think betimes, and take care what you are doing and see that you do not make 300 millions of India your eternal enemies.'

This resolution, if the Government sincerely wants an open door, leaves the door wide open for it. If the Moderate friends wish to rally round the standard of the Khilafat, and round the standard of the liberties of the Punjab and therefore of India, then this resolution leaves the door wide open for them too. If this Government is sincerely anxious to do justice,—if Lord Reading has really come to India to do justice and nothing less,—and we want nothing more,—then I inform him from this platform, with God as my witness, with all the earnestness that I can command, that he has got an open door in this resolution if he means well, but the door is closed in his face if he means ill, no matter how many people go to their graves, no matter what wild career this repression is to go through. There is every chance for him to hold a round-table conference, but it must be a real conference. If he wants a conference at a table, where only equals are to sit and where there is not to be a single beggar, then there is an open door and that door will always remain open. There is nothing in this resolution which any one who has modesty and humility need be ashamed of. This resolution is not an arrogant challenge to anybody, but it is a challenge to authority that is enthroned on arrogance. It is a challenge to the authority which disregards the considered opinion of millions of thinking human beings. It is a humble and an irrevocable challenge to authority which in order to save itself wants to crush freedom of opinion and freedom of association—the two lungs that are absolutely necessary for a man to breathe the oxygen of liberty; and if there is any authority in this country that wants to curb the freedom of speech and freedom of association, I want to be able to say in your name, from this platform, that that authority will perish, unless it repents, before an India that is steeled with high courage, noble purpose and determination, even if every one of the men and women who choose to call themselves Indians is blotted out of the earth. God only knows, if I could possibly have advised you before to go to the round-table conference, I could possibly have advised you not to undertake this resolution of Civil Disobedience, I would have done so.

I am a man of peace. I believe in peace. But I do not want peace at any price. I do not want the peace that you find in stone; I do not want the peace that you find in the grave: but I do want that peace which you find embedded in the human breast, which is exposed to the arrows of a whole world, but which is protected from all harm by the Power of the Almighty God.

II

The following is the revised speech, delivered in opposition to Maulana Hasrat Mohani's proposition on Independence:—

Friends, I have said only a few words (in Hindi) in connection with the proposition of Mr. Hasrat Mohani. All I want to say to you in English is that the levity with which that proposition has been taken by some of you has grieved me. It has grieved me because it shows a lack of responsibility. As responsible men and women, we should remember what we did only an hour ago. An hour ago, we passed a resolution which actually contemplates a final settlement of the Khilafat and the Punjab wrongs and transference of the power from the hands of the bureaucracy into the hands of the people by certain definite means. Are you going to rub the whole of that position from your mind by raising a false issue and by throwing a bombshell in the midst of the Indian atmosphere? I hope that those of you who have voted for the previous resolution will think fifty times before taking up this resolution and voting for it. We shall be charged by the thinking portion of the world that we do not know really where we are. Let us understand too our limitations. Let Hindus and Mussalmans have absolute, indissoluble unity. Who is here who can say to-day with confidence, "Yes, Hindu-Muslim Unity has become an indissoluble factor of Indian Nationalism?" Who is here who can tell me that the Parsis and the Sikhs and the Christians and the Jews and the untouchables about whom you heard this afternoon—who will tell me that those very people will not rise against any such idea? Think, therefore, fifty times before you take a step which will redound not to your credit, not to your advantage, but which may cause you irreparable injury. Let us first of all gather up our strength, let us first of all sound our own depths. Let us not go into waters whose depths we do not know, and this proposition of Mr. Hasrat Mohani lands you into depths unfathomable. I ask you in all confidence to reject the proposition, if you believe in the proposition that you passed only an hour ago. The proposition now before you rubs of the whole of the effect of the proposition that you passed only a moment ago. Are creeds such simple things like clothes which a man can change at will? For creeds people die and for creeds people live from age to age. Are you going to change the creed which, with all deliberation and after great debate in Nagpur, you accepted? There was no limitation of one year when you accepted that creed. It is an extensive creed; it takes in all, the weakest and the strongest, and you will deny yourselves the privilege of clothing the weakest amongst yourselves with protection if you accept this limited creed of Maulana Hasrat Mohani which does not admit the weakest of your bretheren. I therefore ask you in all confidence to reject his proposition.

2nd March 1922

GOVERNMENT DENIALS

(I)

FLOGGING IN PRISONS

To

The Editor, Young India.

Dear Sir,—In continuation of my letter No. 402/C. dated the 17th February, 1922, I invite your attention to an article in the form of a letter from Mr. Mahadev Desai, which you headed 'Flogging in Prisons' and which you published in your issue of the 19th January last. In the course of that letter, no less than six cases of flogging are mentioned and the implication is that political prisoners were involved. In two instances, the names of certain persons are mentioned. They are Kailash Nath and Lachhmi Narayan Sharma. Enquiries have been made from the Superintendent of the Central Prison, Naini, with the result that the letter which you have published proves to be a series of glaring misstatements. I am concerned to deal only with the alleged floggings. Since June 1921, up to date, only two persons have been flogged in that jail. They were No. 13974 Kanhoi and 14370 Tara, both of whom were undergoing sentences of ten years' rigorous imprisonment for dacoity. Both of these persons received 25 stripes on the 7th January last for instigating to mutiny within the jail, being the ringleaders of a disturbance which took place on the night of the 6th preceding. The summary of the evidence was entered according to rule in the punishment register maintained in the jail. Neither of the two prisoners suffered any ill-effects from the flogging. I am able to affirm categorically that neither

Kailash Nath or Lachhmi Narayan, whose names were mentioned by the writer of the letter which you published, have never been flogged in the Naini Jail, nor were they given any punishment whatsoever, with the exception of No. 1488, Kailash Nath, who was 'warned' for refusing to work, when undergoing a sentence for rigorous imprisonment. As the highly coloured and false statements which have been made in this letter are causing considerable uneasiness in the public mind, I beg that you will give a prominent place to this denial in an early issue.

Lucknow,
18-2-22

Yours faithfully,
J. E. Gondge
Publicity Commissioner.

[The categorical denial is wholly unacceptable. Not till a full impartial investigation is made, can any contradiction of statements made by a public man of unimpeachable character be accepted, especially when the contradiction comes from interested quarters. I draw attention to the fact that the *Independent* of Allahabad publishes the statement that a prison official admitted to a Congressman the fact of the flogging of Mr. Lachhmi Narayan. There is just a chance that the prison authorities are quibbling when they deny 'flogging'. The letter published in *Young India* is a translation. The Gujarati word is the same for whipping, flogging and caning. I have known the habit of officials denying unofficial corporal punishments. I hope the Government do not wish the public to infer that if there is no record of corporal punishments in the jail register, it has not been administered. The contradiction I am publishing certainly makes me more uneasy than before, for it betrays an intention to persist in the inhumanity and to hush it by denials. The Publicity Commissioner ill-performs his duty by sending unsupported contradictions by accused parties.—M. K. G.]

(2)

DEHRA DUN INCIDENT

To

The Editor, Young India.

Dear Sir,—In continuation of my letter No. 390/C, dated the 14th February 1922, I beg to draw your further attention to the fact that you quoted as the 7th item of "lawless repression" in your rejoinder to the Government of India communiqué, "the shooting of a boy at Dehra Dun and the forcible dispersal of a public meeting at that place". Whether intended by you or not, the obvious innuendo is that Government officials shot the boy. It is presumed that you are referring to the shooting incident on the 24th December, 1921, when a certain young European named Madden shot a Muhammadan youth. Madden is not a Government servant. The circumstances have been fully reported in the Press. The incident arose out of a personal quarrel and the promptest measures were taken to arrest Madden, the Superintendent of Police and the Joint Magistrate themselves going out at 10 p. m. The Civil Surgeon at the Magistrate's request came down in the night to see the injured boy. Madden was tried after the Xmas holidays and committed to sessions on charges under sections 307, 326 I. P. C. I venture to hope that you will correct in as explicit terms as possible the misrepresentation of fact which has been so widely advertised in your letter to the Government of India. Secondly, you have been undoubtedly misinformed as to the alleged cruel, forcible dispersal of a public meeting. The facts are as follows:—

(1) Volunteer processions had become an extreme nuisance in Dehra Dun and their behaviour on several occasions had been highly provocative.

(2) They were prohibited within certain areas by the Superintendent of Police with the Magistrate's assent, in the interests of non-co-operators themselves, as the temper of certain members of the public was being sorely tried.

(3) The local extremist organ "The Garhwali" had commented upon the unwisdom and folly of these demonstrations.

(4) The volunteers decided to defy the orders of the Superintendent of police and, to make their defiance more aggressive, posted a notice at the Police Station that they would have the procession on the 15th January. It is understood that emissaries were sent to the villages to make the demonstration more imposing. This challenge had to be taken up on penalty of seeing all authority set at naught and grave disorder ensuing. Events at Bareilly and Gorakhpur have proved that there are serious potentialities of disorder and lawlessness in these demonstrations.

(5) The meeting was dispersed with very little force. No one was hurt.

I trust that, considering the importance of the public pronouncement in which you made these allegations, you will see your way to give full publicity to this explanation.

Lucknow, Yours faithfully,
15th February. J. E. Gondge

[The Publicity Commissioner has certainly 'caught' me, regarding the shooting incident. I should have been more precise and stated that the shooting was not by a Government servant. I now see that the mention itself was irrelevant and unjust to the Government. The shooting in question cannot in any way be as part of lawless repression. I tender my apology for the error which, I assure the authorities, was wholly unintentional.

The other contradiction, however, does not appeal to me at all. I deny the necessity in the first instance of the use of force. In the second instance the force used was out of all proportion to the requirements, if my correspondent's description is to be relied upon. The public will not trust the interested official denial. I hope that the mistake about the shooting will be used to discredit or underrate the account of the forcible dispersal. The mistake about the shooting was a thoughtless confusion of facts and their consequent mis-application.—M. K. G.]

(3)

A PEEP INTO A BOMBAY JAIL

With the compliments of the Director of Information, Bombay—

In the issue of "Young India" for January 19th an extract was printed from the "Hindu" dealing with the alleged ill-treatment of a certain "Rahmat Rasool, a Punjabi Martial law prisoner," in the Hyderabad Central prison. Enquiries show that the allegations made are unfounded. The article appears to refer to a Gujarati prisoner, named Himat Rasool, who was sentenced by the Ahmedebad Special Tribunal to transportation for life for cutting telegraph wires, setting fire to the telegraph office and rioting at Ahmedabad on 11th April 1919. The charges made and the actual facts relating thereto are as follows:—

On their arrival in this jail from the Andamans, in November last, no meals were given them for three days until the medical officer saw them and got them meals."

The prisoners (who arrived on December 6th) were seen daily both by the medical officer and the Superintendent, but they refused to take *jowari* diet as they wanted wheat diet. This was given them on Dec. 8th.

"Whenever the Superintendent approached them, they were required to raise their hands as a Muslim does, in prayer, with the greeting "Sarkar is one". This immoral rule, interfering with the fundamental principles of Islam, Rahmat Rasool refused to obey, telling the Superintendent that for him God alone is one and that he can raise his hand in prayer before God alone, when the Superintendent proudly replied that he, as representative of Government, was his God in Jail."

This is a pure invention. When the Superintendent or any official visits the prisoners, the latter stand with their hands open, the arms being at right angles to the elbows and the elbows in at the sides. The object of this is to show that there is nothing concealed in the hands with which an assault can be attempted. This attitude is obviously not that of a Muslim, raising his hands in prayer, and the procedure to which no objection has ever been raised, is common to all jails. It is absolutely untrue that the Superintendent used the words attributed to him.

"The prisoner refused to be led away from the path of religion, with the result that his religiousness was rewarded with the five-fold punishment of 30 stripes, 6 months' solitary confinement, six months' gunny clothing, 6 months' cross fetters and 6 months' bar fetters".

The facts are that on Dec. 13th, the prisoner refused to stand up when ordered, became very excited and was grossly impertinent to the Superintendent. He was awarded, not the punishment alleged, but gunny clothing for one month and bar fetters for three months. Since the arrival of this prisoner in jail, he has been eleven times awarded punishments, including 30 stripes and cross bar fetters for ten days for gross insubordination and persistently refusing to work. He is at present undergoing a punishment of three months' separate confinement, awarded him in the Andamans for refusing to work and refusing to obey orders. His history sheet describes him as "a man of violent temper".

20th February 1922

[I venture to call this a brazen defence of a brutal punishment. It tells the public in so many words, "We have done it and we propose to continue." As I did not publish the incident for the edification of the Government, I remain unperturbed by the shameless admission. The reader will please note that in all this communique there is no denial of a single material particular. It makes no difference, whether the name or description of the prisoner is correctly given. The facts that the prisoner had to starve for three days, that he had to stretch forth his hands in a humiliating fashion, that he had gunny clothing for one month, bar fetters for three and thirty stripes and that he is now undergoing '*separate*' confinement for three months is sufficient corroboration of the allegations of the *Hindu*. I am prepared to assume that every prisoner who receives punishment is, in official parlance, a man of violent temper'.—M. K. G.]

DEATH DANCE

(BY M. K. GANDHI)

Why is there this chorus of condemnation of the doubling of the salt tax and other taxes on the necessaries of life? Wonder is expressed that now there is no apology ever offered for the terrific military charges of sixty-two crores. The fact is, it is impossible to offer apology for the inevitable. The military charges must grow with the growing consciousness of the nation. The military is not required for the defence of India. But it is required for the forcible imposition of the English exploiters upon India. That is the naked truth. Mr. Montagu has bluntly but honestly stated this. The retiring President of the Bengal Chamber of Commerce has said it and so has the Governor of Bombay. They want to trade with us not upon our terms but upon their terms.

It is the same thing whether it is done with the kid glove on or without it. The councils are the kid glove. We must pay for the glove. The reforms hang upon us like an incubus. They cover a multitude of defects including the blood-sucking salt tax.

They say to us, 'We propose to hold India whether you wish it or keep from fighting one another without the protecting power of the British arms.' And so, being afraid to die at the hands of our brothers, we are content to live as bond men.

It would be a thousand times better for us to be ruled by a military dictator than to have the dictatorship concealed under sham councils and assemblies. They prolong the agony and increase the expenditure. If we are so anxious to live, it would be more honourable to face the truth and submit to unabashed dictation than to pretend that we are slowly becoming free. There is no such thing as slow freedom. Freedom is like a birth. Till we are fully free, we are slaves. All birth takes place in a moment.

What is this dread of the Congress but the dread of the coming freedom? The Congress has become a grim reality. And therefore it has to be destroyed law or no law. If only sufficient terror can be struck into the hearts of the people, the exploitation can last another century. It is another question whether India itself can last that time under the growing strain or whether the people must, during that time, die like flies. When a man begins to eat a cocoanut, he is not called upon to be tender to the kernel. When he has carved off the last bit he throws away the shell. We do not consider it a heartless performance. No more does the trader consider what he takes from the helpless buyer. A heartless performance, there never is any heart about it. The trader takes all he can and goes his way. It is all a matter of bargain.

The Councillors want their fares and extras, the ministers their salaries, the lawyers their fees, the suitors the decrees, the parents such education for their boys as would give them status in the present life, the millionaires want facilities for multiplying their millions and the rest their unmanly peace. The whole revolves beautifully round the central corporation. It is a giddy dance from which no one cares to free himself and so, as the speed increases, the exhilaration is the greater. But it is a death-dance and the exhilaration is induced by the rapid heart beat of a patient who is about to expire.

The expenditure is bound to grow so long as the dance continues. I should not be surprised if the increase is also laid upon the broad shoulders of Non-co-operators.

For them, there is only one lesson. They may look upon the increase with philosophic calmness, if they will be but true to their creed. The only way they can prevent it, the only way it will ever be prevented is the way of non-violence. For, the greatest part of Non-co-operation is withdrawal from the organised violence on which the Government is based. If we want to organise violence to match that of the Government, we must be prepared to incur greater expenditure even than the latter. We may not convince all the dancers of the fatal doom awaiting them, but we must be able to convince the masses who take part in it and sell their freedom to buy the so-called peace. This we can only do by showing them that non-violence is the way to freedom—not the forced non-violence of the slave, but the willing non-violence of the brave and the free.

30th March 1922

FROM BADA DADA

Writing on the conviction of Mahatma Gandhi, Sjt. Dwijendranath Tagore says :—

" The present Government appears to me to be bound, hand and foot, by the evil precedence of the high-handed British rulers of the past, and the short-sighted ill-advisers of the present times, so that it is incapable of doing towards the people of India anything that is wise, good, just and humane. On the contrary, it is always ready to do anything that is unwise, evil, unjust and inhuman, at the bidding of a handful of mercantile adventurers and those favourite priests of Jehova, whose god is the merciless God of Joshua and his gang, rather than the Heavenly Father of Jesus Christ, so far as it can do so with impunity. Hence it is useless to expect anything good or great at the hands of the present Government. The only way which is open to us is to choose from amongst ourselves a resolute and capable man for our captain who is endowed by Providence with sufficient wisdom, goodness, energy and divine grace to steer the storm-tossed vessel—India as we see it to-day—to a safe harbour. And this man is, I doubt not, Mahatma Gandhi.

Yours Sincerely,
Dwijendranath Tagore.

HAKIMJI'S CONGRATULATIONS

Mrs. Gandhi has received the following telegram from Hakimji :—

Country's truest servant, your dear husband's conviction for no other offence than his uncompromising devotion to motherland, can't fail to give most powerful impetus to our vital national activities and is sure to prove in the future foundation of Swaraj. I, therefore, congratulate not only yourself and your family, but the whole of India on Mahatma's conviction.

Ajmal Khan.

30th March 1922

WHAT SHALL WE DO NOW ?

Now that Mahatmaji has been arrested and is no longer free in body to help us with his advice, people are asking the above question among themselves—*What shall we do now?*

The answer has been given by Mahatmaji himself, in his final request to non-co-operators as embodied in his article—" *If I am arrested* "—in the latest issue of *Young*

India (March 9, 1922), on the day previous to his arrest. This is what he has asked us to do in the circumstances which have overtaken us. "There should be no *hartals*, no noisy demonstrations, no processions. I would regard the observance of perfect peace on my arrest as a mark of high honour paid to me by my countrymen. *What I would love to see, however, is the constructive work of the Congress going on with clock work regularity and the speed of the Punjab Express.* I would love to see people who have hitherto kept back, voluntarily discarding all their foreign cloth and making a bonfire of it. Let them fulfil the whole of the constructive programme framed at Bardoli, and they will not also only release me and other prisoners, but they will also inaugurate Swaraj and secure redress of the Khilafat and the Punjab wrongs. Let them remember the four pillars of Swaraj,—Non-violence, Hindu-Moslem-Sikh-Parsi-Christian-Jew Unity, total removal of untouchability, and of hand-spun and hand-woven *Khaddar* completely displacing foreign cloth."

A similar question was put to Buddha when He was about to leave His body and enter on His final Nirvan in the 80th year of His age. The disciples were weeping and asked him: WHO SHALL TEACH US WHEN THOU ART GONE? Buddha's answer was as follows:—

"Do not let yourselves be troubled, do not weep. Why shall I preserve this body of flesh *when the body of the excellent Law wilt endure?* I am resolved; having accomplished my purpose and attended to the work set before me, I look for rest.

"Seeking the way, you must exert yourselves and strive with diligence. It is not enough to have seen me; walk as I have commanded you; free yourselves from the tangled net of sorrow; walk in the path with steadfast aim. A sick man may be cured by the healing power of medicine and will be rid of all his ailments without beholding the physician. He who does not do what I command sees me in vain. This brings no profit. A man may dwell beside me, and yet, being disobedient, will be far away from me; yet he who obeys the *Dharma* will always enjoy the bliss of my presence." *(From pages 217-218 of Gospel of Buddha by Dr. Paul Carus, 6th edition, 1898).*

Those who have been in intimate touch with Mahatmaji, living in the same house with him, following him in his tours throughout the length and breadth of India, attending public meetings and conferences almost every two hours, sitting up late nights with him when he was beseiged by representatives of different sections of the community for advice and guidance, and in the Working Committees and in the sessions of the Congress and of the All-India Congress Committees besides seeing him writing endlessly in connection with his two weeklies and his daily correspondence, know full well the amount of hard work he has had to do, to what great strain his physical frame has been put. Truly, if we, his followers, are not spoilt children and our hearts are not hearts of stone, we must seek at all costs not only to please him and obey his last words and requests, but we must feel supremely pleased in the thought that at any rate he will have physical rest inside the prison-walls. So long as his body was free, he was not given a moment's rest by us, but now we should be better able to understand and appreciate the following words from his pen which concluded his article "If I am arrested—" "Fourthly and selfishly, it (Mahatmaji's arrest and imprisonment) "will give me a quiet and physical rest which perhaps I deserve."

Of course to many of us, a prison is a prison—something namely, which is extremely disagreeable. But to Mahatmaji, as to all free innocent souls fighting the war of right against governmental wrong-doing, a prison is the true abode of freedom, while also to others like some of us who are undisciplined and are given to bursts of passion—jail-life is extremely disciplinary in every respect, if only we know when and how to resist humiliations of the spirit, degrading our manhood, which is the divine in us.

30th March 1922

MR. GANDHI'S MESSAGE TO THE PARSIS

Mr. Gandhi addressed the following message to the Parsis from the Sabarmati Jail, through Mr. B. F. Bharucha :—How can I forget to write to you? Please tell my Parsee sisters and brothers never to lose faith in this movement. It is impossible for me to give up my confidence in them. There is no other programme before me than that of Khadi and Charkha, Charkha and Khadi. Hand-spun yarn must be as current among us as are small coins. To attain this object, we can put on no other cloth than hand-spun and hand-woven Khadi. So long as India is not able to do this much, Civil Disobedience will be futile, Swaraj cannot be attained, and Khilafat and the Punjab wrongs are impossible to be righted. If this conviction is driven home to you, keep on turning out yarn and using Khaddar. Be expert spinners.

Bande Mataram from
Mohandas.

13th April 1922

A LETTER FROM MAHATMA GANDHI

Mahatma Gandhi has sent the following letter to Mr. C. F. Andrews from Sabarmati Jail, in answer to a letter expressing deep regret that on account of the railway strike, he was not able to leave his work and come to him before the trial was over:—

Sabarmati Jail, March 17.

"My dear Charlie, I have just got your letter. You were quite right in not leaving your work. You should certainly go to Gurudev, and be with him as long as he needs you. I would certainly like your going to the Ashram (Sabarmati), and staying there awhile, when you are free. But I would not expect you to see me in jail; I am as happy as a bird! My ideal of a jail life—especially that of a civil resister,—is to be cut off entirely from all connection with the outside world. To be allowed a visitor is a privilege—a civil resister may neither seek, nor receive a privilege. The religious value of jail discipline is enhanced by renouncing privilege. The forthcoming imprisonment will be to me more a religious than a political advantage. If it is a sacrifice, I want it to be the purest.

With love, Yours,

Mohan.

13th April 1922

THE SECRET OF BAPU

(To realise the full significance of the observance of the 18th as a national day, we must bear in mind the great personality for whom we observe it and the noble ideals and principles that he stands for. "A lover of

Bapu" draws a living pen-picture of Mahatma Gandhi under the heading "The Secret of Bapu". "Bapu" means father and is the name by which Mahatma Gandhi is known amongst his devoted admirers. We draw special attention of our readers to the faithful and excellent pen-picture which we publish below.—Editor).

The secret of Bapu's hold upon the Indian masses is that Bapu loves them from the very bottom of his soul, as perhaps no man living has done. That love is also the secret of his incessant, interminable labours on their behalf. That love also explains Bapu's strange hankering for a peaceful renunciation of the body through the process of a prolonged fasting and prayer, when he conceived himself unworthy of the great trust that had been reposed on him. That explains again the internal agony which Bapu felt at the Chauri Chaura and the Bombay tragedies, and his longing to be sent to jail to suffer the severest punishment in some small expiation of the sins and crimes of those for whom he had laboured, but whom he had not been able to redeem. He would put on his khaddar loin-cloth in sheer love and devotion to a poverty-stricken, helpless people towards whom his heart went out in an endless prayer, and an endless ecstacy of suffering.

Bapu cannot bear the sight of evil and suffering, wherever they may be found. But he is no patriot in the technical sense of the term. He would not lift his little finger against anybody, even against the oppressor and the tyrant. For, Bapu cannot forget that he is his brother, only misled, mistrained, vicious,—aye, wicked. Bapu is a patriot, humanitarian and lover of God, all in one. For, he has no sense of hatred against any individuals or individual, because he considers himself as one of them. Bapu is a lover of India; for, the Indian people at the present moment are the most long-suffering of peoples, poverty-stricken, emasculated, downcast and helpless ; and because also, India to him when she has once been set on her feet, would represent a civilisation which shall be a beacon of light to humanity.

Bapu's sufferings and agonies on behalf of India are almost divine, because they have not the least tinge of hatred in them; and on that account are proving and shall prove to be paramount factors in saving India's soul. Therefore, the Lord is crucifying the lover for the sake of the beloved. His passionate devotion to Hindu-Muslim unity and his passionate repudiation of untouchability are, to those who have looked into Bapu's character, born of his innate love for man, whether friend or foe, high or low. There is nothing of the artificiality of civilised politics about Babu's politics; although the latter has promoted, and shall always promote, a political cause. In truth, in Babu's view, lofty ethics—that spirit of love and humanity which manifests itself in endless suffering and sacrifice for others, if applied to the solution of our present day social, economic and political problems—are capable of setting the world on its feet. The attainment of his political Swaraj for India is, to Babu, a new and a loftier method of saving a down-trodden world, wallowing in the mire of selfish greed and earth hunger.

If these fundamental qualities of character do not entitle Bapu in his own estimation, to be called a Mahatma, or a Great Soul, it is because, like the greatest of all true souls, Bapu has no consciousness of his own greatness. Bapu is all love and pity and tenderness, and is lost in the ocean of the divine life, even in the midst of his harrowing labours amongst us. Such greatness of soul is truly transcendent, and lesser souls like ourselves can only look at his virtues from our own angle of vision. Nevertheless, Bapu's soul draws us from afar as would a star of transcendent brilliance draws the most recalcitrant amongst us towards him, even against our own selves, and we are helplessly carried along. Bapu is a force—a moral and spiritual force—that will live for all time and will affect the destiny of peoples and nations, even though he may not have succeeded in lifting within the short space at his disposal the weight of a wearied world. For Bapu has behind him the *SHAKTI* of the Lord to reinforce him and his labours, and may be, he may even be, His chosen instrument.

A Lover of Bapu.

18th March 1923

THE GREAT STATE-TRIAL

(By N. C. Kelkar)

I feel indebted to Mahadeobhai Desai for asking me to sketch my impressions of the great Gandhi trial to which I was an eye-witness on the 18th March 1922. For it helps me to recall a vision which shall remain one of the cherished reminiscences of my life. Never were romance and reality rolled into a more vital unity than in that sublime spectacle.

As a member of the Working Committee of the Congress, I had that day the privilege of occupying one of the reserved seats in the Court-House. But the 'courthouse' was only one term in a whole series of misnomers on that occasion. The reader can well imagine what ideas the name of a State-trial brings in its train. But here everything was completely reversed. This State-trial was not so much a trial *by* the State as a trial *of* the State itself. And all else was naturally consonant.

The court-house was not the architectural, ill-lighted, awe-inspiring hall that, I fancy, it proverbially is in great State-trials. This was a mean, white-washed, inelegant, insipid room of the true barrack fashion. A hundred people could easily overcrowd it. From the interloper, who, for want of an admission ticket, spied with one eye from the farthest window, up to the Judge who presided over the trial, was one continuous assembly of human forms, knit together, as it were, by a real physical nexus. No one, high or low, among the hundred there could keep his distance.

The judge, I thought, was the most pathetic figure among them all in that memorable trial. Never was he charged with a more unpleasant duty. Never did he feel as he did on that day that an accused under judgement could be really superior to the judge himself. The bloom on Mr. Bloomfield's face had faded. A hectic pallor had taken its place. Neither the natural correctness of conduct nor the consciousness of prestige could keep off the creeping nervousness from him. For once in his official life a Civilian English Sessions Judge nodded respectful salutation to a native in the dock before he himself took his seat on the Bench. For once were the judicial words of a penal sentence belied by the tributary words of human admiration. "Would I not rather sit at your feet and learn a little of your nobility than send you to jail for six years?"—words like these might easily have come from the inner lips of Mr. Bloomfield when he stole a parting glimpse of Mahatma Gandhi.

The apologetic Advocate-general obviously felt quite

out of his element in conducting that State-trial. There was no tangled skein of a secret plot which his skill should unravel in the opening address. He felt the mockery of leading evidence where every thing was avowed and admitted. He winced at reading the articles charged, as every word in them was a bold indictment of the Government he represented, and left some unanswerable reproach sticking to the reader's soul, inspite of his assumed professional scornful manner. He regretfully missed the contentious opposition which he delights to meet in the Law Court every day, as it provides good sport for the keen file of his intellect or legal acumen. For once perhaps did Mr. Advocate-general also feel that the fat fees he would charge were simply wasted on him.

And what shall I say of the accused himself? Clad only in a Khadi enlargement of the proverbial fig-leaf, there was Mahatma Gandhi, with submission to none and yet with good-will to all, the grand accused, whom it was Mr. Bloomfield's rare privilege to try and judge. When he was brought from the jail to the court-house his guard looked more like an escort of honour. With his nimble feet he stepped into the court-room, and with one universal smile he at once shed a halo of the holy spirit of the blessed passive resister upon the whole assembly, from which even his prosecutors could not extricate themselves. But I doubt whether they really did not like to share in that glory. The accused was not only supremely serene but looked even festively joyful to a degree. Was it his trial or his own bridal ceremony? But he was even more jealous of his happiness than a bride-groom in that he had not even a single 'best man' by his side. No Counsel in robes or without robes appeared for him. He was himself his own Counsel.

And paradoxical as it may seem, also his own accuser. He needed no file of witnesses, no tomes of law-books, and no encumbering paraphernalia of authorities. A single type-writ sheet contained the whole of his defence, the greater part of it, however, being devoted rather to a justification and an aggravation of the offence than a defence in any shape or form.

Did he plead guilty to the charge? Yes, by all means. He was only eager that the great categorical question be put that he might answer it away, like a shot. For once in his life, Mr. Advocate-General realised that his task of prosecution could be a *thankful* task, and the convicting judge that, he could be complimented upon leniency *vis-a-vis* a penal sentence of six years' imprisonment.

Mahatma Gandhi thus succeeded in completely subduing all the latent or patent dramatic elements in the great State-trial by simply reversing the familiar points of view in the affair. And like a skilful railway pointsman, he shunted the train of the trial from the track of vulgar terror to that of refined sublimity. The hidden surprise upon, and the consequent humiliation of, the Prosecutor and the Judge might have turned the noble drama into a farce, if there were not elements of grandeur in it too pronounced to be turned into ridicule.

Great as were the efforts made by Mahatma Gandhi to keep the trial free from feeling, the Judge could not help giving it an emotional touch when he mentioned the name of Tilak in passing the sentence and trying to justify its severity by a precedent. And then Mahatmaji too could not help striking the sympathetic chord and declaring that he only felt honoured by the parallel cited. Swiftly did the memories of another great State-trial of fourteen years ago rush into the mind of every one present; and the Judge proved an unconscious wizard so to convert the dead past into the living present by one key-word. There must be surely some magic charm in a sentence of six years' imprisonment that it should be regarded by Government as an effective amulet for the salvation of India, and two heroes like these—Tilak and Gandhi—should accept it as such in terms and spirit. Yes, by common consent imprisonment of six years for men like these could certainly do much to cure India of its present maladies!

I wonder if Mr. Bloomfield did not leave the Court with a secret feeling of self-reproach. Mr. Advocate-General was happier for not being elevated to the Bench, for he could actually shake hands with the accused, and thus earn the needed atonement for even such small animus as might remain to his debit, after the remarkably fair and even gentle treatment he had given to the Mahatma and his co-accused. And the Police officers in attendance for once felt completely floored. Their usual fussy business of looking after a convict this day was gone. They need not hurry him out, and they would not have done it even if they could. With the disappearance of the judge and the Advocate-General from the Court-room the assembly was turned into a social gathering, the Police being simply ignored.

And then commenced the re-enactment of a scene with which I had been familiar for about a couple of years before. There was Mahatmaji sitting in the centre with a *melee* of men women and children, engrossed in talking to Mahatmaji and being talked to by him in return, with all the welcome, because enjoyable, interventions of wit, wisdom and repartee. I heard Mahatmaji affectionately chaffing a young dandy of five years on wearing a suit of foreign cloth and a fashionable necktie. He mildly reproched an old title-hunter advising him to get rid of his habit at least at that ripe age. By silent inspiration of courage he arrested the tears before they could moisten, and in his opinion tarnish, the eyes of some affectionate follower here; and to another there, more stern and practical, he would give a useful hint for further strenuous work alloted to him. The ladies felt caressed by his blessings, and the men felt they got a gift of strength by shaking his supple but saintly hands.

In half an hour the grand levee was over. One by one the gathering in the Court-house was dissolved. And even when the police escorted Mahatmaji back in the ominous motor-van of the jail, we all felt the trial yet vividly remaining behind of a spirit of rare devotion and self-sacrifice, which could not be suppressed by the proceedings of the State-trial for the moment, or even by the threatened absence of the hero, figuring in them, for six long weary years.

Four years ago, when I first read the prospectus of the Satyagrah-ashram founded by Mahatma Gandhi, the one word in it which attracted my attention most was the pledge of fearlessness prescribed for its inmates by this disciple of Gopal Krishna Gokhale. That, I said, must be the really more salient feature in the political design of this Ashram than the drastic code of puritanism that served as an adorning embroidery. And as I left the premises of the improvised Court-house I said to myself, 'Verily has this pledge been fulfilled.' Mahatmaji had by his personal example that day cast a true type of fearlessness which neither long time nor short memories can ever efface.

6th September 1923

THE KEY TO YERRAVDA

When the heart sinks and the head reels to think of the purposeless riots in various places in the U. P., there is one thing which soothes the troubled soul. It is the return of Moulana Mahomed Ali.

Dr. Kitchlew came and placed the issue before the country in words clear and emphatic. 'The situation is so bad that we cannot do without Mahatmaji. Not Swaraj, not Hindu-Moslem unity; let Mahatmaji's release be our first concern'—that has been the burden of all of his speeches. Lalaji too has placed the issue in the forefront, and has emphasised that the programme he suggests should be considered only in Mahatmaji's absence. And so has Moulana Mahomed Ali—but in a manner all his own, in a manner supremely captivating. His telegram to the revered mother Kasturibai—probably the first thing that he did immediately on his discharge —will remain in history for all time: "Searching Key of Yeravda prison with trust in God and in my fellow countrymen". And he has repeated his heart's desire to many another, asking them not to trouble him with further querries. The music and other demonstrations of welcome jarred on his ears; they were too much to bear in the absence of Bapu. As one thinks of this enthusiasm of devotion, almost beyond all telling, he is most irresistibly put in mind of Bharata of old, declaring before all his grievous distress,—the absence of Rama. All pleasures and palaces, the Ayodhya of his happy days, even the mothers and kinsmen, to say nothing of the offered, *gadi*,—all was naught to him without Rama. 'Permit me to join or bring back Rama, unless I see him the fire in my soul cannot be quenched;

the fierce longing of my eyes cannot be assuaged.' There is just this little difference. That he would get to see Rama, Bharata had no doubt; but he was not sure that he would bring him back. The key to Rama's recovery was with Rama as Bapu's recovery is with us. Even as Bharata rated himself for the exile of Rama, Mahomed Ali rates himself and his fellow men. It is we, he says, who have kept him in; let us, with trust in God, get him out.

One reads various prophecies about Kaliyuga, the present age, in ancient Sanskrit books. We read of the irreligion and immorality and iniquity, the diverse crimes against God and man, that man's race in India, at any rate, will in the Black Age perpetrate. It may be all true in proportion to one's quickness of perception and sensitiveness of conscience. But one thing the ancient sages' vision failed to prophesy is that a Muslim Mahomed Ali will be so devoted to a Hindu Gandhi, that he can find no rest or peace without him. Blessed we who have filled our eyes with their vision, with that friendship and brotherhood which ennoble and adorn both Hindiusm and Islam. The mad mobs in Saharanpur, Agra and other places may be too blinded with petty passions and animosities to see the significance of the return of Mahomed Ali and of his passionate cry. But it cannot long continue to be lost on them. In his return and the rallying cry that he has raised lies the key to Hindu-Muslim unity. Devotion to a great personality is indeed the key to all self-improvement, self-elevation, all unity—certainly to Hindu-Muslim unity. The strength of Islam and Christianity is the devotion to the Prophet and the Prince of Glory, cherished by every adherent of the respective religions. The strength of the religion of Indian Unity will be the devotion each bears to the greatest men of faiths different from his. For the sign of the purity and strength of a faith, as of a nation, is the thought and act of its best and most representative man. That devotion binds Mahomed Ali to Mahatmaji and Mahatmaji to Mahomed Ali. Take up anyone of Mahatmaji's speeches in those days when he used to go about with the bigger and the younger brothers. Every one of them you will find prefaced with an exhortation to the people to see Hindu-Muslim unity embodied in his attachment to the brothers. Attachment to the brothers meant to him attachment to Islam and he wanted the people to see the greatness of the faith in the greatness of its representative adherents. Even so does Mahomed Ali to-day. His ardent cry for the release of Mahatmaji, his passionate declaration that Mahatmaji is dearer to him than his brother, is an exhortation to all, especially to the erring brethren of his faith, to see the greatness of Hinduism in the greatness of Gandhi and to forget the little things about them that stir up their prejudices and their animosities. In his self-surrender to Allah, he says that he will think that his task is unfulfilled if he fails to bring about Hindu-Moslem unity. But it is not difficult to see that in the search for the key to Yeravda is the solution of Hindu-Muslim unity.

Where then is the key? Dr. kitchlew in his straight, plain manner answered: 'Satyagraha'. The poetic Moulana gave a suggestive reply: 'I adhere to Mahatmaji's *programme* of non-violent Non-co-operation. There is absolutely no change in my views.' In the course of a reply to a telegram from Mr. Raza Ali he said:—

"If co-operation was *haram* according to the Islamic law two years ago, it cannot become *halal* to-day unless the *Jazirut-ul-Arab* is once more under an absolutely independent and exclusive Muslim sovereignty and the Khilafat's relationship with the Muslim world is recognised according to the Islamic law. Have you been able to persuade the British Government to respect these religious requirements?"

The key then is not to be found in co-operation, not in the Councils, but in the way that the Master had shown. He knows he cannot insult Mahatmaji by seeking to release him with the help of Councils that do not represent his country—that will not represent it until we have Swaraj. He knows that the thing nearest his heart was exactly the one nearest to his own heart, viz., *Kurbani.* That is his life breath and he knows that it was Mahatmaji's life breath. In a passage of matchless vigour, Mahatmaji has revealed the miracle of *Kurbani*:—

"It is the magnitude of Irish sacrifice which has been the deciding factor. The late President Kruger, when with a handful of his undisciplined countrymen hurled his ultimatum against the British Empire, said he would stagger humanity. He meant that he would sacrifice every Boer man, woman and child and leave not a single Boer heart to subdue. And England yielded when she was choked with the bloody feast that the Boers had provided for her. And even so Ireland has been staggering humanity for many a long year. And England has yielded when she is no longer able to bear the sight of blood pouring out of the thousands of Irish arteries. I know for certain that it is no legal subtleties, discussions on academic justice or resolutions of Councils and Assemblies that will give us what we want. We shall have to stagger humanity even as South Africa and Ireland have been obliged to. Only instead of repeating South African and Irish histories, non-co-operators are learning from the living examples of these two nations the art of spilling their own blood without spilling that of their opponents.

Mahadeo Desai.

[K]

AT THE HOSPITAL

On 13th January 1924, the whole of India was painfully surprised when the following statement issued by the Director of Information, Bombay :

Owing to his being found to be suffering from abdominal pain and fever, Mr. Gandhi was removed from Yerrowada Jail on Saturday morning and taken to the Sassoon Hospital, Poona.

An operation was performed in the evening and Mr. Gandhi was found to be suffering from suppurating appendix. The Civil Surgeon reports that Mr. Gandhi has stood the operation very well.

At the request of the Civil Surgeon and also by the wish of Mr. Gandhi, Dr. Dalal was asked to proceed to Poona.

A later Press Communique issued the same day by the Director of Information stated : Mr. Gandhi's condition this morning was as good as could be expected. His temperature was normal and the Doctors are so far quite satisfied with the result of the operation.

A special supplement of the "Navjivan" issued the same day at Ahmedabad says that Miss Anusya visited last Tuesday Indulal Yagnig in the Yerrowada Jail and learnt from him that Mr. Gandhi was suffering since Saturday from fever which once rose to 102 degrees. Therefore Mr. Ramdas Gandhi enquired by wire about his father's health to which the following reply was received last Friday : "Your father is suffering from ordinary fever. No cause for anxiety. You can see him when you like."

The Superintendent of the Yerrowada Jail wired yesterday evening saying "Your father removed to the Sassoon Hospital, Poona."

MR. SASTRI'S STATEMENT

The Right Hon'ble V. S. SrinivasaSastri, P. C., issued the following statement to the press the same day 13th January 1924:

I was called suddenly to the Sassoon Hospital yesterday night to see Mahatma Gandhi. In view of the profound interest that the matter would have for the public I venture to make the following statement:—

"Dr. V. B. Gokhale came to me about 8-45 p. m. just as I was finishing my dinner and told me how the Yerrowada authorities had removed Mr. Gandhi to the Sassoon Hospital where he was in charge. He was about to be operated on for appendicitis. As the case was serious the patient had been asked whether he would like any doctor friends of his to be sent for. He had mentioned Doctor Dalal of Bombay and Doctor Jiviraj Mehta who was in Baroda. Both had been wired to and attempts had been made but in vain to get at Doctor Dalal by means of the phone. Meanwhile in view of the patient's temperature and pulse it had been decided to perform the operation immediately and he was asked whether he would like to have any friends brought to see him. He mentioned me Doctor Phatak of the Non-co-operation Party and Mr. N. C. Kelkar. Doctor Gokhale and I started at once and took Doctor Phatak on the way, Mr. Kelkar being away at Satara.

On my entering the room we greeted each other and I enquired how he felt as to the operation. He answered firmly that the doctors had come to a definite conclusion and he was content to abide by it, and in reply to further inquiry he said that he had full confidence in the medical men about him and that they had been very kind and very careful. Should there arise any public agitation he added that it should be made known that he had no complaint whatever to make against the authorities and that so far as the care of his body went their treatment left nothing to be desired. Then I enquired if Mrs. Gandhi had been informed of his condition. He said that she did not know the latest developments but she knew that for sometime he had not been well and he expected to hear from her. He then made enquiries of my wife and of my colleagues in the Servants of India Society, viz., Messrs. Devadhar, Joshi, Patwardhan and Kunzru. He asked: "Have your frequent journeys out of India benefited your health?" Doctor Phatak then read a draft statement to be signed by Mr. Gandhi conveying his consent to the operation. After hearing it once, Mr. Gandhi put in his spectacles and read it himself. Then he said he would like the wording to be changed and asked Colonel Maddock who was in the room what he thought. The Colonel said Mr. Gandhi knew best how to put it in appropriate language. His own suggestion would be of much value.

Then he dictated a lengthy statement* which I took down in pencil. It was addressed to Colonel Maddock who was to perform the operation. The letter acknowledged the exceeding kindness and attention which he had received from Col. Maddock, the Surgeon General, and other medical men and stated he had the utmost confidence in Colonel Maddock, officers and attendants. It proceeded to thank the Government for their consideration in owing him to send for his own doctors but

* See p. 1370.

as they could not be got, in spite of the best attempts made by Colonel Maddock and as delay would in the opinion of the Colonel involve serious risk, he requested him to perform the operation at once.

When it was finished I read it out to him once. Then he called Colonel Maddock to his side and I read it again at his desire. Colonel Maddock was quite satisfied and remarked: "Of course you know best how to put in proper language." He then drew up his proper posture for signing the paper, which he did in pencil. His hand shook very much and I noticed that he did not dot the "I." At the end he remarked to the doctor: "See how my hand trembles. You will have to put this right." Colonel Maddock answered: "Oh! We will put tons and tons of strength into you."

As the operation room was being got ready the doctors went out and I found myself nearly alone with the Mahatma. After a remark or two of a purely personal nature I asked him whether he had anything particular to say. I noticed a touch of eagerness as he replied as though he was waiting for an opportunity to say something. "If there is an agitation," he said, "for my release after the operation, which I do not wish, let it be on proper lines. My quarrel with the Government is there and will continue so long as the originating causes exist. Of course there cannot be any conditions. If the Government think they have kept me long enough they may let me go, that would be honourable if they think I am an innocent man and that my motives have been good. While I have a deep quarrel with the Government, I love the Englishmen and have many friends amongst them. They may release me. But it must not be on false issues. Any agitation must be kept on proper non-violent lines. Perhaps I have not expressed myself quite well but you had better put it in your own inimitable style."

I mentioned the motions of which notice had been given in the Assembly and added that, though Government might in other circumstances have opposed it, I expected that they would take a different line.

I then pressed him again for a message to his people, his followers or the country. He was surprisingly firm on this subject. He said he was a prisoner of Government and he must observe ths prisoners' code of honour scrupulously. He was supposed to be civilly dead. He had no knowledge of outside events and he could not have anything to do with the public. He had no message.

. . . .

Briskly at this point the nurse came in with some articles of apparel for him,and signalled to me to depart. In a few minutes he was shifted to the operation room. I sat outside marvelling at the exhibitions I had witnessed of high-mindedness, forgiveness, chivalry and love transcending ordinary human nature, and what a mercy it was that the Non-co-operation movement should have had a leader of such serene vision and sensitiveness to honour.

The Surgeon-General and the Inspector-General of Prisons were also there. I could see from their faces how anxious they were at the tremendous responsibility that lay on them. They said that the patient had borne the operation very well indeed, that some puss had come out and that it was a matter of congratulation that the operation had not been delayed any longer. The patient had had morphia and was expected to sleep soundly for some time longer when we dispersed.

I learnt from the Doctor this morning that the patient's condition was thoroughly satisfactory.

I have read out this statement to Doctor Phatak who approves of it and adds that his inquiry as to a message elicited the same sort of answers.

Sassoon Hospital, Poona, Jan. 12 1924.

Dear Col. Maddock,

I know that you know the history of my illness during the past 6 months. You have been extraordinarily kind to me. You, the Surgeon-General and other medical gentlemen have come to the conclusion that any delay in performing the operation described by you to me involves considerable risk. You were kind enough to tell me that the Government had authorised you to send for any of my special medical friends. I therefore suggested the names of Dr. Dalal and Dr. Jivraj Mehta. You have tried your utmost to secure their presence but then you have not been able to get at either of them. I have the fullest confidence in you and regard being had to the serious nature of the case, I would ask you please to go on with the operation without delay.

I am,
Yours sincerely,
(Sd.) M. K. Gandhi.

7th February 1924

AT THE SASSOON HOSPITAL

God in his infinite mercy has spared for us our Bapu, however little we might deserve him. When the news first reached me on the 13th, my guilty conscience began to whisper to me that the stock of my *punyam* was over, and unless the good luck of the rest of my countrymen came to my aid, I would not have the privilege of seeing Bapu. But the privilege did come indeed, after full twenty-six months. I saw him ten days ago. In the flesh, he was hardly half himself, it was nothing less than torture to expect him to speak. But you could not stop him from torturing himself. He felt he must speak to us, at whatever cost, and he began telling us how he came to be removed to the Sassoon Hospital. He surely knew that we had all the details from Devadas and others. But he must shower extra affection on us by narrating the whole tale himself. We listened mutely wondering what we had done to deserve this excess of affection.

But if any one had asked me to write anything about Bapu that day I would not have had the heart to do it. He was so emaciated, so shrivelled up, that you could not bring yourself to be composed enough to say or write anything about his condition. But, thank God, he began picking up unexpectedly fast, and I am happy to say that I feel now able to say something about what is happening in this the greatest of our places of pilgrimage to-day.

These have been days which will live in our annals. The Nation had the good fortune to see its revered leader at work, to see him mould heroes out of clay whilst at work. It had yet to see his gospel go forth from his sick-bed and see it translated into act before his eyes. It has done so during the past fortnight. It is a living atmosphere of love of which you begin to feel the effects, as you approach the room which happens to possess to-day the light that trancends the bounds of time and space.

I have had the privilege, as unmerited probably as the

one I had two years ago, of being with him these ten days, though not the privilege of serving him. That privilege is being entirely monopolised by the hospital nurses. One of them is an Englishwoman of long experience. He cannot help smiling as she approaches him. One day she comes talking about her pet dogs, and draws Bapu in a conversation about the different varieties of dogs and their usefulness. Another day she talks about her experience in English and African hospitals, and tells him how she has lived throughout her life the lesson that her Doctors taught her of never trying to be popular. A third she decorates the room with the finest flowers and asks Bapu to admire her work. There was another nurse much younger, but equally fond of Bapu, who prided herself on having Mr. Gandhi as her first "private" patient after passing out as a trained nurse. "Nursing is not always a joy, at times it is a task", she used to say, "but it has been a pure joy and a privilege to nurse Mr. Gandhi. The Doctor comes and tells me, 'you did not use to print your reports like this ever before' and I tell him straightaway, 'Nor had I such a patient before.'" Another day she told me, 'my friends were chaffing me for getting fond of Mr. Gandhi; I told them they would do the same if they had the privilege of serving him.'

And the Surgeon's love for him is as undisguised as the nurses'. The Civil Surgeon has had letters and telegrams pouring on him to congratulate him for the way in which he was serving Mahatmaji, and it is not without a blush that he says, "how am I to reply to all of them? Shall I do it through the Press?"

I do not know if any one attending Bapu has the slightest consciousness that he is serving a state prisoner. A compelling love chokes all other consciousness.

But why? Even he who has to look upon him as a prisoner seemed scarcely different in his manner from the rest. Col. Murray, the Yerravda Superintendent, came to see Bapu the other day. "Do you think Mr. Gandhi, I have neglected you? No, I thought I should not disturb you. And as I see you now after some days I find you very much better. The Colonel also assures me you are quickly improving. Your friends remember you. Mr. Ganni especially asked me to tell you that he still gets up at 4 o'clock. Every one of them is happy, and misses you—I hope they do so permanently." His sweetness was touching. "Thank you Col. Murray," said Bapu, "but I assure you nothing will please me better than to be up and doing and be under your kind care once again at Yerravda." You never could tell, if you did not know him, that a jail Superintendent was speaking to one of his prisoners, and you could almost visualise the atmosphere of love created by Bapu in his prison cell at Yerravda.

But I must say something about Bapu's health, rather than go on talking about his alchemy of love. He looks still emaciated, but he is better than he might have been as he told Mr. Rajagopalachariar, the other day, rating him for his ill-health, adding "and you are worse than you ought to be." His weight which at its best was 112 lbs, in jail cannot be now very much over a maund, though it is difficult to be precise, as he is still in bed, and cannot be moved out of it. There is no doubt, however, that he is getting stronger every day. There is a chain hanging down from the top of his bed of which he gets a hold to enable him to sit up or turn in bed. 'That's for my gymnastics' he said to a friend the other day. The fingers are still shaky, but not so much as before. His nourishment is nearly half his usual quantity, and consists of about 2 pounds of milk, a couple or two oranges and grapes. The bowels open without the help of the enema, though a mild purgative is at times necessary. Above all he gets most restful sleep of the kind he has never had during the last few years. For even the days in jail were of 'toil unsevered from tranquillity.' From my talks with the Surgeon I can say that there is now no cause for anxiety, though the convalescence will certainly be prolonged and even indefinite.

And need I say anything about the torrents of love that have taken their course to Poona from all the parts of India? Devadas who should be privileged to be with his father for all the time has to content himself serving him by attending to the numerous letters and telegrams coming day and night inquiring after Bapu's health. But the telegrams and letters do not exhaust the affections. One day the residents of far off Tanjore write to say that they did their *archanas* and *abhishekams* in a particular Mandir, and send on the sacred ashes and *kumkum* for Mahatmaji another day comes a letter from Kashi telling Devadas that special *japas* were performed in the temple of Mrityunjay Mahadeo (the Conqueror of Death), that hundreds of Brahmins will be continuing their *anushthanams* until Mahatmaji gets better, and they do not omit to send the sacred water of the Ganges and the sacred ashes also. Hindus from Shiyali, Tirupur, and Dindigul vie in their love with their Mussalman brothren of Nagore who send special *tabarruk* (prasadam) of some *Aulia*. A Parsi sister writes offering her blood if the Surgeons thought it necessary to put in blood in Mahatmaji, while an English lady writes detailed instructions about Bapu's diet, and Mrs. Gokhale from Bombay writes to say that she will spin an extra couple of hours every day, now that Mahatmaji cannot spin.

One of the constant visitors at the hospital—and of these there is no end, my duty here being only that of standing at the gate to keep them away—is an Englishman, an old military pensioner who makes it a point to come every other day with a boquet of flowers, and gets into Bapu's room unobstructed by any one. It is simply impossible to stop him. Impatiently he rushes to Bapu, shakes his hand, and delivers his message of cheer in a few seconds and walks away, "Cheer up old man! I see that you are very much better than yesterday. I know you must get better. How old are you? Fifty five. Oh it is nothing, You know I am 82, Get better, please do." One day he stopped and asked, "can I do anything for you Mr, Gandhi?" "No," said Bapu, "Please pray for me." "That I will but tell me if I can do anything for you. Please do tell me. Believe me to be your brother." To which Bapu replies with a smile, "Believe me I have amongst my friends a number of Englishmen whom I regard as more than my brothers." The man is deeply touched, moves out assuring us that he prays thrice every day that Mr. Gandhi may live up to his age, and also telling us that many Englishmen pray for him, and many officers inquire after him.

The picture will be incomplete if I did not say a word about the illustrious leaders who are now flocking to Poona to see their leader. They did not come untill now, as they knew it would not be well to disturb him. A man like Mr. Jayakar says, "I will now come, but will only have his darshan from a distance," and Pt. Jawaharial assures Devadas that he would come last of all. The big brother comes, and insists that Mahatmaji should not talk to him, fumbles about on Mahatmaji's bed for his legs, which he finds with some difficulty, opens out the covering, and kisses them. Shankerlal and others like him, are choked with tears and Pandit Motilalji has no heart to get away without bidding him good bye a second time, and deliberately misses a train. Lalaji comes eager to have a talk with him, but stands aside, almost inspite of himself, so that he may not draw him into a talk with him. He visits him again before leaving Poona. There is something in him which is struggling to find expression. Probably it checks the tears, or the tears check it. But ultimately it succeeds and bursts out. But Bapu with his inimitable smile says, "Lalaji, the joke is too big for my stomach. I would have a hearty laugh, but for the wound and the stiches." Lalaji, who would have gone otherwise with a heavy heart, goes away with a much lighter heart, not without assuring others also that we may not be sad now, but rejoice that God in His infinite mercy has blessed us.

Poona, 29-1-24, Mahadev Desai.

P. S.

The above reached too late for the last issue. I should have followed up with more impressions. But the news of the release must crowd out everything. I must warn the public that the A. P. I. telegram saying that Mahatmaji is quite well is far from the truth. And may I also say that the fact that Maulana Mahomed Ali had asked Mahatmaji to visit Ajmer immediately on discharge from the hospital alarmed me? He is still in bed, though he can just toddle in his room. It will be months before he gets fit and strong again. Let the country give him a long period of undisturbed rest and labour and pray that he may be long preserved to us.

6-2-24 M. D.

21st February 1924

THE TRUE RULER OF INDIA

(By C. F. Andrews)

On my arrival from England, I was quite shocked when I saw the emaciated form of Mahatma Gandhi in the Sassoon Hospital at Poona. Those have been with him however informed me that I should have been far more greatly shocked if I had seen his condition only a few days before. At once I felt the truth of Rabindra Nath Tagore's words, that each day he was kept a prisoner was a day of humiliation for the rulers of the country. No order had yet come for his release and the Viceroy's speech contained no hint of it. To me it had seemed almost incredible that Christmas Day had passed as the day of peace and good-will, without such a simple and natural act of peace and good-will being done.

Now at last, as I write, the news has come. The release has been announced. Although its lateness detracts somewhat from its value, yet if it brings with it any change of heart in the rulers, it is welcome. The future alone will show.

Those who were near the sufferer in the hospital had many things to tell me about the kindness he had received. The Civil Surgeon's goodness, which had been so full of courage and skill, the nurses' tender care, the utter absence of all official restraint,—these represented a different gesture from the repression of former days. They had prepared the way for the final act of release.

It has been Mahatma Gandhi's supreme faith that there is a nobler element in man that may be won over by love. For this reason, he began his Non-co-operation movement, not in bitterness but in love. For this reason, he spoke with the frankness of true love to the judge who condemned him to prison. For this reason, he wrote in the columns of *Young India* again and again explaining to the rulers the object which he had in view, so that there might be no possible misunderstanding. But, in spite of it all, it was nothing less than a tragedy in England to find how he had been misunderstood.

If the question is asked, what is the sum and substance of the charge which Mahatma Gandhi laid against the British Government in India, it may be summed up in a single phrase. He charged them with the oppression of the poor. In the statement which he made at his trial, his condemnation of the British Raj was this: They had oppressed the poor. The hungry skeleton-like figures, which Mahatma Gandhi had seen in Orissa and elsewhere, had haunted his mind till he could never forget them, by night or by day. He went so far as to offer to co-operate again, if the British rulers would join with him in a campaign to destroy the drink and drug traffic and to build up the industrial village-life by the encouragement of *Khaddar*. But such simple work of lowly service was beyond the ken of the present rulers. They must do their work in their own patronising way or not at all. The gorgeous magnificence of an Imperial Delhi obsessed their minds. They neglected to take note of the plain fact that all this magnificence would only be an added burden to the poor. They spent fabulous sums upon it, until the treasury was empty, and then doubled the burden of the salt tax in order to prevent a deficit. The crores of rupees spent on building a New Delhi over the ruins of old Delhi could not be sacrificed. The one necessary of life to the many millions of half-starving people must be taxed instead.

There is a weakness due to long ages of subjection which has invaded the mind of India itself and supports this vulgar craving for a display of pomp and power such as New Delhi affords. Mahatma Gandhi has called it a 'slave mentality'. It may be seen in our own day in the gaping crowds that frequent the race courses, whenever they are patronised by Viceroys and Governors in state procession. Extravagant durbars, royal visits, imperial pageants, British Empire Exhibitions, all draining away the wealth of the country, have become more frequent of late in order to captivate the waning attention of the common people. But the spiritual mind of India is not captivated by things so tawdry as these. Rather it pays silent homage to this one tired sufferer in the hospital at Poona, who has looked into the face of death without fear. For there is a ruler of India here, in this hospital, Mahatma Gandhi, whose sway is greater than all imperial power. His name will be remembered and sung by the village people long after the names of the modern governors in their palaces at New Delhi are forgotten. When all the buildings of Raisina have crumbled into ruins, such as those around the Kutub Minar and Taghlakabad, the name of Mahatma Gandhi will still be taught by mothers to their little children as one of the greatest of India's saints and saviours.

For there is a spiritual palace which Mahatma Gandhi has built up out of an eternal fabric. Its foundations are deeply and truely laid in the Kingdom of God. No oppression of the poor has gone to build it. Love and devotion and service to the poor are its golden decorations. No military pomp reigns within its borders, but only the peaceful harmony of human souls. No race or colour distinctions have any place in it. No clash of religious controversy mars its silence. Its empire is the heart.

Difficult indeed it is for me to snatch myself away from this hospital room with its patient, now that once the vision has been seen, the *darshan* for which I have waited so long in my journey across the sea. I came to the hospital at Poona with the expectation of going afterwards to Delhi. But the spirit within me has leapt up in revolt, as though it were impossible now to make any such proposal. For, here I have seen a vision which makes all thoughts of doing anything political at Delhi fade away. It might have been possible to have gone to Delhi, if I had not visited this hospital. But to go now, after this, would be almost like—I hardly know how to put it—a sacrilege. I could journey to Sabarmati Ashram; I could go to Shantiniketan; but not into the midst of the turmoil of politics at Delhi. Let me keep pure the vision which God has given me. For when such a gift has come, there is nothing else in life except to hold it fast.

NATIONAL PRAYER ON 18TH

Maulana Mohamed Ali, President of the Congress, issued the following message to his countrymen under date January, 15:

"Ever since news was received from Poona that Mahatma Gandhi was removed from Yerrawada Jail to the Sassoon Hospital for a surgical operation, the nation has been waiting for further news of his health with bated breath. The shock to the nation was almost too great even for prayers though what every feeling has all this time suffered is itself one long prayer to heaven. But the time has now come that we should organise ourselves to offer a national prayer, beseeching Almighty God to grant complete and speedy recovery to India's greatest son. Friday, 18th inst., being Gandhi Day, seems to be the most suitable day for the purpose. Mussalmans will no doubt offer prayers in their mosques after Friday Service, but I suggest that the joint national prayer of men and women of all communities should be offered precisely at 5 p. m., standard time all over India and that mass meetings should be organised everywhere for this purpose. I trust my suggestion will meet with the Nation's approval and that steps will be taken immediately to act upon it."

WORKING COMMITTEE

At a meeting of the Congress Working Committee held at Bombay on January 30, 31, and February 1, the following resolutions were passed and business transacted, besides many others dealing with Congress administration:—

GANDHI MONTH

> The Working Committee of the Indian National Congress is deeply thankful to merciful Providence that Mahatma Gandhi has passed safely through his recent grave illness and that his further services in the cause of freedom have thus been vouchsafed to the nation. The Committee appeals to the nation that in order to prepare for a great struggle to be carried on all over the country to wrench from Government his and the nation's freedom and establish Swarajya, a supreme effort should be made to strengthen the Congress organisation in every respect and for this purpose the month beginning from 18th February and ending on 18th March next should be observed as the Gandhi month and devoted to intensive national work by every man and woman desiring the emancipation of the country. The

Working Committee calls upon all Indians to put forth the utmost endeavour to cloth the nation in Khaddar, to enrol Congress members and to collect money for the Tilak Swarajya Fund. All Congress Committees are called upon to organise work at once in order to carry out the above resolution.

THE RELEASE ORDER

There was intense excitement in the hospital this morning when the news came that Mahatmaji had been released, telegraphed the special correspondent of the *Hindu* on February, 5, 1924, who was one intimately in touch with Mahatmaji:

The news reached the hospital in this manner. Mr. C. F. Andrews had gone early to the hospital and had been laughing and joking with Mahatmaji as he usually does each morning since his return from England. Mahatmaji enjoyed this and they were there engaged together when quite unexpectedly Colonel Maddock, the Doctor, came in and said to Mahatma Gandhi: "I am so glad to see you looking so well this morning." Mahatmaji introduced Mr. Andrews to him and they shook hands.

Then Colonel Maddock said: "I am so glad to tell you that I have some very good news to give you and I wanted myself to be the first to bring it to you. The order came last night by special messenger and here it is. You are unconditionally released."

The Mahatma remained entirely quiet and unmoved and said to Colonel Maddock: "Perhaps you would not mind reading to me the order."

When Colonel Maddock had read the order through, Mahatmaji smiled at the Colonel and said: "I hope you will not mind my remaining your guest and your patient a little longer." This, he said laughingly, and the Colonel replied, with a smile: "I hope you will continue to obey all my instructions as a doctor."

Mahatmaji promised to do so. Then he turned to the Colonel and thanked him for all his exceeding kindness.

The scene was one that was wonderful to witness. There was a complete absence of any excitement and the main feature of Mahatmaji's attitude as he received the news with his characteristic smile and accepted the overpowering greetings from Mr. Andrews and all his other friends, including Maulana Shaukat Ali who happened to be in Poona, was that it was like the absence of all excitement which characterised the night of February, 10, two years ago when he received the news of a different nature with the same self-possession as a brave soldier of Satyagraha.

The doctors who have paid him hurried visits by turns since his release have had a glimpse of him in his unfettered freedom and have seen how unmoved he has been with the excitement all around him. They have acknowledged all his wishes with more than usual courtesy. Colonel Maddock, after dressing his wound with his own hands again this morning, expressed satisfaction at his progress. At the same time he gave a very strict warning that nothing must be done to tire the distinguished patient. He must be given all the rest and repose possible and must sleep whenever he could manage to do so both at night and during the day, for the tired body sorely needed rest.

Mahatmaji read through a message which Mr. Andrews has sent to the Associated Press at Mahatmaji's request. He passed it after it had been read. From this message it will be seen how important rest is for the patient and how there is need of patience on the part of the general public so that there may not be the slightest relapse on account of the tiring visits of a multitude of friends which must be altogether avoided.

Telegrams begin to pour in almost immediately after the Colonel's visit.

Mahatma Gandhi has asked Mr. C.F. Andrews to go at once to Sabarmati in order to give there a message from Mahatmaji himself to the students and teachers and dwellers in the Ashram. He has already started, but will return immediately because his presence will be required again in Poona when Mahatmaji's message has been delivered. The first message that Mahatmaji sent was to the Parsee Rustomjee in Durban which will at once be telegraphed all over South Africa and will give there the joyful news.

MR. ANDREWS' STATEMENT

The news of Mr. Gandhi's release has been received, stated an Associated Press message issued on 5th February 1924, with great satisfaction by all sections of public and to-day it is the absorbing topic of conversation.

Mr. Gandhi had a long talk with Mr. C. F. Andrews this morning. It is learnt that he will remain in hospital for at least another fortnight.

Mr. Gandhi or none of his party had learnt anything of his release till 7-30 a.m. It was Col. Maddock who first informed him of the good news. Mr. C. F. Andrews was present at the occasion and he has issued a graphic statement of his impression which will be wired from Bombay. Mr. Gandhi has been removed to Division No. 9 nursing home which are private apartments this noon. He has a separate spacious room and nurse is in attendance. Everything now has a cheery atmosphere and visitors are pouring in hundreds. Mr. Gandhi interviewed stated that he intends to issue a statement tomorrow.

Mr. C. F. Andrews has communicated the following statement to the Associated Press concerning Mr. Gandhi:

"I was present at the Sassoon Hospital this morning about 7-30 A.M. and found Mahatma Gandhi very bright and cheerful after a good night's rest. While we were talking, Col. Maddock, who has been in charge of the patient in the hospital, came in and announced to Mahatmaji the news of his unconditional release and congratulated him upon it most heartily. He then read out to him the words of the official message and said that it had come on Monday night by a special messenger. Therefore he had taken the earliest opportunity of coming to him as he wished to be the first man to bear the news that he was now free.

Mahatma Gandhi remained quiet for a few moments and then said to Col. Maddock with a smile: "I hope you will allow me to remain your patient and also your guest for a little longer". The Doctor laughed and told him that he trusted that his patient would go on obeying his orders as a Doctor and that he himself might have the very great pleasure and satisfaction of seeing him thoroughly restored to health.

Later on, in that morning after dressing the wound, Col. Maddock gave warning that the recovery of the patient which was going on so well might be seriously thrown back if any unnecessary excitement or tiredness was caused in the next few days by the visits of those who wished to see him. The kindest thing in the world would be for everyone, except those who were nursing him, to give him all the rest possible at this critical time in his recovery. It had to be remembered that the wound, which had to be made while performing the operation, was not fully healed, and a little over-tasking of the strength of the patient might throw the recovery back. The next fortnight would be the time when every reserve of strength would be needed in order the wound might be fully healed. Everything had gone well up to the present but it was imperative that no unnecessary risks shall be incurred.

Mahatma Gandhi was removed by the Doctor's orders into another room with an outside verandah where he could be able to get the full benefit of the sunshine and open air.

Telegrams began to pour in upon him from an early hour. The first telegram reached the hospital very soon after Col. Maddock had left.

I would wish, if I may be permitted to do so after all I have seen in the hospital concerning Mahatma Gandhi's health, to add my own urgent request to the warning given by the doctor for, while undoubtedly, Mahatma Gandhi has recovered wonderfully hitherto, he is still in a weak condition and it must be remembered that the healing of the wound has still to go on and anything that in the slightest degree might bring about a relapse must be avoided. Every day of complete rest which he can now obtain, especially during the next fortnight will mean an immense difference for the future. It would be the greatest kindness possible if those to whom his health is most precious would strictly observe the doctor's instructions until the recovery has been fulfilled.

It will also be quite impossible for Mahatmaji to grant interviews to press correspondents.

After writing out this statement, I read it over to Mahatma Gandhi himself at his own request and he has passed it for the press.

MAHATMAJI'S STATEMENT

Mahatmaji has addressed the following to Moulana Mahomed Ali, President of the Indian National Congress :—

My dear Friend and Brother,

I send you, as the President of the Congress, a few words which I know our countrymen expect from me on my sudden release. I am sorry that the Government have prematurely released me on account of my illness. Such a release can bring me no joy, for I hold that the illness of a prisoner affords no ground for his release.

I would be guilty of ungratefulness if I did not tell you and through you the whole public that both the goal and the hospital authorities have been all attention during my illness. Colonel Murray, the Superintendent of the Yerrowada Prison, as soon as he suspected that my illness was at all serious, invited Colonel Maddock to assist him and I am sure promptest measures were taken by him to secure for me the best treatment possible. I could not have been removed to the David and Jacob Sassoon Hospital a moment earlier. Colonel Maddock and his staff have treated me with the utmost attention and kindness. I may not omit the nurses who have surrounded me with sisterly care. Though it is now open to me to leave this Hospital, knowing that I can get no better treatment anywhere else, with Colonel Maddock's kind permission, I have decided to remain under his care till the wound is healed and no further medical treatment is necessary.

The public will easily understand for sometime to come I shall be quite unfit for active work and those who are interested in my speedy return to active life will hasten it by postponing their natural desire to see me. I am unfit, and shall be for some weeks perhaps, to see a number of visitors. I shall better appreciate the affection of friends if they will devote greater time and attention to such national work as they may be engaged in and especially to hand spinning.

My release has brought me no relief. Whereas before release I was free from responsibility save that of conforming to goal discipline and trying to qualify myself for more efficient service, I am now overwhelmed with a sense of responsibility I am ill-fitted to discharge. Telegrams of congratulation have been pouring in upon me. They have but added to the many proofs I have received of the affection of our countrymen for me. It naturally pleases and comforts me. Many telegrams however betray hopes of results from my service which stagger me. The thought of my utter incapacity as to cope with the work before me humbles my pride.

Though I knew very little of the present situation in the country, I know sufficient to enable me to see that, perplexing as the national problems were at the time of the Bardoli resolutions, they are far more perplexing to day. It is clear that without unity between Hindus, Mahomedans, Sikhs, Parsis and Christians and other Indians all talk of Swaraj is idle. This unity which I fondly believed in 1922 had been nearly achieved has, so far as Hindus and Mussalmans are concerned, I observe, suffered a severe check. Mutual trust has given place to distrust. An indissoluble bond between the various communities must be established if we are to win freedom. Will the thanksgiving of the nation over my release be turned into a solid unity between the communities? That will restore me to health far quicker than any medical treatment or rest cure. When I heard in the gaol of the tension between Hindus and Mahomedans in certain places, my heart sank within me. The rest I am advised to have will be no rest with the burden of disunion preying upon me. I ask all those who cherish love towards me to utilise it in furtherance of the union we all desire. I know that the task is difficult but nothing is difficult if we have a living faith in God. Let us realise our own weakness and approach Him and He will surely help. It is weakness which breeds fear and fear breeds distrust. Let us both shed our fear, but I know that even if one of us will cease to fear we shall cease to quarrel. Nay, I say that your tenure of office will be judged solely by what you can do in the cause of union. I know that we love each other as brothers. I ask you therefore to share my anxiety and help me to go through the period of illness with a lighter heart.

If we could but visualise the growing pauperism of the land and realise that the spinning wheel is the only remedy for the disease, the wheel will leave us little leisure for fighting. I had during the last two years ample time and solitude for hard thinking. It made me a firmer believer than ever in the efficacy of the Bardoli programme and therefore in the unity between the races, the charka, the removal of untouchability and the application of non-violence in thought, word and deed to our methods as indispensable for Swaraj. If we faithfully and fully carry out this programme, we need never resort to Civil Disobedience and I should hope that it will never be necessary, but I must state that my thinking prayerfully and in solitude has not weakened my belief in the efficacy and righteousness of Civil Disobedience. I hold it as ever before to be a nation's right and duty when its vital being is in jeopardy. I am convinced that it is attended with less danger than war and whilst the former when successful benefits both the resister and the wrong-doer the latter harms both the victor and the vanquished.

You will not expect me to express any opinion on the vexed question of return by Congressmen to Legislative Councils and the Assembly. Though I have not in any way altered my opinion about the boycott of Councils, Law Courts and Government Schools, I have no data for coming to a judgment upon the alterations made at Delhi and I do not propose to express any opinion until I have had the opportunity of discussing the question with our illustrious countrymen who have felt called upon in the interests of the country to advise removal of the boycott of legislative bodies.

In conclusion, may I, through you, thank all the very numerous senders of congratulatory messages. It is not possible for me personally to acknowledge each message. It has gladdened my heart to see among the messages many from Moderate friends I have. Non-co-operators can have no quarrel with them. They too are well-wishers of their country and serve to the best of their lights. If we consider them to be in the wrong, we can hope to win them over only by friendliness and patient reasoning, never by abusing. Indeed, we want to regard Englishmen too as our friends and not misunderstand them by treating them as our enemies and if we are to-day engaged in a struggle against the British Government, it is against the system for which it stands, not against the Englishmen who are administering the system. I know that many have failed to understand

always bear in mind the distinction and in so far as we have failed we have harmed our cause.

I am your sincere friend and brother,
(Sd). M. K. Gandhi.

Poona 7th February 1924

AN INTERVIEW BEFORE RELEASE

"Yuga Dharma," an Ahmedabad literary vernacular magazine, edited by Dr. Sumant Mehta, published in the form of a letter an account of a visit the Editor had with Mahatmaji before his release, when the latter was a patient in the Sassoon Hospital, Poona.

Dr. Sumant enquired of Mahatmaji how it was that such a disease could attack a man like him (Mahatmaji), who was self-restricted (Sanyasin). Mahatmaji replied that, though he was moderate in food for many years, he had not yet been abstemious as he ought to have been. "I am sure," said Mahatmaji, " that my body does not need much food. In fact very little food is required when one has to undergo mental work and a good deal of concentration. Perhaps my weight might have been decreased by being abstemious. But my body would have been surely improved."

Mahatmaji was of opinion that there was no necessity of pulse as food for those who are used to brain work.

As regards the amelioration of the depressed classes, Mahatmaji expressed the necessity of working in the villages by encamping there.

He did not at all believe the rumour that there is a depression in the workers of Gujarat.

In a further conversation, Mahatmaji said: "I have plunged into politics simply in search of Truth. When I went to jail, I had fixed my programme for full six years. I have dictated a little about South Africa to Indu Lal, but my thoughts about the Gita are still to be dictated and I want to show how to epitomise the Mahabharata. I also think of writing my auto-biography. Still I have to do much."

On Dr. Sumant commenting on the new Labour Government in England by saying that there were still people who hope to get sweets from the Labour Government, Mahatmaji answered with a rather grave voice: 'People do not leave off the hope of getting help from outside. Who can give Swaraj? We have to take it. What about the depressed classes and what about solving the problem of Hindu-Muslim unity? What help can the Labour Government give you as regards these questions? Your future lies in your own hands. If you get sweet balls they will be made of stones."

Dr. Sumant concludes his letter after describing some conversation with Mahatmaji about Indu Lal Yagnik.

28th February 1924

TO THE AKALIS

Dear countrymen,—It was with great distress that I heard about the shooting of an Akali Jatha on the orders of the Administrator of Nabha State resulting in several members being killed and many more wounded. In reply to telegrams beyond sending a message of sympathy I had no wish to say or do anything more. It is contrary to the wish of Col. Maddock who has covered me with every form of kindness during my illness that I am undertaking a moderate amount of activity in the shape of informing myself of the prevailing situation in the country. But the following telegram just received from Zira namely "Come, unminding health condition soon, Akali Jatha" compels me to say something in connection with the tragedy just mentioned. I do not happen to know the sender of the telegram but had it been at all possible for me I would certainly have gone down in reply to the message. The wound being yet unhealed any such journey is a physical impossibility. I am therefore doing the next best thing. I need hardly assure the Akali Sikhs of my sympathy in the loss of so many brave men and many more being wounded.

Without the full facts before me I am unable to say whether the march of a large number of men in order to pay devotion to the shrine of Gangsur at Jaito was or was not justified. But I would ask the Akali Sikhs not to send any more Jathas without further deliberation and consultation with those leaders outside the Sikh community who have hitherto been giving them advice. It would be well to stop and watch developments arising out of the tragedy. One of telegrams received by me tells me that the Jatha was and remained throughout strictly non-violent. You have from the very commencement claimed that your movement is perfectly non-violent and religious. I would like every one of us to understand all the implications of non-violence. I am not unaware of the fact that non-violence is not your final creed. It is therefore doubly incumbent upon you to guard against any violence inthought or word creeping in the movement.

Over 25 years of the practice of non-violence in the political field has shown me as clearly as daylight that in every act of ours we have to watch our thoughts and words in connection with the movement in which we may be engaged. Non-violence is impossible without deep humility and the strictest regard for truth, and if such non-violence has been possible in connection with the movement not termed religious, how much easier it should be with those like you who are conducting a strictly religious movement. I have deemed it necessary to reiterate what I used to say about non-violence before my imprisonment, because I have observed during my brief study of the events of the past years that we who claim to be engaged in a non-violent movement have not fully and in thought and speech, conformed to our creed during the past two years as we certainly did not during the previous years. I am sorry to have to say that what I wrote about ourselves in the pages of "Young India" during the three months prior to my arrest holds truer to-day with us than it did then. I have not the slightest doubt in my mind that had we practised non-violence in the sense I mean during all these five years we would not only have achieved our common goal, but there would be to-day no differences and quarrels between Hindus and Mussalmans.

In drawing your attention therefore to the necessity of non-violence in your special struggle about your Gurdwaras I do not wish to be understood to mean that there had been a greater disregard of the essentials of non-violence amongst you than the other communities. But a word of caution is more necessary in your case because you have never flagged. You have been incessantly active in the pursuit of your special goal. I would therefore have you to search yourselves and if you find that you have not been true to the standard you set before yourselves to cease further demonstration for the time being and perform the necessary cleaning process before beginning anew. I doubt not that your efforts will be crowned with success.

I remain your friend and servant,

Poona, Feb. 25. (Sd.) M. K. Gandhi.

A MISCONCEPTION CLEARED

Mr. Gandhi, with a view to clear some misunderstandings about his letter to the Akalis, stated as follows to a Press representative on February 28:

I have just read a paragraph on the news column of the "Chronicle" of the 29th February about the Jaito tragedy in which it is suggested that my open letter to the Akali Sikhs is based on wrong information supplied to me and that, in this respect, people mostly suspect Lala Lajpat Rai. In justice to Lalaji I wish to state that before he saw me I had read all I could about the tragedy and that when the telegram inviting me to go to the Punjab was received, I had made up my mind before Lalaji had seen that telegram, that I should make some such statement as ultimately I did make. As the telegram asking me to come down from Akali Jathas was received from Tira and I did not know anybody there and as I was anxious that the advice I tendered should reach the Akali Sikhs as early as possible, I adopted the method of the open letter. My letter was based purely on the information gleaned by me from the papers and the knowledge acquired by me after my release about the state of the spirit of non-violence in thought, word and deed in the country. Lalaji did see the letter and under his pressure I struck out a large number of passages which otherwise I would have retained and which were stronger than the final letter. Lalaji further pressed me to end the letter at the clause advising the Akali Sikhs not to send another Jatha before deliberation with non-Sikh advisers, but as I felt that a general reference to the implications of non-violence at this moment was of vital importance, I was obliged respectfully to differ from Lalaji's advice and retained the passages regarding non-violence.

27th March 1924

THE CLASS AREAS BILL

Mr. Gandhi has issued the following statement to the Press on 23rd March :

The following cablegram has been received from Capetown signed by Mr. Pather, General Secretary, South African Indian Congress:—

"South African Indian community submits notwithstanding strongest protests Union Government determined carrying through Class Areas Bill violating pledges given. Bill indefensible. Foreigners, also Euro-Africans, Malays and Natives being exempted. Bill will apply only to India. Euro-Africans, Malays, and Natives assembled in thousands Capetown assured Mrs. Sarojini Naidu of support to Indians in opposition to Bill. Indians will never submit segregation. Inform India. Please take such action as you think best. Mrs. Sarojini Naidu has made deep impression and won many hearts. Mrs. Naidu deferred leaving South Africa until 30th April owing great demand on her in interest of the cause."

This is startling news, almost too bad even for South Africa, to be believed. I have already endeavoured to show why the Cape was to be excluded from the operation of the measure. If the information cabled by Reuter as to the exclusion of the Cape is correct, there is something wrong in the foregoing cable, or the information contained in it is applicable to the other three Provinces only, namely, Orangia, Transvaal and Natal. The position then will be that, so far as the Cape is concerned, the Cape Indians will still remain exempted from the operation of the measure, whereas in the other Provinces the measure will apply only to Indians. There is no difficulty about understanding the exemptions, because the idea of segregation of Natives and Malays in the extreme sense is new. Every European household has natives of South Africa as domestic servants. Malays, as I have shown in a previous communication, are a negligible quantity except in the Cape. We have, therefore, the naked truth before us that the Bill in question is aimed merely at Indians and that it connotes not only segregation but indirect expulsion. Mrs. Sarojini Naidu's visit to South Africa and her inspiring presence there will undoubtedly steel the hearts of the Indian settlers for further effort. Her presence is also bringing Europeans and Indians on the same platform. Let India, however, not be lulled into a sense of false security, because of the commanding presence of Mrs. Naidu in the midst of the sorely tried Indian settlers; after all, the cultured Europeans of South Africa are gentlemen, and I have little doubt that Mrs. Naidu is receiving all the attention that is due to her for her many and matchless gifts, but the South African Europeans have also a fixed and determined anti-Indian policy. General Smuts is a finished diplomat. On due occasion he can speak honeyed words, but he knows his mind, and let there be no mistake that unless India can make an effort adequate to the situation, the Bill will be carried through the Union Parliament in spite of Mrs. Naidu's resourcefulness.

MAHATMAJI AND JUHU

A message to the "A. B. Patrika," dated Poona, Feb. 28, stated:

A deputation consisting of Mr. Jairamdas Doulatram, Kaki Abdul-Rehman Seth Isserdas and Mr. R. K.

Sidhva waited upon Mahatma Gandhi this morning requesting him to come to Karachi to restore his health. Mahatmaji was lying in bed and received the deputation cheerfully.

Mr. Sidhva acted as spokesman and said: 'Your health will be immensely improved on the sea beach of Karachi where the weather is excellent."

Mahatmaji replying said: "I would wish I could come to Karachi to gain health because I know Clifton is an excellent place but I wish to remain in a central place so that friends would not find it inconvenient to see me from places far off. Hence I have decided to stay in Andheri near the sea.

Mr. Sidhva: "We look to your health first and those intending to see you could come even from thousands of miles. So you should come to Karachi. People are more anxious about your health."

Mahatmaji: "It is true, friends could come to see me from any distance but I don't want to trouble them. I had an invitation from Ceylon also and although I have not seen Ceylon, I am told it is a beautiful and lovely place but for the convenience of visitors with whom I have to consult often, I have decided to remain near Bombay. I had once decided to live at Dadabhoy Naoroji's house and I was glad that I would be staying in the house of persons under whom I had learnt politics.

A TOUCHING SCENE

A Correspondent wrote to the "Bombay Chronicle" from Poona on March 10:—

The students of the B. J. School of Medicine, Poona, had the unique privilege of paying their respects to

Mahatmaji and Mrs. Gandhi, on the eve of their departure from Poona. The staff of the Sassoon Hospital, including Col. Maddock, Major Coullie, Dr. Shikare, the Sister-in-charge, was present on the occasion.

The students presented Mahatmaji with a garland made of "Khadi" and expressed their heart felt wishes for Mahatmaji's rapid recovery. They also prayed for his long life and prosperity and expressed their thanks to Col. Maddock for his skill in operation.

At the express request of the students, Mahatmaji addressed a few words to the gathering. He said:

"You will excuse me for I am speaking, sitting on the chair, but my health does not permit me to stand. You have asked me to speak to you on the eve of my departure from Poona, but I am unfit to do so. I am doing Civil Disobedience to the commands of Col. Maddock, but it will be injustice if I would not speak a few words.

Col Maddock has become my friend since he was sent to Yerrawda to examine me by the Government. I was not willing for the operation, but Col. Maddock impressed upon me in such a way that I was obliged to keep my full confidence in him. I had full faith in his skill. I am not an expert to certify so, but it is the fact. I am still glad to hear from you that he is a friend of mine. I hope that Col Maddock will spend his leisure time in the cause of humanity, wherever he may go.

Non-violent Non-co-operation means sympathy and good feeling towards every man. It will grieve me much if I know others saying that I have ill-feeling towards any individual or person. It will also grieve me much after my death. I cannot keep silent without mentioning the kind attitude and help rendered to me by the staff, nurses, sisters and students. I have no sufficient words to repay their help. I am very glad that I am assured by you that you will use 'Swadeshi cloth.' I do not mean that Swadeshi means ill-feeling towards any man. My stay in the hospital will be one of the treasures in my remembrance and I will carry it to the end of my life.

In fine, I pray God to give long life and prosperity to Col. Maddock and Mrs. Maddock wherever they are. I thank you all for giving me this opportunity."

REMOVAL TO SEA-SIDE

Mr. C. F. Andrews communicated the following statement to the Associated Press on March 11:

The removal of Mr. Gandhi to sea-side at Andheri north of Bombay was undertaken last night with as little discomfort and inconvenience as possible. Everything passed off quietly and though the journey was a very tiring one for the patient it was not too much for his strength. What is needed now more than anything else is complete rest both of body and mind. The weather at the sea-side on the Bombay coast is cooler and fresher than at Poona at this time of the year and it is hoped that after the difficult journey which has now been successfully accomplished the change of air will make recovery more rapid. It need to be remembered however that because the physical weakness was very great when the operation was performed, full recovery of physical strength and vigour must necessarily be slower than in ordinary cases.

13th March 1924

A DYING GIRL'S GIFT TO MAHATMAJI

Om

The Vias Ville,
Lahore, 18-2-24.

I am enclosing herewith a currency note for Rs. 100 in compliance with the wishes of my youngest daughter Bibi Sarla Devi aged 16 years who died on the 6th instant. She heard the news of your release before her demise and was most happy for this. The girl used to keep pretty good health before going to Simla in April last. She was not only brisk in her long walks and was of very jovial and cheerful temperament. She was endowed with a strong commonsense and realised full well what her obligations were to herself, her family and her beloved country. She took the vow of Khadi in August 1921 before her mother and eldest sister, though against the wishes of the former, who was of opinion that it was perhaps unsafe for the unmarried girls to take such vows as they might not keep them up after their marriage. The girl pooh-poohed this argument of her mother. As ill-luck would have it, the eldest sister died on the 30th July 1922 after protracted illness of four months and poor Sarla fell ill on the 17th of August last. She was confined to bed for over five months and before her last breath said to her mother, whose heart was already lacerated in consequence of the demise of two adult sons and one daughter, that she was glad to have been enabled to stick to her vow of Khadi and that all her clothes should be given to orphan girls. After this she turned her eyes towards me and said with a fainting voice that a sum of Rs. 100 should be placed at your disposal as her dying contribution towards the Swaraj

Fund. Oh! how the poor girl longed to see her motherland restored to her lost grandeur and freedom. May God fulfil her desire!

Barkatram Thapur.

MAHATMAJI INTERVIEWED

The following is the text of the interview that the "Evening News of India" had with Mahatma Gandhi:

"I do not hope for very much from the Labour Government not because it is worse than a Conservative or a Liberal Government, but because of the traditions handed down from generation to generation which no Government, no matter however powerful, can in a day rid of." With these words Mr. M. K. Gandhi summed up his impressions of the Labour Government to a representative of the "Evening News of India," who visited him at Narotam Morarji's bungalow at Juhu on March 20.

Everybody in Bombay knows Juhu—that long palm-fringed beach where bathing parties resort to during week-ends. Latterly, however, Juhu has become more than a Mecca of pleasure-seekers; since Mr. Gandhi's arrival it has changed into a place of political pilgrimage. Nothing makes this clearer than the increased traffic on the roads leading to and from the beach. When the "Evening News" representative motored out this morning, he encountered several cars in his journey across the flats, and when he reached the vicinity of Narotam Morarji's bungalow, signposts were placed at convenient intervals to direct visitors, and the deeply rutted road bore evidence of heavy traffic.

Mr. Gandhi, although he is now able to take occasional walks, still spends the most of the day in bed, and he was sitting up in his couch, naked to the waist as is his custom, when he received our representative this morning. His closely cropped hair is liberally sprinkled with grey, but otherwise he is looking quite well and is evidently making good progress towards recovery.

In answer to questions, Mr. Gandhi very willingly gave a few details of his daily routine. He gets up at four o'clock, a practice which he invariably follows. After family prayers in which the household join, he reads religious literature for a time and then goes off again in a short sleep. At six he has his breakfast of milk—Mr. Gandhi confessed with a twinkle in his eye that he was following scrupulously Colonel Maddock's instructions regarding food--and afterwards, still following his old medical advisers' advice, he takes a walk on the verandah and treats his wound to a sun-bath. Immediately after this, he attends to his correspondence, both English and Gujarathi. In order to deal with the former he has been provided with shorthand typists who greatly facilitate his work. His time until mid-day is occupied by correspondence, the study of political problems and the seeing of important political and other friends by appointment. Early in the afternoon he has his bath and at four o'clock is ready to see the very large number of visitors who call on him.

In the evening, about six, Mr. Andrews takes him for a walk along the sea-shore, and this walk has now been prolonged to about forty minutes. The day's work is over by about eight, at which hour Mr. Gandhi usually retires for the night. "Later on," he explained, "I hope to take up spinning once I am able to sit up without fatigue."

"What do you think of the new Labour Government?" was one of the first political questions which our representative put to Mr. Gandhi. Mr. Gandhi evidently did not think much of it. "It has a precarious existence," he began. "It has to depend on the good-will of the other parties, and if it isn't to break in pieces, it has to conciliate its very exacting constituents and follow out its special domestic programme I have no doubt that in trying to acquire the support of the majority of the House in pushing through its domestic programme, it will not hesitate to sacrifice its principles regarding Imperial policy affecting India, or Indians in South Africa and Kenya. In fact, I should not be surprised, seeing it is so weak if the Labour Government does worse even than its predecessors so far as Indian policy is concerned."

Mr. Gandhi concluded by admitting that he was not much perturbed over the Labour Government, because India had to rely upon her own strength and resources. "When she becomes irresistible," he added, "I have no manner of doubt that any Government, whether Labour, Conservative or Liberal, will fall in with India's demands."

On the subject of Council entry and recent events in the Central Provinces and in the Assembly, Mr. Gandhi frankly confessed he could say nothing. The Swarajist leaders are coming down from Delhi to see him at the end of the month, and he cannot give any opinion on their actions until he has discussed the whole position with them. After having done this, he will be in a position to formulate his policy.

Interrogated regarding the Colonies Committee, which has just sailed in connection with the Kenya question, Mr. Gandhi thought that the Committee could do a great deal if it was not fettered by too many restrictions. "Whether the personality of the Committee is strong enough to assert itself is very difficult to say" he added.

"Speaking apart from my views as a non-co-operator, I cannot help noticing the absence of Mr. Sastri, Sir Tej Bahadur Sapru and Mr. Andrews from the Committee. They are the men who have studied the question and know it in all its bearing, while Mr. Andrews is an expert. I cannot help saying that these omissions are glaring and inspire me with distrust as to the Committee's findings."

Mr. Gandhi gave an interesting explanation of the South African Government's decision to omit the Cape Provinces from the operation of the Class Areas Bill. "This," he said, "is merely an instance of selfishness on the part, principally, of the Dutch population. Nearly all the house work in the Cape is done by Malay women, and if the Segregation Act came into force, these Malay women would be affected by it. This would mean depriving a major part of the white population of its domestic help, which would give no end of inconvenience. Consequently, as the Indian population of the Cape is small--about 10,000 in all—the Cape people decided that they are not worth worrying about as far as segregation is concerned in view of the difficulties which segregation would bring in its train."

In the course of the conversation, Mr. Gandhi paid a tribute to Colonel Maddock—"who was more than my doctor; he is my friend"—and to Mr. Andrews—or "Charlie Bhai" as he is familiarly known—who is his right hand man at Juhu and who writes articles incessantly from morning till night.

"I hope when India gets Swaraj, you will not pack us poor but honest European journalists back home," laughingly remarked our representative. "Nothing is further from my mind," replied Mr. Gandhi with a bright smile as he shook hands. As our representative took his departure, Mrs. Gandhi, who is her husband's chief nurse, was quietly and efficiently propping him up in bed in order that he might take his second ration of bread and milk.

27th March 1924

TRUE LOVE TO BETTER ACCOUNT

Brothers and Sisters,

This request is addressed to those brothers and sisters, who come to see me or desire to see me.

I have already issued a request through the Press that those who cannot help seeing me, may visit me during the evening between four and five. My visitors are either unaware of this request or even though aware of this request cannot restrain themselves from seeing me and continue coming in at irregular hours. The result is bad for me. The little service I can render is affected adversely.

I possess very little vitality. I want to use that little for purposes of service alone. Next week I wish to resume the burden of editing "Young India" and "Navjiwan." For this purpose I want complete solitude. If my day is to be wholly passed in receiving and pleasing my visiting brothers and sisters, my whole energy will be taken up by it and it will be impossible for me to conduct these weeklies as I wish them to be.

Moreover, a visit to me can possibly do no good to my brothers and sisters. It is no doubt the symbol of their love for me, but this seems to me to assume rather an exaggerated form. I consider love to be a great force. Its use should be made in the service of the nation rather than in seeing me. This is my prayer. Whatever is to be spent for the purpose of coming to see me, may be spent up for the production and propagation of Khaddar. The time taken up in visiting me, may be spent profitably in

(1) spinning or carding

(2) spreading Khaddar, and

(3) teaching one's neighbour to spin or to card.

Those who are not prepared to do it and who cannot restrain themselves from visiting may come between five and six in the evening on all days except Monday. I shall see them *en masse*, not individually.

Again, I pray to all visitors to bring the yarn spun by themselves. It will be used in the weaving of Khaddar. The money will be spent in spreading Khaddar.

I am sure, brothers and sisters, that you will accept this prayer of mine. I shall feel obliged in that case and my time will be spared for the services of my country.

M. K. Gandhi.

Juhu 24th March 1924.

"AT THE FEET OF MAHATMAJI"

Mr. D. B. Divanji writes to the "Voice of India" under date April 4:

With the previous permission of Mahatmaji, a party of the students and teachers of the Bombay Rashtriya Sala (Gujarati Section) went to Juhu for his Darshan on Friday the 2nd instant. After a short prayer sung by the music teacher of the school the students of music gave a treat of their music to Mahatmaji. Lalit then sung the favourite song of Mahatmaji describing the qualities of a true Vaishnava. The Acharya then read out the address specially prepared for that occasion and written on a piece of Khaddar woven out of the yarn spun by the students themselves. After this the following articles prepared by the students in the school were presented to Mahatmaji :—

(1) Flower-pot—made of clay (2) Incense-burner—made of clay (3) Waste-paper basket—made of cane (4) A mat for carding—made of cane (5) Holder and pencil-stand —made of wood (6) Book stand—made of wood (7) Book case—made of wood (8) Puja-pat—made of wood (9) Travelling Bag—made of wood and Khadi (10) Slivers prepared by the students (11) Garlands of yarn spun by the school.

Then Mahatmaji addressed a few words to the students and teachers to the following effect :—

I need not say to you that I am happy to see you all to-day. I am thankful to you for the little presents you have offered me. Two at least of these presents convey a special meaning to me at present. The mat for carding and the slivers prepared by you remind me that I must immediately take up the work of spinning and carding. I assure you that when I am engaged in doing that work, I feel Swaraj approaching nearer and nearer. Therefore I request you all to pray for my complete and immediate recovery in order that I may be able to take up work as early as possible. I desire that you also should devote yourself to the spinning wheel and I am sure you will also feel that it brings Swaraj nearer and nearer. If we concentrate upon the constructive programme we are sure to get all we want. You must have heard the beautiful song of Poet Narasimha Mehta sung by Lalitji. I wish you understand the meaning of such religious songs and I appeal to you that you will make all efforts to translate the noble ideals of such poems into your actions. But I warn you that even for teachers it is a very difficult thing to act according to the ideals inculcated in these beautiful songs.

I' remember that when I first visited your school, I told you that you had much to learn in the art of music. To-day I again have heard some of the students singing, but I am sorry to remark that you have not as yet made sufficient progress to earn my certificate. However, I do hope that when I next visit your school after my complete recovery, you will make yourself fit for passing —though complete mastery over that art may not be possible for you even then.

Then Mahatmaji left his seat and the small gathering dispersed.

3rd April 1924

FOR THE READERS PAST AND PRESENT OF 'YOUNG INDIA'

(BY M. K. GANDHI)

It is not without much hesitation that I resume the editorship of *Young India*. I do not know whether my health can yet sustain the energy required for conducting the paper. But I cannot foresee. I can only dimly understand God's purpose in bringing me out of my retirement in Yerrowada. In taking up the editorial control of *Navajivan* and *Young India* I am following the Light as far as I see It.

Nor have I any new message to deliver to the reader. I had hoped for release by an act of a Swaraj Parliament and to be able to take my humble share in serving Free India. That was not to be.

We have yet to attain freedom. I have no new programme. My faith in the old is just as bright as ever if not brighter. Indeed one's faith in one's plans and methods is truly tested when the horizon before one is the blackest.

Though therefore so far as my mind can perceive, there will be no new method or policy developed in the pages of *Young India*, I hope they will not be stale. *Young India* will be stale when Truth becomes stale. I want to see God face to face. God *I know* is Truth. For me the only certain means of knowing God is non-violence—*Ahimsa*—love. I live for India's freedom and would die for it, because it is part of Truth. Only a free India can worship the true God. I work for India's freedom because my Swadeshi teaches me that being born in it and having inherited her culture, I am fittest to serve *her* and *she* has a prior claim to my service. But my patriotism is not exclusive; it is calculated not only not to hurt any other nation but to benefit all in the true sense of the word. India's freedom as conceived by me can never be a menace to the world.

But if it is not to be such a menace, the means adopted for gaining it must be strictly non-violent. My interest in India's freedom will cease if she adopts violent means, for their fruit will be not freedom but slavery in disguise. And if we have not yet attained our freedom, it is because we have not been non-violent in thought, word and deed. It is true that non-violence has been adopted as a policy *i.e.,* because we are convinced that by no other means can *India* achieve her freedom. Our policy is not, must not be, a camouflage. We may not harbour violence under cover of non-violence. Whilst we claim to be non-violent for a particular purpose and a particular period, our thought and word must accord with our practice for that purpose and that period. Even so does an honest gaoler act towards a condemned man. He protects his life at the peril of his own till the date of the extreme penalty. He thinks and speaks of his safety. He is, for the time and the person, non-violent in thought, word and deed.

We pledged ourselves to be non-violent towards each other and our opponents whether administrators or co-operators. We were to appeal to their hearts and evoke the best in them, not play upon their fear to gain our end. Consciously or unconsciously the majority of us -the articulate portion—have not been true to our pledge. We have been intolerant towards our opponents. Our own countrymen are filled with distrust of us. They simply do not believe in our non-violence. Hindus and Mussalmans in many places have provided an object lesson not in non-violence but in violence. Even the 'changers' and the 'no-changers' have flung mud against one another. Each has claimed the monopoly of truth and with an ignorant certainty of conviction sworn at the other for his helpless stupidity.

The pages of *Young India* can only, therefore, illustrate the utility and the necessity of non-violence in dealing with the questions that engage public atten-tion. So much for the central policy of *Young India*.

A word as to the business side. Some of the readers will recollect that I announced that when at the instance of Mr. Shankerlal Banker and other friends, I took up the editing of *Young India*, I told the public that it was run at a loss and that I would be obliged to give it up if the loss continued. I do not believe in publishing newspapers indefinitely at a loss or by means of advertisements. If a paper supplies a felt want, it must pay its way. The subscription list however ran up steadily week by week and it began to yield profits. But during the last two years as the reader is aware, the list has fallen from 21,500 to 3,000 and it is now being run at a loss. Happily *Navajivan* has made up for it. But even that method is wrong. *Young India* must stand on its own bottom or fall. It is likely that if I still retain the personal affection of the old readers, *Young India* will soon pay its way. But I have mentioned the loss not only to acquaint the public with the true state of affairs but also as an introduction to an important announcement.

When Messrs. Banker and Yajnik suggested that the Gujarati *Navajivan* which was then a monthly, should be turned into a weekly and edited by me and when I undertook the responsibility, I announced that it would be given up if it proved a loss and that if there were profits, they would be utilized for some public purpose. *Navajivan* soon became profitable but at the instance of Sheth Jamnalalji, *Hindi Navajivan* was commenced. It too had just begun to pay its way when my arrest took place and the circulation steadily fell. It is now again being issued at a loss. But in spite of these losses the large circulation of *Navajivan* and other publications enable the management to devote Rs. 50,000 to public work. Swami Anandanand who is managing the *Navajivan* press has left it entirely to me to allocate the money and as I know no other and better method of utilising it, I propose to devote the sum through the agency of the Provincial Congress Committee to the spread of the spinning wheel and Khadi in Gujarat including Kathiawad. Preference will be given to their spread among poor women and the suppressed classes. It is due to my co-workers that I should inform the public that with some of them the work is a labour of love. Where they receive payment, it is just enough for their wants. The result of such work is before the public. I know that if from the sweeper upward I could secure selfless workers, with the efficient management I have the good fortune to have to-day, it would be possible to show a better surplus.

I should also like to add that if *Young India* again shows profits, as it did before my imprisonment, they will be distributed for all-India work. If any profits are derived from *Hindi Navajivan*, they will be devoted to the spread of Hindi.

3rd April 1924

MY MISSION

(BY M. K. GANDHI)

Pandit Ghasita Ram, "President, all-India Sub Assistant Surgeons' Association, Punjab Province, Amritsar," sent to the Editor some days ago 'an open letter' addressed to me. After omitting from it laudatory phrases and sentences of good wishes, and after correcting obvious grammatical errors, the letter reads:

"I am a Brahman, doctor and an old man like you. It will not be out of courtesy if I, in this triple capacity, offer you a piece of counsel. If you see wisdom and truth in it and if it appeals to your commonsense and sentiments, kindly take it to heart.

You have seen much of the world; you have read much of it. Consequently you possess a wonderful experience of it, but in this world of mortals none till now has been able to accomplish the task he has undertaken in his life-time. For instance Buddha in spite of his high morality could not convert the whole of India into Buddhism.

Shankaracharya in spite of his high intellectuality

could not make all India Vedantist. Christ in spite of his high spirituality could not bring into the fold of Christianity the whole Jewish nation. I do not think, and I am not prepared to believe for a single moment about the accomplishment of your task. Still in face of these historical facts if you believe in its accomplishment in your lifetime, then Sir, I venture to say that it is nothing but a dream.

This world is a place of trials, troubles, and turmoils. The more a man sinks into it the more he is restless and eventually he loses his spiritual calmness and peace of mind. Consequently the Mahatmas of olden time kept themselves aloof from the worldly worries, anxieties and cares and strove to gain perfect peace and true quality of mind and enjoyed an everlasting happiness and bliss thereby.

The Jail life has brought a great change in your life and vigour and the disease has reduced you much. Therefore in the fitness of things, you may live a calm life and spin the thread of your remaining days in a certain solitary cave in the meditation of God, and in realization of your own self in perfect spiritual tranquility and calmness, because your health will not allow you to bear the burden of the worldly cares any more. It shall not be out of place to mention that you are absolutely convinced of the goodwill, mercy and sympathy of good officers. That very system of European medicines and surgery which you condemned more than once, has saved you from the jaws of monstrous death. The English officers helped you in time of your trouble and needs.

"A friend in need is a friend indeed." Now it remains for you to show your true friendship and to become the true ally of the British Raj in gratitude for the safety of your life and your release from the jail. If anyhow you cannot do so by your words and deeds, then pray do not come into the arena of political activity but still if your restless soul does not allow you to sit in rest, then in this Bhumi —the motherland of great sages and saints, Rishis and Munis—take up the task of spiritualising your brother Indians, teach them a lesson of true realisation of the self. By doing so, instead of gaining this Kingdom of Earth, you will gain the Kingdom of Heaven."

In my opinion, the writer is desperately in earnest and merits an answer on that account if for nothing else. But it enables me, too, to clear up certain misapprehensions about my mission in life.

Let me first however dispose of the advice about my views on medicine. I have not *Indian Home Rule* before me, but I recollect sufficient to be able to say that I have nothing to revise about the views set forth there. If I had written it for English readers and in English, I would have put the same thought in a manner that would have been more acceptable to the English ear. The original is in Gujarati and was written for the Gujarati readers of *Indian Opinion* of Natal. Moreover what is written there has reference to an ideal state. It is a common error to think that condemnation of measures involves that of men. Medicine does often benumb the soul of the patient. It may therefore be considered evil but not therefore necessarily medicine-men. I had precious medical friends when I wrote the book and did not hesitate to seek their advice in times of need. That was, as the writer implies, inconsistent with my belief regarding the use of medicine. Several friends have said to me the same thing in so many words. I plead guilty. But that is to admit that I am not a perfect man. Unfortunately for me I am far from being perfect. I am a humble aspirant for perfection. I know my way to it also. But knowing the way is not reaching its end. If I was perfect, if I had acquired full control over all my passions even in thought, I should be perfect in body. I am free to confess that daily I am obliged to expend a great amount of mental energy in acquiring control over my thoughts. When I have succeeded, if I ever do, think what a store-house of energy would be set free for service. As I hold that appendicitis was a result of infirmity of thought or mind, so do I concede that my submission to the surgical operation was an additional infirmity of mind. If I was absolutely free of egoism, I would have resigned myself to the inevitable; but I wanted to live in the present body. Complete detachment is not a mechanical process. One has to grow into it by patient toil and prayer. As for gratitude, I have more than once publicly expressed my gratitude to Col. Maddock and his staff for the kindness with which they overwhelmed me. But there is no connection between the kind treatment I received from Col. Maddock and the system of Government I condemn. Col. Maddock himself would think little of me, if I revised my views about Dyerism because he, Col. Maddock, was a competent surgeon and did his duty as such. Nor have I any cause to be thankful to the Government for providing me with best surgical assistance or for prematurely releasing me. The former they were bound to provide for every prisoner. The latter has embarrassed me. I knew my course in prison whether well or ill. Outside the prison-walls, although I am slowly regaining my health, I do not know with certainty how to shape my course.

Now for the central point of the letter, the confusion in the writer's mind has arisen because of his misconception of the work of the prophets he names and of an awkward (for me) comparison between them and me. I do not know that Buddha did not accomplish his task which was to reach *Nirvana*. Tradition has it that he did. Conversion of others was a bye-product, if one may so describe a sacred function. The Gospels record it of Jesus that he testified on the Cross of his own work--'It is finished.' Nor has their work of love died after them. The truest part of it will live for ever. The two or three thousand years that have gone by since their ministry, are but a speck in the vast time circle.

I do not consider myself worthy to be mentioned in the same breath with the race of prophets. I am a humble seeker after truth. I am impatient to realise myself, to attain *Moksha* in this very existence. My national service is part of my training for freeing my soul from the bondage of flesh. Thus considered, my service may be regarded as purely selfish. I have no desire for the perishable kingdom of earth. I am striving for the kingdom of Heaven which is *Moksha*. To attain my end it is not necessary for me to seek the shelter of a cave. I carry one about me, if I would but know it. A cave-dweller can build castles in the air whereas a dweller in a palace like Janak has no castles to build. The cave-dweller who hovers round the world on the wings of thought has no peace. A Janak though living in the midst of 'pomp and circumstance' may have peace that passeth understanding. For me the road to salvation lies through incessant toil in the service of my country and therethrough of humanity. I want to identify myself with everything that lives. In the language of the Gita I want to live at peace with both friend and foe. Though therefore a Mussalman or a Christian or a Hindu may despise me and hate me, I want to love him and serve him even as I would love my wife or son though they hate me. So my patriotism is for me a stage in my journey to the land of eternal freedom and peace. Thus it will be seen that for me there are no politics devoid of religion. They subserve religion. Politics bereft of religion are a death-trap because they kill the soul.

3rd April 1924

PLEA FOR PATIENCE

(BY M. K. GANDHI)

Some correspondents are anxious for my views on Council entry and Hindu-Muslim questions. Others are equally insistent that I make no hasty pronouncement. I am myself most eager to express my opinion on both these questions but I want to avoid all avoidable mistakes. I owe a duty to those who differ from me. They are valued co-workers. They love their country just as much as I claim to do. Some of them have recent sacrifices to their credit to which I can lay no claim. They have a longer first-hand experience of the country than I have. Their opinions therefore deserve all the respect and consideration that are due to their position and ability. Above all, I must not embarrass them by any ill-considered opinion. Their's is a thankless task. The Government have rejected every advance made by them. The former have stood defiant behind their armed entrenchments even in such trifles (to them) as the removal of the prohibition against

Mr. Horniman and the release of Moulana Hasrat Mohani. In these circumstances, it would be improper on my part without the utmost consideration to say anything that may in any way disturb the plans the Swarajists may develop for meeting the emergency. I am trying to grasp the situation and understand their view-point. Nothing can possibly be lost by patience. Haste may cause unnecessary mischief.

The same may be said of the Hindu-Muslim question with greater emphasis. It is a problem that requires the most delicate handling. Every thought has to be examined. Every word weighed. A hasty adjective may cause an explosion. Though therefore I hold decided views on the question and am most anxious to express them, I must forbear. Both Hindus and Mussalmans occupying front positions in the community are asking me not to say a word without fully studying the situation. I have a letter which goes so far as to say that I shall know little until I have travelled and seen things for myself. Without going so far with my correspondents, I give my assurance to them and all who think with them that I shall not write or say a word without a careful and prayerful study of the question. For me the attainment of Swaraj depends not upon what the English Cabinet thinks or says but entirely upon a proper, satisfactory and lasting solution of the thorny problem. Without it all before us is dark. With it Swaraj is within immediate reach.

Whilst therefore these conferences are going on, I respectfully urge those who are interested in my opinion on these important questions to go on with the constructive programme. Every yard of yarn spun or khaddar woven is a step towards Swaraj. Every one who refrains from harbouring an evil thought of his Hindu or Mussalman brother as the case may be contributes to the solution. Every writer in the Press who economises his adjectives and ceases to impute motives or inflame public opinion makes easy the path to a proper solution. The other day the *Times of India* published illuminating extracts from the vernacular press showing the present mentality of some writers. They tell us how not to do the thing. Granting that a Hindu or a Mussalman utters a hasty word, it is no business of a pressman who wishes well to his country immediately to advertise it. It would be criminal to exaggerate such blunders. I am not sure that the statements advertised in those extracts were even made by the parties concerned. No expression of opinion from anybody is needed to demonstrate the necessity of being accurate, of curbing our tongues and checking our pens.

10th April 1924

AM I UNFAIR?

(BY M. K. GANDHI)

I have the good fortune to possess friends who keep me on the right path when I am inclined or likely to stray away from it. One such friend thought that in my letter last week to the readers of *Young India*, I was less than fair to the Government of Bombay inasmuch as I declined to render thanks to them for having given me best medical assistance and made the path to recovery easy by freely permitting friends to visit me. In my friend's opinion, the treatment was a sign of change of heart due to the advent of the new Governor. I have deeply thought over my friend's argument and I am reluctantly obliged to adhere to the conclusion that I owe no thanks for the best medical assistance and the facilities given to friends to visit me, unless thanks are due to a Government every time it does its duty. I have made ample acknowledgement of the fact that Government did for me during my illness all that it could reasonably be expected to do in respect of a prisoner. But I am unable to render thanks to the Government as such in the same sense that I have rendered them to Col. Maddock, Col. Murray and Major Jones. They need not have been as kind as they were and I would still have to acknowledge that they had done all they could be expected to do in their respective spheres. The personal element was a factor in these gentlemen's conduct towards me, and I was bound to give them my thanks. To finish this part of the argument, if I may state it without indelicacy, I may say that my scrupulously correct conduct as a prisoner had not a little to do with the happy relations that subsisted between the officials and indeed also the Government and myself. I state this merely to emphasise the truth tested by me on scores of trying occasions that uniformly correct conduct will disarm the fiercest opposition, prejudice and suspicion.

Now for the supposed change of heart, I wish I could see it. I am longing for it. The reader may know that the slightest real change of heart will make me capitulate without delay. But it will have to be very real. The Government have failed even in so simple a test as the release of Maulana Hasrat Mohani, and the removal of the ban against Mr. Horniman. I own that from a strong believer I have become an equally strong unbeliever in this Government. I am however sane enough to be able to perceive a sincere change of heart. It has been suggested that Sir George Lloyd would not have treated me during my illness as His Excellency Sir Leslie

Wilson has done. I do not believe it. In spite of Sir George Lloyd's utter dislike of me, he would have given me the same medical assistance and facility that were given to be by the present Governor. Indeed it was he who sent Col. Maddock to examine me when I first became at all seriously ill in the Yerrowada goal about eight months ago. Col. Maddock was asked to visit me weekly during convalescence and send the Governor weekly reports. I have a higher opinion of the British officials than most people imagine. They have a high sense of duty. Only the honesty of an ordinary official does not travel beyond the line of policy. It is no fault of his. He is heir to a system handed down for generations—a system which is based on exploitation of the weak by the strong. The official breaks down when the system which sustains him is in jeopardy. But it is my belief that no other human being will do better under that system. The sooner therefore it is destroyed or radically altered the better for us all.

17th April 1924

SCHOOL MASTERS AND LAWYERS

(BY M. K. GANDHI)

"I hope you have by this time been able to consult friends who were led to modify, at Delhi, the Congress resolution regarding the Triple Boycott. What final decision have you come to? Are you going to preach them over again in the same form?

"As to the boycott of Councils, I may not say anything; the leaders of the Swaraj Party might have clearly laid before you facts and arguments. The work they are doing and are likely to do is before you. As to the boycott of schools and colleges it has, if I may say from my own experience, completely failed. I may refer to my own case. Here there are two full-fledged High Schools, attended by more than 500 pupils each, while the National High School has barely 30 boys on the roll. We have tried all possible ways and means for canvassing boys, but have failed. I have been convinced that people are not prepared for this boycott.

"As to the third boycott, there were only a very few lawyers who gave up their practice. Now almost all have rejoined. The number of court-going people never diminished. The *Lavad* Courts established by national workers never thrived and have since died. These courts having had no power to enforce their decisions, and the people being not trained to submit, cannot be expected to attain any palpable success.

"Under these circumstances what are we—who boycotted our further education and prospects at the clarion call of the Congress to sacrifice for the sake of the country only one year—to do? We have sacrificed not only one year but three. We established national schools for the people and the people heed them not. The sacrifice of the workers is not appreciated. Are not the national schools with such poor attendance a useless waste of the public money, energy and life? Does it not mean that our efforts and plans are premature? Our sacrifice gives no satisfaction to ourselves too. It is often a hindrance to patriotism or national enthusiasm. Khaddar is dearer than mill-cloth and our means are poor. Though elected delegates to the Congress we cannot attend or have to refuse the seat for want of the necessary money required for travelling and other expenses. We have to earn money not for luxury but as a necessity. But our ways are blocked by the Congress.

"I have a family to support and a delicate constitution, and hence cannot bear the hardships of village propaganda. The Congress has practically no work at present. What I think is that the Congress should arrange for the maintenance of workers and admit only those whom it can support. It should give permission to all others to follow their own pursuits patriotically and be soldiers of the militia (irregular army) ready at the country's call whenever required. Such people will enter Government and semi-Government schools and teach their prescribed books and lessons with a patriotic angle of vision. They will join the bar and show to the people at every step what a waste of time and money the Courts are. They will enter the millitary and refuse to fire on their own brethren. And so on. I know not what you intend to do after your recovery. In the meanwhile I seek your advice. I think that I am doing no better service to the people and to the country by remaining the head master of the national school here which is not appreciated and supported by the public. May I complete my law education and join the bar and do what humble services I can to the Motherland? Will you advise the Congress to remove these boycotts and advise some other ways and means for attaining freedom? Or are you going to take up these boycotts in right earnest again? May we wait?

P. S. It is no question of conscience and Religion. I look at Non-co-operation only as a means."

The foregoing letter sums up succinctly the argument advanced by my correspondent and visitors against the boycott of schools and law courts. As usual the sting is in the tail. The post script yields the secret of unbelief in the boycott. One need not regard everything as a matter of conscience or religion to be able to stick to it through thick and thin. Even one's means may be so vital that giving them up may mean death. Lungs are the means whereby we breathe and sustain life. They are not life. But their destruction is destruction of life itself. No one questions that Non-co-operation is a means. The questions are:—Is Non-co-operation as conceived in 1920 the only means of reaching our goal? The Congress decided that it was. But the Congress merely represents the opinion of the delegates for the time being. Some of us evidently consider that it was a mistake to think that it was the only means. Some others think that it was one of the means and many more should have been adopted at the same time. Yet others, though they disbelieved in it, adopted it out of regard for the decision of the majority and because they think that the decisions of the Congress have a mandatory character and bind the minority whether in matters of principle or detail. Yet others adhere to the opinion formed by them in 1920 that Non-co-operation as then conceived is the only means for achieving our goal. I belong to the last category and it will be my humble duty from time to time to show why it is the only means. My correspondent evidently belongs to the opposite school.

I have repeatedly observed that no school of thought can claim a monopoly of right judgment. We are all liable to err and are often obliged to revise our judgments. In a vast country like this, there must be room for all schools of honest thought. And the least therefore that we owe to ourselves as to others is to try to understand the opponent's view-point and, if we cannot accept it, respect it as fully as we would expect him to respect ours. It is one of the indispensable tests of a healthy public life and, therefore, fitness for Swaraj. If we have no charity and no tolerance, we shall never settle our differences amicably and must therefore always submit to the arbitrament of a third party, *i. e.,* to foreign domination. I invite the reader, then, to share with me the respect that is due to the view set forth by my correspondent, and if he belongs to the correspondent's school of thought, to bear with me, even though I cannot see eye to eye with him.

In my opinion, the boycott of schools and law courts has been both a failure and a success. It has been largely, not wholly, a failure in that schools and law courts have not been effective or even appreciably deserted. But it has been a success in that the halo surrounding Government schools and law courts has disappeared. People believe, much more now than they did before, in the necessity of independent national schools and settlement of disputes by panchayats. Lawyers and Government schoolmasters have lost much of the artificial prestige they enjoyed five years ago. I count these as no small gains. Let me not be misunderstood, I do not undervalue the sacrifices and devotion to the country of schoolmasters and lawyers. Dadabhai and Gokhale were schoolmasters. Pherozeshah Mehta and Budruddin Tyabji were lawyers. But I would not have even these distinguished countrymen of ours to claim the exclusive monopoly of wisdom or ability to guide. The spinner, the weaver, the farmer, the artisan, the trader have just as much right to shape the destiny of the country as the member of the so-called liberal professions. As the latter have represented the arm of authority, we have been awed by them and to that extent they have accustomed us to think that we can satisfy our wants only through the Government instead of teaching us that the Government is a creation of the people and merely an instrument for giving effect to their will. The false prestige of privileged classes has suffered a shock from which I hope it will never recover.

That national schools and panchayats have not flourished, as they might have, is due to a variety of causes, some avoidable and others unavoidable. We have been new to the work and therefore we have not known how to go about it. For me therefore, the poverty of results is not a cause for disappointment but for greater and more enlightened effort. Our failures we can convert into so many steps to success.

The village work frightens us. We who are town-bred find it trying to take to the village life. Our bodies in many cases do not respond to the hard life. But it is a difficulty which we have to face boldly, even heroically, if our desire is to establish Swaraj for the people, not substitute one class rule by another, which may be even worse. Hitherto the villagers have died in their thousands so that we might live. Now we might have to die so that they may live. The difference will be fundamental. The former have died unknowingly and involuntarily. Their enforced sacrifice has degraded us. If now we die knowingly and willingly, our sacrifice will ennoble us and the whole nation. Let us not flinch from the necessary sacrifice, if we will live as an independent self-respecting nation.

The difficulty with the Non-co-operating lawyers is greater still. They have unfortunately been used to a highly artificial life totally out of harmony with their national surroundings. I regard it as a crime that any lawyer or doctor should charge or get, say Rs. 1,000 per day or for that matter even Rs. 100 per day. It is no answer to the indictment that it is the monied men who pay and there can be no harm, but it may be all to the good, if lawyers take money from the rich people and use a part for the public good. If the profession was disinterested and charged only enough for maintenance, the monied men would also have to revise their budget. As it is, we seem to be moving in a vicious circle.

If under Swaraj we shall have to make the town life correspond to the village life, we shall be bound to simplify the town mode of life. The beginning has to be made now. Why should lawyers feel so utterly helpless as they seem to do now? Is starvation the only alternative if they cannot resume practice? Is it impossible for a resourceful lawyer to turn his attention to weaving or any other honourable toil?

It is difficult for me to advise Non-co-operating lawyers and schoolmasters. If they believe in the boycott, they should face all difficulties and continue the boycott. If they do not believe in it, they can without any disgrace attaching to their action rejoin the profession. As I do not believe in the mandate theory, I do not consider it to be obligatory on any schoolmaster or lawyer to refrain from rejoining Government schools or law-courts because of the continuance of the boycott resolution. I would still advocate the retention of the boycott, to be worked out not by propaganda for emptying Government schools and courts (that was done and had to be done during 1920 and 1921) but by the constructive method of establishing and popularising national schools and panchayats.

8th May 1924

IS IT NON-CO-OPERATION?

(BY M. K. GANDHI)

The argument has been advanced that with the failure (in my opinion wrongly assumed) of the boycott of titles, schools, law-courts, and Councils, Non-co-operation is dead. The critics see nothing of Non-co-operation in the slow and unexciting Khaddar programme. They forget that the four-fold boycott is like a scaffolding which is absolutely necessary till the whole structure is ready. It does not matter that the institutions, which are the symbols of the authority we seek to destroy, continue to exist so long as *we* do not make use of them. The fact is that we cannot erect our structure without the scaffolding of the four-fold boycott. And we must succeed if we can work the Congress organisation without the aid of these institutions and even in spite of them. Moreover, let us not forget that our boycott is not four-fold, but five-fold. The fifth is by far the most important *i.e.*, boycott of foreign (not merely British) cloth.

The boycott is the negative, though on that account none the less useful, part of our programme. Khaddar, national schools panchayats, Hindu-Muslim unity, and uplift of the untouchable, the drunkard and the opium eater, is the positive part of our programme. The greater our progress in it, the greater will be the progress towards the boycott and therefore, towards Swaraj. Nature abhors a vacuum. Therefore, construction must keep pace with destruction. Even if all the titled friends gave up their titles, and if schools, courts and Councils were entirely deserted, and being thus embarrassed, the Government abdicated in our favour, and if we had no constructive work to our credit, we could not conduct

Swaraj. We should be entirely helpless. I often wonder whether it is sufficiently realised that our movement is not one for mere change of personnel but for change of the system and the methods. Full Khaddar programme is, therefore, to me full Swaraj. The English interest in India is selfish and in conflict with the national interest. It is anti-national, because of the illegitimate cotton interest. To boycott, therefore foreign cloth, is to sterilise the English and all other foreign interests. Boycott merely of British cloth may harm the British, but can lead to no construction in India. Boycott of British cloth will be a jump out of the frying pan into fire. Not before the foreign piece-goods trade is entirely replaced by home-spun, will the bleeding process cease. Boycott of foreign cloth, therefore, is the centre of our boycott programme. This central boycott cannot succeed until we universalise Khaddar. In order to achieve the desirable end we will need to employ all our resources to the fullest extent. We shall need men, money and machinery *i.e.*, organisation. We cannot universalise Khaddar without Hindu-Muslim unity, without removing untouchability. To make Khaddar successful is to *demonstrate* our capacity for self-government. Khaddar is a people's programme, for success in which all, high and low, rich and poor, Hindu and non-Hindu, must take part.

But say the sceptics, 'How can Khaddar bring Swaraj? Will Englishmen then retire in our favour?' My answer is,—yes and no. Yes, because Englishmen will then find that their interest must be coincident with that of India. They will then be content to remain in India as her servants, for they will have then found that they cannot *impose* their custom upon us. When, therefore, Khaddar becomes successful, Englishmen's hearts will have been changed. They will regard it then as an honour to be our allies instead of regarding it as they do now their right to be our masters. My answer is 'No,' if we intend to drive out Englishmen and ruin *every* English interest, legitimate or otherwise. Such is not the goal of the non-violent movement. Non-violence has its limits. It refuses to hate or generate hatred. Indeed by its very nature, it is incapable of so doing. 'But' the sceptics further argue, 'Suppose the English refuse to revise their system and insist upon holding India by the sword, what can universal use of Khaddar do?' In thus doubting the efficacy of Khaddar, they forget that Khaddar is an indispensable preparation for Civil Disobedience. And this, every one admits, is an irresistible force. Without the universal adoption of Khaddar, I see no chance whatsoever of universal civil, *i.e.*, non-violent, disobedience. Any single district that can be fully organised for Khaddar is, if it is also trained for suffering, ready for Civil Disobedience. And I have not a shadow of doubt that even one district thus organised can make itself irresistible even though the whole might of the Government may be matched against it.

'Who shall bell the cat?' is the last question. That question is, however, irrelevant to the present inquiry. The question I set out to answer was whether constructive programme *i.e.*, Khaddar could be considered part of Non-co-operation. I have attempted to prove that it is an integral part of Non-co-operation in its positive aspect.

MAHATMA GANDHI AND THE SWARAJIST

The following statement was issued to the Press by Mahatma Gandhi on 23rd May 1924:

After having discussed with the Swarajist friends the vexed question of entry into the Legislative Assembly and the Councils by the Congressmen, I am sorry to have to say that I have not been able to see eye to eye with the Swarajists. I assure the public that there has been no lack of willingness or effort on my part to accept the Swarajist position. My task would be much simpler if I could identify myself with it. It can be no pleasure to me to oppose even in thought the most valued and respected leaders, some of whom have made great sacrifices in the cause of the country and who yield to no one in their love of freedom of the motherland, but in spite of my efforts and willingness I have failed to be convinced by their argument.

Nor is the difference between them and myself one of mere detail. There is an honest and fundamental difference. I retain the opinion that Council-entry is inconsistent with Non-co-operation as I conceive it. Nor is this difference a mere matter of interpretation of the word "Non-co-operation", but relates to the essential mental attitude resulting in different treatment of vital problems. It is with reference to such mental attitude that the success or the failure of the triple boycott is to be judged and not merely by a reference to the actual results attained. It is from that point of view that I say that to be out of the Legislative bodies is far more advantageous to the country than to be in them. I have, however, failed to convince my Swarajist friends, but I recognise that so long as they think otherwise, their place is undoubtedly in the Councils. It is the best for us all.

It was hardly to be expected that the Swarajists could be convinced by the arguments I advanced in the course of the conversations. They are, many of them, amongst the ablest, most experienced and honest patriots. They have not entered the Legislative bodies without full deliberation and they must not be expected to retire from the position until experience has convinced them of the futility of their method.

The question, therefore, before the country is not an examination and determination of the merits of the Swarajist view and mine. The question is, what is to be done now regarding Council-entry as a settled fact? Are the Non-co-operators to keep up their hostility against the Swarajist method or are they to remain neutral and even help, wherever it is possible or consistent with their principles.

The Delhi and Cocanada resolutions have permitted those Congressmen who have no conscientious scruples to enter the Councils and the Assembly, if they wanted to do so. In my opinion, the Swarajists are therefore justified in entering the Legislative bodies and expecting perfect neutrality on the part of the "No Changers" Thye are also justified in resorting to obstruction because such was their policy and the Congress laid down no conditions as to their entry. If the work of the Swarajists prospers and the country benefits, such an ocular demonstration cannot but convince honest sceptics like me of our error and I know the Swarajists to be patriotic enough to retrace their steps when experience has disillusioned them. I would therefore be no party to putting any obstacles in their way or to carrying on any propaganda against the Swarajists' entry into the Legislatures, though I cannot actively help them in a project in which I do not believe. The purpose of the Delhi and Cocanada resolutions was to allow the Swarajists a chance of trying the method of Council-entry and that purpose can be served only if the "No Changers" with scrupulous honesty allow the Swarajists full liberty to pursue their programme in the Councils unfettered by any obstruction from them.

With regard to the method of work in the Councils, I will say that I would enter a Legislative body, if only I found that I could at all use it to advantage. If, therefore, I enter the Councils, I should, without following a general policy of obstruction, endeavour to give strength to the Constructive Programme of the Congress. I should therefore move resolutions requiring the Central or the Provincial Government as the case may be:

(1) To make all their cloth purchases in handspun and handwoven khaddar;

(2) To impose a prohibitive duty on foreign cloth;

(3) To abolish the drink and drug revenue and at least correspondingly reduce the army expenditure.

If the Government refuse to enforce such resolution when carried in the Legislatures, I should invite them to dissolve them and take the vote of the electors on the specific point. If the Government would not dissolve, I should resign my seat and prepare the country for Civil Disobedience. When that stage is reached, the Swarajists will find me ready to work with and under them. My test of fitness for Civil Disobedience remains the same as before.

During the state of probation, I should advise the "No-Changers" not to worry about what the Swarajists are doing or saying and to prove their own faith by prosecuting the Constructive Programme with undivided energy and concentration. The Khaddar and the National schools are enough to occupy every available worker who believes in quiet, honest and undemonstrative work. The Hindu-Muslim problem too will tax the best energy and faith of the workers. The "No Changers" can justify their opposition to Council-entry only by showing the results of their application through the Constructive Programme even as the pro-changers must justify their entry by results. The "No Changers" are in one respect in an advantageous position for they can secure the co-operation of the Pro-changers. The latter have declared their faith in the Constructive Programme but their contention is that by itself, the Constructive Programme cannot enable the country to reach the goal. In the prosecution, however, of the Constructive Programme outside the Legislatures, all "No Changers," Pro-changers and others can, if they will, work in unison through their respective organisations if necessary.

The statement is incomplete without an examination of the working of the Congress organisation. I hold drastic and definite views in the matter, but I must reserve their expression for a future, though early occasion.

29th May 1924

CONGRESS ORGANISATION

(BY M. K. GANDHI)

As I have said in my statement to the Press on the question of Councils-entry, it is not complete without an examination, in the light of my views, of the working of the Congress organisation. The difference between the Swarajists and myself is honest and vital. I believe that the frank recognition of honest differences will accelerate the country's progress as a patched up compromise designed to hide differences would have retarded it. Each party is now free to give the fullest play to its views unhampered by any consideration save that of the common cause.

It is, therefore, necessary to consider the way the Congress organisation is to be worked. It is clear to me that it cannot be jointly worked just as a government cannot be jointly and efficiently carried on by two parties with opposite views. I hold the boycott of titles etc., to be an absolutely integral part of the Congress programme. The boycott has two objects; first, to persuade those who hold titles etc., to give them up; secondly, to keep the Congress pure from the influence of the institutions boycotted. If the first had been immediately successful, we should have attained our goal at once. But the second is equally necessary, if we are ever to reach our goal through the programme of non-violent non-co-operation. For me the boycott is national so long as the National Congress enforces it in its own organisation. It cannot undermine the influence, the glamour and the prestige of Government institutions, if it cannot be run without the presence in it, of administrators, of title-holders, lawyers, school-masters and councillors who represent as it were, the voluntary branch of the Government administration. The idea running behind the programme of Non-co-operation was that if we could honestly, non-violently and successfully work the Congress organisation without such influence, and nay, even in spite of it, that fact by itself would be enough to give us Swaraj. Our numerical superiority is so great that an effective boycott carried out by the National organisation must make the Congress an irresistible power. It follows, therefore, that the executive organisation of the Congress must not contain titled persons, Government school-masters, practising lawyers and members of legislative bodies and persons who use foreign cloth or cloth manufactured even in our mills, and those who deal in such cloth. Such persons can become Congressmen, but cannot and should not become members of executive organisations. They can become delegates and influence the Congress resolutions, but once the Congress policy is fixed, those who do not believe in that policy, in my opinion, should stand out of the executive bodies. The All India Congress Committee and all the local executive committees are such bodies, and they should contain only those members who whole-heartedly believe in and are prepared to carry out the policy. I am the author of the introduction into the Congress organisation of the system of single transferable votes. But experience has shown that so far as the executive organisations are concerned it cannot work. The idea that all opinions should be represented on these bodies must be abandoned if the executive committees are to become bodies for the purpose of carrying out the Congress policy for the time being.

One of the most important reasons why we have not been wholly successful is that the members of these executive bodies have not believed even in the Congress creed. I stand where I did when I wrote my impressions of the All India Congress Committee, which met at Delhi soon after the Bardoli resolutions were passed by the Working Committee. I saw then as clearly as possible that many members, if not indeed the majority, did not believe in non-violence and truth as an integral part of the Congress creed. They would not allow that 'peaceful' meant 'non-violent' and that 'legitimate' meant 'truthful.' I know that to-day there is more of the violent and the untruthful spirit in us than we had in February 1922. I would, therefore, urge that those who do not believe in the five boycotts and non-violence and truthfulness should resign from the Congress executive bodies. That is why I have said in my statement on the

Councils' entry that the constructive programme should be worked by different parties through their respective organisations. The thorough believers, if there are any, in the five boycotts and non-violence and truth, have no organisation other than the Congress. The most natural thing in my opinion, therefore, is for the Swarajists to work the constructive programme through their own organisations. So far as I can see, their method of working must be different from that of the boycotters. If they are to make the Councils-entry successful, they must devote the whole of their energy to that purpose, and therefore they can help the constructive programme by working it mainly through the Councils and the Assembly.

I, for one, can be no party to a tug of war in which each party tries to capture the Congress executive. That war may be fought out, if at all necessary, without heat and bitterness at the forthcoming sessions in December. The Congress is the debating and legislative body. The permanent organisation are purely executive bodies to give effect to the resolutions of the Congress. I am in a desperate hurry. I believe implicitly in the full and undiluted non-violent non-co-operation programme as passed by the Congress and no other. If I can get really non-violent and truthful workers who share my belief in the boycotts, in the potency of Khaddar, in Hindu-Muslim unity and in removal of untouchability, I would again feel Swaraj coming to us much quicker than most of us think possible. But if we wrangle on in the All India Congress Committee, we can only discredit and obstruct one another. Each party honourably and without jealousy and ill-will working separately (because they cannot do otherwise) can help one another.

I trust that all the members of the All India Congress Committee will attend the forthcoming meeting. If we can discuss the plan of action in a calm manner without imputing motives and make the composition of the All India Congress Committee homogeneous, we can do a tremendous amount of work during the forthcoming six months. I would respectfully invite each member to consider for himself or herself where he or she is in respect of the programme. If they do not believe in the programme as it is and in its capacity unaided to secure Swaraj, and if they really voice the feelings of their electors, I would not hesitate to advise the Committee even to take the risk of revising and radically altering the programme in anticipation of endorsement next year. No doubt for such a drastic change there must be a clearly made out case, there must be real public opinion behind it. Granted these two conditions, I have no doubt that in spite of anything to the contrary in the constitution, it is the duty of the All India Congress Committee to reverse the Congress policy at the risk of incurring condemnation and show useful and substantial work at the end of the year. Stagnation must be avoided at all cost.

After I had finished the foregoing, it was pointed out to me that it was possible that my views might tend to make Swarajists appear weaker than or inferior to the No-Changers in the estimation of the masses. Nothing can be further from my thought than any such idea. There is no question of quality. It is purely a question of temperamental differences. I have written simply with an eye to effective working of the Congress executives. That working is possible only if the executives are run only by one party. If the Swarajist view is more popular, the executive bodies should be solely in their hands. The Congress must always represent the popular view whatever it may be, whether good or bad. And it is the duty of those who hold contrary views not necessarily weak or inferior, to stand out and work on the popular mind from outside. The No-Changers will be belying their trust if they regard pro-changers as, in any way, inferior to them by reason of their holding different views.

It has been further pointed out to me that in arguing for exclusive control of the executives, I am departing from the spirit, if not the letter, of the Delhi resolution reaffirmed at Cocanada. I have read both the resolutions carefully. In my opinion the Delhi resolution and more specially the Cocanda resolution does not contemplate joint control of the executives. The Cocanada resolution is not a mere reaffirmation, but it emphasises the principle of non-violent non-co-operation. But even if my reading of the resolutious is incorrect, my argument remains unimpaired. Mine is only an opinion to be accepted or rejected by the members of the A. I. C. C. And it is actuated by the sole consideration of expeditious working. I feel that both the parties can effectively help each other only if they work separately.

CHRONOLOGICAL INDEX OF THE WRITINGS OF MAHATMA GANDHI

PREPARED BY

MISS ELIZABETH S. KITE, *New York*

For the Year 1919

For the Year 1919—(*Continued*)

For the Year 1920

For the Year 1920—*(Continued)*

For the Year 1920—*(Continued)*

For the Year 1921

For the Year 1921—*(Continued)*

For the Year 1921—*(Continued)*

For the Year 1921—*(Continued)*

For the Year 1922

For the Year 1922—*(Continued)*

For the Year 1924

INDEX

D

T